Direct Social Work Practice

Theory and Skills

Fifth Edition

Related Titles from Brooks/Cole

Bentley, Kia J., and Walsh, Joseph
***The Social Worker and Psychotropic Medication:
Toward Effective Collaboration with Mental Health Clients,
Families, and Providers***
ISBN: 0-534-34004-0

Corey, Gerald, and produced by Haynes
***The Art of Integrative Counseling and Psychotherapy
(2 Video Set)***
ISBN: 0-534-34099-7

Cournoyer, Barry
The Social Work Skills Workbook, Second Edition
ISBN: 0-534-33875-5

Doweiko, Harold
Concepts of Chemical Dependency, Third Edition
ISBN: 0-534-33904-2

Gilliland, Burl, and James, Richard K.
Crisis Intervention Strategies, Third Edition
ISBN: 0-534-34568-9

Homan, Mark S.
***Promoting Community Change: Making It Happen in
the Real World***
ISBN: 0-534-14250-8

Hutchins, David E., and Cole, Clair G.
Helping Relationships and Strategies, Third Edition
ISBN: 0-534-34526-3

Kaiser, Tamara L.
Supervisory Relationships: Exploring the Human Element
ISBN: 0-534-34559-X

Lauver, Philip, and Harvey, David R.
The Practical Counselor: Elements of Effective Helping
ISBN: 0-534-34349-X

Long, Vonda
***Communication Skills in Helping Relationships:
A Framework for Facilitating Personal Growth***
ISBN: 0-534-33869-0

Long, Vonda
***Facilitating Personal Growth in Self and Others
(Workbook)***
ISBN: 0-534-33870-4

Lum, Doman
***Social Work Practice and People of Color:
A Process-Stage Approach, Third Edition***
ISBN: 0-534-33854-2

Okun, Barbara F.
***Effective Helping: Interviewing and Counseling Techniques,
Fifth Edition***
ISBN: 0-534-34173-X

Reid, Kenneth E.
***Social Work Practice with Groups: A Clinical Perspective,
Second Edition***
ISBN: 0-534-34548-4

Rivas, Robert F., and Hull, Grafton H.
Case Studies in Generalist Practice
ISBN: 0-534-20232-2

Sue, Derald Wing; Ivey, Allen E.; and Pedersen, Paul B.
Theory of Multicultural Counseling and Therapy
ISBN: 0-534-34037-7

Tice, Carolyn, and Perkins, Kathleen
***Mental Health Issues and Aging: Building on the Strengths
of Older Persons***
ISBN: 0-534-20754-5

Wehrly, Bea
***Pathways to Multicultural Counseling Competence:
A Developmental Journey***
ISBN: 0-534-33849-6

Westra, Matthew
Active Communication
ISBN: 0-534-34007-5

Direct Social Work Practice

Theory and Skills

Fifth Edition

Dean H. Hepworth
Professor Emeritus, University of Utah
and Arizona State University

Ronald H. Rooney
University of Minnesota

Jo Ann Larsen
Private Practice
Salt Lake City

Brooks/Cole Publishing Company

I(T)P® An International Thomson Publishing Company

Pacific Grove • Albany • Belmont • Bonn • Boston • Cincinnati • Detroit • Johannesburg
London • Madrid • Melbourne • Mexico City • New York • Paris • Singapore
Tokyo • Toronto • Washington

Sponsoring Editor: *Lisa Gebo*
Marketing Team: *Jean Thompson and Christine Davis*
Editorial Associate: *Terry Thomas*
Production Coordinator: *Fiorella Ljunggren*
Production: *HRS Electronic Text Management*
Manuscript Editor: *Suzanne Ingrao*

Interior Design: *HRS Electronic Text Management*
Cover Design: *Roy R. Neuhaus*
Interior Illustration: *HRS Electronic Text Management*
Indexer: *James Minkin*
Typesetting: *HRS Electronic Text Management*
Printing and Binding: *Quebecor Printing, Fairfield*

For more information, contact:

BROOKS/COLE PUBLISHING COMPANY
511 Forest Lodge Road
Pacific Grove, CA 93950
USA

International Thomson Publishing Europe
Berkshire House 168–173
High Holborn
London WC1V 7AA
England

Thomas Nelson Australia
102 Dodds Street
South Melbourne, 3205
Victoria, Australia

Nelson Canada
1120 Birchmount Road
Scarborough, Ontario
Canada M1K 5G4

International Thomson Editores
Seneca 53
Col. Polanco
11560 México, D. F., México

International Thomson Publishing GmbH
Königswinterer Strasse 418
53227 Bonn
Germany

International Thomson Publishing Asia
221 Henderson Road
#05–10 Henderson Building
Singapore 0315

International Thomson Publishing Japan
Hirakawacho Kyowa Building, 3F
2-2-1 Hirakawacho
Chiyoda-ku, Tokyo 102
Japan

Printed in the United States of America.
10   9   8   7   6   5

Library of Congress Cataloging-in-Publication Data

Hepworth, Dean, H.
    Direct social work practice : theory and skills/Dean H.
Hepworth, Ronald H. Rooney, Jo Ann Larsen. — 5th ed.
        p.   cm.
    Includes biographical references and index.
    ISBN 0-534-25104-8
    1. Social service   I. Rooney, Ronald H., [date].   II. Larsen, Jo Ann.
HV40 . H53   1997   96-34253
361.3'2—dc20   CIP

Brief Contents

Contents

Chapter 14
Enhancing Clients' Problem Solving, Social Skills, Assertiveness, and Stress Management 405

CHAPTER 19
MANAGING INDIVIDUAL, FAMILY, AND ORGANIZATIONAL BARRIERS TO CHANGE 556

Preface

As this fifth edition is being published, we social workers and our constituencies face pressing challenges. To face those challenges, we draw on a *cherished tradition* of commitment to social justice, maximum feasible self-determination, and the affirmation that all people are worthy of dignity and respect and are entitled to resources. This cherished tradition is now evolving into a vision of a *desired future* that includes expanded commitment to the enhancement of client strengths and empowerment. Empowerment as a goal builds on our commitment to self-determination by helping our clients realize self-defined goals through the acquisition of skills and resources (Hartman, 1993).

In between this cherished tradition and this vision of a desired future is a *troubled present* that is often antithetical to both. Specifically, our troubled present often includes an emphasis on cost containment and the "management" of care in which practice decisions are no longer the exclusive domain of client and practitioner. This managed care environment resurrects the medical model (Strom, 1992) at the very time we have incorporated strengths and empowerment into our vision.

Also, we can no longer assume that the majority of those who come into contact with a social worker are applying voluntarily for a service. In fact, the majority of our potential clients are referred by others or are under legal pressure to seek contact. Such potential clients do not ask "Who am I? Where am I going? Why am I here?" as does the applicant. Involuntary clients more frequently ask "Who are you? Why are you here? When will you leave?" (Rooney, 1992).

Finally, a change in the national political environment has meant that efforts to balance the budget entail major hardships to many of social work's traditional constituencies. Too often political leaders use terms such as *empowerment* to mean reducing dependency on welfare without assuring adequate supports for child care, job training, and placement (Simon, 1994). We find that social work's commitment to social justice and distribution of resources clashes directly with efforts to cut welfare and roll back affirmative action. In the ambivalence toward lower socioeconomic groups in our society, we find that our traditional clienteles are often perceived as a drain on scarce national resources rather than as a source of underdeveloped, untapped resources.

We could deal with the challenges of the troubled present in many different ways—for example, by choosing to ignore them. Too often we social work faculty and textbook writers choose to preach to students "This is what you *should* do, if only supervisors in the misguided, short-sighted practice settings would allow you." We could also ignore the present by relying too much on our trusty counseling skills in dealing with dislocation of power and resources. It is insufficient to focus on client feelings about loss of resources—"How do you feel about having your welfare benefits ended?"—without in fact acting to assist clients in the recovery of resources. Or we could cling to our cherished tradition and our vision of a desired future alone—a decision that would hardly solve the problems we are dealing with.

In our book, we choose to meet these challenges by encouraging students, practitioners and instructors to rely on our tradition and vision, supported by practical guidelines drawn from research and practice wisdom. We ask ourselves how we can act with clients and consumers to facilitate empowerment, to gain resources for clients, and to mobilize strengths in a manner that is true to both our heritage and our future. We have tried to achieve a balance between social work theory and the practice skills that translate theory into action. Our original motivation to write a textbook was to respond to students' persistent pleas for learning experiences that would help them cope with the concrete challenges encountered in direct work with various clients. In addition to presenting theory, then, we have continued to delineate many basic skills essential to effective practice and have included relevant skill development exercises and modeled responses, many adapted from actual practice situations we have encountered during our combined 80 years of direct social work practice.

We are joined in this edition by Ron Rooney, a professor at the University of Minnesota with extensive experience in public and private direct practice settings and expertise in work with involuntary clients. Before undertaking the revision of the book, we received many suggestions from reviewers of the previous edition. We incorporated many of their suggestions and express our gratitude to them for their thoughtful recommendations.

Structural Changes

We have eliminated what was Chapter 12 in the fourth edition on work with involuntary clients and infused content from that chapter throughout the book. Consequently, Chapter 13 in the previous edition becomes Chapter 12 in this fifth edition, and so on. Content on role socialization has been moved from Chapter 12 to Chapter 5 to provide a context for the discussion on the use of communication skills. The chapters on work with families and groups (Chapters 11 and 17) have been expanded to include task groups and involuntary groups, and examples in Chapters 10 and 16 now draw on work with families in settings such as health care and work with the elderly.

Changes in Content

Work with Referred and Legally Mandated Clients
Rather than assume that the majority of potential clients are applicants for service, this edition integrates throughout the topic of legally mandated and referred clients with materials about voluntary clients. In Chapter 4, barriers to client acceptance are examined anew from normalizing perspectives drawn from strategic self-presentation theory and reactance theory, which are helpful in reframing manipulation, helplessness, and noncompliance. In addition, Chapter 5 now sets the stage for exploring communications skills by discussing role socialization, including an example of how to introduce contact with a legally mandated client. Chapter 7 now includes examples of problem identification with applicants, referrals, and legally mandated clients. In Chapter 12, the topic of contracting has been expanded to include both voluntary and involuntary clients. In addition, content on confrontation now includes a broader continuum of interventions and is adapted to involuntary circumstances in Chapter 18. Resistance is reframed as opposition to change in Chapter 19, with useful perspectives from reactance theory. Finally, Chapter 20 now includes adaptations of the termination process to involuntary clients.

Varied Case Examples and Settings   Social work students and practitioners operate in a variety of settings that include those for which providing therapy is the primary function. Reflecting managed care realities, a case study in Chapter 2 and an ethical dilemma vignette in Chapter 4 now illustrate the involvement of third parties in decisions such as payment for inpatient hospitalizations. The communications skills described in Chapters 5 and 6 are also useful in settings such as work with the elderly, discharge planning, hospital social work, and chemical dependency situations, among others. To reflect applications to these settings, Chapter 5 now includes an elderly-client example and a domestic-violence example; Chapter 6 includes

elderly-client examples, health-care examples, and a teenaged-mother and child welfare example. A major case study from a health-care setting is now used to describe the utility of family assessment methods in Chapter 10. Similarly, Chapter 11 broadens the scope from therapeutic groups to other social work groups including involuntary and task groups. Chapter 17 also includes expanded content on work with task groups.

Greater Focus on Client Strengths and Empowerment To reflect our greater emphasis on a strengths perspective, Chapter 1 begins with a case study that introduces a dual focus on problems or concerns and on strengths and resources. Chapters 1 and 4 include new material from the Council on Social Work Education Accreditation Guidelines and from the proposed revision of the National Association of Social Work Code of Ethics. Social work students have sometimes had difficulties in focusing their assessments and integrating a strengths-oriented assessment process. To help them, Chapter 8 now introduces assessment in an agency context and presents priorities in assessment. Also, the chapter places greater emphasis on identifying strengths in assessments and includes an example emphasizing strengths.

Theoretical Orientation

In this text, we address human problems from an ecological systems framework. Thus, a major feature of the book is the inclusion of material germane to various systems and subsystems typically implicated in problems encountered by social workers. They include individuals, couples, families, groups, and various environmental systems.

To equip students with a broad range of skills, we present a systematic-eclective (pluralistic) perspective of practice. Both demanding and rigorous, this perspective enables practitioners to choose from various theories, practice models, and interventions those that best match the unique needs of each client. To the extent possible, we have included models, interventions, and techniques that are empirically grounded. Moreover, we have included interventions and techniques applicable to modifying environments, improving interpersonal relationships, and enhancing individuals' biophysical, cognitive, emotional, and behavioral functioning. The text thus has a truly multidimensional approach to both assessment and interventions.

Organization of the Book

This edition of the book retains its basic structure, consisting of four parts. The first part introduces the reader to the profession and to direct practice and provides an overview of the helping process. Part 1 concludes with Chapter 4, which is concerned with the cardinal values of social work and how they are operationalized in practice.

Part 2, which is devoted to the beginning phase of the helping process, opens with a chapter that focuses on relationship-building skills in the context of socialization to roles. Chapter 6 shifts the focus to theory and skills entailed in eliciting vital information from clients, exploring problems in depth and providing direction, focus, and continuity to sessions. Chapter 7 deals with barriers to communication, and Chapters 8–12 are concerned with assessing problems and strengths of individuals, families, and groups; forming groups; enhancing motivation; and formulating goals and negotiating contracts.

Part 3 is devoted to the middle phase (goal attainment) of the helping process. It begins with Chapter 13, which is concerned with planning and implementing change-oriented strategies, including the task-centered approach, crisis intervention, and cognitive restructuring. Chapter 14 delineates numerous interventions and skills, including teaching independent problem-solving skills, social skills, assertiveness, and stress management. In Chapter 15, the focus shifts to modifying environments, developing resources, empowering clients, serving as case managers, employing advocacy, and engaging in social planning. Chapter 16 deals at length with methods of enhancing family relationships. The focus of Chapter 17 is on theory and skills entailed in work with social work groups. Chapter 18 is concerned with the implementation of additive empathy, interpretation, confrontation, and related interventions. Part 3 concludes with Chapter 19, which discusses manifestations and methods of dealing with relational reactions and other obstacles to change, methods of coping with opposition to change, and strategies for dealing with them in the context of individuals, families, and organizations.

Part 4 consists of Chapter 20, which deals with the terminal phase of the helping process. This chapter covers five different types of termination, as well as the valuation of the outcomes, the consolidation and maintenance of gains, and the prevention of relapse.

Acknowlegments

We would like to thank the following colleagues for their help in providing useful comments and suggestions. From the University of Minnesota: Constance Fabumni, Michael Graham, Linda Jones, Megan Morrissey, Maura Sullivan, and Kimberly Strom-Gottfried from Augsburg College; Tony Bibus and Rosemary Link. We also wish to thank Elena Izaksonas for her careful searches of the literature that undergirded much of the updated material.

We are very grateful to the reviewers of this edition, whose constructive criticisms and suggestions have been extremely helpful. They are Bonnie Belcastro of Edinboro University, C. Penny Bilofsky of Rutgers University, Carolyn Carter of Arizona State University, Carolyn Dillon of Boston University, Jean R. Frank of St. Edward's University, Bruce D. Friedman of Wayne State University, Eunice C. Garcia of the University of Texas at Austin, JoDee Keller of Pacific Lutheran University, Eva Kopacz of the University of Alaska–Anchorage, Irene Luckey of Rutgers University, James I. Martin of the University of Texas at Arlington, Mary Ruffolo of Syracuse University, and Joseph Walsh of Virginia Commonwealth University.

Finally, this edition could not have been developed without the support, challenge, and inspiration provided by Glenda Dewberry Rooney of Augsburg College and by Glenda and Ron's son, Chris.

Dean H. Hepworth
Ronald H. Rooney
Jo Ann Larsen

A postscript to Dean and Jo Ann:
Many thanks for the opportunity to join your team and continue the cherished tradition of this book toward our desired future through our troubled present.

R.H.R.

Part 1

Introduction

Chapter 1 ▢ ▢ ▢

The Challenges of Social Work

Chapter 1 introduces the mission of social work and the purposes of social work services, illustrates the roles played by social workers within the organizational context for such services, and identifies the value perspectives that guide social workers. These topics are introduced and exemplified through the following case example.

....

Case Example

Jane Percy, 39, the single-parent mother of Jerald, 13, telephoned The Arch, a social service agency that works with runaway and homeless youth as well as "throwaways" (children banished from the home). The Arch provides some brief placements of children with the goal of reuniting children with their families as soon as possible. Agency services usually include time-limited, in-home counseling in which resources and problems are identified and follow-up services after reunification are developed.

Ms. Percy told the intake worker that she was very upset and needed help with Jerald, who was getting into trouble. Most recently Jerald had been throwing rocks from an overpass onto cars on the expressway near the housing project in which they lived. Ms. Percy had attempted to keep Jerald at home after school and out of trouble, but he had stayed away from the home for several nights in the past month, though he was currently at home. Jerald is biracial, with an African American father, whom he does not see, and a Caucasian mother. The housing development included a higher percentage of African American families than the surrounding communities. Ms. Percy was dating a Caucasian man who made comments about Jerald she described as racist . She reported that they felt like excluded minorities and that Jerald had been hanging out with a group of African American boys at school.

During the intake worker's initial assessment, she found that Ms. Percy's apartment in the housing development offered the benefit of low rent, but public transportation was infrequent and inconvenient for getting to shopping centers and for buying groceries. Frequent bus services were available for commuters to and from the central city, but few routes were available within Ms. Percy's community. Consequently, she rode a bicycle to work and took cabs for groceries.

....

Social workers advocate for poor, disadvantaged, disenfranchised, and oppressed peoples (Barber, 1995). Hence, social workers are likely to work with many persons such as Jane Percy and her neighbors. Social work's domain has steadily expanded, and social workers serve in such diverse settings as governmental agencies, schools, health care centers, family and child welfare agencies, mental health centers, business and industry, correctional settings, and private practice. Social workers work with people of all ages, races, ethnic groups, socioeconomic levels, religions, sexual orientations, and abilities (see Table 1-1).

Social workers themselves variously describe their work as rewarding, frustrating, satisfying, discouraging, stressful, and most of all, challenging.[1] Consider, for example, the difficulties suggested by Jane Percy's example. You might take a couple of minutes to list the potential problems and concerns raised in her case. List also the possible strengths and resources that could be explored.

PROBLEMS AND CONCERNS; POTENTIAL STRENGTHS AND RESOURCES

Ms. Percy is asking for help in reducing her stress, guidance in parenting her son Jerald, including dealing with his absenting from the home. During the intake worker's initial assessment, several additional potential issues have emerged that may or may not be Ms. Percy's concerns or require action. For example, Ms. Percy and her neighbors lack adequate transportation for shopping; she may be interested in a group for biracial children or single parents or parents of biracial children; there may be a lack of recreation opportunities or access to them; and Ms. Percy's male friend seems to have a racist attitude toward Jerald. Social work assessments frequently include (1) exploration of multiple concerns expressed by potential clients, (2) circumstances that might involve legally mandated intervention, and (3) other potential problems that emerge from the assessment. Such assessments also include strengths and potential resources. The fact that Ms. Percy was employed,

---

TABLE 1-1 GROUPS OF PEOPLE SERVED BY SOCIAL WORKERS

- Persons who are homeless.

- Families that have problems of child neglect or sexual, physical, or spousal abuse.

- Couples that have serious marital conflicts.

- Families including single-parent families that have serious conflicts manifested by runaways, delinquency, or violence.

- People afflicted with AIDS and their families.

- Individuals and families whose lives have been disrupted by punishment for violations of the law.

- Unwed, pregnant teenagers.

- Persons who are gay, lesbian, or bisexual who face personal or family difficulties.

- Individuals or families whose lives are disrupted by physical or mental illness or disability.

- Persons who abuse drugs or alcohol and their families.

- Foster parents and children whose parents are deceased or who have been unable to safely care for them.

- Immigrants and minority persons who lack essential resources.

- Persons with severe physical, developmental, or physical disabilities and their families.

- Aging persons no longer able to care for themselves adequately.

- Persons who are migrants and transients who lack essential resources.

- Children (and their families) who have school-related difficulties.

- Persons who experience high stresses related to traumatic events or to major life transitions such as retirement, death of loved ones, children who leave home, or coming out for gay, lesbian, and bisexual persons.

coping with the many stresses of single parent-hood, and seeking help were considered potential strengths.

The Mission of Social Work

The perspectives taken by social workers in their professional roles will influence how Ms. Percy's concerns are conceptualized and addressed. According to the National Association of Social Workers (NASW), "the primary mission of the social work profession is to enhance human well-being and help meet basic human needs, with particular attention to the needs of vulnerable, oppressed, and poor people"(NASW, 1994). Similarly, the Council on Social Work Education (CSWE), the organization which accredits undergraduate and masters degree social work programs, describes the social work profession as "committed to the enhancement of human well-being and to the alleviation of poverty and oppression" (CSWE, 1994). These statements place social work as a helping profession (to enhance human well-being), but do so with a special focus on the alleviation of poverty, oppression, and service to vulnerable people.

We shall delineate core elements that lie at the heart of social work wherever it is practiced. These core elements can be subsumed under the following four dimensions:

1. The purposes of the profession.
2. Values and ethics.
3. Knowledge base of direct practice.
4. Methods and processes employed.

In this chapter, we consider each of the first three dimensions. The fourth dimension is discussed in Chapter 3 in order to draw the big picture of the helping process and to set the stage for the remainder of the book.

Purposes of Social Work

Social work practitioners serve clients toward specific objectives while the means of accomplishing them vary according to the unique circumstances of each problematic situation. The activities of all practitioners share common goals that constitute the purpose and objectives of the profession. These goals unify the profession and assist members in avoiding the development of perspectives limited to particular practice settings. To accomplish the purpose of the profession, practitioners must be willing to assume responsibilities and engage in actions that go beyond the functions of specific social agencies and their designated individual roles as staff members. For example, staff at the Arch may assist Ms. Percy with problems such as transportation and recreation programs for Jerald which are not directly related to the agency's function of providing counseling and brief, out-of-home care.

CSWE describes the social work profession as receiving its sanction from public and private auspices, as the primary profession in the provision of social services, and **as practiced in a wide range of settings** (CSWE, 1994, p. 135). CSWE describes social work as having four purposes.

1. "The promotion, restoration, maintenance, and enhancement of the social functioning of individuals, families, groups, organizations and communities by helping them to accomplish tasks, prevent and alleviate distress, and use resources"(ibid., p. 135). This purpose suggests that Ms. Percy and Jerald might be assisted in restoring and maintaining their relationship including nurturing and discipline, guidance, and protection. Also, she can help him navigate the development of his identity, friendships, school, and growing up without hurting himself or others. They might be helped to accomplish such tasks and alleviate their distress through providing

access to resources both within the agency and without. As social workers work with multiple-client systems, the client system may evolve from Ms. Percy as client to including the family unit with Jerald as client, to work with either or both through groups, and to work with the community around expressed needs.

Social workers perform preventive, restorative, and remedial functions in pursuit of this purpose. *Prevention* involves the timely provision of services to vulnerable persons, promoting social functioning before problems develop and includes programs and activities such as family planning, well-baby clinics, parent education, premarital and preretirement counseling, and marital enrichment programs. For example, Ms. Percy might be linked to ongoing support groups for single parents, parents of biracial children, a Big Brothers program or peer group for Jerald. *Restoration* is aimed at assisting clients in the restoration of functioning that has been impaired by physical or mental difficulties. Included in this group of clients are those with varying degrees of paralysis caused by severe spinal injury, people afflicted with severe mental illness, persons with developmental disabilities, persons with deficient educational backgrounds, and people with many other types of disability. *Remediation* entails the elimination or amelioration of existing social problems. Clients in need of remedial services form the largest group served by social workers and include all of the groups listed on Table 1-1 as well as many others. Many of the potential clients in this category are not persons like Ms. Percy who have applied for a service, but rather persons referred by others such as family members, neighbors, and doctors who have perceived a need, and others who are legally mandated to receive services (Rooney, 1992).

Enhancing social functioning involves addressing common human needs that must be adequately met to enable individuals to achieve a reasonable degree of fulfillment and to function as productive and contributing members of society. Essential resources and opportunities must be available to meet human needs, and social workers are vitally involved in resource utilization and development. Rosenfeld (1983) defines the domain of social work practice as constituted by incongruities or discrepancies between needs and resources that various systems and social institutions have not dealt with adequately.[2] Social workers aim "to match resources with needs to increase the 'goodness of fit' between them, largely by harnessing potential provider systems to perform this function" (p. 187). Tapping resources essential to meeting human needs generally involves enhancing transactions between people and their social or physical environments. To further clarify the transactions between individual needs and environmental resources, social workers consider certain basic needs and the loci of resources that correspond to those needs. These interactions are graphically demonstrated in Table 1-2, showing that human beings are extremely dependent on the environment for the fulfillment of basic needs. Social work practice thus is directed to the interface between people and their environments.

Problems at the interface between people and these environments are not exclusively caused by environmental deficiencies. Many clients whom practitioners serve have difficulties that impair their ability to utilize available resources. For example, recreation and socialization programs may be available for Ms. Percy and Jerald, but they may lack knowledge of these resources or how to gain access to them. Practitioners, therefore, often must focus their efforts on helping clients to gain interpersonal skills to reduce the mismatch between their clients' needs and environmental resources (see Table 1-2).

2. "The planning, formulation and implementation of social policies, services, resources, and programs needed to meet basic human needs and support the development of human capacities" (CSWE, 1995, p.135). This purpose suggests that

TABLE 1-2 HUMAN NEEDS AND RELATED LOCI OF RESOURCES

HUMAN NEEDS	LOCI OF RESOURCES
Positive self-concept: Identity Self-esteem Self-confidence	Nurturance, acceptance, love and positive feedback provided by significant others (parents, relatives, teachers, peer group)
Emotional: Feeling needed and valued by others Companionship Sense of belonging	Parents, marital partner, friends, siblings, cultural reference groups, social networks
Personal fulfillment: Education Recreation Accomplishment Aesthetic satisfaction Religion	Educational, recreational, religious, employment, and other social institutions
Physical needs: Food, clothing, housing Health care Safety Protection	Economic, legal, and health care institutions; formal social welfare systems, law enforcement, and disaster relief organizations

while some social workers provide direct services to clients such as Ms. Percy and Jerald, others act indirectly to influence the environments supporting the client, developing and maintaining the social infrastructure that assist clients in meeting their needs.

3. "The pursuit of policies, services, resources, and programs through organizational or administrative advocacy and social or political action, to empower groups at risk and to promote social and economic justice." This purpose is also reflected in the second value in the draft of the revised social work Code of Ethics: "Social workers challenge social injustice" (NASW, 1995, p. 5). This value points social workers to the pursuit of social change on behalf of vulnerable or oppressed people on the basis of poverty, discrimination, and other forms of injustice. The focus of efforts on populations at risk should increase the power of such persons to influence their own lives.

The curriculum policy statement of CSWE also requires that social work education programs "provide an understanding of the dynamics and consequences of social and economic justice, including all forms of human oppression and discrimination...[and include] strategies of intervention for achieving social and economic justice and for combating the causes and effects of institutionalized forms of oppression" (CSWE, 1994, p. 140). If resources and opportunities are to be available to all members of society, laws, governmental policies, and social programs must assure equal access of citizens to resources and opportunities. Social workers promote social justice by advocating for clients who have been denied services, resources, or goods to which they are entitled. Social workers also actively engage in efforts to combat racism, sexism, and other forms of discrimination that block equal access of clients to resources to which they are entitled. For example, racism and lack of political and economic power may be one of the reasons why Ms. Percy and her neighbors do not have adequate access to transportation.

The preceding purpose focuses social work efforts also on populations at risk. Social work educational programs "must present theoretical and practice content about patterns, dynamics, and consequences of discrimination, economic deprivation, and oppression. The curriculum must provide content about people of color, women, and gay and lesbian persons. Such content must emphasize the impact of discrimination, economic deprivation and oppression on these groups. Each program must include content about populations at risk that are particularly relevant to its mission. In addition to those mandated above, such groups include but are not limited to those distinguished by age, ethnicity, culture, class, religion, and physical or mental ability "(CSWE, 1994, p. 140).

In promoting social and economic justice with populations at risk, social workers in direct practice also join with other social workers and groups in promoting social action and legislation that remedy and redress wrongs resulting from unfair decisions and dysfunctional policies and practices. Moreover, they advocate for programs and resources to increase opportunities and enhance the welfare of disadvantaged people; they advocate especially for groups of people who are unable to effectively advocate for themselves, such as persons with developmental disabilities or severe mental illness. For example, the social workers at the Arch joined with other local groups in advocating for more accessible services for the residents of Ms. Percy's neighborhood.

The objective of promoting social and economic justice merits a renewed commitment by social workers in view of more conservative trends in the political climate that have occurred over the past two decades (Specht & Courtney, 1994). According to Walz and Groze (1991), this trend has partially deflected the focus of social work away from the needs and concerns of poor and disadvantaged people. Waltz and Groze have urged that the profession adopt a "clinical activist model" of practice that emphasizes the role of social workers as advocates "on behalf of those exploited or harmed by today's social system" (p. 503).

4. "The development and testing of professional knowledge and skills related to these purposes." The social work profession engages in ongoing efforts to expand the knowledge base to assist clients such as Ms. Percy and Jerald and others so as to provide services which are efficient, ethical, and effective. This purpose is also reflected in the sixth value in the proposed revision of the NASW Code of Ethics: "Social workers practice within their areas of competence and develop and enhance their professional expertise" (NASW, 1995). This value commits individual social work practitioners to continual efforts to increase their professional knowledge and skills and "aspire to contribute to the knowledge base of the profession."

SOCIAL WORK VALUES

All professions have value preferences that give purpose and direction to people who practice within them. Indeed, the purpose and objectives of social work and other professions emanate from their respective value systems. Professional values, however, are not separate from societal values; rather, professions espouse selected societal values, and society in turn gives sanction to professions through supportive legislation, funding, delegation of responsibility for certain societal functions, and mechanisms for ensuring that those functions are adequately discharged. Because a profession is linked to certain societal values, it tends to serve as society's conscience with respect to those particular values.

Values represent strongly held beliefs about how the world should be, how people should normally behave, and about preferred conditions of life. Broad societal values in the United States are reflected in the Declaration of Independence, the Constitution, and the laws of the land, which declare and ensure certain rights of the people. Societal values are also reflected in governmental entities and programs designed to safeguard the rights of people and to promote the common good. Interpretations of values and rights, however, are not always uniform, as reflected, for example, in heated national controversies over the right to bear arms, the right of women to have abortions, efforts to secure universal health coverage, and attempts to link work with welfare (Ewalt, 1994).

The values of the profession of social work similarly refer to strongly held beliefs about the rights of people to free choice and opportunity. They also refer to the preferred conditions of life that enhance people's welfare, how members of the profession should view and treat people, about preferred goals for people, and how those goals should be reached. In the following sections, we consider the five values and purposes which guide social work education. The values are italicized and the content that follows each is our commentary.

1. *Social workers' professional relationships are built on regard for individual worth and dignity, and are advanced by mutual participation, acceptance, confidentiality, honesty, and responsible handling of conflict* (CSWE, 1994, p. 139). This value is also reflected in several parts of the Proposed Revision of the Social Work Code of Ethics. The first value of that revision states that " Social workers' primary goal is to serve" (NASW, 1995, p. 5). This means that service to others is elevated above self-interest and that social workers use their knowledge, values, and skills to help people in need and to address social problems. The second value states that they serve others in a fashion such that "social workers respect the inherent dignity and worth of the person." Every person is unique and has inherent worth; therefore, social worker interactions with people as they pursue and utilize resources should enhance their dignity and individuality, enlarge their competence, and increase their problem-solving and coping abilities. People who employ social work services are often overwhelmed by their difficulties and have exhausted their coping resources. Many, such as Jane Percy, come to services feeling stressed by a multitude of problems. In addition to attempting to help clients such as Ms. Percy reduce her stress, practitioners provide service to clients in a variety of ways: assist them to view their difficulties from a fresh perspective, consider various remedial alternatives, foster awareness of strengths and mobilize both active and latent coping resources, enhance self-awareness, and teach problem-solving strategies and interpersonal skills.

Social workers perform these functions while recognizing "...the central importance of human relationships"(NASW, 1995, p. 5) This principle suggests that social workers engage people as partners in purposeful efforts to promote, restore, maintain, and enhance client well-being.

Finally, this value is also reflected in the Revised Code of Ethics principle that "...social workers behave in a trustworthy manner"(ibid., p. 6). This principle suggests that social workers practice consistent with the profession's mission, values, ethical standards and promote ethical practices in the organizations with which they are affiliated (ibid., 1995, p. 6).

2. *Social workers respect the individual's right to make independent decisions and to participate actively in the helping process* (ibid., p. 139). People have a right to freedom insofar as they do not infringe on the rights of others; therefore, transactions with people in the course of seeking and utilizing resources should enhance their independence and self-determination. Too often in the past, social workers and other helping professionals have focused on " deficit, disease and dysfunction" (Cowger, 1994). The current emphasis on empowerment and strengths leads us to attempt to assist clients in increasing their personal potential and political power such that clients can improve their life situation (Gutierrez, 1990). Consistent with this value, we present in this book an empowerment and strength-oriented perspective to working with clients. We have further devoted Chapter 14 to a modality that enhances clients' problem-solving capacities and have included in this and other chapters content that delineates ways of assisting clients to expand their interpersonal and other coping skills.

3. *Social workers are committed to assisting client systems to obtain needed resources.* People should have access to the resources they need to meet life's challenges and difficulties as well as access to opportunities to realize their potentialities throughout their lives. Our commitment to client

self-determination and empowerment is hollow if clients lack access to the resources necessary to achieve their goals (Hartman, 1993). People often have little knowledge about various available resource systems needed to reach their goals, so practitioners often perform the role of broker in referring people to resource systems such as public legal services, health care agencies, child welfare divisions, mental health centers, centers for elderly persons, and family counseling agencies. In some instances, individual clients or families may require goods and services from many different providers, and may lack the language facility, physical or mental capacity, experience, or skill in availing themselves of essential goods and services. Practitioners then may assume the role of case manager, which involves not only providing direct services but also assuming responsibility for linking the client to diverse resources and ensuring that the client receives needed services in a timely fashion. Both the broker and case manager roles are discussed in the next Chapter and in Chapter 15. The Arch assisted Jane Percy by providing her information about their own counseling and support programs for herself and Jerald, as well as those provided by other agencies.

Clients sometimes need resource systems that are not available, and in these cases, practitioners must carry out the role of program developer by assisting in creating and organizing new resource systems. Examples of such efforts include the following: working with citizens and public officials to arrange transportation to health care agencies for the elderly, persons with disabilities, and indigent people; developing neighborhood organizations to campaign for better educational and recreational programs; organizing tenants to assert rights to landlords and housing authorities for improved housing and sanitation; and organizing support groups, skill development groups, and self-help groups to assist people in coping with difficult problems of living. In the Percy's case, a supervisor at the Arch became part of a task force which advocated for increased bus services to support the many persons in the housing project who did not have cars.

Social workers also frequently pursue this goal by facilitating access to resources. Social workers perform the role of facilitator or enabler in carrying out the following functions: enhancing communication among family members; coordinating efforts of teachers, school counselors, and social workers in assisting troubled students; assisting groups to provide maximal support to members; opening channels of communication between co-workers; including patients or inmates in the governance of institutions; facilitating teamwork among members of different disciplines in hospitals and mental health centers; and providing for consumer input into agency policy-making boards. Later chapters deal specifically with content intended to assist students and practitioners in accomplishing this objective. The Arch specifically attempted to assist Ms. Percy and Jerald in improving their relationship. In assisting her with providing male role models for Jerald, they helped her make contact with Jerald's father and family. In addition, they helped Ms. Percy consider the implications of her own and her male friend's attitudes toward people of color on Jerald's developing identity as a multiracial person considered African American by others.

4. *Social workers strive to make social institutions more humane and responsive to human needs.* Although direct practitioners work primarily in providing direct service, they also have a responsibility to work toward improving the quality of life by promoting policies and legislation that enhance physical and social environments. Problems of individuals, families, groups, and neighborhoods can often be prevented or ameliorated by laws and policies that prohibit contamination of the physical environment and that promote enrichment of both physical and social environments. Therefore, direct social workers should not limit themselves

to remedial activities but should also seek to discover environmental causes of problems and to sponsor or support efforts aimed at enhancing the environments of people. We discuss this topic at greater length in Chapters 15 and 19.

Social workers also enact this value when they assume the role of expediter or troubleshooter by scrutinizing the policies and procedures of their own and other organizations to determine if clients have ready access to resources and if services are delivered in ways that enhance the dignity of clients. Complex application procedures, needless delays in providing resources and services, discriminatory policies, inaccessible agency sites, inconvenient service delivery hours, dehumanizing procedures or behaviors by staff—these and other factors may deter clients from utilizing resources or subject them to demeaning experiences. Systematically obtaining input from consumers is a method of monitoring an organization's responsiveness to clients. Advocacy actions with and on behalf of clients are sometimes required to secure services and resources to which clients are entitled. (See elaboration in Chapters 15 and 19). The Arch made a short-term decision in light of the transportation problems in the housing project to make an agency van available to assist clients in getting to appointments and shopping for groceries.

Practitioners additionally support this value through performing roles as coordinator, mediator, or disseminator of information. For example, as a case manager, a practitioner may coordinate medical, educational, mental health, and rehabilitative services provided a given family by multiple resource systems. Mediational activities may be required to resolve conflicts between agencies, minority and majority groups, and neighborhood groups. Dissemination of information regarding legislation or the availability of new funding sources that potentially affect the relationships between public and private agencies may strengthen interactions between these resource systems.

Practitioners must also maintain liaison with key organizations to facilitate mutual awareness of changes in policies and procedures that affect ongoing relationships and the availability of resources.

5. *Social workers demonstrate respect for and acceptance of the unique characteristics of diverse populations.* This value acknowledges the fact that social workers perform their services with populations characterized by great diversity including"…groups distinguished by race, ethnicity, culture, class, gender, sexual orientation, religion, physical or mental ability, age, and national origin" (CSWE, 1994, p. 140). The value suggests that the social worker must be informed and respectful about differences. They must educate themselves over time as a part of lifelong learning since there can be no "how-to" manual that will guide the practitioner in understanding all aspects of diversity. The value suggests that the practitioner must continually update his or her knowledge about the strengths and resources associated with individuals from such groups to increase the sensitivity and effectiveness of services.

Values and Ethics

Realization of the above values should be the mutual responsibility of individual citizens and of society. Society should foster conditions and provide opportunities for citizens to participate in the policy determining processes of society. Citizens should fulfill their responsibilities to society by actively participating in those processes.

Considered individually, the preceding values and mission are not unique to social work. Their unique combination, however, differentiates social work from other professions. Considered in their entirety, these ingredients make it clear that social work's identity derives from its connection with the institution of social welfare, which, according to Gilbert (1977), represents a special helping mechanism devised to aid those who suffer from the variety of ills found in industrial society. "Whenever other major institutions, be they familial, religious, economic, or educational in nature, fall short in their helping and resource-providing functions, social welfare spans the gap" (p. 402).

These five values represent the ultimate values or prized ideals of the profession and, as such, are stated at high levels of abstraction. As Siporin (1975) and Levy (1973, 1979) have noted, however, there are different levels of professional values. At an intermediate level, values pertain to various segments of society, as for example, characteristics of a strong community. At a third level, values are more operational, referring to preferred behaviors. For example, the ideal social work practitioner is a warm, caring, open, and responsible person who safeguards the confidentiality of information disclosed by clients. Because you, the reader, have chosen social work, it is probable that most of your personal values coincide with the cardinal values espoused by the majority of social work practitioners. But at the intermediate and third levels of values, you may not always be in harmony with specific value positions taken by the majority of social workers. During the Vietnam War, the majority of social workers favored withdrawal from Vietnam, but support of that position by members of the profession was by no means unanimous. The same might be said of other controversial issues, such as the right to work, legalization of marijuana, tax-supported abortion, and capital punishment.

Self-determination refers to the right of people to exercise freedom of choice in making decisions. Issues such as the above may pose value dilemmas for individual practitioners because of conflicts between personal and professional values. In addition, conflicts between two professional values and/or principles are common. For example, when considered in relationship to the issue of legalized marijuana, the value of the right to self-determina-tion collides with the concept that it is good to promote the health and well-being of others.

Public positions taken by the profession that emanate from its values also sometimes stand in opposition to attitudes of a large segment of society. Consonant with its value that all people should have adequate economic resources to ensure a minimal standard of living, NASW, the National Association of Social Workers, has supported legislation for a guaranteed annual income for all citizens. Yet such legislation has not been supported by the majority of representatives in Congress. Similarly, professional support for universal health coverage has not been supported by the Congress (Webber, 1995).

With respect to diverse value preferences among social workers, we advocate the value that social workers should be sufficiently flexible to listen to many differing value positions on most moral and political issues. Different value positions do not necessarily reflect divergence among social workers on the five values delineated earlier. Rather, such differences reflect that there are many possible means of achieving given ends, and rigid assumptions about preferred means to an end often crumble when put to the test of hard experience. Consistent with our value preference for flexibility, we reaffirm our commitment to the value that social workers, whatever their beliefs, should assert them in the forum of professional organizations such as NASW (the National Association of Social Workers). We maintain further that social workers should accord colleagues who differ on certain value positions the same respect, dignity, and right to self-determination that would be accorded clients. Differences on issues may be frankly expressed. Those issues can be clarified and cohesiveness among professionals fostered by debate conducted in a climate of openness and mutual respect.

Conflicts between personal and/or professional values on the one hand and the personal values of a client or group on the other hand sometimes occur. Not infrequently, students (and even seasoned practitioners) experience conflict over value-laden, problematic situations such as incest, infidelity, rape, child neglect and/or abuse, spouse abuse, and criminal behavior. Because direct practitioners encounter these and other problems typically viewed by the public as appalling and because personal values inherently shape attitudes, perceptions, feelings, and responses to clients, it is vital that you be flexible and nonjudgmental in your work. It is equally vital that you be aware of your own values, how they fit with the profession's values, and the impact they may have on clients whose values differ from your own or whose behavior offends you.

Because values are critical determinants of behavior in interaction with clients and other professional persons, we have devoted Chapter 4 to practice situations involving potential value dilemmas, including exercises to assist you in expanding your awareness of your personal values. Chapter 4 also deals at length with the relationship-enhancing dimension of respect and contains exercises to assist you in responding respectfully to value-laden situations that are potentially painful for both you and your clients.

Social Work's Code of Ethics

An essential attribute of legitimate professions is a code of ethics consisting of principles that define expectations of its members. A code of ethics specifies rules of conduct to which members must adhere to remain in good standing within a professional organization. A code of ethics thus defines expected responsibilities and behaviors as well as proscribed behaviors. Central to the purposes of a code of ethics is its function as a formalized expression of accountability of (1) the profession to the society that gives it sanction, (2) constituent practitioners to consumers who utilize their services, and (3) practitioners to their profession. Consequent to its function in promoting

accountability, a code of ethics serves additional vital purposes, including the following:

1. Safeguards the reputation of a professional by providing explicit criteria that can be employed to regulate the behavior of members.
2. Furthers competent and responsible practice by its members.
3. Protects the public from exploitation by unscrupulous or incompetent practitioners.

Most states now have licensing boards which certify social workers for practice and review allegations of unethical conduct (Land, 1988). Similarly, local and state chapters of the National Association of Social Workers establish committees of inquiry to investigate alleged violations of the profession's Code of Ethics, and national committees provide consultation to local committees and consider appeals of decisions made by local chapters. We have blended the values in the draft of the revised code of ethics above in our presentation of the five values stated by CSWE.

KNOWLEDGE BASE OF SOCIAL WORK PRACTICE

One of the core elements of social work practice is its undergirding knowledge base. Although much of the knowledge base is borrowed from other disciplines in the social and behavioral sciences, that knowledge is assembled in unique ways. Moreover, many of the profession's basic concepts are unique to social work. The profession's universe of knowledge can be subsumed under the following five categories, which are regarded as core curriculum areas by the Council on Social Work Education (CSWE).

1. *Human behavior and the social environment.* Knowledge about "...human bio-psycho-social development, including theories about the range of social systems in which individuals live (families,

groups, organizations, and communities) (CSWE, 1994, pp. 139–140) is required to function effectively as a social worker. Such knowledge includes human growth and development with particular emphasis on the life tasks encountered by individuals during different developmental stages is essential to practitioners. To assess and to work with human problems, practitioners must be aware of needs and resources associated with each developmental phase. They must also become aware of how these needs are identified and met in different cultures. Knowledge of ecological systems theory, which we discuss later in this chapter, is also essential, as is knowledge about the forces that motivate behavior in groups and organizations. Because of its mission in enhancing the social functioning of people, social work is particularly concerned with the knowledge of factors that contribute to developmental difficulties. Knowledge of these factors, which commonly involve inadequate physical and emotional resources, is essential to planning and implementing effective preventive and remedial programs. Social work's focus on the person in a situation is reflected in the interactive way that this study includes content about "...the ways in which systems promote or deter people in the maintaining or achieving optimal health and well-being" (ibid., p. 141).

2. *Social welfare policy and services.* Content in this curriculum area "...must be presented about the political and organizational processes used to influence policy, the process of policy formulation, and the frameworks for analyzing social policies in light of principles of social and economic justice (CSWE, 1994, p. 141). The emphasis accorded by social work to the body of knowledge concerned with social policy most sharply differentiates social work curricula from those of related disciplines. This broad body of knowledge embodies the complex factors involved in the formulation of social policies that shape and guide planning of human service systems at all levels of government and in the private sector as well. To practice in full accordance with the mission and ethics of the profession, social workers have a responsibility to participate in the development of and to utilize social policies that enhance the social functioning of individuals, families, groups, and communities.

The study of social welfare policy and services must occur in the context of the profession's commitment to social and economic justice. Social work must address the consequences of oppressed conditions (Longres, 1991). Knowledge of inequities in the distribution in America of opportunities, resources, goods, and services, and the impact of these inequities on minority and disadvantaged groups are essential to social work practitioners (Brill, 1990).

3. *Social work practice methods.* "...emphasize mutuality, collaboration, and respect for the client system...content on practice assessment focuses on the examination of client strengths and problems in the interactions among individuals and between people and their environments...to enhance the well-being of people and to ameliorate the environmental conditions that affect people adversely...practice with clients from differing social, cultural, racial, religious, spiritual, and class backgrounds, and with systems of all sizes (CSWE, 1994, p. 141).

To accomplish the mission and objectives of the profession, practitioners need knowledge and practice skills that enable them to enhance the social functioning of clients. Knowledge of and skills in practice methods vary according to the level of client system served by practitioners. The levels have been designated as micro, mezzo, and macro. Effective practice requires knowledge related to all three levels of practice, but schools of social work commonly offer "concentrations" in either micro or macro practice and require less preparation in the other methods. Curricula of schools vary, of course, and some schools have "generalist" practice curricula, which require students to achieve balanced preparation in all three levels of practice.

Undergraduate programs and the first year of graduate programs have generalist practice curricula, which are aimed at preparing students for working with all levels of client systems. The practice methods that correspond to the three levels of practice are as follows:

- *Micro level practice.* At this level, the population served by practitioners includes various client systems, including individuals, couples, and families. Practice at this level is designated as direct (or clinical) practice because practitioners deliver services directly to clients in face-to-face contacts. Direct practice, however, is by no means limited to such face-to-face contacts as we discuss in Chapter 2.

- *Mezzo level practice* is defined as "...interpersonal relations that are less intimate than those associated with family life; more meaningful than among organizational and institutional representatives; [including] relationships between individuals in a self-help or therapy group, among peers at school or work or among neighbors." (Sheafor, Horejsi, & Horejsi, 1994, pp. 9–10). Mezzo events are "the interface where the individual and those most immediate and important to him/her meet" (Zastrow, & Kirst-Ashman, 1990, p. 11). Mezzo intervention hence is designed to change the systems that directly affect clients, such as the family, peer group, or classroom.

- *Macro level practice.* Still further removed from face-to-face delivery of services, macro practice involves the processes of social planning and community organization. On this level, social workers serve as professional change agents who assist community action systems composed of individuals, groups, or organizations to deal with social problems. Practitioners at this level may work with citizen groups or with private, public, or governmental organizations. Activities of practitioners at this level include the following: (1) Development of and work with community groups and organizations; (2) Program planning and development; (3) Implementation, administration and evaluation of programs (Meenaghan, 1987).

Administration entails assuming leadership in human service organizations directed to enabling the effective delivery of services in accordance with the values and laws of society. Definitions of administration vary, but according to Sarri (1987), "administration is the sum of all the processes involved in: 1. Formulation of policy and its translation into operative goals. 2. Program design and implementation. 3. Funding and resource allocation. 4. Management of internal and interorganizational operations. 5. Personnel direction and supervision. 6. Organizational representation and public relations. 7. Community education. 8. Monitoring, evaluation, and innovation to improve organizational productivity" (pp. 29–30).

Direct practitioners are necessarily involved to some degree in administrative activities, as we discuss in the next chapter. Further, many masters degree direct practitioners become supervisors or administrators later in their professional careers. Knowledge of administration, therefore, is vital to direct practitioners at the masters degree level, and courses in administration are frequently part of the required masters degree curriculum in social work.

Although many direct practitioners engage in little or no macro level practice, those who work in rural areas where practitioners are few and specialists in social planning are not available may work in concert with concerned citizens and community leaders in planning and developing resources to prevent or combat social problems.[3]

4. *Research.* "The research curriculum must provide an understanding and appreciation of a scientific, analytic approach to building knowledge for practice and to evaluating service delivery in all areas of practice" (CSWE, 1994, p. 108). Knowledge of research is indispensable to scientific and scholarly inquiry, which in turn is the driving force behind advancement of knowledge. To keep abreast of knowledge, practitioners must be able to utilize information gained from research studies. This requires knowledge of research designs and the ability to discriminate between conclusions based on empirical data and others that are unwarranted. Moreover, direct service practitioners require knowledge of single-subject experimental

designs to be able to evaluate the effectiveness of their own practice from time to time.

5. *Field practicum.* "The field practicum is an integral component of the curriculum in social work education. It engages the student in supervised social work practice and provides opportunities to apply classroom learning in the field setting" (CSWE, 1994, p. 142). Graduates of social work programs consistently report that their experiences in the field practicum is integral to their learning how to practice as responsible professionals. Your learning on content in your classroom courses and from this book will be greatly enhanced by the opportunity to apply your knowledge, values, and skills in the field and receive modeling and appropriate feedback from your field instructor.

PRACTICING COMPETENTLY: AN ETHICAL REQUIREMENT

As reflected above in the profession's proposed revision of the Code of Ethics, "social workers practice within their areas of competence and develop and enhance their professional expertise" (NASW, 1995). Consequently, attaining and maintaining competence in practice is an ethical requirement of social workers. To meet this requirement, aspiring social workers must achieve proficiency in a broad range of activities. The rationale for this requirement is compelling because much is at stake for consumers of social work services. Furthermore, who would question that clients have the right to expect competent services from those who represent themselves to the public as experts in their field of practice? Competent practice is defined as "fitting, suitable for the purpose; adequate; properly qualified; having legal capacity or qualification." To assess professional competency, however, is far from simple because competency in practice embodies knowledge, values, skills, and attitudes essential to fulfill one's professional role skillfully. Ingredients essential to perform one's role adequately vary according to the demands of each situation. A practitioner may thus be competent in providing certain types of service, such as marital or family therapy, and not in others, such as correctional services or protective services to children who have been abused or neglected. Furthermore, the elements of competent practice in various settings evolve as a result of expanding knowledge, emerging skills, and the changing demands of practice. Competency must thus be viewed within a temporal context, for a practitioner may achieve competence at one time only to suffer steady erosion of that competence by failing to keep abreast of ever-expanding knowledge and skills.

Because of the broad scope of social work activities embodied in the three levels of practice, it is highly doubtful that without extensive study beyond the master's level, practitioners can achieve advanced expertise in all levels of practice. This reality is reflected in the curricula of schools of social work, which typically require master's level students to select one level of practice or "concentration" for intensive study. Our primary aim in writing this book was to assist students and practitioners to achieve and to advance their professional competence. This is not a modest objective, as social work practice theory has been in a state of vigorous ferment for the past 25 years.

This ferment has resulted from three major sources: (1) Analyses of earlier research studies that cast doubt on the effectiveness of traditional social work interventions (Fischer, 1976, Mullen & Dumpson, 1972); (2) Emerging theories and empirically proven interventions; and (3) Ever-constricting sources of funding for social work programs that has produced strident demands for accountability and cost effectiveness of services. The knowledge base of social work practice has expanded rapidly, and empirical research has infused the profession with welcome stimulation and scientific vitality. Whereas students of the

1970s entered the profession during a time when earlier research findings had cast serious doubt on the efficacy of social work interventions, subsequent research studies have provided more support for the effectiveness of social work practice in helping clients (Reid & Hanrahan, 1982; Rubin, 1985; Thomlison, 1984). Moreover, practitioners have available an ever-widening array of interventions they can employ for many different human problems. Our objective of assisting students and practitioners to achieve competence presented a formidable challenge. We responded by including principles of effective practice identified by prominent theoreticians, researchers, and educators. Our task was further complicated by the fact that competence embodies much more than possessing knowledge of practice theory; competent practitioners must be able to transform that knowledge into action. Social work educators have been increasingly occupied with identifying and defining competencies (skills) in explicit terms and with developing technologies for assisting students to master these skills. We have incorporated these technologies in this book.

Evolving Theory and Competence

Possessing skills alone does not ensure competence, for without an undergirding knowledge base a practitioner would be little more than a technician. To analyze problems, persons, and situations, to plan remedial interventions, and to implement appropriate techniques requires an adequate grasp of practice theory and knowledge about human behavior in the social environment. The social work practitioner uses skills in the context of understanding the systems and contexts in which problems take place. Direct practice theory involves a complex domain within which rapid expansion in recent years has supplied much needed vigor, but not without painful growing pains. Much of the new theory has not expanded the

margins of preexisting theory but has tended to be incompatible with and to replace the older theory. Incorporating new theory, therefore, has posed some challenging dilemmas to schools of social work, responses to which are discussed in the following section.

Trend Toward Integrating Practice Models

Because human beings present a broad array of problems of living, no single approach or practice model is sufficiently comprehensive to adequately address them all. Moreover, techniques associated with one practice model may be applied equally effectively by practitioners who espouse other models. Indeed, although some practitioners identify largely with only one practice model, few only apply interventions and techniques that originated from a single practice model. Single-model practitioners do a disservice to themselves and their clients by attempting to fit all clients and problems into their chosen model. Practitioners should select interventions and techniques that best fit certain types of problems and clients (Berlin & Marsh, 1993).

Practice theories vary widely in their world views, targets of intervention, specifications of techniques, methods of assessment, length of interventions, and other important dimensions. Some interventions are thus more relevant to and cost effective for certain problems than are others. Moreover, except for a limited number of problems, no single theory has proven to be more effective than other practice theories, although some interventions have proven to be effective and others ineffective in treating certain problems. All theories may thus be viewed as possessing some part of the universe of truth.

The proliferation of theories in the social sciences, social work, and allied disciplines has ushered in a new era that offers the potential of enabling practitioners to select specific interventions proved effective for specific problem situations. To achieve this potential presents a formidable challenge, however, since available knowledge is often fragmented. To integrate the many theories and interventions, a generic framework capable of encompassing such theories and interventions is essential. Fortunately, such a unifying framework, the ecological systems model (Germain, 1979, 1981; Meyer, 1983; Pincus & Minahan, 1973; Siporin, 1980), is available.

Ecological Systems Model   Adaptations of this model, originating in biology, makes a close conceptual fit with the "person-in-environment" perspective that was dominant in social work until the mid-1970s. Although that perspective accorded recognition to the impact of environmental factors upon human functioning, an inordinate emphasis had been accorded to internal factors in assessing human problems and a perception of the environment as constraining the individual that did not sufficiently acknowledge the individual's actions to effect the environment. This heavy emphasis, which resulted from the prominence and wide acceptance of Freud's theories in the 1920s and 1930s, reached its zenith in the 1940s and 1950s. With the emergence of ego psychology, systems theory, theories of family therapy, expanded awareness of the importance of ethnocultural factors, and emphasis on ecological factors in the 1960s and 1970s, increasing importance was accorded to environmental factors and to understanding ways in which people interact with their environments.

Systems models were first created in the natural sciences. Meanwhile, ecological theory developed from the environmental movement in biology. Ecological systems theory in social work adapted concepts from systems and ecological theories. Two concepts of ecological theory that are especially relevant to social workers are habitat and niche. Habitat refers to the places where organisms live and, in the case of humans, consists of the physical and social settings within particular cultural contexts. When habitats are rich in resources required for growth and development, human beings tend to thrive. When habitats are deficient in vital resources, physical, social, and emotional development and ongoing functioning may be adversely affected. For example, a substantial body of research indicates that supportive social networks of friends, relatives, neighbors, work and church associates, and pets mitigate the damaging effects of painful life stresses. By contrast, people with deficient social networks may respond to life stresses by becoming severely depressed, resorting to abuse of drugs or alcohol, engaging in violent behavior, or by coping in other dysfunctional ways.

The concept of niche refers to statuses or roles occupied by members of the community. One of the tasks in the course of human maturation is to find one's niche in society, which is essential to achieving self-respect and a stable sense of identity. Being able to locate one's niche, however, presumes that opportunities congruent with human needs exist in society, a presumption that may not be valid for members of society for whom equal opportunities do not exist because of race, ethnicity, gender, poverty, age, disability, sexual identity, and other like factors.

An objective of social work, as noted earlier, is to promote social justice, the accomplishment of which expands opportunities for people to create appropriate niches for themselves. Ecological systems theory posits that individuals are engaged in constant transactions with other human beings and with other systems in the environment and that these various persons and systems reciprocally influence each other.

Further, each system is unique, varying in characteristics and ways of interacting (e.g., no two individuals, families, groups, or neighborhoods are the same). People thus are not mere reactors to environmental forces. Rather, they act on their environments, thereby shaping the responses of other people, groups, institutions, and even the physical environment. For example, people make choices about where to live, whether to upgrade or to neglect their living arrangements, and whether or not to initiate or support policies that combat urban decay, safeguard the quality of air and water, provide adequate housing for the elderly poor, and the like.

Adequate assessments of human problems and plans of interventions, therefore, must consider the reciprocal impact of people and environmental systems. The importance of considering the reciprocal interaction between people and their environments in formulating assessments has been reflected in changing views over the past decade of various human problems. Disability, for example, is now defined in psychosocial terms rather than in medical or economic terms, as had previously been the case. As Roth (1987) has clarified, "What is significant can be revealed only by the ecological framework in which the disabled person exists, by the interactions through which society engages a disability, by the attitudes others hold, and by the architecture, means of transportation, and social organization constructed by the able-bodied" (p. 434). Disability is thus minimized by goodness of fit between needs of people with physical or mental limitations and environmental resources that correspond to their special needs (e.g., rehabilitation programs, special physical accommodations, education, and social support systems).[4]

It is clear from the ecological systems perspective that the satisfaction of human needs and mastery of developmental tasks require the availability of adequate resources in the environment and positive transactions between persons and their environments (e.g., effective learning by a student requires adequate schools, competent teachers, parental support, adequate perception and intellectual ability, motivation to learn, and positive relationships between teachers and students). Gaps in the environmental resources, limitations of individuals who need or utilize these resources, or dysfunctional transactions between individuals and environmental systems block the fulfillment of human needs and lead to stress or impaired functioning. Reduction or removal of the stress requires coping efforts aimed at gratifying the needs, or stated another way, achieving adaptive fit between person and environment. People, however, often do not have access to adequate resources, or they lack effective coping methods. Social work involves assisting such people to find ways to meet their needs by linking them with or developing essential resources or by enhancing their capacities for utilizing resources or coping with environmental forces.

Assessment from an ecological systems perspective obviously requires knowledge of the diverse systems involved in interactions between people and their environments. These systems include the following: subsystems of the individual (biophysical, cognitive, emotional, behavioral, motivational); interpersonal systems (parent–child, marital, family, kin; friends, neighbors, cultural reference groups, and others in people's social networks); organizations, institutions, and communities; and the physical environment (housing, neighborhood environment, buildings, other artificial creations, water, and weather and climate). These various systems and their interactions are considered in Chapters 8–11.

A major advantage of the ecological systems model is that it is so broad in scope that typical human problems involving health care, family relations, inadequate income, mental health difficulties, conflicts with law enforcement agencies, unemployment, educational difficulties, and so on can all be subsumed under this model, enabling the practitioner to analyze the complex variables involved in such problems. Assessing the sources of problems and determining the focuses of interventions are the first steps in applying the ecological systems model.

Pincus and Minahan have adapted systems models to social work practice, suggesting that a client system includes those persons who are requesting a change, sanction it, are expected to benefit from it, and contract to receive it (Pincus & Minahan, 1973; Compton & Galaway, 1994). Jane Percy fits the first part of this definition since she requested a change. Potential clients who request a change are described as applicants. Her son Jerald has not requested a service, though he might be expected to benefit from it. Many persons like Jerald come into contact with social workers without requesting a service. Additional terms are needed for potential clients related to their various routes to social work contact. Referrals are persons who are referred by other professionals and family members. Jerald is a referral, referred by his mother. Contacted persons are approached through an outreach effort (Compton & Galaway, 1994). Some referred and contacted persons may not experience pressure from that contact which was not sought out. Others experience the contact as pressure, though not legally binding, and may be considered nonvoluntary clients (Rooney, 1992). Still others have contact with a practitioner through current or impending legal pressure and might be considered legally mandated clients. Rather than immediately bestow the label client on all persons who have contact with a social worker, it is better to consider them as potential clients and be aware of their route to such contact and their response to that contact.

The next step is to determine what is to be done vis-à-vis the pertinent systems involved in the problem situation. In this step, the practitioner surveys the broad spectrum of available practice theories and interventions. To be maximally effective, interventions, of course, must be directed to all systems that are critical in a given problem system.[5] The target system represents people and problems which must be influenced to reach goals (Compton & Galaway, 1994, p. 133). When a client desires assistance on a personal problem, the target and client systems overlap. Frequently, however, clients request assistance with problems outside themselves. In such instances, that problem

becomes the center of a target system. For example, if part of the contract with Ms. Percy entails assessment of conditions and her responses to them which have produced stress, the client system and target system would overlap. Even when there is overlap, it is important to focus on the PROBLEM which is the overlap rather than on the entire person as the target. Frequently, the target system relates to problems outside the person. For example, the lack of recreational opportunities for Jerald suggests inclusion of the YMCA and possible school and scouting programs. The action system refers to those persons with whom the practitioner needs to cooperate to accomplish a purpose. Meanwhile, the agency system includes the practitioners and service systems involved in work on the agreed upon problems (Compton & Galaway, 1994).

Social systems also vary in the degree to which they are open and closed to new information or feedback. Closed systems have relatively rigid boundaries preventing the input or export of information while open systems have relatively permeable boundaries permitting more free exchange. Thus families may vary from being predominantly closed to new information to excessively open. In fact, all families and human systems exhibit a tension with efforts to maintain stability and boundaries in some areas while seeking and responding to change in others. For example, at this point the boundary linking Ms. Percy and Jerald as a family is tenuous while Ms. Percy's part of the system is open in seeking solutions to problems occuring to them. Systems theorists also suggest that change in one part of a system often affects other parts of the system. For example, work with Ms. Percy on the problem she identified of high stress may affect her parenting of Jerald. The principle of equifinality suggests that the same outcome can be achieved from different starting places. For example, starting on any problem which motivates both Ms. Percy and Jerald, no matter what the problem, may eventuate in better relations between them. Meanwhile, the principle of multifinality suggests that beginning from the same starting points may end in different outcomes. For example, starting on work with Ms. Percy's difficulties parenting Jerald may enhance her coping ability more generally and lead to a variety of additional targets for change, such as parenting, support, transportation, returning for more education and training, and recreation. While such system models are often seen as useful in providing concepts for describing person–situation interactions, others have suggested that they have limitations in providing the basis for specific intervention prescriptions (Whittaker & Tracy, 1989).

To make judicious choices and to implement chosen interventions skillfully requires knowledge of numerous practice theories and techniques and a rigorous approach to selecting those that are most appropriate for a given client. Systematic eclecticism (Beutler, 1983; Beutler & Clarkin, 1990; Fischer, 1978; and Siporin, 1979) is such a rigorous approach to practice. A systematic eclectic practitioner adheres exclusively to no single theory but rather selects models and theories that best match a given problem situation and accords highest priority to techniques that have been empirically demonstrated to be effective and efficient.

Systematic eclecticism requires the practitioner to keep abreast of emerging theories and research findings. In our judgment, this approach to practice holds the highest promise of being effective with a broad range of clients and problems. The theoretical base of this book, therefore, is systematic eclecticism practiced under the umbrella of ecological systems theory. The systematic eclectic approach to practice would be fairly straightforward if clear guidelines for selecting theories and interventions were available, but the state of the art in social work has not reached that level of sophistication. However, significant progress has been made in the early 1990s (Beutler & Clarkin, 1990; Burman & Allen-Meares, 1991), and in Chapter 13 we discuss pertinent criteria that have been identified.

Six general criteria also exist to guide social workers in deciding which theories and interventions to study in depth.

1. The extent to which a given theory has been supported by empirical research is a central criterion. Obviously, theories whose tenets have been affirmed through research and whose efficacy has likewise been established are preferable to theories that have not been subjected to rigorous empirical testing. A number of writers have stressed the importance of basing direct practice upon empirical research. This has prompted controversy over a period of several years, with other writers cautioning that adherents of empirically based practice have taken an extreme position that discounts the importance of other approaches to expanding knowledge.[6]

2. When two interventions both have been proven effective, the intervention that produces results with the least expenditure of time, money, and effort is the more efficient and is preferable to the other.

3. The extent to which interventions and techniques subsumed under the theory are specifically delineated. Theories that are largely composed of abstractions fail to inform practitioners as to how to implement theory in actual practice situations and therefore have limited value. Psychoanalytic theory has been criticized for that reason. Behavior modification, by contrast, is characterized by the high degree of specificity with which its procedures are delineated.

4. *Ethical and value implications of interventions.* Practitioners should avoid interventions that subject the client to emotional trauma or humiliation, that violate confidentiality, or that otherwise conflict with the profession's code of ethics. Assessing whether the information source emphasizes health and strengths versus pathology relates to the value emphasis on strengths in social work. A similar value leads to preference for methods that emphasize collaborative work with clients versus practitioner manipulation.

5. The practitioner's level of knowledge and skill with respect to given interventions. It is vital that the practitioner be well grounded in knowledge of interventions, including the rationale of an intervention, indications and contraindications for employing it, cautions to be observed, guidelines for appropriate timing, and specific procedures for implementing it. Interventions are best learned under careful supervision, and practitioners have an ethical responsibility not to apply them in a haphazard manner or to subject clients to the risk of trial-and-error learning.

6. Finally, the recognition of both a personal and a societal context within materials from outside the field selected as sources is a criterion consistent with the person–situation focus of social work (Compton & Galaway, 1994, p. 99).

Because this book rests on a systematic eclectic approach to direct practice, we have drawn from and integrated numerous behavioral theories and models of practice extant in social work and other helping professions. These theories and models include the task-centered system, cognitive therapy, behavior modification, client-centered therapy, ego psychology, role theory, social learning theory, decision theory, crisis intervention, existential theory, solution-oriented therapy, and several models of family therapy. We refer to these theories and models in the book, and you will study some of them in depth during your professional education.

NOTES

1 See, for example, Wallace and Brinkerhoff (1991) and Jayaratne and Chess (1984).

2 This view was first posited by Gordon (1962) and later reaffirmed by Gordon and Schutz (1977).

3 For a brief but informative overview of social planning and community organization, see the article by Gilbert and Specht (1987), the source of the foregoing information.

4 In this regard, the critical importance of environmental resources to rehabilitation of patients with major paralyses caused by severe spinal cord injuries has been illustrated and documented in a study reported by Mackelprang and Hepworth (1987).

5 These and other principles of ecological systems theory are discussed at greater length in an informative article by Allen-Meares and Lane (1987).

6 For a discussion of issues involved and of a rationale for empirically based practice see Ivanoff, et al. (1987). For a contrasting analysis of issues and limitations of empirical practice as the dominant approach to direct practice see Witkin (1991).

Chapter 2

Direct Practice: Domain, Philosophy, and Roles

DOMAIN

Prior to 1970, social work practice was defined by methodologies or by fields of practice. Social workers were thus variously identified as caseworkers, group workers, community organizers, child welfare workers, psychiatric social workers, school social workers, medical social workers, and so on. The terms *direct practice* and *clinical practice* are relatively new in social work nomenclature. The profession was unified in 1955 by the creation of the National Association of Social Workers (NASW) and, with the inauguration of the journal *Social Work*, the gradual transformation from more narrow views of practice to the current broader view was under way. This transformation accelerated during the 1960s and 1970s when social unrest in the United States led to challenges and criticisms of all institutions, including social work. Minority groups, organized groups of poor people, and other oppressed groups accused the profession of being irrelevant to their pressing needs. These accusations were often justified because many social workers were engaged in narrowly focused and therapeutically oriented activities that did not address the social problems of concern to oppressed groups (Specht & Courtney, 1994).

Casework had been the predominant social work method during this period. Casework involved the activities of a caseworker, in widely varying settings, aimed at assisting individuals, couples, or families to cope more effectively with problems that impair social functioning. Group work had also evolved as a practice method, and group workers were practicing in settlement houses, neighborhoods, on the streets with youth gangs, in hospitals, correctional institutions and other settings. Although the target units served by group workers were larger, their objectives did not address broad social problems. It was clear that urgent needs for broadly defined social services could not be met through the narrowly defined remedial (therapeutic) efforts of the casework and group work methods.

The efforts of Gordon (1965) and Bartlett (1970) to formulate a framework or common base for social work practice comprised of purpose, values, sanction, knowledge, and common skills resulted in a broadened perspective of social work. This new perspective was not oriented to methods of practice and fostered the use of the presently employed generic term *social work practice*.

GENERALIST PRACTICE

The Council on Social Work Education responded by adopting a curriculum policy statement stipulating that to meet accreditation standards, social work educational programs must have a curriculum containing foundation courses that embody the common knowledge base of social work practice. Both undergraduate (BSW) and graduate (MSW) programs embody such foundation courses and thus prepare students for generalist practice. BSW curricula, however, are designed primarily to prepare generalist social workers and avoid specialization in practice methods.

The rationale for generalist programs, as we discussed in Chapter 1, is that practitioners should view problems holistically and be prepared to plan interventions that address all systems implicated in clients' problems (also referred to as client systems). Similarly, client goals and needs should suggest appropriate interventions rather than be led by interventions into exploring compatible goals. Client systems range from micro systems (individuals, couples, families, and groups) to macro systems (organizations, institutions, communities, regions, and nations).

Connecting client systems to resource systems that can provide needed goods and services is a paramount function of BSW level social workers. Many BSW programs, in fact, are oriented to preparing students to assume the role of case manager, a role that focuses on linking clients to resource systems. We alluded to this role in Chapter 1 and discuss it briefly again later in this chapter and more extensively in Chapter 15.

The first year (foundation year) of MSW programs also prepares graduate students for generalist practice. Although a few MSW programs are oriented to preparing students for "advanced generalist practice," the large majority of second-year curricula in the MSW programs are designed to permit students to select specializations or "concentrations" that may be in methods of practice or in fields of practice (e.g., substance abuse, aging, child welfare, work with families, health care, or mental health). Methods of practice typically are denoted as *micro* or *macro*, the former referring to direct practice and the latter to social policy, community organization and planning to bring about

social and economic justice. MSW students thus are prepared for both generalist and specialized practice.

Both similarities in orientation and differences in function between BSW and MSW social workers and the importance of having practitioners at both levels are highlighted in the following case example, in which the different levels of practice are indicated by initials that correspond to BSW and MSW levels. Please note also that similarities and differences exist on a continuum such that some MSW social workers perform some of the tasks described as related to the BSW practitioner and vice versa.

Case Example

Mrs. C, a recipient of AFDC public assistance, called her social worker, Ms. BSW, to report that she felt she was "falling apart" and needed to talk. Ms. BSW made a home visit the following day and found Mrs. C in a highly agitated state. Mrs. C reported that three days ago she had been visiting with a neighbor who had been attending a group for adult women who were sexually abused as children. The neighbor had related the "horror stories" of several group participants as well as her own. The day following the visit with her neighbor, Mrs. C found herself flooded with memories of being sexually abused by her stepfather during her childhood. Experiencing the memories for the first time was extremely painful, and Mrs. C began feeling worthless, depressed, and having thoughts of taking her life. She wondered if she should be hospitalized but didn't know what she would do with her three children if she were to go to the hospital. She was apprehensive that being hospitalized would be traumatic to her children, especially to her seven-year-old son, Joe, who had been doing poorly in school and had been clinging to her since her divorce from her husband 6 months ago.

Ms. BSW listened carefully and after exploring further Mrs. C's feelings of depression and thoughts of suicide explained that she would contact the mental health center regarding alternatives for treatment. She also inquired about Mrs. C.'s insurance coverage. Ms. BSW assured her that they would plan together for assistance with her children and offered to contact Joe's school regarding his poor performance, if that were agreeable with Mrs. C, who gratefully assented.

Interventions Ms. BSW phoned the mental health center and talked with Ms. MSW, a social worker assigned to the inpatient unit. Ms. MSW arranged for an appointment with Mrs. C the same day and explored her troubling thoughts, depression, and suicidal impulses. In consulting with the psychiatrist in charge and reviewing reimbursement guidelines from Mrs. C's health plan, it was determined that she did not meet the criteria of imminent danger required for hospitalization but might be helped quickly through participation in an out-patient group (Strom, K. 1992).

Part of Mrs. C's treatment would consist of participating in an out-patient therapy group led by Ms. MSW for women sexually abused as children. Previous experience indicated Mrs. C would benefit by expressing her troubling feelings in a supportive environment provided by the group to regain her equanimity. Moreover, this experience would bolster her damaged self-esteem. Further, Ms. MSW helped Mrs. C see that her seeking help in this time of need was evidence of a coping strength. Because Ms. MSW shared the same holistic orientation to problem assessment and an emphasis on strengths as Ms. BSW from similar training in her first year of graduate school, they consulted together about how best to support and assist in empowering Mrs. C and her family while she was a part of this out-patient group. Other types of intervention were discussed with Mrs. C., including having a friend or relative stay with her for a few days or she to stay with the friend with child care arranged. Mrs. C preferred to have a friend stay with her. Ms. MSW taught Mrs. C some coping skills for handling thoughts of suicide and a plan for addressing them should they arise

again. Home visits and regular calls were also planned to help her get through the crisis period.

Ms. BSW contacted the school the following day and talked with the school social worker, Mr. MSW, regarding Joe's difficulties in school. She explained that the school difficulties and Joe's clinging behavior appeared temporally associated with Mrs. C's divorce. Mr. MSW said he would explain the situation to the teacher and would recommend that Joe be given special attention. He also explained that he was leading a group of children from families in transition and would include Joe in the group.

DIRECT PRACTICE

Direct practice includes work with individuals, couples, families and groups. Direct practitioners perform many roles besides delivering face-to-face service; they work in collaboration with other professionals, organizations, and institutions, and act to advocate with landlords, agency administrators, policy-making boards and legislatures, among others.

The term *clinical practice* is commonly used interchangeably with direct practice, but the terms may have different meanings for different people. Proponents of the term have emphasized that clinical social work entails liberating, supporting, and enhancing people's adaptive capacities and increasing the responsiveness of physical and social environments to people's needs. The *Register of Clinical Social Work*, in defining clinical social work suggests that client problems are identified and intervention plans agreed upon with the client and that "the plan is supported by securing historical facts and clues to the latent forces within the individual's personality"[1] (Register of Clinical Social Workers, 1976, p. xi). Some people think of clinical practice as limited to psychotherapy done in mental health settings, independent practice settings, or similar settings. Opponents of the term suggest that it has connoted a focus on disease and pathology rather than health and strengths. Direct practice encompasses a full range of roles, including acting as a psychotherapist. Subsequently in this book, we use the terms direct practice or clinical practice in the broad sense to refer to practice done in any of the diverse settings in which micro services are delivered. Services delivered by direct practitioners may be addressed to most of the troubling situations encountered by human beings and may be delivered in any of the diverse settings listed at the beginning of Chapter 1.

Central to assisting people with difficulties is knowledge of and skill in problem solving. Problem solving requires knowledge and skills in assessing human problems and in locating, developing, or utilizing appropriate resource systems. Skills in engaging clients, mutually planning relevant goals, and defining roles of the participants are also integral parts of the problem-solving process. Similarly, the practitioner must possess knowledge of interventions and skills in implementing them. A more extensive review of the helping process is contained in the next chapter, and the entire book is devoted to explicating theory and skills related to direct practice with clients.

Direct practitioners of social work must be knowledgeable and skilled in interviewing and in assessing and intervening in problematic interactions involving individuals, couples, families, and groups. Knowledge related to group process and skill in leading groups are also essential, as are skills in forming natural helping networks, functioning as a member of an interdisciplinary team, and negotiating within and between systems. The negotiating function entails skills in mediating conflicts and advocating and obtaining resources, both of which embody high levels of interpersonal skills.

Questions as to whether direct practitioners do or should engage in psychotherapy are still raised by some who regard psychotherapy as the exclusive province of psychology and psychiatry. These individuals argue that only psychoanalysts are trained to work with the unconscious mind and that social workers should limit their function to casework or counseling. Others have questioned whether engaging in psychotherapy is appropriate for a profession whose mission focuses on social justice. However, Jerome Wakefield argues that social work is distinguished as a profession by its goal of pursuing minimum distributive justice for its clients and that social workers can appropriately utilize psychotherapy as a method in pursuit of this goal (Wakefield, 1995). In our opinion these debates are moot. Currently many practitioners in social work and other helping professions practice psychotherapy which draws on additional theory bases such as behavioral and family systems models, hence the emphasis on work with the unconscious which presumes a psychoanalytic theory is less relevant. In fact, more social workers are employed in mental health centers (which deal in psychotherapy) than members of any other core helping profession (Taube & Barrett, 1983).

A PHILOSOPHY OF DIRECT PRACTICE

As a profession evolves, its knowledge base expands and practitioners gain experience in applying abstract values and knowledge to specific practice situations. Instrumental values thus gradually evolve, and as they are adopted, they become principles or guidelines to practice. Such principles express preferred beliefs and attitudes about the nature and causes of human problems, the capacity of humans to deal with problems, desirable goals, desired qualities in helping relationships, vital elements of the helping process, roles of the practitioner and client, characteristics of effective group leaders, the nature of the human growth process, and so on.

Over many years, we have evolved a philosophy of practice from a synthesis of principles gained from sources too diverse to acknowledge, including our own value preferences. We thus offer as our philosophy of direct practice the following principles (see Figure 2-1):

A PHILOSOPHY OF DIRECT PRACTICE

1. The problems experienced by social work clients stem from lack of resources and lack of knowledge and skills (societal, systemic, and personal sources), either alone or in combination.

2. As social work clients are often afflicted with poverty, racism, sexism, discrimination, and lack of resources, social workers negotiate systems and advocate for change to ensure clients access to rights, resources, and treatment with dignity.

3. People are capable of making their own choices and decisions. Although controlled to some extent by their environment, they are able to direct their environment more than they realize. Social workers aim to assist in the empowerment of their clients by helping them gain the ability to make decisions that affect their lives and increase their working toward changing environmental influences that adversely affect clients individually and as members of groups.

4. As social service systems are often funded on the basis of individual dysfunctions, social workers often play an educational function in sensitizing service delivery systems to more systemic approaches to problems emphasizing health, strengths, and natural support systems.

5. Frequently, social workers deal with involuntary clients whose behavior is self-defeating or has incurred legal consequences. While people have a right to their own values and beliefs, sometimes their behaviors violate the rights of others and the social worker assists these clients in facing these aspects of their difficulties. As such involuntary clients are often not seeking a helping relationship but rather wishing to escape one, negotiation is frequently called for.

6. Some clients apply for service and wish to experience change through a social worker's assistance. Such clients are often helped by having an accepting relationship, with appropriate self-disclosure, which will allow them to seek greater self-awareness and to live more fully in the reality of the moment.

7. All clients, whether voluntary or involuntary, are entitled to be treated with respect, dignity, and with choices facilitated.

8. Client behavior is goal directed although these goals are often not readily discernible. Clients are, however, capable of learning new skills, knowledge, and approaches to resolving difficulties. Helping professionals are responsible for helping clients discover their strengths and affirming their capacity for growth and change.

9. While current problems are often influenced by past relationships and concerns, and though limited focus on the past is sometimes beneficial, most difficulties can be alleviated by focusing on present choices and by mobilizing strengths and coping patterns.

Figure 2-1   Principles of a Philosophy of Direct Practice

ROLES OF DIRECT PRACTITIONERS

During recent years, increasing attention has been devoted to the various roles that direct practitioners perform in discharging their responsibilities. In Chapter 1, we referred to a number of these roles. In this section, we summarize these and other roles and refer to sections of the book where we discuss certain roles at greater length. We have categorized the roles based in part on a schema presented by Lister (1987) (see Figure 2-2).

Figure 2-2   Roles Social Workers Play

I. Direct Provision of Services

Roles subsumed under this category are those in which practitioners meet face-to-face with clients or consumer groups in providing services. These include the following:

1. Individual casework or counseling.

2. Marital and family therapy (may include sessions with individuals, conjoint sessions, and group sessions).

3. Group work services (may include support groups, therapy groups, self-help groups, task groups, and skill development groups).

4. Educator/disseminator of information. The practitioner may provide essential information in individual, conjoint, or group sessions or may make educational presentations to consumer groups or to the public. For example, practitioners may conduct educative sessions concerned with parenting skills, marital enrichment, stress management, or various aspects of mental health or health care.

Roles involved in the direct provision of services are primary in the work of most practitioners, especially roles 1-3 listed above. Because this book is aimed at preparing practitioners to provide such direct services, we shall not elaborate on these roles in this section.

II. System Linkage Roles

Because clients often need resources not provided by a given social agency and lack knowledge of or ability to utilize other available resources, social workers often perform roles in linking people to other resources. System linkage roles include the following:

1. *Broker.* To perform the role of broker (i.e., an intermediary who assists in connecting people with resources), practitioners must have a thorough knowledge of community resources so that they can make appropriate referrals. Familiarity with the policies of resource systems and working relationships with key contact persons are essential to successful referrals. The preceding case example of Mrs. C. being referred by Ms. BSW to the mental health center was an example of performing the broker role.

Before some people are able to avail themselves of resources, they may require the practitioner's assistance in overcoming fears and misconceptions. Practitioners also have responsibilities in developing simple and effective referral mechanisms and ways of monitoring whether clients actually follow through on referrals. To assist you in gaining skills in referring clients to needed resources, we present relevant guidelines in Chapter 3.

2. *Case manager/coordinator.* Some clients lack the ability, skills, knowledge, or resources to follow through on referrals to other systems. In such instances, social workers may serve as *case manager*, a person designated to assume primary responsibility for assessing the needs of a client, arranging and coordinating the delivery of essential goods and services provided by other resources, and working directly with the client to ensure that the

goods and services are provided in a timely manner. Case managers must maintain close contact with clients (including sometimes acting to provide direct casework services) and with other service providers to ensure that plans for service delivery are in place and are subsequently delivered as planned. It is noteworthy that in the case manager role, practitioners function at the interface between the client and the environment more than in any other role.

Because of dramatic increases in recent years in the numbers of people needing case management services (e.g., homeless, elderly, and chronically mentally disabled people), numerous articles have appeared in the literature concerned with those who need such services, issues related to case management, and various functions of case managers. Because we discuss these topics at some length in Chapter 15, we defer discussion of them to that chapter.

3. *Mediator/arbitrator.* Occasionally breakdowns occur between clients and service providers so that clients do not receive needed services to which they are entitled. For example, a client may be denied badly needed public assistance, food stamps, or health care. Service may be denied, however, because of arbitrary decisions of a provider, because clients did not adequately represent their eligibility for services, or because of strains that sometimes develop between clients and service providers that precipitate withdrawals of requests for services by clients or withholding of services by providers.

In such instances, practitioners may serve as mediators with the goal of eliminating obstacles to service delivery. *Mediation* is a process that "provides a neutral forum in which disputants are encouraged to find a mutually satisfactory resolution to their problems" (Chandler, 1985, p. 346). In serving as a mediator, you must carefully listen to and draw out facts and feelings from both parties to determine the cause of the breakdown. It is important not to take sides with either party until

you are confident that you have accurate and complete information. When you have determined the nature of the breakdown, you can plan appropriate remedial action aimed at removing barriers, clarifying possible misunderstandings, and working through negative feelings that have impeded service delivery. This process entails the use of communication skills that are delineated in subsequent chapters of this book.

In recent years, knowledge of mediation skills has evolved to a high level of sophistication, and a small but increasing number of practitioners are working independently or in tandem with attorneys to mediate conflicts between divorcing partners regarding child custody, visitation rights, and property settlements. These same skills can be used to mediate personnel disputes, labor–management conflicts, and to mediate between victims and offenders (Umbreit, 1993).

4. *Client advocate.* Serving as an advocate for a client or group of clients has been a role assumed by social workers since the inception of the profession. The obligation to assume this role has been reaffirmed most recently in the draft of the revised NASW Code of Ethics, which includes advocacy among the activities performed by social workers in pursuit of the professional mission (NASW, 1995, p. 2). With respect to linking clients with resources, advocacy is the process of working with and/or on behalf of clients to obtain services and resources that would not otherwise be provided. We discuss circumstances under which this might occur and appropriate remedial measures at length in Chapter 19. We also discuss skills involved in advocacy (including social action for groups of clients) in Chapter 15.

III. System Maintenance and Enhancement

As staff members of social agencies, practitioners bear responsibility for evaluating structures, policies, and functional relationships within agencies that impair effectiveness in service delivery. Roles that relate to fulfilling this responsibility include:

1. *Organizational analyst.*[2] Discharging this role entails pinpointing factors in agency structure, policy, and procedures that have a negative impact on service delivery. Knowledge of organizational and administrative theory is essential to performing this role effectively. We focus on this role in Chapter 19 in the section "Organizational Resistance." Students will also learn more about organizational dynamics in courses concerned with organizational theory.

2. *Facilitator/expediter.* After pinpointing factors that impede service delivery, practitioners have a responsibility to plan and implement ways of enhancing service delivery. This may involve providing relevant input to agency administrators, recommending staff meetings to address problems, working collaboratively with other staff members to bring pressure to bear on resistant administrators, encouraging and participating in essential in-service training sessions, and other similar activities. In Chapter 1, we saw how the social worker from the Arch working with Ms. Percy was able to convince agency administrators to make the agency van available to clients to bring them to appointments and to facilitate their shopping for groceries.

3. *Team member.* In many agency and institutional settings, (e.g., mental health, health care, and rehabilitation settings) practitioners function as members of clinical teams that collaborate in assessing clients' problems and delivering services. Teams commonly consist of a psychiatrist or physician (usually the team leader), a psychologist, a social worker, a nurse and perhaps a rehabilitation counselor, occupational therapist, and/or a recreational therapist, depending on the setting. Members of the team have varying types of expertise that are tapped in formulating assess-

ments and planning and implementing therapeutic interventions.

As team members, social work practitioners often contribute knowledge related to family dynamics and engage in therapeutic work with family members. Dane and Simon note that social workers performing in host settings in which the mission and decision making are dominated by non-social workers often experience a discrepancy between their professional mission and the values of the employing institution. They can act, however, to sensitize team members to strengths and a more holistic approach while exercising their knowledge of resources and expertise in linking clients with resources(Dane & Simon, 1991). Social workers also are expected to apply their knowledge of community resources in planning for the discharge of patients and facilitating their reentry into the community following periods of hospitalization. In so doing, social workers bring their systems and strengths perspectives to teams that are sometimes more deficit focused. Social workers are also increasingly involved in collaborative work across systems, such as schools and child welfare which require knowledge of and ability to work in several systems (Bailey-Dempsey, 1995). As team members, social workers also often serve as case managers in coordinating discharge planning for patients who would otherwise be unable to function adequately in the community (Dane & Simon, 1991; Kadushin & Kulys, 1993).

4. *Consultant/consultee. Consultation* is a process whereby an expert enables a consultee to deliver services more effectively to a client by increasing, developing, modifying, or freeing the consultee's knowledge, skills, attitudes, or behavior with respect to the problem at hand. Although social workers both provide and receive consultation, there has been a trend over the past decade for MSW social workers to serve less as consumers of consultation and more as providers. BSW social workers may provide consultation regarding the availability of specific community resources but

more often are consumers of consultation when needing information about how to work effectively in problem solving that entails complex situations and behaviors.

Social workers assume the consultee role when in need of expert knowledge from doctors and nurses, psychiatrists, psychologists, and other social workers who possess high levels of expertise related to certain types of problems (e.g., substance abuse, child maltreatment, sexual problems, and other problems that require advanced knowledge).

Social workers serve as consultants to members of other professions and to other social workers in need of their special expertise including the role of supervisor. For example, they may provide consultation to school personnel who need assistance in understanding and coping with problem students; to health care providers who seek assistance in understanding a patient's family, or ethnic and cultural factors; to court staff regarding matters that bear on child custody decisions and decisions about parole and probation; and in many other similar situations.[3]

IV.   Researcher/Research Consumer

Practitioners face responsibilities in both public and private settings to select interventions which can be evaluated and to evaluate the effectiveness of their interventions, and to systematically monitor the progress of their clients. Implementing these processes requires practitioners to conduct and make use of research.

Actual research conducted by direct practitioners sometimes involves single-subject (also denoted as single-system) designs. This type of research design enables practitioners to obtain measures of the extent (frequency and severity) of problem behaviors before implementing interventions aimed at eliminating or reducing the problem behaviors (e.g., substance abuse, aggressive or vio-

lent behavior, overeating) or increasing the frequency of behaviors that are absent or insufficient (e.g., doing homework, engaging in prosocial behaviors, setting realistic and consistent limits with children, sending positive messages, abstaining from drinking).[4] These measures provide a baseline against which the results of implementing interventions can be assessed by applying the same measures periodically during the course of the interventions, at termination, and at follow-up (Reid, 1994). Perhaps more frequently, practitioners use some form of *Goal Attainment Scaling* that calls for rating goal achievement on a scale with points designated in advance.[5]

Unless practitioners employ such designs to evaluate their practice, they must rely on clinical judgment, which is subject to error and bias. Assessing progress through repeated measures, by contrast, enables both client and practitioner to discern small changes that might otherwise be underestimated or to determine that interventions are not producing the desired changes and a different approach is indicated.

V.   System Development

Direct practitioners sometimes have opportunities to improve or to expand agency services based on assessment of unmet client needs, gaps in service, needs for preventive services, or findings of one's own or other research studies that indicate more promising results achieved by interventions other than those currently employed. Roles that relate to system development include:

1. *Program developer.* As we noted earlier, practitioners often have opportunities to develop services in response to emerging needs of clients. Such services may include educative programs (e.g., for immigrants or unwed pregnant teenagers), support groups (e.g., for rape victims, adult children of alcoholics, and victims of incest), and skill develop-

ment programs (e.g., stress management, parenting, and assertiveness training groups).

2. *Planner.* In small communities, rural areas, and boom towns that lack access to community planners, direct practitioners may need to assume a planning role, usually in concert with community leaders. In this role, the practitioner works both formally and informally with influential people to plan programs in response to unmet and emerging needs. Varying from one area to another, such needs may include child care programs, transportation for the elderly and disabled, and recreational and health care programs, to name just a few.

3. *Policy and procedure developer.* Participation of direct practitioners in formulating policies and procedures typically is limited to agencies in which they provide direct services to clients. This degree of participation is largely determined by the style of administration within a given agency. Able administrators generally solicit and invite input from professional staff as to how the agency can more effectively respond to consumers of services. Because practitioners serve in the "front lines" they are in a strategic position to evaluate clients' needs and how policies and procedures serve or fail to serve the best interests of clients. It is impor-

tant, therefore, that practitioners seek to be actively involved in decision-making processes related to policies and procedures.

In rural areas and small communities, direct practitioners often participate in policy development concerned with the needs of a broad community rather than the needs of a circumscribed target group. In such instances, practitioners must draw from knowledge and skills gained in courses in social welfare policy and services and community planning.

4. *Advocate.* Just as practitioners may advocate for an individual client, they may also join client groups and other social workers and allied professionals in advocating for legislation and social policies aimed at providing needed resources and enhancing social justice. We discuss skills in advocacy and social action in the concluding section of Chapter 15.

As we have indicated previously, knowledge and skills related to some of the foregoing roles are taught in segments of the curriculum that lie outside direct practice courses. To do justice in one volume to the knowledge and skills entailed in all these roles is impossible; consequently, we have limited our focus primarily to the roles subsumed under Figure 2-2, providing direct service.[6]

NOTES

1 Carel Germain, quoted in Goldstein (1983).

2 We have adapted this term from Weissman, Epstein, and Savage (1987).

3 The principles and skills involved in consultation are beyond the scope of this book. Those interested in pursuing this topic further will find Dougherty's 1990 book informative. A quarterly journal, *Consultation: An International Journal*, published by Human Science Press, is also an excellent reference.

4 Although we discuss single-subject research in Chapters 12 and 20, adequate treatment of this topic is beyond the scope of this book. Most students of direct practice learn the role of researcher in research courses, especially courses in clinical research, for

which several excellent textbooks are available. See Jordan, Corcoran, and Fischer.

5 Kiresuk, T.J. & Sherman, R.E. (1968). Goal attainment scaling: A general method for evaluating community mental health programs. *Community Mental Health Journal.* Vol. 4, 443-453. Kiresuk, T.J., Stelmachers, E.T. & Schultz, S.K. (1982). Quality assurance and goal attainment scaling. *Professional Psychology,* Vol. 13, 145-152

6 Weissman, Epstein, and Savage (1983) have written an excellent book concerned with many of the administrative roles involved in direct practice.

Chapter 3 □□□

Overview of the Helping Process

COMMON ELEMENTS AMONG DIVERSE THEORISTS AND PRACTITIONERS

Direct practitioners working with individuals, couples, families, groups, and other systems draw on contrasting theories of human behavior, use different models of practice, implement diverse interventions, and serve widely varying clients. Despite these varied factors, all direct practitioners work to assist clients in coping more effectively with problems of living and improving the quality of their lives. People are impelled by either internal or external sources to secure social work services because current solutions are not working in their lives. Some persons are hence *applicants* who request services of a social worker to deal with these internal or external problems (Alcabes & Jones, 1985). In many other instances, the need for help has been identified by teachers, doctors, employers, or family members, and they initiate contact at the behest of these others. Such persons might be best considered *referrals* because they are not applicants. There is variation, then, among referrals, as some perceive pressure to seek help while others perceive assistance in finding the appropriate help. Still others are at least initially *involuntary clients* as they respond to requirements to seek help as a result of a current or impending legal mandate. Applicants, referrals, and respondents are all potential clients if they can negotiate a contract addressed to some of their concerns. The helping process thus is aimed at assisting people to regain equilibrium and to achieve growth in problem-solving ability by developing new resources or employing untapped resources in ways that reduce tension and achieve mastery over problems.

Whatever their approach to assisting clients, most direct practitioners employ a problem-solving process. Further, they use communication skills in their work with different systems involved in clients' problems.

The first portion of this chapter is devoted to an overview of the helping process and its three distinct phases, and subsequent portions of the book are organized to correspond to these phases. The latter part of this chapter focuses on the structure and processes involved in interviewing. Later chapters deal with the structure, processes, and skills involved in modifying the processes of families and groups.

THE HELPING PROCESS

As noted above, involuntary clients are the majority of those seen in many social work settings. Such persons are not seeking a helping process but rather responding to pressure from others to seek help. With such persons, helping processes include an exploration of the pressures that led to contact and an examination of how a helping process as perceived by the potential client can be initiated. Rather than presume that we are dealing with voluntary clients who have applied for service under no external pressure, it is more appropriate to consider first the possibility that the potential client is responding to pressure. This exploration of roles, expectations, and pressures influencing contact is known as *role socialization.*

Beyond this socialization phase, virtually all social work theorists agree that the helping process consists of three major phases. Each of the phases has distinct objectives, and the helping process generally proceeds successively through these phases. These phases, however, are not sharply demarcated by the activities and skills employed. The activities and skills of the three phases differ more in frequency and intensity than in kind. The processes of exploration and assessment, for example, are central during Phase I, but these processes continue in somewhat diminished significance during subsequent phases of the helping process. The three major phases are:

- Phase I   Exploration, engagement, assessment, and planning.
- Phase II   Implementation and goal attainment.
- Phase III Termination, planning maintenance strategies, and evaluation.

Phase I: Exploration, Engagement, Assessment, and Planning

This phase lays the groundwork for subsequent implementation of interventions and strategies aimed at resolving clients' problems and promoting problem-solving skills. Processes involved and tasks to be accomplished during Phase I include the following:

1. Exploring clients' problems by eliciting comprehensive data about the person(s), the problem, and environmental factors including forces impinging on the referral for contact.

2. Establishing rapport and enhancing motivation.

3. Formulating a multidimensional assessment of the problem, identifying systems that play a significant role in the difficulties, and identifying relevant resources that can be tapped or must be developed.

4. Mutually negotiating goals to be accomplished in remedying or alleviating the problem and formulating a contract.

5. Making referrals.

We briefly discuss each of these five processes in the following sections and refer to portions of the book that include extensive discussions of these processes.

1. *Exploring clients' problems by eliciting comprehensive data about the person(s), the problem and environmental factors including forces impinging on the referral for contact.* Contact begins with an initial exploration of the circumstances which have led to contact. Since self-referred persons are the minority of clients served in many settings, and even those who self-refer often do so at the suggestion or pressure of others, it should not be assumed that potential clients at this stage are really applicants or voluntary clients (Cingolani, 1984). Further, they may be anxious about the prospect of seeking help and lack knowledge about what to expect. For many, the social worker will have information from an intake form or referral source about the circumstances which have brought them into contact.

These many possibilities can be explored by asking "What brings you here? How can we help you?" These questions should elicit a beginning elaboration of the concern or pressures which the potential client sees as relating to his or her contact. The social worker can hence begin to determine to what extent the motivation for contact was initiated by the potential client him or herself and to what extent the motivation is in response to external forces.

The social worker should also give a clear, brief description of his or her own view of the purpose of this first contact and encourage an exploration of how the social worker can be helpful.

2. *Establishing rapport and enhancing motivation.* Effective communication in the helping relationship is crucial, for unless practitioners succeed in engaging clients, they may be guarded in revealing vital information and feelings and, even worse, may not return after the initial session. Engaging clients successfully means establishing rapport, which involves reducing the level of threat and gaining the trust of clients in the practitioner's helpful intent. A condition of rapport is that clients perceive a practitioner as understanding and genuinely interested in their well-being. To gain such a positive perception with clients whose race or ethnicity differs from the social worker's, the practitioner must attend to relevant cultural factors and vary interviewing techniques accordingly, as we discuss later in this chapter and throughout the book. Further, when potential clients have been referred by others, they will need to be reassured that they are clients and not merely targets for change.

Potential clients who are not applicants or genuinely self-referred frequently have misgivings about the helping process. They don't perceive themselves as having a problem and often attribute the source of difficulties to another person or to untoward circumstances. Such clients confront practitioners with the challenging task of (1) neutralizing negative feelings, (2) attempting to help potential clients understand problems attributed by others and assessing the advantages and disadvantages of dealing with those concerns,

and (3) creating an incentive to work on acknowledged problems. Skillful practitioners often succeed in tapping into the motivation of such involuntary clients, thus affirming the principle from systems theory that motivation is substantially influenced by the interaction between clients and practitioners.

In still other instances, clients freely acknowledge problems and do not lack incentive for change but assume a passive role, expecting practitioners to magically work out their difficulties for them. Practitioners must be able to avoid taking on the impossible role that some clients would ascribe to them. Instead they should impart a belief in clients' abilities to work as partners in searching for remedial courses of action and to mobilize clients' energies in implementing tasks essential to successful problem resolution.

Indispensable to success in the helping process are acknowledgment of a problem and adequate motivation on the part of clients to actively work toward its solution. Potential clients do not lack motivation; they sometimes lack motivation to work on the problems and goals perceived by others. In addition, motivation relates to a person's past experience which leads him or her to expectations that behaviors will be successful or failures in attempting to reach goals. Hence, those with limited expectations for success often appear to lack motivation. The work of social workers is then often directed to attempting to increase motivation by assisting clients to discover that their actions can be effective in reaching their goals (Gold, 1990).

Practitioners, therefore, must possess skills for tapping in to client motivation and assisting those who readily acknowledge a problem but lack willingness to expend the required effort or to bear the discomfort generally involved in effecting essential change. A major task in this process is then to provide information to the potential client about what to expect from a helping process. This socialization process includes identifying the kinds of concerns the social worker and agency can help with, client rights including confidentiality and circumstances in which it might be abridged, and information about what behavior to expect from the practitioner and client (Videka-Sherman, 1988).

The task for clients in groups is twofold, for they must develop trust not only in the practitioner but in other group members as well. If group members vary in race, ethnicity, or social class, the group leader must be sensitive to such cultural determinants of behaviors and assume a facilitative role in breaking down related barriers to rapport not only between himself or herself and individual group members but also among group members.

Establishing rapport requires that practitioners manifest a (1) nonjudgmental attitude; (2) acceptance; (3) respect for clients' right of self-determination; and (4) respect for clients' worth and dignity, uniqueness and individuality, and problem-solving capacities (discussed at length in Chapter 4). And finally, practitioners foster rapport when they relate with empathy and authenticity, which involves facets of both attributes and skill. Both these skills are considered in later chapters of this book.

3. Formulating a multidimensional assessment of the problem, identifying systems that play a significant role in the difficulties, and identifying relevant resources that can be tapped or must be developed. Establishing rapport and exploring clients' problems are processes that practitioners implement concurrently. Moreover, these processes are mutually reinforcing. Astute exploration not only yields rich data but also cultivates rapport by inspiring confidence in the practitioner.

Similarly, empathic communication not only conveys understanding and fosters rapport but also elicits expanded expressions of feelings, enabling practitioners to evaluate the role clients' emotions play in their difficulties. Certain responses thus serve dual functions, and the processes of relationship building and problem exploration not only proceed concurrently but also overlap.

Problem exploration is a critical process, for comprehensive information must be gathered before all the dimensions of a problem and their interaction can be understood. Exploration begins by attending to the emotional states and immediate concerns manifested by clients. Gradually, the practitioner broadens the exploration to encompass relevant systems (individual, interpersonal, and environmental) and explores in depth aspects of the problem that appear salient. During the process of exploration, the practitioner is also alert to and highlights strengths manifested by clients, realizing that these strengths represent a vital resource to be identified and tapped later during the goal-attainment phase.

Skills that are employed in the exploratory process with individuals, couples, families, and groups are delineated later in this chapter and at length in subsequent chapters. To explore problematic situations thoroughly, practitioners must also be knowledgeable about the various systems commonly involved in human difficulties, topics considered at length in Chapters 8–11.

Problem exploration skills are put into use as part of the assessment process that begins from the first contact with clients and is ongoing. During interviews, practitioners weigh the significance of clients' behavior, thoughts, beliefs, emotions, and of course, information revealed. These moment-by-moment assessments guide the practitioner in deciding what aspects of the problem to explore in depth, when to explore emotions more deeply, and so on, as we discuss at greater length later in this chapter. In addition to this ongoing process of assessment, the practitioner must formulate a working assessment from which flow the goals and contract upon which Phase II of the problem-solving process is based.

An adequate assessment includes analysis of the problem, the person(s), and the ecological context. Focus in assessment is critical. Given temporal limitations, there are layers of assessment. At the first layer, attention must be devoted to issues of client safety, legal mandates, and client wishes for service. The rationale for this threefold set of priorities is that client wishes should be governing in circumstances in which there are not legal mandates impinging on choices or dangers to self or others.

Analysis of the problem specifies the nature of the difficulties, which may involve inadequate resources; decisions about a crucial aspect of one's life; difficulties in individual, interpersonal, or societal systems; or interactions between any of the preceding factors. Analysis of the problem also involves judgments about the duration and severity of a problem as well as the extent to which the problem is susceptible to change, given the clients' potential coping capacity and the permeability of the problematic situation to change. In considering the nature and severity of problems, practitioners must also weigh these factors against their own competencies and the types of services provided by the agency. If the problems call for services that are beyond the agency's function, such as prescribing medication or rendering speech therapy, referral to another professional person or agency may be indicated.

Analysis of the individual system includes assessment of the client's wants and needs, coping capacity, strengths, and limitations, and motivation to work on the problem(s). In evaluating the first two dimensions, the practitioner must assess such factors as flexibility, judgment, emotional characteristics, degree of responsibility, capacity to tolerate stress, ability to reason critically, and interpersonal skills. These factors, which are critical in selecting appropriate and attainable goals, are discussed at length in Chapter 9.

Assessment of ecological factors entails consideration of the adequacy or deficiency, success or failure, and strengths or weaknesses of salient systems in the environment that bear on the client's problem. Ecological assessment thus is aimed at identifying systems that must be strengthened, mobilized, or developed in response to the client's unmet needs. Systems that often bear on clients' needs include marital, family, and social support systems (e.g., kin, friends, neighbors, coworkers, peer groups, and ethnic reference groups); child care, health care, and employment systems; various institutions; and the physical environment.

Cultural factors are also vital in ecological assessment, for personal and social needs and means of satisfying them vary widely from culture to culture. Moreover, resources that can be tapped to meet clients' needs also vary according to cultural contexts. Some cultures have indigenous helping persons, such as folk healers, religious leaders, and relatives from extended family units who have been invested with authority to assist clients in times of crisis. These persons can often provide valuable assistance to practitioners.

Assessment of the client's situational context further involves consideration of the circumstances as well as actions and reactions of participants in problematic interaction. Knowledge of circumstances and specific behavior of participants before, during, and after troubling events is crucial to understanding the forces that shape and maintain problematic behavior. Assessment, therefore, requires that practitioners elicit detailed information about actual transactions between people.

Whether making assessments of individuals per se or of individuals as subsets of marital dyads, families, or groups, it is important to assess the functioning of these larger systems. These systems have unique properties including power distribution, role definitions, rules, norms, channels of communication, and repetitive interactional patterns. Such systems also manifest both strengths and problems that strongly affect and shape the behavior of constituent members. It follows that individual difficulties tend to be related to systemic dysfunction, and interventions must therefore be directed to the system as well as to the individual.

Assessments of systems are based on varied data-gathering procedures. With couples and families, practitioners may or may not conduct individual interviews, depending on their theoretical biases, practice styles, and impressions gained during preliminary contacts with family members. If exploration and assessment are implemented exclusively in conjoint sessions, the processes are similar to those of individual interviews except that interaction between the participants assumes major significance. Whereas information gained in individual interviews is limited to reports and descriptions by clients, requiring the practitioner to make inferences about actual interaction within relevant systems, practitioners view interaction directly in conjoint interviews and group sessions. The practitioner is alert to strengths and dysfunction in communication and interaction and to the properties of the system (see Chapters 10 and 11). Assessment therefore focuses heavily on styles of communication employed by individual participants, interactional patterns among members, and the impact of individual members on processes that occur in the system. These factors are weighed in selecting interventions aimed at enhancing functioning at these different levels of the larger systems.

Finally, a working assessment involves synthesizing all relevant information gained in the exploration process. To enhance the validity of the assessment, it is desirable to involve clients in the process by soliciting their perceptions and assisting them in gathering data about their perceived difficulties as well as sharing impressions with them and inviting affirmation or disconfirmation of those impressions. It is also beneficial to further highlight their strengths and to identify other relevant resource systems that can be tapped or need to be developed to accomplish remediation of the difficulties. When the practitioner and client(s) reach agreement about the nature of the problems involved, they are ready to enter the process of negotiating goals, assuming that clients are adequately motivated to advance to Phase II of the helping process.

4. *Mutually negotiating goals to be accomplished in remedying or alleviating the problem and formulating a contract.* If the practitioner and the individual client, couple, family, or group have reached agreement concerning the nature of the difficulties and the systems that are involved, the participants are ready to negotiate individual and/or group goals. This is a mutual process aimed at identifying what needs to be changed and what related actions need to be taken to resolve or ameliorate the problematic situation. We briefly discuss the process of goal selection in this chapter and at length in Chapter 13. If agreement is not reached about the appropriateness of services or clients choose not to continue, then services may be terminated.

After goals have been negotiated, participants undertake the final task of Phase I: formulating a contract. The contract (see Chapter 12), which is also mutually negotiated, consists of a formal agreement or understanding between the practitioner and client that specifies the goals to be accomplished, relevant strategies to be implemented, roles and responsibilities of participants, practical arrangements, and other factors. When the client system is a couple, family, or group, the contract also specifies group goals that tend to accelerate group movement and to facilitate accomplishment of group goals.

Mutually formulating a contract is a vital process because it demystifies the helping process and clarifies for clients what they may realistically expect from the practitioner and what is expected of them; what they will mutually be seeking to accomplish and in what ways; and what the problem-solving process entails. While most straightforward with voluntary clients or applicants, developing contracts which are voluntary at least in part is also a feasible goal for nonvoluntary clients.

5. *Making referrals.* Exploration of clients' problems often reveals that resources or services beyond those provided by the agency are needed to remedy or ameliorate presenting difficulties. This is especially true of clients who present a broad array of needs. In such instances, referrals to other resource and service providers may be necessary. Moreover, clients may lack the knowledge,

skills, or resources needed to avail themselves of resources that are badly needed. Social workers may assume the role of case manager in such instances (e.g., persons with severe and persistent mental illness, developmental and physical disabilities, foster children, and infirm elderly clients).

Linking clients to other resource systems requires careful handling if clients are to follow through in seeking and obtaining essential resources. The following guidelines will assist you in making referrals:

1. Ascertain the client's readiness for a referral by eliciting his or her feelings, which may involve doubts, apprehension, and misconceptions about seeking service elsewhere. Clients are most likely to follow through with a referral if they see a need for it. Frequently, however, mandated and nonvoluntary clients are referred for services such as chemical dependency evaluations which they have not sought and do not perceive a need for (Rooney, 1992). It is appropriate to explain the rationale for a referral, including the potential benefits of pursuing it and potential costs of deciding not to follow through. Client choice should be emphasized including options such as not pursuing the referral and accepting consequences, pursuing the referral for one's own reasons, or deciding to do it for the reasons suggested by others.

2. When the decision has been made by the client to pursue a resource, determine together what resource best matches the client's wishes. In this regard, it is important to present two or more choices, if available, as nonvoluntary clients respond better to choices, even when constrained, than to the perception of lack of choice (Rooney, 1992). To accomplish this, you must be knowledgeable about various resources within your community. You must also be familiar with agencies' policies and procedures as well as the quality of service provided by both agencies and private practitioners. Implementing this guideline presupposes you have developed a list of resources and maintain ongoing liaison with agencies so that your knowledge about their operations is current. It is your obligation to share relevant information with clients so that they can render informed judgments.

3. As you explore possible options for referral, respect the client's right to self-determination but offer your recommendation as to which resource is likely to be most beneficial. As Weissman (1976) has indicated, "Throwing the decision back on the client is an abrogation of professional responsibility under the guise of 'participation'" (p. 52).

4. Avoid making false promises or conveying unrealistic reassurance about what another agency can do in assisting the client. It is realistic, however, to express optimism about clients' potential to benefit from the services of another agency or practitioner.

5. Although you should clarify the function and methods of the agency selected, avoid specifying what the next practitioner will do. Practitioners have different styles and employ different methods. If you prescribe what other practitioners should do, you impose a handicap on them and set clients up for disappointment.

In addition to the preceding guidelines, practitioners can enhance the rate of achieving successful connections between clients and resources in the community by following five discrete steps. Weissman (1976) has defined these "connection techniques" and has reported impressive findings on the rate of successful referrals. The steps range in the client competency and motivation presumed. For example, the first step is often sufficient for highly competent and motivated clients. Steps 2–5 provide varying levels of assistance to clients lacking resources to make the referral without further assistance. These steps are as follows:

1. Write out the necessary facts about contacting the resource, including such information as name and address of the resource, how to obtain an appointment, how to reach the resource, and what the client may expect upon arriving. The initiative in making an appointment and following through resides with the client.

2. Provide the client with the name of a specific contact person. To avoid disappointment and discouragement if the contact person is not available, provide alternate names.

3. If the client's problem is complex, provide the client with a brief written statement, addressed to the resource, detailing the problem and the services desired by the client. Involve the client in composing the statement.

4. Have the client call the resource from your office to make an appointment. You may choose to place the call to ensure that the client reaches the contact person and then turn the conversation over to the client.

5. When clients manifest apprehension or diffidence about going to the resource alone, it may be advisable to arrange for a family member or friend to accompany the client. In exceptional circumstances, you may wish to accompany the client yourself. Behavioral rehearsal may also be employed to prepare the client.

After following the preceding steps, your responsibility to facilitate the referral does not end. You may ask the client to report back after making the contact or may personally initiate a contact to secure a progress report. Your continued interest and efforts may make the difference between a successful and unsuccessful referral.

Phase II: Implementation and Goal Attainment

After mutually formulating a contract, the practitioner and client(s) enter the heart of the problem-solving process—the implementation and goal-attainment phase, also denoted as the action-oriented or change-oriented phase (terms that are used interchangeably in this book). Phase II involves translating plans formulated between the practitioner and individual clients, couples, families, or groups into actions. The participants thus combine their efforts in working toward the goal accorded highest priority. This process begins by dissecting the goal into general tasks which identify general strategies to be employed in pursuit of the goal. These general tasks are then subdivided into specific tasks which designate what the client practitioner plans to do between one session and the next (Epstein, 1988; Reid, 1992; Robinson, 1930; Taft, 1937).[1] Tasks may relate to the individual's personal functioning or to interaction with others in the client's environment, or they may involve interaction with other resource systems, such as schools, hospitals, or law enforcement agencies. The processes of negotiating goals and tasks are discussed in Chapter 12.

After mutually formulating goals with clients, practitioners select and implement interventions designed to assist clients in accomplishing their goals and subsidiary tasks. Interventions should directly relate to the problems and to the consequent goals that were mutually negotiated with clients and derived from accurate assessment. Helping efforts often fail when social workers employ global interventions without considering clients' views of their problems and without attending to the uniqueness of such problems.

Enhancing Self-Efficacy   Research findings (Bandura, 1977; Kazdin, 1979; Zeiss, Lewinsohn, & Munoz, 1979) have strongly indicated that a major source of gain in the helping process is an increased sense of self-efficacy on the part of clients. *Self-efficacy* refers to an expectation or belief that one can successfully accomplish tasks or perform behaviors associated with specified goals. Note that the concept also overlaps with notions of individual empowerment. The most powerful means for enhancing self-efficacy is to assist clients in actually performing certain behaviors prerequisite to accomplishing their goals. Another potent technique is to draw awareness of clients to their strengths and to accredit incremental progress of clients toward goal attainment. Moreover, family and group members represent potent resources for enhancing self-efficacy. Practitioners can develop and tap these resources by assisting families and groups to accomplish tasks that involve perceiving and accrediting strengths and progress of group and family members. We consider other sources of self-efficacy and relevant techniques in Chapter 14 and to a lesser extent in other chapters.

Monitoring Progress   As work toward goal attainment proceeds, it is important to monitor progress on a regular basis. The reasons for this are fourfold:

1. *To evaluate the effectiveness of change strategies and interventions.* Practitioners are increasingly required to document the efficacy of services to satisfy third party funders of services in a system of managed care. If an approach or intervention is not producing desired effects, practitioners should determine the reasons for this and/or consider negotiating a different approach.

2. *To guide clients' efforts toward goal attainment.* Evaluating movement toward goals enhances continuity of focus and efforts and promotes efficient use of time.

3. *To keep abreast of clients' reactions to progress or lack of progress.* When they believe they are not progressing, clients tend to become discouraged and may lose confidence in the helping process. By evaluating progress periodically, practitioners will be alerted to negative client reactions that might otherwise undermine progress.

4. *To concentrate on goal attainment and evaluate progress.* These will tend to sustain clients' motivation to work on their problems.

Methods of evaluating progress vary from eliciting subjective opinions to using various types of measurement. These and other matters related to evaluating progress on an ongoing basis are discussed in Chapter 12.

Barriers to Goal Accomplishment   As clients strive to accomplish goals and related tasks, progress is rarely smooth and uneventful. Rather, clients encounter obstacles and experience anxiety, uncertainties, fears, and other untoward reactions as they struggle to solve problems. Furthermore, family or group members or other significant persons may undermine clients' efforts to change by opposing such changes, by ridiculing the client for seeing a practitioner, by making derisive comments about the practitioner, or otherwise making change even more difficult for the client. (For this reason, it is vital to involve significant others in the problem-solving process whenever feasible.) Because of the potency of barriers to change, practitioners must be perceptive to manifestations of clients' struggles and skillful in assisting them to surmount these obstacles.

Barriers to goal accomplishment are frequently encountered in work with families and groups. Such barriers include personality factors that limit participation of certain group members, problematic behaviors of group members, or processes within the group that impede progress. These matters are addressed in later chapters.

Still other barriers may involve organizational resistance within systems whose resources are essential to goal accomplishment. Denial of resources or services (e.g., health care, rehabilitation services, and public assistance) by organizations, or policies and procedures that unduly restrict clients' access to resources may require the practitioner to assume the role of mediator or advocate. A major portion of Chapter 19 in Part 3 of this book is devoted to ways of overcoming organizational resistance.

Relational Reactions   As practitioners and clients work together in solving problems, emotional reactions on the part of either party toward the other may impair the effectiveness of the working partnership and pose an obstacle to goal accomplishment. Clients, for example, may have unrealistic expectations or may misperceive the intent of the practitioner. Consequently, clients may experience disappointment, discouragement, hurt, anger, rejection, longings for closeness, or many other possible emotional reactions that may seriously impede progress toward goals. Marital partners, parents, and group members may also experience relational reactions to other members of these larger client systems, resulting in problematic interactional patterns within these systems. Not uncommonly, such relational reactions are manifestations of inappropriate attitudes and beliefs learned from relationships with parents or significant others; in many other instances, however, the practitioner or members of clients' systems may unknowingly behave in ways that understandably foster unfavorable relational reactions on the part of individuals or family or group members. In either event, it is critical to explore and resolve the relational reaction. Otherwise, clients' efforts may be diverted from working toward goal accomplishment, or even worse, clients may prematurely withdraw from the helping process.

Practitioners are also susceptible to relational reactions. Practitioners who relate in an authentic manner provide clients with experience that is transferable to the real world of the client's social environment. They communicate that they are human beings not immune to making blunders and experiencing emotions and desires in relationships with clients. It is vital that practitioners be aware of unfavorable reactions to clients and be knowledgeable about how to manage them. Otherwise, they may be working on their own problems rather than the client's, placing the helping process in severe jeopardy. Chapter 18 is designed to assist practitioners in coping with potential relational reactions residing with the client(s), the practitioner, or both.

Enhancing Clients' Self-Awareness As clients interact in a novel relationship with a practitioner and risk new interpersonal behaviors in marital, family, or group contacts, they commonly experience emotions (or physical manifestations of emotions) that may be pleasing, frightening, confusing, and even overwhelming. Though managing such emotional reactions may require a temporary detour from goal-attainment activities, such activities frequently represent rich opportunities for growth in self-awareness. Self-awareness is the first step to self-realization. Many voluntary clients wish to understand themselves more fully, and they can benefit from being more aware of feelings that have previously been buried or denied expression. Practitioners can facilitate the process of self-discovery by employing additive empathic responses during the goal-attainment phase. Additive empathic responses focus on deeper feelings than do reciprocal empathic responses (referred to earlier in the discussion of Phase I). This technique can be appropriately applied in individual and conjoint interviews as well as in group sessions. Addi-

tive empathy, explicated at length in Chapter 18, is of particular value in assisting clients to get in touch with their emotions and to express them clearly to significant other persons.

Another technique that can be employed in fostering self-awareness is confrontation, a major topic of Chapter 18. This technique is employed to assist clients in becoming aware of growth-defeating discrepancies in perceptions, feelings, communications, behavior, values, and attitudes, and to examine such discrepancies in relation to stated goals. It is also used in circumstances when clients act to violate laws or threaten their own safety or that of others. Confrontation must be offered in the context of goodwill, and it requires high skill.

Use of Self As helping relationships become strong during the implementation and goal-attainment phase, practitioners increasingly use themselves as tools to facilitate growth and accomplishment. Relating spontaneously and appropriately disclosing one's feelings, views, and experiences provide for clients an encounter with an open and authentic human being. Modeling authentic behavior encourages clients to reciprocate by risking authentic behavior themselves, thereby achieving significant growth in self-realization and in interpersonal relations. Indeed, when practitioners model authentic behavior in groups, members often follow suit by assuming like behavior. Practitioners who relate in an authentic manner provide clients with experience that is transferable to the real world of the client's social relationships. A contrived, detached, and sterile "professional" relationship, by contrast, lacks transferability to other relationships. Obviously these factors should also be covered in the training process for practitioners.

Assertiveness involves dealing tactfully but firmly with problematic behaviors that impinge on the helping relationship or impede progress toward goal attainment. For example, when clients act in ways which are contrary to their goals or potentially harmful to themselves or others, the practitioner must deal with these situations. Further, practitioners must relate assertively to larger client systems at times; for example, to focus on the behavior of group members that hinders the accomplishment of goals. To passively permit dysfunctional behavior to continue is tantamount to contributing to that same behavior. Using oneself to relate authentically and assertively is a major focus of Chapter 5.

Phase III: Termination and Evaluation

The terminal phase of the helping process involves four major aspects: (1) assessing when individual and group goals have been satisfactorily attained and planning termination accordingly, (2) effecting successful termination of the helping relationship, (3) planning for maintenance of change and continued growth following termination, and (4) evaluating the results of the helping process. Deciding when to terminate is relatively straightforward when time limits are specified in advance as part of the initial contract, as is done with the task-centered approach. Decisions about when to terminate are also simple when individual or group goals are clear-cut (e.g., to get a job, obtain a prosthetic device, arrange for nursing care, secure tutoring for a child, implement a specific group activity, or hold a public meeting).

In other instances, however, goals involve growth or changes that have no limits, and judgments must be mutually made about when a satisfactory degree of change has been attained. Examples of such goals include increasing self-esteem, communicating more effectively, becoming more outgoing in social situations, and resolving conflicts more effectively. Actually, judgments about termination that involve such goals are much less difficult when goals have been explicitly specified in terms of behavioral indexes of desired levels of growth, a matter discussed in Chapters 12 and 20. It is increasingly the case that

decisions about termination and extension involves third parties as managed care funders must be consulted in decisions about how much service is enough (Corcoran & Vandiver, 1996).

Successfully Terminating Helping Relationships
Responses to termination by practitioners and clients are often positive, reflecting pride and accomplishment from both (Fortune, Pearlingi, & Rochelle, 1992). Clients whose contact with the practitioner was mandated or otherwise pressured may experience a sense of relief at getting rid of pressure or outside scrutiny. As voluntary clients share personal problems and are accompanied through rough emotional terrain by a caring practitioner, they often feel close to the practitioner. Consequently, termination tends to produce mixed feelings for clients. They are likely to feel strong gratitude to the practitioner. They are also likely to experience a sense of relief over no longer having to go through the discomfort associated with exploring problems and making changes (not to mention the relief from paying fees when fees are charged). Although clients are usually optimistic about the prospects of confronting future challenges independently, they sometimes experience a sense of loss over terminating the relationship with the practitioner. Moreover, uncertainty about their ability to cope independently often is mixed with their optimism.

When engaged in the helping process over a lengthy period of time, clients sometimes develop a strong attachment to a practitioner, especially if the practitioner has fostered dependency. For such individuals, termination involves a painful process of letting go of a relationship that has met significant emotional needs. Moreover, these clients often experience apprehension about facing the future without the reassuring strength represented by the practitioner. Group members often similarly experience painful reactions as they face the loss of supportive relationships with the practitioner and group members as well as a valued resource that has assisted them to cope with their problems. To effect termination with individuals or groups that minimizes psychological stress requires both perceptiveness to manifestations of emotional reactions and skills in helping clients to work through such reactions. This subject is discussed in Chapter 20.

Planning Change—Maintenance Strategies In recent years, practitioners have been increasingly concerned over the need to develop strategies that maintain change and continue growth after formal service is terminated (Rzepnicki, 1991). These concerns have been prompted by disconcerting findings to the effect that a significant portion of clients revert to previous dysfunctional behavior patterns following termination. Consequently, strategies for maintaining change are receiving increasing attention (see Chapter 20).

Evaluating Results The final aspect of the problem-solving process is to evaluate the results. Evaluation is important because it enables practitioners and agencies to respond to demands for accountability from funding sources and consumers of service. Furthermore, by evaluating results, practitioners are able to test the efficacy of interventions employed and to monitor their own successes, failures, and progress in achieving favorable outcomes.

Until recent years, practitioners were unable to evaluate outcomes because research studies required large numbers of clients, substantial expense, and sophistication in both research design and statistical analysis. Moreover, group research designs are of little value in assessing individual outcomes. Fortunately, a new approach to outcome research (single-subject design) has evolved in recent years, making it feasible for practitioners to go far beyond subjective evaluation of outcomes. Single-subject research is convenient, involves little or no expense, appeals to most clients, and can be employed with minimal research expertise. A discussion of single-subject research is included in Chapter 12.

Ideally, evaluation should not end with termination. Planning for follow-up sessions not only makes it possible to evaluate the durability of results, but also facilitates the termination process by indicating the practitioner's continuing interest in clients, a matter we discuss in Chapter 20.

INTERVIEWING PROCESS: STRUCTURE AND SKILLS

Direct practitioners employ interviewing as the primary vehicle of influence, although administrators and social planners also rely heavily on interviewing skills to accomplish their objectives. Interviews vary according to purpose, types of setting, characteristics, and number of participants. For example, interviews may involve interaction between a practitioner and individuals, couples, or family units. Interviews are conducted in offices, homes, hospitals, prisons, automobiles, and other diverse settings. Despite the numerous variables that affect interviews, certain factors are essential to all effective interviews. The following discussion identifies and discusses these essential factors and highlights relevant skills.

Physical Conditions

The physical climate in which an interview is conducted determines in part the attitudes, feelings, and degree of cooperation and responsiveness of people during interviews. Conditions conducive to productive interviews include:

1. Adequate ventilation and light.
2. Comfortable room temperature.
3. Ample space (to avoid a sense of being confined or crowded).
4. Attractive furnishings and decor.
5. Chairs that adequately support the back.

6. Privacy.
7. Freedom from distraction.
8. Open space between participants.

The first five items obviously are concerned with providing a pleasant and comfortable environment and need no elaboration. Privacy is vital, of course, because people are likely to be guarded in revealing personal information and expressing feelings if other people can see or hear them. Interviewers also find it awkward and have difficulty in concentrating or expressing themselves when others can hear them. Settings of course vary in the extent to which practitioners can control these conditions. In some settings, it may be impossible to ensure complete privacy. Even when interviewing a patient in a hospital bed, however, privacy can be maximized by closing doors, drawing curtains that separate beds, and requesting nursing staff to avoid nonessential interruptions. Privacy during home interviews may be even more difficult to arrange, but people will often take measures to reduce unnecessary intrusions if interviewers stress that privacy enhances the productivity of sessions. Similarly, practitioners working in public social service settings often work in cubicle offices. They can often, however, conduct client interviews in special interview rooms.

Because interviews often involve intense emotional involvement by participants, freedom from distraction is a critical requirement. Telephone calls, knocks on the door, and external noises can impair concentration and disrupt important dialogue. Moreover, clients are unlikely to feel important and valued if practitioners permit avoidable intrusions. Still other sources of distraction are crying, attention seeking, and restless behavior of clients' infants or children. Small children, of course, cannot be expected to sit quietly for more than short periods of time; hence it is advisable to encourage parents to make arrangements for the care of children during interviews (except when it is important to observe interaction between parents and their children). Because requiring such arrangements can create a barrier to service utilization, many practitioners and agencies maintain a supply of toys for such occasions.

Having a desk between an interviewer and interviewee(s) emphasizes the authority of the practitioner and creates a barrier that is not conducive to open communication. Although there may be instances in which an interviewer believes that maximizing authority will promote objectives, most practitioners strive to foster a sense of equality. Hence, they arrange their desks so that they can rotate their chairs to a position where there is open space between them and their clients. Others prefer to leave their desks entirely and use other chairs in the room when interviewing.

The Structure of Interviews

Interviews in social work have purpose, structure, direction, and focus. The purpose is to exchange information systematically with a view toward illuminating and solving problems, promoting growth, or planning strategies or actions aimed at improving the quality of life for people. The structure of interviews varies somewhat from setting to setting, client to client, and from one phase of the helping process to another. Indeed, skillful interviewers adapt flexibly both to different contexts and to the ebb and flow of each individual session. Thus, each interview is unique. Still, effective interviews conform to a general structure, manifest certain properties, and reflect use of certain basic skills by interviewers. In considering these basic factors, we shall begin by focusing on the structure and processes involved in initial interviews.

Establishing Rapport

Before discussing how to begin exploring clients' difficulties, it is important to focus on achieving rapport. Rapport with clients fosters open and free communication, the hallmark of effective interviews. Achieving rapport enables clients to gain trust in the helpful intent and goodwill of the practitioner to the extent they are willing to risk revealing personal and sometimes painful feelings and information. Some clients readily achieve trust and confidence in a practitioner, particularly when they have the capacity to form relationships easily. Voluntary clients often want to know "Who am I and why am I in this situation?" whereas involuntary clients have less reason to be initially trusting and want to know "Who are you and when will you leave?" (Rooney, 1992).

Establishing rapport begins by greeting the client(s) warmly and introducing oneself. If the client system is a family, you should introduce yourself to each family member. In making introductions and addressing clients, it is important to extend the courtesy of asking clients how they prefer to be addressed; doing so conveys your respect and desire to use the title they prefer. Although some clients prefer the informality involved in using first names, practitioners should be discreet in using first-name introductions with all clients because of their diverse ethnic and social backgrounds. For example, some adult blacks interpret being addressed by their first names as indicative of a lack of respect (Edwards, 1982; McNeely & Badami, 1984).

With many clients, practitioners must surmount formidable barriers before establishing rapport. It is important to bear in mind that the majority of clients have had little or no experience with social work agencies and enter initial interviews or group sessions with uncertainty and apprehension. Many did not seek help initially or view having to seek assistance with their problems as evidence of failure, weakness, or inadequacy. Moreover, revealing personal problems is embarrassing and even humiliating for some people, especially those who have difficulty in confiding in others.

Cultural factors compound potential barriers to rapport even further. For example, Asian Americans who retain strong ties to cultural traditions have been conditioned not to discuss personal or family problems with outsiders. Revealing problems to others may be perceived as a reflection of personal inadequacy and as a stigma upon an entire family. The resultant fear of shame may thus impede the development of rapport with clients from this ethnic group (Kumabe, Nishida, & Hepworth, 1985; Lum, 1992; Tsui & Schultz, 1985). African Americans, Native Americans, and Hispanics may also experience difficulty in developing rapport because of distrust that derives from a history of being exploited or discriminated against by other ethnic groups (Longres, 1991, Proctor & Davis, 1994).

Clients' difficulties in communicating openly tend to be even more severe when their problems involve allegations of socially unacceptable behavior, such as child abuse, moral infractions, or criminal behavior. In groups, the pain is further compounded by having to expose one's difficulties to other group members, especially in early sessions when the reactions of other members represent the threat of the unknown.

One means of fostering rapport with clients is to employ a "warm-up" period. This is particularly important with ethnic minority clients for whom such openings are the cultural norm, including Native Americans, persons with strong roots in the cultures of Asia and the Pacific basin, and Hispanics. Aguilar (1972), for example, has stressed the importance of warm-up periods in work with Mexican Americans:

When Mexican Americans meet to negotiate or arrange affairs, the first step is to set the climate or ambience. A preliminary period of warm, informal, personal conversation precedes the discussions of the concerns that brought them together. Jumping into the middle of serious and controversial affairs—as many people in the United States are inclined to do—seems confusing and even discourteous to most Mexican Americans (Aguilar 1972, p. 67).

Native Hawaiians and Samoans also typically expect to begin new contacts with outside persons by engaging in "talk story," which also involves warm, informal, and light personal conversation similar to that described by Aguilar. To plunge into discussion of serious problems without a period of talk story would be regarded by members of these cultural groups as rude and intrusive. Practitioners who neglect to engage in a warm-up period are likely to encounter passive-resistant behavior from members of these cultural groups.

A warm-up period and a generally slower tempo are also critically important with Native Americans, as Hull (1982) has emphasized: "The social worker who is all business and who attempts to deal with an Indian family as she or he might with a non-Indian family may be rebuffed, since forcing or hurrying relationships with Native Americans does not work. A variety of casual behaviors including small talk, comments addressed to all family members regardless of age, and patience are important if the Indian is to feel comfortable with the worker" (p. 346).[2]

Consistent with this recommendation, Palmer and Pablo (1978) suggest that practitioners who are most successful with Native Americans are low-key, nondirective individuals.

Warm-up periods are also important in gaining rapport with adolescents, many of whom are in a stage of emancipating themselves from adults and who are also frequently referred by those adults. Consequently, they may be wary of practitioners, and this is a particularly strong tendency among those who are delinquent or who are otherwise openly rebelling against authority. Moreover, adolescents who have had little or no experience with social workers have an extremely limited grasp of practitioners' roles. Many adolescents are at least initially involuntary and perceive social workers as adversaries, fearing that their role is to punish or to exercise power over them.

With the majority of clients, a brief warm-up period is usually sufficient. When barriers discussed in the preceding do not apply, introductions and a brief discussion of a timely topic (unusual weather, a widely discussed local or national event, or a topic of known interest to the client) adequately foster a climate conducive to exploring clients' concerns. Most clients, in fact, expect to plunge into discussion of their problems early on, and their anxiety level heightens if practitioners delay getting to the business at hand. This is particularly true with involuntary clients who did not seek the contact. With these clients, rapport often develops rapidly if practitioners respond sensitively to their feelings and skillfully give direction to the process of exploration by sharing the circumstances of the referral, thus defusing the global sense of threat experienced by many.

Respect for clients is critical to establishing rapport. Early in this chapter and in Chapter 1, we stressed the importance of respecting clients' dignity and worth, uniqueness, capacities to solve problems, and other factors. An additional aspect of respect is common courtesy. Being punctual, attending to clients' comfort, listening attentively, remembering clients' names, and assisting clients who have limited mobility convey the message that the practitioner values the client and esteems the client's dignity and worth. Courtesy should never be taken lightly.

Verbal and nonverbal messages from practitioners that convey understanding and acceptance of clients' feelings and views also facilitate the development of rapport. This does not mean agreeing with or condoning clients' views or problems but rather apprehending and affirming clients' rights to their own views, attitudes, and feelings. Attentiveness to feelings that clients manifest both verbally and nonverbally and empathic responses to these feelings convey understanding in a form that clients readily discern. Empathic responses clearly convey the message, "I am with you. I understand what you are saying and experiencing." The "workhorse" of successful helping persons, empathic responding is important not only in Phase I but in subsequent phases as well. Mastery of this vital skill (discussed extensively in Chapter 5) requires consistent and sustained practice.

Authenticity, or genuineness, is still another practitioner quality that facilitates rapport. Being authentic during Phase I of the helping process involves relating as a genuine person rather than assuming a contrived and sterile professional role. Authentic behavior by practitioners also models openness, the effect of which is to encourage clients to reciprocate by lowering their defenses and relating more openly (Doster & Nesbitt, 1979). Further, encounters with authentic practitioners provide clients with a relationship experience that more closely approximates relationships in the real world than do relationships with people who conceal their real selves behind a professional facade.

A moderate level of authenticity or genuineness during early interviews fosters openness most effectively (Giannandrea & Murphy, 1973; Mann & Murphy, 1975; Simonson, 1976). At this level, the practitioner is spontaneous and relates openly to the extent of being nondefensive and congruent. The practitioner's behavior and responses match her or his inner experiencing. Being authentic also permits the constructive use of humor. Relating with a moderate level of authenticity, however, precludes a high level of self-disclosure. Rather, the focus is on the client, and the practitioner reveals personal information or shares personal experiences judiciously. During the change-oriented phase of the helping process, however, practitioners engage in self-disclosure when they believe that doing so may facilitate the growth of clients. Self-disclosure is discussed at length in Chapter 5.

Rapport is also fostered by not employing certain types of responses that block communication. To avoid responses that hinder communication, practitioners must be knowledgeable about such types of responses and must eliminate them from their communication repertoires. Toward this end, we have devoted Chapter 7 to identifying various types of responses and interviewing patterns that inhibit communication and to describing strategies for eliminating them.

Beginning practitioners often fear that they will forget something, not observe something crucial in the interview that will lead to dire consequences, freeze up with tongue tied, or talk endlessly to reduce their anxiety (Epstein, 1985). Practice interviews such as those presented in subsequent chapters will assist in reducing this fear. Awareness that referred clients need to know the circumstances of the referral while clarifying choices, rights, and expectations before they are likely to wish to have rapport with the practitioner also helps.

Starting Where the Client Is   Social work researchers have suggested that motivational congruence or the fit between client motivation and what the practitioner attempts to provide is a major factor in explaining more successful findings in studies of social work effectiveness (Reid & Hanrahan, 1982). Starting with client motivation helps practitioners in establishing and sustaining rapport and in maintaining psychological contact with clients. If, for example, a client appears in emotional distress at the beginning of an initial interview, the practitioner focuses attention on the client's distress before proceeding to explore the client's problematic situation. An example of an appropriate focusing response would be, "I can sense you're having a difficult time. Could you share with me what you're experiencing at this moment?" Discussion of the client's emotions and related factors tends to reduce the distress, which might otherwise impede the process of exploration. Moreover, responding sensitively to clients' emotions fosters rapport as clients begin to regard practitioners as concerned, perceptive, and understanding persons.

Beginning practitioners sometimes have difficulty in starting where the client is because they are worried they will not present quickly and clearly the services of the agency, thus neglecting or delaying exploration of client concerns. Practice will allow them to relax and recognize that they can meet the expectations of their supervisors and others by focusing on client concerns while sharing content about the circumstances of referrals and their agency's services.

Starting where the client is has critical significance with involuntary clients. Because these clients are compelled by external sources to see practitioners, they often enter initial interviews with negative, hostile feelings. Practitioners, therefore, should begin by eliciting these feelings and focusing on them until they have subsided. By responding empathically to negative feelings and conveying understanding and acceptance of them, skillful practitioners often succeed in neutralizing these feelings, which enhances clients' receptivity to exploring their problem situations. Such feelings can often be reduced by clarifying choices available to the involuntary client. If practitioners fail to deal with clients' negativism, they are likely to encounter persistent oppositional responses. These responses are frequently labeled as resistance, opposition to change, and lack of motivation. It is useful to reframe these responses by choosing not to interpret them with deficit labels and replacing them with expectations that oppositional attitudes and behavior are normal when something the involuntary client values is threatened (Rooney, 1992).

Language also poses a barrier with many ethnic minority clients who may have a limited grasp of the English language that could cause difficulty in understanding even commonplace expressions. With ethnic minority clients and others whose educational backgrounds have been limited, practitioners must slow down the pace of communication and be especially sensitive to nonverbal indications that clients are confused. To avoid embarrassment, ethnic minority clients sometimes indicate that they understand messages when, in fact, they are perplexed.

Using Interpreters   When ethnic minority clients have virtually no command of the English lan-

guage, effective communication requires the use of an interpreter of the same ethnicity as the client, making it possible to bridge both cultural value differences and language differences. To work effectively together, however, both the practitioner and interpreter must possess special skills. Interpreters must be carefully selected and trained to understand the importance of the interview and their role in the process, and to interpret cultural nuances to the practitioner. Skilled interpreters thus assist practitioners by translating far more than verbal content, including nonverbal communication, cultural attitudes and beliefs, subtle expressions, emotional reactions, and expectations of clients. To achieve rapport it is also essential for practitioners to convey empathy and establish an emotional connection with the ethnic minority client. The interpreter thus "must have the capacity to act exactly as the interviewer acts—express the same feelings, use the same intonations to the extent possible in another language, and through verbal and nonverbal means convey what the interviewer expresses on several levels" (Freed, 1988, p. 316).[3]

The practitioner should explain the interpreter's role to the client and ensure the client of neutrality and confidentiality on the part of both the practitioner and the interpreter. Obviously these factors should also be covered in the training process for interpreters.

Successful transcultural work through an interpreter requires that the practitioner be acquainted with the history and culture of the client's and the interpreter's country of origin. Practitioners must also adapt to the slower pace of interviews. When practitioners and interpreters are skilled in working together in interviews, effective working relationships can evolve and many clients experience the process as beneficial and therapeutic. As implied in this brief discussion, interviewing through an interpreter is a complex process requiring careful preparation of practitioners and interpreters.

Exploration Process and Skills

When clients manifest readiness to discuss their problem situations, it is appropriate to begin the process of problem exploration. Messages typically employed to initiate the process are:

"Could you tell me about your situation?"

"I'm interested in hearing about what brought you here."

"Tell me about the difficulties you've been having, and we can think about them together."

Clients will generally respond by beginning to relate their problems. The practitioner's role at this point is to draw out the client(s), to respond in ways that convey understanding, and to seek elaboration of information needed to gain a clear picture of factors involved in clients' difficulties. Some clients, particularly applicants, spontaneously provide rich information with little assistance. Others, especially referred and involuntary clients, may be hesitant; many struggle with their emotions; and many have difficulty finding words to express themselves.

Because referred clients may perceive that they were brought here by the concerns of others, they often respond by recounting those external pressures. The practitioner can assist in this process by sharing his or her information about the circumstances of the referral.

To facilitate the process of exploration, practitioners employ a number of skills, often blending two or more in a single response. One type of skill, furthering responses, encourages clients to continue verbalizing. *Furthering responses* include minimal prompts (both verbal and nonverbal) and accent responses. Furthering responses, which convey attention, interest, and an expectation that the client continue verbalizing, are discussed in Chapter 6.

Other responses facilitate communication (and rapport) by providing immediate feedback that assures clients that practitioners have not only heard but also understood their messages. *Para-phrasing* is employed to provide feedback that the practitioner has grasped the content of a client's message. In using paraphrasing, the practitioner rephrases (with different words) what the client has expressed. *Empathic responding*, by contrast, provides feedback that the practitioner is aware of emotions the client has experienced or is currently experiencing.

Both paraphrasing and empathic responding, which are discussed in Chapters 5 and 6, are especially crucial with clients who have limited language facility, including ethnic minority and developmentally disabled clients. When language barriers exist, practitioners should be careful not to assume that they correctly understand the client or that the client understands the practitioner. Further, with ethnic clients who have been culturally conditioned not to discuss personal or family problems with outsiders, practitioners need to make special efforts to grasp intended meanings. Many of these clients are not accustomed to participating in interviews and tend not to discuss their concerns openly. Rather, they may send covert (hidden) messages and expect practitioners to discern their problems by reading between the lines. Practitioners thus need to use feedback more extensively with these clients to determine if their perceptions of intended meanings are on target. Using feedback to ascertain that the practitioner has understood the client's intended meaning and vice versa can avoid unnecessary misunderstandings. Further, clients generally appreciate efforts of practitioners to reach shared understanding, and they interpret patience and persistence in seeking to understand as evidence that the practitioner respects and values them. It is not the ethnic minority client's responsibility, however, to educate the practitioner. [4]

On the other hand, what the practitioner thinks he or she knows about the minority client's culture may be an inappropriate stereotype because individuals and families vary on a continuum of assimilation and acculturation with majority culture norms (Congress, 1994). Based on a common Hispanic value, the practitioner might say, "Can you call on other family members for assistance?"

Exploring Expectations Before exploring problems, it is important to determine clients' expectations, which vary considerably and are influenced by socioeconomic level, cultural background, level of sophistication, and previous experience with helping professionals. In fact, socialization which includes clarifying expectations about the roles of clients and practitioners has been found to be associated with more successful outcomes, especially with involuntary clients (Rooney, 1992; Videka-Sherman, 1988). In some instances, clients' expectations diverge markedly from what practitioners can realistically provide. Unless practitioners are aware of and deal successfully with such unrealistic expectations, clients may be keenly disappointed and disinclined to continue beyond the initial interview. In other instances, referred clients may have mistaken impressions about whether they can choose to work on concerns as they see them as opposed to the views of referral sources such as family members. By exploring expectations, however, practitioners create an opportunity to clarify the nature of the helping process and to work through clients' feelings of disappointment. Being aware of clients' expectations also assists practitioners to vary their approaches and interventions according to clients' needs and expectations, a matter discussed at greater length in Chapter 5.

Eliciting Essential Information

During the exploration process, practitioners assess the significance of information revealed as clients discuss problems and interact with the practitioner, group members, or significant others. Indeed, judgments about the meaning and significance of fragments of information guide practitioners in deciding which aspects of a problem are salient and warrant further exploration, how ready a client is to explore certain facets of a problem more deeply, what patterned behaviors of the client or system interfere with effective functioning, when and when not to draw out intense emotions, and so on.

The direction of problem exploration proceeds from general to specific. Clients' initial accounts of their problems are typically general in nature ("We fight over everything," "I don't seem to be able to make friends," or "We just don't know how to cope with Scott. He won't do anything we ask," or "Child protection says I don't care for my children."). Clients' problems, however, typically have many facets, and accurate understanding requires careful assessment of each one. Whereas open-ended responses, such as those illustrated earlier, are effective in launching problem explorations, other types of responses are used to probe for the detailed information needed to identify and unravel the various factors and systems that contribute to and maintain the problem. Responses that seek concreteness are employed to elicit such detailed information. There are many different types of such responses, each of which is considered at length in Chapter 6. Another type of response needed to elicit detailed factual information (also discussed in Chapter 6) is the closed-ended question.

Focusing in Depth

In addition to possessing discrete skills to elicit detailed information, practitioners must be able to maintain focus on manifest problems until they have elicited comprehensive information. Adequate assessment of problems is not possible until a practitioner possesses sufficient information concerning the various forces (involving individual, interpersonal, and environmental systems) that interact to produce the problems. Focusing skills (discussed at length in Chapter 6) involve blending the various skills identified thus far as well as summarizing responses.

During the course of exploration, practitioners should elicit information that will enable them to answer numerous questions, the answers to which are crucial in understanding various factors that bear on the clients' problems, including ecological factors. These questions (discussed in Chapter 8) serve as guideposts to practitioners and provide direction to interviews.

Employing Outlines

In addition to answering questions that are relevant to virtually all interviews, practitioners may need to elicit data that will answer questions pertinent to the function of specific practice settings. Outlines that embody essential questions to be answered can be extremely helpful to beginning practitioners. It is important, however, to use outlines flexibly and to focus on the client, not the outline. Examples of outlines and suggestions for using them are contained in Chapter 6.

Assessing Emotional Functioning

During the process of exploration, practitioners must be keenly sensitive to clients' moment-to-moment emotional reactions and to the part that emotional patterns (e.g., inadequate control of anger, depression, and widely fluctuating moods) play in their difficulties. Emotional reactions during the interview (e.g., crying, intense anxiety, anger, and hurt feelings) often impede problem exploration and require detours aimed at assisting clients to regain equanimity. It must be noted that anxiety and anger exhibited by involuntary clients may be as much influenced by the circumstances of involuntary contact as by more enduring emotional patterns.

Emotional patterns that powerfully influence behavior in other contexts may also be problems in and of themselves that warrant careful exploration. Depression, for example, is a prevalent problem in our society and one that responds well to proper treatment. When clients manifest symptoms of depression, the depth of the depression and risk of suicide should be carefully explored. Empathic communication is a major skill employed to explore emotional patterns.

Factors to be considered, instruments that assess depression and suicidal risk, and relevant skills are discussed in Chapter 9.

Exploring Cognitive Functioning

Because thought patterns, beliefs, and attitudes are powerful determinants of behavior, it is important to explore clients' opinions, and interpretations of circumstances and events deemed salient to their difficulties. Often, careful exploration reveals that misinformation, distorted meaning attributions, mistaken beliefs, and dysfunctional patterns of thought (such as rigid, dogmatic thinking) play a major role in clients' difficulties. Messages commonly employed to explore the thinking of clients include the following:

1. How did you come to that conclusion?
2. What meaning do you make of . . . ?
3. How do you explain what happened?
4. What are your views (or beliefs) about that?

The significance of cognitive functioning and other relevant assessment skills are discussed further in Chapter 9.

Exploring Substance Abuse, Violence, and Sexual Abuse

Because of the prevalence and magnitude of problems associated with substance abuse (including alcohol), violence, and sexual abuse in our society, the possibility that these problems contribute to or are the primary source of clients' difficulties should be routinely explored. Because of the significance of these dysfunctional behaviors, we have devoted major sections to them in later chapters.

Negotiating Goals and a Contract

When practitioners and clients believe they have adequately explored the problems, they are ready to enter the process of planning. By this point (if not sooner), it should be apparent whether other resources and/or services are needed. If it appears other resources are needed or are more appropriate, the practitioner may initiate the process of referring clients elsewhere. If clients' problems match the function of the agency and clients express readiness to proceed further in the helping process, it is appropriate to begin negotiating a contract. When involuntary clients are unwilling to participate in a helping process, their options are clarified here. They can choose to return to court, choose not to comply and risk legal consequences, choose to comply minimally or choose to work with the practitioner on problems as they see them in addition to legal mandates (Rooney, 1992). Goals specify the end results that will be attained if the problem-solving efforts are successful. Generally, after participating together in the process of exploration, practitioners and clients share common views as to end results or changes that are desirable or essential. In some instances, however, practitioners may recognize the importance of accomplishing certain goals that clients have overlooked and vice versa.

Practitioners introduce the process of negotiating goals by explaining the rationale for formulating them. If formulated in explicit terms, goals give direction to the problem-solving process, and serve as progress guideposts and as outcome criteria for the helping efforts. To employ goals effectively, practitioners need skills in involving clients in selecting attainable goals, in formulating general task plans for reaching these goals, and in developing specific task plans to guide practitioner and client efforts between sessions.

When more than one goal is entailed in resolving a problematic situation, as is usually the case, practitioners assist clients in assigning priorities to goals so that immediate efforts can be directed to the most burdensome aspects of the problem. Giving clients major responsibility for selecting goals enhances their commitment to actively participate in the problem-solving process by ensuring that goals are of maximal relevance. Even involuntary clients can often choose the order of goals to be addressed or participate in the process of that choice. Essential elements of the goal selection process are delineated in Chapter 12.

Ending Interviews

Both initial interviews and the contracting process conclude with a discussion of "housekeeping" arrangements and an agreement about next steps. During this final portion, practitioners focus on the length and frequency of sessions, who will participate, the means of accomplishing goals, the duration of the helping period, fees, date, and time of next appointment, pertinent agency policies and procedures, and other relevant matters. The contracting process is discussed at length in Chapter 12.

When you have completed the interview processes, as detailed above, or when the time allocated for the interview has elapsed, it is appropriate to conclude the interview. Messages appropriate for ending interviews include the following:

1. I see our time has run out today. Let's stop here and we'll begin next time by reviewing our experience in carrying out the tasks we discussed.

2. Our time is running out, and there are still some areas we need to explore. Let's arrange another session when we can finish our exploration and think about where you'd like to go from there.

3. We have just a few minutes left. Let's summarize what we accomplished today and what you and I are going to work on before our next session.

Goal Attainment

During Phase II of the helping process, interviewing skills are used to help clients accomplish their goals. Much of the focus during this phase is on identifying and carrying out actions or tasks clients must implement to accomplish their goals. Preparing clients to carry out actions is crucial to successful implementation. Fortunately, effective strategies of preparation are available (see Chapter 14).

As clients undertake the challenging process of making changes, it is important that they maintain focus on a few selected priority goals until they have made sufficient progress to warrant shifting to other goals. Otherwise, they may jump from one concern to another, dissipating their energies without achieving significant progress. The burden, therefore, falls on the practitioner to provide structure for and direction to the client. Toward this end, skills in maintaining focus during single sessions and continuity between sessions are critical (see Chapter 6).

As noted earlier, barriers to goal attainment commonly occur during the helping process. Typical individual barriers include obstacles such as fears associated with change and/or behavior and thought patterns that are highly resistant to change efforts because they serve a protective function (usually at great psychological cost to the individual). With couples and families, barriers include entrenched interactional patterns that resist change because they perpetuate power or dependence, maintain safe psychological distance, or foster independence (at the cost of intimacy). In groups, common barriers involve dysfunctional processes that persist despite repeated efforts by leaders to replace these patterns with others that are conducive to group goals and to group maturation.

Additive empathy, a skill referred to earlier, is used with individuals, couples, and groups to recognize and to resolve emotional barriers that are blocking growth and progress. Confrontation is a high-risk skill used to assist clients in recognizing and resolving resistant patterns of thought and behavior. Because of the sophistication involved in using these techniques effectively, we have devoted Chapter 18 to them and have provided

relevant skill-development exercises. Additional techniques for managing barriers to change (including relational reactions) are discussed in Chapter 19.

Termination

During the final phase of the helping process, the focus shifts to consolidating gains achieved by clients, planning maintenance strategies, managing emotional reactions to the impending separation, and evaluating results. Each of these processes is discussed in Chapter 20.

Because relapse is high with certain client groups, most notably in cases involving substance abuse, marital difficulties, chronic mental illness, and overeating, developing maintenance strategies is of critical importance. Increasing attention has been accorded to developing and testing such strategies, which we discuss in Chapter 20.

Evaluating results (outcomes) also has assumed increasing importance, as we discussed in earlier chapters. Measuring progress at termination by using the same instruments or strategies employed in obtaining baseline data is thus an integral part of the termination process. Determining the durability of gains achieved at one or more follow-up points is also part of effective evaluation.

SUMMARY

In this chapter, we have viewed the three phases of the helping process from a global perspective and have briefly considered the structure and processes involved in interviewing. Table 3-1 depicts in summary form constituent parts of the helping process and their interrelationships with various interviewing processes.

The remaining parts of the book focus in detail on the three phases of the helping process and on various subsidiary interviewing skills and interventions.

TABLE 3-1 PHASES OF THE HELPING PROCESS AND CONSTITUENT ACTIVITIES AND PROCESSES

PHASES		
Phase I (Exploration, Assessment, and Planning)	Phase II (Implementation and Goal Attainment)	Phase III (Termination and Evaluation)
Establishing rapport (using appropriate warm-up period)	Partializing goals into subgoals and tasks	Evaluating readiness for termination
Starting where the client is	Selecting and implementing interventions	Mutually planning termination
Exploring the client's problem and the ecological context: exploring the problem in depth, maintaining focus, eliciting information needed to answer critical questions	Planning task implementation Enhancing self-efficacy Maintaining focus within sessions	Effecting positive termination of relationship Planning strategies to maintain change and continued growth Evaluating results
Responding to clients' emotional reactions	Maintaining continuity between sessions	Conducting follow-up evaluation
Determining if problems match the agency's function	Monitoring progress	
Making referrals when indicated	Resolving barriers to change: enhancing awareness by employing additive empathy, managing relational reactions, and resolving resistance to change by employing confrontation and other techniques	
Exploring clients' expectations		
Enhancing deficient motivation		
Formulating a multidimensional assessment		
Negotiating goals and ranking them by priority	Employing self-disclosure and assertiveness to facilitate change	
Defining roles		
Formulating a contract		

NOTES

1 The idea of specific phases and their accompanying tasks in structuring casework was originally developed by Jessie Taft and Virginia Robinson and the Functional School . They were later elaborated by Reid (1992) and Epstein (1988) in the task-centered approach.

2 An interesting model of developing rapport through sharing tribal backgrounds is depicted in the instructional videotape "Ethnic Sensitive Practice with Involuntary Native American Client" avail-

able from Rooney at the School of Social Work, University of Minnesota.

3 We recommend Freed's (1988) article, which addresses the complexities and cites many useful references.

4 Personal communication, Lila George, Department of Social Work, Bemidji State University, 1993.

Chapter 4

Operationalizing the Cardinal Social Work Values

THE INTERACTION BETWEEN PERSONAL AND PROFESSIONAL VALUES

In this chapter, we present the cardinal values of the profession and demonstrate how these values apply to specific practice situations. As you read this chapter, you will have opportunities to place yourself in complex situations that challenge you to analyze your values and to assess their compatibility with social work values. You will also be presented with situations that pose value dilemmas even to seasoned practitioners.

Personal values greatly influence what you actually do in the helping process, for your beliefs and attitudes inevitably influence your feelings and behavior with clients. For this reason, it is critical that you develop an appreciation of the significant role your values play in your daily encounters with clients. To the extent that you are unaware of these values, you are likely to attempt, sometimes unknowingly, to impose them on your clients. There are five major ramifications associated with imposing values on clients, the first of which is that imposing values is antithetical to the client's right to self-determination.

The second ramification is that until clients have internalized new values, behaving contrary to deeply held values may create intense feelings of guilt, as illustrated in the following example.

....

Case Example

Mr. R, a single man, age 35, who lived with his aging parents and was very devoted to them, sought counseling because of conflicts between his personal needs and those of his parents. He had recently become interested in a widow but could tell that his parents were hurt because of the amount of time he was spending with her. They had said nothing, as was typical, but they related coolly to him. He didn't wish to hurt them but felt they should understand that he needed to live his own life. The practitioner appropriately supported his thrust for independence but, in addition, pushed Mr. R to confront his parents directly with their unrealistic expectations and to express his intentions of living his own life. The practitioner further indicated that, in devoting himself to his parents, Mr. R had done himself a strong injustice, and the practitioner suggested it was high time he rectified the situation. Upon the strong urging of the practitioner, Mr. R agreed to confront his parents, although he was apprehensive. His parents responded with unexpected understanding to the confrontation. Mr. R could sense their hurt and disappointment, however, and felt extremely guilty. Attempts to relieve his guilt failed, and he rapidly became depressed and preoccupied with thoughts that life was not worth living.

The third ramification is that many clients resent and oppose attempts to impose values upon them—some to the extent that they discontinue seeing a practitioner, as in the following instance reported by a student who had been a participant observer in an interview conducted by an experienced practitioner.

Case Example

Mrs. W, a widow, had sought professional help for depression that had persisted following her husband's death one year earlier. In this, the fifth interview, Mrs. W expressed a deep sense of loss associated with her husband's death. She said that she and Mr. W had been very close and had enjoyed a mutually fulfilling sexual relationship. She missed their sexual relationship and was frustrated because she believed only married people should engage in sexual relations. She had dated several men, most of whom had made sexual overtures. She was inclined to respond positively on a few occasions but believed to do so would be wrong. The practitioner responded that she was an adult and that there was nothing wrong with sex between consenting adults. The practitioner further suggested she needed to discard her outmoded ideas and enjoy herself more. Mrs. W hesitantly replied that she wasn't sure she could or wanted to do that. She subsequently canceled her next appointment and did not return for additional interviews.

The fourth ramification of imposing values is that practitioners must be aware of their own values in order to assist clients who themselves are having value conflicts. Otherwise, they may unwittingly impose their own values rather than engage clients in careful exploration and analysis of issues and consequences involved in various courses of action associated with differing value preferences. Of course, clients' problems may derive from self-defeating behaviors associated with dysfunctional values, and practitioners have a responsibility to assist them to come to this realization so that they can make choices, having awareness of the values involved and of the probable outcomes of those choices. In such instances, the practitioner's motivation is constructive, for it is based on the client's needs. By contrast, attempting to convert clients to one's values because of a conviction that these values are right meets the needs of the practitioner, not the client.

The final ramification is that the practitioner may sometimes represent organizational or cultural values which are in conflict with a client's culture.

Case Example

Mrs. D, 75, a Native American woman, was released from a hospital with a chronic kidney condition, but otherwise good health. While making a home visit, the social worker found that Mrs D lived in a one-room home with a dirt floor and no indoor plumbing. The walk to the outhouse was at least a half block away. There was, however, a house with indoor plumbing on the property which the Bureau of Indian Affairs built for her several years earlier. Was this evidence that she was incapable of making rational decisions about her well-being? A culturally competent worker might know that she was choosing to live in a traditional fashion and the dirt floor had spiritual meaning for her, not unlike the cross hanging over the bed of a Catholic. Mrs. D considered the walk to the outhouse good exercise rather than a problem, and had lived in these conditions her entire life. She stored the pottery she made in the government housing. Such a culturally competent worker would discover that Mrs D's extended family visited her regularly, and brought her food when she was unwell.

THE CARDINAL VALUES OF SOCIAL WORK

To assist you in operationalizing the cardinal values of social work and to reflect those values in your responses to specific practice situations, we delineate in the subsequent sections the following values and concepts that flow from the profession's cardinal values.

1. All human beings deserve access to the resources they need to deal with life's problems and to develop their potentialities.

2. All human beings have intrinsic worth and dignity.

3. The uniqueness and individuality of each person is of value.

4. Given appropriate resources, human beings are capable of growth and change and should be supported in increasing their choices in solving their problems and directing their lives.

We have included value clarification exercises designed to expand your awareness of your personal values and of the implications of these values for your social work practice. Finally, we have provided skill development exercises in the latter portion of the chapter to give you practice in formulating responses to specific situations that involve implementing the values and concepts discussed earlier.

1. All human beings deserve access to the resources they need to deal with life's problems and to develop their potentialities.   An historic and defining feature of social work is the profession's focus on individual well-being in a social context. Fundamental to social work is attention to environmental forces that create, contribute to, and address problems in living (NASW, 1995, p. 2). Consequently, "Social workers are committed to assisting client systems to obtain needed resources (CSWE, 1994, p. 139). To implement this value requires that you develop commitment to the value, knowledge of and skill in employing community resources, and willingness to develop and implement policies and programs that effectively meet human needs.

Social workers generally express firm commitment to this value; yet when applied to certain situations, that commitment sometimes dwindles. In these situations, conflicting beliefs and personal biases come into play, and ultimate attitudes may indicate that a competing belief supersedes one's commitment to assist a client in obtaining resources.

To enhance your awareness of the extent to which you meet the five previous ramifications, we describe several situations. We suggest that you explore your personal feelings and attitudes regarding these situations by engaging in the following activity.

Imagine yourself in interviews with the clients involved in each of the following situations. Try to picture yourself and your client as vividly as possible. Imagine the client making the request for the resource described and think of the response you would make. Be aware of your feelings and of possible discomfort or conflict. Then contemplate how your response is or is not consistent with the social work value in question. If the client has not requested a resource, but the need for one is apparent, consider what resource might be developed and how you might go about developing it.

Situation 1   You are a practitioner in a public assistance agency that has special funds available to assist clients to purchase essential eyeglasses, dentures, hearing aids, and other prosthetic items. Your client, Mr. Y, who lives in a large apartment complex for single persons, is disabled by a chronic psychiatric disorder. He requests special aid in purchasing new glasses. He says he accidentally dropped his old glasses and they were stepped on by a person passing by. However, you know from talking to his landlord earlier that Mr. Y broke his glasses while inebriated.

Situation 2   During a home visit to a large impoverished family in the central city, you observe Eddy, a teenage boy, drawing pictures of animals. The quality of the drawings reveals an exceptional talent. When you compliment him, he appears shy, but his faint smile expresses his delight over your approval. Eddy's mother then complains that he spends most of his time drawing, which she thinks is a waste of time. Eddy's face registers pain and discouragement at her remarks.

Situation 3   During a routine visit to an elderly couple who are recipients of public assistance, you discover that the roof on their home leaks. They have had small repairs on several occasions, but the roof is old and worn out. They have had bids for reroofing, and the lowest bid was over $2,500. They ask if your agency can assist them with funding. State policies permit expenditures for such repairs under exceptional circumstances, but much red tape is involved, including securing special approval from the county director of social services, the county advisory board, and the state director of social services.

Situation 4   A number of low-income families in your community have been forced to move to housing beyond their means by real estate development companies that have been demolishing older apartment houses to construct high-rise condominiums. In the last session of the state legislature, a bill to provide low-interest mortgage funds for low-income families was defeated by a narrow margin. The legislature will be convening next month.

Situation 5   Mr. M sustained a severe heart attack three months ago. His medical report indicates that he must limit future physical activities to light work. Mr. M has worked as a freight handler for trucking firms and has no other special skills. Not working, he feels useless and worried about how he can provide adequately for his wife and three children.

Situation 6   During the course of an interview with Laurie, a teenage girl in foster care, you learn that her younger sister, age 15, has been having serious difficulties with her parents and has confided in Laurie that she plans to run away and support herself through prostitution. An older male has promised to set her up in an apartment and refer customers to her.

Represented in the preceding vignettes are needs of clients for resources or for opportunities to develop potentials or needed skills. Possible obstacles to responding positively to these needs, according to the sequence of the vignettes, are as follows: (1) judgmental attitude by a practitioner, (2) failure of significant others or of a practitioner to recognize a potential that might be developed, (3) unwillingness to support a request because of the red tape and effort required, (4) unwillingness by practitioners and others to actively support needed legislation, (5) ignorance of both practitioner and client of potential rehabilitation services, and (6) judgmental attitude or failure to intervene assertively in a timely manner. As you read the vignettes, you may have experienced some of these reactions or additional ones. Such reactions, which are not uncommon among learners, may result from personal values that you have not scrutinized. If you experienced negative reactions to these situations, you need not be unduly alarmed. However, these reactions are indications of your need for expanded self-awareness and additional experience.

2. *All human beings have intrinsic worth and dignity.* This value is reflected in both the proposed revision of the NASW Code of Ethics and Council on Social Work Education accreditation guidelines. Value III of the proposed revision says "Social workers respect the inherent dignity and worth of the person," while M6.5.1 of the accreditation guidelines includes the statement that "Social workers' professional relationships are built on regard for individual worth and dignity."

This cardinal value means that social workers believe that all human beings have intrinsic worth, whatever their past or present behavior, beliefs, lifestyle, or status in life. As they perform their responsibilities, practitioners should affirm the dignity and self-worth of those whom they serve. Universally accepted among the helping professions, this value embodies several related concepts, which have been variously denoted as unconditional positive regard, nonpossessive warmth, acceptance, and respect.

Although this value derives largely from Judeo-Christian and humanistic moral beliefs, it also has pragmatic implications associated with the helping process. Before people will risk sharing personal problems and expressing deep emotions, they must first feel fully accepted and experience the goodwill and helpful intent of practitioners. Keep in mind that many people feel highly vulnerable in requesting or accepting assistance, fearing they may be perceived as inadequate or as failures. Vulnerability is even greater when clients' alleged behavior involves moral infractions, cruelty, child neglect, dishonesty, and other behaviors generally violating societal norms. Such allegations often coincide with involuntary status, so that such potential clients enter helping relationships with their antennas finely attuned to possible condemning reactions by practitioners. Usually these clients have been criticized, rebuked, and condemned previously by others, and their anticipation and fear of being judged by the practitioner are readily understandable.

The social worker's role is not to judge but to seek to understand clients and their difficulties and to assist them to search for solutions. The role of judging falls under the purview of legal and ecclesiastical authorities. Social workers thus should avoid making judgments as to whether clients are good, bad, evil, worthy, guilty, or innocent. Similarly, it is inappropriate for social workers to seek to determine the extent to which clients are to blame for their difficulties. In this regard, it has been our observation that experienced practitioners who have rendered service to many people with diverse problems are less judgmental than are neophytes. This difference can be attributed to the fact that seasoned practitioners have learned through experience that the more one understands the life experience of others, however appalling their behavior may be, the more understanding and accepting one becomes of them.

As you work with clients, therefore, seek to view them as persons in distress and avoid perceiving them according to labels, such as lazy, irresponsible, delinquent, rapist, alcoholic, or prostitute. As you learn more about your clients, you will find that many of them have suffered various forms of deprivation and have themselves been victims of abusive, rejecting, or exploitative behavior. Remember also that many clients lacked sustained love and approval during critical periods of development, the result of which is a diminished sense of self-worth. Consistent respect and acceptance on your part tends to exert a corrective influence in assisting them to gain self-esteem, which is vital to sound mental health.

Withholding judgments does not mean that social workers condone or approve of illegal, immoral, abusive, exploitative, or irresponsible behavior. Social workers have their own values and moral codes and are offended by child neglect, rape, brutal crimes, and like behaviors to much the same extent as are other persons. Moreover, social work as a profession and social workers as individuals have responsibilities to assist people to live according to the laws of society.

The objective of not blaming people for their difficulties should not be construed to mean that social workers avoid assisting clients to take responsibility for the part they play in their difficulties. Indeed, change is possible in many instances only as clients gain awareness of the part they play and seek to modify their behavior accordingly. The difference between blaming and defining ownership of responsibilities lies in the fact that the former tends to be punitive, whereas the latter emanates from positive intentions to ameliorate difficulties.

The implication of the preceding discussion is that you as a practitioner are confronted with the challenges of maintaining your own values (except those that hinder relating effectively to people) without imposing them and of divesting yourself of possible tendencies to judge people whose behavior may be offensive to you and to others. Still another challenge is to develop composure to the extent that you do not manifest embarrassment or dismay when people discuss value-laden problems associated with socially unacceptable behavior. The value clarification exercises provided in the following section will assist you in identifying particular areas of vulnerability.

To the extent that you fall short of the goal of developing an openness and ability to accept people whose behavior runs counter to your values, your range of effectiveness will be diminished, for it is difficult if not impossible to conceal negative feelings toward others. Even if you are able to mask negative feelings toward certain clients, you are likely to be unsuccessful in helping them, for clients are quick to discern insincerity. In seeking to expand your capacity for openness and acceptance, you may find it helpful to view association with others whose beliefs, lifestyles, and behaviors differ strikingly from your own as an opportunity to enrich yourself as you experience their uniqueness. Truly open people relish such opportunities, viewing differentness as refreshing and stimulating. Furthermore, gaining understanding of the forces that motivate people can also be intriguing and enlightening. By prizing the opportunity to relate to all types of people and by seeking to understand them, you will gain a deeper appreciation of the diversity and complexity of human beings. In so doing, you will become disinclined to pass judgments and will achieve personal growth in the process.

Value Clarification Exercises

The following exercises will assist you in expanding awareness of values and attitudes that may impair your effectiveness in affirming the dignity and worth of certain clients. In each situation, imagine yourself in an interview or group session with the client(s). If appropriate, you can role-play the situation with a fellow student, changing roles so that you can benefit by playing the client's role as well. As you engage in imagination or role-playing, be aware of your feelings, attitudes, and behavior. After each situation, contemplate or discuss the following:

1. What feelings and attitudes did you experience? Were they based on what actually occurred or did they emanate from preconceived beliefs about such clients?
2. Were you comfortable or uneasy with the client? What were your partner's perceptions of your attitudes as reflected in your behavior?
3. What values were reflected in your feelings, attitudes, and behavior?

Situation 1   Your client is a 35-year-old married male who was ordered by the court to secure mental health services following his arrest for making obscene telephone calls. He appears uncomfortable and blushes as you introduce yourself.

Situation 2   You are just starting your first group session with a group of males being treated for AIDS in a health center.

Situation 3   You are a child welfare worker, and your client is a 36-year-old father whose 13-year-old daughter ran away from home after he enticed her into having sexual intercourse on several occasions during the past two months. She reported to you earlier that he has been molesting her since she was six years old.

Situation 4 Your 68-year-old client has been receiving chemotherapy for terminal cancer at your hospital for the past month. Appearing drawn and dramatically more emaciated than last month, she reports she has been increasingly suffering with pain and believes her best course of action is to take an overdose of sleeping pills.

Situation 5 You are a probation officer, and the judge has ordered you to complete a presentence investigation of a woman arrested for being an accomplice in a con game employed to bilk elderly people out of their savings.

Situation 6 You have been working for eight weeks with Mr. X, who initially sought help for marital difficulties. His wife left him four weeks ago, and he has continued seeing you for anxiety and depression. He confides he has been pushing drugs for 18 months and has wanted to stop but doesn't know how he could produce a comparable income.

Situation 7 You are interviewing parents for inclusion in a group formed to help the members control violent outbursts toward their children. You introduce yourself to Mr. O, who was referred by the hospital following admission of Isabel, his four-year-old daughter. Isabel sustained a broken leg and rib injuries when Mr. O threw her against the wall in a fit of rage.

If you experienced discomfort or negative feelings as you read or role-played any of the above situations, your reactions were not unusual. Most people (even social work students) are repulsed by some of the problematic behaviors embodied in the situations described. Trying to look beyond the behaviors to see clients as individuals in distress is a formidable challenge. However, by focusing selectively on the person rather than the behavior, you can gradually overcome inclinations to label

people negatively and learn to see them in full perspective.

When practitioners warmly accept clients as they are, consistently manifesting care and concern, they increase the likelihood that the clients will gradually lower their defenses. A climate of trust and mutual respect usually evolves, and clients increasingly sense and appreciate practitioners' goodwill. Acceptance is conveyed by listening attentively; by responding sensitively to feelings manifested by the client; by facial expressions, voice intonations, and gestures that convey interest and concern; and by extending courtesies and attending to the client's comfort.

Acceptance is probably conveyed most strongly by consistent efforts to understand clients and their difficulties. Verbal following by the practitioner, especially in the form of empathic responding, conveys a commitment to understand. Though you may not always fully understand all of your client's messages, genuine efforts on your part to do so will be discerned and appreciated. Careful efforts to explore the client's problems also convey interest, commitment to understand, and a desire to assist clients with difficulties.

As we have noted, acceptance is also conveyed through practitioner warmth. Although the element of warmth is difficult to define, it is generally agreed that a warm person is attentive, yet calm and relaxed, and speaks with a well-modulated voice that reflects the nuances of feeling manifested by a client. Monotonic speech, by contrast, tends to be interpreted as indicating boredom, whereas rapid and staccato speech has an excited quality that fosters tension.

Although you can do little to modify the pitch of your voice, you can increase your warmth by listening to recordings of your interviews and identifying both positive and negative patterns in your speech. If, for example, you wished to convey genuine concern for a client at a particular point in a session and your voice intonations failed to adequately convey that concern, you may benefit by engaging in practice that involves varying your voice inflections until you attain the desired intonation. Feedback from colleagues after role-playing exercises can also help you to identify strengths as well as areas for improvement in reflecting warmth.

With respect to warmth, a caveat is in order. Excessive efforts to be warm may achieve effects opposite to those desired. Some clients, especially those who habitually maintain considerable distance from others to protect themselves from imagined hurt, are frightened by lavish friendliness and warmth. Other people may view effusive warmth as inappropriate, insincere, or seductive. This is especially true when dealing with referred and involuntary clients who did not seek the contact. Clients vary in the extent to which they welcome or tolerate emotional closeness, and it is vital to avoid pressuring for a degree of intimacy that exceeds their level of tolerance. A warm, pleasant demeanor, augmented by genuine demonstrations of interest and concern, fosters a positive helping relationship and is appreciated by clients; gushy friendliness, by contrast, offends some people.

Other Threats to Acceptance and Respect

In addition to differences in values between you and your clients and possibly stereotypes and prejudices that you may have toward certain client groups (we discuss stereotypes and prejudices more fully later), other threats in the form of certain behavioral patterns of clients may severely test your tolerance and your capacity to affirm the dignity and worth of clients. These types of behaviors, of course, are by no means limited to clients, and when confronted in other walks of life, such behaviors tend to produce negative interactions and to strain relationships. Because acceptance of and respect for clients are indispensable to the helping process, it is important that you develop awareness of your reactions to these behaviors and

evolve patterns of response that safeguard the helping relationship.

Because practitioners vary widely in their personalities, each will be vulnerable to responding negatively to certain types of behavior and not to others. We have not attempted to identify all the kinds of behavior that pose threats to acceptance and respect but have limited our focus to those most commonly encountered. We will present both the troubling behavior and normalizing perspectives to assist in understanding them. It should be noted that all of the following are more likely to occur with involuntary than with voluntary clients.

1. Helplessness.
2. Silence and withdrawal.
3. Aggressive and sullen behavior.
4. Manipulative and exploitative behavior.
5. Self-effacing behavior.
6. Noncompliant behavior or treatment nonadherence.

Helplessness   The threat posed by helpless behavior is that a practitioner will underestimate the strengths and capacities of clients and thereby foster and reinforce dependency by assuming responsibility for solving a client's difficulties. The following are typical examples of helplessness:

Mother of adolescent son: I just don't know what to do with Larry. He's so demanding and loses his temper when I don't let him have his way. I'm just lost in knowing what to do. He's a good boy, but he's so strong willed [cries and wrings hands]. Please talk with him and help him see how he's just killing his poor mother. I'm at my wit's end.

Aged single woman: I live in a place that is all I can afford and I get beaten up coming home with groceries. I've got nowhere to go and nobody else to take care of me. What can you do to help me?

There are many possible explanations for helpless behavior. One is that the potential client has little experience with helping professionals and anticipates that his or her role is to accept advice from an expert. In instances in which the client is mandated to receive services, they may believe that "throwing themselves at the mercy" and in no way threatening practitioners is likely to help them reach their goals. Social psychologists use the term *Self-presentation strategies* to describe such efforts to manage the impression that others have of us in order to better reach our goals (Friedlander & Schwartz, 1985). Clients are most likely to attempt such tactics when stakes are high and they do not trust that they can get what they wish from a practitioner by asking for it. Still a third explanation is learned helplessness. When over a period of time, people come to feel that they cannot influence events important to them, they stop trying (Seligman, 1975).

In such instances, taking the initiative in response to pressure from clients manifests disrespect for their strengths and fosters unrealistic expectations that you are all-powerful and capable of dispensing ready-made solutions to their difficulties. Moreover, by unrealistically assuming the burden of solving clients' problems, you negate the cardinal value of self-determination.

After failing to cope successfully with problems, many clients, of course, seek help precisely because they feel helpless and overwhelmed. Rather than inviting dependency, however, your tasks in such instances are to engender hope, enhance motivation, and enlist active participation in the search for remedial courses of action. This is done by clarifying role expectations for clients and ourselves. For example, responding to the message of the aged woman cited previously who implores the practitioner to give her answers to her problems, the worker might say:

"You are telling me that you live in a dangerous situation and may wonder if just talking about it is going to help. I don't have easy answers to the problems of your safety and housing. Together we can take a look at these problems and start on the ones that look most resolvable. You are the expert in your life and I can't know what will work for you in handling these problems. I know that together we can make progress by cutting this overwhelming situation into pieces."

Clients who participate actively in the problem-solving process, who see themselves as the cause of change, are more likely to be committed to follow through on mutually selected courses of action than are those who passively depend on practitioners (Feld & Radin, 1982). Adopting a strength-oriented perspective and conveying expectations of responsible, independent behavior also foster hope, self-respect, and commitment to implement strategies for change.

Practitioners should be aware of the special threat to acceptance and respect involved in work with immigrants and ethnic minority groups who remain closely tied to their cultures of origin. Handicapped by an inability to communicate in English and overwhelmed by the alien and complex bureaucracies of American society, many of these people manifest dependency and helplessness that reflect their situational context rather than personality deficiencies. It is important to keep in mind that most of these clients functioned adequately and were productive citizens in their native lands. Their seeming helplessness thus belies latent strengths that can be mobilized by according them respect, assisting them through the maze of bureaucratic procedures, and linking them with support systems that can enable them to gain greater language facility and knowledge of available resources and their rights.

Unduly catering to dependency that is a realistic response to an alien environment may foster or prolong dependency. Aiding such clients to mobilize their coping capacities, teaching them new skills, working in partnership with them to develop support networks, and providing direct assistance as needed strengthen their adaptation to their new environment.

Silence and Withdrawal   The threat represented by silence and withdrawal is similar to that posed by excessive dependency and helplessness. When confronted with silence or withdrawal, beginning practitioners tend to respond by assuming inordinate responsibility for maintaining verbalization.

Although silence tends to produce a certain amount of tension, to cope with that tension by consistently taking the initiative tends to result in nonproductive monologue by the practitioner and to produce a sense of frustration. Moreover, constantly assuming the initiative for conversation establishes a pattern in sessions that may be difficult to change, since clients will understandably assume that this is the norm and will passively wait for you to break periods of silence. With other clients, your assuming the initiative provides them with leverage to control the interview. Still other clients may deliberately use silence in a hostile manner, realizing that they can produce anxiety in the practitioner by remaining silent.

For the above reasons, it is important that you learn to tolerate silence without undue discomfort. Although few pauses occur in successful interviews, it is not realistic to expect constant verbalization. Pauses naturally occur when either clients or practitioners need a moment to reflect on an idea or feeling or when clients have exhausted a given topic and need to gather thoughts before proceeding to a different one. Such natural pauses usually are short-lived and do not warrant interruption on your part. Moreover, clients vary in levels of verbalization and in verbal facility. Some clients reveal rich information with minimal prompting, whereas others lack verbal skills or find it difficult to reveal personal information. With the latter type of client, you will need to be active in eliciting information, as silence may engender acute anxiety, especially with clients who are insecure and hypersensitive. These clients may misinterpret silence as indicative of lack of interest or rejection on your part. Passivity is no more desirable than is constantly assuming the initiative. It should be noted, however, that there are instances when it is appropriate to give a client permission to be silent (for example, when the client is discussing painful material or pondering an issue) by employing a message such as, "Take your time—I know this is painful for you to discuss."

In addition to the meanings cited above, silence may also be a manifestation of opposition to change or of strong emotions (positive or negative) experienced toward the practitioner. These dynamics generally occur later in the helping process; skills needed to manage these phenomena are discussed in Chapter 19. For the present, it is sufficient to point out that prominent silence is a signal that you need to shift the focus to exploring underlying thoughts and feelings that, if not resolved, may become a major barrier to progress.

In the final analysis, decisions about breaking silence must be made according to the type of client and the situational context. Our point is that you must be sufficiently flexible to remain silent or to break silence according to the client's best interest. Otherwise, you may unwittingly deprive clients of opportunities to assume an appropriate measure of responsibility for maintaining verbalization in individual and group sessions. Equally important, you may undermine the helping relationship by establishing communication patterns that foster dependency and passivity.

Aggressive and Sullen Behavior   Perhaps the greatest threats to relating to clients with acceptance and respect are aggressive and sullen behavior, which are often encountered with delinquent youth and inmates of correctional institutions but are by no means limited to these populations. Aggressive behavior may consist of verbal attacks in the form of challenges to your integrity, competence, or motives, or it may involve insults directed at your status, appearance, speech, or other aspects of personal demeanor. Clients' anger may emanate from many sources. Some clients tend to be angry people, and little or no provocation is required to trigger angry outbursts. Such behavior is often most clearly a sign that the potential client views the counseling situation as dangerous. Verbal or physical intimidation may be a form of self-presentation strategy as described above which is designed to regain power in a potentially threatening situation.

Another explanation for such aggressive behavior is that the potential client is experiencing reactance or a threat to valued freedoms (Brehm, 1976). Reactance is most likely to occur when the client feels that undesirable changes will be forced on him or her regardless of his or her wishes (Brehm & Brehm, 1981). Instead of focusing on the client's negative reaction, it is useful to ask: "Reacting *to what*? What valued freedom is being threatened?." Hence, reactance can often be reduced by focusing on constrained choices, alternatives for meeting requirements, spelling out specifically what must change and what freedoms remain.

Whatever the source, the natural reaction to provocative messages is to feel defensive and to counter anger with anger or to set the other person straight. Similarly, when an involuntary client sits sullenly, avoiding eye-to-eye contact except for an occasional glare, the natural reaction is to express irritation or to admonish the client to shape up. Such defensive reactions or counterattacks only tend to inflame the situation and perpetuate an escalation, leading to more attacks and counterattacks. Such an excalation is often self-defeating, as it does not deal with problems at hand and may lead to worsening conditions. However, few clients have the process skills to halt an escalation by saying, "Why don't we slow down here? It's clear that you and I are both saying things we don't mean."

How then should you respond to aggressive and provocative behavior? First, it is vital to master your natural tendency to respond defensively. Recognizing that the client's hostility may be displaced from other sources can assist you not to personalize verbal attacks or sullen behavior, thus freeing you from feeling threatened and enabling you to respond facilitatively. To resolve the hostility, it is important to assist clients to drain off angry feelings. This is best accomplished by employing empathic responses, which not only foster expanded expression of feelings but also convey respect and understanding for the client. Clients' anger may also emanate from their understandably perceiving certain social work roles or functions as threatening (e.g., investigating a complaint of child neglect). In such instances, practitioners must be empathically responsive to such feelings. By fostering a release of hostile feelings, empathic responses tend to defuse anger, permitting a more rational exploration of the factors associated with the client's feelings.

It is important to recognize that you are not expected to become a perpetual target for client abuse. If responding empathically for a period of time fails to mellow the client or if the situation is otherwise timely, you may wish to authentically (but unabrasively) describe the impact of the client's provocative or abusive behavior upon you (see Chapter 5). It is vital that clients receive descriptive feedback about their aggressive and provocative behavior, particularly if it seems to be an ongoing, repetitive style of behavior that is also manifested in significant relationships. One of the reasons why provocative behavior is often maintained in the client's repertoire is that others have responded defensively rather than authentically describing the negative reaction the client's behavior causes in them and the damaging effect it has upon the relationship. Further, if rapport between the practitioner and client is sufficiently developed and the client is amenable, the practitioner may wish to explore with the client the possibility of modifying the provocative behavior through subsequent change efforts.

To respond openly and nondefensively to expressions of angry feelings is difficult for practitioners who have not as yet evolved effective ways of coping with their own angry feelings. Research (Bandura, Lipsher, & Miller, 1960) has indicated that practitioners who avoid expressing their own negative feelings in social interactions tend to avoid aggressive expressions of clients by ignoring them, changing the subject, or employing other avoidance behaviors. In such instances, unfortunately, clients are left to struggle with negative feelings by themselves, often to the detriment of the helping process. Self-awareness is thus essential to responding facilitatively to aggressive behavior. You will find exercises for dealing with aggressive behavior, as well as modeled responses, in the last portion of this chapter.

Manipulative and Exploitative Behavior   Similar to aggressive behavior in their effect on practitioners are manipulative and exploitative behaviors on the part of certain clients (Hepworth, 1993). These behaviors also engender natural reactions of anger at being deceived or ripped off. In some instances, the anger also stems in part from disgust with oneself for being gullible or for making errors in judgment that lead to exploitation. One beginning practitioner, for example, went to some lengths to provide a positive experience for a delinquent who was permitted temporary leave from a state correctional institution. The practitioner took the youth shopping for new clothes, to the movies, and generally extended himself in the youth's behalf. When they returned to the institution, the youth expressed profuse gratitude. Shortly thereafter, the social worker's sense of satisfaction and dedication turned to bitterness and near fury when he discovered his "grateful" client had stolen his keys to the institutional facilities.

To affirm the worth and dignity of clients who engage in manipulative behavior strains the capacity for acceptance of even the most altruistic and patient practitioners. Accepting the person, however, does not mean condoning or disregarding the exploitative behavior. In such instances, practitioners should confront the client in a genuine manner, expressing their feelings of disappointment with tact. This involves relating authentically and employing confrontation and other skills judiciously.

Rather than jeopardizing the helping relationship, facilitative confrontations ultimately strengthen it, for they demonstrate that clients are of sufficient worth and importance that the practitioner will not passively permit them to engage in behavior that can result in their loss of freedom and engender condemnation and social ostracism from others as well. Indeed clarifying how they can reach their own goals, how you can help them, and how manipulative behavior will prevent them from reaching those goals is an important way of fostering agreement on the goals pursued (Rooney, 1992, p. 143).

Self-Effacing Behavior   Some clients engage in practitioner flattery and/or excessive put-downs of their own competence. Such behavior can be interpreted in several ways. One hypothesis is then that the behavior suggests that the client has low self-esteem. A second is that the client perceives the practitioner to control an important resource which he or she believes can not simply be asked for in order to receive it. A third is that such patterns are at times culturally supported in some cultures and institutional settings, which expect clients to show very high respect for professionals.

With the first hypothesis, we note that some clients have strong feelings of inadequacy and worthlessness, such that they tear themselves down, constantly apologize for themselves, and attempt to win the approval of others, including practitioners, by ingratiating behavior and flattery.

With the second hypothesis, self-presentation theory once again can help us understand the use of insincere influence methods as a means toward reaching important goals. Readers who can recall seeking a job which they very much want and need to have, may recall using a variety of strategies, not all of which were candid, to assist in making a good impression. For example, when asked to describe a weakness, how many of us choose to say, "I sometimes get overwhelmed with my work and let things like paperwork slide," rather than,

"I am so committed to helping clients directly that I sometimes let that take precedence over paperwork."

Self-presentation theorists describe a range of such strategies including ingratiation (flattery and agreeing with the opinions of the other), self-promotion (emphasizing one's own competence) and moral examplification (emphasizing one's moral worthiness) (Rooney, 1992, p. 140). While all these terms carry a disreputable taint, it is interesting to note that job-seeking manuals *teach* most of them but reframe them in more positive terms such as "selling your strengths." Consequently, if you sense that insincere efforts are being made to influence you, you might ask yourself, "Does the client think that I control a resource that is very important to him or her?" Knowing that you and I and others are likely to use self-presentation strategies around goals very important to us such as getting an attractive job is a useful way of connecting to whether the client perceives that you could influence an important resource such as child custody, needed financial resources, or a favorable court recommendation.

Finally, it should be considered that some clients have learned cultural expectations that professionals are to be treated with great deference and respect. The same is also true in some institutional settings which reward such behavior and discourage assertive behavior such as selecting goals other than those approved by the institution. In such circumstances, it is important for the practitioner to understand how such behavior has been learned and rewarded while indicating through role expectations how the client is expected to take an active, honest part in solving problems.

When the timing is appropriate, it is important to assist clients to observe their own self-effacing behavior, its repetitive nature, and the impact of their actions on themselves and others. The practitioner does this with the objective of helping clients to take action to alleviate such self-defeating behaviors and to assume more functional and assertive ways of relating.

For those clients who engage in this behavior as a repetitive pattern, it is crucial that you respond to these clients by affirming their worth and dignity as well as their strengths and problem-solving capacities. The threat to implementing these values is that practitioners may also take such clients for granted because of their lack of assertiveness and self-deprecating behavior. When they must juggle their schedules, it is not uncommon for practitioners to be tardy for appointments, to cut interviews short, or to change the appointment times of such clients rather than others. It is important to recognize that although these clients typically acquiesce when inconvenienced, they nevertheless experience hurt, disappointment, and resentment. Moreover, they tend to interpret being taken advantage of as evidence of their lack of worth.

Practitioners can convey respect and foster self-respect by helping them to believe in their right to expect more from others. Practitioners can nurture assertive behavior by tuning in to and empathizing with more genuine feelings that often lie beneath the client's manifest obsequious behavior. Such empathic responding validates negative feelings and enables clients to get in touch with these emotions that have previously been suppressed or denied expression. Gradually, as clients risk expressing negative feelings without being rebuked or rejected, they learn that the practitioner and others can value them quite apart from their complying with the real or imagined expectations of others. And finally, if practitioners are courteous and empathic, conveying the expectation that clients have a perfect right to respect, clients will gradually gain self-respect.

Noncompliant Behavior or Treatment Nonadherence   Still another pattern of behavior that poses a threat to responding to clients with acceptance and respect is passive noncompliant behavior. Meichenbaum and Turk suggest that noncompliant behavior be reframed to the term treatment nonadherence (Meichenbaum & Turk,

1987). They suggest that nonadherence problems range from consistent failure to comply with instructions to inappropriate compliance and that the term treatment noncompliance places blame on clients rather than leaving open the cause for the behavior in the transaction between client and professional. Clients, for example, may fail to keep agreed-upon appointments with practitioners, physicians, or prospective employers, or may fail to follow through in carrying out vital actions they have agreed to perform (e.g., following a prescribed medical regimen for a child). The most direct hypothesis to explain such behavior is that the practitioner is mistakenly presuming a shared goal or agreement or the means to reach it. A second hypothesis from reactance theory is that the client is reasserting his or her freedom to decide what to do by choosing not to carry out the expected behavior (Brehm, 1976). Clients are free to refuse to carry out tasks which might indeed be in their best interest as seen by others if such tasks are not legally mandated. The practitioner can return to review whether goals are shared or have been imposed on the client and, if the client accepts the goal, review whether there may be other means which the client chooses to reach the goal, or choose to accept the consequences of not complying with the recommended actions.

Treatment nonadherence in certain cultural contexts, however, has an entirely different meaning. For example, among some Filipinos, it is common to regard openly disagreeing with another person or declining an invitation to another's home as rude and offensive. Consequently, persons of this cultural orientation may overtly agree to comply with certain arrangements or planned courses of action but express their actual intentions through passive nonadherence. Failure to understand the cultural significance of such behavior can lead to inaccurate assessments and to lack of respect for these clients. However, practitioners who are knowledgeable about culturally mediated behavior carefully and sensitively explore clients'

beliefs about causes of problems and are keenly alert to nonverbal negative reactions that signal the need to explore feelings further and to defer making plans or suggestions until clients are likely to be genuinely receptive. As clients gain trust, practitioners also assist them to resolve inhibitions about expressing themselves more openly by clarifying for the clients that they welcome disagreement and open expression of feelings and views, rather than being offended by such behavior. By thus clarifying the cultural differences in expectations, practitioners assist these clients to risk new behaviors. Changes in actual behavior, of course, occur only gradually because such values and beliefs are deeply embedded.

3. *The uniqueness and individuality of each person is of value.* Intertwined with acceptance and nonjudgmental attitude is the equally important value that every person is unique and that social workers should affirm the individuality of those whom they serve. Human beings, of course, are endowed with widely differing physical and mental characteristics; moreover, their life experiences are infinitely diverse. Consequently, people differ from one another in appearance, beliefs, physiological functioning, interests, talents, motivation, goals, values, emotional and behavioral patterns, and many other factors.

To affirm the uniqueness of another person, you must be committed to the value just discussed and also enter the other person's world, endeavoring to understand how that person experiences life. Only through attempting to walk in the shoes of another person can you gain a full appreciation of the rich and complex individuality of that person. Affirming the individuality of another, of course, goes far beyond gaining an appreciation of the other person's manifold perspectives of life. One must be able to convey awareness of what the other is experiencing moment by moment and affirm the validity of that experience.

Affirming the validity of another's experience does not mean agreeing with or condoning that person's views and feelings. Part of your role as a practitioner is to help people to disentangle their confusing, conflicting thoughts and feelings; to align distorted perceptions with reality; and to differentiate irrational reactions from reality. To fulfill this role, you must retain your own separateness and individuality. Otherwise, you may overidentify with clients, thereby losing your potential for providing fresh input. Affirming the experiences of another person, then, means validating those experiences, thus fostering that person's sense of personal identity and self-esteem.

Appreciation for uniqueness goes beyond individual characteristics to include those which occur through membership in a group. As CSWE suggests, "Social workers demonstrate respect for and acceptance of the unique characteristics of diverse populations"(CSWE, 1994). Those populations include, but are not limited to, "groups distinguished by race, ethnicity, culture, class, gender, sexual orientation, religion, physical or mental ability, age, and national origin"(CSWE, 1994, p. 140). Further, the proposed revision of the NASW Code of Ethics includes as evidence of culturally competent practice that a practitioner "have a knowledge base of their clients' cultures and be able to demonstrate competence in the provision of services that are sensitive to clients' culture and to differences among people and cultural groups" (NASW, 1995, p. 8).

Opportunities for affirming individuality and sense of self-worth are lost when practitioners are blinded to the uniqueness of clients by prejudices and stereotyped perceptions of the groups to which they belong. Although prejudices may be either favorable or unfavorable, we are using the term to refer to unfavorable judgments or feelings toward persons or groups that are made on the basis of preconceived opinions rather than actual experience. Prejudices commonly are directed toward people who differ from one's own reference group on dimensions such as race, ethnicity, gender, religion, sexual orientation, socioeconomic level, political persuasion, and lifestyle. Such

prejudices generally are associated with misconceptions caused by limited and inaccurate information and little or no interaction with members of a particular group. We have observed various social work students, for example, who manifest irrational fears of talking with delinquents, elderly clients, or mental patients, perceiving them as strange, different, or otherwise vaguely threatening. Interestingly, social workers themselves have been the objects of stereotyping, being labeled by some people as do-gooders or flaming liberals.

Prejudices tend to diminish or to disappear when people have frequent personal contacts with members of a particular group. As they are subjected to the test of actual experience, supposed or even real differences among people tend to shrink due in large measure to the fact that people become more aware of how much greater are their similarities than their differences. Thus liberated from their prejudices, people are able to see others formerly regarded as members of an alien group as worthwhile and interesting individuals in their own right.

Stereotypical perceptions are closely related to prejudices in that they also derive from preconceived fixed opinions about other people on the basis of their membership in particular groups. For example, some people view long-haired males as rebellious, irresponsible, immoral, and addicted to drugs. While these labels may well be applicable to some such individuals (and to short-haired males and females as well), they are entirely inappropriate for others.

As such, stereotypes are also antithetical to the value of affirming the uniqueness and individuality of other people. Although stereotypes do not necessarily involve negative judgments about others, they do involve conventional views and inaccurate perceptions that may obscure practitioners' awareness of clients' potentialities. Consequently, practitioners may unwittingly restrict efforts to assist clients to actualize these potentials or, even worse, may block clients' efforts to develop themselves more fully.

Stereotypes of greatest significance to social workers involve perceptions of persons of color, sex roles, the elderly, people with disabilities, and various groups whose lifestyles diverge markedly from the cultural majority. Stereotypical perceptions of minority groups are endemic in our culture, as attested to by the popularity of ethnic jokes that typically degrade and demean people of African, Mexican, Italian, Polish, Irish, Native American, and Jewish extraction.

You may counter the detrimental effects of stereotypes by seeking to gain extensive knowledge about the culture of your clients. If you manifest a genuine interest in and respect for a culture, members of that culture will usually be receptive to your efforts to expand your knowledge. Conducive to this objective and to working effectively in cross-cultural relationships is the same value cited earlier, namely, affirming the worth and uniqueness of other cultures. If you work extensively with a cultural group that speaks another language, it is highly desirable to learn to speak that language. The ability to converse in the client's language facilitates developing a working relationship and enhances understanding of clients and their cultures. By being open to and prizing the differences among cultures, you will be broadened and enriched. You may even internalize certain values of other cultures that appear more valid than your own.

Research findings further emphasize the importance of affirming the worth and uniqueness of other cultures. In an outcome study of casework with Chicano clients, Gomez, Zurcher, Farris, and Becker (1985) found that the factor that correlated most highly ($r = .43$) with clients' satisfaction with services was the practitioner's skill in "the development and reinforcement of positive feelings about clients' self-concept as Mexican-Americans" (p. 481). Probably this finding is also applicable to work with other ethnic minority groups.

You may have little opportunity to learn about their cultures firsthand, but you can gain knowledge by reaching out to fellow students who are members of different ethnic groups and by studying the substantial literature pertaining to different cultures. (Many universities devote portions of their libraries to ethnic literature.) You might also participate in programs related to specific minorities, such as black studies programs. Opportunities for developing resources also exist within your student body, as, for example, organizing a program for cultural enrichment within your student organization.

Sex-role stereotypes have been a major concern to social workers in recent years, and the professional organization has vigorously attempted to abolish discriminatory practice associated with these stereotypes. Sex-role stereotypes may also have a detrimental impact on the helping process. Research findings concerning the extent to which social work students and practitioners have stereotypical sex-role perceptions have generally indicated that the profession (females particularly) have made substantial strides in supplanting traditional, anachronistic role perceptions with egalitarian views. The findings are not conclusive, however, and the challenge remains to foster the individuality of both men and women rather than to view them in fixed, sex-linked ways. To meet this challenge, you will need to make individual efforts, for as Davenport and Reims (1978) stress, "Clinicians also must be aware that their attitudes are influenced by factors external to their training, and they cannot assume that professional training in and of itself will address or correct potential bias" (p. 308).

Stereotypical perceptions of elderly persons may also distort assessment, limit goals, and restrict helping efforts with this neglected group of Americans. Individual problems in social functioning may incorrectly be attributed to the infirmities of age. Similarly, reversible health problems associated with inadequate nutrition or need for medication may be dismissed as merely symptomatic of advanced age. Depression associated with unfulfilled common human needs for affection, meaningful activities, companionship, and sexual gratification may likewise be overlooked. Considering the many losses (energy, health, employment, loved ones, status, reduced income) and stresses commonly associated with old age, it is a sad commentary that only 2 to 3% of all persons seen in community mental health centers in our country are over age 65 (Butler, 1975).

Strengths of elderly persons are also frequently overlooked, resulting in faulty assessment and restricted goal planning. Common stereotypes held by many Americans tend to relegate elderly persons to a rocking-chair status or to playing bingo in senior citizens' centers. The capacity to grow, to develop new skills, and to be productive, however, does not abruptly cease when people reach retirement age. Toseland (1977), for example, has reported research findings that document the capacity of elderly persons to master problem-solving skills and to enhance social skills. Elderly couples also frequently need and can benefit from marital therapy and from sex therapy (Sander, 1976).

Stereotypes about persons with physical and developmental disabilities also skew perceptions of practitioners toward clients' incapacities rather than toward their capacities, strengths, and potentialities. Many people still view those with disabilities as objects of curiosity and pity. Haney and Rabin (1984), for example, characterize negative societal attitudes as the major obstacle to resocialization of persons paralyzed by severe spinal cord injury. Some of these persons report that others stare at them, continually causing them to feel they are on display. Intrusive questions about their disabilities, unsolicited help, and comments made within earshot, such as, "I'd rather be dead than like that" abridge the rights of these and others with disabilities (Weinberg, 1983).[1]

Societal attitudes toward persons with developmental disabilities are perhaps even more negative than toward persons with physical disabilities. Moreover, the public holds misconceptions that persons with developmental disabilities have little or no awareness of their handicaps and are indif-ferent to the terms used to refer to them. The fact is that persons with developmental disabilities, like people with severe physical disabilities, experience anguish when stared at and asked intrusive questions. The effects of stigmas toward this group and implications for overcoming them have been discussed by Dudley (1987).

Social workers and other health care professionals can join people with disabilities in seeking to overcome negative societal attitudes toward them (it is important to work with them in a manner which manifests respect for their capacities and fosters development of the same). Practitioners, of course, should begin by taking inventory of their own perceptions and attitudes. Beyond this they should advocate for policies that provide opportunities for people with disabilities and that bring them into the mainstream of American society. Social policy implications related to this goal have been discussed by Coudroglou and Poole (1984).

Social workers must also be aware of and rectify prejudices and stereotypes associated with groups of people whose lifestyles and sexual orientations diverge from dominant cultural norms. In our pluralistic society, many people also have fixed ideas about the desirable type of family unit—the traditional nuclear family (consisting of father, mother, and children)—and look askance at other types of living arrangements. Social workers must avoid such preconceived judgments and affirm many different types of family structures and must render services impartially.

Prejudices toward and stereotypical views of gay, lesbian, and bisexual persons are especially rampant in our society. Research findings (Wisniewski & Toomey, 1987), unfortunately, reveal "preliminary empirical support" (p. 455) that a substantial percentage of social workers manifest signs of homophobia (i.e., fear and anxiety and perhaps disgust toward gays, lesbians, and bisexuals). One-third of 77 clinical social workers surveyed in Columbus, Ohio, earned scores on the Index of Attitudes Toward Homosexuals (Hudson & Ricketts, 1980) that classified them as homophobic. Obviously these findings are of concern because practitioners with fears of or negative attitudes toward gays, lesbians, and bisexuals are unlikely to be effective in work with such clients or with others for whom they hold similar negative attitudes.

A later study (Gillman, 1991) of 353 social workers in Philadelphia, however, reported more encouraging findings, suggesting that increased education and exposure to information has improved attitudes toward homosexuals. These findings indicated relatively positive attitudes toward gays, lesbians, and bisexuals with 86% of the respondents viewing homosexuality as an acceptable lifestyle and 94% stating they were comfortable with the idea of having a gay neighbor.

Attitudes of social workers toward working with gays, lesbians, and bisexuals with HIV/AIDS were less favorable, with about one-third of the respondents manifesting reluctance to work with an HIV-infected client. Their reluctance, however, was far more related to not wanting to work with terminally ill clients and to their lack of knowledge about AIDS than to negative attitudes toward homosexuals. Interestingly, the more knowledgeable social workers were about AIDS the less opposed they were to working with people with AIDS. Findings of this and other studies cited by Gillman suggest that "social workers have many fears and misconceptions about AIDS that might impede empathic and competent service delivery to clients" (Gillman, 1991, p. 599). The need for relevant educational programs is apparent in light of projections that HIV/AIDS will eventually affect the professional lives of all social workers (Shernoff, 1990). Support of persons with AIDS by social workers is vitally needed, because these persons may feel isolated from society at the very time their need for social and emotional support is greatest.

Societal prejudices and discrimination toward gays, lesbians, and bisexuals have influenced many of this group to choose to remain in the closet rather than risk losing their jobs, friends, and sta-

tus and subjecting themselves to ostracism and abuse (Roberts, Severinsen et al., 1992). Such prejudices create serious difficulties for families with a gay, lesbian or bisexual member, and these families therefore have particular needs for social services (Hall, 1978; Lewis, 1980; Wyers, 1987). The challenge to social workers is to acknowledge the existence of families with gay, lesbian, and bisexual members and to recognize their special identities and needs (Hall, 1978, p. 384).

Hall's challenge should be preceded by still another step—being aware of one's prejudices or stereotypes. It is natural to have biases or stereotypes regarding certain groups of people within our society; in fact, it is probably impossible to be entirely free of preconceived attitudes toward certain groups of people. If you are open to considering that you have certain biases, however, you are in a position to strive to overcome them.

Value Clarification Exercises

The following exercises will assist you in expanding your awareness of prejudices or stereotypes you may have that could impair your effectiveness in working with certain clients. In each situation, imagine yourself in an interview or group session with the client(s). Try to picture the client as vividly as possible and try to be aware of your feelings, attitudes, and behavior. After each situation, contemplate or discuss with peers the following:

1. What feelings and attitudes did you experience?
2. Have you experienced like reactions to similar persons in the past?
3. What possible prejudices or stereotypes were reflected in your body reactions, feelings, or attitudes?

Most students discover they do have some active or residual biases, and this is no cause for alarm. It is a basis of concern, however, for if you do not alter such negative attitudes, they will impair your effectiveness in working with related practice situations.

Situation 1 Two women in their mid-20s request help in resolving difficulties in their relationship. One complains the other is jealous and overly possessive. The other replies that her partner is insensitive to her needs and feelings. They have lived together in a lesbian relationship for two years.

Situation 2 As an adoption worker in a children's service agency, you have just learned that Mr. and Mrs. Y, a Caucasian couple in their 30s, have applied for adoption of a black infant.

Situation 3 You are a social worker in a large university hospital that pioneered surgical techniques for changing males into females. After learning that many patients who have undergone such operations have difficult problems in adjusting socially, the director of social services has requested that you lead a group of such individuals.

Situation 4 You are an African American outreach worker operating in a housing project which includes low income people from many racial and ethnic groups and many elderly persons. One elderly Caucasian woman who has expressed appreciation for the help you have provided in linking her to transportation and home-delivered meals services tells you repeatedly that she is afraid living in this area with so many coloreds.

Unfortunately, many people lack awareness of their prejudices and stereotypes, deceiving themselves into believing they are entirely free of such unfavorable attitudes. Indeed, some practitioners mistakenly pride themselves on possessing no biases, and their naïveté in this regard limits their openness to experiencing themselves, let alone other people who are strikingly different from them. Never really able to come to terms with their prejudices, they tend to alienate others who perceive and respond negatively to subtle manifestations of their prejudices. Still others perceive themselves as champions of victims of discrimination and, blinded by their zeal, erroneously attribute problems rooted in other sources to the effects of discrimination. Such zeal often emanates from unconscious overcompensation for guilt about living in a racist society. Overcompensation and overidentification with the oppressed can result in offering special privileges and relaxing standards of behavior beneath those expected by minorities themselves. As such, overidentification can impair effective work as much as prejudices and stereotypes.

It is thus clear that self-awareness is key to liberating oneself from prejudices and stereotypical perceptions. Self-awareness notwithstanding, practitioners occasionally encounter situations in which a client's behaviors or goals evoke such negative reactions that a positive helping relationship cannot be attained. For example, practitioners who have extreme feelings about rape or who are intensely opposed to abortions may find it difficult to accept a rapist as a client or to offer help to a person seeking an abortion. In such instances, it is important to acknowledge such feelings to oneself and to explore the possibilities of a transfer to another practitioner who can accept both the client and the goals. When a transfer is possible, it is vital to clarify for clients that the reason for transfer is not personal rejection of them but that they deserve the best service possible and that the practitioner cannot provide that service because of value conflicts. Such an explanation conveys goodwill and safeguards the self-esteem of clients. Frequently such a transfer is not possible, and the practitioner is responsible for being up front with the client about their difficulties while committing themselves to carrying out their ethical and professional responsibilities. Practitioners who frequently encounter difficulties in accepting clients probably tend to be inflexible and consequently have a limited range of effectiveness. Such practitioners owe it to themselves and to future clients to seriously consider if they have chosen the appropriate profession.

4. *Given appropriate resources, human beings are capable of growth and change and should be supported in increasing their choices in solving their problems and directing their lives.* As stated by CSWE, "social workers respect the individual's right to make independent decisions and to participate actively in the helping process"(CSWE, 1994, p. 139). This value embodies the beliefs that clients have the capacity to grow and change and to develop solutions to their difficulties, as well as the right and capacity to exercise free choice responsibly. These values are magnified when practitioners adopt a strengths-oriented perspective, looking for positive qualities and undeveloped potentialities rather than limitations and past mistakes (Saleeby, 1992; Cowger, 1994). Such a positive perspective engenders hope and courage on the client's part and nurtures self-esteem as well. These factors, in turn, enhance the client's motivation, which is indispensable to a successful outcome.

The positive effects of accrediting strengths and highlighting increments of progress were manifested in a fourth interview with a client who had entered counseling because of frequent periods of depression. She began the interview by complaining that she had been depressed over the weekend. Her depressed mood during the interview, in part, seemed to derive from discouragement over being unable to control the feelings of depression. After carefully reviewing the events that occurred over the weekend and the client's response to them, the practitioner made several observations that reflected improvement in the client's coping with her depressed feeling. The client had not deemed it necessary to call the practitioner for support, as she had done previously. The depression was also less intense and of a shorter duration than usual. Further, rather than going to bed as she typically did when depressed, the client had actively tried to ward off the depression by taking a walk, going to a movie, and going for a ride with her husband. Accrediting these efforts, the practitioner expressed the impression that the client appeared to be moving from the position of feeling helpless about coping with her depressed mood to a position of actively taking steps to counter it. The client was pensive for a few moments and then replied she hadn't thought of it that way, but it was true. Her mood brightened perceptively as she realized the progress she had made.

Belief in the capacity of others to change is critically needed, for people's perceptions of themselves and their problems are strongly influenced by feedback from others. Thus, if you view clients positively and express the belief that they can work out their problems, they are likely to adopt a similar outlook. Of course, your view must be realistic in the sense that clients' situations are susceptible to change and that clients possess the capacity to implement whatever actions are required. Otherwise you may engender false hope that ultimately will lead to discouragement and perhaps to justifiable resentment toward you. Most problem situations can be remedied to some extent, however, and the large majority of clients have the capacity to take constructive actions on their problems.

Ethical principles which follow from commitment to the value of supporting choices include self-determination, informed consent, protection of confidentiality, and privileged communication. In the proposed revision of the NASW Code of Ethics, these principles are subsumed under the social workers' ethical responsibilities to clients. As stated in subsection 1.01, "Social workers' primary responsibility is to promote the welfare of clients. However, social workers' responsibility to the larger society or specific legal obligations may on limited occasions supersede the loyalty owed clients and clients should be so advised"(NASW, 1995, p. 7). Next, we will describe each principle in more detail, including those circumstances in which they are limited.

Self-Determination

Before considering how social workers affirm self-determination, a definition is in order. Biestek

(1957) has defined self-determination as "the practical recognition of the right and need of clients to freedom in making their own choices and decisions" (p. 103). Self-determination is a value accorded high priority by social work, as attested to by the following section from the draft of the Revised NASW Code of Ethics, which is subsumed under Major Principle I pertaining to the social worker's ethical responsibility to clients: "Social workers respect and promote the right of clients to self-determination and assist clients in their efforts to identify and clarify their goals. Social workers may limit clients' right to self-determination when, in their professional judgment, clients' actions or potential actions pose a serious, foreseeable, and imminent risk to themselves or others"(NASW, 1995, p. 7).

The extent to which you affirm self-determination rests in large measure on your perceptions of the helping role and of the helping process. If you consider your major role to be that of providing solutions or dispensing advice freely, you may foster dependency, demean clients by failing to recognize and affirm their strengths, and relegate them to a position of passive cooperation—or passive resistance, as often occurs under such circumstances.[2] Such domineering behavior is counterproductive; not only does it discourage open communication but, equally important, it denies clients the opportunity to gain strength and self-respect as they actively struggle with their difficulties. Fostering dependency generally leaves people weaker rather than stronger and is a disservice to clients.

The type of relationship that affirms self-determination and fosters growth is a partnership wherein practitioner and client (whether individual, couple, or group) are joined in a mutual effort to search for solutions to problems or to promote growth. As enablers, practitioners assist clients to view their problems realistically, to consider various solutions and their consequences, to implement change-oriented strategies, to understand themselves and others more fully, to gain aware-

ness of previously unrecognized strengths and opportunities for growth, and to resolve obstacles to change and growth. Although these facilitative functions often prove invaluable to clients, the ultimate determinant of the outcome of the shared venture resides, as it should, with the client.

Just as fostering self-determination enhances client autonomy, paternalism (i.e., preventing self-determination based on a judgment of the client's own good) infringes on autonomy. Paternalistic behavior rests on the assumption that a practitioner has a right to interfere with a client's right to choose because she or he knows better than the client what is for the client's good. As Abramson (1985) clarifies, however, a practitioner who takes paternalistic actions for a client is obliged to justify such actions and carries responsibility for the burden of proof. Abramson acknowledges four conditions in which paternalism may be justifiable:

1. When the client is a child and is assumed to lack the capacity to make an informed decision.

2. When the client is considered mentally incompetent or lacking in rationality to the extent of being unable to comprehend the results of decision making.

3. When the consequences of an act are far reaching and are irreversible (such as a suicide attempt).

4. When temporary interference with liberty ensures future freedom and autonomy.

Abramson cautions practitioners to be judicious in employing paternalistic actions and builds a strong philosophical and pragmatic case for encouraging self-determination.[3]

Involuntary clients partially forfeit their right to freedom of choice by violating laws, infringing on the rights of others, or failing to adequately discharge responsibilities in providing for others. Illustrated in the following list are a few acts of commission or omission that may constrain self-determination:

1. Criminal acts that result in incarceration.

2. Child abuse that results in loss of custody.

3. Status offenses, such as running away from home or habitual truancy, that require court intervention.

4. Unethical acts that result in loss of the privilege to practice one's profession.

5. Physical or emotional neglect of a child, including exposing the child to immoral acts.

6. Refusal to secure medical services vital to a child's health, requiring court intervention to ensure that services are provided.

7. Violations of moral laws resulting in excommunication from religious organizations.

Self-determination may also be constrained by the incapacity to exercise one's freedom of choice. In such instances, people lose the opportunity rather than the right to exercise self-determination. Typical constraints include physical or mental incapacity (e.g., being unable to function autonomously because of hospitalization), immobility because of unavailable transportation, or mental incompetence caused by organic brain disease or other forms of trauma to the brain. As stated in the proposed revision of the NASW Code of Ethics: "When the social worker must act on behalf of clients who are not able to make informed decisions or who have been adjudged legally incompetent, social workers should safeguard the interests and rights of those clients" (NASW, 1995, p. 13). In such instances, social workers have an obligation to reduce the losses of self-determination to a minimum by mobilizing resources that restore opportunity (e.g., arranging transportation so that immobile people can exercise their right to vote or to participate in social activities) or providing a proxy who can represent the client's interests or make essential decisions.

Even when clients have reduced capacity for exercising self-determination, social workers should act to ensure that they exercise their capacities to the fullest feasible extent. For example, based on research findings, Abramson (1988) concluded that discharge planning for hospitalized elderly patients who are severely ill or have mild senile dementia should include the patient whenever possible. These findings indicated that some patients afflicted with mild dementia still manifested capacity to participate in decision making, although moderate or severe dementia seriously impeded participation. Depression also did not appear to limit participation of elderly patients in planning their post-hospital arrangements.

Including elderly patients in discharge planning not only safeguards their right to self-determination, but also reduces the likelihood of negative reactions to relocation, according to studies summarized by Abramson. Abramson also reported results of studies indicating that in discharge planning for elderly patients, social workers spent substantially more time with family members than with patients, even though many of the patients manifested the physical and mental capability of making decisions for themselves. Clearly social workers in hospital settings should carefully evaluate whether they are, in fact, maximizing their elderly patients' rights to self-determination in discharge planning.

Even more severe circumstances, such as being terminally ill and comatose or in great pain, deprive those people of their right to self-determination in making decisions as to whether to be permitted to die or have their lives extended through "heroic" life-sustaining procedures and devices such as intravenous feedings, dialysis, and respirators. In such instances social workers can ensure patients' rights to self-determination by educating patients and their families to employ advance directives, which provide instructions to health care personnel regarding what medical interventions are acceptable. These directives become operative when the patient no longer is capable of making decisions because of being comatose or otherwise precluded from making autonomous decisions.

Advance directives can take the form of living wills or authorizing an individual to act as durable power-of-attorney. The latter procedure is broader in scope and more powerful than a living will.

The person designated to be durable power-of-attorney is authorized to make decisions as if he or she were the patient when grave illness or accident has obliterated the patient's autonomy.

Less powerful steps can also be taken to safeguard people's right to self-determination in matters of life and death.[4] Operationalizing clients' rights to self-determination sometimes can pose perplexing challenges. Adding to the complexity is the reality that in certain instances values of a higher order supersede the right to self-determination, which we discuss in a later section dealing with value dilemmas in social work practice.[5]

Value Implementation Exercises

To challenge your thinking about how you might affirm the value of self-determination in practical situations, we have provided exercises that consist of problematic situations actually encountered by the authors or colleagues. As you read each exercise, analyze alternative courses of action that are available. Consider how you would work with the client to maximize self-determination, taking care also to promote the best interests of the client. You may also wish to suggest discussion of these situations in class.

Situation 1   In your work for the state welfare department, you oversee the care of numerous nursing home residents whose expenses are funded by the state. Two of your clients, both in their 20s, reside in the same nursing home and have told you that they are eager to get married. The administrator of the home strenuously protests that the two are retarded and, if they marry, might produce a child they could not properly care for. Further, she has stressed that she has no private room for a couple and that if the two marry, they will have to leave the nursing home.

Situation 2   A runaway 15-year-old adolescent who is four months pregnant has contacted you

several times in regard to planning for her child. In her last visit, she confided to you that she is habituated to heroin. You have expressed your concern that the drug may damage her unborn child, but she does not seem worried nor does she want to give up use of the drug. You also know that she obtains money for heroin through prostitution and is not attending school.

Situation 3   While making a visit to Mr. and Mrs. F, an elderly couple living in their home on their own savings, you discover that they have hired several home health aides who have stolen from them and provided such poor care that their health and nutrition are endangered. When you discuss with them your concern about the adequacy of their care, they firmly state that they can handle their own problems and do not want to be put in a nursing home.

Situation 4   As a rehabilitation worker, you have arranged for a young woman to receive training as a beautician in a local technical college, a vocation in which she expressed intense interest. Although initially enthusiastic, she now tells you that she wants to discontinue the program and go into nursing, indicating that her supervisor at the college is highly critical of her work and that the other trainees tease her and talk about her behind her back. You are torn about what to do, knowing that your client tends to antagonize other people with her quick and barbed remarks. You wonder if, rather than changing programs, your client needs to learn more appropriate ways of communicating and relating to her supervisor and co-workers.

Providing Informed Consent

Self-determination is supported when clients are able to provide genuinely informed consent about the services they are to receive. Frequently agencies utilize standardized consent forms which are couched in language that may be difficult for clients to understand. According to the proposed revision to the NASW Code of Ethics, "Social workers are responsible for soliciting such consent through explaining in clear and understandable language the purpose of service, risks entailed, costs, alternatives, clients' right to refuse or withdraw consent, and the time frame covered by the consent" (NASW, 1995, p. 7). In addition, with clients who are not literate or who have difficulty with the primary language used in the practice setting, social workers are responsible for providing a detailed verbal explanation or arranging for an interpreter or translator.

Sometimes clients are temporarily or permanently incapable of providing informed consent because of the conditions described by Abramson (such as being a child or having a mental incapacity). In such circumstances "social workers should protect clients' interests by seeking permission from an appropriate third party, and inform clients consistent with their level of understanding. Social workers should take reasonable steps to enhance clients' ability to give informed consent" (NASW, 1995, p. 7).

Finally, some clients receive services involuntarily. In those instances, "social workers should provide information about the nature and extent of services, and of the extent of clients' right to refuse service "(ibid., 1995).

Safeguarding Confidentiality

Another way in which social workers convey respect and affirm the worth of clients is by preserving the confidentiality of private information disclosed during the course of the helping process. Confidentiality is vital to the helping process for practical, ethical, and legal reasons. Practitioners, therefore, must be knowledgeable about the various facets of this critical value.

From a practical standpoint, confidentiality is a sine qua non of the helping process, for without

assurance of confidentiality, it is unlikely that clients would risk disclosing private aspects of their lives that, if revealed, could damage their reputations. This is especially true when clients' problems involve marital infidelity, deviant sexual practices, illicit activities, child abuse, and the like. Implied confidentiality, if not explicitly requested by clients, is an assurance that such personal revelations will never be revealed to others by the practitioner.

Social workers are bound by the revised NASW Code of Ethics to safeguard confidentiality, as indicated in the following:

(a) "Social workers should respect clients' right to privacy. Social workers should not solicit private information from client unless it is essential to providing a service"(NASW, 1995, p. 9).

(b) "The social worker may disclose confidential information when appropriate with a valid consent from a client or a person legally authorized to consent on behalf of a client."

(c) "Social workers should protect the confidentiality of all information obtained in the course of professional service, except for compelling professional reasons." Those reasons include when disclosure is necessary "to prevent serious, foreseeable, and imminent harm to a client or other identifiable person or when laws or regulations permit or require disclosure without a client's consent" (ibid., p. 9).

(d) "Social workers should inform clients about the disclosure of confidential information, to the extent possible, and when feasible, before the disclosure is made."

(e) "Social workers should discuss with clients and other interested parties the nature of confidentiality and limitations of clients' rights to confidentiality (ibid., p. 10).

(f) "The social worker should obtain informed consent of clients before taping, recording, or permitting third-party observation of their activities" (ibid., p. 10).

Social workers thus have a profound responsibility to safeguard confidentiality. An unjustified breach of confidentiality is a violation of justice and is tantamount to theft of a secret with which one has been entrusted (Biestek, 1957). Maintaining strict confidentiality requires a strong commitment, for clients sometimes reveal information that is shocking, humorous, bizarre, or "juicy." To fulfill your responsibility in maintaining confidentiality, it is vital to guard against disclosing information in inappropriate situations, the most common of which include the following: discussing with family and friends, having gossip sessions with colleagues, dictating within the listening range of others, discussing client situations within earshot of other staff, and making remarks about clients in elevators or hallways. Violation of the client's right to confidentiality could result not only in loss of right to practice but also in a malpractice suit.

The right to confidentiality is not absolute, however, for confidential information is often stored in case records that are typed by stenographers, or entered into a computer data bank. Moreover, case situations are sometimes discussed with supervisors and consultants and may be presented at staff conferences. Disclosing information in these instances, however, is for the purpose of enhancing service to clients, who will generally consent to these uses when the purposes are clarified. The client has a right to be informed that such disclosures may occur, and practitioners have a responsibility to conceal the identity of the client to the fullest extent possible and also to reveal no more personal information than is absolutely necessary.

Obligations of Other Staff Persons   Others who have access to confidential information are similarly obligated to preserve confidentiality. Such persons include supervisors, administrators, volunteers, members of other disciplines, secretarial and clerical staff, consultants, board members, researchers, legal counsel, and outside persons who may review records for purposes of quality assurance, peer review, or accreditation. It is thus essential that social workers promote policies that ensure stringent measures to protect confidentiality and carefully orient and hold employees of the agency to their ethical responsibilities.

Obtaining Informed Consent When Providing Confidential Information   Practitioners are often requested by other social workers, members of other disciplines, or other agencies to provide confidential information pursuant to the client's contacts with these other parties or agencies. In these instances, it is important that such information be provided only with the written, informed consent of clients, which releases the practitioner and agency from liability in disclosing the requested information. Even when informed consent is obtained, however, it is important that information be revealed selectively according to the essential needs of the other party.

There are exceptions when information can be revealed without informed consent, such as a bona fide emergency in which a client's life appears at stake. In other instances, however, it is prudent to obtain legal counsel before disclosing confidential information without a written consent for release of information.

Confidentiality versus Other Rights   In certain instances, the client's right to confidentiality may be less compelling than the rights of other people who could be severely harmed or damaged by actions planned by the client and confided to the practitioner. For example, if a client plans to commit kidnapping, injury, or murder, the practitioner is obligated to disclose these intentions to the intended victim and to law enforcement officials so that timely preventative action can be implemented. Indeed, if practitioners fail to make appropriate disclosure under these circumstances, they are extremely liable to civil prosecution for negligence. In recent years, for example, practitioners have lost court cases in which they have been tried for negligence in failing to warn intended victims of harmful actions threatened by clients.

Confidentiality in Child Abuse Rights of others also take precedence over the right to confidentiality in instances of child abuse and/or neglect. In fact, all 50 states now have statutes making it mandatory for professionals to report suspected or known child abuse. Moreover, all statutes governing the mandatory reporting of child abuse contain a criminal clause for failure to report. It is noteworthy that practitioners are protected from both civil and criminal liability for breach of confidentiality resulting from the legal mandate to report (Butz, 1985). Without such immunity, as Butz indicates, involved professionals would be placed in a double bind.

Although afforded immunity from prosecution for reporting, practitioners are still confronted with the difficult challenge of preserving the helping relationship after having breached confidentiality.[6]

When child-abusing parents are being treated by a social worker for substance abuse, conflicting state and federal statutes place professionals in a quandary. On one hand, they are mandated by state law to report child abuse under threat of penalty; on the other hand, if they report cases involving parents who are substance abusers, they may be prosecuted either criminally or civilly by federal authorities for breaching federal confidentiality requirements set forth in the federal alcohol and drug abuse confidentiality acts. In her discussion of the complex issues involved, which are far from resolved, Saltzman (1986) cites a federal policy statement that authorizes substance abuse workers covered by the federal acts to report child-abuse parents who are also substance-abuse patients if they first obtain a court order. Although seeking a court order may be cumbersome and time consuming, Saltzman recommends that such orders be sought to avoid violating federal law (Saltzman, 1986, p. 475).

Confidentiality in Rural Subcultures Social workers and other professionals may also find themselves in a different sort of quandary involved in reporting child abuse that occurs in rural subcultures. As Long (1986) reports, "On Indian reservations and in small rural towns it is often impossible to prevent community awareness of abuse victims, abuse perpetrators, and abuse informants. Despite the best efforts of health care professionals involved, abuse perpetrators may learn of an informant through informal channels or through tribal court procedures" (p. 133). Further, the sense of loyalty to one's clan members may take precedence over the commitment to protect an informant and the need to protect an abused child. Consequently, tribal sanctions may be more severe in relation to the informant than to the abuser. Long provides documentation of case situations in which both informant and victim were physically beaten, verbally abused, and harassed by clan members. Definitions of abuse also differ from culture to culture, and within certain subcultures even severe abuse (according to common standards) may not be considered a problem by the victim or other family members.

Subcultural differences are by no means limited to members of ethnic minority groups. Long provides additional documentation of how closely knit Anglo health care practitioners discounted reports of child abuse perpetrated by a colleague and hindered effective intervention. Clearly, loyalty to the professional "clan" protected a member of the clan and hampered efforts to protect the child.

What course of action should practitioners take when community (subcultural) definitions of child abuse diverge from generally accepted standards, and when clan loyalties may result in punishment to informants and victims rather than perpetrators? We concur with Long's (1986) recommendations that we "must look beyond legal guidelines and discipline-specific prescriptions." If professionals are to be both genuinely helpful and realistically effective, there is often a need to make compromises related to treatment ideals. Thoughtful evaluation is required to allow for treatment strategies that can fit and be useful within a given subcultural context, and which still maintain the ethical and legal principles (p. 136).

Privileged Communication   Still another constraint on clients' rights to confidentiality is the fact that this right does not necessarily extend into courts of law. Unless social workers are practicing in one of the states that grant privileged communication, they may be compelled by courts to reveal confidential information and to produce confidential records. Bernstein (1977) therefore recommends that social workers practicing in states without statutes that grant privileged communication explain to clients that practitioners "can be subpoenaed in court, records in hand, and forced under penalty of contempt to testify under oath, as to what was said between the parties and what was recorded concerning such exchanges" (p. 264).[7] Bernstein further recommends that, "To avoid even a hint of malpractice, the social worker should explain the problem of privileged communication ... and should have in each client's file a document carefully drafted by an attorney and signed by the client acknowledging the possibilities" (p. 268).

Although increasing numbers of states have granted social workers privileged communication, many still do not. Because social workers have expanded their roles and provide more mental health services than do other professionals, the need for privileged communication is greater than ever before (Levick, 1981; VandeCreek, Knapp, &

Herzog, 1988). The writers just cited suggest that social workers in states that do not grant privileged communication should lobby legislators for a statute that grants that protection to clients.

It is important to note that because laws that grant privileged communication were created for the protection of the client, the privilege belongs to the client and not to the professional (Schwartz, 1989). In other words, if the practitioner were called on to take the witness stand, the attorney for the client could invoke the privilege to prohibit testimony of the practitioner (Bernstein, 1977). The client's attorney can also waive this privilege, in which case the practitioner would be obligated to disclose information as requested by the court.

Another important factor regarding privileged communication is that the client's right is not absolute (Levick, 1981). If, in a court's judgment, disclosure of confidential information would produce benefits that outweigh the injury that might be incurred by revealing that information, the presiding judge may waive the privilege. Occasionally, the privilege is waived in instances of legitimate criminal investigations, because the need for information is deemed more compelling than the need to safeguard confidentiality (Schwartz, 1989). In the final analysis, then, courts make decisions on privilege on a case-by-case basis.

Because the privilege resides with clients they may waive the privilege voluntarily. A client also waives or forfeits the privilege when he or she discloses "confidential" information (e.g., positive test results for AIDS) to other parties, such as friends or roommates. Viewed as public disclosure, such disclosure removes the need for the privilege (Schwartz, 1989). In still other instances clients may be mandated to waive the privilege, as when they file charges against a certified social worker involving confidential communications.

Perlman (1988) has reviewed general principles of confidentiality that bear on privileged communication. Of great importance to social workers is the principle that although a number of federal laws affect client rights to confidentiality, individual states control most of the law on client privilege. Perlman cautions social workers to master the relevant rules by studying the law of the state in which they practice. She adds, "With general knowledge of confidentiality principles alone, a social worker cannot be certain of making informed decisions" (p. 425).

A final caution is that state legislatures may amend a statute and "at any time the court may deliver an opinion that modifies its meaning" (pp. 425–426). It is thus prudent for social workers to devise a system to remain current with the law and with pertinent court decisions. One effective means of doing so is for state chapters of NASW to maintain ongoing dialogue with state legal organizations.[8]

It is also important to recognize that not only practitioners, but group members as well may be subpoenaed to testify in legal proceedings that involve another group member. Group members, of course, have the same obligation to preserve confidentiality of information revealed by other group members and should be so informed early in the process of group development. Because of the nature of group therapy, each member becomes a therapeutic agent for other group members. Unfortunately, privileged communication has not been extended to group members even in states that grant such privileges to social workers (Bernstein, 1977). The group practitioner thus has a responsibility to inform group members that their right to confidentiality does not extend into legal courts. It would be inimical to group process, however, to place heavy emphasis on this constraint, for as Bernstein notes, group members could hardly be expected to interact freely "with a judicial cloud hanging over their heads" (p. 267). Therefore, in explaining the matter to group members, it is desirable to emphasize

that the possibility of being subpoenaed is remote. Indeed, the authors are unaware of a single instance in which this has occurred.

Confidentiality in Various Types of Recording

Because case records can be subpoenaed and because clients and other personnel have access to them, it is essential that practitioners work toward the development and implementation of policies and practices that provide maximal confidentiality. To this end, practitioners should observe the following:

1. Record no more than is essential to the functions of the agency. Identify observed facts and distinguish them from opinions.

2. Omit details of clients' intimate lives from case records; describe intimate problems in general terms.

3. Do not include verbatim or process recordings in case files.

4. Employ private and soundproof dictation facilities.

5. Keep case records in locked files and issue keys only to those who require frequent access to the files.

6. Do not remove case files from the agency except under extraordinary circumstances with special authorization.

7. Do not leave case files on desks where janitorial personnel or others might have access to them.

8. Use in-service training sessions to stress confidentiality and to monitor observance of agency policies and practices instituted to safeguard confidentiality.

Practitioners sometimes record live interviews or group sessions so that they can later analyze interactional patterns or group process as well as scrutinize their own performance with a view toward improving skills and techniques. Recording is also used extensively for instructional sessions between students and practicum instructors. Still another use of recordings is to provide first-hand feedback to clients by having them listen to or view their actual behavior in live sessions.

Before recording sessions for any of the preceding purposes, practitioners should obtain written consent from clients on a form that explicitly specifies how the recording will be used, who will listen to or view the recording, and when it will be erased. In no instance should a recording be made without the knowledge and consent of the client. Clients vary widely in their receptivity to having sessions recorded, and if they manifest reluctance, their wishes should be respected. Practitioners who tape sessions assume a heavy burden of responsibility in safeguarding confidentiality, for live sessions are extremely revealing. Such recordings should be guarded to ensure that copies cannot be made and that unauthorized persons do not have access to them. When they have served their designated purpose, tapes should be promptly erased. Failure to heed these guidelines may constitute a breach of professional ethics.

Used for training purposes, tapes of live interviews are extremely valuable, enabling instructors and trainees to analyze moment-by-moment transactions. Such learning experiences are indispensable in developing mastery of specific skills. To avail yourself of this rich learning opportunity you must, of course, first gain consent from clients to tape sessions. The chances of gaining consent are enhanced by discussing the matter openly and honestly, taking care to explain the client's right to decline. If approached properly, the majority of clients consent to taping. Indeed, it has been our experience that students are more uncomfortable with taping than are clients. The following is an example of an interchange that involves a practitioner's request for taping an interview. Obviously, not all requests proceed as smoothly as this example, but in our experience, students' hesitancy to introduce the matter is usually the biggest obstacle.

Practitioner: "Mrs. F, to be as helpful to you as possible, I'd like, with your permission, to tape-record our interviews so that I can review them with my supervisor, who may have suggestions as to other ways I can be helpful. How do you feel about that possibility?"

Mrs. F: Gee, I don't know [*laughs uncomfortably*]. I think I'd probably be a little self-conscious. Uh, what do you do with the tape?

Practitioner: I'm sensing some concern on your part and assure you you're in no way obligated. In answer to your question, after my supervisor and I have gone over the tape together, I erase it. We're very careful with the tape, and if you agree to the taping, I'd want to have a written agreement with you that specifies how the tape will be used and when it will be erased. But before we go any further, I'm wondering about your feeling self-conscious. I don't want to create a problem for you.

Mrs. F: I'm sure I'd get over being self-conscious. If it would help you, I'm agreeable.

Practitioner: I appreciate your honesty and willingness [*laughs*]. You know, I'm a little self-conscious myself at first. But I have found that taping is very helpful to me. Most important, though, is that you feel good about it.

Mrs. F: It's no problem for me. Let's go ahead.

Practitioner: Good. I have the consent form right here. I'll go over it with you.

Legal Implications for Keeping Case Records

Although social work has historically embraced clients' rights to confidentiality, implementation of this ethical principle has been more stringent in recent years as a result of the federal Privacy Act of 1974, which was enacted to safeguard people against "harmful disclosures of information whether through inaccurate information being used in irrelevant circumstances or through inaccurate information being used in important decisions affecting individuals" (Schrier, 1980, p. 452). Although this act applies only to the federal government, many states have passed corresponding statutes or have used provisions of the law as criteria in adjudicating civil cases that involve alleged violations of people's rights to privacy. The act specifies duties for agencies that maintain record-keeping systems, including the following: (1) maintaining only information relevant and necessary to the agency's purposes, (2) collecting as much information as possible from the client directly, (3) informing clients of the agency's authority to gather information, whether disclosure is mandatory or voluntary, the principal purpose of the use of the information, the routine uses and effects, if any, of not providing part or all of the information, (4) maintaining and updating records to assure accuracy, relevancy, timeliness and completeness, (5) notifying clients of the release of records owing to compulsory legal actions, and (6) establishing procedures to inform clients of the existence of their records, including special measures if necessary for disclosure of medical and psychological records and a review of requests to amend or correct the records (Schrier, 1980, p. 453).

The proposed revisions to the NASW Code of Ethics reflects most of these provisions. Under Section 1.08 on Access to Records, "social workers should provide clients with reasonable access to records concerning them" (NASW, 1995, p. 11).

Item 6 in the preceding list establishes clients' rights of access to their records, which is consistent with provisions of the federal Freedom of Information Act of 1966. Where federal funds are involved and where states have enacted similar legislation, agencies and institutions are obligated to grant clients access to their case records. These statutes, of course, have major implications for record-keeping procedures.[9]

Social workers have reacted to the right-to-access law in mixed ways. Many strongly resisted making records available to clients, arguing that they could no longer be candid in recording and could include only innocuous information. Some private agencies that were not subject to the laws responded positively by modifying recording procedures and inviting clients to review their records. According to Freed (1978), "The few agencies,

hospitals, and clients that have tried sharing social work records with clients have found that the practice contributes favorably to the casework process and promotes the therapeutic goal by enhancing the client's trust and the openness of the relationship" (p. 460). Others similarly reported favorable results from sharing case records with clients whose problems involved marital and family difficulties. Interestingly, the experience of most agencies is that clients do not wish to see their records. The revised NASW Code of Ethics states that client access to social work records concerning them should be limited "only in very limited circumstances when there is compelling evidence that such access would cause serious harm to the client. Only that portion of the record should be withheld" (NASW, 1995, p. 11).

Because case recording procedures have been tightened and to avoid strains with clients and even a possible lawsuit, Freed (1978) recommends that practitioners carefully distinguish objective from subjective information, use descriptive terms rather than professional jargon, and avoid using psychiatric and medical diagnoses that have not been verified. Further, information gained in confidence from other sources should not be made a part of the record unless permission is obtained from parties who provided the information. And finally, if there is reason to believe the client may be harmed by knowing what is in the record, the practitioner is obligated to share this opinion with the client. In our opinion, the changes that have resulted from both of the acts cited have enhanced the rights of clients by avoiding misuse of records and have compelled practitioners to be more prudent, rigorous, and scientific in keeping case records.

Managing Ethical Dilemmas

Social workers sometimes experience quandaries in deciding which values or ethics should take precedence when a conflict exists between two legitimate values or ethics. In the foregoing discussions of self-determination and confidentiality, for example, we cited examples of how these rights of clients and ethical obligations of social workers are sometimes superseded by higher-order values (e.g., the right to life, safety, and well-being). Thus, clients' right to confidentiality must yield when they confide that they have physically or sexually abused a child or otherwise reveal intentions or plans to engage in harmful acts that would jeopardize the health or safety of other persons. Moreover, in your practice you may recognize that certain policies or practices of your employing agency may be detrimental to clients and you may be conflicted about your ethical obligations to advocate for changes because doing so may jeopardize your employment or pose a threat to relationships with certain staff members.

Conflicts involving such ethical dilemmas can confront social workers with agonizingly difficult decisions. Reamer (1989), however, has presented general guidelines that can assist you in making these decisions. Here we present our versions of certain of these guidelines and illustrate instances of their application.

1. The right to life, health, well-being, and necessities of life takes precedence over rights to confidentiality and opportunities for additive "goods" such as wealth, education, and recreation. We have previously alluded to the application of this principle in instances of child abuse or plans to do physical harm to another person. In such instances the rights of both children and adults to health and well-being take precedence over clients' rights to confidentiality. Similarly, a neglected child's rights to health and well-being take precedence over parents' rights to confidentiality and self-determination.

2. An individual's basic right to well-being takes precedence over another person's right to privacy, freedom, or self-determination. Put another way,

in the language of the courts (which have consistently upheld this principle), individual rights end when the public peril begins. The rights and needs of infants and children to receive medical treatments thus supersede parents' rights to withhold medical treatment because of religious beliefs. Similarly, several states have adopted rules that stipulate "the duty to warn," requiring professionals to warn potential victims and to inform law enforcement officials when clients reveal plans to do physical harm to others.

3. People's right to self-determination takes precedence over their right to basic well-being. This principle asserts the right of people to carry out actions that appear contrary to their best interests, providing they are competent to make an informed and voluntary decision with consideration of relevant knowledge, and as long as the consequences of their decisions do not threaten the well-being of others. This principle affirms the cherished value of freedom to choose and protects the rights of people to make mistakes and to fail.

It is important to recognize that this principle must yield to principle 1 when an individual's decision might result either in his or her death or severe damage to his or her physical or mental health. For example, when a client is at high risk of committing suicide, a social worker has an ethical (and legal) obligation to take preventative action. Otherwise, the social worker is vulnerable to a malpractice suit.

Still another example of an exception to this principle involves homeless mentally ill persons, as documented by a relevant research study conducted by Belcher (1988). In this study, Belcher found that of 132 patients discharged from a state hospital in Ohio in the mid-1980s, 47 (36% of the sample) became homeless during the 6 months of the study period. Of these 47 persons, 33 were identified as chronically mentally ill and chronically homeless. According to Belcher these persons "were characterized by long histories of chronic mental illness and continuing problems with severe psychotic behavior, which gradually led to inabilities to understand the world and to increased distancing from normative society" (p. 400).

During the study period, the mental conditions of a number of these persons deteriorated to the extent that they became out of touch with reality and neglected their hygiene, dress, and eating; in fact, the very survival of some was at stake. Clearly, the mental status of these persons precluded them from being able to exercise self-determination competently, and their health and well-being should have taken precedence over their right to self-determination. A sad commentary is that, despite their dire circumstances, mental health personnel resisted hospitalizing them because they did not regard them as dangerous (that is, suicidal or homicidal).

4. Persons' rights to well-being may override laws, policies, and arrangements of organizations. Ordinarily, social workers are obligated to comply with the laws, policies, and procedures of social work agencies, other organizations, and voluntary associations. When a policy is unjust or otherwise harms the well-being of clients or social workers, however, violation of the laws, policies, or procedures may be justified.

Examples of this principle include policies or practices that discriminate against or exploit certain persons or groups. An agency, for example, might employ clients (or social workers for that matter) on a part-time, hourly, or other basis to avoid having to pay costs for Social Security or unemployment benefits. Reamer (1989) also cites the example of a consortium of private agencies that might conspire to create a monopoly on services provided a certain group of clients, thus stifling competition and inflating the cost of services. In these and similar situations the well-being of affected groups takes precedence over compliance with the laws, policies, and arrangements at issue.

Although Reamer's guidelines are a valuable resource in resolving value dilemmas, applying them to the myriad situations that social workers encounter still involves uncertainties and ambiguities, a reality that practitioners must accept. For example, it is often extremely difficult to assess the degree of risk a client's behavior poses to the health and safety of the client or others.[10]

Ethical Dilemmas and AIDS Some of the most perplexing ethical dilemmas are related to issues regarding the rights of persons with AIDS and the rights of other people. Reamer (1989) has identified and discussed three major issues: (1) mandatory testing, (2) the client's right to confidentiality versus the rights of mates and other sexual partners to safeguard their health, and (3) rights of self-determination, the full exercise of which may jeopardize the health of others.

The issue of mandatory testing for athletes, health care personnel, and other groups has prompted heated legislative debate about whether such a requirement would enable health care professionals to track the incidence of the disease more effectively, curtail its spread, educate and protect the public, and assist those who are infected. Those in opposition argue that mandatory testing would require vast expenditures with little gain and would generate some false positive results, which would cause affected persons to suffer needless emotional trauma. Reamer (1989) takes the position that social workers "must oppose mandatory testing that exacerbates discrimination and emotional trauma, and discourages individuals from seeking treatment" (p. 462).

With respect to clients' right to confidentiality, extensive debates have also been publicized in the media. At issue is the conflict between clients' rights and the rights of others (mates, other sexual partners, and children of persons with AIDS) to health (and even to life). These conflicts affect social workers and health care personnel when they learn a client or patient has AIDS. Does a spouse have the right to know that his or her mate has AIDS? Do present and/or future sexual partners have a right to know? One may well respond in the affirmative because life and health take precedence over confidentiality. On the other hand, how can future sexual partners be warned? Could their rights to health be better protected through the use of condoms?[11]

Equally confounding issues arise regarding self-determination. Should prostitutes suspected of having AIDS be permitted to continue their trade? Should social workers assertively discourage clients exposed to the AIDS virus from engaging in sex, even when they are willing to take precautionary measures? Should a pregnant woman who has been exposed to the AIDS virus be encouraged to abort? These and other difficult questions have been raised by Reamer and others. Answers to these questions are difficult at best, and can be reached only through active and open debate, a challenge issued by Reamer.[12]

Skill Development Exercises in Confidentiality and Ethical Dilemmas

The following exercises will give you practice in applying to specific practice situations the concept of confidentiality and the guidelines for resolving ethical dilemmas. These situations include some of the most difficult ones that we and our colleagues have encountered in practice. You will note that in few of the situations is the appropriate response or course of action cut and dried. After reading each situation, consider the following:

1. Do you experience conflicting pulls regarding possible courses of action?

2. How can you best discharge your ethical responsibility in the situation?

3. When an ethical dilemma is involved, what guideline to resolve the dilemma is applicable?

Situation 1   A male client confided in an individual marital therapy session several weeks ago that he is gay, although his wife does not know this. The client's wife, whom you have also seen conjointly with him, calls you today troubled over the lack of progress in solving marital problems, and asks you point-blank whether you think her husband could be gay.

Situation 2   You are forming a youth group in a state correctional facility. You know from past experience that youths sometimes make references in the group to previous offenses that they have committed without being apprehended. You also know that they may talk about plans to run from the institution or about indiscretions or misdemeanors they (or others) may have committed or plan to commit within the institution, such as smoking marijuana or stealing institutional supplies or property from peers or staff.

Situation 3   In conducting an intake interview with a client in a family agency, you observe that both of her young children are withdrawn. Further, one of the children is badly bruised, and the other, an infant, appears malnourished. Throughout the interview, the client seems defensive and suspicious and also ambivalent about having come for the interview. At one point, she states that she feels overwhelmed with her parenting responsibilities and is having difficulty in coping with her children. She also alludes to her fear that she may hurt them but then abruptly changes the subject. As you encourage her to return to the discussion of her problems with the children, your client says she has changed her mind about wanting help, takes her children in hand, and leaves the office.

Situation 4   You have seen a husband and wife and their adolescent daughter twice regarding relationship problems between the parents and the girl. The parents are both extremely negative and blaming in their attitudes toward their daughter, believing their troubles would be over if she would just "shape up." Today, during an individual interview with the girl, she breaks into tears and tells you that she is pregnant and plans to "go somewhere" with her boyfriend this weekend to get an abortion. She pleads with you not to tell her parents, who she feels would be extremely angry if they knew.

Situation 5   In a mental health agency, you have been working with a male client who has a past history, when angered, of becoming violent and physically abusive. He has been under extreme psychological pressure lately because of problems relating to a recent separation from his wife. In an interview today, he is extremely angry, clenching his fists as he tells you that he has heard that his wife has initiated divorce proceedings and plans to move to another state. "If this is true," he loudly protests, "she is doing it to take the kids away from me, and I'll kill her rather than let her do that."

Situation 6   As a private practitioner, some of your clients rely on health maintenance organizations to fund their counseling services. If you are on the list of cooperative providers, it is likely that the organization will make referrals to you. If you are not on the preferred list, you may never get referrals from them. It is the policy of one organization you work with that progress reports on work with clients be submitted to them by voice mail. Your client is addressing sensitive issues and is very concerned about "who else will know" about his situation with particular concern about his employer. Recent experiences have increased the severity of his condition and you must share this with the care manager to get further treatment sessions approved. You have concerns about the confidentiality of a voice mail transmission and would prefer to discuss the imformation directly with the utilization reviewer. You, however, get the message that this is the organizational policy and, if you cannot abide by it, you are unlikely to get approval for continuing treatment and unlikely to receive further referrals from them.

Skill Development Exercises in Operationalizing Cardinal Values

To assist you in developing skill in operationalizing the cardinal values in specific practice situations, we have provided a number of exercises with modeled responses. As you read each one, note which of the values is (are) germane to the situation and whether one of the six threats to acceptance and respect is involved in the client's messages. To refresh your memory, the values and threats are as follows:

Values

1. All human beings deserve access to the resources that they need to deal with life's problems and to develop their potentialities.

2. All human beings have intrinsic worth and dignity.

3. The uniqueness and individuality of each person are of value.

4. Given appropriate resources, human beings are capable of growth and change and should be supported in increasing choices in solving their problems and directing their lives.

Threats to Acceptance and Respect

1. Helplessness.

2. Silence and withdrawal.

3. Aggressive and sullen behavior.

4. Manipulative and exploitative behavior.

5. Self-effacing behavior.

6. Noncompliant behavior or treatment non-adherence.

Next, assume you are the client's practitioner and formulate a response that implements the relevant social work value. After completing each exercise, compare your response with the modeled response that follows the exercises. Bearing in mind that the modeled response is only one of many possible acceptable responses, analyze it and compare it with your own. By carefully completing these exercises, you will improve your competence in operationalizing the cardinal values in the varied and challenging situations encountered in direct social work practice.

Client Statements

1. **Group member** [*in first group session*]: Before I really open up and talk about myself, I need to be sure what I say isn't blabbed around to other people. [Turning to practitioner.] How can I be sure that won't happen?

2. **Rural mother** [*living in dilapidated but neatly kept home; her children are shabbily dressed but appear healthy*]: You city folk don't seem to understand that you don't have to have a fancy home and a lot of luxuries to have a good life and raise healthy kids.

3. **Adolescent delinquent in correctional institution** [*after practitioner introduces self*]: So you want to help me, huh? I'll tell you how you can help. You can get me out of this damn place—that's how!

4. **Female client, age 21** [*to mental health practitioner*]: Yeah, I know that kicking the habit was a victory of sorts. But I look at my life and I wonder what's there to live for. I've turned my family against me. I've sold my body to more rotten guys than I can count—just to get a fix. I've had VD three times. What do I have to offer anyone? I feel like my life has been one big cesspool.

5. **Teenage male** [*in a group session in a correctional setting*]: [*Takes off shoes and sprawls in his chair. His feet give off a foul odor, and other members hold noses and make derisive comments. He responds defensively.*] Hey, get off my back, you creeps. What's the big deal about taking off my shoes?

6. **Female** [*initial interview in family counseling center*]: Before I talk about my marital problems, I need to let you know I'm a Seventh Day Adventist. Do you know anything about my church? I'm asking because a lot of our marital problems involve my religion.

7. **Client** [*as interview ends and time of next appointment is discussed*]: Oh, just work me into your schedule where it's convenient for you. Just let me know when you want me to come, and I'll get here somehow.

8. **Female client** [*sixth interview*]: Maybe it sounds crazy, but I've been thinking this last week that you're not really interested in me as a person. I have the feeling I'm just someone for you to analyze or to write about.

9. **Mexican American male client** [*in fifth group session, the members of which are largely Anglos*]: I have the feeling that you people look down on my people. It really pisses me off.

10. **Teenage female delinquent** [*caught with contraband in her possession by supervisor-counselor in correctional institution*]: Please don't report this, Mrs. Wilson. I've been doing better lately, and I've learned my lesson. You won't need to worry about me. I won't mess with drugs anymore.

11. **Client** [*observing practitioner taking notes during initial interview*]: I'm dying to know what you're writing down about me. But I guess I'm afraid too—wondering if you think I'm a nut.

12. **Single female client, age 29** [*in mental health center*]: I just heard about a job that opened up on the outskirts of town. It'd be right down my alley, but I'd have to drive because there's no bus service that comes within three miles. I don't drive, and I don't want to learn. I've always been afraid I might have an accident and kill someone. Everyone tells me I should learn to drive.

13. **Male parolee, age 27, who has a reputation as a con artist** [*in mandatory weekly visit to parole offi-*

cer]: Man, you've really got it made. Your office is really cool. I admire your taste in furnishing it. But then you deserve what you've got. You've probably got a terrific wife and kids, too. Is that their picture over there?

14. *Male client, age 34* [*in third interview*]: I'm really uptight right now. I've got this tight feeling I get in my chest when I'm nervous. [Pause.] Well, I guess I'll have to tell you if I expect to get anything out of this. [Hesitant.] You know the marital problems we've talked about. Well, Janice doesn't know this, but I'm gay. [Blushes.] I've tried—I've really tried, but Janice doesn't turn me on. I have to think about men to even get an erection. She thinks something's wrong with her, but it's not her fault. [Chin quivers.]

15. *Female, age 68* [*to geriatric worker in county-sponsored housing complex*]: It's been hard since Ralph died a year ago. I didn't know how many things I depended on him for. Like taking me places. I just feel like I'm chained down now because I don't drive. I still have our car, and it's only three years old—just sitting in storage. Ralph always prodded me to learn to drive, and I wish I had now. Do you think I'm too old to learn? I'm no spring chicken, you know.

16. *Black male probationer* [*to white therapist*]: You're so damn smug. You say you want to help me, but I don't buy that crap. You don't know the first thing about black people. Man, I grew up where it's an accomplishment just to survive. What do you know about life in the hood, man?

Modeled Responses

1. "Ginny raises a good point that concerns all of you. So that you can feel more comfortable about sharing personal feelings and experiences with the group, we need an understanding that each of you will keep what is shared in the strictest confidence. I can assure you that I'll keep information confidential myself, but I am interested in hearing from the rest of you regarding the question that Ginny is asking."

2. "Sounds like you're concerned I might look down on you because I'm from the city. I can tell it's important to you to take good care of your children. I want you to know too that rather than being critical, I'm impressed with how clean you keep your house. You know, I don't see us as being all that different because I live in the city and you live in the country. We're a lot more alike than different. I respect you as a person."

3. "I guess that's what I'd want also if I were in your situation. As a matter of fact, that's what I want for you, too. But we both know the review board won't release you until they feel you're prepared to make it on the outside. I can't get you out, but with your cooperation I can help you to make changes that will get you ready for release."

4. "I can see you're really down on yourself and feel pretty worthless. While it's true you've done a lot that you feel bad about, it's important not to let your past ruin your future. Where you're going is a lot more important than where you've been. I'm impressed you kicked the habit. That's a giant step in the right direction. If you just hang in there, you can gradually rebuild your life, and with that you'll feel a lot better about yourself."

5. "I think we need to look as a group at how we can give Jim some helpful feedback rather than making fun of him. Let's talk about what just happened. Maybe you could begin, Jim, by sharing with the group what you're feeling just now."

6. "I have to confess I know just a little bit about your religion. Understandably you're wondering if I can appreciate your problems. I can assure you I'll do my best to understand if you're willing to take a chance with me. You might have to educate me a little bit, but I'm a willing learner. The most important thing, though, is your feelings about it. How do you feel about sharing your problems with me under these circumstances?"

7. "I appreciate that, but your time's important too. Let's see if we can find a mutually convenient time. I have openings at ____ and _____ . Would any of those times be convenient for you?"

8. "That sounds like a painful feeling to have—that I'm not personally concerned with you as an individual. I'd like to explore that with you further because that's not at all how I feel about you, and I'm uncomfortable being seen that way. I'd like to understand more how I've come across to you and how you've reached that conclusion."

9. "Arturo, I'm pleased you could share these feelings because I've noticed you've been pretty quiet in our sessions and I have wondered why. I'd like to know more about you as a person. Perhaps you could tell the group a little more about what you've been experiencing."

10. "I'm sorry you're still involved with drugs, Joy, because of the trouble it's caused you. I don't like to see you get into trouble but I have no choice—I have to report this. If I didn't, I'd be breaking a rule myself by not reporting you. That wouldn't help you in the long run. Frankly, I'm going to keep worrying about you until I'm satisfied you're really sticking to the rules."

11. [*Chuckling*] "So you're wondering what I think of you. Well, you surely don't come across like a nut. Actually what I'm writing down is what we're talking about. What you tell me is important, and notes help to refresh my memory. You're welcome to look at my notes if you like. Actually, I would be interested in hearing a little more about your thoughts regarding what I might think of you."

12. "I can understand your desire not to harm anyone, but it sounds as though you have to pass up some choice opportunities because of your fear.

I respect your right to decide for yourself about learning to drive. But it strikes me that you're letting yourself be at the mercy of that fear. Fears like that can be mastered, and if you're inclined to work on your fear of driving, I'd be happy to explore it with you."

13. "As a matter of fact it is, and I think they're pretty terrific. But we're here to talk about you, Rex. I'd like to hear how your job interview went at _____ ."

14. "This has been very painful for you: sharing this problem with me. You've kept this inside for a long time, and I gather you've been afraid I'd condemn you. I'm pleased you brought it up so that we can work on it together. And rest assured I won't sit in judgment. It took some real courage on your part to talk about this, and I respect you for that."

15. "If you have the determination, I see no reason why you couldn't learn. There are some excellent instructors available in the adult education program. To be honest, I'm delighted you're considering it. You'd feel more independent, and it would open up a lot of possibilities. But what you feel is most important. What goes on inside you when you think about it?"

16. "I'd be phony if I said I understood all about being black and living in your neighborhood. But you're wrong about my being smug. I am interested in you, and I'd like to understand more about your life. How have you come to the conclusion that I can't help you?"

NOTES

1 Yuker (1988) has edited a volume concerned with societal attitudes toward people with disabilities.

2 After goals have been mutually identified and roles in helping the relationship clarified, practitioners need not be hesitant to offer advice, for their expertise and input give impetus and direction to change efforts. Our point is that giving advice should not be the primary means of assisting

3 From an existential stance, Weick and Pope (1988) have taken an even stronger position about the hazards of permitting erosion of the principle of self-determination.

4 Issues related to such situations and pertinent guidelines for social workers in working with patients and their families are discussed at length in an article by Nicholson and Matross (1989), the source of the foregoing information.

5 For a citical analysis of issues related to self-determination, see Rothman (1989).

6 Butz (1985) discusses related issues at length and makes a number of recommendations. To do justice to his discussion, however, would exceed space limitations, and we therefore refer you to his article.

7 Privileged communication is a legal right that protects clients from having confidence revealed publicly from the witness stand during legal proceedings. Statutes that grant privileged communication exempt certain professions from being legally compelled to reveal content disclosed in the context of a confidential relationship.

8 To grasp further the complexities of privileged communication, we urge you to study carefully the articles by Schwartz (1989) and Perlman (1988) .

9 Schrier (1980) discusses these issues at length. We strongly recommend that you read Schrier's article

10 Simple and clear-cut guidelines for solving ethical dilemmas are not available, but Biggs and Blocher (1987), Reamer (1989), Rhodes (1986), Wells and Masch (1986), have written books specifically aimed at assisting practitioners with ethical dilemmas.

11 Responses are highly debatable, as attested to by Bahou and Gralnick's (1989) scathing response to Reamer's article. See also Roberts et al. ,1992 (cited above) and Rosenberger, Judith and Wineburgh, Marsha (1992). Working with denial: A critical aspect in AIDS risk intervention. *Social Work in Health Care* 17, 2, 11–26.

12 We encourage those who would like to study these issues in depth to read a book devoted to the subject by Reamer (1992) .

Part 2

Exploring, Assessing, and Planning

Part 2 of this book deals with processes and skills involved in the first phase of the helping process. We introduce this part by focusing in this chapter on setting the context and developing skills for building effective working relationships with clients, one of the two major objectives of initial interviews. We shift our focus in Chapter 6 to skills entailed in accomplishing the second major objective: to thoroughly explore clients' difficulties. In Chapter 7, we identify verbal and nonverbal patterns of communication that impede the development of effective working relationships.

In Chapters 8 and 9, we focus specifically on the process of assessment, dealing in Chapter 8 with an explanation of the process, sources of information, delineation of clients' problems, and questions to be addressed during the process. In Chapter 9, we focus on the multidimensionality of ecological assessment, delineating the intrapersonal, interpersonal, cultural and environmental systems and how they reciprocally interact to produce and maintain problems.

In Chapter 10, the focus narrows to an examination of family systems. We discuss various types of family structures and consider the various dimensions of family systems that must be addressed in assessing family functioning, including the cultural context of families.

In Chapter 11, the focus changes to groups. We discuss purposes of groups, selection of group members, arrangements to be made, and how to begin group process. We then focus on various factors to be considered in assessing the functioning of groups.

Part 2 concludes with Chapter 12, which deals with negotiating goals and contracts with both voluntary and involuntary clients. Included in this chapter are theory, skills, and guidelines that address these processes, which lay the foundation for the process of goal attainment.

Chapter 5

Relationship-Building Skills: Communicating with Empathy and Authenticity

Social work relationships occur in a context. Potential clients have contact with a social worker usually through an agency setting, public or private. An important step in beginning to develop such a relationship is to clarify what the potential client can expect from the contact.

ROLES OF THE PARTICIPANTS

Clients often have little understanding of the helping process and may have expectations that are discrepant from those of the practitioner, which may impair the helping process. The findings of two classic research studies (Aronson & Overall, 1966; Mayer & Timms, 1969) revealed that unacknowledged discrepancies in expectations produced dissatisfactions and higher rates of discontinuance from therapy of lower-class clients as compared to middle-class clients. Moreover, Perlman (1968) found that she and two other social workers were able to lower the drop-out rate of clients during the intake process by concentrating on eliciting clients' conceptions and expectations of the helping process and by clarifying discrepancies between expectations and what realistically could be offered. Equally important, Perlman found that

the rate of return could be predicted more accurately when it was determined whether or not clarity of expectation and mutual agreement were achieved in the interviews. The potency of using a "role induction interview" to increase the continuance of clients beyond the initial interview has been demonstrated by Hoehn-Saric, Frank, Imber, Nash, Stone, and Battle (1964). Clients prepared by role induction continued contact at a higher rate and fared better in treatment than control clients who received no special preparation. Similar findings have been reported by Zwick and Atkinson (1985), who used a videotape for "pretherapy orientation." The following guidelines will assist you to achieve similar positive results in role clarification.

1. Determine the clients' expectations. The varied expectations that clients bring to initial sessions include lectures, magical solutions, advice-giving, changing other family members, and so on. In the previously cited study conducted by Perlman, only 6 of the 26 clients had realistic expectations of what the practitioner might do with or for them. With minority clients, especially those who are inexperienced with professional helping relationships, sensitively exploring expectations and modifying one's role when indicated are critical.

Clients sometimes convey their expectations without prompting from a practitioner. For example, after reciting the difficulties created by her son, a mother declared, "We were hoping you could talk with him and help him understand how much he is hurting us." Notice that the mother's "hope" involved a request for specific action by the practitioner. When clients thus express their expectations spontaneously, you have the opportunity to deal with those that are unrealistic. Frequently, however, clients do not openly express their expectations, and you will need to elicit them. It is important not to probe too far into expectations until you have established rapport, because the client's request often turns out to be a most intimate revelation. Seeking disclosure too soon thus may put clients on the defensive. The practitioner thus should seek to weave exploration of clients' expectations into the natural flow of the session sometime after clients have had ample opportunity to report their difficulties and to discern the sensitive understanding and goodwill of the practitioner.

If voluntary clients have not spontaneously revealed their requests and timing appears appropriate, you can elicit their requests by asking a question similar to one of the following:

"How do you hope (or wish) I (or the agency) can assist (or help) you?"

"As you thought about coming, what were your ideas as to the nature of help you wanted?"

For potential clients who were referred or mandated for service, such requests may be elicited by asking:

"We have explored the reasons why you were referred/required to seek our service. But I would like to know what *you* hope to gain from this process."

2. Briefly explain the nature of the helping process, and define your relationship as partners seeking a solution to their difficulties. Clients commonly hope that practitioners will give them advice that they can implement and thereby quickly remedy their problematic situations. They will relinquish these unrealistic expectations with a minimum of disappointment and discouragement in favor of a more realistic understanding if you clarify how you can actually be of help and why it would be futile to approach their problems in the manner they expected. It is very important to convey your intent to help clients find the best possible solution and to clarify that offering advice prematurely would likely be a disservice to them. In the absence of such an explanation, clients may erroneously conclude you are unwilling to meet their expectations because of a lack of concern for them. In this regard, Mayer and Timms (1969) found that clients who were dissatisfied with service for interpersonal problems reasoned that the counselor's failure to give concrete advice stemmed from a lack of interest and desire to help. Taking the time to explore expectations and to clarify how you can help thus prevents clients from drawing unwarranted negative conclusions that may result in discontinuance.

At this point, it is important to clarify that we are not arguing against the value of advice. Our point is that to be effective, advice must be based on adequate knowledge of the dynamics of a problem and of the participants in it. Such a grasp is unlikely to be achieved in an initial session. You can assist many clients to modify unrealistic expectations and clarify your respective roles through a message similar to the following:

"I can sense the urgency you feel in wanting to solve your problems. I wish I could give advice that would lead to solving them. You've probably already had plenty of advice, because most people offer advice freely. It has been my experience, though, that what works for one person (couple or family) may not work at all for another.

"As I see it, our task is to work together in considering a number of possible options so that you can decide what solution fits best for you and your situation. In the long run, that's what will work best for you. But it takes some time and a lot of thought."

Notice that the preceding role clarification embodies the following essential elements referred to earlier: (1) acknowledging and empathizing with the client's unrealistic expectation and sense of urgency, (2) expressing helpful intent, (3) explaining why the client's unrealistic expectation cannot be fulfilled, and (4) as part of the practitioner's expertise, clarifying the helping process and defining a working partnership that places responsibility on the client for actively participating and ultimately making choices as to the courses of action to be taken in solving problems.

When clients seek help for marital problems, they commonly view the partner as the source of difficulties and have the unrealistic expectation that the marital therapist will influence the partner to shape up. Because this expectation is so pervasive, we often elicit partners' expectations early in the initial session (individual or conjoint) and clarify the helping role, thereby setting the stage for more productive use of the exploration to follow. Clarifying the process early in the session tends to diminish mutual blaming and competing. Moreover, partners are less likely to respond defensively when the practitioner refuses to be drawn into the "blame game" and focuses instead on assisting each person to become aware of his or her part in the difficulties. The following excerpt of an actual session typifies our approach to role clarification with marital partners:

Practitioner: How much understanding do you have about how marital therapy works?

Husband: Not very much, really. We just know we need help because we're fighting all the time. [*Wife nods in agreement.*]

Practitioner: Perhaps it would be helpful if I took just a few minutes to explain how I work with couples. Would that be agreeable with you?

Husband and wife [*both nod affirmatively*]: Yes, we'd like that.

Practitioner: OK, then, I'll explain it as best I can and give you a chance to ask any questions. It's important that all three of us have the same understanding about what we're going to be doing. [*Couple nod in understanding.*] As I see it, my role is to help each of you to better understand yourself and your partner.

Marital problems usually are caused by the fact that the needs of one or both partners aren't being met adequately. Lots of factors can block the meeting of important needs, and when they do, problems in relationships develop. My job is to help each of you to understand your partner's needs better and to be more aware of your own needs so that you can express them clearly to your partner. Accomplishing that means you have to communicate in such a way that you really understand each other better. So another part of my job is to help you to communicate more effectively.

Wife: Good! We need that. Our communication is really bad. We can't seem to talk without getting into a fight.

Practitioner: Well, we'll need to work on that. Part of my job will be to help you see what's going wrong in your communication and to help you get back on track by learning new ways of communicating. In some ways, that means I'll function much as a teacher at times.

Husband: That's OK. If it will help, I'm willing to learn.

Practitioner: That willingness will be a real asset. Another thing that's important to understand is that I can't help by getting involved in assigning blame to one of you or the other. It's been my experience that most marital partners believe the other person is causing the difficulties, and many of their struggles involve blaming each other. Usually it isn't one or the other who's at fault. Both partners contribute to the difficulties, and my task is to assist each of you to see the part you play in them. It's important that you understand this. Otherwise, you might think I'm siding with your partner when I focus on your part. I won't be taking sides, but if it feels to you like I am, please let me know. Otherwise, you're likely to resent me, and I won't even be aware of it. To work effectively together we'll have to be open with each other. I'll be open with you, but I have to expect the same of you. [*Pause.*]

Further clarification of the roles of the participants will occur later in the session as the participants negotiate goals and formulate a contract.

Implied in the above excerpt is another aspect of the client's role—to be open in sharing feelings, thoughts, and events. By explaining the rationale for openness and by expressing your intent to communicate openly, you enhance clients' receptiveness to this factor. The following illustrates one way of explaining this aspect of the client's role:

"For you to benefit to the fullest, you will need to be as open as possible with me. That means not holding back troubling feelings, thoughts, or events that are important. I can understand you and your difficulties only if you're open and honest with me. Only you know what you think and feel; I can know only as you share with me. Sometimes it's painful to share certain thoughts and feelings, but often those are the very feelings that trouble us the most. If you do hold back, you'll need to remind yourself you may be letting yourself down. If you're finding it difficult to share certain things, let me know. Discussing what's happening inside you—why it's difficult—may make it easier to discuss those painful things.

"I'll be open and honest with you, too. If you have any questions or would like to know more about me, please ask. I'll be frank with you. I may not answer every question, but I'll explain why if I don't."

To enhance clients' participation in the helping process, it is also important to emphasize that they can accelerate their progress by working on their difficulties between appointments. Some clients mistakenly believe that change will result largely from what occurs in sessions. In actuality, the content of sessions is far less significant than how clients apply information gained. The following excerpt illustrates clarifying this aspect of a client's responsibility:

"We'll want to progress toward your goals as rapidly as possible. One way you can hasten your progress is by working hard between our sessions. That means carrying out tasks you've agreed to, applying what we talk about in your daily life, and making mental notes or actually writing down thoughts, feelings, and events that relate to your problems so we can consider them in your next session. Actually, what you do between sessions is more important in accomplishing your goals than the session itself. We'll be together only a brief time each week. The rest of the week you have opportunities to apply what we talk about and plan together."

Still another aspect of the client's role involves keeping appointments. This factor is obvious, but discussing it emphasizes clients' responsibilities and prepares them to cope constructively with obstacles that may cause them to fail or to cancel appointments. The following is an example of a message that clarifies this aspect of the client's role:

"As we work together, it will be most important for you to keep your appointments. Unforeseen things such as illness happen occasionally, of course, and we can change appointments when this happens. At times, however, you may find yourself feeling discouraged or doubting if coming here really helps. It's also possible you may feel upset over something I've said or done and find yourself not wanting to see me. I won't knowingly say or do anything to offend you, but you may have some troubling feelings toward me anyway. The important thing is that you not miss your appointment, because when you're discouraged or upset we need to talk about it. I know that may not be easy, but it will help you to work out your troubled feelings. If you miss your appointment, you may find it even harder to return."

A final factor conveys that difficulties are inherent in the process of making change. Clarifying this reality further prepares clients for the inevitable resistance they will experience. By anticipating these difficulties, clients are enabled to conceive of resistances as natural obstacles that must be surmounted, rather than yielding to them or feeling defeated. An explanation about these predictable difficulties similar to the following clarifies the vicissitudes of the change process:

"We've talked about goals you want to achieve. Accomplishing them won't be easy. Making changes is seldom accomplished without a difficult and sometimes painful struggle. People usually have ups and downs as they seek to make changes. If you understand this, you won't become unduly discouraged and feel like throwing in the towel. I don't mean to paint a grim picture. In fact, I feel very hopeful about the prospects of your attaining your goals. At the same time, it won't be easy, and I don't want to mislead you. The important thing is that you share your feelings so that we can keep on top of them."

Over the years, numerous clients have reported retrospectively that they appreciated explanations similar to the preceding. When the going became rough and they began to waver in pursuing their goals, they recalled that such discouragement was natural and, rather than discontinuing, mustered the determination to persevere.

In addition to clarifying the client's role, it is vital to clarify your own role. Again, it is desirable to stress you will be a partner in helping clients to understand their difficulties more fully. Because you have an outside vantage point, you may be able to assist them to see their difficulties in a new perspective and to consider solutions they may have overlooked. We recommend that you clarify further that although you will be an active partner in considering possible remedial actions, the final decisions rest with them. You will help them to weigh alternatives, but your desire is to see them develop their strengths and to exercise their capacities for independent action to the fullest possible extent. It is also important to emphasize that one of your functions is to assist them in focusing on strengths and the incremental growth they achieve. Stress that although you will actively assume this function in the initial stage of the helping process, you will be encouraging them to learn to recognize their own strengths and growth independently.

Another aspect of the helping role that you should clarify for clients is that you will assist them in anticipating obstacles they will encounter in striving to attain their goals and will help them formulate strategies to surmount these obstacles. Clarifying this facet of your role further reinforces the reality that change is difficult but you will be

with and behind them in offering support and direction.

There are special hurdles in developing productive working relationships between practitioners and potential clients in mandated settings since the mandated client did not seek the contact and often perceives it as contrary to his or her interests. Notice how in the following dialogue, the practitioner begins to develop expectations about a collaborative relationship.

Client: I didn't like the earlier workers because they came into my house telling me what I can do and can't do. One thing I don't like is someone telling me what I can do with my kids and what I can't.

Practitioner: It sounds like you have had a negative experience with earlier workers.

Client: Yeah, I did. I did not like it at all because they were telling me what I should do.

Practitioner: I'm going to have a different approach with you because I don't feel that I know it all; you know best about the situation occurring in your own family and in your own life. I will want you to tell me about the problems you are concerned about and how we together can best resolve those.

Client: Ok.

Practitioner: So my job will be to develop a case plan with you. I won't be the one to say "this is what you need to do"; I want you to have input in that and to say "well I feel I can do this." I will be willing to share ideas with you as we decide what to work on and how to do it. I will need to include any court mandated requirements, such as our need to be meeting together, in the agreement. However, I want you to have a lot of say in determining what we work on and how.

THE FACILITATIVE CONDITIONS

The practitioner uses communication skills as building blocks to assist in the development of a productive working relationship. The present chapter is concerned with two of the three skills embodied in what have been variously referred to as the facilitative conditions or core conditions in helping relationships. These conditions or skills were originally denoted by Carl Rogers (1957) as empathy, unconditional positive regard, and congruence. Other terms have since evolved, and we shall refer to the conditions as empathy, respect or nonpossessive warmth, and authenticity or genuineness. Because we addressed nonpossessive warmth or respect at length in Chapter 4, we limit our focus in this chapter to empathy and authenticity.

Research (primarily in psychology) has documented that the conditions are associated with positive outcomes. One important study by a social worker (Nugent, 1992) has further documented the effectiveness of these conditions in facilitating positive helping relationships. It is thus vital that social workers master these skills. While particularly useful in treatment situations with voluntary clients, we will describe ways that such skills can be building blocks in both involuntary relationships and other situations such as discharge planning that do not have therapy as the primary focus (Bennett, Legon, & Zilberfein, 1989).

EMPATHIC COMMUNICATION

This skill involves the ability of the practitioner to perceive accurately and sensitively inner feelings of the client and to communicate understanding of these feelings in language attuned to the client's experiencing of the moment. The first dimension of empathy, that of empathic recognition, is a precondition of the second dimension, that is, demonstrating through accurate reflection of feelings that the practitioner comprehends the client's inner experiencing.

Empathic communication plays a vital role in nurturing and sustaining the helping relationship and providing the vehicle through which the practitioner becomes emotionally significant and influential in the client's life. In mandated circumstances in which involuntary clients are not seeking a helping relationship, conveying empathic understanding reduces threat and defensiveness, conveys interest and helpful intent, and creates an atmosphere conducive to behavior change. In addition, many clients live in environments which constrict resources and opportunities; practitioner empathy to the social and economic context of problems is an important adjunct to empathy with personal experiencing (Keefe, 1978).

In responding to clients' feelings, practitioners must avoid being misled by conventional facades used to conceal emotions. Thus, the empathic communicator responds to feelings that underlie such messages as "Oh, no, it doesn't really matter," or "I don't care what he does!" These messages often mask disappointment or hurt as do such messages as "I don't need anyone" when experiencing painful loneliness, or "I don't let anyone hurt me" when one is finding rejection hard to bear. To enter the client's private world of practical experience, the practitioner must also avoid making personal interpretations and judgments of the client's private logic and feelings that, in superficial contacts, might appear as weak, foolish, or undesirable.

Being empathically attuned involves not only grasping the client's immediately evident feelings but, in a mutually shared, exploratory process, identifying underlying emotions and discovering the meaning and personal significance of feelings and behavior. In getting in touch with camouflaged feelings and meanings, the practitioner must tune in not only to verbal messages but to more subtle cues, including facial expressions, tone of voice, tempo of speech, and postural and gestural cues that amplify and sometimes contradict verbal meanings. Such nonverbal cues as blushing, crying, pausing, stammering, changing voice intonation, clenching jaws or fists, pursing the lips, lowering the head, or shifting the posture often reveal the presence of distressing feelings and thoughts.

Empathic communication also involves "stepping into the shoes of another," in the sense of attempting to perceive the world of experience of the other person. When clients feel pressure from referral by others or are in other ways involuntary, such empathy includes conveying the perception that the practitioner understands and is aware of that pressure and how it feels. The listener, however, must remain outside, avoiding being overwhelmed by the fears, anger, joys, and hurts of that person, though deeply sensing the meaning and significance of these feelings for the other. "Being with" the client involves the practitioner's focusing intensely on the client's affective state without losing perspective or taking on the emotions experienced by the client.

When a person experiences feelings in common with another person and is similarly affected by whatever the other person is experiencing, the former usually responds sympathetically rather than empathically. Sympathetic responding, which depends on emotional and intellectual accord, involves supporting and condoning the other person's feelings (e.g., "I'd feel the same way you do if I were in your position" or "I think you're right"), whereas empathic responding involves understanding the other person's feelings and circumstances without taking that person's position (e.g., "I sense you're feeling…" or "You seem to be saying…"). When practitioners support clients' feelings, clients may feel no need to examine their behavior or circumstances and may not engage in the process of self-exploration so vital to growth and change; rather, in such instances, clients look to the practitioner to change the behavior of other persons who play a significant role in their problems. Retaining separateness and objectivity thus is a critical dimension in the helping process, for when practitioners assume the client's feelings and positions, they lose not only vital perspective but the ability to be helpful as well.

Being empathic involves more than recognizing clients' feelings. Practitioners must also respond verbally and nonverbally in ways that affirm their understanding of clients' inner experiencing. It is not unusual for a person to experience empathic feelings for another without conveying them in any way to the second party. High-level empathy requires skill in verbally and nonverbally demonstrating understanding. A common mistake made by practitioners is to tell the client, "I understand how you feel." Rather than producing a sense of being understood, such a response often creates doubts in the client's mind about the practitioner's perceptiveness because specific demonstration of understanding is lacking. Indeed, use of this response may mean that the practitioner has not explored the client's feelings sufficiently to fully grasp the significance of the problematic situation. To convey unmistakably, "I am with you; I understand," the practitioner must respond empathically. Use of this skill creates an ambience of acceptance and understanding in which the client is more likely to risk sharing deeper and more personal feelings.

Later in the chapter, we present theory and exercises for developing skill in empathic responding. Initially, we provide a list of affective words and phrases to assist you in expanding your vocabulary so that you can meet the challenge of responding to the wide range of emotions experienced by clients. We also provide exercises to assist you to refine your ability to perceive the feelings of others—a prerequisite to the mastery of empathic communication. To assist you to discern levels of empathy, a rating scale for empathic responding is included, accompanied by examples of varying levels of practitioner responses and exercises. These exercises will assist you to gain mastery of empathic communication at an effective working level.

DEVELOPING PERCEPTIVENESS TO FEELINGS

A vital and universal aspect of human experiencing, feelings or emotions exert a powerful influence on behavior and often play a central role in the problems of clients. Applicants or voluntary clients have often sought the helping relationship with openness and hope that they will explore both their concerns and their related feelings. Involuntary clients experience strong feelings but have not sought a helping relationship for dealing with them (Cingolani, 1984). Hence, use of the skills sometimes takes a slightly different course with them, as a goal is to express empathy with the *situation* the involuntary client experiences and the feelings related to them.

Responding to the broad spectrum of emotions and feeling states presented by clients requires that the practitioner be fully aware of the diversity of human emotion. Further, the practitioner needs a rich vocabulary of words and expressions that not only reflect client feelings accurately but also capture the intensity of those feelings. For example, there are dozens of descriptive feeling words to express anger, including furious, aggravated, vexed, provoked, put out, irritated, impatient—all of which express different shades and intensities of this feeling. When used judiciously, such words serve to give sharp and exact focus to the feelings of clients.

Possessing and utilizing a rich vocabulary of affective words and phrases that accurately reflect client feelings is a skill that often is not developed by even experienced practitioners. It is important to realize that high-level empathic responding involves first a thinking process and, second, a responding process. A deficient vocabulary of feelings limits practitioners' ability to conceptualize and hence to reflect the full intensity and range of feelings experienced by clients.

It has been our experience that beginning practitioners have a limited range of feeling words from which to draw in conveying empathy. Although there are literally hundreds of feeling words that may be used to capture feelings, learners often limit themselves to, and use to excess, a few catch-all terms, such as upset or frustrated, losing much of the richness of client messages in the process.

The accompanying lists illustrate the wide range of expressions available for practitioners' use in responding to clients' feelings. It must be noted that using feeling words discriminately is important not only in empathic responding but indispensable in relating authentically as well. Becoming a competent professional involves a maturing process whereby practitioners develop not only the capacity to deeply share the inner experiencing of others, but also a way to express their own personal feelings constructively.

Affective Words and Phrases

Competence, Strength

convinced you can	confident
sense of mastery	powerful
potent	courageous
resolute	determined
strong	influential
brave	impressive
forceful	inspired
successful	secure
in charge	in control
well-equipped	committed
sense of accomplishment	daring
feeling oats	effective
sure	sense of conviction
trust in yourself	self-reliant
sharp	able
adequate	firm
capable	on top of it
can cope	important
up to it	ready
equal to it	skillful

Happiness, Satisfaction

elated	superb
ecstatic	on cloud nine
on top of the world	organized
fantastic	splendid
exhilarated	jubilant

terrific	euphoric	horrible	terrible
delighted	marvelous	hopeless	gloomy
excited	enthusiastic	dismal	bleak
thrilled	great	depressed	despondent
super	in high spirits	grieved	grim
joyful	cheerful	brokenhearted	forlorn
elevated	happy	distressed	downcast
lighthearted	wonderful	sorrowful	demoralized
glowing	jolly	pessimistic	tearful
neat	glad	weepy	down in the dumps
fine	pleased	deflated	blue
good	contented	lost	melancholy
hopeful	mellow	in the doldrums	lousy
satisfied	gratified	kaput	unhappy
fulfilled	tranquil	down	low
serene	calm	bad	blah
at ease		disappointed	sad
		below par	

CARING, LOVE

adore	loving
infatuated	enamored
cherish	idolize
worship	attached to
devoted to	tenderness toward
affection for	hold dear
prize	caring
fond of	regard
respect	admire
concern for	taken with
turned on	trust
close	esteem
hit it off	value
warm toward	friendly
like	positive toward
accept	

DEPRESSION, DISCOURAGEMENT

anguished	in despair
dreadful	miserable
dejected	disheartened
rotten	awful

INADEQUACY, HELPLESSNESS

utterly	worthless
good for nothing	washed up
powerless	helpless
impotent	crippled
inferior	emasculated
useless	finished
like a failure	impaired
inadequate	whipped
defeated	stupid
incompetent	puny
inept	clumsy
overwhelmed	ineffective
like a klutz	lacking
awkward	deficient
unable	incapable
small	insignificant
like a wimp	unimportant
over the hill	incomplete
immobilized	like a puppet
at the mercy of	inhibited

insecure — lacking confidence

unsure of self — uncertain

weak — inefficient

unfit

ANXIETY, TENSION

terrified — frightened

intimidated — horrified

desperate — panicky

terror-stricken — paralyzed

frantic — stunned

shocked — threatened

afraid — scared

stage fright — dread

vulnerable — fearful

apprehensive — jumpy

shaky — distrustful

butterflies — awkward

defensive — uptight

tied in knots — rattled

tense — fidgety

jittery — on edge

nervous — anxious

unsure — hesitant

timid — shy

worried — uneasy

bashful — embarrassed

ill at ease — doubtful

uncomfortable — self-conscious

insecure — alarmed

restless

CONFUSION, TROUBLEDNESS

bewildered — puzzled

tormented by — baffled

perplexed — overwhelmed

trapped — confounded

in a dilemma — befuddled

in a quandary — at loose ends

going around in circles — mixed-up

disorganized — in a fog

troubled — adrift

lost — disconcerted

frustrated — floored

flustered — in a bind

torn — ambivalent

disturbed — conflicted

stumped — feeling pulled apart

mixed feelings about — uncertain

unsure bothered — uncomfortable

undecided — uneasy

REJECTION, OFFENSIVENESS

crushed — destroyed

ruined — pained

wounded — devastated

tortured — cast off

betrayed — discarded

knifed in the back — hurt

belittled — abused

depreciated — criticized

censured — discredited

disparaged — laughed at

maligned — mistreated

ridiculed — devalued

scorned — mocked

scoffed at — used

exploited — debased

slammed — slandered

impugned — cheapened

mistreated — put down

slighted — neglected

overlooked — minimized

let down — disappointed

unappreciated — taken for granted

taken lightly — underestimated

degraded — discounted

shot down

ANGER, RESENTMENT

furious — enraged

livid — seething

could chew nails

burned up

bitter

vengeful

indignant

hostile

have hackles up

upset with

agitated

got dander up

dismayed

disgusted

turned off

miffed

irked

ticked off

chagrined

cross

infuriated

fighting mad

hateful

galled

resentful

irritated

pissed off

had it with

bent out of shape

annoyed

bristle

uptight

bugged

put out

ruffled

perturbed

teed off

griped

impatient

violent

LONELINESS

all alone in the universe

abandoned

forsaken

lonely

estranged

remote

apart from others

left out

lonesome

aloof

isolated

totally alone

forlorn

alienated

rejected

alone

shut out

excluded

distant

cut off

GUILT, EMBARRASSMENT

sick at heart

humiliated

degraded

mortified

branded

like two cents

guilty

crummy

unforgivable

disgraced

horrible

exposed

could crawl in a hole

ashamed

remorseful

really rotten

lost face

foolish

silly

egg on face

wrong

at fault

responsible for

lament

demeaned

ridiculous

stupid

regretful

embarrassed

in error

goofed

blew it

Use of the Lists of Affective Words and Phrases

The lists of affective words and phrases may be used with the exercises at the end of the chapter to assist you in formulating responses that capture the nature of feelings expressed by clients. Note that involuntary clients are more likely to initially experience the emotions of anger, resentment, guilt, embarrassment, rejection, confusion, tension, inadequacy, helplessness, depression, and discouragement. After you have initially responded to "feeling messages," check the lists to determine if there are other words and phrases that might more accurately capture the client's feelings. Also, scan the lists to see if the client's message involves feelings in addition to those you identified. The lists may similarly assist you in checking out the accuracy of your reflective responses as you review taped sessions.

We suggest you read the lists aloud several times to aid you in making the feeling words and phrases part of your working vocabulary. We further recommend that you memorize five or six words or phrases in each category to further your mastery of feeling language. Developing an alertness to affective words used in the communication media, in conversations with acquaintances, or in reading material and repeating them to yourself will also assist you in expanding your feeling vocabulary. You will increasingly employ words that you rarely, if ever, used before. As you broaden your vocabulary you will experience growing confidence in your ability to formulate feeling responses in sessions. A further benefit will be that your feeling responses will assist your clients to experience their emotions more keenly, thereby pinpointing some of the distress they are feeling.

Acquisition of a wider range of emotional vocabulary is a step toward expressing greater empathy for clients. You are conveying your understanding and compassion for what they are experiencing. Since many clients want to change their situations as well as their feelings about it, conveying empathy is the first step toward helping them work on those concerns.

Although the lists of affective words and phrases are not exhaustive, they encompass many of the feelings and emotions frequently encountered in the helping process. Feeling words are subsumed under 11 categories, running the gamut from emotions that express intense anguish and pain, such as grieved, terrified, bewildered, enraged, powerless, to such positive feeling states as joy, elation, ecstasy, bliss, and pride in accomplishment. Given the emphasis on clients' strengths in this book, care has been taken to include a grouping of terms to assist practitioners in capturing clients' feelings related to growth, strengths, and competence.

Feeling words in each category are roughly graduated by intensity, with words conveying strong intensity grouped toward the beginning of each category and words denoting moderate to mild intensity toward the end. In responding to client messages, the practitioner should choose feeling words that accurately match the intensity of the feelings the client is experiencing. To illustrate, picture an African American client in a drug after care program who has returned to work as a meter reader. He reports that when he knocked on the door in a largely Caucasian suburb intending to read the meter, the elderly Caucasian woman would not let him in, despite his wearing his picture identification name tag on his uniform. "I was so low down and depressed. What can you do? I am doing my thing to keep straight and I can't even do my job because I'm Black." Such a response appropriately calls for an intense response

by the practitioner: "Sounds like you felt demeaned and humiliated that you couldn't do your job because of this woman's fear of Black people. You felt discriminated against, disrespected, yet you did not let these humiliating feelings carry you back to drug use—you kept your head on course, keeping straight, and not being stopped by other people's perceptions."

In addition to using words that accurately reflect the intensity of the client's feelings, it is important to respond with a tone of voice and nonverbal gestures and expressions that similarly reflect the intensity of feelings conveyed by the verbal response. Further, the proper intensity of affect may also be conveyed by using appropriate qualifying words. For example, "You feel (somewhat) (quite) (very) (extremely) discouraged by your low performance on the entrance test."

Clients' messages may also contain multiple feelings. Consider, for instance, the following client message: "I don't know what to do about my teenage daughter. I know that she's on drugs, but she shuts me out and won't talk to me. All she wants is to be out with her friends, to be left alone. There are times when I think she really dislikes me."

Feeling words that would capture the various facets of this message include: confused, bewildered, alarmed, troubled, overwhelmed, lost, desperate, worried, frightened, alienated, rejected, and hurt. A response that included all of these feeling words would be extremely lengthy and overwhelming to the client; however, a well-rounded empathic response should embody at least several of the surface feelings, such as worried and confused, and with appropriate timing, the practitioner might also bring deeper-level feelings in focus, as explained in the following paragraphs.

Notice in the preceding client message that many feelings were implied but not explicitly expressed by the client. Some of these emotions would likely be just beyond the client's level of awareness but could easily be recognized if they were drawn to the client's attention. For example, the client might emphatically confirm a practitioner response that sensitively identifies the hurt, rejection, and even anger inherent in the client's message. Yet without the practitioner's assistance, the client might not develop full awareness of those deeper-level feelings.

In responding to client messages, you must be able to distinguish between readily apparent feelings and probable deeper feelings. In the early phase of the helping process, the practitioner's objectives of developing a working relationship and creating a climate of understanding are best accomplished by using a reciprocal level of empathy—that is, focusing on the client's immediately evident feelings. As the client perceives your genuine effort and commitment to understand, that experience of being "empathically received" gradually creates a low-threat environment that obviates the need for self-protection.

Note, however, that clients from oppressed groups, such as the client in the above situation, may rightly feel both better understood by the practitioner as well as continue to feel disillusioned by an alien environment. It is important to acknowledge those feelings about the environment. Cingolani writes of the "negotiated relationship" with such clients in place of the "helping relationship" (Cingolani, 1984). But even in negotiated relationships, increased trust is essential. That trust may be gained, however, by actions outside the session that indicate that the practitioner is trustworthy and has the client's best interest at heart, as well as verbal conveyance of empathy in the session. Similarly, Ivanoff, Tripodi and Blythe (1994) suggest that too much emphasis on empathy can feel manipulative to involuntary clients (p. 21).

With voluntary clients, the resultant climate of trust sets the stage for self-exploration, a prerequisite to self-understanding, which in turn facilitates behavior change. This positive ambience prepares the way for the use of "additive" or "expanded" levels of empathy to reach for underlying feelings, as well as hidden meanings and goals of behavior. However, attempting to explore underlying feelings during the early phase of the helping process

is counterproductive. Uncovering feelings beyond the client's awareness before a working relationship is firmly established tends to mobilize opposition and may precipitate premature termination. Involuntary clients in a negotiated relationship may never desire such uncovering of deeper feelings and may find exploration for them to be intrusive (p. 21).

EXERCISES IN IDENTIFYING SURFACE AND UNDERLYING FEELINGS

In the following exercise, identify both the apparent surface feelings and the probable underlying feelings embodied in the client's message. Remember that most of the feelings in the messages are only implied, as clients often do not use feeling words. As you complete the exercise, read each message and write down the feelings involved. Then scan the lists of affective words and phrases to see if you can improve your response. After you have responded to all four messages, check the feeling words and phrases you identified with those given by the authors at the end of the chapter. If the feelings you identified were similar in meaning to those of the authors, consider your responses accurate. If they were not, review the client messages again to see if you can identify clues about the client's feelings that you overlooked.

Client Statements

1. *Elderly client:* I know my children are busy, but I haven't seen them for ages. They don't even bother to call.

   Apparent feelings:

   Probable deeper feelings:

2. *Client:* I don't know if my husband loves me or not. He says he cares, but he doesn't pay much attention to me, particularly when we're with other people. Sometimes he even seems ashamed of me.

   Apparent feelings:

   Probable deeper feelings:

3. *Client:* When I was a teenager, I thought that when I was married and had my own children, I would never yell at them like my mother yelled at me. Yet, here I am doing the same things with Sonny. [*Tearful.*]

Apparent feelings:

Probable deeper feelings:

4. *African American client in child welfare system:* The system is against people like me. People think that we drink, beat our kids, lay up on welfare, and take drugs.

Apparent feelings:

Probable deeper feelings:

Exercises at the end of this chapter for formulating reciprocal empathic responses will also assist you in increasing your perceptiveness to feelings.

ACCURATELY CONVEYING EMPATHY

Empathic responding is a fundamental yet complex skill that requires systematic practice and extensive effort to achieve competency. Skill in empathic communication has no limit or ceiling; rather, this skill is always in the process of "becoming." In listening to their taped sessions, even highly skilled professionals discover feelings they overlooked. Many practitioners, however, do not fully utilize or selectively employ empathic responding, failing to grasp the versatility of this skill and its potency in influencing clients and fostering growth in moment-by-moment transactions.[1] In fact, some practitioners dismiss the need for training in empathic responding, mistakenly believing themselves to be empathic in contacts with clients.

Research findings indicate that beginning social work students relate at empathic levels considerably lower than the levels necessary to work facilitatively with clients (Fischer, 1978; Larsen, 1975). These findings are not totally unexpected, for comparatively few people are inherently helpful in the sense of relating naturally with high levels of empathy or any of the other core conditions.

Although people achieve varying degrees of empathy, respect, and genuineness through life experiences, to attain high levels of these skills appears to require rigorous training.

Research scales that operationalize empathy conditions have been developed and validated in extensive research studies (Truax & Carkhuff, 1967). These scales, which specify levels of empathy along a continuum ranging from high- to low-level skills, represented a major breakthrough not only in operationalizing essential practitioner skills but also in establishing a relationship between these skills and successful outcomes in therapy.

The empathic communication scale has been particularly helpful to social work educators in assessing pre- and post-levels of empathy of trainees in laboratory classes (Larsen & Hepworth, 1978; Wells, 1975). The scale has been further employed to assist students to distinguish between high- and low-level empathic responses and has been used by peers and instructors in group training to assess levels of students' responses. Students then receive guidance in reformulating low-level responses to bring them to higher levels.

The Carkhuff (1969) empathy scale, which consists of nine levels, has been widely used in training and research, and similar versions of this scale can be found in the literature. Although we have found nine-point scales valuable as training aids, they have proven somewhat confusing to students, who have difficulty in making the fine distinctions between levels. For this reason, we have adapted the nine-level scale described by Hammond, Hepworth, and Smith (1977) by collapsing it to the five-level scale reproduced in the next section.

On the following empathic communication scale, level 1 responses are generally made by practitioners who are preoccupied with their own rather than the client's frame of reference and as such completely fail to match the client's feelings. At this low level of responding, practitioners' responses are usually characterized by the ineffective communication styles identified in Chapter 7. Responses at level 2 convey an effort to understand but are partially inaccurate or incomplete. At level 3, the midpoint, practitioners' responses are essentially interchangeable in affect with the surface feelings and expressions of the client. This midpoint, widely referred to as "interchangeable" or "reciprocal" responding in the literature, is considered the "minimally facilitative level" at which an effective and viable process of helping can take place. Above the midpoint, the practitioner's responses add noticeably to the surface feelings and, at the highest level, add significantly to client expressions. At these higher levels of empathic responding, the practitioner accurately responds to clients' full range of feelings at their exact intensity and is "with" clients in their deepest moments. Level 4 and 5 empathic responses, which require the practitioner to infer underlying feelings, involve mild to moderate interpretations.

Empathic Communication Scale

Client statement [*African American male to child welfare worker*]: "I don't trust you people. You do everything you can to keep me from getting back my son. I have done everything I am supposed to do and you people always come up with something else."

Level 1: Low-Level Empathic Responding   At this level, the practitioner communicates little or no awareness or understanding of even the most conspicuous of the client's feelings; practitioners' responses are irrelevant and often abrasive, hindering rather than facilitating communication. Operating from a personal frame of reference, the practitioner changes the subject, argues, gives advice prematurely, lectures, or uses other ineffective styles that block communication, often diverting clients from their problems and fragmenting the helping process. Furthermore, the practitioner's nonverbal responses are not appropriate to the mood and content of the client's statement.

When practitioners relate at this low level, clients often become confused or defensive, reacting by discussing superficialities, arguing, disagreeing, changing the subject, or withdrawing into silence. Thus, the client's energies are diverted from exploration and/or work on problems.

Level 1 Responses   "Just carry out the case plan and you are likely to succeed." (*Giving advice*.)

"Just think what would have happened if you had devoted more energy in the last year to carrying out your case plan: You would have been further along." (*Persuading with logical argument; negatively evaluating client's actions*.)

"How did you get along with your last social worker?" (*Changing the subject*.)

"Don't you think it will all work out in time?" (*Leading question, untimely reassurance*.)

"Why, that's kind of an exaggeration. Just work along with me and before you know it things will be better." (*Reassuring, consoling, giving advice*.)

The preceding examples illustrate various ineffective styles of communication used at this low level. Notice that messages reflect the practitioner's own formulations concerning the client's problem, rather than capture the client's inner experiencing. Such responses stymie clients, blocking their flow of thought and producing negative feelings toward the practitioner.

Level 2: Moderately Low-Level Empathic Responding   The practitioner responds to the surface message of the client but erroneously omits feelings or factual aspects of the message. At this level, the practitioner may also inappropriately qualify feelings (e.g., "somewhat," "a little bit," "kind of") or may inaccurately interpret feelings (e.g., "angry" for "hurt," "tense" for "scared"). Responses may also emanate from the practitioner's own conceptual formulations, which may be diagnostically accurate but not empathically attuned to the client's expressions. Although level 2 responses are only partially accurate, they do convey an effort to understand and, for this reason, do not completely block the client's communication or work on problems.

Level 2 Responses   "You'll just have to be patient. I can see you're upset."

The word *upset* only vaguely defines the client's feelings, whereas feeling words such as angry, furious, discounted more accurately reflect the inner experiencing of the client.

"You feel angry because your case plan has not been more successful to date. Maybe you are expecting too much too soon; there is a lot of time yet."

In this case, the listener begins to accurately capture the client's feelings but then moves to an evaluative interpretation ("you expect too much too soon") and inappropriate reassurance.

"You aren't pleased with your progress so far?"

This response focuses on external, factual circumstances to the exclusion of the client's feelings or perceptions regarding the event in question.

"You feel like things aren't going too well."

This response contains no reference to the client's immediately apparent feelings. Beginning practitioners often use the lead-in phrase "You feel like... ," without noticing that, in employing it, they have not captured the client's feelings.

"You're disappointed because you haven't gotten your son back?"

This response, although partially accurate, fails to capture the client's anger and distrust of the system, wondering whether any of his efforts are likely to succeed.

"I can see you're angry and disappointed because your efforts haven't been more successful so far, but I think you may be expecting the system to work too quickly."

Although the message has a strong beginning, the empathic nature of the response is negated by the listener's explanation of the reason for the client's difficulties. This response represents a form of sidetaking, that is, justifying the actions of the child welfare system in suggesting that too much is expected of it.

The preceding responses illustrate many of the common errors made by practitioners in responding empathically to client messages. Although some part of the messages may be accurate or helpful, notice that all the responses in some way ignore or subtract from what the client is experiencing.

Level 3: Interchangeable or Reciprocal Level of Empathic Responding   Practitioner's verbal and nonverbal responses at this level convey understanding and are essentially interchangeable with the obvious expressions of the client, accurately reflecting factual aspects of the client's messages and surface feelings or state of being. Reciprocal responses do not appreciably add affect or reach beyond the surface feelings, nor do they subtract from the feeling and tone expressed. Factual content of the client's message, though desirable, is not required; if included, this aspect of the message must be accurate. Level 3 responses facilitate further exploratory and problem-focused responses by the client. The beginner does well in achieving skill in reciprocal empathic responding, which is an effective working level.

Level 3 Responses   "You're really angry about the slow progress in your case and are wondering if your efforts are likely to succeed."

"I can tell you feel very let down and are asking yourself, will I ever get my son back?"

Essentially interchangeable, these responses express accurately the immediately apparent emotions in the client's message. The content of the responses is also accurate, but deeper feelings and meanings are not added. The second also illustrates a technique for conveying empathy that involves changing the reflection from the third to the first person, and speaking as if the practitioner were the client.

Level 4: Moderately High-Level Empathic Responding   Responses at this level are somewhat additive, accurately identifying implicit underlying feelings and/or aspects of the problem. The practitioner's response illuminates subtle or veiled facets of the client's message, enabling the client to get in touch with somewhat deeper-level feelings and unexplored meanings and purposes of behavior. Level 4 responses thus are aimed at enhancing self-awareness.

Level 4 Responses "You feel very frustrated with the lack of progress in getting your son back. You wonder if there is any hope in working with a new worker and this system which you feel hasn't been helping you."

This response conveys not only immediately apparent feelings and content, but also is noticeably additive in reflecting the client's deeper feelings of suspicion of institutional racism.

Level 5: High-Level Empathic Responding Reflecting each emotional nuance, and using voice and intensity of expressions finely attuned to the client's moment-by-moment experiencing, the practitioner accurately responds to the full range and intensity of both surface and underlying feelings and meanings. The practitioner may connect current feelings and experiencing to previously expressed experiences or feelings, or may accurately identify implicit patterns, themes, or purposes. Responses may also identify implicit goals embodied in the client's message, which point the direction for personal growth and pave the way for action.

Responding empathically at this high level facilitates the client's exploration of feelings and problems in much greater breadth and depth than at lower levels.

Level 5 Responses "Not succeeding in getting custody of your son by now has angered and frustrated you very much. I'm sensing that you're unsure of whether any efforts will succeed and maybe thinking the 'system is stacked against me'. You want to be able to trust that your efforts are likely to succeed and that I and this child welfare system will do all we can to assist you."

Significantly additive, this response goes well beyond the surface feelings in reflecting the keen disappointment of the client and his underlying fear that he may never regain custody of his son. In addition, the latter part of the response includes an action or goal statement that paves the way for further exploration of the problem. The latter is critical. Client suspicions of institutional racism and the lack of responsiveness of the system are not alleviated exclusively or even primarily by empathic statements, however well formed. The key for engaging client motivation would be demonstrating that the practitioner and agency will respond in a reliable, trustworthy fashion in their actions.

EXERCISES TO DISCRIMINATE LEVELS OF EMPATHIC RESPONDING

The following exercises in rating varied responses for their level of empathy are designed to assist you in refining your ability to determine the helpfulness of responses. These exercises will prepare you for subsequent practice in formulating empathic messages. Three client statements are given, followed by a number of possible responses. Using the empathic scale, rate each response. Rating messages will be less difficult if, using the list of affective words and phrases, you first identify the feelings contained in the client's message. After you have rated each response, compare your rating with those of the authors at the end of the chapter. Referring to the rating scale, analyze the responses you rated inaccurately, trying to pinpoint the reason for the authors' ratings.

Client Statements

1. *Female public assistance recipient, age 80 [to social worker concerning her request to move to a special apartment complex provided for ambulatory elderly persons]:* Goodness, the more I think of moving, the more scared I get. I have neighbors here who look

after me, and I won't know a soul there. I'm afraid I'll be all alone.

Level Responses:

_____ 1. "It's pretty scary to you, leaving your neighbors and familiar surroundings. But there will be a lot of friendly people there and things to do. Besides, they fix one hot meal for you every day."

_____ 2. "Don't worry, you'll make friends in no time, and you'll wish you'd moved sooner."

_____ 3. "Did you sign those application papers I left with you a few days ago?"

_____ 4. "Just thinking about moving worries you because you'll be leaving your own neighborhood and friends. Even though your life would be much easier, you're unsure you'll be better off in other ways."

_____ 5. "So I gather in some ways you'd rather stay right where you are rather than gamble on a change."

_____ 6. "Lots of other people in the new apartments were just as scared as you before they moved, but I don't know a single one who's sorry now."

_____ 7. "It sounds as though you have some pretty mixed feelings about moving. Part of you wants to go because you could live more comfortably, but another part of you is afraid you'll feel alone and lost and wants to cling to people you know care about you."

_____ 8. "Are you saying we just ought to forget the whole thing?"

2. **Male, age 16** [*in weekly visit to social work probation officer*]: I don't see the sense in having to come here every lousy week. I haven't been in a trouble now since I went to court a month ago. You should know by now you can trust me.

Level Responses:

_____ 1. "A month isn't very long, you know. And how can I be sure you're staying out of trouble?"

_____ 2. "I gather you'd rather not have to see me. I can understand that, but the judge ordered it and you'd be in trouble with him if you didn't meet the conditions of your probation."

_____ 3. "Has it been a month since you went to court? I didn't think that it had been that long."

_____ 4. "You'd prefer not coming here and feel you've earned my trust."

_____ 5. "Having to come here each week gripes you, and I gather you're irritated with me for encouraging you to follow the judge's order."

_____ 6. "Look, you got yourself into this mess so don't complain to me if you don't like it. Maybe you'd like to talk the judge into changing his mind."

_____ 7. "It irritates you to have to come here each week. You'd like to get me off your back."

_____ 8. "You're confused about why you have to come here and wish you didn't have to."

3. **Group member** [*in hesitant, quiet voice*]: It's really hard for me to say what I want to say in this group. When I do start to talk, I get tongue-tied, and my heart starts beating faster and faster. I feel like some of you are critical of me.

Level Responses by group members or group leader:

_____ 1. "Yeah, I feel that same way sometimes, too."

_____ 2. "It is frightening to you to try to share your feelings with the group. Sounds like you find yourself at a loss for words and wonder what others are thinking of you."

_____ 3. "I know you're timid, but I think it's important that you make more of an effort to talk in the group, just like you're doing now. It's actually one of the responsibilities of being a group member."

_____ 4. "You get scared when you try to talk in the group."

_____ 5. "I sense that you're probably feeling pretty tense and tied up inside right now as you talk about the fear you've had in expressing yourself. Although you've been frightened of exposing yourself, I gather there's a part of you that wants to overcome that fear and become more actively involved with the rest of the group."

_____ 6. "What makes you think we're critical of you? You come across as a bit self-conscious, but that's no big deal."

_____ 7. "You remind me of the way I felt the first time I was in a group. I was so scared, I just looked at the floor most of the time."

_____ 8. "I wonder if we've done anything that came across as being critical of you."

DEVELOPING SKILL IN RESPONDING WITH RECIPROCAL EMPATHY

Reciprocal or interchangeable empathic responding (level 3) is a basic skill used throughout the helping process to acknowledge client messages and to encourage exploration of problems. In the initial phase, empathic responding serves the vital purpose in individual, conjoint, and group sessions of facilitating the development of a working relationship and fostering the climate of understanding necessary to communication and self-disclosure, thereby setting the stage for deeper exploration of feelings during subsequent phases. Additive empathic responses, that is, those rated as a 4 or 5 on the empathic scale, exceed the level of feelings and meanings expressed by clients and are thus reserved, in large part, for the later phases of the helping process.

Since reciprocal responding is an essential skill used frequently to meet the objectives of the first phase of the helping process, we recommend you first seek beginning mastery of responding at level 3; extended practice of this skill should significantly increase your effectiveness in establishing viable helping relationships, interviewing, and gathering data. In the remainder of this chapter, we provide guidelines and practice exercises that will help you in mastering reciprocal responding. Although responding at additive levels is an extension of the skill of reciprocal responding, the former is an advanced skill that can be used in varied ways to achieve specific objectives and, for this reason, has been grouped with other change-oriented or "action" skills presented in Part 3 of the book.

Constructing Reciprocal Responses

To reach level 3 on the empathic scale, you must be able to formulate responses that accurately capture the content and the surface feelings in the client message. It is also important to frame the message so that you do not merely restate the client's message. The following paradigm, which identifies the various elements of an empathic or reflective message, has proven useful for conceptualizing and mastering the skill of empathic responding:

$$\text{You feel} \underline{\quad\quad} \begin{array}{c} \text{about or} \\ \text{because} \end{array} \underline{\quad\quad}$$

(Accurately identifies feelings of client)

(Accurately describes situation or event referred to by client)

As shown, the response focuses exclusively on the client's message and does not reflect the practitioner's conceptualizations. The following excerpt from a session involving a practitioner and a 17-year-old female illustrates the use of the preceding paradigm in constructing an empathic response:

Client: I can't talk to my father without feeling scared and crying. I'd like to be able to express myself and to disagree with him, but I just can't.

Practitioner: Sounds as though you just feel panicky when you try to talk to your father. I gather you're discouraged because you'd like to feel comfortable with your dad and able to talk openly with him without falling apart.

Many times client messages contain conflicting or contrasting emotions, such as the following: "I like taking drugs, but sometimes I worry about what they might do to me."

In such cases, each contrasting feeling should be highlighted: You feel _____, yet you also feel _____. For example: "I sense that you feel torn because while you find taking drugs enjoyable, you have nagging thoughts that they might be harmful to you."

Remember that in order to respond empathically at a reciprocal level, you must use language clients will readily understand. Abstract, intellectualized language and professional jargon are barriers to communication that should be avoided. It is also important to vary the language you use in responding. Many professionals tend to respond with stereotyped, repetitive speech patterns, commonly using a limited variety of communication leads to begin their empathic responses. Such leads as "you feel..." and "I hear you saying..." repeated over and over not only are distracting to the client but also seem phony and contrived. Such stereotyped responding draws more attention to technique than to message.

The list of varied introductory phrases will help you expand your repertoire of possible responses. We encourage you to read the list aloud several times and to review the list frequently while practicing the empathic communication training exercises in this chapter and in Chapter 19 on additive empathic responding. The reciprocal empathic response format ("You feel ____ because ____") is merely a training aid to assist you in focusing on the affect and content of client messages. The leads list will help you respond more naturally.

LEADS FOR EMPATHIC RESPONSES

Could it be that...	You're feeling...
I wonder if...	I'm not sure if I'm with you but...
What I guess I'm hearing is...	You appear to be feeling...
Correct me if I'm wrong, but I'm sensing...	It appears you feel...
Perhaps you're feeling...	Maybe you feel...
Sometimes you think...	Do you feel...
Maybe this is a longshot, but ...	I'm not sure that I'm with you; do you mean...

I'm not certain I understand; you're feeling ...

As I hear it, you...

Is that the way you feel?

Let me see if I'm with you; you...

The message I'm getting is that...

If I'm hearing you correctly...

So, you're feeling...

You feel...

It sounds as though you are saying...

I hear you saying...

So, from where you sit ...

I sense that you're feeling...

Your message seems to be, "I ____"

I gather you're feeling...

If I'm catching what you say...

What you're saying comes across to me as...

It seems that you...

Is that what you mean? What I think I'm hearing is...

I get the impression that...

As I get it, you felt that...

To me it's almost like you are saying...

So, as you see it...

I'm picking up that you...

I wonder if you're saying...

So, it seems to you...

Right now you're feeling...

You must have felt...

Listening to you, it seems as if...

You convey a sense of ...

As I think about what you say, it occurs to me you're feeling...

From what you say, I gather you're feeling...

Exercises designed to help you to respond to clients with level 3 reciprocal empathic responses are found at the end of the chapter. Contained in the exercises are a variety of client statements taken from actual work with individuals, groups, couples, and families in diverse settings.

In addition to completing the skill development exercises, we also recommend that you keep a record of the number of empathic responses you employ in sessions over several weeks to determine the extent to which you are applying this skill. We also suggest that either you or a knowledgeable associate rate your responses and determine the mean level of empathic responding for each session. If you find (as most beginning practitioners do) that you are underutilizing empathic responses or responding at low levels, you may wish to set a goal to improve your skill.

Employing Empathic Responding

In early sessions, empathic responding should be used frequently as a method of developing rapport and "staying in touch" with the client. Responses should be couched in a tentative manner to allow for inaccuracies in the practitioner's perception. Further, checking out the accuracy of responses with appropriate lead-in phrases, such as "Let me see if I understand…" or "Did I hear you right?" is helpful in communicating a desire to understand and a willingness to correct misperceptions.

In initially using empathic responses, learners are often leery of the flood of emotions that sometimes occurs as the client, experiencing none of the usual barriers to communication, releases feelings often pent up for months or years. It is important to understand that empathic responses have not "caused" such feelings but rather have facilitated their expression, thus clearing the way for the client to explore and to consider such feelings more rationally and objectively.

You may worry, as do many beginning practitioners, about whether you will "damage" the client or the helping relationship if your empathic responses do not always accurately reflect the client's feelings. Perhaps even more important than accuracy, however, is the "commitment" to understand conveyed by genuine efforts to perceive the client's experience. If you consistently demonstrate your goodwill and intent to help through attentive verbal and nonverbal responding, occasional lack of understanding or faulty timing will not damage the relationship. In fact, efforts to clarify the client's message will usually enhance rather than

detract from the helping process, particularly if you respond to corrective feedback in an open, nondefensive, and empathic manner.

MULTIPLE USES OF EMPATHIC COMMUNICATION

Earlier in the chapter, we referred to the versatility of empathic communication. In this section, we delineate a number of ways in which you can employ reciprocal empathic responding.

1. *Establishing relationships with clients in initial sessions.* As discussed previously, the use of empathic responding actively demonstrates the practitioner's keen awareness of clients' feelings and creates an atmosphere wherein the latter will risk and explore personal thoughts and feelings. Numerous researchers have established that when practitioners relate empathically, clients are more likely to continue contact than when little empathy is conveyed.

Over a span of many years, many studies have emphasized the critical nature of empathic communication to successful work with virtually every type of client. For example, Miller (1983) has stressed the vital nature of empathy in work with problem drinkers, and Zingale (1985) has focused on the importance of empathy with a broad spectrum of clients.

Research studies (e.g., Banks, Berenson, & Carkhuff, 1967; Cimbolic, 1972; Santa Cruz & Hepworth, 1975) also indicate that empathic communication, along with respect and genuineness, facilitate the development of effective working relationships when practitioners and clients are from different ethnic or cultural backgrounds. These findings are particularly meaningful in view of the fact that social workers typically work with diverse populations that include ethnic minorities and clients from low socioeconomic backgrounds. To employ empathy with maximal effectiveness to transcultural relationships, practitioners must be aware of and sensitive to cultural factors.

The importance of knowledge of cultural factors was documented almost 40 years ago by the research findings of Mayer and Timms (1969), who studied clashes of perspectives between clients and social workers. Based on their findings they concluded: "It seems that social workers start where the client is psychodynamically but they are insufficiently empathic in regard to cultural components" (p. 38).

Although empathic communication is important in bridging cultural gaps, it can be used to excess with many Asian Americans and American Indians. Many members of these groups tend to be lower in emotional expressiveness than other client groups and may react with discomfort and confusion if a practitioner relies heavily on empathic communication. Still, it is important to "read between the lines" and to sensitively respond to troubling emotions that these clients do not usually express directly. Like other clients, they are likely to appreciate sensitive awareness by a practitioner to painful emotions associated with their difficulties.

We again emphasize the importance of assuming a more directive, active, and structured stance with Asian Americans. As Tsui and Schultz (1985) have clarified, "A purely empathetic, passive, nondirective approach serves only to confuse and alienate the [Asian] client" (p. 568). The same can be said of many American Indian clients.

2. *Staying in touch with clients.* Reciprocal empathic responding operationalizes the social work principle of "starting where the client is" and keeps practitioners attuned to clients' current feelings. Although employing many other skills and techniques, the practitioner utilizes and returns to empathic responding to keep in touch with the client. In that sense, empathic communication is a fundamental intervention prerequisite to the use of other interventions. Writing to this point, Gendlin (1974) uses the analogy of driving a car

to refer to the vital role of empathy in keeping in touch with clients. Driving involves much more than watching the road. A driver does many things, including steering, operating the brakes, signaling, and watching signs. One may glance at the scenery, visit with others, and think private thoughts, but watching the road must be accorded highest priority. When visibility becomes limited or hazards appear, all other activities must cease and one must attend exclusively to observing the road and conditions that may pose hazards. Just as some drivers fail to maintain proper lookout and become involved in accidents, some practitioners also fail to attend sufficiently to changes in clients' moods and reactions, mistakenly assuming they know their frame of mind. As a consequence, practitioners may fail to discern important feelings of clients, who may perceive them as disinterested or insensitive and subsequently disengage from the helping process.

3. *Accurately assessing client problems.* Extensive evidence indicates that the levels of empathy offered by practitioners correlate with levels of self-exploration by clients. High-level empathic responding thus increases clients' exploration of self and problems. As the practitioner moves "with" clients by frequently using empathic responses in initial sessions, clients begin to unfold their problems and to reveal events and relevant data. Figuratively speaking, clients then take practitioners where they need to go by providing information crucial to making an accurate assessment. Such an approach contrasts sharply with sessions in which history-taking is emphasized and where practitioners, following their own agendas rather than the clients', spend unnecessary time asking hit-or-miss questions and gathering information often extraneous to the problem.

4. *Responding to the nonverbal messages of clients.* Clients often convey through their facial features, gestures, and body postures feelings they do not express verbally. In the course of a session, for

instance, a client may become pensive, or show puzzlement, pain, or discomfort. In such instances, the practitioner may convey understanding of the client's feeling state and verbalize the feeling explicitly through a reflective response that attends to the emotion suggested in the client's nonverbal expressions. For instance, in response to a client who has been sitting dejectedly with her head down for several minutes after having reported some bad grades, a practitioner might say: "At this moment you seem to be feeling very sad and discouraged, perhaps even defeated." Further, in group or conjoint sessions, the practitioner might reflect the nonverbal messages of several, or all, of the members—for example: "I sense some restlessness today, and we're having a hard time staying on our topic. I'm wondering if you're saying, 'We're not sure we want to deal with this problem today.' Am I reading the group correctly?" Empathic responses that accurately tune into clients' nonverbal experiencing will usually prompt clients to begin exploring feelings they have been experiencing. Making explicit the nonverbal messages of clients is an important skill discussed in several chapters in the book.

5. *Making confrontations more palatable.* Confrontation is employed in the change-oriented phase to expand clients' awareness and to motivate them to action. They are most appropriate when clients are contemplating actions that are unlawful, or dangerous to themselves or others. They are also appropriate when such actions conflict with goals and values a client has chosen for him or herself. However, even well-timed confrontations may be met with varying degrees of receptivity. Concern as well as prudence dictate that the practitioner determine the impact of confrontations upon clients and implement a process of making these interventions more palatable. This may be accomplished by employing empathic responses attuned to client reactions immediately following confrontations. As practitioners listen attentively and sensitively to client expressions, defensiveness

abates, and clients often begin to engage in processing new information and thinking through and testing the validity of ideas, embracing those that fit and rejecting others that seem inapplicable. Blending confrontation and empathic responses is a particularly potent technique for managing group processes when the practitioner must deal with a controversial issue or distractive behavior that is interfering with the work of the group.

6. *Handling obstacles presented by clients.* Client opposition to what is happening in a session is sometimes healthy. What is often interpreted as unconscious resistance may be a negative reaction to poor interviewing and intervention techniques or to client confusion, misunderstanding, or even inertia. It is thus important to carefully monitor client reactions and to deal directly and sensitively with their related feelings. Instances frequently occur in sessions in which clients' verbal or nonverbal actions indirectly comment on what is occurring in the helping process. For instance, the client may look at her watch and ask how long the session is going to take, shift body position away from the practitioner, begin tapping a foot, or stare out the window. In such cases, when it appears the client is disengaging from the session, an empathic response that reflects the client's verbal and/or nonverbal message may be used effectively to initiate discussion of what is occurring. Shifting to what is happening in the here-and-now is an important skill that we further elaborate in later chapters.

Practitioners are also often confronted with excessively verbal clients who talk rapidly and move quickly from one topic to another. Overly verbal clients present a particular challenge to beginning practitioners, who must often overcome the misconception that interrupting clients is rude. Because of this misconception, novice interviewers sometimes spend most of an initial session listening passively to verbal clients without providing any form or direction to the helping process. Further, beginning practitioners may also allow clients to talk incessantly because they mistakenly view this as constructive work on problems. Quite the contrary, verbosity often keeps the session on a superficial level and interferes with problem identification and exploration.

It is important that practitioners provide structure and direction, thereby conveying an expectation that specific topics will be considered in depth. Much more will be said about this in later chapters. However, for the present, it is important to underscore the necessity of using empathic responses with verbal clients as a preliminary effort to slow the process and to provide some depth to the discussion. For example, a practitioner might interject or intervene with: "I'd like to interrupt to check if I'm understanding what you mean. As I get it, you're feeling... ," or "Before you get into talking about that, I would like to make sure I'm with you. You seem to be saying..." or "Could we hold off discussing that for just a minute? I'd like to be sure I understand what you mean. Would you expand on the point you were just making?"

7. *Managing anger and patterns of violence.* During individual or group sessions, clients (especially those who were not self-referred and may be involuntary) often experience surges of intense and conflicting feelings, such as anger, hurt, or disappointment. In such instances, empathic responding is a key tool for assisting them to work through those feelings. As empathic responses facilitate expanded expression of these feelings, clients engage in a process of ventilating, clarifying, and experiencing different feelings, gradually achieving a mellowing of emotions and a more rational and thoughtful state of being. Employed to focus sharply on clients' feelings, empathic responding thus efficiently manages and modifies strong emotions that represent obstacles to progress. As the practitioner successfully handles such moments and clients experience increased self-awareness and cathartic benefits, the helping relationship is strengthened.

Empathic responding is particularly helpful in dealing with hostile clients and is indispensable when clients are angry with the practitioner, as illustrated in the following example: "What you're doing to help me with my problems doesn't seem to be doing me any good. I don't know why I keep coming."

At such moments, the practitioner must resist the temptation to react defensively, for such responses further antagonize the client and exacerbate the situation. Responding by challenging the client's perception, for instance, would be destructive to the helping relationship. The purpose of the practitioner's responses should be to understand the client's experiencing and feelings and to engage the client in fully exploring those feelings. Keeping this in mind, consider the impact of the following reciprocal empathic response: "You're very disappointed that things aren't better, and are irritated with me, feeling that I should have been more helpful to you."

This response accurately and nondefensively acknowledges the client's frustration with the situation and with the practitioner. By itself, the preceding response would not be sufficient to mellow the client's ire and to free the client to consider the problem more fully and rationally. Carefully following feelings and remaining sensitively attuned to the client's experiencing by employing empathic responses for several minutes usually assists both the practitioner and client to understand more clearly the strong feelings that prompted the client's message and to adequately assess the source of those feelings. Attending to the emotions expressed does not mean that the content is discounted. The practitioner can follow the empathic response above by saying: "I'd like to explore more with you about the parts of our work that have not felt worthwhile to you."

When faced with angry clients in group and conjoint sessions, it is critical that the practitioner empathically reflect not only the negative feelings and positions of the clients who are manifesting the anger but also reach for and reflect the feelings or observations of members who may be experiencing the situation differently. Utilizing empathic responses in this manner assists the practitioner in gathering information that will elucidate the problem, in helping angry members air and examine their feelings, and in putting other points of view before the group for consideration. Further, employing empathic responding at such moments also encourages a more rational discussion of issues involved in the problem and thus sets the stage for possible problem solving.

The principles just discussed also apply to clients who are prone to violent behavior. Such clients often come to the attention of social workers because they have abused their children and/or spouses. People who engage in violence often do so because of underlying feelings of helplessness and frustration and because they lack skills and experience in coping with troubling situations in more constructive ways. Some have short fuses and weak emotional controls, often coming from backgrounds in which they vicariously learned violence as a mechanism of coping. Using empathy to defuse their intense anger and to tune in to their frustrations is an important first step in work with such clients (Lane, 1986). Other clients have difficulties with anger and express it only when under the influence of alcohol or other substances. Assisting them to experience and to ventilate anger when sober and in control is a major approach employed to assist such clients to learn constructive ways of coping with anger (Potter-Efron & Potter-Efron, 1992). Assisting clients to control anger, of course, involves use of other interventions, as we discuss in later chapters.

8. *Utilizing empathic responses to facilitate group discussions.* Practitioners may facilitate discussion of specific issues in conjoint or group sessions by first identifying a desired topic and then utilizing empathic (or paraphrasing) responses to reflect the observations of various group members in relation to that topic. The practitioner may also reach for responses from members who have not contributed and then employ empathic responses (or paraphrases) to acknowledge their observations. Utilized frequently in this manner, empathic responding encourages (and reinforces) clients' participation in group discussions.

TEACHING CLIENTS TO RESPOND EMPATHICALLY

Clients often have difficulties in relationships because their styles of communication include many barriers that prevent them from accurately hearing messages or conveying understanding to others. An important task of the practitioner thus involves teaching clients to respond empathically, a task accomplished in part by modeling, which is generally recognized as a potent technique for promoting client change and growth. People who manifest problems associated with distorting or ignoring messages of others (as frequently occurs in marital, family, and other close relationships) vicariously benefit by observing the practitioner listen effectively and respond empathically. Moreover, clients who are hard to reach or who have difficulties in expressing themselves gradually learn to recognize their own emotions and to express themselves more fully as a result of the practitioner's empathic responding.

Teaching clients empathic communication skills also can entail assuming an educative role. A number of approaches to assisting mates (married or otherwise) who are having serious conflicts embody teaching them to gain and to express empathy for each other. A similar approach has been employed in Parent Effectiveness Training (Gordon, 1970) for over two decades. Still another approach to increasing empathy for children by parents at risk for child abuse has successfully employed a cognitive component designed to assist these parents to attribute less negative meanings to behaviors otherwise perceived by the parents as deliberately provocative (Whiteman, Fanshel, & Grundy, 1987).[2]

Practitioners' roles as educators require them to intervene actively at opportune moments to enable clients to respond empathically, particularly when they have ignored, discounted, or attacked the contributions of others in a session. With respect to this role, we suggest that practitioners consider taking the following actions:

1. Teach clients the paradigm for empathic responding introduced in the chapter. If appropriate, ask them to engage briefly in a paired practice exercise similar to the one recommended for beginning practitioners at the end of the chapter. Utilizing topics neutral to the relationship, have each person in turn carefully listen to the other for several minutes, and afterwards evaluate with participants the impact of the exercise on them.

2. Introduce clients to the list of affective words and phrases and to the leads list contained in this chapter. If appropriate, you may wish to have clients assume tasks during the week to broaden their feeling vocabulary similar to those recommended for beginning practitioners.

3. Intervene in sessions when clients ignore or fail to validate messages, a situation that occurs frequently in work with couples, families, and groups. At those moments, facilitatively interrupt the process to ask the sender to repeat the message and the receiver to paraphrase or capture the essence of the former's message with fresh words, as illustrated in the following example:

16-year-old daughter: I don't like going to school. The teachers are a bunch of jerks, and most of the kids just laugh and make fun of me.

Mother: But you've got to go. If you'd just buckle down and study, school wouldn't be half so hard for you. I think...

Practitioner [*interrupting and speaking to mother*]: I can see that you have some real concerns about Janet's not going to school, but for a moment, I'm going to ask you to get in touch with what she just said to you by repeating it back to her.

Mother [*looking at practitioner*]: She said she doesn't like school.

Practitioner: That's close, but turn and talk to Janet. See if you can identify what she's feeling.

Mother [*turning to daughter*]: I guess it's pretty painful for you to go to school when you don't like your teachers and you feel shut out and ridiculed by the kids.

Janet [*tearfully*]: Yeah, that's it... it's really hard.

Notice that the mother did not respond empathically to her daughter's feelings until the practitioner intervened and coached her. This example thus illustrates the importance of persevering in teaching clients to "hear" the messages of others, a point we cannot overemphasize. Clients often have considerable trouble mastering listening skills because habitual dysfunctional responses are difficult to discard. This is true even when clients are highly motivated to communicate more effectively and when practitioners actively intervene to assist them.

4. Give positive feedback when you observe clients listening to each other or, as in the preceding example, when they respond to your coaching. In the example cited, for instance, the practitioner might have responded to the mother as follows: "I liked the way you responded because your message accurately reflected what your daughter was experiencing. I think she felt you really understood what she was trying to say." It is also helpful to ask participants to discuss what they experienced during the exchange and to highlight positive feelings and observations.

AUTHENTICITY

Although theoreticians generally agree that empathy and respect are vital to developing effective working relationships, they do not agree about the amount of openness or self-disclosure practitioners should offer. Theorists who espouse traditional psychoanalytically oriented theory have advocated that practitioners should relate to clients in a professionally detached manner, although one psychoanalyst, Bernstein (1972), contends that psychoanalysts have gone to an undesirable extreme in emotionally detaching themselves from their patients. He adds, "if an analyst is a healthy, mature, gentle human being, his human response to the expression of a need for help … is a feeling of compassion" (p. 163). The findings of a study by Grunebaum (1986) further indicate that emotional detachment by practitioners can actually be harmful to clients. In a study of 47 patients who believed they had been harmed by psychotherapy, 18 attributed the harm to coldness, distance, and rigidity by the therapist. It is noteworthy that the patients in this study were all mental health professionals who had sought psychotherapy for themselves.

Taking an opposing position to the traditional view, humanistic writers maintain that practitioners should relate openly and authentically as "real" persons. These writers argue that relating in a prescribed "professional" role presents clients with a sterile, contrived relationship that fails to model openness and authenticity, inhibits clients' growth, and fails to provide clients with an experience in relating that is transferable to the real world.

With respect to empirical evidence, numerous research studies cited by Truax and Mitchell (1971) and Gurman (1977) indicated that empathy, respect, and genuineness were correlated with positive outcomes. Critical analyses of these studies and conflicting findings from other research studies have led experts to question these earlier findings and to conclude that "a more complex association exists between outcome and therapist 'skills' than originally hypothesized" (Parloff, Waskow, & Wolfe, 1978, p. 251). However, authenticity or genuineness and the other facilitative conditions are still viewed as central to the helping process.

Authenticity is defined as the sharing of self by relating in a natural, sincere, spontaneous, open, and genuine manner. Being authentic, or genuine, involves relating personally so that expressions are spontaneous rather than contrived. Practitioners' verbalizations are also congruent with their actual feelings and thoughts. Authentic practitioners thus relate as real persons, expressing their feelings and assuming responsibility for them rather than denying the feelings or blaming the client for causing

them. Authenticity also involves being nondefensive and human enough to admit errors to clients. Realizing that they expect clients to lower their defenses and to relate openly (thereby increasing their vulnerability), practitioners themselves must model humanness and openness and avoid hiding behind a mask of "professionalism."

Relating authentically does not mean that practitioners indiscriminately disclose feelings. Indeed, authentic expressions can be abrasive and destructive. Yalom and Lieberman (1971), for example, found in a study of encounter groups that attacks or rejections of group members by leaders or other members produce many psychological casualties. Practitioners should thus relate authentically only when doing so is likely to further therapeutic objectives. This qualification provides considerable latitude and is only intended to constrain practitioners from (1) relating abrasively (even though the practitioner may be expressing genuine feelings) and (2) meeting their own needs by focusing on personal experiences and feelings rather than those of the client.

With respect to the first constraint, practitioners must avoid misconstruing authenticity as granting free license to do whatever they wish, especially with respect to expressing hostility. The second constraint reiterates the importance of practitioners' responding to clients' needs rather than their own. Moreover, when practitioners share their feelings or experiences for a therapeutic purpose, they should immediately shift the focus back on the clients. Keep in mind that the purpose of relating authentically, whether with individuals, families, or groups, is to facilitate growth of clients, not to demonstrate one's own honesty or authenticity.

Types of Self-Disclosure

The aspect of authenticity denoted as self-disclosure has been variously defined by different authors (Chelune, 1979). For this discussion we define it as the conscious and intentional revelation of information about oneself through both verbal expressions and nonverbal behaviors (e.g., smiling, grimacing, or shaking one's head in disbelief). Viewed from a therapeutic perspective, self-disclosure encourages clients to reciprocate with trust and openness. In fact, numerous studies (Doster & Nesbitt, 1979) document that client self-disclosure is correlated with practitioner self-disclosure.

Danish, D'Augelli, and Hauer (1980) have identified two types of self-disclosure, *self-involving statements and personal self-disclosing*. The former type includes messages that express the practitioner's personal reaction to the client during the course of a session. Examples of this type would be:

"I'm impressed with the progress you've made this past week. You applied what we discussed last week and have made another step toward learning to control angry feelings."

"I want to share my reaction to what you just said. I found myself feeling sad for you because you put yourself down unmercifully. I see you so differently from how you see yourself and find myself wishing I could somehow spare you the torment you inflict on yourself."

"You know, as I think about the losses you've experienced this past year, I marvel you've done as well as you have. I'm not at all sure I'd have held together as well as you have."

Personal self-disclosing messages, by contrast, center on struggles or problems the practitioner is currently experiencing or has experienced that are similar to the client's problems. The following are examples of this type of self-disclosure:

(To couple) "As you talk about your problems with your children, it reminds me of similar difficulties I had with mine when they were that same age" (goes on to relate his experience).

(To individual client) "I think all of us struggle with that same fear to some degree. Earlier this week I..." (goes on to relate events in which she experienced similar fears).

Research findings comparing the effects of different types of self-disclosure have been mixed (Dowd & Boroto, 1982; McCarty & Betz, 1978; Reynolds & Fischer, 1983). Given the sparse and inconclusive findings, practitioners should use personal self-disclosure judiciously. Logic suggests that self-disclosures of current problems may undermine the confidence of clients, who may well wonder how practitioners can presume to help others when they haven't successfully resolved their own problems. Moreover, focusing on the practitioner's problems diverts attention from the client, who may conclude that the practitioner prefers to focus on his/her own problems. Self-involving disclosures, by contrast, appear to be low risk and relevant to the helping process.

TIMING AND INTENSITY OF SELF-DISCLOSURE

Still another aspect of self-disclosure involves timing and level of intensity, ranging from superficial to highly personal statements. Giannandrea and Murphy (1973) found that moderate self-disclosing by practitioners, rather than high or low levels, resulted in clients higher rate of return for second interviews. Simonson (1976) has reported similar findings. It is thus logical to assume that practitioners should avoid sharing personal feelings and experiences until rapport and trust have been achieved and clients have demonstrated readiness to engage on a more personal level. The danger in premature self-disclosure is that such responses can threaten clients and lead to emotional retreat at the very time when it is vital to reduce threat and defensiveness. The danger is especially great with clients from other cultures who are unaccustomed to relating on an intense personal basis. For example, in a study comparing the reactions of American and Mexican undergraduate students to self-disclosure, Cherbosque (1987) found that the Mexican students perceived counselors who did not engage in self-disclosure as more trustworthy and expert than those who did. This researcher concluded, therefore, that practitioners who work with Mexican Americans need to maintain a degree of formality that is unnecessary with Anglo clients. We believe that this caution is also applicable to American Indian clients. Formality, however, should not preclude honesty, for Gomez et al. (1985) have reported that manifesting honesty and respect and communicating genuine concern were positively correlated with satisfaction levels of Chicano clients treated as outpatients in a mental health system.

With respect to Asian Americans, Tsui and Schultz (1985) indicate that self-disclosure by practitioners may facilitate the development of rapport:

> Personal disclosure and an *appropriate* [italics ours] level of emotional expressiveness are often the most effective ways to put Asian clients at ease. Considering the generally low level of emotional expressiveness in Asian families, the therapist is, in effect, role modeling for the client and showing the client how the appropriate expression of emotion facilitates the treatment process. (p. 568)

Asian American families, of course, vary as their members range in acculturation and familiarity with values such as self-disclosure.

As clients manifest trust, practitioners can appropriately relate with increased openness and spontaneity, assuming, of course, that authentic responses are relevant to clients' needs and do not shift the focus from the client for more than brief periods. Even when trust is strong, practitioners should exercise moderate self-disclosure, for beyond a certain level authentic responses no longer facilitate the helping process (Truax & Carkhuff, 1964). Practitioners must exercise discretion in employing self-disclosure with severely mentally ill clients. Shimkunas (1972) and Doster, Surratt, and Webster (1975) report higher levels of symptomatic behavior (e.g., delusional ideation) by paranoid schizophrenic patients following personal self-disclosure by practitioners. Superficial self-disclosure, by contrast, did not produce increases in disturbed behavior.

With respect to social workers' actual use of self-disclosures, it is heartening to note that a recent study (Anderson & Mandell, 1989) indicated that self-disclosure gained increased acceptance by social workers between 1978 and 1989. Moreover, they were adhering to the guidelines advocated in this and other relevant references. As expected, however, psychodynamically oriented practitioners were less likely to use self-disclosure than were other practitioners.

A Paradigm for Responding Authentically

Beginning practitioners (and clients) learn the skill of relating authentically more readily if they have a paradigm for formulating effective messages. Note in the following paradigm that there are four elements of an authentic message:

(1) "I" ( )	**About**	**Because**
(2) Specific feeling	(3) Neutral description	(4) Impact of situation upon
or wants	of event	sender or others

The following example (Larsen, 1980), involving a social work student's response to a message from an institutionalized youth, illustrates the use of the paradigm. The student describes the situation: "Don and I had a tough go of it last week. I entered the living unit only to find that he was angry with me for some reason, and he proceeded to abuse me verbally all night long. This week, Don approached me to apologize."

Don: I'm really sorry about what happened the other night, I didn't mean nothing by it. You probably don't want nothing more to do with me.

Student: Well, you know, Don, I'm sorry it happened, too. I was really hurt and puzzled that night because I didn't understand where all your anger was coming from. You wouldn't talk to me about it, so I felt frustrated and I didn't quite know what to do or make of it. And you know, one of my real fears that night was that this was going to get in the way of our getting to know each other. I didn't really want to see that happen.

In the preceding message, note that the student uses all the elements of the paradigm, identifying specific feelings (hurt, puzzlement, frustration, fear), describing the events that occurred in a neutral, nonblaming manner, and identifying the impact she feared these events might have upon their relationship.

As you consider the paradigm, note that we are not recommending that you use it in a mechanistic and undeviating "I-feel-this-way-about…" response pattern. Rather, we suggest you learn and combine the elements of the paradigm in various ways as you practice constructing authentic messages. Later, as you incorporate authentic relating within your natural conversational repertoire, you will no longer need to refer to the paradigm.

This paradigm is also applicable in teaching clients to respond authentically. We suggest that you present the paradigm to clients and guide them through several practice messages, assisting them to include all the elements of the paradigm in their responses. For example:

SPECIFIC "I" FEELINGS	DESCRIPTION OF EVENT	IMPACT
I get frustrated	when you keep reading the paper while I'm speaking	because I feel dicounted and very unimportant to you.

It is important to stress with clients the need to use conversational language when they express authentic messages. Also emphasize, however, that they should talk about their own feelings and opinions. Otherwise, they may slip into accusative forms of communication as they vary their messages.

Guidelines for Responding Authentically

As you practice authentic responding and teach clients to respond authentically in their encounters with others, we suggest you keep in mind the following guidelines that relate to the four elements of an authentic message.

1. *Personalize messages by using the pronoun "I."* When attempting to respond authentically, both practitioners and clients commonly make the mistake of starting their statements with "You." This introduction tends to focus a response on the other person rather than on the sender's experiencing. Beginning messages with "I," however, encourages senders to own responsibility for their feelings and to personalize their statements.

Efforts by practitioners to employ "I" statements when responding can profoundly affect the quality of group processes, increasing the specificity of communications and the frequency of "I" statements by clients. As a general rule, groups (including couples and families) are likely to follow a practitioner's communication style.

Just as groups tend to follow suit when practitioners frequently use "I" messages, they also imitate counterproductive behaviors of the practitioner, including communicating in broad generalities, focusing on issues external to the individual, or relating to the group in an interrogative or confrontational manner.

The behavior of practitioners thus may not necessarily be a good model for clients to emulate in real life. Practitioners must be careful to model the skills they wish clients to acquire. Practitioners should master relating authentically to the extent that they automatically personalize their messages and constructively share their inner experiencing with clients. To facilitate personalizing messages, practitioners can negotiate an agreement with individuals or groups specifying that clients will endeavor to incorporate the use of "I" statements in their conversational repertoires. Thereafter, it is critical to intervene consistently to assist clients to personalize their messages when they have not done so.

2. *Share feelings that lie at varying depths.* To achieve this, practitioners must reach for feelings that underlie their immediate experiencing. Doing so is particularly vital when practitioners experience strong negative feelings (dislike, anger, repulsion, disgust, boredom) toward a client, for an examination of the deeper aspects of feelings often discloses more positive feelings toward the client. Expressing these feelings preserves the client's self-esteem, whereas expressing superficial negative feelings often poses a threat to the client, creating defensiveness and anger. In expressing anger (and perhaps disgust) toward a client who is chronically late for appointments, the practitioner may first connect his feelings of anger to feeling inconvenienced. In reaching for deeper feelings, the practitioner may discover that the annoyance derives from disappointment that the client is not fully committed to the helping process. At an even deeper level may lie hurt in not being more important to the client. Further introspection may also discover a concern that the client may be manifesting similar behavior in other areas of life that could adversely affect relationships with others.

Utilizing an example of boredom, Gendlin (1967) illustrates the process a practitioner might go through to analyze feelings toward a client and to discover positive aspects of this experiencing that can be safely and beneficially shared with the client. Rather than just blurting out, "You bore me" or "Why do you never say anything important?" Gendlin recommends that practitioners advance their own experiencing for a few moments in a chain of "content mutation and explication": "I am bored... This isn't helping him... I wish I could help... I'd like to hear something more personal... I really would welcome him... I have more welcome on my hands for him than he lets me use... but I don't want to push away what he does express..." The resulting therapist expression

now will make a personal interaction, even if the client says nothing in return. The therapist will say something like: "You know, I've been thinking the last few minutes, I wish I'd hear more from you, more of how you really feel inside. I know you might not want to say, but whenever you can or want, I would like it" (p. 90).

By employing the process just described, the practitioner may discover multiple (and sometimes conflicting) feelings that may be beneficially shared with the client, as illustrated in the following message:

[*To mother.*] "I've been experiencing some feelings in the session I want to share with you because it may shed some light on what others may experience with you. I was wanting to tell you that it appears you often come to Robert's [*son's*] rescue in the session and that at times you seem to protect him from the consequences of his own actions, but I held back and began to feel a slight knotting in my stomach. Then it hit me that I was afraid you'd be hurt and offended and that it might have a negative impact on our relationship. As I think about it just now, I'm aware that sometimes I feel I'm walking on eggshells with you, and I don't like that because it puts distance between us. Another reason I don't like it is because I think I'm underestimating your ability to handle constructive feedback. I think you're stronger than you come across at times. [*Slight pause.*] Could you share what you're feeling just now about what I said?"

Sharing multiple emotions also assists practitioners to manage situations in which they experience frustration or anger with clients. Dyer (1969) cites an example of feeling extremely angry at a client and simultaneously feeling guilty about having that feeling. Rather than sharing just the anger, Dyer shared the multiple emotions he was experiencing, including his wish not to feel angry and his desire to discuss and resolve his feelings. In such instances, a practitioner could also express underlying caring for the client and highlight the importance of understanding the dynamics involved so that both might learn from the situation. It is critical, of course, to analyze what changes need to be made by the client and/or practitioner to prevent future recurrences.

Like prospective practitioners, clients are prone to focus on one aspect of their experiencing to the exclusion of deeper and more complex emotions. Clients often have difficulty, in fact, pinpointing any feelings they are experiencing. In either case, practitioners should persevere to help clients broaden their awareness of their emotions and to express them openly, as illustrated in the following excerpt. The practitioner speaks to the husband:

Practitioner: When you told your wife you didn't want to take her to a movie and she said you were a "bump on a log"—that you never seemed to want to do anything with her—what feelings did you experience?[3]

Husband: I decided that if that's what she thought of me, that's what I'd be.

Practitioner: Can you get in touch with what you were feeling? You told me a little bit about what you thought, but what about what's happening inside? Try to use feeling words to describe what you're experiencing.

Husband [pause]: I felt that if she was going to get on my back ...

Practitioner [gently interrupting.]: Can you use a feeling word like "bad," or "hurt," or "put down"? What did you feel?

Husband: OK. I felt annoyed.

Practitioner: So you experienced a sense of irritation. Good. I'm pleased you could get in touch with that feeling. Now see if you can get to an even more basic feeling. Remember, as we've talked about before, anger is usually a surface feeling that camouflages other feelings. What was under your annoyance?

Husband: Uhhh, I'd say frustrated. I just didn't want to sit there and listen to her harp at me. She never quits.

Practitioner: I would like to check out something with you. Right now, as you're talking about this, it seems you're experiencing a real sense of discouragement and perhaps even hopelessness about

things ever changing. It's as though you've given up. Maybe that's part of what you were feeling Saturday.

Husband: Yeah, I just turn myself off. Doesn't seem to be anything I can do to make her happy.

Practitioner: I'm glad that you can recognize the sense of despair you're feeling. I also appreciate your hanging in there with me for a minute to get in touch with some of your feelings. You seem to be a person whose feelings run deep, and at times expressing them may come hard for you. I'm wondering how you view yourself in that regard.

In the preceding excerpt, the practitioner engaged in extensive coaching to assist the client to get in touch with his underlying feelings. Deeper than the feelings of annoyance and frustration the client identified lay the more basic emotions of hurt and being unimportant to his wife.[4] By providing other spontaneous "training sessions," the practitioner can help him to identify his feelings more readily, to find the feeling words to express them, and to begin formulating "I" statements.

3. *Describe the situation or targeted behavior in neutral or descriptive terms.* In their messages, clients often omit reference or make only vague reference to situations that prompted their responses. Moreover, they may convey their messages in a blaming manner, engendering defensiveness that overshadows other aspects of self-disclosure. In either event, self-disclosure is minimal and respondents do not receive information that could otherwise be of considerable value. Consider, for example, the low yield of information in the following messages:

"You're a neat person."

"You should be more conscientious."

"You're progressing well in your work."

"You have a bad attitude."

All the preceding messages lack supporting information that respondents need to identify specific aspects of their behavior that is competent and warrants recognition or is substandard or dysfunctional. Practitioners should thus assist parents, spouses, or others to provide higher-yield feedback by including behavioral references. Examples of such messages are as follows:

[*Parent to six-year-old girl*]: "I've really appreciated all that you've done tonight by yourself. You picked up your toys, washed your hands before dinner, and ate dinner without dawdling. I'm so pleased."

"I'm very disappointed with your behavior right now. You didn't change your clothes when you came home from school; you didn't feed the dog; and you haven't started your homework."

Note in the last example that the parent sent an "I" message and owned the feelings of disappointment rather than attacking the child for being undependable.

When responding authentically, practitioners should also carefully describe specific events that prompted their responses, particularly when they wish to bring clients' attention to some aspect of their behavior or to a situation of which they may not be fully aware. The following practitioner's message illustrates this point:

"I need to share something with you that concerns me. Just a moment ago, I gave you feedback regarding the positive way I thought you handled a situation with your husband. [*Refers to specific behaviors manifested by client.*] When I did that, you seemed to discount my response by [*mentions specific behaviors*]. Actually, this is not the first time I have seen this happen. It appears to me that it is difficult for you to give yourself credit for the positive things you do and the progress you are making. This, in fact, may be one of the reasons that you get so discouraged at times. I wonder how you view your behavior in this regard."

Practitioners constantly need to assess the specificity of their responses to ensure that they give clients the benefit of behaviorally specific feedback and provide positive modeling experiences for them. It is also vital to coach clients in giving specific feedback whenever they make sweeping generalizations and do not document the relationship between their responses and specific situations.

4. *Identify the specific impact of the problem situation or behavior on others.* Authentic messages often stop short of identifying the specific impact of the situation upon the sender or others, even though such information would be very appropriate and helpful. This element of an "I" message also increases the likelihood that the receiver will adjust or make changes, particularly if the sender demonstrates that the receiver's behavior is having a tangible effect on him or her. Consider a practitioner's authentic response to a male member of an adult group:

"Sometimes I sense some impatience on your part to move on to other topics. [*Describes situation that just occurred, documenting specific messages and behavior.*] At times I find myself torn between responding to your urging us "to get on with it" or staying with a discussion that seems beneficial to the group. It may be that others in the group are experiencing similar mixed feelings and some of the pressure I feel."

Note that the practitioner first clarifies the tangible effects of the client's behavior upon himself and then suggests that others may experience the behavior similarly. Given the practitioner's approach, it is likely that others in the group will also give feedback. The client is then free to draw his own conclusions about the cause-effect relationship between his behaviors and the reactions of others and to decide whether he wishes to alter his way of relating in the group.

In addition to documenting the impact of specific behaviors of clients on themselves, practitioners can also identify the negative impact of a client's behavior on the client (e.g., "I'm concerned about [*specific behavior*] because it keeps you from achieving your goal"). Further, they may document the impact of a client's behavior on others (e.g., wife) or the relationship between the client and another person (e.g., "It appears that your behavior creates distance between you and your son").

Clients often have difficulty in clarifying the impact of others' behavior on themselves. A mother's message to her child, "I want you to play someplace else," establishes no reason for the request nor does it specify the negative impact of the behavior on her. If the mother responds in the following authentic manner, she clearly identifies the tangible effect of her child's behavior: "I'm having a hard time getting through the hallway because I keep stumbling over toys and having to go around you. I've almost fallen several times, and others might also. I'm worried that someone might get hurt, so I'm asking you to move your toys to your room."

The preceding illustration underscores our point that when clients clarify how a situation affects them, their requests do not appear arbitrary and are more persuasive; hence, others are likely to make appropriate accommodations. We suspect that an important reason why many clients have not changed certain self-defeating behaviors before entering the helping process is that others have previously attacked or pressured them to change, rather than authentically and unabrasively imparting information that highlights how the clients' behavior strikes them. Others have also often attempted to prescribe behavioral changes that appear to be self-serving (e.g., "Come on, stop that sulking") instead of relating their feelings (e.g., "I'm concerned that you're down and unhappy. I'd like to help but I'm not sure how"). Such responses do not strike a responsive chord in clients, who may equate making changes with putting themselves under the control of others (by following their directives), thereby losing their autonomy.

In the following excerpt, note how the practitioner assists Carolyn, a group member, to personalize her statements and to clarify her reaction to the behavior of another member who has been consistently silent throughout the first two sessions:

Carolyn: We've talked about needing to add new guidelines for the group as we go along. I think we ought to have a guideline that everyone should talk in the group. [*Observe that the member has not personalized her message but has proposed a solution to meet a need she has not identified.*]

Practitioner [*to Carolyn*]: The group may want to consider this guideline, but for a minute, can you get in touch with what you're experiencing and put it in the form of an "I" statement?

Carolyn: Well, all right. Janet hasn't talked at all for two solid weeks, and it's beginning to really irritate me.

Practitioner: I'm wondering what else you may be experiencing besides irritation? [*Assists member to identify feelings besides mild anger.*]

Carolyn: I guess I'm a little uneasy because I don't know where Janet stands. Maybe I'm afraid she's sitting in judgment of us—I mean, me. And I guess I feel cheated because I'd like to get to know her better, and right now I feel shut out by her.

Practitioner: That response helps us to begin to get to the heart of the matter. Would you now express yourself directly to Janet? Tell her what you are experiencing and, particularly, how her silence is affecting you.

Carolyn [*to Janet*]: I did wonder what you thought about me since I really opened up last week. And I do want to get to know you better. But, you know, underneath all this, I'm concerned about you. You seem unhappy and alone, and that makes me uncomfortable—I don't like to think of your feeling that way. Frankly, I'd like to know how you feel about being in this group, and if you're uneasy about it, as you seem to be, I'd like to help you feel better somehow.

In the preceding example, the practitioner assisted Carolyn to experience a broader range of feelings and to identify her reaction to Janet's silence. In response to the practitioner's intervention, Carolyn also expressed more positive feelings than were evident in her initial message—a not infrequent occurrence when practitioners encourage clients to explore deeper-level emotions.

Engaging one member in identifying specific reactions to the behavior of others provides a learning experience for the entire group, and members often expand their conversational repertoires to incorporate such facilitative responding. In fact, there is a correlation between the extent to which practitioners assist clients to acquire specific skills and the extent to which clients acquire those same skills.

CUES FOR AUTHENTIC RESPONDING

The impetus for practitioners to respond authentically may emanate from (1) clients' messages that request self-disclosure or (2) practitioners' decisions to share perceptions and reactions they believe will be helpful. In the following section, we consider authentic responding that emanates from these two sources.

Authentic Responding Stimulated by Clients' Messages

Requests from Clients for Personal Information

Clients often confront students and practitioners with questions aimed at soliciting personal information such as "How old are you?" "Do you have any children?" "What is your religion?" "Do you and your wife ever fight?" and "Are you a student?" It is natural for clients to be curious and to ask questions about a practitioner in whom they are confiding, especially when their wellbeing and future are at stake.

Self-disclosing responses may or may not be appropriate, depending on the practitioner's assessment of the client's motivation for asking a particular question. When questions appear to be prompted by a natural desire for information, such responses are often very appropriate. Seemingly innocuous questions, however, may camouflage deep concerns or troubling feelings. In such instances, providing an immediate answer may be countertherapeutic because doing so may close the door to exploring and resolving clients' concerns and feelings. Clients are thus left to struggle with their feelings alone, which may seriously impair progress or cause premature termination. To illustrate, consider the following excerpt taken from an initial session involving a 23-year-old student and a 43-year-old woman who requested help for marital problems:

Client: Are you married?
Student: No, but I'm engaged. Why do you ask?
Client: Oh, I don't know. I just wondered.

Given the context of an older adult with a much younger student, the client's question was likely motivated by the concern that the student might lack life experience essential to understand her marital difficulties or the competence needed to assist her in resolving them. In this instance, immediate authentic disclosure by the student was inappropriate because it did not facilitate exploration of the feelings underlying the client's inquiry.

An exchange such as the preceding may yield information vital to the helping process if the practitioner avoids premature self-disclosure. It is sometimes very difficult to distinguish between situations in which the questions of clients are motivated by a natural desire for information or by hidden concerns or feelings. As a rule of thumb, when you have questions about clients' motivation for making personal inquiries, *precede disclosures of views or feelings with either open–ended or empathic responses.* Responding in this manner significantly increases the probability that clients will reveal their real concerns. Notice what happens when the practitioner utilizes an empathic response before responding authentically:

Client: Are you married?
Student: I gather you're wondering if I can understand and help you with your difficulties in light of the fact that I'm much younger than you.
Client: Well, I guess I was thinking that. I hope that doesn't offend you.

Student: To the contrary—I appreciate your frankness. It's natural that you want to have confidence in your counselor. I know there's a lot at stake for you. Tell me more about your concerns.

In the preceding excerpt the student responded to the probable concern of the client and struck pay dirt. Such astuteness tends to foster confidence by clients and greatly facilitates the development of a therapeutic partnership. The fact that the student "leans into" the situation by inviting further exploration rather than skirting the issue may also be read by the client as an indicator of the student's own confidence in his or her ability to help. After fully exploring the client's concerns, the student can respond with an authentic response identifying personal qualifications, as illustrated in the following message:

"I do want you to know that I believe I can be helpful to you. I have studied marriage counseling at some length, and I have counseled other clients whose difficulties were similar to your own. I also consult with my supervisor regularly. However, the final judgment of my competence will rest with you. It will be important for us to discuss any feelings you may still have at the end of the interview as you make a decision about returning for future sessions."

Questions That Solicit the Practitioner's Perceptions   Clients may also pose questions that solicit the practitioner's opinions, views, or feelings. Typical questions include, "How do I compare to your other clients?" "Do you think I need help?" "Am I crazy?" or "Do you think there's any hope for me?" Such questions can be challenging, and practitioners must again consider the motivation behind the question and judge as to whether to disclose their views or feelings immediately or to employ either an empathic or open-ended response. As practitioners do disclose their perceptions, however, their responses must be congruent with their inner experiencing. In response to the question, "Do you think there's any hope for me?" the practitioner may congruently respond with a message that blends elements of empathy and authenticity:

"Your question tells me you're probably afraid you're beyond help. Although you do have some difficult problems, I'm optimistic that if we work hard together things can improve. You've shown a number of strengths that should help you make changes, including [*reviews strengths*]. A lot, of course, will depend on whether you're willing to commit to making changes you think would improve your situation and to invest the time and effort necessary to achieve your goals. In that respect, you're in control of the situation and whether things change for the better. That fact is something that many people find encouraging to know."

It is not necessary to answer all questions of clients in the service of authenticity. If you feel uncomfortable about answering a personal question or deem it inadvisable to do so, you should feel free to decline answering. In so doing, it is important to explain your reason for not answering directly, again utilizing an authentic response. If a teenage client, for example, asks whether the practitioner had sexual relations before she married, the practitioner may respond as follows:

"I need to share with you some thoughts I have about answering your question. Frankly, I'd rather not reveal that information to you inasmuch as that area is a very private part of my life. I'm doubtful that knowing that personal information about me would be helpful to you in the long run. However, I'm also aware of feeling apprehensive that you might feel embarrassed or put down by my response, and I don't want that to happen. Asking me, that took some risk on your part. I have an idea that your question probably has to do with a struggle you're having, although I could be wrong. I would appreciate your sharing your thoughts about what I've said and telling me what sparked your question." The practitioner should then utilize empathic responding and open-ended questions to explore the client's reaction and motivation for asking her question.

Authentic Responding Initiated by Practitioners

Authentic responding initiated by practitioners may take several forms, which are considered separately in the following sections.

Disclosing Past Experiences
As we previously indicated, such responses should be used sparingly, be brief, relevant to the client's concerns, and well timed. In relating to a particular client's struggle, a practitioner may indicate, "I remember I felt very much like that when I was struggling with…" Practitioners may also cite personal perceptions or experiences as reference points for clients, as, for example, "I think that is very normal behavior for a child. For instance, my five-year-old…" A fundamental guideline that applies to such situations is that practitioners should be certain they are focusing on themselves to meet the therapeutic needs of clients.

Sharing Perceptions, Ideas, Reactions, and Formulations
A key role of the practitioner in the change-oriented phase of the helping process is to act as a "candid feedback system" by revealing personal thoughts and perceptions relevant to client problems (Hammond et al., 1977). The function of such responding is to further the change process in one or more of the following ways:

1. To heighten clients' awareness of dynamics that may play an important part in problems.
2. To offer a different perspective regarding issues and events.
3. To aid clients in conceptualizing the purposes of their behavior and feelings.
4. To enlighten clients on how they affect others (including the practitioner).
5. To bring clients' attention to cognitive and behav-

ioral patterns (both functional and dysfunctional) that operate at either an individual or group level.
6. To share here-and-now affective and physical reactions of the practitioner to clients' behavior or to processes that occur in the helping relationship.
7. To share positive feedback concerning clients' strengths and growth.

After responding authentically to achieve any of these purposes, it is vital to invite clients to express their own views and draw their own conclusions. *Owning* perceptions rather than using under-the-table methods to influence clients to adopt particular views or to change in ways deemed desirable by the practitioner (e.g., "Don't you think you ought to consider…") relieves clients of the need to behave deviously or to defend themselves from the tyranny of views with which they do not agree.

Sharing perceptions with clients involves some risk that clients may misinterpret the practitioner's motives and thus feel criticized, put down, or rebuked. Clarifying helpful intent before responding diminishes the risk somewhat. Nevertheless, it is vital to be observant of clients' reactions that may indicate a response has struck an exposed nerve.

To avoid damaging the relationship (or to repair it), the practitioner should be empathically attuned to the client's reaction to candid feedback, shifting the focus back to the client to determine the impact of the self-disclosure. If the client appears to have been emotionally wounded by the practitioner's authentic response, the practitioner can use empathic skills to elicit troubled feelings and to guide subsequent responses aimed at restoring the relationship's equilibrium. Expressions of concern and clarification of the goodwill intended by the response are also usually facilitative: "I can see that what I shared with you hit you pretty hard—and that you're feeling put down right now. [*Client nods but avoids eye contact.*] I feel badly about that because the last thing I'd want is to hurt you. Please tell me what you're feeling."

Openly (and Tactfully) Sharing Reactions When Put on the Spot Clients sometimes create situations that put practitioners under considerable pressure to respond to messages that bear directly on the relationship, such as when they accuse a practitioner of being uninterested, unfeeling, irritated, displeased, critical, inappropriate, or incompetent. Clients may also ask pointed questions (sometimes before the relationship has been firmly established) that require immediate responses. The first statement of one female client in an initial interview, for example, was, "I'm gay. Does that make any difference to you?" In the opening moments of another session, a pregnant client asked the practitioner, "How do you feel about abortion?"

Over the years, students have reported numerous such situations that sorely tested their ability to respond facilitatively. In one instance, a male member of a group asked a female student leader for her photograph. In another, an adolescent boy kept taking his shoes off and putting his feet (which smelled very bad) on the practitioner's desk. By reflecting on your practice experience, you too can no doubt pinpoint instances in which the behavior of clients caused you to squirm or produced butterflies in your stomach. Experiencing discomfort in sessions (sometimes *intense* discomfort) may be an indication that something is going awry that needs to be addressed. It is thus important to reflect on your discomfort, seeking to identify events that seem to be causing or exacerbating that discomfort (e.g., "I'm feeling very uneasy because I don't know how to respond when my client says things like, 'You seem to be too busy to see me,' or 'I'm not sure I'm worth your trouble.'"). After privately exploring the reason for the discomfort, the practitioner might respond:

"I'd like to share some impressions about several things you've said in the last two sessions. [*Identifies client's statements.*] I sense you're feeling pretty unimportant—as though you don't

count for much—and that perhaps you're imposing on me just by being here. I want you to know that I'm pleased you had the courage to seek help in face of all the opposition from your family. It's also important to me that you know that I want to be helpful to you. I am concerned, however, that you feel you're imposing on me. Could you share more of those feelings with me?"

Notice that in the preceding response the practitioner specifically identifies the self-defeating thoughts and feelings and blends elements of empathy and authenticity in the response.

Situations that put practitioners on the spot also include clients' angry attacks, as we discuss later in the chapter. Practitioners must learn to respond authentically in such situations. Consider a situation in which an adolescent attacks a practitioner in an initial interview, protesting, "I don't want to be here. You counselors are all losers." In such instances, practitioners should share their reactions, as illustrated in the following:

"It sounds as though you're really ticked off about having to see me and that your previous experiences with counselors have been bummers. I respect your feelings and don't want to pressure you to work with me. I am concerned and uncomfortable, however, because you apparently have lumped all counselors together and that makes me a loser in your eyes. If you close your mind to the possibility that we might accomplish something together, then the chances are pretty slim I can be helpful. I want you to know that I am interested in you and that I would like to know what you're up against."

Intertwining empathic and authentic responses in this manner often defuses clients' anger and encourages them to think more rationally about a situation.

Sharing Feelings When Clients' Behavior Is Unreasonable or Distressing Although practitioners should be able to take most client behaviors in stride, there are times when they experience justifiable feelings of frustration, anger, or even hurt. In one case, a client acquired a practitioner's home phone number from another source and began calling frequently about daily crisis situations, although discussions of these events could easily have waited until the next session. In another instance, a tipsy client called the practitioner in the middle of the night "just to talk." In yet another case, an adolescent client let the air out of a practitioner's automobile tires. In such situations, practitioners should share their feelings with clients—*if they believe they can do so constructively.* In the following recorded case example, note that the student interweaves authentic and empathic responses in confronting a Hispanic youth in a correctional institution who had maintained he was innocent of hiding drugs that staff had found in his room. Believing the youth's story, the student went to bat for him, only to find out later he had lied. Somewhat uneasy at her first real confrontation, the student tries to formulate an authentic response; ironically, the youth helps her to be "up-front" with him:

Student: There's something I wanted to talk to you about, Randy … [*Stops to search for the right words.*]

Randy: Well, come out with it, then. Just say it straight.

Student: Well, remember last week when you got that incident report? You know, I really believed you were innocent. I was ready to go to the hearing and tell staff I was sure you were innocent and that the charge should be dropped. I guess I'm feeling kind of bad because when I talked to you, you told me you were innocent, and, well, that's not exactly the way it turned out.

Randy: You mean I lied to you. Go ahead and say it.

Student: Well, yes, I guess I felt kind of hurt because I was hoping that maybe you had more trust in me than that.

Randy: Well, Susan, let me tell you something. Where I come from, that's not lying, that's what we call survival. Personally, I don't consider myself a liar. I just do what I need to do to get by. That's an old trick, but it just didn't work.

Student: I hear you, Randy. I guess you're saying we're from two different cultures, and maybe we both define the same thing in different ways. I guess that with me being Anglo, you can't really expect me to understand what life has been like for you.

Several minutes later in the session, after the student has further explored the client's feelings, the following interchange occurs:

Student: You know, Randy, I want you to know. One is that when social workers work with clients, they have what they call confidentiality, so I won't be sharing what we talk about without your permission in most cases. An exception to this relates to rule or law violations. I can't keep that confidential. The other thing is that I don't expect you to share everything with me. I know there are certain things you don't want to tell me, so rather than lying about something that I ask you about, maybe you can just tell me you don't want to tell me. Would you consider that?

Randy: Yeah, that's OK. [*Pause*] Listen, Susan, I don't want you to go around thinking I'm a liar now. I'll tell you this, and you can take it for what it's worth, but this is the truth. That's the first time I've ever lied to you. But you may not believe that.

Student: I do believe you, Randy. [*He seems a little relieved and there is a silence.*]

Randy: Well, Susan, that's a deal, then. I won't lie to you again, but if there's something I don't want to say, I'll tell you I don't want to say it.

Student: Sounds good to me. [*Both start walking away.*] You know, Randy, I really want to see you get through this program and get out as fast as you can. I know it's hard starting over because of the incident with the drugs, but I think we can get you through. [*This seemed to have more impact on Randy than anything I had said to him in a long time. The pleasure was visible on his face, and he broke into a big smile.*]

Noteworthy in this exchange is that the practitioner relied almost exclusively on the skills of authenticity and empathy to bring the incident to a positive conclusion. Ignoring her feelings would have impaired the student's ability to relate facilitatively to the client and would have been destructive to the relationship; focusing on the situation, on the other hand, was beneficial for both.

Sharing Feelings When Clients Give Positive Feedback   Practitioners sometimes have difficulty responding receptively to clients' positive feedback about their own attributes and/or performance. We suggest that practitioners model the same receptivity to positive feedback they ask clients to demonstrate in their own lives, as illustrated in the following exchange between a client and a practitioner:

Client: I don't know what I would have done without you. I'm just not sure I would have made it if you hadn't been there when I needed you. You've made such a difference in my life.

Practitioner: I can sense your appreciation. I'm touched by your gratitude and pleased you are feeling so much more capable of coping with your situation. I want you to know, too, that even though I was there to help, your efforts have been the deciding factor in your growth.

POSITIVE FEEDBACK: A FORM OF AUTHENTIC RESPONDING

Because positive feedback plays such a vital role in the change process, we have allocated this separate section to do justice to the topic. Practitioners often employ (or should employ) this skill in supplying information to clients about positive attributes or specific areas in which they manifest strengths, effective coping mechanisms, and incremental growth. In so doing, practitioners enhance motivation to change and foster hope for the future. Many opportune moments occur in the helping process when practitioners experience warm or positive feelings toward clients because of the latter's actions or progress. When appropriate, practitioners should share such feelings spontaneously with clients, as illustrated in the following messages:

"I'm pleased you have what I consider exceptional ability to 'self-observe' your own behavior and to analyze the part you play in relationships. I think this strength will serve you well in solving the problems you've identified."

"I've been touched several times in the group when I've noticed that, despite your grief over the loss of your husband, you've reached out to other members who needed support."

[*To newly formed group*]: "In contrast to our first session, I've noticed that this week we haven't had trouble getting down to business and staying on task. I've been pleased as I've watched you develop group guidelines for the past 20 minutes with minimal assistance from me, and I had the thought, This group is really moving."

The first two messages accredit strengths of individuals, and the third lauds a behavioral change the practitioner has observed in a group process. Both types of messages sharply focus clients' attention on specific behaviors that facilitate the change process, ultimately increasing the frequency of such behaviors. Given consistently, positive messages also have the long-range effect of helping clients who have low self-esteem to develop a more positive image of self. When positive feedback is utilized to document the cause-effect relationship between their efforts and positive outcomes, clients also experience satisfaction, accomplishment, and control over their situation. Positive feedback can have the further effect of increasing clients' confidence in their ability to cope. We have occasionally had experiences with clients who were on the verge of falling apart when they came to a session but left feeling able to manage their problems for a while longer. We attribute their increased ability to function in part to authentic responses that documented and highlighted areas in which they were coping and successfully managing problems.

Taped sessions of students and practitioners often reflect a dearth of authentic responses that underscore clients' strengths or incremental growth, which is unfortunate because, in our experience, clients' rates of change often correlate with the extent to which practitioners focus on these two vital areas. As practitioners consistently focus on clients' assets and the subtle positive changes that often occur in early sessions, clients invest more effort in the change process. As the rate of change accelerates, practitioners can focus more extensively on clients' successes, identifying and reinforcing their strengths and functional coping behaviors.

Practitioners face several challenges in accrediting clients' strengths and growth, including enhancing their ability to recognize and express fleeting positive feelings when clients manifest strengths or progress. Practitioners must also learn to document events so that they can provide information about specific positive behaviors. Still another challenge and responsibility is to teach clients to give positive feedback to each other, strategies for which we discuss in Chapter 16.

To increase your ability to discern client strengths, we recommend you and your clients construct a profile of their resources. This may be done with individuals, couples, families, or groups, preferably early in the helping process. In individual sessions, the practitioner should ask the client to identify and list all the strengths she or he can think of. The practitioner also shares observations of the client's strengths, adding them to the list, which is kept for ongoing review to add further strengths as they are discovered.

With families, couples, or groups, practitioners may follow a similar procedure in assessing the strengths of individual members, but they should ask other group members to share their perceptions of strengths with each member. The practitioner may also wish to ask couples, families, or groups to identify the strengths and incremental growth of the group per se periodically throughout the helping process. After clients have identified their strengths or those of the group, the practitioner should elicit observations regarding their reactions to the experience. Often they may mutually conclude that clients have many more strengths than they have realized. The practitioner should also explore discomfort experienced by clients as they identify strengths, with the goal of having them acknowledge more comfortably their positive attributes and personal resources.

We further suggest that you carefully observe processes early on in sessions and note subtle manifestations of strengths and positive behavioral changes, systematically recording these in your progress records. The following observations are taken from the progress records of a practitioner regarding the strengths of several members of a group formed for young adults with cerebral palsy:

Lorraine: Expresses caring and concern for feelings of other members; acts as "interpreter" between members with difficult speech patterns and myself; speaks for herself when appropriate; exhibits leadership in the group; can carry out tasks both in the group and outside; open to change.

Ken: Accepts his physical limitations; is concerned for members' feelings and problems; expresses love and affection freely; has many friends; gets along remarkably well with father and sister; is patient and easygoing; sense of humor; encourages group members to participate; actively involved in every session; listens attentively.

Dale: Helps keep group on designated topic when one member strays or focuses too much on self; expresses opinion and feelings somewhat openly and freely; can present positive aspects of situations, sometimes in a different light than others; can be persistent, even patient; is able to "hear" another's honest, sincere response to his behavior (positive and negative); at times can be very open and nondefensive; can admit to mistakes and has the ability to keep to tasks when he wants to accomplish things.

In your progress records, note not only the strengths and incremental growth of clients but also whether you (or group members) focused on those changes. Keep in mind that changes often occur very subtly within a single session. For instance, clients may begin to discuss problems more openly during the later part of a session, tentatively commit to work on a problem they refused to tackle earlier, show growing trust in the practitioner by confiding high-risk information about themselves, or own responsibility for the first time for their part in problems. Groups and families may likewise manifest growth within short periods of time. It is thus vital to keep your antenna finely attuned to such changes so that you do not overlook clients' progress.

RELATING ASSERTIVELY TO CLIENTS

Still another aspect of relating authentically entails relating assertively to clients when a situation warrants such behavior. Reasons for relating assertively are manifold. To inspire confidence and influence clients to follow their lead, practitioners must relate in a manner that projects competence. This is especially important in the initial phase of the helping process in which clients usually covertly test or check out practitioners to determine whether they can understand their problems and appear competent to help them.

In conjoint or group sessions, clients may also entertain the question of whether the practitioner is strong enough to protect them from destructive interactional processes that may occur in sessions. (Family or group members, in fact, generally will not fully share, risk, or commit to the helping process until they have answered this question affirmatively through consistent observation of assertive actions by the practitioner.) If practitioners are relaxed and demonstrate through decisive behavior that they are fully capable of handling clients' problems and of providing the necessary protection and structure to control potentially chaotic or volatile processes, clients generally relax, muster hope, and begin to work on problems. If the practitioner appears incapable of curtailing or circumventing dysfunctional processes that render clients vulnerable, clients will have justifiable doubts as to the advisability of placing themselves

in jeopardy and, consequently, may disengage from the helping process.

Skill in relating assertively is also prerequisite to implementing confrontation, a major technique that practitioners employ to surmount opposition to change. But practitioners must employ confrontation with sensitivity and finesse, as the risk of alienating clients by using this technique is high. All forms of assertiveness, in fact, must be conveyed in a context of goodwill and empathic regard for clients' feelings and self-esteem.

In the following discussion, we identify guidelines that can assist you to intervene assertively with clients:

Making Requests and Giving Directives   To assist clients to relate more facilitatively and to solve problems, practitioners frequently must make requests of them, some of which involve relating in new ways during sessions. These requests may include asking clients to do any of the following:

1. Speak directly to each other rather than through the practitioner.
2. Give feedback to others in the session.
3. Respond by checking out meanings of others' messages, take a listening stance, or personalize messages.
4. Change the arrangement of chairs.
5. Role-play.
6. Make requests of others.
7. Assume tasks to respond in specified ways within sessions.
8. Agree to carry out defined tasks during the week.
9. Identify strengths or incremental growth of themselves or others in the group or family.

In making requests, it is important to express them firmly and decisively and to deliver them with assertive nonverbal behavior. Practitioners often err by couching their requests in tentative language, thus conveying doubt to clients as to whether they expect them to comply with requests.

The contrast between messages couched in tentative language and those couched in firm language can be observed in the illustrations that follow.

TENTATIVE REQUESTS	FIRM REQUESTS
Would you mind if I interrupted...	I would like to pause for a moment...
Is it OK if we role-play?	I'd like you to role-play with me for a moment.
Excuse me, but don't you think you're getting off track?	I think we're getting off track. I'd like to return to the subject we were discussing just a minute ago.
Could we talk about something Kathy just said?	Let's go back to something Kathy just said. I think it's very important...

Many times practitioners' requests of clients are actually *directives*, as are those under the column, "Firm requests." In essence, directives are declarative statements that place the burden on clients to object if they are uncomfortable, as the following message illustrates: "Before you answer that question, please turn your chair toward your wife. [*Practitioner leans over and helps client to adjust chair. To wife.*] Will you please turn your chair, also, so that you can speak directly to your husband? Thank you. It's important that you be in full contact with each other while we talk."

If the practitioner had given clients a choice (e.g., "Would you like to change your chairs?"), they might not have responded affirmatively. We thus suggest that when you want clients to behave differently in sessions, you simply state what you would like them to do. If clients verbally object to directives or manifest nonverbal behavior that may indicate reservations, it is vital to respond empathically and to explore the basis of their opposition. Such exploration often resolves fears or misgivings, freeing clients to engage in requested behavior.

Maintaining Focus and Managing Interruptions

Maintaining focus is a vital task that takes considerable skill and assertiveness on the practitioner's part. It is often essential to intervene verbally to focus or refocus processes when interruptions or distractions occur. At times, practitioners also respond assertively on a nonverbal level to prevent members from interrupting important processes that may need to be brought to positive conclusion, as illustrated in the following excerpt from a family session:

Kim [*14 years old, in tears, talking angrily to her mother*]: You hardly ever listen. At home, you just always yell at us and go to your bedroom.

Mrs. R: I thought I was doing better than that...

Mr. R [*interrupting his wife to speak to practitioner*]: I think it's hard for my wife because...

Practitioner [*holds up hand to father in a "halt" position, while continuing to maintain eye contact with mother and daughter. To Kim*]: I would like to stay with your statement for a moment. Kim, please tell your mother what you're experiencing right now.

Interrupting Dysfunctional Processes   Unseasoned practitioners often permit dysfunctional processes to continue for long periods either because they lack knowledge of how to intervene or because they think they should wait until clients have completed a series of exchanges. In such instances, practitioners fail to fulfill one of their major responsibilities, that is, to *guide* and *direct* processes and to influence participants to interact in more facilitative ways. Remember that clients often seek help because they cannot manage their destructive interactional processes, and permitting them to engage at length in their usual patterns of arguing, cajoling, threatening, blaming, criticizing, and labeling each other only exacerbates their problems. Rather, the practitioner should intervene, teaching them more facilitative behaviors and guiding them to implement such behaviors in subsequent interactions.

If you decide to interrupt ongoing processes, do so decisively so that clients listen to you or heed your directive. If you intervene nonassertively, your potential to influence clients (particularly aggressive clients) will suffer, since being able to interrupt a discussion successfully manifests your power or influence in the relationship (Parlee, 1979). If you permit clients to ignore or to circumvent your interventions to arrest dysfunctional processes, you yield control and assume a "one-down" position in relationship to the client.

With respect to interrupting or intervening in processes, we are advocating assertive, not aggressive behavior. You must thus be sensitive to vested interests of clients, for even though you may regard certain processes as unproductive or destructive, clients may not. The timing of interruptions is thus vital. If it is not critical to draw clients' attention to what is happening immediately, you can wait for a natural pause. If such a pause does not occur shortly, you should then interrupt. You should *not* delay interrupting destructive interactional processes, however, as illustrated in the following excerpt:

Wife [*to practitioner*]: I feel the children need to mind me, but every time I ask them to do something, he [*husband*] says they don't have to do it. I think we're just ruining our kids, and it's mostly his fault.

Husband: Oh—well—that shows your lack of intelligence.

Practitioner: I'm going to interrupt you because finding fault with each other will only lead to mutual resentment.

Observe that the practitioner intervenes to refocus the discussion after only two dysfunctional responses on the clients' part. If participants do not disengage immediately, the practitioner will need to use body movements that interfere with communication pathways or, in extreme instances, an exclamation such as "time out!" to interrupt behavior. When practitioners have demonstrated their intent to intervene quickly and decisively, clients will usually comply immediately when asked to disengage.

"Leaning into" Clients' Anger We cannot overstate the importance of openly addressing clients' anger and complaints. Unless practitioners are able to handle themselves assertively and competently in the face of such anger, they lose the respect of most clients and thus their ability to help them. Further, clients may use their anger to manipulate practitioners just as they have done with others. To help you respond assertively in managing clients' anger, we offer the following suggestions:

Respond empathically to reflect clients' anger and, if possible, other underlying feelings (e.g., "I sense you're angry at me for ____ and perhaps disappointed about ____").

- Continue to explore the situation and the feelings of participants until you understand the nature of the events that have caused the angry feelings. As you do so, you may find that anger toward you dissipates and that clients begin to focus on themselves, assuming appropriate responsibility for their part in the situation at hand. The "real problem," as often happens, may not directly involve you.

- As you explore clients' anger, authentically express your feelings and reactions if it appears appropriate (e.g., "I didn't know you felt that way… I want to hear how I might have contributed to this situation. There may be some adjustments I'll want to make in my style of relating… I'm pleased that you shared your feelings with me").

- Apply a problem-solving approach (if appropriate) so that all concerned make adjustments to avoid similar occurrences or situations in the future. If a particular client expresses anger frequently and in a dysfunctional manner, you may also focus on the client's style of expressing anger, identify problems this may cause him/her in relationships with others, and negotiate a goal of modifying this response pattern.

Saying No and Setting Limits

Some practitioner tasks are quite appropriate; for example, negotiating for clients and conferring with other parties and potential resources supplement and facilitate client action (Epstein, 1992, p. 208). In contracting with clients, practitioners must occasionally decline requests or set limits.

This is sometimes difficult for beginning practitioners, who may be zealous in their desires to render service and to demonstrate willingness to help others. Commitment to helping others is a desirable quality, but it must be tempered with judgment as to when acceding to clients' requests is in the best interests of both practitioner and client. Certain clients may have had past experiences which lead them to believe that practitioners will do most of the work required out of sessions. Clients are often more likely to become empowered by increasing their scope of actions than by practitioners doing things for them that they can learn to do for themselves. Consequently, if practitioners unthinkingly agree to take on responsibilities which the client can now or could in the future perform, they may reinforce passive client behavior.

Setting limits has special implications when practitioners work with involuntary clients. Cingolani has noted that practitioners engage in negotiated relationships with such clients in which roles of compromiser and mediator and enforcer are called for in addition to the more comfortable counselor role. For example, when an involuntary client requests a "break" related to performance of a court order, the practitioner must be clear about the choices and consequences of those choices which the client may make as well as clarify what to expect from the practitioner.

Rory, *member of domestic violence group:* I don't think that it is fair that you report that I didn't meet for eight of the ten group sessions. I could not get off work for some of those sessions. I did all I could do.

Practitioner: You did attend seven of the sessions, Rory, and made efforts to attend others. However, the contract you signed which was presented in court stated that you must complete eight sessions in order to be certified as completing the group. I do not have the power to change that court order. Should you decide to comply with the court order, I am willing to speak with your employer to urge him to work with you to arrange your schedule so that you can meet the court order.

Note that in this response the practitioner made clear that he would not evade the court order, that if Rory chose to comply with it, he would be willing to act as a mediator to assist him with difficulties in scheduling with the employer.

Being tactfully assertive is no easier for practitioners who have excessive needs to please others than it is for clients. These practitioners have difficulty declining requests or setting limits when doing so is in the best interests of clients. We therefore recommend that such practitioners engage in introspection and study carefully the section of Chapter 15 that deals with cognitive factors involved in nonassertive behavior. Further, such practitioners may benefit by setting tasks for themselves related to increasing their assertiveness. Participating in an assertiveness training group and delving into the popular literature on assertiveness may also be highly beneficial.

Following are a few of the many situations in which you may need to decline requests of clients:

1. When clients invite you to participate with them socially.

2. When clients ask you to grant them preferential status (e.g., set lower fees than specified by policy).

3. When clients request physical intimacy.

4. When clients ask you to intercede in a situation they should handle themselves.

5. When clients request a special appointment after having broken a regular appointment for an invalid reason.

6. When clients make requests to borrow money.

7. When clients request that you conceal information about violations of probation, parole, or institutional policy.

8. When spouses request that you withhold information from their partners.

9. When clients disclose plans to commit crimes or acts of violence against others.

10. When clients ask you to report false information to a draft board, employer, or other party.

In addition to declining requests, you may need to set limits with clients in situations such as the following:

1. Making excessive telephone calls to you at home or the office.
2. Canceling appointments without advance notice.
3. Expressing emotions in abusive or violent ways.
4. Habitually seeking to go beyond designated ending points of sessions.
5. Continuing to fail to abide by contracts (e.g., not paying fees or missing appointments excessively).
6. Making sexual overtures toward you or other staff members.
7. Coming to sessions when intoxicated.

Part of maturing professionally involves being able to decline requests, set limits, and feel comfortable in so doing. As you gain experience, you will realize increasingly that in holding clients to reasonable expectations you help as much as when you provide a concrete action for them. Modeled responses for refusing requests and for saying no to clients are found among the exercises to assist practitioners to relate authentically and assertively.

Situations also occur in which it is important that practitioners assert themselves with other social workers and members of other professions. Lacking experience and sometimes confidence, beginning practitioners often tend to be in awe of physicians, lawyers, psychologists, and more experienced social workers. Consequently, they may relate passively or may acquiesce to plans or demands that appear unsound or unreasonable. Although it is critical to be open to ideas of other professionals, beginning practitioners should also risk expressing their own views and asserting their own rights. Otherwise, they may know more about a given client than other professionals but fail to contribute valuable information in joint case planning.

Beginning practitioners should also set limits and assert their rights in refusing to accept unreasonable referrals and inappropriate assignments.

Assertiveness may also be required when other professionals deny resources to which clients are entitled, refer to clients with demeaning labels, or engage in unethical conduct. Assertiveness, indeed, is critical in assuming the role of client advocate—a role we discuss at length in Chapter 15.

EXERCISES IN RESPONDING AUTHENTICALLY AND ASSERTIVELY

The following exercises will assist you in gaining skill in responding authentically and assertively. Read each situation and client message and formulate a written response as though you are the practitioner in the situation presented. Then compare your written responses with the modeled responses provided in the following section, keeping in mind that the modeled responses are only examples of many appropriate responses.

You will find additional exercises that involve authentic and assertive responding under exercises in confrontation in the final portion of Chapter 18 and in exercises concerned with managing relational reactions and resistance in the final section of Chapter 19.

Client Statements and Situations

1. *Marital partner* [*in third conjoint marital therapy session*]: It must be really nice being a marriage counselor—knowing just what to do and not having problems like ours.
2. *Female client, age 23* [*in first session*]: Some of my problems are related to my church's stand on birth control. Tell me, are you a Catholic?
3. *Client* [*fifth session*]: You look like you're having trouble staying awake. [*Practitioner is drowsy from having taken an antihistamine for an allergy.*]
4. *Adult group member* [*to practitioner in second session—group members have been struggling to determine the agenda for the session*]: I wish you'd tell us what we should talk about. Isn't that a group leader's function? We're just spinning our wheels.

5. *Male client* [*sixth session*]: Say, my wife and I are having a party next Wednesday, and we thought we'd like to have you and your wife come.

6. *Client* [*calls 3 hours before scheduled appointment*]: I've had the flu the past couple of days, but I feel like I'm getting over it. Do you think I should come today?

7. *Client* [*scheduled time for ending appointment has arrived, and practitioner has already moved to end session. In previous sessions, client has tended to stay beyond designated ending time*]: What we were talking about reminded me of something I wanted to discuss today but forgot. I'd like to discuss it briefly, if you don't mind.

8. *Client* [*has just completed behavioral rehearsal involving talking with employer and played role beyond expectations of practitioner*].

9. *Female client* [*10th interview*]: I've really felt irritated with you during the week. When I brought up taking the correspondence course in art, all you could talk about was how some correspondence courses are rip-offs and that I could take courses at a college for less money. I knew that, but I've checked into this correspondence course, and it's well worth the money. You put me down, and I've resented it.

10. *Client* [*seventh session*]: You seem uptight today. Is something bothering you? [*Practitioner has been under strain associated with recent death of a parent and assisting surviving parent, who has been distraught.*]

11. *Client* [*sends the following message as the final session of successful therapy draws to a close*]: I really want to thank you for your help. You'll never know just how much help you've been. I felt like a sinking ship before I saw you. Now I feel I've got my head screwed on straight.

12. *Male delinquent on probation, age 15* [*first session*]: Before I tell you much, I need to know what happens to the information. Who else learns about me?

13. *Public assistance recipient* [*during office interview*]: You've told me in the past I should report any income I receive. Well, I've been doing some part-time work for the past 6 months and making about $200 a week. I was hoping you wouldn't report it, though, because they'll cut my monthly check if you do. It's too small now.

14. *Male welfare recipient, age 47* [*with problem of alcoholism*]: I was wondering if you could lend me five bucks to get my coat out of hock. I'll pay you back when I get my check.

15. *Practitioner* [*forgot to enter an appointment in daily schedule and, as a result, failed to keep a scheduled appointment with a client. Realizing this the next day, she telephones her client.*]

Modeled Responses

1. [*Smiling.*] "Well, I must admit it's helpful. But I want you to know that marriage is no picnic for marriage counselors either. We have our rough spots, too. I have to work like everyone else to keep my marriage alive and growing."

2. "I gather you're wondering what my stand is and if I can understand and accept your feelings. I've worked with many Catholics and have been able to understand their problems. Would it trouble you if I weren't Catholic?"

3. "You're very observant. I have been struggling with drowsiness these past few minutes, and I apologize for that. I had to take an antihistamine before lunch, and a side effect of the drug is drowsiness. I want you to know my drowsiness has nothing to do with you. If I move around a little, the drowsiness passes."

4. "I can sense your frustration and your desire to firm up an agenda. If I made the decision, though, it might not fit for a number of you and I'd be assuming the group's prerogative. Perhaps it would be helpful if the group followed the decision-by-consensus approach we discussed in our first session."

5. "Thank you for the invitation. I'm complimented you'd ask me. Although a part of me would like to come because it sounds like fun, I must decline your invitation. If I were to socialize with you while you're seeing me professionally, it would dilute my role, and I couldn't be as helpful to you. I hope you can understand my not accepting."

6. "I appreciate your calling to let me know. I think it would be better to change our appointment until you're sure you've recovered. Quite frankly, I don't want to risk being exposed to the flu, which I hope you can understand. I have a time open day after tomorrow. I'll set it aside for you if you'd like in the event you're fully recovered by then."

7. "I'm sorry I don't have the time to discuss the mat-

ter today. Let's save it for next week, and I'll make a note that you wanted to discuss it. We'll have to stop here today because I'm scheduled for another appointment."

8. "I want to share with you how impressed I was with how you asserted yourself and came across so positively. If you'd been with your boss, he'd have been impressed too."

9. "I'm glad you shared those feelings with me. And I can see I owe you an apology. You're right, I didn't explore whether you'd checked into the program, and I made some unwarranted assumptions. I guess I was overly concerned about your not being ripped off because I know others who have been by taking correspondence courses. But I can see I goofed because you had already looked into the course."

10. "Thank you for asking. Yes, I have been under some strain this past week. My mother died suddenly, which was a shock, and my father is taking it very hard. It's created a lot of pressure for me, but I think I can keep it from spilling over into our session. If I'm not able to focus on you, I'll stop the session. Or if you don't feel I'm fully with you, please let me know. I don't want to shortchange you."

11. "Thank you very much. As we finish, I want you to know how much I've enjoyed working with you. You've worked hard, and that's the primary reason you've made so much progress. I'm very interested in you and want to hear how your new job works out. Please keep in touch."

12. "Your question is a good one. I'd wonder the same thing if I were in your situation. I keep the information confidential as much as I can. We keep a file on you, of course, but I'm selective about what I put in it, and you have the right to check the file if you wish. I do meet with a supervisor, too, and we discuss how I can be of greatest help to clients. So I might share certain information with her, but she keeps it confidential. If you report violations of the law or the conditions of your probation, I can't assure you I'll keep that confidential. I'm responsible to the court, and part of my responsibility is to see that you meet the conditions of your parole. I have to make reports to the judge about that. Could you share with me your specific concerns about confidentiality?"

13. "I appreciate your sharing this information, knowing your check might be cut. I wish your check could remain the same because I know it's not a lot. I don't really have any choice about reporting the income, though, because I'd be putting my job in jeopardy. I will look into policies to see how we can keep your cut to a minimum and help you to realize as much benefit as possible from working."

14. "Let's think about some other ways of your getting by until you get your check. It would complicate our relationship if I loaned you money, and I don't want that to happen. Sometimes the thrift store will lend a coat on credit. Have you considered that?"

15. "Mr. M, I'm very embarrassed calling you because I realized just a few minutes ago I blew it yesterday. I forgot to enter my appointment with you in my schedule book last week and completely forgot about it. I hope you can accept my apology. I want you to know it had nothing to do with you."

SKILL DEVELOPMENT EXERCISES IN EMPATHIC COMMUNICATION

The following exercises, including a wide variety of actual client messages, will assist you in gaining mastery of reciprocal empathic responding (level 3). Read the client message and compose on paper an empathic response that captures the client's surface feelings. You may wish to use the paradigm, "You feel ____ about (or because) ____ in organizing your response before phrasing it in typical conversation language. Strive to make your responses fresh, varied, and spontaneous. To expand your repertoire of responses, we strongly encourage you to continue using the lists of affective words and phrases.

After formulating your response, compare it with the modeled response provided at the end of the exercises. Analyze the differences, being particularly aware of the varied forms of responding and the elements that enhance the effectiveness of your own and/or the modeled responses.

Because 29 different exercises are included, we recommend that you not attempt to complete them in one sitting, but space them across several sessions. Consistent practice and careful scrutiny of your responses are essential in gaining mastery of this vital skill.

Client Statements

1. *Father of developmentally disabled child, age 14* [*who is becoming difficult to manage*]: We just don't know what to do with Henry. We've always wanted to take care of him, but we've reached the point where we're not sure it's doing any good for him or for us. He's grown so strong—we just can't restrain him anymore. He beat on my wife last week when she wouldn't take him to the 7–11 late at night—I was out of town—and she's still bruised. She's afraid of him now, and I have to admit I'm getting that way too.

2. *Chicano* [*living in urban barrio*]: Our children do better in school if they teach Spanish, not just English. We're afraid our children are behind because they don't understand English so good. And we don't know how to help them. Our people been trying to get a bilingual program, but the school board pay no attention to us.

3. *Female client, age 31:* Since my husband left town with another woman, I get lonely and depressed a lot of the time. And I find myself wondering whether something is wrong with me or whether men just can't be trusted.

4. *Mother* [*to child welfare protective services worker on doorstep during initial home visit*]: Who'd want to make trouble for me by accusing me of not taking care of my kids? [*Tearfully.*] Maybe I'm not the best mother in the world, but I try. There are a lot of kids around here that aren't cared for as well as mine.

5. *Male ninth-grade student* [*to school social worker*]: I feel like I'm a real loser. In sports I've always had two left feet, and when they choose up sides, I'm always the last one chosen. A couple of times they've actually got into a fight over who doesn't have to choose me.

6. *Member of abused-women's group at YWCA:* That last month I was living in mortal fear of Art. He'd get that hateful look in his eyes, and I'd know he was going to let me have it. The last time I was afraid he was going to kill me—and he might

have if his brother hadn't dropped in. I'm afraid to go back to him. But what do I do? I can't stay here much longer!

7. *Male, age 34* [*to marital therapist*]: Just once I'd like to show my wife I can accomplish something without her prodding me. That's why I haven't told her I'm coming to see you. If she knew it, she'd try to take charge and call all the shots.

8. *African American man* [*in a group session*]: All I want is to be accepted as a person. When I get hired, I want it to be for what I'm capable of doing—not just because of my skin color. That's as phony and degrading as not being hired because of my skin color. I just want to be accepted for who I am.

9. *Client in a state prison* [*to rehabilitation worker*]: They treat you like an animal in here—herd you around like a damn cow. I know I've got to do my time, but there are some times I feel like I can't stand it any longer—like something's building up in me that's going to explode.

10. *Client* [*to mental health worker*]: I don't have any pleasant memories of my childhood. It seems like just so much empty space. I can remember my father watching television and staring at me with a blank look—as though I didn't exist.

11. *Patient in hospital* [*to medical social worker*]: I know Dr. Brown is a skilled surgeon, and he tells me not to worry—that there's very little risk in this surgery. I know I should feel reassured, but to tell you the truth, I'm just plain panic-stricken.

12. *Female member, age 29* [*in marital therapy group*]: I'd like to know what it's like with the rest of you. Hugh and I get into nasty fights because I feel he doesn't help me when I really need help. He tells me there's no way he's going to do women's work! That really burns me. I get to feeling like I'm just supposed to be his slave.

13. *Male college student, age 21:* Francine says she's going to call me, but she never does—I have to do all the calling, or I probably wouldn't hear from her at all. It seems so one-sided. If I didn't need her so much I'd ask her what kind of game she's playing. I wonder if she isn't pretty selfish.

14. *Caucasian student, age 14* [*to school social worker*]: To be really honest, I don't like the black kids

in our school. They pretty much stay to themselves, and they aren't friendly to whites. I don't know what to expect or how to act around them. I'm antsy when they're around and—well, to be honest—I'm scared I'll do something they won't like and they'll jump me.

15. *Single female, age 27* [*to mental health worker*]: I've been taking this class on the joys of womanhood. Last time the subject was how to catch a man. I can see I've been doing a lot of things wrong. But I won't lower myself to playing games with men. If that's what it takes, I guess I'll always be single.

16. *Married male, age 29* [*to marital therapist*]: Sexually, I'm unfulfilled in my marriage. At times I've even had thoughts of trying sex with men. That idea kind of intrigues me. My wife and I can talk about sex all right, but it doesn't get better.

17. *Married female, age 32* [*to family practitioner*]: I love my husband and children and I don't know what I'd do without them. Yet on days like last Thursday, I feel I could just climb the walls. I want to run away from all of them and never come back.

18. *Married blind female* [*to other blind group members*]: You know, it really offends me when people praise me or make a fuss over me for doing something routine that anyone else could do. It makes me feel like I'm on exhibition. I want to be recognized for being competent—not for being blind.

19. *Male teacher* [*to mental health practitioner*]: I have this thing about not being able to accept compliments. A friend told me about how much of a positive impact I've had on several students over the years. I couldn't accept that and feel good. My thought was, "You must be mistaken. I've never had that kind of effect on anyone."

20. *Lesbian, age 26* [*to private practitioner*]: The girls at the office were talking about lesbians the other day and about how repulsive the very thought of lesbianism was to them. How do you think I felt?

21. *Male member of alcoholics group:* I don't feel like I belong in this group. The rest of you seem to have better educations and better jobs. Hell, I only finished junior high, and I'm just a welder.

22. *Patient* [*to a medical social worker*]: Maybe it doesn't seem important to other people, but I don't like having to share a room with a heavy smoker. When I went through the admissions interview, I specifically requested that I not be put in a room with a smoker.

23. *Male, age 30* [*to private practitioner*]: Sometimes I can't believe how bent out of shape I get over little things. When I lose a chess game, I go into orbit. First, I'm furious with myself for blundering. It's not like me to make rank blunders. I guess I feel humiliated, because I immediately want to start another game and get even with the other guy.

24. *Male client, age 72* [*to medical social worker*]: Since I had my heart attack, I've just had this feeling of foreboding—like my life's over for all practical purposes. I feel like I'm just an invalid—of no use to myself or anyone else.

25. *Male applicant* [*to public assistance worker*]: This is a very hard thing for me to do. I never thought I'd have to turn to welfare for help. But what do you do when you're backed into a corner? I've looked for jobs everywhere, but there's none to be had.

26. *Child, age 15, in foster care* [*to child welfare worker*]: I've had it with them [the foster parents]. They want me to work all the time—like I'm a slave or something. If you don't get me out of here, I'm going to run.

27. *Family member, age 13* [*in initial family group session*]: Yeah, I can tell you what I'd like to be different in our family. I'd like to feel that we care about each other, but it's not that way. Every time I go in the house, Mom nags me, and Dad doesn't say anything—he doesn't seem to care. Sometimes I feel there's no point in going home.

28. *Married woman* [*in initial interview with marital therapist*]: I think this is just a complete waste of time. I didn't want to come and wouldn't be here if my husband hadn't forced me. He's the one who should be here—not me.

29. *Married woman* [*in YWCA adult women's group*]: This past week I've felt really good about how things are going—like I've finally got my act together. I've handled my emotions better, and for the first time in a long time, I've felt like an intelligent human being.

Modeled Responses

1. "So you're really on the horns of a dilemma. You've wanted to keep him at home, but in light of his recent aggressiveness and his strength, you're becoming really frightened and wonder if other arrangements wouldn't be better for both you and him."

2. "I can see you're worried about how your children are doing in school and believe they need a bilingual program."

3. "It's been a real blow—your husband leaving you for another woman—and you've just felt so alone. And you find yourself dwelling on the painful question, 'Is something wrong with me, or is it that you just can't trust men?'"

4. "This is very upsetting for you. You seem to be saying that it's not fair being turned in when you believe you take care of your children. Please understand I'm not accusing you of neglecting your children. But I do have to investigate complaints. It may be I'll be able to turn in a positive report. I hope so. But I do need to talk with you further. May I come in?"

5. "So I gather you feel you really got shortchanged as far as athletic talents are concerned. It's humiliating to you to feel so left out and be the last guy chosen."

6. "It sounds as though you lived in terror that last month and literally feared for your life. You were wise to remove yourself when you did. A number of other women in the group have had similar experiences and are facing the same dilemma about what to do now. As group members, each of us can be helpful to other group members in thinking through what's best to do now. In the meantime, you have a safe place to stay and some time to plan."

7. "Sounds like you get pretty annoyed, thinking about her prodding and trying to take charge. I gather it's important right now that you prove to her and to yourself you can do something on your own."

8. "I gather you're fed up with having people relate to you as a color or a minority, instead of being accepted as an individual—as yourself."

9. "If I understand you, you feel degraded by the way you're treated—as though you're less than a human being. And that really gets to you—sometimes you find yourself seething with resentment that threatens to boil over."

10. "From what you say, I get a picture of you just feeling so all alone as you were growing up—as though you didn't feel very important to anyone—especially your father."

11. "So intellectually, you tell yourself not to worry—that you're in good hands. Still, on another level you have to admit you're terrified of that operation. [*Brief pause.*] Your fear is pretty natural, though. Most people who are honest with themselves experience fear. I'd be interested in hearing more about your fears."

12. "So the two of you get into some real struggles over differences in your views as to what is reasonable of you to expect from Hugh. And you seem to be saying you very much resent his refusal to pitch in—like it's not fair to have to carry that burden alone. Hugh, I'd be interested in hearing your views. Then we can hear how other members deal with this kind of situation."

13. "Sounds like part of you is saying you have a right to expect more from Francine: that you don't feel good about always having to be the one to take the initiative. You also seem to feel you'd like to confront her with what she's doing, but you're uneasy about doing that because you don't want to risk losing her."

14. "So, you're uncomfortable around them and just don't know how to read them. I gather you kind of walk on eggs when they're around for fear you'll blow it and they'll climb all over you."

15. "There is a lot of conflicting advice around these days about how men and women should relate to each other and it is hard to figure out what to believe. You know you don't want to play games, and yet that is what the class is telling you to do if you don't want to be single."

16. "Things don't get better despite your talks, and you get pretty discouraged. At times you find yourself wondering if you'd get sexual fulfillment with men, and that appeals to you in some ways."

17. "So even though you care deeply for them, there are days when you just feel so overwhelmed you'd like to buy a one-way ticket out of all the responsibility."

18. "Are you saying you feel singled out and demeaned when people flatter you for doing things anyone could do? It ticks you off, and you wish people would recognize you for being competent—not being blind."

19. "In a way you seem to be saying you don't feel comfortable with compliments because you feel you don't really deserve them. It's like you feel you don't do anything worthy of a compliment."

20. "You must have felt extremely uncomfortable and resentful believing that they would condemn you if they knew. It must have been most painful for you."

21. "Ted, you seem to feel uncomfortable, like you don't fit with the other group members. I gather you're feeling the rest of the members are above you, and you're concerned they won't accept you."

22. "I can see you'd be pretty irritated then, ending up with a smoker, especially after making a specific request as you did. I can understand your feelings, and I'll look into having this corrected. Thanks for letting me know."

23. "When you lose, lots of feelings surge through you—anger and disappointment with yourself for goofing, loss of face, and an urgency to prove you can beat the other guy."

24. "So things look pretty grim to you right now. As though you have nothing to look forward to and are just washed up. And you're apprehensive that things might get worse rather than better."

25. "It sounds like you've struggled hard to make it on your own and that it's been painful to admit to yourself you needed help. I'm sensing you're feeling some embarrassment about having to ask for help."

26. "You sound pretty burned up right now, and I can sense you feel there has to be a change. I'd like to hear more about exactly what has been happening."

27. "Am I getting it right, that you feel picked on by Mom and ignored by Dad? And you'd like to feel they really care about you. You'd like more love shown by family members for each other."

28. "You're feeling pretty angry with your husband for forcing you to come. I gather you're pretty resentful right now at having to be here and just don't see the need for it."

29. "That sounds great. You seem delighted with your progress—like you're really getting on top of things. And most of all you're liking yourself again."

Answers to Exercise in Identifying Surface and Underlying Feelings

1. *Apparent feelings:* unimportant, neglected, disappointed, hurt. *Probable deeper feelings:* rejected, abandoned, forsaken, deprived, lonely, depressed.

2. *Apparent feelings:* unloved, insecure, confused, embarrassed, left out or excluded. *Probable deeper feelings:* hurt, resentful, unvalued, rejected, taken for granted, degraded, doubting own desirability.

3. *Apparent feelings:* chagrined, disappointed in self, discouraged, letting children down, perplexed. *Probable deeper feelings:* guilty, inadequate, crummy, sense of failure, out of control, fear of damaging children.

Answers to Exercises to Discriminate Levels of Empathic Responding

CLIENT STATEMENT

1	
RESPONSE	**LEVEL**
1.	2
2.	1
3.	1
4.	3
5.	2
6.	2
7.	4
8.	1

CLIENT STATEMENT

2		**3**	
RESPONSE	**LEVEL**	**RESPONSE**	**LEVEL**
1.	1	1	1
2.	3	2	4
3.	1	3	2
4.	2	4	2
5.	4	5	5
6.	1	6	1
7.	3	7	2
8.	2	8	2

Suggested Classroom Skill Development Exercises in Empathic Communication

1. The instructor presents a discrete client message to students who anonymously formulate responses on index cards or slips of paper. The instructor then collects the written responses and reads the messages to the class. After reading each individual message, the instructor and group members, on the count of three, simultaneously indicate their rating of the message by all raising a hand and displaying the number of fingers that correspond to their respective ratings. Student and instructor then discuss the strengths and weaknesses of the response in question before moving to the next one.

2. Students pair off, and one shares a personal concern with the other for 3 to 5 minutes. The other assumes the role of social worker, practicing empathic responses that convey understanding of the feelings experienced by the other. It is important that the person who is sharing feelings gives corrective feedback when the "practitioner" is off target. After the interaction is complete, the paired students can benefit from discussing their respective experiences and giving appropriate feedback to each other. Students should then reverse roles, again following the same instructions. After the paired prac-

tice, the instructor may wish to lead a group discussion of the students' collective experience.

3. *(In the classroom or practicum, for students in units of five or six.)* Ask one student in each unit to play the role of client. The "client" then proceeds to relate his or her difficulties message by message. After each message, the students take turns responding empathically as if each were the practitioner at a given moment. The other students rate the message given by raising an appropriate number of fingers to designate the level of response. Responses may be briefly discussed, and feedback from the client is particularly helpful. After a few minutes, rotate the client role to a different student so that all students have equal learning opportunities.

4. The instructor may wish to give the following assignments to students in the classroom or practicum one week and discuss student observations related to the assignments the following week:

   a. As you interact with others and observe others interact during the week, notice how infrequently people send empathic messages. Also observe the types of messages that are sent and how these messages influence the course of conversations.

   b. As you interact with your spouse, parents, children, friends, and fellow students, practice listening carefully and responding with empathic messages when appropriate. Be alert to how empathic messages draw others out and to the feeling tones that these responses create.

Notes

1 The selective use of this skill to achieve specific therapeutic objectives is discussed briefly later in this chapter and in Chapter 19.

2 See also a more recent article which describes less empathic responding by high-risk mothers to crying children by Milner et al., (1995).

3 In categorizing her husband as a "bump on a log," the wife makes a sweeping generalization that fits her husband's behavior into a mold. Although the practitioner chose to keep the focus momentar-

ily on the husband, it is important that he helps the couple to avoid labeling each other. Strategies for intervening when clients use labels are delineated in a later chapter.

4 We suggest that you teach clients the concept that anger usually overlays other feelings and systematically assist them to identify the multiple emotions they are experiencing when they express anger, an approach that is illustrated in the above excerpt.

Chapter 6

Verbal Following, Exploring, and Focusing Skills

MAINTAINING PSYCHOLOGICAL CONTACT WITH CLIENTS AND EXPLORING THEIR PROBLEMS

Researchers and theoreticians agree that verbal following by practitioners is critical in communication with clients (Finn & Rose, 1982; Katz, 1979; Mayadas & O'Brien, 1976; Schinke, Blythe, Gilchrist, & Smith, 1980). Verbal following involves the use of and, at times, blending of discrete skills that enable practitioners to maintain psychological contact on a moment-by-moment basis with clients and to convey accurate understanding of their messages. Moreover, embodied in verbal following behavior are two performance variables that are essential to satisfaction and continuance on the part of the client:

1. *Stimulus-response congruence*: the extent to which practitioners' responses provide feedback to clients that their messages are accurately received.

2. *Content relevance*: the extent to which the content of practitioners' responses is perceived by clients as relevant to their substantive concerns.

First conceptualized by Rosen (1972), who detailed empirical and theoretical support for their relationship to client continuance, these two variables received further validation as critical practitioner behavioral responses in findings of a study by Duehn and Proctor (1977). Analyzing worker–client transactions, these authors found that practitioners responded incongruently to clients' messages much more frequently with clients who terminated treatment prematurely than with clients who continued treatment. (Incongruent messages fail to provide immediate feedback to clients that their messages have been received.) Further, practitioners gave a lower proportion of responses that matched the content expectations of "discontinuers" than they did with "continuers." These authors concluded that responses that are relevant and accurately attend to client messages gradually increase moment-by-moment client satisfaction with interactions in the interview. On the other hand, continued use of questions and other responses not associated with previous client messages and unrelated to the client's substantive concerns contribute to consistent client dissatisfaction. When content expectations of clients are not fulfilled, clients prematurely discontinue treatment. Effective use of such attending behaviors should facilitate motivational congruence, or the fit between client motivation and practitioner goals, which has been shown to be associated with better outcomes in social work effectiveness studies (Reid & Hanrahan, 1982). Employing responses that directly relate to client messages and concerns thus enhances client satisfaction, fosters continuance, and also greatly facilitates the establishment of a viable working relationship.

The importance of explaining the relevance of questions to Asian Americans seen for mental health problems has been emphasized by Tsui and Schultz (1985): The practitioner must explicitly educate the client about the purpose of questions regarding clinical history, previous treatment information, family background, and psychosocial stressors. The linkage of these issues to their current symptoms is not clear to many Asian clients. Many Asian clients conceive of mental distress as the result of physiological disorder or character flaws. This issue must be dealt with sensitively before any sensible therapeutic work can be effected (pp. 567–568). Similarly, clients who are members of oppressed groups may perceive questions as interrogations not designed to help them with their own concerns, so the rationale for such questions must be explained.

In addition to enabling practitioners to maintain close psychological contact with clients, verbal following skills serve two other important functions in the helping process. First, these skills yield rich personal information, allowing practitioners to explore clients' problems in depth. Second, these skills enable practitioners to focus selectively on facets of clients' experiencing and on dynamics in the helping process that facilitate positive client change.

In the following pages, we introduce you to skills for verbally following and exploring clients' problems. Several of these skills are easily mastered. Others require more effort to acquire. We provide exercises in the body of the chapter to assist you in acquiring proficiency. Although empathic responding is the most vital skill for verbally following clients' messages, we have not included it in this chapter since it was discussed in the preceding one. Later, however, we discuss the blending of empathic responses with other verbal following skills to advance your ability in focusing upon and fully exploring relevant client problems.

VERBAL FOLLOWING SKILLS

Briefly, the discrete skills highlighted in this chapter include the following types of responses:

1. Furthering.
2. Paraphrasing.
3. Closed-ended questions.
4. Open-ended questions.
5. Seeking concreteness.
6. Providing and maintaining focus.
7. Summarizing.

Furthering Responses

Furthering responses indicate practitioners are listening attentively and encourage the client to verbalize. They are of several types:

1. Minimal prompts, which signal the practitioner's attentiveness and encourage the client to continue verbalizing, can be either nonverbal or verbal. Nonverbal minimal prompts consist of nodding the head, using facial expressions, or employing gestures that convey receptivity, interest, and commitment to understanding. The nonverbal prompts implicitly convey the message, "I am with you; please continue."

Verbal minimal prompts consist of brief messages that convey interest and encourage or request expanded verbalizations along the lines of the previous expressions by the client. These messages include, "Yes," "I see," "But?" "Mm-mmm" (the so-called empathic grunt), "Tell me more," "And then what happened?" "And?" "Please go on," "Tell me more, please," and other similar brief messages that affirm the appropriateness of what the client has been saying and prompt him or her to continue.

2. Accent responses (Hackney & Cormier, 1979) involve repeating, in a questioning tone of voice or with emphasis, a word or a short phrase. If, for instance, a client says, "I've really had it with the way my supervisor at work is treating me," the practitioner might use the short response, "Had it?" to prompt further elaboration by the client.

Paraphrasing Responses

Paraphrasing involves using fresh words to restate the client's message concisely. Responses that paraphrase are more apt to focus on the cognitive aspects of client messages (i.e., emphasize situations, ideas, objects, persons) than on the client's affective state, although reference may be made to obvious feelings. Below are three examples of paraphrasing:

Elder client: I don't want to get into a living situation in which I will not be able to make choices on my own.

Practitioner: So independence is a very important issue for you.

Client: I went to the doctor today for a final checkup, and she said that I was doing fine.

Practitioner: She gave you a clean bill of health, then.

Client: I just don't know what to think about the way my girlfriend treats me. Sometimes she seems so warm—like she really likes me—and at other times she acts really cold.

Practitioner: Her hot and cold behavior really confuses you.

When employed sparingly, paraphrases may be interspersed with other facilitative responses to prompt client expression. Used to excess, however, paraphrasing produces a mimicking effect. Paraphrases may also be utilized when practitioners want to bring focus to an idea or situation for client consideration. However, paraphrasing is inappropriate when clients are preoccupied with

feelings. In such cases, practitioners need to relate with empathic responses that accurately capture clients' affect and assist them to reflect on and sort through feelings. Sometimes practitioners may choose to direct discussion from feelings for therapeutic purposes. For instance, a practitioner may believe that a chronically depressed client who habitually expresses discouragement and disillusionment would benefit by focusing less on feelings and more on actions to alleviate distress. When the practitioner chooses to de-emphasize feelings, paraphrases that reflect content are helpful and appropriate.

Exercise in Paraphrasing

In the following exercise, formulate written responses that paraphrase the messages of clients. Remember, paraphrases usually reflect the cognitive aspects of messages, rather than feelings. Modeled responses to these exercises are found at the end of the chapter.

Client Statements

1. *Client:* I can't talk to people. I just completely freeze up in a group.

2. *Woman:* I think that in the last few weeks I've been able to listen much more often to my husband and children.

3. *Client:* Whenever I get into an argument with my mother, I always end up losing. I guess I'm still afraid of her.

4. *Husband:* I just can't decide what to do. If I go ahead with the divorce, I'll probably lose custody of the kids—and I won't be able to see them very much. If I don't, though, I'll have to put up with the same old thing. I don't think my wife is going to change.

5. *Elder client:* It wasn't so difficult to adjust to this place because the people who run it are helpful and friendly and I am able to make contacts easily—I've always been a people person.

6. *Mother* [*speaking about daughter*]: When it comes right down to it, I think I'm to blame for a lot of her problems.

Open- and Closed-Ended Responding

Generally used to elicit specific information, *closed-ended questions* define a topic and restrict the client's response to a few words or a simple yes or no answer. Typical examples of closed-ended questions are:

"When did you obtain your divorce?"

"Do you have any sexual difficulties in your marriage?"

"When did you last have a physical examination?"

"Is your health insurance Medicare?"

Although closed-ended questions restrict the client and elicit limited information, many instances occur in which these responses are both appropriate and helpful. Later in the chapter we discuss how and when to use this type of response effectively.

In contrast to closed-ended responses, which circumscribe client messages, *open-ended responses* invite expanded expression and leave the client free to express what seems most relevant and important. For example:

Practitioner: You've mentioned your daughter. Tell me how she enters into your problem.

Client: I don't know what to do. Sometimes I think she is just pushing me so that she can go live with her father. When I ask her to help around the house, she won't, and says that she doesn't owe me anything. When I try to insist on her helping, it just ends up in an ugly scene without anything being accomplished. It makes me feel so helpless.

In the preceding example, the practitioner's open-ended response prompted the client to expand on the details of the problems with her daughter, including a description of her daughter's behavior, her own efforts to cope, and her present sense of defeat. The information contained in the message is typical of the richness of data obtained through open-ended responding.

Some open-ended responses are unstructured, leaving the topic to the client's choosing ("Tell me what you would like to discuss today," or "What else can you tell me about the problems that you're experiencing?"). Other open-ended responses are structured in that the practitioner defines the topic to be discussed but leaves clients free to respond in any way they wish ("You've mentioned feeling badly about the incident that occurred between you and your son. I'd be interested in hearing more about that.") Still other open-ended responses fall along a continuum between structured and unstructured in that they give the client leeway to answer with a few words or to elaborate with more information ("How do you feel about that?" or "How willing are you to do this?").

Practitioners may formulate open-ended responses either by asking a question or by giving a polite command. For example, when a terminally ill cancer patient said, "The doctor thinks I could live about six or seven months now; it could be less, it could be more; it's just an educated guess is what he told me," the practitioner could respond by asking, "How are you feeling about that prognosis?" or "Would you tell me how you are feeling about that prognosis?". Polite commands have the effect of direct questions in requesting information but are less forceful and involve greater finesse. Similar in nature are embedded questions that do not take the form of a question but embody a request for information. Examples of embedded questions are: "I'm curious about..." "I'm wondering if..." and "I'm interested in knowing..." Open-ended questions often start with what or how. Why questions are often unproductive inasmuch as they ask for reasons, motives, or causes that are either obvious, obscure, or unknown to the client. Asking how ("How did that happen?") rather than why ("Why did that happen?") often elicits far richer information regarding client behavior and patterns.

Exercises in Identifying Open- and Closed-Ended Responses

The following exercises will assist you to differentiate between closed and open-ended messages. Identify each statement with either a C for closed or O for open. Turn to the end of the chapter (p.176) to check your answers.

1. "Did your mother ask you to see me because of the problem you had with the principal?"
2. "When John says that to you, what do you experience inside?"
3. "You said you're feeling fed up and you're just not sure that pursuing a reconciliation is worth your trouble. Could you elaborate?"
4. "When is your court date?"

Now read the following client messages and respond by writing open-ended responses. Avoid using why questions. Examples of open-ended responses to these messages can be found at the end of the chapter.

Client Statements

1. *Client:* Whenever I'm in a group with Ralph, I find myself saying something that will let him know that I am smart too.
2. *Client:* I always have had my parents telephone for me about appointments and other things. I might foul up.
3. *Terminally ill cancer patient:* Some days I am really angry because I'm only 46 years old and there are so many more things I wanted to do. Other days, I feel kind of defeated like this is what I get for smoking two packs a day for 25 years.
4. *Teenager* [*speaking of a previous probation counselor*]: He sure let me down. And I really trusted him. He knows a lot about me because I spilled my guts out.

In the following sections, we explain how you can blend open-ended and empathic responses to keep a discussion focused on a specific topic. In

preparation for that, respond to the next two client messages by formulating an empathic response followed by an open-ended question that encourages the client to elaborate on the same topic.

5. *Unwed teenage daughter seeking abortion brought in by her mother who wishes to discuss birth alternatives:* I feel like you are all tied up with my mother, trying to talk me out of what I have decided to do.
6. *Client:* Life is such a hassle, and it doesn't seem to have any meaning or make sense. I just don't know whether I want to try figuring it out any longer.

The difference between closed-ended and open-ended responses may seem obvious to you, particularly if you completed the preceding exercises. It has been our experience, however, that beginning and even seasoned practitioners have difficulty in actual sessions in discriminating whether their responses are open- or closed-ended, in observing the differential effect of these two types of responses in yielding rich and relevant data, and in deciding which of the two types of responses is appropriate at a given moment. We recommend, therefore, that as you converse with your associates, you practice drawing them out by employing open-ended responses and noting how they respond. We also recommend that you use the form provided at the end of the chapter to assess both the frequency and the appropriateness of your closed- and open-ended responses in several taped client sessions.

Discriminate Use of Open- and Closed-Ended Questions

Beginning practitioners typically ask an excessive number of closed-ended questions, many of which block communication or are inefficient or irrelevant to the helping process. When this occurs, the session tends to take on the flavor of an interrogation, with the practitioner bombarding the client with questions and taking responsibility for maintaining verbalization. Notice what happens, for example, in the following excerpt from a recording of a practitioner interviewing an institutionalized youth.

Practitioner: I met your mother yesterday. Did she come all the way from Colorado to see you?

Client: Yeah.

Practitioner: It seems to me that she must really care about you to take the bus and make the trip up here to see you. Don't you think so?

Client: I suppose so.

Practitioner: Did the visit with her go all right?

Client: Fine. We had a good time.

Practitioner: You had said you were going to talk to her about a possible home visit. Did you do that?

Client: Yes.

When closed-ended responses are used to elicit information in lieu of open-ended responses, as in the preceding example, many more discrete interchanges will occur, but the client's responses will be brief and the yield markedly lower.

Open-ended responses often elicit the same data as closed-ended questions but in addition draw out much more information and elaboration of the problem from the client. The following two examples contrast open-ended and closed-ended responses that address the same topic with a given client. To appreciate the differences in the richness of information yielded by these contrasting responses, compare the likely client responses elicited by such questions to the closed-ended questions used above.

1. *Closed-ended:* "Did she come all the way from Colorado to see you?"

   Open-ended: "Tell me about your visit with your mother."

2. *Closed-ended:* "Did you talk with her about a possible home visit?"

   Open-ended: "How did your mother respond when you talked about a possible home visit?"

Occasionally, beginning practitioners also use closed-ended questions to explore feelings, but responses from clients typically involve minimal self-disclosure, as might be expected. Rather than encouraging expanded expression of feelings, closed-ended questions limit responses, as illustrated in the following example:

Practitioner: Did you feel rejected when she turned down your invitation?

Client: Yeah.

Practitioner: Have there been other times when you've felt rejected that way?

Client: Oh, yeah. Lots of times.

Practitioner: When was the first time?

Client: Gee, that's hard to say.

Had the practitioner employed empathic and open-ended responses to explore the feelings and thoughts associated with being rejected, the client would likely have revealed much more.

Because open-ended responses elicit more information than closed-ended ones, frequent use of the former increases the efficiency of data gathering. The richness of information revealed by the client, in fact, is directly proportional to the frequency with which open-ended responses are employed. Frequent use of open-ended responses also fosters a smoothly flowing session; consistently asking closed-ended questions, by contrast, often results in a fragmented, discontinuous process.

Closed-ended questions are used chiefly to elicit essential factual information. Skillful practitioners use closed-ended questions sparingly, since clients usually reveal extensive factual information spontaneously as they unfold their stories, aided by the practitioners' open-ended and furthering responses. Employed little during the first part of a session, closed questions are used more extensively later to elicit data that may have been omitted by clients, such as names and ages of children, place of employment, date of marriage, medical facts, and data regarding family of origin.

In obtaining factual data such as the preceding,

the practitioner can unobtrusively weave into the discussion closed-ended questions that directly pertain to the topic. For example, a client may relate certain marital problems that have existed for many years, and the practitioner may ask parenthetically, "And you've been married how many years?" Similarly, a parent may explain that a child began to truant from school when the parent started to work six months ago, to which the practitioner may respond, "I see. Incidentally, what type of work do you do?" It is vital, of course, to shift the focus back to the problem. If necessary, the practitioner can easily maintain focus by using an open-ended response to pick up the thread of the discussion. For example, the practitioner may comment, "You mentioned that Ernie began truanting when you started to work. I'd like to hear more about what was happening in your family at that time."

Because open-ended responses generally yield rich information, they are used throughout initial sessions. They are used most heavily, however, in the first portion of sessions to open up communication and to invite clients to reveal problematic aspects of their lives. The following open-ended polite command is a typical opening message: "Could you tell me what it is you wish to discuss, and we can think about it together." Because such responses convey interest in clients as well as respect for clients' abilities to relate their problems in their own way, they also contribute to the development of a working relationship.

As clients disclose certain problem areas, open-ended responses are also extensively employed to elicit additional relevant information. Clients, for example, may disclose difficulties at work or in relationships with other family members. Typical open-ended responses that will elicit clarifying information are:

"Tell me more about your problems at work."

"I'd like to hear more about the circumstances when you were mugged coming home with the groceries."

It may sometimes be necessary to employ closed-ended questions extensively to elicit information if the client is unresponsive and withholds information or has limited conceptual and mental abilities. However, in the former case it is vital to explore the clients' immediate feelings about being in the session, which often are negative and impede verbal expression. Focusing on and resolving negative feelings, which we discuss in Chapter 12, may pave the way to using open-ended responses to good advantage. Using closed-ended messages as a major interviewing tool early in sessions may be appropriate with some children, but the use of open-ended responses should be consistently tested as the relationship develops.

When you incorporate open-ended responses into your repertoire, you will experience a dramatic positive change in interviewing style and confidence level. To assist you to develop skill in blending and balancing open-ended and closed-ended responses, we have provided a recording form that you may wish to use in examining your own interviewing style (see Figure 6-1). Utilizing the form, analyze several recorded individual, conjoint, or group sessions over a period of time to determine changes you are making in employing these two types of responses. The recording form will assist you in determining the extent to which you have used open- and closed-ended responses. In addition, however, you may wish to review your work for the following purposes:

1. To determine when relevant data are missing and whether the information might have been more appropriately obtained through an open- or a closed-ended response.

2. To determine when your use of closed-ended questions was irrelevant, ineffective, or distractive to the data-gathering process.

3. To practice formulating open-ended responses you might use in place of closed-ended responses to increase client participation and elicit richer data.

PRACTITIONER'S RESPONSE	OPEN-ENDED RESPONSES	CLOSED-ENDED RESPONSES
1.		
2.		
3.		
4.		
5.		
6.		
7.		

Directions: Record your discrete open- and closed-ended responses and place a check in the appropriate column. Retain a copy of the form so that you can monitor your progress in appropriately using open- and closed-ended responses from week to week.

Figure 6-1   Recording Form for Open- and Closed-Ended Responding

Seeking Concreteness

People (including clients and beginning practitioners) are inclined to think and talk in generalities and to use words that lack precision when speaking of their experiences. In order to communicate one's feelings and experiences so that they are fully understood, however, a person must be able to respond concretely, that is, with specificity. Responding concretely involves utilizing words that describe in explicit terms specific experiences, behaviors, and feelings. In the following message, the respondent expresses his experiencing in vague and general terms: "I thought you gave a good speech." By contrast, he might have described his experience in precise language: "As you delivered your speech, I was impressed with your relaxed manner and your clear articulation of the issues." To test your comprehension of the concept of concreteness, assess which of the following messages give descriptive information concerning what a client experiences:

"I have had a couple of accidents that wouldn't have happened if I had full control of my hands. The results weren't that serious but they could be."

"I'm uneasy right now because I don't know what to expect from counseling, and I'm afraid you might think that I really don't need it."

"People don't seem to care whether other people have problems."

"My previous experience with counselors was lousy."

"I really wonder if I'll be able to keep from crying and to find the words to tell my husband that it's all over—that I want a divorce."

"You did a good job."

You could probably readily identify which of the preceding messages contained language that increased the specificity of the information conveyed by the client. In developing competency as a practitioner, one of your challenges is to consistently recognize clients' messages expressed in abstract and general terms and to assist them to reveal highly specific information related to feelings and experiences. Such information will assist you to make accurate assessments and, in turn, to plan interventions accordingly.

The second challenge is to assist clients to learn how to respond more concretely in their relationships with others, a task you will not be able to accomplish unless you are able to model the dimension of concreteness yourself.

The third challenge is to describe your own experience in language that is precise and descriptive. It is thus not enough to recognize concrete messages; you must familiarize yourself with and practice responding concretely to the extent that it becomes a natural style of speaking and relating to others. The remainder of our discussion on the skill of seeking concreteness is devoted to assisting you in meeting the three challenges.

Types of Responses That Facilitate Specificity of Expression by Clients Practitioners who fail to move beyond general and abstract messages often have little grasp of the specificity and meaning of a client's problem. Eliciting highly specific information that minimizes errors or misinterpretations, however, is a formidable challenge because clients typically present impressions, views, conclusions, and opinions that, despite efforts to be objective, are biased and distorted to some extent. Further, as we have already mentioned, clients are prone to speak in generalities and to respond with imprecise language, and thus their messages may be interpreted differently by different people. To help you to conceptualize various ways you may assist clients to respond more concretely, in the following sections we have identified, discussed, and illustrated different facets of responses that seek concreteness, including:

1. Checking out perceptions.
2. Clarifying the meaning of vague or unfamiliar terms.
3. Exploring the basis of conclusions drawn by clients.
4. Assisting clients to personalize their statements.
5. Eliciting specific feelings.

6. Focusing on the here and now, rather than on the distant past.
7. Eliciting details related to clients' experiences.
8. Eliciting details related to interactional behavior.

In addition to discussing the preceding categories, we have included 10 skill development exercises, the completion of which will further bring your comprehension of concreteness from the general and abstract to the specific and concrete.

Checking Out Perceptions Responses that assist practitioners to clarify and to "check out" whether they have accurately heard clients' messages (e.g., "Do you mean…" or "Are you saying …") are vital in building rapport with clients and in communicating the desire to understand their problems. Such responses also minimize misperceptions or projections in the helping process. Benefits also accrue to clients from practitioners' efforts to understand, in that clarifying responses assist clients in sharpening and reformulating their thinking regarding feelings and other concerns and thus encourage self-awareness and growth.

At times, perception-checking is necessary because clients convey messages that are incomplete, ambiguous, or complex. Occasionally, practitioners encounter clients who repetitively communicate in highly abstract or metaphorical styles, or other clients whose thinking is scattered and whose messages often just do not "track" or make sense. In such instances, practitioners must sometimes spend an inordinate amount of time sorting through clients' messages and clarifying perceptions.

At other times, the need for clarification is not because of confusing, faulty, or incomplete client messages but because the practitioner has simply not fully attended to a client's message or comprehended its meaning. It is important to realize that fully attending moment by moment throughout a session requires intense concentration. Further, it is impossible to fully focus on and comprehend the essence of every message in group and family meetings where myriad transactions occur and competing communications bid for the practitioner's attention. Thus, it is important that you develop skill in using clarifying responses to elicit ongoing feedback regarding your perceptions and to acknowledge freely your need for clarification when you are confused or uncertain. Rather than reflecting personal or professional inadequacy, your efforts to accurately grasp the client's meaning and feelings will most likely be perceived as signs of your genuineness and your commitment to understand.

Perception-checking may be accomplished by asking simple questions that seek clarification or by combining your request for clarification with a paraphrase or empathic response that reflects your perception of the client's message (e.g., "I think you were saying _____ . Is that right?"). Examples of various clarifying messages include the following:

"You seem to be really irritated, not only because he didn't respond when you asked him to help but because he seemed to be deliberately trying to hurt you. Is that accurate?"

"I'm not sure I'm following you. Let me see if I understand the order of the sequence of the events you described…"

"Would you expand on what you are saying so that I can be sure that I understand what you mean?"

"Could you go over that again and perhaps give an illustration that might help me to understand?"

"I'm confused. Let me try to restate what I think you're saying."

"As a group, you seem to be divided in your approach to this matter. I'd like to summarize what I'm hearing, and I would then appreciate some input regarding whether I understand the various positions that have been expressed."

In addition to clarifying their own perceptions, practitioners need to assist clients in conjoint or group sessions to clarify their perceptions of the messages of others who are present. This may be accomplished in any of the following ways:

1. By *modeling* clarifying responses, which occurs naturally as practitioners seek to check out their own perceptions of clients' messages.

2. By *directing* clients to ask for clarification. Consider, for example, the following response by a practitioner in a conjoint session: "You [*mother*] had a confused look on your face, and I'm not sure that you understood your daughter's point. Would you repeat back to her what you heard and then ask her if you understood correctly?"

3. By *teaching* clients how to clarify perceptions and by reinforcing their efforts to "check out" the messages of others, as illustrated in the following responses:

[*To group*]: One of the reasons families have communication problems is that members don't hear accurately what others are trying to say, and therefore, they often respond or react on the basis of incorrect or inadequate information. I would like to encourage all of you to frequently use what I call "checking out" responses such as, "I'm not sure what you meant. Were you saying…?" to clarify statements of others. As we go along, I'll point out instances in which I notice any of you using this kind of response.

[*To family*]: I'm wondering if you all noticed Jim "checking" out what his dad said…. As you may recall, we talked about the importance of these kinds of responses earlier. [*To dad*] I'm wondering, Bob, what you experienced when Jim did that?

Clarifying the Meaning of Vague or Unfamiliar Terms

In expressing themselves, clients often employ terms that have multiple meanings or use terms in idiosyncratic ways. For example, in the message, "My husband is cruel to me," the word cruel may have different meanings to practitioner and client. Until establishing what this term means to a particular client, a practitioner cannot be certain whether the client is referring to physical abuse, criticism, nagging, withholding affections, or other possibilities. The precise meaning can be clarified by employing one of the following responses:

"In what way is he cruel?"

"I'm not sure what you mean by cruel. Could you clarify that for me?"

"I can tell that is painful for you. Could you give me some examples of times he has been cruel?"

Many other adjectives also lack precision, and it is therefore important to avoid assuming that the client means the same thing you mean when you employ a given term. The terms oversexed, dependent, irresponsible, selfish, careless, and similar terms conjure up meanings that vary according to the reference points of different persons. Exact meanings are best determined by asking for clarification or for examples of events in which the behavior alluded to actually occurred.

Exploring the Basis of Conclusions Drawn by Clients Clients often present views or conclusions as though they are established facts. For example, the messages, "I'm losing my mind," or "My wife doesn't love me anymore," involve views or conclusions that the client has drawn. To accurately assess the client's difficulties, additional information upon which the views or conclusions are based must be elicited. This information is valuable in assessing the thinking patterns of the client, which are powerful determinants of emotions and behavior. For example, a husband who believes his wife no longer loves him will behave as though his belief represents reality. The practitioner's role, of course, is to unravel distortions and to challenge erroneous conclusions in a facilitative manner.

Examples of responses that would elicit clarification of the basis of views and conclusions embodied in the messages cited earlier include the following:

"How do you mean—losing your mind?"

"How have you concluded you're losing your mind?"

"What leads you to believe your wife no longer loves you?"

"How have you come to the conclusion that your wife doesn't love you anymore?"

It should be noted that entire groups may hold in common erroneous conclusions or biased or distorted information about any variety of subjects, and in such instances, the practitioner has the challenging task of assisting members to reflect upon and to analyze their views. Examples of the conclusions or distortions that the practitioner may need to assist group members to assess include the following:

"We can't do anything about our problems. We are helpless and others are in control of our lives."

"We are innocent victims."

"People in authority are out to get us."

"Someone else is responsible for our problems."

"They [members of another race, religion, group, etc.] are no good."

We further discuss the practitioner's role in challenging distortions and erroneous conclusions and identify relevant techniques that may be used for this purpose in several chapters of the book.

Assisting Clients to Personalize Their Statements The relative concreteness of a specific client message is related in part to the focus or subject of that message. Client messages fall into several different classes of topic focus (Cormier & Cormier, 1979), each of which emphasizes different information and leads into very different areas of discussion:

1. *Focus on self*, indicated by the subject "I" (e.g., "I'm disappointed that I wasn't able to keep the appointment").

2. *Focus on others*, indicated by subjects, such as "they," "people," "someone," or names of specific persons (e.g. "they haven't fulfilled their part of the bargain").

3. *Focus on the group or mutual relationship between self and others*, indicated by the subject "we" (e.g. "We would like to do that").

4. *Focus on content*, indicated by such subjects as events, institutions, situations, ideas (e.g., "School wasn't easy for me").

Clients are more prone to focus on others, on content, or to speak of themselves as a part of a group rather than to personalize their statements by using "I" or other self-referent pronouns, as illustrated in the following messages: "Things just don't seem to be going right for me," "They don't like me," or "It's not easy for people to talk about their problems." In the last example, the client means that it is not easy for her to talk about her problems; however, in talking about this concern, she uses the term people, thus generalizing the problem and obscuring her struggle.

In assisting clients to personalize statements, practitioners have a two-fold task:

1. To model, to teach, and to coach clients to use self-referent pronouns ("I," "me") in talking about concerns rather than using topic focuses that do not clearly show the affective relationship between individuals and their concerns. For example, in response to a vague client message that focuses on content rather than self ("Everything at home seems to be deteriorating"), the practitioner can gently ask the client to reframe the message by starting the response with "I" and giving specific information about what she is experiencing. It is also helpful to teach clients the difference between messages that focus on self—"I (think) (feel) (want)…"—and messages that are *other*-related ("You…" "they…" "we…" "it…" "someone…") or *subject*-related (objects, things, ideas, or situations). Although teaching clients to use self-referent pronouns when talking about their concerns is a substantive task, clients derive major benefits, since not owning or taking responsibility for feelings and speaking about problems in generalities and abstractions is perhaps one of the most prevalent causes of problems in communicating.

2. To focus frequently on the client, use the client's name or the pronoun "you." Beginning practitioners are apt to attend to client talk about other people, distant situations, the group at large, various escapades, or other events or content that give little information about self and the relationship between self and situations or people. Notice in the following illustration that the practitioner's response focuses on the situation rather than on the client:

Client: My kids want to shut me up in a nursing home.

Practitioner: What makes you think that?

In contrast, consider the following message, which personalizes the client's concern and explicitly identifies the feelings she is experiencing:

Practitioner: You're really frustrated and disappointed with your children for feeling that you would be better off in a nursing home. You would like to be part of the decision about what would be a safe environment for you.

A practitioner may employ various techniques to assist clients to personalize messages; in the preceding example, however, the practitioner utilized an empathic response. In this instance, this skill is invaluable to the practitioner in helping the client to focus on self. Remember that personalizing feelings is an inherent aspect of the paradigm for responding empathically ("You feel _____ about/because _____"). Thus, a client can make a statement in which there are no self-referent pronouns, and by utilizing empathic responding, the practitioner may assist clients to "own" their feelings.

Eliciting Specific Feelings Even when clients personalize their messages and express feelings, practitioners often need to elicit information to clarify what they are experiencing, for certain "feeling words" denote *general feeling states* rather than *specific feelings*. For example, in the message, "I'm really *upset* that I didn't get a raise," the term *upset* helps to clarify the client's general frame of mind but fails to specify the precise feeling. "Upset" in this instance may refer to feeling disappointed, discouraged, unappreciated, devalued, angry, resentful, or even feeling incompetent or inadequate over not having been granted a raise. The point is that until practitioners have elicited additional information, they cannot be sure of how being "upset" is actually experienced by the client. Other feeling words that lack specificity include *frustrated, uneasy, uncomfortable, troubled,* and *bothered.* When clients employ such words, you can pinpoint their feelings by employing responses such as the following:

"How do you mean, upset?"

"I'd like to understand more about that feeling. Could you clarify what you mean by frustrated?"

"In what way do you feel bothered?"

Focusing on the Here and Now Still another aspect of concreteness embodies responses that shift the focus from the past to the present—the here and now. Messages that relate to the immediate present are high in concreteness, whereas those that center on the past are low. Some clients (and practitioners) are prone to discuss past feelings and events. Precious opportunities for promoting growth and understanding may slip through the fingers of practitioners who fail to focus on emotions and experiences that unfold in the immediacy of the interview. Focusing on feelings as they occur will enable you to observe reactions and behavior firsthand, thus eliminating bias and error caused by reporting feelings and experiences after the fact. Furthermore, the helpfulness of your feedback is greatly enhanced when this feedback relates to the client's immediate experience.

An example of concreteness in such situations is provided in the following excerpt:

Client [*choking up*]: When she told me it was all over, that she was in love with another man—well, I just felt—it's happened again. I felt totally alone, like there just wasn't anyone.

Practitioner: That must have been terribly painful. [*Client nods; tears well up.*] I wonder if you're not having the same feeling just now—at this moment. [*Client nods agreement.*]

Not only do such instances provide direct access to the client's inner experience, but they may also produce rich benefit as the client shares deep and painful emotions in the context of a warm, accepting, and supportive relationship. Here-and-now experiencing that involves emotions toward the practitioner (anger, hurt, disappointment, affectional desires, fears, and the like) is designated as *relational immediacy.* Skills pertinent to relational immediacy warrant separate consideration and are dealt with in Chapter 19.

Focusing on here-and-now experiencing with groups, couples, and families, discussed at length in Chapter 16, is a particularly potent technique for assisting members of these systems to clear the air of pent-up feelings. Further, interventions that focus on the immediacy of feelings bring covert issues to the surface, thus paving the way for the practitioner to assist members of these systems to clearly identify and explore their difficulties and (if appropriate) engage in problem solving.

Eliciting Details Related to Clients' Experiences
As previously mentioned, one of the reasons why concrete responses are essential is that clients often offer vague statements regarding their experiences. For example: "Some people in this group don't want to change bad enough to put forth any effort." Compare this to the following concrete statement in which the client assumes ownership of the problem and fills in details that clarify its nature:

"I'm concerned because I want to do something to work on my problems in this group, but when I do try to talk about them, you, John, make some sarcastic remark. It seems that then several of you [gives names] just laugh about it and someone changes the subject. I really feel ignored then and just go off into my own world."

Aside from assisting clients to personalize their messages and to "own" their feelings and problems, practitioners have the task of asking questions that elicit illuminating information concerning the client's experiencing, such as that illustrated in the preceding message. In this regard, questions that start with "how" or "what" are often helpful in assisting the client to give concrete data. To the client message, "Some people in this group don't want to change bad enough to put forth any effort," the practitioner might ask, "Specifically what has been happening in the group that leads you to this conclusion?"

Eliciting Details Regarding Interactional Behavior

Concrete responses are also vital in accurately assessing interactional behavior. Such responses pinpoint what actually occurs in interactional events, that is, what circumstances preceded the events, what was said and done by the participants, what specific thoughts and feelings were experienced by the client, and what consequences followed the event. In other words, the practitioner elicits details of what happened, rather than settling for clients' views and conclusions. An example of a concrete response to a client message follows:

Client: Well, Fred blew his cool as usual last night. He really read me the riot act, and I hadn't done one thing to deserve it.

Practitioner: Could you recall exactly what happened—what led up to this situation and what each of you said and did. To understand better what went wrong, I'd like to get the details as though I had been there and observed what happened.

In such cases, it is important to keep clients on topic by continuing to assist them to relate the events in question, using responses such as "Then what happened?" "What did you do next?" or "Then who said what?" If dysfunctional patterns become evident after exploring numerous events, practitioners have a responsibility to share their observations with clients, to assist them to evaluate the impact of the patterned behavior, and to assess their motivation to change it.

Specificity of Expression by Practitioners

Seeking concreteness applies not only to the communication of clients but to that of practitioners as well.

In this role, you will frequently explain, clarify, give feedback, and share personal feelings and views with clients. As a budding practitioner who has recently entered a formal professional educational program, you, too, may be prone to speak with the vagueness and generality that characterize much of the communication of the lay public. When such occurs, clients and others may understandably misinterpret, draw erroneous conclusions, or experience confusion about the meaning of your messages. Consider, for example, the lack of specificity in the following actual messages of practitioners:

"You seem to have a lot of pent-up hostility."

"You really handled yourself well in the group today."

"I think a lot of your difficulties stem from your self-image."

Vague terms, such as *hostility*, *handled yourself well*, and *self-image*, tend to leave the client in a quandary as to what the practitioner actually means. Moreover, conclusions are presented without supporting information, thus requiring the client to accept them at face value, to reject them as invalid, or to speculate as to the basis of the conclusions. Fortunately, some clients are sufficiently perceptive, inquisitive, and assertive to request greater specificity, but many are not.

Contrast the preceding messages to the following in which the practitioner responds to the same situations but this time with messages that have a high degree of specificity:

"I've noticed that you've become easily angered and frustrated several times as we've talked about ways you might work out child custody arrangements with your wife. This appears to be a very painful area for you. I would like to know just what you have been feeling."

"I noticed that you responded several times in the group tonight, and I thought you offered some very helpful insight to Marjorie when you said…. I also noticed you seemed to be more at ease than in previous sessions."

"We've talked about your tendency to feel inferior to other members of your family and to discount your own feelings and opinions in your contacts with them. I think that observation applies to the problem you're having with your sister that you just described. You've said you didn't want to go on the trip with her and her husband because they fight all the time, and yet you feel you have to go because she is putting pressure on you. As in other instances, you appear to be drawing the conclusion that how you feel about the matter isn't important."

When practitioners speak with specificity, clarify meanings, personalize statements, and document the sources of conclusions, clients are much less likely to misinterpret or project their own feelings or thoughts. Clients are clear about what is expected of them and how they are perceived, as well as how and why practitioners think and feel as they do about various matters discussed. Equally important, clients vicariously learn to speak with greater specificity as practitioners model sending concrete messages.

Both beginning and experienced practitioners face the additional challenge of avoiding the inappropriate use of jargon, which has pervaded professional discourse and has become rampant in social work literature and case records. The use of jargon confuses rather than clarifies meanings for clients. The careless use of jargon with colleagues also fosters stereotypical thinking and is therefore antithetical to the cardinal value of individualizing the client. Furthermore, labels tend to conjure up images of clients that vary from one practitioner to another, thus injecting a significant source of error into communication. Consider, for example, the lack of specificity in the following messages that are rich in jargonese:

"Mrs. N manifests strong passive-aggressive tendencies."

"Sean displayed *adequate impulse* control in the group and *tested the leader's authority in a positive manner*."

"Hal needs assistance in gaining greater *self-control*."

"The group members were able t*o respond to appropriate limits.*"

"Ruth appears to be *emotionally immature* for an eighth-grader."

To accurately convey information about clients to your colleagues, you must explicitly describe their behavior and document the sources of your conclusions. Keeping in mind the preceding vague message, "Ruth appears to be emotionally immature for an eighth-grader," consider how much more accurately another practitioner could perceive your client if you conveyed information in the form of a concrete response: "The teacher says Ruth is quiet and stays to herself in school. She doesn't answer any questions in class unless directly called upon, and she often doesn't complete her assignments. She also spends considerable time daydreaming or playing with objects." By describing behavior, you avoid biasing your colleague's perceptions of clients through conveying either vague impressions or erroneous conclusions.

It has been our experience that mastery of the skill of communicating with specificity is gained only through extended and determined effort. The task is complicated by a typical lack of awareness by beginning practitioners of the vagueness and generality of their communication. We recommend that you carefully and consistently monitor your recorded sessions and your everyday conversations with a view toward identifying instances in which you did or did not communicate with specificity. Such monitoring will enable you to set relevant goals for yourself and to chart your progress. We also recommend that you enlist the assistance of your practicum instructor in providing feedback about your performance level on this vital skill.

Exercises in Seeking Concreteness   In the preceding discussion, we identified guidelines for formulating concrete responses. To review, you achieve specificity by:

1. Checking out perceptions.

2. Clarifying the meaning of vague or unfamiliar terms.

3. Exploring the basis of conclusions drawn by clients.

4. Assisting clients to personalize their statements.

5. Eliciting specific feelings.

6. Focusing on the here and now.

7. Eliciting details related to clients' experiences.

8. Eliciting details related to interactional behavior.

In the following exercises, formulate written responses that will elicit concrete data regarding clients' problems. You may wish to combine your responses with either an empathic response or a paraphrase. Reviewing the above guidelines as you complete the exercise will assist you in formulating effective responses and will help you to clearly conceptualize the various dimensions of this skill as well. After you have finished the exercises, compare your responses with the modeled responses following the last client statement.

Client Statements

1. *Adolescent* [*speaking of his recent recommitment to a correctional institution*]*:* It really seems weird to be back here.

2. *Client:* You can't depend on friends; they'll stab you in the back every time.

3. *Client:* He's got a terrible temper—that's the way he is, and he'll never change.

4. *Client:* My supervisor is so insensitive, you can't believe it. All she thinks about is reports and deadlines.

5. *Client:* I was upset after I left your office last week. I felt you really didn't understand what I was saying and didn't care how I felt.

6. *Client:* My dad's 58 years old now, but I swear he still hasn't grown up. He always has a chip on his shoulder.

7. *Elder client:* My rheumatoid arthritis has affected my hands a lot. It gets to be kind of tricky when I'm handling pots and pans in the cooking.

8. *Client:* I just have this uneasy feeling about going

to the doctor. I guess I've really got a hang-up about it.

9. *African American student* [*to African American practitioner*]*:* You ask why I don't talk to my teacher about why I'm late for school. I'll tell you why. Because she's white, that's why. She's got it in for us blacks, and there's just no point talking to her. That's just the way it is.

10. *Client:* John doesn't give a damn about me. I could kick the bucket, and he wouldn't lose a wink of sleep.

Modeled Responses

1. "In what way does it seem weird?"

2. "I gather *you* feel that your friends have let you down in the past. Could you give me a recent example in which this has happened?"

3. "Could you tell me more about what happens when he loses his temper with you?" or "You sound like you don't have much hope that he'll ever get control of his temper. How have you concluded he will never change?" [*A practitioner might explore each aspect of the message separately.*]

4. "Could you give me some examples of how she is insensitive to you?"

5. "Sounds like you've been feeling hurt and disappointed over my reaction last week. I can sense you're struggling with those same feelings right now. Could you tell me what you're feeling at this moment?"

6. "That must make it difficult for you. Could you recall some recent examples of times you've had difficulties with him?"

7. "When you say that handling the pots and pans is kind of tricky, can you tell me about recent examples of what has happened when you are cooking?"

8. "Think of going to the doctor just now. Let your feelings flow naturally. [*Pause.*] What goes on inside you—your thoughts and feelings?"

9. "So you see it as pretty hopeless. You feel pretty strong about Ms. Wright. I'd be interested in hearing what's happened that you've come to the conclusion she's got it in for blacks."

10. "So you feel like you're nothing in his eyes. I'm wondering how you've reached that conclusion?"

Summarizing Responses

The technique of summarization embodies four distinct and yet related facets. Although employed at different times and in different ways, each facet serves the common purpose of tying together functionally related elements that are manifested in a fragmented fashion at different points in the helping process. These four facets include:

1. Highlighting key aspects of discussions of specific problems before changing the focus of the discussion.
2. Making connections between relevant aspects of lengthy client messages.
3. Reviewing major focal points of a session and assignments clients plan to work on before the next session.
4. Recapitulating the highlights of a previous session and reviewing clients' progress on assignments during the week for the purpose of providing focus and continuity between sessions.

These facets of summarization are considered in the following sections.

Highlighting Key Aspects of Problems During the phase of an initial session in which problems are explored in moderate depth, summarization can be effectively employed to tie together and highlight essential aspects of a problem before proceeding to explore additional problems. The practitioner may summarize how the problem appears to be produced by the interplay of several factors, including external pressures, overt behavioral patterns, unfulfilled needs and wants, and covert thoughts and feelings. Connecting these key elements assists clients in gaining a more accurate and complete perspective of their problems. Employed in this fashion, summarization involves fitting pieces of the problem together to form a coherent whole. Seeing the problem in a fresh and more accurate perspective is beneficial, as it expands clients' awareness and can generate hope and enthusiasm for tackling a problem that has hitherto seemed insurmountable.

Summarization that highlights problems is generally employed at a natural point in the session when the practitioner believes that relevant aspects of the problem have been adequately explored and clients appear satisfied in having had the opportunity to express concerns. The following example illustrates this type of summarization:

The client, an 80-year-old widow, has been referred to a Services to Seniors program for exploration of alternative living arrangements because of her failing health, isolation, and recent falls. As the practitioner has helped her explore alternative living arrangements, several characteristics that would be important for her in an improved living situation have been identified. Highlighting the salient factors, the practitioner summarizes:

"So it sounds as if you are looking for a situation in which there is social interaction but your privacy is also important to you: you want to maintain your independence."

Summarizing responses of this type serve as a prelude to the process of formulating goals, as goals flow naturally from problem formulations. Moreover, highlighting various dimensions of the problem facilitates the subsequent delineation of subgoals and tasks that must be accomplished to achieve an overall goal. In the preceding situation, to explore an improved living situation, the client above would be helped to explore the specific form of privacy (whether living alone or with someone else) and social interaction (how much and what kind of contact with others).

Summarizing salient aspects of problems is a valuable technique in sessions with groups, couples, and families, enabling the practitioner at timely moments to highlight the difficulties experienced by each member. In a family session with a pregnant adolescent and her mother, for example, the practitioner might say:

[*To pregnant adolescent*]: "You feel as if deciding what to do about this baby is your decision: It's your body and you have decided that an abortion is the best solution for you. You know that you have the legal right to make this decision and want to be supported in making it. You feel as if your mother wants to help but can't tell you what decision to make."

[*To mother*]: "As you spoke, you seemed saddened and very anxious about this decision your daughter is making. You are saying, "I care about my daughter, but I don't think she is mature enough to make this decision on her own." As you have noted, women in your family have had a hard time conceiving, and you wish that she would consider other options besides abortion. So you feel a responsibility to your daughter, but also to this unborn baby and the family history of conceiving children."

Such responses synthesize in concise and neutral language the needs, concerns, and problems of each participant for all other members of the session to hear. When summarization of this type is employed frequently, it underscores the fact that all participants are struggling with and have responsibility for problems that are occurring, thus counteracting the tendency of families to view one person as the exclusive cause of family problems.

Summarizing Lengthy Messages Clients' messages range from one word or one sentence to lengthy and sometimes rambling monologues. Although the meaning and significance of brief messages are often readily discernible, lengthy messages confront the practitioner with the challenge of encapsulating and tying together diverse elements that may possess marked complexity. Linking the elements together often highlights and expands the significance and meaning of the client's message. For this reason, such messages

represent one form of additive empathy, a skill discussed in Chapter 18.

Because lengthy client messages typically include emotions, thoughts, and descriptive content, you will need to be perceptive to how these dimensions relate to the focal point of the discussion. To illustrate, consider the following message of a mildly brain-damaged and socially withdrawn 16-year-old female—an only child who is extremely dependent on her overprotective but subtly rejecting mother:

"Mother tells me she loves me, but I find that hard to believe. Nothing I do ever pleases her; she yells at me when I refuse to wash my hair alone. But I can't do it right without her help. `When are you going to grow up?' she'll say. And she goes bowling with her friends and leaves me alone in that creaky house. She knows how scared I get when I have to stay home alone. But she says, `Nancy, I can't just baby-sit you all the time. I've got to do something for myself. Why don't you make some friends or watch TV or play your guitar? You've just got to quit pitying yourself all the time.' Does that sound like someone who loves you? I get so mad at her when she yells at me, it's all I can do to keep from killing her."

Embodied in the preceding message are the following elements:

1. Wanting to be loved by her mother yet feeling insecure and rejected at times.

2. Feeling inadequate about performing certain tasks, such as washing her hair.

3. Feeling extremely dependent upon her mother for certain services and companionship.

4. Feeling afraid when her mother leaves her alone.

5. Feeling hurt (implied) and resentful when her mother criticizes her or leaves her alone.

6. Feeling intense anger and wanting to lash out when her mother yells at her.

The following is a summarizing response that ties these elements together:

"So you find your feelings toward your mother pulling you in different directions. You want her to love you, but you feel unloved and resent it when she criticizes you or leaves you alone. And you feel really torn because you depend on her in so many ways, and yet at times, you feel so angry you want to hurt her back for yelling at you. You'd like to have a smoother relationship without the strain."

In conjoint interviews or group sessions, summarization can also be used effectively to highlight and to tie together key elements and dynamics embodied in transactions, as illustrated in the following transaction and summarizing responses of a practitioner:

Wife [*to husband*]: You're just never home when I need you. I need your help making decisions about the children. We've got this big activity coming up with Susan this weekend. And where are you going to be? [*Said with animation and sarcasm.*] Deer hunting—of course!

Husband [*bristling and defensive*]: You're damned right! You make it sound like a crime. I suppose you expect me not to go deer hunting just because you can't make a decision. Once a year I get to do something I really enjoy, and you bitch about it. Why shouldn't you make decisions? I didn't marry you to make your decisions for you. Making decisions about the children is your job. Why don't you learn to stand on your own two feet for a change?

Practitioner: Let's stop here and think about what each of you is saying. [*To wife.*] You're feeling overwhelmed in coping with the children alone. I gather the bottom line of what you're saying is that your husband is very important to you, and you want to work together as a team in dealing with matters related to the children. [*Wife nods in agreement as husband listens attentively.*] [*To husband.*] And I gather you're reading your wife's message as an attempt to pass the buck to you. You also sounded as though you felt attacked and read her message as an attempt to deny you an opportunity to enjoy yourself. [*He vigorously nods affirmatively.*][*To both.*] Each of you seems to be feeling a lack of caring and understanding by the other, but these needs get buried under your criticism and attempts to defend yourselves.

Let's explore further what each of you is needing from the other.

The practitioner's summarization employs additive empathy in identifying needs that underlie the negative and destructive messages exchanged by the spouses. Going beyond the negative surface feelings, the practitioner summarizes implied messages and needs, the exploration of which may lead to increased understanding and to positive feelings rather than mutual recriminations.

On occasion, client messages may ramble to the extent that they contain numerous unrelated elements that cannot all be tied together. In such instances, your task is to extract and focus on those elements of the message that are most relevant to the thrust of the session at that point. Utilized in this manner, summarization provides focus and direction to the session and averts aimless wandering. With clients whose thinking is loose or who ramble to avoid having to focus on unpleasant matters, you will need to interrupt on occasion to assure some semblance of focus and continuity. Otherwise, the interview will be disjointed and unproductive. Skills in maintaining focus and continuity are discussed at length later in the chapter and in Chapter 13.

Reviewing Focal Points of a Session   During the course of an individual, conjoint, or group session, it is common to focus on more than one problem and to discuss numerous factors associated with each problem. Toward the end of the first or second session, therefore, depending on the length of the initial exploration, summarization is employed to review key problems that have been explored and to highlight themes and patterns that relate to these problems. Because summarizing themes and patterns expands the client's awareness of dysfunctional patterns and his or her role in the difficulties manifested (assuming the client affirms the validity of the summarization), use of this skill opens up promising avenues for growth and change.

In fact, through summarizing responses, the practitioner can review problematic themes and patterns that have emerged in the session and test the client's readiness to consider goals aimed at modifying these dysfunctional patterns. The following is an example of such a message:

"As we explored the stresses that appear to precede your periods of depression, the theme of your discounting yourself by trying so hard to meet unreasonable demands of your family members struck me as very significant, and you seemed to agree. As we begin to consider goals, I wonder what you think about working toward the goal of giving your own needs higher priority and learning to say 'No!' and feeling good about it when others make demands that conflict with your needs?"

Providing Focus and Continuity Summarization can also be utilized by the practitioner at the beginning of an individual, group, or conjoint session to review work that clients have accomplished in the last session(s) and to set the stage for work in the present session. At the same time, the practitioner may wish to identify a promising topic for discussion or to refresh clients' minds concerning work they wish to accomplish in that session. In addition, summarization can also be employed periodically to synthesize salient points at the conclusion of a discussion or utilized at the end of the session to review the major focal points. In so doing, the practitioner will need to place what was accomplished in the session within the broad perspective of the client's goals. By considering how the salient content and movement manifested in each session fit into the larger whole, both the practitioner and clients are more likely to maintain a sense of direction and to avoid needless delays caused by wandering and detours that commonly occur when continuity within or between sessions is weak.

Used as a "wrap-up" when the allotted time for a session is nearly gone, summarization also assists the practitioner to draw a session to a natural con-clusion. In addition to highlighting and linking together the key points of the session, the practitioner reviews with clients plans for performing tasks that they have agreed to accomplish before the next session. Upon concluding the session in such a manner, all participants are clear about where they have been and where they are going in relation to the goals toward which their mutual efforts are directed.

Analyzing Your Verbal Following Skills

After taking frequency counts over a period of time of some of the major verbal following skills (empathy, concreteness, open-ended and closed-ended responses), as suggested in this chapter, you are ready to assess the extent to which you employ, blend, and balance these skills in relation to each other. Employing the form for verbal following (Figure 6-2), categorize each of your responses from a recorded session. As you analyze your relative use and blending of responses alone or with your practicum instructor, determine whether you think certain types of responses were used either too frequently or too sparingly. Further, think of steps that you might take to correct any imbalances in your utilization of skills for future sessions.

FOCUSING: A COMPLEX SKILL

Skills in focusing are critical to effective social work practice for several reasons, the first of which is purely pragmatic. Clients and practitioners spend limited time together, and it is critical that they use that time fruitfully by focusing on topics and employing processes that produce maximal yield. Practitioners, therefore, are responsible for giving direction to the helping process and avoiding wandering that unnecessarily consumes valuable time. Indeed, one feature that differentiates effective helping relationships from general social relationships is that the former are characterized

CLIENT MESSAGE	OPEN-ENDED RESPONSES	CLOSED-ENDED RESPONSES	EMPATHIC RESPONSES	LEVEL OF EMPATHY	CONCRETE RESPONSES	SUMMARIZING RESPONSES	OTHER TYPES OF RESPONSES
1.							
2.							
3.							
4.							
5.							
6.							
7.							

Directions: Categorize each of your responses from a recorded session. Where responses involve more than one category (blended responses) , record them as a single response, but also check each category embodied in the response. Excluding the responses checked as "other," analyze whether certain types of responses were utilized too frequently or too sparingly. Set tasks for youself to correct imbalances in future sessions. Retain a copy of the form so that you can monitor your progress in mastering verbal following skills over an extended period of time.

Figure 6-2   Recording for Verbal Following Skills

by sharp focus and continuity, whereas the latter are relatively unstructured.

Another reason why focusing skills are vital is that clients have limited perspectives of their problems and look to professionals for expertise and guidance in concentrating their efforts in areas likely to produce desired results. Moreover, many of us (both clients and practitioners) tend to be scattered in our thinking and dissipate energies by rapidly shifting focus from one topic to another. Practitioners perform a valuable role by assisting them to focus on problems in greater depth and to maintain focus until they accomplish desired changes.

Still another vital reason for developing focusing skills is that families and groups often engage in dysfunctional processes that not only cause interactional difficulties but also hinder groups

from focusing effectively on their problems. To enhance family and group functioning, therefore, practitioners must be able to refocus the discussion any time interactional processes cause families and groups to prematurely shift away from the topic at hand.

To assist beginning practitioners to learn how to focus effectively, we consider the various functions of focusing skills, which are as follows:

1. Selecting topics for exploration

2. Exploring topics in depth

3. Maintaining focus and keeping on topic

Knowledge of these functions assists you to focus sharply on relevant topics and elicit sufficient data to formulate an accurate problem assessment—a prerequisite for competent practice.

Selecting Topics for Exploration

Areas relevant for exploration vary from situation to situation. However, clients who belong to the same populations, such as delinquents, unwed mothers, nursing home residents, persons with mental retardation, patients in psychiatric institutions, or families in the same stage of life development, generally share many problems in common. Before meeting with clients whose probable difficulties differ from client populations with which you are familiar, you can prepare yourself to conduct an effective exploration by developing (in consultation with your practicum instructor or field supervisor) a list of relevant and promising problem areas to be explored. This preparation will assist you to avoid the tendency of beginning practitioners to focus on areas irrelevant to clients' problems and thus to elicit numerous bits of inconsequential information. In initially interviewing an institutionalized youth, for example, you could more effectively select questions and responses if you knew in advance that you might explore the following areas. As the institutionalized youth is an involuntary client, part of this exploration would include the youth's understanding of what parts of his work are nonnegotiable requirements, and what parts could be negotiated or free choices (Rooney, 1992).

1. Client's own perceptions of problem areas.
2. Client's perceived strengths and resources.
3. Reasons for being institutionalized and brief history of past problems related to legal authority and to use of drugs and alcohol.
4. Details regarding client's relationships with individual family members, both as concerns and sources of support.
5. Brief family history.
6. School adjustment, including information about grades, problem subjects, areas of interest, and relationships with various teachers.
7. Adjustment to institutional life, including relationships with peers and supervisors.
8. Peer relationships outside the institution.
9. Life goals.
10. Reaction to previous experiences with counseling.
11. Motivation to engage in counseling relationship and to work on concerns.

Similarly, if you plan to interview a self-referred depressed middle-aged woman, the following topical areas could assist you in conducting an initial interview. As she is self-referred, she is likely to be more voluntary than the institutionalized youth above. High attention would be paid to identifying the specific concerns which have led her to seek help.

1. Concerns as she sees them, including nature of depressive symptoms.
2. Client perception of her strengths and resources.
3. Health status, date of last physical examination, and medications being taken.
4. Onset and duration of depression, previous depressive or manic episodes.
5. Life events associated with onset of depression (especially losses).
6. Possible suicidal thoughts, intentions, or plans.
7. Dysfunctional thought patterns (self-devaluation, self-recrimination, guilt, worthlessness, helplessness, hopelessness).
8. Previous coping efforts, previous treatment.
9. Quality of interpersonal relationships (interpersonal skills and deficiencies, conflicts and supports in marital and parent–child relationships).
10. Reactions of significant others to her depression.
11. Support systems (adequacy and availability).
12. Daily activities.
13. Sense of mastery vs. feelings of inadequacy.
14. Family history of depression or manic behavior.

As noted previously, problem areas vary, and outlines of probable topical areas likewise vary accordingly. A list of areas for exploration in an initial session with a couple seeking marriage counseling or with a group of alcoholics will include a number of items that differ from those in the first list. Note, however, that items 1, 2, and 8 through 11 would likely be included in all exploratory interviews with individual clients and would be equally applicable to preparatory interviews with prospective group members.

In using an outline, you should avoid following it rigidly or using it as a crutch, for you may otherwise destroy the spontaneity of sessions and block clients from relating their stories in their own way. Rather, you should encourage clients to discuss their problems freely and play a facilitative role in exploring in greater depth problems that emerge. You must use outlines flexibly, reordering the sequence of topics, modifying, adding, or deleting topics, or abandoning the outline altogether if using it hinders communication.

You should note that you cannot always anticipate fruitful topical areas, for although clients from the same population share many commonalities, their problems also have unique aspects. It is thus important to review tapes of sessions with your practicum instructor or a field supervisor for the purpose of identifying other topical areas you should explore in future sessions.

Exploring Topics in Depth

A major facet of focusing involves centering discussions on relevant topics to assure that exploration moves from generality and superficiality to more depth and meaning. Practitioners must have skills that enable them to explore problems thoroughly, for success in the helping process depends on clear and accurate definitions of problems.

Selectively attending to specific topics is challenging for beginning practitioners, who often wander in individual or group sessions, repeatedly skipping across the surface of vital areas of content and feelings and eliciting largely superficial and sometimes distorted information. This is illustrated in the following excerpt from a first session with an adolescent in a school setting:

Practitioner: Tell me about your family.

Client: My father is ill and my mother is dead, so we live with my sister.

Practitioner: How are things with you and your sister?

Client: Good. We get along fine. She treats me pretty good.

Practitioner: How about your father?

Client: We get along pretty well. We have our problems, but most of the time things are okay. I don't really see him very much.

Practitioner: Tell me about school. How are you getting along here?

Client: Well, I don't like it very well, but my grades are good enough to get me by.

Practitioner: I notice you're new to our school this year. How did you do in the last school you attended?

Notice that by focusing superficially on the topics of family and school, the practitioner misses opportunities to explore these potential problem areas in the depth necessary to illuminate the client's situation. The exploration thus yielded little information of value, in large part because the practitioner failed to employ responses that focus in depth on topical areas. In the following sections, we further delineate skills discussed earlier in the chapter that considerably enhance a practitioner's ability to maintain focus on specific areas.

Open-Ended Responses Practitioners may employ open-ended responses throughout individual, conjoint, and group sessions to focus unintrusively on desired topics. Earlier we noted that some open-ended responses leave clients free to choose their own topics and that others focus on a topic but encourage clients to respond freely to that topic. The following examples, taken from an initial session with a depressed mother of eight children, illustrate how practitioners can employ open-ended responses to define topical areas that may yield information vital in grasping the dynamics of the client's problems.[1]

1. "What have you thought that you might like to accomplish in our work together?"

2. "You've discussed many topics in the last few minutes. Could you pick the most important one and tell me more about it?"

3. "You've mentioned that your oldest son doesn't come home after school as he did before and help you with the younger children. I would like to hear more about that."

4. "Several times as you've mentioned your concern that your husband may leave you, your voice has trembled. I wonder if you could share what you are feeling."

5. "You've indicated that your partner doesn't help you enough with the children. You also seem to be saying that you feel overwhelmed and inadequate in managing the children by yourself. Tell me what happens as you try to manage your children."

6. "You indicate that you have more problems with your 14-year-old daughter than with the other children. Tell me more about Janet and your problems with her."

In the preceding illustrations, the practitioner's open-ended questions and responses progressively moved the exploration from the general to the specific. Note also that each response or question defined a new topic for exploration. To encourage in-depth exploration of the topics thus defined, the practitioner must blend open-ended questions with other facilitative verbal following responses that focus on and elicit expanded client expressions.

After having defined a topical area by employing an open-ended response, the practitioner may deepen exploration by weaving other open-ended responses into the discussion. If the open-ended responses shift the focus to another area, however, the exploration suffers a setback. Note in the following illustration that the practitioner's second open-ended response shifts the focus away from the client's message, which involves expression of intense feelings:

Practitioner: You've said you're worried about retir-ing. I'd appreciate your sharing more about your concern. [*Open-ended response.*]

Client: I can't imagine not going to work every day. I feel at loose ends already, and I haven't even quit work. I'm afraid I just won't know what to do with myself.

Practitioner: What are your thoughts about doing some traveling? [*Open-ended response.*]

Even though open-ended responses elicit information about clients' problems, they may not facilitate the helping process if they prematurely lead the client in a different direction. If practitioners utilize open-ended or other types of responses that frequently change the topic, they will gain information that is disjointed and fragmented. As a result, assessments will suffer from large gaps in the practitioner's knowledge concerning clients' problems. As practitioners formulate open-ended responses, they must be acutely aware of the direction that responses will take.

Seeking Concreteness Earlier we discussed and illustrated the various facets of seeking concreteness. Because seeking concreteness enables practitioners to move from the general to the specific and to explore topics in depth, it is a key focusing technique. By focusing in depth on topical areas, practitioners are able to discern, and to assist clients to discern, dysfunctional thoughts, behavior, and interaction. We illustrate in subsequent sections how practitioners can effectively focus on topical areas in exploratory sessions by blending concreteness with other focusing skills. In actuality, the majority of responses that practitioners typically employ to establish and maintain focus are blends of various types of discrete responses.

Empathic Responding Empathic responding serves a critical function by enabling practitioners to focus in depth on troubling feelings, as illustrated in the next example:

Client: I can't imagine not going to work every day. I

feel at loose ends already, and I haven't even quit work. I'm afraid I just won't know what to do with myself.

Practitioner: You seem to be saying, "Even now, I'm apprehensive about retiring. I'm giving up something that has been very important to me, and I don't seem to have anything to replace it." I gather that feeling at loose ends, as you do, you worry that when you retire, you'll feel useless.

Client: I guess that's a large part of my problem. At times I feel useless now. I just didn't take time over the years to develop any hobbies or to pursue any interests. I guess I don't think that I can do anything else.

Practitioner: It sounds like you regret not having developed other interests in the past and are afraid that now you may lack the ability to develop in other areas. Maybe you're wondering if it's too late.

Client: Yes, that's right. But it isn't just that. I'm really dreading being at home with time on my hands. I can just see it now. My wife will want to keep me busy doing things around the house for her all the time. I've never liked to do that kind of thing.

Observe in the preceding example that the client's problem continued to unfold as the practitioner utilized empathic responding, revealing rich information in the process.

Blending Open-Ended, Empathic, and Concrete Responses to Maintain Focus

After employing open-ended responses to focus on a selected topic, practitioners should use other responses to maintain focus on that topic. In the following excerpt, observe how the practitioner employs open-ended and empathic responses to explore problems in depth, thereby enabling the client to move to the heart of her struggle. Notice also the richness of the client's responses elicited by the blended messages.

Practitioner: As you were speaking about your son, I sensed some pain and reluctance on your part to talk about him. I'd like to understand more about what you're experiencing. Could you share with me what you are experiencing right now? [*Blended empathic and open-ended response that seeks concreteness.*]

Client: I guess I haven't felt too good about coming this morning. I almost called and canceled. I feel I should be able to handle these problems with Jim [*son*] myself. Coming here is like having to admit I'm no longer capable of coping with him.

Practitioner: So you've had reservations about coming [*paraphrase*]—you feel you're admitting defeat and that perhaps you've failed or that you're inadequate—and that hurts. [*Empathic response.*]

Client: Well, yes, although I know that I need some help. It's just hard to admit it, I think. My biggest problem in this regard, however, is my husband. He feels much more strongly than I do that we should manage this problem ourselves, and he really disapproves of my coming in.

Practitioner: So even though it's painful for you, you're convinced you need some assistance with Jim, but you're torn about coming here because of your husband's attitude. I'd be interested in hearing more about that. [*Blended empathic and open-ended response.*]

In the preceding example, the practitioner initiated discussion of the client's here-and-now experiences through a blended open-ended and empathic response, following this with other empathic and blended responses to explore the client's feelings further. With the last response, the practitioner narrowed the focus to a potential obstacle to the helping process (the husband's attitude toward therapy), which could also be explored in a similar manner.

Open-ended and empathic responses may also be blended to facilitate and encourage discussion from group members about a defined topic. For instance, after using an open-ended response to solicit group feedback regarding a specified topic ("I'm wondering how you feel about..."), the practitioner can employ empathic or other facilitative responses to acknowledge the contribution of members who respond to the invitation to comment. Further, by utilizing open-ended responses, the practitioner can successively reach for comments of individual members who have not contributed ("What do you think about..., Ray?").

In the next example, the practitioner blends empathic and concrete responses to facilitate in-depth exploration. Notice how these blended responses yield behavioral referents of the problem. The empathic messages convey sensitive awareness and concern for the client's distress. The open-ended and concrete responses focus on details of a recent event and yield valuable clues that the client's rejections by women may be associated with insensitive and inappropriate social behavior, awareness of which is a prelude to formulating relevant goals. Goals thus formulated are highly relevant to the client.

Client: [*Single male, age 20.*] There has to be something wrong with me, or women wouldn't treat me like a leper. Sometimes I feel like I'm doomed to be alone the rest of my life. I'm not even sure why I came to see you. I think I'm beyond help.

Practitioner: You sound like you've about given up on yourself—as though you're utterly hopeless; but apparently part of you still clings to hope and wants to try. [*Empathic response.*]

Client: What else can I do? I can't go on like this, but I don't know how many more times I can get knocked down and get back up.

Practitioner: I sense you feel deeply hurt and discouraged at those times. Could you give me a recent example of when you felt you were being knocked down? [*Blended empathic and concrete response.*]

Client: Well, a guy I work with got me a blind date for a dance. I took her, and it was a total disaster. I know I'm no Prince Charming, but you'd think she could at least let me take her home. After we got to the dance, she ignored me the whole night and danced with other guys. Then, to add insult to injury, she went home with one of them and didn't even have the decency to tell me. There I was, wondering what had happened to her.

Practitioner: Besides feeling rejected, you must have been mad as blazes. When did you first feel you weren't hitting it off with her? [*Blended empathic and concrete response.*]

Client: I guess it was when she lit up a cigarette while we were driving to the dance. I kidded her about how she was asking for lung cancer.

Practitioner: I see. What was it about her reaction, then, that led you to believe you might not be in her good graces? [*Concrete response.*]

Client: Well, she didn't say anything. She just smoked her cigarette. I guess I really knew then that she was upset at me.

In the next example, observe how the practitioner blends empathic and concrete responses to elicit details of interaction in an initial conjoint session. Such blending is a potent technique for eliciting specific and abundant information that bears directly on clients' problems. While responses that seek concreteness elicit details, empathic responses enable practitioners to stay attuned to clients' moment-by-moment experiencing, thereby focusing on feelings that may present obstacles to the exploration.

Practitioner: You mentioned having difficulties communicating. I'd like you to give me an example of a time when you felt you weren't communicating effectively, and let's go through it step by step to see if we can understand more clearly what is happening.

Wife: Well, weekends are an example. Usually I want to go out and do something fun with the kids, and John just wants to stay home. He starts criticizing me for wanting to go, go, go.

Practitioner: Could you give me a specific example? [*Seeking concreteness.*]

Wife: Okay. Last Saturday I wanted for us all to go out to eat and to a movie, and John wanted to stay home and watch TV.

Practitioner: Before we get into what John did, let's stay with you for a moment. There you are, really wanting to go to a movie—tell me exactly what you did. [*Seeking concreteness.*]

Wife: I think I said, "John, let's take the kids out to dinner and a movie."

Practitioner: Okay. That's what you said. How did you say it? [*Seeking concreteness.*]

Wife: I expected him to say no, so I might not have said it the way I just did.

Practitioner: Turn to John, and say it the way you may have said it then. [*Seeking concreteness.*]

Wife: Okay. [*Turning to husband.*] Couldn't we go out to a movie?

Practitioner: There seems to be some doubt in your voice as to whether or not John wants to. [*Focusing observation.*]

Wife: [*Interrupting.*] I knew he wouldn't want to.

Practitioner: So you assumed he wouldn't want to go. It's as though you already knew the answer. [*To husband.*] Does the way your wife asked the question check out with the way you remembered it? [*Husband nods.*]

Practitioner: After your wife asked you about going to the movie, what did you do? [*Seeking concreteness.*]

Husband: I said, nope! I wanted to stay home and relax Saturday, and I felt we could do things at home.

Practitioner: So your answer was short. Apparently you didn't give her information about why you didn't want to go but just said no. Is that right? [*Focusing observation.*]

Husband: That's right. I didn't think she wanted to go anyway—the way she asked.

Practitioner: What were you experiencing when you said no? [*Seeking concreteness.*]

Husband: I guess I was just really tired. I have a lot of pressures from work, and I just need some time to relax. She doesn't understand that.

Practitioner: You're saying, then, "I just needed some time to get away from it all," but I take it you had your doubts as to whether she could appreciate your feelings. [*Husband nods. Turning to wife.*] Now, after your husband said no, what did you do? [*Blended empathic and concrete response.*]

Wife: I think that I started talking to him about the way he just sits around the house.

Practitioner: I sense that you felt hurt and somewhat discounted because John didn't respond the way you would have liked. [*Empathic response.*]

Wife [*nods*]: I didn't think he even cared what I wanted to do.

Practitioner: Is it fair to conclude, then, that the way in which you handled your feelings was to criticize John rather than to say, "This is what is happening to me?" [*Wife nods.*] [*Seeking concreteness.*]

Practitioner [*to husband*]: Back, then, to our example, what did you do when your wife criticized you? [*Seeking concreteness.*]

Husband: I guess I criticized her back. I told her she needed to stay home once in a while and get some work done.

The practitioner above has asked questions to enable the couple to provide a guide to the sequence of their interaction in a way that elicits key details and provides insight into unspoken assumptions and messages.

EVALUATING USE OF FOCUSING AND EXPLORING SKILLS

To gain mastery of focusing skills and other verbal following and exploring skills, it is important that you "track" the categories of your responses to determine the extent to which you are exploring problem areas in depth. By examining a portion of a session transcribed in verbatim form, you can diagram the session to identify topical areas, to determine the depth of exploration of each, and to analyze the categories of responses used. In an initial session you may find that your first attempts at interviewing take this form:

FIFTEEN-MINUTE SEGMENT OF INTERVIEW

t1	t2	t3	t4	t5	t6	t7	t8	t9	t10
OER	OER	OER	OER	OER	OER	OER	OER	OER	P
OER		OER	MP	P	MP	OER		OER	
						MP			
						CEQ			

Key: t=Topical area.
   CEQ=Closed-ended question.
   OER=Open-ended response.
   MP=Minimal prompt.
   P=Paraphrase.

In the preceding diagram, note that the practitioner used a limited number of verbal following skills and changed topics frequently, thus exploring subjects only superficially. This type of interviewing explains why beginners sometimes complain that they "just couldn't get anywhere" in sessions or that clients discussed their problems in vague terms. Such difficulties, of course, may also result in part from behaviors of clients that interfere with practitioners' efforts to focus, as we discuss later. Often, however, the practitioner's interviewing style is largely responsible for the low yield of information and the sketchy picture of the client's situation.

If you use open-ended responses to focus on selected areas and employ verbal following skills to maintain focus on these topics, a profile of a 15-minute segment of an interview would likely resemble the following:

t1	t2	t3	t4	t5
OER	OER	ER/OER	OER	CEQ
MP	ER	CEQ	ER	OER
ER	ER	ER	OER/SC	ER
A	ER	ER	ER	A
ER		ER	ER	ER
SC		MP	CEQ	
ER		P	ER	
SR		SC	A	
			SR	

Key: t=Topical area.
   ER=Empathic response.
   CEQ=Closed-ended question.
   OER=Open-ended response.
   MP=Minimal prompt.
   P=Paraphrase response.
   A=Accent response.
   SC=Seeking concreteness.
   SR=Summary response.

A diagram of an actual initial session, of course, is unlikely to be as tidy as our illustration. Other types of responses (e.g., information-giving responses) might be intermixed with exploring and focusing responses. Further, practitioners expend considerable time and effort in sessions on activities such as negotiating goals and contracting.

We recommend that you diagram and analyze segments of actual and simulated sessions many times, with the goal of assessing your focusing patterns. Doing so will assist you to make appropriate modifications in style so that you achieve the second type of profile.

Although individual sessions are easier to diagram than group or conjoint sessions, it is possible to diagram the latter to determine the extent to which you focused and assisted members of the group to focus or to refocus on pertinent topics.

Managing Obstacles to Focusing

Occasionally you may find that your efforts to focus selectively and to explore topical areas in depth are unsuccessful in yielding pertinent information. Although you have a responsibility in such instances to assess the effectiveness of your own interviewing style, you should also analyze clients' styles of communicating to determine to what extent their behaviors are interfering with your focusing efforts. As we noted in an earlier chapter, a common reason why clients seek help is that they have, but are not aware of, patterned communications or behaviors that cause difficulties in relationships. In addition, involuntary clients who do not yet perceive the relationship as helping may be inclined to avoid focusing. Also manifested in their contacts with practitioners, these repetitive behaviors can impede communication; the pursuit of practice objectives; and, pertinent to this discussion, exploration of problems. The following list includes common types of client communications that may challenge your efforts to focus in individual, family, and group sessions:

- Responding with "I don't know."
- Changing the subject or avoiding sensitive areas
- Rambling from topic to topic.
- Intellectualizing or using abstract or general terms.
- Diverting focus from the present to the past.
- Responding to questions with questions.
- Interrupting excessively.
- Failing to express opinions when asked.
- Producing excessive verbal output.
- Using humor or sarcasm to evade topics or issues.
- Verbally dominating the discussion.

You can counter repetitive client behaviors and communications that divert the focus from exploring problems by tactfully drawing them to clients' attention and assisting clients to assume behaviors that are compatible with practice objectives. It is important to recognize that until practitioners assist group members to modify behaviors that repetitively impede effective focusing and communication, groups will not move to the phase of group development wherein most of the work related to solving problems is accomplished.

Practitioners may use a number of different techniques for managing and modifying client behaviors that impede exploration. Some of these techniques include requesting the client to communicate or behave differently; teaching, modeling, and coaching clients to assume more effective communication styles; reinforcing facilitative responses; and selectively attending to functional behaviors.

Intervening to Help Clients Focus or Refocus

Communications that occur in group or conjoint sessions are not only myriad and complex but may also be distractive or irrelevant. Consequently, the practitioner's task of assisting members to explore defined topics fully, rather than meander from subject to subject, is a challenging one. Related techniques that practitioners can employ are highlighting or clarifying issues or bringing clients' attention to a comment or matter that has been overlooked. In such instances, the objective is not necessarily to explore the topic (although that may subsequently occur) but, rather, to stress or elucidate important content. The practitioner thus focuses clients' attention on communications and/or events that occurred earlier in the session or immediately preceded the practitioner's focusing response, as illustrated in the following messages:

[*To son in session with parents*]: Ray, you made an important point a moment ago that I'm not sure your parents heard. Would you please repeat your comment?

[*To individual*]: I would like to return to a remark made several moments ago when you said. I didn't want to interrupt then, but I think perhaps the remark was important enough that we should return to it now.

[*To family*]: Something happened just a minute ago as we were talking. [Describes event.] We were involved in another discussion then, but I made a mental note of it because of how deeply it seemed to affect all of you at the time. I think we should consider what happened for just a moment.

[*To group member*]: John, as you were talking a moment ago, I wasn't sure what you meant by…. Could you clarify that for me and for others in the group?

[*To group*]: A few minutes ago, we were engrossed in a discussion about…, yet we have moved away from that discussion to one that doesn't really seem to relate to our purpose for being here. I'm concerned about leaving the other subject hanging because you were working hard to find some solutions and appeared to be close to a breakthrough.

Because of the complexity of communications in group and family sessions, some inefficiency in focusing process is inescapable; however, the practitioner can sharpen the group's efforts to focus and encourage more efficient use of time by teaching focusing behavior. We suggest that practitioners actually explain the focusing role of the group and identify behaviors, such as attending, active listening, and asking open-ended questions, emphasizing that by utilizing these skills members facilitate exploration of problems. Practitioners can also foster use of these skills by giving positive feedback to group or family members when they have adequately focused on a problem, thus reinforcing their efforts.

Traditionally, practitioners have not conceived of their roles as including the *teaching* of focusing and exploring behaviors but rather have used indirect approaches, that is, guidance and modeling to encourage groups to center on specific topics or problem areas. In the past, then, groups have gradually learned these behaviors by imitating practitioners' efforts to identify and explore problems and by responding to their encouragement. As a result, in group contexts focusing has often been inefficient and haphazard, typified by members neglecting important problem areas, exploring issues superficially, and allocating an inordinate amount of time to a few group members.

Although group members usually have difficulty in learning how to focus, they should be able to delve deeply into problems by the third or fourth session, given sufficient guidance and education by practitioners. Such efforts by practitioners tend to accelerate movement of groups to maturity, a phase in which members achieve maximum therapeutic benefits. A characteristic of a group in this phase, in fact, is that members explore issues in considerable depth rather than skim the surface of many topics.

Modeled Responses to Exercise in Paraphrasing

1. "You just get so uptight in a group you don't function."

2. "So you've made some real progress in tuning in to your husband and children."

3. "Because your fears really block you when you argue with your mother, you consistently come out on the short side."

4. "You're really torn and wonder if not seeing the children very often is too high a price to pay for a divorce. You seem pretty clear, though, that if you stay with her, there won't be any improvement."

5. "So people's helpfulness here and your own skills in meeting people have helped your adjustment here."

6. "So the bottom line, as you see it, is that you're responsible for many of her problems."

ANSWERS TO EXERCISE IN IDENTIFYING CLOSED- AND OPEN-ENDED RESPONSES

STATEMENT	RESPONSE
1.	C
2.	O
3.	O
4.	C

Modeled Open-Ended Responses

1. "Could you tell me more about your wanting to impress Ralph?"

2. "What are you afraid you'd do wrong?"

3. "I'm so pleased for you. Tell me more about your job."

4. "So you have mixed feelings of resentment and guilt. Can you tell me more about those feelings?"

5. "It sounds like you feel ganged up on and really resent it. I'd like to understand those feelings better.

Could you tell me about when you last felt I took her side?"

6. "Sounds like you're feeling lost and confused about whether you want to try finding yourself. I gather you've been confused about what's been happening to you recently. I'd like to hear more about that."

Classroom Exercises for Developing Verbal Following Skills

1. (*Open- versus closed-ended responses.*) Instruct students to pair off and assign one member of each pair to play the role of "social worker." Each social worker is then instructed to conduct a three-minute interview with the other student, who is to share a real-life problem, preferably one that is not deeply personal. Instruct the social worker to employ closed-ended responses exclusively during the interview. At the conclusion of the three-minute interval, ask the students to reverse roles and conduct another three-minute interview. When the role-playing is complete, invite students to share their reactions to the consistent closed-ended responses as they attempted to disclose their problems.

2. Follow the same instructions for (1) above, except that in this exercise instruct the student in the social worker role to employ open-ended responses while interviewing the other student concerning the same problem discussed previously. After the students have reversed roles, ask them to compare their reactions to the interviews conducted using open-ended and closed-ended interviewing techniques.

3. (*Seeking concreteness.*) Play a 15-minute segment of an actual or simulated interview, stopping the tape after each message of the client. Discuss the degree of specificity in each message and identify additional information that may be needed to achieve greater clarity. Evaluate the efficacy of the practitioner's responses in eliciting clarifying information and consider other responses that may have been more productive.

4. (*Paraphrasing.*) Have the students pair off and alternate playing social worker and client in five-minute role-playing situations. Instruct students to practice paraphrasing while playing the social worker role. Students in the client role may discuss actual stressful situations in their lives or in the lives of others with whom they are closely associated. Before having the students engage in practice, the instructor may model paraphrasing with a student volunteer in the client role.

5. (*Recognizing and assessing verbal following skills.*) Transcribe a 15-minute segment of an actual or simulated audiotaped initial interview. Make copies of the typed transcription and distribute to class members. (A taped interview may be substituted for a typewritten session if desired.) Using a list of the various types of following skills delineated in this chapter, have the students analyze each response of the interviewer, identifying the type of response employed. Discuss the appropriateness of each response, and analyze its effect as reflected in the client's subsequent response. Analyze whether responses facilitated the client's expression and yielded rich or limited data. Note instances in which other responses could have been used to greater advantage. (Not all of the interviewer's responses will be verbal following responses. Some, for example, may involve explanations or answers to questions.)

Classroom Exercises for Developing Skill in Focusing

1. After dividing the class into pairs, have each pair record role-played five-minute interviews,

exchanging roles at the end of five minutes. Each student thus will play the roles of social worker and client discussing actual or simulated problems. In the practitioner's role, students are to explore one problem area in depth, employing open-ended, empathic, furthering, concrete, and closed-ended responses. After the role-playing, instruct students to review their tapes, identifying the types of responses used and ascertaining the extent to which they maintained focus and achieved depth in exploring one topical area.

2. Ask students to role-play and record actual or simulated problems in pairs for 15-minute interviews, exchanging roles so that both have opportunities to play the role of social worker. After the role-playing, instruct students to review their tapes, diagramming their focusing patterns as illustrated earlier in this chapter. Using the diagram, students should next determine the extent to which they explored topics in depth. Based on this analysis, students should be encouraged to set specific goals aimed at enhancing their skill in focusing by using certain techniques more frequently and eliminating the use of other counterproductive types of responses. Ask students to retain their diagrams for future comparisons.

3. After further practice in developing focusing skills over one week, ask students again to record 15-minute role-played interviews, exchanging roles as specified in (2) above. Students are to diagram their interviews and compare the present diagram with that completed one week earlier. Instruct students to determine the extent to which they have progressed in achieving their goals specified as part of exercise (2) and to specify additional goals that will enhance mastery of their skill.

4. Ask students to form groups according to the types of client populations they are working with in their practicum settings. Instruct the groups to develop interviewing guides that can be employed to assure that they explore relevant topical areas during initial interviews in these settings. Ask the students to compare their guidelines, citing similarities and differences.

5. Divide students into small groups and assign one student to be the leader of a five-minute taped discussion on a topic of the group's choosing. Ask the leader to facilitate discussion and to assist the group to stay on topic by utilizing empathic responding and the other verbal following skills delineated in this chapter. Ask each small group to review its tape and make observations related to the forces that occurred in the group that fostered or impeded focusing by the group. Further, ask group members to give leaders feedback as to their effective and ineffective use of skills. You may wish to do this exercise several times to give others in each group an opportunity to test their focusing skill.

NOTES

1 You will note that several of these messages could also be categorized as seeking concreteness. Messages that seek concreteness and open-ended messages are not mutually exclusive, and often overlap considerably.

Chapter 7 □ □ □

Eliminating Counterproductive Communication Patterns

IMPACTS OF COUNTERPRODUCTIVE COMMUNICATION PATTERNS

As beginning practitioners, you bring a desire to learn to be helpful and a commitment to improve. That desire and commitment will not directly translate into flawless skills that help all clients improve and appreciate your abilities. Instead, your learning will include making mistakes that make you wonder if you will ever do it all, or without great effort. Our experience is that even the most successful practitioners were once beginners, and learning from mistakes is an integral part of learning.

We focus in this chapter on verbal and nonverbal communication patterns that inhibit the helping process. The communication repertoires of aspiring practitioners usually include halting beginning practice of new skills and some response patterns that inhibit the free flow of information and negatively affect helping relationships. Such responses impede progress each time they occur, eliciting, for example, defensiveness, hostility, or silence. Consistent use of such responses can block growth, precipitate premature terminations, or cause deterioration in clients' functioning. The findings of a research study by Nugent (1992) have documented the inhibitory impact on helping relationships of the types of responses discussed in this chapter. Attaining competence, therefore, requires learning to avoid such messages and behaviors. This chapter will enable you to identify and eliminate from your repertoire such counterproductive verbal and nonverbal communications.

ELIMINATING NONVERBAL BARRIERS TO EFFECTIVE COMMUNICATION

Nonverbal behaviors strongly influence interactions between people. The importance of this medium of communication is underscored by numerous research findings that counselors' nonverbal interview behavior contributes significantly to ratings of counselor effectiveness. Nonverbal cues, which serve to confirm or to deny messages conveyed verbally, are in large part beyond the conscious awareness of participants. In fact, nonverbal cues may produce "leakage" by transmitting information the sender did not intend to communicate. Facial expressions, such as a blush, a sneer, or a look of shock or dismay, convey much more about the practitioner's attitude toward the client than what is said. In fact, if there is a discrepancy between the practitioner's verbal and nonverbal communication, the client is more likely to discredit the verbal, for people learn through myriad transactions with others that nonverbal cues more accurately indicate feelings than do spoken words.

Physical Attending

Beginning practitioners are often relatively unaware of their nonverbal behaviors, and they may not as yet have learned to consciously use these behaviors to advantage in conveying caring, understanding, and respect. Therefore, mastering physical attending, a basic skill critical to the helping process, is an initial learning task. Physical attentiveness to another person is communicated by receptive behaviors, such as facing the client squarely, leaning forward, maintaining eye contact, and remaining relaxed. Attending also requires practitioners to be fully present, that is, to keep in moment-to-moment contact with the client through disciplined attention.

Cultural Nuances of Nonverbal Cues

To consciously use nonverbal behaviors to full advantage in transcultural relationships, practitioners must be aware that different cultural groups ascribe varied meanings to certain nonverbal behaviors. Eye-to-eye contact, for example, is expected among communicating persons in mainstream American culture. People who avoid eye-to-eye contact, in fact, may be viewed as untrustworthy or evasive. Many Native Americans, however, regard direct gazing as an intrusion of privacy, and it is important, therefore, to employ minimal eye-to-eye contact with this cultural group.[1]

A practitioner's failure to understand the significance of the nonverbal behavior of Asian clients may pose a major barrier to effective communication. Many Asian clients tend to view helping professionals as authorities who can solve their problems (often presented as physical symptoms) by providing advice. Because Asian cultural patterns prescribe deference to authority, the Asian client may speak little unless spoken to by the practitioner, who may mistakenly perceive what the client regards as being respectful as being passive, silent, and ingratiating. Consequently, "Long gaps of silence may occur as the client waits patiently for the therapist to structure the interview, take charge, and thus provide the solution" (Tsui & Schultz, 1985, p. 565). Such gaps in communication engender anxiety in both parties that may undermine the development of rapport and defeat the helping process. Further, failure to correctly interpret the client's nonverbal behavior may lead the practitioner to conclude erroneously that the client has flat affect (i.e., little emotionality). Given these potential hazards, practitioners must be more active and directive with Asian clients, and they must focus on role expectations, a matter we discuss at more length in Chapter 13.

Other Nonverbal Behaviors

Barriers that prevent the practitioner from staying in psychological contact with the client can be caused by preoccupation with judgments or evaluations about the client or by inner pressures to find immediate solutions to the client's problems. Reduced focus on the client can also result from being preoccupied with oneself while practicing new skills. Further, extraneous noise, a ringing phone, an inadequate interviewing room, or lack of privacy can also interfere with the practitioner's being psychologically present.

Lack of concern for the client can also be conveyed by numerous undesirable behaviors and revealing postural cues. For example, staring vacantly, looking out the window, frequently glancing at the clock, yawning, fidgeting convey inattention; trembling hands or rigid posture may communicate anger or anxiety. These and a host of other behavioral cues that convey messages such as a lack of interest, disapproval, shock, or condemnation are readily perceived by most clients, many of whom are highly sensitive to criticism or rejection in any form.

Taking Inventory of Nonverbal Patterns of Responding

To assist you in taking inventory of your own styles of responding to clients, we have listed desirable and undesirable nonverbal behaviors in Table 7-1. You will probably find that you have a mixed bag of nonverbal responses, some of which have the potential to enhance helping relationships and foster client progress and others that often indicate beginning practitioner nervousness which may block your clients from freely disclosing information and otherwise retard the flow of the helping process. You thus have a threefold task: (1) to assess your repetitive nonverbal behaviors; (2) to eliminate nonverbal styles that hinder effective communication; and (3) to sustain and perhaps increase desirable nonverbal behaviors.

TABLE 7-1 INVENTORY OF PRACTITIONER'S NONVERBAL COMMUNICATION

DESIRABLE	UNDESIRABLE
Facial expressions:	
Direct eye contact (except when culturally proscribed)	Avoidance of eye contact
Warmth and concern reflected in facial expression	Staring or fixating on person or object
Eyes at same level as clients	Lifting eyebrow critically
Appropriately varied and animated facial expressions	Eye level higher or lower than client's
Mouth relaxed; occasional smiles	Nodding head excessively
	Yawning
	Frozen or rigid facial expressions
	Inappropriate slight smile
	Pursing or biting lips
Posture:	
Arms and hands moderately expressive; appropriate gestures	Rigid body position; arms tightly folded
Body leaning slightly forward; attentive but relaxed	Body turned at an angle to client
	Fidgeting with hands
	Squirming or rocking in chair
	Slouching or placing feet on desk
	Hand or fingers over mouth
	Pointing finger for emphasis
Voice:	
Clearly audible but not loud	Mumbling or speaking inaudibly
Warmth in tone of voice	Monotonic voice
Voice modulated to reflect nuances of feeling and emotional tone of client messages	Halting speech
Moderate speech tempo	Frequent grammatical errors
	Prolonged silences
	Excessively animated speech
	Slow, rapid, or staccato speech
	Nervous laughter
	Consistent clearing of throat
	Speaking loudly
Physical proximity:	
Three to five feet between chairs	Excessive closeness or distance
	Talking across desk or other barrier

There is a checklist at the end of this chapter for use in training or supervision to obtain feedback on nonverbal aspects of attending. Given opportunity to review a videotape of your performance in actual or simulated interviews and/or to receive behaviorally specific feedback from supervisors and peers, you can adequately master physical aspects of attending in a relatively brief time. Review of your taped performance may reveal that you are already manifesting many of the desirable physical attending behaviors listed in Table 7-1. Further, you may possess personal nonverbal mannerisms that are particularly helpful to you in establishing relationships with others, such as a friendly grin or a relaxed, easy manner. As you take inventory of your nonverbal behaviors, elicit feedback from others regarding both your desirable and undesirable nonverbal behaviors. When appropriate, increase the frequency of positive behaviors that you have identified and especially cultivate the quality of warmth, which we discussed in Chapter 3.

As you review videotapes, pay particular attention to your nonverbal responses at those moments when you experienced pressure or tension, which will assist you in determining whether your responses were counterproductive. All beginning interviewers experience moments of discomfort in their first contacts with clients, and nonverbal behaviors are an index of their comfort level. As you review your work, you may notice that under pressure you respond with humor, fidget, change voice inflection, assume a rigid body posture, or manifest other nervous mannerisms. Making an effort to become aware of and to eliminate obvious signs of anxiety is an important step in achieving mastery of your nonverbal responding.

ELIMINATING VERBAL BARRIERS TO COMMUNICATION

Many types of ineffective verbal responses prevent clients from exploring problems and sharing freely with the practitioner. We are assisted here by reactance theory which suggests that clients will act to protect valued freedoms. Such freedoms can include the freedom to one's own opinions and inclination to action. When such valued freedoms are threatened, clients will often withdraw, argue, or move to a superficial topic. The following list identifies common verbal barriers that usually have an immediate negative effect upon communications and thus prevent clients from revealing pertinent information and working on problems:

1. Moralizing.
2. Advising and giving suggestions or solutions prematurely.
3. Trying to convince client about right point of view through logical arguments, lecturing, instructing, arguing.
4. Judging, criticizing, or placing blame.
5. Analyzing, diagnosing, making glib or dogmatic interpretations.
6. Reassuring, sympathizing, consoling, excusing.
7. Using sarcasm or employing humor that is distractive or makes light of clients' problems.
8. Threatening, warning, or counterattacking.

The negative effect of certain types of responses is not always apparent because the client does not manifest untoward reactions at the time or because the retarding effect upon the helping process cannot be observed in a single transaction.

In order to assess the effect of responses, then, the practitioner must determine the frequency of detrimental responses and evaluate the overall impact of such responses on the helping process. Frequent use of some types of responses by the practitioner indicates the presence of counterproductive patterns of communication such as the following:

9. Using questions inappropriately.
10. Interrupting inappropriately or excessively.
11. Dominating interaction.
12. Fostering safe social interaction.
13. Responding infrequently.

14. Parroting or overusing certain phrases or clichés.
15. Dwelling on the remote past.
16. Going on fishing expeditions.

Individual responses that fall within these patterns may or may not be ineffective when employed singularly; when employed extensively in lieu of varied response patterns, however, such responses inhibit the natural flow of a session and limit the richness of information revealed.

Verbal Barriers to Effective Communication

1. Moralizing and Sermonizing by Using "Shoulds" and "Oughts"

"You shouldn't have done that."

"You're too young to get married."

"You should try to understand your parents' position. They really have your welfare at heart."

"You ought to pay your bills."

Sometimes practitioners have strong views about appropriate ways of looking at client problems and resolving them. However, moralizing, sermonizing, admonishing, or otherwise passing judgment is an unethical and ineffective way to be helpful to clients in making choices. Should and ought messages, which imply that clients have a duty to some vague, external authority, have often been used effectively by significant others in clients' lives to make them feel guilty or obligated. Moralizing responses by practitioners have the same effect, eliciting feelings of guilt and resentment. Such messages also communicate lack of trust—"I'll tell you what to do because you're not wise enough to know." When experiencing such criticism and lack of confidence in their ability and judgment, clients are unlikely to be receptive to assessing their own positions or to considering others. We know from reactance theory that such efforts are likely to boomerang as clients act to protect their freedom to think and act by opposing such pressures.[2]

2. Advising and Giving Suggestions or Solutions Prematurely

"I suggest that you move to a new place since you have had so many difficulties here."

"I think you need to try a new approach with your daughter. Let me suggest that …"

"I think it would be best for you to try using time-out…"

"Since your boyfriend is such a loser, why don't you try to make some relationships with other men?"

Clients often seek advice, and appropriately timed advice can be an important helping tool. However, untimely advice often elicits opposition for similar reasons as moralizing efforts considered above. Interestingly, even when clients solicit advice in early phases of the helping process, they often react negatively when they receive such advice because recommended solutions based on superficial information often do not address their real needs. Further, because clients often are burdened and preoccupied with little-understood conflicts, feelings, and pressures, they are not ready to take action on their problems. For these reasons, after offering premature advice, practitioners may observe clients replying with responses such as "Yes, but I've already tried that," or "That won't work."

Practitioners often dispense advice prematurely because they feel pressure to provide quick answers or solutions for clients who unrealistically expect magical answers and instant relief from problems that have plagued them for long periods of time. Beginning practitioners also experience inner pressure to dispense solutions to clients' problems, mistakenly believing that their new role demands that they, like physicians, prescribe a treatment regimen. They thus run the risk of giving advice before they have conducted a thorough exploration of the problem. Instead of dispensing wisdom, however, a major role of practitioners is to create and shape processes with clients in which they engage in mutual discovery of problems and solutions, work that will take time and concentrated effort.

In the helping process, the timing and form of recommendations are all important. Generally, advice should be offered sparingly, only after thoroughly exploring a problem and clients' ideas regarding possible solutions. At that point, practitioners may serve as consultants, tentatively sharing ideas regarding solutions to supplement those developed by clients. Pressures from clients to influence practitioners to dispense premature knowledge would deprive them of developing effective solutions to these problems. Practitioners should also stress clients' roles in helping to discover and to "tailor-make" solutions that fit their unique problems.

Client expectations that they will receive early advice may also occur if practitioners have not appropriately clarified roles and expectations about mutual participation in generating possible solutions to further the growth and self-confidence of clients. Assuming a position of superiority and quickly providing solutions for problems without encouraging clients to formulate possible courses of action fosters dependency and stifles creative thinking. Freely dispensing advice also minimizes or ignores clients' strengths and potentials, and many clients may be expected to respond with inner resentment. In addition, clients who have not been actively involved in planning their own courses of action may lack motivation to implement the advice given by practitioners. Further, when advice does not remedy a problem, as it often doesn't, clients may blame practitioners and disown responsibility for an unfavorable outcome.

3. Trying to Convince Client About Right Point of View Through Lecturing, Instructing, Arguing

"Let's look at the facts about drugs."

"Remember that you have some responsibility for solving problems, too."

"Taking that course of action will only get you in more difficulty."

"That attitude won't get you anywhere."

Clients sometimes consider courses of action which appear to practitioners to be unsafe, illegal, or contrary to client goals. However, attempting to convince clients through arguing, instructing, and the like often provoke the kind of boomerang effect described above. According to reactance theory, clients will attempt to defend valued freedoms when these are threatened. For some clients (especially adolescents for whom independent thinking is associated with a developmental stage), deferring to or agreeing with practitioners is tantamount to giving up individuality or freedom. In vigorously attempting to persuade clients to another point of view, practitioners also often foster power struggles, thereby perpetuating dynamics that have previously occurred in clients' personal relationships. By arguing, practitioners also ignore feelings and views of clients, focusing instead on "being right," which may engender feelings of resentment, alienation, or hostility. Hence such efforts are both unethical and ineffective. Persuasion in the sense of helping clients to have accurate information from which to make decisions with informed consent can be an ethical intervention. When clients contemplate actions which are contrary to their own goals, or will endanger themselves or others, then an effort to persuade can be an ethical intervention. Such efforts should not be focused on the one "pet" solution of the practitioner, as suggested above, but rather should assist the client in examining the advantages and disadvantages of several options, including those with which the practitioner may disagree (Rooney, 1992). Hence, the effort is not to convince, but rather to assist clients in making informed decisions.

4. Judging, Criticizing, or Placing Blame

"You're wrong about that."

"Running away from home was a bad mistake."

"One of your problems is that you're not willing to consider another point of view."

"You're not thinking straight."

Responses that evaluate and show disapproval are detrimental to clients and to the helping process. Clients usually respond defensively and sometimes counterattack when they experience criticism by practitioners; further, they often cut off any meaningful communication with practitioners. Intimidated by a practitioner's greater expertise, some clients also accept negative evaluations as accurate reflections of their poor judgment or lack of worth or value. In making such negative judgments about clients, practitioners violate the basic social work values of nonjudgmental attitude and acceptance.

5. Analyzing, Diagnosing, Making Glib or Dramatic Interpretations; Labeling Clients' Behavior

"You're behaving that way because you're angry at your husband."

"Your attitude may have kept you from giving their ideas a fair chance."

"That is passive-aggressive behavior."

"You are really hostile today."

Used sparingly and appropriately timed, interpretation of the dynamics of behavior is a potent change-oriented skill (see Chapter 19). However, even accurate interpretations that focus on purposes or meanings of behavior substantially beyond clients' levels of conscious awareness engender resistance and are doomed to failure. When stated dogmatically (e.g., "I know what's wrong with you," or "how you feel," or "what your real motives are"), interpretations also present a threat to clients, causing them to feel exposed or trapped. When a glib interpretation is thrust upon them, clients often expend their energies disconfirming the interpretation, explaining themselves, or making angry rebuttals rather than working on the problem at hand.

Using social work jargon, such as fixation, transference, resistance, reinforcement, repression, passive, or neurotic, and a host of other terms to describe the behavior of clients in their presence is also destructive to the helping process, often confusing or bewildering clients and creating resistance. These terms also oversimplify complex phenomena and psychic mechanisms and stereotype clients, thereby obliterating their uniqueness. In addition, these sweeping generalizations provide no operational definition of clients' problems, nor do they suggest avenues for modification of behavior. If clients accept practitioners' restricted definitions of their problems, they may then define themselves in the same terms as those used by practitioners (e.g., "I am a passive person," or "I have a schizoid personality"). This type of stereotypic labeling often causes clients to view themselves as "sick" and their situations as hopeless, thus providing them a ready excuse for not working on problems.

6. Reassuring, Sympathizing, Consoling, Excusing

"You'll feel better tomorrow."

"Don't worry, things will work out."

"You probably didn't do anything to aggravate the situation."

"I really feel sorry for you."

When used selectively and with justification, well-timed reassurance can engender much needed hope and support.[3] In glibly reassuring clients that "things will work out," "everybody has problems," or "things aren't as bleak as they seem," however, practitioners avoid exploring clients' feelings of despair, anger, hopelessness, or helplessness. Situations faced by clients are often grim, with no immediate analgesics or relief at hand. Rather than glossing over clients' feelings and seeking to avoid discomfort, it is the task of practitioners to explore distressing feelings and to assist clients in acknowledging painful realities.

Reassuring clients prematurely or without genuine basis often serves the purposes of practitioners more than of clients and, in fact, may represent efforts by practitioners to dissuade clients from their troubling feelings. Such reassurance thus serves to restore the comfort level and equilibrium of practitioners rather than to help clients. Rather than fostering hope, glib reassurances also convey a lack of understanding of clients' feelings and raise doubts about the authenticity of practitioners, causing clients to react with thoughts such as "It's easy for you to say that, but you don't know how very frightened I really am," or "You're just saying that so I'll feel better." In addition, responses that excuse clients (e.g., "You're not to blame") or sympathize with their position (e.g., "I can see exactly why you feel that way; I think I would probably have done the same thing") often have the effect of unwittingly reinforcing inappropriate behavior or reducing clients' anxiety and motivation to work on problems.

7. Using Sarcasm or Employing Humor That Is Distractive or Makes Light of Clients' Problems

"Get up on the wrong side of the bed?"

"It seems to me that we've been all through this before."

"You really fell for that line."

"You think you have a problem."

Humor is an important therapeutic tool, bringing relief and sometimes perspective to work that may otherwise be tense and tedious. Excessive use of humor, however, is distractive, keeping the content of the session on a superficial level and interfering with therapeutic objectives. Sarcasm often emanates from unrecognized hostility that tends to provoke counterhostility in clients.

8. Threatening, Warning, or Counterattacking

"You better ... or else!"

"If you don't ... you'll be sorry."

"If you know what's good for you, you'll ..."

Sometimes clients consider actions which would endanger themselves or others or are illegal. In such instances, alerting clients to potential consequences is an ethical and appropriate intervention. However, conveying threats of the sort described above often produces a kind of oppositional behavior which exacerbates an already strained situation. Still, even the most well-intentioned practitioners may bristle or respond defensively under the pressure of verbal abuse, accusatory or blaming responses, or challenges to their integrity, competence, motives, or authority. Practitioners conducting group sessions with adolescents, for instance, can testify that provocative behavior of this client population may defeat even herculean efforts to respond appropriately.

Whatever the dynamics behind provocative behavior, a defensive response by practitioners is counterproductive, often duplicating the destructive pattern of responses that clients have typically elicited and experienced from others. To achieve competence, therefore, it is important that you master your own natural defensive reactions and evolve effective ways of dealing with negative feelings. Empathic communication, for example, produces a cathartic release of negative feelings, defusing a strained situation, and permitting a more rational emotional exploration of factors that underlie clients' feelings.

9. Stacking Questions

In exploring problems, practitioners should use facilitative questions that assist clients to reveal detailed information about specific problem areas. However, when practitioners ask several questions in succession, they diffuse their focus on specific content areas, confusing and distracting clients, as illustrated in the following messages:

"When you don't feel you have control of situations, what goes on inside of you? What do you think about? What do you do?"

"Have you thought about where you are going to live? Is that one of your biggest concerns, or is there another that takes priority?"

Adequately answering even one of the foregoing questions would require an extended response by a client. Rather than focusing on one question, however, clients often respond superficially and nonspecifically to the practitioner's multiple inquiry, omitting important information in the process. Stacked questions thus have "low yield" and are unproductive and inefficient in gathering relevant information.

10. Asking Leading Questions

Leading questions are those with hidden or under-the-table agendas designed to induce clients to agree with a particular view or to adopt a solution that practitioners deem to be in clients' best interests. For example:

"Do you think you've really tried to get along with your wife?"

"You don't really mean that, do you?"

"Aren't you too young to move out on your own?"

"Don't you think that arguing with your mother will provoke her to come down on you as she has done in the past?"

In actuality, such leading questions often obscure legitimate concerns that practitioners should discuss with clients. Practitioners conceal their feelings and opinions about such matters, presenting them obliquely in the form of solutions (e.g., "Don't you think you ought to…") in hope that the leading questions will lead clients to desired conclusions. It is an error, however, to assume that clients will not see through such maneuvers. Clients, in fact, often discern the practitioner's motives and inwardly resist having views or directives imposed upon them under the guise of leading questions. Nevertheless, to avoid conflict or controversy with the practitioner, they may express feeble agreement or may simply divert the discussion to another topic.

By contrast, when practitioners authentically assume responsibility for concerns they wish clients to consider, they enhance the likelihood that clients will respond receptively. In addition, questions can be raised which are not slanted to imply the "correct" answer from the practitioner's viewpoint. For example, "How have you attempted to come to agreement with your wife?" would

not contain the indication of the "right" answer found in the first question above. Similarly, the last question above could be rephrased "I am not clear how you see arguing with your mother as likely to be more successful than it has been in the past."

11. Interrupting Inappropriately or Excessively

Beginning practitioners are often excessively worried about covering all items on their and their agency's agenda ("What will I tell my supervisor?"). To ensure focus on relevant problem areas, practitioners must at times interrupt clients. To be effective, however, interruptions must be purposive, well timed, and smoothly executed. Interruptions are detrimental to the helping process when they are abrupt or divert clients from exploring pertinent problem areas. Frequent untimely interruptions tend to annoy clients, stifle spontaneous expression, and hinder exploration of problems.

12. Dominating Interaction

At times, practitioners may dominate interaction by talking too much or by excessively asking closed-ended questions, thus assuming the initiative for discussions rather than placing this responsibility with clients. Domineering behaviors by practitioners also include frequently offering advice, pressuring clients to improve, presenting lengthy arguments to convince clients, frequently interrupting, and so on. Some practitioners are also prone to behave as though they are all knowing, failing to convey respect for clients' points of view or capacities to solve problems. Such dogmatic and authoritarian behavior discourages clients from expressing themselves and fosters a one-up, one-down relationship in which clients feel at a great disadvantage and resent the practitioner's supercilious demeanor.

Practitioners should monitor the relative distribution of participation by all persons (including themselves) who are involved in individual, family, or group sessions. Although clients naturally vary in their levels of verbal participation and assertiveness, all group members should have equal opportunity to share information, concerns, and views in the helping process. Practitioners have a responsibility to ensure this opportunity.

As a general guideline, clients should consume more "speaking time" than practitioners in the helping process, although during initial sessions with many Asian American clients practitioners must be more directive than with Anglo clients, as we discussed earlier. Sometimes practitioners defeat practice objectives in group or conjoint sessions by dominating interaction through such behaviors as speaking for members, focusing more on some members than others, or giving speeches.

Even practitioners who are *not* particularly verbal may dominate sessions that include reserved or nonassertive clients as a means of averting their own discomfort with silence and passivity. Although it is natural to be more active with reticent or withdrawn clients than with those who are more verbal, practitioners must avoid dominating the interaction. Using facilitative responses that draw clients out is an effective method of minimizing silence and passivity.

When review of one of your taped sessions reveals that you have monopolized interaction, it is important that you explore the reasons for your behavior. Identify the specific responses that were authoritarian or domineering and the situations that preceded those responses. Also examine the clients' style of relating for clues regarding your own reactions, and analyze the feelings you were experiencing at the time. Based on your review and assessment of your performance, plan a strategy to modify your own style of relating by substituting facilitative responses for ineffective ones. It may also be necessary to focus on and to explore the passive or nonassertive behavior of clients with the objective of contracting with them to increase their participation in the helping process.

13. Fostering Safe Social Interaction   Channeling or keeping discussions focused on safe topics that exclude feelings and minimize self-disclosures is inimical to the helping process. Social chit-chat about the weather, news, hobbies, mutual interests or acquaintances, and the like tends to foster a social rather than a therapeutic relationship. In contrast to the lighter and more diffuse communication characteristic of a social relationship, helpful, growth-producing relationships are characterized by sharp focus and specificity.

In the main, safe social interaction in the helping process should be avoided. It is important to note two qualifications to this general rule: (1) discussion of safe topics may be utilized to assist children or adolescents to lower defenses and risk increasing openness, thereby assisting practitioners to cultivate a quasi-friend role with such clients; (2) a brief discussion of conventional topics may be appropriate and helpful as part of the getting acquainted or warm-up period of initial sessions or during early portions of subsequent sessions.[4] A warm-up period is particularly important when engaging clients from ethnic groups for which such informal openings are the cultural norm, as we discussed in Chapter 3.

Even when you try to avoid inappropriate social interaction, however, some clients may resist your attempts to move the discussion to a topic that is relevant to the problems they are experiencing and to the purposes of the helping process. Techniques for managing such situations are found in later chapters of the book.

14. Responding Passively   Monitoring the frequency of your responses in individual, conjoint, or group sessions is an important task. As a practitioner, you have an ethical responsibility to utilize fully the limited contact time you have with clients in pursuing practice objectives and promoting their general well-being. Relatively inactive practitioners, however, usually ignore fruitful moments that could be explored to promote clients' growth and allow the focus of a session to stray to inappropriate or unproductive content. To be maximally helpful, practitioners must give structure to the helping process by developing contracts with clients that specify respective responsibilities of both participants, engaging clients in a process of identifying and exploring problems, formulating goals, and delineating tasks to alleviate clients' difficulties. To provide form and direction to the helping process, thereby maximizing change opportunities, you must be consistently active in structuring your work with clients.

Inactivity by practitioners contributes to counterproductive processes and failures in problem solving. One deleterious effect, for example, is that clients lose confidence in practitioners when practitioners fail to intervene by helping them with situations that are destructive to themselves or to others. Confidence is particularly eroded by the failure of practitioners to intervene when clients communicate destructively in conjoint or group sessions.

Although practitioners' activity per se is important, the quality of their moment-by-moment responses is also critical. Practitioners significantly diminish their effectiveness by neglecting to utilize or by underutilizing facilitative responses.

15. Parroting or Overusing Certain Phrases or Clichés

Parroting a message often irritates clients, prompting at times a response of "Well, yes, I just said that." Rather than merely repeating clients' words, it is important that practitioners use fresh words that capture the essence of clients' messages and place them in sharper perspective. Practitioners generally should also refrain from punctuating their communications with superfluous phrases. The distracting effect of such phrases can be observed in the following message: "You know, a lot of people wouldn't come in for help. It tells me, you know, that you realize that you have a problem, you know, and want to work on it. Do you know what I mean?"

Frequent use of such phrases as "you know," "okay?" ("Let's work on this task, okay?"), and "stuff" ("We went to town, and stuff"), or "that's

neat," can be very annoying to some clients (and practitioners, for that matter). Further, if used in excess, the same may be said of some of the faddish clichés that have permeated today's language, such as "awesome," "rad," "dork," "cool," "nerd," or "dude."

Another mistake practitioners sometimes make is to "overrelate" to youth by using adolescent jargon to excess. Adolescents tend to perceive such communication as phony and the practitioner as inauthentic, which hinders rather than facilitates the development of a working relationship.

16. Dwelling on the Remote Past

Practitioners' verbal responses may focus on the past, present, or future. Helping professionals differ regarding the amount of emphasis they believe should be accorded to gathering historical facts about clients. Focusing largely on the present is vital, however, for clients can change only their present circumstances, behaviors, and feelings. Permitting individuals, groups, couples, or families to dwell on the past may reinforce diversionary tactics employed to avoid dealing with painful aspects of present difficulties and with the need for change. It is important to recognize that often implied in messages about the past are feelings the client is currently experiencing related to the past. For example:

Client [*with trembling voice*]: He used to make me so angry.

Practitioner: There was a time when he really infuriated you. As you think about the past, even now it seems to stir up some of the anger and hurt you felt.

Thus, changing a client's statement from past to present tense often yields rich information about clients' present feelings and problems. The same may be said of bringing future-oriented statements of clients to the present (e.g., "How do you feel now about the future event you're describing?"). The point is that it is not only possible but also often productive to shift the focus to the present experiencing of clients even when historical facts are being elicited to illuminate client problems.

17. Going on "fishing" expeditions. A danger for beginning (and many experienced) practitioners is pursuing content which is tangentially related to client concerns, issues of client and family safety, or legal mandates. Such content may relate to pet theories of practitioners or agencies and be puzzling to clients if their connection to the concerns which have brought them into contact is not clear. Consequently, it is recommended that practitioners explain the relevance of questions in new areas far afield from client concerns, safety, and mandates.

GAUGING THE EFFECTIVENESS OF YOUR RESPONSES

The preceding discussion should assist you in identifying ineffective patterned communications you may have been employing. Since most learners typically ask closed-ended questions excessively, frequently change the subject, and recommend solutions before completing a thorough exploration of clients' problems, you should particularly watch for these patterns. In addition, you will need to monitor your interviewing style for idiosyncratic counterproductive patterns of responding.

The manual that is provided for instructors who use this book contains classroom exercises designed to assist students to recognize and eliminate ineffective responses. Further, since identifying ineffective styles of interviewing requires selective focusing upon the frequency and patterning of responses, you will find it helpful to analyze extended segments of taped sessions using the form, "Assessing Verbal Barriers to Communication," found at the conclusion of the chapter.

One way of gauging the effectiveness of your responses is to carefully observe clients' reactions immediately following your response. Because of

the number of clients involved in group and family sessions, you will often receive varied and nonverbal cues regarding the relative effectiveness of your responses to engage clients in these systems. As you assess your messages, keep in mind that a response is probably helpful if clients respond in one of the following ways:

- Continue to explore the problem or stay on the topic.

- Express pent-up emotions related to the problematic situation.

- Engage in deeper self-exploration and self-experiencing.

- Spontaneously volunteer more personally relevant material.

- Verbally or nonverbally affirm the validity of your response.

By contrast, a response may be too confrontive, poorly timed, or off target if clients respond in one of the following ways:

- Verbally or nonverbally disconfirm your response.

- Change the subject.

- Ignore the message.

- Appear mixed up or confused.

- Become more superficial, more impersonal, more emotionally detached, or more defensive.

- Argue or express anger rather than examining the relevance of the feelings involved.

In analyzing practitioner–client interactions, it is important to keep in mind that the participants mutually influence each other. Thus, a response by either person in an individual interview affects the following expressions of the other person. In group and conjoint sessions, the communications of each person, including the practitioner, also affect the responses of all other participants; in a group situation, however, the influence of messages on subsequent responses of other members is sometimes difficult to detect because of the complexity of the communications.

With respect to the mutual-influence process, beginning interviewers often reinforce unproductive client responses through responding indiscriminately or haphazardly or letting pass without comment positive responses that support practice objectives or reflect growth. Novice practitioners are also sometimes jolted as they realize the extent to which they have allowed clients to control sessions through dysfunctional or manipulative behaviors. As a beginning practitioner, then, it is extremely important that you monitor and review your moment-by-moment transactions with clients with a view toward avoiding getting caught in ongoing ineffective or destructive communication perpetuated by yourself and the client.

Although beginning practitioners encounter ineffective patterns of communication in individual interviews, they are even more likely to encounter recurring dysfunctional communications in groups or in conjoint sessions with spouses or family members. In fact, orchestrating an effective conjoint interview or group meeting often proves a challenge to even advanced practitioners because of clients' rampant use of ineffective communications, which may engender intense anger, defensiveness, and confusion among family or group members.

In summary, you have a twofold task of monitoring, analyzing, and eliminating your own ineffective responses while observing, managing, and modifying ineffective responses by clients—a rather tall order. Although modifying dysfunctional communication of clients requires advanced skill, you can eliminate your own barriers in a relatively short time. You can accelerate your progress by also eliminating ineffective styles of responding and testing out new skills in your private life. It is unfortunate that many practitioners compartmentalize and limit their helping skills to work with clients and continue to use ineffective styles with professional colleagues, friends, and families.

It is our experience that practitioners who have not fully integrated the helping skills in their private lives do not relate as effectively to their clients as do practitioners who have fully implemented and assimilated them as a part of their general style of relating in all situations. It is our conviction, in fact, that to adequately master essential skills and to fully tap their potential in assisting clients, practitioners must promote their own interpersonal competence and personality integration, thereby modeling for the client the self-actualized or fully functioning person. Pursuing this personal goal prepares practitioners for one of their major tasks or roles: teaching clients new skills of communicating and relating.

THE CHALLENGE OF LEARNING NEW SKILLS

Because of the unique nature of the helping process, establishing and maintaining a therapeutic relationship requires highly disciplined efforts. Moment by moment, transaction by transaction, the practitioner must sharply focus on the needs and problems of clients. The success of each transaction is measured by the practitioner's adroitness in consciously applying specific skills to move the process toward therapeutic objectives.

Interestingly, one of the major threats to learning new skills emanates from student fear that in relinquishing old styles of relating they are giving up an intangible, irreplaceable part of themselves. Similarly, students who have previously engaged in social work practice may experience fear related to the fact that they have developed methods or styles of relating that have influenced and "moved" clients in the past; thus, giving up these response patterns may mean surrendering a hard-won feeling of competency. These fears are often exacerbated when the focus of instruction and supervision in the classroom and practicum is predominately upon eliminating errors and ineffective interventions and responses rather than on developing new skills or increasingly employing positive

ASSESSING VERBAL BARRIERS TO COMMUNICATION

Directions: In reviewing each 15-minute sample of taped interviews, tally your use of ineffective responses by placing marks in appropriate cells.

15-MINUTE TAPED SAMPLES	1	2	3	4
1. Moralizing, sermonizing ("shoulds," "oughts")				
2. Advising prematurely				
3. Convincing, lecturing, instructing, arguing, intellectualizing				
4. Judging, criticizing, or blaming				
5. Analyzing, diagnosing, making glib interpretations; labeling behavior				
6. Reassuring, sympathizing, consoling, excusing				
7. Using sarcasm or employing distractive humor				
8. Threatening, warning, counterattacking				
9. Using excessive closed-ended questions				
10. Stacking questions				
11. Asking leading questions				
12. Using phrases repetitively (e.g., "OK," "you know," "that's neat"). List:				
13. Going on "fishing" expeditions				
Other responses that impede communication. List:				

ASSESSING PHYSICAL ATTENDING BEHAVIORS

	COMMENTS
1. Direct eye contact 0 1 2 3 4	
2. Warmth and concern reflected in facial expression 0 1 2 3 4	
3. Eyes on same level as clients' 0 1 2 3 4	
4. Appropriately varied and animated facial expressions 0 1 2 3 4	
5. Arms and hands moderately expressive; appropriate gestures 0 1 2 3 4	
6. Body leaning slightly forward; attentive but relaxed 0 1 2 3 4	
7. Voice clearly audible but not loud 0 1 2 3 4	
8. Warmth in tone of voice 0 1 2 3 4	
9. Voice modulated to reflect nuances of feelings and emotional tone of client messages 0 1 2 3 4	
10. Moderate tempo of speech 0 1 2 3 4	
11. Absence of distractive behaviors (fidgeting, yawning, gazing out window, looking at watch) 0 1 2 3 4	
12. Other 0 1 2 3 4	

Rating Scale:
0=Poor, needs marked improvement.
1=Weak, needs substantial improvement.
2=Minimally acceptable, room for growth.
3=Generally high level with few lapses.
4=Consistently high level.

responses or interventions with clients. Learners may thus receive considerable feedback about their errors but receive inadequate input regarding their effective responses or styles of relating. Consequently, they may feel vulnerable and stripped of defenses (just as clients do) and experience more keenly the loss of something familiar.

As a learner, it is important that you develop your capacity to openly and nondefensively consider constructive feedback regarding ineffective or even destructive styles of relating or intervening. However, it is also important that you assume responsibility for eliciting positive feedback from educators and peers regarding the positive moment-by-moment responses you make. Remember that supervision time is limited and that responsibility for utilizing that time effectively and for acquiring competency necessarily rests equally with you and your practicum instructor. It is also vital that you take steps to monitor your own growth systematically by reviewing audio and videotapes, by taking frequency counts of desired and undesired responses, and by comparing your responses against guidelines for constructing effective messages contained in the book. Perhaps the single most impor-

tant requirement for you in furthering your competency is to assume responsibility for advancing your own skill level by consistently monitoring your responses and practicing proven skills.

Most of the skills delineated in this book are not easy to master. Competent practitioners have spent years in perfecting their ability to sensitively and fully attune themselves to the inner experiencing of clients, in furthering their capacity to share their own experiencing in an authentic, helpful manner, and in developing a keen sense of timing in employing these and other skills.

In the months ahead, as you forge new patterns of responding and test your skills, you will experience growing pains, that is, a sense of disequilibrium as you struggle to respond in new ways and, at the same time, to relate warmly, naturally, and attentively to your clients. You may also feel at times that your responses are mechanistic and experience a keen sense of transparency, that is, "The client will know that I'm not being real." If you work intensively over several months to master specific skills, however, your awkwardness will gradually diminish, and you will incorporate these skills naturally into your repertoire.

NOTES

1 It is important not to set up artificial dichotomies that do not represent actual behaviors. Emma Gross argues that too frequently writers have inappropriately generalizied across Native American cultures. See Gross (1995).

2 See consideration of reactance theory, pp. 129–136 in Rooney (1992).

3 When utilized, reassurance is best directed to client's capabilities. Appropriate reassurance can be effectively conveyed through the skill of positive feedback described in Chapter 5.

4 Although the relationship practitioners offer clients may have elements of friendship in it, practitioners must be careful to be more than friends by channeling the focus to clients' problems.

Chapter 8 □ □ □

Multidimensional Assessment

THE CRITICAL ROLE OF ASSESSMENT

Assessment is the basis for contracting, goal setting, and intervention planning. Indeed, the effectiveness of selected interventions, and ultimately the case outcome, depend in large measure upon the accuracy of the assessment.

Historically, assessment was referred to as "diagnosis" or "psychosocial diagnosis," but we avoid the term diagnosis because of its association with symptoms, disease, and deficits. However, a clinical diagnosis, despite these implications, is often required in many managed care settings as a requirement for funding services (Strom, 1992). An assessment does include what is wrong, often including a clinical diagnosis, but the broader meaning of the term leaves room for evaluating strengths, resources, healthy functioning, and other positive factors that can be tapped not only in resolving difficulties but also in promoting growth, enhancing functioning, actualizing potentials, and developing new resources.

DEFINING ASSESSMENT

Assessment can be defined in two ways. In the first, it refers to a process occurring between practitioner and client in which information is gathered, analyzed, and synthesized into a multidimensional formulation. In settings in which social work is the primary profession, the social worker often makes the assessment independently or consults with colleagues or a member of another discipline and often completes the assessment in one or two sessions.

The second use of the term refers to a process whereby potential clients interact with practitioners and organizations to determine if their needs and wants can be appropriately dealt with by the organization (Specht & Specht, 1986a). That is, the assessment of potential client concerns often occurs in the context of the organization's goals, capacities, and resources as well as the client's. In this organizational view, assessment begins with a determination of need for service: Does the potential client (whether applicant, referral, or involuntary client) have a need which meets the function of the setting or organization? If such a need is discovered, then the assessment proceeds to exploration of eligibility. In the context of managed health care, this often entails an exploration of the kind of insurance coverage or payment plan available for the potential client. If the potential client is eligible, then an exploration of client resources and ability to make use of agency services follows aiming toward the development of a contract (Specht & Specht, 1986) (see Figure 8-1).

In settings in which social work is not the only or not the primary profession (often called *secondary settings*), the social worker may be a member of a clinical team (e.g., child guidance, mental health, medical and correctional settings), and the process of assessment may be a joint effort of a psychiatrist, social worker, psychologist, nurse, and perhaps members of other disciplines. In such settings, the social worker typically compiles a social history and contributes knowledge related to marital and family dynamics. The process of assessment in such settings ordinarily is longer because of the length of time required for team members to complete individual assessments and to meet as a group to reach a collective assessment.

Before describing the variety of topics about which the practitioner might seek information, it is important to say once again that the purpose of assessment is to gain necessary information in order to make a decision about whether the potential client can be served by the practitioner and setting and, if so, to develop a contract and inter-

vention plan. While a variety of systems and factors may impinge on a potential client's concerns, it is critical that assessment be focused on these three key issues:

1. *What are the problems or concerns as seen by potential clients?* The social work profession places high priority on client self-determination and assisting clients, where possible, in reaching their own goals on problems of greatest concern to them.

2. *What (if any) legal mandates are current or impending such that the potential client and practitioner must consider them?* Some potential clients have a semivoluntary or mandated relationship with the practitioner such that some items must be considered by legal mandate. For example, in addition to other potential client concerns, a child protection worker must assess the danger of child abuse or neglect whether or not those are client concerns.

3. *What (if any) potentially serious or dangerous health or safety concerns might require practitioner and potential client attention?* As described in Chapter 4, among the ethical priorities of social work practice are exploring serious dangers to the health and safety of potential clients and their families which represent "serious, foreseeable, and imminent harm" (NASW, 1995, p. 9). In some cases these dangers, such as in the case of potential elder abuse, may reach a point in which actions may be taken for client protection. In other cases, when such dangers do not reach a sufficient threshold of danger to the potential client or others, the potential client can choose to consider them or avoid them.

These three central foci permit the practitioner to proceed to assess additional systems and aspects with consideration of their pertinence to the development of an action plan. Without such a focus, it is quite possible to gather large amounts of information about elements which turn out to be tangential to potential client concerns, mandates, or safety issues, and both lose valuable time and the potential client in the process.

A second layer of assessment then follows of four major types: exploration of problems and challenges, exploration of potential strengths and resources, examination of developmental needs and life transitions, and exploration of systems impinging on client concerns and circumstances.

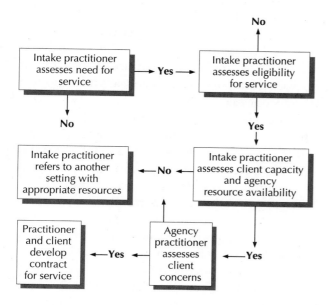

Figure 8-1 The Agency Assessment Sequence *(Source: Adapted from Harry and Riva Specht (1986). Social work assessment: route to clienthood. Part I (November), 525–532. Part 2 (December), 587–593.)*

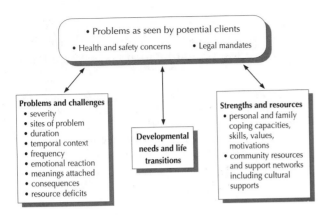

Figure 8-2   Assessment Focus

In the context of exploring problems and challenges, specific data about problems are gathered, including sites where the problems occur, their severity, duration, temporal context, frequency, consequences, emotional reaction, and meanings attached. In addition, personal and family limitations related to resolving problems are explored. In the context of exploring strengths and resources, data are obtained on the coping capacities of clients and significant others (usually family members), their strengths, skills, values and motivations. Practitioners also explore related life transitions and developmental needs and wants. Finally, relevant systems involved in clients' problems are explored (including client and family interaction), and an assessment is made of the nature of reciprocal transactions between clients and these systems, resources (including community and cultural supports) that are available or are needed to remedy or ameliorate problems (see Figure 8-2).

ASSESSMENT AS AN ONGOING PROCESS

At this point, it is important to differentiate between assessment as an ongoing process and as a product. Practitioners engage in the process of assessment from the time of an initial contact with clients to the terminal contact, which may be weeks, months, or even years later. Assessment thus is a fluid and dynamic process that involves receiving, analyzing, and synthesizing new information as it emerges during the entire course of a given case. In the first session, practitioners generally elicit abundant information and must assess its meaning and significance as it unfolds.[1] This moment-by-moment assessment guides practitioners in deciding which information is salient and merits deeper exploration. When they have gathered sufficient information to illuminate the problems, practitioners analyze it and, in collaboration with clients, integrate the data into a tentative formulation of the problem. Many potential clients do not proceed with the practitioner beyond this point. If their concerns can be best handled through a referral to other resources, if they do not meet eligibility criteria, or they choose not to continue, contact often stops here. Specht and Specht (1986b) have emphasized that the relationship in this initial assessment and eligibility process should hence not be considered as necessarily leading to a therapeutic relationship (Specht & Specht, 1986b). Communications skills as described in previous chapters are very important in assessment but not necessarily as precursors to a therapeutic relationship.

Should practitioners and potential clients move from the exploratory phase to on-going contact involving a contract for services and full client status, assessment continues, although on a somewhat diminished scale. Not uncommonly, clients disclose new information as problem solving progresses, casting the problems initially presented into a new perspective. Some clients, for example, withhold vital information that they fear may evoke criticism or condemnation from the social worker until they are reasonably confident of the latter's goodwill and helpful intent. Many preliminary assessments thus prove inaccurate and must be discarded or drastically revised.

The process of assessment continues even during the terminal phase of service. During final interviews, the practitioner carefully evaluates the client's readiness to terminate, assesses the presence of residual difficulties that may cause future difficulties, and identifies possible emotional reactions to termination. The practitioner also considers possible strategies to assist the client to maintain improved functioning or to achieve additional progress after formal social work service is concluded.

Assessment as a Product

As a product, assessment involves an actual formulation or statement at a given time regarding the nature of clients' problems and other related factors delineated earlier. A formal assessment thus involves analysis and synthesis of relevant data into a working definition of the problem that identifies various associated factors and clarifies how they interact to produce and maintain the problem. Because assessments must constantly be updated and revised, it is helpful to think of an assessment as a complex working hypothesis based on the most current data.

A formal assessment is generally made and recorded following an exploration of the client's problems, and tentative goals to be accomplished are based on this assessment. Another assessment could be made at any subsequent time during the course of service, but this is seldom done except in preparation for supervisory sessions, consultations, or case presentations, or to complete an agency record. Rather, assessment thereafter consists of gradually reshaping and modifying the initial assessment as new information emerges.

EMPHASIZING STRENGTHS IN ASSESSMENTS

Changes in practice have lagged far behind the change in terms from diagnosis to assessment, for social workers persist in formulating assessments that emphasize the pathology and dysfunction of clients—despite the time-honored social work platitude that social workers work with strengths, not weaknesses (Cowger, 1994; Saleeby, 1992). Saleeby suggests that this focus derives from a focus on the moral defects of despised, deviant and often poor clients (Saleeby, 1992, p.3) The problem was located in the individual and it was the professional's job to "fix" the problem or problem person. A focus on strengths is consonant with the value stance of the profession, facilitates partnership through sharing power and deemphasizes stigmatizing diagnostic categories that often reinforce passivity (Cowger, 1992, pp. 140-141).

The marked tendency of practitioners to focus on pathology has several important ramifications, the first of which is that to tap client strengths effectively, practitioners must be sensitive to them and skillful in utilizing them in the service of accomplishing case goals. The findings of at least one research study (Maluccio, 1979) strongly suggest that social workers underestimate client strengths. In this study of comparisons between clients' and caseworkers' perceptions of the outcomes of interventions, Maluccio found that the former "presented themselves as proactive, autonomous, human beings...able to enhance their functioning and their competence," whereas the latter viewed them as "reactive organisms with continuing problems, underlying weaknesses, and limited potentialities" (p. 399). Given this finding, it is probable that the caseworkers studied focused their efforts extensively on perceived weaknesses.

The findings of this study also revealed that clients were more satisfied with the outcomes of service than were the caseworkers, who manifested concerns about residual pathology, especially with clients who terminated prematurely. These findings have been supported by the findings of Presley (1987) and Toseland (1987), both of whom found that clients who did not return after one session often terminated service "prematurely" for reasons other than dissatisfaction (often because they felt they had benefited from the session and needed no further help). Presley thus concluded that "therapists may have a more fragile image of the client than appears warranted" (p. 607).

Again, one must wonder if preoccupation with dysfunction reinforced in many settings distorts social workers' perceptions and predisposes them to believe that clients should continue to receive service longer than is necessary. In this regard, Maluccio concluded: "There is a need to shift the focus in social work education and practice from problems or pathology to strengths, resources, and potentialities in human beings and their environments" (p. 401). We strongly concur!

A second ramification is that selectively attending to pathology impairs a social worker's ability to discern clients' potentials for growth. Although social workers fervently espouse the belief that human beings have the right and opportunity to develop their potentialities, their tendency to focus on pathology has the effect of undermining that very value commitment. To implement this value fully, social work practitioners must achieve more balanced perceptions of their clients by attuning themselves to strengths and potentialities as well as to dysfunction and pathology. By thus broadening their perspectives of clients, social workers may also enhance the efficacy of their interventive efforts. As Cowger says "clinical practice based on empowerment assumes that client power is achieved when clients make choices that give them more control over their presenting problem situations and in turn their own lives (Cowger, 1994, p. 263.)

The importance of discerning and focusing on strengths of Chicano clients has been documented by the findings of Gomez et al. (1985). A major finding of this outcome study was that supporting clients' strengths was one of the behaviors of practitioners that significantly correlated ($r = .33$) with helpfulness to clients. Concerning the impact of supporting strengths these authors concluded, "In supporting clients' strengths, workers project an honest belief in the clients' ability to deal with problems. This display of belief in the clients' potential strengthens their own belief of the possibilities in the undertaking" (p. 481).

A third ramification of attending excessively to pathology concerns the fact that a large proportion of clients need help in enhancing their self-esteem. Troubled by self-doubts, feelings of inadequacy, and even feelings of worthlessness, their lack of self-confidence and self-respect underlies many dysfunctional cognitive, emotional, and behavioral patterns, including fears of failure, depression, social withdrawal, alcoholism, and hypersensitivity to criticism—to name just a few. To assist clients to view themselves more positively, social workers and the settings in which they are employed must first view their clients more positively. Indicative of the consequent challenge to helping professionals is Berwick's (1980) observation pertaining to work with parents of children who fail to thrive because of nonorganic reasons associated with inadequate parental nurturance. After cautioning practitioners to avoid the tendency to blame the parents, Berwick notes:

> Self-esteem is already at a low ebb in many of the parents of these children, and the success of the hospital in nourishing a child when the mother has failed only serves to accentuate the pain of failure....Even in the few cases that require foster care, the health care team's task is to seek strengths and to develop a sense of competence in both the parents and the child that will permit a synchronous nurturant relationship to emerge. (p. 270)

Why does this preoccupation with pathology persist despite increasing exhortations which emphasize strengths? Bricker-Jenkins in a study of the implementation of a practice model which focused on client wishes in a public service setting, has suggested that supervisors were uncomfortable with the degree to which clients were able to set so much of their own agendas (Bricker-Jenkins, 1992, p.126). Similarly, part of the explanation for a preoccupation with pathology is the funding basis of many managed health care insurance packages which often require a clinical diagnosis of an individual and hence assume a medical model of treatment. To assist in emphasizing strengths and empowerment in the assessment process, Cowger (1994, p.265) suggests that practitioners

1. Give preeminence to client understanding of the facts.
2. Discover what the client wants.
3. Assess personal and environmental strengths on multiple levels.

We will bear these guidelines in mind as we present additional sources of information.

SOURCES OF INFORMATION

Information that is considered in the assessment process may derive from several sources, of which the following are the most common:

1. Background sheets or other forms that clients complete.
2. Verbal report by clients (i.e., accounts of problems, expressions of feelings, views, thoughts, events, and the like).
3. Direct observation of nonverbal behavior.
4. Direct observation of interaction between marital partners, family members, and group members.
5. Collateral information from relatives, friends, physicians, teachers, employers, and other professionals.
6. Psychological tests.
7. Personal experiences of the practitioner based on direct interaction with clients.

Verbal Report

Of these major sources, client verbal report is generally the primary source of information. Verbal report consists of descriptions of problems, expressions of feelings, reporting of events, presentation of views, and the like. Clients' feelings and reports should always be respected as indicating their understanding of their circumstances. Verbal report, however, is an indirect source of information because it is provided after the fact rather than through direct observation of problematic behavior, events, feelings, or views. As with other information sources, verbal report often needs to be augmented because of possible faulty recall, biases, and limited self-awareness on the part of clients. It is often useful to additionally elicit highly specific details of the client-perceived behaviors and events through focusing in depth and seeking concreteness.

Direct Observation of Nonverbal Behavior

Direct observation of clients' nonverbal behavior adds additional information, for people generally lack awareness of their nonverbal behavior and it is therefore less subject to conscious control than is verbal report. Nonverbal cues are valuable indicators of emotional states and reactions such as anger, hurt, embarrassment, and fear. It is thus vital to develop an acute perceptiveness to nonverbal cues, such as tone of voice, tears, clenched fists, voice tremors, quivering hands, tightened jaws, pursed lips, variations of countenance, and gesticulations. The doors to many rich discussions of emotional reactions have been opened by empathic responses directed to nonverbal cues (e.g., "Your eyes are telling me you feel very sad right now. Could you put into words what you're experiencing at this moment?").

Observation of Interaction

Direct observation of interaction between spouses, family members, and group members often is extremely enlightening. Students (as well as seasoned practitioners) frequently are amazed at the striking differences between impressions concerning interaction of clients gained from self-report and from subsequent direct observation of their actual interaction. Enactment can be employed by practitioners to observe interaction firsthand rather than to rely on verbal report. Use of this technique involves having clients reenact a conflictual event during a live session. Participants are instructed to recreate the situation exactly as it occurred, using the same words, gestures, and tones of voice as in the actual event. Before giving the instructions, however, it is important to provide an explanation for making the request, such as the following:

> To understand what produced the difficulties in the event you just described, I'd like you to recreate the situation here in our session. By seeing what both of you do and say and how you do it, I can get an accurate picture of what actually happens. I'd like you to recreate the situation exactly as it happened. Use the same words, gestures, and tone of voice as you did. Now, where were you when it happened, and how did it start?

Most clients are willing to engage in enactment, but encouragement is sometimes needed. Enactment can also be used in contrived situations to see how a couple or family interact in situations that involve decision making, planning, role negotiation, child discipline, or other like activities. Practitioners will need to exercise their creativity in designing situations likely to generate and clarify the types of interaction the practitioner desires to observe.

Direct observation of spontaneous behavior or of enacted situations is not without flaws, for clients often understandably attempt to create a favorable impression and behave differently than they have in actual situations. Practitioners can counter this possibility after enacted situations by asking to what extent the behaviors of participants corresponded with their behavior in actual situations. It is wise to elicit views of all participants to ascertain the authenticity of reported discrepancies. Reported discrepancies that are validated by participants are highly informative.

It is also important to recognize that an office setting is not a natural arena for family interaction and that behavior of family members may be strongly influenced by this unnatural environment. As a corrective measure, it is desirable to visit clients in their homes, if possible. In fact, one of the strengths of an emerging form of practice, in-home, family-based services, is the opportunity to observe first-hand family difficulties rather than rely on second-hand accounts (Ronnau & Marlow, 1995). Observations of living conditions, incidentally, may also reveal problems that would otherwise not come to light.

Direct observation is also subject to perceptual errors by the observer. A method to compensate for this error is to employ more than one observer and to determine the degree of congruence between observations made independently by different observers. This corrective measure, however, requires time and is generally not feasible in practice. Despite the flaws of direct observation, information gained by this means adds significantly to that gained from verbal report.

Client Self-Monitoring

Client self-monitoring is a potent source of information (Kopp, 1989). Involvement in self-monitoring not only produces rich and quantifiable data, but also assists in empowering the client during the assessment process by actively obtaining some of the information considered in treatment planning as a collaborator rather than a passive participant.

Self-monitoring can involve clients in writing descriptions and recording feelings, behaviors, and thoughts associated with occurrences of their targeted problems. The first step in self monitoring is to recognize the occurrence of the event (e.g., events that lead to anger outbursts, temper tantrums by children, heated disputes, episodes of drinking or overeating). The next step is to chart or graph the information to determine the baseline of the behavior.

A major advantage of using self-monitoring is that by focusing their attention, clients gain insights about their situations. Moreover, as they discuss their recorded observations they "spontaneously operationalize goals and suggest ideas for change" (Kopp, 1989, p. 278).[2] The targeted behaviors can then be quantified, which assists in monitoring progress.

Collateral Sources of Information

Information is also sometimes provided by relatives, friends, physicians, and others who possess essential information about relevant aspects of clients' lives. Information from such collateral sources is subject to the same limitations of other indirect sources. Nevertheless, persons who are not directly implicated in the problematic situation may provide information that illuminates otherwise obscure dynamics of problematic behavior.

Unfortunately, practitioners often overlook collateral sources, thereby losing potentially valuable information. However, it is not necessary or even desirable to contact collateral sources routinely, and you must exercise prudence in deciding when such information is needed. Furthermore, client consent is required, except in the case of bona fide exigencies. It is prudent to obtain written consent from clients with agency "release of information" forms.

Although clients occasionally will request that you contact others to gain their views, you will often need to initiate such discussions. If you explain that you can best serve the client by gaining a well-rounded picture of the problematic situation and that others often can identify factors that may otherwise be overlooked, clients will often consent to and even welcome such collateral contacts.

In weighing the validity of information obtained from collateral sources, it is important to consider the degree to which collateral persons are emotionally involved with clients. Those most emotionally involved, such as members of the immediate family, tend to be emotionally biased and hence more subjective. Similarly, persons who have something to gain or to lose pending case decisions (e.g., custody of a child, property settle-

ment, or the burden of caring for a chronically mentally ill person) tend to be less credible than persons more emotionally removed from case situations. And finally, information from persons whose emotional or mental stability is questionable or whose behavioral patterns have been erratic must be carefully scrutinized. Skepticism is justified in such circumstances.

Psychological Tests

Still another possible source of information consists of psychological tests including self-report inventories (e.g., personality inventories; fear, social skill, and depression inventories) and behavioral checklists, such as problem behavior, behavioral skills, and family verbal behavior checklists. Also an indirect source of information, psychological tests represent a useful and expedient way of quantifying data and behaviors. To use them effectively, however, practitioners must be well grounded in knowledge of test theory and specific tests. Many tests, for example, have low reliability and validity and should be used with extreme caution, if at all. In the hands of unqualified persons, psychological tests may be grossly misused. Because social workers generally have limited knowledge and experience in the realm of psychological testing, they are well advised to strictly observe the old caveat, "A little learning is a dangerous thing." If testing is needed or test results are available, social workers may wish to seek consultation from qualified psychologists in interpreting the results appropriately.

It is advantageous for social workers who practice in settings where psychological tests are extensively employed to gain knowledge of the testing. A valuable resource to those who would like to gain expertise in using a number of tests developed for social workers and allied professionals is the Walmyr Assessment Scales (Hudson, 1992).[3] Included in this package are scales that measure the following: depression, self-esteem, clinical stress, anxiety, alcohol involvement, peer relations, sexual attitudes, homophobia, marital satisfaction, sexual satisfaction, nonphysical abuse of partner, physical abuse of partner, parental attitude toward children, children's attitudes toward both mother and father, sibling relations, family relations, children's behavior, and a general screening inventory. Another excellent resource is Corcoran and Fischer's (1987) comprehensive review of instruments that can be used to assess various aspects of clients' functioning.

Computer-Assisted Assessment

Technological advances have led to still another promising aid in assessment. Nurius and Hudson (1988, 1993) have reported on the development of a microcomputer-based evaluation tool that includes all of the Walmyr Assessment Scales listed in the preceding section. The scales are contained both on diskettes (Nurius & Hudson, 1993) and in the Walmyr Assessment Scales Scoring Manual (Hudson, 1992); thus clients can complete the scales manually or on a personal computer, according to their preferences. The computer program is user friendly. Clients can complete a single scale and scoring can be done in about five minutes. Practitioners can also add any measure that is designed to assess the degree or severity of a client problem. Moreover, the computer program accommodates different types of scales including single-item, self-anchored, multi-item, multidimensional rating scales, checklists, and others.

Computer-aided assessment deserves the attention of practitioners. Clients reportedly respond well to this technology. The greatest potential for use of this tool derives from the computer's ability to process, integrate, and synthesize data from expanded sources of information. The computer's objectivity also reduces evaluative errors caused by subjective interpretations of data by practitioners.

Personal Experience Based on Direct Interaction

A final source of information is *personal experience* based on direct interaction with clients. You will react in varying ways to different clients, and your reactions may be useful in understanding how other people react to these clients. For example, you may experience certain clients as withdrawn, personable, dependent, caring, manipulative, seductive, assertive, overbearing, or determined. Client behavior is often influenced by the situation of contact with the practitioner. For example, potential clients referred by others or mandated for service can be expected to behave in a more guarded fashion than persons who have applied for a service. However, some patterns may be manifested which also occur in their general social relationships. Hence, your own reaction may be a vital clue to understanding their possible difficulties or successes in interpersonal relationships. For example, a client who reports that others take him for granted and make unreasonable demands upon him may make inordinate efforts to please a practitioner and may manifest self-deprecating behavior. The practitioner's experience with the clients provides clues to at least part of the source of their problems.

The Importance of Self-Awareness

Initial impressions, of course, can be misleading and must be supported by additional contacts with clients. Moreover, such impressions are subjective and may be influenced by your own interpersonal patterns and perceptions. Before drawing even tentative conclusions, it is important that you scrutinize your reactions to identify possible biases, distorted perceptions, or behavior on your part that may have contributed to clients' behavior. If you tend to be domineering or represent an agency which may have a reputation (deserved or not) for intrusiveness (such as child protective service), many clients respond with passivity or counteraggressiveness that is atypical. Similarly, overly challenging or confrontive behavior on your part may produce defensiveness or withdrawn behavior that is in part a natural reaction to your inappropriate behavior.

Your perceptions of and reactions to clients may also be distorted by your own life experiences. For example, if you had painful experiences as a child with a controlling and critical parent, you may react negatively to clients who manifest similar qualities and may have difficulty perceiving their strengths and uniqueness. If you were abused or sexually molested as a child, you may have a tendency to overidentify with victims of child maltreatment and to feel hostile toward perpetrators of abuse. If you had an alcoholic parent, you may also unknowingly experience discomfort or feelings of rejection toward alcoholic clients. There are, of course, many other types of life experience that distort perceptions of and judgments regarding clients. Self-awareness thus is indispensable to drawing valid conclusions about your experiential reactions to clients. Just as part of your role with clients is to assist them to disentangle reaction from reality, you have a similar obligation toward yourself.

THE MULTIDIMENSIONALITY OF ASSESSMENT

Human problems, even those that appear to be simple, often involve a complex interplay of many factors. Rarely do sources of problems reside solely within an individual or within that individual's environment. Rather, reciprocal interaction occurs between a human being and the external world. One acts upon and responds to the external world, and the quality of one's actions affects reactions and vice versa. For example, a parent may complain about poor communication with an adolescent child, attributing the difficulty to the fact that the adolescent is sullen and refuses to talk about most things. The adolescent, however, may complain that it is pointless to talk with the parent because the latter consistently pries, lectures, or criticizes. Each participant's complaint about the other may be accurate, but each unwittingly behaves in ways that have produced and now maintain their dysfunctional interaction. Thus, the behavior of neither person is the sole cause of the breakdown in communication in a simple cause-effect (linear) fashion. Rather, it is their reciprocal interaction that produces the difficulty; the behavior of each is both cause and effect, depending on one's vantage point.

The multidimensionality of human problems is also a consequence of the fact that human beings are social creatures, dependent upon other human beings and upon complex social institutions to meet their needs. Basic needs such as food, housing, clothing, and medical care require adequate economic means and the availability of goods and services. Educational, social, and recreational needs require interface with societal institutions. Needs to feel close to and loved by others, to have companionship, to experience a sense of belonging, and to experience sexual gratification require satisfactory social relationships within one's marriage or partnership, family, social network, and community. The extent to which people experience self-esteem depends on certain individual psychological factors and the quality of feedback from other people.

Bearing in mind previous caveats about focus on client concerns, legal mandates, and safety issues, assessment of the concerns of a client system (individual, couple, or family) thus requires extensive knowledge about that system as well as consideration of the multifarious systems (e.g., economic, legal, educational, medical, religious, social, interpersonal) that impinge upon the client system. Moreover, to assess the functioning of an individual entails evaluating various aspects of that person's functioning. For example, one may need to consider dynamic interactions among the biophysical, cognitive, emotional, cultural, behavioral, and motivational subsystems and the relationships of those interactions to problematic situations. With a couple or family client system, the social worker finds it useful to attend to communication and interactional patterns as well as to each member of the system. Although not all of the various systems and subsystems cited above are likely to play significant roles in the problems of any given client system, overlooking relevant systems results in assessment that is partial at best and irrelevant or erroneous at worst. Interventions based on incomplete or inaccurate assessments, therefore, are likely to have limited remedial effects, to be ineffective, or even to produce detrimental results. Conversely, interventions that are based on accurate and comprehensive assessments are more likely to be effective.

Choices and priorities in assessment occur given client concerns and agency purpose and resources. To reiterate, one part of assessment is to determine if the potential client can or should receive services from the practitioner and his or her agency. A second part is then to gather information that will assist in the formulation of a contract and treatment plan to deal with identified problems and concerns. To assist you to formulate assessments that consider the many dimensions of human problems, we consider in this chapter the major questions that you will need to answer in formulating an assessment. In the next chapter, we address multidimensional assessment of individuals and of the environment. In Chapter 10, we focus on assessment of interpersonal systems, with particular emphasis upon marriages and families. In Chapter 11, we consider assessment within the context of growth groups.

THE PROBLEM

In your initial contacts with potential clients, you take the first step in uncovering the sources of their problems and engaging them in planning appropriate remedial measures.

Applicants typically seek help because they have exhausted their coping efforts and/or lack resources required for satisfactory living. They have often found that, despite earnest efforts, their coping efforts are futile or seem to aggravate the problematic situation. In many such instances, applicants have erred in defining their problems, and their solutions ironically have become problems in and of themselves. An applicant, for example, may make heroic efforts to please others—a spouse, parent, or employer—to no avail. The problem, however, may not be an inability to please others but rather a pattern of striving excessively to please others. Leaning over backwards to win approval of others tends to be self-defeating because one thereby devalues oneself in the eyes of others and invites being taken for granted. Having exhausted their coping efforts, such applicants may turn to a professional person, expecting that the latter will somehow assist them to discover a solution to their problem.

Problem identification takes a somewhat different course when the potential client has been referred or is an involuntary client. Referred clients may approach services willingly, assisted by the referral from a professional, friend, or family member familiar with your own or your agency's services. However, many referred clients acquiesce passively because someone else thinks that they "need help." Their initiation of contact does not necessarily imply willingness to accept services.

Meanwhile, involuntary clients are further down the continuum of voluntarism, reluctantly "seeking help" because of coercion from family members or some official power structure. Involuntary clients often do not perceive themselves as having problems or portray pressure from the referral source as the problem. Typically used by such clients is the following message, "I don't know why I should have to come. My wife is the one with the problems, and she's the one who should be here." When the source of motivation thus lies outside the client, the parameters of the problem are less readily identifiable. In such instances, after attempting to understand and reduce the client's negativism about being pressured to seek help, the practitioner engages the client in an exploration of the latter's life situation, the goals of which are to determine if wants or areas of dissatisfaction on the client's part can be identified and if motivation can be engendered to work toward enhancing the client's satisfaction in pertinent areas. When and if the client acknowledges a problem, the boundaries of the problem become clear, and the exploration then proceeds in a normal fashion.

IDENTIFYING THE PROBLEM

Early in a session, often after introductions have been made (or after a warm-up period), the practitioner invites potential clients to describe their problems or concerns. Applicants typically respond to such overtures by giving a general account of their problems. The problem identified by clients typically involves a deficiency of something needed (e.g., health care, adequate income or housing, companionship, harmonious family relationships, self-esteem) or an excess of something that is not desired (e.g., fear, guilt, temper outbursts, marital or parent–child conflict, or addiction). In either event, applicants are in a state of disequilibrium and experience both tension and troubled emotions. The emotions thus are often a prominent part of the problem configuration, which is one reason why empathic communication is such a vital skill.[4] The presenting problem as viewed by the applicant is highly significant because it reflects his or her immediate perceptions of the problem and is the focal point of their motivation for seeking help.

Those potential clients referred by others sometimes encounter the fact that the referral source (often a doctor, employer, family member or school official) has a view of the problem and recommendations for a treatment plan. It is important to clarify with referred clients that they can choose to work on problems of concern to them, not necessarily the concerns of the referral source (Epstein, 1992).

In the case of involuntary clients under threat of a legal mandate, choices are also available. While the consequences of avoiding a court order or impending legal action may be serious, involuntary clients may choose to do so and accept the consequences. More importantly, involuntary clients frequently have their own views of concerns which do not correspond with their legal pressures and may in fact include "getting them off my back" (Rooney, 1992). It is frequently possible to engage involuntary clients in contracts which are at least partially voluntary through finding and including their motivation in the contract.

Problem definition is client centered with all types of potential clients. To be sure, clients generally modify their perceptions of their problems as they explore factors of which they previously had little or no awareness. Moreover, potential clients do not always initially reveal their most troubling problems because to do so may be highly embarrassing or may risk condemnation. Our point is that you must be carefully attuned to clients' definitions of their problems, for to proceed to work exclusively on problems they do not acknowledge is to risk losing their motivation. Several reviews of studies of casework effectiveness have suggested that more successful outcomes are associated with motivational congruence, or a fit between practitioner and client views of the problem (Reid & Hanrahan, 1982; Videka-Sherman, 1988).

The presenting problem is also of vital significance because it suggests areas to be explored subsequently. If the presenting problem described by parents involves truancy and rebellious behavior of an adolescent, the exploration will include the family, school, and peer systems. As the exploration proceeds, it may also be useful to explore the marital system if there is some indication that difficulty in the marital relationship is negatively affecting the parent–child relationship. If learning difficulties appear to contribute to the truancy, the cognitive and perceptual subsystems of the adolescent may also need to be assessed as part of the problem. The presenting problem thus identifies systems that are constituent parts of the problem. Finally, it should be noted that truancy and rebellious behavior reflect the presenting problem as seen by parents. If their view alone is accepted, then the adolescent is transformed from potential client to problem bearer or target. While such behavior is likely to be an important focus, it is important also to explore the adolescent's view, to enhance the possibility of collaboration and becoming a client.

Clarifying Ecological Factors

As clients describe their difficulties, they identify other people and larger systems involved in their problematic situations. The configuration of the client(s), the social milieu, and relevant systems that interact to produce and maintain the problem constitute the ecological boundaries of the problem. To understand more fully how the client(s) and other involved systems interact to produce and maintain the problem, you must elicit specific information that pertains to the functioning and interaction of these various systems.

Systems with which clients commonly transact include:

1. The family and extended family or clan.
2. The social network (friends, neighbors, co-workers, religious leaders and associates, club members, and cultural groups).
3. Public institutions (educational, recreational, law enforcement and protection, mental health, social service, health care, employment, economic security, legal and judicial, and various governmental agencies).

4. Personal service providers (doctor, dentist, barber or hairdresser, bartender, auto mechanic, etc.).

Individuals have more or less ongoing transactions with the systems listed under (1) and (2) above and have less frequent transactions with other systems listed under (3) and (4), depending on circumstances and the individual's stage of development. The challenge is to include in the assessment those systems that reside in the ecological boundaries of the client's problem. Relevant systems are those that contribute to the client's difficulties or that can be tapped to resolve them (Congress, 1994).

To assist you in considering social systems germane to the problems of clients, refer to Figure 9-1 in the latter part of Chapter 9, wherein we discuss assessment of these factors more extensively.

Ecomaps have been found to be a useful way to visually depict such information and to include clients in the collection of information. Key systems such as nuclear and extended family are portrayed as circles intersecting with the client system. Additional circles or elements may include school, friends, organizations, and neighborhood (Hartman & Laird, 1983). Ecomaps will be further explored in Chapter 9.

Assessing Developmental Needs and Wants

As we noted earlier, clients' problems commonly involve unmet needs and wants that derive from lack of goodness of fit between these needs and resources in the environment. (Recall from Table 1-2 in Chapter 1 the close link between individual needs and sources of need gratification in the social milieu or in the environment.) Determining unmet needs, then, is the first step to identifying resources that must be tapped or developed. If resources are available but clients have been unable to avail themselves of the resources, it is important to determine the barriers to resource utilization. Some people, for example, may suffer from loneliness not because of an absence of support systems but because their interpersonal behavior alienates others and leaves them isolated. Still other clients may *appear* to have emotional support available from family or others, but closer exploration may reveal that these potential resources are unresponsive to clients' needs. Reasons for the unresponsiveness typically involve reciprocal unsatisfactory transactions between the participants. The task in such instances is to assess the nature of the dysfunctional transactions and to attempt to modify them to the benefit of the participants—often a complex and difficult task.

Human needs include the universal necessities (adequate nutrition, clothing, housing, and health care). *Needs* are critical and must be met at least partially for human beings to survive and maintain sound physical and mental health and well-being. As we use the term, wants involve strong desires that motivate behavior and that, when fulfilled, enhance satisfaction and well-being. Although fulfillment of wants is not essential to survival, some wants develop a compelling nature, rivaling needs in their intensity—for example, people who are compelled to seek power, wealth, and prestige or people who are compelled to gain acceptance by others at any price. For illustrative purposes, we provide the following list of examples of typical wants involved in presenting problems.

TYPICAL WANTS INVOLVED IN PRESENTING PROBLEMS

To have less family conflict.	To have more freedom.
To feel valued by one's spouse.	To handle conflict more effectively.
To be self-supporting.	To control one's temper.
To achieve greater companionship in marriage.	To overcome depression.
To gain more self-confidence.	To get someone or something off my back.
To have more friends.	To make a difficult decision.
To be included in decision making.	To master fear or anxiety.
To gain release from an institution.	To cope with children more effectively.
To stay out of trouble.	

In determining clients' unmet needs and wants it is essential to consider the *developmental stage* of the individual client, couple, or family. For example, the psychological needs of an adolescent for acceptance by peers, for sufficient freedom to develop increasing independence, for development of a stable identity, including a sexual identity, are markedly different from the typical needs of elderly persons for health care, adequate income, social relationships, and meaningful activities. As with individuals, families go through developmental phases that also include both tasks to be mastered and needs that must be met if the family is to provide a climate conducive to the development and well-being of its members.

Different theorists conceptualize developmental stages for individuals in different ways and use different terms, but the following stages correspond with those generally identified:

Infancy	Late teenage
Preschool	Early adulthood
School age	Middle age
Early teenage	Old age

Families also have discrete stages of development, but we defer discussion of them until Chapter 10, which is concerned with assessment of families. Although knowledge of the needs and tasks associated with each developmental stage is critical, we will not provide a detailed list of needs, for that content is germane to human behavior courses and textbooks.[5]

Although clients' presenting problems often reveal obvious needs and wants (e.g., "Our unemployment benefits have expired and we have no income"), it is often necessary to infer what is lacking. Presenting problems may reveal only what is troubling clients on the surface, and careful exploration and empathic "tuning in" are required to identify unmet needs and wants. Marital partners, for example, may initially complain that they disagree over virtually everything and fight constantly. From this information, one could safely conclude they want a more harmonious relationship; exploring their feelings on a deeper level, however, may reveal that their ongoing disputes are actually a manifestation of unmet needs of both partners for expressions of love, caring, appreciation, or increased companionship.

Translating complaints and problems into needs and wants is often helpful to clients, many of whom have dwelled on the troubling behavior of other participants in the problem systems and have not thought in terms of their own specific needs and wants. The presenting problem of one client was that her husband was married to his job and spent little time with her. When the practitioner responded, "I gather then you're feeling left out of his life and want to feel important to him and valued by him," she replied, "You know, I hadn't thought of it that way, but that's exactly what I've been feeling." The practitioner then encouraged her to express this need directly to her husband, which she did. He listened attentively and responded with genuine concern. This was the first time she had expressed her needs directly. Previously, her messages had been complaints and his usual response had been defensive.

Identifying needs and wants also serves as a vital prelude to the process of negotiating goals. Goals, of course, often embody specified changes in problematic behavior on the part of participants that will enhance the degree of need gratification and satisfaction for those who are part of the problem system. Expressing goals in terms that address needs and wants also enhances the motivation of clients to work toward goal attainment, as the payoff for goal-oriented efforts is readily apparent to them.

Although goals generally relate to unmet wants and needs, clients' wants are sometimes unrealistic when assessed against the capacity of the client and/or opportunities in the social environment. (One mildly brain-damaged and slightly retarded young adult, for example, wanted to become a nuclear physicist.) Moreover, wanting to achieve a desired goal is not the same as being willing to expend the time and effort and to endure the discomfort required to attain that goal. These are matters that warrant extensive consideration and, as such, are central topics in Chapter 13.

Stresses Associated with Life Transitions

In addition to developmental stages that typically correspond to age ranges, individuals and families commonly must adapt to other major transitions that are less age specific. Some transitions (e.g., geographical moves and immigrations, divorce, and untimely widowhood) can occur during virtually any stage of development. Many such transitions can be traumatic and the adaptations required may temporarily overwhelm the coping capacities of individuals or families. For example, losses or separations from a person, homeland, or familiar role are highly stressful for most persons and often temporarily impair social functioning.

Again the environment plays a crucial role in facilitating people's adaptation to major transitional events. People with strong support networks (e.g., close relationships with family, kin, friends, and neighbors) generally have less difficulty in adapting to traumatic changes than do those who lack strong support systems. Assessments and interventions related to transitional periods, therefore, should consider the availability or lack of essential support systems.

The following are major transitions that commonly beset adults:

Work, career choices and changes	Untimely widowhood
Marriage	Postparenthood years

Parenthood	Retirement
Geographic moves and migrations	Health impairment
Separation and divorce	Institutionalization
Single–parenthood status	Death of a spouse and being single

In addition to the above transitions, others affect specialized groups. For example, gay and lesbian persons have difficult decisions to make about to whom and under what conditions they will reveal their sexual identity. Cain has identified six circumstances in which gay men decide to come out and suggests useful guidelines for helping gay men assess the benefits and risks associated with coming out (Cain, 1991). Similarly, biracial children often experience intense pressures to "choose" their racial identity as adolescents.

Assessing whether clients are in the throes of a developmental phase or transitional period is vital because clients' presenting problems often involve "being stuck" as a result of failing to master tasks essential to adapting successfully to developmental or transitional periods of life. Practitioners can play a vital role in identifying essential tasks and assisting clients to master them, a role central to the modality of crisis intervention, which we discuss in Chapter 13.

KEY FACTORS TO BE ADDRESSED IN ASSESSMENT

Accurate and complete assessments must address key factors implicated in clients' problems, some of which we identified earlier in this chapter. Using these factors as a guideline will assist you to conduct thorough explorations and to formulate adequate assessments.

To illustrate the significance and application of many of the factors, we have related them to problems of high concern to social workers, namely child maltreatment (neglect and physical and/or sexual abuse) and spouse abuse. This concern derives from the fact that increasing numbers of families served by social workers have manifested difficulties associated with these problems.

Bricker-Jenkins (1992) points out that such problems are a particular challenge for the application of a strengths perspective: "risk assessment procedures, for example, have become increasingly refined and predictive to some degree; however, that predictive power is achieved by focusing narrowly on individual and family dysfunction. After analyzing and thoroughly documenting dysfunction, workers are then expected to focus and ally themselves with family strengths to achieve casework goals" (p. 125). To assist in addressing this challenge, we will present examples including strengths assessments from family preservation services.

In 1989, an estimated 2.4 million cases of suspected child neglect and abuse were filed nationwide, and an estimated 1,225 children were fatally injured (National Committee for Prevention of Child Abuse, 1990). Although precise data on the incidence of child sexual abuse are not available, estimates are that one out of three females and one of six males will be victims of sexual abuse through body contact by age 18 (Spungen, Jensen, Finkelstein, & Satinsky, 1989).

With respect to spouse abuse, government reports indicate that an average of 1,500 women are killed each year by husbands or lovers and more than 2 million are badly injured in quarrels (U.S. Department of Justice, 1986; U.S. Federal Bureau of Investigation, 1988). Moreover, Gelles and Cornell (1990) state that "researchers generally report that intrafamilial homicide accounts for between 20% and 40% of all murders" (p. 67). These figures, however, do not tell the whole story, because many cases of spouse abuse go unreported.

Manifestations of the Problem(s)

Voluntary clients typically describe manifestations of their presenting problems, but you will generally need to elicit additional detailed information before you can adequately assess the problem.

Involuntary clients, however, often see their problems differently from referral sources. Consequently, when the physical and mental health and safety of others are in jeopardy as in instances of alleged child maltreatment and spousal abuse, these issues must be assessed in addition to the involuntary client's view of the problem. For these reasons we focus on indicators of these problems in the following sections.

Indications of Neglect and/or Physical Abuse

Parental neglect is manifested by a number of factors, including the following: low birth weight and/or stunted growth; an emaciated appearance; lethargy; repeated requests by children for food from neighbors, teachers, and others; unlaundered, ill-fitting, shabby, and worn-out clothing; lack of protective clothing and footwear during cold weather; consistently grimy faces and hands, and disheveled hair; head lice; frequent colds and runny noses; and complaints from neighbors about children being left alone or begging for food.

Indications of physical abuse include frequent and severe bruises (in various stages of healing) from being choked, grabbed, shaken, slapped, or squeezed; wounds and scars from being scalded or burned; lacerations around the mouth; old and new bone fractures; eye and head injuries; intra-abdominal injuries; and bite marks (Wolff, 1990).

The effects of child abuse involve far more than physical injuries, for abused children suffer emotional scars, impaired social relationships, and damaged self-esteem. These effects hinder social and emotional development and often persist into adulthood. Common behavioral manifestations of these effects are wariness and distrust of adults, apprehension when other children cry, extremes in either aggressiveness or passivity, fear of parents and/or of going home, difficulties in forming relationships with others, hypervigilant behavior in the presence of others, attention deficits, silence and withdrawal, anxious and clinging attachment to adults, inability to play spontaneously and freely, and aggressive outbursts toward other children (Fatout, 1990).[6]

Reporting Child Abuse When there are strong indications that child abuse has occurred, social workers are mandated by state laws to report the abuse to authorized child protection agencies, whose function it is to investigate the situation and to take appropriate action to ensure the health and safety of the child (as discussed in Chapter 4). Ramifications of the legal mandate to report both physical and sexual abuse have been discussed by Besharov (1990) and Watson and Levine (1989).

Indications of Child Sexual Abuse Sex-abuse victims seldom reveal their experiences of abuse spontaneously. Many keep it a secret because of threats by the perpetrator and feelings of guilt and shame. Many others dissociate themselves from the experience and "perceive it as insignificant or unrelated to current difficulties" (Kilgore, 1988, p. 228). Often abuse comes to light as children tell other children, who tell their parents, who then bring it to the attention of authorities. (The legal mandate to report sexual abuse, of course, is the same as for physical abuse.) It is thus critical that social workers be knowledgeable about manifestations of sexual abuse, which are multidimensional and involve the several domains. It is important to recognize that one cannot conclude that sexual abuse has occurred from any single item on the list.

Immediate Physical Indications Pain or itching in the genital area; bruises or bleeding in the genitalia or anal regions; swelling or inflamed vulva, cervix, or perineum; torn, stained, or bloody underclothing; semen around genitalia, clothing, or mouth.

Ongoing Physical Indications Continuing injuries to the genitalia or rectum, urinary infections, venereal disease, AIDS, chronic stomachaches, chronic bowel complaints, eating disorders, pregnancy.

Emotional Indications   Depression, guilt/shame, low self-esteem, panic states, social withdrawal, phobias, vague physical complaints, hysteria.

Interpersonal Indicators   Pseudomaturity or regressive immaturity, aggressiveness or excessive compliance, poor relations with peers, either clinging or hypervigilance to being touched.

Cognitive/Perceptual Indicators   Detailed knowledge about sex, nightmares, inability to concentrate at school, learning delays and disabilities, hallucinations, recurrent illusions.

Behavioral Indicators   Excessive or inappropriate masturbation, exhibitionistic behavior, sexual abuse of other children, suicide gestures, running away, lying, stealing, excessive bathing, self-mutilation, fire setting, promiscuity, prostitution, withdrawal or hyperactivity, bedwetting or soiling, delinquency, age-inappropriate thumb sucking.[7]

Use of Anatomical Dolls   Anatomical dolls have been increasingly used in child sexual abuse investigations as a way of evaluating children's statements about being sexually molested. Such use has been described as both promising and controversial. Credibility is a central issue, and the courts have been skeptical about children's abilities to recall events accurately and to distinguish between fantasy and reality. There appears general agreement that professionals who employ anatomical dolls should be rigorously trained in this approach and should follow standardized procedures. There is also general agreement that information gained from using anatomical dolls should not be regarded as sufficient evidence of child abuse, but rather as one of many sources of information needed to establish that child sexual abuse has, in fact, occurred.[8]

Assessment of Strengths in Family Preservation Services

The seriousness of the above problems has understandably led to an emphasis on child welfare and safety with sometimes less emphasis on the family context. Family-centered services have been defined as "an approach to the delivery of social services that focuses on families rather than individuals. Services in the family-based context are intended to strengthen and maintain client families and to prevent family dissolution and out-of-home placement of children. The resources of the agency are focused on assisting client families in regaining or maintaining family autonomy" (Hutchinson et al., 1983). The approach is characterized in assessment by a focus on utlizing family strengths and the environment (Maluccio, 1990). That is, in addition to assessing indicators of actual or potential child harm, assessments include parenting skills and abilities. In addition to deficits, such assessments include records of what the parent is doing well. The family preservation movement that parents are generally doing the best they can and want the best for their family, and do not mean harm for them. As expressed by (Marckworth,1990) "We can help clients define problems as behaviors to be changed rather than using labels that give us and them no direction for change. Then we can see client strengths and articulate them to clients. We can also teach clients to identify strengths for themselves so that they can build on those strengths...to see that people are doing the best that they can, we must focus on cues from clients about how hard they are trying and how much they care about each other. We must look for those environmental factors that are contributing to client stress and forming barriers to change" (Marckworth, 1990, pp. 30–31).

Assessing Strengths and Obstacles

Charles Cowger has developed a matrix framework for assessment in which two dimensions are portrayed. On a vertical axis, potential strengths and

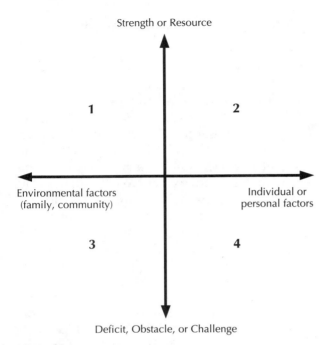

Strength or Resource

1   2

Environmental factors
(family, community)

Individual or
personal factors

3   4

Deficit, Obstacle, or Challenge

Figure 8-3   Framework for Assessment   (*Source:* Adapted from
Charles D. Cowger, Assessment of Client Strengths (New York:
Longman, 1992), pp.139–147 in Saleeby, Dennis (ed.), *The Strengths
Perspective in Social Work.*)

resources are depicted at one end and potential
deficits, challenges, and obstacles at the other. The
horizontal axis ranges from environmental (family
and community) to individual factors. The framework provides a useful way to press us to move
beyond the frequent preoccupation with personal
deficits (quadrant 4), to include personal strengths
and environmental strengths and obstacles
(Cowger, 1992) (see Figure 8-3).

To assist in examining how such a matrix can be
helpful in producing a more complete assessmant,
the following case will be presented and examined
for points in assessment.

....

Case Example

Tom is 20, Caucasian, and has been in the mental
health system since he was 9 years old. He was
raised by his mother and never knew his father. He
had many problems during childhood and was
placed in residential facilities on at least three occasions. His primary childhood diagnosis was conduct disorder and he periodically assaulted others
during adolescence. Records consistently indicate
that Tom and his mother had a very stressful relationship. Tom's maternal grandparents were
somewhat involved in his life, and he thinks highly of them. He reports feeling much love and support from them while he was growing up.

Tom was placed in a juvenile facility when he
was 17 after hospitalization on a mental health
unit where he desplayed psychotic behaviors and
was, at times, violent. Just prior to turning 18,
Tom entered the adult mental health system. At
that time he was transferred from a residential
juvenile facility to an adult facility where he currently resides.

Tom is hoping to move into an apartment with
his significant other (Sarah) in the near future. He
currently has several diagnoses including obsessive-
compulsive disorder, bipolar disorder, anxiety disorder, and learning disorder. Although medication
seems to control his psychotic thoughts, he continues to be easily frustrated and to have verbal outbursts. His overall IQ is 84, and he continues to
attend special education classes at his high school,
which he can do until his twenty-second birthday.
He has had considerable difficulty maintaining part-
time employment, even when the jobs involved support from his school program. His level of
independent living skills is assessed at well below the
minimum needed to live independently. He has difficulty completing household tasks, including cooking and cleaning, without much assistance. He has
had difficulty in managing his money. Tom has
learned to use public transportation, although he is
easily frustrated about remembering which bus to
take and will sometimes take a cab home despite a
lack of funds to pay the fare. Tom has consistently
refused assistance in any of these areas, reporting
that he does not need assistance.

Tom and Sarah met at a mental health facility
and have known each other for about six months.
Sarah has somewhat better independent living

skills and reports that she will help Tom with cooking and taking the bus, among other things. Neither is currently employed, but both plan to get jobs to support themselves. They are now asking for assistance from staff in moving into an apartment together.

....

To assist in using the assessment framework, the information above has been applied to the matrix. For example, quadrant 4 (individual deficits, challenges, or obstacles) includes the behavioral consequences and difficulties related to his multiple diagnoses. His difficulties with independent living skills and tendencies toward violence are concerns in relation to his living plans. Sarah may be in danger of domestic violence. In addition, without birth control, they may become pregnant soon. His low IQ may impede his learning of necessary independent living skills. The stressful relationship with his mother is of long standing. Finally, Tom is not open to help about these concerns, focusing instead on his desire to move in with Sarah.

Moving to quadrant 3 (environmental, including family and community deficits, obstacles, and challenges), we are alerted to the stressful relationship with his mother and her probable lack of support for his plan. Choosing to live in the community will probably mean that his treatment will be primarily based on medication rather than mental health counseling. In addition, the mental health system is often lacking in resources to support independent living. Employment opportunities commensurate with his skills may be limited.

When we move above the horizontal axis to consider potential strengths and resources, we become alerted to additional factors equally essential to the assessment. In quadrant 1 (potential community resources and strengths), we note that Tom's grandparents have been a valuable source of support in the past and could possibly be again. Sarah supports their joint plan. The high school is able to continue to support him in continuing his education. Staff in his current facility and voca-

tional services can assist Tom with acquiring more independent living skills. Finally, Tom's mother may be engaged in assisting Tom in making his plans succeed.

In quadrant 2 (potential personal strengths and resources), we are struck by the fact that Tom has a clear goal which he is highly committed to. He has begun work on many independent living skills, is taking the bus, and is motivated to work. Tom has developed a caring relationship with Sarah, one which she is willing to commit to a more permanent relationship. His medication is assisting him in controlling psychotic thoughts.

Cowger's framework for assessment alerts us to the fact that a useful assessment is not limited to either deficits or strengths, and that the environmental dimension is important as well as the personal. Use of the four quadrants provides us with information that can assist in pursuing goals, mindful of obstacles and challenges.

To further assist you in perceiving personal strengths, we have identified in the following list a number of strengths often manifested by clients in initial sessions. We urge you to cultivate your sensitivity to these and other manifestations of these crucial client resources:

1. Facing problems and seeking help, rather than denying or otherwise avoiding confronting them.
2. Risking by sharing problems with the practitioner—a stranger.
3. Persevering in attempting to keep a family together under difficult circumstances.
4. Expressing feelings and views openly rather than being guarded.
5. Exercising resourcefulness and creativity in making the most out of limited resources or managing and surviving upon a meager income.
6. Making sacrifices on behalf of children and others.
7. Seeking to further knowledge, education, and skills.
8. Expressing loving and caring feelings to family members.
9. Asserting one's rights rather than submitting to injustice.

10. Attempting to meet one's debts and obligations despite financial adversity.

11. Seeking to be independent.

12. Seeking to understand the needs and feelings of others.

13. Demonstrating capacity to be introspective and to shift thinking or realign perceptions when presented with new information or alternate views of situations.

14. Owning responsibility for one's own action and showing interest in making changes in *self* rather than focusing extensively on the changes one thinks others should make.

15. Demonstrating capacity for self-control.

16. Demonstrating ability to make individual value judgments.

17. Manifesting emotional capacity to function effectively in stressful situations.

18. Demonstrating ability to abstract and to make connections between causes and effects.

19. Demonstrating ability to form close relationships with others.

20. Demonstrating ability to consider alternative courses of actions and the needs of others when solving problems.

Participants and Systems Implicated in the Problem

The presenting problem usually identifies key persons, and further exploration reveals other persons, groups, or organizations that are participants in the client's difficulties. An accurate assessment must consider all the elements and how they interact to produce difficulties. Furthermore, an effective plan of intervention should embody these same elements, recognizing that it is not always feasible to involve everyone who is a participant in a given problematic situation. Some participants, for example, may refuse to become involved.

How Participants Interact

To understand how the interaction of participants results in difficulties, it is essential to understand the contributions of each to the problem situation. This requires detailed information about the behavior of all participants, including what they say and do before, during, and after problematic events. Detailed information regarding these factors is vital, for analysis of them illuminates circumstances associated with the problematic behavior, how each person affects and is affected by others, and consequences of events that tend to perpetuate problematic behavior. It is important to keep in mind that human behavior is purposive and can be understood by analyzing the forces that motivate people to behave as they do. Motivational forces consist of both external events (that is, those that are visible to others) and covert forces (that is, inner thoughts, beliefs, emotions, wishes, and images) as well as physiological and psychological states.

With regard to external events, certain circumstances or behaviors typically precede problematic behavior. One family member may say or do something that precipitates an angry, defensive, or hurt reaction by another. Events that precede problematic behavior are referred to as antecedents. Antecedents often give valuable clues as to the behavior of one participant that may be provocative or offensive to another, thereby triggering a negative reaction, followed by a counter negative reaction, thus setting the problematic situation in motion.

What each participant does and says during the problematic event must also be determined, for the response of each participant is a stimulus to other participants, and the nature and intensity of these responses tend to intensify, perpetuate, or even mitigate the dysfunctional interaction. One person may blame or insult another, and the latter may respond by yelling, making a counteraccusation, or calling the first party an unprintable name. We examine this interaction and patterns in depth in Chapter 10.

Determining the environmental consequences associated with problematic behaviors also may elucidate factors that perpetuate dysfunctional behaviors. Certain actions or responses increase the frequency of (reinforce) behaviors that precede them, and effective intervention must therefore be aimed at modifying such consequences. Tantrum behavior may be unwittingly perpetuated by parents who yield to their children's demands. Pouting by a marital partner may similarly be reinforced by pleading with the pouter to talk or consistently apologizing even though apologies may not be warranted. Recognizing the dynamic significance (effects) of such response patterns often enables practitioners to assist clients in developing new response patterns that break dysfunctional cycles and gradually reduce the frequency of the problematic behaviors.

Analyzing the antecedents of problematic behavior, describing the behavior in specific terms, and assessing the consequences or effects of the problematic behavior provide a powerful means of identifying factors that motivate dysfunctional behavior and are appropriate targets of interventions. This straightforward approach to analyzing the functional significance of behavior has been designated by numerous authors as the ABC model (A = antecedent, B = behavior, C = consequence). Although it is far less simple than it may seem, the ABC model provides a coherent and practical approach to understanding behavior, particularly when it is supplemented by consideration of cognitive factors.

Patterns of Communication/Interaction in Spouse Abuse Because episodes of spouse abuse are commonly preceded by gradual buildup from tension that may derive in part from dysfunctional patterns of communication/interaction, it is vital to assess this dimension carefully. It is also vital to elicit detailed information about how each partner contributes to and reacts to arguments that culminate in violence. Moreover, to fully understand the reactions of the partners, it is essential to explore the cognitive meanings each attaches to the messages and behavior of the other. Doing so elucidates sensitive areas and dynam-

ics underlying defensive and attacking reactions by the partners.

In eliciting details of interaction, requesting each partner to reveal what she or he said, thought, and did tends to yield information that reveals problematic behaviors that become targets of change efforts. For example, the woman may have superior verbal skills that she employs to belittle the man or otherwise gain an edge, which the man counters by threats, intimidating tactics, and finally greater physical strength.

Other interactional patterns of particular relevance include power inequities, power struggles, lack of shared decision making, and dependency associated with fear of abandonment on the part of the woman. Because abusing partners manifest many patterns of violence, effective treatment requires accurate assessment of the patterns. Pittman (1987) identifies major patterns, which are as follows:

1. Men Who Are Insensitive to the Needs of Others Insensitive to others and having almost total lack of empathy, these men relate to women and, in fact, all people as though they are objects and not human beings. They brutalize wives, children, and others as though they are objects to be used and dominated. Many drink and when they do they are even worse. Most women do not marry or remain with such men for long, unless they are vulnerable to domination by such men as a result of warping experiences in childhood that involved being abused by this type of man.

2. Men with an Overdeveloped Sense of Gender As with some child sexual abusers, these men believe they should be powerful, successful, adored, desired, and served; but they know such is not the case. They see themselves as powerless and fear they are inadequate. To attempt to overcompensate for feelings of failure and inadequacy, they use violence to gain a sense of power and portray themselves as powerful, even though the sense of power is short-lived.

3. Men Who Believe They Should Control Their Wives   These men cling to outmoded beliefs that men should be dominant and should punish their wives for displeasing them or usurping their authority. Men from fundamentalist religions are especially prone to this pattern (Denton, 1989).

4. Both Partners Engage in Escalating Conflict   Interaction with these couples is characterized by competitiveness, with both partners seeking to gain a one-up position. Heated arguments are common. In some instances a spouse who has been under tension may have an outburst of rage that is triggered by a mild provocation. These couples have ongoing dysfunctional patterns of interaction that must be addressed in treatment planning.

Unmet Needs and Wants

Because we discussed the significance of this factor at length earlier in this chapter, we will limit our discussion to basic unmet needs involved in families with identified child maltreatment or spouse abuse. Neglected children obviously have unmet needs to live in a secure nurturing environment wherein they receive adequate and consistent physical care, proper nourishment, emotional sustenance (attention, affection, approval, and encouragement), and supervision. Abused children have these same needs but in addition need a safe family environment that is free of violence, intimidation, and sexual molestation. Children who are maltreated have the needs of all children—to be loved, valued, and protected by parents who want them and who are committed to safeguarding their health and well-being.

In addition to needing a safe and secure relationship with their partners, abused spouses need to feel valued and respected by their partners. Both partners may have needs for skills in managing emotions and engaging in constructive problem solving. A need for increased self-esteem is also common among both abused women and their abusive partners, many of whom were themselves abused as children.

Social Needs of Single Parents   Numerous studies over the past two decades have consistently revealed that one-parent families, the vast majority headed by women, are at risk of child maltreatment when the parents lack supportive networks and are socially isolated. A review of the literature by Seagull (1987) revealed a clear relationship between parental social isolation and child neglect and a weaker relationship between isolation and physical abuse. Moreover, parents with the greatest need for developing and maintaining close, supportive relationships may be those least capable of forming such supportive relationships (Lovell & Richey, 1991).

Unmet social needs of isolated parents give rise to frustrations. For single-parent mothers, these frustrations very often are compounded by deficient financial resources that make it impossible to meet the needs of the family adequately. Because isolated single parents spend an inordinate amount of time with their children, it is understandable that they are vulnerable to venting their frustrations on their children or to leaving them unattended while pursuing involvement in activities outside the home. Social support of parents and social skills thus are factors that should be addressed in child abuse and neglect cases (using the guidelines provided in Chapter 9).

Developmental Stage and/or Life Transition

Because we also discussed this factor earlier, we will limit discussion to the groups we have selected for particular focus. Physical and/or sexual abuse of children can occur anywhere in the developmental cycle from infancy through adolescence. The effects of physical abuse can severely block social and emotional development, as we noted earlier. Normal opposition of two year olds to parental guidance is sometimes interpreted as willful by parents who become involved in child abuse. Sexual curiosity of preschoolers is sometimes interpreted as budding promiscuity by adults who engage in sexual abuse. Such abuses often cause developmental regression in children and interfere with normal completion of developmental tasks.

Severity of the Problem

Determining the severity of problems can be useful in determining whether clients have the capacity to continue functioning in the community or whether hospitalization or other strong supportive or protective measures are needed. Moreover, determining the level of stress can assist in determining the frequency of sessions and the need to mobilize support systems. The large majority of clients are able to function adequately so that weekly or even less frequent sessions suffice.

When clients are severely depressed and potentially suicidal, however, hospitalization may be required until they manifest significant improvement. Similarly, people whose functioning is temporarily impaired by extreme anxiety and loss of emotional control, such as people who are experiencing acute post-traumatic stress disorders (Patten, Gatz, Jones, & Thomas, 1989), may require short-term hospitalization.

Acute stress reactions also sometimes occur because of crises in people's lives (such as rape or unexpected loss of a job) that temporarily overwhelm their coping capacities. Relaxation procedures, combined with short-term crisis intervention (see Chapter 14), may enable such clients to regain their equilibrium. Frequent sessions over a short period are commonly employed in such situations.

Exploring the level of stress through interviewing techniques often suffices in evaluating the client's level of stress. You may wish to quantify the level of stress, however, by using a scale devised for this purpose. The Index of Clinical Stress (Hudson, 1992) is a convenient, self-administered scale of proven reliability (Abell, 1991). Other instruments developed to assess depression and suicidal risk are discussed in the next chapter.

Assessing Risk in Child Maltreatment Assessing severity of child abuse and risk of reabuse is a critical task of child protective service workers, who bear responsibility for ensuring the safety of abused children. Agreement about indicators of high risk, however, is by no means unanimous. A recent study (McDonald & Marks, 1991) of eight risk-assessment instruments currently in use throughout the country identified 88 different factors. Of the 88 variables identified, 15 were included in the majority of instruments, and these variables were subsumed under six domains. The six domains and the 15 variables (stated in terms of indication of high risk) are as follows:

1. Parent characteristics
   (1) Poor mental health
   (2) Poor physical health
   (3) Low capacity for child care
   (4) Inadequate physical health care of child
   (5) Inadequate supervision of children
   (6) Failure to cooperate with the agency

2. Environmental factors
   (7) Inadequate support for the caretaker
   (8) Neglect of physical safety in the home

3. Parent-child interactions
   (9) Unrealistic expectations of child

4. Child characteristics
   (10) Presence of physical disabilities
   (11) Poor personal hygiene
   (12) Inadequate and inappropriate clothing

5. Maltreatment
   (13) Past sexual abuse
   (14) Chronic and abusive physical discipline

6. Perpetrator
   (15) Ready access to the child

Of the 88 variables included in the eight instruments, fewer than one-half have been subjected to empirical scrutiny, according to McDonald and Marks (1991). Further, only three such studies have been reported in the literature. Based on the findings of these studies, a number of factors have been reported useful in differentiating reabusing (high risk) from nonreabusing (low risk) cases. The following list contains factors indicative of high risk. Factors indicative of low risk are the converse of those listed.

High Risk

- More than one child
- History of severe and frequent abuse
- Much time spent with child
- Poor parental coping skills
- Low capacity to use resources
- Previous placement of child
- Single parent
- Negative social relationships
- Younger caretaker
- Younger child
- Greater access to child
- Limited physical and mental abilities of child

Obviously, the state of the art in predicting recurrence of child abuse is not sophisticated and additional research is badly needed.

When the risk of recurrence is high, steps may be required to place the child in a safe environment (e.g., with relatives or foster parents). Because of the damaging effects of uprooting children from their homes, however, efforts are made to keep children in their homes whenever feasible, and to employ intensive, home-based services to lower the risk of reabuse by enhancing families' functioning, as we discuss in Chapter 16.

Meanings Clients Ascribe to Problems

Despite the utility of the ABC model, assessments of the forces that motivate clients' behaviors are incomplete until the clients' perceptions and definitions of the problem are carefully considered. It is increasingly recognized that the meanings people attribute to events (meaning attributions) are as important as the events themselves, a fact recognized by the ancient Greek stoic philosopher Epictetus (first century A.D.) who asserted, "Men are disturbed not by the things which happen to them but by their opinions about the things." You, your clients, other participants in problems, and external observers thus may view problem situations in widely varying ways. Determining the views of the major actors will enhance your understanding of the motivation of each, for people behave according to the meaning a situation has for them. Moreover, to apply the principle of starting where the client is, you must first know clients' perceptions of the causes of problematic behavior (Goldstein, 1983).

Determining meaning attributions is also vital because clients' beliefs about factors that cause problems often represent barriers to changes that must be made if problems are to be ameliorated. Such meaning attributions thus tend to maintain problematic behavior and can also be regarded as targets of change (Hepworth, 1979). Hurvitz (1975, pp. 228–229) has categorized meaning attributions that pose obstacles to change, which in modified form with examples are as follows:

1. *Pseudoscientific explanations*: "Our biorhythms don't mesh, and there's nothing we can do about it; we're just not good for each other." "Jenny [*an adopted child*] just has bad blood. Her mother was a prostitute."

2. *Psychological labeling*: "Mother is a paranoid; I've only lied to her a few times." "I think Larry is just hyperactive."

3. *Beliefs that other major actors lack the ability or desire to make essential changes*: "I know he says he wants our marriage to work, but I know better. He wants a divorce, and he's trying to provoke me into giving him a reason for it." "She'll never change. She never has. I think we're wasting our time and money."

4. *Unchangeable external factors*: "There's no point in talking to my teacher. She's got it in for me and doesn't even try to understand." "As long as his

father's alive, we don't have a chance of making it. His father just seems to have a hold on him."

5. *Misconceptions about innate qualities that cannot be changed:* "I was born a loser. There's no point in talking about learning to be a mechanic. I'd just wash out." "I know he has a right to expect me to be a better sexual partner. I wish I could be, but I've never had any sexual desires, and I never will."

6. *Unrealistic feelings of helplessness:* "There's nothing I can do. Gloria is such a strong person that she defeats me at every turn." "What can I do? I'm completely at the mercy of Hal. If I don't settle on his terms, he'll take the children away from me."

7. *Reference to "fixed" religious or philosophical principles, natural laws, or social forces:* "Sure, I already have as many children as I want. But I don't really have a choice. The church says that birth control is evil." "She calls all the shots because that's just how women are. They just see men as someone to bring home a paycheck."

8. *Assertion based upon presumed laws of human nature:* "All children tell lies at that age. It's just natural. I did when I was a kid." "Sure, I've had trouble with people in authority. When people get authority, they try to step on others. It's just human nature."

9. *Allegations about limitations of significant others involved in the problem:* "He's just dense. I've tried every way I know how to get through to him, but he's too dense to understand my feelings." "I think she must be a little stupid. Anyone with any brains would know how to balance a checkbook."

Fortunately, many clients manifest meaning attributions that are not inimical to change. Some clients are open and even eager to examine the part they play in problematic situations. Others readily acknowledge their parts and desire to modify their behavior. When obstacles such as those listed above are encountered, however, it is vital to explore them and to resolve them before attempting to negotiate change-oriented goals or to implement interventions. Until such barriers are removed, clients do not assume responsibility for their part in problems and typically and understandably resist having goals or interventions imposed upon them, for from their vantage point the practitioner is barking up the wrong tree.

To elicit meaning attributions from clients, you must employ appropriate exploratory responses following clients' accounts of their problems. Appropriate responses include the following:

"What meaning do you make of his behavior?"

"What were the reasons for your parents grounding you?"

"What conclusions have you drawn about why your landlord evicted you?"

"What are your views as to why you didn't get a promotion?"

Meaning attributions are also relevant to child maltreatment and spouse abuse. Young children who have been physically abused lack the maturity and perspective to recognize that their parents' abusive behavior derives from multiple sources related to traumas from the past, frustrations in the present, and dysfunctional coping patterns. Instead, they may blame themselves for being bad, unlovable, or deserving of their parents' abusive behavior. Similarly, children who are sexually abused commonly blame themselves for their parents' sexual molestation and view themselves as bad or worthless as a result. Even many abused spouses who were deprived and abused as children mistakenly view spouse abuse as the norm and need assistance in believing they have a right to be respected and treated as an equal. In each of the preceding instances, determining the meaning that clients attribute to abusive behavior is a crucial step to enabling them to adapt a more realistic perspective and to liberate themselves from the torment of blaming themselves for the egregious behavior of their parents or spouses.

Sites of Problematic Behavior

Determining where problematic behavior occurs may provide clues to understanding factors that trigger problematic behavior. Children may throw tantrums in certain locations and not in others. As a result of repeated experiences, they soon discriminate where certain behaviors are tolerated and where they are not. Adults may experience anxiety or depression in certain environmental contexts and not in others. One couple, for example, invariably experienced breakdown in communication in the home of one spouse's parents. Some children manifest problematic behavior at school but not at home, or vice versa. Determining where problematic behavior occurs will assist you in identifying areas that warrant further exploration aimed at pinpointing factors associated with the behavior in question.

Identifying where problematic behavior does not occur is also of value in some instances, for as Brown and Levitt (1979) explain, such understanding may identify sources available to the client for temporary relief of painful states, such as fear, anxiety, depression, loneliness, and insecurity. One client may be assisted to gain temporary respite from overwhelming anxiety by visiting a cherished aunt. In other instances, clients may actually gain permanent relief from intolerable stress by changing employment, discontinuing college, or moving out of relationships when tension or other unpleasant feeling states are experienced exclusively in these contexts.

The Temporal Context of Problematic Behaviors

Determining when problematic behaviors occur often yields valuable clues to factors that play a critical role in clients' problems. Onsets of depressive episodes, for example, may coincide with the time of year when a loved one died or when a divorce occurred. Family problems may also occur, for example, when the father returns from work, at bedtime for the children, at mealtimes, or when children are (or should be) getting ready for school. Similarly, couples may experience severe conflict when one spouse is working the midnight shift, a few days before the wife's menstrual period, after participation by either spouse in activities that exclude the partner, or when one or both

drink at parties. Clues such as the foregoing illuminate the nature of stresses associated with problems and suggest fruitful areas for detailed explorations of the behaviors of participants in the problem system.

Determining the temporal context of child maltreatment may also elucidate factors that are pertinent to planning treatment. Parents may experience severe stress associated with certain times or events. For example, abuse may occur after intense marital conflict, after visits of in-laws, or after heavy drinking. Abuse may also follow provocative behavior by children, rejection by a lover, or a period of unemployment for a male (Jones, 1990).

Child sexual abuse may also occur at certain times, as, for example, when the adult male is alone with the child while the mother is at work. Sexual abuse may also occur when the adult male (or female) sleeps with, wrestles with, or bathes with a child. Knowing when and where the abuse occurs enables practitioners and clients to develop strategies to prevent reoccurrences.

Cycles of Spouse Abuse A number of writers (cited by Douglas, 1991) have identified varied cyclical patterns of violence, which should be considered in assessing violence. (Our discussion is based on the article by Douglas.) Spouse abuse tends to recur, and repeat victims account for more than half of the cases reported over several years' time.

The cycle begins with a tension-building phase followed by dramatic escalation that culminates in a battering episode. In this period of acute crisis the social worker sees the female, who is bruised or more seriously injured and who is angry, hurt, and frightened to the extent she may be determined to end the relationship. The abusing partner typically responds by expressing remorse and promising not to resort to violence in the future. Although they initially blame each other, each recognizes to a degree that he or she contributed to the development of tensions that preceded the violence. Often both partners desire reconciliation, making pledges to each other and believing it will not happen again. A honeymoon period ensues, and calm is temporarily restored.

Tensions again gradually build, however, as a result of external stressors or unresolved difficulties in the relationship. Stressful incidents increase in both intensity and severity. The stage is now set for another rapid escalation of tension and violent outburst.

If couples are seen before the cycles have become well established, they may be receptive to and able to learn and apply new and functional patterns of communication and conflict resolution. Without intervention, however, patterns of conflict gradually become set, centering around recurring themes and unresolved issues. "As the themes are replayed, the intensity of their actions increase, resulting in increased physical and verbal abuse" (Douglas, p. 527). Underlying issues surface over even minor conflicts and positive feelings in the relationship are eroded. Aversive communication increases, caring messages are sent infrequently, if at all, and commitment to the relationship is diminished to the extent the relationship may be in jeopardy.

In the "severe" stage, violence may be used by one partner "to maintain dominance and power by intentionally inflicting fear, humiliation and injury on the partner" (Douglas, p. 528). In this stage, violence is frequent and severe, and partners have fallen into set roles of perpetrator and victim. The situation is dangerous at this point, and the children, too, may be at risk for abuse. In this advanced stage, the family violence is unlikely to be a secret and the family may have had repeated involvement with police, health care institutions, and social agencies. Motivation of partners to seek counseling is usually lacking when the patterns have evolved to this degree of severity. However, the very severity of the violence may induce battered women to seek assistance from shelters. Such involvement often leads to court orders for perpe-

trators, and treatment is offered as an alternative to prison sentences.

Frequency of Problematic Behaviors

The frequency of problematic behavior is an index to both the pervasiveness of a problem and its impact on the participants. Clients who constantly nag or criticize family members, who drink to excess habitually, or who frequently express anger in violent ways severely impair family functioning by producing tension, conflict, and fear and eroding self-esteem of family members. Services for such clients and their families may need to be more intensive than for clients whose dysfunctional behaviors are less frequent or intermittent. Similarly, clients who report feeling depressed constantly may require more vigorous treatment measures than those who experience episodic periods of depression. Determining the frequency of problematic behaviors thus helps to clarify the degree of dysfunctional behavior and the extent to which it impairs the daily functioning of clients and their families.

Assessing the frequency of problematic behaviors also provides a baseline on behaviors targeted for change. Making subsequent comparisons of the frequency of the targeted behaviors enables you to evaluate the efficacy of your interventions, as we discuss in Chapter 13.

Duration of the Problem

Another important dimension vital to assessing problems relates to the history of the problem. Knowing when the problem developed and under what circumstances assists in further evaluating the degree of the problem, formulating psychosocial dynamic factors associated with the problem, determining the source of motivation to seek assistance, and planning appropriate interventions. Often significant changes in people's life situations, including even seemingly positive ones, disrupt their equilibrium to the extent that they are unable to adapt to changes. An unplanned pregnancy, loss of employment, job promotion, severe illness, birth of a first child, move to a new city, death of a loved one, divorce, retirement, severe disappointment—these and many other life events may cause severe stresses. Careful exploration of the duration of problems often discloses such antecedents to dysfunctional behavior. These antecedent events often are equally as significant as the immediate problematic situation and warrant careful exploration to determine residual emotions and problems that must be addressed.

Antecedent events that immediately precede decisions to seek help are particularly informative. Designated as precipitating events, these antecedents often give valuable clues to critical stresses that might otherwise be overlooked. Spouses and parents often report their problems have existed longer than a year. Why they chose to ask for help at a particular time is not readily apparent, but knowing why may cast their problems in a somewhat different light. For example, careful exploration revealed that a couple who identified their problem as fighting incessantly for the past four years did not decide to seek help until the wife began working outside the home for the first time, just two weeks before they called for an appointment. Similarly, parents who complained about their teenage daughter's long-standing rebelliousness did not seek assistance until they became aware (one week before calling the agency) that she was engaging in an affectional relationship with a woman six years her senior. In both these instances, the precipitating events would not have been disclosed had the practitioner not sought to answer the critical question of why they were seeking help at this particular time.

Precipitating events can usually be determined by asking clients to identify reasons for seeking assistance at a particular time. In some instances, clients themselves will not be fully aware of their reasons, and it may be necessary to explore what events or emotional experiences were occurring shortly before their decision to seek help.

Determining the duration of problems is also vital in assessing clients' levels of functioning and in planning appropriate interventions. Exploration may reveal that a client's adjustment has been marginal for many years and that the immediate problem is only an exacerbation of long-term multiple problems. In other instances, the onset of a problem may be acute and clients may have functioned at an adequate or high level for many years. In the first instance, modest goals and long-term intermittent service may be indicated; in the second instance, short-term crisis intervention may be sufficient to restore clients to their previous level of functioning.

Duration of Child Maltreatment and Spouse Abuse   When child maltreatment has extended over a lengthy period of time, the effects on a child's development will ordinarily be even more severe than the effects of short-term maltreatment. Ongoing maltreatment produces cumulative effects because psychological damage during one phase of development impairs a child's capacity to master developmental tasks during subsequent phases of development (including adulthood). Remedial measures aimed at building trust in others, enhancing self-esteem, developing social skills, and ameliorating the warping effects on sexual adjustment may need to be intensive and prolonged.

Patterns of spouse abuse sometimes begin as early as courtship or on a honeymoon (Pirog-Good & Stets, 1989). For one or both partners, violence may be part of a lifestyle learned early from parents who engaged in ongoing violence. With such couples, violence continues until one or both partners decide the violent behavior is no longer tolerable or when pressure from an external source (e.g., law-enforcement officials, religious leaders, or extended family) motivates them to change.

Sometimes violence toward a spouse erupts suddenly with no previous history. As such it may be a response of desperation that may bewilder and distress both partners. Most often, a significant change in the life of the perpetrator or in the marriage is the precipitant (e.g., infidelity, unemployment, or wife going to work). Short-term crisis intervention may be all that is needed to stabilize the marriage in such instances.

Possible Alcohol or Substance Abuse

Given the prevalence of problems associated with abuse of alcohol or other substances in our country, it is generally appropriate to evaluate the possibility of substance abuse as part of the assessment process. As noted earlier, alcohol abuse is frequently implicated in problems of child maltreatment and spouse abuse. It is vital, therefore, to evaluate that possibility before formulating treatment plans. Focus on the alcohol abuse must be given priority; otherwise, efforts to reduce risk of reabuse by seeking to enhance family functioning are unlikely to be fruitful. We discuss a number of useful instruments that can be used to screen for alcoholism in the next chapter.

Clients' Emotional Reactions to Problems

When people encounter problems in living, they typically experience emotional reactions to those problems. It is important to explore and assess such reactions for three major reasons. First, people often gain relief from expressing troubling emotions related to their problems. Common reactions to typical problem situations are worry, concern, resentment, hurt, fear, and feeling overwhelmed, helpless, or hopeless. Being able to ventilate such emotions in the presence of an understanding and concerned person is a source of great comfort to many persons. Moreover, releasing pent-up feelings often has the effect of relieving oneself of a heavy burden. In fact, ventilating

emotions may have a liberating effect for persons who tend to be out of touch with their emotions and have not acknowledged to themselves or others that they even have troubled feelings.

A second reason for exploring and assessing emotional reactions is that, because emotions strongly influence behavior, the emotional reactions of some people impel them to behave in ways that exacerbate or contribute to difficulties. In some instances, in fact, people create new difficulties as a result of emotionally reactive behavior. In the heat of anger, some persons overreact and physically abuse children and/or spouses. Other individuals may be verbally abusive, behaving in ways that frighten, offend, or alienate family members or other significant people. Powerful emotional reactions may thus be an integral part of the overall problem configuration.

The third major reason for assessing emotional responses is that intense reactions often become primary problems, overshadowing the antecedent problematic situation. Some people develop severe depressive reactions associated with problematic situations. A mother may become depressed over an unwed daughter's pregnancy; a man may react with depression to unemployment or retirement; and culturally dislocated persons may become depressed following relocation, even though they may have fled intolerable conditions in their homeland. Other individuals may react to problematic events with feelings of helplessness or panic that cause virtual paralysis. In such instances, interventions must be addressed to the overwhelming emotional reactions as well as to the problematic situation that triggered them.

Maltreated children may respond to episodes of abuse by feeling depressed, fearful, and overwhelmed, and viewing their situation as unsolvable. Some manifest suicidal tendencies as a result of feeling helpless and hopeless about their situations. Older children may resent an offending parent and may act out their frustrations by running away from home. The emotional reactions of wives to being abused are similar to those just described.

Coping Efforts and Needed Skills

Further light is shed on clients' difficulties by determining how they have attempted to cope with their problems. The coping methods they employ give valuable clues to their levels of stress and of functioning. Exploration may reveal that a client has marked deficits in coping skills, relying upon rigid patterns that often prove dysfunctional. Some clients employ avoidance patterns through withdrawing or attempting to numb or fortify themselves by using drugs or alcohol. Other clients attempt to cope with interpersonal problems by resorting to aggressive, domineering behavior or by placating or becoming submissive. Still other clients manifest flexible and effective coping patterns but collapse under unusually high levels of stress that would overwhelm even the strongest persons. By contrast, other clients depend heavily upon others to manage problematic situations for them.

Exploring how clients have attempted to cope with problems sometimes reveals that they have struggled effectively with similar problems in the past but are no longer able to do so. In such instances, it is important to explore carefully what has changed. For example, a person may have been able to cope with the demands of one supervisor but not with a new one who is more critical and aloof.

Changes in clients' levels of functioning also occasionally reduce their capacity to cope. Severely depressed clients commonly overestimate the difficulty of their problems and underestimate their coping abilities. Some clients are also able to cope effectively in one setting but not in another. Interestingly, some people slay various and sundry dragons at work with dispatch but find themselves unable to cope with the needs and emotions of family members. Some schoolteachers are able to be firm and consistent with challenging pupils but

are at a loss as to how to deal effectively with their own children. And finally, some social workers have marvelous ability to listen to and understand their clients only to find they simply cannot understand the "irrationality" of their own spouses. The point is that by exploring the different circumstances, meaning attributions, and emotional reactions of clients, you will be able to identify subtle differences that account for the varied effectiveness of their coping patterns in different contexts.

Another aspect of assessment is to identify the skills clients must possess to ameliorate their difficulties. Knowledge of needed skills enables you to negotiate appropriate and feasible goals aimed at assisting clients to develop skills not already possessed. To improve parent-child relationships, for example, clients may require the development of listening and negotiating skills. Socially inhibited clients may similarly need to learn skills in approaching others, introducing themselves, and engaging others in conversation. To enhance marital relationships, partners often need to learn communication and conflict management skills. To cope effectively with people who tend to exploit them, still other clients must acquire assertiveness skills.

Parenting Skills Deficiencies in parenting skills can be a major factor that contributes to child abuse. As we noted earlier, many abusing parents were abused by their own parents and thus had poor models for parenting. Consequently, they learned dysfunctional parenting behaviors and are deficient in knowing how to cope with challenging behaviors that confront all parents. In disciplining their children, they tend to employ physical punishment, which sometimes escalates to violent behavior and culminates in abuse. It is thus apparent in such instances that interventions must be designed to enhance parenting skills, dimensions of which are discussed in Chapters 15 and 17.

Anger Control Deficient anger control is still another factor that can contribute to child and spouse abuse. Some adults have relatively low tolerance for frustration and are subject to fits of rage when frustration in coping with children or partners exceeds their level of tolerance. In such instances interventions aimed at increasing their frustration tolerance and managing anger should be included in the overall intervention strategies.

In assessing anger control it is important to determine circumstances and specific stressors that trigger anger, as interventions will be aimed at reducing clients' sensitivity to such provocative stimuli. Moreover, it is important to elicit clients' thoughts about and interpretations of events that precede violent outbursts, as these factors play a key role in anger control strategies. We discuss such a strategy in the last part of Chapter 14 in the section "Stress Inoculation Training."

By identifying skills needed to resolve problems, you can formulate appropriate interventions. Fortunately, skill development programs exist for a number of skills commonly needed by clients, which we discuss in Part 3.

Cultural, Societal, and Social Class Factors

As we noted in earlier chapters, ethnocultural factors influence how people feel about requesting assistance, how they view their problems, how they communicate, how they perceive the role of the professional person, and how they view various approaches to solving problems. It is thus vital that you be knowledgeable about these factors and competent in responding accordingly. We discuss cultural factors at length in Chapter 9.

Socioeconomic and Ethnocultural Factors in Child Abuse
Studies summarized by Garbarino and Ebata (1983) have consistently indicated that of families in the United States where child abuse allegations have occurred, a disproportionately high percentage comes from the less educated, the poor, and minority groups, with black children being overrepresented. Social class is, however, an intervening factor in child abuse reporting. Families with greater resources are less likely to have instances of abuse reported.[9] Similarly, the fact that race and ethnicity are often correlated with poverty and social class does not suggest that these factors make an independent contribution to predicting child abuse beyond the stresses and frustrations associated with living in conditions of poverty and oppression.

With respect to child-rearing practices, ethnicity plays a major role. Samoans, for example, believe in and practice corporal punishment, whereas Japanese utilize emotional punishment. Further studies of some Hispanic groups have indicated that they view child abuse as more serious than neglect, preferring indirect means of controlling children and disfavoring corporal punishment.[10] The fact is that no cultures approve of child abuse or neglect. They vary, however, in their definitions of what constitutes abuse or neglect and what constitutes acceptable child-rearing practices. Problems occur when personal or cultural beliefs about acceptable practices conflict with larger community legal standards defining abuse or neglect.

The implication of the factors just discussed is that poor families are especially vulnerable to child abuse and neglect. Social workers, therefore, should consider interventions (including advocacy and social action) aimed at improving the socioeconomic statuses and parenting skills of these families.

Cultural and Social Class Factors in Spouse Abuse

As with child abuse, reported incidence of spouse abuse is higher among the poor and among minority groups. The stress-producing factors of low income, inadequate housing, unemployment, inadequate health care, discrimination, and limited opportunity produce frustrations that result in the tendency for high levels of violence toward spouses as well as children.[11]

It is also common knowledge that violence of husbands toward wives is higher in cultures that relegate women to subordinate positions in relationship to men, as occurs in many countries of the Mideast and Asia. Power is gender-linked to a far greater degree in those countries than in some parts of the United States, and a woman who challenges the power and authority of her husband places herself at risk of being abused. Latino families generally are also often patriarchal with the male having far greater power and authority than the female. The incidence of wife abuse thus is somewhat higher among these families, and even more so when poverty is present and/or when the males place a high value on masculine characteristics, ranging from male genital prowess to towering pride and fearlessness.

Societal Factors in Family Violence   Societal factors also play a role in family violence. The history of violence in the United States and the saturation of our media (especially movies, television, and comic books) with violence no doubt contribute to the high incidence of violent actions inside and outside the family. Davis (1991) has written a brief but thought-provoking article that places violence of parents toward children and husbands toward wives in historical perspective. We urge you to read it.

External Resources Needed

When clients request services it is essential to determine if the services requested match the functions of the agency and if the staff possesses the skills required to provide high-quality service. Often when clients apply for services from an agency or practitioner, they have made their selection based on knowledge gained from others who have used the services of the agency or practitioner. In either instance, the service requested may match the services available, and external resources may not be needed.

Many clients, however, have inadequate or erroneous information about an agency's functions or eligibility requirements and/or need services in addition to those provided by an agency, such as medication, rehabilitation services, or special education services. Specific service needs of clients also may be better provided by staff members of other agencies that specialize in certain services (e.g., sex therapy, divorce counseling, and rape crisis counseling), and referral may be indicated to ensure that the client receives the highest quality of service. In such instances, the practitioner performs a broker or case manager role. Performing these roles effectively requires knowledge of community resources or at least knowledge of how to obtain relevant essential information. Fortunately, many large communities have community resource information centers that are of great value to both clients and professionals in locating needed resources. To familiarize you with typical resources available in large communities, we have compiled a list (see Table 8-1), which is intended to be illustrative and not comprehensive.

In certain instances, in addition to the public and private resources listed in the table, two other major resources should be considered. The first is self-help groups, which have been extremely helpful to some individuals with personal problems. Eschewing professional leadership, members of these groups look to themselves to help each other, and the rapid expansion of such groups in recent years attests to their value. Self-help groups typically provide emotional support and the opportunity to share with and benefit from others who have had to cope with similar problems.

A second major resource, which is often overlooked, consists of natural support systems that may be tapped to counter isolation and difficulties in coping with disruptions caused by transitional stresses. Natural support systems include the family, relatives, friends, neighbors, coworkers, and close associates from school, church, and other social groups.

Some family therapists have developed innovative ways of tapping support systems collectively

TABLE 8.1   Types of Community Resources

Need	Resources
Income maintenance	Public assistance; Old Age, Survivors, Disability, and Health Insurance (OASDHI); Unemployment Compensation; Worker's Compensation; church welfare programs; food stamps
Housing	Special housing programs for the elderly, other low-income persons and homeless; housing outreach programs; Salvation Army; YMCA, YWCA, migrant housing
Healthcare	Tax-funded hospitals, local public and private health centers, Shriners hospitals, veteran's hospitals, Medicare, Medicaid, visiting nursing services, convalescent homes, rehabilitation programs, home health sevices.
Child services	Day-care centers, child-guidance clinics, child welfare divisions, shelter homes, Children's Service Society, church programs, Headstart program, adoption agencies, school social sevices, special education and developmentally disabled programs, children's treatment centers, crippled children's services
Vocational guidance and rehabilitation	Job service, public vocational rehabilitation programs, veteran's services, Job Corps, Fountain House and like facilities for mentally disabled persons
Mental health care	Mental health centers, hospitals with psychiatric units, substance abuse centers, private practitioners
Legal services	Legal service societies (United Way), public defender, county attorneys, American Civil Liberties Union
Marital and family therapy	Family service centers (United Way), division of family services (public), ministers, church-affiliated services, private practitioners, mental health centers
Youth services	YMCA, YWCA, public and private recreational programs, local youth service programs, residential treatment programs, youth group homes, juvenile courts, Youth Authority programs
Recreation	Public and private recreation programs and centers, senior citizens centers, arts and handicrafts programs
Transportation	Traveler's Aid Society, local governmental programs, volunteers

through an intervention termed network therapy. These therapists contend that much of the dysfunctional behavior labeled as mental illness derives from feelings of alienation from one's natural social network, which consists of all human relationships that are significant in a person's life, including natural support systems. Employing network therapy, these practitioners mobilize 40 to 50 significant people who are willing to come together in a period of crisis for one or more members of the network. The goal is to unite their efforts in tightening the social network of relationships for the purpose of offering support, reassurance, and solidarity to troubled members and other members of the social network. Mobilizing social networks is in keeping with the best traditions of social work.

In instances of cultural dislocation, natural support systems may be limited to the family, and practitioners may need to mobilize other potential resources in the community. Assisting refugees poses a challenge, for a cultural reference group may not be available in some communities. The language barrier poses an additional obstacle, and practitioners may need to search for interpreters and other interested parties who can assist these families in locating housing, gaining employment, learning the language, adapting to an alien culture, and developing social support systems.

In still other instances, people's environments may be virtually devoid of natural support systems. Consequently, environmental changes may be necessary to accomplish a better fit between needs and resources, a topic we consider at greater length in the next chapter.

QUESTIONS TO BE ANSWERED IN ASSESSMENT

To assist you in determining if you have considered all of the factors discussed in the preceding sections, we have encapsulated the factors in the following questions. You can employ these questions as a checklist to ensure you have not overlooked a significant factor in your assessment.

1. What are the concerns and problems of potential clients as they perceive them?

2. What current or impending legal mandates (if any) are relevant to the situation?

3. What serious or imminent health or safety issues are relevant to the situation?

Questions 4 to 17 pertain to further specifcation of problems. They do not imply a priority for a problem focus over explorations of strengths and resources which follow in questions 18–22. As suggested in the strengths matrix described above, assessment of strengths, resources and limitations or challenges are required for a full assessment.

4. What are specific indications or manifestations of the problem(s)?

5. What persons and systems are implicated in the problem(s)?

6. How do the participants and/or systems interact to produce and maintain the problem(s)?

7. What unmet needs and/or wants are involved in the problem(s)?

8. What developmental stage or life transition is entailed in the problem(s)?

9. How severe is the problem and how does it affect the participants?

10. What meanings do clients ascribe to the problem(s)?

11. Where do the problematic behaviors occur?

12. When do the problematic behaviors occur?

13. What is the frequency of the problematic behaviors?

14. What is the duration of the problem(s)?

15. What are the consequences of the problem?

16. Have other issues, such as alcohol or substance abuse, physical or sexual abuse, affected the functioning of the client or family members?

17. What are the clients' emotional reactions to the problem(s)?

18. How have the clients attempted to cope with the problem, and what are the required skills to resolve the problem?

19. What are the skills and strengths of the clients?

20. How do ethnocultural, societal, and social class factors bear on the problem(s)?

21. What support systems exist or need to be created for the clients?

22. What external resources are needed by clients?

OTHER FACTORS IN ASSESSMENT

In addition to the key factors discussed in the preceding sections, still other dimensions must be explored and evaluated before an adequate assessment can be completed. These factors include:

1. The individual functioning of clients, including several key intrapersonal subsystems.

2. The motivation of clients to work on specified target problems.

3. Dynamics involved in couple and family systems.

4. Environmental factors that impinge upon the participants in the problem system.

In addition to these factors, which we discuss in the next two chapters, the role of clients in formulating assessments is also critical. Clients' views are a valuable resource in formulating assessments, a resource often ignored, as Prager (1980) has noted:

> Clients traditionally have had little if any real input into these professional areas of practice (diagnosis, rehabilitation, and evaluation)…it is almost paradoxical that, although mental health clients have spent a good part of their lives learning and implementing skills in relationships and communication, help is still largely defined, planned, and evaluated for them, not by them. (p. 5)

If you involve clients in the assessment process to the fullest extent possible, by inviting their views and responding to them with respect, they are likely to respond similarly to your views. On the other hand, if you attempt to impose your judgments on clients, they are likely to resist either openly or covertly. What we are advocating, then, is an open and mutual process that culminates in a synthesis of your own and your clients' views. The result of such mutuality is likely to be more accurate assessments and greater investment of clients in the assessments as well as in the planning and contracting processes.

NOTES

1 It is also crucial to engage the client in the helping relationship while eliciting data; otherwise, you may gain data but lose the client in the process.

2 The potency of this method in producing insight and change with a mother who had a severe problem in controlling anger has been reported by Nugent (1991).

3 For more information, contact Walter Hudson, Ph.D., at the School of Social Work, Arizona State University, Tempe, AZ 85287-1802.

4 The importance of having skills in relating to and identifying the emotions and unmet needs of partners with marital difficulties has been discussed by Denton (1991). Moreover, it is noteworthy that one approach to marital therapy has been denoted as Emotionally Focused Therapy (James, 1991), attesting to the vital role of emotions in interpersonal problems.

5 For those interested in reading more about the relationship between developmental needs and environmental resources, we recommend an article by Vigilante and Mailick (1988).

6 Besharov (1990) has provided extensive guidelines for recognizing various indications of child abuse.

7 The source of the above-listed manifestations is the Diagnostic and Statistical Manual (3rd ed., Revised). Washington, D.C.: American Psychiatric Association, 1987.

8 These and other issues related to use of anatomical dolls have been amply discussed by Lie and Inman (1991).

9 For an extensive discussion of research and theory concerning violence in black families, see Hampton, 1990.

10 For a cross-cultural analysis of family violence, see Levinson's (1989) book.

11 See also Hurst (1995).

Chapter 9 □ □ □

Assessing Intrapersonal and Environmental Systems

THE INTERACTION OF MULTIPLE SYSTEMS IN HUMAN PROBLEMS

Problems, strengths, and resources encountered in direct social work practice result from interaction of the intrapersonal, interpersonal, and environmental systems. Rarely are they confined to one of these broad systems, for functional imbalance in one system typically contributes to imbalance in others. Individual difficulties (e.g., feelings of worthlessness and depression) invariably influence how one relates to other people; interpersonal difficulties (e.g., marital strain) likewise affect individual functioning. Similarly, environmental deficits (e.g., inadequate housing or social isolation) affect individual and interpersonal functioning.

The reciprocal impacts among the three major systems, of course, are not limited to the negative effects of functional imbalance and system deficits. Assets, strengths, and resources also have reciprocal positive effects. A strong environment may partially compensate for intrapersonal difficulties; similarly, strong interpersonal relationships between parents and children may provide positive experiences for the latter that more than compensate for an otherwise impoverished environment.

To adequately assess the many forces that inter-act to produce problems, it is essential to be well grounded in knowledge about the three major systems that are typically involved in problems. Therefore, we devote this and the next two chapters to assisting you to grasp more fully the complexities of these systems. This chapter deals with the intrapersonal (within the person) and environmental systems; the next chapter is focused on interpersonal systems (between people), with particular emphasis on marital and family systems.

THE INTRAPERSONAL SYSTEMS

In assessing the social functioning of individuals, practitioners often make global judgments, such as "at best this person's level of functioning is marginal." Such a global statement, however, has limited usefulness, for it fails to specify areas in which functioning is marginal (and emphasizes deficits). We will attempt in this chapter to provide you with models which are more useful by clearly specifying strengths, resources, and challenges. Some individuals, of course, uniformly function at high or low levels, but variability is more often the case. Assessment of the individual considers biophysical, cognitive/perceptual, emotional, behavioral, cultural, and motivational factors. However, your written assessment should emphasize only salient factors in understanding the functioning of individuals who are part of the client system.

BIOPHYSICAL FUNCTIONING

Biophysical functioning is vital to and affects both individuals and families. Biophysical functioning encompasses physical characteristics, health factors, and genetic factors, and we consider each of these factors separately. Because drug and alcohol use and abuse embody biophysical components, we also address assessment of use of these substances, realizing that systems other than biophysical are also implicated.

Physical Characteristics and Presentation

The physical characteristics and appearance of clients may be either assets or liabilities. In Western society, physical attractiveness is highly valued, and unattractive people are disadvantaged in the realms of social desirability, employment opportunities, and marriageability. Further, the findings of at least one study (Farina, Burns, Austad, Bugglin, & Fischer, 1986) indicate that physical attractiveness facilitates the readjustment of discharged psychiatric patients. It is thus important to be observant of distinguishing physical characteristics that may affect social functioning. Particular attributes that merit attention include body build, posture, facial features, gait, and various physical anomalies that may distort the self-image or pose a social liability.

How clients present themselves is also important. Clients who walk slowly, manifest stooped posture, talk slowly and without animation, lack spontaneity, and show minimal changes in facial countenance as they talk may be depressed. Dress and grooming often reveal much about a person's morale, values, and lifestyle. While lack of sufficient income is a key issue, people who wear shabby, inappropriate, or neglected clothes, have disheveled hair, poor grooming, and the like are often considered depressed or mentally ill. By contrast, clients who, despite financial difficulties or other untoward circumstances, are neatly dressed and well groomed may be seen as manifestations of ongoing efforts to cope successfully and to create a favorable appearance.

Other factors associated with appearance that merit attention include hand tremors, facial tics, rigid or constantly shifting posture, and tense muscles of the face, hands, and arms. These physical manifestations often indicate a high degree of tension or anxiety that warrants exploration. It is normal, of course, for clients to manifest a certain degree of anxiety, especially in initial sessions. This is especially true for referred and legally mandated clients who have not requested the session and are understandably apprehensive about the practitioner's goals and the personal consequences of the session (e.g., assessment of possible child abuse).

Physical Health

Ill health can contribute to depression, sexual difficulties, irritability, low level of energy, restlessness, anxiety, inability to concentrate, and a host of other difficulties. It is therefore important for practitioners to routinely consider state of health as they explore clients' problems. One of the first assessment activities is then to determine if clients are under medical care and, if not, when they last had a medical examination.

Possible Brain Disorder Practitioners should rule out medical sources of difficulties by referring clients for medical examinations when appropriate before attributing problems solely to psychosocial factors. Practitioners have occasionally employed psychotherapy to treat dramatic increases in irritability, sudden losses of emotional control, and other personality changes to discover too late that these changes were caused by brain tumors or other organic ailments. To avoid such tragedies, practitioners should be cautious and avoid drawing premature conclusions about the sources of problems when there is even a remote possibility that medical factors may be involved.[1]

Groups Vulnerable to Health Problems   Assessing the health of clients is especially important with groups known to underutilize medical care. These groups include people who live in poverty, ethnic minority groups, elderly people, immigrants (including refugees), foster children, unwed pregnant adolescents, homeless people, people with AIDS, and persons who lack health insurance.

Health care needs of elder adults are among the greatest of the special groups. According to Morrison (1983), "Of people 65 years and older residing outside of institutions, 85 percent reported at least one chronic disease and 50 percent reported some limitations in functional capacity related to chronic health problems" (p. 161). Health problems of aging people of color are especially acute because a disproportionate percentage of this group are in the lower socioeconomic strata. A high representation of health problems amenable to early detection and treatment is found among aged people of color, particularly among males. Relatively higher rates of disease and death due to influenza, pneumonia, and respiratory conditions such as bronchitis, emphysema, and asthma are found among older nonwhite males, whereas nonwhite women show higher mortality rates for diabetes. Health education and preventive measures aimed at early detection and lifestyle modification are needed to reduce illness and death due to these conditions.

Assessment of the health of elderly persons also frequently entails evaluating the capacity for self-care and the need for care in an institutional setting such as a nursing home. Frequently involved in such assessments are evaluations of the capacity for managing daily living activities, mental function, and physical capacity.[2]

Prenatal care for pregnant adolescents is critically important because of the high risk of adolescent childbearing (e.g., high rate of premature births and handicapped offspring). Pregnant adolescents are notoriously difficult to involve, however, and require special efforts and approaches by practitioners. Research findings reported by Joyce, Diffenbacher, Greene, and Sorakin (1983) indicate that women who delivered babies at a metropolitan hospital without prenatal care attributed their failure to receive prenatal care more often to internal factors than to external factors. Internal factors include fear of doctors, depression, denial of pregnancy, and unplanned pregnancy, whereas external factors consisted of inadequate finances, transportation problems, lack of child care, long waiting periods, or difficulties getting appointments.[3]

Because lack of prenatal health care can damage the health of both the adolescent and the unborn child, both preventative and remedial health care programs are urgently needed.[4] A recent study revealed that service delivery systems could influence client beliefs about weight gain, nutrition, and anemia through the development of posters, calendars, and brochures (Alcalay, Ghee & Scrimshaw, 1993).[5] The needs of adolescents and their children, of course, continue after the birth of the child. Moroz and Allen-Meares (1991) have written an article concerned with assessing such needs and offering individualized services. It is also important to recognize that different cultures view and react to adolescent pregnancy in different ways (Dore & Dumois, 1990).

A high percentage of people of color live in poverty and are highly vulnerable to health problems. The Hispanic group is the fastest growing minority; yet, according to researchers, lack of health care insurance for many of the jobs that they hold effectively bars them from good medical care (Associated Press, 1991). An alarming finding is that rates of diabetes among Hispanics are triple the rates for non-Hispanic whites. Moreover, hypertension, measles, lead poisoning, tuberculosis, alcoholism, cirrhosis, and AIDS are more prevalent, as are injuries and violent deaths.

Clearly social workers must be alert to needs for health care among people of color and refugee populations. Following the war in Vietnam, for example, the influx of Asian refugees showed high rates of tuberculosis, malaria, hepatitis, and intestinal parasites. Similar high rates of disease might be expected in refugees of other third world countries, such as Haiti. Compounding the health problems of refugees is a lack of financial resources to purchase medical care and limited knowledge of Western medical care and of the complex health care provider systems in the United States. Relocation of refugees in localities that have few or no residents from their native lands also creates a sense of isolation, which, combined with the stresses previously cited, often lead to depression. Added to these burdens are difficulties in communicating.

Many homeless people also manifest urgent needs for both medical and dental care and case management services. Because many homeless persons are severely mentally ill and do not seek social services, outreach is often required before case managers can connect with them and secure health care services and other essential services for them (Bush, Langford, Rosen, & Gott, 1990).

People with AIDS have unique health care needs. Because the disease is terminal, patients have psychosocial needs that go beyond those of people with other illness. Needs for health care and social support are critical, but "Ambivalent community responses to AIDS, especially to its sex-and-drug-related aspects, has often meant that patients are not afforded the same benefits as others with terminal illnesses" (Moynihan, Christ, & Silver, 1988, p. 380).

Moreover, as a result of medical advances, life has been prolonged for many people with AIDS, resulting in increasing numbers of patients who develop cognitive symptoms ranging from mild cognitive disturbance to moderate and severe AIDS dementia complex (ADC). Symptoms of ADC result from HIV-related infection of the brain and central nervous system, which can produce "organic affective disorder marked by grandiosity, loss of sexual inhibition, and impulsivity" (Lee & McGill, 1991, p. 473). These behavioral symptoms pose a challenging problem in management, because the unique and severe behaviors often associated with ADC do not fit with existing hospital and community resources. Lee and McGill (1991) have proposed that social workers advocate for additional resources that will meet the housing and service needs of these patients and will provide a continuum of care.

Difficulties for people with AIDS are even more acute in rural areas, because rural citizens expect greater conformity to community norms and are less tolerant of diversity. Therefore, those who are gay or lesbian, to avoid being stigmatized in rural communities, often maintain a low profile and conceal their sexual orientation (Rounds, 1988). The distance to health care facilities and reluctance of health care professionals to treat AIDS patients in rural communities is another formidable obstacle. Implications for social workers for dealing with such organizational difficulties, for assuming organizing roles in both rural and urban areas, and for functioning as case managers in serving the needs of people with AIDS are discussed in Chapter 15.

Assessment involving AIDS extends beyond determining the needs of the persons afflicted by the disease. Partners and family members also are severely affected by the caretaking process and the impending death of the afflicted person (Dane, 1991). Shelby (1992) has written a comprehensive book that provides guidelines for interventions with well partners of persons with AIDS. Kelly and Sykes (1989) have discussed the needs of family members and caretakers for support and the use of support groups to assist them to cope with the complex and painful emotions experienced in having a loved one afflicted with the disease and mourning the impending death.

Lockhart and Wodarski (1989) have also provided data about increasing numbers of children and adolescents afflicted with AIDS. They are even more in need of support and service because they have less well developed coping mechanisms to contend with the ostracism, rejection, and isolation that commonly confront persons with AIDS.

Cultural Factors in Illness

Determining clients' views of causes of illness, physical aberrations, disabling conditions, and mental symptoms is an important task in assessment, for the degree of clients' receptiveness to medical diagnoses and treatment will depend on their credibility from the client's perspective. In modern Western society, despite the increasing acceptance by professionals of the systems perspective, most people continue to attribute illness to physical causes (i.e., infections, toxins, degenerative processes, heredity, improper nutrition, chemical imbalance, lack of exercise, or other unknown physical factors). People thus tend to be receptive to diagnoses and treatments that match their expectations. Mainstream Americans, for example, are familiar with and accept antibiotics, vitamins, hormones, diverse medications, surgical procedures, radiation therapy, chemotherapy, exercise, and proper rest. By contrast, the majority of mainstream Americans reject acupuncture, herbal therapy, and spiritualistic rituals as legitimate treatments.

Differing from members of the mainstream culture, many ethnic minority clients espouse markedly different beliefs about the causes of ill health or other physical afflictions. Consequently, their expectations regarding diagnoses and treatment may differ sharply from those presented by Western health care professionals. In this regard, Low (1984) has noted: "Numerous cases of ethnic differences in expectations of treatment, behavior and compliance can be traced to cultural distinctions embedded in belief systems and norms of culturally appropriate behavior" (p. 13).

When major discrepancies exist between clients' expectations and physicians' diagnoses and recommendations for treatment, clients tend to covertly reject diagnoses and fail to comply with treatment regimens, often producing confusion and consternation for health care professionals who lack sophistication in understanding the powerful influence of cultural beliefs. Experienced practitioners in health care settings can attest to many instances of clients' noncompliance with medical recommendations based on clashes between diverse cultural and Western medical beliefs concerning causes of illness and physical afflictions. One of the many case examples reported by Kumabe et al. (1985) highlights the significance of cultural factors:

Case Example

Living in Hawaii after migrating from the Philippine Islands five years earlier, the parents of a small child had resisted having surgical repair of their child's cleft lip and palate even though the costs would be paid by insurance. After carefully exploring both the circumstances that preceded the birth of the child and the parents' beliefs regarding the cause of the condition, the social worker learned that the parents attributed the child's condition to punishment from God for their use of withdrawal as a contraceptive measure during sexual intercourse. The father's uncle, who lived with the family, asserted they had interfered with God's will by practicing contraception. The withdrawal method, he claimed, caused deformed babies; because sexual intercourse was never completed, a baby could never be completed either. Fortunately, the practitioner recognized the futility of attempting to dissuade them from their belief and instead referred them for a consultation with a physician of their ethnicity. The Filipino physician readily gained their trust and assisted them to accept that their child's condition was congenital and unrelated to their sexual practices. This consultation paved the way to having the corrective surgery performed and liberated the parents from oppressive guilt.

....

Cultures that differ sharply from mainstream American culture may attribute illness and other physical afflictions to factors and forces that are discounted or lightly regarded by scientifically oriented Western medical authorities. Hispanic concepts of disease (discussed by Green, 1982), for example, derive from several sources including medieval Spanish traditions brought to the New World by colonizers, the influence of indigenous Indian groups, elements of Anglo traditions made popular through advertising and the mass media, and scientific medical knowledge.

Like traditional Hispanic culture, the traditional culture of many Native American tribes includes concepts of illness and cure that are in conflict with scientific medical knowledge. Good health requires living in balance with nature, which in turn depends on adhering to a strict set of cosmic laws. The world as viewed by some Indian shamans[6] is made up of both physical and spiritual elements, and every sickness has both a physical and spiritual cause. The philosophy of an Indian shaman concerning health and sickness, as quoted by Lake (1983), is that

> A healthy person lives by the laws of Nature. An unhealthy person has violated the laws, or he/she can be the recipient of misapplied laws by another's violation through inheritance or witchcraft. Ignorance is no excuse to the Creator's cosmic laws irregardless [sic] of age, sex, race, nationality, creed, or religion. Healing therefore means the individual must be recreated, reconnected, and/or balanced with Nature; or put back into harmony with the Universal laws and function.[7] (p. 33)

Folk Healers It is important for all practitioners to be knowledgeable about the significance of folk healers and shamans in diverse cultures throughout the world. As Canda (1983) points out, shamanism exists on every continent and on the islands in the oceans. Beliefs in supernatural forces, such as witchcraft, evil spirits, curses, and hexes, are widespread among ethnic minority persons, especially those who are poorly educated, from low socioeconomic levels, and closely tied to cultures whose belief systems are rooted in traditional folkways.

Folk healers and shamans are especially important to some persons of color who have recently experienced cultural dislocation. As Delgado (1977) has pointed out, "Supernatural beliefs tend to persist when they offer solutions to significant human problems" (p. 425). Because people who are uprooted are beset with intense stresses as they attempt to adapt to a strange land, they may increase their reliance on spiritualism as a means of coping with these stresses. With respect to Puerto Ricans, Delgado reports:

> If a Puerto Rican in need of assistance is offered a choice between a medium and a social worker he will probably choose the medium. Social workers lack the prestige given to spiritualists whose roles are sanctioned by the entire society to which they and their clients belong. (p. 453)

Because of the significance of folk healers and shamans in the lives of many persons of color, practitioners should view these indigenous practitioners as resources. Canda (1983), for example, cites references that report successful informal arrangements between medical professionals and nature healers in the Cook Islands, Nigeria, and Puerto Rico. Kumabe et al. (1985) have also described cases in which social workers have orchestrated the efforts of medical professionals and folk healers in successfully treating ethnic minority clients in Hawaii.[8]

Family Factors Attitudes of key family members should also be considered in assessing health problems. In most cultures, the family decides whether or not a member is ill, the meanings of illnesses, and how family members should cope with illness. Moreover, cultural values and lifestyle of a family affect the course of a patient's illness and recovery. The family influences decision making during each phase of a member's illness, beginning with the initial steps involved in seeking medical care, the response to the diagnosis, and the compliance or noncompliance with the treatment recommendations.

Practitioners must also assess how illness of a member affects the functioning of a family. The illness of a member, particularly of a parent, creates imbalance in a family system, often requiring adjustment in role performance by family members. Further, outside resources (e.g., financial aid, homemaking services, or visiting nursing service) may be required to assist families to maintain their equilibrium.[9]

Social Support and Health Care

Because other systems affect clients' health, practitioners should also explore the nature of clients' interaction with these systems. Social support systems are particularly important, especially marital and family relationships. Gallo (1982), for example, studied the relationship between the adequacy of social support networks and health of the elderly and reported a high correlation. Research on psychosocial kinship systems also indicates that support networks are critical to sound mental health. Cutler and Madore (1980) report that the support systems of most people usually contain 20 to 30 people, whereas those of neurotics consist of about one-half that number, and those of psychotics are limited to approximately four or five. Hepworth, Farley, and Griffiths (1988) also emphasize the importance of social support systems in assessing the functioning of potentially suicidal adolescents. We discuss assessment of social support systems later in this chapter.

ASSESSING USE AND ABUSE OF ALCOHOL AND DRUGS

Rauch suggests that it is important (especially in health care settings) to determine if clients regularly use drugs. Even beneficial drugs can produce side effects that affect the functioning of various biopsychological systems. Drowsiness, for example, is a side effect of many drugs. Changes in sexual functioning may also result from use of certain medications used to treat high blood pressure. A jaundiced appearance, rigid gait, zombie-like countenance, tongue-thrusting, and various involuntary muscle contractions may result from excessive dosages of major tranquilizing drugs used to treat certain forms of psychosis, and medical evaluation of dosage may be needed. Other problems may be associated with the excessive use of minor tranquilizers used to treat anxiety and tension. And these are but a few of the myriad side effects of commonly used drugs. Other health problems may respond favorably to drugs (e.g., premenstrual syndrome, menopausal difficulty, severe depression, attention deficit disorders and hyperactivity in children, and epileptic seizures), and referral to a physician or health care facility may be indicated.

Alcohol abuse is a problem that can severely impair health, disrupt or destroy family life, and create serious community problems. Conservatively estimated to afflict from 9 to 10 million Americans, alcoholism can occur in any culture, of course, but the problem is widespread among Native Americans. Alcoholism is also associated with high incidence of suicide, homicide, and spouse and child abuse, all of which are prominent problems among the Native American population.

Effects of Alcohol Abuse on the Fetus

Another serious problem associated with alcohol abuse involves adverse effects on offspring produced by alcohol consumption during pregnancy. The effects range from full-blown fetal alcohol syndrome (FAS) to fetal alcohol effects (FAE). At the extreme end of a range of potential effects of alcohol on a fetus, FAS (found in infants of chronic alcoholic mothers who have four to six drinks per day) involves prenatal and postnatal growth retardation, central nervous system involvement, and abnormalities in shape and size of the head and/or facial features (dysmorphology). One of the most serious features of FAS is mental retardation (FAS children in the United States have an average IQ of 65), and the damage is irreversible.

The severity of FAE effects (found in mothers who are social drinkers) varies according to the amount of alcohol consumed, but the risks associated with two drinks daily include miscarriage, prenatal growth retardation, behavioral deficiencies, and various anomalies. With increased consumption, partial effects of FAS may develop. In addition, some newborns manifest withdrawal effects from alcohol such as irritability, tremulousness, alcohol on the breath, transient seizures, and jitteriness.

Because of the potentially severe damage to developing fetuses of excessive alcohol consumption, practitioners should routinely question prospective mothers about their use of alcohol during pregnancy. By taking a history of consumption of beer, wine, and liquor during pregnancy (focusing on frequency, quantity, and variability), practitioners can delineate clients' drinking patterns. Numerous screening tools for alcoholism are also available, as we discuss later. It is now recommended that all women avoid drinking during pregnancy. If the prospective mother drinks more than two or three drinks daily or more than five drinks on any occasion, practitioners should strongly encourage involvement in a treatment program.

Use of Alcohol by Women

Women who drink have patterns more like nonaddicted women than men. They are more likely to abuse prescription drugs, to consume them in isolation, and to have had the onset of abuse after a traumatic event such as incest, and racial or domestic violence (Nelson Zlupko, Kauffman & Dore, 1995).[10] Women who drink are likely to come from families in which drugs and alcohol were used. Women are less likely than men to enter and complete treatment programs, and availability of child care while in treatment is a major obstacle. Since guilt and shame tend already to be high among alcohol-abusing women, aggressive confrontation designed to break through denial tends to be counterproductive. Treatment approaches that focus on strengths, including coping tools such as identifying characteristics of an unhealthy environment which has triggered drug usage and familiarizing women with a context of oppression are recommended for better serving the needs of this population (ibid., 1995).

Dual Diagnosis in Alcoholism

As Turnbull (1988) stresses, alcoholism can be a primary or secondary disorder, which is true of men as well as women. Mulinski (1989) cites studies indicating that of persons in the community with substance-abuse problems, from 21 to 39% also meet criteria for other psychiatric disorders. Moreover, of hospitalized male alcoholics, as many as two-thirds manifest symptoms of one or more other psychiatric diagnoses. Mulinski thus discusses the importance of distinguishing between symptoms and syndromes and establishing primary and secondary diagnoses so that treatment plans can be formulated accordingly.

Biopsychosocial Factors in Alcoholism

Based on recent research, it is increasingly evident that alcoholism is a multidimensional disorder and that adequate assessment entails consideration of genetic, personality, psychological, and psychosocial factors. Wallace (1989) has discussed these factors at length, and we urge you to read his article. Space limitations permit us to discuss pertinent factors only in a cursory fashion.

The family histories of alcoholic patients indicate that roughly 80 to 85% have had an alcoholic parent or grandparent, strongly suggesting genetic factors may be implicated in alcoholism. Studies of children born to alcoholic parents but raised in different environments indicate genetic vulnerability to alcoholism. Studies cited by Wallace indicate that certain males are biogenetically predisposed to alcoholism. In particular, Type 2 alcoholism (characterized by early onset beginning in the teens) appears to be a sex-linked male disorder almost entirely genetic in nature. Taking careful family histories about drinking patterns of parents and grandparents thus is critical in identifying males at risk of developing alcoholism. By identifying such persons, practitioners can preventively counsel them as to the risk of becoming alcoholic.

Personality, psychological, and psychosocial factors related to alcoholism are especially relevant to social workers. Type 2 alcoholics are believed to be high in novelty seeking behaviors, and low in traits denoted as harm avoidance and reward dependence. Moreover, they are not oriented to seeking social approval and quickly give up actions that do not produce immediate gratification.

Alcoholics seldom acknowledge alcohol use problems, rationalize offensive behaviors, blame others and their situations for difficulties, develop grandiose ideas about their abilities and importance, and selectively attend to aspects of situations and communications that minimize discomfort and safeguard self-esteem.

The sociocultural environments of alcoholics should also be assessed, as environmental factors appear to account for as much variance in treatment outcomes as do intake characteristics and treatment activities combined (Wallace, 1989, p. 331). Socializing with other alcoholics, frequenting bars, or associating with others who encourage drinking clearly foster continued drinking. By contrast, associating with sober people who express caring, discourage drinking, do not permit the alcoholic to lean on or to exploit them, and do not protect the alcoholic from the consequences of drinking and behaving irresponsibly foster abstinence.

Using Interviewing Skills to Assess Possible Alcoholism

Social workers are often involved with problem drinkers at the point in the cycle referred to as precontemplation. This is at a point prior to which the problem drinker has not acknowledged a problem or sought help (Barber, 1995). Griffin (1991) emphasizes the need to manifest nonjudgmental acceptance while interviewing people who may be alcoholic. Doing so can be difficult because they may not see alcohol use as a problem and often attempt to conceal it by lying, arguing, distorting, attempting to intimidate, diverting the interview away from discussion of their drinking, or verbally attacking the worker. Despite these aversive behaviors, the worker needs to express empathy and sensitivity to the client's feelings, realizing the behaviors are often a subterfuge behind which lie embarrassment, guilt, shame, ambivalence, and anger.

Being direct and seeking concreteness can facilitate exploration and instigate confrontation. When inquiring as to alcohol consumption, the worker should be forthright in explaining why that line of questioning is being pursued. Asking indirect questions tends to support the client's evasion and tends to be unproductive. Because the effects of alcoholism tend to pervade all aspects of an alcoholic's life, it is important to explore all of the social systems that play a key role in the client's life.

Family and History   Because of the importance of genetic factors in alcoholism, as discussed previously, it is important to include use of alcohol by parents, grandparents, uncles, and aunts as a part of the exploration of family history. In exploring family life, it is important to determine both the quality and frequency of interaction with other family members. It is also vital to explore the frequency and nature of quarrels and whether they increase during drinking episodes. The possibility of violence toward other family members should be explored, not only with the client but also with other family members.

Employment History Exploration of job changes, job satisfaction, problems with coworkers and supervisors, absenteeism from work, and working at a job below the client's educational or skill level may indicate job difficulties associated with alcoholism. Frequent job changes or being fired are clues that the client may have missed work frequently because of binges and/or may have been drinking on the job.

Social Life Discussing the client's social life—the types of friends and activities and places of socialization—may also disclose the centrality of alcohol in the client's life. Whether key persons in the client's social network drink with the client is also indicative of possible alcoholism.

Legal Difficulties A record of arrests for driving under the influence of alcohol, and especially revocation of a driver's license, are strong indicators of alcoholism, as are other illegal activities such as forgery or theft, disorderly conduct, and fighting in or around bars.

Health Factors Because of erratic eating, malnutrition is common among alcoholics. Malnutrition often is manifested by an emaciated appearance. Hand tremors are also common.

Drinking Patterns Drinking in the morning, drinking to escape the effects of a hangover, drinking alone, drinking to reduce anxiety or to fortify oneself before facing an anxiety-producing situation are patterns characteristic of alcoholics. Blackouts (i.e., being unable to remember where one was or what happened the night before) are also an indication of alcoholism. Being unable to stop with one or two drinks, of course, is a primary indicator of alcoholism. Clients with drinking problems are more likely to respond well to such factual questions than global questions such as "Does alcohol control your life?"

Using Instruments and Procedures to Assess Alcoholism

A number of easy-to-use instruments are available to assess possible alcoholism. The Walmyr Scales (Hudson, 1992) contain an Alcohol Abuse Scale. Another widely employed test is the Michigan Alcoholism Screening Test (Selzer, 1971). Still another scale is the Alcohol Use Profile (Hystad, 1989). All of these scales are self-administering and can be completed, scored, and interpreted in a short time.

A weakness of self-administering instruments such as those listed above is that subjects can fake their responses. To circumvent this difficulty, behavioral methods that rely on systematic interview procedures are also used to assess alcohol consumption. The Comprehensive Drinking Profile (CDP; Marlatt & Miller, 1984) is widely used for this purpose. For a comprehensive analysis of factors related to assessment of addictive disorders (in addition to alcoholism), we recommend Donovan and Marlatt's (1988) book, which also describes and evaluates pertinent instruments and procedures.

ASSESSING DRUG ABUSE

Because of widespread publicity, the public is aware of the dangers and tragic consequences resulting from drug abuse and overdose. Less well known by the public but extremely familiar to social workers are the ravages to individual lives and the disruption and suffering experienced by families of both alcohol and drug abusers.

People abuse many types of drugs. Because immediate care may be essential in instances of acute drug intoxication and because drug abusers often attempt to conceal their use of drugs, it is important that practitioners know the indications of abuse of commonly used drugs. Table 9-1 lists by category the most commonly abused drugs and their indications.

In addition to the indications of abuse of specific drugs listed above, common general indications include the following:

- Changes in attendance at work or school.
- Decrease in normal capabilities (work performance, efficiency, habits, etc.).
- Poor physical appearance, neglect of dress and personal hygiene.
- Use of sunglasses to conceal dilated or constricted pupils and to compensate for eyes' reduced ability to adjust to sunlight.
- Unusual efforts to cover arm and hide needle marks.
- Association with known drug users.
- Need to steal or engage in prostitution to raise cash to support drug habit.

In assessing the possibility of drug abuse, it is important to elicit information not only from the

TABLE 9-1   INDICATIONS OF ABUSE OF COMMONLY USED DRUGS

TYPE OF DRUG	TYPICAL INDICATIONS
1. Depressants (downers) including Quaalude, Doriden, and various barbiturates	Intoxicated behavior with no odor of alcohol, staggering or stumbling, falling asleep at work, slurred speech, dilated pupils, difficulty concentrating.
2. Stimulants (amphetamines, including methamphetamine or "speed")	Excessively active, irritable, argumentative, nervous, dilated pupils, long periods without eating or sleeping.
3. Cocaine (also a stimulant)	Energetic, euphoric, fixed and dilated pupils, possible tremors (euphoria quickly replaced by anxiety, irritability and/or depression, sometimes accompanied by hallucinations and paranoid delusions).
4. Narcotics (opium, heroin, morphine, codeine)	Scars on arms or backs of hands from injecting drugs, fixed and constricted pupils, frequent scratching, loss of appetite (but frequently eat sweets). May have sniffles, red, and watering eyes, and cough until another "fix," lethargic, drowsy, and alternate between dozing and awakening ("nodding").
5. Marijuana (a hallucinogen)	In early stages, may be euphoric and appear animated, speaking rapidly and loudly with bursts of laughter; pupils may be dilated and eyes bloodshot; may have distorted perceptions and experience hallucinations; in later stages, may be drowsy.
6. Other hallucinogens (LSD, STP, DOM) mescaline, DTM, DET	Behavior and mood vary widely, may sit or recline quietly in trance-like state or appear fearful or even terrified; dilated pupils in some cases; may experience nausea, chills, flushes, irregular breathing, sweating, or trembling of hands; may be changes in sense of sight, hearing, touch, smell, and time.

suspected abuser (who often attempts to conceal their use) but also from persons who are familiar with the habits and lifestyle of the individual.

When exploration reveals that a client is a drug abuser (or alcoholic), referral to a drug treatment center (some mental health centers and hospitals have drug abuse units) often is indicated. Staff members of these centers have special skills needed to work effectively with these often difficult clients. Moreover, drug abuse centers often employ group methods that are particularly relevant for work with drug abusers (Alcoholics Anonymous and Narcotics Anonymous are well-established, group-oriented self-help programs.)

It is also important to assess problems of drug abuse from a systems perspective. Explorations of family relationships often reveal that drug abusers feel alienated from other family members. Moreover, family members often unwittingly contribute to the problems of both alcoholics and drug abusers. Consequently, many professionals regard problems of drug abuse as manifestations of dysfunction within the family system. Keep in mind that drug abusers affect and are affected by the family system.

Just as the effects of alcoholism pervade key social systems of clients, so do the effects of drug abuse and addiction. The information provided earlier related to systems affected by alcoholism is equally relevant to and should be considered in assessing drug abuse. Moreover, because of the commonalities between alcohol abuse and drug use, the guidelines for employing interviewing skills to assess alcoholism are also applicable to assessing drug abuse.

Use of Instruments and Procedures to Assess Drug Abuse

As with alcoholism, the Walmyr Scales (Hudson, 1992) also include one specifically designed to assess drug abuse, the Drug Use Scale. Another widely employed scale is the Drug Abuse Screening Test (DAST; Skinner, 1982). Both of these scales are self-report scales that are easily completed and scored in a brief period. For extensive analysis and discussion of factors in assessing abuse of various drugs and of diverse instruments and procedures related thereto, we again refer you to the authoritative book by Donovan and Marlatt (1988).

Conveying Assessment Findings to Clients

During assessment interviews with possible alcoholic or drug-abusing clients, the worker should include exploration of whether the client is alcoholic or is depending on or abusing drugs. When sufficient information has emerged to enable the worker to make such a judgment, the worker should first review details elicited about the impact of the substance-abusing behaviors on the various aspects of the client's life, as reviewed during the interview, and invite the client's views about the extent of the problem. The worker can also delineate objective behavioral criteria accepted as indicators of alcohol or drug abuse and ask the client how his/her behavior compares with these criteria. Problem drinkers are more likely to respond to feedback conveyed empathically and nonjudgmentally with specific information about how consumption is affecting this person's life. Such feedback is more likely to be accepted when the source is seen as a medical practitioner or specially qualified to assess consequences of use (Barber, 1995).

The worker should also express forthrightly his or her own conclusions, including an estimate of the severity of the problem. It is also appropriate to explain treatment options and to express guarded optimism that with hard work and persistence the client can overcome the dependency or addiction. It is important not to paint a rosy picture and to explain that the process will be lengthy and painful at times (Griffin, 1991).

Genetic Factors

As we discussed earlier, genetic factors play a major role in Type 2 alcoholism. Genetic factors are also implicated in manic–depressive disorder, certain forms of mental retardation, and perhaps in schizophrenia and other emotional (affective) disorders, although the role of genes in the latter disorders is controversial. Many other biophysical disorders have genetic roots including cleft lip, cleft palate, club foot, diabetes mellitus, spina bifida, congenital scoliosis, hemophilia, Duchenne's muscular dystrophy, Huntington's disease, neurofibromatosis, cystic fibrosis, sickle-cell anemia, and Tay-Sachs disease.

According to Rauch (1988), social workers will likely have increased involvement with people who have genetic concerns. Adoption workers, for example, should be concerned about the genetic histories of adoptees, and both prospective adoptive parents and adoptees have the right to know about genetic risk factors of adoptees. In light of recent developments on national and state levels, Rauch suggests that in the future, "adoption agencies will face expectations to provide a full and competent family genetic history, genetic evaluation of the potential adoptee, and genetic counseling for the adopting parents when warranted" (p. 393).

Social workers may provide services to others who have genetic concerns such as people seeking premarital counseling and people who are afflicted with or have relatives afflicted with congenital disorders. In such instances, social workers are unlikely to be equipped to provide genetic counseling themselves, but they can perform the broker role by connecting clients with those who possess requisite expertise. Public and voluntary genetic services including comprehensive clinical genetic centers exist throughout the United States and a national directory of services is available through the U.S. Department of Health and Human Services (DHHS Publication No. HRS-D-MC 86-1) in Washington, D.C.

Psychiatric Diagnoses

In certain settings that file for insurance payments (e.g., mental health and private practice), practitioners are required to make psychiatric diagnoses for various types of developmental and mental health disorders. The disease model undergirding psychiatric diagnosis places lesser emphasis on the broader systems, empowerment and strengths oriented view than the social work profession's view of assessment (Kirk & Kutchins, 1995). Kirk and Kutchins conducted a survey of clinical social workers that indicated that their use of the DSM was primarily for reimbursement purposes rather than as a useful guide to treatment and medication (Kirk & Kutchins, 1988; Kutchins & Kirk, 1988).

While reliability of diagnoses has been problematic, psychiatric diagnoses are sometimes crucial in identifying conditions which have been shown to be amenable to psychopharmacological and other treatment. To render such diagnoses, practitioners must be able to use the Diagnostic and Statistical Manual (DSM IV) published by the American Psychiatric Association). Content related to psychiatric diagnosis, however, is taught in advanced behavior or practice courses and is beyond the scope of this book. However, clients with certain diagnoses may pose a suicidal risk or may urgently need medications to control severe symptoms; all social workers, therefore, must be able to diagnose these disorders, which we discuss later in this chapter under the section "Assessing Affective Disorders." It is essential for social workers who work in settings requiring assessment for such diagnostic conditions to see the client as a person who may have a psychiatric condition: The client is not the condition.

COGNITIVE/PERCEPTUAL FUNCTIONING

Assessing how clients perceive their worlds of experience is critically important, for people's perceptions of others, themselves, and events largely determine how they feel and respond to life's experiences in general and to their problematic situations in particular. Perceptions, of course, do not exist apart from meanings that are ascribed to them; hence, we have considered perceptual and cognitive functioning as a single entity. The meanings or interpretations of events, rather than the events themselves, motivate human beings to behave as they do, as we noted in the preceding chapter. Furthermore, every person's world of experience is unique. Perceptions of identical events or circumstances thus vary widely according to the complex interaction of belief systems, values, attitudes, state of mind, and self-concepts, all of which in turn are highly idiosyncratic. It follows that to understand and to influence human behavior you must first be knowledgeable about how people think.

People's thought patterns, of course, are influenced by numerous factors, including intellectual functioning, judgment, reality testing, coherence, cognitive flexibility, values, mistaken beliefs, self-concept, and dynamic interaction between cognition, emotions, and behavior. In the following sections, we briefly consider these factors.

Intellectual Functioning

Evaluating the intellectual capacity of clients is essential to gearing your verbal expressions to a level that clients can readily comprehend, assessing their strengths and difficulties, negotiating goals, and planning tasks that are commensurate with their capacities. In most instances, a rough estimate of level of intellectual functioning is sufficient. Criteria that you may employ include clients' abilities to grasp abstract ideas, to express themselves fluently, and to analyze or think logically. Additional criteria include level of educational achievement and vocabulary employed, although these factors must be considered in relationship to the clients' previous educational

opportunities and/or possible learning difficulties. Some adults with average or higher intellectual capacity may be unable to read or write because of learning disabilities or poor instruction. It is important to avoid confusing unfamiliarity with the language for non-native speakers with problematic intellectual functioning.

When clients have marked intellectual limitations, it is vital that you employ a vocabulary consisting of easily understood words. You should avoid abstract explanations and utilize feedback to ascertain that clients have grasped intended meanings, for to avoid embarrassment, many intellectually impaired clients will pretend to understand when they do not. Greater time and patience are therefore required with these clients. Employing concrete examples of concepts frequently assists such clients to understand complex ideas.

Intellectual capacity, of course, establishes the upper limits of goals that clients can reasonably be expected to accomplish. To encourage clients to pursue goals that exceed their capacities is to risk failure, which can be devastating when they already are painfully aware of their limitations. This caution is particularly relevant to educational and vocational planning. Failures in these ventures may so discourage clients that they lose confidence in their abilities and simply quit trying.

Judgment

Some clients (and nonclients, for that matter) who have adequate or even keen intellect encounter severe difficulties in life because of deficiencies in judgment. Clients with poor judgment may experience more difficulties than those with intellectual deficiencies because the former may get themselves into one jam after another. By contrast, some people with intellectual limitations manifest strengths and live stable and productive lives by exercising prudence in making decisions and governing their behavior. Typical manifestations of deficiencies in judgment involve consistently living beyond one's means, entering get-rich schemes without carefully exploring possible ramifications, quitting jobs impulsively, leaving small children unattended, getting married with little knowledge of the partner, failing to safeguard or maintain personal property, squandering resources, and the like.

Deficiencies in judgment generally come to light as you explore clients' problematic situations and patterns in detail. Often it is apparent that clients act with little forethought, fail to consider probable consequences of their actions, or engage in wishful thinking that things will somehow work out. Other clients manifest repetitive dysfunctional coping patterns that lead predictably to unfavorable outcomes. Failing to profit from past mistakes, these clients appear to be driven by intense impulses that overpower consideration of the consequences of their actions. These impulse-ridden clients may lash out at authority figures or write bad checks, both of which may provide immediate gratification but ultimately lead to loss of jobs, arrest, or other adverse consequences.

Reality Testing

This factor is a critical index to a person's mental health. Strong functioning on this dimension involves:

1. Being properly oriented to time, place, and person.
2. Reaching appropriate conclusions about cause and effect relationships.
3. Perceiving external events and discerning the intentions of others with reasonable accuracy.
4. Differentiating one's own thoughts and feelings from those that emanate from others.

Relatively few clients manifest disorientation, but those who do usually are severely mentally disturbed, under the influence of drugs, or suffering from a pathological brain syndrome. Disorientation is usually readily discernable, but when doubt exists, questions about the date, day of the week, current events that are common knowledge, and recent events in the client's life will usually clarify the matter. Clients who are disoriented typically respond inappropriately, sometimes giving bizarre answers. For example, in responding to a question about his daily activities, a recluse reported that he engaged in conversation with his 18 pet dogs.

Choosing to blame circumstances and events rather than take personal responsibility for actions is a common response of persons in the process of becoming labeled as deviant (Rooney, 1992). For example, in explaining reasons for their arrest, delinquents frequently place responsibility outside of themselves by attributing the cause to cops who have it in for them or to a bum rap. One client who stole an automobile externalized actions for his behavior by blaming the owner for leaving the keys in the car. Some clients blame their employers for losing their jobs, even though they habitually missed work for invalid reasons. Still others attribute their difficulties to the fact that fate decreed them to be losers. It is a welcome strength when clients own responsibility for their actions.

Perceptual patterns that involve distortions of external events are fairly common among clients and may cause severe difficulties in interpersonal relationships—the domain in which perceptual distortions most frequently occur. Mild distortions may be associated with stereotypical perceptions (e.g., "All policemen are cruel and punitive" or "The only interest men have in me is sexual"). Moderate distortions often involve marked misinterpretations of the motives of others and may severely impair interpersonal relationships (e.g., "My boss told me I was doing a good job and that there is an opportunity to be promoted to a job in another department; he wants to get rid of me" or "My wife says she wants to take an evening class, but I know what she really wants. She wants to have an affair because she's not satisfied with me.") In instances of extreme distortions, people may manifest delusions that others plan to harm them and on rare occasions take violent actions to protect themselves from their imagined persecutors. Bizarre killings of innocent strangers are sometimes the actions of deranged people attempting to protect themselves from imagined communists, CIA agents, the federal government, or other feared groups.

Dysfunction in reality testing of psychotic proportions is involved when people project onto others repressed thoughts and impulses that if owned by themselves would obliterate self-esteem and create unbearable anxiety. Self-esteem is thus safeguarded to some degree when, rather than acknowledging thoughts as their own, people "hear" voices (auditory hallucinations) telling them to murder, steal, or commit rape or criticizing them for being utter failures. The cost of such extreme measures to preserve some semblance of self-esteem is the loss of personality integration, for such persons lack the capacity to distinguish between thoughts and beliefs that emanate from themselves and those that originate from external sources. Although dysfunction in reality testing may be rooted in psychological causes such as those just discussed, current theories hold that thought disorder more often results from biochemical and neurological dysfunction, some of which may be linked with genetic factors. Whatever the source, it is vital to recognize such severe cognitive dysfunction, for clients thus affected usually require medication and/or hospitalization.

Coherence

Practitioners occasionally encounter clients who manifest major thought disorders characterized by rambling and incoherent speech. Successive thoughts of these persons may be highly fragmented and disconnected from one another, a phenomenon denoted as looseness of association in the thought processes. Thought disorder of this type is a prominent feature of the mental disorder designated as schizophrenia. Severe thought disorder, of course, pervades virtually all aspects of social functioning, often incapacitating a person from performing appropriate social roles. (Incoherence, of course, may also be produced by acute

drug intoxication, and practitioners should be careful to rule out this possibility.)

A number of scales are available for assessing mental illness. Schneider and Struening (1983) have developed a behavioral rating scale that is particularly useful for social workers. An advantage of this scale is that it focuses on specific skills required for daily living.

Cognitive Flexibility

Receptiveness to new ideas and the ability to analyze many facets of problematic situations are conducive not only to effective problem solving but to general adaptability as well. Cognitive flexibility is manifested by clients who seek to grow, to understand the part they play in their difficulties, and to understand others; such clients also can ask for assistance without believing it is an admission of weakness or failure. Many people, however, are rigid and unyielding in their beliefs, and their inflexibility poses a major obstacle to progress in the helping process.

A common pattern of cognitive inflexibility is thinking in absolute terms (e.g., a person is good or evil, a success or a failure, responsible or irresponsible—there is no in-between). Clients who think this way are prone to be critical of others who fail to measure up to their stringent expectations. Difficult to live with, many such people appear at social agencies because of marital difficulties or problems in parent–child relations. Improvement often requires helping them to examine the destructive impact of their rigidity, to broaden their perspectives of themselves and others, and to "loosen up" in general.

Negative cognitive sets also include biases and stereotypes that render clients unable to relate to members of certain groups (e.g., authority figures, ethnic groups, and the opposite sex) as individuals. Severely depressed clients evince tunnel vision, viewing themselves as helpless and/or worthless and the future as dismal and hopeless.

These clients also selectively attend to their own negative attributes, leaving no way to feel good about themselves.

Values

An integral part of the cognitive-perceptual subsystem, values strongly influence human behavior, often playing a key role in problems presented by clients. For this reason, you should seek to identify clients' values, assess the role they play in their difficulties, and consider ways in which their values can be used to create incentives to modify their problematic behaviors. Further, you have an ethical responsibility to respect the rights of clients to cling to their values and to make choices consistent with them—an obligation that requires awareness of their values.

Many values, of course, are a product of cultural conditioning. Practitioners therefore must have knowledge about the values of clients' cultural reference groups to avoid making errors in assessment. Traditional Native American values, for example, differ sharply from mainstream values on the following (Native American values are listed first): (1) harmony with nature versus mastery of nature, (2) orientation to the present versus orientation to the present and future, (3) orientation to "being" activity versus orientation to "doing" activity, and (4) primacy of family and group goals versus primacy of individual goals. In a study comparing 36 practicing Native American MSW social workers with Anglo American counterparts, DuBray (1985) found the two groups differed significantly on all these value orientations except (3), despite the fact that the Native American social workers had completed six years of college education. DuBray concluded, therefore, that Native Americans prefer traditional value orientations and resist assimilation into the dominant culture. Gross has recently suggested that while a traditional value orientation may be preferred by many, there is reason to believe that actual preferences occur on a continuum with considerable diversity among individuals in any given culture with respect to value preferences (Gross, 1995).

Value conflicts often lie at the heart of clients' difficulties, as, for example, being torn between a desire for independence on one hand and a desire to be a homemaker on the other. Other clients may be engaged in a tug-of-war between a desire for liberation from an oppressive marital partner and a belief that marriage should be maintained at all costs. Value conflicts may also be central to difficulties between spouses. One partner may strongly value having children, whereas the other partner may reject this value. Conflicts between marital partners over religious values and clashes in beliefs between parents and adolescent children concerning premarital sexual behavior or the importance of education and achievement are also prevalent.

Being aware of clients' values is also prerequisite to employing these values to create incentive for changes in dysfunctional behavior. Clients may express strong commitment to certain values and yet engage in behavior that is in direct opposition to their purported values. When clients are assisted to measure their behavior against the yardstick of values they themselves have identified, they often realize for the first time that their behavior is inconsistent and self-defeating. For example, an adolescent who has protested that his parents should trust him agrees that being trusted is important to him. The practitioner then clarifies that his persistent lying to his parents defeats any possibility of his meriting their trust. Only by changing his behavior can he realistically expect them to trust him.

Awareness of client values is critical to ethical persuasion. Clients are more open to influence around instrumental values (means to ends) than they are around terminal values (ultimate goals)(Rooney, 1992). Cognitive dissonance may be aroused when inconsistency between thoughts or values and behavior is discovered. You can determine clients' relevant values by exploring what matters most to them, how they believe spouses should relate to one another, how they think children should be disciplined, and so on. Examples of questions that will clarify clients' values are as follows:

"You say you believe your parents are old-fashioned about sex; what are your beliefs?"

"If you could be married to an ideal wife, what would she be like?"

[*To a couple*]: "What are your beliefs as to how couples should make decisions?"

"So you feel you're not succeeding in life. To you, what does being successful involve?"

Misconceptions

Clients commonly hold mistaken beliefs about human relationships, sex roles, authority, and countless other facets of life. Increasing emphasis has been accorded to these beliefs, and one prominent school of psychotherapy (rational-emotive therapy) posits the tenet that beliefs mediate both emotions and behavior (Ellis, 1962). A central premise in this approach is that mistaken beliefs lie at the heart of human maladjustment. In Table 9-2, we have listed a few common misconceptions as well as contrasting functional beliefs.

Because misconceptions lie at the roots of many human problems, it is vital to learn to identify them and to include them in assessments. Goals often involve modifying key misconceptions, the accomplishment of which paves the way to behavioral change.

The Self-Concept

Convictions, beliefs, and ideas about the self have been generally recognized as one of the most crucial determinants of human behavior. Raimy (1975) and many other theorists have concluded "that beliefs about the self that are consonant with reality lead to adjusted behavior, whereas inappropriate beliefs lead to maladjusted behavior" (p. 9). It is thus a strength and is conducive to mental health to have high self-esteem and to be realistically aware of one's positive attributes, accomplishments, and potentialities as well as one's limitations and deficiencies. A healthy person can accept limitations as a natural part of human fallibility without being distressed or discouraged. People with high self-esteem, in fact, can joke about their limitations and failings.

Many human beings, however, are tormented with feelings of worthlessness, inadequacy, and helplessness. These and other like feelings pervade their functioning in diverse negative ways, including the following:

- Underachieving in life because of imagined deficiencies.
- Passing up opportunities because of fears of failing.
- Avoiding social relationships because of fears of being rejected.
- Permitting oneself to be taken for granted and exploited by others.
- Ingratiating oneself to others.
- Being self-conscious or retiring in social situations to avoid looking stupid.
- Gravitating in social relationships to low-status persons.
- Drinking to excess or taking drugs to fortify oneself because of feelings of inadequacy.
- Devaluing or discrediting one's worthwhile achievements.
- Becoming depressed.
- Failing to defend one's rights.

Extremely low self-esteem also is a primary contributor to mental illness. Certain manifestations of mental illness appear to be dysfunctional efforts to compensate for extremely low self-esteem. Some psychotic patients, for example, delude themselves into believing they are someone else—usually a person of power and status such as Jesus

TABLE 9-2   EXAMPLES OF COMMON MISCONCEPTIONS AND FUNCTIONAL BELIEFS

MISCONCEPTIONS	FUNCTIONAL BELIEFS
It is a disaster if I displease someone, and I must suffer.	I can't be constantly at the mercy of others' reactions to me, or I will be extremely vulnerable to hurt. Pleasing myself is more important than pleasing others.
I am completely at the mercy of circumstances beyond my control and totally powerless.	Although many circumstances are beyond my control, there is much I can do to improve my situation.
The world is a dog-eat-dog place. No one really cares about anyone except themselves.	There are all kinds of people in the world, including those who are ruthless and those who are caring. If I seek the latter, I will find them. The world will be a better place if I strive to be a caring person.
All people in authority use their power to exploit and control others.	People in authority vary widely. Some usurp others' rights; others are benevolent. I must reserve judgment, or I will indiscriminately resent all authority figures.
Men's only interest in women is to dominate them and use them for sexual pleasure.	Men are as different from one another as are women. Healthy men and women are interested in sex but not necessarily to use others for selfish pleasure.
To be worthwhile, a person must be thoroughly competent and successful in every endeavor.	Everyone has a range of talents and will do better in some endeavors than in others. No one is perfect, and disappointments are bound to occur from time to time.
It's a terrible blow to lose in competition.	Although it makes me feel good to win, there must be a loser for every winner. There is accomplishment in losing gracefully as well as in winning.
To be worthwhile, one must be the center of attention and admired by everyone.	Self-esteem that depends on constant attention is tenuous. Stable self-esteem comes from within; therefore I must learn to esteem myself.
It is virtuous to sacrifice, suffer, and deprive oneself in promoting the welfare of others.	Although it is desirable to assist others and to be concerned about them, I owe it to myself to seek personal satisfaction also. There is no virtue in unnecessary suffering.

Christ, the Virgin Mary, Napoleon, or some other historical giant. Others project their feeling of worthlessness and hear voices that say, "You're no good" or "You're rotten."

Because clients with poor self-concepts often desperately need help in enhancing their self-esteem, it is vital to assess this dimension of their functioning. Often clients will spontaneously discuss how they view themselves. When they do not, an open-ended response, such as "Tell me how you see yourself," will often elicit rich information. Because many people have not actually given much thought to the matter, they will hesitate or reply, "I'm not sure what you mean; what did you have in mind?" Persistence on your part will usually be rewarded. A further response, such as "Just what comes into your head when you think about the sort of person you are?" is usually all that is needed.

Instruments have also been developed to measure self-esteem. The Index of Self-Esteem, one of the Walmyr scales (Hudson, 1992), can be completed by clients in a matter of minutes. It is also easily scored and interpreted.

Interaction Between Cognition, Emotions, and Behavior

As is apparent in the foregoing discussion, cognitive functioning embraces many critical factors that interact with other variables to influence social functioning. Cognition, for example, plays a powerful role in mediating emotional arousal. Cognitive/perceptual sets, particularly the self-concept, influence both emotions and behavior. Because theoreticians and researchers have increasingly realized the significance of cognitive factors, they have in recent years developed and empirically tested a number of cognitive-behavioral interventions that have widespread application. Accordingly, we have devoted portions of Chapters 13 and 14 to these interventions.

EMOTIONAL FUNCTIONING

Emotions powerfully influence behavior and are of high concern to social work practitioners. Strong emotions or states of feeling often play a central role in the problems of people who seek help. Some persons, for example, are emotionally volatile and engage in violent behavior while in the heat of anger. Others are emotionally unstable, struggling to stay afloat in a turbulent sea of emotion. Some people become emotionally distraught as the result of stress associated with the death of a loved one, divorce, severe disappointment, or another blow to self-esteem. Still others are pulled in different directions by opposing feelings and seek help to resolve their emotional dilemmas. To assist you in assessing emotional functioning, we devote the following sections to vital aspects of this dimension.

Emotional Control

People vary widely in the degree of control they exercise over their emotions, ranging from emotional constriction to emotional excesses. Prominent in the former are individuals who are unexpressive and withholding in relationships. Out of touch with their emotions, they do not permit themselves to feel joy, hurt, enthusiasm, and other emotions that invest life with zest and meaning. Such persons are comfortable intellectualizing but retreat from expressing or discussing feelings. They often favorably impress others with their intellectual styles, but sometimes have difficulties maintaining close relationships because their emotional detachment thwarts fulfilling the needs of others for intimacy and emotional stimulation.

Clients who manifest emotional excesses may have a "short fuse" and react intensely to even mild provocations. Clients who physically abuse family members, for example, lose control of anger and express it in violent ways. Others overreact to stress with tears, panic, depression, helplessness, and the like. Still others have difficulties in interpersonal relationships because they are excessively grouchy, irritable, or morose.

Cultural Factors In considering emotional excesses, cultural factors should be considered, for cultures vary widely in approved patterns of emotional expressiveness. It is generally accepted, for example, that people of Italian extraction are more emotionally reactive than are Asian and English people, who are known for their emotional reserve. Hispanics also tend to be emotionally reactive, as Queralt (1984, p. 118) indicates in his description of Cubans: "Uninhibited emotionality and a hedonistic tendency that manifests itself through love of comfort, of life, and of pleasure, sensuality, playfulness, lightness, and gaiety are important Cuban traits." Hispanics also vary in emotional expressiveness when they switch from speaking Spanish to English. According to Queralt:

Hispanics generally offer more carefully weighted, rational, and intellectualized messages in English and more emotional messages in Spanish...Hispanics may come across as relatively guarded and businesslike in English, and yet, when switching to Spanish, they frequently become much more open, expansive, informal, jovial, friendly, jocose, explosive, negative, or positive. It is as if two personalities resided in the same person at once. (p. 119)

In assessing cultural factors, however, it is vital to differentiate individual from cultural factors, for a wide range of emotional expressiveness exists among members of specific cultural groups. Individual patterns thus must be weighed against cultural norms.

Emotional health in any culture, however, involves having control over the emotions to the extent that one is not overwhelmed by them. Emotionally healthy persons also enjoy the freedom of experiencing and expressing emotions appropriately. It is also a strength to be able to bear painful emotions when beset by stress without denying or masking feelings or being incapacitated by them. Further, emotionally healthy persons are able to discern the emotional states of others, empathize, and discuss painful emotions openly without feeling unduly uncomfortable—recognizing, of course, that a certain amount of discomfort is natural. And finally, it is a strength to be able to mutually share deeply personal feelings in intimate relationships.

Range of Emotions

Another aspect of emotional functioning involves the ability to experience and to express a wide range of emotions that befit the diversity of situations encountered by human beings. Some people's emotional experiencing is confined to a limited range, which often causes interpersonal difficulties. A marital partner, for example, may have a "blockage" of tender emotions, causing the partner to feel rejected, insecure, or deprived of deserved affection. Some individuals are unable to

feel joy or to express many pleasurable emotions—a dysfunction denoted as anhedonia. Still others have been conditioned to block angry feelings, blame themselves, or placate others when friction develops in relationships. Because of the blocking of natural emotions, they often experience extreme tension or physiological symptoms such as asthma, colitis, and headaches when involved in situations that normally would engender anger. And finally, some people, to protect themselves from unbearable emotions, evolved psychic mechanisms early in life that blocked experiencing rejection, loneliness, and hurt. Often such blockage is reflected by a compensatory facade of toughness and indifference, combined with verbal expressions such as "I don't need anyone" and "No one can hurt me."

Emotionally healthy people experience the full gamut of human emotions within normal limits of intensity and duration. It is thus a strength to experience joy, grief, exhilaration, disappointment, and all the rest of the full spectrum of emotions. When clients manifest emotional blockages that inhibit resolution of the problems they are seeking help with, the practitioner has the task of enabling them to get in touch with the blocked emotions.

Appropriateness of Affect

Direct observation of the affect (emotionality) manifested by clients often discloses valuable information about their emotional functioning. Some anxiety or mild apprehension is natural in initial sessions (especially for involuntary clients and those referred by others), as contrasted to intense apprehension and tension at one extreme or complete relaxation at the other. Spontaneous experiencing and expressing of emotion that befits the content of material being discussed is indicative of healthy emotional functioning. It is thus a strength to be able to laugh, to cry, to express hurt, discouragement, anger, and pleasure when these feelings match the mood of the session. Such spontaneity indicates that clients are in touch with emotions and can express them appropriately.

Inordinate apprehension manifested through muscle tenseness, constant postural shifts, hand wringing, lip biting, and other like behaviors usually indicate a client is fearful, suspicious, or exceptionally uncomfortable in unfamiliar interpersonal situations. Such extreme tenseness may be expected in involuntary situations. In other cases, it may be characteristic of a client's demeanor in other interpersonal situations.

Clients who appear completely relaxed and express themselves freely in a circumstance which would normally suggest apprehension or anxiety may reflect a denial of a problem and may indicate a lack of motivation to engage in the problem-solving process. Further, charming demeanor may be a reflection of skill in projecting a favorable image when it is advantageous to do so. In some situations, as in sales or promotional work, such charm may be an asset. Such behavior sometimes is a person's coping style to conceal being self-centered, manipulative, and exploitative in relationships. Such individuals often engender anxiety in those who are victimized by their manipulativeness, but they themselves typically lack anxiety that is prerequisite to wanting to change their own behavior.

Emotional blunting or apathy frequently is indicative of severe mental disorder. It is important to consider this possibility when clients discuss in a detached matter-of-fact manner traumatic life events or conditions, such as murder of one parent by another, deprivation, or physical and/or sexual abuse. When such emotional blunting appears in tandem with thought disorder, a strong likelihood exists that the client is psychotic and in need of careful psychiatric evaluation.

Inappropriate affect can also be manifested in other forms, such as laughing when discussing a painful event (gallows laughter) or wearing a constant smile regardless of whatever is being discussed. Elation or euphoria that is incongruent with one's life situation, combined with constant and rapid shifts from one topic to another (flight of ideas), irritability, expansive ideas, and constant motion also suggest dysfunction denoted as manic behavior. Although manic behavior is relatively rare, it is important to recognize manifestations of it, for manic clients urgently need medication and/or hospitalization to safeguard their health or protect them from impulsive and irrational actions, such as squandering resources on foolish investments.

Cultural Factors In transcultural work, appropriateness of affect must be considered in light of the impact of cultural differences. As Lum (1992) has indicated, minority persons may feel uncomfortable with nonminorities but mask their emotions as a protective measure. Moreover, in the presence of nonminority practitioners, minority persons may control painful emotions according to culturally prescribed behavior. An Asian American, for example, may react with politeness, quietness, and friendliness in the face of an overwhelming and threatening situation.

ASSESSING AFFECTIVE DISORDERS

In the earlier section concerned with psychiatric diagnoses, we referred to DSM-IV, the manual widely employed as a guide for formulating psychiatric diagnoses. Generally speaking, psychiatric diagnoses have limited value to social workers, because they are largely descriptive, provide little information about causality, and aid little in formulating treatment plans (Beutler & Clarkin, 1990). Certain affective disorders (i.e., disorders of mood), however, are exceptions, namely, bipolar major affective disorders (also known as manic-depressive illness) and unipolar major affective disorders (severe depression). Research findings cited by Rauch, Sarno, and Simpson (1991) have consistently provided evidence that genetic factors are implicated in these disorders, so that the diagnoses do inform us, at least partially, as to causative factors. Treatment of persons with these diagnoses generally includes medication (often with concurrent cognitive or interpersonal psychotherapy) so that these diagnoses also provide direction in treatment planning. Moreover, persons with these disorders can pose suicidal risk and other serious risk factors. For these reasons, we discuss diagnosis of the major affective disorders in the following sections.

Bipolar Affective Disorders

The dominant feature of this disorder is the presence of elevated mood (mania) with or without intervening periods of depression. During the period of elevated mood, at least three of the following seven symptoms must persist (American Psychiatric Association, 1987, p. 217):

- Inflated self-esteem or grandiosity.
- Decreased need for sleep.
- More talkative than usual or pressure to keep talking.
- Flight of ideas or subjective experience that thoughts are racing.
- Distractibility.
- Increase in goal-directed activity (either socially, at work or school, or sexually) or psychomotor agitation.
- Excessive involvement in pleasurable activities which have a high potential for painful consequences, e.g., unrestrained buying sprees, sexual indiscretions, or foolish business investments.

Full-blown manic episodes require that symptoms be sufficiently severe to cause marked impairment in job performance or relationships, or to necessitate hospitalization to protect patients or others from harm.

When a practitioner has reason to believe that a client may have a bipolar major affective disorder, it is important to inquire whether the client has experienced the symptoms listed above. Rauch, Sarno, and Simpson (1991) list specific questions that can be asked to screen for mania and we urge you to read their article.

If exploration seems to indicate a client has the disorder, immediate psychiatric consultation is needed; first, to determine if hospitalization is needed, and second, to determine the need for medication. This disorder is biogenetic, and various compounds containing lithium carbonate produce remarkable results in stabilizing and maintaining these persons. Close medical supervision is required, however, because lithium compounds have a relatively narrow margin of safety.

Major Unipolar Affective Disorders

This type of disorder, in which persons experience recurrent episodes of depressed mood, are far more common than bipolar disorders. Major depression differs from the blues in that dysphoria (painful emotions) and the absence of pleasure (anhedonia) are present. The painful emotion commonly is related to anxiety, mental anguish, an extreme sense of guilt (often over what appears to be relatively minor offenses), and restlessness (agitation).

To be assigned a diagnosis of major depressive episode, a person must have had at least five of the following nine symptoms for at least two weeks (American Psychiatric Association, 1987, pp. 222–223):

- Depressed mood...most of the day, nearly every day.
- Markedly diminished interest or pleasure in all, or almost all, activities.
- Significant weight loss or weight gain when not dieting...or decrease or increase in appetite.
- Insomnia or hypersomnia nearly every day.
- Psychomotor agitation or retardation.
- Fatigue or loss of energy nearly every day.
- Feelings of worthlessness, or excessive or inappropriate guilt.
- Diminished ability to think or concentrate, or indecisiveness.

- Recurrent thoughts of death...recurrent suicidal ideation with a specific plan, or a suicide attempt or a specific plan for committing suicide.

Again, Rauch, Sarno, and Simpson (1991) provide specific questions you can ask to determine if a client meets the above criteria. In addition, there are a number of scales available to assess the presence and degree of depression. They include the Depression Scale in the Walmyr Scales (Hudson, 1992), the Beck Depression Inventory (Beck, Ward, Mendelson, Mock, & Erbaugh, 1961), and the Zung Self-Rating Depression Scale (Zung, 1965). All of these scales are easy to complete, to score, and to interpret. All are also highly correlated with each other.

When assessment reveals clients are moderately or severely depressed, psychiatric consultation is indicated to determine the need for medication and/or hospitalization. Antidepressive medications have proven to be effective in accelerating recovery from depression and work synergistically with cognitive or interpersonal psychotherapy. Electroconvulsive therapy (ECT) is also effective with certain types of depression. Elderly persons who are depressed, a group often overlooked, may improve dramatically when treated with antidepressives or ECT.

In assessing depression, it is important to identify precipitants of the depressive episode. Commonly an important loss or series of losses have occurred, and clients may need assistance in working through grief associated with these losses and developing compensatory sources of companionship and support.

Assessing Suicidal Risk

When clients manifest severe depressive symptoms, it is critical to evaluate suicidal risk so that precautionary measures can be taken when indicated. With adults the following factors are associated with high risk of suicide:

- Feelings of despair and hopelessness.
- Previous suicidal attempts.
- Concrete plans to commit suicide (when, where, and how).
- Ruminations about suicide.
- Lack of support systems.
- Feelings of worthlessness.
- Belief others would be better off if one were dead.
- Ruminations about wanting to join loved ones who are deceased.

Careful exploration of the above factors will assist you in assessing suicidal risk. In addition, the following scales can be used to evaluate suicidal risk: the Hopelessness Scale (Beck, Resnik, & Lettieri, 1974), the Scale for Suicide Ideation (Beck, Kovacs, & Weissman, 1979), and the Suicide Probability Scale (Cull & Gill, 1991). When suicide is a distinct possibility, psychiatric evaluation and/or hospitalization should be considered.

Assessing Depression and Suicidal Risk with Children and Adolescents

Children and adolescents, too, may experience depression, and suicide can be a risk with these groups. The rate of suicide for adolescents, in fact, has tripled over the past 30 years; half a million young people between ages 15 and 24 attempt suicide each year and 5,000 of them succeed. It is thus important to recognize both symptoms of depression in adolescents and behavioral manifestations reported by parents. Based on a careful study of severely depressed adolescents, researchers (Ryan et al., 1987) identified common symptoms. The following list, which contains only symptoms that were present in 35% or more of the cases, orders the symptoms from the highest frequency (60%) to the lowest (35%):

1. Depressed mood.
2. Anhedonia.
3. Fatigue.

4. Negative self-image.

5. Mood reactivity.

6. Decreased concentration.

7. Suicidal ideation.

8. Insomnia.

Because parents often do not realize their child is depressed, it is important to alert them to the following additional behavioral manifestations (Gold, 1986, p. 10):

- Deterioration in personal habits.
- Decline in school achievement.
- Marked increase in sadness, moodiness, and sudden tearful reactions.
- Loss of appetite.
- Use of drugs or alcohol.
- Talk of death or dying (even in a joking manner).
- Sudden withdrawal from friends and family.

Given the mood swings and tempestuousness typical of adolescence, the above warning signs should be regarded as indications of serious depression only when they persist for ten days or longer. If a child manifests several of these symptoms, psychiatric consultation is advisable. Suicidal risk is highest when the adolescent, in addition to the above-listed symptoms of severe depression, manifests feelings of hopelessness, has recently experienced a death of a loved one, had severe conflict with parents, lost a close relationship with a key peer or a sweetheart, and has no support system. Studies (Fowler, Rich, & Young, 1986) of suicides by adolescents have indicated that moderate to heavy drinking and/or drug abuse were implicated in at least 50% of the suicides.[11]

With respect to depression in children, the manifestations vary little from those listed for adolescents, although the order of frequency varies somewhat. One notable difference is that separation anxiety (fear of being separated from the parents) appears in 34% of severely depressed children.

BEHAVIOR FUNCTIONING

In direct practice, change efforts typically are aimed at modifying behavioral patterns that impair the social functioning of clients and others involved in the problem. As you assess behavior, it is important to keep in mind that one person's behavior does not influence another person's behavior in simple linear fashion. Rather the behavior of all participants reciprocally impacts upon and shapes the behavior of others.

Because behavioral change is commonly the target of interventions, you must be skillful in discerning and assessing both dysfunctional and functional patterns of behavior. With respect to direct observation in individual sessions, you will be able to observe certain social and communication patterns of clients, as well as some personal habits and traits. In conjoint interviews and group sessions, you will be able to observe these types of behavioral patterns and in addition can observe the functioning of clients on the dimensions of power/control and nurturance/support.

In assessing behavior, it is helpful to think of problems as consisting of excesses or deficiencies on the part of clients. With respect to the former, interventions are aimed at the goal of diminishing or eliminating behavioral excesses, which include temper outbursts, excessive talking, arguing, overachieving, and consummatory excesses (e.g., overeating, immoderate drinking, and excessive sexual indulgence). With regard to deficiencies, interventions are employed to assist clients to acquire skills and behaviors needed to function more effectively. The behavioral repertoires of clients, for example, may not include skills in expressing feelings directly, engaging in social conversation, listening to others, solving problems, managing finances, planning nutritional meals, being a responsive sexual partner, handling conflict, and other skills that are essential to effective social functioning.

In addition to identifying dysfunctional behavioral patterns, it is important to be aware of those that are effective and represent strengths. To assist you in assessing both dysfunctional and functional patterns of behavior, we have listed, according to major behavioral categories, numerous patterns of behavior (see Table 9-3). Although the list is extensive, it is by no means comprehensive, nor are the categories all-inclusive. We have, however, included those patterns that most frequently create interpersonal difficulties. As you review the list, you may question whether a few patterns are functional or dysfunctional. This determination, of course, depends on the situational context within which the behavior occurs. Aggressive behavior may serve a self-protective function in a prison environment but may be dysfunctional in family relationships or in most groups. In compiling the list, our frame of reference encompassed typical marital, family, and group contexts.

You will note that the list consists of many adjectives and verbs that are very general and are subject to different interpretations. In assessing behavior, therefore, it is vital to specify actual problem behaviors. For example, rather than assessing a client's behavior as abrasive, a practitioner might specify that the client constantly interrupts his fellow workers, insults them by telling them they are misinformed, and boasts about his own knowledge and achievements. When dysfunctional behavior is thus pinpointed, the changes that must be made become clear.

An adequate assessment of behavior, of course, goes beyond identifying dysfunctional behaviors. You must also determine the antecedents of behaviors—when, where, and how frequently they occur—and specify the consequences of the behaviors as well. Further, you should explore thoughts that precede, accompany, and follow the behavior, as well as the nature of and intensity of emotions associated with the behavior. We identified these factors in the preceding chapter and earlier in this chapter.

We have also limited the dysfunctional behaviors embodied in the list to individual patterns of behavior. The list does not include dysfunctional patterns of interaction between two or more persons in marital, family, and group contexts. However, we devote the following chapter to this important topic.

MOTIVATION

Evaluating and enhancing the motivation of clients are integral parts of the assessment process. Clients who don't believe that they can influence their environments may manifest a kind of learned helplessness (Gold, 1990, p. 51). In order to assess motivation, the practitioner needs to understand the person and his or her perception of the environment.

Motivation, of course, is a dynamic force that is strongly influenced by ongoing interaction with practitioners, who thus bear the responsibility not only to assess initial motivation but also to enhance motivation that lacks strength or direction. By relating facilitatively and determining clients' wants and goals, practitioners often succeed in engendering incentives and engaging clients. Conversely, clients who initially are adequately motivated may lose that motivation if their encounter with a practitioner is negative. It is to be expected that family and group members will range along a continuum of motivation.

As Reid (1978) has pointed out, motivation consists of two critical aspects. The first aspect is the direction of the motivation; that is, toward what goals is the client motivated? Clients are generally motivated to fulfill certain wants or needs. In evaluating the directionality of motivation, the central issue concerns whether or not clients' wants are realistic and achievable. Some clients seek to accomplish goals that exceed their capacity (e.g., vocational goals that require aptitude well beyond that possessed by the client). Others express wants

TABLE 9-3   BEHAVIORAL PATTERNS

DIMENSIONS OF BEHAVIOR	DYSFUNCTIONAL PATTERNS	FUNCTIONAL PATTERNS (STRENGTHS)
Power/ control	Autocratic, overbearing, aggressive, ruthless, demanding, domineering, controlling, passive, submissive; excludes others from decision making.	Democratic, cooperative, assertive; includes others in decision making, stands up for own rights.
Nurturance/support	Self-centered, critical, rejecting, withholding, demeaning, distant, punitive, fault-finding, self-serving; insensitive to or unconcerned about others.	Caring, approving, giving, empathic, encouraging, patient, generous, altruistic, warm, accepting, supportive; interested in others.
Responsibility	Undependable, erratic; avoids responsibility, places pleasure before responsibility, externalizes responsibility for problems, neglects maintenance of personal property.	Dependable, steady, consistent, reliable; follows through, accepts responsibility, owns part in problems, maintains personal property.
Social skills	Abrasive, caustic, irritable,insensitive, aloof, seclusive, sarcastic, querulous, withdrawn, self-conscious, ingratiating; lacks social delicacy.	Outgoing, poised, personable, verbally fluent, sociable, witty, courteous, engaging, cooperative, assertive, spontaneous, respectful of others, sensitive to feelings of others; has sense of propriety.
Coping patterns	Rigid, impulsive, rebellious; avoids facing problems, uses alcohol or drugs when under stress, becomes panicky, lashes out at others, sulks.	Flexible; faces problems, considers and weighs alternatives, anticipates consequences, maintains equilibrium, seeks growth, consults others for suggestions, negotiates and compromises.
Personal habits and traits	Disorganized, dilatory, devious, dishonest, compulsive, overly fastidious, impulsive; manifests poor personal hygiene, has consummatory excesses, has irritating mannerisms.	Planful, organized, flexible, clean, efficient, patient, self-disciplined, well-groomed, honest, open, sincere, temperate,considerate, even-dispositioned, punctual.
Communication	Mumbles, complains excessively, nags, talks excessively, interrupts others, tunes others out, stammers, yells when angry, withholds views, defensive, monotonic, argumentative, taciturn, verbally abusive.	Listens attentively, speaks fluently, expresses views, shares feelings, uses feedback, expresses self spontaneously, considers others' viewpoints, speaks audibly and within tolerable limits.
Accomplishment/ independence	Unmotivated, aimless, nonproductive, easily discouraged, easily distracted, underachieving; lacks initiative,seldom completes endeavors, workaholic, slave to work.	Ambitious, industrious, self-starting, independent, resourceful, persevering, successful in endeavors, seeks to advance or to improve situations.
Affectional/sexual	Unaffectionate, reserved, distant, sexually inhibited, promiscuous, lacking sexual desire, engages in deviant sexual behavior.	Warm, loving, affectionate, demonstrative, sexually responsive (appropriately).

that require changes beyond the sphere of influence of the client and/or practitioner (e.g., "I want you to persuade my wife to drop her divorce action and to reconcile with me" or "I want you to get my kids back; they need me and are not happy in that foster home"). In such instances, it is important to tactfully assist clients to recognize the unrealistic nature of their wants and to direct them toward realistic goals that are relevant to their problematic situation (e.g., "Only the judge has the authority to return your children to you, but I'm very willing to assist you in making whatever changes are necessary to meet the conditions he has specified for the return of your children").

The second aspect concerns the strength of motivation. Clients often manifest wants but lack the willingness or current skill to participate actively in planning and implementing remedial actions. Many clients have misconceptions about the helping role, imputing to the practitioner magical power for solving their difficulties. Others are willing to participate but mistakenly perceive their role as compliantly carrying out the practitioner's directives. Still others manifest strength and independence by correctly perceiving the practitioner as a partner and facilitator and by assuming responsibility for mutually exploring their problems and for planning and implementing remedial measures.

PRECIPITATING EVENTS AND MOTIVATION

All potential clients, both applicants and persons who are referred, are motivated. Their motivation frequently differs, however, from the problems attributed to them by others. By carefully exploring life events that precipitate applicants' decisions to seek service, you can often discern both the direction and strength of their initial motivation. When applicants decide to seek service shortly after critical events and request assistance in modifying behavior or circumstances associated with these events, their motivation is likely to be adequate in both direction and strength.

When potential clients' decisions to seek assistance result from a referral in the form of an ultimatum from a family member or employer, their motivation to work on the problems attributed to them by the referral source is likely to be less strong. To differentiate such referred clients from applicants, Rooney has described such clients as nonvoluntary to reflect their response to external, nonlegal pressure and to suggest that they are the "invisible involuntary" because the nonlegal pressure they experience is often hidden or ignored by the practitioner (Rooney, 1992). For example, though a couple requested marital therapy, the intake practitioner discovered that in fact their "request" was precipitated by an ultimatum from the husband's mother, with whom they were living, to get help or move out. Further exploration revealed that intense verbal arguments between the couple had precipitated the mother's ultimatum. As such nonvoluntary clients frequently lack motivation to work on the problem attributed to them by the referral source, practitioners should first act to clarify available choices. In this case, the couple could choose not to continue with the pressured request for services, to ignore the recommendation of the referral source, or to work on concerns of their own (ibid.). Such a clarification focuses attention on problems acknowledged by clients rather than those attributed by others (Reid, 1978). Consequently, it is possible to find problems for which there is adequate motivation both in strength and direction if attention is devoted to those problems acknowledged by clients. Frequently nonvoluntary clients will choose to get rid of or reduce the pressure. In this case, the couple did not view themselves as in need of marital treatment. They did, however, wish to remain living with the mother for the time being. After assurances that these arguments had not escalated to physical violence, the couple agreed to work on verbal means for reducing conflicts partly motivated by their wish to avoid eviction from the mother's home.

Meanwhile, mandated clients whose contact with helping professionals is impelled by legal mandate or the threat of such rarely acknowledge the same problems as do the sources of the legal mandate. For example, parents who are alleged to have abused or neglected their children rarely acknowledge child abuse or neglect as their concern. Similarly, mandated clients in correctional institutions rarely acknowledge the same problems as those for which they have been imprisoned. Rooney describes strategies whereby practitioners can seek to discover acknowledged problems with mandated clients and link them to mandated pressures (Rooney, 1992). We will discuss these strategies in Chapter 12.

CULTURAL FACTORS

In this and previous chapters, we have discussed many cultural factors related to various aspects of the helping process. In this section, we focus on general cultural factors that are relevant to the process of assessment. Many other cultural factors are discussed in subsequent portions of the book.

Cultural Norms

Knowledge of the norms related to a client's culture of origin is indispensable when the client's cultural background is markedly different from your own. Without such knowledge, you may make serious errors in assessing both individual and interpersonal systems, for cognitive, emotional, behavioral, and interpersonal patterns that are deemed functional in one cultural context may be deemed problematic in another and vice versa. Further, such errors in assessment may lead to selecting interventions that aggravate rather than diminish clients'

problems. For example, encouraging relatively unacculturated Hispanic women to assert themselves to their husbands may subject them to violent behavior because such behavior is contrary to cultural norms. Similarly, to suggest that an Asian American woman should stand up to or distance herself from controlling in-laws would be potentially damaging because of the cultural norm that dictates respect for older persons and maintaining strong family ties (see Lum, 1992 for an extensive discussion of cultural norms and values).

Cultures vary widely in their prescribed patterns of child care, child rearing, adolescent roles, mate selection, marital roles, and care of the aged—to name just a few. In Anglo-American culture, for example, there has been a major trend toward equality of the sexes, resulting in the prevailing view that domineering behavior by husbands is dysfunctional. While there are feminists among American Hispanics and in Middle-Eastern cultures, autocratic behavior by husbands and dependent behavior by wives is often the norm.

Patterns of communication between marital partners also vary widely from culture to culture. Among certain Native American tribes, husbands and wives tend to communicate more with members of their same sex than with each other. Similarly, the extent of communication between parents and children varies substantially from culture to culture.

Differentiating Individual and Culturally Determined Patterns

Although knowledge about the client's culture is vital in transcultural work, practitioners must guard against stereotyping clients on the basis of that knowledge. Considerable variation exists among subgroups of identified ethnic groups, and overgeneralizations about members of these groups may obscure rather than clarify the meanings of individual behavior. For example, there are over 400 different tribal groups of Native Americans in the United States, and these groups speak over 250 distinct languages (Edwards, 1983). Comparisons of Plains tribes with Native Americans of the Southwest have revealed sharply contrasting cultural patterns and patterns of individual behavior as well as marked differences in the incidence of certain social problems (May, Hymbaugh, Aase, & Samet, 1983). Cubans, Puerto Ricans, and Mexican American groups also differ widely from one another although they are much more alike than different because of their common Hispanic heritage (Queralt, 1984). Filipinos also embody diverse cultural groups who speak eight major different languages and 75 or more different dialects (Ponce, 1980). Obviously, Asian Americans also represent many different cultures that share certain characteristics but also differ significantly from one another. In this regard, Gould (1988) negates the myth that Asians and Pacific Islanders are model minorities that take care of their own and should not qualify for the title of disadvantaged. Data reveal that after four years of living in the United States, almost one-third of Indochinese refugees live below the poverty line and 55% of the households still need public assistance. Moreover, these groups manifest problems of wife abuse, physical and mental health problems, and victimization in the forms of violence, vandalism, harassment, and intimidation.

Within homogeneous cultural groups, wide variations also exist among individuals. Being knowledgeable about the cultural characteristics of a given group is necessary but insufficient for understanding the behavior of individual members of the groups. As with members of the cultural majority, each member of an ethnic minority group is unique. Practitioners, therefore, must consider each ethnic minority client as an individual, for dysfunctional or deviant behavior as viewed from the perspective of the cultural majority may be similarly viewed by members of ethnic minority groups. The task confronting practitioners, therefore, is to differentiate between behavior that is culturally mediated and that which is a product of individual personality. Possession of in-depth knowledge about a given cultural group facilitates making such differentiations, but when in doubt, practitioners are advised to consult with well-informed and cooperative members of the ethnic group in question. Kumabe et al. (1985), for example, have reported an instance involving a neglectful Southeast-Asian refugee mother who appeared to be depressed. After making extended and futile efforts to assist this mother, the practitioner consulted with another refugee and learned that the mother (who spoke little English) was mentally retarded rather than depressed. Further, she had manifested child neglect in her native community before coming to the United States.

Degree of Acculturation

In assessing the functioning of ethnic minority clients, it is important to consider the degree to which they have been socialized into the mainstream culture. Ethnic minority clients are actually members of two cultures, and their functioning must be considered in relationship to both their culture of origin and the majority culture. Clients from the same ethnic group may vary widely in the degree of their acculturation, which depends upon a number of factors. Foremost is the number of generations that have passed since the original emigration from the native land. Ordinarily, first-generation minority clients adhere closely to their traditional beliefs, values, and patterns of behavior. By the third generation, however, clients have usually internalized many of the patterns of the dominant culture although they typically maintain many traditional patterns of family relationships.

Even when considering the degree of acculturation of an ethnic minority client, errors can be made if practitioners fail to attend to a client's uniqueness. For example, although unacculturated

Asian Americans are generally regarded as emotionally unexpressive and preferring structure and direction by practitioners, Sue and Zane (1987) report that "many... seemed quite willing to talk about their emotions and to work well with little structure" (p. 39).

Still, the significance of the different generations to Japanese Americans is reflected in the fact that this ethnic group specifies by linguistic terms each generation of descendants from the original immigrant group. The terms Issei, Nisei, and Sansei thus refer to first, second, and third generations, respectively. Mass (1976) has discussed characteristics, patterns, and problems of each of these groups. Lott (1976) has presented a similar discussion of different generations of Filipino immigrants.

Other factors also affect the degree of "bicultural" socialization and interactions of ethnic minority clients with mainstream society. One writer (De Anda, 1984, p. 102) identified and discussed six such factors:

1. The degree of commonality between the two cultures with regard to norms, values, beliefs, perceptions, and the like.
2. The availability of cultural translators, mediators, and models.
3. The amount and type (positive or negative) of corrective feedback provided by each culture regarding attempts to produce normative behaviors.
4. The conceptual style and problem-solving approach of the minority individual and their mesh with the prevalent or valued styles of the majority culture.
5. The individual's degree of bilingualism.
6. The degree of dissimilarity in physical appearance from the majority culture, such as skin color, facial features, and so forth.

Culturally sensitive assessment thus carefully considers the degree of biculturalism manifested by a client. Rogler, Malgady, Costantino, and Blumenthal (1987) dramatize this point by reporting how treatment plans with an individual Hispanic client may span the continuum from "most His-panic" to "most Anglo." Fortunately, an excellent scale, the Acculturation Scale for Mexican Americans (Cueller, Harris, & Jasso, 1980), is available to assess acculturation of Mexican Americans. Formulated in both the English and Spanish languages, the scale has won plaudits by Hispanics for its construction and correct use of the Spanish language. Still another scale, the Latino Bicultural Assessment Questionnaire (Camayd-Freixas & Amaro, 1984), has been designed for use with any Latino population.

Other authors (Kumabe et al., 1985) have reported that varying degrees of acculturation occur among members of the same family and same generation. These authors also discuss and illustrate the complexities involved in acculturation when parents are from different ethnic minority backgrounds, as for example, a Japanese American married to a Filipino American. The socialization of children to such parents is tricultural. Such permutations are not uncommon in truly pluralistic societies such as Hawaii, where people often refer to their ethnic heritage as smorgasbord. Transcultural work is the rule rather than the exception in such communities, and effective practice requires extensive knowledge of the cultures represented.

Biculturalism and Mental Health

Controversy has fermented for many years as to whether policies should encourage minority members to retain their cultural roots, to assimilate into mainstream society, or both. Many factors, of course, enter into the debate, including whether one adopts the majority or minority perspective. Chau has noted that most cross-cultural change efforts have focused on psychological adaptation of the minority person to the majority culture (Chau, 1990). These efforts often reflect an ethnocentric assumption that the minority person needs to gain from strengths of the majority culture. When the assumptions shift from ethnocentrism to cultural pluralism, change efforts can reflect a two-way interaction in which attention is devoted to strengths different cultures can bring to each other, strengthening both host and minority cultures.

From the standpoint of mental health, one important study sheds some light on the matter. Studying the mental health of Cuban Americans, Gomez (1990) measured the degree of biculturalism of the study groups and then determined the relationship between the degree of biculturalism and the psychological well-being, self-esteem, marital adjustment, and job satisfaction of the subjects. The findings indicated that the more bicultural the subjects were, the higher their psychological well-being and self-esteem. Further, among married subjects there was a relationship between biculturalism and higher marital adjustment. Findings related to job satisfaction were less impressive. These findings further support the need for social workers to assess the biculturalism of clients, to sensitize themselves to minority cultures, to encourage clients to maintain ties to their cultural roots, and to assist them in adapting to mainstream culture.

Fluency with the English Language

Degree of bilingualism is also a major factor that practitioners should consider in assessments involving ethnic minority clients. Clients whose command of English is very limited often have great difficulty in formulating and explaining their problems in a different language. Often an interpreter is needed to bridge the language gap. If an interpreter is not available, it is important to speak in simple terms and to proceed at a slower pace. Clients need ample time to process messages, and practitioners must exercise care in checking out whether clients have grasped the intended meaning of their messages.

Limited fluency in language can also block ethnic minority clients from access to essential community resources (especially clients isolated from their cultural reference groups). Inability to converse with others and to take advantage of the vast information provided through newspapers, radio, and television thus not only produces social isolation but also deprives people of information essential to locating and utilizing essential resources. However, many cities in the United States and parts of the country now have Spanish television and social services available in Spanish.

Problem-Solving Methods

In assessing the functioning of ethnic minority clients and planning interventions, it is important to be aware that members of different cultures define problems in different ways (Green, 1982, pp. 44–47). Behavior that is regarded as normal in one culture may be viewed as deviant in another. For example, as seen from an Asian American perspective, individualism and aggressive competition (which characterize mainstream society) conflict with traditional Asian respect for authority and filial piety toward parents and ancestors (Ho, 1976, p. 196). Similarly, among Hispanic families the commonly close degree of involvement among family members shows a tendency toward what might be regarded as dysfunctional "enmeshment" (see Chapter 10) among Anglo American families (Queralt, 1984, p. 117).

Approaches to problem solving also vary among different cultures. Within the mainstream culture, an analytical cognitive style appears to be the most highly valued approach to defining most problems and searching for solutions to them (De Anda, 1984). Certain ethnic minority groups, however, rely on approaches based on group values to coping with problems which differ from the individually focused style of the mainstream culture. All cultures exert pressures on individuals to follow prescriptive courses of action in given problematic situations. Novel and creative solutions which differ from cultural assumptions are discouraged in such circumstances, and deviation from those culturally prescribed rules may generate anxiety and/or guilt for clients strongly influenced by their cultures.

Variations among cultures are also common with respect to key persons who normally become involved in efforts to solve problems. In most Native American tribal groups, for example, family members actively seek counsel from elderly members of the extended family unit in coping with family problems. The wisdom of the elderly is highly valued, and elderly members of the tribe are accorded much respect (Hull, 1982). When sought for counsel, elderly Native Americans often pass along their wisdom in the form of storytelling, "which does not insult the intelligence or integrity of the listener because one is always free to ignore unacceptable suggestions" (Hull, 1982, p. 343). Asian Americans similarly look to the extended family for direction in problem-solving situations and value the wisdom of the elderly.

Achieving Credibility

Practitioners whom clients consider likable, trustworthy, and deemed to have the client's best interest at heart are most likely to be perceived by clients to be positive sources of influence (Rooney, 1992). These factors may be facilitated by cultural similarity between client and practitioner. However, practitioners who are culturally similar to their clients may differ from them in other important ways such as values, education, and level of acculturation. In fact, a Southeast Asian child welfare worker reported that his job was easier with Caucasian clients than with Southeast Asian clients who expected that cultural similarity would override professional allegiances and legal mandates. Davis and Gelsomino report in a study of cross-cultural contact that Caucasian practitioners were

more likely to explore psychological problems and internal difficulties with minority clients than were minority practitioners working with minority clients (Davis & Gelsomino, 1994). The study suggests that minority practitioners were more likely to take seriously structural problems and less likely to focus exclusively on internal difficulties.

Cross-cultural contact also occurs between minority practitioners and clients from the majority culture. While the minority practitioner is usually more familiar with the majority culture than majority culture practitioners are with minority cultures, clients often challenge the credibility of minority practitioners (Proctor & Davis, 1994). Cultural differences between practitioner and client are often ignored in a color blind assumption that services are not affected by those differences. Proctor and Davis indicate that trust is enhanced when the practitioner addresses the client by terms preferred by the client (often including the title Mr./Mrs./Ms. and the last name with African American clients) and describes the helping process and the rationale for questions in the assessment process. In addition, the practitioner should not attempt to hide ignorance of client values, but rather acknowledge differences and take on the learner role (ibid.). Finally, the practitioner should directly ask clients about their experiences with practitioners from a different culture rather than expect clients to raise the issue.

Credibility is also ascribed to a practitioner by reason of education, position, role, age, gender, and other factors emphasized in the client's culture: factors over which a practitioner has little control. Credibility can also be achieved, however, through favorable experiences by clients with practitioners who foster respect, confidence, trust, and hope. Sue and Zane (1987) hypothesize that practitioners foster credibility by following three major guidelines:

1. The practitioner must conceptualize the problem in a manner that is consistent with the client's belief systems. Imposing upon client's problem formula-

tions that are antagonistic to client's belief systems may block achievement of credibility.

2. Expectations of change efforts to be made by clients must be compatible with their cultural values. For example, encouraging an Asian client to express anger directly to a father would require the client to violate a deeply embedded value and would be perceived by the client as destructive and inappropriate.

3. Treatment goals must be consonant with clients' perceptions of desired objectives. When goals reflect the practitioner's agenda rather than the client's, credibility may not be achieved and clients may disengage from the helping process.

Although the above guidelines are applicable to all client groups, they are particularly relevant to ethnic minorities. Prerequisite to adhering to these guidelines, of course, is possessing knowledge about the belief systems and values of a given ethnocultural group.

Providing Immediate Benefits

Sue and Zane (1987) maintain that in addition to establishing credibility, gift giving is also vital in transcultural work. The term "gift giving" is used symbolically rather than literally and refers to enabling clients to experience a direct benefit from treatment, as soon as possible, preferably in the first session. These authors use the term "gift" because "gift giving is a ritual that is frequently a part of interpersonal relationships among Asians" (p. 42). Explanations to clients that benefits of the helping process will be forthcoming in the future are insufficient, according to Sue and Zane. Rather, ethnic minority clients, especially Asians, who tend to be skeptical of Western forms of treatment, need demonstration of the direct relationship between activities in the helping process and the alleviation of problems.

What kind of gifts (immediate benefits) can the practitioner provide? One important gift cited is *normalization* (also denoted as universalization), which refers to "a process by which clients come to realize that their thoughts, feelings, or experi-

ences are common and that many individuals encounter similar difficulties" (p. 42). Use of this supportive technique tends to reduce anxiety associated with the mistaken belief that one's difficulties are strange and different and reflect one's being different and less adequate than others. Other gifts that the practitioner can offer include stress relief procedures, concrete assistance, depression relief, clarification of factors producing difficulties, reassurance (when it is reality based), hope, plans for skill training, discussion of promising coping measures, and setting of relevant goals. As with credibility, we believe that "gift giving" is also applicable to nonminority clients, but even more so with minority clients.[12]

Attitudes Toward External Help

Behavior of members of certain ethnic minority groups is strongly influenced by their attitudes toward asking for help and by the type of help needed. To the Japanese, for example, "The need for mental health services has always been seen as shameful" (Mass, 1976), and people with psychological problems are viewed with disdain as weaklings. Koreans take a similar stance toward mental problems. According to Harvey and Chung (1980), "Koreans find mental illness in a family a source of shame and regard mental illness as a form of deviant and harmful behavior, the causes of which are variously attributable to supernatural forces, such as the displeasure of ancestral spirits, spirit intrusion, somatic-natural conditions, and psychological distresses originating in interpersonal disharmony" (p. 147). Such beliefs share much in common with those of Native Americans, but the approach to treatment differs markedly. Whereas Native Americans turn to indigenous folk healers (e.g., a medicine man), Koreans consider family care as the most logical and effective treatment inasmuch as the cause is believed to be interpersonal disharmony in the family.

In light of attitudes such as those just reported,

clients from the ethnic groups cited can be expected to manifest shame and apprehension during an initial interview. Practitioners must be sensitive to the causes of such reactions for two important reasons. First, the client's manifest behavior is likely to be atypical, and assessment of the client's functioning without this knowledge could lead the practitioner to draw erroneous conclusions. Second, such untoward emotional reactions about seeking help can be formidable barriers to establishing trust and rapport. Awareness of clients' feelings, however, enables the practitioner to respond to them with empathy and understanding, which enhances the possibility of working through the feelings.

Negative experiences of certain ethnic minority groups with the dominant culture and particularly with the government also dispose members of these groups to approach helping agencies with skepticism and even hostility. In light of efforts of the federal government first to annihilate Native Americans and then to assimilate them, their distrust of the government is understandable (Diorio, 1992; Hull, 1982). Similarly, skepticism toward Anglo Americans by African Americans, Hispanics, and Asian Americans is a natural consequence of their histories of being exploited and victimized by overt racism and/or institutionalized racist practices. Behavior of these individuals in transcultural relationships must be assessed accordingly. Moreover, practitioners must be prepared to deal with distrust, fear, and even hostility in transcultural relationships.

Cultural Resources

By attending to cultural factors, you may be able to locate or develop indigenous cultural resources that can be tapped to assist clients who are strangers in another culture and who, because of poverty, language barriers, limited experience, and lack of information, do not know what to do or whom to see when confronted with major stress.

Other more experienced and sophisticated members of a given cultural group often are willing to assist such clients to find their way through the maze of bureaucratic structures. Indigenous nonprofessionals have also been employed as staff members to serve as client advocates and to provide direct outreach services to impoverished minority clients (Budner, Chazin, & Young, 1973). Valuable services performed by indigenous nonprofessionals include assuming the role of advocate and interpreter (in both language and policy), assisting people to utilize resources within a given agency, intervening with other social systems to obtain timely responses to needs of clients, providing direct services (e.g., homemaking, baby-sitting, shopping, and escorting clients to various agencies), discussing problems in times of crisis, and rendering technical assistance (e.g., completing forms, writing letters, and establishing eligibility for services).

Indigenous nonprofessionals have also organized tenant groups among impoverished minority members to obtain essential repairs of facilities and to use legal means of assuring that landlords comply with housing laws. Participating in such groups not only results in improved living conditions but also counters the sense of helplessness and creates cultural reference groups that combat the social isolation commonly experienced by poverty-stricken minority persons.

Knowledge of cultural factors may also assist you in connecting clients with still other valuable resources indigenous to their cultures. Jung (1976) and Homma-True (1976), for example, have described indigenous resources that exist in Chinatowns in two large American cities. Similar resources exist in pockets of ethnic groups located in many other large urban cities.

Extended family members are also an important resource to be considered in work with ethnic minority clients. Filipinos, for example, have a strong sense of loyalty that extends far beyond the nuclear family. Many Filipinos, therefore, have many people to whom they can turn for support and assistance in crisis situations (Ponce, 1980). The same is true of Native Americans (Lewis & Ho, 1975), Asian Americans (Homma-True, 1976), African Americans (Jones, 1983), Hawaiians (Kumabe et al., 1985), Samoans (Wong, 1983), and Hispanics, although Queralt (1984) indicates "The value of the extended family for Hispanics has probably been overrated" (p. 117). The extent of availability of extended family support for ethnic minority families, of course, varies according to the number of generations a given family is removed from the original family of immigration. That availability is also influenced by geographic distance, placing heavy demands on long distance telephone conversations and occasional reunions.

ENVIRONMENTAL SYSTEMS

The environment was a central concern of pioneers in social work in the late 1800s and early 1900s, but had receded into the background of social work theory by the 1920s, being overshadowed by the impact of evolving theories related to individual functioning, most notable of which was Freudian psychoanalysis. Emphasis on the individual continued to the 1960s and 1970s, when it was supplemented by interactional and systems theory (including theories of family therapy). Although theoreticians did not exclude the environment from their formulations, they accorded it minor significance. The emphasis on the person, and to a lesser extent on interpersonal transactions, undoubtedly was a consequence of the fact that theories pertaining to individual and interpersonal functioning were far more developed than theories pertaining to the environment.

A strong resurgence of interest in the environment commenced in the early 1970s. Strongly influenced by ecological theory, systems theory, and by the increased emphasis placed on the environment by prominent ego psychologists, Germain and Gitterman (1973), Meyer (1970), and Siporin (1975) advocated a perspective of social work practice that revolved around systems theory and ecological theory. These theorists incorporated this perspective in their practice textbooks, and acceptance of the ecological perspective has steadily expanded. In addition, milieu treatments came into prominence in many residential and institutional settings.

The ecological perspective does not represent a swing of the pendulum from primary focus on the person to the other extreme of primary focus on the environment. Rather, assessment focuses on the transactions between the two, and problem-solving efforts may be directed toward assisting people to adapt to their environments (e.g., training them in interpersonal skills), altering environments to meet the needs of clients more adequately (e.g., enhancing both the attractiveness of a nursing home and the quality of its activities), or a combination of the two (e.g., enhancing the interpersonal skills of a withdrawn, chronically ill person and moving the person to a more stimulating environment).

In assessing clients' environments, attention should be limited to those aspects of the environment that are salient to the problem situation. Relevant factors vary according to the needs of specific clients, which in turn are determined by clients' personalities, states of health, stages of development, interests, aspirations, and other related factors. You should thus tailor your assessments of clients' environments to their varied life situations, weighing clients' unique needs against the availability of essential resources and opportunities within their environments.

Health and Safety Factors

For elderly persons, a safe environment is a primary consideration, for these persons are easy prey for thieves, gangs, and even rapists. Some elderly persons who live in high-crime areas virtually confine themselves to their apartments because of fears of being mugged, beaten up, or killed. Often such persons need assistance in moving to safer areas, but it is difficult for some to leave familiar neighborhoods, friends, and living arrangements to which they have become attached. In some instances, social workers have organized neighborhoods to increase the security of residents by forming "block watch" groups and by organizing elderly groups to check up on each other and to develop strategies for notifying the police when a threat to security appears. Organizing elderly groups in this way serves an empowering function that counters feelings of helplessness.

Assessing health factors also includes considering sanitation, space, and heat. Some large families will be found crammed into two or three drafty rooms without adequate beds and bedding. Privacy is impossible. Further, rats infest some buildings, posing a threat to the health and safety of infants. In such instances it is clear that steps must be taken to improve living conditions, often a difficult challenge given the scarcity of adequate low-cost housing. Elderly persons may qualify for government-subsidized housing facilities, which not only provide adequate housing but social opportunities as well. In other instances, landlords may be negligent in conforming to building standards and in maintaining plumbing so that sanitation is compromised. Joining clients in advocacy actions to force landlords to fulfill their obligations to tenants may be indicated in such instances.

Environmental Resources Universally Needed

Although clients' needs vary widely, certain environmental resources are universally needed. We have therefore compiled the following list of basic environmental needs, which you can employ in evaluating the adequacy of clients' envi-

ronments. The list, of course, must be individualized to each client.

1. Adequate social support systems (e.g., family, relatives, friends, neighbors, organized groups).
2. Access to specialized health care services (e.g., physicians, dentists, physical therapists, hospitals, nursing homes).
3. Access to day care services (for working mothers and single-parent families).
4. Access to recreational facilities.
5. Mobility to socialize, utilize resources, and exercise rights as a citizen.
6. Adequate housing that provides ample space, sanitation, privacy, and safety from hazards and pollution (both air and noise).
7. Adequate police and fire protection and a reasonable degree of security.
8. Safe and healthful work conditions.
9. Adequate financial resources to purchase essential resources.
10. Adequate nutritional intake.
11. Predictable living arrangements with caring others (especially for children).
12. Opportunities for education and self-fulfillment.
13. Access to legal resources.
14. Access to religious organizations.
15. Employment opportunities.

Identifying Relevant Social Systems

Embodied in the preceding list of resources are a number of social systems that provide goods and services needed by clients. Diverse social systems either are part of the problem configuration or represent resources needed to improve the goodness of fit between personal and family needs on one hand and environmental resources on the other. To enable you to identify pertinent social systems, we have constructed a diagram (see Fig. 9-1) that depicts interrelationships between individuals and families and other systems (Hartman, 1994).[13]

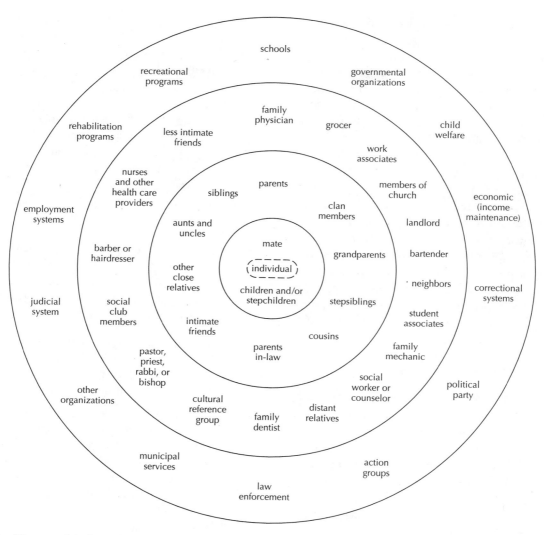

Figure 9.1 Diagram of Ecological Social Systems

Systems that are central in a person's life are in the center of the diagram. These systems typically play key roles as both sources of difficulties and resources that may be tapped or modified in problem solving. Moving from the center to the periphery in the areas encompassed by the concentric circles are systems that are progressively more removed from individuals and their families. There are exceptions, of course, as when an individual feels closer to an intimate friend or a pastor than to family members. Moreover, as clients' situations require frequent contacts with institutions or organizations (e.g., child protective services, income maintenance programs, and judicial systems), those institutions no longer occupy a peripheral position because of the intense impact they have upon individuals and families at such times. Reciprocal interactions thus change across time, and diagrammatic representation of such interactions should be viewed as snapshots that are accurate only within limited time frames. The challenge in formulating such ecological diagrams of your clients' social networks is to include the salient boundaries of the clients' situation and to specify how the systems interact, fail to interact, or are needed to interact in response to clients' needs.

The nature of positive interactions, negative interactions, or needed resources can be depicted by using different colored lines to connect the individual or other family members to pertinent systems, where specified colors represent positive, negative, or needed connections and interactions with those systems. If colored lines do not appeal to you, different types of lines—single, double, broken, wavy, dotted, or cross-hatched—can be used.

Social Support Systems (SSSs)

Social support systems (SSSs) are increasingly recognized as playing a crucial role in determining the level of social functioning of human beings. Theorists, of course, have long recognized the critical importance of a nurturing environment to healthy development of infants and children. In recent years, however, it has become clear that adults, too, have vital needs that can be met only through a nurturant environment. The literature is replete with articles that accord paramount importance to major deficiencies in SSSs available to people who manifest diverse problems of living. Moreover, articles concerned with strategies for remedying varied problems of clients likewise place heavy emphasis on mobilizing SSSs.

Before considering client groups that are particularly vulnerable to breakdown in social functioning in the absence of adequate SSSs, it is important to clarify the vital needs of people that are met through SSSs. Based in part on a list developed by Weiss (1974), we propose that people in the personal networks of individuals (i.e., partner, family members, close kin, friends, and work associates) provide the following:

1. Attachment, provided by close affectional relationships that give a sense of security and sense of belonging.
2. Social integration, provided by memberships in a network of persons that share interests and values.
3. The opportunity to nurture others (usually children), which provides incentive to endure in the face of adversity.
4. Physical care when persons are unable to care for themselves due to illness, incapacity, or severe disability.
5. Validation of personal worth (which promotes self-esteem), provided by family and colleagues.
6. A sense of reliable alliance, provided primarily by kin.
7. Guidance, child care, financial aid, and other aid in coping with difficulties that arise.

Stresses associated with certain problem situations can be so severe that, without consistent and reliable responsiveness from SSSs to the needs specified in the preceding paragraph, afflicted persons may experience serious breakdowns in functioning. Moreover, the severity of stress in certain situations may result precisely from temporary or permanent disruption of major sources of social support. Such stressful situations commonly involve losses through death of loved ones, divorces, children leaving home, job termination, retirement, severance of valued relationships, and so on. In a study comparing depressed people who did and did not attempt suicide, for example, Slater and Depue (1981) found that loss of important social support through "exit" events (losses such as those just enumerated) played an important role in initiating suicide attempts. These researchers also concluded that the presence of SSSs tends to buffer the impact of exit events and thereby reduces suicidal risk.

It is thus apparent that, at best, absence of adequate SSSs renders people vulnerable to major maladaptation to external stress and, at worst, is itself a primary source of stress, as with people who are socially isolated or feel alienated from society. By contrast, the presence of adequate SSSs tends to reduce the impact of stressful situations and facilitates successful adaptation. SSSs thus represent a vital resource that practitioners should consider as they assess problems of living. Moreover, social workers increasingly employ interventions that tap the potential of dormant SSSs and mobilize new SSSs in assisting clients to cope with life's stresses.

SSSs are of particular significance with certain client groups who are vulnerable to serious maladaptation because of deficiencies in their social environments. Previously, we cited clients who have sustained losses of important relationships. Another group consists of single parents or parents who receive little companionship and emotional support from their spouses and kin. Because of the heavy demands of child care and limited time and opportunity to participate socially, these parents often are unable to meet their own needs for nurturance. Consequently, such parents feel empty, frustrated, and resentful about ongoing demands for child care, and receive little personal need gratification. Children can thus become objects of their frustrations and resentments, which can lead to child abuse, as we discuss in Chapter 10.

Single, elderly people, especially those who have no children or whose children are unresponsive to their needs, are another group for whom SSSs are highly relevant. Often having restricted financial resources and limited mobility, elderly persons can become socially isolated to the extent that life becomes barren and empty. Depression is common among such persons. Such elderly persons often improve physically and mentally when they move from an isolated environment to one that provides increased activity, improved nutrition, and more frequent social contact. Other elderly persons may have multiple afflictions including chronic illness, infirmity, and impaired vision and hearing. Needs of these persons can be so pervasive that social workers or others can best serve as

case managers in coordinating the utilization of essential resources, which may include financial, medical, recreational, transportation, nutritional, nursing, and other services.

Chronic psychiatric patients also typically suffer from deficient SSSs. These people lack interpersonal and coping skills essential to maintaining themselves independently in the community, thus requiring practitioners to take an active role in mobilizing multiple resources including SSSs. Practitioners or others can also best serve these clients as case managers (Harris & Bergman, 1987; Rapp & Chamberlain, 1985).

Many caregivers of people who require intensive and continuous care also have urgent needs for SSSs and respite. People who require such care include those who care for frail elderly persons, victims of Alzheimer's disease in advanced stage, severely disabled persons, dying persons, and people with severe mental illness. We will address this topic at greater length in Chapter 14.

Another group extremely vulnerable to problems associated with deficient SSSs consists of people who experience geographical and/or cultural dislocation. Refugees and immigrants often have acute needs that extend even beyond the need for SSSs, including housing, health care, work training, and language training needs (Mayadas, 1983; Montero & Dieppa, 1982; Timberlake & Cook, 1984). Among refugees are groups with unique needs that also must be considered, including unaccompanied women and children, elderly and disabled persons, and persons who are disabled by acute illnesses.

Other vulnerable client groups who have special needs dependent on adequate SSSs include pregnant adolescents (O'Leary et al., 1984), teenaged mothers and parents (Barth & Schinke, 1984; Brindis, Barth, & Loomis, 1987; De Anda & Becerra, 1984), victims of child abuse (Gagliano, 1987), widows and widowers (Lieberman & Videka-Sherman, 1986), families of the mentally ill (Zipple & Spaniol, 1987), terminally ill patients

(Arnowitz, Brunswick, & Kaplan, 1983), children of divorced parents (Bonkowski, Bequette, & Boomhower, 1984), developmentally disabled persons (Hill, Rotegard, & Bruininks, 1984), disabled (Kennard & Shilman, 1979; Mackelprang & Hepworth, 1987), transients (Breton, 1984), and persons who have newly moved into communities, particularly rapidly expanding communities (boomtowns). Boomtowns typically have loosely knit social networks, and human service programs tend to lag well behind the needs of citizens. These communities present challenging opportunities to social workers in collaborating to develop natural support networks and to plan service delivery systems that are responsive to the unique needs of each community.

Negative Social Support Systems

To this point, we have highlighted the positive aspects of SSSs. The presence of certain types of SSSs, however, may foster and sustain dysfunctional behavior, and practitioners must be alert to this possibility as they assess problem systems. For example, families with overprotective parents thwart the development of autonomy and personal responsibility in their children. Children from such families often fail to develop social skills, problem-solving skills, and the ability to relate in a mature give-and-take manner. Unrealistic expectations of others and excessive dependency are typical manifestations of people reared in such cloistered environments. Urban gangs are also negative support systems that foster violence and criminality.

Negative social support systems also play a vital role in fostering and maintaining substance abuse. Through an analysis of the social network of street drug addicts, Fraser and Hawkins (1984) found that these persons are not isolated or lonely but rather report sharing intimate relationships with people whom they like to see. The relationships, however, largely include other drug abusers. Based

on their findings, these authors concluded: "Most drug users are enmeshed in a subculture that rewards hard drug abuse and that endures through residential treatment" (p. 94). Bates (1983) similarly characterizes the social milieu of the Skid Row alcoholic as fostering continued drinking and lacking ingredients essential to competent adult functioning. Fine, Akabas, and Bellinger (1982) believe that problem drinking is also fostered in workplaces that "embody the norms and values of a culture of drinking" (p. 437). Clearly, then, assessment of problems of substance abusers must address the social networks of these clients, and interventions must be directed to replace these networks with cultures of sobriety.

Assessing Reciprocal Interactions Between Individuals and SSSs

In formulating assessments, practitioners must consider the reciprocal interaction between individuals and their SSSs. The responsiveness of SSS members to individuals and families under stress depends in great measure on the nature of previous interactions between these systems. For example, people who have been warm, sensitive, and generous in responding to the needs of others are far more likely to receive nurturant social support in times of distress than are people who typically relate to others in a complaining, aggressive, or withholding manner. Further, people vary widely in their perceptions of the adequacy of social support in times of adversity. Certain people believe they receive inadequate succor from others irrespective of its quality and quantity. A study of the perceptions of social support received in times of adversity by persons diagnosed as having neuroses, for example, led Henderson (1982) to conclude: "The crucial property of social relationships, insofar as neurosis is concerned, is not their availability...but how adequate they are perceived to be when individuals are under adversity" (p. 227). With such individuals, therefore, intrapsychic and personality factors are likely to be strong determinants of how they perceive the adequacy of SSSs. SSSs of clients thus cannot be adequately assessed apart from the clients themselves.

Instruments to Assess SSSs

A number of instruments have been developed to assess the personal SSSs of clients. One such instrument is the Interview Schedule for Social Interaction (Henderson, Duncan-Jones, Byrne, & Scott, 1980). Others include the Social Support Network Inventory (Flaherty, Gaviria, & Pathak, 1983), and the Perceived Social Support Network Inventory (Oritt, Paul, & Behrman, 1985). An instrument that is especially practical for social workers is the Social Network Grid (Tracy & Whittaker, 1990). This instrument yields the following information:

1. Key persons in clients' social networks.
2. Areas of life in which the support occurs.
3. Specified types of support provided by each person.
4. The degree to which support persons are critical.
5. Whether the support is reciprocal or unidirectional.
6. The degree of personal closeness.
7. The frequency of contacts.
8. Length of the relationship.

Completion of the grid, for which Tracy and Whittaker provide explicit instruction, yields rich information for both the practitioner and the client. Students who have used it report favorable reactions from clients, who describe feeling more positive as they gain expanded awareness of the social support they receive or can tap.[14]

Chronically Ill and Elderly Clients

Some writers and researchers have focused their attention on environmental resources needed by specific client populations. Building on Germain's (1977) earlier work, Coulton (1979, 1981), for example, studied the person–environment fit of chronically ill patients suffering from such serious ailments as kidney failure, spinal cord injuries, cancer, diabetes, and arthritis. Based on interviews with these patients, Coulton identified a number of environmental needs (1979, pp. 8–9). Although several of these needs are specific to the population Coulton studied, virtually all of them also appear to be highly relevant to elderly and physically handicapped persons. As you review the list, notice the balanced focus on the person and the environment.

1. Having sufficient opportunities for social relationships.
2. Having sufficient opportunities to express feelings.
3. Having sufficient sources of emotional support.
4. Meeting expectations of self and others.
5. Being able to fulfill responsibilities.
6. Having opportunities to engage in interesting productive activities and achieve goals.
7. Fulfilling the demands of certain situations (e.g., job, social events).
8. Getting information to allow some certainty about the future.
9. Having knowledge about their physical condition, community resources, etc.
10. Knowing where things are, what to expect, how to behave in new settings.
11. Having sufficient financial resources to meet demands and obligations.
12. Having help with physical and self-care needs.
13. Having the means to maintain physical mobility.

In her article, Coulton illustrates each type of need as reflected by actual statements of patients. From these statements, it was apparent that although the needs cut across all of the patients' environments and were more adequately met in some environments than others, patients varied widely in their degrees of perceived need. Individual patients emphasized certain needs more than others, and their expectations in regard to specific needs also varied considerably. With respect to social relationships, for example, Coulton observed, "it was not the absolute amount of contact...but whether the contact seemed to be what they needed" (1979, p. 10). This finding, of course, is consistent with Henderson's (1982) view that perceived adequacy of social support is more important than the availability of support. Again, the point is that accurate assessment requires careful individualizing of each client's needs.

Environmental Needs of Disabled Adults and Children

The importance of environmental factors listed earlier in this section to the social functioning of disabled persons is vividly illustrated by the needs of paraplegics and quadraplegics, whose needs encompass virtually all of those listed. A research study by Mackelprang and Hepworth (1987) of the adjustment of these persons following spinal injury, hospitalization, and rehabilitation efforts indicated that those who attain maximal independence have higher levels of social functioning on several criteria than do those who are dependent on others for various aspects of daily living. Because paraplegics are paralyzed in their lower limbs and quadraplegics in both upper and lower limbs, achieving maximal independence requires major environmental changes, including housing that provides special access through ramps or lifts, specially equipped kitchens and bathrooms, electric wheelchairs, and environmental control units and devices adapted for other activities of daily living such as eating and grooming. Moreover, opportunities for vocational training, employment, and socialization are essential to the well-being of these persons. Most of those who have the advantage of these special arrangements function amazingly well and report higher levels of satisfaction with their lives than do those who lack these advantages.

The number of people with work-limiting health conditions who may require assistance in obtaining and maintaining gainful employment is estimated to be over 20 million adults between ages 18 and 64. Of this group about one-half report they are so severely disabled they cannot work at all (Mudrick, 1991). Obviously, for those able to work, opportunities must be available and special arrangements may be required by employers to accommodate the functional impairments of these people. When such accommodations are made, many disabled people are not, in fact, disabled as far as their capacity to perform required tasks in the workplace. Some, in fact, outperform people without functional impairments.

Opportunities for people with disabilities to secure employment were enhanced by the Rehabilitation Act of 1973, which prohibits employment discrimination against qualified individuals with a disability. The Americans with Disabilities Act (ADA) of 1990, which became effective on January 1, 1992, goes even further in requiring employers to make reasonable accommodations to facilitate the employment of an otherwise qualified individual with a disability. The ADA mandates employers to make arrangements that provide access to the workplace, which may require an entrance ramp, a widened doorway, or more flexibility in work hours and tasks (e.g., time off for treatment for persons with chronic illnesses or drug or alcohol addictions). Employers may be exempted from making accommodations that impose undue hardship on them. Disabled clients who are qualified for certain jobs thus have many rights, and when discrimination denies those rights, social workers should explore with clients undertaking advocacy actions to secure their rights.

People with disabilities often require special therapy, education and training, and services arranged for and funded by state rehabilitation programs to qualified persons. Work in rehabilitation programs is well suited for social workers, who must be knowledgeable about various types of disabilities, relevant resources in the community or region, and relevant laws, policies, and procedures.[15]

Children with handicaps are vulnerable to parental rejection, impaired social development, learning difficulties, and low self-esteem. Moreover, parents of handicapped children may need services in coping with their feelings about having a handicapped child and in providing a nurturant climate for such a child. Bernier (1990) and Kratochvil and Devereux (1988) have written about the impact on parents of having a handicapped child and on the implications of counseling these parents. Discussing environmental needs, Siegel and Roberts (1989) have authored an article about recruiting foster families for disabled children, and Malekoff, Johnson, and Klappersack (1991) have addressed the need for collaboration between professionals and parents on behalf of children with learning disabilities. Seligman (1991) has written about the impact on grandparents of having grandchildren with disabilities and how grandparents can be a resource to parents. And finally, Thompson and Hupp (1991) have authored a book concerned with prevention of developmental disabilities in families that live in poverty.

Assessing Homeless Persons

Homelessness is a social problem that has reached alarming proportions in recent years. Estimates of the number of homeless in the United States vary from 250,000 to 300,000 on the lower extreme to 3 million (Connell, 1987). Although homelessness is not a new problem, its scope and the people who make up this population are new. Whereas until the 1970s homeless persons consisted largely of white male chronic alcoholics who lived in the Skid Rows of large cities, homeless people now also consist of unemployed individuals and families who have been evicted from housing, runaway/throwaway youth, women who have left home to avoid domestic violence, and those released from jails and hospitals without adequate financial means (Hagen, 1987a). Substantial proportions of homeless people are now minorities (First, Roth,

& Arewa, 1988), women (Hagen, 1987b), and families (Phillips, DeChillo, Kronenfeld, & Middleton-Jeter, 1988). Reasons for homelessness include marked escalation in the cost of housing and a dearth of low-cost housing, the mental health deinstitutionalization movement that returned mental patients from centralized state hospitals to communities (funds intended to provide for these patients were subsequently drastically curtailed), substance abuse, and economic recession, resulting in a high rate of unemployment and domestic conflicts.

Because of the heterogeneity of this population, accurate assessment of causes of homelessness and the needs of these people is of paramount importance. Although the need for emergency shelter is shared by all homeless people, other needs may vary widely. For example, the frequency of severe medical and psychiatric illnesses is far greater than for the general population. In addition to common illnesses that afflict the general population, homeless people manifest a much higher incidence of "trauma, infestations such as scabies and lice, problems arising from exposure, nutritional and vitamin deficiencies, and peripheral vascular diseases such as cellulitis and leg ulcers" (Surber et al., 1988, p. 116). Careful assessment and individualization of clients may thus reveal any of the following needs, which were identified in a study by Hagen (1987a) of needs of the homeless in Albany, New York and its environs: food, financial assistance, alcohol treatment, mental health assessment, drug treatment, employment, educational/vocational training, legal assistance, transitional/supportive living, and long-term counseling. Further, because many homeless people (especially the chronically mentally ill, substance abusers, and runaway/throwaway youth) have very limited coping and interpersonal skills, case management services are often needed to ensure that services are actually provided.

Careful assessment of homeless families, which constitute approximately 20% of the nation's homeless (Bassuk, Rubin, & Lauriat, 1986), must also consider the functioning of both parents and children. In a study of single-female-headed homeless families in New York City, Phillips et al. (1988) found that 96% of the families experienced failure in the mother's functioning and 51% experienced failure in a child's functioning. Further, in addition to having no access to housing other than emergency shelter, these families had experienced other life stresses within the previous year including "serious illness of a close family member (30 percent), death of a close family member (25 percent), pregnancy (33 percent), and separation from a husband or boyfriend (31 percent)" (p. 50). The support systems of these families were also woefully inadequate. Clearly these families manifest urgent and multiple needs that must be carefully assessed. (We discuss assessment of family functioning in Chapter 10.)

From the foregoing discussion, it is clear that the problems of homeless people are a prime manifestation of how human problems must be viewed as resulting from transactions between people and their environments. It is also clear how the problems of the homeless have resulted increasingly in the expansion of the case management direct practice role. Responding to the needs of the homeless is a major challenge to communities, to social work, and to allied disciplines. We describe interventions employed with the homeless in Chapter 16.

SUMMARY

In the preceding sections, we discussed assessment of physical, cognitive/perceptual, emotional, and behavioral functioning, as well as motivation and cultural and environmental factors. Although we presented each of these factors as discrete entities, we again emphasize that these factors are neither independent nor static. Rather, the various functions and factors interact dynamically over time, and from the initial contact, the practitioner is a part of that dynamic interaction. Each of the factors is therefore subject to change, and the practitioner's tasks are not only to assess the dynamic interplay of these multiple factors but also to instigate changes that are feasible and consonant with clients' goals.

We also reemphasize that assessment involves synthesizing relevant factors into a working hypothesis about the nature of problems and their contributory causes. You thus need not be concerned in every case with assessing all the dimensions identified thus far. Indeed, an assessment should be a concise statement that embodies only pertinent factors.

We also remind you that the scope of this chapter was limited to intrapersonal and environmental dimensions. We purposely excluded marital, family, and group systems, not because they are not important components of people's social environments but because they generally are the hub of people's social environments. To work effectively with interpersonal systems, however, requires an extensive body of knowledge about these systems. Therefore, we devote the next two chapters to assessing marital and family systems and growth-oriented groups.

NOTES

1 An excellent book that offers practitioners procedures for screening suspected brain dysfunction and determining whether to refer for further evaluation has been written by Berg, Franzen, and Wedding (1987).

2 Fortunately, an excellent resource exists (Kane & Kane, 1981) that reports on many instruments available to aid in assessing all aspects of the functioning of elderly persons.

3 O'Leary, Shore, and Wieder (1984) and Joyce et al. (1983) discuss considerations involved in reaching and working with this unique population.

4 An excellent resource related to the needs of this population is a book by Voydanoff and Donnelly (1990).

5 An excellent reference concerning the health care needs and implications thereof for health care delivery systems is a book edited by Brickner, Scharer, Conanan, Elvy, and Savarese (1985).

6 A shaman is a sacred specialist who utilizes a technique of ecstatic trance to communicate with spirits and other powerful forces, natural and supernatural. The shaman acquires sacred power from the spiritual realm to heal and to enhance the harmony between the human community and the nonhuman environment (Canda, 1983).

7 Lake (1983) lists the cosmic laws as identified by a Yurok Indian shaman, and we recommend this article to those interested in learning more about Indian medical beliefs and practices.

8 Delgado (1977) has presented eight recommendations that can be extremely useful to practitioners in working with clients who believe in the efficacy of spiritualist folk healers.

9 Kumabe et al. (1985) have extensively discussed cultural nuances involved in the reciprocal effects of illness and disability and family functioning.

10 See Steinmetz (1992) for an article about FAS, including photographs comparing a normal fetus with one damaged by excessive alcohol consumption by the mother. Detailed information about FAS and FAE has been presented in articles by Giunta and Streissguth (1988) and Anderson and Grant (1984). Anderson and Grant (1984) have discussed such treatment programs, and Giunta and Streissguth (1988) have discussed the needs of caregivers of children with FAS, as well as related family needs and community services and resources.

11 For a more complete discussion of adolescent suicide, including treatment implications, we recommend an article by Hepworth, Farley, and Griffiths (1988).

12 In the preceding, we have highlighted major ethnic and cultural factors that are salient to the process of assessment. Space limitations, however, preclude dealing comprehensively with this important topic. Other authors (Devore & Schlesinger, 1981; Green, 1982; Jenkins, 1981; Sue & Moore, 1984; Wright, Saleebey, Watts, & Lecca, 1983) have devoted entire books to ethnocultural factors.

13 For further explication of ecomaps, see Hartman, pp. 153–165, in Compton and Galaway, 1994.

14 With respect to issues involved in the measure of social support, evaluation of eight related instruments, and guidelines for practitioners, we recommend an article by Streeter and Franklin (1992).

15 For an excellent overview of social work in such settings, we recommend the article by Mudrick (1991), the source of much of the foregoing information.

Chapter 10

Assessing Family Functioning in Diverse Family and Cultural Contexts

THE EVOLUTION OF FAMILY SYSTEMS

The family has highest significance among the various systems of concern to social work. The family performs essential caretaking functions including "meeting the social, educational, and health care needs" of its constituent members (Hartman, 1981, p. 10). It is largely through the family that character is formed, vital roles are learned, and children are socialized for responsible participation in the larger society. Further, it is primarily through family interaction that children develop (or fail to develop) vital self-esteem, a sense of belonging, and interpersonal skills. Conflicts are created here for some low-income and minority families who find that such efforts to enhance self-esteem are met with a lack of support in the larger society for the creation of roles such as jobs which enhance responsible participation.

Because families play key roles in meeting (or failing to meet) the needs of constituent members, practitioners must be skilled in assessing the functioning of families. That task has never been more challenging, for over the past decade there has been a marked growth in both the proportion and diversity of ethnic groups in the United States (Ho, 1987; Mindel, Habenstein, & Wright, 1988). The increasingly culturally pluralistic population in this country challenges practitioners from all cultures to become culturally sensitive to diverse ethnic groups and to extricate themselves from viewing their values and lifestyle as the "standard of reference for all other groups" (Maretzki & McDermott, 1980).

Likewise, practitioners face the challenge of assessing families during the evolution of the "traditional" family into other, more accommodating family forms. "It is a phenomenon of our times that people have discovered so many other ways to come together as 'family,'" observes Meyer (1990). Yet, she asserts, many social workers and others have not yet fully recognized these new family forms as "permanent features of the American landscape" (p. 4).

To best assess and serve families, Meyer urges that practitioners free themselves of personal and professional biases that force modern family types into preformed nuclear family patterns, thus creating an illusion of clinical pathology. Rather, practitioners can usefully conceptualize the modern "family" as "Two or more people who are joined together by bonds of sharing and intimacy." This flexible, "no-fault" definition will aid practitioners to "meet clients on their own turf, in their own terms, within their own self-definitions" and to "provide help in many forms to people who live as they live, for their own reasons, swept up as they are in the tides of social change" (Meyer, 1990, p.16).

Social workers practice with families in a variety of settings and with a range of problems. In some instances, they work with whole families in formally designated family therapy designed to have an impact on family structure. In many other instances, social workers practice with family members related to a specific problem and agency function. For example, social workers in health and elderly care settings often work together on specific health, safety, and independence issues of the elderly and infirm. They also work in child welfare settings related to the health and safety of children and the preservation of families. While the family therapy literature provides a rich, informative resource for such work, elements from that perspective must be used selectively when therapy is not the agency function or the family concern (Reid, 1985).

Families served by social workers frequently encounter a hostile or indifferent environment with major deficits in health care, day care, after-school care, rigid work schedules and insufficient income, unsafe neighborhoods, and schools. Further there is often little enforcement of child support, inadequate welfare payments, or pressures to seek work without sufficient health and child care benefits.

With these challenging tasks in mind, we have written this chapter to assist practitioners in developing skills in family assessment and in adopting both a "cultural variant" and a "family variant" perspective allowing them to assess families within their own idiosyncratic context. In the introductory part of this chapter, we present a systems framework for assessing families, inasmuch as each family is an entity in which each of its parts or elements interacts with each other in a predictable, organized fashion. We then discuss vital dimensions of family assessment that will aid practitioners to identify functional and dysfunctional family patterns. Later, in Chapter 15, we build on this chapter but shift the focus to ways of engaging couples and families and to interventions aimed at enhancing their interaction and problem solving.

A SYSTEMS FRAMEWORK FOR ASSESSING FAMILY FUNCTIONING

Family members influence and are influenced by every other member, creating a system that has properties of its own and that is governed by a set of implicit "rules" specifying roles, power structure, forms of communication, and ways of negotiating and solving problems.[1]

Because each family is a unique system, practitioners must develop a systems framework or a perceptual "set" that will enable them to analyze and to understand the behavior of individuals in relation to the ongoing operations of the family group. Therefore, we have devoted this section to vital concepts that will assist you in viewing the family as a system and prepare you for family assessment. In the interest of addressing the importance of family assessment in settings in which formal family therapy is neither requested nor the function of the agency, we will introduce family assessment concepts through application in a case study in a health care setting.

Case Example

Carlos Diaz, 66, lives with his 16-year-old son John in a subsidized apartment on the second floor of a three-story building. Mr. Diaz is diabetic, is visually impaired but not legally blind, and has a history of heavy alcohol use, though he has been abstinent for seven years. Mr. Diaz's companion of 18 years, Ann Mercy, recently died of a massive stroke. Ann Mercy provided emotional support, gave Mr. Dias his insulin injections, and managed the household. Mr. Diaz has difficulty walking, has fallen several times in the past year, and is now hesitant to leave his apartment. In addition to John, Mr. Diaz has eight children from an earlier marraige who live in nearby suburbs, though only one, Maria, calls him regularly. Mr. Diaz's physician considers his current living arrangement dangerous because of the stair climbing and is concerned about his capacity to administer his own insulin. A medical social worker convenes a family meeting with Mr. Diaz, John, his daughter Maria, and stepdaughter Anita.

Systems Impinging upon Family Functioning

Problems occur in a person or family and situation context. In this case, the problems occur in part because of the living situation of Mr. Diaz, his access to alternative living environments, and the availability of a continuum of care which might include in-home supports. Mr. Diaz's income and insurance coverage will also influence alternatives available to the family. Such systems factors should always be accorded prominence to avoid assumptions that problems are caused by factors internal to the family system and resolved by interventions addressed to those internal factors.

Family Homeostasis

As systems, families develop mechanisms to maintain balance or homeostasis in their structure and operations. All families restrict the interactional repertoires of members to a limited range of familiar behaviors and develop mechanisms for restoring equilibrium whenever it is threatened (in much the same way that the thermostat of a heating system governs the temperature of a home). Minuchin (1974) speaks of this tendency of families to maintain preferred patterns as long as possible and to offer resistance to change beyond a certain range of specific behaviors:

Alternative patterns are available within the system. But any deviation that goes beyond the system's threshold of tolerance elicits mechanisms which reestablish the accustomed range. When situations of system disequilibrium arise, it is common for family members to feel that other members are not fulfilling their obligations. Calls for family loyalty and guilt-inducing maneuvers then appear. (p. 52)

When the medical social worker convenes the Diaz family, she discovers that the previous equalibrium in Mr. Diaz's life and health care has been disrupted by the death of Ann Mercy. Maria is concerned about Mr. Diaz's capacity to care for himself and his son John. Ann's daughter Anita from a previous marriage has taken Ann's possessions including a washing machine without Mr. Diaz's knowledge or approval.

Mr. Diaz fears that his children want to place him in a nursing home and to take John out of his care. He states emphatically that he can administer his own insulin, can cook, clean and vacuum, though he has not done these tasks for many years.

Mr. Diaz's wishes can be seen as an effort to protect his independence and restore as much of the equilibrium as possible. Meanwhile, family members (except son John) and the doctor doubt his capacity to assume these duties.

Family Rules

Family homeostasis is maintained to the extent that all members of the family adhere to a limited number of rules or implicit agreements that prescribe the rights, duties, and range of appropriate behaviors within the family. Rules are formulas for relationships or guides for conduct and action in the family. Unwritten and covert, rules represent a set of prescriptions for behavior that define relations and organize the ways in which family members interact. Since rules are implicit (i.e., unwritten laws governing behavior that are often beyond the participants' level of awareness), they must be inferred from observing family interaction and communication. Examples of implicit rules that dictate the behavior of members in relation to vital family issues include: "Father has the final say," "It's okay to talk about sex in front of everyone but Mother," "Don't say what you really feel," and "It is important to respect the personal property and privacy of other family members."

Families do, of course, formulate rules that are openly recognized and explicitly stated, such as "Teenagers are to be in the house by 10 at night," "Children are limited to two hours of TV a day," "There will be no swearing in this house," and "Children don't talk back to parents." In assessing family systems, the practitioner is most interested in implicit rules that guide a family's actions because, to the extent these rules are dysfunctional, they may have insidious effects on the family (e.g., inflicting severe emotional damage on members, limiting the family's ability to accommodate to changing circumstances, and restricting choices and opportunities for growth). Because rules are implicit, their damaging impact on the lives of families often goes unrecognized, and members become caught in situations in which their behavior is dictated by forces of which they are unaware. By thus adhering to dysfunctional "rules," family members often perpetuate and reinforce the very problematic behaviors of which they complain.

Although rules govern the processes of families from any cultural origin, they differ drastically from one culture to another. In the traditional Asian culture, for example, major rules governing family processes are similar to the following:

- Do not bring attention to yourself.
- Respect your elders.
- Avoid shaming your family at all costs.
- Bring honor to your family.
- The duty of children is to listen and obey.
- Share what you have with your relatives.
- A wife's duty is to her husband.
- Always defer to authority.

You probably recognize that these rules differ significantly from typical rules of families in West-ern society, for Western culture stresses competitiveness, assertiveness, and individualism and limits obligations to the nuclear family.

Two of these rules, however, appear to be acting in the Hispanic Diaz family: (1) Respect your elders and (2) the duty of children is to listen and obey. Mr. Diaz appears to be perceiving a threat to his autonomy both physically and as head of the family.

Functional and Dysfunctional Rules With respect to the preceding discussion, it is vital to recognize that the implicit rules or "norms" found in a family system may be either functional or dysfunctional. Rules that may have destructive consequences for families include the following:

"Dad can express his needs and wants, but other members of the family can't express theirs unless they correspond with those of dad."

"Be careful what you say around mom. She might get upset."

"Self-control is evidence of strength. Don't let people see your weaknesses by showing affection or anger."

"Avoid serious discussions of family problems."

"Don't take responsibility for your own behavior. Always put the blame on someone else."

"Don't be different from other family members."

"It is important to win arguments. Losing an argument means losing face."

If rules are functional, however, they enable the family to respond flexibly to environmental stress, to individual needs, and to the needs of the family unit. Functional rules thus contribute to the development of capable, adaptive, and healthy family members. Examples of functional rules include the following:

"Everyone in this family counts—their ideas and feedback are important."

"It is acceptable to be different—family members don't always have to agree or to like the same things."

"It is important to show your positive feelings toward others in the family."

"It is desirable to talk about any feelings—disappointments, fears, hurts, anger, criticisms, joys, or achievements."

"It is important to work out disagreements with other family members."

"It is OK to admit mistakes and to apologize—other family members will understand and will respond with support."

As you observe processes, then, keep in mind that all families have both functional and dysfunctional rules and behavior and that identifying both types of rules is critical to making a balanced assessment of family functioning. Remember also that family systems are operated by a relatively small set of rules governing relationships. Understanding families' rules enhances assessment of family systems. Inasmuch as families are rule-governed, many behaviors or communications you observe will likely be stylized or patterned. Be alert to repetitive sequences of behavior in all areas of family life; behaviors that are crucial to the operations of the family will appear over and over. You thus will have many opportunities to observe stylized behavior that is an integral part of the family's functioning.

In the Diaz family, the medical social worker observed that the rule that "Dad has the final say, though others may contribute ideas" could be a functional rule if those contributions are focused on helpful solutions that support his independence.

Violation of Rules   When rules are violated and new behaviors are introduced into its system, a family may employ habitual modes of restoring conditions to a previous state of equilibrium, thereby keeping the system "on track." These modes often take the form of negative feedback to members, filled with "shoulds," "oughts," and "don'ts" intended to modify or eliminate behaviors that deviate from the norm. Irregularities in the system may also be counteracted by family members through anger, depression, silence, guilt induction, or other such forms of behavior. To grasp the potency of a system in limiting or eliminating proscribed behaviors, note in the following example the pressure exerted by Mr. Diaz to his step–daughter to adhere to the rule of "Dad has the final say."

Anita: I have taken Mom's things including the washing machine because they were hers, she bought them. I want things to remember her by, and she said I could have them.

Mr. Diaz: You have no right to come in here and take things that belonged to your Mother *and* me. You show no respect for your stepfather.

Anita: You were often a burden to Mom with your drinking and providing for your insulin. It is clear that you can't take care of John and something has to be done.

Mr. Diaz: You cannot come into this house and take things and decide how things will be done.

Anita: If you don't agree, I can go to court to get custody of John.

In the preceding scene, Anita and Mr. Diaz do not agree on the rule that "Dad has the final say" because Anita does not consider Mr. Diaz to be her father.

If the family has a rule that anger may not be expressed in any physically or verbally aggressive manner, family members may stop speaking and ignore an offending member until the latter offers an apology. If the family's rule is that all members should have a sense of humor about negative things that happen to them, a member who fails to see the irony of his situation may be kidded by other family members until he laughs. Further, if the family abides by the rule "the family comes first and friends and activities second," other family members may make guilt-inducing remarks if a member plans an activity that excludes the family on "family" days (such as, "Don't you want to be with us on our day?").

The preceding examples of rules may remind you of incidents in your own nuclear or extended family in which your behavior was regulated, reinforced, or extinguished by the behaviors of other members of those systems. As you contemplate your own experiences, perhaps you can begin to appreciate more fully the potent influence of the family in shaping and continuing to influence the lives, behaviors, and problems of clients, even years after they have physically departed from their families of origin.

Flexibility of Rules   The opportunity to influence rules or to develop new rules varies widely from family to family. Optimally functioning families have rules that permit the system to respond flexibly to change and to evolve new rules compatible with changing needs of family members. Dysfunctional systems, on the other hand, have rigid rules that prevent members from modifying their behavior over time in response to changing circumstances and pressures, thus crystallizing relationships and stereotyping roles.

With respect to flexibility of rules, Becvar and Becvar (1988) introduce the concepts of morphostasis and morphogenesis. Morphostasis describes a system's tendency toward stability, a state of dynamic equilibrium. Morphogenesis refers to the system-enhancing behavior that allows for growth, creativity, innovation, and change.

A system must be able to find a balance, remaining stable in the context of change and changing in the context of stability, say Becvar and Becvar. In a healthy system, the rules allow for a change when such change is needed to meet individual and family needs. As you assess family systems, then, you must not only identify a family's rules and operations, but also determine the degree of flexibility (or rigidity) of the rules and of the system itself. This may be observed in part by assessing the degree of difficulty a family has in adjusting and maintaining a dynamic state of balance in response to potentially disruptive developments that occur during its life cycle, such as individual maturation, emancipation of adolescents, marriage, birth, aging, and death (as in the case of Ann Mercy). Strains on families often occur

when a first child is born, a grandparent comes to live with the family, an adolescent reaches puberty, the last child "leaves the nest," a wife goes to work, or a breadwinner retires. Pressures on families are also caused by ongoing developmental changes of children who press for redefinition of family rules and often pursue interests and values alien to those embraced traditionally by the family. These pressures, write Goldenberg and Goldenberg (1991), cause "disequilibrium within the family system, a sense of loss, and perhaps a feeling of strangeness until new transactional patterns restore family balance" (p. 40). Finally, extreme stress can occur in families from minority cultures whose values, beliefs, and perceptions clash with those of the majority culture.

In addition to assessing the stresses on rules caused by developmental changes and internal events (inner forces), you must also assess the extent to which a family's rules allow the system to respond flexibly to dynamic societal stresses (outer forces), such as those that may occur with the loss of job by a breadwinner, relocation of the family, the occurrence of a natural disaster that affects the family, or the drastic uprooting of the family experienced by political refugees. Ambiguous definitions of role expectations emanating from evolving norms and changing lifestyles in the larger society also cause strains on family systems. Yankelovich (1981) has identified 20 major changes in the norms guiding American life over the past several decades that are transforming the institutions of the workplace and the family. Among the shifting norms that carry the greatest significance for the culture are those relating to sexuality, childbearing, and marriage. In sharp contrast with the past, marriage and parenthood are now rarely viewed as necessary, and people who do not choose these roles are no longer considered social deviants. Further, with the norms affecting whether a wife should work outside the home having reversed themselves in the past several decades, more and more women are seeking employment, the male/female division of labor in the family is changing dramatically, and the dual-earner family has become a common phenomenon. Such rapidly changing cultural norms put significant stress on many families.

Adding to the complexity of these dynamics and confusing role changes are stresses incurred by new immigrant families, who must also face vast contrasts between themselves and the Western culture. The process of immigration and cultural transition represents, for example, a severe blow to Asian/Pacific families because it requires of them a large number of life changes over a short period of time, including material, economic, educational, and language transitions. Such transitions are required at the same time families are experiencing losses of extended family and familiar environments and support systems (Ho, 1987).

Responding successfully to inner and outer stressors requires constant transformation of the rules and behaviors of family members to accommodate to necessary changes while maintaining family continuity. Families often seek help because of an accumulation of events that have strained the coping ability of the entire family or of individual members. Studying life-change patterns, Holmes and Rahe (1967) discovered that if individuals encounter too many life changes in too short a period of time, the chances of those persons becoming physically ill, experiencing accidental injury, or suffering emotional disorders (such as depression) substantially increase. Ironically, even when the changes are for the better— marriage, birth of a child, a better job, a move to a bigger house, a luxurious vacation, or a windfall inheritance—if they are in sufficient degree, they may overwhelm the coping mechanisms of individual members or an entire family system. The concept that the family is a vulnerable system that may break down under accumulated stress is consonant with that of Minuchin (1974), who views many families who enter therapy as "families in transitional situations, suffering from the pains of

accommodation to new circumstances" (p. 60). Minuchin, in fact, reserves the label of pathology for those families who "in the face of stress increase the rigidity of their transitional patterns and boundaries and avoid or resist any exploration of alternatives" (p. 60).

It appears that most families have some maladaptive behaviors and rules that do not allow the system to respond readily to dynamic inner and outer forces. In an authoritative study designed to identify the vital characteristics of optimally functioning families, Lewis, Beavers, Gossett, and Phillips (1976) distinguished five levels of family functioning—optimal, adequate, midrange, borderline, and severely disturbed. But rather than families sorting neatly into discrete categories, these researchers pointed out that families fall along a continuum in regard to their functioning, with the most flexible, adaptive, goal-achieving systems at one end and the most inflexible, undifferentiated, and ineffective systems at the other. Elaborating on the implications of this research in a second volume, Beavers (1977) contends that, in terms of relative size of population, moderately dysfunctional families probably comprise the largest group, that is, greater than the family groups at either end of the continuum. The "normal" family in our society thus probably has some maladaptive features, and the "optimally functioning family," as defined by Lewis et al. (1976), is actually an atypical phenomenon.

The Diaz family may fall in the midrange of this continuum, because they have both rigid and more flexible rules. The rule that "Dad has the final say" is a rigid rule with his biological children. However, the rule that "Taking care of family members is a primary obligation" is functional in the sense that it has meant that both Maria and John, two of his biological children, wish to assist him to continue independently in a manner safe for his health and well-being. Maria offers to help him find a first floor apartment near her and to learn, with John, how to administer his insulin.

Content and Process Levels of Interaction

To make adequate family assessments and to identify important rules and behaviors, it is also vital to grasp the concepts of content and process levels of interaction. Pretend for a moment that the following brief scenario occurs in your office in a family agency as you conduct an initial interview with Mr. and Mrs. Barkley. In response to your inquiry as to the problems they are experiencing, Mr. B glances at his wife and then indicates that she has been depressed and "sick" for some time, and they have come to the agency seeking help for "her" problem. As you look at Mrs. B, she nods her assent. You are concerned at this moment with what the couple is saying to you (the content of the discussion); however, you are also keenly interested in assessing the underlying intent or meaning of messages and in observing the manner in which the spouses are relating or behaving as they talk about their problems. In other words, you are also observant of the process that occurs as the couple discusses content. You therefore make mental note of the fact that the husband served as spokesman for his wife (with her tacit approval) and that the problem as defined by both spouses resides with the wife. Both spouses thus disregarded any impact of the problem on the husband, any possible part he might play in reinforcing or exacerbating the wife's depression or other problematic behavior, or any problems the husband might be experiencing. Essentially, with respect to roles, the couple has presented the wife as the "problem person," and the husband as the practitioner's "consultant." Several important interactional behaviors thus occurred at the process level in the opening gambits of the session, revealing information about the manner in which the spouses define their problem and how they relate and pointing to promising avenues for exploration in assessing their problems.

Families' rules are often revealed at the process level—a level often ignored by beginning practitioners as they selectively attend to what clients are "saying." Learning to sharpen one's observational powers to attend to what people are doing as they discuss problems is crucial to assessing and intervening effectively in family systems. Otherwise, the practitioner can easily get caught up at the content level and, for example, continue to explore the etiology of Mrs. B's "depression" (with the husband as information-giver and Mrs. B as the passive, identified patient) while ignoring stylized behaviors of the couple that play a vital part in their problems.

Sequences of Interaction

In order to assess family rules adequately, practitioners must also pay attention to sequences of interaction that occur between members. All families play out scenarios or a series of transactions in which they manifest redundancies in behavior and communication. Analysis of interactional sequences may reveal functional or dysfunctional coping patterns utilized by members or by the entire family system. In troubled families, however, the scenarios are often destructive, serving to reinforce maladaptive behavior and dysfunctional rules. Observation of these destructive interactional sequences yields rich information concerning communication styles and dysfunctional behavior of individuals and the manner in which all family members reinforce dysfunctional interactions.

The following excerpt from the first minutes of a first session with the Diaz family—Mr. Diaz, daughter Maria, son John, and stepdaughter Anita—illustrates habituated sequential behaviors that have a powerful impact on the system. The medical social worker, as described above, has convened the family to consider health and safety alternatives for Mr. Diaz.

Anita [*to practitioner.*]: Carlos can't maintain himself or John. John runs wild, with no appropriate adult supervision, and Carlos can't take care of himself now that Mother has died. [*Anita looks earnestly at the practitioner while Mr. Diaz sits stolidly, arms fold-ed, glowering straight ahead.*]

Maria [*to practitioner.*]: Dad is having trouble with John and hasn't taken care of himself all these years with Ann Mercy doing the cooking and cleaning and injecting his insulin. [*To Mr. Diaz.*] Dad, I respect you and want to help you in any way, but things just can't continue like they are.

Mr. Diaz [*to practitioner.*]: These children "no tienen respeto," they don't give me the respect they should give the Father of this family. They want to put me in a nursing home and take John away from me.

Anita: Maybe that would be for the best since you can't take care of yourself or John.

Maria [*to practitioner.*]: Dad is used to having his own way and we do respect him, at least I do, but he won't listen to how some things have to change.

Mr. Diaz: Maria, you have been a good daughter, and I am surprised at your behavior. I would think that you would stick by your Father if anyone would.

John: Dad, you know I stick by you. And I can help with some things too. I want to stay with you. We have been getting along ok and I want to be a good son and take care of you.

Anita: John, you have been running the streets, in trouble with the law, taking money from your father. You are no help to him, and he can't be a good parent to you.

Maria: John, I know you want to help, and you are close to your Dad. But you have made a lot of problems for him and I too wonder if you can take care of him or he of you.[2]

In the preceding example, the family plays out discordant thematic interaction that, with slight variation, can be observed over and over in the family's transactions.[3] It is as though the family is involved in a screenplay, and once the curtain is raised, all members participate in the scenario according to the family script. It is important to understand that the family script has no beginnings or endings; that is, anyone may initiate the scenario by enacting his or her "lines." The rest of the members almost invariably follow their habituated styles of relating, editing their individual scripts slightly to fit different versions of the scene being acted out by the family. In the scenes, the

subjects discussed will vary, but the roles taken by individual members and the dysfunctional styles of communicating and behaving that perpetuate the scenario fluctuate very little.

In the preceding scenario, notice the sequencing of the transactions that took place:

- Anita speaks forthrightly about her concerns about John and Mr. Diaz's capacity for parenting him. Responding nonverbally (folding his arms and glowering straight ahead), Mr. Diaz declines to participate openly.

- Maria affirms some of Anita's concerns but also speaks directly to her Father, affirming her respect for him as Father and head of the family.

- Mr. Diaz asserts that his children "no tienen respeto" and that their motivation is to put him away.

- Anita does not deny that a nursing home might be the best solution.

- Maria reasserts her respect for her father yet notes that some things will have to change.

- Mr. Diaz addresses Maria and questions whether she is in fact showing proper respect for him as her Father.

- John joins the fray and tries to identify himself as a good son with "respeto."

- Anita puts John in his place by doubting whether he has acted as a good son or whether Mr. Diaz can be a good parent to him.

- Maria supports John's claim to wish to be a good son but agrees that there are problems with Mr. Diaz and his care of John that remain.

In witnessing this and other similar scenarios of the Diaz family, the practitioner may identify patterned behaviors and "rules" governing family interaction that may not be apparent when observing single transactions. For example:

- Anita, perhaps because she is a stepdaughter, does not acknowledge the family rule of "respeto" and challenges Mr. Diaz's wishes and capabilities.

- Maria does acknowledge Mr. Diaz's place in the family and tries to show appropriate respect while acknowledging that problems do exist.

- John attempts to present a strong coalition with Mr. Diaz by identifying his wishes to maintain the current situation.

- Mr. Diaz addresses the practitioner and Maria, ignoring Anita, who has violated a family rule.
- Anita and Mr. Diaz invariably disagree.
- Maria attempts to mediate, affirming Mr. Diaz's position and the rule, while acknowledging problems.

Sifting out the habituated interactional responses in family processes enables the practitioner to focus interventions strategically on the family's limited number of destructive processes.[4]

By analyzing the rules and patterns involved in the interaction, the practitioner has many entry points for intervening in the family processes to assist the family in coming to a decision. Despite the agreement between the stepsisters (Maria and Anita) that Mr. Diaz cannot continue to live his life as he has and that change is required, Mr. Diaz's role is not altogether clear at this point. Mr. Diaz and John appear to be allied as the two males in the family, protective of one another. It is important to recognize that there are many family situations such as the Diaz family in which family rules and patterns are significant; however, the function of the agency is not family treatment nor is this the client's request. Nonetheless, family rules and patterns are playing a part in the problem and its potential resolution.

Employing "Circular" Explanations of Behavior

In our previous discussion, we viewed the behavior of the Diaz family from a systems framework, establishing the repetitive nature of interactional behavior and the reciprocal influence of all actors on the behaviors of other family members. In so doing, we applied a circular concept of causality to the Diaz family, demonstrating that each member's behavior becomes a stimulus to all other involved members of the system. Further, interactions with the environment including the neighborhood, the availability of a continuum of services, play a part in the maintenance of problems. This may be contrasted to a linear explanation of the causes of behavior in which A event causes B event, B event causes C, and so forth. To illustrate the difference between these two conceptual frameworks for viewing the causality of behavior, we turn once again to the Diaz family. Employing a linear explanation of behavior, one would say, "When Anita attacks Mr. Diaz, he defends himself." A circular explanation of behavior would involve the following: "When Anita attacks Mr. Diaz, he defends himself, and Maria acts to mediate, both supporting Mr. Diaz and Anita. The mediation is not accepted and the charges and countercharges between Anita and Mr. Diaz continue with John attempting to ally with his father. Further, the whole problem is maintained by a lack of adequate services to resolve the difficulties."

Tomm (1981) underscores that circular and linear concepts of causality reflect contrasting approaches employed by practitioners in assessing and intervening in family processes. He points out, however, that the circular explanation is systemic and preferred by systems-oriented practitioners, not only because it offers a more adequate description of behavior but also because it offers more alternatives for intervention. In the preceding example, for instance, a practitioner who operated from a linear orientation might intervene to stop Anita from attacking Mr. Diaz, whereas a practitioner who employed a circular explanation of the causes of behavior might target the entire circular pattern for intervention. Further, a social worker sensitive to the role of the environment would also assist family members in looking at environmental causes and solutions.

Tomm emphasizes that a preference for circularity influences the practitioner's interviewing style in the assessment (and intervention) process.

Utilizing a circular perspective, Tomm notes that there are three types of differences that may be usefully explored in family assessment. These include differences between individuals (e.g., "Who gets angry the most?"), differences between relationships (e.g., "What is the difference between the way Mr. Diaz treats Anita compared to how he treats Maria?"), and differences between time periods (e.g., "How did she get along with Mr. Diaz last year as compared to now?"). By orienting the assessment to solicit information regarding differences, Tomm points out, the practitioner elicits more relevant data and does so more efficiently than would occur by obtaining linear descriptions.

Beginning practitioners tend to employ linear rather than circular perspectives when explaining behavior and to view interactional processes as "action-reaction" cycles, often assigning responsibility or blame for problems to one or more members whose problematic behavior is conspicuous. When not attuned to the repetitive nature of dysfunctional interactions, however, practitioners sharply reduce their ability to help family members, who often need the help of an expert in removing themselves from destructive interactional patterns. They also often ignore the role of the larger environment in maintaining and resolving problems.

Not unlike beginning practitioners, family members also tend to explain behavior using a linear orientation, often assigning arbitrary beginnings and endings to sequences of interaction in ways that define other members as villains and themselves as victims. Mr. Diaz, for instance, viewed himself as an innocent victim of Anita's disrespectful behavior and defined her as the person who needed to change in the family. "Punctuating" interactional sequences in this manner, according to Sluzki (1975) "constitutes an optical illusion...the chicken-egg puzzle is arbitrarily solved by designating one of the participants as the initiator and the other as reactor" (p. 378). To counteract this linear perspective, practitioners must punctuate interactions in ways that define the responsibility of all family members in contributing to and maintaining dysfunctional interactions.

Assessing Problems Employing a Systems Framework

The utilization of a systems view of family problems has implications for gathering relevant data in the assessment process. Many clients, even those designated as villains by other family members, see themselves as victims of the actions of significant others or of external forces over which they have no control. Most often they initially enter counseling prepared to "complain" about those who are "causing" their problems, rather than to engage in efforts to change themselves. Because of their selective perception of the "causes" of events, they often do not offer information that assists practitioners to formulate a clear picture of how these problems may be reinforced and exacerbated either by the client or by significant others in the family system. It is important that practitioners have an appropriate conceptual framework and accompanying skills to identify themes within the family's processes and to elicit relevant data about the family system. Otherwise, practitioners may unwittingly adopt clients' definitions of "who has the problem," focus interventions on changing the behavior of these selected persons, and neglect the influence of other significant family members upon the problems in the systems.

It should be noted that although systemic interactional patterns that restrict and mold clients' behavior are woven throughout the fabric of many client problems, practitioners often do not have the opportunity of observing these firsthand. Family members, for instance, may refuse service or be unavailable because of geographical location. In this case, a family member who lived at a distance (Anita) was available briefly. It was unclear whether she would be involved with the family beyond this session as a participant in problem solving. At other times, it may not be expedient to involve key actors who play significant roles in the problems of clients. It is vital to remember when clients describe problems, however, that they often talk extensively about difficulties they are experiencing in relationships with family members or with significant others who are not present. Thus, when you cannot directly observe interactional processes, you have the important task of eliciting highly specific information from clients that will aid you in assessing the interpersonal patterns and rules of the family system. This is best accomplished by carefully exploring a number of critical incidents that illustrate problematic behaviors manifested in the family system. In order to identify underlying family patterns, you must elicit descriptive information about the behaviors and communications of all involved actors and establish the sequencing of discrete transactions and events that occurred before, during, and after the identified incident. Inasmuch as clients tend to summarize critical incidents, thereby omitting vital details, it is helpful to explain to them that you are searching for family styles of relating and to underscore the importance of carefully identifying each discrete event or transaction that occurred in any critical incident targeted for exploration. We recommend that you request clients to give a verbatim account of an event so that you see what happened as clearly as if you had been present.

Even when clients define their problems as involving some members of a family and not others, it is critical to explore family relationships to the extent that you can identify key interactional patterns and the nature of alignments among various subsystems of the family. In such explorations, it is not uncommon to discover that other persons besides parents (e.g., sibling, stepfather, grandparents) play significant roles in contributing to the problem behaviors of a child brought to an agency. Based on information gained in exploring family affiliative ties and rules, you will often need to "redefine" and expand the problem system to include more actors than originally identified by clients.

In assisting clients to understand the need for an overall assessment of family relationships when they initially believe that only one or two members

are involved in problems, it is helpful to explain that the family is a "system" and to stress that the entire family is affected by, and may even exacerbate, problems experienced by one member. Further, you should stress that the causes of problems usually reside largely in interactions that involve various members of the family rather than with individual family members. As underscored by Wile (1978), "family members are as likely to be relieved and grateful as they are to be threatened and resistant when a problem they had attributed to the 'identified patient' is redefined as a general family problem" (p. 16). Wile stresses, however, that this approach holds only to the extent that the practitioner's approach is nonaccusatory and that the practitioner clarifies for the whole family how all involved members are caught in difficult conflicts or dilemmas related to the problematic family situation.

DIMENSIONS OF FAMILY ASSESSMENT

In explicating integral concepts of a systems framework for viewing family functioning in our earlier discussion, we have set the stage for family assessment. In this section, we present dimensions of assessment that represent guidelines for exploring and organizing the massive data you will gather in working with family systems. These dimensions will also assist you in bringing patterned interaction into bold relief and will prepare you to evaluate functional and dysfunctional aspects of family operations—a critical preliminary step to planning interventions to assist a family in problem solving.

The following list contains the dimensions that we consider at length in the chapter.

1. Family context.
2. Outer boundaries of family systems.
3. Internal boundaries and family subsystems.

4. Family power structure.
5. Family decision-making processes.
6. Family affect and range of feelings expressed.
7. Family goals.
8. Family myths and cognitive patterns.
9. Family roles.
10. Communication styles of family members.
11. Family strengths.
12. Family life cycle.

In employing these dimensions to formulate assessments and plan interventions, we recommend you utilize the following format:

1. Identify the dimensions that are most relevant to your clients. Although the dimensions apply to the processes of all couples and families, some may not be pertinent when viewed in the perspective of the presenting complaint and the nature of the help requested by the family. For example, a family may seek help because of stress caused by the advanced senility of an aged relative living in the home. Initial exploration may reveal no major deficits in functioning (e.g., ineffective style of decision making) that are contributing to the family's problem. Thus, the practitioner would narrow the assessment to an exploration of factors that contribute to the specific problem identified by the family.

2. Utilize the dimensions to guide your exploration of family behavior. After the first session, review the dimensions and develop relevant questions to further your exploration in subsequent sessions.

3. Utilize the dimensions as guidelines for compressing new data into themes and patterns. Determine the family's or couple's rules or habitual ways of relating in relation to *each* relevant dimension. For example, ask yourself what the family's rules are in relation to decision making, communicating, and the other dimensions. Refer to appropriate discussions in the book for guidelines that will help you pinpoint specific rules.

4. Based on the relevant dimensions, develop a written profile of functional and dysfunctional behaviors of *individual* members of the system. For example, with respect to the dimension of communication, a family member may often paraphrase messages of others and personalize statements (functional behaviors). The same family member may be prone to interrupt and to talk excessively, thus monopolizing the session at times (dysfunctional behaviors). Developing a profile of these two types of behavior for each family member will serve as a conceptual framework not only for assessing behaviors but for planning interventions as well.

5. Employ the dimensions to assess relevant behaviors of the *entire family*, developing a profile of salient functional and dysfunctional behaviors that are manifested by the system itself. Again utilizing the dimension of communication, functional behaviors of a family may include occasional listening responses and responses that acknowledge the contributions of others (e.g., "You did a good job"). In contrast, dysfunctional responses manifested by the same family may include labeling of members (e.g., "You're dumb") and frequent expressions of anger toward others.

Family Context

The family context includes its access to basic resources, such as food, health care, housing, financial aid, or job training, and their ability to secure such resources. Assisting families to meet their "survival" needs must often take precedence, in fact, over interventions to change family dynamics or to teach marital or parenting skills. Such interventions are simply not relevant to families who are in dire need of basic sustenance.

Paramount to gathering data and assessing families is the task of accurately viewing the family within the context of its cultural milieu, sexual orientation, and family form. The practitioner's challenge in even deciding who makes up the family is illustrated by McPhatter (1991), who observes:

In exploring the structure of a family, the worker should not make assumptions about family composition and type based on traditional definitions of family. For example, typical American families include single mothers with children, single fathers with children, grandparent(s) with children, foster parents with children, and extended family members and nonblood relatives who are significant to the family. (p. 16)

The fact that the definition of "family" differs greatly from culture to culture adds even more complexity to the practitioner's assessment task. Although the dominant American definition focuses on the intact nuclear family, for Italians there is no such thing as the "nuclear" family, observes McGoldrick (1982a), "To them family means a strong tightly knit three-or four-generational family, which also includes godparents and old friends. The Chinese go beyond this and include in their definition of family all their ancestors and all their descendants" (p. 10).

Though the contexts of families differ dramatically, it is commonplace for practitioners "to commence, maintain, and terminate treatment without having the slightest appreciation, knowledge, or respect for the larger contextual issues (e.g., race, culture, gender, ethnicity) that subsequently impact treatment. This oversight often results in ... a 'neglect of context' that is replete throughout the field of family therapy" (Hardy, 1989, pp. 17–18). The consequence to families is that practitioners "may filter out their inner resources, values, intelligence, spirituality, and wisdom; and most importantly, (they) may underestimate the influence of the social settings in which they live" (Saba et al., 1989, p. 2).

It is vital, then, that practitioners have a working knowledge of the family: its reality, culture,

biculturalism, ethnic status, language, social class, customs, history, and sexual orientation. Once having attained this perspective, they can employ what Norton (1978) and McPhatter (1991) call a "dual perspective." This perspective involves "the conscious and systematic process of perceiving, understanding and comparing simultaneously the values, attitudes of the larger societal system with those of the client's immediate family and community system"—a vital aspect in assessing the social context of a family's presenting problems (McPhatter, 1991, pp. 14–15).

The usefulness of utilizing a "dual perspective" to identify the points of conflict between the family and larger systems can be seen, for example, in the assessment of same-sex couples. Such couples live in the context of "homophobia" in the larger culture, "defined operationally as the fear and hatred of same-sex intimacy, love, sexuality, and relationships, and of those individuals and institutions that participate in, affirm, and support same-sex relating." As a consequence, these couples risk jobs, freedom, custody of children, and homes if identified in the larger culture (Brown & Zimmer, 1986, pp. 451–452).

A "dual perspective" is an absolute must in assessing the rich variety of family cultures, for family behavior makes sense "only in the larger cultural context in which it is embedded" (McGoldrick, 1982a, p. 4). Such a perspective also aids practitioners to avoid being "triggered" by ethnic characteristics they may have regarded negatively or being caught in an ethnocentric view that their group values are more "right" or "true" than others (McGoldrick, 1982a, p. 25).

Utilizing a dual perspective, practitioners can view the functionality of a family's behavior within the context of what is "normal" for that particular family's culture, for what is dysfunctional in one culture may not be in another. Gwyn and Kilpatrick (1981) and Weaver (1982), for example, stress that the black culture is a distinct culture, and nonblack practitioners can often mistake black behavior patterns and lifestyle for dysfunction.[5] With respect to Latino families, Bernal and Flores-Ortiz (1982) also caution practitioners to be clear about the use of such terms as "enmeshment," "fusion," and "undifferentiated ego mass," for "the healthy interdependence of Latino families may appear as pathological fusion to the non-Latino observer" (p. 363). Numerous other authors offer similar cautions against practitioners imposing their own cultural biases on the ethnic families they serve. When such occurs, practitioners may intervene in ways that actually disrupt family functioning. Red Horse, Lewis, Feit, and Decker (1978), for instance, report several case examples of practitioners making grave errors in intervening with Native American families. Not understanding the culture of these families, practitioners can punish Indian families for acting normally and can cause "irreparable alienation between family and human service professionals" (p. 68).

Ironically, even when practitioners understand the culture of various ethnic groups, the danger exists of stereotyping minority people. It is thus imperative that practitioners realize that members of minority groups may differ considerably from descriptions of typical behavior of such groups. Queralt (1984), for example, dispels the myth that there is a "typical Hispanic." Although Spanish-speaking people share some aspects of Hispanic heritage, similar language, and variations of a Catholic ideology, they nonetheless belong to diverse cultures and nationalities and vary in many other respects. Queralt also emphasizes that the normative values of a minority group are not necessarily professed by each and every member of that group. It would be difficult, for example, to find Cubans who showed absolute conformity with traditional Cuban-Hispanic values. Further, as Queralt points out, the values of cultural groups are not fixed but are always evolving and may be impacted by the degree of acculturation to mainstream society. The implications of Queralt's observations are critical to practitioners, for each

family system is unique, and practitioners must be able to individualize each family within its cultural context.

As practitioners assess the processes of families from various cultural groups, they must also be aware of the extent to which a family has become acculturated into the mainstream culture, as we discussed in Chapter 8. All ethnic minority groups in the United States who have migrated or come as refugees face issues related to acculturation. The problems Asian refugees face in acculturating to mainstream society are extreme and plainly visible to practitioners. However, as McGoldrick (1982a) observes, even families who have migrated several generations ago continue to experience the complex stresses of migration, "having been forced to abandon much of their ethnic heritage…and thus hav(ing) lost a part of their identity." Such stresses "may be 'buried' or forgotten, but they continue…to influence the family's outlook" (p. 12).

In assessing the functioning of families of immigrants, practitioners must gain information concerning the family's migration and look for the continuing stresses on the family of accommodating to two (and sometimes more) cultures. The amount of disruption to Asian, Cuban, or other refugee families who have been uprooted from their homelands and have suffered losses in all aspects of their lives is particularly extreme (Queralt, 1984).

Immigrants experience family disruption as factors such as migration, the mass media, and the new-found independence of working women call traditional values into question (Ghali, 1982). The migratory experience often causes family disruption also because migration-related tasks such as finding work, preparing food, clothing, shelter, and learning a new language often preempt the completion of family development tasks (Bernal & Flores-Ortiz, 1982).

Practitioners must assess the family's relative effectiveness in coping with its situation and rejuvenating its "connectedness" or roots with its cultural reference group. Timberlake and Cook (1984), for example, describe the coping efforts of Vietnamese refugees to rebuild their lives:

> Family units react to the life crisis of uprooting and separation by seeking to mend or to reconstitute their traditional structures as rapidly as possible…families split apart during evacuation and resettlement work hard at rebuilding a social network by incorporating distant relatives, friends, and even strangers who are also refugees. (Indeed, the phenomenon of having literally been in the same boat seems to generate strong mutual support among refugees.) As more members are incorporated into the family unit…the Vietnamese extended family (is) gradually restored. (p. 110)

Outer Boundaries of Family Systems

As living systems that are part of still larger systems, families necessarily have diverse transactions with the environment. Families differ widely, however, in the degree to which they are open to transactions with other systems and in the flexibility of their outer boundaries. By flexibility, we mean the extent to which outsiders are permitted or invited to enter the family system, members of the family are allowed to invest emotionally and to engage in relationships outside the family, and information and materials are exchanged with the environment. As identified by Kantor and Lehr (1975), there are three prototypical bounding arrangements of families—open, closed, and random. Each of these types involves distinctive styles of relating to the outer environment.

Closed Family Systems   Those who hold authority in families perform the bounding functions in such a way that they create discrete family space that exists apart from the larger space of the neighborhood and community. The closed family system thus is characterized by strict regulation that limits transactions with the external environment and restricts incoming and outgoing people, objects, information, and ideas. Locked doors,

tight parental control over input from the media, supervised excursions, close scrutiny of strangers, trespass prohibitions, high fences, and unlisted telephones are typical features of closed family systems. The tight boundaries of closed systems serve the function of preserving territoriality, protecting the family from undesired intrusions, safeguarding privacy, and even fostering secretiveness. Authorities in the family maintain tight control of traffic at the family's perimeter, and the bounding function is never relinquished or shared with outsiders or even with family members who have not been assigned the role of performing bounding functions.

Open Family Systems   In this type of system, the bounding movements of individual members are regulated by the process of group consensus. Consequently, family boundaries are flexible, extending the territory of the family into the larger community space as well as bringing external culture into the family space. Individuals are permitted the freedom to regulate their own incoming and outgoing traffic to the extent that they do not adversely affect other family members or violate the family norms. Features of open family systems include having numerous guests in the home, visiting with friends, participating in external activities, belonging to outside groups, participating in community affairs, and permitting free information exchange with minimal censorship of the media. Open boundaries within a family fosters beneficial interchange with other members of the community; indeed, guests are not only welcome but are viewed as contributing to the well-being of the family.

Random Family Systems   Within this category, family members develop individual bounding patterns in establishing and defending their own and their family's territory. There are no family bounding patterns per se, and there may be as many bounding guidelines as there are members in the family; in effect, the random family's bounding pattern is a conglomerate of individual styles. Individual styles collide at times, but there are no fixed patterns, and family members therefore feel no need to modify their styles. Features of family life that are normally confined to a family's space may also occur outside the household. For example, conflicts and affectional expressions may occur in public as well as in the privacy of the home. Random bounding also deemphasizes defending the territorial perimeter of the family, so that limits on entry or exit to the family are not imposed. Indeed, random families tend to extend and broaden prerogatives for entry and exit not only to members but also to guests and strangers.

Knowledge of the three prototypes of family structure discussed in the preceding sections should assist you in identifying the bounding patterns of families you encounter in practice. Bear in mind that these three types of family structures are only prototypes and that the actual bounding patterns of families may include aspects of all these types of structures: No living system is ever truly closed. It is vital, therefore, to assess each family's unique style of transacting with the environment. Remember also that although the bounding pattern of the open system is most conducive to meeting the emotional and social needs of individual members, the strengths as well as the liabilities of bounding patterns must be assessed within the context of each family's unique needs and styles.

In assessing the bounding patterns of families, practitioners must also assess the extent to which relatives or nonrelatives are included in the family's bounding patterns. In Anglo families, for example, practitioners may find grandparents, a live-in boyfriend or girlfriend, or a godparent, who wield considerable influence in the family's affairs. In assessing families from other cultures, practitioners will often find an extended family system that includes many kin who have well-defined obligations and responsibilities to each other. The Puerto Rican (or Hispanic) definition of family, for example, goes way beyond the family of origin, encompassing not only those related by blood and marriage but including those who are tied to it as well through custom (Mizio, 1974).

Assessing the bounding patterns in stepfamilies may prove particularly difficult, as frequently there is lack of agreement between stepfamily members as to who is in the household. "As a result, there is boundary ambiguity in many parts of the stepfamily—between households and between parenting adults, as well as within households where intergenerational boundaries may be problematic and personal space a complicated matter" (Visher & Visher, 1988, p. 203). We found this to be the case in the Diaz family earlier, as there was not agreement about the stepdaughter Anita's role in the on-going decisions of the family about her brother John and stepfather.

Use of family genograms, in which the practitioner pictorially diagrams a family's history and constellation over several generations, can provide important data on bounding patterns when working with any type of family (McGoldrick & Gerson, 1985). Visher and Visher (1988) particularly recommend the use of a genogram in work with stepfamilies, as it provides information about previous marriages, the length of the single-parent household phases, and details about the shifts in the living arrangements of the children. It also "gives a picture of where family members have been and the direction in which they need to go" (p. 32).

Internal Boundaries and Family Subsystems

All families develop networks of coexisting subsystems formed on the basis of gender, interest, generation, or functions that must be performed for the family's survival (Minuchin, 1974).[6] Members of a family may simultaneously belong to a number of subsystems, entering into separate and reciprocal relationships with other members of the nuclear family, depending on the subsystems they share in common (e.g., husband/wife, mother/daughter, brother/sister, father/son) or with the extended family (e.g., grandmother/granddaughter, uncle/nephew, mother/son-in-law). Each subsystem can be thought of as a natural coalition between participating members. As Sluzki (1975) states, "intimacy…necessarily includes a coalitionary component" (p. 69). Many of the coalitions or alliances that families form are situation-related and temporary in nature. A teenager may be able to enlist her mother's support in asking her father's permission for a special privilege or for new clothing. A grandmother living in a home may voice disagreement with her daughter and son-in-law regarding a particular decision involving one of their children, thus temporarily forming a coalition with the affected child. Such passing alliances are characteristic of temporary subsystems (Goldenberg & Goldenberg, 1991). We noticed this in the situational alliance of the Diaz stepsisters above.

Other subsystems, particularly the spouse, parental, and sibling subsystems, are more enduring in nature. According to Minuchin (1974), the formation of stable, well-defined coalitions between members of these vital subsystems is, in fact, critical to the well-being and health of the family. Unless there is a strong and enduring coalition between husband and wife, for instance, conflict reverberates throughout a family, and children are often co-opted into one warring faction or another as parents struggle for power and control. For optimal family functioning, according to Minuchin, the boundaries of these three subsystems must be clear and defined well enough to allow members sufficient differentiation to carry out functions without undue interference but permeable enough to allow contact and exchange of resources between members of the subsystem and others. Minuchin, in fact, points out that the clarity of the subsystem boundaries is of far more significance in determining family functioning than the composition of the family's subsystem. According to Minuchin, a parental subsystem that includes a grandmother or a parental child may function quite adequately, for

instance, if the lines of responsibility are clearly defined.

The relative integrity of the boundaries of the spouse, parental, and sibling subsystems is determined by related rules of the family. A mother clearly defines the boundary of a parental subsystem, for instance, in telling her oldest child not to interfere when she is talking to a younger child about assigned chores that the child has left undone. The message, or "rule," then, is that children are not allowed to assume parenting roles with other children in the family. The mother, however, may delegate responsibility for parenting to her oldest child when she leaves the home. Nevertheless, the "rules" regarding who does the parenting and under what circumstances clearly delineate the boundaries of the parental and sibling subsystems.

Culture also plays a determining role in family subsystems. For example, traditionally, many Native American tribes did not consider people to be functional adults until they were in their mid-fifties or a grandparent. For this reason grandparents were assigned the child-rearing responsibilities and thus the parenting subsystem included grandparents and grandchildren, rather than parents and their own children (Tafoya, 1989).

The clarity of boundaries within a family is a useful parameter for evaluating family functioning. Minuchin (1974) conceives of all families as falling somewhere along a continuum of extremes in boundary functioning, the opposite poles of which are disengagement (diffuse boundaries) and enmeshment (inappropriately rigid boundaries). Family closeness in an enmeshed family system is defined as everyone thinking and feeling alike. Membership in such families requires a major sacrifice of autonomy, thereby discouraging members from exploration, independent action, and problem solving. Members of disengaged families, on the other hand, tolerate a wide range of individual variations by members but are apt to lack feelings of family solidarity, loyalty, and a sense of belonging. Members of such families find it difficult to give or to get support from other family members. Family organization in such systems is unstable and chaotic, with leadership often shifting moment to moment. In disengaged families, only high-level stresses upon one family member appreciably affect other members or activate the family's supportive systems. These systems, in fact, tend not to respond when a response is appropriate (parents may not worry when their adolescent child stays out all night). At the enmeshed end of the continuum, one member's behavior immediately affects others, reverberating throughout the family system. Members tend to respond to any variations from the accustomed with excessive speed and intensity, with parents becoming very angry, for instance, if a child does not eat everything on his plate.

Enmeshment and disengagement as processes are not necessarily dysfunctional. According to Minuchin, every family experiences some enmeshment or disengagement in its subsystems as a family goes through developmental phases. During a family's early developmental years, mother and young children may represent an enmeshed subsystem, with father in a peripheral position. Adolescents gradually disengage from the parental-child subsystems as they get ready to leave home. But continued operations by a family at either extreme of the continuum may signal the presence of maladaptive patterns and rules that hinder the growth needs of members. Many relatively dysfunctional and highly intractable coalitions between members occur in families who adopt enmeshed styles of relating. Mother and child in a highly enmeshed subsystem may form a coalition against father. In another instance, a mother may relinquish many of her parenting functions to become a member of a sibling subsystem as manifested by a mother's descriptive message—"I treat my daughter just like my sister." A "parental" child may join an executive subsystem, forming a destructive coalition with the parents against other children in the family. Or a

woman may "parent" both her grown daughter and the daughter's children, thus interfering with her own offspring's parental functioning. An entire family may also shun one member whose behavior deviates from the family's prescribed norms.

In disengaged families, by contrast, coalitions may be formed between some members, but these alliances are apt to be fragile and transitory, based on immediate gratification of the needs of family members who abandon the alliance once their needs are temporarily satisfied or the coalition no longer serves their purposes. In disengaged families, it is the relative lack of opportunity to form stable alliances that is detrimental to the growth needs of individuals. The resulting "disconnectedness" of this transactional family style leaves members isolated and alienated from each other and unable to utilize family resources or emotional supplies. Disengaged families suffer from structural underorganization, a feature often characteristic of low socioeconomic families, as Aponte (1977) notes:

> Family members often lack contextual support for their individual development and for the elaboration of the interpersonal structure of their family relationships. Families trapped within ghettoized, powerless communities struggle against great odds, not only in dealing with their social circumstances but in developing the basic emotional and social tools for ordinary living. They may well be "underorganized" in the sense that the social structures within the families may be relatively few, relatively inflexible, and relatively discontinuous. (pp. 101–102)

In assessing the various structural arrangements of a family, attend to the alignments between family members and outsiders that tug at family loyalties and cause acute family stress. Grandparents living outside the home may take the side of children in family disputes and provide a refuge for them, which may interfere with parents and children working out their difficulties. A 15-year-old girl may begin to keep company with an older man and, despite her parents' objections, may continue to see him surreptitiously. Ignoring his wife's protestations, a husband may also keep late hours and spend an inordinate amount of time with a "best friend," going to bars, playing poker, and the like. Further, either spouse may begin an affair with another person while continuing in the marital relationship.

Even practitioners may form inappropriate alliances with clients that interfere with family members working together on their problems. In one instance a woman had had 30 years of intermittent therapy with several practitioners. Although many of her problems were marriage related, her husband had seen these practitioners only twice, each time to consult with them about his wife's problems rather than to participate in any change process. Although this example is extreme, clients are often seen individually for therapy when their problems either emanate from or are exacerbated by marital or family relationships.

Family Power Structure

Closely related to the process of forming subsystems and negotiating coalitions in a family are the vicissitudes of power relationships in the system. Power can be thought of as the capacity of one member to induce change in the behavior of another family member. The more "need fulfilling" resources one person has in a family in relation to other members, the more power that person wields in the family. Needs include requirements for economic support, social rank, love, affection, and approval while resources include the ability to provide these need-fulfilling elements to another person. All families develop a power structure that defines the relative influence that each member has upon other members of the system and who will participate in what way in decision making. It is through this power structure that systems are able to maintain the behavior of individuals within acceptable limits and to provide leadership to assure that maintenance functions of the family will be carried out, thus maximizing the possibility of survival of the group.

Distribution and Balance of Power   Families are often viewed as having single monolithic power structures—either the husband or the wife makes all the decisions, or both participate equally. In actuality, multiple power structures exist in families. Wives may be more influential in some decisions and husbands in others, depending on expertise or jurisdictional "agreements" among spouses. Since both partners share in the family's decision-making process (although possibly to an unequal extent), it is important to determine who may be the most influential in which decisions and how the balance of power is distributed in the family.

To the extent that children are able to influence decisions made by the husband and wife executive subsystem or to assume "decider" roles themselves, they also play a part in the family's power structure. Minuchin (1974) has observed that some families develop a "parental child" who cares for siblings in the absence of parents. If the child has been delegated appropriate authority, the family system may function smoothly and the child may develop responsibility and capability beyond his or her years. If parents abdicate their responsibilities or do not explicitly delegate authority, however, the child may be forced to assume control and decision-making functions beyond his or her developmental capacity, producing stresses that often result in adolescent rebellion and mishandling of younger siblings.

Culture plays a powerful role in defining the allocation of power in families. Consider, for example, Zborowski and Herzog's (1952, p. 138) description of a Jewish woman: "She was a perfect Jewish woman, clear, patient, hardworking, and silent, submissive to God and to her husband, devoted to her children…her own well-being was unimportant." Many cultures are male oriented and clearly define the female's role as subordinate to that of the male, stripping her of any power.

Because of many complex factors, including industrialization, the higher level of education of women and their entrance into the work force, and the equal rights movement, families in Western society are moving toward more egalitarian definitions of male–female roles; however, many families continue to suffer stress because of the difficulty in resolving discrepancies between traditional and new egalitarian definitions of male–female roles. As immigrant families enter the United States, they too face resolution of the same issues.

Stuart (1980) uses a "power-gram" to assess the power imbalances in a marriage and to ascertain the various decision-making areas in which individual spouses have authority to make decisions or share vested power. In determining how power is apportioned in the marriage, Stuart provides spouses with a list of areas in which couples commonly make decisions (p. 266) that includes the following items:

1. Where couple lives.
2. What job husband takes.
3. How many hours husband works.
4. Whether wife works.
5. What job wife takes.
6. How many hours wife works.
7. Number of children in the family.
8. When to praise or punish children.
9. How much time to spend with children.
10. When to have social contacts with in-laws and relatives.
11. When to have sex.
12. How to have sex.
13. How to spend money.
14. How and when to pursue personal interests.
15. Whether to attend church and, if so, which church to attend.

Individual spouses are then asked to rate each of the preceding according to who usually has the responsibility for making decisions in each area, using the following scale:

1. Almost always husband.
2. Husband, after consulting wife.
3. Both share equally.
4. Wife, after consulting husband.
5. Almost always wife.

Once ratings have been obtained, individual spouses are once again asked to rate the decision-making areas according to desired authority ratings; that is, the extent to which each would like authority to make decisions to be distributed among the partners. Finally, couples are asked to negotiate a desired balance of power in areas identified as being of primary importance to them in the relationship. Thus, both partners are able to indicate their view of the present and desired balance of power and, with the partner, to negotiate new decision-making rules.

Shifts in Power   In assessing family systems, it is also critical to understand that the power base of a family may shift with inner and outer stressors bringing upon the system pressures to which the family must accommodate. For instance, the contribution of an independent income increases the wife's power in a family; further, the higher the wife's education relative to her husband's education, the greater her power. Thus, as many more women enter the occupational world or seek higher levels of education as a result of current changing social conditions, dynamic changes are occurring in the balance of power in families. The power base in a family may also shift as a result of other factors. The influence or authority of a power figure may diminish if that person does not provide effective leadership in times of crisis. On the other hand, if the power figure successfully handles a crisis, that person's authority in a family may perceptibly increase.

Shifts in power often occur when new stepfamilies are formed. Factors associated with adults holding more power are: having custody of the children; being older; being male; being better educated; having a higher income; providing more financial support of children/stepchildren; and having interpersonal alliances—any of which may change in a new marriage. Finally, children in step-families may acquire more power than in their nuclear family, where both parents were in one household. As a result, these children acquire a standing in the hierarchy that is greater than that of at least one (or more) of the adults (Visher & Visher, 1988).

With immigrant families, shifts in power can occur when the male cannot secure employment in the new country. For example, in Puerto Rican families, the sense of being a *macho completo* (complete male) goes hand in hand with being a provider or protector of his family. When the male cannot find work and his wife, who can more easily secure employment, takes a job as a domestic or perhaps a sewing machine operator, the role reversal causes tremendous strains on the family, realigning the power base of the family and often causing the wife to have contempt for the husband she can no longer view as "macho" (Mizio, 1974).

Families encounter many stressful situations (e.g., loss of a job, reduced coping capacity caused by mental illness, debilitation resulting from an accident, or a wife's entering the work force) that may challenge the balance of power and cause realignments in the power base of the family. In fact, the emotional impact of these stressors and the tumultuous upheaval caused as family members struggle for power and control in a transitional situation may play a key role in a family's difficulties. In assessing family systems, therefore, you must not only determine how power has been distributed in the family but also whether changing conditions of the family are "threatening" the established power base. You must also assess the extent to which the family's "rules" allow the system to reallocate power flexibly and to adjust roles to meet the demands of the family's changing circumstances. Finally, you

must assess how husband and wife view the relative vestment of power in the family, for even if power is unequally distributed, both may be well satisfied with the arrangement. Under such circumstances, unless power dynamics play a significant role in family problems, it is not appropriate to seek to make adjustments in this area.

Covertly Held Power   It is important to keep in mind that power in a family may be held at a covert as well as an overt level. For instance, one partner may be formally acknowledged as the power figure in the family, a position usually accorded to the person in the family (traditionally the husband) who has more economic resources, social status, or skills in managing enterprises and thus more power over family decisions. However, power can be usurped from this power figure or from the husband–wife executive subsystem through various covert coalitions that may be formed in the family. A strong alliance between a child and a grandmother, for instance, may substantially weaken the power base of the parents. Similarly, in a male–dominated patriarchial family, a power bloc made up of mother and daughter may undermine the authority of the father.

Although almost all cultures appear on the surface to be male dominated, practitioners should avoid making premature decisions concerning which member or members of the family hold the power. At a covert level, women often maintain a central and powerful role in the family, despite subservient role definitions. Speaking of traditional Mexican American families, for example, Falicov (1982) observes that while there is outward compliance with the cultural ideal of male dominance and female submission, this is sometimes "a social fiction." Observers often fail to notice a culturally acceptable but less obvious norm—that of *hembrismo* or *marianismo*, "the undercover power and family centrality of the self-sacrificing mother" (p. 139).

The covert power that women hold in some cultures despite their subservient status has been referred to as a paradox by some authors. Speaking of Italian women, Rotunno and McGoldrick (1982, p. 347) observe that, "Although men are the central authority figures...and women are considered the servers of men...the mother...plays a very powerful role, especially in her son's affections (as his wife will hardly fail to notice)." The same type of paradox in the Jewish culture has also been observed by Herz and Rosen (1982):

> Wives were often referred to contemptuously and viewed as inferior to their husbands. On the other hand, they were extremely powerful in the primary role that they played in the home. In actual daily living they took the lead and made basic decisions about the destiny of their families. This is, of course, a paradox: women are powerful, while at the same time compelled to deny that they are. (p. 374)

Persons also exercise covert power in a family through use of emotional or physical symptoms. Haley's (1963) description of the interpersonal dynamics involved in a classic case of handwashing compulsion illustrates how power in a relationship may accrue to a person manifesting symptomatology and how symptoms, as interpersonal events, may be used to define and control relationships. In Haley's case, a woman sought therapy because she felt compelled to wash her hands and to take showers numerous times a day. Exploring the problem with the woman and her husband (a couple who had recently emigrated from Germany to the United States), the practitioner found that they were engaged in a bitter struggle over this compulsion. The husband, tyrannical about all details of the couple's life, constantly demanded his own way and insisted that his wife respond obediently to him at all times. Trying to gain control over his wife's symptomatic behavior, the husband constantly forbade her to wash her hands, followed her around to make sure that she was not washing them, and timed her showers and rationed her soap. Although unable to openly oppose her husband on any issue—except the handwashing—the wife defeated her husband's maneuvers by pointing out that she had no control over her compulsion. Further, through this symptom, she was able to avoid responding to other requests he made of her. For example, the husband liked the kitchen clean and the dishes done promptly, but his wife could not do the dishes because, once she placed her hands in the dishwater, she was compelled to go on washing them. Further, although her husband insisted on a spotlessly clean house, she could not clean the house because she was busy washing her hands.

Through her handwashing compulsion, the wife gained the upper hand in her relationship with her husband, and as Haley points out, although the husband insisted on being master of his house, "He was dethroned by the simple washing of a pair of hands" (p. 14).

Children as well as adults may gain control in a family through extreme symptomatology. Such children receive at least momentary gratification through the attention they receive for their fits, withdrawal periods, runaways, psychotic episodes, and so on. Also, as persons who carry the labels "sick," "bad," or "different," these children require special consideration. Further, the role of deviant often exempts them from responsibilities and relieves them from the necessity of coping with reality beyond the limits that the family sets for them.

It should be noted that although a person with symptomatic behavior may have considerable leverage and power in a family, all members of the family tacitly support the perpetuation of symptoms through their own behavioral contributions to family patterns that have developed. Vogel and Bell (1960) astutely observe the role of parents in supporting the dysfunctional behavior of their children:

> In all instances, while the parents explicitly criticized the child and at times even punished him, they supported in some way, usually implicitly, the persistence of the very behavior which they criticized. This permission took various forms: failure to follow through on threats, delayed punishment, indifference to and acceptance of the symptom, unusual

interest in the child's symptom, or considerable secondary gratification offered the child because of this symptom.(p. 390)

Assessing Power   A number of factors, then, must be addressed in assessing with families the power base and the manner in which power is distributed. This may include who holds the "balance of power"; who, if anyone, is the formally designated leader; to what extent power is covertly held by members who have aligned to form a power bloc; and to what extent covert power accrues to individual members who are manifesting extreme symptomatology in the family. The role of a family's culture in determining the distribution of power, of course, must also be considered.

Keep in mind that family struggles over power issues and the resulting destructive coalitions that are formed are manifested in families' processes. Observation of family interaction often reveals "an affect-laden process in which coalitions are being proposed, accepted, modified, locked, tested, qualified, broken, rejected, and betrayed in a constant flowing process" (Sluzki, 1975, p. 69) as warring factions compete for power and for definition of the relationship (i.e., who has control over whom). Key information about these processes may be gleaned by keeping the following questions in mind when viewing family operations:

1. Who does what and who comments on it?
2. Who speaks for whom?
3. Who speaks first?
4. Who speaks at the same time as someone else?
5. Who interrupts whom?
6. Who agrees with whom?
7. Who does the most speaking?
8. Who decides who decides?
9. Whose ideas are usually adopted when the family engages in decision making?
10. Who seems to hold the ultimate authority for making decisions, regardless of who originated the ideas the family is considering?

Bear in mind that all families must address power issues and allocate power in some manner—it is the functionality of the power structure in meeting individual psychological needs and promoting the health of the system that must be determined in assessing this dimension of family functioning. Assessment questions that address the functionality of the power structure include:

1. Is the family's power structure stable, allowing the system to carry out its maintenance functions in an orderly manner, or does the power base shift as members compete for power?

2. Does the power base reside within the executive subsystem or within covert coalitions in the family?

3. Are members of the family content with the relative distribution of power?

Family Decision-Making Processes

Closely tied to issues of power is the family's style of decision making. Families range in extremes from leaderless groups in which no one has enough power to determine and direct activities or to organize decision-making processes to families in which virtually absolute power to make decisions is rigidly held by one member. Although effective deliberation and decision making are critical in determining the well-being of the system and its responsivity to individual family members, most families do not consciously select a modus operandi for making family decisions. Rather, the family's style of decision making usually evolves in the formative stages of development of the system, often patterned after decision-making approaches modeled by parents in the families of origin of the marital partners. Further, the persisting conflicts experienced by troubled families can often be traced largely to the inability of marital partners over the years to resolve, at a covert level, incompatible expectations (emanating from role models they have experienced) regarding the distribution of power and the manner in which decisions should be made in the family. As children are added to the system, they too may be pulled into the conflict as neither parent is fully successful in wresting power from the other.

In order to assess the functionality of decision-making processes found in families, it is important to understand vital ingredients that are inherent in effective problem solving with family systems:

1. Effective decision making requires open feedback and self-expression among members. Classifying all interpersonal systems as either closed or open, Satir (1967) contrasts these two modes in relation to the relative autonomy of individual members and their freedom to express themselves within these systems. Members of closed systems are expected to have the same opinions, feelings, and desires and, thus, must be very cautious about what they say. Open and congruent self-expression is viewed as deviant or "crazy" by other members of the system, and differences are treated as dangerous, requiring members to close themselves off from others in order to remain in the system. On the other hand, an open system permits its members to converse freely and relate to each other without fear of negative judgment. Differences are viewed as natural and welcomed by all. Further, members use such mechanisms as compromise, agreeing to disagree, or taking turns to negotiate and resolve differences. In the open system, members can say what they think and feel without fear of destroying themselves or others in the system. In systems that do not allow feedback regarding feelings, preferences, and opinions, members are stifled, pressured to ignore their own needs and wishes and to conform, without complaint, to maladaptive processes in the system. Without open feedback and self-expression, decision-making processes are not responsive to needs of individual members that emerge as the system goes through transitional developmental phases that demand adaptation to inner and outer stresses and crises.

2. Effective decision making requires a philosophical or attitudinal set on the part of each family member that all members of the system "count," that is, that each member's needs will be taken into consideration in decision making that will affect that member. Satir (1967) has identified four exhaustive solutions to what she calls the "self-other" dilemma in relationships that apply to decision-making processes in families:

a. In the first position, the person discounts the wants of self ("I count myself out"). Operating from this position, people handle differences by submitting, agreeing, placating, apologizing, or in other ways discounting their own needs (regardless of how they really feel) when negotiating with others.

b. In the second position, a person discounts the wants of the "other" ("I count you out"). In this position, persons may behave by finding fault, blaming, and disagreeing with others, thus leaving no room for negotiating differences.

c. In the third position, the person discounts the wants of both ("Let's count us both out"). Operating from this position, persons may exclude both themselves and others by being irrelevant, changing the subject, leaving the situation, or behaving in other ways that make it impossible to negotiate differences openly with others.

d. In the fourth position, a person takes into account the wants of other parties involved ("I count myself in but try to make room for others"). In this position, a person openly and clearly negotiates differences with others and permits or invites others to do the same.

Satir describes the fourth position as the only "growth-producing" solution to negotiation of differences between self and others. This alternative allows individual members to flourish while remaining a part of the system—and vitalizes and energizes the system itself. By contrast, the other three positions may promote individual survival at the expense of others in the family and cause conflict, intrigue, and resentment in the system that divert energies from productive tasks and block the family's developmental progress.

These positions can be viewed as interpersonal patterns or styles of individual family members that are consistently expressed in the family. In decision making (as well as other interpersonal events), individual family members and the family as a unit may "count in" some members and "count out" others. Before a family may become an optimally nurturing environment for individual growth, all members must be "counted in" in the sense that their needs are considered when important decisions affecting them are made in the family. Members of the family are likely to contribute productively when they know that every member "counts" and that needs, rather than power, are at issue in the decision-making process. In traditional patriarchal families, the issue of the wife's feeling "counted in" in the decision-making process (even if both spouses agree that the husband should have the final say) is of obvious importance. Further, although children should have considerably less power than parents in a family and often should not be vested with decision-making authority in problem-solving processes, they should have the opportunity to express themselves or to give feedback in relation to decisions that affect them. Examples of such decisions include activities in which the family engages, responsibilities assigned them in the home, and personal leisure time activities in which they engage.

3. Effective decision making requires members of a family system to think in terms of needs rather than solutions. Members of families are often conditioned by life experiences to see problem solutions in terms of dichotomies—"either we do things your way or mine; one of us has to lose"— a narrow approach to problem solving that centers on competing solutions, preventing negotiation and compromise. "Do what I want, think what I

think, feel what I feel"—in other words, "Do things my way"—is often the position taken by individual family members as they attempt to coerce or coax others to adopt their solutions to life's problems. Operating from the principle that love and total agreement go together, they, in effect, take the position, "If you love me, you will do what I want. If you don't, you are bad" (Satir, 1967). Taking a trivial example of a couple attempting to negotiate differences when A wants to go out for a hamburger and B wants to go out for a chicken dinner, Satir describes (p. 14) how persons with dysfunctional communication styles disagree:

a. We find them vacillating and postponing: "Let's decide later what to eat."

b. We find them trying to coerce: "We are going to eat hamburgers!"

c. We find them trying to delude each other: "They are both food, so let's eat hamburger."

d. We find them trying to undermine each other: "You don't really like chicken" or "You must be crazy to like chicken."

e. Always we find them accusing and evaluating morally: "You are bad and selfish for not wanting to eat hamburger. You never do what I want. You have mean intentions toward me."

A couple with functional styles of disagreeing, on the other hand, would be more likely to solve their problems by taking turns, by finding an alternative that pleases them both, or by going their separate ways—one to eat chicken, the other to eat hamburger. In focusing immediately on "win-lose" solutions when there is a problem, family members prevent any creative and conflict-free negotiations that emanate from and meet the needs of all involved. Needs include basic conditions (e.g., to be trusted, to be considered) that must be addressed in order to arrive at a satisfactory solution. In the preceding example, for instance, a basic need of the couple may be to spend the evening together, and a viable solution must necessarily take this need into consideration.

4. Effective decision making requires the ability of family members to generate alternatives, which is closely parallel to group brainstorming in which members generate options, no matter how far-fetched, without criticism or censorship. Individuals manifest this skill when they draw from a repertoire of ideas that is not merely variations on a single theme but rather different categories of solutions to a given problem. The issue is whether the individual thinks in terms of options: "I could do this, or that, or I could even do that" or, in contrast, characteristically forecloses without considering alternative routes (Spivack, Platt, & Shure, 1976, p. 5).

In the assessment process, then, one of your tasks may be to determine to what extent families identify alternatives in contrast to quarreling over competing solutions.

5. Effective decision making requires ability on the part of family members to weigh alternatives. Decisions may be made in families after information gathering, input by members, and deliberation; or decisions may be made impulsively without gathering or weighing relevant information or without considering the needs of family members in relation to possible solutions.

6. Effective decision making also requires that the family organize to carry out decisions through assignments to individual members. Planning to implement a decision is just as important as making the decision initially. Some systems are so disorganized and chaotic that members have great difficulty either in making a decision or implementing it. In other systems, members lack motivation to carry out decisions because their input was not elicited or considered in the decision-making process. Thus, even when decisions have been made in the system, the process may break down at the point of implementation. Ascertaining the extent to which families can implement as

well as make decisions is a key task in assessing family functioning.

7. Effective decision making also requires the system to allow for negotiation and adjustment of earlier decisions based on new information and emerging individual and family needs. Some systems, of course, are much more responsive and flexible in relation to this item than others.

In assessing the family's decision-making style, then, you should elicit information and view the processes you observe in relation to the preceding criteria. Keep in mind that you are looking for functional as well as dysfunctional patterns in each of these areas. Keep in mind, too, that the decision-making skills we have described encourage optimum family functioning as it is perceived in Western culture. These decision-making skills are usually lacking in troubled families and are often underdeveloped even in well-functioning families in Western culture. Such skills are also often lacking in families from different ethnic backgrounds, for many cultural groups have no frame of reference for "joint decision making," and, in fact, espouse cultural values prescribing behavior that is in direct contradiction to the methods of decision making we discuss here and in Chapter 13. Including family members in decision making and assuring that the needs of all are satisfied is a Western culture ideal advocated by helping professionals and social scientists. Although we espouse the need for families to learn skills in decision making, practitioners must assess whether introducing these skills to family members will facilitate family functioning or cause family disruption by disturbing patterns that are deeply engrained and culturally sanctioned. Hence, collaboration with families in the assessment process is essential.

Family Affect and Range of Feelings Expressed

In their authoritative research on characteristics of distressed and optimally functioning families,

Lewis et al. (1976) stress that feelings expressed in a family are intimately related to the structure of the system. In systems that have rigid, inflexible boundaries, unclear structure, and the lack of differentiation of members, the prevailing mood may be one of despair, hopelessness, depression, anxiety, hostility, guilt, cynicism, or apathy. Commenting on this phenomenon in a later volume, Beavers (1977) speculates on the reason for the negative affective climate that permeates such severely dysfunctional families:

> I believe *expectations*, that is, the results one expects from human encounters, are central to these observations. Severely dysfunctional family members believe that encounters inevitably produce a destructive result, that human interaction is necessarily oppositional. To appreciate this expectancy is to understand the result of disturbed communication patterns: the prevention of genuine encounter. It also explains the pervasive, unpleasant feeling tone, since the choice is either to avoid conflict and to be alone or to engage in encounters that threaten the self, relationships, and the family system. (p. 50)

By contrast, Beavers points out that optimally functioning families have a permeating atmosphere of optimism, empathy, warmth and affect, goodwill, and positive emotional tone, based on the expectation that human encounters produce satisfaction and that responsiveness to others and clear expressions of feelings will be rewarded.

Although observation of the system as a whole will reveal a "family character" in regard to mood or tone, expressions of individual affect may vary within the range tolerated by the family system. Further, individuals from different families develop diverse styles in relation to the range and intensity of feelings expressed. Some individuals, for example, seem emotionally numb or almost void of feelings, experiencing great difficulty "getting in touch with" any inner emotions. Other persons may readily express one particular kind of feeling, such as anger or feelings of despair or guilt, but not be able to reveal tender and vulnerable feelings. Still other persons are able to experience and

express a wide range of feelings with little difficulty. While some individuals are placid and slow to register emotions, others respond intensively to the slightest stress or turn of events. While some persons are "incurable optimists," others are intractably depressed or pessimistic or experience extreme mood swings between optimism and despair. Culture, of course, plays a key role in determining a person's expressiveness, as in the case of many Native Americans who are taught to carefully monitor their anger and not express it openly for fear of hurting others (Tafoya, 1989).

The extent to which family members are able to express caring and love for each other is a vital dimension of assessment. Clients vary dramatically in their ability to "own" or to express verbally their tender feelings of caring to other family members. For instance, in response to a question of whether she ever told her daughter that she loved her, one client declared emphatically, "I could never do that!" Manifesting caring through touch or other nonverbal manifestations is also very difficult for some clients. Many parents, for instance, rarely touch or hug their children once they are old enough to dress, feed, and care for themselves. Since members of family systems vary in their ability to tolerate and express verbal and nonverbal affection and in their preferred modes of expressing tender feelings, you will need to weigh a family's style in relation to the following questions to gauge the amount of change that may be necessary or feasible:

1. To what extent are care and affection expressed verbally and nonverbally and by whom?

2. To what extent are caring behaviors perceived and/or appreciated by intended recipients?

3. To what extent are individual members dissatisfied with low levels of caring messages from others in the family?

4. To what extent do individual members of the family feel they would like to increase caring messages to others or to be the recipients of such messages?

5. How flexible are individual members and the system as a whole in making adjustments in this area? What are the tolerable limits?

Family affect and the range of feelings expressed can be quantitatively affected by the presence of clinical depression in one or more members. Angry outbursts and irritability, mood swings, excessive emotionality, or gloomy or overly elated mood states, for example, are among the prevalent symptoms of unipolar or bipolar depression. In assessing such characteristics, the practitioner should not assume that they are simply features of individual or family affect, or that family members have good reason to be depressed and thus depression will subside with effective treatment. In cases in which depression is an inherited biological disorder, without pharmacological intervention therapy may simply produce better-informed and sometimes better-adjusted but still depressed persons. Even in cases in which depression is situationally caused, it may linger for months or years even with the best of treatment. This is because the depression becomes physical and somewhat self-perpetuating in nature, i.e., under chronic stress a malfunction in the brain's regulation of the chemicals or neurotransmitters occurs, causing a short-circuiting of the electrical impulses that transfer information in the brain. This chemical process is not easily reversed, particularly when the intense environmental stressors that impelled the client to seek treatment remain unabated.

In assessment, practitioners must recognize that depression of one or more family members may severely affect family functioning, being capable of eroding communication and driving schisms in relationships. In the case of genetic depression, several family members can carry the disorder, and the distress of individuals can severely increase family conflict and tension. Thus, as Rauch et al. (1991) indicate, screening for affective disorders should be a routine part of the initial assessment of families, and practitioners should know how to monitor mood-disordered clients (and/or their significant others).

Family Goals

The family is a social organization in which members typically cooperate and coordinate their efforts in order to achieve certain goals. According to Briar (1964), family goals spring from two primary sources. First, families usually adopt and have in common goals established by society; that is, socializing children, transferring major cultural patterns essential to the maintenance of society, and meeting certain personal needs of family members. Second, marital partners bring individual goals with them into the family.

Goals that families espouse may be openly recognized by the family or they may be covert and even beyond the family's awareness. "We want to put all the kids through college" or "We want to retire by the time Ted's 45 years old" are examples of explicit goals held by a family. Covert or unrecognized goals that may have a profound influence on a family system might be, "We have to be at the top of the social ladder" or "We have to present the picture of being an ideal family." Briar points out that goals often are not explicit, and that when families are in crisis, the system's goals and their ordering often become more apparent, for at these times families may be forced to choose between competing goals and values. Briar observes, for example, that a wide variety of responses would be observed if one were to study a number of families confronted with a sudden and drastic reduction in income:

> One family, for example, will give first priority to the expenditure of its limited financial resources to maintaining a very adequate diet for the children and will sacrifice other things in order to do so. Another family will sacrifice other things, even food, in order to make sure that the children are exceptionally well dressed. Such differences, which at first seem erratic and even irrational, often are comprehensible when the prior goals and aspirations of the family are understood. (p. 250)

In most families, members vary in regard to the goals each considers important and the value each attaches to common goals. As in any organization, a family functions best when there is a high degree of consensus concerning family goals and provision within the system to negotiate and to take into consideration the unique needs, aims, and wishes of individuals. Briar, in fact, observes that, "The degree of consensus which develops among family members regarding the ranking of family goals can be a crucial factor in the family's ability to cope appropriately with crises" (p. 248). Because goals often are not explicit, however, differences among family members in relation to major goals and expectations may not be worked through, creating dissension and disappointment within the group. Further, because of pressures from the most powerful or influential members of the group, the family may give lip service to particular goals, although several or the majority of the members may not agree in principle with them. These families then become particularly vulnerable to breakdown under stress.

Many interactional patterns in families evolve in part to achieve goals. Briar, in fact, observes that if practitioners examine the family's interactions without considering the goals of the system, they may miss the meaning of patterns they identify. To illustrate this and other points that we have discussed throughout this section, consider the following case example of a covertly held goal around which family energies are extensively organized.

Case Example

In the White family, an overriding goal of the family was to "keep the house clean," a goal set and maintained by Mrs. White, who felt constant inner pressure to keep her house tidy in order to avoid criticism from her own mother and other relatives. Often depressed, Mrs. White spent much of her time in her room and participated only infrequently in the house-cleaning; however, she kept constant pressure on her younger daughters, ages 14 and 16, to keep the house clean and orderly. To her two older girls, attending school and holding down part-time jobs, however, she gave permis-

sion to participate only minimally in housecleaning chores because "they're tired when they come home and need time to relax and study." Seeing the older girls often excused from housecleaning (even when they left messes), the two younger girls were extremely resentful and often complained bitterly to their father about the situation. Further, they attacked the older girls with accusations such as "You don't act like you're members of the family" or "You don't care about anybody around here." Assuming the role of their absent mother, they monitored the older sisters, pointing out the messes they had created and ordering them to clean them up, which the older girls always refused to do. Feeling mistreated and misunderstood, the older daughters defended themselves and counterattacked by name-calling and threatening. Trying to maintain peace, Mr. White consistently served as a mediator between the warring factions and often picked up or cleaned the house to avoid the inevitable disputes that would arise when chores were assigned to his daughters. Whenever his wife intermittently emerged from her room, Mr. White also felt compelled to serve as mediator between her and the daughters because she usually found something out of order and would angrily blame one of the younger daughters for "not doing her job."

In our illustration, all of the White family adhered to the mother's goal of keeping the house clean. Because the younger girls experienced much more pressure than the older girls, however, more of their energies were invested in carrying out or in persuading other members of the family to implement this goal. The unequal distribution of pressure in the family had shaped the alliances that were in place at the time this family initially sought therapy. Only as the practitioner carefully explored and clarified the family goal and rules associated with it were family members able to recognize the extent to which their behaviors revolved around this goal.

In summary, then, we offer the following questions to assist you in assessing family goals for both strengths and difficulties:

1. To what extent do clear goals guide the family organization?

2. To what extent are members aware of the overriding goals of the family?

3. To what extent is there shared consensus among members regarding major goals and the priorities assigned to these goals?

4. To what extent is family conflict caused by the lack of consensus regarding primary goals of individual family members?

5. How functional are commonly held goals in meeting the needs of individual members and promoting the well-being of the group as a whole?

6. To what extent are dysfunctional interactional patterns related to covert goals espoused by the family?

To the extent that goals are clear, that consensus exists regarding major goals, and that goals serve the needs of the individual members and of the group, families manifest key strengths on this dimension of family functioning.

As a word of caution, practitioners must view the family's goals in the family's cultural context and avoid the hazard of assessing the goals against those deemed desirable in Western culture. For example, Montiel (1973, p.25) cites biased descriptions of "deficiencies" of Mexican American families found in literature that is culture- and class-bound: "Parents indulge male children, which limits their desire to achieve; do not encourage independence; teach their children lax habits; do not stress education; are oriented to the present; speak only Spanish; and think too much about their own misfortunes." To avoid such biased evaluations, then, it is important not to view a family as deficient because it does not espouse mainstream American goals. Rather, it is important to determine the goals of such families and to assess them in the context of their cultural reference groups.

Family Myths and Cognitive Patterns

Earlier in this chapter, we discussed family rules and emphasized how they pervade all aspects of family life. Rules have both a behavioral and a cognitive component; that is, the behaviors manifested by family members flow from and are inextricably related to shared cognitive perceptions or myths about each other, the family unit, and the world at large. These shared perceptions may be congruent with the views of neutral outside observers or may be distortions of reality, that is, ill-founded, self-deceptive, well-systematized beliefs uncritically held by members. Such distortions are often part of the beliefs or myths subscribed to by the family that help shape, maintain, and justify interactional patterns and relationships, as the following case excerpt illustrates.

Over the past four years, 10-year-old Jeffrey Richards has been in constant difficulty with his teachers at school because of open defiance of classroom rules, argumentative behavior, and physical skirmishes with other children. As a result of these problems, Mr. and Mrs. Richards have changed Jeffrey's enrollment from one school to another several times during the past three years. Sharing the cognitive set that "the world is out to get us," Mr. and Mrs. R view teachers and principals alike as punitive and vindictive and their son as "misunderstood." Given this perceptual set, they regard each school contact as a battleground in which they must argue, protest their rights, and defend their son. Continually bombastic, they alienate school personnel, pushing them to take extreme stands on issues that might otherwise be mutually negotiated if the parents were amenable. Further, the parents' constant negative and angry comments at home regarding Jeffrey's teachers and his school reinforce and foster their son's negative classroom behavior.

In the preceding example, the dysfunctional behaviors and cognitive processes of the Richards family are mutually reinforcing. The myths determine the behavior, which predictably elicits negative responses from school personnel. In turn, the family's negative encounters with the school reinforce and confirm their perceptions of the world as dangerous and their view that authoritarian figures cannot be trusted and are out to get them.

Other myths may also prevail in family systems, shaping the behavior and interactions among family members or with outsiders, including the following:

"Things are permanent and unchangeable in our family. No matter what we do, we are powerless to change our circumstances. We are victims of fate."

"Mother doesn't care about the kids; Dad does."

"Problems in the family will take care of themselves."

"It's a sign of weakness to apologize."

"It's important to get even with people who hurt you."

"People (or a certain category of people) are no good."

Among the most destructive myths are persistent beliefs that single out one member as being different or deviant from the group, causing untold damage in human development. Assigned labels such as sick, bad, crazy, or lazy, a family member often becomes the scapegoat for the family, carrying the blame for problems and obscuring the fact that other members also carry responsibility for transactions and communications that go awry.

In many families (even relatively healthy ones!), members may carry permanent labels, such as "black sheep of the family," "intellectual one," "baby of the family," "strict parent," "family pet," "clown," "good child," or "dumb." These labels stereotype roles of family members, causing other members to relate to them on the basis of a presumed single characteristic and to overlook a wide range of attributes, attitudes, and feelings. With only a narrow range of behavioral options open to them, the growth of these members may be stifled. It should be noted that even positive labels (e.g., talented, handsome, bright) may separate and estrange a member of the family from others, for other members may resent the inordinate amount of attention, praise, and recognition accorded to the labeled member, whom they perceive as the favored one or pet of the family.

Note that culture determines many of the cognitive patterns held by families. Cuban immigrants, for example, show a significantly greater fatalistic orientation than Anglo-Americans, frequently using linguistic expressions that allude to destiny, life, luck, God's will, and "what was written" (Queralt, 1984, p. 118). Just as Cubans have a fatalistic orientation, each cultural group has characteristics that influence members' view of their world. Noninterference as a way of being, a value characteristically held by Native Americans and Alaska Native families, alters their perception of the world (Attneave, 1982). Deference to authority, a cultural value espoused by Asians, also influences the cognitive patterns developed by members of that culture.[7]

Family Roles

Each person in a family carries many roles that are integrated into the family's structure and represent certain expected, permitted, and forbidden behaviors. Although family roles may be assigned on the basis of legal or chronological status, traditionally in the Western culture many roles have been delegated to family members on the basis of gender. Thought to be more aggressive than women, males have been viewed as more suited for instrumental roles, such as earning money or making decisions. Women, by contrast, have been thought to be more cooperative, emotional, and tender and suited for expressive activities, such as providing nurturance, caring for children, expressing affection, and the like. However, forces associated with the sexual revolution that have taken place during the past several decades are changing and equalizing the roles and status of the sexes, freeing both men and women to assume roles once thought to be biologically determined and to be the territorial prerogative of one sex or the other.

In many marriages, the pervasive movement to

equalize sexual roles has called into question traditional perceptions of marital roles, particularly in families in which previously unemployed wives have entered the work force. Consequently, many couples have had to change their living styles drastically. Couples have coped with these profound changes in various ways, some clinging tenaciously to traditional roles despite significant changes in their life situations and the world around them. Other marital partners have welcomed role changes and have made marked accommodations and changes in role definitions. Still other partners have experienced major disruptions in their relationships, culminating in severe conflicts and even divorce.

The extreme fatigue women experience in dual-career couples because of role overload is emphasized by Hochschild (1989). Of her eight-year research with dual career couples, she observes: "I discovered that women worked roughly fifteen hours longer each week than men. Over a year, they worked an extra month of twenty-four-hour days a year. Over a dozen years, it was an extra year of twenty-four hour days" (p. 3). In her study, women "talked about sleep the way a hungry person talks about food" (p. 9). Hochschild documents the intense strain on marriage in which men "helped out" but did not carry an equal share of the role load.

The stresses upon women in particular in today's world are further discussed by Larsen (1991) in *I'm a Day Late and a Dollar Short... And It's Okay! A Woman's Survival Guide for the '90s*. Maintaining that women are driven by unconscious, embedded cultural conditioning emanating from the traditional woman's role, Larsen identifies six characteristics of women who try to do too much too well: the Caretaker, the Juggler, the Perfectionist, the Guilt Sponge, the Pleaser, and the Depleted Woman. Unrecognized and unchecked, these characteristics cause epidemic stress, burnout, and depression in women.

Same-sex couples also experience particular difficulties with role definition, having very different sets of dynamics and issues than their heterosexual counterparts, as Brown and Zimmer (1986) note:

> In a same-sex couple, both partners possess the benefits and drawbacks of an essentially similar pattern of gender-role socialization. Whatever complementarity of roles that such socialization may create in a heterosexual couple is absent in most same-sex relationships. Rather, both partners are well-socialized members of their own, same gender. (p. 450)

Dealing with gender-role socialization multiplied by two causes role confusion in such couples. In addition, in the process of rejecting both traditional female and male roles, some lesbian couples are likely to experience more conflicts when it comes to the expression of behaviors in relationships that are typically gender-role determined for heterosexual adults (Brown & Zimmer, 1986).[8]

In accurately assessing the extent to which role performance and definitions are factors in problems of families, you must consider many factors including those associated with the sex-role revolution. To assist you in considering these various factors, we provide the following list of questions that bear on role assessment in families:

1. To what extent are role assignments in the family made on the basis of gender rather than factors such as abilities, interests, and available time of individual members to perform various roles? Assigned by gender, marital roles may be inequitable in relation to the available time spouses have to perform them. Further, marital problems are often caused by one or both partners operating from a marital "contract" made years ago specifying "traditional" roles that are no longer functional in light of changing family circumstances. "You said you'd never go to work!" or "You said I'd never have to work!" are common indictments made by marital partners where the wife either wants or is forced to seek employment.

2. How clearly defined are roles in the family? Role strain may occur between marital partners when

roles are ambiguous or too global, fostering dissension as a result of differing perceptions of expected role performance. Further, as we pointed out earlier, role boundaries between children and parents may be blurred. In extreme cases, such roles may even be reversed. Boszormenyi-Nagy and Spark (1973) refer to this process as parentification of children, a situation in which children are forced to take care of childlike parents and/or younger siblings at the sacrifice of their own childhood.

Role strain may also occur when there are changes in ordinal positions of children in new stepfamilies. Visher and Visher (1988) observe that children often suffer role loss in stepfamilies where the "household composition may change every day of the week" (p. 100). Losses are incurred in part because certain role expectations tend to accompany a child's position in the family with, for example, the oldest expected to be mature and responsible and the youngest expecting to be more "cared for" than the older siblings. Likewise, roles in stepfamilies are ambiguous for everyone and individuals are pulled by competing loyalties (Visher & Visher, 1988).

3. How satisfied are marital partners with their prescribed roles, and to what extent is each willing to consider adjustments when dissatisfaction is a key factor in family problems? Further, how flexible is the entire family system in readjusting roles in response to everyday pressures and changing circumstances? Role dysfunction may occur as members are pressed into rigidly defined roles that drastically restrict their range of behaviors. Rigidly defined roles place family members in a bind, for they must either accommodate, sacrificing their individuality in the process, or rebel, losing favor and alienating themselves from other family members. Rigid role prescriptions offer families little opportunity to adjust flexibly to outer pressures. Further, ill-defined roles make it difficult for systems to adjust adequately to changing circumstances or to mobilize under crisis situations.

4. How adequately do spouses perform in their designated roles as marital partner and parent?

5. To what extent do one or both marital partners receive messages from significant others outside the family (parents, other relatives, friends) regarding what their role definitions "ought to be"? What effect does this input have on the system?

6. To what extent are pressures and stresses caused in the family by role overload, a state of affairs caused when marital partners play too many roles at home and at work for the time and energy they have available?

As you consider the preceding guidelines in assessing the functioning of a family, you will probably note a number of family strengths. Marital partners may have clearly defined their roles, for example, and be functioning quite adequately as parents. Or if partners are dissatisfied with their roles, they may recognize the need to make adjustments during marital therapy and readily try to accommodate to the other partner. Our point is that in the assessment process it is important to recognize and accredit the many strengths that couples and families may manifest with respect to role functioning—strengths that may otherwise be obscured by their presenting difficulties.

As you assess the processes of any family, you must necessarily take into consideration the role of culture in determining the definition of roles and the distribution of labor in the family, for each culture has different expectations or norms concerning male–female roles. Wong (1983), for instance, describes female and male roles in Samoa:

In Samoa, men are dominant in rank and women are subordinate such that women "stay put" on their home grounds and men move about. ...The women are assigned work which is considered light (mat-weaving) and men perform work which is heavy (preparing the umu). Women's tasks are usually focused around the household compound or village center (housekeeping and sanitation), whereas the activities of men are away from the household compound and village center (hunting and plantation work). (p. 28)

Because each culture has its own definition of male–female roles, practitioners must determine these roles for ethnic minority families, assess their "goodness of fit" with the needs of family members, and determine to what extent families are amenable to change culturally determined roles that adversely affect family functioning.

Communication Styles of Family Members

One theme that cuts across many cultural groups is that of patterns discouraging the open expression of feelings. Although Western culture espouses the value that openness and honesty are the best policies, the reality is that most people have considerable difficulty in asserting themselves or in confronting others, particularly in ways that are facilitative rather than destructive. Because of strongly embedded norms, people in many other cultures are much less open than even those in Western society. In Asian culture, for example, free participation and exchange of opinions contradict Asian values of humility and modesty (Ho, 1987). In Hawaiian culture, "it is totally unacceptable to resolve conflicts openly and through confrontation" (Young, 1980, p. 14). The Irish, too, have communication patterns that differ from the Western ideal as McGoldrick (1982b) observes:

> The Irish often fear being pinned down and may use their language and manner to avoid it. The affinity of the Irish for verbal innuendo, ambiguity, and metaphor have led the English to coin the phrase "talking Irish" to describe the Irish style of both communicating and not communicating at the same time. (p. 315)

Problems experienced by some families, then, may partially arise because of cultural prohibitions against openness, and in some instances, practitioners can assist clients to understand their cultural norms and make decisions as to whether they are willing to change communication patterns and

styles that negatively affect relationships. In other instances, practitioners may need to work more subtly to bring about enough openness in the system to promote the growth of family members. Falicov (1982) describes such an indirect approach in working with Mexican Americans:

> When feelings are subtly elicited by the therapist, Mexican Americans respond much more openly than when they are asked to describe and explain their feelings and reactions. An experiential communication approach with emphasis on "telling it like it is" or "baring one's soul" or interpretations about nonverbal behavior will be threatening insofar as it challenges inhibitions about personal disclosure and supports symmetrical interactions. (p. 148)

Whether or not family communication patterns are culturally influenced or determined, they may be faulty, causing significant problems and pain for family members. Practitioners thus must be prepared to assess the impact of a family's communication styles upon the problems of members. To do so, they must be aware of the complexities of communication and prepared to assess the functionality of members' communication styles across a number of dimensions, as illustrated in the following discussion.

Congruence and Clarity of Communication

Family members convey messages through verbal and nonverbal channels and qualify those messages through other verbal and nonverbal messages. A task of practitioners, therefore, is to assess the *congruency* of communications, that is, whether there is correspondence between the various verbal and nonverbal elements of messages. According to Satir (1967) and other communication theorists, messages may be qualified at any one of three communication levels:

1. *Verbal level:* When people explain the intent of their messages, they are speaking at a metacommunication level. For example:

   "I was trying to see if you agreed with me."

   "I thought you were feeling bad, and I was trying to comfort you."

Contradictory communications occur when two or more oppositional messages are sent in sequence via the same verbal channel:

"I love you…I hate you."

"You should follow my advice…You need to make your own decisions."

2. *Nonverbal level:* People qualify their communications through many nonverbal modes, including gesture, facial expressions, tone of voice, posture, intensity of eye contact, and the like. Nonverbal messages may:

   a. Reinforce verbal messages.

      A mother smiles at her child and says, "I love you."

      A husband says to his wife that he is pleased that she has found a new job, and his countenance conveys his genuine pleasure.

   b. Contradict or modify verbal expressions.

      A lover says, "Come closer, darling, let's make love," and then stiffens.

      With a bored look on his face, a friend says, "Of course I'm interested in what you've been doing lately."

   c. Contradict or modify nonverbal expressions.

      A person behaves seductively but pulls back when the other makes affectional overtures.

      A visitor puts on his coat to leave and then lingers in the doorway.

3. *Contextual level:* The situation in which communication occurs also reinforces or disqualifies the verbal and nonverbal expressions of a speaker. For example, a mother leans over to her misbehaving child during church services and threatens, "If you don't stop that, I'm going to spank you *right now!*" The context or situation in which she sent the message, then, inherently disqualifies her verbal expression.

Functional communicators identify discrepancies between levels of communication and seek clarification when a person's words and expressions are disparate. They also are receptive to feedback and clarify their own communications when they have sent incongruent messages. Vital to assessment, then, is the task of ascertaining the extent to which there is congruence between the *verbal*, *nonverbal*, and *contextual* levels of messages on the part of individuals in a family system. The more distressed the system and the more symptomatic the behavior, the more likely that surface messages are contradicted by other communications that leave family members bewildered, angry, hurt, and in binds from which they see no way of extricating themselves.

In addition to considering the congruence of communications, it is important to assess the *clarity* of messages. Laing (1965) uses the term *mystification* to describe how some families befuddle or mask communications and obscure the nature and source of disagreements and conflicts in their relationships. Mystification of communications can be accomplished by myriad kinds of maneuvers, including disqualifying another person's experience ("You must be crazy if you think that"), addressing responses to no one in particular when the intent of the speaker is to relay a message to a certain person, employing evasive responses that effectively obscure knowledge of the speaker, or utilizing sarcastic responses that have multiple meanings and are hard to decipher (Lewis et al., 1976). A more exhaustive listing of response categories that represent obstacles to communication and may serve to cloud communications is provided and delineated in the following section.

Barriers to Communication   In Chapter 7, we identified a number of barriers to communication that, when utilized by practitioners, block client communication and impede therapeutic progress. Likewise, clients often repetitively respond with these and other similarly destructive responses in their communications with others, preventing meaningful exchanges and creating conflict and tension in relationships. In the following list, we include categorical responses that obstruct open communication and prevent genuine encounters in relationships:

1. Prematurely shifting the subject or avoiding topics.
2. Overgeneralizing.

3. Asking excessive questions.

4. Sympathizing, excusing, or giving false reassurance.

5. "Mind reading," diagnosing, interpreting.

6. Dwelling on negative historical events in a relationship.

7. Underresponding.

8. Failing to express opinions.

9. Verbally dominating interaction.

10. Speaking in a categorical, "black-and-white," "I'm-right-you're-wrong" manner.

11. Agreeing or disagreeing excessively.

12. Giving advice frequently.

13. Negatively evaluating, blaming, name-calling, or criticizing.

14. Directing, ordering, threatening, admonishing.

15. Using caustic humor, excessive kidding, or teasing.

Assessment of problematic communication of couples and families must also include behaviors on a nonverbal level including, for instance, glaring, turning away from a family member, turning red in the face, fidgeting, shifting posture, pointing a finger, raising the voice, looking with menacing expressions or with expressions of disgust or disdain. As we emphasized in the previous section, the practitioner also needs to be aware of discrepancies between verbal and nonverbal levels of communication.

All families have communication barriers within their conversational repertoires. Members of some families, however, monitor their own communications and adjust their manner of responding when they have had a negative impact on another person. Indeed, such families have "rules" that prevent many kinds of negative communications, for example, "We do not yell or call people names in our family," or "It is important to listen attentively when someone is talking to you." Other families have destructive entrenched styles of communication that pervade many of their exchanges, and members manifest little awareness of their aversive styles. Further, members of these families tend to assume little responsibility for the negative impact of their communications upon others and resist giving up destructive modes of communication in favor of others that are more facilitative. As you observe the communication styles of families, then, it is important to assess: (1) the presence of patterned negative communication, (2) the pervasiveness of such negative patterns, and (3) the relative ability of individual members of the system to modify habituated communication styles.

In addition to assessing the preceding factors, it is also vital to ascertain the various combinations of styles that occur repetitively as individual members of the system relate and react. For instance, in a marital relationship, one partner may frequently dominate, criticize, or accuse the other, whereas the other may defend, apologize, placate, or agree, as adapted from the following exchange between two marital partners (Larsen, 1982):

Wife: You never spend time with Jody [*their child*]. It's more important to you to ride the internet with your computer and talk to people you don't even know.

Husband: I do spend time with her [*gives example*]. You just don't ever notice.

Wife: I do notice. You spend precious little time with her. You can hardly wait to get back to your computer.

Husband: Last Saturday I spent several hours with her. [*Begins to elaborate on how he spent the time.*]

In the preceding exchange, the wife consistently attacks the husband, who just as consistently defends his position, thus manifesting a "fault-defend" pattern of marital communication (Thomas, 1977). Such patterns that involve exchanges of different types of behavior have been designated as complementary patterns. In such instances, the conflictual issues or content discussed changes, but the stylized categories of communication of each partner and the manner in which they orchestrate their scenario remains unchanged. Further, repetitions of the same type of partner-to-partner interchanges will be manifested across many other areas of the couple's interaction.

The thematic configurations that occur in marital communication are limited in number and vary from couple to couple. For instance, rather than the fault-defend pattern just illustrated, spouses may engage in reciprocal or symmetrical patterns in which each attacks, blames, and continually finds fault with one another, i.e., a fault-fault pattern. Another marital pair may "collude" by talking only about superficial matters or matters extraneous to the relationship, thereby consistently avoiding disagreements or openly sharing feelings or complaints.

Assessing the communications of entire families is much more complex than assessing couple communication because of the greater number of relationships involved. Each person in the family has stylized ways of communicating that interface in patterned ways with the thematic communications of other family members. For example, a father may continually serve as a spokesperson or "mind reader" for others in the family (e.g., "You don't really feel that way" or "Randy, you're not hungry: You just like to eat"). Stylized reactions of family members to the father's patterned behavior may range from objections to the mind-reading activity ("That's not how I feel!") to nonverbal withdrawal (e.g., turning away from the father, slumping in chair), or tacit approval ("We always see eye to eye").

Receiver Skills A third critical dimension of communication is the degree of receptivity or openness of family members to the inner thoughts and feelings of other members in the system. Receptivity is manifested by the use of certain "receiving skills," which we will discuss shortly. Before considering these, however, it should be stressed that, in severely disturbed families, members rarely validate through attentive, supportive, or encouraging responses the unique perceptions and responses of others. Rather, the reactions of members are often in the form of ridicule, negative evaluation or depreciation of character, or other critical or disparaging remarks that consistently punish or invalidate the expression of personal thoughts and feelings of members. In such families, members also engage frequently in "dual monologues"; that is, they communicate simultaneously without acknowledging the responses of others. In healthy families, by contrast, members invite, welcome, and acknowledge the views and perceptions of each other. Members also feel free to express agreement or disagreement openly, knowing that even though so doing may sometimes spark conflict or argument, their rights to varying perceptions of events are protected within the system.

When comparing processes of optimally functioning families with those of troubled families, it becomes evident that the former possess several categories of verbal and nonverbal responses that are noticeably absent in the latter. Included in these responses are messages that convey understanding, demonstrate respect for the uniqueness of the sender's experience, and invite further expression and exploration. Facilitative responses that convey such understanding and acceptance are as follows:

1. Physical attending (i.e., direct eye contact, receptive body posture, attentive facial expressions).

2. "Listening" or paraphrasing responses by family members that restate in fresh words the essence of a speaker's message (for example, "You seem to be saying that ...," or "I sense you're feeling...").

3. Responses by receivers of messages that elicit clarification of messages (e.g., "I'm not sure what you meant. Will you tell me again?" "Am I right in assuming you meant...?").

4. Brief responses that prompt further elaboration by the speaker ("Oh," "I see," "Tell me more.").

In assessing communication styles of families, you must gauge the extent to which individual members (and the group at large) utilize the facilitative categories of communication identified in the preceding list. Many distressed families almost entirely lack these response categories in their communication repertoires. Fortunately, educative interventions can be employed to assist members to develop these communication skills.

Sender Skills   A fourth critical dimension of communication is the extent to which members of families can share their inner thoughts and feelings with others in the system. Lewis et al. (1976) refer to this quality as "I-ness," that is, "the ability of individual family members to express themselves clearly as feeling, thinking, acting, valuable, and separate individuals and to take responsibility for thoughts, feelings, and actions" (p. 57). Operationalized, "I-ness" involves messages in the first person (commonly referred to as "I" messages) that openly and congruently reveal either pleasant or unpleasant feelings, thoughts, or reactions experienced by the speaker— "I (feel, think, want) _____ because_____."Healthy families allow members to be candid, open, and congruent. Feelings are shared freely, and people can apologize and admit mistakes. By contrast, in disturbed families, communications are characteristically indirect, vague, and guarded, and individuals fail to take responsibility for feelings, thoughts, or their own participation in events. Rather, members of these families are likely to use "you" messages that obscure or deny responsibility for the speaker's feelings or attribute responsibility for the feelings to others (e.g., "You've got me so rattled, I forgot"). Such messages are often replete with injunctions (shoulds and oughts) concerning another's behavior or negatively evaluate the receiver of the message (e.g., "You're really lazy, Jenny" or "You shouldn't feel that way.").

Responses That Acknowledge Strength and Achievement and Accredit Growth   Critical to the development of high self-esteem in individual family members are messages from others that consistently validate a person's worth and potential. Such responses are rare in most troubled family systems. Rather, the communication repertoires of such families are characterized by constant negative messages that put down, evaluate, blame, attack, criticize, or otherwise humiliate or invalidate the experiences of the members of these systems. Children's self-esteem is particularly vulnerable to such destructive communication processes. Unless children frequently receive positive messages from others outside of the family that disconfirm the negative and destructive messages, they gradually internalize the deficient view of self portrayed by parents and siblings. Further, as a result of incessant repetitions of destructive messages, children may develop negative behaviors that match the predictions contained in the parents' messages (e.g., "You're just like your father; you'll never succeed at anything.") Finally, children often become conditioned to the extent that they ignore or discount all positive messages that are incongruent with their negative views of self, thereby perpetuating the defective and flawed self-image mirrored by others. These negative views of self and the tendency of children to "deflect positives" and to "play out" in life the negative and ominous predictions of significant others become an inherent part of their adult character traits.

By contrast, members of healthy family systems put more emphasis upon positive attributes of members and what they can become rather than on deficiencies and dire predictions. Members of such systems, for example, view mistakes not as failures, but as opportunities for growth. When family members consistently respond with messages that validate the inherent worth and unique achievements of others in the system, the self-esteem of participants continues to grow, and the strong concept of self that a child develops in such a nourishing environment becomes relatively impervious to the storms of adult life.

Healthy families have many ways of validating the worth of members, including warm physical expressions (touching, hugging, tousling hair, and the like), direct verbal expressions of caring (e.g., "I love you"), verbal and nonverbal attentiveness to messages from others, and attention by members to activities in which others in the family are engaged (e.g., father notices his young son playing with a baseball and begins teaching him to throw and catch the ball). To a certain extent, most healthy families are also able to accredit the strengths, growth, and positive actions of the members of the system, although the capacity of even these families to observe and to give positive feedback on these vital areas is usually somewhat underdeveloped.

Family Strengths

All families, even those that function marginally, have a range of individual and group strengths that you should identify during the assessment process. However, because of the deeply entrenched focus on pathology in the helping professions, practitioners sometimes must revise their perceptional "sets" in order to discern undergirding strengths of the family that are not evident at first glance. Highlighting what is going right and what is working in troubled families is difficult because members of these families usually dwell on problems and troubles. Thus, in assessments that involve families or couples, observing and accrediting the strengths inherent in the system requires deliberate and disciplined effort on your part.

In assessment, you also need to pay particular attention to the strengths of families from various cultural groups. Many of these groups have suffered historic discrimination or, as political refugees, have suffered extreme losses, including the loss of identity that accompanies loss of homeland, reference and support groups, and social and vocational roles that come with being political refugees. Often demoralized by discrimination, crippled by family disruption, and handicapped by difficulties with language, lack of education or job skills, and lack of resources or knowledge of how to obtain them, many minority families often feel powerless to cope with overwhelming circum-

stances. Yet these families have many strengths, and it is vital that practitioners identify these strengths and use them in the treatment process to empower families to accomplish desired changes. Speaking of black families, Weaver (1982), aptly captures the challenge practitioners face in accrediting and utilizing strengths to promote the well-being of troubled families from all cultures:

> It is crucial to begin with the strengths of the family system; families move on strengths, not weaknesses. There is inherent strength in the design of every family and the social worker must help families use their own strengths in making choices and decisions that will enable them to achieve their own goals. (p. 103)

A study of the cultural backgrounds of families may reveal some of the strengths commonly found in members of their culture, including, for example, the commitment of many cultures to take care of their extended kin. The Hawaiians' generous hospitality, the Native Americans' attitude of working in harmony with natural forces, the Jewish commitment to learning and achievement, and the German work ethic (manifested in respect for thoroughness, solid craftsmanship, and attention to detail) all represent significant strengths indigenous to each cultural group.

A mark of "successful" or "acculturated" ethnic families is that they show a strong interest in keeping alive the folkways, arts and crafts, language, and values associated with their heritage (Ho, 1987). Likewise, a mark of success of any family is that of preserving family ties through religious, seasonal, holiday, work, or entertainment rituals.

You should be able to identify many strengths of families and couples by observing their processes carefully. Examples of vital strengths include being willing to talk about problems or to accept help, demonstrating commitment to tackle painful issues, expressing caring feelings for family members, attempting to observe and discover the system's processes, or manifesting willingness to make adjustments or changes that will benefit the family.

The Family Life Cycle

The last criterion for assessing families involves the developmental stages through which families as a whole must pass. Based on the seminal work of Duvall (1977) and other theorists, Carter and McGoldrick (1988) offer a conceptual framework of the life cycle of the middle-class American family. This model, involving the entire three- or four-generational system as it moves through time, includes both predictable development events (e.g., birth, marriage, retirement), and those unpredictable events that may disrupt the life cycle process (e.g., untimely death, birth of a handicapped child, divorce, chronic illness, war, etc.).

Carter and McGoldrick identify six stages of family development, all of which address nodal events related to the comings and goings of family members over time. These stages include "the unattached young adult," "the new couple," "the family with young children," "the family with adolescents," "the family which is launching children," and "the family in later life." To master these stages, families must successfully complete certain tasks. The "unattached young adult," for example, must differentiate from the family of origin and become a "self" before joining with another to form a new family system. The "new couple" and the families of origin must renegotiate their relationships with each other. The "family with young children" must find the delicate balance between over- and under-parenting. In all the stages, problems are most likely to appear when there is an interruption or dislocation in the unfolding family life cycle, signaling that the family is "stuck" and having difficulty moving through the transition to its next phase.

Variations in life cycle are, of course, likely to occur in today's world, particularly in the lives of reconstituted families. As Meyer (1990) notes:

> The ground rules have changed as far as the timing and sequence of events are concerned. Education, work, love, marriage, childbirth, retirement are now out of synch. There is no expectation that one phase follows another in linear fashion. In this world, life events are not pre-ordained. They are more likely atomistic, mixed-and-matched, responsive to self-definition and opportunity. (p. 12)

Variations also occur in the family life cycle among cultures. Every culture marks off stages of living, each with its appropriate expectations, defining what it means to be a man or woman, to be young, to grow up and leave home, to get married and have children, and to grow old and die.

NOTES

1 Although our discussion centers largely on families, the concepts presented are pertinent to couples as well.

2 The practitioner in this case was Marilyn Luptak, MSW, and Ph.D. student at the University of Minnesota.

3 Although families may engage in destructive sequences of interaction such as the preceding as they first begin to discuss problems, it is vital that practitioners actively intervene early in sessions to prevent these scenarios from being played out and to assist family members to assume more facilitative ways of communicating about their problems.

4 Note that clients may discuss an endless variety of topics or content issues, but their processes contain only a limited number of rules or stylized behaviors.

5 That nonblack practitioners often mistakenly view black cultural differences as dysfunction is understandable when viewed in light of Jones's (1983, p. 419) observation that "the black family is often viewed strictly as an impoverished version of the American white family, characterized by disorganization and a 'tangle of pathologies.'"

6 Information from this section was drawn in part from a discussion by Goldenberg and Goldenberg (1991) of Minuchin's structural approach.

7 For an expanded discussion of family myths, see "Personal, Marital, and Family Myths" by Bagarozzi and Anderson (1989).

8 For an expansion of information on role issues faced by same-sex couples, see Card (1990); Barret and Robinson (1990); and Bozett (1987). Levy (1992) and Cain (1991) also add dimension to the subject of role issues of lesbians and gay men.

Chapter 11

Forming and Assessing Social Work Groups

Social workers frequently practice with groups. Toseland and Rivas define group work as "goal-directed activity with small groups of people aimed at meeting socio-emotional needs and accomplishing tasks. This activity is directed to individual members of a group and as a whole within a system of service delivery" (Toseland & Rivas, 1995, p. 12). This definition suggests that all social work practice with groups is aimed at reaching specific goals. Those goals may focus on helping individuals to make changes. They may also focus on the group as a whole as a unit of change or the group as a mechanism for influencing the environment. Among the former are treatment groups aimed at enhancing the socio-emotional well-being of members through provision of social skills, education, and therapy. Among the latter are task groups focused on completion of a project or development of a product. Practitioners in task groups work with other professionals in formats such as consultation groups and teams to facilitate client service.

Competent group leaders of both kinds of groups have a threefold task: (1) to create effective groups that serve the purposes for which they were designed; (2) to accurately assess individual and group dynamics within those groups; and (3) to intervene effectively to modify processes central to the achievement of the group's goals.

Skillfully conceiving a group and formulating a group's purpose, structure, and composition must precede all else, as these processes lay the groundwork for both effective assessment and intervention and the ultimate success of the group. Without careful forethought in creating group structure and atmosphere, all assessment and intervention efforts are for naught, for there is no solid foundation to support them. Accurate assessment of group processes also precedes and undergirds effective interventions.

This chapter provides a framework that will enable leaders to effectively form groups and accurately assess group processes. Ultimately, this chapter lays the foundation for effective group interventions, the subject of Chapter 17.

Before focusing on these objectives, we briefly discuss the types of groups that practitioners create and lead in practice settings.

CLASSIFICATION OF GROUPS

The groups with which social work practitioners are often associated fall into two categories: treatment groups and task groups, each with several subtypes, which we consider below:

Treatment groups have the broad purpose of increasing the satisfaction of members' socioemotional needs. Task groups, on the other hand, are established to accomplish a task, produce a product, or carry out a mandate (Toseland & Rivas, 1995, p. 15). Treatment and task groups can be contrasted in a number of basic ways. In treatment groups, communications are open and members are encouraged to actively interact. In task groups, on the other hand, communications are focused on the discussion of a particular task. Roles in treatment groups evolve as a result of interaction while they may be assigned in task groups. Procedures in treatment groups are flexible or formal, depending on the group, whereas in task groups there are usually formal agendas and rules.

Treatment and task groups further differ with respect to self-disclosure, confidentiality, and evaluation. In treatment groups self-disclosure is expected to be high, proceedings are kept within the group, and success is based on members' success in meeting treatment goals. By contrast, in task groups self-disclosure is low, proceedings may be private or open to the public, and the success of the group is based on members accomplishing its task or mandate, or producing a product.

Toseland and Rivas (1995) further refine their classification of treatment groups by employing subtypes determined by the following four primary purposes served by such groups:

1. *Support*—groups that help members cope with life stresses by revitalizing coping skills to more effectively adapt to future life events. For example, school children meeting to discuss the effect of divorce or persons with cancer discussing the effects of the disease and how to cope with it (ibid., p. 21).

2. *Educational*—groups that have the primary purpose of helping members learn about themselves and their society (e.g., an adolescent sexuality group).

3. *Growth*—groups that stress self-improvement, offer-

ing members opportunities to expand their capabilities and self-awareness and make personal changes (e.g., a marital enhancement group for married couples). Growth groups focus on promoting socioemotional health rather than remediating socioemotional illness (ibid., p. 26).

4. *Therapy*—groups that help members change their behavior, cope with or ameliorate their personal problems, or rehabilitate themselves after a social or health trauma (e.g., a drug addiction group). While support is emphasized in therapy groups, they focus on remediation and rehabilitation.

5. *Socialization*—groups designed to facilitate transitions through developmental stages, from one role or environment to another, through improved interpersonal relationships or social skills. Such groups often employ program activities, structured exercises, role plays, and the like (e.g., a social club for formerly institutionalized persons).

Self-help groups can be distinguished from treatment and task groups by the fact that they have central shared concerns such as coping with addiction, cancer, or obesity. Although a practitioner might have aided in establishing a self-help group, the group itself is led by nonprofessionals who are struggling with the same issues as members of the group. The emphasis of such groups is on interpersonal support and creating an environment in which individuals may once again take charge of their lives. Such groups offer support for such shared problems as addictions, aggressive behavior, mental illness, disability, death of children, gambling, weight control, family violence, sexual orientation, and AIDS, among others. It is the practitioner's task to offer support and consultation to such groups without taking them over.

Toseland and Rivas (1995) emphasize that in actual practice much overlap exists in the functions and objectives of the different types of groups. There are also underlying principles that apply to all forms of group work practice. We will begin with the creation and assessment of treatment groups before proceeding to task groups.

FORMATION OF TREATMENT GROUPS

The success or failure of a treatment group rests to a large extent on the thoughtful creation of groups and the careful selection and preparation of members for the group experience. Approaches to achieve the initial conditions essential to positive group outcome are presented in this section.

Establishing Group Purpose

Clarifying the overall purpose(s) of a group is vital, for the group's objective(s) influences all the processes that follow. Further, as Levine (1967) underscores: "Clarity about the purpose for which the group is formed provides a framework for observation, assessment, and action [and] provides a base for the group members to develop a bond and a means for attaining their common goals" (p. 2). Thus, clearly delineating the basic purpose of a group provides the base upon which specific goals and objectives may be constructed. General group purposes may include overarching goals such as the following:

1. To provide through a forum for discussion and education an opportunity whereby divorced women with small children who live in a rural area may explore and seek solutions to common problems, such as a sense of alienation, scarcity of resources, and lack of opportunities for adult companionship.

2. To provide an opportunity for members to learn assertiveness skills and to practice applying them in real-life situations.

3. To establish a governing council for nursing home residents through which they may participate in decision making that affects them and the quality of life in the home.

4. To assist incarcerated adolescents to adhere to written contracts that specify behavioral changes upon which release is contingent, including improvements in school performance, behavior toward peers and staff, and the like.

The overall purpose of a planned group should be established by the practitioner in consultation with agency administrators prior to forming the group. Goals subsequently negotiated by the group should reflect the perspectives of the agency, the client(s), and the practitioner.

The Agency and Practitioner's Perspectives

Because of the agency's key role in determining and/or influencing purpose, practitioners must assure that agency objectives are reflected in the group's overall purpose. However, the agency and practitioner may not always share a common perspective regarding desired goals for a new group. Differences in the views of the agency and practitioner may occur, for instance, because of the latter's personal or professional orientation or because of preferences of either the agency or the practitioner for particular theories, ideologies, or techniques not espoused by the other. For example, one of the authors was asked to form a group of women who were perceived to overuse tranquilizers in an out-patient mental health setting. Rather than focus on the negative identity of drug abuser, the author formed a women's growth group.

In the preformation period, then, practitioners must be clear about their own objectives for a proposed group and must engage in dialogue with administrators and staff for the purpose of eliciting their views concerning group purpose. In cases where agency and practitioners' goals differ, practitioners must address such disparities with administrators and bargain for a general group purpose that is agreeable to both parties.

The Client's Perspective

At the point of entry to a group, the client's goals may differ considerably from either those of the agency or the practitioner's. This is particularly true when potential members have been referred by others or are mandated to participate in the group (Rooney, 1992). Schopler and Galinsky (1974) emphasize that the client's goals may be influenced by many internal or external forces:

> The expectations held by significant others (e.g., husband, mother, teacher) for the client may ...influence the client's perspectives of his problem and his motivation to do something about it. His capabilities provide resources and define limits for work on his problems and his contributions to the group. Further, as he enters the group, each client has some idea, however vague, of what the worker, agency, and group will be like...based on personal experiences from school, work, and friendship groups and from reports of others. Thus, various factors determine what goals the client sees as relevant and what goals he thinks are attainable. (p.128)

The practitioner must then carefully explore clients' expectations of the group and help them to develop individual and collective goals that are realistically achievable. The practitioner must further work to negotiate between individual, group, and agency purposes. For example, in an alternative to prostitution group for which potential members make a constrained choice to participate or risk prosecution, it is important to acknowledge members' goal of avoiding prosecution as central while recognizing that exploring alternative life styles is a non-negotiable condition for participation in the group (Rooney, 1992). Other perspectives in voluntary groups must not supersede clients' goals, as clients are the consumers of the service offered. The need to highlight and preserve clients' goals is reflected in the findings of Levinson (1973). Levinson identified several common patterns concerning the consequences of agreement or disagreement of purpose between the practitioner and group members. When the purposes of practitioners and members were in accord or when the purposes of the two diverged but the practitioner went along with the group's purpose, groups tended to operate optimally. However, when the practitioner advocated pur-

poses that were rejected by members, groups prematurely dissolved.

Establishing Specific Individual and Group Goals

After having established an overall purpose for the group and convened the group, the practitioner engages members in formulating specific goals at both individual and group levels. Individual goals embody the hopes and objectives of members as they enter the group. Group goals, on the other hand, "are the emergent product of the interaction of all participants together, the organizer and the members, as they express their ideas and feelings about the reasons for the existence of the group and its anticipated outcomes. Group goals include, therefore, rationale, expectations and objectives toward which the group puts its collective efforts" (Hartford, 1971, p. 139).

The following list contains examples of specific goals that may be formulated at either individual or group levels:

1. To discern strengths and incremental growth in one's self and in others and to give and receive positive feedback in relation to the same.

2. To expand awareness of one's own behavior (or the group's processes).

3. To identify one's own self-defeating behaviors and to replace these with more functional behaviors.

4. To develop problem-solving skills that enhance decision making in both individual and group contexts and to apply them to specific problems.

5. To relate to others with increased authenticity.

6. To become more liberated from external imperatives, that is, "shoulds," "oughts," and "musts."

7. To learn how to make direct requests for what one wants.

8. To learn how to hear accurately the messages of others and to convey one's understanding of these messages to others.

9. To grow in self-acceptance and to explore hidden potentials and creativity.

10. To increase one's capacity to care for others and to manifest that caring.

11. To learn to express thoughts, feelings, needs, and ideas to others.

12. To develop trust in one's own judgment.

Conducting a Preliminary Interview

Before convening a group, practitioners often meet individually with potential group members for the purpose of establishing rapport, exploring relevant concerns, and formulating initial contracts with those motivated to join the group, and clarifying constrained choices for involuntary clients. Conducting individual interviews is essential to composing a group carefully, which entails selecting members according to predetermined criteria and including those who have specific behavioral or personality attributes thought to be beneficial for the purposes of the group. Further, when composing a group of involuntary clients (e.g., delinquents, court-referred parents, or felons), having an individual interview is a vital first step in assisting potential members to identify acknowledged as well as attributed problems and to clarify constrained choices.

Pregroup meetings with potential members assist practitioners to gain essential information that may be of substantial value in selecting and directing interventions to those members in early sessions. (Because of the time limitations in regular group sessions, such vital information may not otherwise emerge for several weeks.) Further, conducting preliminary interviews enables practitioners to enter initial group sessions with a previously established relationship with each member, a distinct advantage given the fact that leaders must attend to multiple communication processes at both individual and group levels. In addition, previous knowledge about individual members facilitates grasping the meaning of the behavior of those members in the group, thus enabling practitioners to focus more fully on group processes and

the task of assisting members to develop relationships with each other. Establishing rapport with the leader prior to initial sessions also enables members to feel more at ease and to open up more readily in the first meeting.

Objectives that practitioners may wish to accomplish in preliminary interviews include the following:

1. Orienting potential members to proposed goals and purposes of the group, its content and structure, the philosophy and style of the leader in managing group processes, and the respective roles of the leader and group members. It is important with involuntary groups to distinguish between non-negotiable rules and policies such as attendance expectations and general themes to be discussed and negotiable norms and procedures such as arrangements for breaks, food, and selection of particular topics and their order. The practitioner should elicit the client's reactions and suggestions that would enable the group to better serve the client's needs. Orientaion should also include a sharing of the time, place of meetings, length of sessions, and the like. In addition, the practitioner may wish to emphasize commonalities that the client may share with other persons considering group membership, such as problems, interests, concerns, or objectives.

2. Eliciting the client's view of prior group experiences, including the nature of the client's relationship with the leader and other members, the client's style of relating in the previous group, the goals that the client accomplished, and the personal growth that was achieved. You should anticipate negative reactions from involunary group members, recognize them as expectable, yet emphasize ways they can make use of their decision to participate in the group to reach their own goals as well as mandated goals.

3. Eliciting, exploring, and clarifying clients' problems, and identifying those that are appropriate for

the proposed group. In some instances, either because clients are reluctant to participate in the group or because their problems appear to be more appropriately handled through other treatment modalities or community agencies, you may need to refer them to other resources. With respect to treatment approaches, Garvin (1981) emphasizes that "the client's choice of individual, group, or family services should be an informed one based on information regarding different forms of interpersonal helping and what they are like" and suggests employing media aids such as films, tapes, or even comic books to portray what happens in the agency's groups (p. 75). Garvin also emphasizes that some clients' problems are better addressed within a family than a group context. To determine which modality is mutually preferable, Garvin identifies the following three criteria (p. 74):

a. Is the problem maintained by processes operating in the family as a system? (See Chapter 10.)

b. How will the family respond to changes the individual may choose to make, and will these responses support or retard such changes?

c. Does the individual wish to involve the family, and is the family amenable to such involvement?

4. Exploring the client's hopes, aspirations, and expectations regarding the proposed group (e.g., "What would you like to be different in your life as a result of your attending this group?").

5. Identifying specific goals that the client wishes to accomplish, discussing whether these goals can be attained through the proposed group, and determining the client's views as to whether the group is an appropriate vehicle for resolving personal problems. It is critical, of course, to respect a client's right not to participate in a voluntary group. Garvin, Reid, and Epstein (1976) emphasize the need to put "high priority on the client's autonomy, particularly his right to freedom from

imposed or deceptive treatment." These authors recommend employing a specific contract that protects each client from "help for a condition he may not wish to change or from treatment for an unacknowledged problem" (pp. 242–243). With involuntary groups, sharing personal goals that prior members have chosen such as going back to school in addition to mandated goals such as seeking alternatives to prostitution can assist in enhancing the attractiveness of the group.

6. Mutually developing a profile of the client's attributes and determining any that the client might like to enhance through work in the group.

7. Identifying and exploring potential obstacles that might prevent clients from participating in or receiving desired benefits from the group, including reservations they may have about attending the group. Other obstacles may include shyness or nonassertiveness in group situations, opposition from significant others about entering the group, a heavy schedule that would likely preclude attending all group meetings, or problems in finding baby-sitters. After exploring obstacles, it is appropriate to assist clients in generating possible alternatives that might obviate these obstacles. In some cases, obstacles may preclude clients from group participation.

8. Ensuring that the screening for the group is a two-way process. Potential members should have the opportunity to interview the group leader and to determine whether the group is appropriate for their problems and interests.

Group Composition

In most instances, an overriding factor in selecting group members is whether a candidate is motivated to make changes and is willing to expend the necessary effort to be a productive group member. Another factor is the likelihood of a person's compatibility with other members in the group. Practitioners also usually address the following in determining the composition of groups: sex, age, marital status, intellectual ability, education, socioeconomic status, ego strength, and type of problem (Flapan & Fenchel, 1987).

Homogeneity versus heterogeneity of these characteristics is a vital issue in composing a group. Significant homogeneity in personal characteristics and purpose for being in the group is necessary to facilitate communication and group cohesion. Without such homogeneity, members will have little basis for interacting with each other. Toseland and Rivas (1984), for example, identify levels of education, cultural background, degree of expertise relative to the group task, and communication ability as characteristics vital to creating homogeneity in groups.

On the other hand, some diversity among members with respect to coping skills, life experience, and levels of expertise fosters learning and introduces members to differing viewpoints, lifestyles, ways of communicating and problem solving. To attain the end product of providing "multiple opportunities for support, mutual aid, and learning," a treatment group, for example, might be composed of members from different cultures, social classes, occupations, or geographic areas. Heterogeneity is a vital variable in the membership of task groups that ensures sufficient resources to provide for an efficient division of labor when dealing with complex tasks (Toseland & Rivas, 1995, p. 158). The challenge is to attain a workable balance between homogeneity and heterogeneity.

Corey (1990) cautions against including members in voluntary groups whose behavior or pathology is extreme, inasmuch as some people "quite literally drain the energy of the group so that little is left for productive work" and interfere significantly in the development of group cohesion:

This is particularly true of individuals who have a need to monopolize and dominate, of hostile people or aggressive people with a need to act out, and of people who are extremely self-centered and who seek a group as an audience. However, such oppositional behavior may be a common denominator in some groups such as those addressed to domestic violence and drug addiction (Milgram & Rubin, 1992). Others who should generally be excluded from most groups are people who are in a state of extreme crisis, who are suicidal, who have sociopathic personalities, who are highly suspicious, or who are lacking in ego strength and are prone to fragmented and bizarre behavior (p. 89).

A decision to include or exclude a client has much to do with the purposes of the group. For example, an alcoholic might be excluded from a personal growth group but appropriately included in a homogeneous group of individuals who suffer from various types of addictions. Similarly, angry clients are expected in a domestic violence group.

Garvin (1987) warns against including in a treatment group a member who is very different from others, for the danger is that this person…will be perceived as undesirable or, in sociological terms, deviant by the other members. When the difference is based on some attribute such as age or race, the members may avoid communicating with this person, thus creating a group isolate. When the difference is based on a behavior such as topics discussed, personal disclosure, or social skills, the members may become critical of the individual and then scapegoat the person, who will then develop negative feelings toward the group, avoid its influence, and eventually drop out (p. 64).

When there is the likelihood that group composition will lead to creating a deviant member, Garvin recommends enrolling another member who "is either similar to the person in question or who is somewhere in the 'middle,' thus creating a continuum of member characteristics" (p. 65). Speaking of gender, and of ethnic groups that may be oppressed economically or socially such as blacks, Asians and Pacific Islanders, Hispanics, or Native Americans, Garvin also cautions against composing a group in which a person, by virtue of such gender or ethnicity, represents a small minority of one or two within the group, as these persons may experience considerable discomfort and have little in common with the rest of the group. For example, some agencies have found that there are advantages to creating groups for women who have chemical dependencies, as their issues often differ from men (Nelson-Zlepko, Kaufman, & Dore, 1995)

Open versus Closed Groups

Groups may either have an open format, in which the group remains open to new members, or a closed format in which no new members are added once the group gets under way. An open format itself presents different models (Henry, 1988; Reid, 1991), including the drop-in (or drop-out) model in which members are self-selecting, entry criteria are very broad, and members attend whenever they wish for an indefinite period. Another is the replacement model, in which the leader immediately identifies someone to fill a group vacancy, and a third is the re-formed model, in which group members contract for a set period of time, during which no new members are added but original members may drop out. At the end of the contract period, a new group is formed consisting of some old and some new members.

The choice of format depends on the purpose of the group, the setting, and the population served. An open format provides the opportunity for new members to bring fresh perspectives to the group and offers immediate support for those in need, who can stay as long as they choose. At the same time, the instability of such a format discourages members from developing the trust and confidence to openly share and explore their problems, a strong feature of the closed-ended group. Frequent changes of membership may also disrupt the work of the open-ended group. Advantages associated with a closed group include higher group morale, more predictability of role

behaviors, and an increased sense of cooperation among members. A disadvantage, however, is that if too many members drop out, the group process is drastically affected by the high attrition.

Group Size

The size of the group depends in large part on the purpose, the age of clients, the type of problems to be explored, and the needs of members. Five to twelve members is usually an optimum number for a group with an emphasis on close relationships (Reid, 1991). Bertcher and Maple (1985) observe: "In general, the group should be small enough to allow it to accomplish its purpose, yet large enough to permit members to have a satisfying experience."

Frequency and Duration of Meetings

Closed groups benefit from having a termination date at the outset, which encourages productive work. Regarding the possible lifespan of a group, Corey (1990) notes:

> The duration varies from group to group, depending on the type of group and the population. The group should be long enough to allow for cohesion and productive work yet not so long that the group seems to drag on interminably. (p. 92)

For a time-limited therapy group, Reid (1991) recommends approximately 20 sessions, stating that this length provides adequate time for cohesiveness and a sense of trust to develop. Reid recommends the use of time limits, noting that if the leader errs in estimating the length of time needed, "there is an end point in which the group can be reformulated as opposed to it going on indefinitely" (p. 189).

Formulating Group Guidelines

Developing consensus concerning guidelines for behavior (e.g., staying on task) among group members is a vital aspect of contracting in the initial phase. Although in the literature group guidelines are sometimes termed *group rules*, we recommend using the former term because the latter suggests regulations imposed upon a group rather than guidelines voluntarily developed by members to guide the group's processes and actions. In formulating guidelines with the group, the practitioner takes the first step in shaping the group's evolving processes to create a "working group" capable of achieving specific objectives. Attempts to formulate guidelines often fail to achieve this intended effect for three major reasons.

First, a practitioner may establish parameters *for* the group, merely informing members of behavioral expectations to which they are expected to adhere. While non-negotiable requirements such as attendance are often part of involuntary groups, overemphasis on such control may convey the message, "This is my group, and this is how I expect you to behave in it," which may negate later actions by the practitioner to encourage members to assume responsibility for the group. Without consensus among members concerning desirable group guidelines, power struggles and disagreements may ensue as to the appropriateness of certain behaviors. Further, members may not feel bound by what they consider the "leader's rules" and may, in fact, deliberately test them, creating a counterproductive scenario. Members may thus cast the practitioner in the role of "authoritarian parent" and assume the role of "errant children."

Second, the practitioner may discuss group guidelines only superficially and neglect either to identify or to obtain commitment to guidelines. Such neglect by a group leader is unfortunate, for the extent to which members delineate specific and functional parameters greatly influences the extent to which they will modify their behavior in future sessions to conform to adopted guidelines or to achieve stated group objectives.

Third, even when the group adopts viable guidelines for behavior within the group, the practitioner may erroneously assume that members will

subsequently conform to these guidelines. To the contrary, there is often little relationship between contracted behaviors and actual behaviors. Establishing group guidelines merely sets guideposts against which members may measure their current behavior. Practitioners must consistently intervene to assist members to adhere to guidelines and to consider discrepancies between contracted and actual behaviors before negotiated behaviors actually become normative.

Because formulating guidelines is a critical process that substantially influences the success of a group, we offer the following suggestions to assist you.

1. If there are non-negotiable agency rules (e.g., adolescents often are not allowed to smoke in correctional settings), you should present the rules, explain their rationale, and encourage discussion of them (Behroozi, 1992). Confidentiality is often a non-negotiable rule. The rationale for ensuring that issues discussed in the group will not be shared outside the group should be explained.

2. Introduce the group to the concept of *decision by consensus* on all negotiable items (explained later in this section), and solicit agreement concerning adoption of this modus operandi for making decisions *prior* to formulating group guidelines.

3. Ask group members to share their vision of the kind of group they would like to have by responding to the following statement: "I would like this group to be a place where I could…" Reach for responses from all members, and once this has been achieved, summarize the collective thinking of the group. Offer your own views of supportive group structure that assists members to work on individual problems or to achieve group objectives.

4. Ask members to identify guidelines for behavior in the group that will assist them to achieve the kind of group structure and atmosphere they desire. You may wish to brainstorm possible guidelines at this point, adding your suggestions. Then, through group consensus, choose those that seem most appropriate.

Depending on the setting and purpose of your group, you may need to develop guidelines that pertain to the following group behaviors. Guidelines adopted by many groups regarding these behaviors have proven conducive to achieving individual and group objectives.

Group Format   Pursuing ill-defined objectives within a structure that provides few guidelines for efficient use of time can defeat the best-intentioned leader or group. Developing a group structure during the initial phase that embodies the following activities, however, assists leaders and members to focus their energies on therapeutic objectives actively and efficiently.

1. Define group and individual goals in behavioral terms and rank them according to priority.

2. Develop an overall plan that organizes the work to be done within the number of sessions allocated by the group to achieve its goals.

3. Specify behavioral tasks to be accomplished outside the group each week that will assist individuals to make desired changes.

4. Achieve agreement among members concerning weekly format and agenda, i.e., how time will be allocated each week to achieve goals. For instance, a group might allocate its weekly two hours to the following format:

15 MIN.	1½ HOURS	15 MIN.
Reviewing and monitoring tasks	Focusing on relevant content and formulating tasks	Evaluating group sessions

Other than non-negotiable policies in involuntary groups, avoid imposing structure upon a group; rather, assist the group to evolve a format that will facilitate achieving the group's proposed objectives. The structure adopted by your group should also be flexible enough to accommodate to group processes and to the needs of members. To ensure its continued functionality, review the format periodically throughout the life of the group.

We are not recommending that your group adopt all of the preceding suggestions, but we stress the need for a clearly conceptualized format that provides the means for evaluating the ongoing process of group members. Our position is based on a conviction that, regardless of the treatment modality utilized, clients have a right to receive help within a format that provides for accountability in the form of continuing and concrete feedback concerning their progress.

Group Decision Making   Effective deliberation and decision making are critical in determining the productivity and success of a group. To achieve its objectives, every group ultimately develops methods of making decisions. Left to their own devices, however, groups may evolve counterproductive decision-making processes. Some groups, for example, permit the power for making decisions to be vested in a few members, "counting in" some members and "counting out" others. This modus operandi perpetuates conflict and intrigue in the group, causing unrest and resentments that divert energies from productive tasks and block developmental progress.

Members of newly formed groups have varying styles of making decisions and do not know how to make decisions effectively as a group. As a result, most treatment groups learn problem solving through extended trial-and-error processes, gradually gaining from their mistakes (we hope). Most groups, however, can quickly learn to adopt a model of *decision by consensus*, given effective leadership in educating the group. Further, equipping groups with an effective decision-making model in the early stages of development can expedite group process and assist groups in more readily achieving an advanced level of group functioning. Our decision-by-consensus method can be taught early in the first group session according to the following sequence:

1. Explaining that groups need a decision-making method that gives each person an equal vote and "counts everyone in."

2. Gaining group acceptance of this method of making decisions.

3. Explaining steps for effective decision making (these steps are discussed in Chapter 14).

4. Identifying the leader's function in assisting the group to make decisions that meet the needs of all members.

5. Using the decision-by-consensus approach in setting up the initial contract and focusing explicitly on the process to enhance group awareness of the use of this approach.

Help-Giving/Help-Seeking Roles   Groups formed to assist individuals with personal problems benefit from clarification of what might be termed *help-giving* and *help-seeking* roles. Although the two terms are self-explanatory, you may wish to assist the group to operationalize these roles by considering behaviors embodied in them. The help-seeking role, for example, incorporates such behaviors as making direct requests for help, authentically sharing one's feelings, being open to feedback and demonstrating willingness to test new approaches to problems. The help-giving role involves such behaviors as listening attentively, refraining from criticism, clarifying perceptions, summarizing, maintaining focus on the problem, and pinpointing strengths and incremental growth. A critical aspect of the help-giving role you should clarify for group members is the necessity of exploring personal problems of fellow members carefully before attempting to solve them. Otherwise, groups tend to move quickly to giving advice and offering evaluative suggestions about what a member "ought" or "ought not" to do. You can further help the group to adopt these two roles by highlighting instances in which members have performed in either of these helping roles, accrediting them accordingly.

Visitors   A group convened for treatment purposes should develop explicit guidelines specifying whether and under what conditions visitors may attend group meetings. If the group has an open format, allowing frequent changes in membership, the presence of a visitor will have little impact. However, in closed groups (i.e., ones that do not usually add members once the group has convened), visitors can have a devastating effect on group processes, causing members to refrain from sharing feelings and problems openly and creating resentments toward the member (or practitioner) who invited the visitor and thereby violated the integrity of the group. Anticipating with members the possible impact of visitors upon the group and establishing procedures and conditions under which visitors may attend sessions can avert group turmoil as well as embarrassment for individual members.

New Members   Procedures for adding and orienting new members may also need to be established. In some cases, the group leader may reserve the prerogative of selecting members. In other instances, the leader may permit the group to choose new members, with the understanding that choices should be based on certain criteria and that the group should achieve consensus regarding potential members. In either case, procedures for adding new members and the importance of the group's role in orienting them should be clarified.

Individual Contacts with the Practitioner   Whether you encourage or discourage individual contacts with members outside the group depends on the purpose of the group and the anticipated consequences or benefits of such contacts. In some cases, individual contacts serve to promote group objectives. For example, in a correctional setting, planned meetings with an adolescent between sessions provide opportunities to focus on the youth's problematic behaviors in the group and to develop an individual contact with the youth to modify them and support strengths. In the case of marital therapy groups, however, individual contacts initiated by one spouse may be a bid for an alliance with the practitioner against the other partner or may be perceived as such by the other spouse. If you have questions regarding the advisability of having individual contacts outside the group, you should thoroughly discuss these questions with members and mutually develop guidelines pertaining to this matter.

Cleanup Making group decisions regarding cleanup before having to contend with a messy room is an effective strategy that encourages members to assume responsibility for themselves and for the group. Resentments fester, and subgroupings destructive to group cohesiveness tend to form when some members consistently stay to help with cleanup and others do not.

Use of Recorder You should always gain the group's permission before recording a group session. Further, before asking for a decision you should provide information concerning the manner in which the recording is to be utilized outside the session. Reservations regarding recording the session should be thoroughly aired, and the group's wishes should be respected.

Use of Profanity Some practitioners believe that group members should be allowed to use whatever language they choose in expressing themselves. However, profanity may be offensive to some members, including the practitioners, and the group may wish to develop guidelines concerning this matter. For some groups, the practitioners might be the only ones offended, and imposition of the practitioners' preferences might inhibit the group.

Attendance Discussing the problems that irregular attendance can pose for a group before the fact and soliciting commitment from members to attend regularly can do much to solidify group attendance in future group sessions. Involuntary groups often have attendance policies permitting a limited number of absences and late arrivals. Further, late arrivals and early departures by group members can be minimized if the group develops relevant guidelines in advance. Allowances on an individual basis are needed, of course, to accommodate the schedules of members in special instances with the understanding that these situations should be rare. To expedite adherence to a group contract regarding a time frame, you should start and end meetings promptly and extend meetings only after the group has made the decision to do so. Although you may sometimes feel the press of unfinished business at the end of a meeting, holding group members beyond the scheduled time without their consent violates the group contract and may create resentment.

Eating, Drinking, Smoking Opinions vary among group leaders concerning these activities in groups. Some groups and leaders believe these activities distract from group process; others regard them as relaxing and actually beneficial to group operation. You may wish to elicit views from members concerning these activities and develop guidelines with the group that meet member needs and facilitate group progress.

Programming At times, group formats include activities or exercises. Unfortunately, however, such programming does not always directly relate to the group's purpose; further, the activities or exercises in which the group participates may not be discussed by members for the purpose of learning from the experience or relating it to behavioral changes members wish to achieve. Thus, when programming is utilized, practitioners need to discuss with members the manner in which such activities can be best utilized to meet specified objectives and to plan with them ways of evaluating and generalizing the group's experience.

Remember that guidelines are helpful only to the extent that they expedite the development of the group and should be reviewed periodically to assess their functionality in relationship to the group's stage of development. Outdated guidelines, of course, should be discarded or reformulated. Further, when a group's behavior is incompatible with group guidelines, it may be advisable to describe what is happening in the group (or request that members do so) and, after thoroughly reviewing the situation, ask the group to consider whether the guideline in question is still viable. If used judiciously, this strategy not only helps the group to reassess guidelines but also places responsibility for monitoring adherence to guidelines with the group, where it belongs. Leaders who unwittingly assume the role of "enforcer" place themselves in an untenable position, for group members tend to struggle against what they perceive as authoritarian control on the leader's part.

ASSESSING GROUP PROCESSES

In group assessment, practitioners must attend to processes that occur at both the individual and group levels, including emerging themes or patterns they must necessarily consider as they intervene to enhance the functioning of individuals and the group as a whole. In the following section, procedures for making accurate assessments of the processes of both individuals and groups are delineated. Such assessments must be set within a systems framework that allows practitioners to see the patterning of individual and group behaviors.

A Systems Framework for Assessing Groups

Like families, groups are social systems characterized by repetitive patterns. The operations within all social systems share an important principle, namely, that persons who comprise a given system gradually limit their behaviors to a relatively narrow range of patterned responses as they interact with others within that system. Groups thus evolve implicit rules or norms that govern behaviors, shape patterns, and regulate internal operations. Employing a systems framework in assessing the processes of groups, leaders attend to the patterned interactions of members, infer rules that govern those interactions, and weigh the functionality of the rules and patterns.

Knowledge that group processes can be conceptualized and organized into response patterns enables leaders to make systematic, ongoing, and relevant assessments. This knowledge can be comforting to inexperienced group leaders, who often feel they are floundering in group sessions. Some beginning group leaders, in fact, are greatly relieved and gain considerable confidence as they realize it is possible to "make sense" out of group process.

As leaders observe groups to discern patterned behaviors, they must concurrently attend to behavior manifested by individuals and by the group itself. Observing processes at both levels is difficult, however, and leaders sometimes become discouraged when they realize they attended more to individual dynamics than to group dynamics (or the converse), causing their formulations of either individual and/or group patterns to be vague or incomplete. We thus discuss strategies for accurately assessing both individual and group patterns in the remainder of the chapter.

Assessing Patterned Behaviors of Individuals

Some of the patterned behaviors group members manifest are *functional*, that is, enhance the well-being of individual members and the quality of relationships. Other patterned behaviors are dysfunctional in that they erode the self-esteem of members and are destructive to relationships. Many members of growth groups, in fact, join such groups because certain of their patterned dysfunctional behaviors produce distress in interpersonal relationships for themselves and others. Often, of course, these members are not aware of the patterned nature of their behavior nor of the fact that some of these entrenched behaviors cause interpersonal problems. Rather, group members often regard other persons as the source of their difficulties.

A major role of leaders in growth groups, then, is to aid members to become aware of their patterned behavioral responses, to determine the impact of these responses on themselves and others, and to choose whether to change such responses. To carry out this role, leaders must formulate a profile of the recurring responses of each member.

Understanding Content and Process   To formulate accurate assessments of individual behavioral responses, you must apply the concepts of *content* and *process*, which we discussed in the preceding chapter. To refresh your memory, content refers to verbal statements and related topics that members discuss, whereas process involves the ways members relate or behave as they interact in the group and discuss content. To expand your understanding of the concept of group process, consider for a moment the following description of a member's behavior in two initial group sessions:

> In the first group meeting, John moved his chair close to the leader's. Several times when the leader made statements, John expressed agreement. In the second group meeting, John again sat next to the leader and used the pronoun "we" several times, referring to opinions he thought were jointly held by himself and the leader. Later, John tried to initiate a conversation with the leader concerning what he regarded as negative behavior of another group member in front of that member and the rest of the group.

This example describes how John is behaving and communicating rather than what he is saying, and thus it deals with process rather than content.

It is at the process level that leaders discover many of the patterned behavioral responses of individuals. The preceding example reveals John's possible patterned or thematic behaviors. For example, we might infer that John is jockeying to establish an exclusive relationship with the leader and bidding for an informal position of co-leader in the group. Viewed alone, none of the discrete behaviors in the preceding excerpt provides sufficient information to justify drawing a conclusion as to a possible response pattern. Viewed collectively, however, the repetitive responses warrant inferring that a pattern does, in fact, exist.

Identifying Roles of Group Members   In identifying patterned responses of individuals, leaders also need to attend to various roles members assume in the group. Members, for example, may assume *leadership* roles that are formal (explicitly sanctioned by the group) or informal (emerge as a result of group needs). Further, a group may have several leaders who serve different functions or who head rival subgroups.

Some members may assume *task-related* roles that facilitate the group's efforts to define problems, to implement problem-solving strategies, and to carry out tasks. These members may propose goals or actions, suggest procedures, request pertinent facts, clarify issues, or offer an alternative or conclusion for the group to consider. Other members may adopt *maintenance* roles that are oriented to altering, maintaining, and strengthening the group's functioning. Members who take on such roles may offer compromises, encourage and support the contributions of others, or suggest group standards. Some members of involuntary groups often emerge as spokespersons around concerns of the group. Rather than confront such a person as a negative influence, it is often useful to explore whether, in fact, that person is bringing to the fore issues which have been discussed outside of the group. In short, that person may in fact be acting as an informal group leader who can be joined in wishing to make the group succeed (Breton, 1985). Still other members may assume self-serving roles by seeking to meet their own needs at the expense of the group. Such members attack the group or its values, stubbornly resist the group's wishes, continually disagree with or interrupt others, assert authority or superiority, display lack of involvement, pursue extraneous subjects, or find various ways to call attention to themselves.

Members may also carry labels assigned by other members, such as "clown," "uncommitted," "lazy," "dumb," "silent one," "rebel," "overreactor," or "good mother." Such labeling stereotypes members, making it difficult for them to relinquish the set of expected behaviors or to change their way of relating to the group. Hartford (1971, p. 218) elaborates:

> For instance, the person who has become the clown may not be able to make a serious and substantial contribution to the group because, regardless of what he says, everyone laughs. If one person has established a high status as the initiator, others may not be able to initiate for fear of threatening his position. If one has established himself in a dependency role in a pair or subgroup, he may not be able to function freely until he gets cues from his subgroup partner.

One or more members may also be assigned the role of scapegoat, bearing the burden of responsibility for the group's problems and the brunt of consistent negative responses from other members. Such individuals may attract the scapegoating role because they are socially awkward and repeatedly make social blunders in futile attempts to elicit positive responses from others (Balgopal & Vassil, 1983; Klein, 1970). Or they may foster the role because they fail to recognize nonverbal cues that facilitate interaction in the group and thus behave without regard to the subtle nuances that govern the behavior of other members (Balgopal & Vassil, 1983; Beck, 1974). Individuals may also unknowingly perpetuate the scapegoating role they have assumed in their nuclear families. Although group scapegoats manifest repetitive dysfunctional behaviors that attract the hostility of the group, the presence of the scapegoating role signals a group phenomenon (and pattern), the maintenance of which requires the tacit cooperation of all members.

Individuals may also assume the role of an isolate, the characteristics of which Hartford (1971) described:

> The social isolate is the person who is present but generally ignored by the others. He does not seem to reach out to others or he reaches out but is rejected. His lack of affiliation with others in the group may be due to lack of capacity on his part to get along with others, or he may differ in values, beliefs, and lifestyle from others enough to be deviant. He is not generally the scapegoat for if he were, he would be getting attention, however negative. The true isolate is ignored, his contributions go unnoticed, his opinions are not asked for. (p. 208)

It is important to identify roles that members assume because such roles profoundly affect the group's capacity to respond to the individual needs of members and its ability to fulfill treatment objectives. Further, identifying roles is vital because members tend to play out in treatment groups the same roles that they assume in other social contexts. Members need to understand the impact of enacting dysfunctional roles on themselves and others. Some members, of course, assume roles that strengthen relationships and are conducive to group functioning. By highlighting these positive behaviors, leaders enhance members' self-esteem and also place the spotlight on behaviors other members may emulate.

Developing Profiles of Individual Behavior In assessment, group leaders need to develop accurate behavioral profiles of each individual. To carry out this function, leaders record functional and dysfunctional responses of members manifested in initial sessions. Operating from a strengths perspective, it is important to record and acknowledge such functional behaviors as the following.

Functional Behaviors

1. Expresses caring for group members or significant others.
2. Manifests organizational or leadership ability.
3. Expresses self clearly.
4. Cooperates with and supports others.
5. Assists in maintaining focus and helping the group accomplish its purposes.
6. Expresses feelings openly and congruently.
7. Accurately perceives what others say (beyond surface meanings) and conveys understanding to them.

8. Responds openly and positively to constructive feedback.

9. Works within guidelines established by the group.

10. "Owns" responsibility for behavior.

11. Risks and works to change self.

12. Counts in others by considering their opinions, including them in decision making, or valuing their differences.

13. Participates in discussions and assists others to join in.

14. Gives positive feedback to others concerning their strengths and growth.

15. Accredits own strengths and growth.

16. Expresses humor facilitatively.

17. Supports others nonverbally.

Dysfunctional Behaviors

1. Interrupts, speaks for others, rejects others' ideas.

2. Placates, patronizes.

3. Belittles, criticizes, or expresses sarcasm.

4. Argues, blames, attacks, engages in name-calling.

5. Verbally dominates group "air time."

6. Gives advice prematurely.

7. Expresses disgust and disapproval nonverbally.

8. Talks too much, too loudly, or whispers.

9. Withdraws, assumes role of spectator, ignores, shows disinterest.

10. Talks about tangential topics or sidetracks in other ways.

11. Manifests distractive physical movements.

12. Is physically aggressive or "horses" around.

13. Clowns, mimics, or makes fun of others.

14. Aligns with others to form destructive subgroups.

15. Intellectualizes or diagnoses (e.g., "I know what's wrong with you").

16. Avoids focusing on self or withholds feelings and concerns pertinent to personal problems.

Table 11-1 is a record of a women's support group that illustrates how leaders can develop accurate behavioral profiles of each member by keeping track of the functional and dysfunctional behaviors manifested by members in initial sessions. The profile of group members' behaviors in Table 11-1 identifies specific responses manifested by individuals in the group but does not necessarily identify their *patterned* or *stylized* behaviors. Recording specific responses of individuals at each session, however, aids in identifying recurring behaviors and roles members are assuming. With regard to roles, for example, a glance at the preceding profiles suggests that Dixie is vulnerable to becoming an isolate in the group.

Identifying Growth of Individuals Because growth occurs in subtle and diverse forms, a major role of leaders is to document (and to assist the group to document) the incremental growth of each member. To sharpen your ability to observe growth of individuals, we suggest that you develop a record-keeping format that provides a column for notations concerning the growth members make from one session to the next or across several sessions. Without such a recording system, it is easy to overlook significant changes and thus miss vital opportunities to substantiate the direct relationship between their efforts to change and the positive results they attain.

The Impact of Culture Assessment of individual functioning, of course, must be tempered by the individual's cultural background. Tsui and Schultz (1988) stress that "the group norms comprising the so-called therapeutic milieu are actually Caucasian group norms that, in themselves, resist intrusion and disruption from minority cultures" (p. 137). Thus, the behavior of a minority group member might be significantly negatively influenced by a group composed largely of Caucasians who try to assimilate the minority member into what they see as the therapeutic milieu.

Gaining Information from Other Sources In addition to direct observation, information concerning the behavioral styles of members can be obtained from many other sources. In the forma-

TABLE 11-1 EXAMPLES OF BEHAVIORAL PROFILES OF GROUP MEMBERS

NAME	DESCRIPTIVE ATTRIBUTES	FUNCTIONAL BEHAVIOR	DYSFUNCTIONAL BEHAVIOR
June	35 years old Legal secretary 8-year-old son Divorced five years	Gave positive feedback several times Expressed feelings clearly Outgoing and spontaneous; adds energy to group	Ruminated several times about the past Sometimes interrupted others and dominated discussion
Raye	29 years old Homemaker Three children	Articulate Sharp at summarizing feelings of group Expressed ambivalence about attending group	Seemed to have self-doubt concerning validity of own opinions
Janet	34 years old Clerical supervisor Divorced one year	Initiated group discussion of several topics	Was dogmatic and unyielding about several of her opinions Became angry several times during session; appears to have short fuse
Pam	35 years old Truck driver Six children Divorced three years	Joined in discussions Accredited self for several strengths	Responses indicate she labels and puts down her children Twice challenged the comments of others
Dixie	30 years old Homemaker Two children Divorce in progress	Stated she came to group despite considerable apprehension Artist; exhibits paintings	Very quiet in session Acts intimidated by group Sat in chair slightly outside circle
Rachael	30 years old Unmarried	Readily shared problems Responsive to others Able to describe feelings Articulate	Seemed to pull the group toward feeling sorry for her through constant story-telling
Karen	31 years old Homemaker Three children Divorced one year	Seemed eager to work on problems Talked about self introspectively	Several times appeared to appease others rather than expressing how she really felt about issues
Elaine	45 years old Cafeteria worker Two teenagers Divorce in progress	Listened attentively to others Nodded approvingly when others spoke	Did not speak up in group

tion phase of the group, for example, leaders can elicit pertinent data in preliminary interviews with the prospective member or from family members, agency records, or practitioners who have referred members to the group. Within the group, leaders may also glean substantial data concerning patterned behavior of members by carefully attuning to and exploring members' descriptions of their problems and interactions with others.

Assessing Cognitive Patterns of Individuals

Just as group members develop patterned ways of behaving, they develop patterned cognitions, that is, typical or habituated ways of perceiving and thinking about themselves, other persons, and the world around them. Such patterned cognitions are manifested in the form of silent mental speech or internal dialogue that individuals utilize to make meaning of life events. To use an analogy, it is as though various types of events in a person's life trigger a tape recording in his or her mind that automatically repeats the same messages over and over, coloring the person's perceptions of events and determining his or her reality. Examples of negative internal dialogue that tend to create problems for group members include repeated messages such as "I'm a failure," "I'll never be able to succeed," and "Other people are better than I am."

Patterned cognitions and behavior are inextricably related and reciprocally reinforce each other. The following example of a group member's problem illustrates the marriage between cognitions and behavior and the insidious effect that negative cognitions may have on a client's life:

Jean, a 25-year-old dental assistant, entered an adult support group because of problems at work that were jeopardizing her position. As Jean reported her problems to the group, the following situation unfolded: Jean was experiencing severe negative reactions toward her employer, Dr. A. An attractive young dentist, Dr. A was the "darling" of the large dental organization for which Jean worked. Watching Dr. A, who was single, pursue other young women in the office, Jean concluded that he was disinterested and "bored" with her and that she was doing an inadequate job. As Jean worked daily with Dr. A, she made repeated statements to herself such as "He doesn't like me," "He'd rather have someone else as an assistant," and "There's something wrong with me." Jean worked at hiding her growing resentment toward Dr. A but ultimately could not contain her feelings. Defensive and easily riled because of what she constantly said to herself, Jean repeatedly snapped at Dr. A in front of patients. Angered and confused by Jean's irritable behavior, Dr. A began to grow annoyed himself and to relate to Jean more and more coolly. Jean interpreted Dr. A's behavior as evidence that she was correct in her conclusion and that he did not like her and that she was inadequate not only as an assistant but as a person as well.

Because patterned behavioral and cognitive responses are inextricably interwoven and perpetuate each other, leaders must be able to intervene in groups to modify dysfunctional cognitions. Preliminary to intervening, however, leaders must fine-tune their perceptual focus to identify the thematic cognitions that are manifested in members' verbal statements. The following statements, for example, reveal conclusions members have drawn about themselves and others:

- Husband [*about wife's behavior*]: She doesn't allow me to smoke in the house. (My wife is in charge of me.)
- I can't tell people how I feel. (If I do, they'll reject me or I will hurt them.)
- Member of alcoholics group: If I can't trust my wife, how can I stop drinking? (My fate rests in the hands of someone else.)

In the same manner that group leaders observe and record functional and problematic behavioral responses of members, they can record the cognitive themes or patterns of members. Returning to the example of the women's support group cited earlier, note the cognitive responses of several members recorded by the leader in the same session, as illustrated in Table 11-2.

Leaders can help group members identify cognitive patterns during problem exploration by asking questions such as, "When that happened, what did you say to yourself?" "What conclusions do you draw about others under those circumstances?" or "What kind of self-talk did you use to make yourself depressed when that happened?" Leaders can also teach groups to recognize manifestations of patterned cognitions. As the group grasps the significance of internal dialogue and attends to cognitive patterns manifested by members, leaders should accredit the group's growth by giving members descriptive feedback concerning their accomplishments.

Identifying Patterned Group Behavior

To heighten your awareness of functional and dysfunctional patterned behaviors that may occur in

TABLE 11-2 Examples of Cognitive Themes of Group Members

Name	Functional Cognitions	Problematic Cognitions
June	It's OK to risk talking about feelings. Other people will usually treat those feelings with respect and be responsive. I can do things to make myself feel better. I can get help from this group.	I've been hurt by the past . I don't think I'll ever get over it. I will always blame myself for what happened. I can't stop myself from talking so much. I always do that when I get anxious.
Raye	I care about other people. I want to help them. I'm willing to risk by staying in this group because I know I need help.	Other people's opinions are more important than mine. If I express my opinion, other people may disagree with me and/or think I'm not very bright. People in this group may not like me.
Janet	I have personal strengths. There are some good things about me. I'm a survivor. I can take care of myself.	My ideas, beliefs, positions are right; those of other people are wrong. I have to be right (or others won't respect me). You can't trust other people; they will hurt you if they can. The less you disclose about yourself, the better.

groups, we provide contrasting examples of such behavior in Table 11-3.

The functional behaviors in the table are characteristic of a mature therapeutic group. However, note that facilitative group behaviors may emerge in the initial stages of development. These behaviors are usually fleeting, for the group must accomplish a number of developmental tasks, such as building trust and defining common interests and goals, before attaining the supportive and productive behaviors of the group's working stages. Brief or short-lived positive behaviors manifested early in groups include behaviors such as the following:

- The group "faces up to" a problem and makes a necessary modification or adjustment.
- The group responds positively the first time a member takes a risk by revealing a personal problem.
- Members of the group are supportive toward other members or manifest investment in the group.
- The group moves in a positive direction without the leader's guidance or intervention.
- The group works harmoniously for a period of time.

- Members effectively make a decision together.
- Members adhere to a specific group guideline, such as maintaining focus on work to be accomplished.
- Members give positive feedback to another member or observe positive ways the group has worked together.
- The group responsibly confronts a member who is dominating interaction or interfering in some way with the group's accomplishing its task.
- Members pitch in to clean up after a group session.

The preceding list of positive behaviors, of course, is by no means exhaustive. Once practitioners fine-tune their observational skills to register positive group behavior, they will catch glimpses of many newly developing behaviors that enhance a group's functioning. Practitioners can then intervene to facilitate the group's adoption of such functional behaviors. Their challenge, of course, is to focus on these fleeting behaviors before the moment is lost by authentically disclosing positive feelings and by documenting in behavioral terms the positive movement they have observed (Larsen, 1980).

TABLE 11-3   EXAMPLES OF GROUP BEHAVIOR

PROBLEMATIC GROUP BEHAVIOR	FUNCTIONAL GROUP BEHAVIOR
Members talk on a superficial level and are cautious about revealing their feelings and opinions.	Members openly communicate personal feelings and attitudes and anticipate that other members will be helpful.
Members are readily critical and evaluative of each other; they rarely acknowledge or listen to contributions from others.	Members listen carefully to each other and give all ideas a hearing.
Dominant members count out other members in decision making; members make decisions prematurely without identifying or weighing possible alternatives.	Decisions are reached through group consensus after considering everyone's views and feelings. Members make efforts to incorporate the views of dissenters rather than to dominate or override these views.
Members focus heavily on negatives and rarely accredit positive behaviors of others.	Members recognize and give feedback regarding strengths and growth of other members.
Members are critical of differences in others, viewing them as a threat.	Members recognize the uniqueness of each individual and encourage participation in different and complementary ways.
Members compete for the chance to speak, often interrupting each other.	Members take turns speaking. Members use "I" messages to speak for themselves, readily owning their own feelings and positions on matters.
Members do not personalize their messages but instead use indirect forms of communication to express their feelings and positions.	Members encourage others to speak for themselves. Members adhere to guidelines or behavior established in initial sessions.
Members speak for others. Members display disruptive behavior incompatible with group guidelines. Members resist talking about the here and now or addressing personal or group problems. Distractive behaviors may include distractive maneuvers such as fingering objects, whispering, and throwing spitballs.	The group is concerned about its own operations and addresses obstacles that prevent members from fully participating or the group from achieving its objectives. Members assume responsibility for the group's functioning and success.
Members show unwillingness to accept responsibility for themselves or the success of the group and tend to blame the leader when things are not going well.	The group manifests commitment by staying on task, assuming group assignments, or working out problems that impair group functioning.
Members dwell on past exploits and experiences and talk about issues extraneous to group purpose. Members also focus on others rather than themselves.	Members concentrate on the present and what they can do to change themselves.
Members show little awareness of the needs and feelings of others; emotional investment in others is limited.	Members are sensitive to the needs and feelings of others and readily give emotional support. Members also express their caring for others.

The group may also manifest transitory negative behaviors in initial sessions. As noted above, many of these behaviors can also be seen as expectable in the early phases of group development. These behaviors may signal evolving group patterns that are not firmly "set" in the group's interactional repertoire. Counterproductive behaviors that may evolve into patterns include any of the examples of dysfunctional behavior listed earlier in Table 11-3.

Just as we have suggested that you employ a record-keeping system for recording the functional and dysfunctional responses of individual members, we also recommend using the same type of system for recording the functional and dysfunctional behaviors of the group itself, adding a column to record the growth or changes that you note in the group's behavior.

Identifying Group Alliances

As members of new groups find other members with compatible attitudes, interests, and responses, they develop patterns of affiliation and relationship with these members. As Hartford (1971) points out, subgroup formations that evolve include pairs, triads, and foursomes. Foursomes generally divide into two pairs but sometimes shift to three and one. Groups as large as five may operate as a total unit, but generally these groups begin to develop subdivisions influencing "who addresses whom, who sits together, who comes and leaves together, and even who may meet or talk together outside of the group" (Hartford, 1971, p. 204).

Subgroupings that invariably develop do not necessarily impair group functioning. Group members, in fact, often derive strength and support from subgroups that enhance their participation and investment in the larger group. Further, it is through the process of establishing subgroups, or natural coalitions, that group members (like family members) achieve true intimacy. Problems arise in groups, however, when members develop exclusive subgroups that disallow intimate relationships with other group members or inhibit members from supporting the goals of the larger group. Competing factions can often impede or destroy a group.

To work effectively with groups, leaders must be skilled in identifying subdivisions and assessing their impact on a group. To recognize these sub-

divisions, leaders may wish to construct a sociogram of group alignments. Credited to Moreno and Jennings (Jennings, 1950), a sociogram graphically depicts patterned affiliations and relationships between group members by using symbols for people and interactions. Hartford (1971, p. 196) illustrates a sociogram that captures the attractions and repulsions among group members. (See Figure 11-1).

Sociograms are representations of alliances in a group at a given point, because alliances do shift and change, particularly in early stages of group development. Charting the transitory bondings that occur early in group life can be invaluable to leaders in deciding where and when to intervene to modify, enhance, or stabilize relationships between members.

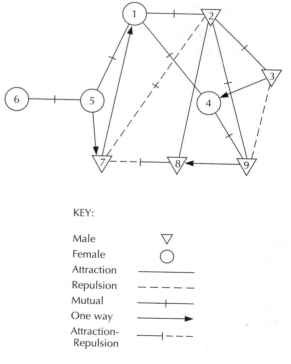

KEY:

Male	▽
Female	◯
Attraction	——
Repulsion	– – –
Mutual	——|——
One way	——▶
Attraction-Repulsion	——|– –

Figure 11-1 Sociogram Capturing the Attractions and Repulsions Among Group Members (*Source:* Margaret Hartford, *Groups in Social Work* (New York: Columbia University Press, 1971), p. 196. By permission of Columbia University Press.)

We suggest you construct a sociogram of members' interactions after every session until you are confident that group relationships have stabilized in positive ways that support the group's therapeutic objectives. Be creative with your sociograms. You may wish to use different colors to show attractions, repulsions, or strength of relationships or to place members closer together or farther apart to convey emotional closeness or distance. Avoid trying to capture in a single sociogram the exact nature of relationships each member has with every other one in the group, as the drawing will become overly complicated. Rather, depict only the major subgroupings in the group and identify the relationships in which major attractions or repulsions are occurring.

Identifying Power and Decision-Making Styles

Groups as well as families develop ways of distributing power among members. To ensure their needs are not discounted, some members may make bids for power and discount other members. Others tend to discount themselves and permit more aggressive members to dominate the group. Still others value power and actively pursue it as an end in itself. Involved in power struggles, groups may initially fail to make decisions on an "I count-you count" basis. Further, subgroups may try to eliminate opposing factions from the group or align themselves with other members or subgroups to increase their power. Groups, in fact, are sometimes torn apart and meet their demise because unresolved power issues prevent the group from meeting the needs of some members.

Power struggles that arise in groups are often caused by members aggressively competing over solutions to a problem. Interested members or factions may vigorously advocate opposing solutions that they are not willing to relinquish. Given these conditions, some members will win and some will lose because ultimately only one of the competing factions can prevail.

Similar to assessing families, when assessing groups practitioners need to identify the current capacity of members to share power and resources equally among themselves and to implement problem-solving steps that ensure "win-win" solutions (see Chapter 13). Increased ability of the group to "count in" all members must necessarily occur for the group to advance through stages of development into maturity. Members are more committed to implementing decisions if they think they have had a fair say in making those decisions. Leaders can thus accelerate the group's progress through the various stages by assuming a facilitative role in teaching and modeling facilitative decision making and assisting members to adopt explicit guidelines for making decisions in initial sessions.

GROUP NORMS, VALUES, AND COHESION

Of central importance to group assessment are *group norms*, a term that refers to implicit expectations and beliefs shared by members concerning how they or others should behave under given circumstances. Norms are regulatory mechanisms that give groups a measure of stability and predictability by providing members with information concerning what they can expect from each other. Norms may define *specific* behaviors of individuals that are appropriate or permissible or define the *range* of behaviors that are acceptable in the group. Group norms are thus similar to the family "rules" discussed in the previous chapter.

Just as families have processes for dealing with rule violations, groups also develop sanctions to reduce behaviors that are considered deviant and to return the system to its prior equilibrium (Lieberman, 1980). For example, an implicit group norm may be that the opinions of the informal leader are not to be challenged by other group members. If a new group member treads on this norm by questioning the opinion of the informal leader, other members may side with the informal leader against the "upstart," pressuring him or her to back away.

People often learn about the norms of particular groups by observing situations in which norms have been violated. Speaking of group members, Toseland and Rivas (1984, p. 67) note that, as members watch the behavior of others, "soon it becomes clear that sanctions and social disapproval result from certain behavior and that praise and social approval result from other behaviors." Once members realize that sanctions are applied to certain behaviors, they usually attempt to adapt their behavior to avoid disapproval or punishment. Sanctions are powerful regulators of behavior, as Lieberman (1980, p. 501) has observed: "Ordinarily, sanctions do not need to be exerted frequently or vigorously; rather, the anticipation of sanctions is often as effective in controlling deviant behavior as is actual application."

The extent to which members adhere to norms often varies. Some norms are flexible, and the psychological "costs" to members of violation are low or nonexistent. In other instances, the group's investment in norms is significant and group reac-

tion is severe when members violate such norms. The relative status of members, that is, the evaluation or ranking of each member's position in the group relative to the others, also determines the extent to which members adhere to norms, as Toseland and Rivas (1984, pp. 68–69) observe:

> Low-status members are the least likely to conform to group norms since they have little to lose by deviating. This is less likely if they have hopes of gaining a higher status. Medium-status group members tend to conform to group norms so that they can retain their status and perhaps gain a higher status. High-status members perform many valued services for the group and generally conform to valued group norms when they are establishing their position. However, because of their position, high-status members have more freedom to deviate from accepted norms.

Norms may or may not support the treatment objectives of a group and should be viewed as to whether they are beneficial or detrimental to the well-being of members and the overall treatment objectives of the group. Examples of norms that may be functional and problematic are presented in Table 11-4.

TABLE 11-4   Examples of Group Norms

FUNCTIONAL	PROBLEMATIC
Risk by spontaneously revealing personal content about yourself.	Keep the discussion centered on superficial topics; avoid risking or self-disclosing.
Treat the leader with respect and seriously consider the leader's input.	Play the game "Let's get the leader." Harass, criticize, or complain about the leader whenever the opportunity arises.
Focus on working out personal problems.	Spend time complaining about problems and don't commit the energy necessary to work them out.
Allow members equal opportunity to participate in group discussions or to become the focus of the group.	Let aggressive members dominate the group.
Talk about any subject pertinent to your problem. Communicate directly to other group members.	Don't talk about emotionally charged or delicate subjects.
Talk about obstacles that get in the way of achieving the group's goals.	Direct comments to the leader. Ignore obstacles and avoid talking about group problems.

All groups develop norms, and once certain norms are adopted, they influence the group's response to situations and determine the extent to which the group offers its members therapeutic experiences. A major leader's role, therefore, is to identify evolving group norms and influence them in ways that create a positive ambience for change. Discerning them is often difficult, however, inasmuch as such norms are subtly embedded in the group process and can be inferred only from the behavior occurring in the group. Leaders may be able to identify norms by asking themselves key questions such as the following:

1. What subjects can and cannot be talked about in the group?

2. What kinds of emotional expressions are allowed in the group?

3. What is the group's pattern with regard to working on problems or staying on task?

4. Do group members consider it their own responsibility or the leader's to make the group's experience successful?

5. What is the group's stance toward the leader?

6. What is the group's attitude toward feedback?

7. How does the group view the contributions of individual members? What kind of labels and roles is the group assigning to them?

Asking such questions also enables leaders to increase their observations of redundant or patterned behavior of members. This is a vital point, for patterned behaviors are always undergirded by supporting norms. Another strategy for identifying norms is to explain the concept of norms to group members and to ask them to identify the guiding "rules" that influence their behavior in the group. This strategy enables members to bring to a conscious level the group norms that are developing and to make choices concerning norms that will increase therapeutic possibilities.

In addition to norms, every treatment group will create a set of values held in common by all or most of the group's members that include ideas, beliefs, ideologies, or theories about the truth,

right or wrong, good or bad, and beautiful or ugly or inappropriate (Hartford, 1971). Examples of such values include the following:

- This is a "good" group and worth our commitment and investment of time. (Or, this is a "dumb" group. We're not going to get anything out of it.)

- It is "bad" to betray confidences to outsiders.

- People who belong to different groups (e.g., authorities, persons of a different race, religion, status) are "bad" or inferior.

- It is undesirable to show feelings in the group. It is fun to try to outwit authority figures (particularly applicable to groups of juvenile or adult offenders).

Just as the group's "choice" of norms significantly affects its capacity to offer a therapeutic milieu, so does the group's "choice" of values. Similar to norms, values can be categorized as functional or dysfunctional when viewed in light of the group's therapeutic objectives. Values that encourage work on personal problems or self-disclosure, acceptance of others, and a positive attitude toward the group, for example, are functional to the group's development. By contrast, values that discourage self-disclosure, create barriers in relationships or negative attitudes toward the group, or prevent members from working on problems are obviously dysfunctional.

In initial phases, leaders must also assess and foster the development of cohesion in groups. Defined as the degree to which members are attracted to each other, cohesion is correlated, under certain conditions, to productivity, participation in and out of the group, self-disclosure, risk taking, attendance, and other vital concerns (Rose, 1989; Stokes, 1983). Cohesion in groups positively affects member's satisfaction and personal adjustment. Further, cohesiveness leads to increased self-esteem, more willingness to listen to others, freer expression of feeling, better reality testing, greater self-confidence, and the effective use of other members' evaluations in enhancing a member's own development (Toseland & Rivas, 1995; Yalom, 1985).

Cohesion is inextricably linked to norm development in a beginning group. Norms that interfere with both group formation and cohesion include, for example, irregular attendance, frequent tardiness, pairing off, excessive interpersonal aggression, excessive dependence on the leader, dominance of interaction by a few members, and general passivity in the interaction (Rose, 1989). The presence of such norms, which indicate low levels of cohesion, requires the attention of the group and group leader, for to ignore such variables is to discourage group development and, indeed, to jeopardize the very group itself.

TASK GROUPS

Task groups are organized to "find solutions to organizational problems, to generate new ideas, and to make decisions" (Toseland & Rivas, 1995, p. 29). Among task groups are teams, treatment conferences, and staff development groups. Other task groups are formed to meet organizational needs such as committees, cabinets, and boards of directors. Finally, task groups to meet community needs include social action groups, coalitions, and delegate councils (Toseland & Rivas, 1995). Task groups focus on producing products, developing policies, and making decisions rather than on the personal growth of members (Ephross & Vassil, 1988). Social workers can often act to enhance the quality of client services through focusing treatment conferences on client concerns, emphasizing client strengths and resources (Toseland, Ivanoff, & Rose, 1987). Too frequently, such groups do not include clients and family members and hence focus on professional consensus while ignoring the potential of mutual involvement of clients and family members (ibid., p. 91).

Important early tasks in forming and assessing task groups are planning for the group and structuring initial sessions to address the purpose of the group.

Planning for Task Groups

While members of treatment groups are recruited for the specific purpose of the group, membership in task groups may be constrained by organizational bylaws or dictated by organizational structure (Toseland & Rivas, 1995, p. 144). For example, members of a delegate council may be elected by constituents and an organization may decide by role who should participate in a treatment conference. However constituted, task groups are assisted by a clear focus on the goals of the group. For example, a treatment conference may have the purpose of coordinating efforts of members of a team to assist consumers in safely reaching their goals. The purpose of a task group may be originally generated by practitioners, agency staff, or members. For example, a staff member might propose a delegate council in a half-way house, the director of an agency might propose a committee to generate alternate sources of funding for the agency, or residents of a housing development might suggest a social action group to deal with poor housing conditions (ibid., p. 149).

Members of a task group should have the interest, information, skills, and power needed to accomplish the purpose of the group. The specific purpose suggests sources for the group. For example, a group formed to study the impact of managed care on a service delivery might include consumers, providers, and representatives from insurance groups. Membership should be large enough and sufficiently diverse to represent constituencies affected by the focus of the group and possess adequate skills and knowledge for addressing the purposes.

Beginning the Task Group

The agenda for a beginning session of a task group is similar to that of a treatment group. That agenda includes facilitating introductions, clarifying the purpose of the group, discussing ground rules, helping members feel a part of the group, setting goals, and anticipating obstacles (ibid., p. 177). An opening statement, including the agency's function and mission as it relates to the group purpose, should be shared in order for members to understand why they have been called together. Members can then be assisted to find out commonalities in their concerns and experiences and shared goals for group participation. Some members may know each other from previous roles and have positive or negative preconceptions from that past. They can be asked to pair up with someone they do not know to share their interests and perspective on the purpose of the group. In sharing after such pairing, a list of potential resources and perspectives for addressing the group purpose can be generated.

Developing group rules then follows including the importance of confidentiality. For example, premature release of information can hinder work of the group (ibid., p. 184). Such rules in task groups usually include proceeding with formal written agendas developed prior to the group.

Members can be encouraged to submit formal items to be included in future agendas. Such agendas usually include approval of minutes, reports from committees and administrators, work on current business, and new business. Items can be further classified into three categories: information, discussion, and action. Such agendas should be given to team members several days prior to the session with sufficient information for members to be able to adequately discuss items.

Task groups then proceed to goal setting. Such goals include those mandated by the external purpose of the group, such as reviewing managed care arrangements in the agency. In addition, the group may generate its own goals which might include generating a list of best practices which meet consumer, provider, and funder needs and a detailed description of situations which are most problematic for meeting the needs of any of these groups. Individual goals might then include interviewing members of these constituent groups prior to the next session.

Chapter 12 □ ◻ □

Negotiating Goals and Formulating a Contract

THE RATIONALE FOR CONTRACTS

If problems are explored sufficiently and agreement is reached as to the nature of the problems and the systems involved and the appropriateness of the practitioner and agency for addressing those problems, the practitioner and client(s) are ready to formulate a *contract*. Contracting is the natural culmination of the first major phase and the introduction of the change-oriented (goal attainment) phase—the heart of the helping process. Contracts specify goals to be accomplished and the means of accomplishing them, clarify the roles of the participants, and establish the conditions under which assistance is provided. An initial contract thus is an agreement that guides practitioners and clients in their joint efforts to achieve specified objectives. While most appropriate with voluntary clients, semivoluntary contracts can also be negotiated with involuntary clients (Rooney, 1992).

Research findings attest to the value of social work contracts. Wood (1978) reviewed numerous outcome studies of direct practice and reported that in a substantial number of those reporting negative outcomes, explicit contracts were not employed by practitioners. Studies that reported positive outcomes typically utilized contracts. Reid and Hanrahan (1982) have suggested that the contracts in the studies with more successful outcomes were characterized by motivational congruence. Motivational congruence is the fit between client motivation and what the practitioner attempts to provide (ibid.).

To use contracts to maximal advantage, you must be aware of their component parts and be skillful in systematically negotiating them. The purpose of this chapter is to assist you to gain knowledge and skill in utilizing contracts effectively. In the first portion, we discuss the process of negotiating goals. The remainder of the chapter is committed to other components of the contract and to the actual process of mutually formulating a contract.

GOALS

The importance of formulating goals has been emphasized in social work literature for many years. Marked advances in formulating goals occurred as a result of research studies that extended from the mid-1960s to the late 1970s. Based on a landmark research study, Reid (1970) concluded that practitioners were overly general in specifying goals, leading to "unrealistic aspirations and to repeated shifts in direction" (p. 145). Wood (1978) drew similar conclusions, cautioning that setting vague or unreasonably high goals "is to subject clients to a cruel and destructive experience in disappointment, frustration, and erosion of their confidence in their own capacities" (p. 453). Wood also found many instances in which goals were set in advance without consulting clients. In such instances, poor outcome could well have resulted from the fact that the clients and practitioners were working toward different ends (poor motivational congruence).

The Purpose of Goals

Goals specify what clients wish to accomplish. Inherent in goals are desired changes in clients' life situations that correspond to wants and needs identified when problems were explored and assessed. Goals thus are inextricably connected with and flow directly from the assessment process. Indeed, as you explore clients' wants and needs, you are engaging in preliminary goal selection work. When clients are involuntary, some goals may be agreed to as ways of satisfying a legal mandate.

Goals serve the following valuable functions in the helping process. They:

1. Ensure that practitioners and clients are in agreement about objectives to be achieved.
2. Provide direction and continuity to the helping process and prevent needless wandering.
3. Facilitate the development and selection of appropriate strategies and interventions.
4. Assist practitioners and clients in monitoring their progress.
5. Serve as outcome criteria in evaluating the effectiveness of specific interventions and of the helping process.

Utilizing goals to perform the preceding functions requires knowledge of the types of goals, criteria for selecting them, and knowledge of and skill in negotiating goals, each of which we consider in the following sections.

Types of Goals

Goals may be categorized in a broad sense as discrete, on one hand, and ongoing or continuous, on the other. Discrete goals consist of one-time actions or changes that resolve or ameliorate problems. Examples include obtaining a needed resource (e.g., public assistance or medical care); making a major decision (e.g., deciding whether to keep an unborn infant or place it for adoption); or making a change in one's environment (e.g., changing living arrangements). Ongoing goals, by contrast, involve actions that are continuous and repetitive, and progress toward such goals is therefore incremental. Examples of ongoing goals include managing conflict effectively, expressing feelings openly, asserting one's rights, setting limits with children, controlling anger, and participating in group discussions.

Another factor that determines the types of goals is the systems or subsystems that will be the focus for change. With individual clients, this focus typically involves intrapersonal subsystems as well as the client's interaction with the social and physical environment. Goals with individual clients commonly involve changes in both overt and covert behaviors. Common examples include changes in *cognitive functioning* (e.g., reducing the incidence of self-depreciating thoughts); changes in *emotional functioning* (e.g., reducing the frequency and intensity of depressive feelings); or *behavioral changes* (e.g., reducing or eliminating consumption of alcohol). Goals may also include changes in interpersonal behavior (e.g., asking someone for a date or engaging others in conversation).

When the target system is a couple, family, or

group, goals typically embody changes on the part of all relevant participants in the system. In these larger systems, goals may be held in common by members of the system (shared goals) or may involve agreed-upon exchanges of different behavior (reciprocal goals). Examples of *shared* goals include marital partners agreeing to listen to one another without interrupting or to adopt a certain strategy of decision making. Family members and group members may agree to pursue a shared goal of supplanting critical, demeaning messages to others with positive, emotionally supportive messages. The distinguishing feature of shared goals is that all members are committed to change their behaviors in essentially the same way.

With *reciprocal* goals, members of a system seek to solve interactional problems by exchanging different behaviors. For example, a couple may seek help because they communicate infrequently and are becoming increasingly distant emotionally. The wife may complain that her husband seldom talks with her, and he may counter that he gradually stopped talking with her because she seldom listened and instead criticized him and ridiculed his points of view. After exploring their problem, the couple may agree to a shared goal of increasing their verbal exchanges and further agree to reciprocal individual subgoals that include attentive listening by the wife and increased verbal sharing by the husband. Reciprocal goals thus tend to be *quid pro quo* in nature; that is, each person agrees to modify personal behavior contingent upon corresponding changes by the other.

Guidelines for Selecting and Defining Goals

Because goals serve several vital functions (listed earlier), it is important to select and define them with care. The following guidelines will assist you in advancing your proficiency in formulating goals.

Goals Must Relate to the Desired End Results Sought by Voluntary Clients   To be adequately motivated, voluntary clients must believe that accomplishing selected goals will enhance their life situations by resolving or mitigating their problems. Clients are thus likely to pursue only those goals in which they are emotionally invested; therefore, practitioners who define goals unilaterally or attempt to impose goals on clients are unlikely to enlist their cooperation. In fact, clients are likely to respond by agreeing superficially or by terminating prematurely. In negotiating goals, you should have no hidden agendas and should accord the voluntary client the final decision in selecting appropriate goals. This does not mean that you should assume a passive role in negotiating goals. To the contrary, clients will look to you for guidance in selecting goals, and you have a responsibility to share your expertise in this regard. We discuss your role in negotiating goals in a later section.

Goals for Involuntary Clients Should Include Motivational Congruence Wherever Possible   Work on problems on which there is motivational congruence, that is, aimed toward personally meaningful goals, is more likely to succeed and result in longer-lasting change than motivation which is primarily devoted to escaping punishments or gaining rewards (Rooney, 1992). Consequently, practitioners should seek to limit involuntary goals to legal mandates and include goals perceived by involuntary clients. Involuntary clients often express their own views of problems or situations that resulted in the mandated referral. Typically their views diverge from those of the legal authority or person(s) who mandated the referral. The "agreeable mandate" strategy in such instances is to search for common ground that bridges the differing views. Reframing the definition of the problem in such a way that adequately addresses the concerns of the client as well as the referral source reduces reactance and makes a workable agreement possible.

This strategy occurred in a case involving a husband whose wife threatened to "call it quits" if he didn't seek professional help. The client could not accept that he was the sole cause of the problem, but through skillful handling did acknowledge that the relationship was "rocky" and that he was "uptight." He was receptive to entering marital therapy rather than individual therapy if his wife would participate. Another example would be reframing the problem of a rebellious adolescent referred by the parents as a family problem that requires participation of other family members.

Bargaining can also be used through a "Let's make a deal" strategy in which the private concerns of the involuntary client can be included with the problem that precipitated the referral. For example, a patient in a mental institution may reject the view that he has problems with sexual impulses, but may express concerns over being inhibited in social situations. The practitioner may agree to focus on the latter if the patient will agree to explore the former. The potency of this strategy derives from being able to offer a payoff to a client (create an incentive).

With some involuntary clients, none of the preceding strategies is viable and the only recourse left to the practitioner is to appeal to clients' desire to be free of the restraints imposed by the mandating referral source. In such a strategy, a goal of getting rid of the mandate or outside pressure is included (Rooney, 1992). For example, some involuntary clients are motivated to "get child protection out of my hair," to escape what they consider an aversive presence.

Goals Should Be Defined in Explicit and Measurable Terms To provide direction in the helping process, goals must specifically define the desired end results so that all participants are clear about changes to be accomplished within the problem

system. In other words, each actor should be able to specify what she or he will be doing differently or what environmental factors will be changed. Goals should thus be defined in specific rather than general terms. Yet some goals defined by practitioners have been so nebulous (e.g., "to improve the Youngs' marital relationship," or "to increase the solidarity of the Williams family") that "drift" (Reid, 1970) or wandering in the helping process occurs and a substantial number of clients report being unclear about what a practitioner has been seeking to assist them to accomplish.

Appropriately stated, goals specify both overt and covert changes to be accomplished and should be measurable. Overt behavioral changes (e.g., "Jimmy will complete his homework each evening before watching television") can be observed by others, making precise measurement possible. Covert changes (e.g., curtailing derogatory thoughts about one's self) are also measurable, but only by the client. Measures of covert behavior thus are more subject to error as a result of inconsistent self-monitoring, the effects of self-monitoring on the target behavior, and other factors.

The lists presented in Table 12-1 will further assist you in discriminating between global and explicit goals. Included in the lists are goals that involve both overt and covert behaviors. Notice that explicit goals refer to specific behaviors or environmental changes that suggest the nature of corresponding remedial interventions.

Goals can be expressed at various levels of abstraction. Since clients and practitioners tend to define goals generally, you will need to practice in defining goals with increased specificity. Goals should be considered as the desired end product of a change effort. For example, completing an academic program with a GED is a goal.

It is important to distinguish a goal as the desired outcome of intervention efforts from general tasks, or the instrumental strategies used to attempt to reach those goals (Reid, 1992). For

TABLE 12-1 GOALS AND GENERAL TASKS

GOALS	GENERAL TASKS
1. Gain increased control over emotions	1. Reduce frequency and intensity of anger outbursts by discerning cues that elicit anger, using internal dialogue that quells anger, and employing relaxation procedures that counter anger
2. Improve social relations	2. Approach others and initiate and maintain conversation by employing listening skills and furthering responses
3. Enhance social environment	3. Explore living arrangements in a center for elderly persons that provides social activities
4. Enhance self-esteem	4. Arrest habitual negative self-statements by engaging in self-dialogue about their destructive consequences; align performance expectations with realistic criteria; attend to strengths and positive qualities; silently express self-approval when merited
5. Improve quality of parenting	5. Demonstrate competence and responsibility in assuring continuous child care, planning and preparing nutritious meals, and maintaining adequate sanitary and hygienic conditions
6. Increase social participation in a group context	6. Resolve fears of "looking stupid," initiate discussion of personal views, ask questions, participate in group exploring and problem-solving activities
7. Improve marital communication	7. Express needs and wants to each other, listen without interrupting and check out meaning attributions, increase frequency of positive messages, avoid competitive interactions, reduce critical and blaming messages
8. Relate more comfortably with desired romantic partners	8. Explore and resolve fears of rejection, introduce self and initiate conversations, ask for date, engage in appropriate activities

example, goals are listed in Table 12-1 in the left column and general tasks are described in the right column. For example, a parent may want to set a goal of reducing tantrum behavior from three times to once a day. Using time outs would be a general task toward this goal. Using time outs is not in itself a goal because it is valued primarily as a way of reaching the client goal.

Another aspect of defining a goal explicitly involves specifying essential behavioral changes of all persons in the target system with respect to shared or reciprocal goals. Observing this guideline en-

sures that all participants are clear about the part they play in accomplishing the overarching goal that relates to the broader system. For example, if a global or *ultimate* goal in family therapy is to reduce conflict and to achieve closer and more harmonious family relationships, family members must be clear about their individual goals in relationship to the larger system. The same principle applies in marital therapy and other small groups.

A final aspect of defining goals explicitly is to specify the degree or extent of change desired by clients. With goals that involve ongoing behavior, growth is potentially infinite, and it is desirable, therefore, to determine the extent of change sought by the client. The advantage of specifying desired levels of change is that practitioners and clients mutually agree to the ends sought by the latter. For example, clients who seek to enhance their social skills and to expand their social participation commonly aspire to varying levels of goal accomplishment. One client may be satisfied with being able to engage minimally in occasional conversations limited to co-workers and relatives, whereas another may aspire to engage openly and actively in a broad array of social situations. Marital partners who seek to reduce the frequency and intensity of conflict likewise differ in their definitions of acceptable levels of goal attainment. Some couples seek total elimination of intense conflicts that involve yelling, name-calling, and other destructive behaviors. Other couples seek only to reduce the frequency of aversive interactions.

Goals Must Be Feasible   Selecting unachievable goals sets up clients for failure that may produce discouragement, disillusionment, and a sense of defeat. Therefore, it is vital to consider both the capacity of clients for accomplishing goals and possible environmental constraints that militate against goal accomplishment. In most instances, clients possess the capacity to accomplish goals they set for themselves, and it is desirable to affirm the validity of their goals and to express belief in their capacity to attain them. Occasionally, you will encounter clients who are grandiose or who deny personal limitations that are obvious to others. In these instances, you can perform a valuable service by sensitively and tactfully assisting them to lower their aim to the upper range of what is realistically achievable. Sometimes funding priorities in settings sets limits to the range of goals. For example, assisting clients to return to daily functioning or survive in a less restrictive setting may be the goal of the setting.

In many cases involving involuntary clients, you may encounter agencies and judges who have grandiose expectations about what clients can accomplish in a short time period. Some practitioners seeking to mollify other agencies and court personnel have been inclined to develop "kitchen sink" contracts often including everything but the kitchen sink, committing the client to simultaneous treatment and support groups, training programs, and work expectations. It is unethical to set up clients to fail. Prioritizing goals for a particular contract period with focus on legal mandates and items of greatest significance to the presenting problem can enable the involuntary client to have a reasonable opportunity to develop and demonstrate skill and capacity (Rooney, 1992).

With respect to environmental constraints, it is important to weigh opportunities, the receptiveness and capacity of significant others to change along desired lines, economic and employment conditions, group and community attitudes, and other related factors. The following examples illustrate the importance of considering environmental opportunities. A client may wish to move from a convalescent facility to the residence of relatives, but the latter may be unwilling or unable to provide the accommodations and care needed. Practitioners may agree to help the client attempt to secure the assistance and support of key outside resources and agents needed to reach goals. If such support is critical to the success of the goal and cannot be attained, then agreeing to the goal would be unethical and setting up the client to fail.

Goals Should Be Commensurate with the Knowledge and Skill of the Practitioner   You should agree to joining clients in working toward only those goals for which you have requisite knowledge and skill or which you can gain in the course of contact. Certain problems and goals require high levels of expertise that you may not yet have attained, and it is your responsibility to clients, the profession, and yourself not to undertake interventions for which you lack competence. Certain problems, for example, require competence in family therapy, sex therapy, behavior modification, and specialized knowledge of emotional disorders and treatment techniques.

If you are receiving supervision from a person who possesses the requisite competence, it can be ethical to contract for goals beyond your competence, for you have access to the guidance needed to enable you to render the essential service. Otherwise, you are ethically bound to undertake only goals commensurate with your competence and to refer clients who require service beyond your competence to other qualified professionals. The question should be raised, of course, as to what course of action one should follow if qualified professionals are not available, as often occurs in rural areas. Under these circumstances, the choice may be between no service or less than optimal service. In our judgment, practitioners are justified in extending service in such cases under two provisions. First, practitioners are obligated to explain their limitations with regard to the goals in question, enabling the client to decide on an informed basis whether to proceed. Second, the practitioner should be confident that undertaking the goals does not place clients or others at risk. With severely depressed clients, for example, the risk of suicide may preclude undertaking treatment without medical consultation and without arranging precautionary measures with significant others. A similar risk may exist when clients have a history of violent behavior that poses a threat to others. Consultation and hospitalization should be considered before undertaking treatment in such instances.

Goals Should Be Stated in Positive Terms That Emphasize Growth   Defining goals in ways that stress growth highlights beneficial changes or gains that will accrue in the lives of clients as a result of attaining goals. In formulating goal statements, stipulating negative behaviors that must be eliminated tends to draw attention to what clients must give up. Even though clients ordinarily welcome relinquishing dysfunctional behavior (e.g., tearing themselves down, fighting, and eating or drinking to excess), they may feel a sense of impending loss, for even though such behaviors produce stress and problems, clients are accustomed to living with them. Psychologically defining goals in terms of gains rather than losses tends to enhance motivation and to mitigate opposition to change. Examples of contrasting negative and positive goal statements are included in Table 12-2.

Avoid Agreeing to Goals about Which You Have Major Reservations   Instances sometimes occur in which it is neither ethical nor wise to enter into agreements to pursue certain goals. Clients may request your assistance in pursuing goals that are incompatible with one of your major values. Values, of course, are highly individual, but many practitioners have serious reservations about working with clients whose life philosophies, moral values, or sexual practices diverge markedly from their own. For example, because of deeply held religious or moral beliefs, some practitioners may not work effectively with people who are considering abortions, or planning to relinquish custody of children to pursue personal interests. If clients pose goals about which you have strong reservations, it is generally wise to refer them to another professional person who is comfortable in working toward such goals, if such a person is available. It is important to explain your reason for making the referral, being careful to safeguard the client's self-esteem. For example: "I'm sorry I can't join you in working toward that goal. You and I have different values, and mine would get in the way of giving you the help you're seeking. I'm not faulting you for being different from me. We're all different, and that's how it should be. I do want to help you

TABLE 12-2   NEGATIVE AND POSITIVE GOAL STATEMENTS

NEGATIVE	POSITIVE
1. To reduce the frequency of criticism among family members	To increase the family members' awareness of each other's strengths and to increase the frequency of positive messages
2. To eliminate pouting between marital partners	To deal with disagreements openly, promptly, and constructively
3. To eliminate subgroupings and non-participatory behavior by group members	To unite efforts of group members in working collectively and to draw each member into participation
4. To eliminate or reduce the frequency of drinking binges	To achieve ever-increasing periods of sobriety, taking one day at a time
5. To eliminate yelling at the children and resorting to physical punishment	To consistently apply new ways of influencing and disciplining children, such as utilizing "time out" procedures, increasing positive feedback, and employing a problem-solving approach with them

obtain the service you need, however, and if it's agreeable with you, we can explore that together." In cases in which a referral cannot be made, reservations about the kind of help you may be able to provide should be shared up front.

Occasionally, you may also have reservations about clients' goals that appear to be potentially harmful to the physical or mental well-being of themselves or others. An adult may have a goal of using devious means to regain custody of children in foster placement. A pregnant adolescent may seek to enlist your assistance in planning to entrap an unwary male into marrying her. In these and similar situations, you would be justified in declining to assist clients in their planned ventures. In such instances, candidly but tactfully explain the basis of your misgiving, expressing your willingness to consider other goals.

Goals Must Be Consistent with the Functions of the Agency   Explorations of problems and clients' wants sometimes disclose desired changes that are incompatible with the functions of the agency. For example, after exploring a couple's problems in a family service agency, it may be ap-

parent that the couple's primary need relates to vocational counseling, a service not provided by the agency. Similarly, in hospital settings, clients often manifest problems that require services beyond the scope of the hospital's function, such as marital therapy, mental health services, or financial assistance. In such instances, it is appropriate to assist the client to secure the needed services through referral to another agency.

The Process of Mutually Selecting and Defining Goals

Having considered the rationale of employing goals and delineating criteria for selecting and defining them, we are now ready to consider the actual process of negotiating goals. This process consists of several activities that may be implemented in the following sequence, adapting the sequence to the circumstances of each case.

1. Determine clients' readiness to negotiate goals.

2. Explain the purpose of selecting and defining goals.

3. Elicit goals from clients, suggest other potential

goals, and then mutually select those that are appropriate.

4. Include mandated goals with involuntary clients.

5. Define the goals explicitly, and specify the extent of change desired by clients.

6. Determine the feasibility of targeted goals, and discuss potential benefits and risks associated with them.

7. Assist clients in making a choice about committing themselves to specific goals. When involuntary clients have mandated goals, make sure they have informed consent about the consequences of not working on those goals.

8. Rank goals according to clients' priorities. Also prioritize any mandated goals.

To clarify how to implement these steps, we will briefly discuss each one in the following sections.

Determine Clients' Readiness   When you believe you have explored clients' problems sufficiently, it is appropriate to determine if your clients concur with your opinion and are ready to negotiate goals.[1] A message similar to the following may be used to assess clients' readiness: "You've provided a good description of your problems and situation, and I feel I have a pretty good grasp of them. I wonder if you feel ready to talk about some specific goals at this point or if you feel we need to discuss some additional information first." If the client conveys readiness, you can advance to the next step.

Explain the Purpose of Goals   Explaining the purposes of goals increases clients' receptivity to the process and fosters their participation. It has been our experience that clients respond positively to such explanations, readily grasping and appreciating the significance of goals in the problem-solving process. Usually a brief explanation is all that is needed. Your explanation, of course, should be consistent with the functions of goals listed early in

this chapter and should emphasize the importance of clients' participation and ultimate authority in selecting voluntary goals. An example of such an explanation follows:

"We've been exploring your problems at some length, and you've indicated a number of things you'd like to be different in your life (or marriage or family). I'd like to think with you now about some specific goals you'd like to accomplish. Selecting goals assures that we're all trying to accomplish the same results. They also provide a sense of direction and serve as guideposts to make sure we stay on track. With goals, we can also evaluate your progress and determine how successful we've been in our work together. It's important that the goals represent the changes that are most important to you. I have some ideas about goals, which I'll share with you. Actually they'll likely be much the same as yours. When we have taken a look at all of them, we'll sort out the goals you regard as most important."

When the client is involuntary, the statement might include:

"As we have been talking about the problems we have been legally mandated to work on and your own views of those problems as well as your own concerns, it would help us focus our efforts if we can spell out what we are trying to accomplish here. As you know, participation in a parent training group as well as an assessment of your parenting after you complete the program are part of your court order. You can choose between different programs from an approved list we have. In addition, you have discussed your desire to return to school. This is not a mandated goal and we can decide together the best way to approach this goal that you wish for yourself."

If clients appear confused or manifest misgivings about proceeding further, you will need to explore their feelings and perhaps clarify further the function of goals. If clients respond positively, you are ready to advance to the next step.

Jointly Select Appropriate Goals   While involuntary clients have some mandated goals, the practitioner can help them as well as voluntary clients in identifying goals they would like to achieve. An effective way of assisting them is to employ messages similar to the following:

"If we succeed in our work together, how will you think and behave differently?"

"If your family could be the way you would like it to be, what would you as family members be doing differently?"

"It's been very evident in our session so far that both of you want to improve your marriage. I'd like to hear from each of you as to specific improvements you'd like to achieve."

"Now the court would like to see changes in your parenting as we have discussed. What kinds of changes do you want to see on your own, regardless of the court?"

Notice that each message requests clients to identify specific changes desired, which paves the way to the next step. If clients have difficulty identifying goals, you can prompt them by making reference to problems and wants identified during the exploratory process and suggest they consider changes related to those problems and wants. The following is an example of such a prompting message. In Chapter 10, Mr. Diaz reported wanting to maintain some independence in his living arrangements and medical regimen: "As you talked about your feeling that your family wanted to infringe on your freedom, you mentioned that you thought you could be capable of administering your own medication with your son's help. I wonder if you might like to work toward getting the kind of help necessary for you and your son to administer the medication?"

With a little encouragement, most clients will identify key goals. We recommend that as they define goals you write them down, explaining that because goals are extremely important, you are keeping a record of them.

As clients verbalize goals, you may need to interject comments that seek clarification or to suggest rewording a goal to clarify its meaning or enhance its specificity. It is important, however, not to take liberties with clients' goals but to gain their approval of rewordings. It has been our experience that if you offer suggestions tentatively and respectfully, clients welcome them.

Clients often identify most or all of the goals and general tasks that must be accomplished to obviate their problems. Frequently, however, because of your external vantage point, general task strategies will occur to you that clients have overlooked or omitted. Consequently, you have a responsibility to introduce these methods for reaching client goals for clients' consideration. In introducing such general tasks, it is important to offer them as suggestions and to explain your reason for offering them, referring to related information revealed earlier in the session.

Define the Goals Explicitly   After mutually selecting goals, you are ready to refine them by defining them explicitly and determining the extent of change desired by the client or required by legal mandate. If you were successful in the previous step, this task may require little or no further attention. If the goals were expressed in somewhat general terms, however, you will need to increase their specificity. Examples of messages you can employ to enhance the specificity of goals were presented in the preceding section. You may need to supplement these messages with suggestions of your own as to pertinent behavioral changes that would operationalize general goals.

With respect to determining the desired extent of changes, you can employ messages similar to the following:

"You say you want to improve your housekeeping. What standards do you want to achieve?"

"You have set decreasing your anxiety as a goal. What would be signs for you that you have achieved that?"

[*To elderly client*]: "You say that you want to maintain your independence in any kind of new living arrangement. What kinds of independence do you want to insure in a new place?"

[*To family members*]: "Your goal of wanting to do more things together as a family appears to be well worth pursuing. What is the extent of family-centered activities you would like to achieve?"

Determine the Feasibility of Goals and Discuss Their Potential Benefits and Risks   Before settling upon goals, it is important to ascertain their feasibility and to assess the benefits and risks associated with them. To assist clients in evaluating the feasibility of questionable goals, you can employ responses similar to the following:

"What obstacles do you foresee that might block you from achieving this goal?"

"That sounds like a very ambitious goal. I can sense how you'd like to accomplish it, but I'd hate to see you struggle for a goal that may be out of reach. Let's think about what you'd have to do to accomplish your goal."

Discussing benefits that will derive from attaining goals tends to enhance clients' commitment to exerting vigorous efforts to achieve them. A response similar to the following assists in identifying such benefits:

"What benefits do you expect to reap by achieving this goal?"

[*To marital partners*]: "How will your marriage be enhanced by achieving this goal?"

[*To family members*]: "In what ways will your family life improve by successfully accomplishing this goal?"

You also have an obligation to ensure that clients weigh possible risks associated with attaining goals. Enhanced functioning sometimes entails growth pains and negative as well as positive consequences. Examples of the former include losing a job by being assertive with an unjust employer, being rejected when making social overtures, experiencing increased pressure and family conflict

by going to work, and suffering from anxiety and discomfort by exposing painful emotions to family and group members.

Clients have a right to be aware of potential risks, and you may be vulnerable to lawsuits if you neglect your obligation in this regard. Because clients may lack awareness of certain risks, you may need to draw their attention to them. Clients may also be aware of risks you have overlooked, and it is therefore important to inquire as to risks they may anticipate.

Assist Clients to Make a Choice about Committing Themselves to Specific Goals   After discussing the benefits and risks of pursuing specific goals, the next step is to weigh these potential consequences and to reach a decision about making a commitment to strive to attain the goals in question. In most instances, benefits are likely to outweigh risks, and clients will manifest adequate readiness to contract to work toward the goals. A simple but effective means we have employed to assess clients' readiness is to ask them to rate this factor on a scale from 1 to 10, where 1 represents "extremely uncertain and not at all ready" and 10 represents "optimistic, eager to start, and totally committed." Most clients report their readiness in the range of 6–8, which usually indicates sufficient willingness to proceed with the contracting process. When clients rate their readiness at 5 or lower, they usually are unready to proceed.

Occasionally, clients manifest marked ambivalence, indicating the need to explore their reservations further. Should this occur, we recommend that you accept their misgivings and avoid attempting to convince them about the desirability of proceeding further. It is important, of course, to determine if their misgivings are realistic or are based on irrational fears (e.g., a parent may be hesitant to pursue a goal of setting consistent limits for a child because of fears of losing the child's love, or a sexually inhibited woman may fear that if she lets herself experience sensual feelings she will lose control of herself and become a slave to sexual impulses). When you encounter exaggerated fears you should assist the client to realize that the fears may be an important dynamic in the problem and that it would be unfortunate to decide against working to accomplish a worthwhile goal on the basis of unrealistic fears. Rather, the client may choose to pursue the goal of resolving the fears before undertaking related goals. Negotiating such an intermediate goal reduces the threat of the primary goal and enhances the readiness of the client to enter a working contract.

With involuntary clients, commitment to mandated goals may be expected to not be in the highest range. While the practitioner can empathize with the feeling of pressure to work on a goal that is not desired, the client can choose to approach it in his or her own way, to get a personal benefit from it, or choose to avoid it and risk legal consequences (Rooney, 1992).

When voluntary clients manifest continued ambivalence, it is appropriate to suggest that they may desire additional time to ponder a decision. We recommend that you express your willingness to think with them further about the matter inasmuch as discussing feelings and concerns with another person often serves to clarify issues and to resolve feelings. Again, we emphasize the importance of not exerting pressure upon voluntary clients to continue. It has been our experience that voluntary clients who reluctantly submit to pressure often fail to return for scheduled sessions. Voluntary clients thus tend to exercise their right to self-determination when practitioners unwittingly fail to respect this right fully.

Rank Goals According to Clients' Priorities

After clients have established goals and have committed themselves to working toward them, the final step in goal negotiation is to assign priorities to the goals. (Usually clients select from two to five goals.) The purpose of this step is to ensure that beginning joint-change efforts are directed to the goal that is most important to clients. When mandated goals are included, these can also be prioritized since simultaneous efforts on all may not be possible and some contain greater consequences than others. This step further ensures maximal responsibility and participation in the process by clients, thereby enhancing their motivation to work on goal attainment. As a lead-in to the ranking process, we recommend a message similar to the following: "Now that you've settled upon these goals, it's important to rank them according to priority. I suggest you start with the goal most important to you; then you can rank the others as you see fit. We'll get to all of them in time but we want to be sure to start with the most important one."

With involuntary clients, this message might be: "While we are coming to agreement about the priority of those goals most important to you, we also need to consider the priority of those goals that are mandated. Your court order states that you need to complete a chemical dependency evaluation immediately, so that is one that is a top priority. However, exploring educational and employment possibilities might be delayed a bit until this has begun, and you can choose which one of those you want to explore first."

When the target system involves more than one person, different members may accord different priorities to goals. Further, members may have individual goals as well as shared or reciprocal goals. If the target system is a couple, a group, or a family it is desirable to have goals that pertain both to individuals and to the larger system. With larger systems, it is desirable to have lists of goals for both individuals and the systems and to rank the goals for each person and the system. Where differences exist in ranking goals for a system, you may need to assist members to negotiate rankings.

BASELINE MEASUREMENT AND EVALUATION

As we noted in Chapters 1 and 3, evaluation of the outcomes of treatment with clients is or should be an important component of direct practice. Demands from funding sources and administrators for accountability have increasingly required service providers to furnish evidence of the efficacy of their work with clients. Until recent years, direct practitioners have tended to resist these demands, as indicated by the findings of Gingerich (1984) to the effect that a small percentage of social workers actually evaluated their practice. A study by Penka and Kirk (1991), however, revealed marked improvement in the intervening years, perhaps resulting from a combination of even more strident demands for accountability and an increasing number of social work graduates who possess the competency and inclination to employ evaluation procedures. The majority of practitioners included in the study engaged in general evaluation with their clients, although their evaluations tended to lack quantitative measurement. Consistent with this trend, we predict that similar studies in the future will reveal marked increases in quantitative evaluation.

Quantitative Baseline Measurement

Quantitative evaluation embodies the use of procedures that measure the frequency and/or severity of target problems. Measurements taken before implementing change-oriented interventions are termed *baseline* measures because they provide a baseline against which measures of progress and measures at termination and follow-up can be compared. These comparisons thus provide quantitative data that make it possible to evaluate the efficacy of work with clients.

Measuring Overt Behavior   Baseline measures can be of either overt or covert behaviors. Overt behaviors are observable and as such, lend themselves to frequency counts. For example, if family members negotiated a shared goal of increasing the frequency of positive messages sent to each other, you might instruct them to keep a daily tally of the number of such messages they convey for a period of one week. The daily average thus would serve as a baseline against which progress could be measured. Similar baselines can be determined for behaviors that involve eliminating temper tantrums, overeating, speaking up in social situations, expressing troubling feelings, listening to one's children, and a myriad of other possible target behaviors. Such measures quantify problem behaviors and make it possible to ascertain both weekly progress and ultimate outcomes of change efforts. In addition, clients are enabled to discern small incremental changes that might otherwise escape detection, which often sustains and enhances their motivation.

Frequency counts may be made by clients, by observers, or by practitioners themselves (when the target behavior occurs in conjoint or group sessions). Because it is convenient, practitioners often have clients record personal behaviors that occur outside the therapeutic sessions. Baselines obtained through self-monitoring, however, are not true measurements of behavior under "no treatment" conditions, for self-monitoring itself often produces therapeutic effects. For example, monitoring the rate of a desired behavior may influence a client to increase the frequency of that behavior. Similarly, measuring the rate of negative behavior may influence a client to reduce its frequency. These effects of self-monitoring on the behavior being monitored are termed *reactive effects*. Viewed by a researcher, reactive effects are a source of contamination that confound the effects of interventions being tested. From a clinician's viewpoint, however, self-monitoring may be employed to advantage *as an intervention* precisely because reactive effects tend to increase or decrease certain target behaviors.[2] Although desired changes may result from self-monitoring of either positive or negative behaviors, selecting positive behaviors is preferable because doing so focuses on strengths related to goals.

When baseline measures are taken of current overt behaviors, repeated frequency counts across specified time intervals are typically employed. The time intervals selected should be those during which the highest incidence of behavioral excesses occur or times in which positive behaviors are desired. It is also important to obtain measures under relatively consistent conditions. Otherwise the measure may not be representative and reflect the true picture accurately (Proctor, 1990).

Retrospective Estimates of Baseline Behavior

Baseline measurements are obtained before change-oriented interventions are implemented, either by having clients make retrospective estimates of the incidence of behaviors targeted for change or by obtaining data before the following session. Although less accurate, the former method often is employed because change-oriented efforts need not be deferred pending the gathering of baseline data. This is a key advantage, for acute problems often demand immediate attention and delaying intervention for even one week may not be justifiable. On the other hand, delaying interventions for one week while gathering baseline data often does not create undue difficulty, and the resultant data are likely to be far more reliable than mere estimates.

When determining the baseline of target behav-

ior by retrospective estimates, it is common practice to ask the client to estimate the incidence of the behavior across a specified time interval, which may range from a few minutes to one day, depending on the usual frequency of the target behaviors. Time intervals selected for frequent behaviors, such as nervous mannerisms, should be relatively short (e.g., 15-minute intervals). For relatively infrequent behaviors, such as temper tantrums, intervals may consist of several hours.

Measuring Covert Behaviors

Baseline data can also be obtained for covert behaviors, such as troubling thoughts or feelings (e.g., irrational fears, depressed states, or self-depreciating thoughts). Clients may make frequency counts of targeted thoughts or rate degrees of emotional states. Where goals involve altering feelings, such as anger, depression, loneliness, and anxiety, it is desirable to construct self-anchoring scales (Bloom, 1975) that denote various levels of an internal state. To do this, employ a five- or seven-point scale that represents varying levels of internal states ranging from absence of the troubling feeling or thought on one end to maximal intensity on the other. To "anchor" such scales, ask clients to imagine themselves experiencing the extreme degrees of the given internal state and to describe what they experience. You can then use the descriptions to define at least the extremes and the midpoint of the scale. Developing scales in this manner quantifies internal states uniquely for each client. In constructing self-anchoring scales, it is important to avoid mixing different types of internal states, for even though emotions such as "happy" and "sad" appear to belong on the same continuum, they are qualitatively different, and mixing them will result in confusion. Figure 12-1 depicts a seven-point anchored scale.

Clients can employ self-anchoring scales to record the extent of troubling internal states across

1	2	3	4	5	6	7
Least anxious (calm, relaxed, serene)			Moderately (tense, uptight, but still functioning with effort)		Most (muscles taut, can't concentrate or sit still, could climb the wall)	

Figure 12-1   A Sample of a Self-Anchored Scale for Anxiety

specified time intervals (e.g., three times daily for seven days) in a manner similar to that of making frequency counts of overt behaviors. In both instances, clients keep tallies on the target behaviors. A minimum of 10 separate measures is generally necessary to discern patternings of data, but urgent needs for intervention sometimes require practitioners to settle for less.

Guidelines to Obtaining Baseline Measures

In employing baseline measures, it is vital to maximize the reliability and validity of your measurements (Berlin and Marsh, 1993). Otherwise, your baseline measures and subsequent comparisons with measures will be flawed. Adhering to the following guidelines will assist you in maximizing reliability and validity:

1. Define the target of measurement in clear and operational terms. Reliability is enhanced when behavior (overt or covert) targeted for change is specifically defined. Global descriptions and sloppy specifications of behaviors block accurate measurement.

2. Be sure your measures relate directly and specifically to the goals targeted for change. Otherwise, the validity of your measurements at baseline and subsequent points will be highly suspect. For example, when clients' problems embody low self-esteem, measures designed to tap self-esteem should be

employed. If a mother's child care and organization of household tasks are deficient, measures should be devised that directly specify behavioral changes that are deemed essential. Similarly, measures of violent behavior and alcohol abuse should correspond to frequency of angry outbursts (or control of anger in provocative situations) and consumption of alcohol (or periods of abstinence), respectively.

3. Because clients typically present more than one problem and because individual problems may embody several dimensions (e.g., depressed affect, low self-esteem, and low assertiveness are frequently components of depression), you will often need to use multiple measures.

4. Measures should be obtained under relatively consistent conditions. Otherwise, changes may reflect differences in conditions rather than in goal-related behaviors.

5. Baseline measures are not feasible with discrete goals, for evaluating the efficacy of helping efforts in such instances is a clear-cut matter; either clients accomplish a goal or they do not. By contrast, progress toward ongoing goals is incremental and not subject to fixed limits. Employing baseline measures and periodic measures, therefore, effectively enables both practitioners and clients to discern incremental changes that might otherwise be overlooked.

Measuring with Self-Administered Scales

Self-administered scales are also useful for obtaining baseline data. Many psychological scales are available, but the Walmyr assessment scales (Hudson, 1992) are especially useful for social workers. Designed by Hudson and fellow social workers, the 22 separate scales (most of which we listed in Chapter 8) tap many of the dimensions relevant to social workers. Ease of administration, scoring, and interpretation, as well as acceptable reliability and validity are among the advantages of these scales.[3]

Self-administered scales also quantify measurement of target problems, and although they are subjective and less precise than behavioral counts, they are particularly useful in measuring covert behavioral states (e.g., anxiety, depression, self-esteem, and clinical stress) and perceptions of clients about their interpersonal relationships. As with measures of overt behaviors, selected scales can be administered before implementing treatment and thereafter at periodic intervals to monitor progress and to assess outcomes at termination and follow-up. It is interesting to note that unlike behavioral self-monitoring (i.e., counting behaviors or thoughts), subjective self-report through self-administered instruments such as those just discussed are less likely to produce reactive effects (Applegate, 1992).

Receptivity of Clients to Measurement

Some practitioners may be hesitant to ask clients to engage in self-monitoring or to complete self-report instruments because they are concerned that clients will resist or react negatively. Research studies by Applegate (1992) and Campbell (1990)

indicate such concerns are not justified. These researchers found that clients generally were receptive to formal evaluation procedures, and Campbell found, in fact, that clients preferred being involved in evaluation to having evaluations limited to practitioner's opinions. Moreover, Campbell found that practitioners were able to estimate accurately their clients' feelings about different types of evaluation procedures.

Monitoring Progress

After obtaining baseline measures of targets of change, the next step is to transfer the data to a graph on which the horizontal axis denotes time intervals (days or weeks) and the vertical axis denotes frequency or severity of target behaviors. Simple to construct, such a graph makes it possible to evaluate the progress of clients and the efficacy of interventions. Figure 12-2 is an example of such a graph, which depicts the incidence of anxiety before and during the implementation of change-

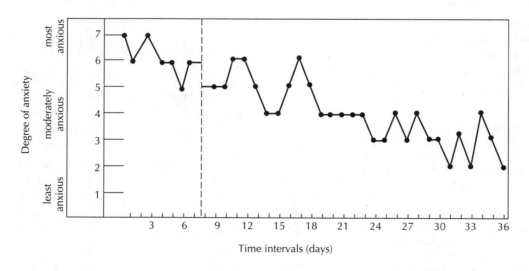

Figure 12-2   Sample of Graph Recording Extent of Anxiety during Baseline and Intervention Periods

oriented interventions. Note that the baseline period was seven days and the time interval selected for self-monitoring was one day. Interventions were employed over a period of four weeks. From the graph, it is apparent that the client experienced some ups and downs (as usually occurs), but marked progress was achieved.

In monitoring progress through repeated measures, it is critical to employ the same procedures and instruments employed in obtaining baseline measures. Otherwise, meaningful comparisons cannot be made. It is also important to continue to adhere to the guidelines listed in the preceding section. Repeated measurement of the same behavior at equal intervals enables practitioners not only to assess progress but to determine variability in clients' behavior and to assess the impact of changes in the clients' life situation. For example, by charting measures of depression and self-esteem from week to week it is possible to discern either positive or negative change that corresponds to concurrent stressful or positive life events. Visible representation on graphs of measured changes thus not only enables clients to view discernible evidence of progress but also to gain awareness of how specific life events affect their emotional states or behavior.

Monitoring progress provides still further advantages. Measures afford guidelines to both client and practitioner as to when treatment can be terminated. For example, when the observable behaviors of neglectful parents improve to the degree that they conform to explicit criteria, termination is justified. Similarly, when measurements of depression of a depressed client drop to the range of nonclinical depression, termination may be indicated. Results of monitoring can substantiate progress for payers to justify continued coverage. A final advantage is that if interventions are not achieving measurable results after a reasonable trial period, the practitioner can explore possible rea-

sons for this lack of progress and negotiate the use of different interventions when indicated.

OTHER PURPOSES OF EVALUATION

The process of evaluation described in the foregoing sections is essentially a form of single-subject or single-system research. This basic approach can also be used for other research purposes, including testing the effectiveness of specific interventions and comparing the effectiveness of different interventions. Proctor (1990) has discussed issues related to the purpose and design of single-system research (some of the preceding information was based on her article). When used strictly for research purposes, stringent guidelines should be followed, and doing so may conflict with delivering services in an optimal fashion (Gambrill & Barth, 1980; Thomas, 1978). Further, rigorous research employing single-subject design requires knowledge beyond the scope of this book.[4]

FORMULATING A CONTRACT

When you have completed the process of negotiating goals with clients, you are ready to formulate a *contract*. Writers generally agree that a contract should include the following elements:

1. Goals to be accomplished (ranked by priority).
2. Roles of the participants.
3. Interventions or techniques to be employed.
4. Time frame and frequency and length of sessions.
5. Means of monitoring progress.
6. Stipulations for renegotiating the contract.
7. Housekeeping items, such as beginning date, provisions for canceling or changing scheduled sessions, and financial arrangements.

Although it is the final discrete activity of the

first phase of the helping process, contracting continues throughout the entire course of the helping venture. Goals are fluid and should be expanded or modified as situations change and new information comes to light. Hence, goals are not to be set aside at the time of contracting only to be returned to at termination; they provide a focus for work in ongoing sessions. Time limits, types of intervention employed, frequency of sessions, and participants in the helping process may be altered according to the changing circumstances of each case. It is for these reasons that item 6, providing stipulations for renegotiating contracts, is included in the list of essential elements of a contract. Ongoing explicit understandings between practitioners and clients are vital. Keeping the contract updated also conveys continuing respect for the client and enhances ongoing motivation and cooperation. The initial contract thus is only preliminary and must be tailored to fit the changing circumstances of each case.

Practitioners construct contracts with varying degrees of formality. Public agencies often require signed service agreements. Such *written contracts* specify each of the items listed and provide space for entering details. The clients and practitioners sign the contract, giving it much the same form as a legal contract. The rationale for using a written contract is that it emphasizes the commitments both clients and practitioners make and minimizes the possibility of misunderstandings. The document, of course, is not legally binding, and this should be clarified verbally or stipulated in the written contract. Otherwise clients may believe they are justified in filing suit for malpractice if they do not achieve the goals of the contract. Some practitioners prefer *verbal contracts*, which include all of the same provisions but without the sterility and finality of a written contract. A third solution is to include a partially verbal and partially written contract with the latter including the basics of problems and goals identified, role expectations, time limits, and provisions for revision. If a written contract is not used, questions of informed consent arise. If you or your agency choose not to use written contracts, we recommend that you record in your notes the goals and their priority rankings, which makes them available for review and emphasizes the seriousness of goal setting. Research comparing the efficacy of written versus verbal contracts with respect to process and outcome measures disclosed no superiority of one method of contracting over the other (Klier, Fein, & Genero, 1984).

We now consider elements 2 through 7 in greater depth. Item 1 (goals) was considered earlier in this chapter.

Roles of Participants

We reviewed the verbal process of socialization to client and practitioner roles in Chapter 5. Those should be reviewed in the contracting process and, in the case of mandated clients or public agency practice, specified in writing. The written contract provides an opportunity for such clients to model the mutual accountability of all parties. The practitioner should spell out what he or she and their agency are committing themselves to providing. For example, the agency may agree to provide child care during sessions or transportation to certain appointments. Similarly, if the client has agreed to participate in a parenting group, that would be specified.

Interventions or Techniques to Be Employed

This aspect of the contract involves specifying interventions and techniques that will be implemented to accomplish goals. During initial contracting it is often possible to specify interventions only on a somewhat global level, such as individual, conjoint, or family sessions or a mixture of them. You can, however, specify you will be discussing problematic situations and considering alternate remedial courses of action, which is common to virtually all problem-solving efforts.

In some instances, depending on your assessment, you can discuss interventions with greater specificity. You may thus specify such interventions as relaxation training; identifying and eliminating irrational thoughts, beliefs, and fears (cognitive restructuring); role-playing and behavioral rehearsal; self-management techniques; and developing skills (e.g., communication, assertiveness, problem solving, and conflict resolution).

Whenever you consider implementing interventions, it is vital to discuss them with clients, to present a brief overview of the intervention, to elicit clients' reactions, and to gain their consent. Bear in mind that contracting is ongoing.

Temporal Conditions

Another integral aspect of the contract involves the duration of the helping process and the frequency and length of sessions. With respect to duration, there are basically two patterns—time-limited service (also known as planned short-term service) and open-ended service. The former pattern involves a specified maximum number of sessions (usually within a limited time frame), whereas the latter pattern does not specify time limits. Both patterns have existed in social work for many decades. The open-ended pattern is historically tied to the diagnostic school of casework, which developed from roots in Freudian psychoanalytic theory. Time limits were introduced by Otto Rank, a contemporary of Freud, and were adopted by the functional school of social work, which emerged in the 1930s.

More recently, time limits were incorporated as a major component of the task-centered system of social work, a model of practice that emerged in 1972 (Reid & Epstein, 1972). This model, which has gained wide acceptance, was developed as a result of compelling research evidence. Reid and Shyne conducted a study designed to compare the efficacy of time-limited casework with open-ended casework, and the results indicated that clients who received service under the former method achieved results that equaled (and sometimes exceeded) those achieved under the latter pattern. Moreover, the results were as durable, as measured six months following termination of service (Reid & Shyne, 1969).

The use of time limits is supported by grounds other than the research cited above. From a strictly logical standpoint, it can be persuasively argued that most humans tend to intensify their efforts to accomplish a given task when a deadline exists, as, for example, last-minute cramming that students do before an examination. Time-limited service thus employs time as a dynamic to counter the human tendency to procrastinate.

Still another argument supportive of time limits is that even in planned long-term treatment, most of the gains are achieved early in treatment (i.e., by the fifth or sixth session). Moreover, whatever the intended length, most treatments turn out to be relatively brief, as indicated by the findings of several studies, some of them national in scope. The National Center for Health Statistics, for example, reported in 1966 an average of fewer than five contacts for the almost 1 million psychiatric patients seen during that year. Even more impressive is the fact that if only those patients who actually began treatment are considered, the median duration of treatment is between five and six sessions.

The advantages of time-limited interventions have far-reaching implications for practitioners, including the following:

1. Time-limited service is cost-effective. Results equal

to those of open-ended service can be achieved at much less cost.

2. More clients can be served under time-limited patterns. The problem of waiting lists can be reduced appreciably when agencies adopt time-limited services as the primary pattern of service delivery (as many have).

3. Time limits foster optimism of clients when practitioners express confidence that improvement is possible in a short time.

4. Time-limited service facilitates the process of termination by introducing it during the preliminary contracting phase.

5. Time limits sharply demarcate the problem-solving process into the beginning, middle, and ending phases.

6. Funding sources are more willing to approve and pay for time-limited than open-ended treatment because of the specificity of goals and the limitation of time (Corcoran & Vandiver, 1996).

In addition to the preceding implications, two others warrant discussion. First, by adopting time-limited intervention as the primary mode of service delivery, an agency can accommodate more clients over a span of time, which enhances the likelihood of being able to provide service when it is needed most. This is a crucial advantage, for research indicates that delays in providing service negatively affect results. Based on a review of three research studies that uniformly reported negative correlations between delays of actual beginnings of service following intake and attained outcomes, Orlinsky and Howard (1978) concluded: "The message to the therapist appears to be that [patients] should be seen as promptly as possible" (p. 312).

The second additional implication concerns the matter of employing time-limited service with disadvantaged clients, who represent the major population served by social workers. Based on research findings, Lorion (1978) and Reid (1978) concluded that working-class clients better utilize and prefer structured and time-limited interventions.

Indeed, both the earlier research that provided the impetus for developing the task-centered system and later research that undergirds subsequent refinements of the system have been conducted largely with working-class clients.

The task-centered system has broad applicability to client populations. Indeed, adaptations have been tested for most settings in which social workers practice (Reid, 1987, 1992). Further, the approach has been adapted to and tested with groups (Fortune, 1985a; Garvin, 1985; Larsen & Mitchell, 1980) as well as with families (Fortune, 1985b; Reid, 1985).

Are time limits effective with ethnic minority groups? Based on a previously cited outcome study of mental health services provided to Chicano clients, Gomez et al. (1985) concluded: "the short-term casework services provided had a positive effect on the problems of Chicano clients and … clients were highly satisfied with the services" (p. 482).

Time limits, of course, are not appropriate for all client populations or situations. For clients whose goals involve or whose problems are related to deeply ingrained personality dysfunction, long-term therapy may be essential. In addition, problems correlated with poverty such as chronic neglect require longer range investment of agency resources and advocacy than short-term treatment provides. Time limits with institutionalized mentally ill patients or chronically mentally ill outpatients for whom practitioners have ongoing responsibility are impractical, except when circumscribed problems of living are defined as goals. For example, the latter may involve multiple short-term contracts related to specific problems and episodes. Similarly, time limits with assigned clients who are legally confined to correctional institutions or who are on probation or parole for extended periods of time are also inappropriate. Even in these instances, however, time limits may be used selectively to assist clients to achieve circumscribed goals.

The lengths of time limits vary across different theories or models of social work, counseling, and psychotherapy. Because of the extensive use of and substantial research with the task-centered system, a social work model, we recommend following the time limits commonly employed under this system. Most task-centered contracts specify from 6 to 12 sessions over a time span from two to four months (Reid, 1987). Given this flexibility, you can negotiate with the client for the specific number of sessions. Both clients' preferences and your best estimate of the number of sessions required should be considered. The advantage of determining clients' preferences, of course, is that mutuality in contracting is enhanced and clients are more likely to react positively to time limits when they have participated in selecting them.

Another aspect of time structuring pertains to the frequency of sessions. In social work, weekly sessions are the norm (except in instances cited below), although more frequent sessions may be employed in cases that require intensive support and monitoring. Provision can also be made in contracts for spacing sessions further apart during the terminal phase of the helping process.

To enhance mutuality in contracting, it is generally desirable to elicit clients' preferences related to the frequency of sessions. Occasionally, clients may request more frequent sessions than appear justified, and you will need to express your recommendations. It has been our experience that most clients look to the practitioner for recommendations and readily agree to them.

When intensive home-based family preservation service (see Chapter 16) or intensive outpatient crisis stabilization is the intervention selected, marked divergence from usual patterns of service delivery occurs. In such instances, service is intensive with each family, and practitioners may have a caseload of six or fewer cases. Many hours weekly are spent with each family and the practitioner is on call on a 24-hour basis. The period of intensive service, however, is generally limited to a few weeks.

A final time factor concerns the length of each session. Research offers no solid guidelines as to superior arrangements. A 50-minute session for individuals is the prevailing norm, but more time (usually one and one-half to two hours) is frequently allotted to intake sessions and to regular family and group sessions. Because some children, adolescents, and elderly clients have difficulty tolerating 50-minute sessions, shorter but more frequent sessions are a common variation. Finally, setting requirements in schools, hospitals, and other settings often influence the length of sessions. For example, contacts in a hospital setting may last 15 or 20 minutes, depending on the condition of the patient and the goals to be achieved.

Means of Monitoring Progress

Stipulating in the contract how progress will be monitored serves the vital function of fostering an action-oriented mind-set that is conducive to change. Maintaining an expectancy of change enhances motivation and actualizes a positive self-fulfilling prophecy.

When baseline measures on target problems have been obtained, the preferred method of monitoring progress is to use the same measuring devices at specified intervals, as we noted in an earlier section. If baseline data are not available, a crude method of attempting to quantify progress is to ask clients to rate their progress on a scale of 1 to 10 where 1 represents no progress and 10 denotes complete achievement of a given goal. Comparing their ratings from one time to the next gives a rough estimate of clients' progress.

Another method of assessing progress is to depict it graphically. Calibrated drawings of thermometers with a scale from 1 to 10 can be employed for each goal, and clients can color in the thermometers to reflect their progress. This method is particularly appealing to children and developmentally disabled adults, who derive satisfaction in coloring in the units as they achieve progress. The dramatic effect is further enhanced when accompanied by recognition from the practitioner and significant others.

The frequency of monitoring sessions should be negotiated. We find that clients often ask for recommendations and that spending a few minutes every other session to evaluate progress works out well. Some clients may prefer to take a few minutes each session, whereas others may prefer to discuss progress less frequently. We recommend that you be flexible but not allow more than three sessions between discussions of progress. Less frequent monitoring dilutes the benefits achieved by highlighting growth and by maintaining focus on desired changes.

Stipulations for Renegotiating the Contract

Because contracting continues during the entire helping process, it is important to clarify for clients that conditions in the contract are subject to renegotiation at any time. Circumstances change, new facts emerge, assessment evolves, and progress occurs (we hope). These and other changing factors require that the contract be constantly updated to maintain its relevance and fit. We therefore recommend that you explain that any participant in the helping process (including you) may request modifications in the contract at any time. Such an explanation further highlights the expectancy of change and enhances full mutuality in the helping process. When contracting with involuntary clients, any circumstances such as evidence of new legal violations which would cause a unilateral change in the contract should be specified.

Housekeeping Items

The final element involved in formulating a contract includes establishing a beginning date, clarifying provisions for canceling or changing scheduled sessions, and firming financial arrangements (when fees are required). With respect to changes in appointments, it is important to stress that clients are responsible for time that has been set aside for them. Should legitimate circumstances warrant changing or canceling an appointment, they should generally provide advance notice of at least 24 hours so that the time can be rescheduled for others. Ordinarily, it is desirable (and indeed often essential) to charge clients for appointments they fail to keep, inasmuch as the time was allocated for them. Explicitly discussing these matters emphasizes the importance of attending sessions; tends to avoid misunderstandings; and reduces the frequency of changes, cancellations, and failed appointments.

Discussing financial arrangements is painful for many students, who often are not comfortable in requiring others to pay for their services. This discomfort is understandable in light of the fact that students generally are inexperienced and unsure of the value of their services. Still, many agencies have policies that require payment for services, and the majority of clients expect to pay for them. Moreover, students receive supervision that enhances the quality of their services, and many provide services of high quality.

Students should bear in mind that part of competency is being able to handle financial arrangements effectively, which requires discussing them openly and without apology. Recognizing that clients expect to discuss fees may assist you in dealing with this matter more comfortably. Your responsibility, of course, does not end after negotiating the contract. If clients fail to pay fees according to the contract, you should explore the matter with them promptly. Procrastinating only makes it more difficult. Moreover, failure to pay fees may result from negative feelings toward the

AGREEMENT FOR PROFESSIONAL SERVICES

_____   _____   _____
            Name   Name   Name

_____   _____   _____
           Address   Name   Name

I. I (we) have discussed my (our) situation with _____ and hereby agree to work collaboratively in achieving certain goals that will enable me (us) to improve my (our) situation. I
   (we) agree that to achieve these goals I (we) will share my (our) experiences, life events, and
   reactions to them. I (we) agree that I (we) will participate actively in planning and carrying out
   assignments that we will mutually plan for the purpose of achieving these goals. The initial goals
   we have agreed upon are as follows:

   1. _____
   2. _____
   3. _____
   4. _____
   5. _____

   I (we) understand that we may add to or change these goals in the course of our work together.

II. I (we) agree that the format of our sessions will be:

   _____
   (individual   conjoint marital or family,   group, or combination)

   I (we) understand that each session will last about _____ beginning on _____ and
                                                             (time)   (date)
   ending by _____ for a total of _____ sessions.
                (date)

III. I (we) agree that I (we) will participate in evaluating my (our) progress each _____ ses-
                                                                                       (no.)
   sions by means of _____._____
                                      (specify measurement procedure)

   I (we) also agree to participate in follow-up evaluation after we have completed our work together.

IV. I (we) have discussed the fee for the professional service and agree to the fee of _____ per session, which I (we) will pay _____
                                              (specify arrangements)

V. I (we) have reviewed all of the above terms of agreement and on this date _____ agree to
   abide by them.   (date)

_____   _____   _____
            Name   Name   Name

_____   _____   _____
            Name   Name   Name

VI. I (we) understand that this agreement can be renegotiated at any time.

VII. I have read the above terms of agreement and pledge to do my best to assist the client(s) to
   achieve the goals listed and others that we may subsequently agree upon.

_____   _____
       Professional's signature   Date

Figure 12.3   Sample Contract

practitioner, financial strains, or irresponsibility in meeting obligations, any of which merits immediate attention.

Sample Contract

To assist you in developing contracts, we have included a sample contract (see Figure 12-3) that includes most of the components discussed in preceding sections. You will note that only a brief reference is made to the client's role in Section I of the contract, and the practitioner's role has been excluded. These aspects of the contract are excluded because they should be explicated in length as part of the verbal agreement. Delineating roles in a written agreement would result in an excessively long document.

NOTES

1 The time required for an adequate exploration varies but usually ranges from 45 minutes to 90 minutes. Initial conjoint interviews typically require about 30 minutes more than individual interviews.

2 In fact, Paquin (1981) has written about using self-monitoring for this purpose in marital and family therapy.

3 Many other scales, of course, are also available, a number of which are described in the book by Corcoran and Fischer (1987).

4 For those interested in studying single-subject research, Bloom and Fischer (1982), Jayaratne and Levy (1979), and Tripodi and Epstein (1980) have written informative texts.

Part 3

The Change-Oriented Phase

After formulating a contract, the participants enter phase two of the problem-solving process—the goal attainment or change-oriented phase. In this phase, practitioners and clients plan and implement strategies to accomplish the goals selected. Implementing these strategies involves employing interventions and techniques specified in the contract and contracting to use others as changing circumstances dictate. Before considering these factors further, however, a preview of Part 3 is in order.

A PREVIEW OF PART 3

Chapter 13 begins with a discussion of planning goal-attainment strategies, followed by a section on a general practice model, namely the task-centered system. We next consider crisis intervention, a practice model related to the task-centered system but applied in somewhat more specific situations. The chapter concludes with focus on cognitive restructuring, a still narrower model that is highly useful in addressing the cognitive component of diverse problems and that is often com-

bined with other interventions, as we shall see in Chapter 14. In subsequent chapters of Part 3, we explicate a number of widely used interventions, many of them empirically grounded. We also identify others that we cannot delineate because of limited space but list references so that you can study them independently. Given the large number of treatment models in the helping professions and an even larger number of specific interventions, it is not possible to include all of them in a single volume. Chapter 14 is devoted to widely used interventions employed to increase clients' vital coping skills in independent problem solving, interpersonal relationships, assertiveness, and managing stress. Chapter 15 focuses on environmental interventions and social planning. In Chapter 16, we delineate interventions employed to enhance functioning of families. Chapter 17 then focuses on group interventions. Techniques employed to expand self-awareness and to pave the way to change (additive empathy, interpretation, and confrontation) are considered in Chapter 18. Part 3 concludes with Chapter 19, which is concerned with skills in managing barriers to change of individuals, families, groups, and organizations.

Chapter 13 □ □ □

Planning and Implementing Change-Oriented Strategies

PLANNING GOAL-ATTAINMENT STRATEGIES

As we emphasized in Chapter 12, it is vital to include clients in planning strategies to accomplish goals. Besides safeguarding clients' rights to self-determination, including clients in selecting interventions enhances the likelihood of their cooperation. This is also true with involuntary clients, even when choices are constrained. For example, a court order to secure a chemical dependency assessment may be non-negotiable. However, choices are available in selecting the particular program from which an assessment will be secured. Clients who do not understand an intervention and its relevance to their problems and goals are unlikely to be invested in the change effort and may cooperate in a halfhearted fashion or not at all. To achieve cooperative participation, *interventions must make sense to the client*. Involving clients in planning strategies, of course, does not mean discussing strategies in detail or even identifying all strategies that will be employed. Clients are generally satisfied with a brief explanation of the rationale for and descriptions of strategies.

Effective interventive strategies must flow from the assessment of the problem and must be the most relevant and promising means of achieving the goals posited in the contract. To avoid mismatches between interventions on one hand and problems and goals on the other, it is important that interventions be relevant to the target system or subsystems and to clients' specific problems.[1]

MATCHING INTERVENTIONS TO TARGET SYSTEMS

To achieve effective outcomes, interventions must be directed to the systems implicated in problems and must be appropriate for those systems. To accomplish this is no small task, for one must be knowledgeable about the broad array of interventions and techniques and skillful in selecting and employing them. Many of these interventions are appropriate only for individual problems, some are appropriate for modifying dysfunctional interactions in families and groups, and still others relate to modifying the environment. It is important, therefore, to select and employ interventions that match systems targeted for change. Mismatches tend to lead to negative outcomes, often in the form of premature terminations by clients. For example, if a client's depression appears to be caused by social isolation associated with an impoverished physical and social environment, employing an intervention aimed at enhancing the client's self-awareness (i.e., an insight-oriented therapy) is inappropriate. Similarly, planning separate sessions for marital partners when their marital problems appear to be produced largely by dysfunctional communication and interaction makes little sense unless there are compelling reasons for not seeing the partners conjointly. And finally, implementing an intervention aimed solely at assisting a child-abusing parent to gain emotional control when that parent's loss of control appears to be triggered by overwhelming stresses associated with inadequate finances, poor housing, responsibilities for many children, lack of support systems, and severe marital conflict is tantamount to prescribing an aspirin for severe bacterial infection.

MATCHING INTERVENTIONS TO PROBLEMS

It is also vital in treatment planning to match interventions to problems, a task that is facilitated when empirical evidence has proven that a certain intervention is effective with a specified problem. Unfortunately, we are still a long way from possessing comprehensive empirical knowledge to guide treatment selection. Significant progress has been made in recent years, however, and even more rapid progress is likely to occur with increasing numbers of social workers engaging in practice research. In this and other chapters, we delineate certain interventions and cite empirical support for their use with certain problems. For example, cognitive therapy is known to be effective in treating depression, certain behavioral skills training programs have proven to be effective in treating people whose problems derive from deficiencies in basic interpersonal and problem-solving skills, and educationally focused group interventions have proved effective in treating men who have abused their spouses (see Chapter 19).[2]

MATCHING INTERVENTIONS TO DEVELOPMENTAL PHASES

Because clients vary in levels of achieved maturity, it is vital to match interventions to their developmental phases. Young children typically lack the capacity to think abstractly, so play therapy, structured group activities (with leaders employing behavior modification techniques), mutual story telling directed at enhancing coping skills and teaching moral principles (Gardner, 1971), and skill development groups are commonly employed. When parent–child interactional difficulties appear to underlie rebelliousness, truanting, substance abuse, antisocial behavior, and other related problems, family therapy may be the treatment of choice. Parent training groups are also increasingly employed to assist parents to enhance their skills in communication, setting limits, negotiation, and problem solving. In some instances, severe family problems associated with children and adolescents require interventions involving environmental changes. Residential treatment, inpatient psychiatric treatment, confinement in correctional facilities, and other such programs may be required. Severe problems of child neglect/abuse may necessitate temporary or permanent removal of a child to a safe environment.

We will not attempt to discuss interventions appropriate for all developmental phases. It is sufficient to reemphasize that you should carefully consider the developmental stages of individuals and families in planning interventions.

MATCHING INTERVENTIONS TO STRESSFUL TRANSITIONS

As we indicated in Chapter 8, clients' problems are often associated with overwhelming stresses precipitated by major life transitions. Crisis intervention and the task-centered system, which we discuss in this chapter, are models that have general application to transition problems. In recent years support groups have also been used extensively to cope with transition problems. These groups include divorce groups, rape crisis groups, groups for parents whose children have died, groups for farm families in crisis (Van Hook, 1987), groups for wives who learn their husbands are gay or bisexual (Auerback & Moser, 1987), and groups for widows and widowers (Lieberman & Videka-Sherman, 1986), to mention just a few.

MATCHING INTERVENTIONS TO ETHNOCULTURAL GROUPS

As we have stressed in previous chapters, accurate assessment of the problems of ethnic minority persons requires knowledge of both their culture and their degree of acculturation. The same is true when planning interventions. Long-term insight-oriented interventions, for example, are ineffective for the many Hispanic clients (Rogler et al., 1987), whereas short-term interventions are more effective (Gomez et al., 1985). Folk stories (*los cuentos*) have been used effectively in work with Hispanic children (Rogler et al., 1987).

A useful guideline to planning interventions with ethnic minority persons (and other clients, for that matter) is to solicit their views as to what needs to be done to remedy their difficulties. Their suggestions will be in harmony with their beliefs and values. Moreover, their views about essential changes are often on target; they lack only the "know-how" required to accomplish the changes. Deficiencies in the latter are often associated with limited knowledge about available resources and about the complexities of our service delivery systems. Determining clients' views enables the practitioner to suggest interventions that clients will perceive as relevant and to couch the rationale for selecting them in terms that make sense to clients. Including clients in the planning of interventive strategies enhances their cooperation, as we noted previously.

Another important factor to consider in planning interventions with ethnic minority clients is the importance in some cultures of family ties and the extended family. Citing the fact that in Mexican American culture the family is the primary source of identity and of support in times of crisis, Rothman, Gant, and Hnat (1985) recommend that family therapy, including the extended family or *familia*, should be considered regularly. These authors recommend that "with the agreement of the client, members of the family should be used as resources, as advocates, and in other supportive ways" (p. 202). Further, because of the patriarchal family structure and the esteemed position of elders, they recommend involving extended family elders in treatment, according them due respect.

THE TASK-CENTERED SYSTEM

The task-centered approach to attaining goals is both systematic and efficient. The approach is based on advances in methods that have resulted from the advent of short-term interventions over the past 33 years and particularly the task-centered system, which has evolved over the past 24 years. Prior to the 1960s, open-ended, long-term interventions (for intrapersonal and interpersonal problems) were the prevailing norm in social work practice and in allied disciplines. Practice theories posited the belief that attempts to produce change are opposed by countervailing forces, including unconscious resistances, inertia, fear of the unknown, and vicissitudes in the helping relationships. Resistance to change was viewed as a powerful force that required an extended time to resolve.

In the 1960s, authors began to challenge the prevailing views of resistance and advocated that the lengthy time often required for successful treatment could result from defective treatment methods. Masserman (1965) took the position that resistance may be a healthy response to poor treatment technique. Wolberg (1965) specifically criticized the practice in long-term therapy of "permitting the patient to wallow in resistance until he somehow muddles through," noting that "Where time is of no object the therapist can settle back comfortably and let the patient pick his way through the lush jungles of his psyche" (p. 235). Wolberg further faulted long-term therapists for their passivity and their failure to provide direction.

Recognizing that the sources of resistance included defects in the helping process was a theoretical milestone, for it opened the door to major changes in the process that held promise of accelerating the rate of clients' progress. Short-term therapies subsequently evolved rapidly, achieving in the 1960s a strong momentum that has continued to the present. Numerous research studies also disclosed with unanticipated consistency that brief therapies were as effective as long-term therapies and, in some instances, more effective (Wells, 1982; Wells & Gianetti, 1990).

Early short-term therapies, however, were not systematic and provided few guidelines to practitioners (with the exception of time limits) as to how they should provide direction to the helping process. Wolberg (1965) acknowledged this dilemma when he lamented that "The most pressing problem that confronts us today in short-term therapy is that we do not possess an adequate methodology. We apply the same tactics that we find useful in prolonged treatment" (p. 128). The development of the task-centered system, a social work method characterized by highly specified tactics of intervention, was a tailor-made solution to this problem. This system has the key advantage of providing a framework that accommodates interventions and techniques from many practice models.

The task-centered system has been adapted to many of the settings in which social workers practice and its efficacy has been empirically established with many different client populations (Reid, 1987), as we noted in Chapter 12. Nevertheless, we are not recommending wholesale adoption of the system. Indeed, time limits, which are central to the system, are not feasible for certain types of clients and problematic situations, as we noted earlier. However, many of the tactics of the system can be employed to increase the efficiency of other types of interventions. Progress can often be accelerated in open-ended interventions, for example, by maintaining sharp focus and continuity—another key aspect of the system. In fact, the *major components of task accomplishment— namely, preparation, implementation, and follow- up—undergird all the more specific change-oriented interventions.*

Developing General Tasks

We discussed in Chapter 12 the distinction between goals and general tasks, or those strategies planned to reduce problems and reach goals (Reid, 1992; Epstein, 1990). These general tasks consist of discrete actions to be undertaken by the client and, in some instances, by the practitioner. The tasks may be covert as well as overt. Cognitive tasks may include dismissing irrational fears of being ridiculed when one expresses a view or reminding oneself that it is not a disaster to make ordinary mistakes inasmuch as all humans occasionally make mistakes.

Partializing goals is not a new technique in social work practice; indeed, partialization has long been a basic tenet of practice theory (Perlman, 1957, pp. 147–149). Yet, in reviewing seven outcome studies of intensive services rendered to welfare recipients by public agency workers, Wood (1978, p. 443) noted that social workers in successful projects were apparently more skillful in partializing problems and goals than were workers in unsuccessful projects. It thus appears that partialization is underutilized by at least some practitioners.

Even goals formulated with a high level of specificity often are complex and involve multiple actions that must be completed in proper sequence. Because of this complexity, many clients feel overwhelmed and are unable to break their ultimate goals into constituent parts that are less intimidating. As they dissect them into bite-sized portions, guided by practitioners, they become emboldened to undertake discrete corrective actions (tasks), which lead to goal accomplishment. This process is hence consistent with social work values reflecting commitment to empowerment in facilitating client capacity and ability to make decisions and effecting events in their lives.

Partializing thus involves developing goals and then dissecting them into general tasks that specify explicit actions prerequisite to goal accomplishment. To illustrate this process, we consider three varied goals and identify general tasks associated with them.

1. The ultimate goal of a single mother is to regain custody of children removed from her custody because of neglect. As the practitioner and the mother explore conditions that must be met to regain custody, they develop the following general tasks:

    a. Improve conditions in the home by developing and following a house-keeping schedule developed in collaboration with the practitioner.

    b. Institute acceptable hygienic and nutritional standards (enlist services of a public health nurse to provide instruction and temporary supervision).

    c. Improve parenting effectiveness by participating in a parenting class and in a parents' group.

    d. Explore and develop support systems that will make child care available, thereby freeing time to socialize in the evenings.

2. The ultimate goal of a couple is to reduce the incidence and severity of marital conflict. The goal is partialized into the following general tasks:

    a. To reduce criticism and put-downs that provoke defensiveness and recriminations.

    b. To avoid venting anger on one another; to explain that one is angry but not express raw anger; to identify and express feelings underlying anger, such as hurt or disappointment, or feeling discounted.

    c. To identify sources of anger and to learn and apply effective conflict resolution skills.

    d. To work together in identifying problems and employing problem-solving strategies.

    e. To increase positive, supportive messages (compliments, approval, affection, and appreciation).

3. The goal is to improve sanitation in an apartment house by bringing pressure to bear on a recalcitrant landlord to fulfill his obligations. General tasks include the following:

    a. Talk with other tenants and mobilize an action group.

    b. Plan meetings of the tenants to enlist leaders and develop strategies.

    c. Explore legal resources and obtain legal counsel.

    d. Present a formal grievance to the landlord and express intention of resorting to legal means to force him, if necessary, to make needed improvements.

    e. File a complaint with the health department and initiate court action, if necessary.

From the above examples, it is apparent that general tasks may involve actions on the part of the client, the practitioner, or both. In the first illustration, for example, the practitioner may assume responsibility for enlisting the services of a public health nurse. In the third example, the practitioner may explore possible legal resources, subsequently involving the client or representatives of the tenants' group in talking with legal counsel.

Partializing Group Goals

The same processes also pertain to a family or a treatment group. In such cases, the entire group may engage in formulating relevant general tasks to accomplish an identified group objective. For example, to achieve a group goal of preparing for discharge from a psychiatric hospital, a group of adult men and women may decide on the following courses of action:

- Visit the halfway house to which they will be discharged, and discuss facets of the program, such as daily schedule, living arrangements, rules concerning behavior, and the format of the bi-weekly group therapy sessions.

- Investigate leisure time community resources, such as theaters, restaurants, and facilities for recreation.

- Invite several discharged patients who are successfully living in the community to share their experiences with the group.

- Plan several activities in the community, such as shopping or going out to dinner, and discuss the reactions of group members upon return to the hospital.

After partializing goals into general tasks, the next step is to order the general tasks so that they flow from one to another in a natural sequence, as was done in the preceding example of the goal of improving sanitation.

General tasks sometimes tend to be disconnected, however, and do not fall into logical sequence, as is true in the preceding illustration of the goal of assisting a mother to regain custody of her child. In such instances, you must determine which subgoal is of most immediate concern to the client and focus your beginning change efforts on that subgoal. For example, depending on the single parent's own priorities, actions in developing support systems to make child care available might be tabled or, if free time was an urgent desire, might become a priority. However, you should note one caution: It is important to settle upon a specific task that poses excellent chances for successful accomplishment by the client. Success with one general task engenders confidence and courage to tackle another; failure produces discouragement and undermines confidence in the helping process.

Formulating Specific Tasks

Even general tasks can prove to be overwhelming to hard-pressed clients. The key to the task-centered system is then to divide general tasks into specific agreements about client and practitioner actions to attempt between one session and the next. A general task such as "seek employment" must be cut into specific tasks such as "develop a resume´" and "contact employment service." For example, the single mother (above) may be unable to begin work on all of these general tasks in the first week. She might agree to draft a housekeeping schedule to share with the practitioner in the following week. The practitioner might then agree to contact the public health nurse to arrange a first home visit. The practitioner might also bring in descriptions of parenting classes and groups available for the following session at which time the client would decide which ones to contact first. Specific tasks may consist of either behavioral or cognitive actions that require effort (and often discomfort) on the client's part. The following lists illustrate both behavioral and cognitive forms of specific tasks.

Behavioral Tasks

a. To phone for information about a rehabilitation program.

b. To convey feelings of hurt to a significant person.

c. To study each day for a specified length of time.

d. To follow a schedule for completing household tasks.

e. To give positive feedback to a family member at least three times daily.

Cognitive Tasks

a. To meditate for 30 minutes daily.

b. To engage in cognitive rehearsal involving talking to an employer.

c. To keep a daily tally of self-demeaning thoughts over three one-hour intervals.

d. To recognize manifestations of anger arousal before they mount out of control.

e. To spend 15 minutes in the morning anticipating difficulties that may develop at work and mentally rehearse coping responses.

Essential tasks are sometimes readily apparent. Further, clients themselves sometimes propose tasks, and if such tasks are realistic, it makes good sense to endorse them because clients are likely to be committed to tasks they themselves identify. In many instances, however, tasks are less readily apparent, and it becomes necessary to explore alternate ways of accomplishing a general task. The challenge is to select a promising alternative that optimally fits a particular client.[3]

An effective way of identifying alternatives is to brainstorm with clients. Brainstorming involves the creative process of mutually focusing efforts on generating a broad range of possible options from which clients can choose. (We discuss brainstorming at greater length in the next chapter.) Although useful in any context, brainstorming is particularly fruitful in yielding alternatives in work with groups or families. If clients overlook options, it is important to suggest additional ones to ensure a broad range of alternatives. We have found that practitioners often need to assume the initiative, as many clients fail to generate alternatives. Keep in mind that if clients were able to formulate detailed and effective remedial courses of action, they likely would not have needed assistance in the first place. Clients generally are receptive to suggested tasks, and research indicates little difference in the rate with which they accomplish tasks suggested by practitioners as compared to those they propose themselves (Reid, 1978, p. 251).

It is important that you be sensitive to clients' reactions to tasks that you propose, for further research (Reid, 1978) indicates that "the degree of the client's apparent commitment or expressed willingness to work on the task was positively related to task progress" (p. 250). Although clients may be just as committed to tasks you introduce as to their own, if you attempt to "assign" tasks, thereby failing to enlist their commitment, it is unlikely they will expend their best efforts in im-

plementing tasks, if indeed they undertake such tasks at all. Reactance theory suggests that clients may be inclined to protect valued freedoms when they perceive little choice. The same principle applies in working with groups or families. Persons in these systems may be quick to come up with tasks they think other individual members should assume. Thus, it is important for the group leader to protect individual members' right to choose— without pressure—which tasks they will undertake and, indeed, whether they will undertake any tasks. A common mistake of beginning practitioners is to conclude erroneously that clients oppose change when, in fact, they oppose tasks imposed upon them. Such opposition often manifests a healthy assertion of individuality.

To demonstrate how specific tasks flow from general tasks, we return to one of the examples we cited earlier. Don and Jean identified a goal of reducing their marital conflict by communicating more effectively. By exploring the specific ways they would communicate differently if they accomplished their goal, the practitioner assisted them to break the goal down into several general tasks, one of which was, "We will express ourselves without antagonizing each other." Further exploration of how they antagonized each other revealed that in discussing various topics, Jean often felt her husband demeaned her by invalidating her opinion, which "gets my hackles up." Don agreed her complaint was legitimate and expressed a desire to avoid putting her on the defensive. He explained, however, that he had been very unhappy at work where he was deriving little satisfaction and sense of accomplishment. Jean acknowledged his difficulties, complaining that, "He often comes home from work looking very glum, which tends to cast a dark cloud over the family." He agreed this was true, adding he didn't feel very important to anyone. He explained further, "I need strokes, and if she would give me some strokes I would have a brighter attitude and be less inclined to put her down." Jean said if this would help she would be happy to give him some strokes, which wouldn't be difficult because of his many good qualities.

The practitioner observed that each was giving the other valuable information that if acted upon could assist them in achieving their general task of expressing themselves without antagonizing each other. After exploring their feelings and ascertaining that both were receptive to making changes in line with the discussion, the practitioner and the clients formulated the following reciprocal tasks:

1. When Jean expresses her opinions, Don will listen attentively without criticizing or belittling her. He will also endeavor to be more positive when he comes home after work.

2. Jean will be more attentive and supportive of Don, expressing affection and greater interest and concern over his frustrations at work.

Both Jean and Don agreed to keep daily tallies of the number of times they performed the actions inherent in their respective tasks, willingly committing themselves to increase the frequency of these actions to at least twice daily during the first week.

To illustrate further, let us consider another general task—to talk with other tenants and mobilize an action group—taken from a preceding example. This general task already embodies an action strategy but can be partialized still further by developing plans for contacting specific tenants, including setting a time frame for accomplishing the tasks and preparing the presentation to be made to other tenants. Specified at this level, both the practitioner and clients are clear about the task to be accomplished before the next session (assuming the clients manifest commitment to the task).

Notice that the preceding tasks have been formulated in terms of positive behaviors that clients are to perform rather than behaviors from which they are to refrain. Positively framed tasks that specify undertaking desired behaviors highlight growth and gains that clients will achieve. By contrast, tasks that specify eliminating negative behaviors focus exclusively on what clients are to give up. Clients tend to be more enthusiastic about tasks oriented to growth and achievement, and

accomplishing such tasks often motivates them to undertake even further changes.

Certain situations present opportunities for combining tasks that involve decreasing the frequency of dysfunctional behaviors and increasing the frequency of related functional behaviors. A parent, for example, may agree to implement tasks that involve decreasing nagging and increasing expressions of approval when a child performs assigned duties. Similarly, a client may agree to dismiss negative thoughts about a spouse and to increase the frequency of thoughts about the spouse's positive attributes. Still another example may involve reducing time spent brooding over disappointments and increasing time spent in recreational activities with friends.

The process of partializing goals into general tasks and ultimately into specific tasks occupies a substantial portion of the time in the early portion of the change-oriented phase. Much time is also spent in preparing to accomplish one or more tasks before the next scheduled session. We clarify the rationale for this in later sections of this chapter.

Although it is often appropriate to identify more than one task, it is important to identify and carefully plan implementation of at least one before concluding a session. In fact, many clients ask for "homework assignments." Mutually identifying tasks and planning implementation of them in each session sharpen the focus on change and facilitate progress by maintaining action-oriented involvement of clients between sessions. Without such actions, sessions become primarily verbal, and little or no change may occur between them. The ongoing focus upon task accomplishment, by contrast, concentrates, intensifies, and accelerates the helping process.

Planning Task Accomplishment

After settling upon one or more tasks, the next step is to assist clients in preparing to implement each task. Skillfully executed, this process augments clients' motivation for undertaking tasks and substantially enhances the probability of successful outcomes. A systematic approach termed the *task implementation sequence* (TIS) has been described by Reid (1975), who reported research findings to the effect that clients were more successful in accomplishing tasks when TIS was employed than when it was not.

The TIS involves a sequence of discrete steps that encompass major ingredients generally associated with successful change efforts. Although Reid recommends that the TIS be applied systematically, he also cautions practitioners to be sufficiently flexible to permit adaptation to the circumstances of each case. Reid's caution, of course, also applies to modifying the TIS to fit a group format. The TIS thus embodies the following steps:

1. Enhance clients' commitment to carry out a specific task.
2. Plan the details of carrying out the task.
3. Analyze and resolve obstacles that may be encountered.
4. Have clients rehearse or practice the behaviors involved in carrying out the task.
5. Summarize the plan of task implementation, and convey both encouragement and an expectation that the client will carry out the task.

Before considering each of the preceding steps, it is important to recognize that the accomplishment of a task often poses a formidable challenge to clients. It would be simplistic to assume that merely agreeing to carry out a task assures that the client has the knowledge, courage, interpersonal skill, and emotional readiness to implement a task successfully. Clients who possess these ingredients are unlikely to need the assistance of the practitioner in the first place. Moreover, if a client is ill-prepared to undertake a task, the probable outcome will be failure either to attempt the task or to complete it successfully. Either outcome is likely to cause the client to feel discouraged and to experience lowered self-esteem and subsequent difficulty in facing the practitioner. Opposition can thus be engendered, which might be manifested by not keeping the next appointment or diverting attention from the pertinent task.

Having clarified the challenges inherent in tasks, let us consider each step in more detail.

1. Enhancing Commitment to Carry Out a Task

Directly aimed at enhancing motivation to carry out a task, this step involves clarifying the relevance of tasks to clients' goals and identifying benefits that will result from carrying out tasks. The rationale of this step is that to follow through with tasks, clients must perceive gains that outweigh potential costs (including anxiety and fear) associated with risking new behavior. Because change is difficult, involving apprehension, discomfort, and uncertainty, this step is especially critical when clients' motivation to carry out a given task is questionable.

In many instances, the potential gains of carrying out a task are obvious, and it would be pointless to dwell on this step. The potential gains of applying for a job interview or securing essential information about eligibility for financial assistance are self-evident. The benefits of other tasks, however, are less apparent, and a discussion of them may be essential for the client to grasp the relationship between the task and the goals. Benefits of following a medical regimen may not be clear if a client's physician has not explained the need for the regimen and the consequences of not following it. Similarly, the benefits of keeping a daily log on self-defeating thoughts may be unclear to a client who does not see the connection between this task and an ultimate goal of overcoming depression.

It is preferable to begin implementing step one by asking clients to identify benefits they will gain by successfully accomplishing a task. Clients are usually able to identify obvious benefits but may overlook others that are less apparent. Consequently, you may need to bring these benefits to their awareness.

To illustrate this process, we consider an actual case situation involving a male client in his early

20s who was distressed over the fact that when he took his girlfriend on a date they frequently encountered some of her friends, and she often left him standing for lengthy intervals while she conversed with them in a foreign language that he neither spoke nor understood. After exploring his reactions of feeling left out, less important to her than her friends, and frank irritation over her insensitivity to his feelings, he agreed to work on the task of directly but tactfully expressing his feelings to her.

When asked what benefits he would gain by carrying out the task, he replied that he would feel better about dealing with her rather than just feeling irritated and left out. The practitioner agreed, adding he would also feel stronger and experience more self-respect for facing the problem rather than avoiding it. Furthermore, his girlfriend would also likely respect him more, and they would gain experience in dealing with relationship problems. Last, he would be taking an important step toward accomplishing one of his ultimate goals—to resolve his mixed feelings toward his girlfriend.

Just as it is important to identify benefits, it is also essential to consider possible risks of carrying out tasks. (Recall our making this same point in the last chapter with respect to the process of selecting goals.) Again, we recommend you ask clients to identify risks and then add others that occur to you. In the case situation discussed in the foregoing paragraph, the client expressed concern that his girlfriend might take offense and construe his expressing his feelings as an attempt to control her. He described her as independent and somewhat domineering. Further discussion, however, led him to conclude this was not a real risk because he needed to learn to stand up to her in any event. Otherwise, he might be inviting being dominated, and that was unacceptable to him. He definitely wished to carry out the task even though it might introduce some strain in the relationship.

In work with growth groups, practitioners can use group process to good advantage in assisting individual members to weigh the benefits and risks of individual goals. In using group process, it is important to elicit expressions from other group members. Preferably, this should take place after a member considering a potential change has had an opportunity individually to contemplate the relative benefits and risks in assuming a task. As "outside consultants" who often share many of the same situations and dilemmas as the person contemplating the task, other members often make a penetrating analysis of the costs and rewards involved.

In enhancing motivation to change ingrained behaviors, it is sometimes essential to create immediate incentives by planning tangible rewards for carrying out planned actions. One client had a long-established pattern of going on eating binges, during which she would consume large quantities of food, to her later chagrin. She initially viewed herself as helpless to control her impulses to gorge herself, attributing her difficulties to "lack of willpower." Careful assessment had led the practitioner to disagree with her explanation, imputing her problem instead to (1) mistaken and demeaning beliefs about herself and (2) the habituated use of eating as a substitute for gratification she was not gaining through more appropriate modes of behavior.

To enable her to experience success in exercising self-control, the practitioner suggested that she identify something she wanted badly and earn the privilege of acquiring it by modifying her eating habits during the week. (Her previous longest time of maintaining control of her eating was four days.) With a smile, she responded that she had wanted to purchase a pair of leather boots for several months but had not done so because it seemed extravagant. She and the practitioner then negotiated an agreement whereby she could reward herself by buying the boots if she ate only at mealtimes and consumed average portions of food over the week's time. She could also have one small snack each day but only by making a conscious choice to do so and then eating it while sitting at the dining room table. On the other hand, if she indulged in a binge, she would forfeit the right to purchase the boots for at least four months. She appeared excited about the challenge and agreed to share it with her husband, whose knowledge of it would create additional incentive. (He had earlier encouraged her to buy the boots.) If she successfully implemented her task, she was to reward herself further by expressing silent approval and to remind herself she had consciously made decisions to exercise self-control. Further, she was to think of herself as capable of increasing self-control week by week.

In her session one week later, the client's success was mirrored in her countenance as she greeted the practitioner. With obvious pride, she described how she had constantly reminded herself she could exercise self-control, and her success over the week's time gave substance to her thoughts. She described how pleased her husband was with her success and how they had planned to celebrate by going together to purchase the boots. The initial success was the first of a series of similar successes that led to increased self-confidence and to eventual mastery of her excessive eating.

Rewarding oneself (self-reinforcement) to enhance the incentives for completing a task is particularly relevant when changes sought involve yielding pleasures of consummatory excesses and carrying out essential activities that may be perceived as aversive, e.g., studying, cleaning the house, mowing the lawn, doing the dishes, or planning and preparing regular meals. Possible rewards should be considered in light of each client's uniqueness, but the following are typical examples: going to a special movie or artistic production; allocating time to engage in special activities, such as reading a novel, going swimming, or going bowling; visiting or shopping with a special friend; or purchasing an inexpensive but desired item.

Rewards can also be utilized to create incentives for children to complete tasks, such as completing homework assignments, showing caring behaviors to siblings, picking up after themselves, or doing household chores. In addition to negotiating tasks with children, practitioners often establish complementary tasks with parents or other significant persons for the purpose of assisting children in carrying out their tasks or modifying dysfunctional behavioral patterns that involve both children and parents. When rewards are used to create incentives for children, it is important during the early stages of change to provide rewards immediately after children perform desired behaviors. It is also important to reward small changes; otherwise, children may become discouraged and give up, believing they cannot meet the standards expected by parents. Naive parents and practitioners mistakenly assume that elaborate long-range rewards (e.g., get a bicycle in June) will motivate children to make changes. In actuality, even for older children, smaller rewards given soon after the behavior are far more effective as motivators.

In setting up tasks with accompanying rewards for children and parents (or significant others, such as teachers), the following guidelines are helpful:

a. Frame tasks so that what children and parents are to do and when they are to do it are explicitly defined. For example, with an eight-year-old child who frequently argues and complains when parents make requests of him, a task can be formulated so that the child will carry out the requested actions immediately. The task also specifies what the parent is to do in a given circumstance (e.g., make the request in a calm and cheerful manner). And finally, the task specifies the time frame and conditions under which the task is to be performed (e.g., every two hours, twice daily, each Wednesday, for the next four days).

b. Designate points that children can earn for performing specified target behaviors, and establish a method of keeping track of the points (e.g., each time the child responds appropriately to requests, the parent will enter a mark on a chart constructed conjointly by the parents and the children.)

c. Establish a reward for earning a specified number of points for specified periods of time (e.g., if the child earns five points by 8 o'clock each night, he or she will have a choice of playing a short game or having a parent read a story). Whenever possible, it is important to offer "relationship" rewards, as contrasted to ones that are monetary or material.

Relationship rewards involve time spent in an attractive activity with a parent or other significant person. It is also important to invite children to choose the type of reward they wish to earn, since they will choose rewards that have maximal value as incentives.

d. Give a bonus for consistent achievements of tasks over an extended period of time (e.g., if the child achieves a quota of five points each day for seven consecutive days, he or she and the involved parent will celebrate by going out for a hamburger and drink).

e. Teach parents or others to give consistent positive feedback regarding the child's progress and negotiate tasks related to expressing encouragement and approval as the child engages in task-related efforts.

Tasks buoyed by creative rewards can do much to reduce parent–child tensions, motivating both adults and children to focus on developing positive behaviors. One parent, who was consistently embarrassed in restaurants by the disruptive behavior of her five children, readily consented to a task of monitoring her children's positive behaviors during the meal. Also giving her children the task of reporting to her their positive actions, the mother gave them credit by recording one point for each positive action. At the end of the meal, each child had earned enough points (at the rate of a penny a point) to redeem them for an after-dinner treat (something they usually received anyway). Although the mother spent more time recording points than eating, she was ecstatic about the successful outcome of the activity and particularly about the sharp increase in caring behaviors manifested by her children toward each other and toward her during the evening, which, incidentally, generalized to other situations throughout the week. She also reported experiencing more positive feelings toward her children.

2. Plan the Details of Carrying Out the Task

This step is vital in assisting clients to prepare themselves for all the actions inherent in a task. Most tasks consist of a series of actions to be carried out sequentially, including both cognitive and behavioral subtasks. For example, before carrying out an overt action, such as asking a boss for a raise, requesting repairs from a landlord, or submitting to a painful medical examination, clients often benefit by preparing themselves psychologically. This may involve reviewing potential benefits, dismissing needless fears by reminding themselves of reality factors, mustering courage by accrediting themselves for past successes, recalling the encouragement of the practitioner, and praying for strength if they are religiously inclined. By planning such cognitive strategies, clients are better able to cope with the inevitable ambivalence and trepidation associated with implementing new actions.[4]

Planning overt actions involves considering details of actual required behaviors. For example, in the first case cited under step 1, the client would need to consider when he would talk with his girlfriend, how he would introduce the topic, express his feelings, and cope with possible reactions on her part. The more detailed the plans, the greater the likelihood of success. Moreover, by discussing discrete actions, you increase opportunities to elicit cues to misgivings, fears, or skill lacks that must be remedied if clients are to complete tasks successfully.

Task planning may also involve practitioner tasks that must be coordinated with the client's actions. For example, an unemployed and unskilled young adult may be interested in obtaining vocational guidance. A task may be to take tests that assess aptitudes and interests. Task planning may involve telephone calls by the practitioner to locate an appropriate resource and to convey information to the client, as well as subsequent actions by the client to arrange to take the tests and have the results interpreted. Subsequent tasks may involve exploring and arranging appropriate vocational training, locating financial resources, and the like. Practitioner tasks should be undertaken when the practitioner has access to resources or information that will facilitate client work. If the client could benefit from eventually being able to carry out the practitioner task on his or her own, it is useful to walk through the steps together. In other instances, practitioners may accompany or arrange for someone else to accompany the client in performance of a task. In group contexts, a group or family member might also informally assist a designated person in planning and carrying out actions outside the group.

In many instances, it is important to specify carefully the conditions under which the task will be carried out. For example, a sixth-grade boy who constantly disturbs his peers and irritates his teacher through boisterous talk and teasing behavior may accept a task of listening attentively when the teacher is speaking during the one-hour arithmetic class and raise his hand three times to answer questions during that time. He is to carry out this task each day for the next five days. A grandmother who is living with her son and daughter-in-law and whose specialty is monitoring and critically reporting to the parents all of their children's negative behaviors may be asked during a family therapy session to assume a task of reporting *positive* behaviors directly to the children and to the parents. This grandmother may agree to work on this task extensively during the upcoming weekend, a time when all of the children are at home. It has been our experience that if the time for implementing tasks is left indefinite, clients (and practitioners) tend to procrastinate until it is too late to implement requisite actions effectively. Although we have not subjected our impression to empirical testing, we are convinced that clients implement tasks at a higher rate when specific times are stipulated than when they are left indefinite. In determining a time frame, it is also important to elicit feedback from clients regarding the amount of time they feel is needed to accomplish a specific objective rather than to set a time frame arbitrarily.

In selecting and planning tasks pertaining to *ongoing* goals, you should observe an additional caution. Because progress on such goals is incremental, it is vital to begin with relatively simple tasks that are within the clients' capacity to a-

chieve. The chances of clients undertaking more difficult tasks later are much enhanced if they achieve success on initial tasks. Conversely, if they experience failure on initial tasks, their confidence and courage may decline, and they may be reluctant to undertake additional ones. It is thus preferable to have the first task be too easy than too difficult.

3. Analyze and Resolve Obstacles   Based on a recognition of the inevitability of forces that counter the client's thrust for change, this step is aimed at countering these forces.[5] Implementing it involves anticipating and analyzing obstacles that may be encountered as the client seeks to accomplish a task. Employed effectively, this step is a powerful technique for enhancing task accomplishment and for accelerating change.

With commonplace tasks, obstacles are generally minor and can often be readily identified by asking clients what difficulties, if any, they expect to encounter. Included in such tasks are those requiring simple actions, such as telephoning a community agency that the client and the practitioner have just discovered, which holds promise of providing needed assistance. A caveat should be observed, however—what is a simple action for most people may be difficult for a few. Making a telephone call was an overwhelming task for one client. Mildly brain damaged and overprotected by his parents for all his 19 years, the client had depended on them to make telephone calls for him because he feared he would "foul up and sound stupid." In such instances, fears may pose formidable barriers to accomplishing a task and may require careful exploration and working through before they are overcome.

When tasks are complex, obstacles likewise tend to be complex and difficult to identify and resolve. Tasks that involve changes in patterns of interpersonal relationships tend to be multifaceted, encompassing subsidiary but prerequisite intrapersonal tasks as well as a mastery of certain interpersonal skills. Successfully resisting unwanted sexual advances, for example, may involve overcoming powerful fears that refusal to submit will result in utter rejection. The irrational belief that one has nothing to offer other than sex must be supplanted by a belief about one's self that is aligned with reality. The client must also master new behaviors that tactfully but firmly set limits with predatory males.

Clients vary widely in their capacity to anticipate obstacles. Consequently, it is vital to elicit from them (and from members when in a group context) possible obstacles to achieving their planned course of action. Observations regarding obstacles may also be made by the practitioner. In introducing the possibility of relevant obstacles, it is vital to safeguard the client's self-esteem by explaining that obstacles are common to many people. An example of an obstacle that had to be identified involved a withdrawn, late adolescent client whose goal was to mingle socially with others. She was embarrassed and hesitant to reveal that she was afraid of accepting an invitation to visit a friend in her neighborhood because her legs might become rubbery and she might vomit on the neighbor's rug. Similarly, a musically talented male client who wished to play the organ for others was afraid to display his talents because others might perceive him as weird.

As these examples imply, psychological barriers to accomplishing tasks are often encountered regardless of the nature of the target problem. Overlooking such barriers may in some instances cause needless difficulties in the accomplishment of tasks and, in others, result in outright failure. Applying for a job, submitting to a medical examination, talking to a school-teacher, expressing tender feelings—these and a host of other seemingly everyday tasks are charged with strong emotionality for some people and may be threatening.

Prerequisite to the successful accomplishment of a task, therefore, may be a subsidiary task of neutralizing untoward emotions. This can be accomplished often in a brief time by eliciting and clarifying the apprehension, rationally analyzing it, and modeling and rehearsing the behavior re-

quired to implement the task successfully. In other instances, more extensive efforts are required. Whatever time and effort are invested are likely to be rewarded by achieving a higher rate of success in accomplishing tasks. An economy of time is also effected, since failures in implementing tasks further extend the time required for successfully implementing them.

Other cues and techniques may also facilitate identifying obstacles. In discussing plans for implementing a task, you should be alert to nonverbal cues that indicate apprehension on the client's part about undertaking the task. Such cues include looking away from you, speaking diffidently and unenthusiastically about the task, changing the topic, fidgeting atypically, and tightening facial and body muscles. If you detect such reactions, you should further explore the presence of undisclosed barriers or work further on resolving obstacles already identified.

Vital to successful task implementation is the client's readiness to tackle the mutually negotiated task. Such readiness, however, should not be confused with feeling comfortable; it is neither realistic nor desirable to expect clients to feel altogether comfortable with the task. A certain amount of tension and anxiety is to be expected and may positively motivate the client to risk the new behavior embodied in the task. Inordinate anxiety, by contrast, may be a major deterrent to undertaking the task or may impair the client's effectiveness upon attempting it. Obviously, when clients report that they did not carry out a task, you should consider the possibility that the task was premature and that unresolved barriers remain. Another possibility is that the client was inadequately committed to the task, an important factor to be discussed later.

A simple yet effective way to gauge readiness for undertaking tasks is to ask clients to rate their readiness on a scale from 1 to 10, with 1 representing total unreadiness and 10 complete readiness. It is important to explain first that a certain amount of apprehension is natural and should not deter the client from trying out new behaviors;

indeed, relative freedom from apprehension is not achieved before implementing the task but is rather a by-product of successful implementation. This explanation is important because many clients are overly hesitant to risk themselves and needlessly postpone taking actions.

When clients rate their readiness at 7 or higher, you can assume a sufficient degree of readiness and suggest that they appear prepared to undertake the task. Also provide support by expressing restrained confidence that the client can successfully implement the task and by conveying an expectation that the planned actions will be carried out. Exploring the reasons why clients rate themselves at 7 rather than 10 on the readiness scale will often give you vital information concerning potential obstacles to change, including reservations they may have about completing the task.

After identifying barriers to change, you must next assist the client in overcoming them. Barriers encountered most frequently include *deficiencies in social skills and misconceptions and irrational fears* associated with performing tasks. The former is a formidable barrier that must be overcome, for one may lack the skill and experience to know how to carry out a task. In such instances, clients commonly fear bungling a task and appearing ridiculous as a result. Undertaking the task thus is perceived as placing one's self-esteem in jeopardy.

Modeling and behavioral rehearsal in sessions may assist clients to gain the courage and skills necessary to carry out interpersonal tasks. In some instances, however, more intensive interventions may be required, such as personal effectiveness training and assertiveness training.

The second major type of barrier to task accomplishment involves misconceptions and irrational fears that embrace misunderstandings of the self, stereotypic perceptions of others, and intense apprehensions based on distorted and dreaded consequences of actions. Cognitive theorists present a compelling case to the effect that the quality and intensity of emotions experienced in a given situation are largely determined by the perceptions and attributions of meaning associated with that situation. Inordinate fear and apprehension are thus cues that something is amiss in the client's patterns of thought. Your task is to elicit the problematic emotions, to identify their cognitive sources, and to assist clients in aligning their thoughts and feelings with reality. Removing this barrier usually enables clients to move several points higher on the readiness scale.

Resolving misconceptions, perceptual distortions, and irrational fears was once believed to require a lengthy expedition into the unconscious to discover the genesis of such inhibiting forces. In recent years, however, new techniques (see Chapter 14) have been used successfully in eliminating fears and misconceptions rapidly without shifting the focus to the remote past.

4. Have Clients Rehearse or Practice Behaviors Involved in Carrying Out Tasks Certain tasks involve skills clients lack or behaviors with which they have had little or no experience. Step 4 is thus aimed at assisting clients to gain experience and mastery in performing behaviors essential to task accomplishment. Successful experience, even in simulated situations, fosters belief in having the ability to carry out a task effectively. Having an expectancy of success is vital, for as Bandura (1977) has indicated, "The strength of people's convictions in their own effectiveness is likely to affect whether they will even try to cope with given situations" (p. 193). Bandura builds a strong case, documented by research evidence, to the effect that the degree of positive expectation that clients have in their ability to perform tasks effectively determines how much effort they will expend in attempting tasks and how long they will persist in the face of obstacles or aversive circumstances. It follows that a major goal of the helping process is to enhance clients' sense of self-efficacy with respect to the tasks they select.

Research evidence cited by Bandura (1977, p. 195) indicates that, once established, self-efficacy and skills tend to be transferred by clients to other situations that they previously avoided. According to Bandura, people receive information about self-efficacy from four sources: (1) performance accomplishments, (2) vicarious experience, (3) verbal persuasion, and (4) emotional arousal. Of these four sources, performance accomplishment is especially influential because it is based on personal mastery experience.

Major methods of increasing self-efficacy through performance accomplishment include assisting clients to master essential behaviors through modeling, behavior rehearsal, and guided practice, all of which we discuss at length later in this chapter. An example of performance accomplishment would be assisting family members to master certain communication skills during actual sessions.

Vicarious experiences gained by observing others demonstrate target behaviors or perform threatening activities without adverse consequences can also generate expectations in clients that they too can master the target behaviors. Efficacy expectations based on observing the practitioner or others model desired behaviors, however, are likely to be weaker and more vulnerable to change than expectations based on performance accomplishment. Information about one's capabilities based on assumptions that one can perform comparably to a model are hardly as persuasive as direct evidence of personal accomplishment.

Attempting to reassure or convince clients that they can perform new behaviors has limitations as an enduring source of personal self-efficacy. Nevertheless, it can and does contribute to successful performance when accompanied by measures that equip clients for effective action. Verbal persuasion contributes by raising *outcome expectations* rather than enhancing self-efficacy per se.

The fourth source of information about self-efficacy, emotional arousal, is based on the fact that the perceived level of emotional arousal affects how people perform. Clients who are extremely anxious or fearful about performing a new behavior are unlikely to have sufficient confidence that they can perform the behavior competently. Many interventions are therefore directed to reducing anxiety or fear or to influencing clients to *believe* they are not fearful or anxious. Evidence cited by Bandura indicates that to be effective, reductions in emotional arousal must be genuine and not based on deceptive feedback aimed at assuring clients they are not anxious when they are anxious. Emotional arousal obviously is an undependable source of self-efficacy because it too is not related to actual evidence of capability. Perceived self-competence tends to reduce emotional arousal rather than the converse.

Having defined the sources of information about self-efficacy, we return to the topic of behavioral rehearsal. As employed in actual sessions, behavioral rehearsal assists clients to practice new coping patterns under the tutelage of the practitioner. Indications for using behavioral rehearsal include situations that clients feel inadequately prepared to confront. When clients manifest strong uneasiness or appear overwhelmed by the prospects of carrying out a given task, behavioral rehearsal is an effective way of developing requisite skills and reducing the threat posed by the action. Such tasks usually involve interacting with significant other people with whom strain already exists or is expected to develop as a result of the planned actions. Typical examples include asserting one's rights to an authority figure; expressing feelings of hurt or rejection to one's spouse; or making a social overture to a member of the other sex.

Role-playing is the most common mode of behavioral rehearsal. Before engaging clients in rehearsal of desired behaviors, however, practitioners can use role-playing to have clients demonstrate their initial levels of skills, thus enabling practitioners to model skills that build on clients' extant skills. Practitioners frequently model behavior that clients are expected to perform before actually having them rehearse the behavior. Used particularly when the requisite behavior is unfamiliar to the client, modeling has been amply documented as an effective means of enabling clients vicariously to learn new modes of coping behavior, as we noted earlier.

In employing modeling, ask the client to play the role of the *other* person involved in the real-life difficulty and, in doing so, to simulate as accurately as possible the anticipated behavior to be encountered in the actual situation. The role-playing thus enables you to model appropriate responses to behavior that has previously overwhelmed the client. After the role-playing, it is productive to discuss what happened, focusing on the client's reactions and on questions and concerns as well. It is also beneficial to explain your rationale for particular responses and to share difficulties you may have experienced. It has been our experience that in assuming the role of clients, we often gain new insights and fuller appreciation of the difficulties they encounter.

If your coping in the modeling situation falls short of being effective, it is appropriate and even helpful to acknowledge the difficulties you experienced and to consider mutually other possible coping responses. Indeed, it is desirable to model imperfect *coping efforts* rather than *mastery*, for research indicates that clients benefit more from observing a "coping model" (Kazdin, 1979; Meichenbaum, 1977). A coping model manifests the struggles that a person might expect to experience in performing the behavior or activity, including expressing anxiety and hesitation and making errors. Clients identify more easily with and are less threatened by a coping model than one who performs flawlessly or perfectly.

Modeling need not be limited to overt behaviors, for clients may also benefit from modeling of covert coping with cognitive barriers to task accomplishment. Covert modeling involves expressing aloud thoughts and feelings associated with manifest difficulties and demonstrating appropriate ways of coping with related problematic thoughts and feelings. As with modeling of overt behavior, covert modeling should demonstrate coping rather than mastery.

After completing a modeling exercise, the next step is to reverse the roles so that the client rehearses the actual target behavior and you assume the role of the other significant person. In so doing, it is important that you attempt to approximate the anticipated behavior of the other person, including tone of voice, facial expressions, gestures, choice of words, and provocative behavior as modeled earlier by the client. The responses of the client to your simulated behavior provide an opportunity for corrective suggestions and for identifying need for additional practice, as well as for reinforcement and encouragement. Moreover, clients' readiness to tackle situations in real life can best be assessed by observing their behavior in rehearsal. Most important, clients' confidence to carry out tasks is enhanced by practice. You can further enhance clients' self-efficacy by expressing confidence in their ability to carry out the planned task successfully, if your support and encouragement are genuine.

As clients mobilize the strength and courage gained through behavioral rehearsal and face problems head-on rather than avoid them, their previous greatly feared consequences dwindle into realistic perspective. Clients have affirmed the effectiveness of modeling and behavioral rehearsal numerous times for the authors by reporting that their practice during sessions was the single most important factor in assisting them to accomplish their tasks. Behavioral rehearsal, incidentally, need not be confined to sessions. It is often productive to encourage clients to continue rehearsing target behaviors outside the interviews by pretending to engage in real-life encounters.

Modeling and behavioral rehearsal need not be confined to relationships between practitioners and individual clients. Often, a client in a group or family session may be able to provide effective and realistic coping modeling for another group member. Indeed, a rule of thumb in conducting group role-playing sessions is to tap group resources for coping models whenever possible, which enhances the help-giving role of group members.

Closely related to behavioral rehearsal, *guided*

practice is another form of performance accomplishment, which differs from behavioral rehearsal in that it consists of *in vivo* rather than simulated behavior. Using guided practice as a mode of intervention, you assist clients to gain mastery of target behaviors by coaching them as they actually attempt to perform the target behaviors. For example, in conjoint marital sessions, you may assist clients to master skills in solving problems or resolving conflicts by instructing them as they deal with actual problems or conflict situations. Guided practice is particularly relevant to family and group contexts. Skills in brainstorming, active listening, assertiveness, and control of anger—to name just a few—can be effectively learned through guided practice in groups.

Guided practice is an especially potent method of inducing change. The practitioner can observe live behavior and provide immediate corrective feedback as well as encouragement and approval. Observing behavior directly is especially valuable in marital and family sessions, for opportunities exist to intervene immediately when dysfunctional behavior occurs. Such on-the-spot interventions enable you to clarify what is going wrong, to explain more effective ways of coping, and to coach clients in employing more competent behavior.

5. Summarize the Plan of Task Implementation

This final step involves reviewing the various actions clients are to carry out in accomplishing a task. Implementing this step, which is done in the concluding segment of an individual or group session, enables clients to emerge from the session with a clear understanding of what they are to do and in what sequence. To enable clients to gain maximum benefit from this step, we recommend that you ask them to review details of their plan for implementing the task, including strategies for coping with obstacles that may be encountered. By eliciting clients' descriptions of their plans, you can assess whether certain aspects of the plan need to be further clarified. It is often useful to begin by describing your own plans for practitioner tasks: "I

have agreed to do xyz by our meeting next week" followed by a request for a review of client plans: "What is it that you plan to do by next week?" Many clients find it beneficial to have a written list of agreed-upon tasks. Some clients prefer to write their own lists while in other cases, the practitioner can write down the tasks, keeping a carbon copy for their own records. To counter procrastination, it is advantageous to specify the time frame for implementing the plan.

After summarizing the plan of task implementation, it is appropriate to terminate the session. An effective way of closing the session is to express approval of clients' plans and expectations that they implement them. Because results cannot be accurately predicted, however, it is desirable to convey restrained optimism. We recommend you also express interest in hearing about their experience at the beginning of the next session.

Maintaining Focus and Continuity

The strength of the task-centered system lies in its focus on change through task accomplishment and its systematic format that promotes continuity of change efforts. Individual sessions are sharply focused, and continuity is maintained from one session to the next. Each session begins with a review of clients' experiences in implementing tasks that were agreed upon during the previous session. There are two major objectives and benefits of discussing clients' experiences in implementing tasks. First, both clients and practitioners can identify ways in which clients can further improve their effectiveness in performing newly developed behaviors. This discussion may further enhance clients' comfort in coping with problematic situations and suggest additional activities in the session to refine their skills. A second benefit is that the practitioner can explore clients' perceptions of their impact on others and their feelings as they implemented the tasks. This discussion provides an opportunity to identify additional work to be done and prepares the ground for mutually planning future tasks.

Still another benefit of reviewing task implementation is that you can reinforce clients for carrying out planned tasks. When clients report successes, it is appropriate to express your delight, to accredit their strength and progress, and briefly to share in savoring their successes. Your own way of conveying your positive feelings is best, but the following is a typical message:

[*Smiling with pleasure*]: "I'm delighted with how well you did. As I listened to you describe how you talked with your teacher, I was impressed with how clearly you expressed your feelings. Your teacher must have been impressed too, because you shared a part of yourself she hasn't seen before."

In reviewing task accomplishments, it is critical to elicit details as to actions or behaviors that assisted clients in achieving a task. Even when tasks have been only partially completed, it is important to focus on results clients achieved as a consequence of their efforts. In so doing, it is important to connect clients' efforts with the results that they attained, underscoring that in accomplishing specified tasks, they demonstrated ability to shape their own lives. Establishing that clients have more control than they had previously realized is a powerful force for countering feelings of helplessness, hopelessness, and depression that many clients experience.

Although they may report improvements in problem situations discussed in previous sessions, some clients attribute the reasons for these changes to circumstances beyond themselves. Through careful exploration, practitioners often are able to establish that changes occurred (at least in part) through clients' efforts. Establishing such cause-effect relationships is critical to successful outcomes, for clients are thereby enabled to view themselves as actors who have the potential to solve their problems and to enhance their life situations.

After completing a review of task implementation, you mutually plan additional tasks that enable clients to progress closer to their focal goals. In addition to following the steps previously delineated for defining tasks, it is important in working toward accomplishment of *ongoing goals* to plan tasks that involve incremental changes and build on one another. Planning tasks that are graded in difficulty enhances chances of successful accomplishment and tends to increase clients' motivation to exert greater efforts in the change process.

To illustrate gradual progression in developing tasks, we consider an extremely self-conscious, socially inhibited client in his early 20s, who negotiated a goal of being able to socialize with his fellow workers in the shipping department of a large wholesale supply firm. He rarely engaged in discussions with co-workers, his conversations being limited to job-related topics. To accomplish his goal, the following tasks were mutually negotiated and accomplished sequentially as listed:

1. Smile at workers and look them in the eyes upon arriving at work.
2. Verbally greet co-workers each morning and when leaving work say "see you tomorrow." (Expect startled reactions from co-workers.)
3. Greet co-workers and ask "How are you doing, (person's name)?"
4. Ask if he can join co-workers at lunch.
5. Listen to co-workers at lunch and "shut off" thoughts about possible negative impressions they may have of him.
6. Make at least one comment or ask one question at lunch.
7. Make at least three comments at lunch.
8. Make overtures to initiate conversation at other times by picking up on topics discussed at lunch.
9. Share at least one personal view or experience during luncheon discussion.
10. Ask a co-worker to join him for a cold drink at break time.

Extensive planning, including modeling, behavioral rehearsal, and discussion of problematic feelings, was involved in preparing to execute each of the preceding tasks. As the client successfully accomplished the tasks, he decided to risk himself in social relationships away from work and formulated a new goal of asking a woman out on a date. To accomplish this goal, progressive tasks building on those previously listed were negotiated.

In actual practice, progress is rarely as smooth as the preceding implies. Not infrequently clients fail to carry out tasks or to achieve the desired results when they do. Occasionally, unforeseen circumstances such as illness, crowded schedules, and unavailability of others involved in tasks preclude task accomplishment between sessions, necessitating carrying them over to the next week.

Clients may also fail to carry out tasks because of weak commitment to them, emergence of more pressing problems, negative reactions to the practitioner or to the group, or inadequate preparation. In any event, it is vital to explore the reasons carefully, attempting to resolve factors that have blocked implementation if both you and the clients agree the task remains valid. If you determine the task is not valid, it is important to shift your focus to more relevant tasks, as we discuss later. The importance of commitment to the task has been documented by Reid (1977), who cited this factor as "the only consistent statistically significant predictor of task progress" (p. 69).

A lack of commitment is not to be confused with a lack of readiness. In the former, the willingness to change is absent; in the latter, clients possess the willingness but are blocked from acting by other barriers. One frequent cause of a lack of commitment to undertake interpersonal tasks is a covert unwillingness to own one's part of a problem. A spouse or parent may pay lip service to carrying out a specific task but subsequently report feeble excuses for not doing so. Inwardly, unwilling clients often blame others for their difficulties and passively wait for others to initiate corrective actions. In such instances, it is important to explore further the interactions between clients and other actors and to clarify which part of the difficulty is owned by each. Confrontation may also be used to help clients recognize their responsibility for maintaining the undesired status quo by waiting for others to change. If clients exhibit a continued unwillingness to work on tasks, it is appropriate to question their willingness to change.

A lack of commitment to carry out specific tasks is also frequently associated with the efforts of involuntary clients. In these instances, it is the practitioner's responsibility to engage such clients by creating an incentive for change, as we discussed in Chapter 12. Persistent failure to carry out tasks, however, belies expressed intentions; inaction certainly speaks louder than words, and in such instances, the advisability of continuing should be carefully weighed.

In some instances, what appears at first blush to be clients' lack of commitment to tasks may in actuality be a reflection of other more pressing concerns. Clients with multiple problems and limited coping skills may be beset between sessions with difficulties that supersede the focal problem. Such situations require judicious handling, for the practitioner and clients are faced with a difficult decision. On one hand, it is important to be flexible and to shift focus when emerging problems demand immediate attention. On the other hand, some clients are constantly besieged with "crises," and they should be made aware of the consequences of making little progress with any one when there is too much shifting from one to another.

Although you should be flexible in shifting focus, you must avoid letting crises dictate change efforts. Some clients who live from crisis to crisis benefit in the long run by seeing individual tasks through to completion, taking brief detours only to "apply Band-Aids" as needed. By successfully completing individual tasks, they gain increments of positive coping strengths they can apply to other crises.

Clients may not implement tasks in other situations because of overriding problems they have not as yet revealed. Some clients disclose only relatively minor difficulties during initial interviews and defer revealing more burdensome problems until they feel more comfortable in sharing them.

Tasks agreed upon initially thus may not be valid in that they do not relate to the clients' paramount concerns. When this occurs, it is proper to shift the focus to more burdensome difficulties and to formulate new goals and tasks accordingly. It is important, however, to be satisfied that you are shifting focus for valid reasons and not reinforcing a pattern of avoidance.

Frequently tasks fail because they have been inadequately specified: The client did not understand what to do. In other cases, they may be based on adverse beliefs. For example, some parents are hesitant to utilize reward systems, believing that parents should not be bartering with children (Rooney, 1992, p. 241).

A variety of other reasons may be responsible for task failure. In marital therapy, individual spouses often renege on their commitments to carry out tasks because each does not trust the other partner to carry out his or her part of the bargain. Further, during the week, one or both partners may gather "evidence" that the other spouse is uncommitted to the agreed-upon task, thus justifying his or her own noncompletion of it. Adequate preparation for an initial task in marital therapy thus entails exploration of the trust issue and establishment of a contract that each partner will strictly monitor his or her own task regardless of whether the other person does or does not.

When a client's problems involve the family system, it is important to include relevant members of the family in the sessions. Practitioners often defeat their client's objectives (and their own) by limiting their contacts to the individual client when the behaviors of other persons in a system impinge greatly on identified problems. Although at times families will accommodate an individual member who steadfastly achieves and maintains changes in the system, in many instances families defeat the individual's change efforts. Some families are so disorganized or insensitive to individual change efforts that they discourage any positive efforts of individual family members to modify behavior. Further, other families have dysfunction-

al interactional patterns that are so pervasive and intractable that it is extremely difficult for members to make needed behavioral changes without great cost unless adjustments are made in the entire system. In such situations, it is vital to involve all family members in sessions to assess individual needs as well as family dynamics and to include them in goal and task planning.

A factor that practitioners must consider in assisting groups to assume tasks is the group's stage of development. Group members have difficulty accomplishing significant change-oriented tasks in the first two stages of group development. In these stages, members tentatively test out the practitioner, other group members, and the group itself, at the same time attempting to find their own positions. Thus, they sometimes have little psychic energy or commitment to accomplish individual or group tasks. For this reason, tasks should be kept simple, and accomplishing them should not require an inordinate amount of investment by members. For instance, asking a newly formed group of delinquent adolescents in a correctional facility to make changes in their behavior toward staff or peers before they are "emotionally committed" to the purposes of the group is doomed to failure. On the other hand, asking members to assume small tasks during the week so that the group might participate in an attractive activity may appeal to them.

Negative reactions to the practitioner may also block task accomplishment. Such reactions often result when the practitioner assigns tasks unilaterally. Assigning tasks in such a manner tends to activate negative feelings in clients akin to those experienced in childhood toward a parent when unpleasant chores were assigned.

Another factor that may block task accomplishment is failure on the practitioner's part to follow up on task implementation. If practitioners neglect to review the client's experience in implementing a task, the client (or practitioner) may shift the focus to other topics before actually seeing previous efforts through to completion. Such shifts disrupt the continuity of change efforts and foster "drift," which dilutes and prolongs the helping process. For this reason, it is vital to review progress in implementing tasks, preferably at or close to the beginning of each session. Use of a written task sheet facilitates such a review.

A final factor sometimes involved in failures either to attempt or to implement tasks successfully involves inadequate preparation. A practitioner may overestimate the coping skills of clients or may not devote sufficient time and effort to the task implementation sequence, leaving clients ill-prepared to cope with tasks' demands. Actually, it is preferable for clients not to attempt tasks rather than to attempt them and fail because they are not adequately prepared. In the former instance, blows to self-esteem are usually minimal, and additional efforts can be made to prepare a client more adequately. Failure, by contrast, may damage self-esteem and undermine confidence in the helping process.

Even when preparation has been adequate, successful outcomes of task efforts are not ensured. Unanticipated reactions of others, ineffectual task performance, panic reactions, inappropriate task selection based on inaccurate assessment, and adverse circumstances may block goal attainment. To avoid or minimize undue discouragement by clients when results are negative, it is helpful to interpret such results not as failures but as indications of the need for additional information and task planning. Negative results, in fact, sometimes serve a constructive purpose in further elucidating dynamics of problems, thereby enabling clients and practitioners to sharpen their assessment, goals, and tasks.

Evaluating Progress

A final mode of maintaining focus and continuity is to evaluate progress toward goal attainment regularly. We discussed this process in the previous chapter, but here we add the following objectives served by systematically monitoring progress.

1. By eliciting clients' views of their progress or by comparing latest rates of target behavior with the baseline, you maintain focus on goals and enhance continuity of change efforts.

2. Clients gain perspective not only in determining where they stand in relationship to ultimate goals but also to their pretreatment level of functioning. Discerning incremental progress toward goals tends to sustain motivation and to enhance confidence in the helping process and in the practitioner.

3. Eliciting clients' feelings and views regarding progress enables practitioners to detect and to work through feelings of disappointment and discouragement that may impede future progress and lead to premature discontinuance.

4. Practitioners can evaluate the efficacy of their interventions and change strategies. If a given approach fails to yield positive results within a reasonable time, more of the same is unlikely to produce different results. We recommend you apply the maxim, "If what you're doing isn't working, try something different."

5. Indications of marked progress toward goal attainment alert practitioners to possible readiness by clients to shift the focus to another goal or to consider planning for termination if all goals have been substantially achieved.

Evaluation of progress should be conducted in accordance with the agreement negotiated in the contracting process. Progress should be monitored every two to three sessions at a minimum. Methods of assessing progress should also be those negotiated in the contract.

CRISIS INTERVENTION (CI)

Crisis intervention (CI) is another widely employed general interventive strategy or modality. This modality shares much in common with task-centered casework. It: (1) is time limited, (2) focuses on problems of living rather than psychopathology, (3) is oriented to the here and now, (4) involves a high level of activity by the practitioner, (5) employs tasks as a primary tactic of change efforts, and (6) is an eclectic framework that can accommodate various practice theories and interventions. Because crisis intervention addresses urgent crisis situations precipitated by stressful events, maturational crises, and acute transitional situations, its potential use is somewhat more limited than that of task-centered casework.

CI methods were used during the Gulf War to provide immediate responses to traumatic events. The interventions ranged from single session, telephone intervention to intervention with groups (Gilbar, 1992; West, Mercer, & Altheimer, 1993). Social workers are said to be especially qualified to take a leadership role in the organization of such traumatic event debriefing (Bell, 1995). On a more local scale, social workers have taken the lead in developing postventions in the public schools to assist family members and the school community in dealing with the grief caused by student suicide (Komar, 1994).

Tenets of Crisis Intervention Theory

Basic to CI theory is the concept that when people are beset by a crisis, a potential exists for them to cope in ways that are either adaptive or maladaptive. According to CI theorists, most crisis situations are limited to a period of four to eight weeks, during which time people manage to achieve a degree of equilibrium, which may be equivalent to, lower than, or higher than the precrisis level of functioning. The amount of time required before a crisis is resolved depends on the stress; persons coping with cancer surgery are reported to need from four weeks to five years in adjustment and rape victims often require six months to several years to recover (Barth, 1988, p. 92). Life crises can thus be viewed as presenting potential threats that can permanently impair people's level of functioning or as painful challenges that embody opportunities for growth in personal strength and coping capacity. CI theory emphasizes the importance of intervening immediately to assist clients who are overwhelmed by crises. Timely intervention is critical not only to prevent deterioration in

functioning but also to reach people when their defenses are low and their receptiveness to therapeutic interventions are greatest, as occurs during acute periods of crisis.

Most CI theorists accept Caplan's (1964) definition of a crisis as an upset in a steady state (state of equilibrium) that poses an obstacle, usually important to the fulfillment of important life goals or to vital need satisfaction, and that the individual (or family) cannot overcome through usual methods of problem solving. A crisis thus is stressful and disruptive and can adversely affect biological, psychological, and social functioning and can produce disturbed emotions, impair motor functioning, and negatively affect ongoing behavior. Crisis situations have a subjective element, for people's perceptions and coping capacities vary widely. What is severely stressful and overwhelming for one person or family may be stressful but manageable for others. Nevertheless, although crisis situations or events (denoted as hazardous events) are diverse, most people would agree that natural disasters, death of a loved one, disabling or life-threatening illness or injury, cultural dislocation, rape, out-of-wedlock pregnancy, and other like events usually pose a crisis to those involved.

Hazardous events can be experienced as a threat, challenge, or loss. A threat (e.g., possibility of losing a job, spouse, home, or valued status) may involve anticipated loss of an individual's sense of integrity or autonomy. A threat thus involves high anxiety and apprehension about a possible dreaded event. A challenge involves anxiety over the possibility of failure in the immediate future, as, for example, not performing adequately on a new job or failing an examination crucial to one's future. Challenge, of course, also involves motivation to succeed and hope of success. Loss, by contrast, involves an acute sense of deprivation resulting from an event that has already occurred, such as a death, divorce, or move from one's homeland. Loss, therefore, produces depressed affect associated with the grieving process.

CI theory posits that people's reactions to crises

typically involve going through different stages. Theorists differ as to whether three or four stages are involved. Our description involves a synthesis of stages identified by various authors. The first stage involves an initial rise in tension accompanied by shock and perhaps even denial of the crisis-provoking event. To reduce the tension, persons resort to their usual emergency problem-solving skills, and when these fail to alleviate the tension, heightened tension ensues. At this point, the person or family enters the second stage, which is characterized by tension so severe that the person feels confused, overwhelmed, helpless, angry, or perhaps acutely depressed. The length of this phase varies according to the nature of the hazardous event, the strengths and coping capacities of the person, and the degree of responsiveness from social support systems.

As people move from stage 2 to stage 3, they resort to different coping tactics, the outcome of which depends on whether these tactics are adaptive or maladaptive. If the tactics are maladaptive, tension may continue to escalate and the person may suffer a mental breakdown or, in extreme instances, attempt suicide. If the efforts are adaptive, the person regains equilibrium and perhaps achieves a higher level of functioning.

According to CI theory, crisis periods are time limited and people achieve a degree of equilibrium for better or for worse during this time. Consequently, immediate intervention aimed at restoring clients to their precrisis level of functioning or better is crucial. Departures from the traditional weekly 50-minute sessions are common, and some clients may even be seen daily during acute periods of crisis.

Time limits (generally six to eight weeks) are employed in CI, although some clients require even shorter periods of time. Practitioners assume an active role and deliberately employ their authority and expertise to inspire the hope and confidence so badly needed by clients. The temporal focus of CI is on the here and now, and goals are limited to alleviating distress and enabling clients to regain equilibrium. No attempt is made to deal either with precrisis personality dysfunction or intrapsychic conflict, although even minor changes effected through CI may provide the impetus for enhanced personal and interpersonal functioning as well as improved transactions with social support systems.

The heart of CI involves delineating tasks that clients can perform to achieve a new state of equilibrium. Although practitioners are active and directive in defining tasks, clients should be encouraged to participate to the extent of their capability, for their active participation fosters autonomy. Obviously, clients' abilities to participate actively are limited during periods of severe emotional distress but increase as the distress subsides.

After completion of the essential tasks, CI moves into the final major activity, which consists of anticipatory guidance. This activity, which has preventive implications, involves assisting clients to anticipate future crisis situations and to plan coping strategies that prepare them to face future stresses.

Having reviewed the essential concepts of CI, we now turn to procedures for implementing the modality.

The Initial Phase of Crisis Intervention

During the initial phase of CI, the practitioner's objectives are (1) to relieve the client's emotional distress, (2) to complete an assessment, and (3) to plan the strategy of intervention, focusing on relevant tasks the client must perform. The following sections briefly focus on each of these processes.

Relieving Emotional Distress   Drawing out clients' emotions and responding empathically to them often assist clients to unburden themselves of painful and sometimes overwhelming emotions. Practitioners can also provide needed emotional support as they encourage clients to ventilate pent-up emotions by reassuring them that their emotions are a natural reaction to an extremely distressing situation.

When clients in an acute crisis are immobilized by tension and anxiety, deep breathing and progressive muscle relaxation procedures (see Chapter 14) can be helpful in alleviating tension and in assisting clients to gain composure. Practitioners should also consider the need for antianxiety or antidepressant medications in extreme instances.

Use of social support systems may also reduce emotional distress for some clients. Friends and loved ones may provide comfort and compassion that clients sorely need to buffer the devastating impact of certain crises. Clients' church affiliations can also be a source of great emotional support. Local church leaders can often provide solace and guidance and rally the support of church members. Moreover, support groups for diverse crises are available in many communities. Practitioners may need to develop such resources in others.

Assessment Because of the short time involved in CI, practitioners concurrently assess and alleviate clients' emotional distress. Objectives of the assessment involve determining the nature of the crisis situation, its significance to and impact on the client(s), factors or events that precipitated the crisis, adaptive capacities of the client, and resources that can be tapped to alleviate the crisis situation. These factors are crucial to formulating tasks that must subsequently be accomplished.

The nature of a crisis, of course, provides valuable clues as to the sources of clients' distress. Losses, for example, leave people bereft of vital sources of emotional supplies and typically produce grieving reactions. The meanings people attach to losses of close kin vary considerably, however, leading to differing emotional reactions. A client who has been extremely dependent on a spouse may react to the spouse's death not only with grief but also with feelings of helplessness and hopelessness concerning ability to manage independently. A client whose relationship to a deceased spouse or parent was ambivalent and

conflictual may react to the death with feelings of guilt, hostility, or even relief. Practitioners, therefore, must determine the unique meaning of crisis situations to each client. Determining the meaning and significance of precipitating events can be highly therapeutic to clients. Through exploring precipitating events and other factors that bear on clients' reactions, practitioners enable clients to view their situation in a new perspective, which can foster hope. Many clients, in fact, improve dramatically as they gain expanded understanding of the complex forces involved in their crisis situations and their reactions to them.

Assessing clients' capacities for adaptive coping involves not only determining their current level of functioning but also their precrisis level. Obviously, to restore clients to their previous level of functioning, one must first ascertain that level. Knowledge of adaptive capacity is also essential to formulating relevant tasks and selecting appropriate interventive techniques. Practitioners, therefore, must rapidly assess individuals' and families' precrisis functioning.

Cultural Factors and CI Cultural factors are also vital in assessing clients' reactions to crisis situations. Situations deemed as crises vary widely from one culture to another, as do the reactions to them. Divorce or unwed pregnancy, for example, requires considerable adaptation in most cultures but may pose an extreme crisis to first generation Asian Americans because of the social ostracism, loss of face, and shame involved for persons in Asian cultures. The extremity of the stress involved in such situations has led to suicide in some instances.

Refugees from nations that are torn by war and/or political upheaval suffer multiple losses and are especially in need of CI services. Many arrive in the United States stripped of social, economic, psychological, and religious supports. Some are physically ill. Moreover, most are ill-equipped to adapt to American patterns of life such as shopping, transportation, banking, food preparation, use of home appliances, health care systems, and bureaucratic structures. Further compounding these overwhelming stressors is that many refugees do not speak English. Weiss and Parish (1989) have written about the need to adapt crisis intervention to these most vulnerable groups.

CI with Marginally Functioning Persons It is important to note, as Lukton (1982) and others have stressed, that use of CI need not be limited to people who ordinarily are psychologically intact. Target groups for CI have been extended to include marginally functioning people with chronic problems. Moreover, even acutely psychotic people can be helped. A psychotic break, in fact, may be viewed as a way of responding to a crisis state and as an opportunity for developing more effective coping mechanisms and interpersonal skills (Lukton, 1982, p. 277). (With clients whose precrisis functioning was marginal, case management services may be needed to link them with other needed resources.) Crisis teams have also been employed in the public sector (e.g., in hospital emergency rooms, youth service centers, and mental health centers) to provide immediate assistance aimed at stabilizing people and their families and preventing relapses of psychiatric patients.

Assessing Support Systems Another aspect of assessment in CI is to determine clients' social support systems, for "interventions that enhance the natural helping network can be enormously helpful in crisis intervention" (Lukton, 1982, p. 280). Practitioners can enhance natural helping networks by mobilizing family, friends, neighbors, the clergy, or cultural reference groups. Another valuable resource is self-help groups, which consist of people with similar problems. Members of self-help groups provide mutual support and assistance to each other in solving problems.

You will recall we discussed assessment of support systems in Chapter 9. We also discuss support systems at greater length in Chapter 15.

Contracting and Planning Contracting in CI involves basically the same elements as those described in Chapter 12. The overall goal, to restore equilibrium, is applicable to all cases, but general and specific tasks vary according to the nature of the crisis situation and the unique characteristics of each person and/or family. Similar crisis situations, of course, involve similar tasks that must be accomplished, and the literature contains many articles that identify tasks relevant to specific crisis situations such as rape (Holmes, 1981; Koss & Harvey, 1991); having AIDS (Gambe & Getzel, 1989); out-of-wedlock pregnancy (Chesler & Davis, 1980); and cultural dislocation (Golan & Gruschka, 1971). Lukton (1982) has cautioned, however, that in addressing the same types of crisis situations, different writers often identify different tasks. Moreover, the sequence of accomplishing tasks may vary from client to client. Practitioners, therefore, can benefit from available knowledge in determining and negotiating essential tasks but must consider the individuality of each client situation.

In negotiating time limits, it is important to involve clients (thereby increasing their autonomy) by soliciting their views as to how long they believe they will need to "get back on an even keel." Many will suggest just a few weeks, which is the time ordinarily required. Some clients will suggest only two to three weeks and will, in fact, require no more. When clients are reluctant to commit themselves, practitioners can suggest that from four to eight weeks are usually sufficient and ask the client to select a limit, recognizing that fewer sessions may prove ample.

Problems of Transition An exception to the use of the usual time limits involves clients in certain states of transition, such as adapting to the death of a spouse or child, single-parent status following divorce, retirement, and a new country and culture. Golan (1980, 1981), Lukton (1982), and others argue persuasively that traditional CI is not appropriate for such transition states that require "identity transformation and role change that continues long after the acute phase of disorganization is overcome" (Golan, 1981, p. 264). With respect to loss of a child, research cited by Videka-Sherman (1987) indicates that "grief after a child dies lasts a very long time and may actually intensify over the first 1–2 years following the child's death. Social workers must be very careful not to impose unrealistic expectations that acute grief will end in 6 months or even in 1 or 2 years" (p. 109). Weiss and Parkes (1983) report similar findings regarding the time required for spouses to adapt following the death of a mate. In such instances, principles of CI are relevant to the acute phase of disorganization, but extended service is required for clients to adapt to new roles and to develop new sources of emotional supplies. The phases of crisis resolution thus are far longer for this group than earlier believed.

Task Implementation

In facilitating clients' accomplishments of tasks deemed essential to mastery of crisis situations, practitioners should observe the guidelines to task implementation delineated earlier in this chapter. Practitioners assume an active and directive role and give advice to a greater extent than when using other approaches. Still, it is important to foster client autonomy by involving clients in planning for task implementation and by encouraging and reinforcing independent actions whenever feasible.

Space limitations preclude our giving examples of tasks appropriate for specific types of crisis situations. Numerous examples are provided, however, in books and articles that discuss particular types of crisis situations.

Anticipatory Guidance

During the concluding phase of CI (after the crisis has subsided), practitioners engage in anticipatory guidance, an activity of major preventive signifi-cance. This activity is a strong feature of CI, and we urge practitioners to include it in the terminal phase of any practice model. Anticipatory guidance involves assisting clients to anticipate future crises that might develop and to plan effective coping strategies (based on knowledge gained during the preceding period of problem solving) they can employ to avoid being overwhelmed in the future. Relevant strategies might include analyzing sources of distress, recalling and accrediting successful efforts in coping with past crisis situations, anticipating needs, identifying and utilizing support systems and other potential resources, and formulating and implementing essential tasks. It is important, however, not to convey an expectation that clients should be able to manage all problem situations independently in the future. Indeed, during the process of termination, practitioners should express continuing interest, reassure clients that the door is open should they need future help, and explain that the practitioner will be contacting them soon to check on their continued progress.[6]

COGNITIVE RESTRUCTURING

Although the large majority of theories of casework, counseling, and psychotherapy acknowledge the central role of cognition in human behavior, it has only been in recent years that theories and techniques have been developed that can be applied directly and systematically to problems of cognitive dysfunction. Over three decades ago, however, Ellis's (1962) book, *Reason and Emotion in Psychotherapy*, posited the theory of rational-emotive therapy (RET). This work proved to be seminal, and since that time, particularly in the past 22 years, cognitive therapy has burgeoned. Numerous books and articles have been published delineating the significance of mistaken beliefs and faulty patterns of thought in diverse emotional and behavioral problems ranging from childhood and adolescence (Weisz et al., 1987) to old age (Lam et al., 1987). Many of these same publications also describe the application of cognitive therapy (CT) to widely varying disorders. Perhaps the most significant of these publications is *The Cognitive Therapy of Depression* (Beck et al., 1979), a book widely recognized as the definitive work on treatment of depression. Further, research studies have documented that cognitive/behavioral therapy is one of the two major psychotherapeutic approaches that produces outcomes equivalent to those produced by antidepressant medication (Elkin et al., 1986).

Recent articles indicate that social workers have adopted CT as a major treatment modality. Cohen (1985) has reported on the use of CT with criminals; Barth (1985) has described cognitive/behavioral treatment of depression in mothers who maltreat children; and Marshall and Mazie (1987) have delineated a cognitive approach to treating depression. Cognitive behavioral interventions are also a major component of treatment programs for reducing the anger of parents at risk of abusing children (Nugent, 1991; Whiteman, Fanshel, & Grundy, 1987) and for treating male spouse batterers (Eisikovits & Edleson, 1989). Schrodt and Fitzgerald (1987) present a rationale for using CT in work with adolescents. It is thus evident that CT has strong empirical support and has entered the mainstream of interventions employed by social workers.

The basic premise of cognitive theorists is that most social and behavioral dysfunction results directly from misconceptions that people hold about themselves, other people, and various life situations. To be maximally effective therefore, practitioners must become proficient in assessing cognitive functioning and in applying appropriate interventions to enhance cognitive functioning. (We focused on assessing cognitive functioning in Chapters 9 and 11.)

Uses of Cognitive Restructuring

Cognitive restructuring is particularly useful in assisting clients to gain awareness of dysfunctional and self-defeating thoughts and misconceptions that impair personal functioning and to replace them with beliefs and behaviors that are aligned with reality and lead to enhanced functioning. Cognitive restructuring techniques are particularly relevant for problems associated with low self-esteem; distorted perceptions in interpersonal relations; unrealistic expectations of self, others, and life in general; irrational fears, anxiety, and depression; inadequate control of anger and other impulses; and lack of assertiveness. Practitioners have found cognitive restructuring to be especially useful in assisting people with problems of impulse control manifested in child abuse.

Cognitive restructuring is often blended with other interventions (e.g., modeling, behavioral rehearsal, relaxation training, assertiveness training, drug therapy, and desensitization) because combinations of interventions are sometimes more potent in producing change than are single interventions.

Cautions

Although cognitive theorists attribute most dysfunctional emotional and behavioral patterns to mistaken beliefs, they are by no means the only causes. Dysfunction may be produced by various biophysical problems, including brain tissue damage, neurological disorders, thyroid imbalance, blood sugar imbalance, circulatory disorders associated with aging, ingestion of toxic substances, malnutrition, and other forms of chemical imbalance in the body (Lantz, 1978). Consequently, these possibilities should be considered before undertaking cognitive restructuring.

Tenets of Cognitive Therapy

A major tenet of CT is that thinking is a basic determinant of behavior. Thinking consists of statements that people say to themselves, and it is this inner dialogue, rather than unconscious forces, that is the key to understanding behavior.

To grasp this first major tenet accurately, practitioners must clearly differentiate thinking from feeling. Clients (and practitioners, too) often confuse feelings and thoughts, which tends to foster confusion in communication and hinders successful implementation of cognitive restructuring techniques. The confusion is manifested in messages such as, "I feel our marriage is on the rocks," or "I feel nobody cares about me." The word *feel* is used incorrectly in these messages, which do not involve feelings but rather embody views, thoughts, or beliefs. Thoughts per se are devoid of feelings, although they are often accompanied by and tend to generate feelings or emotions. Feelings involve emotions, such as sadness, joy, disappointment, exhilaration, and any of the hundreds of feelings listed in the "Affective Words and Phrases" found in Chapter 5.

To assist clients to differentiate between feelings and cognitions, it is helpful to explain the difference and to provide several examples of both. Thereafter, it is important to intervene when clients fail to distinguish between these functions. It is critical that clients be able to make these distinctions, for self-monitoring of cognitions (discussed later) requires this ability.

A second major tenet of cognitive therapy is that the past is important only in identifying the origins of faulty thinking. It is the present faulty thinking, not the past, that motivates behavior. Furthermore, new patterns of thinking can be learned and problems resolved without determining the origins of faulty thinking. Therefore, the focus of cognitive therapy is largely on the present and the future. Clients are not permitted to use the past as an excuse for present difficulties.

Still another major tenet of cognitive therapy is that to make constructive changes, people must realize that their misconceptions may produce or contribute to many of their problems, and they must assume responsibility for modifying these misconceptions. In our view, this assumption must be tempered with the recognition that many factors contribute to the problems of clients, including inadequate resources and adverse environmental conditions. Still, with clients whose problems are rooted in misconceptions and faulty logic, this tenet is valid. The thrust of this tenet is that as practitioners we must assist clients to assume maximal responsibilities for themselves.

Steps in Cognitive Restructuring

Several discrete steps are involved in cognitive restructuring. Different authors vary slightly in their definitions of these steps, but the similarities are far greater than the differences. The steps we have found most useful are those identified by Goldfried (1977) and Cormier and Cormier (1979). These steps together with guidelines for implementing them are as follows:

1. Assist clients in accepting that their self-statements, assumptions, and beliefs largely mediate (i.e., determine or govern) their emotional reactions to life's events. Assisting clients to accept this explanation is vital, for clients are unlikely to commit themselves to procedures that they view skeptically or reject. To enhance their acceptance, we recommend that you present the rationale for cognitive restructuring and also demonstrate its relevance by citing common life experiences that document how cognitions mediate emotions. Draw examples from your own experiences, if possible, because they will be most meaningful to you. To guide you in assisting clients to accept the rationale, we offer the following example of an explanation provided to a client who was severely inhibited in social situations by feelings of inadequacy and social incompetence.

> For you to achieve your goal of expressing yourself more openly with others, we first need to determine what happens inside you that maintains your fears. That will involve your becoming aware of thoughts you experience in social situations—in other words, what you say to yourself before, during, and after social situations. Generally, such thoughts occur

automatically, and you won't be fully aware of many of them. We also want to discover assumptions and beliefs you have about social situations—beliefs you may have had much of your life. Becoming aware of self-defeating thoughts, assumptions, and beliefs is an extremely important first step in discarding them in favor of others that serve you better.

What you think determines in large measure what you feel and do. For example, if a friend tells me I'm stupid because I bought a new car instead of a used one, I can make various meanings or self-statements related to that message, each of which results in different feelings and actions. Consider, for instance, the different ways I might think about this:

He's probably right; he's a bright guy, and I respect his judgment. Why didn't I think of buying a used car? He must really think I'm a clod. If I think that, I'll feel crummy about myself, probably regret buying a new car, and won't enjoy it as much as I might.

Who does he think he is calling me stupid? He's the one who's stupid. What a jerk! If I think that, I'll feel angry and defensive. I may get in a heated argument over the merits of a new car or a used one.

It's apparent that we have different ideas on that subject. He's entitled to his opinion, although I certainly don't agree with him and do feel good about what I did. I don't like his referring to my decision as stupid, though. No point getting bent out of shape over it, but I think I'll let him know I don't feel good about his putting me down that way. If I think these thoughts, I'm not going to experience negative feelings. I'll feel good about my actions despite the other person's difference of opinion and I won't be unduly influenced by his insensitivity.

There are other meanings I could make, of course, but these should make the point. To enable you to master your fears, we'll explore together statements you make to yourself and how they affect your feelings and behavior. After we've identified thoughts and beliefs that are causing difficulties, we'll begin working on developing others that are realistic and consistent with your goal of expressing yourself more openly in social situations.

When the rationale is presented in a simple, straightforward manner, the majority of clients respond positively. Nevertheless, it is important to elicit clients' reactions to your explanation and to invite discussion. It is important not to proceed with cognitive restructuring until clients manifest receptivity and commitment to implementing the intervention. Clients, indeed, tend to resist changing their beliefs if they feel they are being coerced to adopt the beliefs of someone else.

2. Assist clients in identifying dysfunctional beliefs and patterns of thoughts that underlie their problems.

Once clients accept the proposition that thoughts and beliefs mediate emotional reactions, the next task is to assist them to examine personal thoughts and beliefs that pertain to their difficulties. This step involves detailed exploration of events related to problematic situations, with particular emphasis upon cognitions that accompany distressing emotions. For example, some clients attribute their problems to factors such as fate, inherent personal inadequacy or unlovability, and various forces beyond their control. In identifying key misconceptions, it is vital that you and your client agree as to what beliefs need to be changed. Although there are a number of ways of reaching agreement, the preferred way is to involve clients so that they feel they are actively participating and contributing.

You can begin the process of exploration by focusing on problematic events that occurred during the preceding week or on events surrounding a problem the client has targeted for change. As you mutually explore these events, it is important to elicit specific details regarding overt behavior, cognitions (i.e., self-statements and images), and emotional reactions. Focusing on all three aspects of behavior enables you to assist the client to see the connections between them and to grasp the role of cognitions in mediating feeling and behavior. As clients identify their self-statements and beliefs, they become increasingly aware that automatic thoughts and beliefs they have not subjected to critical analysis are powerful determinants of their behavior. This, in turn, increases their receptivity and motivation to work on tasks involving liberating themselves from these dysfunctional thoughts and beliefs.

As you engage in explorations, it is important to identify thoughts and feelings that occur before, during, and after events. To elicit such self-statements, ask clients to recreate the situation just as it unfolded, recalling exactly what they thought, felt, and actually did. If clients experience difficulty, it may be helpful to have clients close their eyes and "run a movie" of the problematic event, including thoughts and feelings that preceded, accompanied, and followed the event.

Identifying self-statements and assumptions that precede events makes it possible to pinpoint cognitive sets that predispose clients to experience certain emotions and to behave in predictable ways. For example, our socially inhibited client, cited earlier, disclosed she made the following self-statements before a disappointing discussion with fellow workers in the lunchroom.

"I'm not sure I want to join the others. If I do, I'll just sit there and feel left out."

"I'll bet they'd rather I didn't join them. They probably think I'm a real bore."

"I'd better join them, I guess. If I don't, they'll ask me where I was, and I'll have to come up with some lame excuse."

Given these self-statements, the client felt uneasy and apprehensive about joining her co-workers. As typically occurred, these thoughts predisposed her to enter the situation programmed for defeat. Moreover, she was tense and preoccupied with herself as she engaged in self-debate and finally decided to eat with her fellow workers. Such preoccupation is self-defeating because it limits involvement by dominating thinking with fears and worries about making mistakes.

Exploration of self-statements during events reveals that dysfunctional thoughts maintain self-defeating feelings and behavior and drastically reduce personal effectiveness. For example, clients who dwell on worries and are hypervigilant to the possible negative reactions of others are unable to "tune in" fully to discussions and to express themselves in positive ways that create favorable impressions. In other words, it is difficult for them to be fully present and involved because of self-con-

sciousness and fears of exposing their imagined personal inadequacies. To illustrate the destructive impact of such dysfunctional thoughts, let us again consider the self-statements of our socially inhibited client during lunch with her co-workers:

"Well, here I am again, and it's just like it's always been. I'm just out of it."

"I wish I had something interesting to say, but my life's such a drag. They couldn't possibly be interested in anything I might say."

"They're probably wondering why I even join them. I sure don't add anything to the group. I wish I could just disappear."

It is apparent from these and other like self-statements that the client dwells on self-demeaning thoughts. She thinks of herself as having little or nothing to offer, behaves accordingly, and feels unwanted and unworthy to participate actively. Her preoccupation with these thoughts and assumptions about herself block her from engaging in ongoing interaction with her peers.

Clients' self-statements and feelings following events reveal the impact of earlier thoughts and behaviors on subsequent feelings, thereby highlighting further the mediating function of cognitions. Moreover, the conclusions clients draw about the outcomes of events indicate further whether they are able to focus on positive aspects of their behavior and to identify challenges for further growth or whether they merely perceive an event as the latest in a long series of failures caused by their personal inadequacies. The meanings clients make of events, of course, are powerful in shaping their attitudes and feelings toward similar future events, as illustrated by the thoughts and feelings of our familiar client:

"I blew it again. I might as well quit trying. No use kidding myself. I just can't talk with others."

"They didn't really try to include me. It's obvious they could care less about me. They'd probably be pleased if I didn't join them tomorrow."

"I think I won't eat lunch with them anymore. I don't enjoy it, and I'm sure they don't either. Tomorrow I'll just eat by myself."

Clearly, this client's thoughts lead to feelings of utter failure. Without intervention into her circular self-defeating patterns of thought, she will tend to withdraw even further socially. It could be expected that she would experience further self-demeaning thoughts accompanied by depressed feelings.

As you mutually identify self-statements, it is important to assist clients to assess the degree of rationality of these self-statements. Through guided practice in critically analyzing the validity of their thoughts, clients gain experience that prepares them to engage in a similar process outside the sessions. Clients, however, may not acknowledge the irrationality of certain beliefs, especially those that are deeply embedded in their belief systems. Indeed, clients can cling tenaciously to key misconceptions and argue persuasively about their validity. Practitioners must therefore be prepared to challenge or "dispute" such irrational beliefs and to persist in assisting clients to recognize the costs or disadvantages associated with not relinquishing these beliefs.[7]

Techniques that challenge clients to assess the rationality of their beliefs and self-statements include:

1. Asking them how they reached certain conclusions.
2. Challenging them to present evidence supporting dysfunctional views or beliefs.
3. Challenging the logic of beliefs that magnify feared consequences of certain actions.

To illustrate the applications of these techniques, we have provided three self-statements, or beliefs, followed by responses that direct clients to analyze their validity.

1. *Self-statement*: "I've got to study every available moment. If I don't get the highest score on that test, it will be just awful."

   a. "Let's just suppose for a moment you really bombed out on that test. What would it really mean?"

   b. "So if you're not number 1, it will be a catastrophe. I can agree it's nice to be number 1, but why is it such a disaster to be number 2 or number 15 for that matter?"

2. *Self-statement*: "I don't want to tend her children, but if I don't she'll be furious. I don't dare risk displeasing her."

   a. "How have you concluded she'd be furious?"

   b. "Suppose you did risk turning her down and she got furious. Perhaps a question you should answer is whether you are going to let possible unreasonable reactions on her part dictate your behavior."

3. *Self-statement*: "There's no point in my taking a time-out when my wife starts ragging on me. She would see me as trying to escape, and there's no way she would see that I am trying to avoid a potentially violent situation."

   a. "What evidence do you have that she wouldn't believe you?"

   b. "Sounds like you've convinced yourself that she would not understand what you are trying to do. Have you explained to her what we are working on and what you are attempting to change?"

Clusters of misconceptions are commonly associated with dysfunctional behavior. Often it is possible to discern such patterns of thoughts even by the end of one session. By closely following feelings and eliciting accompanying thoughts, you can identify such clusters early. Dysfunctional thoughts typically include the following clusters of misconceptions:

1. About one's self.
2. About others' perceptions and expectations of oneself.
3. Expectations of oneself.
4. Expectations of others.

For illustrative purposes we have provided our conception of a cluster of beliefs associated with having unreasonable self-expectations:

"I must be the best in everything I do."

"It is terrible if I am unsuccessful in any venture."

"I am worthwhile as a person only if I am constantly working."

"I never quite achieve the level of excellence I should."

"When I compare myself with others, I never quite measure up."

"I should be able to succeed in any endeavor; if I don't, it's because I'm incompetent."

"I should be able to accept numerous assignments and perform all at a high level."

"I don't really deserve praise for my accomplishments because they're not that significant."

"If I'm not perfect in everything I do, it is terrible, and I'm a failure."

By identifying clusters or patterns of misconceptions, you can direct your efforts to the theme common to all of them, rather than dealing with each as a separate entity. Common to the cluster identified in the preceding is the theme of setting unrealistic expectations for oneself. By focusing on this central theme, you can conserve efforts, for the related misconceptions are merely derivatives of the central one and lose their potency when the core misconception is resolved.

By gaining practice in identifying and assessing the validity of self-statements and beliefs during sessions, clients achieve readiness to engage in self-monitoring *between* sessions. After the session in which you introduce clients to cognitive restructuring and mutually explore cognitions related to their difficulties, it is timely to negotiate a task that involves self-monitoring of thoughts and beliefs related to problematic events that occur between sessions. Through self-monitoring, clients become increasingly aware of the pervasive nature of their dysfunctional thoughts and recognize the need to cope actively with them. Self-monitoring thus expands self-awareness and paves the way for later coping efforts. Moreover, self-monitoring alone often enables clients to nip self-defeating thoughts in the bud as they realize the irrational nature and destructive impact of these thoughts.

To facilitate self-monitoring, we recommend that you ask clients to keep daily logs to record information in columns, as illustrated.[8]

DATE: TUES., SEPT. 8

Situation or Event	Feelings (rate intensity from 1 to 10)	Beliefs or Self-Statements (rate rationality from 1 to 10)
1. Asked boss for a day off	Scared (7)	He'll be annoyed and critical of me (4)
2. Clerk at drugstore shortchanged me, and I didn't say anything	Annoyed (4); afraid to tell clerk (8); disgusted with self (7)	I ought to tell clerk (9); she'd be displeased and I'd be embarrassed (2); it isn't worth it to risk a hassle (3)

Daily logs are valuable because they focus clients' efforts between sessions; clarify further the connections between cognitions and feelings; and provide valuable information to the practitioner about the prevalence and intensity of dysfunctional thoughts, images, and feelings. Moreover, they stimulate clients to engage in logical analysis of their thoughts. To prevent clients from feeling overwhelmed by the task of keeping a log, suggest they begin by limiting their recording to events related to those identified during the session and that they record only about three such events each day. Otherwise, clients tend to experience the task as unduly burdensome because of the host of troubling thoughts they may have during a given day. As other dysfunctional patterns of thoughts emerge during sessions, the focus of self-monitoring can be shifted as necessary.

In the preceding discussion, we have made passing references to images as an integral part of cognitions. Explorations of cognitions and self-monitoring should include images, for they may also play a key role in mediating emotions. Some clients are immobilized by terrifying images that may involve imagined rape, violence, or actual scenes that seemingly have left a permanent imprint upon their minds. For example, one client found it extremely difficult to engage in sexual relations with her husband because of images and memories associated with a man who had raped her earlier.

3. Assist clients in identifying situations that engender dysfunctional cognitions.
As practitioners and clients review completed log sheets and continue to identify problematic feelings and cognitions associated with stressful events, it is important to note recurring situations and themes. Pinpointing the place where stressful events occur, key persons involved in them, situations that involve tearing oneself down for failing to fulfill self-expectations, and the like enables you and your clients to develop tasks and coping strategies tailor-made for those specific situations. Clients who have difficulties controlling anger may discover that certain situations or types of persons consistently trigger their anger. Other clients may experience depression after having disputes with their husbands or with certain children. Still others may feel inadequate and demean themselves severely after interactions that have involved the slightest hint of criticism by others. Again, awareness of their areas of vulnerability often lowers clients' susceptibility to dysfunctional thoughts and feelings.

4. Assist clients in substituting functional self-statements in place of self-defeating cognitions.
As clients gain expanded awareness of their dysfunctional thoughts, beliefs, and images and recognize how these produce negative emotional reactions, they generally welcome efforts to learn new coping patterns. These coping strategies consist of employing self-statements that are both realistic and effective in eliminating negative emotional reactions and self-defeating behaviors. Although functional self-statements foster courage and facilitate active coping efforts, they are not idealistic and do not ignore the struggles inherent in shifting from habitual, ingrained patterns of thinking, feeling, and behaving to new patterns. In fact, as with coping modeling, coping self-statements embody recognition of the difficulties and anxiety inherent in risking new behavior. To introduce clients to coping self-statements, we recommend an explanation similar to the following:

"Now that you've identified many of your key self-defeating beliefs and thoughts, we're going to focus on how to replace them with new self-statements. It will take a lot of hard work on your part, but as you practice new coping self-statements, you'll find that they will become more and more natural to you until they finally crowd out the old ones."

After providing such an explanation, it is desirable to model coping self-statements that can be substituted for self-defeating thoughts and beliefs. In modeling, it is helpful to explain that you are going to assume the role of the client and are going to think aloud as the client might when coping with a target situation. To illustrate the process, we return to our socially inhibited client and model coping self-statements she might substitute for self-defeating ones *before* joining her co-workers in the lunch room.

"I know a part of me wants to avoid the discomfort of socializing, but it's not going to get any better by withdrawing."

"I don't have to say a lot to be part of the group. If I listen to the others and get my mind off myself, I can involve myself more."

"I can't expect them to draw me into the conversations. It would be nice if they did, but if I'm going to be included I'll have to be responsible for including myself. I can do it even though it's going to take courage and strong effort. It's better than withdrawing and feeling out of it."

Notice in these self-statements that the practitioner models the struggle going on within the client rather than modeling "mastery" self-statements. This is important because coping self-statements lie close to clients' actual experience, whereas mastery self-statements do not. Moreover, the former convey empathy for and understanding of the client's struggle, which in turn inspires greater confidence in the process and in the practitioner.

After modeling coping self-statements, it is appropriate to ask if the client feels ready to practice similar behavior. With a little encouragement, most clients agree to engage in guided practice. To enhance the effectiveness of this practice, we recommend suggesting that clients close their eyes and picture themselves in the exact situation they will be in before engaging in the targeted behavior. When they report they have succeeded in capturing this situation, ask them to think aloud the thoughts they typically experience when contemplating the targeted behavior. Then ask them to substitute coping thoughts and coach them as needed. Give positive feedback as they produce functional statements independently and provide encouragement as they struggle with conflicting thoughts. Expect your clients to express doubt and uncertainty about their ability to master new patterns of thinking and explain that most people experience misgivings as they experiment with new ways of thinking. Continue to practice with them until they feel relatively comfortable in their ability to generate coping self-statements. When clients demonstrate increased confidence in employing coping self-statements before entering a target situation, you can shift to a strategy for the *during* stage. Again, model coping self-statements, of which the following are examples with our same client:

"Okay, so you're feeling anxious. That's to be expected. You can still pay attention and show interest in the others. That's it, look at the others and smile. What they're talking about is interesting. Ask them for clarification if you want to know more. That'll show them you're interested."

"You have some thoughts on the subject they're discussing. Your opinions are worth as much as theirs. Go ahead, take a chance and express them, but look at others as you talk."

After modeling, ask how the client is feeling about what has happened thus far. This is important, for if clients are overly anxious, uncomfortable, or skeptical, you must first deal with these feelings before proceeding further. If they continue to respond positively, you may then ask them to rehearse coping self-statements, following essentially the same format as for the preceding phase.

When clients have demonstrated beginning ability to generate coping self-statements in the during phase, they are ready to enter the *after* phase. Again, it is important to model coping self-statements, of which the following are examples:

"Well, you did it. You stuck it out and even said a couple of things. That's a step in the right direction."

"No one looked down their nose when you expressed yourself. They appeared genuinely interested. Maybe I'm not so bad after all."

"Even though it was sweaty, it went pretty well, even better than I expected. I handled it, and that's an accomplishment. I'll join them again tomorrow and maybe do even better."

After modeling such self-statements, you should again explore the clients' reactions and feelings. If they indicate they are ready, you can then proceed to having them rehearse more coping self-statements. To assist clients to apply coping statements in actual life situations, it is beneficial to negotiate tasks that they can tackle between sessions. It is important, of course, not to rush clients, for undue pressure may threaten or discourage them. Again, we suggest using the Readiness Scale, as defined earlier in this chapter, to gauge their readiness.

Continued self-monitoring by clients is essential as clients implement step 4. Maintaining a daily log, employing the format suggested earlier (but augmented with a fourth column headed with the caption "Rational or Coping Self-Statements"), facilitates active ongoing efforts by clients and requires them to attempt to place situations and events in realistic perspective by identifying coping self-statements they can substitute for self-defeating ones. Furthermore, maintaining a log and implementing tasks foster independent action by clients.

Substituting coping self-statements for self-defeating thoughts or misconceptions is the heart of cognitive restructuring. Because they tend to be automatic and deeply embedded, however, dysfunctional thoughts tend to persist and clients sometimes become discouraged when they do not achieve quick mastery of them. It is important to recognize that step 4 extends across a number of weeks. When clients express discouragement, we find they are reassured when we explain that change is only gradual and that it takes most people several weeks at least before they achieve a satisfactory degree of mastery. Nevertheless, we stress that they can hasten the process by planning at the beginning of each day to anticipate situations they will encounter that present opportunities for using their newly discovered coping skills.

Another technique that equips clients to cope with automatic dysfunctional self-statements is to encourage them at first awareness of such thoughts to nip them in the bud. We explain to clients that their first awareness of such thoughts is a flashing signal that they need to apply coping techniques. One way of coping is "to have a talk with oneself," reminding oneself that it is vital to *make a choice* not to continue thinking dysfunctional thoughts. Permitting such thoughts to continue leads to predictable undesired emotional reactions and reinforces the dysfunctional pattern. By contrast, nipping negative self-statements in the bud averts negative reactions and adds another increment of growth in the quest for mastery.

5. Assist clients in rewarding themselves for successful coping efforts.

For clients who attend only to their failures and shortcomings and rarely, if ever, give themselves a pat on the back, this step is especially important. Aimed at reinforcing coping efforts, this step also assists clients in savoring their progress in learning still another new and functional cognitive pattern.

In implementing this step, it is desirable to explain the rationale of giving oneself credit for progress. The following is an example of such an explanation:

"Louise, now that you've experienced some success in substituting coping self-statements for self-defeating ones, it's important to learn to give yourself credit for your well-deserved accomplishment. By giving yourself a pat on the back, you savor your success and encourage yourself to continue with your efforts. It's also an important way of learning to feel good about yourself. I'm going to help you learn to reward yourself by pretending I'm you and thinking aloud self-statements you might make after a successful coping experience."

After providing such an explanation, you then model several laudatory self-statements of which the following are typical examples:

"You weren't sure you could do it, but you did."

"You didn't back off. You dismissed those negative thoughts and stayed with your game plan."

"That was a big step. Sure, you have a long way to go, but you've made a darn good start, and it feels just great."

As with step 4, you should elicit the client's reactions to your explanation and modeling. If clients appear receptive, instruct them to re-create a recent success and practice making approving self-statements by expressing them aloud. Because positive self-statements are alien to many clients, initially they may feel awkward or self-conscious. Empathic understanding and encouragement on your part will usually prompt them to begin, and they may actually enjoy the experience. Indeed, it is vital to give consistent positive feedback, identifying the small and often subtle increments of growth clients achieve.

To facilitate the transfer of coping skills from sessions to real life, it is important to negotiate tasks with clients that involve making positive self-statements about their progress and about other accomplishments in daily living. Self-monitoring is again a valuable tool. We recommend asking clients to record in their logs all their daily successes, including small ones they may be inclined to overlook, and to record self-statements that give themselves credit for the achievements. This approach can be a powerful means of eliminating patterns of attending selectively to short-comings, failures, and negative experiences.

Limitations of Cognitive Restructuring

In assisting clients to make changes, practitioners must not mistakenly assume that clients can perform new behaviors solely as a result of cognitive changes. Often clients lack social skills and require instruction and practice before they can effectively perform new behaviors, such as making social overtures, expressing personal feelings, engaging in problem solving, and asserting themselves. Cognitive restructuring removes cognitive barriers to change and fosters willingness to risk new behaviors but does not equip clients with requisite skills. In the next chapter, we focus on behavioral interventions that enable clients to learn requisite coping skills. In actual practice, combining these skills with cognitive structuring produces a potent package for effecting desired changes.

NOTES

1 The importance of careful planning in direct practice has been emphasized by Rosen, Proctor, and Livne (1985). For a discussion of components that practitioners should consider in planning treatment strategies, you will find this article useful.

2 To adequately discuss the integration of treatments with diverse clinical problems, however, would require writing a separate volume. In the field of clinical psychology, Beutler and Clarkin (1990) have done just that, and we highly recommend their book. O'Hare (1991) has written a useful article for social workers that provides a framework for integrating research and practice.

3 Reid (1992) has elaborated specific task strategies to address a great variety of client problems and situations.

4 A series of videotapes is available from Ronald Rooney at the University of Minnesota depicting individual and family practice using the task-centered approach.

5 Much of the information in this section is taken from Hepworth (1979).

6 Of necessity, the preceding discussion of CI has been brief. For more extensive expositions of CI, we recommend books by Aguilera and Messick (1982), Golan (1978), and Puryear (1979). For a critique of CI, we recommend Lukton's (1982) article.

7 Walen, DiGuiseppe, and Wessler (1980) present and illustrate comprehensive strategies for disputing beliefs, and we strongly recommend this reference.

8 We wish to acknowledge that this schema is based on one developed by Aaron Beck et al. as presented in *Cognitive Therapy of Depression* (New York: Guilford Press, 1979), appendix.

Chapter 14 □ □□ □□

Enhancing Clients' Problem Solving, Social Skills, Assertiveness, and Stress Management

Humans constantly encounter situations, events, and problems that require coping responses. Effective coping with the diverse demands of daily living requires skills in making decisions, communicating, solving problems, resolving conflicts, and managing stresses. Increasing evidence from research studies suggests that these and other coping skills are essential to sound mental health and behavioral adjustment. Ineffective coping in problematic situations, in fact, can lead to emotional and behavioral disorders that have a severe impact on functioning.

Clients seek professional help when their coping efforts have failed to remedy problematic situations. Varying widely in their coping capacities, some clients possess meager skills and others have rich coping repertoires that have been temporarily overwhelmed by virtually insuperable stresses. It is the former group, however, that most frequently comes to the attention of social workers.

Over the past 20 years, human service practitioners and researchers have increasingly devoted attention to ways of increasing clients' coping capacities by assessing strengths, and resources as well as deficits or challenges (as we described in Chapter 8). Training programs have been developed to assist clients in developing many skills. Four areas of skills training that have broad appli-

cation—problem solving, social skills, assertiveness, and stress management—are the topics of this chapter. Chapter 16 focuses on other interpersonal skills that are vital in families, groups, and other social contexts.

PROBLEM-SOLVING SKILLS

Teaching clients problem-solving skills can equip them to cope more effectively with the myriad difficulties they will encounter in the future. A major advantage of learning problem-solving is that the principles can be readily transferred from one situation to another.

At this point, some clarification is in order. We have previously made repeated reference to the problem-solving process, and you may be confused as to why clients need additional assistance in learning to apply problem-solving strategies. After all, clients and practitioners engage in problem solving, so isn't it logical to assume they learn the process? The answer is that most clients probably do learn something about the problem-solving process, but what they usually learn is likely to be incomplete. In fact, many practitioners have difficulty delineating precisely the elements of independent problem solving. Utilizing problem solving to assist clients in coping with discrete problems and teaching them the principles in preparation for coping independently with future problems are different processes. We propose that practitioners engage in both processes, thereby seeking not only to remedy immediate problems but also to enhance clients' future coping capacities.

Our proposal is not new. About 25 years ago, behaviorally oriented psychologists (D'Zurilla & Goldfried, 1971) advocated that practitioners assist clients to enhance their problem-solving skills. These authors maintained that much of what was viewed as abnormal or disturbed behavior could be viewed as resulting from ineffective behavior that fails to solve life's challenging problems and leads to undesired effects such as anxiety and depression. Support for their view came from the research of Spivack, Platt, and Shure (1976), who reported two major findings. First, deviant or abnormal people manifested inferior skills in problem solving compared to "normal" people. The former group (1) generated fewer possible solutions to hypothetical problem situations than the latter; (2) suggested solutions that often were antisocial; and (3) had very inaccurate expectations about probable consequences of alternate solutions. Other researchers similarly found deficiencies in problem-solving skills among conflicted marriages as compared to nonconflicted marriages (Vincent, Weiss, & Birchler, 1976). Subsequent studies have extended the findings to conduct-disordered adolescents (Tisdelle & St. Lawrence, 1988), antisocial children (Kazdin et al., 1987), depressed children (Weisz et al., 1987), Vietnam veterans with posttraumatic stress disorder (Nezu & Carnevale, 1987), suicidal psychiatric patients (Schotte & Clum, 1987), alcoholics (Jacob et al., 1981), and schizophrenics (Kelly & Lamparski, 1985).

The second major finding of Spivack et al. (1976) was that promising results were obtained in several projects in which youth received systematic training in problem solving. Of particular relevance have been similar results indicating that instruction

in and practice of problem-solving skills assist children with antisocial behavioral patterns (Kazdin et al., 1987), nondelinquent early adolescents (LeCroy & Rose, 1986), predelinquent youth (Kifer et al., 1974), and delinquent adolescents (Tisdelle & St. Lawrence, 1988) to deal with conflictual situations more effectively. Other findings indicate that training in problem solving also assists families to function more harmoniously (Blechman, 1974; Blechman et al., 1976).

Still another study (Nezu, 1985) found that self-appraised effective problem solvers reported less depression, less anxiety, a greater sense of internal control, fewer problems, and less distress than those who appraised themselves as ineffective problem solvers.

It is thus clear that many of the most vexing problems encountered in social work involve clients whose capacities for coping with problems of living are inadequate. The research findings that systematic efforts to remedy these deficiencies have produced higher levels of functioning are most promising.

By mastering a systematic approach to making decisions and solving problems, clients gain the following benefits:

1. Learn a process that promotes collaboration, cohesiveness, and mutual respect among family or group members.

2. Prevent interpersonal conflicts produced by dysfunctional modes of reaching decisions or solving problems.

3. Reduce tension, anxiety, and depression by solving stress-producing problems effectively.

4. Generate a wider range of options for coping, thereby enhancing chances of selecting maximally effective decisions or solutions.

5. Enhance the likelihood that family and group members will commit themselves to implementing options that are selected.

6. Increase confidence, self-efficacy, and self-esteem by acquiring a mode of problem solving that can be employed in future problematic situations.

7. Prevent children from developing dysfunctional coping patterns by including them in effective problem-solving efforts and by teaching and guiding them in employing such efforts.

Embedded in the preceding benefits and central to the rationale for independent problem solving is the preventive function of this intervention. Clients gradually achieve mastery of skills that they can transfer to the real world. Their dependence on practitioners gradually decreases, and their self-reliance increases.

Before delineating problem-solving strategies and methods of assisting clients to learn them, we wish to clarify that theory related to making decisions and solving problems is not limited to the helping professions. Because of the importance of decision making in business management, governmental policy formulation, public administration, and other phases of life, numerous articles and entire books have been devoted to this topic. Across fields, authors agree that effective problem solving involves a systematic approach consisting of several discrete phases, and their views of the basic elements involved in problem solving are similar. The strategy we delineate is a synthesis of our own ideas with those of several authors, most notably Janis and Mann (1977), Gordon (1970), and Jacobson and Margolin (1979). We have adapted this strategy particularly for interpersonal situations typically encountered in families and groups.

PREPARING CLIENTS TO LEARN PROBLEM-SOLVING SKILLS

Before delineating the steps involved in problem solving, we first discuss conditions prerequisite to introducing this intervention. Preparing clients is critical, for unless they are receptive (1) to learning the process and (2) to engaging in collaborative efforts with the practitioner and with each other, employing this intervention is likely to be futile. Early in the helping process, clients often meet neither of these conditions, and practitioners therefore face the challenges of enlisting their willingness to engage in the process and of fostering a collaborative set.

Several strategies can be employed to influence clients to adopt a collaborative set, including the following:

1. Lay groundwork during the initial contracting process.

2. Demonstrate the need to learn problem solving by focusing on the destructive impact of self-defeating interaction.

3. Enhance use of capacities by intervening to increase positive and collaborative interactions.

4. Accredit collaborative efforts and highlight the connections between these efforts and positive outcomes.

5. Define problems as belonging to a system rather than to any one person.

In the following sections, we consider the preceding strategies in greater detail.

Lay Groundwork during the Initial Contracting Process

We consider the learning of problem-solving skills a vital component of most contracts established by the practitioner with couples, families, or groups. As you may recall, in Chapter 11, we encouraged practitioners to develop a contract with new groups to the effect that all members will be "counted in" in decision making and also stressed the need for practitioners to teach decision-making steps to groups in initial sessions. In Chapter 10, we also emphasized that many families have both dysfunctional interactional patterns and ineffective styles of decision making that discount the needs of some or all members—which perpetuates resentment, unrest, and conflict. Thus, opportunities to negotiate the goal of learning to apply effective problem-solving methods often occur when clients are seen in conjoint sessions. For example, we have worked with many couples and families with presenting problems similar to the following:

"Our ideas about childrearing are totally different, which creates constant friction between us and confuses our children."

"We bicker constantly in our family about who should do the dishes, vacuum the rugs, and cut the grass. We just can't seem to work together on anything."

Common to each of the preceding presenting complaints is failure of the participants to work collaboratively in solving problems related to carrying out vital functions within a family. By reflecting these complaints in terms of wants, you focus on the necessity for collaborative problem solving and thus pave the way to negotiating a goal of learning mutual problem solving, as illustrated in the following responses to the above presenting problems:

"You seem to be saying you're working at cross purposes in rearing your children, which causes divisiveness between you and is hard on your children. I gather you're feeling a need to resolve your differences and *to learn to work together as partners.*"

[*To family member*]: "Sounds like the constant bickering creates a strain and leads nowhere. I'm sensing that learning ways of working together as a family in planning to get things done could improve things in your family."

Clients generally respond affirmatively to such messages, indicating some degree of receptivity to learning collaborative problem solving. The practitioner can then suggest that later in the session they may want to consider a goal of learning a problem-solving process that has proven effective in resolving difficulties similar to their own. Subsequently, during the contracting process, clients themselves may select as goals learning to make decisions or to cope with marital or family difficulties without excessive conflict. If clients do not identify such goals, you may make reference to the difficulties they described earlier and again suggest that seeking to develop effective problem-solving strategies may be an effective way of remedying identified problems and of averting similar problems in the future.

Demonstrate the Need to Learn the Problem-Solving Process

This strategy can be employed in tandem with the preceding strategy or can be introduced later at an expedient time. Implementing the strategy in the former instance involves providing an expanded explanation of the benefits of learning to collaborate in problem solving. In the latter instance, after observing clients engage in competitive, unproductive interaction that produces strain, the practitioner capitalizes on their obvious frustration by emphasizing the destructive impact of the interaction, drawing attention to how each participant contributes to the dysfunctional behavior, and presenting a case for learning effective problem-solving strategies. Executed well, such a timely intervention often motivates clients to welcome modifying their contract to include a goal of learning problem-solving strategies. The following illustrates application of this intervention strategy in the third interview with Rose and Gary Wilson, a couple who sought help with difficulties involving intense conflicts in many aspects of their marriage. The practitioner intervenes following a heated interchange between the partners involving Rose's criticism of Gary's handling of their eight-year-old son, Danny:

Practitioner: You're both pretty angry with each other right now, and if you continue along the same lines, you're likely to get even angrier. Let's stop a moment and consider what's happening between you.

Gary: You're damn right I'm mad. She always thinks she has the answers. It's like my opinion couldn't possibly be worth anything.

Rose: That's not true, and you know it. It's just that you expect too much of Danny.

Gary [*shakes head in disgust*]: What's the use? I can't get through to her.

Practitioner: Wait a minute! I know that you both have some strong feelings right now and it is hard to disengage, but it is very important that we look at what's going wrong. Are you willing to do that now? [*They agree.*] Both of you have your ideas about what you need to do with Danny—right? [*Each nods.*] What's happening is that each of you believes you're right and you're trying to convince the other. Then each of you gets uptight because the other doesn't listen and puts your ideas down. So you end up arguing. Am I right? [*They concede this happens.*] You get into a battle of "Who's right," and both of you only lose when you get caught up in that. You get mad at each other, and your communication breaks down just as it did a few moments ago.

Rose: Well, I think you've described it pretty well. But what do we do about it?

Practitioner [*smiling*]: I thought you'd never ask. All kidding aside, what I'd like to suggest is that the two of you consider working toward a goal of learning a method of solving problems that avoids getting into hassles. It involves working together, seeking to understand each other's views, and searching together for solutions that are acceptable to both of you, rather than struggling over who's right. The advantage of learning this method is that you learn to work *with* rather than against each other.

Gary: That'd be different for a change.

Practitioner: Then I take it it has some appeal to you. [*Both nod in agreement.*] Do you feel it might be a goal you'd like to tackle, then?

Rose: I'm game. I think it might really help us. What we're doing now isn't working—that's for sure. How about you, Gary?

Gary: Let's do it.

Obtaining a commitment to work collaboratively is a crucial step in achieving a climate conducive to the change process, but it would be naive to assume that commitment alone is sufficient. Persistent effort is required to break established patterns of interaction. The same applies to formed groups, for members bring with them patterns of communication they habitually employ in other contexts. Furthermore, people can employ only those skills they already possess. Therefore, for some clients, learning to solve problems collaboratively may entail learning a new set of skills. Consequently, the next two strategies are essential in assisting contentious members of systems to achieve a collaborative set.

Intervening to Produce Collaborative Interactions

Tactics involved in this strategy are twofold. First, the practitioner actively intervenes to arrest negative, competitive, and other destructive patterns of interaction. Interrupting such dysfunctional interaction, the practitioner translates or redefines negative, blaming messages into expressions of needs or wants or requests for change. The second tactic involves inducing collaborative interaction by recognizing constructive patterns, teaching clients to express their needs, to listen attentively, to personalize their feelings, and to give positive feedback. The potency of collaborative interaction derives from the fact that enabling clients to engage in such interactions assists them to learn new modes of behavior and to experience the benefits of them. Experiencing the benefits of collaborating enables clients to gain a measure of success and satisfaction from this different mode of relating, which in turn encourages additional efforts to collaborate with other members of the system and with the practitioner. Implementation of the preceding techniques is illustrated in the following excerpt involving parents and an adolescent daughter:

Daughter [*to parents*]: You're on my back all the time. Why don't you get off my case for a change? [*Attacking, blaming message.*]

Father: We wouldn't be on your case if you'd get in at night when you're supposed to. [*Counterattacking message.*]

Daughter: Well, if you'd quit bugging me, maybe I'd feel more like getting in. Besides, you expect me to be home before any of the other kids, and it isn't fair. [*More of same.*]

Mother: I don't think 11 o'clock is unreasonable. [*Defensive response.*]

Practitioner: I'd like to stop and see if we can understand better just what's troubling everyone here. Each of you has some needs that aren't being met, and let's begin by seeing if we can identify what those needs are. I'd like each of you just to listen and try to understand the other person's needs. You may not agree with each other, but I would like to ask you to hold your disagreement for a while. Just try to understand. Let's begin with you, Betty. From what you were saying, I sensed you're wanting more room to move around. You'd like more freedom, am I right?

Notice the destructive interaction among the family members characterized by verbal attacks, blaming messages, defensiveness, and counterattacks. The practitioner intervenes and begins to translate the blaming messages into needs. The practitioner further requests the participants to listen to and to attempt to understand each other's needs. We now pick up the interaction where we left off.

Daughter: Yeah! That's right. I get tired of being nagged all the time.

Practitioner: OK. But let's stay with what you want. Would you tell your parents specifically what positive changes you'd like? Tell them what you'd like them to do, not what you feel they're doing wrong. OK? [*Maintaining focus on her want; suggesting she request positive change.*]

Daughter: I'll try. Well, I'd like you to give me more freedom. I feel you're trying to control me, and I'm able to run my own life. You act like you don't trust me.

Practitioner [*to parents*]: So she's telling you she wants more freedom and wants to be treated as an adult. Was that the message you got? [*Still focusing on her wants; checking out meaning attribution with parents.*]

Father: Yeah, but—

Practitioner: I would appreciate it if we could save the "but" for later. Right now I think it's important to work on understanding your needs. [*To parents*] Let's turn to your needs now. What positive changes would each of you like to see happen?

In this last response, the practitioner assertively intervened to avert sidetracking that would likely follow father's "but." The practitioner maintains focus on the participants' needs, shifting to the parents' needs. Now return to the interaction.

Mother: I'd like Betty to get in earlier. I worry when she stays out late.

Practitioner: That tells me you have some fears. Can you tell Betty what those fears are?

Mother: Betty, I know you're basically a good kid. But I do worry. Even the best of kids can get into trouble when they spend too much time together late at night.

Practitioner [*to Betty*]: Betty, I hope you're hearing what your mother is telling you. She's expressing a concern for you—not distrust or wanting to control you. [*To mother*] Why all the concern? Please tell Betty. I'll tell you in a minute why I ask.

In the last response, notice how the practitioner facilitates understanding and positive interaction by clarifying that mother's fears emanate from positive concern, not from distrust or a desire to control Betty. In the last question, the practitioner seeks to elicit further positive feelings, as reflected in the continuation of the interaction.

Mother: Well, Betty, it's because we—well—you're our only daughter. We love you. We don't want anything bad to happen.

Practitioner: I'll tell you now why I asked. I sensed you were concerned because Betty's so important to you. But I'm not sure that message had gotten through to Betty. [*To Betty*] What you've thought is that your parents have wanted to control you. Do you hear that underneath all of their negative messages is love and concern for you? [*Clarifying further the parents' positive concerns and facilitating positive feedback.*]

Daughter: I do right now. But that isn't what I've been hearing lately. No way!

Practitioner: But you hear it now. How does that make you feel right now? Can you tell your parents? [*Maintaining focus on positive feedback.*]

Daughter: Good. Real good. Like maybe they're not so bad after all.

Practitioner: Well, maybe you're beginning to understand each other a little better. [*To father*] We didn't hear from you, dad. Could you let us know your needs or wants? [*Drawing father into discussion of needs and wants.*]

Father: My wife expressed them pretty well. Not much I could add.

Practitioner: Nevertheless, I'd like Betty to hear it from you. Could you tell Betty your feelings?

Notice in the preceding excerpts that the practitioner identified the needs of each participant, an important step in problem solving discussed at length later in the chapter. Further, the practitioner actively intervened each time the participants began to revert to negative messages. By being attuned to the concerns and underlying love inherent in the mother's statement, the practitioner rechanneled the interaction in positive directions. The practitioner thus elicited feelings of caring, and what began as typical dysfunctional interaction was converted into an embryonic form of collaborative communication. This strategy incidentally provides participants with an initial "success" experience in communicating in a positive manner about problems.

We cannot emphasize too strongly your responsibility as a practitioner in converting negative interaction to positive interaction. Except for making an initial assessment, no constructive purpose is served by passively permitting clients to engage in destructive patterns of communication, whether the target system be a couple, family, or group.

Accredit Collaborative Efforts

This strategy is employed to reinforce spontaneous collaborative behavior on the part of clients and to enhance their awareness of consequent beneficial effects by highlighting connections between positive behavioral changes and its beneficial effects. Although collaborative behavior tends to be self-reinforcing because it produces positive results, expressing recognition and approval of collaborative efforts further reinforces such behavior. Moreover, assisting clients to discern the association between their collaborative behavior and its favorable results further enables them to make choices to interact collaboratively, as illustrated in the following:

Practitioner [*to group*]*:* I'd like to point out something that just happened that pleased me a great deal. You'll recall in our first session you agreed as members to assist one another to understand each other's problems better and to work cooperatively in searching for solutions. I know we struggled in our last session with interruptions and with members trying to talk at the same time. Well, what pleases me is that during these past minutes as Julie shared her problems we really began to work as a group. Everyone listened, no one interrupted, and several of you supported Julie in her struggle to express herself. As a result, Julie appeared to open up and shared more with us. I was really impressed with how you pitched in as a group. Julie, I'd like to hear how it felt to you.

Julie: Well, it was hard at first, but like you said, it got easier. I really felt everyone was behind me. It felt great.

Define Problems as Belonging to the System

When a client reveals a problem, significant others tend to see the problem as residing solely with that person and to disclaim any part in it. From the standpoint of systems theory, however, problems of one member are problems of the system, and other members share responsibility for working out solutions. Moreover, solutions are far more likely to be efficacious if contributions of all members to the problem are considered and if all participate in planning corrective measures. In formed groups, the situation is somewhat different, for members have not contributed to the pre-existing problems of others. In becoming part of the new system, however, each makes a commitment to assist other members, and each member shares responsibility for contributing to the effective functioning of the group. Further, as groups evolve, all participants contribute in some manner to dysfunctional group processes and all have capacities to escape them.

The following are typical examples of how participants mutually contribute to problematic situations:

1. Mrs. Adams complains that her husband spends little time with her. He agrees but explains he spends increasing time away from home because she nags and badgers him constantly.

2. Mr. Sharp expresses a desire for his wife to make sexual overtures. She explains she has desires to do so but when she has made overtures in the past he has rebuffed her. To avoid the resultant hurt, she decided not to take the risk.

3. Parents of 15-year-old Alan complain he seldom talks to them about his daily activities. He agrees but explains when he has shared in the past his parents criticize him or give him lectures.

It is apparent in the preceding examples that all of the participants play a part in the problems. Your task is to assist all parties to recognize their respective parts and to agree to make behavioral changes accordingly. This is not easy, for people tend to be more aware of and to focus more on the distressing behaviors of others than on their own; hence, their tendency is to define solutions in terms of changes *others* need to make. However, by intervening and guiding clients to interact collaboratively, you assist them not only to reveal their respective perceptions of problematic situations but also to listen attentively to others' views. You can further enhance their receptivity to owning their respective parts by explaining that successful change results from each person working to change his or her own behavior, not from trying to change others.

Perhaps the most effective strategy of assisting people to define problems as mutually owned is to appeal to their self-interest. If they can see a payoff for themselves, they will be inclined to participate in seeking a solution. For example, if a husband is helped to consider how his wife's depression or unhappiness negatively affects him, dampening his interaction with her and reducing his own satisfaction and happiness, he is likely to be receptive in helping her to overcome her depression. Through this involvement, he may also be helped to see how he has contributed to her depression. Similarly, if you assist family members to recognize that improved functioning of one person enhances relationships and solidarity within the system, they will be more likely to accept responsibility for participating actively in problem solving.

By defining problems as mutually owned and clarifying the part each participant plays in maintaining them, you enhance the likelihood that participants will be willing to initiate positive behavioral changes. Manifest willingness on the part of one person tends to foster reciprocal willingness by others. No one loses face because no one is defined as the sole cause of the problems. Moreover, impasses tend to dissolve as each person becomes aware that others care enough to acknowledge their parts and to commit themselves to making changes.

INTRODUCING THE PROBLEM-SOLVING PROCESS

After clients have begun to engage in collaborative interactions, have demonstrated beginning awareness of behaviors entailed in such interactions, and have contracted to learn the problem-solving process, it is appropriate to introduce them to the process and then to guide them in applying it to some of their problems. Before defining the formal process, however, it is vital to explain conditions prerequisite to using it effectively. Carefully explaining these conditions and the rationale behind them further enhances receptivity and prepares clients to implement the process successfully.

Introducing clients to the process begins by clarifying its nature with an explanation similar to the following:

"Let's begin by clarifying what the problem-solving process is all about. Basically, it's an approach that will enable you to collaborate in solving problems or in reaching decisions effectively. It involves a number of steps that will assist you to define problems accurately and to generate several possible solutions so that you can select the best possible one. The best option is the one that meets your needs best, so another step involves helping you to identify and understand each other's needs. There are also guidelines that will assist you to work together and to avoid needless and unproductive hassles."

It is also critical to clarify that the process is *effective* and that clients can succeed in applying it but only if they commit themselves to following the steps and guidelines. However strong their good intentions, they will tend to revert to habitual patterns of interaction, and if they permit this to happen, they will likely end up arguing, blaming, or playing "who wins." For this reason, it is vital to differentiate problem solving from other interactions. Clients must understand that when they agree to engage in problem solving they commit themselves to follow the structured pattern of interaction. In sessions, the practitioner will guide them in adhering to these steps and guidelines. Outside the sessions, they must practice carefully to avoid falling into habitual patterns of interaction.

MANAGING INTERACTION DURING PROBLEM SOLVING

Before teaching the actual steps of the problem-solving process, it is important to be prepared to manage clients' interaction and to guide them so that they adhere to the steps and thereby achieve successful results. Toward this end, the practitioner should assist clients to observe the following guidelines:

1. Be specific in relating problems.
2. Focus on the present problem rather than on past difficulties.
3. Focus on only one problem at a time.
4. Listen attentively to others who are sharing problems.
5. Share problems in a positive and constructive manner.

In the following sections we delineate each of these guidelines.

Guideline 1. Be Specific in Relating Problems

To define a problem accurately, it is essential to express it so that others can determine the specific nature of one's concerns or needs. Further, specifying problems with precision avoids the confusion and misunderstanding that may result from expressing them in vague and general terms. You can utilize the skill of seeking concreteness to elicit specific details of clients' problems. Keep in mind that when clients express problems globally, you will need to press for details and clarify the importance of pinpointing difficulties.

Guideline 2. Focus on the Present Problem Rather Than on Past Difficulties

As you help clients to define problems, it is important to maintain focus on the present. Needless and fruitless arguments over circumstances and details tend to ensue when clients dredge up numerous examples of problematic behavior from the past. Details of recent difficulties do help in pinpointing problematic behavior at times, but more than a few examples amount to overkill. We therefore recommend that you develop a contract with clients specifying the need to focus on present problems and that you intervene to refocus the process when clients begin to employ lengthy recitations of past events as verbal ammunition against others.

Guideline 3. Focus on Only One Problem at a Time

Clients often have a tendency to bring up a problem and then rapidly shift to another, which diffuses their effort and impairs the helping process. Shifts in focus (*sidetracking*) may result from deliberate diversionary tactics or occur because some people have difficulty staying on one topic for any length of time.

When clients sidetrack, it is important to intervene and bring them back to the original problem. It is also important to assist them to discern sidetracking by labeling it and clarifying how it blocks problem-solving efforts. You can further assist clients to cope independently by intervening when sidetracking occurs, asking them to identify what they are doing. They will usually correctly identify their shift in focus. An effective method of assisting clients to reduce sidetracking is to negotiate tasks with them to monitor their interaction between sessions, attempting to avoid sidetracking, gently drawing the attention of others to the fact they are sidetracking, and refocusing on the original topic.

Guideline 4. Listen Attentively to Others Who Are Sharing Problems

Implementing this guideline means that others must suspend judgment about the validity of a person's concerns and feelings and hold in check the natural tendency to express contrary views or to advise the person as to what she or he should do to resolve the problem. To ascertain that one fully understands what the other person is saying, it is important to check out perceptions by giving feedback. Summarizing what one has heard is an effective means of providing feedback that enables the person who has shared the problem to determine if others have accurately understood the intended message.

This guideline is critical, for how others respond to the sharing of a problem determines whether a positive and collaborative climate will evolve or whether defensiveness will ensue. Although providing feedback may seem artificial and mechanical, it is a powerful way of enhancing collaborative communication.

You can facilitate clients' implementation of this guideline by instructing those who are to be recipients of a problem-sharing message to listen carefully and attempt to understand the sender's message and feelings. Ask clients to attempt to shut off their own thoughts and to put themselves in the shoes of other persons so that they can be fully attuned to those persons. After they have received the message, ask them to check out with the sender what they have heard; be prepared to intervene should the recipient of the message respond negatively. Coach them in using feedback until both sender and receiver agree upon the intended meaning of the message.

Guideline 5. Share Problems in a Positive and Constructive Manner

The way in which a person presents a problem sets a tone that tends to elicit either concern and collaboration or defensiveness from other participants. In presenting a problem or concern that involves the behavior of another participant, it is important to express the concern without blaming or attacking the other person. Expressing problems in the form of accusations, such as "You're insensitive to my feelings," "You never notice how hard I work," or "You've been staying out too late," tends to engender defensiveness or counter criticism, undermining the process almost before it starts. It is thus important that the person presenting the problem begin by expressing positive intent and by owning personal feelings rather than focusing on what another person is doing wrong. An effective way of introducing concerns is to send a positive, caring message before bringing up a concern. For example, contrast the following two messages and consider the likely impact upon a recipient:

[Pregnant unwed adolescent to mother]: "Mom, you are a good mother and I know you care for me. I don't always show it, but I appreciate that. But I feel like it is my decision whether or not to have this baby, and I need support, not pressure, in making it."

"Mom, you are always getting into my business, and now especially I need you to butt out because this is my baby and my decision."

Clients usually require help in expressing problems without blaming or attacking. When they express their problem or concerns in a negative manner, it is important to intervene immediately to avert destructive interaction. Explaining how blaming messages cause others to bristle or asking recipients of blaming messages to express their reactions assists clients to differentiate between positive messages that involve ownership of feelings and negative, accusatory messages. After making this clarification, coach the client in couching the concern or problem in a positive manner. During the course of subsequent interactions, you will likely need to intervene many times, for the pull of habituated patterns of communication is strong and clients revert to these patterns frequently.

In sharing problems, some clients also need help in learning to avoid making overgeneralized or absolute types of statements, such as "You *never* clean up after yourself," or "I *always* have to remind you to do your chores." Overgeneralizations have a negative effect on communication not only because they are accusatory but also because they are generally inaccurate. Recipients of such messages typically counterattack, seeking to disprove the validity of the accusation. Arguments then ensue and disputes tend to escalate.

When clients send overgeneralized messages, immediate interventions are indicated. We recommend that you stop the interaction, label the message as an overgeneralization (defining what that means), and clarify the destructive impact of such messages. You can then request the sender of the message to send an accurate and positively phrased message, coaching the person as needed.

STEPS FOR PROBLEM SOLVING

In the following sections, we delineate the steps of the problem-solving process and present techniques in assisting clients to master each step. To assist clients in grasping and applying this process,

we recommend that you provide them with a reference sheet that lists the steps.

Before discussing the process with clients, explain that implementing the process does not *ensure* that resultant decisions and solutions will always produce desired results, for outcomes cannot always be predicted with accuracy. Employing the process avoids discord, however, and substantially enhances the chances of achieving favorable outcomes. Realistically, this is all that can be expected, for outcomes are usually determined by the interplay of many factors, some of which cannot be anticipated.

The steps of the problem-solving process are as follows:

1. Acknowledge the problem.
2. Analyze the problem and identify the needs of participants.
3. Employ brainstorming to generate possible solutions.
4. Evaluate each option, considering the needs of participants.
5. Implement the option selected.
6. Evaluate the outcome of problem-solving efforts.

We consider each of these steps in the following sections.

Step 1. Acknowledge the Problem

People often do not face problems until they become so severe that they can be ignored no longer. Furthermore, because facing problems often produces discomfort, some people attempt to rationalize their problems away or to ignore them in the hope they will disappear. While it is true that some problems do clear up without planned corrective action, more often they worsen and expand, sometimes leaving in their wake irreparable damage, great expense, and mental anguish.

Explain this step to clients in a straightforward fashion, emphasizing that in their early stages problems usually are manageable. If ignored, however, problems may escalate severely.

Step 2. Analyze the Problem and Identify the Needs of Participants

This step is crucial, for participants in a problem situation often are prone to prematurely consider solutions before they have accurately analyzed the problem. Consequently, their solutions may be misdirected, resulting in wasted time and energy and causing discouragement. Moreover, clients' ensuing interaction may be adversarial, centering around whose proposed solution should be adopted. In fact, clients often *start* their "problem solving" with arguments over incompatible solutions rather than first assessing needs and then developing creative solutions that meet the needs of all concerned.

As you assist clients to analyze problems, it is important *not* to dwell on their problem at length or to engage in deep probing aimed at discovering the root causes of difficulties. The objective is not to search for causes, for doing so often leads to unproductive speculation. Rather, the purpose in analyzing problems is to discover factors that produce clients' difficulties and to identify the needs of participants that must be met in order to solve the problem to the satisfaction of all persons involved. To define problems accurately, clients must learn to adhere to the following guidelines:

1. Pinpoint problematic behaviors and explicitly express feelings related to them (e.g., "When you go to a bar after work, I resent it and feel unimportant to you").

2. Analyze who owns what part of the problems.

3. Specify needs of the participants germane to the problematic situation.

Earlier we discussed the first two guidelines at length and need not elaborate further on them. The third guideline, however, merits elaboration. Specifying the needs of participants in problem situations is critical for two reasons. First, to be acceptable, any solution must satisfactorily meet the needs of all participants. Therefore, it is logical to identify the needs in advance so that clients can employ them as criteria for assessing possible solutions. Second, by sharing personal needs, clients

are far more likely to be listened to receptively by other participants than by complaining about what others are doing. Identifying needs in problem solving further enhances collaboration because mutually seeking to determine and to understand each other's needs fosters mutual caring and respect. Equally important, identifying needs paves the way for arriving at a solution that best meets the needs of all concerned—the hallmark of effective problem solving.

The following are examples of messages that identify the needs of clients:

"I don't like your going to the bar with your buddies several nights in a row. I feel unimportant to you when you spend so little time with me. I'd like to share more evenings with you."

"It humiliates me when you get on my case in front of my friends. I would like to feel I can bring my friends home without fear of being embarrassed."

Notice that in the preceding messages the sender specifies the problematic behavior, the situational context, the emotional reaction to the behavior, and the unmet needs or wants. In addition, the senders own their own feelings, avoid accusatory comments, and focus on the immediate present.

Identifying needs of participants requires careful structuring of processes and active intervention, particularly in family sessions, for clients are quick to move from needs to accusations and criticisms of others. To avert defensive responses, it is often necessary to help clients reframe negative messages by modeling "I" messages for them and coaching them to alter parts of their subsequent messages so that they accurately identify and own their feelings and express their needs. Further, it is often necessary to guide recipients of "problem" messages to assume an "understanding" stance by using feedback to ascertain if they have grasped the intended meaning of the initial message.

To structure processes in a manner that assists clients to identify and to value the needs of each other, we recommend that you implement the following sequence of actions:

1. Explain that the most effective solution to a problem

is the one that best meets the needs of everyone concerned.

2. Clarify that the needs of every person are important and that no one will be counted out in the problem-solving process. All persons will be asked in turn to identify their needs, and others will be asked to listen attentively and to seek to understand, seeking clarification as needed.

3. Ask for a volunteer to write down needs as they are identified. If no one volunteers, you may request that a person serve as a recorder or do it yourself.

4. Ask each person in succession to identify his or her personal needs, encouraging open discussion and requesting clarification when expressed needs are vague or confusing. Begin with the person who initially identified a problem. Ensure that needs are recorded, and have the recorder check with participants to ascertain that their needs are accurately worded and that none is omitted.

Before participants identify their needs, it is important to ask them not to challenge the needs identified by other participants or to debate whose needs are of highest priority when potential conflicts are apparent. Stress that identifying needs should be limited to just that. Further, clarify that assigning priorities and resolving conflicts come later in the problem-solving process. It is also vital to intervene to stop criticism or arguments, should either occur during discussion of needs.

Although identifying needs is important in problem solving with couples, families, and groups, we have chosen a family system to illustrate this process. The Taylor family has had frequent family squabbles about use of the family automobile. The practitioner sees this as an opportunity to assist the family in learning problem-solving skills, and the parents and their two teenage children, Bert and Renee, both of whom drive, are receptive to learning this process.

The parents define the problem as heated arguments among family members over who will use their automobile on frequent occasions. They say that the children make excessive requests for the car, creating difficulties for them in meeting their obligations. The children mildly protest that they need a car for special activities. The practitioner

intervenes, explaining that all the family members have needs and that the objective is to seek a solution that best meets all their needs. Mr. Taylor nods with understanding and assures Bert and Renee that their needs are important and that they will work together to develop a solution to their liking. The practitioner then explains the importance of recording the needs, and Renee volunteers to serve as recorder. In the ensuing discussion, the following needs are identified:

Bert: Transportation for dates and for going to athletic events held at other schools.

Renee: Transportation to sorority meetings and to go to a drive-in movie or to engage in other recreation with friends.

Mrs. T: Transportation to the hairdresser's once a week and to the grocery store; also needs to visit her widowed mother several times a week and take her on errands.

Mr. T: Transportation for bowling on Tuesday and for usual dinner date on Friday night with Mrs. T; also needs the car to drive to work.

Having identified their needs, the Taylors are ready to advance to step 3. We will rejoin them in step 4.

Step 3. Use Brainstorming to Generate Possible Solutions

To reach sound decisions, participants need to consider a number of possible alternatives. Otherwise, they may limit their deliberations to one or two obvious options and overlook more promising alternatives. *Brainstorming* produces a wide range of possibilities through freewheeling discussion aimed at generating many possible solutions. Therefore, request all participants to stretch their thinking in identifying several creative solutions. If participants are hesitant or unable to suggest many alternatives, it is appropriate for you to offer additional possible solutions. The goal of effective decision making is to arrive at the best possible solution, not one that is merely satisfactory.

To maximize the productivity of brainstorming, it is essential that participants foster a climate of openness and receptivity to each other's ideas. Therefore, you should request that all participants refrain from criticizing or ridiculing suggestions, however impractical or absurd they may seem. Otherwise, participants will be hesitant to share their ideas for fear they will be rejected as stupid or silly. This step encourages the family or group norm that everyone is important and that criticism is detrimental to the system's process.

Brainstorming should be open, spontaneous, and freewheeling. Encourage participants to contribute their ideas, and give them positive feedback when they do so. The goal is to promote enthusiastic participation without evaluating any of the proposed solutions. To facilitate the subsequent process of evaluation, it is desirable to ask the recorder to list each proposed solution on a sheet of paper or on a chalkboard, leaving room on one side to enter ratings, as we illustrate later.

Step 4. Evaluate Each Option, Considering the Needs of Participants

This step is the heart of the decision-making process. If participants satisfactorily complete the preliminary steps, they enter step 4 with a cooperative frame of mind, ready to measure solutions generated in the preceding step against the needs of each participant. The objective of step 4 is to carefully weigh the pros and cons of each solution and to select the one that best meets the needs of all participants. Evaluating solutions in this manner avoids needless and unproductive hassles and employs the decision-by-consensus principle. Because the problem-solving method thus averts power struggles, it has been termed a no-lose method. The final solution has maximal fit for all participants, and each person, in effect, "wins."

To implement this step, guide the participants in evaluating each proposed solution generated. Ask the recorder to read each proposed alternative, and guide the participants in turn to rate the

solution as to whether or not it meets their needs. Ratings can be assigned by using a plus to indicate an acceptable solution, a minus for an unacceptable solution, and a neutral rating (zero) for a solution that meets needs only marginally. An alternative method of rating is to ask participants to assign ratings based on a scale from 1 to 10, where 1 represents "totally fails to meet my needs" and 10 represents "completely meets my needs."

To illustrate this process, we return to the hypothetical case of the Taylor family, listing each alternative generated by the family and rating it according to whether or not it meets the needs of family members, as shown in the following illustration:

POSSIBLE SOLUTIONS	RATINGS			
	Father	Mother	Bert	Renee
1. Buy a second car	−	−	+	+
2. Reduce social and recreational activities that require driving	0	−	−	−
3. Reduce need for car by walking and catching bus when feasible	+	+	+	+
4. Attempt to form car pools for various events	+	+	+	+
5. Double-date more frequently, reducing the times a family car is required	+	+	+	+
6. Meet as a family at the beginning of each month and week to determine members' needs for car and to plan schedule according to priorities negotiated by family	+	+	+	+

Having the family inspect the ratings of alternative solutions reveals that proposals 1 and 2 fail to meet the needs of most family members; after discussion, therefore, the family members eliminate these alternatives from further consideration. Proposals 3, 4, 5, and 6, however, appear to be promising alternatives, since all family members rate them as pluses. The family members conclude these solutions are not in conflict with one another and may be combined to resolve the problem adequately.

As they consider solution number 3, Mr. T indicates he could catch the bus to work instead of driving, except on Wednesdays when he needs the car. Mrs. T volunteers to curtail driving to the grocery store by planning needs for the week and limiting her shopping to weekly visits. She also believes she could reduce trips to her mother's apartment by combining shopping trips with social visits and compensate by phoning her mother more frequently.

With respect to proposed solution number 4, Mr. T expresses his intention to suggest to other members of his bowling team that they form a car pool for bowling nights. Renee and Bert follow suit by volunteering to explore car pools to attend sorority meetings and athletic events. Bert also agrees to comply with solution number 5 by double-dating more often. All agree that proposal number 6 would prevent arguing and result in decisions fair to all family members.

Pleased with the results of their deliberations, the Taylors believe they will be able to meet the transportation needs of each family member. Equally important, they emerge from the problem solving with mutual respect and high family morale.

Choosing an alternative often does not proceed as smoothly as it did for the Taylors, and the stakes are sometimes much higher. Furthermore, two or more alternatives may receive an equal number of plus ratings, and the participants may be forced to choose only one of them. When this occurs, you will need to assist the participants to analyze further the acceptable alternatives. This is best done by having participants identify the pros and cons of each option and assign weights according to the relative importance of each factor. To enhance this process, have the recorder list the pros and cons so that comparisons can be made readily and objectively.

In weighing pros and cons, it is critical to guide participants in considering the likely consequences of each acceptable alternative, keeping in mind the following: "Is a certain decision likely to produce lasting beneficial results by getting to the core of a problem, or is it merely relieving pressure temporarily and postponing an inevitable course of action that will be more difficult later?" "How is a decision likely to affect relationships among the participants?" "Has sufficient information been gained to assess the probable effects of a given solution?" "Have all likely obstacles to the given solution been anticipated?" "Are personal biases producing favoritism for one alternative over another?" You can play an active and vital role by encouraging participants to share their ideas and by supplementing their discussion by pointing out consequences they may have overlooked. Your role in this regard is vital, for clients learn from your modeling. Modeling related to considering consequences of decisions is particularly beneficial, as many clients tend to be impulsive and fail to anticipate probable consequences of their actions.

After participants have weighed the pros and cons of acceptable solutions, ask them to rerate these proposed solutions, employing the scale from 1 to 10 described earlier. (Because all the remaining solutions are acceptable, the "plus-minus" scale is no longer applicable.) On the basis of the new ratings, guide the members in selecting the solution that they have given the highest overall ratings.

Step 5. Implement the Option Selected

After the participants have selected an option, explain that the next step is to implement it with enthusiasm and confidence. After all, they have done their best to reach a sound decision, and they will enhance the chances of achieving a successful outcome by wholeheartedly applying themselves to implementing it. It is important to emphasize this point because some people tend to dwell on uncertainties and to delay actions because of lingering doubts. Others carry out solutions in a halfhearted manner, which sabotages the chances of successfully solving the problem. Many well-conceived solutions fail not because they are defective but because of defective execution, which may result from hesitation, doubt, and fears of bungling.

Step 6. Evaluate the Outcome

Effective problem solving does not end after participants have implemented an alternative. Because of human fallibility and life's vicissitudes, even carefully chosen and well-executed solutions sometimes fail to achieve desired results. Consequently, it is vital that participants systematically monitor the effects of their chosen course of action. Keeping records based on careful and consistent observations assists them in making thorough and objective evaluations and thus determining early on if their solution is working as planned.

To assist clients in evaluating outcomes of solutions, it is important to explain the value of monitoring and to guide participants in developing a mutually acceptable strategy of monitoring. Appropriate strategies may involve keeping daily logs that record the incidence of desired behaviors or, in the case of the Taylor family, maintaining records to determine if the incidence of family squabbles over the car decreased. Similarly, parents who have implemented a strategy to reduce the frequency of a child's temper tantrums can evaluate the effectiveness of their strategy by recording daily over several weeks the frequency of the tantrums.

A less rigorous method of monitoring is to hold regularly scheduled meetings in which participants share their views as to how solutions are working. Groups, for example, may agree to review over a course of several weeks whether strategies developed by members to keep the group on task are indeed proving effective. Scheduled meetings of couples and families also have the advantage of promoting sustained collaborative efforts by participants.

When a solution has not produced positive results over a reasonable trial period, participants can safely conclude their solution is ineffective. This need not cause alarm, as they likely have not assessed the problem accurately or anticipated all the obstacles. Further efforts may identify a more efficacious solution. To assist participants to develop a more effective solution, have them return to step 2 and repeat the process. It is possible their first solution failed because their problem formulation was inaccurate. When participants are confident of their problem formulation, however, ask them to return to step 3 and carefully review other alternate solutions or generate additional ones. Assisting them to follow the guidelines and steps presented earlier will expedite their devising an effective and timely solution to their problem.

EXPEDITING THE DEVELOPMENT OF CLIENTS' PROBLEM-SOLVING SKILLS

Although couples and families may select the development of problem-solving skills as a goal in initial sessions (with the practitioner's help), the practitioner may not actually *teach* members these skills until a later date. With respect to groups, an important aspect of the practitioner's role in an initial session is to assist the group to agree to use a decision-by-consensus method of solving problems and to teach steps for decision-making members. The problem-solving method can be taught to groups, families, or couples using a structured learning experience to facilitate the learning of the steps. Actual practice of the steps, however, should occur in an informal manner that provides for maximum interaction among members. An ultimate goal of the practitioner, in fact, is to help clients learn to apply problem-solving steps spontaneously in their relationships with others.

Clients can be expected to struggle in adhering

to the steps and guidelines at first. Even in couple, family, and group sessions you will need to intervene actively when participants get off track or begin to engage in dysfunctional interactions. By intervening and clarifying the destructive nature of their interaction, you can guide clients to achieve positive outcomes. Gradually, you can give them increasing responsibility for getting back on track by asking family or group members to identify what is going wrong and by challenging them to take corrective action. You can also anticipate with them how they will encounter similar obstacles outside of sessions and participate with them in planning corrective strategies.

When evaluating clients' efforts to employ problem solving, keep in mind that the hard-won ability to make decisions collaboratively with others is a reflection of substantial growth in a number of areas. Clients may falter in their first tentative efforts to apply the problem-solving process because implementation of a decision-by-consensus approach requires extensive adjustments in the individual styles of many members. For example, many families must alter crystallized dysfunctional patterns in order for members to count each other in and to acknowledge and address the needs of members through problem solving. It is also difficult for a newly formed group to orchestrate a problem-solving process that effectively meets the needs of all concerned when members are strangers with no previous experience in mutual problem solving. The ability of formed groups to solve problems consistently in a facilitative manner, in fact, is a sure sign that such groups have achieved the working stage of development.

The following statements illustrate the practitioner's role in facilitating development of problem-solving skills early in initial or group sessions:

1. "As we make this decision, let's consider members' needs first and then develop a number of possible solutions before we decide on a course of action."

2. "The experience we just had is an example of decision by consensus. What did you observe as we went through this process?"

3. "I'm really pleased with the way the group attacked this problem; everyone's needs were considered. We chose our solution from several alternatives, and everyone seems satisfied with the decision."

Thus, by intervening to guide groups through problem solving (message number 1), assisting them to discuss their efforts to make decisions collaboratively (message number 2), and accrediting their increments of growth and success (message number 3), you can assist members in assuming increasing responsibility for self-directed problem solving.

Applying Problem Solving with Individuals

Although our preceding discussion and examples of problem solving related to couples, families, and groups, the steps are equally applicable to work with individuals. Individuals function within an interpersonal context and need to learn skills that apply to that broader arena of life. In enabling individual clients to solve problems, you must also guide them through essentially the same steps as outlined in this chapter.

The step concerned with generating numerous alternatives is particularly vital in working with individual clients. Clients can learn to engage in individual brainstorming, thereby expanding their range of options and avoiding impulsive actions. With clients who tend to act impetuously, learning to generate alternatives, to assess their pros and cons, and to weigh possible consequences of actions may significantly enhance their social functioning by equipping them with new and more effective coping patterns.

FACILITATING TRANSFER OF PROBLEM-SOLVING SKILLS

Enabling clients to apply problem-solving processes in the real world is a challenging task. Because the process embodies a number of discrete concepts and skills and requires both commitment and self-discipline, mastering it requires persistent and determined effort. The benefits more than justify the efforts, and it is important to emphasize to clients the benefits that will gradually accrue if they persevere until they achieve mastery.

As you guide clients through the steps, they gain rudimentary skills in applying the process. These "in-session" activities are merely a means to an end. The ultimate benefit lies in whether clients succeed in applying the process outside the session.

You can assist clients to expand and to transfer their problem-solving facility by negotiating tasks of applying the process to problems that emerge between sessions. Suggest to clients that they agree to assist each other to adhere to the steps and guidelines by gently drawing deviations to their attention and facilitatively suggesting they get back on course. By applying the process independently, they will gain additional practice and will experience rough spots that can be explored and ironed out in their next session.

Applying the process under your tutelage provides additional opportunity for them to refine their skills. As you observe them effectively following the steps and guidelines, you can accredit their progress, thereby enhancing their confidence and reinforcing their efforts.

You will further enhance transfer of the skills to the real world by intervening less frequently and giving less direction as clients demonstrate increasing mastery of the process. By giving them increasing responsibility to monitor their own behavior and to make their own "interventions" when their efforts go awry, you are preparing them for successful independent problem solving. You will, of course, need to continue making timely interventions and to coach them until they are better able to stand on their own feet. But always bear in mind that you achieve ultimate success with clients when they are able to function effectively without your services.

SOCIAL SKILLS TRAINING (SST)

Training in social skills has expanded over the past two decades with many articles and evaluations of SST programs. SST programs have been employed to teach a wide variety of skills for both primary prevention and remediation. SST assists clients by providing them with the opportunity to learn skills needed to function effectively in their current environment, and in anticipated roles relationships and life-cycle stages. In this section, we explain the rationale of SST for prevention and remediation, identify target groups, enumerate various skills, and describe a format that can be employed for teaching various skills.

Rationale for and Uses of SST

Beginning with Rapoport (1961) 35 years ago, prominent social workers have increasingly promoted the development of primary preventive programs in social work. The rationale for preventive programs is that efforts to prevent social dysfunction by equipping people with coping skills reduces the possibilities of later maladjustment, unhappiness, failure to develop potentials, and loss of productivity. Moreover, preventive programs cost much less than remedial programs such as mental health treatment, foster care, substance abuse treatment programs, public assistance, and correctional institutions, to name just a few.

Many research studies document the importance of adequate socialization during childhood and adolescence to adequate adjustment. Children who are deprived of adequate socialization fail to learn certain vital social skills and are at risk to experience a variety of personal and interpersonal difficulties. For example, a study (Weisz et al., 1987) revealed that perceived personal incompetence by children is linked with depression in childhood. Other research studies (summarized in

LeCroy, 1983) have documented the importance of skills in forming peer relationships to the healthy socialization of children. As a consequence of these findings, practitioners have developed preventive skill training programs (LeCroy & Rose, 1986), including one that uses a game format (LeCroy, 1987).

Preventive SST has been employed in middle schools by LeCroy (1983) to teach three primary skills: making requests of others; resisting peer pressure, which is prerequisite for "saying no to drugs"; and maintaining friendships. Jason and Burrows (1983) have developed an SST program for assisting high school seniors to cope with the transition associated with completing high school. Schinke, Blythe, and Gilchrist (1981) have used SST for teaching pregnancy prevention skills to young people in a school setting.

The rationale for SST in remediation programs is similar to that just discussed. Social dysfunction is commonly associated with a lack of social skills essential to achieving self-esteem, forming satisfying interpersonal relationships, and performing various social roles effectively. Limited social skills contribute to difficulties involving loneliness and depression, marital dysfunction, parent–child problems, family breakdown, employment problems, various mental health problems, and other difficulties. As a consequence, SST programs are often included in services provided in diverse practice settings. For example, a training program in social skills aimed at expanding social support for mothers at risk of child maltreatment has been developed by Lovell and Richey (1991). Another program has been developed to assist transient women in learning skills essential for daily functioning (Breton, 1984).

Skills selected for remedial SST are diverse and vary according to the setting and the target problems of clients typically served. Among the more common skills are various parenting skills, assertiveness, listening to others and sending clear messages, personalizing feelings, making requests, initiating and maintaining conversation, making friends, managing anger, and solving problems. With clients who lack many social skills, skills may include personal grooming, using public transportation, ordering meals, making telephone calls, and initiating conversation, to name just a few.

Use with Persons with Disabilites   Skill building is especially relevant for developmentally and mentally disabled persons, for these groups often lack social skills and other coping skills. Vital preventive work can be accomplished by enhancing the parenting skills of developmentally disabled parents. Whitman, Graves, and Accardo (1989) have described such a program for mentally retarded parents. Another parenting skills program has been developed and tested (with promising results) for normal parents of children with developmental disabilities (Gammon & Rose, 1991). Still another program has been designed to enable developmentally disabled persons to develop skills requisite to utilizing transportation they need to secure essential resources (Taylor, 1988).

Assessing Skill Deficits

The first step in employing SST is to determine the skills targeted for training. When deficits are readily apparent this is a simple task. Adolescents who are easily provoked to anger and discharge anger in violent and destructive ways, for example, lack skills in coping with provocation and controlling anger. Socially inhibited people commonly lack skills in making social overtures, maintaining conversation, and asserting themselves. Certain clients will themselves identify problems and request assistance in learning certain social behaviors, for example, accepting compliments or overcoming extreme sensitivity to criticism.

With other clients, however, as with those who lack many skills or those whose deficits are more subtle, assessment is more complex. Parent–child difficulties, for example, may involve a lack of parental skill in providing encouragement and approval, expressing expectations, setting limits, managing demands or tantrums, being firm and consistent, being flexible, or listening to children without lecturing or being critical. Clients with schizophrenia may have many skill limitations that require extensive SST. To identify specific skill deficits of persons with schizophrenia, Curran et al. (1985) recommend administering a scale that covers major areas of psychosocial functioning and identifies stressors to which patients have not adapted adequately. Various other instruments have also been developed by behaviorally oriented marital and family therapists to assess skills of partners in performing various marital roles.[1]

Identifying Components of Social Skills

After selecting a social skill for training, the next step is to break down the skill into its discrete components or subskills. This process is essentially the same as that of dissecting tasks into behavioral units, as discussed in Chapter 13. As with dissecting tasks, the analysis should consider cognitive and emotional components as well as specific behaviors, for fears and uncertainties often must be mastered before clients can effectively perform requisite actions. We will illustrate this process later in this chapter in the section on assertiveness training.

FORMAT FOR TRAINING

SST can be conducted in sessions with individuals or in a group context. We have chosen to focus on the group context; however, you can follow essentially the same format in sessions with individuals because the principles and steps are virtually identical. When using a group, it is important,

of course, to prepare members for the group, as we discussed in Chapter 11. Once the group has been formed, the following steps are typically followed.

1. Discuss the Rationale and Describe the Skill

This first step is critical to successfully engaging members in learning a selected skill. Participants must believe that developing the skill will benefit them. To enhance the relevance for participants we recommend you briefly introduce the skill, alluding in general to situations in which it is applicable, and then elicit from participants specific relevant social situations that have posed difficulties for them and have led to adverse outcomes because of ineffectual coping. For example, if the selected skill is assertively resisting peer pressure you might use a message similar to the following:

"Learning to say 'No!' with firmness and not giving in to pressure from other kids can help you avoid doing things you don't really want to do and things that can get you into trouble. Probably a number of you can recall times you gave in to pressure and later regretted it. I know I can (*gives an example*). How about the rest of you? Could you share times when you wished you had been able to say 'No'?"

As participants share experiences, commend them for risking with the group. After a number of participants have shared experiences, you can further attempt to enhance their motivation by asking if they can think of several benefits of learning the skill. Initiate the discussion by listing an advantage on a chalkboard (e.g., don't get started on drugs and have higher self-respect). Compliment persons who identify advantages and list the advantages on the chalkboard, elaborating on advantages when clarification is needed.

2. Identify the Components of the Skill

Explain that the skill involves a number of different components. Then list each component on the chalkboard, explaining its significance to successfully employing the skill. It is helpful as you do so to involve participants by asking if they have had difficulties with the component being discussed (e.g., the cognitive/emotional component—fearing the reactions of peers if one refuses to participate in a certain problematic activity). Explain that the group will discuss and practice each component.

3. Model the Skill

Recall from an earlier chapter that vicarious learning is the second most potent source of self-efficacy. To tap this source, you can model the component of the skill (using *coping* modeling rather than mastery) or ask if a member of the group will volunteer to model the skill. A critique or discussion by participants regarding their observations of the modelling is often fruitful in highlighting aspects of the target component that contribute to effective and ineffective performance.

4. Role-Play Use of Each Component

Explain that the most effective way of learning a skill is to practice until one feels confident in applying the skill. Therefore, participants will take turns practicing each component and will give feedback to each other to assist in further developing the skill. Ask for a volunteer to begin role-playing and set the stage by prescribing roles they are to play. (You will need to prepare for this step by identifying problematic situations typical of those that participants commonly encounter. You can also enlist the aid of participants in identifying relevant situations.) It is desirable to begin with less difficult situations and, as participants demonstrate the ability to apply the skills, more challenging situations can be role-played. Before beginning the role-playing, ask participants to observe carefully so that they can provide feedback to each other.

5. Evaluate the Role-Play

After each episode of role-playing, invite participants to provide feedback. To foster a climate that is conducive to openness, encourage participants to give positive feedback initially. You may wish to initiate the process or add feedback about positive aspects of the participant's role-play that may have been overlooked.

For maximum benefit, feedback should be addressed to both verbal and nonverbal behaviors. For example, a participant may employ appropriate words but may speak hesitantly with a subdued tone of voice or may avoid eye-to-eye contact with the other protagonist. When such nonassertive behaviors are evident, it is beneficial to have the participant engage in further practice, seeking to modify the behaviors in question. Again, positive feedback should be given for even slight improvements and participants should be requested to evaluate their own performance, focusing on both positive and negative aspects, and to share feelings experienced during the role-play. Discussion of feelings that inhibit performance can be valuable in identifying common barriers to implementing the skill effectively.

6. Combine the Components in Role-Play

After participants have role-played and demonstrated adequate mastery of the various components, have them take turns role-playing the skill itself. Continue to have members give feedback to each other and continue practicing until they manifest self-efficacy with respect to the skill. A simple way of assessing the self-efficacy of participants is to have them rate their readiness to perform the skill in real-life situations on a scale from 1 to 10, where 1 represents a total lack of confidence and 10 represents complete confidence. Ratings of 7 or higher generally indicate adequate mastery.

7. Apply the Skill in Real-Life Situations

This step entails applying the skill in actual social situations, the ultimate test of the skill training efforts. Preparing participants adequately for this crucial step begins with eliciting situations that are likely to occur during the forthcoming week and obtaining the commitment of participants to apply the newly gained skills in these situations. Reviewing components of the skill and practicing application of them further prepares participants. Anticipating difficulties that will likely arise and preparing to surmount them through rehearsing appropriate thoughts and behaviors produces maximal preparation and self-efficacy.

Subsequent debriefing sessions provide opportunities to discuss and analyze the experiences of participants in applying the skill. The practitioner should encourage participants to accredit successes, enthusiastically drawing attention to specific behaviors and cognitions that resulted in successful outcomes. Such focusing draws the attention of participants to their mastery of components targeted for learning and further enhances their self-efficacy.

Not all participants report successes, of course, and even those who achieve successful outcomes may report aspects of their performance that were flawed. Debriefing sessions thus provide opportunities for additional practice in enhancing and refining skills. Step 7 thus may be extended for several weeks, depending upon the needs of participants and the feasibility of doing so.

GAME FORMATS FOR LEARNING SKILLS

Another format for assisting people to learn problem solving and social skills is the use of games specifically developed for those purposes. Use of a game format has a number of advantages, including the following cited by Rabin et al. (1985):

1. Many participants are receptive to this approach because games are expected to be fun.

2. Experimentation with new forms of behavior is natural in the context of a game.

3. Games with easily understood rules exert powerful control over the behavior of players.

4. Well-designed rules promote learning at participants' own pace with a minimum of failures.

5. Skill-training games foster adaptive interdependence of players and minimize the need for a third party.

Because the game format is a recent innovation, empirical support for this approach is scanty. Nevertheless, the rationale for the format appears sound and preliminary findings are promising. Rabin et al. (1985) describe the Marriage Contract Game, which was designed to teach marital partners the skills of successful problem solving and of warm and open communication. Outcome findings of the use of the game with four distressed couples who had requested treatment for a child and were averse to marital therapy indicated these couples learned to solve problems and to communicate positive feelings along the dimensions targeted by the game.

The game format appears particularly promising for work with children because of the high appeal of games to children. LeCroy (1987) has reported that the use of a board game designed to teach social skills that are components of social competence produced results that were equivalent to but not superior to results achieved using a standard social skills group. The game format had been designed partly as a response to difficulties encountered by social workers in involving children in formal skills groups. According to the group leaders who employed the game, children responded positively to the game and group attractiveness and cohesion increased.

Based on the limited experimentation described in the preceding, it appears that expanded use of and testing of the game format are warranted. This format offers a new approach to teaching skills to children and adults who might otherwise be hesitant to participate in formal skills development programs.

ASSERTIVENESS TRAINING

Lack of assertiveness pervades many aspects of interpersonal difficulties, and assertiveness training (AT) as a clinical intervention has been applied in diverse settings to almost every major diagnostic classification or behavioral disorder. Particularly relevant for both battered wives and their abusive husbands, AT achieved popularity with the publication in 1970 of *Your Perfect Right: A Guide to Assertive Behavior* (Alberti & Emmons, 1970, 1974) and has since become a widespread movement in the United States. At least one study has shown that assertiveness by social workers in the place of employment was associated with greater job satisfaction (Rabin & Zelner (1992).

The construct of assertiveness has been defined in various ways. Our definition, which synthesizes some of these definitions and adds our own interpretation, is that assertiveness embodies specific components of behavior that enable individuals to express their opinions, feelings, wants, and preferences in a manner that respects the rights and feelings of others even when such expressions risk aversive consequences such as criticism, disap-

proval, or punishment. Assertiveness is not a unitary construct, as revealed by Bucell (1979), who empirically studied behaviors embodied in various assertiveness inventories. Bucell identified the following relatively distinct types of assertive behaviors or response classes: (1) refuse requests, (2) express unpopular opinions, (3) admit personal shortcomings, (4) accept compliments, (5) express positive feelings, (6) make requests for changes in behavior, and (7) initiate and maintain conversations.

The first step in AT, therefore, is to identify the response class in which training is needed. After doing so you can prepare the client(s) for training following the guidelines and steps delineated earlier in the section on skills training. Training can be implemented either with individuals or in a group context. As with training in other social skills, modeling, behavioral rehearsal, and guided practice are crucial aspects of AT. To avoid redundancy we will not delineate steps involved in AT but refer you to a chapter by Schroeder and Black (1985) that describes in detail AT aimed at teaching conversational behavior.

Cultural Factors

Before discussing assertiveness further, assertiveness training may not be appropriate for clients whose culturally prescribed roles prohibit assertive behavior. Asian American cultures, for example, prescribe deference to authority. Similarly, women from traditional Hispanic, Latino, and Asian culture backgrounds are often expected to be submissive to their husbands. Assertiveness training could compound rather than resolve difficulties for such clients. Nevertheless, ethnic minority clients need to learn to assert their legal rights to resources to which they are entitled. Practitioners, therefore, often must assume an advocacy role in assisting them to gain assertiveness in dealing with bureaucratic structures.

Differentiating Assertiveness from Other Response Styles

In preparing clients for AT, it is important to differentiate assertiveness from the response styles of *aggressiveness* and *nonassertiveness*. We have previously defined assertiveness but add that the basic message relayed by persons who are relating assertively is that they "count" and that their ideas, perceptions, and opinions are important. By contrast, nonassertiveness involves the violation of one's own rights "by failing to express honest feelings, thoughts, and beliefs and consequently permitting others to violate oneself, or expressing one's thoughts and feelings in such an apologetic, diffident, self-effacing manner that others can easily disregard them" (Lange & Jakubowski, 1976, p. 9). Persons who relate nonassertively attempt to appease others and to avoid conflict, conveying through their behavior that their needs, wants, and opinions are not important and that others are superior to them.

The third response style, *aggression*, as defined by Lange and Jakubowski (1976), involves "directly standing up for personal rights and expressing thoughts, feelings, and beliefs in a way which … violates the rights of the other person" (p. 10). Persons who relate aggressively seek to dominate others, ignoring their needs, wants, and feelings.

The idea of relating assertively has had immense popular appeal to the lay public. Many people have problems with nonassertiveness or timidity, frequently permitting themselves to be pushed aside or discounted by others. Unable to express themselves effectively in a wide variety of situations, such persons often feel unappreciated, taken for granted, and exploited by others. Many other persons, who relate aggressively, often suffer the loss of significant relationships because others weary of their abrasive, debasing response styles. Still other persons vacillate between aggressive and nonassertive or passive behavior, failing to develop an effective and comfortable style of relating to others.

Clients often seek (or are coerced to seek) professional assistance because of problems that can be traced to habitual styles of relating aggressively or passively. Experienced over long periods of time, such difficulties may cause or contribute to low self-esteem, depression, or marked anxiety in interpersonal situations.

Congruence between Verbal and Nonverbal Behavior

Nonverbal components of messages may either strengthen and complement an assertive statement or contradict it. Persons who wring their hands, look at the floor, or stammer, for instance, do not appear assertive no matter how assertive the verbal content of their message. Practitioners must thus observe clients' nonverbal behaviors to determine whether these behaviors convey assertiveness, aggressiveness, or nonassertiveness. Common nonverbal behaviors associated with assertive relating and the other two response styles include the following:

ASSERTIVENESS	AGGRESSIVENESS	NONASSERTIVENESS
Relaxed posture	Glares	Evasive or fleeting eye contact
	Tightened fists	
Direct eye contact	Clenched jaws	Nervous gestures
Firm and moderate tone of voice	Pursed lips	Soft, whiny, or pleading voice
Fluent speech pattern	Rigid body posture	Hesitant speech
Appropriately varied facial expressions	Sarcastic or belittling tone of voice	Nervous laughter or throat clearing
Moderately expressive gestures	Loud speech	
	Finger pointing	Clammy hands

Cognitive/Perceptual Obstacles to Assertiveness

Developing assertiveness is not easy for practitioners or clients. Clients often experience extreme tension and paralyzing emotions that block them from asserting themselves despite strong desires to do so. These powerful emotions are generally a product of deeply embedded mistaken beliefs, of which clients usually have limited or vague awareness. Consequently, practitioners need to assist clients to expand their awareness of these irrational beliefs and to replace them with realistic conceptions.

Common misconceptions that inhibit assertiveness include: (1) beliefs that one's obligations to others far outweigh one's own wants or rights, (2) extreme concern with pleasing or impressing others favorably, and (3) extreme fears about the consequences of asserting oneself with others. With respect to beliefs, many clients were conditioned as children to believe that it is bad or selfish to accord equal significance to personal wants and needs as compared to responding to the needs or wants (and sometimes demands) of others. To feel they are "good" persons (or, rather, not *bad* persons), such individuals develop keen sensitivity to the wants of others, sometimes going to extremes to please them, often at great expense to themselves. Saying no (and sometimes even thinking it) automatically triggers feelings of guilt and badness. Sadly, these individuals are so governed by the wants and expectations of others that they are often out of touch with their own needs and wants.

The second and third types of misconceptions are linked with the first. Having an inordinate need to please or impress others derives from the mistaken belief that one's worth as a person is directly proportional to the extent that one gains the approval of others. Often rooted in early life experiences in which parental love and approval were not expressed generously and were contingent upon pleasing the parents, such beliefs link self-esteem exclusively to the reactions of others.

Self-esteem, under such circumstances, is tenuous at best, and it is overwhelming to such persons to risk incurring the displeasure of others. The tacit motto of these persons is, "I am of value only as I win approval from others." The irony in this motto is that persons who seek excessively to please others tend to attain the opposite effect, for others often devalue them. Such persons need to adopt instead the realistic belief that people tend to value those who value themselves and are assertive.

The third type of misconception involves fearing disastrous consequences if one asserts one's right, wants, or feelings. Some people, who were severely punished as children for not conforming to parental demands, experience vague fears of being physically or verbally abused if they assert themselves. Others have conscious fears of being rejected or literally abandoned (as they feared in childhood) if they assert themselves. These feared reactions are of catastrophic proportions, and it is understandable that these people are extremely threatened by the prospects of asserting themselves.

Assisting clients to surmount the obstacles described in the preceding involves an approach that combines cognitive restructuring (see Chapter 13), behavior rehearsal, and stress management (the topic of the next section).

STRESS MANAGEMENT

Stress management is a broad term that refers to varied approaches that share the common objective of enabling people to cope more effectively with the tensions and stresses associated with problems of living. These approaches are employed to assist people to use coping skills that prevent excessive reactions to stressful events and situations. For example, stress management skills enable people to avoid being immobilized by extreme tensions or losing control of emotions or impulses and expressing them in violent ways that can be damaging to others or to themselves. Training in stress management skills thus is widely employed with people who react to stress with excessive anxiety or anger.

The stress management approach we delineate has been denoted as stress inoculation (Meichenbaum, 1977), a multidimensional approach that embodies skills directed to biophysical, cognitive/perceptual, and behavioral components of clients' reactions to stressful situations. We focus first on relaxation training, an integral part of stress inoculation that addresses the biophysical component. Relaxation training, however, is also employed as an intervention in its own right to assist people to reduce anxiety and to keep emotions within manageable limits. To the best of our knowledge, Vattano (1978) was the first social work author to describe muscle relaxation procedures and to recommend this intervention for stress management.

Relaxation Training

Two major physiological components of excessive tension and anger are rapid breathing and tightening of the muscles. Relaxation training targets both of these components through deep breathing and muscle relaxing exercises. Numerous studies have reported that relaxation training has been used successfully to assist clients with problems related to various stress-related physical symptoms (e.g., high blood pressure, tension headaches, insomnia, and anxiety). It has also been effectively employed to reduce the extreme emotional reactions of people in crisis situations, to reduce tension associated with performance anxiety (e.g., before giving talks or taking examinations), and to reduce anger in provocative situations. Relaxation training also occupies a central role in the Lamaze (1958) method of childbirth.

Practitioners may employ relaxation training to particular advantage with clients who:

1. Are chronically tense and anxious.

2. Are acutely anxious as a result of a crisis situation.

3. Are anxious and fearful about various anticipated events or situations.

4. Have tension headaches, migraines, tightness of the chest, breathing difficulties, and other psychophysiological reactions when medical causes have been ruled out.

5. Suffer with insomnia.

6. Have difficulty controlling anger.

7. Are moderately depressed.

Major advantages of relaxation training include the fact that it is a simple procedure that clients can readily learn and can practice at home, which enables them to master the procedure in a few weeks' time. Another advantage is that clients can employ abbreviated forms of muscle relaxation in diverse stressful situations, thereby reducing tension and enhancing coping efforts.

Cautions

Although relaxation training can be employed in diverse situations, it is important to employ this procedure with discrimination, for there are limitations and contraindications associated with this modality. For example, although relaxation training is useful in assisting people to regain emotional control following a crisis, it should not be employed as a substitute for coping with situations that have created or contributed to the crisis. If a crisis is precipitated by sudden loss of a job, family disruption, loss of housing, unplanned pregnancy, or other stress, to achieve *enduring* benefit, you must implement other interventions that address the sources of the crises. When clients are distraught, panicky, or otherwise overwhelmed by intense emotionality, however, muscle relaxation serves as a useful adjunct in assisting them to regain equilibrium, thereby enabling them to begin exploring their problems.

Another caution relates to clients with motor disorders (e.g., cerebral palsy) or muscular or skeletal disorders. These clients should not engage in muscle relaxation exercises without clearance from a physician.

Implementing Relaxation Training

While instructing clients in relaxation, it is important to observe the guidelines spelled out in the following sections.

Explaining the Rationale of the Procedure and Gaining Consent   To gain maximal cooperation of clients, practitioners should explain the purpose of muscle relaxation and obtain their consent. It has been our experience that clients readily and willingly agree to participate in the procedure, for they typically are highly motivated to gain alleviation from the discomfort produced by excessive tension, anxiety, or fear. In explaining the rationale, we recommend you include the following factors:

1. The causes and adverse effects of excessive tension.
2. The beneficial effects of muscle relaxation.
3. The diverse uses of muscle relaxation.
4. The need to develop a "muscle sense"; that is, to recognize the presence of excessive tension.
5. The need to practice to gain mastery of the procedure.

The following is an example of an explanation of the rationale of the procedure:

Life gets pretty hectic at times, causing people to become tense. At such times we often breathe rapidly and tighten our muscles, sometimes without even being aware of it. On occasions being tense and uptight for an extended time can produce muscle spasms, headache, and even gastrointestinal difficulties caused by involuntary contractions of the smooth muscles in the stomach and the intestines.

When people are chronically tense, they may experience other physical reactions such as elevation in blood pressure and heart rate, headaches, and nervous stomach. Excessive muscle tension also burns up energy rapidly and can produce fatigue. Muscle tension can also interfere with sleep. By learning to relax the skeletal muscles, you can counter all of these negative effects.

Muscle relaxation first involves developing awareness of the sensation of tension in your muscles. The procedure heightens awareness of the sensations of tension in various muscle groups, and you'll become keenly aware of the difference between tension and relaxation. You're also going to learn how to instruct your muscles to relax so that when you're aware of tension you can consciously reduce it.

I'm going to instruct you in a procedure that you can practice in your home. By practicing each day, you'll become more and more skillful so that you won't need to relax all of the muscle groups separately. Some people, in fact, learn to relax in a matter of a few seconds but only after much practice. I'll tell you more about how to practice later.

Clarifying Conditions Conducive to Relaxation
Optimal conditions for relaxation training include a comfortable and quiet environment. Further, furniture that permits relaxed posture should be employed, such as a reclining chair or padded chaise lounge. When instructing a group, padded floor mats or blankets may be used if appropriate furniture is not available.

Clients should wear loose-fitting clothing that permits freedom of movement. We recommend that you explain to clients that tightfitting clothing restricts movements and produces discomfort that may be distracting. It is also desirable to suggest that clients make these same arrangements for comfort when they practice relaxation training at home. As they gain facility in relaxing their muscles, the environment becomes less important. Indeed, the ultimate goal is for them to learn to relax in stress-producing situations.

Guidelines for Instructing Clients   To assist you in instructing clients in muscle relaxation, we offer the following guidelines, which involve a synthesis of procedures developed by Jacobson (1929), Bernstein and Borkovec (1973), and ourselves. We recommend that you study these guidelines until you have memorized them and that you practice instructing friends, relatives, or student colleagues in muscle relaxation before applying the procedures with individual clients or groups.

1. Allow sufficient time to apply the procedure. Preliminary discussion, implementation of the procedure, and subsequent discussion and planning usually consume the largest part of a 50-minute session.

2. Explain that when you ask clients to tighten a group of muscles, you do not mean for them to tense the muscles as hard as they can. Tightening muscles to the extreme can strain a muscle; tightening them to the point of uncomfortable tension is sufficient.

3. Explain that to enhance muscle relaxation, clients should breathe deeply, exhaling all the air, and think the word *relax* when you instruct them to relax. (Deep breathing facilitates relaxation as does thinking the word *relax*.) Ask them to practice with you. Model taking three or four deep breaths and exhaling completely. Ask them to do the same, concentrating on the word *relax*. Explain that you will remind them of this procedure with the first two muscle groups, but thereafter you want them to continue this breathing procedure without further reminders.

4. Explain that as clients relax their muscles they may experience warm, heavy, or tingling sensations. They should not be alarmed because these sensations are merely indications that they are succeeding in achieving relaxation.

5. Explain that you will be practicing muscle relaxation along with them. Practicing in concert with clients enhances timing in giving instruction and models appropriate behaviors. Moreover, clients are less likely to feel awkward and self-conscious if you participate with them in applying the procedure.

6. Speak with a relaxing and soothing tone of voice but avoid being dramatic. When you use the word *relax*, express it slowly and softly in a manner that fosters relaxation.

Instructing Clients in Applying the Procedure

After you have completed the foregoing procedures, you are ready to instruct clients in applying relaxation training.

Instructing clients involves five discrete activities (Bernstein & Borkovec, 1973) in the following sequence:

1. Draw the client's attention to the appropriate muscle group.

2. Instruct the client to tense the muscle group (we will list the muscle groups and provide directions for tensing them later).

3. Ask the client to hold the tension (for five to seven seconds) and to be aware of the sensations in the affected muscles.

4. Instruct the client to relax.

5. Instruct the client to be aware of the pleasant feeling of relaxation as contrasted to the discomfort associated with tension (relaxation interval lasts about 10 seconds).

To enhance clients' awareness of varying degrees of muscle tension, we instruct them to tense and to relax each group of muscles three times, reducing the degree of tension during the second and third contractions. We also emphasize the importance of being aware of the sensations of tension and contrasting them with the feelings of relaxation, as we illustrate below in the instructions to clients.

Before actually engaging in muscle relaxation, ask clients to get into a comfortable position. Then explain that you are going to teach them to relax 16 different muscle groups. Ask them to listen closely and to follow your instructions carefully. You are now ready to begin with the muscle groups, which should be relaxed in the sequence listed. (Different authors suggest lists of muscle groups that vary slightly. The list below is the one we have found most useful.) To assist you in giving instructions, we have provided a verbatim example for the first muscle group and partial instructions for the third and fifth muscle groups. We have also listed the remaining muscle groups together with methods of tensing them. Instructions for the remaining muscle groups are essentially the same as for those we have illustrated.

1. *Fingers and hands.* "We're going to begin with your finger and hand muscles. Clench both of your fists tightly as I'm doing but not too tightly. Keep them clenched and be aware of the tension in your fingers, the back of your hand, and your forearm. [*After sev-*

en seconds.] Now r-e-l-a-x. Tell yourself to relax, take a deep breath, and exhale all the air. Let your hand be limp and be aware of the pleasant feelings. [*After 10 seconds.*] Now I want you to make a fist again, but tense your muscles just half as tight as last time. Be aware of where you feel the tension. [*Pause for a few seconds.*] Now relax, breathe deeply, and think the word 'relax.' Let the tension flow out of your fingertips and enjoy the relaxation. [*After 10 seconds.*] Make a fist again, but this time tighten your fingers very lightly so that you can barely feel the tension. Hold your hand in this position and be aware that you can still feel the tension in the same places. [*Brief pause.*] Now relax, take a deep breath, and think the word 'relax.' Just savor the exhilarating feeling of relaxation for a few moments."

2. *Wrist and lower arm.* "Bend your wrists forward toward your head and point your fingers toward the ceiling so that you feel tension in the muscles in the back of your hand and forearm." [*Repeat procedure described with first muscle group, but explain that clients will need to remember to breathe deeply and think the word "relax."*]

3. *Upper arm/biceps.* "Now we're going to work with your upper arm muscles. Make your hands into fists and bring them toward your shoulders, tightening your biceps. Hold the muscles tightly and be aware of the tension in your upper arm. [*After five to seven seconds.*] Now relax and let all the tension drain out of your arms and fingers. Be aware of the pleasurable feeling of relaxation, and just enjoy it for a few moments." [*Repeat procedure after pauses, using reduced degrees of tension as indicated for group 1.*]

4. *Shoulders.* "Shrug both of your shoulders, bringing them close to your ears."

5. *Forehead and eyebrows.* "Now that you've relaxed your shoulders, you should have a refreshing relaxed feeling down both of your arms. Notice the pleasant feeling when your arms are free of tension. Now we'll work on relaxing the muscles of the face. First, wrinkle your brow tightly. Make it furrow as though you are scowling and be aware of the tension in your forehead and eyebrows. [*Pause.*] Now relax. Smooth out your forehead until the muscles are loose. Be aware of the feeling of relaxation and enjoy it a few moments." [*Pause for 10 seconds.*] [*Repeat the preceding twice, tensing the muscles only half as tightly the second time and very lightly the third time as illustrated for group 1. Vary your words to avoid being monotonous.*]

6. *Eyes.* "Close your eyes tightly and be aware of the tension around your eyes."

7. *Jaws.* "Clench your jaws together and study the tension and discomfort in your jaws, cheeks, and temples." [*With clients who wear dentures, you may use alternate exercises of having them push their tongue against the roof of the mouth or thrust their lower jaw forward.*]

8. *Lips.* "Now press your lips together tightly and be aware of the tension all around your mouth."

9. *Back neck muscles.* "Push your head backward into the chair. Be aware of the tension in the back of your neck and in the upper part of your back."

10. *Front neck muscles.* "Now, we're going to work with your front neck muscles. Tilt your head forward so that your chin is tight against your chest. Concentrate on the tension in the front of your neck."

11. *Back.* [*Advise clients who have lower back pain or spinal difficulties to avoid straining their back.*] "Now, turn your attention to your upper back. Arch your back by sticking out your chest and stomach. Study the tension and discomfort in your back."

12. *Chest.* [*Many clients complain of tightness in the chest when they are tense and anxious.*] "Take a deep breath and hold it, thrusting your chest forward. Be aware of the tension in your chest and upper abdomen. [*Pause.*] Now exhale completely and just relax. Enjoy the pleasant feeling of relaxation."

13. *Abdomen.* "Now focus on your stomach area. Pull in your stomach and tighten the muscles of your abdomen so that they feel like a knot."

14. *Upper leg.* [*Take one leg at a time.*] "Lift your right leg and hold it. Get in touch with the tension in your upper leg." [*Repeat with left leg after alternately raising and lowering right leg three times.*]

15. *Lower leg.* "Direct your attention to your lower leg. Now flex your ankle and point your toes at your head. Be aware of the tension in your lower leg."

16. *Feet and toes.* "Arch your foot by tightening your toes and pushing them against the floor. Experience the tension in your toes and in the ball of your foot."

After tensing and relaxing each muscle group three times, the next step is to review each muscle group and to instruct the client to dispel residual tension. To accomplish this, draw attention to each muscle group as follows:

> Now we're going to go over all the muscle groups again. As I name each group, be aware of any tension remaining in those muscles. If you feel tension, focus on those muscles, breathe deeply, and instruct them to relax. Think of the tension draining completely from your body. Let's begin with the toes and feet. If you feel any tension, let it drain out. [*Five-second pause*]

Then repeat the procedure with each muscle group, moving from the muscle groups in the legs to the abdomen, lower back, chest, shoulder, upper arms, lower arms, hands, neck, and ending with the facial muscles. After relaxing the facial muscles, instruct the client to remain relaxed from head to toes and to sit quietly and enjoy being relaxed for a few moments. Note that you instruct the client to relax each group once in the review.

To evaluate the extent of relaxation achieved, ask clients to relate their degree of relaxation on a scale from 1 to 10, where 1 represents complete relaxation and 10 extreme tension. If the client reports an uncomfortable level of tension, you may wish to suggest implementing an additional procedure to deepen the degree of relaxation. Akin to self-hypnosis (Lechnyr, 1980a), this procedure involves instructing the client to take 10 deep breaths as follows:

> Listen very carefully to me, and shut off all other thoughts. Breathe deeply and easily [*model deep breathing*]—that's right. Now I'm going to count to 10 slowly. With each number, you will become more and more relaxed. By the 10th breath, you will be very relaxed and sleepy. Now, one [*pause*], you're becoming more relaxed. Two [*shorter pause*] still more relaxed. [*Continue counting slowly with a soft, soothing voice, suggesting deeper relaxation with each count.*]

When you have finished counting, your client should be deeply relaxed and may be in a light hypnotic trance. Instruct the client to remain relaxed for a few moments and enjoy it fully. After a pause of about 20 seconds, instruct the client as follows:

> I'm going to count backwards from five, and with each count, you will feel more alert. When I reach "one" you will be fully alert and will feel refreshed and relaxed.

When you have finished and the client is alert, explain that in the future the client can employ this procedure independently by breathing easily and deeply and counting from 1 to 10, becoming increasingly relaxed with each count. You may explain that this is a form of self-hypnosis that many people use to relax or to go to sleep.

Post-Training Follow-up After completing the preceding relaxation training procedure, it is important to emphasize again that learning to relax, like any other skill, requires considerable practice. To master the skill, therefore, the client should practice 20 to 30 minutes daily under the conditions specified earlier. After practicing each day, the client should rate the degree of relaxation achieved using the scale described earlier, thereby making it possible to assess progress.

After clients have consistently practiced relaxing the 16 muscle groups for a week or two and report satisfactory progress in achieving relaxation, they are ready to advance to more streamlined forms of muscle relaxation. One such form involves reducing the number of muscle groups from 16 to 4 by combining the muscle groups into major anatomical parts of the body, which include the following:

1. Fingers, hands, lower arms, and upper arms.
2. Face and neck muscles.
3. Shoulders, back, chest, and abdominal muscles.
4. Upper legs, lower legs, feet, and toes.

The instructions for relaxing these four muscle groups are similar to those outlined earlier. Instruct the client to tighten and relax each of the muscle groups three different times, decreasing the degree of tension the second and third time according to the pattern described earlier. Taking a deep breath while simultaneously thinking the word "relax" is also part of the procedure. Counting to 10 while breathing deeply after relaxing all four muscle groups is optional according to the degree of relaxation reported by the client. After completing this procedure, you should again instruct the client to practice relaxing the four muscle groups daily for one week.

When the client reports success in relaxing the four muscle groups, you may employ a still more advanced procedure termed *recall* (Bernstein & Borkovec, 1973). Employing this procedure, the client relaxes the four muscle groups without first tensing them, focusing instead upon recall of the sensations experienced during the previous procedure. In introducing the client to the recall procedure, you can use an explanation similar to the following:

Now we're going to increase your skills in relaxing your muscles without the need to tighten them first. Relax the muscles in your hands and lower and upper arms, and contrast the feeling of relaxation with your memory of what it was like to release the tension in these same muscles as you practiced during the week. Just relax now and enjoy it. If any tension remains, send the message "relax" to the muscles and let the tension flow out of them.

Because muscles are not tightened in the recall procedure, muscle groups are relaxed only once. Counting to 10 while breathing easily and deeply is again optional according to the degree of relaxation the client reports.

When clients have mastered the recall procedure, they are ready to begin applying relaxation procedures as a means of coping with daily stresses. Explain to them that as they become aware of being excessively tense, they can take deep and easy breaths, think the word "relax," and consciously relax tense muscles that are not needed in given situations (e.g., the facial, chest, and abdominal muscles). By consciously practicing and employing muscle relaxation, they are developing a valuable coping tool they can use all their lives. Situations in which clients can employ this skill include the following: driving under nerve-wracking conditions, waiting up for children who stay out late, taking an examination, giving a talk, managing an aversive social situation, talking to a supervisor, overcoming sexual fears, reducing self-consciousness, keeping anger under control, and mastering various types of irrational fears.

Abbreviated Muscle Relaxation Training for Crisis Situations   The procedures described in the preceding sections commonly extend across two to six weeks. When clients are overwhelmed by crisis situations, however, abbreviated muscle relaxation training often provides temporary relief from extreme tension and enables clients to reestablish emotional equilibrium. In such instances, practitioners can assist clients to achieve relaxation during a session by having them practice taking deep breaths, visualize pleasant and tranquil scenes, relax the four major muscle groups, and think appropriate cue words such as "calm," "relax," and "peaceful." Should extreme tension recur between sessions, clients can implement these same procedures. Researchers have experimented with modifications of relaxation procedures including tape-recorded instructions, brief procedures (Marks, 1975), and use of biofeedback in tandem with muscle relaxation. Based on a review of this research, Borkovec and Sides (1979) have concluded that taped relaxation instructions are less effective than therapist-directed instructions. Lehrer (1982) has also concluded that brief procedures (often employing hypnosis) are not as effective as a full course of relaxation training and that biofeedback does not enhance the efficacy of relaxation training.

STRESS INOCULATION TRAINING (SIT)

This intervention involves combining relaxation training, cognitive coping skills, and behavioral rehearsal—skills discussed in this chapter and the preceding chapter. Stress inoculation (SIT), like medical inoculation, strengthens clients' coping skills for stressful situations and then exposes them to stress strong enough to arouse their coping defenses without overwhelming them. As clients progress in mastering coping skills, they are exposed to increasing increments of threat that require greater coping capacity. The potency of the "inoculation" thus increases gradually according to the degree of mastery attained. Numerous and successful applications of SIT have been reported in the literature, the most common of which are reducing tension and fear in anxiety-producing situations, managing anger in provocative situations, and coping with pain associated with physical conditions. In our opinion, SIT can be adapted for effective use in virtually all situations in which reduction of tension and fear and management of emotions and impulses are indicated. For example, SIT can be used to good effect with child or spouse abusers. Wertkin (1985) even has demonstrated that SIT is effective in reducing stress associated with the rigors of graduate social work education.

SIT consists of three major phases: (1) educational, (2) rehearsal, and (3) application. In the following sections, we delineate each of these phases. For illustrative purposes, we consider SIT as employed in anger control.

I. Educational Phase

The purposes of this phase are to provide a rationale for SIT and to present a conceptual framework in lay terms that enables clients to understand their reactions to stressful events. Ordinarily this phase lasts for only one session, and because it consists primarily of instruction, you can employ it in a group context. It is critical to provide a plausible explanation of SIT because clients will not engage wholeheartedly in the procedure unless they understand and accept its logic.

In presenting the rationale for SIT, emphasize that emotional reactions are more than just single-phase reactions. Moreover, mastery of emotions involves being aware of what triggers them, recognizing indications of emotional arousal, and developing new ways of coping with stressful situations that permit appropriate expressions of emotions. The following is an example of such a rationale:

"You've been having difficulty in controlling anger (fear, anxiety, tension) in certain situations. To learn to control your anger, you need to understand it more fully, what triggers it, indications your anger is being aroused, and what you say to yourself and actually do when you're angry. You also need to learn new ways of coping with situations that trigger anger so that you can keep it from mounting out of control. Stress inoculation training is designed to accomplish these various tasks. Our first session will involve exploring all these matters further. Do you have any questions?"

If clients accept the rationale and appear receptive, you can proceed with presenting the conceptual framework. If they raise questions or manifest misgivings, it is important to focus on them, as favorable results depend on gaining willing and active participation by clients. The conceptual framework you present depends on the nature of the stressor causing difficulties. If you are seeking to inoculate clients against fears of public speaking, for example, your conceptual framework will be very different from one relevant to inoculating against stressors that arouse intense anger.[2]

Novaco (1975)[3] conceptualizes anger as an emotional response to stress that is shaped by three subresponses—namely, *cognitive*, *somatic-affective*, and *behavioral*. To grasp how each of these components relates to their anger responses, clients must first grasp the general meaning of the concepts and then discover how these concepts apply to their individual experiences.

The cognitive component relates to self-statements that clients make in the face of provocative situations. These self-statements involve appraising a situation, which includes predicting the behavior of others by gauging their intentions and motives; evaluating one's own self-expectations, personal intentions, and images; weighing the magnitude of a situation; and assessing possible outcomes. Some clients, however, exclude some of the preceding types of self-statements, which contributes to deficient anger control. Failing to consider their own intentions or the magnitude of a situation, some clients lash out wildly and impulsively when confronted with provocative situations. Such clients do not ask themselves, "How can I work this situation *out*?" or "What will be the consequences if I blow my stack?" What clients do *not* say to themselves is often equally important as self-statements they *do* make.

To assist clients to appreciate the importance of self-statements in provocative situations, it is helpful to provide examples of contrasting self-statements that lead predictably to increasing anger or to maintaining self-control. The following are examples you may wish to use:

Destructive self-statements:

"What does that rotten SOB think he's trying to pull off? I'll show him."

"Look at that smirk on her face. She really thinks she put me down. I'll get even with her."

"That arrogant bastard must think he can call all the shots. I'll show him a thing or two."

Constructive self-statements:

"She's really acting like a jerk. I'll have to keep my cool, or it could really get out of hand."

"He's doing everything he can to get my goat. But I can cope. Take deep breaths. That's right, don't let him get to you."

"Boy, this really is sweaty. He's totally unreasonable. But I can handle it. If I lose my cool, it'll be an awful mess."

By discussing examples similar to these, clients usually readily grasp the significance of self-statements. For many clients it is a revelation, as they spontaneously realize for the first time that they make self-statements.

After illustrating the cognitive component of

anger arousal, explain the somatic-affective dimension. (You should complete the explanation of general concepts before assisting clients to apply them to themselves.) This component involves the physiological and emotional manifestations of anger arousal. To assist clients to grasp the significance of this component, we recommend you explain that physical and emotional manifestations of anger serve as signals of the need to employ coping skills. By recognizing these signals, they can head off anger before it reaches unmanageable proportions. It is important to clarify further that the somatic-affective component is important also because mounting tension and emotion tend to increase the intensity of the anger response.

Physiological manifestations of anger arousal include body tension, sweaty palms, increased heart rate, rapid breathing, clenched jaws, pursed lips, gastric upset, and the like. Because people experience tension in somewhat different ways, clients need to develop awareness of their own "signals." Early emotional reactions include irritation, agitation, and feelings of resentment.

The behavioral component of anger arousal may involve withdrawal or antagonistic and aggressive behavior, either of which may produce negative consequences. For example, a person may repeatedly withdraw when a spouse makes verbal attacks, letting resentments fester and accumulate until finally even a minor provocation may trigger a violent and destructive outburst of anger. Other persons may respond aggressively to provocations by counterattacking (e.g., name-calling or counteraccusations), thereby fostering escalation of anger by both participants and culminating in heated interaction and even violence.

Phase I culminates with having clients identify their individual patterns of anger arousal and analyze situations that provoke strong anger responses. More specifically, the practitioner guides clients to determine exact aspects of situations that trigger anger, focusing particularly on self-statements and feelings that are experienced in such situations.[4] An effective way of assisting clients to pinpoint their individual patterns of anger arousal is to have them close their eyes, as though running a movie of provocative events, reporting thoughts, feelings, and reactions they experience. At the conclusion of this first session, clients are asked to carry out tasks of (1) monitoring their self-statements when angry, (2) further analyzing aspects of stressful situations that provoke anger, and (3) listing anger-provoking situations on index cards and ranking them according to the intensity of anger they provoke. These tasks facilitate consolidation of the concepts presented in the session and also set the stage for phase II.

II. Rehearsal Phase

Whereas the educational phase can be conducted in a group context, subsequent phases are generally implemented individually. The rehearsal phase consists of assisting clients to develop coping skills that involve direct action and cognitive restructuring, with special emphasis on self-dialogue. Direct action involves two different aspects: (1) obtaining information about objects or situations that engender fear, pain, or anger; and (2) relaxation training. Before engaging in these activities, it is important to explain the rationale for them and to gain cooperation.

In the case of inoculation against losing control of anger, obtaining information involves analyzing the nature of stressors that provoke anger, building on the preliminary work begun in phase I. As clients report on their task related to analyzing situations that provoke anger, further analysis and discussion occur. The practitioner expands their awareness by assisting them to identify unrealistic appraisals of situations that may lead to unwarranted defensiveness and aggressiveness. Often clients' negative self-statements, according to Novaco (1975), reveal intolerance of mistakes by others,

unrealistic self-expectations about the necessity of success, excessive expectations of others, hypersensitivity to criticism, and a belief that retaliation is essential when one is wronged. Emphasis is placed on meanings clients attribute to situations where they perceive a threat to their self-worth, which in turn often is followed by aggressive or defensive behavior that escalates the degree of negative emotionality. Clients are also assisted to analyze other options that are available (e.g., assertive but nonaggressive behavior). Obtaining information and analyzing it thus tends to neutralize the provocative potential of stressful situations.

The second aspect of direct action, relaxation training, proceeds along the lines discussed earlier in this chapter. Before beginning relaxation training, it is important to explain that you are teaching them the procedure because relaxation is incompatible with tension and anger. Thus, when they anticipate confronting a provocative situation or recognize anger arousal manifestations, they can employ deep breathing and muscle relaxation to mitigate anger.

The cognitive restructuring component of phase II consists of assisting clients *(1) to substitute positive self-statements for their habitual negative, anger-generating self-statements; and (2) to confront provocative situations constructively.* Novaco (1975) and Meichenbaum (1977) concur that self-dialogue related to provocation and anger reactions should be viewed in four stages as follows:

1. Preparing for the provocation whenever possible.
2. The impact and confrontation.
3. Coping with arousal.
4. Subsequent reflection when conflict was resolved successfully or when conflict was unresolved (Meichenbaum, 1977, p. 165).

Numerous positive, stress-reducing self-statements for each of these stages are listed by Meichenbaum and Turk (1976, pp. 6–9). We recommend that you become familiar with these self-statements. In the following, for illustrative purposes, we provide a few examples of self-statements for each of the four stages in stress inoculation for controlling anger:

Preparing for provocation:

"This is going to be upsetting, but I can handle it."

"If I work out a plan, I'll be prepared and won't lose my cool."

"I've learned how to manage my anger—no need to push the panic button."

"Remember, deep breaths and relax. Don't let it get to you."

Impact and confrontation:

"Nothing gained by getting mad. It just makes it worse."

"It's too bad he acts like this. I'm pleased I'm staying in control. Whatever he says doesn't matter. What really matters is that I control myself."

"I'm staying on top of this situation by keeping under control."

Coping with arousal:

"I can feel I'm getting tense. Need to breathe deeply and slow things down."

"I have a right to be irritated but must keep my feelings under control."

"Even though he's making a fool of himself, treat him with respect."

"It takes two to have a fight, and I'm not going to let it happen."

"Don't let him push you around. Express your views, but don't blow it by losing your cool."

"He's really trying to get to me, but I won't let him. I'm in control of the situation."

Reflecting on the provocation:

a. When coping is successful and conflict is resolved

"Chalk that up as a success."

"It paid off."

"I actually got through it without blowing my top. It sure feels good."

"I did better than I thought I could. I really can learn to control my anger."

b. When conflict is unresolved

"Even though it wasn't a total success, it wasn't a lost cause. It takes time to work out sticky problems."

"Don't dwell on it. That only makes it worse. It could have gone a lot worse."

"Can't expect success every time. You did the best you could. Simmer down, don't let it eat at you. Relax, take a deep breath."

Note that in the last stage, self-statements are included for both successful and unsuccessful outcomes. It is important to recognize the possibility of the latter and to inoculate the client for that possibility. After all, despite the best laid plans, people do not always cope successfully; moreover, forces beyond one's control (e.g., refractory behavior by another person) may produce undesired outcomes. By assisting clients to view unsuccessful outcomes as sometimes unavoidable and to construe the same as evidence of the need to persist, rather than as ultimate failure, you inoculate them against being unduly discouraged or overwhelmed by life's occasional disappointments.

After learning the coping skills discussed in the preceding, clients rehearse employing these skills by imagining themselves in the stressful situations they earlier listed on the index cards after completing their first session. They begin with the situation they ranked as least stressful, instructing themselves with coping self-statements, breathing deeply, and relaxing their muscles. The practitioner guides them as necessary. As they gain confidence in their ability to cope successfully with one situation, they advance to the next, thereby gradually increasing the potency of their inoculation. During this process, it is important for the practitioner to express approval of their progress and to encourage them to make reinforcing self-statements also. Clients continue this process until they complete the hierarchy of stressful situations. Homework assignments involving practice of the skills with the imagined stressful situation continue between sessions. Phase II thus extends across approximately three weekly sessions.

III. Application Phase

In this phase, clients apply their newly won coping skills to actual life situations and other imagined stressful situations or engage in simulated stressful situations with the practitioner playing the role of other protagonists. In this last activity, the practitioner should play the role "to the hilt," being suf-

ficiently provocative to challenge the coping skills of clients without overwhelming them. The ultimate proof of effectiveness of the coping skills is coping successfully *in vivo*, and clients' confidence increases as they discover they can indeed cope with situations that previously overwhelmed them.

SIT concludes with instructions to the client to continue practicing the skills indefinitely, thereby maintaining and further enhancing the potency of the inoculation. Ordinarily SIT extends across five or six sessions, although a longer time can be taken if deemed necessary.

NOTES

1 These and related instruments are described in the *Handbook of Measurements for Marriage and Family Therapy* (Fredman & Sherman, 1987).

2 For discussion of conceptual frameworks that pertain to several types of stressors, we refer you to Meichenbaum (1977).

3 We wish to acknowledge that much of the material in this section is based on this reference.

4 If situations that provoke anger responses usually involve family members, relatives, or others with whom clients have frequent contacts, you should also make efforts to involve these significant others to assist them in modifying their provocative behavior.

Chapter 15 ☐ ☐ ☐

Modifying Environments, Developing Resources, and Planning

EFFECTS OF MISMATCHES BETWEEN CLIENTS' NEEDS AND ENVIRONMENTAL RESOURCES

As we described in Chapter 1, the social work profession is "committed to the enhancement of human well-being and to the alleviation of poverty and oppression"(CSWE, 1995, p. 97). Further, social work education must provide students with a framework for "understanding...and the dynamics and consequences of social and economic justice...must provide students with skills to promote social change" (ibid., p. 101). Finally, this focus on promoting social and economic justice must include a context of social work practice with populations-at-risk. Social work programs "must present theoretical and practice content about patterns, dynamics and consequences of discrimination, economic deprivation and oppression. The curriculum must provide content about people of color, women, and gay and lesbian persons...in addition to those mandated above, such groups include, but are not limited to, those distinguished by age, ethnicity, culture, class, religion, and physical or mental ability" (ibid., pp. 101–102).

To approach these goals, we turn our attention in this chapter to interventions employed to enhance the social and physical environments of people. It is increasingly recognized that earlier efforts of social workers in assisting clients to adapt to their environments were often misdirected and that client difficulties may reflect a need to adapt environments to clients' needs. For example, practitioners who treated clients in institutional settings (e.g., mental hospitals and youth correctional centers) came to realize that changes which occurred in a protected environment were often not supported in the home and community environment. Unless clients were worked with to deal with threatening factors and to tap into supportive resources in the home and community environment, gains achieved in treatment were threatened. Consequently, practitioners have devoted increasing attention to client groups that are particularly vulnerable to problems associated with inadequate environmental resources. This concern is reflected by a burgeoning literature related to concerns about and ways of improving clients' environments through innovative direct service, advocacy, and the promotion and development of social policies and programs addressed to populations at risk.

Vulnerable Client Groups and Types of Interventions

Mismatches between clients and their environments result from two major types of circumstances: (1) substantial deficiencies in resources normally needed by people at various developmental stages and (2) unusual needs of people that result from developmental difficulties (e.g., mental retardation, autism, cerebral palsy, learning disabilities, congenital deformities, and deafness), disabilities, mental disorders, degenerative disorders, severe stress, cultural dislocation, and environmental disasters.

TYPE 1: RESOURCE DEFICIENCIES NEEDED AT DEVELOPMENTAL STAGES

Vulnerable populations of the first type include infants, children, and adolescents who are neglected and/or abused and who otherwise receive inadequate parenting; children and adults who live in impoverished environments; people who are denied resources and opportunities because of race, ethnicity, age, sex, or other factors; adults whose spouses or other family members lack the capacity to impart warmth, affection, and respect; and people who lack essential support systems. Vulnerable populations of the second type include children and adults who are afflicted with incapacitating illnesses or suffer from various forms of physical and mental disability; elderly clients who are unable to care for themselves; refugees; and people who have lost their homes and possessions as a result of natural calamities.

Many different forms of intervention can be used to improve the environments of such vulnerable groups. Although these interventions are diverse, they incorporate a limited number of general strategies, which we have classified as follows:

1. Enhancing intrafamilial relationships.
2. Supplementing resources in the home environment.
3. Developing and enhancing support systems.
4. Moving clients to different environments.
5. Using case management.
6. Enhancing interactions between organizations and institutions.
7. Improving institutional environments.
8. Empowering clients.
9. Developing new resources.
10. Employing advocacy and social action.
11. Planning and organizing.

In the following sections, we discuss these strategies and the vulnerable populations to which they apply. Limited space precludes discussing specific interventions in detail, but we have included selected references that explicate them in greater depth.

Before proceeding further, we wish to emphasize that environmental interventions are generally implemented in concert with other interventions. Because problems are multidimensional and involve reciprocal interaction among multiple systems and subsystems, interventions aimed exclusively at the environment may ignore dysfunction in individuals, thereby addressing only part of a problem. Children who are neglected or abused by parents often manifest psychological damage that requires attention aside from efforts to improve the social environment afforded by parents. Moreover, children's behavior impinges on parents and may play a major role in precipitating physical or sexual abuse. Another way of thinking about it is that every actor may be viewed as a central figure or as a part of the environment of other actors, depending on one's vantage point.

Enhancing Intrafamilial Relationships

Within families, the members constitute the primary resource for meeting vital human needs, such as nurturance, guidance, protection, nutrition, health care, affection, and companionship. Often parents and spouses lack the capacity to provide emotional resources needed by other family members. Family members may also interact in destructive ways that impair the ability of members to respond to each other's emotional needs. Family therapy is often the preferred intervention for enhancing the functioning of families. Because we consider this mode of intervention at length in Chapter 16, we shall not discuss it further here.

When parents abuse, neglect, or otherwise fail to provide adequate care and guidance for their children, practitioners often employ multiple interventions to enhance family functioning. Prominent among these interventions are various forms of home-based care, which have been summarized by Kadushin and Martin (1988, pp. 83–142). Home-based care is typically aimed at strengthening parental functioning to prevent placement of children in foster homes or institutional settings. We also discuss home-based family treatment in Chapter 16 and will not elaborate on it here.

In addition to home-based family treatment, other interventions employed to assist families with children at risk of maltreatment include using parent aides (Miller et al., 1984) and homemakers (Kaduchin & Martin, 1988, pp. 143–172); working directly with children (Lamb, 1986); employing group work with parents (Kruger et al., 1979); using Parents Anonymous self-help groups (Moore, 1983); blending social services and social support (Miller & Whittaker, 1988); and employing parent education programs (Barozzi & Engel, 1985).

One-Parent, Remarried, and Gay or Lesbian Families

Certain families are vulnerable to dysfunction because the structures of these families often result in unusually high stresses for both parents and children. The single parent is often beset by financial difficulties and by stresses related to having to fulfill multiple roles that are normally distributed between two parents. Moreover, the single parent has personal and social needs that compete with performing these multiple roles. Garfinkel and McLanahan (1986) have written an informative book concerned with single mothers and their children. Kissman (1991) has also written an informative article (from a feminist perspective) that contains useful guidelines in understanding and working with single-parent families. Greif (1985) has written a book based on surveys of single fathers concerning their experiences extending from the divorce process through different stages of single parenting. Bowen (1987) has also written concerning problems of single fathers.

Stepfamilies also are at risk because of possible stresses associated with the absence of a history of emotional bonding among stepmembers, divided loyalties of children, unclear expectations of family members, possible differences in lifestyles between previous families, questions of turf, and conflicts in role definitions. Visher and Visher (1988) have written an authoritative book that defines therapeutic strategies in work with stepfamilies. Whitsett and Land (1992) have reported research findings that document the stresses of role strain on stepparents (especially stepmothers) and discuss coping strategies employed in these families. Dahl, Cowgill, and Asmundsson (1987) have reported findings based on interviews with remarried families. These authors report the first year for remarried families typically is difficult and that it takes from three to five years before these families achieve cohesiveness and a sense of belonging.

Because of the stigma associated with homosexuality in society and the consequent lack of societal supports, gay and lesbian parents are also vulnerable to stresses that can impair family functioning. We discuss this topic further in Chapter 16, but refer you to articles by Levy (1992) and Faria (1994) that discuss research findings concerning lesbian-headed families and ways of strengthening the coping of lesbian parents.

TYPE 2: UNUSUAL NEEDS OF PEOPLE THAT RESULT FROM DEVELOPMENTAL DIFFICULTIES

Families with Deaf, Physically, Mentally, or Developmentally Disabled Members

Certain families are vulnerable to dysfunction because of unusual needs of members that pose difficulties to parents and other family members. Often overlooked are families with members who have been deaf from birth or who have severe hearing losses. Over 90 percent of deaf children have hearing parents, and a large majority of the parents are unfamiliar with special needs that derive from their disability. Pridgen (1991) has described the needs of deaf persons and discussed community resources to serve these persons and their families.

Families with developmentally disabled (retarded) members also have unusual needs that often require services to prevent or allay family dysfunction. Gammon and Rose (1991) and Kratochvil and Devereux (1988) have discussed programs developed to assist parents of children with developmental disabilities and Whitman, Graves, and Accardo (1989) have described a program designed to assist mentally retarded parents with parenting skills. Barbero (1989) has discussed community-based day treatment programs that enable mentally retarded persons to participate more fully in mainstream society and that lighten the burdens on families of caring for such persons. Resources for families with developmentally disabled children are sparse in rural communities, but Fiene and Taylor (1991) have described a case management approach to meeting the needs of these families.

Children with physical disabilities also are at risk because of possible adverse parental reactions to their conditions or because their unusual developmental needs are not adequately fulfilled. Bernier (1990) has discussed factors pertinent to work with parents of disabled children and Malekoff, Johnson, and Klappersack (1991) have discussed the ways professionals can collaborate with parents of children with learning disabilities.

Most stressful and challenging to families are difficulties encountered in attempting to respond to the needs of severely mentally disabled (chronic schizophrenic) family members. Much research has been done to determine ways of supporting these families, and the psychoeducational approach has proven to be the most effective (Hogarty, 1989). Simon, McNeil, Franklin, and Cooperman (1991) have reviewed five different models of psychoeducational treatment, cited research support, and discussed clinical implications. Day treatment programs and community-based psychosocial rehabilitation programs have also been important resources for both mentally disabled persons and their families (Peterson, Patrick, & Rissmeyer, 1990).

Caregivers of Severely Ill and Elderly Persons

Severely ill and frail elderly persons require extensive care giving by their families that can be emotionally taxing and physically exhausting. With ever-expanding numbers of elderly persons and persons afflicted with severe and sometimes terminal illnesses such as cancer and AIDS, social workers have been increasingly concerned with the needs of both afflicted persons and their caregivers, as attested to by a burgeoning literature concerned with these populations. This literature focuses upon the needs of the patients, the stresses experienced by caregivers, other options available, processes of making decisions to assure adequate care giving, and needs for support systems for caregivers. References related to family caregiving in chronic illness or disability include Biegel, Sales, and Schulz (1991) and Parsonnet and O'Hare (1990). Cates, Graham, Boeglin, and Tielker (1990) have discussed the effects of AIDS on families, and Land and Harangody (1990) have reported on the use of support groups for partners of persons with AIDS. Numerous publications deal with caregivers of elderly persons, including those by Anastas, Gibeau, and Larson (1990); Barusch (1991); Borden (1991); Couper (1989); Kuhn (1990); Pilisuk and Parks (1988); Sistler (1989); and Wilson (1990). A research study comparing the effectiveness of individual and group interventions to support family caregivers of elderly persons has been reported by Toseland, Rossiter, Peak, and Smith (1990). They found that individual interventions were most effective when psychological problems were involved and group interventions were most effective when need for support was the central issue.

SUPPLEMENTING RESOURCES IN THE HOME ENVIRONMENT

By augmenting resources in deficient home environments, it is often possible to meet clients' needs adequately, sparing them and other family members the trauma and possible psychological damage that ensues as a result of separation and/or admission to institutions. Visiting nurses and Meals on Wheels, which delivers hot meals to homebound persons, may make it possible for elderly and/or disabled persons to live independently. Moreover, disabled persons who earlier would have had to reside with others or in institutions are now able to live independently as a result of instruction in self-care, new devices that enable them to perform housekeeping functions, independent living centers, and volunteers who assist them to dress and perform other daily tasks (Mackelprang & Hepworth, 1987; Milofsky, 1980).

Homemaker Service

Homemaker service is a valuable resource when a family has no parent who can adequately perform crucial aspects of the traditional homemaker's role. Homemaker service may involve shopping, cleaning, preparing balanced meals, budgeting, doing the laundry, and teaching these same skills to clients. Homemakers also model effective interpersonal and child management skills, thereby enabling clients to learn the same. Equally important, they offer "on-the-spot availability," permitting them gradually to build trust and provide a "corrective emotional experience" for clients, thereby fostering positive change (Stempler & Stempler, 1981). The authors just cited define the partnership between social workers and homemakers in serving families and provide an excellent example of teamwork in assisting an unstable minority family referred to protective service because of child neglect.[1]

Household Items

Some family units, including single-person households, lack basic resources essential to health and effective home management. Refugees, for example, sometimes struggle to live without adequate cooking utensils, warm clothing, beds, blankets, and even food. However, even long-term residents who struggle on meager incomes have needs for acquiring essential goods or replacing worn-out and often dangerous appliances.

Social workers are in a strategic position to identify items that people living in impoverished conditions urgently need. Beyond identifying such needs, practitioners have a responsibility to initiate remedial actions, which may include drawing the needs of people to the attention of appropriate agencies or engaging in direct efforts to supply the needs of clients. Practitioners may contact church, civic, or private service organizations that provide concrete goods for people in need; request special funds from public assistance agencies; or assist clients in purchasing essential items through various thrift stores that cater to low-income people. In other instances, practitioners may need to organize programs to assist groups of people with extensive needs.

Day Care of Children

With more than one-half of the mothers in the United States in the work force, day care for infants and children has become a necessity for many families. For example, a survey of working mothers in Massachusetts revealed that 45% of all infants (age 2 years or younger) were in some type of nonparental child care (Marshall, 1991). The use of day care, in fact, has reached the extent that Marshall now terms it a "normative experience" for children.

Day care takes many different forms, the most common being the family support network. According to Frankel (1991) 80% of preschool children in day care are cared for in homes with relatives. Of children in structured nonrelative day care, the majority are in family day care homes, i.e., homes run by mothers who take other children (usually no more than five or six) into their homes. Both private- and public-funded structured centers also provide day care. The largest of the latter for preschool children is the federally funded Head Start program, which provides half- to full-day care for about 400,000 lower-income children in the United States. Low-income families generally cannot affort private day care centers, other than those run by mothers.

Day care centers such as Head Start are a valuable resource to working low-income families because they not only provide rich environments for children, but also stimulate children to develop skills in observing, communicating, and interacting with others. Varied day care activities also assist children to increase their physical strength and coordination and to develop a positive self-concept. Day care programs are particularly valuable to working mothers but can be of value to all families by providing learning experiences for children during a period when they learn rapidly, as well as creative and healthy experiences in separation for both parents and children. Moreover, day care programs provide opportunities to identify troubled families and to provide services that can strengthen family functioning (Friedman & Friedman, 1982).

Still another advantage of public day care is that low-income children who are eligible can receive up to two meals and one snack daily, the cost of which is funded through the Child Care Food Program, which is administered through the United States Department of Agriculture.[2]

DEVELOPING AND ENHANCING SUPPORT SYSTEMS

As we discussed in Chapters 8 and 9, many people's problems are caused in large measure by the absence or inadequacy of social support systems. In recent years, social workers have increasingly employed interventions that tap natural and formal support networks and develop new ones that can provide vitally needed resources. It should be noted here that more is not necessarily better. Individual needs and wishes for support systems vary; some persons with serious and persistent mental illness have a low threshold for overstimulation and may appreciate a small, functioning social network more than having a larger number of people involved.

Natural Support Systems

Relatives, friends, neighbors, church organizations, clubs, family physicians, and the like comprise natural support systems. People who have roots in a community generally have established helping networks that respond supportively in times of adversity. However, even local people may have weak kinship ties, lack close friends, and have no linkages with neighbors or other potential support groups. Still other clients are homebound and lack access to many of the support systems that would otherwise be available. Newcomers to boomtowns also lack natural support systems, although they may be able to develop them more readily because they do not have to cross cultural barriers or learn a new language.

Vulnerable Populations and Support Systems

Groups who are not in the mainstream of society lack access to support systems essential to satisfactory social functioning. Isolation from support systems can result from the following factors: living in a sparsely populated rural area, being stigmatized (e.g., persons with AIDS), having limited mobility, and lacking social skills. In the following sections, we discuss support systems for these vulnerable populations.

Rural Isolation   In rural settings, where social services tend to be scant, practitioners must become thoroughly familiar with care-giving persons who are a part of communities' natural helping networks. Such indigenous helping persons include welfare workers, grocers, barbers, insurance agents, ministers, civic leaders, schoolteachers, health department nurses, county officials, and the like. By consulting with the welfare worker or leaders of local service clubs, practitioners can also identify other indigenous care-givers to whom rural residents turn because of their reputations for being helpful to people in times of crisis. Conklin (1980) has discussed the use of indigenous care-givers in rural communities. The effectiveness of natural helpers in rural areas has been documented by Patterson et al. (1988). Cohen and Adler (1986) have discussed the role of social network interventions with an inner-city population, and Mitchell (1986) has reported how volunteers can be used to enhance informal social networks.

An innovative method of countering isolation in rural areas, described by Rounds, Galinsky, and Stevens (1991), is to bring support groups into the homes of residents through telephone conference call technology. The authors cited developed this method for people with AIDS who lacked access to support groups because of geographic isolation. This procedure, of course, can also be employed with other groups. Social workers can also exploit the telephone to assist isolated clients to develop telephone friendships between other individuals who share common situations (e.g., disabilities, widowhood, and debilitating illness). Homebound persons in urban settings can also be linked to one another through telephones.

Culturally Isolated Persons   Refugees and immigrants may totally lack support systems other than their immediate families. The traumatic stresses of geographic dislocation and cultural shock have been well documented, as we noted in earlier chapters, but these stresses are not limited to immigrants. Native Americans and Eskimos who move from reservations or the bush to urban centers may be equally or more isolated, as the gap between their cultures and urban American life may be even greater than it is for immigrants.

Support systems for persons who are geographically and culturally dislocated can often be developed by contacting members of the same cultural group who immigrated earlier. In most large urban areas such groups band together because of shared cultural backgrounds, and many have formed mutual assistance organizations that will assist newly arrived persons to this country.

Organized religions also are potential support systems for immigrants. Buddhism, for example, has a long history of providing human services, and Buddhist mutual assistance associations for Southeast Asian refugees exist in many parts of the country (Canda & Phaobtong, 1992). The same can be said of Jewish and Christian refugee organizations.

Types of support and service needed by immigrants vary according to the stage of their migration. Drachman (1992) has presented a framework for determining services needed by immigrants according to their stage of migration.

Churches as Support Systems   We have discussed how religious organizations are potentially valuable support systems to immigrants, but they can also be rich resources to native clients. Parishes and congregations are natural ecological structures and as such may offer many resources needed by clients such as a reference group, spiritual stimulation, social activities, recreational programs, home visiting, short-term homemaking when clients are ill, and concrete services for elderly and homebound persons. Joseph and Conrad (1980) have defined the potential resources often available in "parish neighborhood communities."

Abusive and Neglectful Parents   Garbarino, Stocking, and associates (1980) and Ballew (1985) have provided practical guidelines on how to mobilize relatives, neighbors, and friends into support systems to assist practitioners in detecting, preventing, and treating cases of child abuse and neglect. Such support systems are not only valuable but virtually essential because practitioners can spend only limited time with clients, whereas members of support systems can often be available at short notice when crises develop and can perform ongoing monitoring that is impossible for professional people.

Research has also disclosed that neglectful mothers often feel lonely and isolated even though they may reside in neighborhoods regarded as normal in supportiveness (Polansky, Ammons, & Gaudin, 1985). Recognizing this problem, Lovell and Richey (1991) developed a social support skill training program that provides support to mothers while they systematically learn social skills essential to forming social relationships with other persons. Beeman's research indicated that parents who are abusive or neglectful are less skilled in use of network supports than otherwise similar community parents who are not abusive or neglectful (Beeman, 1995).

Other researchers (Miller & Whittaker, 1988) have developed "blended" programs to increase social support for families at risk of maltreating their children. Another effective support program consists of parent cooperatives that have mutual exchanges of baby-sitting services. Such arrangements provide welcome respite for parents otherwise confined by constant responsibilities of caring for children.

Other Target Groups   Tapping natural social support networks has proven to be of great value in therapeutic work with varied target groups, including mental health clients (Biegel & Naparstek, 1982; Gottlieb, 1985) and families of persons with AIDS (Kelly & Sykes, 1989). Social support systems are especially needed by schizophrenic clients, whose social networks typically are limited to five to six persons, a mere fraction of the numbers in the networks of mentally healthy persons (Crotty & Kulys, 1985). Other client groups for whom mobilizing of social supports has been effective include the homeless (Hutchinson, Searight, & Stretch, 1986), and the elderly (Sauer & Coward, 1985).[3]

Limitations of Social Support

Although several books have discussed the principles and techniques of network therapy (Froland et al., 1981; Gottlieb, 1981; Rueveni, 1979; and Whittaker, Garbarino, & associates, 1983), systematic exploration of the use of social network concepts is still in its infancy. As McIntyre (1986, p. 421) has reminded us, "Current use of network ideas…is often more akin to metaphor and analogy than to precise meaning and careful testing of concepts, methods, and measures." McIntyre identifies trends, strengths, and gaps in knowledge about social networks, as well as problems and directions for future work. Schilling, Schinke, and Weatherly (1988) also caution that social workers may be overestimating the potential of support networks and that it is unrealistic to suggest that the problems of homeless adults, runaway youths, and mentally ill persons in our communities, who generally lack social supports, can be remedied by simply tapping the reservoirs of natural social supports, which, in fact, do not exist. Schilling (1987) acknowledges the essential nature of social support systems but warns that adverse consequences may result from inappropriate implementation of support-enhancing interventions. To assist practitioners to use such interventions discriminately, Auslander and Litwin (1987) have developed an analytic paradigm that aids in assessing the appropriateness and efficacy of a given intervention.

Self-Help (Mutual Aid) Groups

Widely employed as social support systems, self-help groups consist of people who share common conditions, experiences, or problematic situations and mutually seek to assist each other to enhance their coping capacities related to their common factors. The help these groups provide is available without charge and is based on the experiences of members rather than professional expertise. Knowing that caring others are available is a source of great support to members, especially early in their involvement with the group.

Using Volunteers

Volunteers have long been a resource to social workers for enhancing the environments of clients. Indeed, social work as a profession sprouted from seeds planted by early volunteers. Volunteers are persons who render services to social service agencies and clients without remuneration. The importance of tapping the resources afforded by volunteers greatly expanded in the 1980s as a result of drastic cutbacks in governmental funding of social services. An example is the increased utilization of volunteers to expand the social support networks of clients (Mitchell, 1986).

Volunteers perform a broad spectrum of activities, thereby extending the services delivered by social work agencies. Big Brothers (Royfe, 1960), for example, is a national organization of adult male volunteers who provide one-to-one relationships with male children who do not have fathers in the home. Panzer, Wiesner, and Dickson (1978) have described a similar local program instituted for developmentally disabled children. College students have served as volunteers in providing ongoing relationships with emotionally disturbed children deemed likely to benefit from such relationships (Witkin, 1973). Resourceful social workers have also enlisted high school and college students to tutor children who are doing poorly in school and whose parents lack either the inclination or competence to assist them. Other practitioners have enlisted older neighbors to assist such children and to provide nurturance that is deficient in these children's homes. Such an arrangement not only enriches the lives of children but also meets a need of retired persons to remain contributing members of society.

Volunteers can also perform other significant services, such as preventing child abuse and neglect (Rosenstein, 1978), serving as mentors to abusing parents (Withey, Anderson, & Lauderdale, 1980), transporting clients to and from hospitals, reading to the blind and to children who require long-term hospitalization, entertaining and visiting with nursing-home patients, and providing companionship to the depressed elderly (Frankle & Gordon, 1983) and to dying patients. Still other volunteers have aided minorities and other disadvantaged persons in securing needed services and concrete resources by serving as interpreters, expediters, and advocates.

Golden (1991) has reported on the use of carefully selected mature adults to serve as counselors in communities with too little money and too few services. The volunteers are provided 24 hours of basic training (in lay language) and are thereafter supervised. They have successfully provided counseling services for a broad range of problems, but referrals are made for complex and difficult problems. The program has functioned for over 20 years in Rockland County, New York.

Volunteers have also been employed successfully in enhancing the physical environments of clients. Practitioners have worked through churches, youth organizations, service clubs, labor unions, and schools and universities to recruit volunteers to improve homes and yards—one of many potential activities that volunteers can perform to enhance the environments of clients.

Implementing volunteer programs is no simple matter. Indeed, Feinstein and Cavanaugh (1976) maintain that "the dearth of relevant uses of volunteer skills is due not to the volunteers themselves but to the professionals, who, for the most part, are not equipped or willing to deal with them" (p. 14). A crucial task practitioners face in using volunteers is to provide opportunities that are satisfying and growth producing. In addition to this task, implementing volunteer programs requires skills in recruiting, screening, training, placing, supervising, and maintaining positive collaborative relationships between professional staff and volunteers.

Haeuser and Schwartz (1980) maintain that a good volunteer program requires the leadership of a professional volunteer administrator, who should be expert both in clinical service and in management. Schwartz (1984) has compiled numerous essays that deal with the topic of interaction between volunteers and social agencies. Hunt and Paschall (1984) give many guidelines concerned with implementation of volunteer groups employed to improve mental health services. Many of the guidelines are also applicable to other settings.

Formal Support Systems

Numerous types of social agencies and community resources have evolved in response to the needs of clients for environmental supports. The Salvation Army, for example, provides food and shelter for short periods of time, and organizations such as the YWCA and senior citizens' centers provide opportunities for social interaction, recreation, and education in crafts and hobbies. The Red Cross provides shelter, food, and medical services to victims of natural disasters, fires, and accidents that affect substantial numbers of people. In addition, various types of hospitals, convalescent homes, residential treatment centers, and correctional institutions provide resources for people who require intensive care or special types of environments.

Social agencies also provide support systems composed of groups of clients who have special needs as a result of shared conditions, problems, or developmental crises that have produced marked stress and/or drastically diminished their support systems (e.g., death, divorce, retirement). These groups thus serve a function of mutual support similar to self-help groups. Growth groups differ from self-help groups in that members are selected and a professional serves as a group leader.

MOVING CLIENTS TO A DIFFERENT ENVIRONMENT

This strategy is by far the most drastic one because it involves moving people from familiar environments to ones that range from less familiar to altogether different. Because uprooting people from their usual environments, however undesirable they may be, generally produces trauma in varying degrees, this strategy is employed as a last resort when less drastic strategies are impracticable or have failed to remedy an intolerable environmental situation. This strategy is thus appropriate only when vital resources are not available or cannot be developed sufficiently early in a given environment to safeguard the safety, health, and well-being of vulnerable clients.

Circumstances that justify employing this strategy include the following:

1. Physical abuse or neglect of children or adolesents.
2. Sexual abuse of children.
3. Physical abuse of women.
4. Abuse of elderly parents.
5. Children who are ungovernable.
6. Clients with unusual needs that demand special care.
7. Loss of housing because of eviction or natural disaster.

Note that the first four situations listed involve removal of clients from existing environments because their health, safety, and/or physical and psychological development are in jeopardy. In the case of children, protective service practitioners carry a grave responsibility in safeguarding the health and safety—indeed the lives—of children at risk. When complaints are received or referrals are made (often by physicians or schoolteachers), these practitioners must carefully assess whether children should remain at home while efforts are made to strengthen their parents' functioning or whether the degree of risk warrants an immediate removal of a child to a temporary shelter, to the home of relatives, or to a foster home.

Permanency Planning

When abuse or neglect is flagrant and parents cannot provide essential care, the decision to remove children may be clear-cut. In other instances, the decision may be difficult, because deciding what course of action is in the best interest of children is a complex matter. Children have a powerful need for a sense of rootedness, which develops when they live in a predictable, permanent environment where they are accepted and loved. Transplanting them to foster homes is traumatic, and repeated changes from one foster home to another create insecurity, mistrust of others, hostility, and low self-esteem. Because of evidence that severe psychological damage may ensue when children are shifted from one foster home to another, there has

been a marked emphasis in recent years on *permanency planning*; that is, planning for children whose social environments have been disrupted so as to provide opportunities that enable them to gain a sense of permanence or belonging to a group of people who are committed to each other. Having a sense of permanence enables children to develop enduring human attachments. Such attachments occur, however, only if certain crucial ingredients exist in the relationships between children and parents (or surrogate parents). These ingredients include continuity (ongoing predictive availability of parents to respond to children's needs), stability (absence of major disruption or stress in the parent–child relationship), and mutuality of interaction that reinforces the importance of child to parent and vice versa (Hess, 1982). Permanence is also vital because it provides a framework within which children gradually absorb a value system and develop a sense of identity.[4]

Intensive Home-Based Service

Because of the importance of a sense of permanence to children, child welfare workers strive, whenever feasible, to retain children in their homes by working with parents and family systems to enhance child care by improving the consistency of housekeeping, meal preparation, and hygienic practices; to improve parenting skills; to enhance communication; to cope with stress without resorting to violence; to strengthen marriages; and to eliminate threats to the physical and moral welfare of children. To accomplish these objectives, models of intensive home-based family treatment have been developed in recent years. (We discuss this approach in Chapter 16 and will not discuss it further here.) To enhance family functioning to the extent that abused children can remain or return to their homes generally requires multiple interventions and a multidisciplinary approach that, in addition to social workers, may include physicians, judges, public health nurses, police, clergy, mental health professionals, school personnel, and early childhood educators.

Because of the many disciplines and services essential to successful interventions, practitioners should assume the role of case manager in linking children and their families to relevant service providers. The importance of actively fulfilling this role is emphasized by disquieting findings reported by Turner (1984) to the effect that children who were successfully reunited with their parents following foster care received extensive community services, whereas children who had to be removed again from their parents' care following reunification received much less service. The findings of another study of child placement (Rapp, 1982) also suggest that child care practitioners need to consider and utilize community resources more fully in serving the needs of children and their families.

Reunification

When it is necessary to remove children to substitute care, it is critical for child welfare workers to make intensive efforts to reunite children with their families as soon as possible in order to minimize psychological damage resulting from separation of children from their families and to enhance the likelihood that successful reunification can occur. Although research on reunification services is sparse, the few studies completed (e.g., George, 1990; Katz, 1990) clearly indicate that the probability of successful reunification diminishes as time elapses and especially as the number of placements increases.

With certain families the probability of reunification is low because parents do not change, pose a continued high risk of reabuse, or lack the potential capacity to provide adequate care for their children. The probability of successful reunification with drug-abusing parents is especially low because, as Fein and Staff (1991) note: "Care and nurturing of children, ...seems to be a less demanding priority than is the tug of the addiction" (p. 341).

Even when reunification occurs, outcomes are not necessarily positive. As compared with different placement options, Barth and Berry (1987) found that reunification of children with birth families "fails most often to be free from abuse and to yield developmental well-being" (p. 82). An implication of this disquieting finding is that services to reunified families should be more intensive and longer in duration, extending for as long as two to three years.[5]

Adoption

Adoption is the most intrusive environmental intervention, a nearly complete change of environment for the child. Nevertheless, when natural parents fail to respond adequately to consistent efforts to assist them or lack the capacity to be competent parents, child welfare workers should work toward arranging other permanency-planning outcomes. According to the Adoption Assistance and Child Welfare Act of 1980 (P.L. 96-272), adoption is preferred when reunification is not a viable option. For the reasons cited earlier, time is also of the essence in placing children for adoption. Adoption, of course, is much less difficult to arrange for young children than for older children, and is most difficult for children with significant physical disabilities and medical problems, large sibling groups, and children of minority races (Katz, 1990). The author just cited has impressively demonstrated that when efforts to achieve permanency for children adhere to five permanecy-planning methods that incorporate existing child welfare knowledge, children can either be reunited with their families or placed in adoptive homes in an average time of slightly over one year. The study reported by Katz involved a total of 39 children selected from hard-core families that manifested "chronic mental illness, lengthy history of drug abuse, significant criminal history, diagnosed sexual deviancy, documented severe child abuse, repeated child abuse or neglect, repeated placement of the child or children, or persistent domestic violence" (p. 222). The assumption of the project staff was that the children selected were least likely to return home or to be adopted without intensive and specialized permanency-planning services.

Following the five permanency-planning methods, the project staff were able to achieve permanency for 30 of the 39 children (76%) within an average of 13.1 months. Of the 30 children, 28 were adopted by foster parents and two were reunified with their parents. These findings are most impressive, and we cite the study because it provides evidence that *drift* (movement from one foster home to another) in foster homes can be avoided for the large majority of children removed from their homes if expert and intensive services are employed to bring about permanency.[6]

Citing research findings, Barth and Berry (1987) have concluded that even older child adoptions provide a pleasant contrast to outcomes of reunification, and they refer to such adoptions as a highly favorable form of placement.

Other Placement Options

After adoption, guardianship is regarded as the next preferred option, followed by foster care. Little is known about outcomes involving the guardianship option, but findings regarding long-term foster care are more favorable than had been anticipated. Research evidence indicates that this option does not preclude lifelong attachments. Many children in foster care maintain contact with their siblings and more than one-half relocate and live with one of their birth parents following foster care placement.

Whatever the placement option employed, adults who function as parents need not only support services but also formal training in parenting skills. Based on a review of parent training programs employed in child welfare, Berry (1988) concluded that actual training often was not provided and that disruption in placements could likely be reduced by affording such badly needed training to natural parents, adoptive parents, and foster care parents.

Still other options are available when children must be removed from their homes. One such option is family-centered group care (Finkelstein, 1980). This intervention involves placing a child in a substitute family-like environment but maintaining the focus on the problem family, with the goal of permanently discharging the child as rapidly as possible. Treatment is aimed at enhancing family functioning by opening communication in the family system. Parents visit the residential center at least twice weekly, learning how to communicate more productively and how to gain control of their youngster.

Independent Living for Adolescents

Recognizing that permanency planning options are sometimes impractical for older youths in foster care, child welfare practitioners have increasingly prepared youth for independent living. Trends and needs in programming for independent living have been discussed by Cook (1988), and an entire issue of *Child Welfare* has been devoted to vital topics relevant to this option.[7] Moreover, Sims (1988) has discussed different types of independent living programs, limitations and problems associated with them, and needs of youth that must be met to adequately prepare them for successful transition into adulthood.

Shelter Homes for Battered Wives

Changes to different environments may also be required when wives are battered. Increasingly, communities have developed programs for women that provide temporary shelter, legal services, financial aids, and counseling. Although shelter for battered wives is vital, effective treatment must be multidimensional. Because we discuss such treatment at length in Chapter 19 (we discussed assessment of spouse abuse in Chapter 8), we will not discuss it further here.

Abuse of the Elderly

Elderly persons who are abused by their children or relatives are another population that may require environmental changes. Awareness of this problem has expanded considerably in recent years and legislation has been enacted at federal, state, and local levels to address it.[8] Social workers should expand their knowledge about abuse of the elderly and be aware of resources that relate to needs of this vulnerable group.

Changes to Controlled Therapeutic Environments

It is sometimes necessary to move people to a controlled therapeutic environment when they manifest behavioral or emotional disturbances that preclude them from living in their usual living arrangements. One such group consists of homeless young people who have been cast out or abandoned by their families and have not successfully adapted to substitute care in foster homes or group homes. Case records of these persons are typically replete with reports of emotional and behavioral problems, unsuccessful placements, and involvement with many different professional persons (Morrissette & McIntyre, 1989). Treatment of homeless youth in a residential care facility has been discussed by the authors cited.

Still other residential group homes have the goal of returning children to their homes whenever possible, and toward this end, certain programs involve parents as *treatment partners* (Krona, 1980). Programs vary according to the type of youth and the degree of interest and involvement on the part of parents. When parents are unable to provide suitable environments for their children, group homes have been used successfully as alternatives to institutions. Gordon (1978) has described one such program where the professionals and residents govern the facility by "participatory democracy"—that is, they and the teenagers jointly run the house (p. 362). Mutual respect is cultivated by the staff, and the residents gradually turn to the staff and to each other for emotional support much as children turn to parents and siblings in healthy, functioning, intact homes. The residents thus gradually gain a feeling of permanency in this environment.

Still another type of residential treatment center for severely disturbed adolescents that employs modeling and cognitive-behavioral strategies within a family-style environment has been described by Rosen, Peterson, and Walsh (1980). Whittaker (1979) has also written an authoritative book concerned with residential care for disturbed youth.

Institutional Placement

For adolescents who pose a threat to the safety of others, secure facilities are essential. The current trend is to place delinquent adolescents in alternate community youth centers rather than in large state institutions, as was the practice until recent years. The community centers ideally should provide educational, recreational, and social opportunities as well as therapeutic group experiences that enable residents to engage in problem solving, skill development, and other growth experiences. In addition, programs at such centers should embody work with families aimed at enhancing functioning to the extent that youth can be discharged to their homes whenever feasible. A major advantage of community youth centers is that they are generally located within reasonably short distances from the families of youths, making it possible to maintain close contact.

Special environments are often required for severely emotionally disturbed adults. Many general hospitals and community mental health centers have psychiatric wards, making it possible for patients to receive treatment within their communities. The thrust of such programs is to return patients to their homes as rapidly as possible and to avoid the trauma and stigma of placing them in large state institutions geographically isolated from society. Some patients require care for longer periods than community facilities can provide, necessitating hospitalization in larger state institutions. Even in the latter facilities, however, the orientation is to return patients to their local communities as rapidly as possible.

Physical Environmental Changes

Physical factors sometimes dictate a change in environment. Clients with respiratory disorders may be at risk in environments that are high in air pollution. Other environments may pose problems in sanitation, have inadequate heating or cooling facilities, or pose hazards to the health and safety of children and other vulnerable persons. Some families may be crowded into apartments that lack privacy and adequate sleeping arrangements. It is sometimes possible to remedy certain adverse circumstances by exerting pressure on landlords or governmental officials, but even at best, some situations remain grossly deficient in resources. In such instances, changes in environment may be the only viable alternative.

USING CASE MANAGEMENT

The case manager role, more than any other, entails work at the interface between clients and their environments. Case management, in fact, moved to the forefront of direct social work practice with expanded recognition that the needs of increasing numbers of clients with major disabilities (e.g., frail elderly, and developmentally and mentally disabled persons) were not being met because these people could not negotiate the complex and often uncoordinated human service delivery systems (Austin, 1990). Referring to one such vulnerable group, deinstitutionalized chronic psy-

chiatric patients, both McCreath (1984) and Ely (1985) documented that it was common to find such patients with vital needs unmet because appropriate agencies were not providing the services or because clients had not made their needs known. These and other client groups may lack the physical mobility, mental ability, knowledge of resources, experience, maturity, verbal skills, or assertiveness required to avail themselves of needed resources. The consequences of having vulnerable persons with vital needs unmet are suffering and increased vulnerability to deterioration in functioning.

Vulnerable groups in need of case management typically require extensive services and resources, including those provided by systems of health care, mental health, rehabilitation, education, child protection, housing, employment, and other related systems. Because of the pervasive needs of these clients, it is vital that one of the service providers, typically a social worker, be designated as case manager. Such an arrangement affixes responsibility for planning and orchestrating the delivery of services in a systematic and timely manner. Moreover, designating a case manager empowers one person to arrange meetings with or otherwise communicate with other agencies to identify additional needed services, to avoid duplication of services, to develop unified strategies for dealing with difficult clients, and to avoid working at cross purposes.

Social workers are well qualified to serve as case managers because of their knowledge of community resources, their skills in communication and advocacy, and the purposes and objectives of the profession as defined in Chapter 1. To refresh your memory, the central objectives include (1) helping people to obtain resources, (2) facilitating interactions between individuals and others in their environment, and (3) making organizations and society as a whole responsive to people. Serving as case manager thus is consonant with the spirit of social work.

Varied Roles of Case Managers

Practitioners perform their case management roles somewhat differently according to the type of setting and role definitions within specific agencies. In some community mental health settings, practitioners may function as therapists and as case managers to the same clients (Johnson & Rubin, 1983; Lamb, 1982). By contrast, as members of a hospital interdisciplinary team that plans discharge of psychiatric patients, practitioners may supervise paraprofessionals who actually carry out the case manager role (Altman, 1982). Interestingly, a nationwide survey (Bernstein, 1981) of case managers in 15 community-support projects revealed that 60% of the case managers were trained therapists. Still another survey of directors of mental health centers in Georgia disclosed that 75% of the directors expected case managers to perform therapy (Bagarozzi & Kurtz, 1983).

In other settings, however, case managers perform more of a generalist role and do not provide therapy. They may provide limited counseling, but generally refer clients when therapy requiring a high level of expertise is needed. The actual functions or activities of case managers vary according to the practice setting and the type of clients served. With chronic mentally disabled homeless clients, whose social skills are extremely limited, whose contact with reality is tenuous, and whose needs are pervasive, case managers assume an active and ongoing role in coordinating service delivery until clients are established in adequate housing, receiving essential health care, and receiving the necessities of life.

By contrast, in serving the family of a developmentally disabled child, case management is family focused and the objective is to enable the parents, who generally are competent and able, to assume the role of coordinator themselves. In this instance, the case manager assists them in understanding the needs of the disabled child and in becoming knowledgeable about and to utilize community resources that correspond to the needs of the child. When the parents feel competent in handling the child's needs, service is terminated.[9]

Case management thus is not a unitary type of service, and the literature contains varied conceptualizations of case management (see, for example, Austin, 1990; Moore, 1990; and Roberts-DeGennaro, 1987). All models, however, share the basic premise that central to case management is the function of linking clients with essential resources and empowering clients to function as independently as possible in securing the resources they need. Knowledge of resources, skills in connecting clients with resources (as delineated in Chapter 3), and skills in following up to ensure that clients receive services and resources in a timely fashion thus are common to all case management roles.

Some have asked how case management differs from traditional social work practice. The answer is that all social workers engage in case management in varying degrees, and, as Moore (1990) has aptly put it, "case management is just old-fashioned social work wearing new clothes" (p. 444). *Case management* in a strict sense entails "generalist" practice but in another sense case managers are resource "specialists" who possess knowledge about community resources (in areas of practice defined by the populations they serve) and employ skills in utilizing community resources to benefit their clients.

An Empirically Based Model

In carrying out their roles, case managers do much more than perform the broker role in connecting clients with resources. They must also be competent in implementing all aspects of the problem-solving process. Recognizing that case management cuts across many human service fields and that "nobody quite knows what case management is" (Rothman, 1991, p. 520), Rothman developed an empirically grounded model of case management based on a review of 132 pertinent articles and a survey of 48 case managers. We list the steps of *case management* (as identified by Rothman) and briefly discuss the steps. We do not presume to do justice to Rothman's article and hope our brief discussion will stimulate you to read it.

1. *Access to agency.* Case managers need to facilitate clients' access to the system by being receptive and by arranging appointments as quickly as possible when people are referred to the organization. Outreach efforts may also be required to encourage people in need of case management service to enter the system (e.g., homeless, mentally disabled, and frail elderly people).

2. *Intake.* This step involves exploring clients' problems and needs and determining their eligibility for services and financial resources. Information about the services of the organization are provided and forms are completed as needed. Skills in fostering rapport and eliciting information are employed. Some preliminary planning may be initiated.

3. *Assessment.* Problems are defined more explicitly, and additional collateral information is obtained when needed. The family of the client is carefully assessed to determine their capability in coping with a disabled client and their potential as a support system that can be tapped. Accurate assessment may require collaboration of different professionals from different disciplines in the agency.

4. *Goal setting.* Objectives are determined by obtaining the client's perception of areas needing improvement and the case manager's perceptions. Both short-term and long-term goals are formulated, as, for example, treating acute physical and mental symptoms and securing housing versus engaging in a rehabilitation program and building self-esteem. Goals must be realistically geared to the capacities of clients (which often are very limited).

5. *Planning intervention* or *identifying and indexing resources.* This step is dual in nature because planning interventions (e.g., counseling or therapy and planning services) and linking clients with resources are inextricably connected. Resources needed may not be available at a given time and access to services changes according to the demands made on external agencies at a given time. Identifying resources may entail telephone or personal contacts with agencies. Case managers may have files on available resources and may use them in locating resources. As with assessment, clients should be involved in planning interventions to the fullest possible extent.

6. *Linking clients.* As expected, respondents contacted by Rothman indicated that linking clients with resources was a very common activity. As we suggested in Chapter 3, connecting clients with resources is active and facilitative. As Rothman states, "Preparing the client for linkage involves providing detailed information, anticipating difficulties, role playing, and accompanying clients on the first visit" (p. 524).

7. *Monitoring and reassessment.* This is a vital process aimed at determining if the arrangements implemented are adequately maintaining the client in the community. Adequate monitoring requires a substantial allotment of time, which is used to telephone agencies and staff and to phone and visit clients. Crisis situations are expected and careful monitoring enables case managers to implement timely remedial measures.

   In the context of long-term continuing care, ongoing reassessment is essential. Reassessment can be formal or informal but should be done at periodic intervals. Clients should be actively involved in reassessment, which may entail use of instruments employed in the initial assessment phase to obtain baseline measures on specified aspects of the client's problem situation.

8. *Outcome evaluation.* Where it is appropriate, outcome evaluation entails determining the extent to which goals have been attained (e.g., locating housing, securing medical care, or attaining the capacity to live independently). When baseline measures were employed during the assessment phase, they will be employed again as part of outcome evaluation. Because severely disabled clients often require indefinite service, outcome evaluation is not applicable to such populations.

Other Case Management Functions

Embodied in the preceding steps are a number of other common functions performed by case managers, as identified by Rothman's (1991) research. These functions are listed as follows.

Interagency Coordination   This vital function entails developing effective working relationships with external agencies that will enhance the linkage function. Policies or agreements, either formal or informal, are often formulated to foster mutual understanding and to define procedures for making referrals. Such arrangements often identify contact persons with whom efforts to build congenial working relationships often yield rich dividends by facilitating smooth and mutually advantageous referral and follow-up contacts.

Counseling   This function typically is limited to providing information and giving advice and does not involve probing into the psyche or attempting therapy. Rather it includes "problem solving, reality testing, socialization skills, and practical help in such areas as housing, money matters, parenting and employment" (Rothman, 1991, p. 525).

Therapy   As stated earlier, therapy is a case manager function in many mental health settings. The majority of respondents in Rothman's study indicated that therapy should be focused on the present rather than the past and be aimed at assisting clients in coping with daily problems of living. Therapy might be with individuals or groups. Moreover, respondents indicated that family members should often be involved to reinforce or maintain desired changes.

Advocacy   Recent critics suggest that case management is not necessarily a form of client empowerment (Cnaan, 1994).[10] To ensure that empowerment is part of case management, advocacy is intermittently employed to assist a client to receive services that are being withheld unfairly. We discuss advocacy later in this chapter, and will not elaborate on it here.

Vulnerable Populations Served by Case Managers

To effectively perform the linkage functions of case managers, social workers must have extensive knowledge of the needs of vulnerable populations, of relevant community resources, and of the policies and procedures of agencies that provide essential goods and services.

Although the needs of vulnerable groups served by case managers are generally pervasive, they vary from one group to another and even within broad client groups. (Recall, for example, from Chapter 9 that homeless people are a heterogeneous population with widely varying needs.) Space limitations preclude discussing the needs of each group, but in the following we identify vulnerable groups and relevant references: people with AIDS (Gillman, 1991); pregnant teenagers in school (Weinman, 1989); severely psychiatrically disabled adults (Bush, Langford, Rosen, & Gott, 1990), developmentally disabled children (Fiene & Taylor, 1991); mental health adult patients sexually abused as children (Rose, Peabody, & Stratigeas, 1991); elderly homeless persons (Kutza & Keigher, 1991); developmentally disabled adults (Kaplan, 1992); frail elderly persons (Fauri & Bradford, 1986); homeless (Bean, Stefl, & Howe, 1987); teenage parents (Brindis, Barth, & Loomis, 1987); physically disabled adults (Akabas, Fine, & Yasser, 1982); refugees and immigrants (Drachman, 1992); chronically ill (Harris & Bergman, 1987) and foster children; and multi-need families at risk for child maltreatment and/or neglect (Ballew, 1985; Compher, 1983; Turner, 1984).

Resources needed by the vulnerable groups just listed are not always available, especially in rural communities. Case managers, therefore, must (or should) sometimes serve still another function—that of resource developer. We discuss resource development in a later section of this chapter, and will not address that topic here.

ENHANCING INTERACTIONS BETWEEN ORGANIZATIONS AND INSTITUTIONS

Effectively meeting clients' needs often requires concurrent efforts of several organizations and disciplines, and close collaboration is essential. Joint planning, clear definitions of roles, and on-going dialogue among the principals are required to avoid confusion, monitor progress, and maintain adequate working relationships. These processes are facilitated by case management, as previously noted.

Effective interaction among organizations is also often needed to enhance aspects of the environment of a single client or family or of a group of clients that share a common condition. In the first instance, a practitioner may enhance a child's school environment by assuming a *mediating* role between the home and school. The practitioner may assist the parents to work in closer collaboration with the teacher in enhancing the child's functioning in the school. Similarly, a practitioner may coordinate efforts which permit a client to remain in the community through outpatient and in-home services, avoiding unnecessary in patient or residential care. In the second instance, a practitioner may join with other health care professionals in raising the standards for nursing homes (Coulton, 1981), residential centers, or day care centers. Practitioners may also work with public officials to enhance transportation for the elderly, recreation and education for the developmentally disabled, and so on. Marburg (1983) has reported on successful efforts in establishing effective treatment networks to meet the mental health needs of Native Americans.

Still another area that requires effective interaction among organizations involves assisting clients in making major transitions from one environment to another. For example, when clients are discharged from mental or correctional institutions to the community or to their families, provisions for continued service and support are essential. Otherwise, the client and/or the family or institution may be unprepared or unable to cope with the stress of the adjustments required, and the transition may result in early and traumatic failure for all parties. Ongoing liaison, joint discharge planning, and close management facilitate such transitions.

IMPROVING INSTITUTIONAL ENVIRONMENTS

We have previously referred to a few measures that have been taken to enhance the quality of life in state mental institutions, nursing homes, residential treatment centers, and group homes for youth. In this section, we briefly consider ways of enhancing three major facets of institutional environments—namely, staff, program, and physical facilities.

Staff, of course, are the heart of an institution's environment. When staff are dedicated, caring, responsive to residents' or patients' needs, and congenial with each other, the institutional environment tends to be warm and conducive to growth and well-being on the part of all concerned. By contrast, when staff are impersonal, cool, and abrasive and interact with residents no more than is necessary, an institution's atmosphere tends to be sterile, cold, and conducive to withdrawal, deterioration, and low morale. Selecting staff who are warm, accepting, and genuinely interested in helping others is the first step in developing a supportive institutional environment. Such persons play a key role in fostering client trust.

The program of an institution is also crucial. Stimulating, constructive, and growth-promoting programs tend to enhance the functioning of clients, whereas custodial care that fosters idleness produces the opposite effects. The introduction in the 1950s of socioenvironmental programs in mental institutions contributed to the dramatic results in eliminating wards populated by regressed patients, most of whom were regarded as hopeless.

An important factor in institutional programming involves the extent to which residents can exercise choice and control in their daily living. When people have little control over what happens to them, they tend to become helpless, hopeless, and depressed. To enhance choice and control, progressive institutions foster democratic participation in governance of the institution to the extent that such is feasible. Mental hospitals and correctional institutions thus often have ward or unit councils through which residents have input into decision-making processes. Even some nursing homes have resident councils that foster choice. Mercer and Kane (1979), in fact, have reported a study indicating that nursing home patients in an experimental group who were given choices in caring for a plant and participating in a resident council made improvements beyond a control group in reduction of hopelessness, increased physical activity, and psychosocial functioning.

Other aspects of institutional programs should involve education for youth, intellectual stimulation for adults, training opportunities for prisoners, social skill development programs for residents with deficiencies, and opportunities for social intervention. Art, music, and dance therapies have also been described by numerous authors as methods of fostering expression and creativity in institutions. Kelen (1980) described a study involving an environmental intervention with nursing home patients that involved teaching them to write and appreciate poetry. Patients selected to participate in the experimental intervention manifested increased levels of well-being and self-expression over those who did not.

Other programs employed to enrich activities within nursing homes include having volunteers visit with lonely patients and provide entertainment. Some programs have used human–animal companion bonding. Cooley, Ostendorf, and Bickerton (1979) have described an innovative program for Native Americans in nursing homes that involves bringing in leaders, youth, and publications from the reservation monthly to overcome the isolation of these patients and to provide linkages to their native culture. According to these authors, this program has greatly enriched the lives of these people.

The last major factor involved in enhancing institutional environments involves physical facilities and the use of space. Accommodations that foster social interaction and yet permit privacy are highly desirable. For ambulatory residents, a leisure room with television and various games fosters social interaction and constructive activity. Likewise, facilities that permit vigorous physical activity are essential in correctional institutions.

In nursing homes and hospitals, it is desirable to locate patients close to a window so that they can view the outside world. When patients share rooms, they should be permitted to choose roommates with whom they are compatible. Few things can be more demoralizing than occupying limited space with people who wear on one's nerves. Obviously, many other factors come into play in matching roommates, and perfect matches are seldom achieved. Still, practitioners should be sensitive to patients' needs and should be patients' advocates with administrative staff when mismatches adversely affect their well-being.

EMPOWERING CLIENTS

Certain vulnerable groups of clients are unable to cope effectively with stressful situations and to avail themselves of essential environmental resources because of a sense of powerlessness or helplessness. Just as case managers seek to empower their clients by assisting them to exercise control over their lives to the fullest extent possible, other practitioners should attempt to empower clients who manifest powerlessness for other varied reasons. By empowering we mean enabling clients to gain or regain the capacity to interact with the environment in ways that enhance their needs gratification, well-being, and satisfaction. To gain a sense of power, of course, requires that essential resources be available in the environment. Moreover, a sense of power is closely linked to competence, self-esteem, support systems, and belief that individual actions or actions in concert with others can lead to improvement in one's life situation. These attributes or factors, however, are reciprocally influenced by the quality of the environment. Nutritive environments that produce strong goodness of fit between people's needs and corresponding resources foster these positive attributes. Conversely, poor goodness of fit caused by major environmental deficiencies tends to foster powerlessness, helplessness, low self-esteem, and depression.

Gutierrez suggests that in addition to increasing self-efficacy and developing new skills, empowerment includes development of a critical consciousness about the causes of injustice and powerlessness (Gutierrez, 1994). Groups of people who often experience powerlessness in coping with the environment include the poor and oppressed; immigrants and refugees; persons of color; persons with addictions; groups who are stigmatized and discriminated against or otherwise denied full access to societal resources; and the vulnerable groups previously identified who require case management, a major method of empowerment. Assisting these and other clients who experience powerlessness to develop their latent powers and to exert these powers to obtain needed resources is the goal of empowerment. In the following sections, we discuss methods of empowering certain vulnerable populations, namely women of color, single parents, persons with AIDS, and immigrants.

Empowering Women of Color

We begin with this population because many of its members experience the multiple effects of racism, sexism, and poverty. Moreover, because of these multiple effects, techniques of empowerment with this group are applicable to other vulnerable groups.

According to Wilson (1987), the poverty rate of this group is more than double that of white women (32.3% of all black women and 26.4% of all Latinas live below the poverty line). Consequently, women of color are more likely than white women to have to contend with poor housing, inadequate access to health services, inade-

quate clothing, and little recreation that costs money. Further, Asian and Latino women suffer the effects of oppression by men by reason of the dominant role of men in these cultures.

Gutierrez (1990) has discussed processes of empowering women of color, and much of the following information is based on her article. We have modified her conceptualization somewhat, added our views, and cited other sources of information.

Enhancing Self-Esteem   Empowering women of color (or any vulnerable group) begins with demonstrating respect for the individual and for that person's race or ethnic group. You may recall evidence of the importance of this factor in the research findings of Gomez, Zurcher, Farris, and Becker (1985) cited in Chapter 4. Respect is shown by (1) valuing the client's definition of the problem (thereby conveying belief in the client's ability to identify and understand the problem); (2) defining the helping relationship as one of collaboration (wherein the client will be an equal partner in searching for and developing solutions to the problems); (3) expressing a desire to understand, to respect, and to employ culturally relevant solutions to the client's problem; and (4) identifying and building upon existing strengths of clients.

It is important to keep in mind that many of these clients have latent strengths that may be temporarily obscured (even to themselves) by gradual erosion of self-confidence produced by the oppressive forces cited earlier. Survival itself has required many strengths, and calling attention to such strengths enables many clients to regain or to develop a greater measure of self-respect.

Increasing Self-Efficacy   Enabling clients to cope more effectively by enhancing their sense of self-efficacy or competence in carrying out tasks essential to improving their life situations is a critical aspect of empowerment. Toward this end we recommend a two-pronged approach that involves (1) providing essential information, and (2) teaching them specific skills required to enhance their coping abilities. Prerequisite to effective coping, information can be a powerful enabler to women of color, many of whom lack knowledge of their rights, available resources, bureaucratic structures, and procedures to obtain resources. Further, some lack information about age-appropriate behaviors of children, principles of child rearing, essentials of nutrition, and other basic activities associated with daily living. Providing information individually or through educational groups can be extremely beneficial to these persons. If language is a barrier, using interpreters or group leaders who speak their native language may be essential.

As we noted in Chapter 13, performance accomplishment is the most potent source of self-efficacy. Assisting clients to master essential skills through role playing and guided practice thus are potent ways of empowering them to perform tasks essential to improving their life situations. Employing skill development groups that teach social skills and assertiveness (as discussed in Chapter 14) can be a cost-effective way both of empowering clients and providing a support group.

Developing Group Consciousness   This method empowers clients by placing their problems in a more hopeful perspective. Practitioners assist clients to gain awareness that they are not unique in their struggles but rather are members of a large group negatively affected by political structures and prevailing social attitudes and practices. By redefining women of color as a group who have suffered from discrimination and lack of power, practitioners enable such women to develop a consciousness that makes it possible to direct energies to the causes of their problems. This perspective can thus generate hope and counter feelings of inadequacy, helplessness, hopelessness, and self-blame.

Analyzing Possible Courses of Action   This method involves assisting clients first to analyze the conditions of powerlessness operating in their situation and then to consider possible remedial

courses of action. Practitioners thus can assist clients to consider the social and structural origins of their present situation, as, for example, life circumstances and events that contributed to their disadvantaged position. After such an analysis, it is vital to encourage clients "to think creatively about sources of potential power, such as forgotten skills, personal qualities that could increase social influence, members of past social support networks, and organizations in their communities" (Gutierrez, 1990, p. 152). It is important to emphasize that these sources of potential power can be tapped to improve their life situation.

After identifying their potential sources of power, it is important to challenge clients to consider possible courses of action to improve their life situations. Women of color may be encouraged to seek out and affiliate with support groups, to develop arrangements with other parents for mutually tending each other's children (thereby permitting some free time), to participate in educational and skills training groups, or to organize an advocacy or political action group. (We discuss the last activity later in this chapter.)

Mobilizing Resources for Clients   When clients lack the resources (e.g., essential household items, clothing, language facility, social support, and health care) they need to have a greater sense of power, you may need to perform the role of broker or case manager in securing essential resources. You may also need to join the client in advocacy actions if resources to which clients are entitled are arbitrarily denied them.

Single Parents

As with women of color, assisting single parents to perceive their frustrations and burdens as common to millions of others in similar situations can be empowering. An effective way of accomplishing this is to facilitate development of a support network for single parents or to link them with existing support groups, such as a local chapter of Parents Without Partners (Kissman, 1991). Social support groups counter the painful isolation of single parents and may prevent the frustrations that contribute to child abuse. Support groups are also needed for parents who are going through the stresses of divorce.

Because of the constraints that typically confront single working parents, practitioners may facilitate development of parent cooperatives that pool resources in caring for each other's children. Organizing and advocating for child care programs to assist single parents (and other working parents) can also be empowering.

Empowering People with AIDS

People with AIDS experience stigmatization in our society to the extent of being shamed and denied access to critically needed resources and emotional support. Further, "AIDS has become associated with horrifying negative pictures of incapacitation, abandonment, rejection, hatred, physical and mental deterioration, and deformity" (Haney, 1988, p. 251). These perceptions have a forceful impact on people with AIDS and disempower them by disconnecting them from loved ones and obliterating previous sources of self-esteem and satisfaction such as work activities, social interaction, physical appearance, recreational activities, plans for the future, hopes, and dreams. In addition to suffering these severe losses, people with AIDS tend to experience isolation, alienation, and aloneness, sometimes going into hiding and avoiding medical treatment.

Patrick Haney (1988), who died of AIDS early in 1988, left behind a legacy of guidelines for empowering people with AIDS. The following discussion is based on his article, which was published just a few months after his death.

An important step in empowering people with AIDS (and others who feel powerless) is to modify the mindset of being a victim. Perceiving oneself as a victim fosters passivity and a sense of helplessness. As one anonymous person with AIDS confided to Haney (1988):

> Not buying into the victim mindset is keeping me alive…. At this time in my illness I am not helpless and I am anything but passive in dealing with it. I can look around and I see incredibly courageous men who inspire me with their strength. These men continue to defy the odds and say no to AIDS. They give me hope. They give me strength. (p. 252)

To assist people with AIDS to avoid or to relinquish the victim mindset, practitioners themselves must not believe that people with AIDS are victims. Rather, they are people with AIDS who have the capacity to continue to find meaning and satisfactions in their lives.

Another way of empowering people with AIDS is to focus more on opportunities for making the most of a bad situation and to focus less on the fatalistic aspects of the disease. This does not mean denying the very real and tragic aspects of having AIDS. It is a reality, however, that the life expectancy of people with AIDS has increased substantially over the past few years. Further, it is empowering to focus on making the most of living and not dwelling on dying. In this regard Haney's account of his personal experience is informative and helpful:

> Some of the positive consequences I have experienced…include learning to accept my limitations, learning to cope by getting in touch with my strengths, experiencing a clarity of purpose; learning to live one day at a time; learning to focus on the good in my life here and now; and the incredibly moving experience of having complete support and love from my family, friends, lover, people I hardly know, and sometimes even complete strangers. (p. 252)

The importance of emotional support for people with AIDS cannot be overestimated. If the person with AIDS lacks family and friends who are supportive, social workers must assist them to find people who can provide that support and must, themselves, be caring and supportive. Social workers can also participate in developing support groups, a model of which has been described by Gambe and Getzel (1989). Getzel (1991) has also defined and illustrated survival modes employed by people with AIDS, knowledge of which can enable group leaders to assist members in coping with the devastating impact of being afflicted with this disease. Dane (1989) has also discussed the application of crisis intervention in work with persons with AIDS and their families.

Haney describes the impact of support groups as "incredibly potent." He attributed his overcoming his preoccupation with a "death is inevitable" mindset to participation in such a group:

> I overrode my fears and I'm thankful I did. I met two other persons with AIDS who had been living with their illness for almost three years. These two men were joking, laughing and having a good time. Here were two men with a supposedly fatal disease acting as if nothing were wrong. They were acting like a couple of well people, which really eroded the negative mindset I had. It was the beginning of my learning to cope…I found a place where I belonged. (p. 252)

We cannot do justice to Haney's suggestions in this short space and recommend that you read his brief article. It is significant to note that he found meaning and purpose in his shortened life by founding an AIDS information and referral service and by establishing a support network entitled the Persons With AIDS Coalition. Other formal support networks that employ volunteers have been developed in large cities that have substantial numbers of people with AIDS.[11]

Empowering people with AIDS also requires work with communities aimed at mobilizing various groups, educating community residents, developing service networks, and coordinating services. For an example of what one state (New York) has done to deliver services to persons with AIDS, we recommend an article by Ehrlich and Moore (1990).

Case managers may be needed to ensure continuity of care for people with AIDS. Rounds (1988) has discussed implications of developing resources for people with AIDS in rural communities. Haney (1988) has written a similar article that addresses critical issues related to meeting the needs of people with AIDS who live in the inner city of large urban centers.

Empowering Immigrants and Refugees

As immigrants and refugees are transplanted into an alien society, they may experience a sense of powerlessness, generally after the initial excitement wanes and the realization sets in that hopes and dreams may be unattainable. Many factors contribute to the sense of powerlessness, including "language barriers; unfamiliarity with American customs, rules, and norms; subtle discrimination and prejudice against minorities in society; and most important the loss of social support networks, status, roots, and the 'connectedness' that are found in the native environment" (Hirayama & Cetingok, 1988, p. 42). Moreover, normative interpersonal behaviors from their native culture, such as obedience, acceptance, loyalty, deference to authority, and cooperation, may not serve them well in a culture that prizes assertion, persuasion, candor, and confrontation.

Initial efforts to empower immigrants and refugees typically involve assisting these people to meet basic needs for the necessities of life. One can hardly have a sense of power if one lacks adequate shelter, clothing, food, health care, and money to pay for ongoing necessities. Social workers thus initially provide concrete assistance in locating housing, clothing, bedding, jobs, and temporary income until families can provide for themselves.

Empowering immigrants and refugees also requires teaching them about the majority culture, including facts about housing, transportation, shopping, gaining employment, and banking. Empowering also requires teaching them about societal institutions and resources including health care, education, community services, communication media, pertinent laws, government, political processes, and the like. Another aspect of empowerment entails learning about rights and developing skills in communicating with employers, health care providers, fire department, police, grocers, teachers, neighbors, and so forth. Still another vital aspect involves assisting these people in building social networks of friends, both within and outside of their ethnic reference groups. In this regard, members of pertinent ethnic groups who have earlier successfully adapted to American culture often are excellent resources in assisting immigrants and refugees "to learn the ropes" (Cameron & Talavera, 1976). When such persons are not available, other public-spirited persons (older people are an excellent resource) can often be recruited to befriend, teach, and advocate for refugees and immigrants. Sponsoring organizations often take the lead in such matching with resources. Social workers can also empower these people by assisting them and/or joining them in alliances and coalitions aimed at breaking down organizational barriers to the provision of needed resources. Other ways of empowering Asian immigrants and their families have been discussed by Hirayama and Cetingok (1988).

In addition to efforts designed to assist individuals and communities to adapt to a majority culture, work is needed to realize the strengths and coping skills which these persons and communities can bring to the larger culture (Chau, 1990).

The literature also contains articles concerned with empowering other target groups, but space limitations permit us only to refer you to these publications. Solomon (1976) has written about ways of empowering black people in oppressed communities. Hegar (1989) has discussed empowerment-based practice with children, and Parsons and Cox (1989) and McDermott (1989) have reported on ways of empowering frail elderly persons.

DEVELOPING NEW RESOURCES

In the preceding sections, we have identified numerous resources and interventions that practitioners employ to enrich the environments of clients. However, it is important to keep in mind that these resources have evolved only gradually through the efforts of dedicated people who have recognized the needs of fellow human beings and have exercised leadership in organizing other concerned people to bring needed resources to fruition. Many of these resources are not available in a large number of communities, especially smaller ones. In fact, rural areas, emerging communities, and boomtowns usually have a dearth of resources. Moreover, as physical environments change, technology advances, and political and social circumstances relentlessly change, social workers are constantly confronted with the need to organize new resources in response to existing and evolving needs of people. For example, during the past decade homelessness, violence in the home, increasing numbers of people with AIDS, domestic hunger (Brown, 1988), and crises caused by natural disasters have emerged as major social problems.

Organizing efforts to develop new resources are indicated when it is apparent that significant numbers of people within given ecological boundaries (e.g., neighborhood, community, institutions, ward of a hospital, or parish) have important needs for which matching resources are not available. For example, in rapidly expanding communities, women may be confined and lack social and recreational opportunities (Gaylord, 1979); youth may not have access to recreational facilities or programs; adult males may lack opportunity for recreation other than going to bars; and single parents may lack access to day care programs—to name just a few needs. As a result of these deficiencies, the following social problems typically occur in boomtowns: The incidence of depression among women is high; delinquency skyrockets; rape occurs with alarming frequency; alcoholism and prostitution are rampant; and child abuse and family breakdown occur at high levels.

To prevent or at least to reduce the incidence of such problems, practitioners face the challenge of developing support systems for women, establishing recreational programs for people of all ages, developing indigenous networks to prevent and monitor child abuse, establishing rape crisis programs, developing adult education programs, developing neighborhood support networks, and so on. Practitioners must work closely with existing social service agencies, enlist indigenous leaders in the community, organize task groups that consist of vulnerable persons and advocates, work with elected public officials and private industry, and establish lobbies to influence state legislators when laws or public funds are needed.

The need to organize people and to mobilize resources is by no means limited to rapidly expanding communities. Resources for certain vulnerable groups may be woefully inadequate even in large urban communities. It is in large urban areas, in fact, where social workers and clients have been most involved in mobilizing innovative and vitally needed resources. The problem of developing resources for the homeless in our urban communities, for example, is a challenge of the first magnitude, as we discuss later.

Practitioners play an enabling role in organizing activities, working *with* rather than *for* clients. This is important for the following reasons:

1. The chance of achieving successful results is far greater when clients participate actively in formulating and implementing plans. Because they directly experience the impact of deficient resources, clients can provide valuable information and can often present their plight to responsible authorities in dramatic and forceful ways. Furthermore, there is strength in numbers. Public officials are more likely to be impressed at public meetings when a large number of well-organized people appear to present their case than when only a few social workers and a handful of clients appear.

2. Clients are more likely to use, publicize, value, protect, and enhance resources when they have participated in planning and developing them.

3. Resources are more likely to have optimal fit for consumers when consumers have participated in developing them.

4. Clients gain a sense of power when they realize they participate in improving their circumstances. By asserting their needs, they counter the devastating sense of powerlessness that pervades many of the disadvantaged people in our society. They learn that they do count and do possess power to shape their destiny (O'Connell, 1978).

5. By joining others in working toward a common goal, people gain a sense of unity and belonging. An action group becomes a support network that has intrinsic value to members apart from its express purpose.

As implied in the preceding list, the challenge of developing new resources often entails advocacy and social action, topics we discuss later.

Resources for the Homeless

Of the vulnerable groups, homeless persons perhaps have the greatest needs, although the homeless are a heterogeneous group, as we noted in Chapter 4. Common to all the homeless, however, are needs for shelter and food. In addition, certain homeless people need health care, mental health treatment, medications, jobs, employment counseling, rehabilitation services, and social support.

Resources needed vary according to causes of homelessness, which vary substantially from one community to another. Interestingly, data for 13 cities compiled by the U.S. Conference of Mayors indicated that about two-thirds of the homeless in those cities were minority persons, of whom almost 52% were blacks (First, Roth, & Arewa, 1988). Analysis of the data compiled led to the conclusion that homelessness among minority persons was associated with joblessness, the lack of marketable skills for many minority youth, and expensive or nonexistent low-income housing. Providing shelter, food, and other necessities for this group is vital, but a long-range solution requires social planning efforts at federal, state, and local levels. Beginning efforts have been made, but the problem has not been adequately addressed at higher levels of government. Clearly, policy decisions must address root causes of the problem and must consider issues related to social justice and equality. In this regard, data from interviews with homeless persons in Ohio indicate these people "want to and can be employed if given access to the job market. Social policy efforts should target the employment of these individuals and individuals who are marginally employed and at risk of becoming homeless" (First et al., 1988, p. 123).

Low incomes and insufficient low-cost housing cause homelessness for whites as well as people of color. The federal housing voucher program (which provides supplementary income earmarked for housing) has assisted over 115,000 families in our nation to afford more adequate housing (Office of Policy Development, 1988). An excellent example of social planning, this program is a major step in the right direction, but the large numbers of people who remain homeless indicate the need for additional programs that address the problem of joblessness and marginal employment opportunities.

People who are chronically mentally ill or who are substance abusers also comprise a major group of the homeless. In addition to food and shelter, many of these persons urgently need health care, mental health services, medications, and sometimes psychiatric evaluations and short-term hospitalization. Some of these people, however, are fiercely independent, distrustful, and wary of becoming involved in health care and mental health systems. Community-sponsored shelter programs, subsidized by funding from mental health programs, often employ staff who are skillful in engaging such persons through informal interaction and by using case-management skills to connect these people with resources relevant to their needs. Fortunately, some community leaders, in concert with professionals and committed lay people, have been successful in establishing effective walk-in shelter programs for homeless persons. Staff of these facilities often gradually gain the confidence of these clients and become major sources of social support. Some facilities have also enlisted home-

less persons in groups that function as support systems and serve therapeutic and skill-development functions as well (Breton, 1984; Ely, 1985). The ultimate goals of working with chronically mentally ill homeless people are to locate them in permanent housing; to connect them with mental health programs; and to meet their needs for health care, rehabilitation, and social support.

Belcher (1988) has discussed the needs of homeless mentally ill persons and the gaps in relevant resources. A treatment model that recognizes the needs of this population as well as organizational realities has been proposed by Belcher and Ephross (1989). Koroloff and Anderson (1989) have described an alcohol-free living center for homeless alcoholics, and Blankertz et al. (1990) have discussed practice implications, including outreach efforts, for homeless persons who are both alcoholic and mentally ill. Cohen (1989) has also presented useful guidelines for engaging homeless mentally ill persons.

Emergency shelters have also served single-parent homeless families. In addition to providing for the usual concrete needs of these families for shelter, food, and physical safety, social workers provide treatment that integrates crisis intervention, problem solving, task-centered services, and life-space interviewing. Space limitations preclude elaborating upon this approach, an example of which has been described by Phillips et al. (1988). Overall, evaluation of the results indicated that the majority of the families made significant progress in achieving goals that had been formulated.

Mills and Ota (1989) have also written about homeless women and children (most of them black) in the Detroit area and have discussed policy implications, including policies that provide adequate income-support programs, basic living skills training programs, and mental health services delivery. Johnson and Kreuger (1989) have written an article that addresses homeless women in general.

Homeless youth are still another highly vulnerable population that presents a wide range of problems and needs. Kurtz, Jarvis, and Kurtz (1991) have reported on a regional research study conducted in the southeastern states. Most of the youth lacked stable, supportive families and were victims of a fragmented child welfare system. These authors documented the need for a community-based coordinated continuum of care for homeless youth.[12]

And finally, elderly persons are a small but new segment of the homeless population. Kutza and Keigher (1991) discuss the characteristics and special needs of this high-risk population, as well as the emergency and long-term services needed for this group.

EMPLOYING ADVOCACY AND SOCIAL ACTION

We define advocacy as the process of working with and/or on behalf of clients (1) to obtain services or resources for clients that would not otherwise be provided, (2) to modify extant policies, procedures, or practices that adversely affect clients, or (3) to promote new legislation or policies that will result in the provision of needed resources or services.

Advocacy has long been deemed an obligation of social workers. This obligation is reflected in the profession's code of ethics, which clearly articulates in Article VI the ethical responsibility of social workers to serve as advocates for clients:

> The social worker should act to ensure that all persons have access to resources, services, and opportunities which they require. (Item 2)

> The social worker should advocate changes in policy and legislation to improve social conditions and to promote social justice. (Item 6)

Situations that practitioners encounter, however, can present ethical dilemmas as to what type of advocacy actions are most appropriate. We refer you to an article by Gilbert and Specht (1976) for a discussion of these conflicts.

Case and Class Advocacy

Advocacy embodies two separate yet related facets, the first of which involves working with and on behalf of individual clients or families to assure that they receive benefits and services to which they are entitled and that the services are rendered in ways that safeguard their dignity. Because this aspect of advocacy is on behalf of an individual or family, it is denoted as *case advocacy*, corresponding closely to one dictionary definition of an advocate as "one who pleads the cause of another."

The second aspect of advocacy involves acting to effect changes in policy, practice, or laws that affect all persons in a specific class or group—hence this type is denoted as *class advocacy*. Class advocacy is much broader in scope and, in essence, is a form of *social action*. Although the two types of advocacy are different, they are also highly interrelated. As Holmes (1981) points out, one may serve as a case advocate for a client who has been denied a particular service or benefit because of a dysfunctional policy, but if the advocacy action results in gaining that benefit, a precedent may be set that leads to a change in policy affecting all others in the same position. "In other words, class advocacy may be viewed as an extension of case advocacy" (Holmes, 1981, pp. 33–34). A recent random survey of 353 social workers in Washington state suggests that social workers are involved in both case and class advocacy. Agency goals and functions strongly influence the amount of job-related advocacy and that advocacy tended to be focused on individual cases. Meanwhile, these social workers were often involved in class advocacy in their private lives while serving as volunteers (Ezell, 1994).[13]

Indications for Advocacy

Advocacy may be appropriately employed in numerous situations, including the following:

1. When an agency or staff person refuses to deliver services or benefits to which a client is entitled.

2. When services are delivered in a dehumanizing manner (e.g., when rape victims are humiliated).

3. When clients are discriminated against because of race, religion, creed, or other factors.

4. When gaps in services and benefits cause hardship or contribute to dysfunction.

5. When governmental or agency policies adversely affect people in need of resources and benefits.

6. When clients are unable to act effectively on their own behalf.

7. When numerous people have common needs for which resources are not available.

8. When clients have unusual needs for immediate services or benefits because of a crisis situation (e.g., migrants who are seriously ill or have acute financial needs).

9. When clients are denied civil or legal rights.

10. When procedures or facilities of organizations adversely affect clients.

We discuss a number of the preceding situations at greater length in Chapter 19 under the section "Overcoming Organizational Barriers."

Targets of advocacy may be individuals, agencies or organizations, public officials, courts, legislatures, and divisions of government. Tactics thus must vary considerably according to the target system, and to advocate effectively requires a thorough understanding of how organizations are structured and how they function, including an appreciation of organizational politics (Rothman, 1991). Advocacy can also involve different levels of assertive intensity ranging from discussion at a low level to militancy at a high level, as we discuss later.

Sosin and Caulum (1983) have developed a useful typology of advocacy that assists practitioners in planning appropriate advocacy actions. By determining whether the advocacy situation exists in the context of an alliance, a neutral context, or an adversarial context, practitioners can determine what is to be advocated, what level (individual, administrative, or policy) of advocacy is appropriate, and what strategy should be adopted. Albert (1983) has analyzed the process of advo-

cacy in relationship to rule making by governmental administrative agencies. Viewing the process from a legal framework, this author presents helpful guidelines and identifies opportunities and techniques for intervening into the rule making or regulatory process. Nulman (1983) and Pinderhughes (1983) have written informative articles that discuss empowerment and advocacy for families. Pearlman and Edwards (1982) have discussed ways in which practitioners can organize *client advocacy groups* for the purpose of effecting improvements in neighborhood environments. Rose and Black (1985) have written a book concerned with an advocacy/empowerment approach that seeks to restore a sense of human dignity and personal responsibility to mental patients after their return to the community following hospitalization. Dane (1985) has also discussed the use of professional and lay advocacy aimed at enhancing the education of handicapped children. Several of the preceding authors stress that the *sense of empowerment* clients gain through organized advocacy actions may be more significant than the changes themselves.

Self-Determination and Advocacy

In considering advocacy interventions, practitioners must bear in mind that they should strictly observe the client's right to self determination. If clients do not wish to assert their rights, practitioners are ethically bound to respect their wishes. If clients wish to pursue action, practitioners must be sure they are addressing the client's interests as the client defines them (Kutchins & Kutchins, 1978). Moreover, practitioners should go no further in advocacy activities than the client wishes to go. Practitioners also have a responsibility to discuss with clients possible negative aspects of advocacy activities. For example, because advocacy may involve adversarial interaction with pertinent target systems, the client risks generating antagonism or ill will with others that may be disadvantageous in the future. Implementing advocacy actions also typically involves a certain amount of strain and tension; moreover, a positive outcome cannot be assured. However, in discussing possible adverse consequences, it is important not to be unduly discouraging and to assist the client to weigh pros and cons, leaving the final decision to the client.

Still another caution is that before undertaking advocacy actions, practitioners must be certain that the client's situation justifies assertive action. It is important to be certain that the client's account of being denied resources, discriminated against, or treated shabbily is based on fact and does not involve distortions or omissions. For example, a client who claims to have been denied medical care may not have followed a physician's recommendations. Similarly, a client's complaint of being discriminated against by having to wait a long time in an agency before being seen may be a result of understaffing produced by limited funds rather than discrimination. Other clients who complain about not being treated with dignity may be contributors to their difficulties as a result of provocative behavior. It is prudent to assess situations carefully, thereby avoiding drawing premature and erroneous conclusions that may lead to undesired and embarrassing consequences.

Techniques of Advocacy and Social Action

There are many techniques of advocacy and social action, and deciding which techniques to employ depends on the nature of the problem; the wishes of the client, family, or group; the nature of the system targeted for advocacy actions; the personality and individual style of the practitioner; the political climate; and the extent to which the practitioner's agency will support different interventions. In a given situation, a practitioner may employ several interventions but a rule of thumb is to employ no more than are necessary and to cause no more disruption than is required to achieve a given objective. Although militancy may be required in some instances, it should be employed with discretion, for the price of accomplishing certain gains through militant action may be more than offset by the ill will and possible negative image generated.

The following techniques include those employed most often in advocacy and social action.

1. Conferring with Other Agencies[14] When problems involve denial of resources or dehumanizing treatment by another agency, case conferences may be held with appropriate staff persons or with administrators to present the grievance. It is advantageous to have the client accompany you to avoid presenting information that is actually hearsay. Clients often gain strength from learning to deal head-on with such situations. It is generally prudent to present the client's case in a firm but dignified manner. If the other parties appear indifferent or otherwise are unwilling to take appropriate remedial measures, it may be necessary to serve notice of intention to pursue the grievance further by contacting higher authorities or initiating other more vigorous measures.

2. Appeals to Review Boards Client satisfaction surveys are increasingly used as a form of outcome evaluation. Such surveys sometimes provide information which suggests that clients have been denied services or benefits inappropriately. Most agencies and governmental bodies have procedures of appeal for clients who believe they have been unjustly denied services or benefits. Often successful appeals result in changes in procedures and policies.

3. Initiating Legal Action When clients' rights are violated and the preceding interventions fail to achieve redress, filing a legal suit may be an appropriate alternative. However, clients often lack the resources to hire a private lawyer, and it may be necessary to engage a United Way legal service agency or legal services provided through public funds. Clients, of course, must be willing to testify in court.

4. Forming Interagency Committees

When individual agencies are unsuccessful in effecting essential changes, several agencies may combine their efforts in attacking common problems. Committees may be formed that plan collective action directed at modifying the practices of a problem agency or organization or at filling a gap in community services.

5. Providing Expert Testimony

Social workers may exert a powerful force in influencing the development of public policies or developing resources by speaking forcefully about clients' problems and needs in the political and public arenas. This sometimes also takes the form of letters to the editor and editorials.

6. Gathering Information through Studies and Surveys

The impact of testifying in public is much enhanced when social workers can provide concrete data to support their positions. Conducting studies and surveys and reviewing the literature thus arm the social worker with information that can be employed in responding to the penetrating and hostile questions sometimes raised in public hearings and in direct contacts with public officials and legislators, as we discuss later.

7. Educating Relevant Segments of the Community

Often the strongest enemy to developing progressive policies and programs is ignorance of decision makers about the issues. To educate the public in general and decision makers in particular, all forms of media should be considered, including press campaigns; telephone contacts; local television programs concerned with public issues; panel discussions at local, state, and national conventions; exhibits; and speeches at meetings of influential civic organizations.

8. Contacting Public Officials and Legislators

This can be a powerful way of promoting needed policies and programs. Social workers may contact legislators and public officials directly or may appear at committee meetings to present information that legislators need to make informed judgments. To be effective in these endeavors, social workers must be knowledgeable about how special interest groups influence legislators. Smith (1979) has written an informative article explicating six "generalizations" involved in influencing legislators. We briefly mention just two of these generalizations and strongly urge you to read her entire article.

One generalization is that "Knowledge of legislators' role concepts (or orientations) is crucial in determining their behavior toward interest groups, which is usually congruent with their role concepts" (p. 235). Legislators' behavior can be understood by knowing whether they tend to assume the role of facilitator, resister, or neutral. The facilitator generally is receptive to information from special interest groups and is knowledgeable about their existence. This type of legislator represents the most fertile ground for special interest groups.

The second generalization is that "The provision of technical and political information is a significant influence to which legislators respond in the political process" (p. 235). The need for and value of being equipped with relevant knowledge has been affirmed by studies of legislatures in four states. Significantly, "The most important factor governing the influence of a group and one that outweighed others, was the ability of a group to provide lawmakers with both technical and political information" (p. 235). Obviously, social workers who aspire to influence legislators must first do their homework.

9. Forming Agency Coalitions

This technique involves forming an ad hoc group of agencies that are committed to a specific objective. The advantages of this intervention are twofold. First, decision makers tend to be more influenced when numerous agencies present a united front; second, a given agency is less vulnerable to attack when it is but one of many different organizations joined in a common effort. As Panitch (1974) points out, however, there may be a problem in joining a coalition in that "the issue at hand may become too generalized to meet the wishes of member organizations" (p. 331).

10. Organizing Client Groups This intervention involves forming action groups for social change that consist of consumers who have a mutual problem. The social agency initiates formation of the group, stimulates it to take action, and serves a consultative role in assisting it to obtain information, gain access to selected people, and act in concert with other community groups. Organizing client groups is especially appropriate for minority groups, who often feel impotent from a political standpoint. Lum (1992, p. 202) has reported a vignette illustrating the successful work of a practitioner in organizing African Americans to advocate for rights that had been violated in a public housing project.

11. Developing Petitions This activity is used to call attention of decision makers to an issue and to exert pressure for accountability on a public official by expressing the voice of a constituency.

12. Making Persistent Demands This technique involves going beyond the usual appeal process by bombarding officials with continuous letters and telephone calls. Although this intervention stays within the law, it approximates the use of harassment as a pressure tactic and can cause a rebound effect.

As is apparent, the foregoing interventions include both case advocacy and social action. Effective social action, according to Grinnell and Kyte (1974, p. 482), requires a rational, planned approach that consists of the following steps:

1. Define the problem.
2. Systematically diagnose the people, structure, or system to be changed.
3. Assess both the driving forces that may promote change and the resistance forces that may conceivably retard it.
4. Identify specific goals.
5. Carefully match mechanisms or strategies of social action with the goal desired.
6. Make a feasible schedule for implementing the plan of action.
7. Incorporate in the plan a feedback process for evaluating the changes that the action stimulates.

In addition to these steps, certain ingredients are required for effective social action. Not all individual practitioners possess these ingredients, but O'Connell (1978, p. 199) maintains that effective social action *agencies* possess the following characteristics:

1. A cause worth getting excited about.
2. *Genuine* concern for that cause.
3. An ability to keep the cause in *focus*.
4. Acceptance of *activism* as the way to make things change with no apologies for being activists.
5. *Tenacity*. It is interesting to note that John Gardner, a leader of the Common Cause organization, concluded: "The first requirement for effective citizen action is stamina."
6. Successful advocates really *understand* how their government and service systems are organized *and* changed. Blind emotion may work a few times, but a successful, sustained effort requires know-how.
7. To make a difference in any major cause there is a need for people in real *numbers*. Politicians have learned to look behind angry shouts to see if there are voters behind all that noise. It helps to have power people, and the best combination is to have both the numbers and the power people, but if a choice has to be made, take numbers.
8. The effective social action agency must be *independent*: free to tackle anybody or cooperate with anybody.[15]

SOCIAL PLANNING/COMMUNITY ORGANIZATION

A macro approach to enhancing environments and improving social conditions, the practice method of social planning/community organization (SP/CO), goes beyond typical direct practice activities in that the focal units with which practitioners engage are larger systems such as neighborhoods, citizens groups, representatives of organizations, agency executives, and governmental leaders. The joint efforts of the participants are typically directed to solving social problems ranging in scope from those of various resident groups on one end of the continuum to international problems on the other end. Policies and programs of national scope that have emerged over the past 30 years as a result of intensive planning aimed at social problems include the Community Health Act (1963), the Economic Opportunity Act (1964), the Model Cities Program (1967), the Housing and Community Development Act (1974), the Jobs Training Partnership Act (1983), and the Title XX amendments to the Social Security Act (1974), to name just a few. Current problems on which planners are or should be focusing include homelessness, child and spouse abuse, substance abuse, adolescent pregnancy and child bearing, adolescent runaways, poverty of single-parent families, high rates of unemployment of minorities, and problems of the disabled and chronically mentally ill.

Although practitioners with expertise in SP/CO typically perform planning roles in urban centers and even larger systems, direct practitioners may need to engage in SP/CO activities in rural areas, where experts in planning usually are not available. In rural areas, practitioners may join with community leaders in planning to remedy problems associated with lack of transportation for residents with health care needs, needs for child care, problems of child neglect and/or maltreatment,

needs for recreational programs, isolation of the elderly, and other such problems. It is important, therefore, for all practitioners to have at least rudimentary knowledge of the principles and skills involved in SP/CO.

As with direct practice, the problem-solving process is central to practice involving SP/CO. However, the problem-solving process at the macro level differs widely from that at the micro level, and social workers in SP/CO "seem to have more in common with professionals in other fields who are engaged in the same type of efforts, such as trade unionists, politicians, and city and regional planners" (Gilbert & Specht, 1987, p. 610). Before implementing the problem-solving process, planner-organizers must identify and recruit people who will provide funding and other support to undertake a SP/CO effort, identify a problem to which the planning or organizing efforts will be directed, or agree to work on a problem that has previously been identified. The next step is to select goals and to develop a plan that brings together and mobilizes those who have been recruited, organizational and political support, funding sources, and community support essential to attainment of the goals. Implementing these activities requires some of the same skills employed in direct practice, for example, interviewing skills and the ability to facilitate group development by applying knowledge of interpersonal relationships and group dynamics. Other skills required include those embodied in policy analysis and program evaluation, research methods, management of data, and sociopolitical processes.

Problem Identification and Analysis

Different theorists conceptualize the problem-solving process in SP/CO in different ways, each theorist defining different numbers of stages that vary according to the levels of elaboration of relevant tasks. For our purposes, we use the general four-phase process identified by Gilbert and Specht (1987, p. 613), which consists of (1) identification and analysis of a problem, (2) development of a plan of action, (3) implementation of the plan, and (4) evaluation of its outcome. At this level of abstraction, the process is similar to that of the problem-solving process of direct practice.

The first task in identifying and analyzing the problem is to assess the state of the target system (e.g., neighborhood, community, county, or state). Although conceptual approaches to problem analysis vary, common elements in the frameworks of prominent experts include "the need to identify which social values are threatened by the situation, to carry out a detailed analysis of who is affected and the scale of the problem, and to delineate the etiology of the problem" (Moroney, 1987, p. 598). Further, the analysis also addresses the political environment, assessing the readiness of the target system to deal with the problem and to allocate resources to remedy or mitigate the problem.

Identifying the causes of the problem is central to problem analysis. Although founded in the scientific method, this process varies according to the theoretical premises and values of the problem analysts, as attested to by the varying explanations offered as to the causes of poverty, crime, adolescent pregnancy, and other social problems. Approaches to identifying causes of problems often begin by compiling data regarding the incidence and distribution of the social problems in terms of age, sex, race, income levels, severity, duration, and so on. After the data are analyzed, inferences are made concerning causes of the problem.

Another useful method employed in problem analysis entails applying techniques that produce information used to predict demands for services and fiscal resources needed. These techniques, which include social surveys, estimates of future populations and compositions of the same, as well as trend and probability analyses, are beyond the scope of this book.

Another aspect of problem analysis, which follows the steps described in the preceding paragraphs, is needs assessment. The task involved in needs assessment is to estimate from the focal system the numbers of people at risk and in need of remedial measures. Defining needs, however, is an elusive task because need is a complex concept that can be stated in four different ways: (1) normative need, (2) perceived need, (3) expressed need, and (4) relative need. [See Moroney (1987) for elaboration on these different aspects of needs.] Needs can be assessed by utilizing professional judgment and social surveys (normative needs), by holding public forums (perceived needs), by determining the number and profile of people who seek a service (expressed needs), and by assessing relative need by measuring "differences in levels of services in different geographical areas, weighting each area's statistics to account for differences in population and social pathology" (Moroney, 1987, p. 599). Because each approach deals with a different aspect of need, comprehensive needs assessments employ all four different approaches.

Developing a Plan of Action

After identifying and analyzing a problem, the next phase of SP/CO entails developing a plan of action. Ideally, the concept of rationality is embedded in the process of developing a plan of action. Adhering to this concept, planners objectively use information they have gained to describe, to understand, and to make predictions about phenomena in question. Economic rationality requires determining the single or "best" remedy for the focal problem. Ideally, selecting a remedy thus entails identifying all reasonable strategies, assessing the likely consequences of each strategy, and evaluating each set of consequences. Evaluating the cost-effectiveness of each alternative is also part of the process. This task involves determining which alternative will generate the most favorable ratio between valued input and valued output, or in other words, seeking to achieve maximal return for the least investment.

In fact, planning and organizing based exclusively on the concept of rationality are generally impractical, and decisions about alternatives typically must consider complex factors that include political realities in the focal system, limited funding, and the possible impact of special interest groups. Because of the magnitude of these and other realities, "The technical aspects of designing the 'best' programmatic solutions are de-emphasized in favor of sociopolitical behavior that seeks the agreement of relevant interest groups. From this perspective, interactional tasks such as bargaining, exchange, compromise, and building consensus emerge as the predominant features of the problem-solving process" (Gilbert & Specht, 1987, pp. 614–615). Less than ideal, this approach has been called "incremental decision making" because it seeks to improve upon the shortcomings of present policies rather than to select superior courses of action that are likely to be rejected. In this regard, findings of one research study (Gilbert & Specht, 1979) revealed that mobilization of strong political support correlated highest with positive outcomes of Title XX allocations of resources for the aged. So much for the idealism of rational planning!

Implementation of the Plans

After plans have been accepted, support mobilized, and funding allocated, implementation of the program selected commences. This involves performing internal administrative tasks including selecting, training, and supervising staff; providing for intraorganizational communication and quality control; and establishing policies and procedures that serve the interests of both consumers and staff. Other tasks entail managing external relations with other service organizations, funding sources, consumer groups, governmental entities, employee unions, and so forth. Maintaining positive relationships with these various entities is crucial, for their support is indispensable if a new program is to flourish. Managing external relations thus is a primary activity required of planners and organizers.

Evaluation of Outcome

Evaluation seeks to assess the extent to which programs are successful and to identify ways of improving them. Program evaluation thus involves ongoing systematic monitoring of the program's impact, which requires development and implementation of techniques of data management. Systematic analysis of data enables planners to determine if the program is functioning effectively and accomplishing the goals for which it was planned. Evaluation also enables planners to determine which strategies are most effective under which conditions and with which populations.

Program evaluation requires expertise in research design, techniques of measurement, and statistical analysis. Techniques involved in these processes, however, are sophisticated and beyond the scope of this book. Knowledge requisite to implementing these processes is commonly embodied in research courses that deal with program evaluation.

We should also like to draw your attention to innovative approaches that hold promise for enhancing the effectiveness of planning community programs. The first approach consists of applying developmental research (Thomas, 1989), which is a rigorous, systematic, and distinctive methodology consisting of many techniques and methods taken from other fields and disciplines. Its sophisticated methodology relates to social research and development and model development.

Far less systematic, the second approach has

been implemented in Quebec (Gulati & Guest, 1990). This approach places emphasis on natural helping networks, involves lay citizens in analyzing problems and planning remedial measures, deals with users of service not as client consumers but as partners in the provision of services, facilitates integration and coordination of local programs and services by having them housed in close prox-

imity, focuses on prevention, uses multidisciplinary teams extensively, fosters flexibility in organizational structure, and decentralizes administration so that local communities can develop programs that are responsive to their unique needs. This approach is closer to grass-roots community planning than are planning approaches in the United States.

NOTES

1 For a comprehensive discussion on the varied uses of homemaker services, we recommend a chapter by Kadushin and Martin (1988, pp. 143–172).

2 For an excellent discussion of day care, including different forms, utilization, policies, and issues, we recommend an article by Frankel (1991) and a chapter by Kadushin and Martin (1988, pp. 173–217). For a discussion of issues related to day care for low-income families, articles by Marshall (1991) and Marshall and Marx (1991) are informative.

3 An excellent reference that describes processes of mobilizing social support for all target groups is a book by Gottlieb (1988).

4 A comprehensive discussion of the concepts and methods of permanency planning is presented in a book by Maluccio, Fein, and Olmstead (1986). Seltzer and Bloksberg (1987) have also discussed permanency planning and its effects on foster children.

5 For recent reviews of family reunification, see Maluccio et al. (1995) and Pines, Krieger, and Maluccio (1993).

6 Space limitations precluded describing the five methods that were the key to the positive outcomes, but we strongly urge you to read the article by Katz (1990).

7 *Child Welfare*, LXVII, November/December, 1988.

8 Weaknesses of such legislation and policies as well as needed remedial measures have been discussed by Filinson and Ingman (1989). Other relevant books have been authored by Quinn and Tomita (1986) and Steinmetz (1988).

9 For delineation of a model of case management for serving parents of developmentally disabled children in rural areas, see an article by Fiene and Taylor (1991).

10 For extensive discussion of the varied functions of this role in diverse settings we recommend books by Moxley (1989), Rose (1992), and Vourlekis and Greene (1992).

11 Strategies that sustain and support workers and volunteers have been discussed by Lopez and Getzel (1987), who also provide valuable information about the disease, its impact upon people, and issues and challenges faced by professional workers and volunteers.

12 Morrissette and McIntyre (1989) also discuss the problems of homeless youth in residential care and discuss treatment strategies with this population.

13 The authors wish to acknowledge that much of the discussion related to techniques is based on Panitch (1974).

14 Organizing clients and planning social action embody numerous skills that are beyond the scope of this book. A helpful resource that deals with methods of effecting social change in the political arena is a book by Haynes and Mickelson (1986).

15 Because of limited space, the foregoing discussion of SP/CO is sketchy at best. For more extensive overviews, we refer you to chapters by Gilbert and Specht (1987) and Moroney (1987), the sources of much of the preceding information. These chapters also include extensive references to relevant articles and textbooks that discuss SP/CO in depth.

Chapter 16 ☐ ☐ ☐

Enhancing Couple and Family Relationships

THERAPEUTIC IMPLICATIONS OF CLIENTS' INTERACTIONAL PATTERNS

Social workers deal with families and couples in a variety of settings and for diverse purposes. As Reid expresses it, "social workers may work with...a family in preparation for the discharge of a family member from an institution, may help a mother take action to secure the return of her child from foster care, may have crisis-oriented interviews with distraught parents who have brought their injured child to an emergency room, may help mediate conflict between a family and a manager of a housing project" (Reid, 1985, p. 7). Since social work with families encompasses family therapy but is not restricted to it, we devote this chapter to interventions and techniques you can employ to enhance the interactions between clients and significant others. Mastering the content of this chapter and practicing relevant skills will advance your competence in the following ways:

1. Engaging couples and families (voluntary, referred, or mandated) in the helping process and orchestrating initial sessions.

2. Assisting couples and families to enhance their interaction by increasing positive feedback and "opting for the future."

3. Modifying dysfunctional patterns of interaction.

4. Modifying misconceptions and distorted perceptions that impair interaction.

5. Modifying dysfunctional family alignments.

Though the interventions and techniques that are discussed in this chapter are applied to couples and families, most are also relevant to interventions in treatment groups, a topic discussed in Chapter 17.

INITIAL CONTACTS WITH COUPLES AND FAMILIES

To enhance the functioning of couples and family systems, practitioners must be skilled in engaging members of these systems and in focusing on the systems per se. Because clients generally do not think from a systems perspective, it is important to manage initial contacts in ways that encourage work with couples and families rather than settle prematurely on an individual request for service. In this section, then, we describe ways of handling initial contacts that lay the groundwork for implementing the systems-oriented interventions that we later focus on in this chapter.

The Initial Telephone Contact

If the family has previously been screened for a family approach by an agency intake worker, all that the practitioner may need to do in the initial contact is to work out details related to the appointment.[1] If there has been no previous contact with the caller, the practitioner may need to accomplish several other vital objectives, one of which is to determine whether intervening at a family level may be appropriate. Practitioners can generally explore a family approach whenever a caller complains of difficulties that involve immediate family members or other persons living under the same roof, such as a relative, friend, or live-in partner. When problems involve persons less intimately involved with the caller (e.g., employer, parents who live elsewhere), the practitioner usually makes an initial appointment to see the caller only.

Other critical objectives of the initial telephone contact include reaching an agreement as to who will be attending the first session and establishing rapport with the potnetial client who initiated the call. Striking a balance between conveying empathy for the client and establishing expectations regarding the initial contact is sometimes difficult, but as demonstrated shortly, skills delineated in earlier chapters aid in this task.

The initial contact should be kept short and focused on relevant objectives to avoid becoming entangled in the caller's personal problems. To this end you may wish to utilize the following guidelines:

1. Ask the client to describe the problem *briefly*, and empathically respond to the client's messages—a strategy that not only helps establish rapport but also yields important information. Also elicit information that will help you determine who else is involved in the problem. When you believe you have established beginning rapport and have heard the presenting complaint, summarize the client's view of the problem and relevant feelings and emphasize the client's needs or wants.

2. In the instance of referred or mandated contact, the practitioner should share the outlines of the circumstances of the referral including the source and expressed purpose of the referral. The practitioner should make clear what choices the potential client may make including whether to meet at all (in the case of referred contact) or what might be addressed. Any mandates which might affect potential client choices should be shared (Rooney, 1992).

3. If your exploration reveals that family involvement is appropriate, introduce the client to the "family approach," using a message such as the following:

   In helping people with the kinds of problems you've described, it is often helpful to have other family members come for sessions also. It has been my experience that when one person hurts, other members also usually experience stress and discomfort. Members of the family affect and influence each others' problems. Equally important, changes in one member require changes and adjustments in other family members as well. People accomplish the kinds of changes you're wanting more rapidly when all family members work together than when being seen individually. For this reason, it will be important that other members of the family be involved in the helping process.

4. Specify which family members you want to see in the initial session. Practitioners who espouse a family systems orientation differ in their views as to whether the entire family should be included in the initial session, with some strongly advocating involving *all* members from the beginning. Because inexperienced practitioners commonly encounter difficulties managing initial contacts with entire families (which requires advanced skills), we recommend a less ambitious approach. If a parent identifies a child-related problem, request that both parents or the single parent attend the first session *without* the child (or children) unless the parent strongly objects or there are unusual contraindications (e.g., a child threatening suicide). We also recommend that you include in this session any other adult who serves a parental or executive function in the home (e.g., live-in partner or grandmother). When you make this request, however, convey that you may wish to involve other members of the family in future interviews.

When a caller complains of problems involving a spouse or live-in partner, ask that person to bring the partner to the initial session. Respond, however, to any preference of a caller to be seen alone in a first session by agreeing to this but indicating that a usual next step would be to schedule an individual interview for the other partner, thus giving that person "equal time" and providing the practitioner with a balanced view of the problem.

Some clients comply with requests to bring specific family members to the initial session, but others offer excuses such as, "My husband has to work," "She won't come," or "He's not the one with the problem." These messages often reflect the caller's reluctance to include other members as well as the reluctance of others to attend sessions.

Despite the advantage of seeing both partners, the parents, or other specified family members together, you must respond sensitively to a caller's reactions to your requests. Otherwise, your initial contact may be your last. When clients openly state they do not want to involve other family members, it is important to explore their reasons thoroughly, if not on the phone, then in the first session. You should stress during the exploration that other family members can play an important role in helping to find solutions to problems. If clients do not subsequently modify their position, however, you should "begin where they are" by arranging to see whom they are willing to bring. As Garfield (1981) indicates, "*One wishes for therapists the wisdom to know when family participation is a necessity, the courage to press for it when it is, and the humility to take what they get*" (p. 9).

When clients maintain other family members are unwilling to attend sessions, ask their permission to contact those persons directly. If you gain permission (as will usually happen), you may wish to utilize a telephone approach similar to the following:

Mr. X, this is _____. As you know, your wife has seen me concerning problems involving your relationship. She tells me that you are quite busy but I thought I would give you a personal call to ask you to come. Your participation would be extremely helpful and would give me your perspective on the problem. It would also aid me in helping your wife and may even aid in the resolution of the marital difficulties. Would you be available for an appointment, say, at 4:00 P.M. next Wednesday?

After conveying such a message, you should explore the client's reactions. Although you may wish to reiterate your views that the client's participation in *at least one* session is very important, you should respect a decision of the client not to participate and exert no further pressure. Exerting pressure tends to alienate the client and may destroy future opportunities for involving others. With skillful handling of their contacts with families, practitioners are sometimes able to dissipate strong opposition, thereby making it possible to involve key family members later in the helping process.

Managing Initial Contacts with Parents

Earlier we recommended that beginning practitioners meet with only the parents in initial sessions and include children in subsequent sessions. This strategy gives practitioners more time to become acquainted with the problems of the family and, on the basis of known information, to plan strategies with instructors or supervisors for engaging other members and anticipating problems that may occur later. Having an initial session with parents also provides the opportunity to establish rapport with them, enhancing the potential to influence the parents in later sessions involving children. Practitioners also have an opportunity to assess whether modifications by the parents are needed *before* they meet with children. Some parents, for example, manifest such ingrained and severely dysfunctional styles of relating to their children that initial attempts to see the entire family would be disastrous. Further, having an initial session with parents enables practitioners to clarify the systemic nature of problems and to emphasize the need for parents to concentrate on changing their own behaviors.

When meeting with parents in initial sessions, practitioners can begin to delabel children who are identified as problem bearers. They may also clarify that although the parents may believe that one child is responsible for the family's difficulties, entering the family session in this frame of mind will cause the identified problem bearer to feel defensive and to oppose becoming involved in the helping process. Practitioners can further emphasize that even though one person may cause significant strain in the family, all family members are usually involved in the problem and need to make some changes. Practitioners can thus inform the parents that they will be working in family sessions "to take some heat off" one member of the family and to engage all members in a discussion of changes they would like to make to alleviate *family* problems. Practitioners may need to reassure the parents that they will also be helping the child to change, but they should stress that change is less difficult if the child does not believe that other family members expect him or her to make changes expressly to accommodate them. (A similar strategy is appropriate when the designated problem bearer is an adult.)

Interviewing parents in an initial session also makes it possible to plan how best to bring an identified child into the helping process. Rather than seeing a child individually, for example, a practitioner may wish to interview all the children together or to see the "problem child" with a sibling near his or her age. Seeing the identified patient with others imparts the message that the practitioner views the problem as residing in the system rather than in a problem bearer.

By interviewing parents first, practitioners can also help them to plan how to explain to their children why they are seeking professional help and can coach them in preparing a child. The parents' explanation should clarify that the *family* is having problems (not that the family is having problems *with the child*). The parents should also give children a general explanation of what to expect when the children meet with a practitioner and should listen carefully to reservations they may have about coming to the sessions.

Practitioners can also coach parents to behave constructively when children attend sessions. For example, a practitioner may suggest that parents

try to create a climate conducive to open communication by withholding blaming messages, focusing on positive behaviors of their children, and listening attentively to them. Further, the practitioner can ask each parent to refrain from using dysfunctional communication identified in the initial session. Coaching parents to relate in positive ways to their children in initial sessions is critically important, for a key role of practitioners is to foster positive interactions among family members.

If parents do bring the "problem-bearing" child to an initial session, a practitioner should interview the child first, giving the child a chance to "tell his story" without the practitioner having been biased (as the child perceives it) by information provided by the parents. After interviewing the child, the practitioner should then interview the parents, reserving the latter part of the session for seeing all participants. At this time, the practitioner may wish to emphasize the systemic nature of the family problem, assist members to share individual goals with each other, and formulate family goals.

ORCHESTRATING THE INITIAL FAMILY SESSION

The initial session with couples and families is crucial. Clients' experiences during this session determine in large measure whether they will engage in the helping process and contract to work toward specified goals or whether they will decide against proceeding further. Moreover, clients perceive the initial session as a prototype of the helping process. To lay a solid foundation for future work with families, it is important that practitioners accomplish a number of objectives. We briefly discuss each of these objectives in this section, but first we list them for use as a guide in both planning for and evaluating initial sessions:

1. Establish a personal relationship with individual members and an alliance with the family as a group.

2. Clarify expectations and explore reservations about the helping process.

3. Clarify roles and the nature of the helping process.

4. Clarify choices about participation in the helping process.

5. Elicit the family's perception of the problem(s).

6. Identify needs and wants of family members.

7. Define the problem as a family problem and begin to delabel any identified patients.

8. Begin highlighting individual and family strengths.

9. Ask questions to elicit information about the patterned behaviors of the family.

10. Begin drawing repetitive dysfunctional communications to the attention of family members and discuss whether they wish to change these patterns.

11. Begin assisting members to relate to one another in more positive ways.

12. Communicate hope that the family can change.

13. Establish individual and family goals.

14. Gauge motivation of family members to return for future sessions and negotiate a contract.

15. Negotiate tasks to be accomplished during the week.

16. End the session by summarizing problems discussed, goals formulated, and progress achieved.

You will note these objectives are essentially the same as those identified in earlier chapters of the book. In the following sections, however, we explain how to accomplish these objectives specifically in work with families and couples. The following discussion will also assist you in consolidating knowledge and skills that have been presented earlier.

1. *Establish a personal relationship with individual members and an alliance with the family as a group.* In working with families (or groups), practitioners have a twofold task of establishing personal relationships with each individual while developing a "connectedness" with the family as a unit. To cultivate relationships with family members, practitioners can employ several techniques. The technique of *socializing* involves the use of social chitchat and is used briefly by practitioners at the beginning of the session to reduce tension.

Practitioners can also employ joining or coupling techniques (Minuchin, 1974) to expedite their entrance into the family system. One way practitioners "join" the family is to respect family rules (for example, allowing a husband to be spokesperson for the family), even though they may intervene later to change such rules. Practitioners also convey their acceptance of the family by highlighting strengths or offering support to threatened members. The practitioner uses the family's language and idioms and consciously makes statements that establish similarities or parallels between himself or herself and clients (e.g., "Oh, I had a dog almost like that").

A third technique, *facilitating*, involves the use of empathic responses to establish emotional linkages with individual members. Empathic responding can be particularly useful in developing relationships with reserved family members. For instance, when members do not respond spontaneously to new topics of discussion, a practitioner can solicit a response (e.g., "Jan, I don't think you've said what you experienced when you learned you were coming here. Could you tell me how you felt?"). The practitioner can then respond empathically to what that member says or does. The practitioner thus reaches for the responses of reticent or less assertive clients and "stays" with such clients briefly to encourage them to open up but does not press them. After repeatedly experiencing empathic responses from practitioners that reflect their verbal and nonverbal messages, such clients often begin to participate more actively.

In addition to the preceding strategy, practitioners should also endeavor to distribute time and attention somewhat equally among members, to highlight individual strengths, and to intervene when one member speaks for another or when one member is the target of blaming or put-down messages (techniques for which are discussed later in the chapter). Through such interventions, practitioners demonstrate positive regard for individuals and the value they place on the unique contributions of each.

Practitioners also develop rapport with members by addressing observations and questions to the *family*. For example: "From what you've said, it appears that *all* of you would like others in the family to listen more carefully when you speak." Such responses not only facilitate developing a "connectedness" to family members at a group level but also serve to heighten their awareness that their family often functions as a unit, and that as members of this unit, they have common aspirations, goals, and (at times) shared emotions.

2. *Clarify expectations and explore reservations about the helping process.* Family members have varying and often distorted perceptions of the helping process and may also have misgivings about participating in sessions. To identify obstacles to full participation in these areas (which is prerequisite to establishing a viable contract), it is helpful to elicit the responses of all family members to questions such as the following:

"What were your feelings about coming today?"

"On a scale of 1 to 10, in which '1' represents 'I didn't want to come at all' and '10' represents 'I could hardly wait to get here,' how would you rate yourself?"

"What do you hope might happen in our meetings together?"

"What are your fears about what might happen?"

As you elicit reservations, fears, and even hopes from individual family members, you can broaden the focus to the family by asking, "I'm wondering if others share the same feelings as…" As members acknowledge similar feelings, they often begin to realize that despite feeling some degree of alienation from others in the family, they share certain common concerns—a realization that tends to draw members toward each other. Exploring reservations about participating in the helping process often diminishes negative feelings or enables clients to lay them aside. If certain clients continue to manifest strong opposition to participating, you can address their reluctance by asking them one or both of the following questions and exploring their subsequent responses:

1. "What (if anything) would make you feel better about participating?"
2. "Given how you feel, are you willing to stay for the rest of the session and decide at the conclusion as to whether you will return?"

Manifesting willingness to negotiate the terms under which clients participate and acknowledging their right to make a choice often reduces negativism to the point that they will agree to continue for the remainder of the interview and, at times, to return for further sessions. Bauman (1981) also identifies other strategies of engaging a reluctant member:

> These can include a request for the…adolescent or adult to attend sessions, while being under no obligation to participate. The paradoxical technique of telling the…member not to talk, to read a book, or just be present in the session, places no direct pressure on the person to contribute. It may take as long as eight sessions, but eventually fears can be allayed, leading to full participation. I have noted that silent members are closely attuned to the process, and when a sensitive area is broached, they often forget their defensive stance and join in the process. (p. 19)

3. *Clarify roles and the nature of the helping process.* In exploring misgivings and reservations, practitioners must often explain the nature of the helping process and also clarify both their own and clients' roles. When an explanation is not necessary early in the session, however, practitioners often defer it until they engage clients in negotiating a contract, an activity that takes place in the closing minutes of the meeting.

4. *Clarify choices about participation in the helping process.* In the instance of referred contact, the practitioner can clarify again the message conveyed in telephone contact that the potential client is free to decide whether further contact meets their needs and, if so, what to work on, regardless of the

concerns of the referring source. If contact is mandated, it is necessary to clarify what the practitioner is required to do (such as submit a report) and the parameters of required contact for clients. For example, in addition to mandated concerns, they may choose to deal with other problems of concern to them.

5. *Elicit the family's perception of the problems.* In initiating discussion of problems, practitioners ask questions such as "Why did you decide to seek help?"(in the case of voluntary contact), "What changes do you want to achieve?" or "How could things be better in the family?" Barker (1981) discusses the practitioner's role in structuring initial discussion of the family's problems:

It is usually best to ask the parent [these questions] first, then the children. If both parents are present, the therapist should ask them both and leave it to them to decide who will answer; the process by which they decide who is to speak is often itself of interest to the therapist. By the end of [the problem] stage the therapist should have sought everyone's opinion on each of the problems that have been mentioned and should have enquired how they have tried to solve each one. It is very important to be clear what methods the family has already tried in attempting to overcome their difficulties.(p. 54)

6. *Identify needs and wants of family members.* As practitioners engage the family in a discussion of problems, they listen for needs that are inherent in their messages and can inform clients that they are doing just that, as illustrated in the following explanation:

You're here because some of your wants or needs are not being met in the family. As we discuss the family's problems, therefore, I'm going to ask you to help me identify those needs and wants. In turn, we will consider them as we formulate goals and plan our change efforts.

Even early in the session, the practitioner "reaches" for needs of participants through empathic responses, as illustrated in the following excerpt from a family session:

Jed [*16 years old, to parents*]: You don't ever let me do anything with my friends. [*Feels angry, resentful, cheated, stifled; wants more autonomy and freedom.*]

Practitioner: It sounds to me, Jed, as though you feel boxed in and controlled by your parents—that you'd like more freedom to move around and more trust from them. Am I hearing your needs correctly?

Other family members, perhaps uneasy about where the discussion may lead, may interrupt such messages or in some way discount them. For example, Jed's father (Mr. B) might respond:

"We're just not about to let you run around wherever you want, particularly with that friend who's been coming to the house lately. You'd just get in more trouble."

The practitioner, however, can prevent family members from sidetracking from an exploration of needs by using the technique of temporarily "putting clients on hold." This technique involves blending an empathic response that addresses the participant's feelings with a focusing response that structures the interaction to achieve the immediate objective illustrated in the following excerpt:

I hear your concern about your son—you don't want him to just run loose. I also know you have some important needs that I'd like to discuss in a minute. But first, I'd like to ask you to identify Jed's needs. What do you hear him saying he needs or wants?

As just illustrated, the practitioner works to enable members to acknowledge each other's needs.

In initial discussions of needs, the practitioner also corrects misperceptions often held by some members that a discussion of the needs of one person means that the practitioner will support that person's position. In the following message, for example, the practitioner allays Mr. B's fear that the practitioner may support his son's bid for freedom at his own expense:

"Identifying needs precedes problem solving. When we get to the point of considering solutions, we'll identify options that might help you and Jed with problems you've pinpointed and select ones that meet *both* your needs."

In exploring needs, it is important to identify needs of participants within the context of various family relationships (e.g., husband/wife, mother/daughter). In our illustration below, which we pick up at the point where the practitioner returns to the father's needs, notice that she works to establish *common* needs of father and son:

Practitioner: You probably noticed that I kept the discussion focused on Jed's needs. I did so because it is critical for me to understand what each of you wants. I'd like you to help me to identify *your* needs now. You were saying, "I can't go along with Jed's just running around. That worries me."[2] What needs do you have?

Mr. B: I guess I need to know where he's going—after all, I'm responsible for him. And I need to know he's not getting in trouble when he's gone. There's been too much of that.

Practitioner: Jed, could you hear what your father said?

Jed: He said he needs to know where I am and what I'm doing.

Practitioner: Good. I'm pleased that you could hear his needs so readily. I'm going to try filling in your dad's message. I think he's also saying, "I need those things because I care very much about my son."[3] Is that accurate, Mr. B? [*Father nods.*]

Practitioner: I'd like you to tell that directly to Jed.

Mr. B: I do care. [*Hesitates.*] I've felt shut out of your life for a long time, though.

Practitioner: Tell Jed more about what you're experiencing.

Mr. B: We don't talk anymore, Jed. I miss those close times we used to have when we went hunting and fishing together. It's almost like I've lost a son.

Practitioner: It's like there is a big gulf that separates you from Jed now. You seem to be saying, "I miss him terribly." I think we're getting to a vital need you have—to feel closer to Jed. [*To Jed.*] I'd like you to tell your father what you're experiencing right now.

Jed: I didn't know you felt that way. I haven't ever heard you talk like that before.

Practitioner: See if you can tell your dad how you feel.

Jed: I feel bad. But I can't talk to him. All he does is

bad-mouth my friends. He's always critical of what I'm doing.

Practitioner: Try to talk directly to your dad rather than to me, and tell him what you need from him.[4]

Jed: I'd like to be able to talk to you without always ending up in an argument over my friends.

Practitioner: I think that both you and your dad share a common need there. [*Looks at Mr. B, who nods.*] What about being closer to your dad—do you want that?

Jed: Yeah, I miss the good times we used to have, too.

By identifying and highlighting common needs, the practitioner employs a potent intervention that enables participants to focus on their similarities rather than their differences and to formulate goals they can mutually achieve to improve their relationship.

7. *Define the problem as a family problem and delabel problem bearers.* Earlier in the chapter, we modeled the type of message you can use in clarifying the systemic nature of problems. Continue to maintain that stance throughout the family session, emphasizing that every member's perspective is important; that family members can do much to support the change efforts of other family members; that all members will need to make adjustments to alleviate stress upon the family; and that the family can do much to increase the quality of relationships and the support that each member receives from others.

Despite efforts to influence members to define problems as belonging to the family, you will often encounter a persistent tendency of some members to blame others for problems. Your consequent task is twofold: First, you must monitor your own performance to ensure that you do not collude with some family members in labeling others as problem bearers and as the persons responsible for the family's ills. It is thus essential to model the circular orientation to causality of behavior explicated earlier and to remember that it is simplistic to account for events in family systems on the basis of actions and reactions; rather, family members *reciprocally* influence each other in ways that perpetuate patterns of interaction. A useful rule of thumb when you become aware that you are viewing one or more members as responsible for family problems is to consciously pull back from the immediate interaction in order to gain perspective on how other family members may be contributing to the behavior of the person(s) in question.

Your second task is to *delabel* identified problem bearers and engage members in assuming appropriate ownership for the part they play in the family's problems. One vital strategy for accomplishing these objectives is to explore relationships *between* family members in lieu of focusing on the behavior of individual members. For example, you may center on a dyad (brother/brother), then move to a triad (father/son/son), and finally explore interrelationships involving all four family members (mother/father/son/son). It is also vital to plan interventions to change the relationships among these various subsystems, a subject upon which we elaborate later in this chapter.

Another key strategy for delabeling identified problem bearers is to focus initially on the role of blamers (or plaintiffs) in the difficulties about which they complain. This strategy counteracts the tendency of these family members to attribute blame to others and highlights the fact that they, too, are contributing to the problem. To illustrate this strategy, consider the example of a mother of a chronically mentally ill young man who has decided to try living independently with his girl friend rather than remain in the group home. Rather than turning to the son, the practitioner utilizes such questions as the following to focus on the mother's participation in the problematic situation:

"You've said that your son doesn't listen to you about your concerns related to his plans. When you want to discuss these concerns with him, how do you approach him?"

"When he says he doesn't want to talk to you, how do you respond? What do you experience at such moments?"

After first posing questions to the mother, the practitioner can then divide responses between mother and son and determine the son's participation in the identified problem by asking questions such as the following:

"How does your mother approach you when she wants to share her concerns?"

"What is your reaction to her approach?"

"What might she do differently that would make you feel more like talking to her?"

This line of inquiry emphasizes the reciprocal nature of the problem. Further, the last question enables the practitioner to set the stage for identifying positive behaviors each participant would like from the other. If both are receptive, the practitioner can help them formulate a reciprocal task that each can work on during the week to improve their relationship.

Another way in which practitioners can maintain focus on a plaintiff is to ask that person to change a complaint to a request, as illustrated in the following transaction:

Daughter [*to invalid mother*]: I can hardly go out at night because you drink all that coffee and wet the bed and I have to change the sheets.

Practitioner: Carol, I'd like you to tell your mother what you'd like her to do differently.

This strategy helps to divert focus from an identified problem bearer. In addition, such interventions influence plaintiffs to consider behavior they *would like* and provide valuable information to others concerning desired changes.

Another strategy that practitioners can employ when *parents* complain about their children is to focus on the way the parents work together in coping with problems presented by the child. Such an exploration often reveals disagreements between parents as to how they manage (or should manage) the child, ways in which they may be working at cross-purposes, dysfunctional communication patterns that block them from effectively discussing the problem, ways in which they may use the child as a pawn in their relationship, and the like. If either parent raises questions about the exploration (e.g., "I don't see how talking about our relationship relates to our child's problem"), the practitioner should fully explore the parent's view and elicit concerns the other parent may have. At the conclusion of the exploration, however, the practitioner should emphasize the importance of the parents' being able to communicate and work together in assisting their son with his problems. Before proceeding to other subjects, it is also important to develop a minicontract with parents that specifies that they are willing to examine their own relationship and to consider making beneficial changes.

Another promising strategy for shifting focus from the identified problem bearer and assisting other family members to assume responsibility for making changes themselves is to ask them, "What would you like to change in your way of relating that might encourage your child (or another person) to change …?" Another version of this message is the following:

"I know that you would like_____to make some changes, but you must also have some thoughts about changes you might wish to make that would help you cope more effectively with _____. Could you identify changes of this kind you'd consider making?"

In helping family members to take responsibility for personal changes (rather than waiting for others to change), it is critical to emphasize that members cannot change each other and that each individual can alleviate problems only by concentrating on changing his or her own behavior.

8. *Begin highlighting individual and family strengths.* In work with families, practitioners highlight strengths at *two* levels—the strengths of individual members and of the *family* itself. At the individual level, the practitioner observes the strengths and resources of members, drawing them to the attention of the family (e.g., "I really like your sense of humor. I think it might keep us

from becoming too serious about ourselves in our sessions."). At the family level, the practitioner reports the strengths she or he observes in the way members operate as a group (e.g., "In your family, I sense that even though there are problems, you can count on one another. You seem to have a strong sense of loyalty to each other.").

9. *Ask questions such as the following to elicit information about the patterned behaviors of the family:*

- What brought the family here? Who made the decision and what was the process of deciding?
- Which family members are closest in this family? the least close? How satisfied are you with the closeness you feel to other members of the family?
- Who is the most unhappy in the family? Who is next? and next?
- Who is most likely to argue in the family? least likely? with whom?
- Who is the most likely to help with chores? the least likely?

Base your questions about family patterning on the dimensions of assessment previously identified in the chapter. In cases where the culture of the practitioner varies from that of the family, ask questions related to that culture: What are the traditional ways in which families in your culture have approached the question of authority? the expression of anger? the showing of affection? the making of decisions? Asking questions such as these aids practitioners in entering the family's cultural frame of reference.

10. Begin drawing repetitive dysfunctional communications to the attention of family members and discuss whether they wish to change these patterns. If dysfunctional communications occur during the initial session (as they frequently do), practitioners often intervene to *counteract* their influence without focusing on the dysfunctional communication per se. For example, a practitioner can translate a blaming message into a neutral one by empathically reflecting the feelings and wants of

the sender of the message. Or, when one client speaks for another, the practitioner can intervene to elicit the personal views of the latter. As the session proceeds, the practitioner begins to draw dysfunctional communications to the family's attention through responses such as the following:

"I observed [*describes behavior and situation*] occurring between family members. Did you see the situation in the same way?"

"Did you notice what went wrong as you talked about...?"

Questions such as these help clients to become aware of dysfunctional patterned communications. However, the practitioner also needs to stimulate participants to analyze their behaviors further and to consider whether they wish to modify such communications. This can be accomplished by asking clients questions similar to the following:

"How would you like to address these concerns?"

"How would you like to solve these problems?"

"How would you like to relate differently?"

"How would behaving differently change your relationship?"

"Given the problem the behavior creates in the relationship, how important is it to you to change the behavior?"

Utilizing this line of exploration in initial and subsequent sessions, you can assist family members to define for themselves the relative functionality of behavior and to make choices as to whether they wish to change it. If they choose to modify their behavior, you can negotiate relevant goals that will guide their efforts (and yours) in the helping process.

11. *Begin helping members to relate to each other in more positive ways.* We discuss strategies for accomplishing this objective later in this chapter.

12. *Communicate hope that the family can change.* Although we discussed this topic at length in Chapter 12, we remind you that you can engender significant hope in a family by assisting individual members to see how they can make changes that will reduce pressures. When family members mistakenly believe that the only hope for alleviating their problems involves changes by others (who choose not to change), they feel powerless and helpless—and thus defeated.

13. *Establish individual and family goals based on your earlier exploration of wants and needs.* Goals that flow from this exploration should include individual goals, goals for the entire family, and goals that pertain to subsystems (e.g., "Father and Jed, you indicated you wanted to explore ways of getting closer to each other").

The identification of goals can be facilitated during an initial interview by posing and exploring answers to the "miracle question" utilized by de Shazer (1988, p. 5): "Suppose that one night, while you were asleep, there was a miracle and your marriage (family) became perfect—just the way you wanted. When you woke up in the morning how would the marriage (family) be different?"

When asked this question, most troubled couples or families will describe a "new" miracle relationship as being one in which at least the positive conditions of peace, respect, appreciation, and low-risk, open communication are present. These and other desired conditions identified by clients can then become goal statements, guiding efforts of both the family and the practitioner.

14. *Gauge interest of family members in returning for future sessions and negotiate a contract.* Because family members do not always reveal their feelings openly, never assume that all members want to return for another session (even if you were successful in engaging members and sparking their interest in working on problems). You can employ the scale described earlier to assess the difference between the attitudes of participants at the beginning and end of the session. Also ask about reservations that participants may still have about engaging in the helping process, and after explo-

ration, if reluctant members decide to return for another session, indicate that you will continue in future sessions to discuss their feelings about continuing. It is important to stress that it may take a number of sessions before any family member decides to participate fully or to commit to making changes. If family members are sufficiently motivated to return for another session, specify the time of the next session, who will be involved, and negotiate other elements of a contract as delineated in Chapter 12.

If a member is not willing to meet with the family, contract to see that person individually for one or more sessions if possible. During your meeting(s) endeavor to establish a relationship that provides a positive emotional experience, and use the time to explore and resolve obstacles to participating in family sessions. Paralleling this work, help other family members to identify and modify dysfunctional processes that may discourage the participation of the absent member, and generally prepare them for the return of that person. If that person decides not to participate in person in sessions, help them consider ways they can support the efforts of other family members or, at least not block them.

15. *Negotiate tasks to be accomplished during the week.* Although we discussed tasks at length in Chapter 13, we reemphasize that tasks should directly relate to goals identified by individual members or by the family itself.

16. *End the session by summarizing the problems discussed and goals, tasks, and progress achieved.* Wrapping up the session by summarizing major topics, goals, and tasks highlights what was accomplished in the session, tends to engender hope, and increases the momentum of change efforts.

INTERVENING IN FAMILIES: A CULTURAL PERSPECTIVE

In intervening with clients of a different ethnicity, practitioners, of course, must use a "culturally

sensitive" approach, modifying their expectations and interventions in relation to factors such as the following:

1. *Differences in communication styles.* There are differences in the "pause time" response between native English speakers and many Native American tribes—that is, the unconsciously controlled signaling of when one person finishes and another can begin speaking. For English speakers, this is a one-second pause; for some native tribes it may be 1.5 seconds, enough of a difference that an English-speaking therapist may interrupt the Native American client before he or she can begin, never providing a long enough pause to signal the Native American client that it is his or her turn. Likewise, many Native American clients consider staring and excess eye contact a major breach of etiquette as well as any other action that may be taken as over-fam-iliar, including a "strong, firm" handshake. For those Native American people who have adapted the handshake, it is usually expressed as a very light grasp, sometimes only a brushing of fingers (Tafoya, 1989; Rhoades, 1990).

2. *Hierarchical considerations.* For example, because of age-sex hierarchies in the Chinese culture, Lee (1989) advises that practitioners address questions to the father first, then the mother, then to other adults, and finally to the older and younger children. Also, in a Pacific/Asian family the use of a child who has greater proficiency in language to interpret for the practitioner may undermine the traditional authority of the father (Ho, 1987). In addition, in coming from a culture in which chronological age and familial hierarchy play a significant role, Asian Indian families may view open dialogue between parents and children as insolence and children who "talk back" as contaminated by American culture (Segal, 1991).

3. *Authority of the practitioner.* Many Asian/Pacific Americans, for example, do not understand the practitioner's role and may confuse him or her with a physician. Nevertheless, observes Ho

(1987), they will perceive the practitioner as a knowledgeable expert who will guide them in the proper course of action, requiring that practitioners take a more directive rather than a more passive role. Practitioners should not hesitate to discuss their professional background, for these clients need assurance that the practitioner is more powerful than their illnesses or family problem and will "cure" them with competence and the necessary know-how. Practitioners must thus be active, serving as advocate, friend, and advice-giver in order to ensure the family's continuance in therapy.

4. *Use of first names in counseling.* When working with black clients, Robinson (1989, p. 328) recommends that practitioners use last names until invited by the client to do otherwise: "The racial importance of first names is magnified for the black client because of the historical tradition of calling black people by their first names in situations in which first names would not be permitted if both participants were white."

5. *Appropriate social distance.* An informal and egalitarian approach, second nature to Americans, is actually considered improper in many cultures, including that of Mexican American clients, whose initial encounters tend to be formal, polite, and reserved. Further, "direct questioning, informal use of language and expectations of full disclosure may increase suspicions and sharpen defenses" (Falicov, 1982, p. 148).

6. *Engaging the family.* Techniques of coupling or joining are particularly crucial in involving minority families. Engaging in sufficient warm-up periods, answering clients' questions warmly and directly, and showing a keen interest in the family's cultural background facilitate rapport. In addition, Bernal and Flores-Ortiz (1982) suggest that practitioners welcome clients in their native language and have objects and symbols of the family's culture in their offices and waiting rooms. Home visits are invaluable to practitioners in assessing a family's functioning in its natural environment, enabling them to convey interest in the family by inquiring about portraits, cultural objects, and other items of interest. Attendance at events such as a wedding or family outing, of course, serves the same purpose.

7. *Utilizing an ecological approach with families.* It is imperative that practitioners employ an approach that places equal emphasis on meeting minority families' immediate survival needs (employment, day care, housing). Sager, Brayboy, and Waxenburg (1970, p. 122) observe that the threat to survival leaves families "no time to luxuriate with purely psychic rumination. The actual threat to life is the number one priority. ... Families that face external threat as well as internal psychic danger tend to see their problems largely in terms of environmental perils and obstacles." Practitioners thus must focus on family-environmental interaction, which includes intervening to address problems of housing, public assistance, and unresponsive social institutions and working with the extended family or other key people to reduce dysfunctional interaction and to increase support to a family. Pinderhughes (1982, p. 91), in fact, warns that failure of practitioners to focus on family-environmental interaction "may lead to a distorted understanding of family functioning and to interventions that may be pathogenic."

The preceding are but samples of the variables to which practitioners must attend in serving families of other cultures. Fitting a practice approach to a particular family culture is, of course, a complicated process that requires an examination of many variables and a practitioner who is "on his or her toes." Suffice it to say, it is a quest at best but one worthy of the practitioner's undivided attention.

INCREASING FOCUS ON THE FUTURE AND ON POSITIVES

As practitioners meet with couples or families, they are charged with the responsibility of creating a therapeutic atmosphere. In ways not yet discussed in this book, practitioners have control over the ambience of sessions and the relative power of the therapeutic culture to effectively and efficiently promote change. To that end, whenever appropriate, we encourage practitioners to aid clients to *opt for the future*. One major obstacle to change is the propensity of couples or families to focus on what they don't have or what isn't working rather than on what they would like *in the future*. Thus, in sessions the practitioner frequently asks, "What can you do about this in the future?" and encourages clients to adopt this perspective at home. "Opting for the future" as a guiding concept for client and practitioners can be utilized, for example, in the following manner:

- A discussion of any argument can lead quickly to consideration of what each person is willing to do to prevent a recurrence of that argument *in the future*.

- Any complaint or criticism can be translated by a disgruntled client into information about what changes in others might help *in the future*. Recipients can also give information: "This is what you could do i*n the future* that would aid me in giving you the changes you want."

- Any breakdown in communication can be analyzed from this point of view: "What can we learn from what just happened that we can apply in the future?"

- Conflicts of interest can alert clients to the need to apply "win-win" problem solving: "How can we resolve this problem right now so we can feel good about it *in the future*?"

"Opting for the future," adopted as a philosophy and guideline by clients and practitioners alike as to how they focus on problems and issues, takes the blame out of relating. It is the future, not the past, that is relevant and the future is fresh, hopeful, and untainted by "past crimes."

Opting for the future, of course, requires that each client commit to attending *only* to what *he* or *she* is going to do in the future, rather than monitoring the activities of the other person in that regard. The question each client must answer moment by moment is, "How can I improve on *my* performance in the future?"

Opting for the future also requires that clients monitor and accredit their successes: "What did we do well that gave us the peace or the respect or the closeness we just enjoyed?" And, "How can we repeat that in the future?"

Clients essentially become the monitoring agents of their successes, rather than of their failures. Each client acknowledges the changes he or she sees in the other. And each focuses on what is possible and changeable, rather than on what is impossible and intractable. This puts clients on the same team—advocates rather than adversaries—as they move in concert to create the positive conditions they opt for in their relationship.

Practitioners, of course, help create a hopeful future through their own vision of what is possible and their frequent interventions to remind clients to approach any particular complaint or problem from a futuristic perspective. Practitioners can increase clients' focus on the future by always starting sessions with a question regarding what successes clients have had in achieving goals or tasks, or in creating fresh, positive ways of relating. Clients may resist this at first, for their orientation is to talk about problems. However, if practitioners persevere, even repeatedly putting "problem talk" on hold, until clients have spent significant time acknowledging and savoring even small changes, over time clients will often adopt a practitioner's vision and initiate "change talk" themselves. One possible goal practitioners can encourage clients to adopt, in fact, is that of opting for the future in their transactions at home and counting their successes in that regard each time they return for another session.

Complementing this approach, Weiner-Davis (1992) teaches clients to focus on the "exceptional times" to determine what's working and why, and then encourages them to turn productive behaviors into habits. Focusing on exceptions shrinks problems, she notes, because identifying what they can do is infinitely more hopeful and empowering to clients than noting what they can't do. Focusing on exceptions also demonstrates to clients that they are changeable and that seemingly fixed traits are fluid. Finally, focusing on exceptions supplies clients with a blueprint for describing exactly what they need to do the next time a particular situation occurs.

"Opting for the future," as a guiding philosophy for enhancing relationships, encourages clients to increase their positive feedback to others, a vital therapeutic goal in the change process. Positive feedback from significant others (i.e., expressions of caring, approval, encouragement, affection, appreciation, and other forms of positive attention), of course, is a vital source of nourishment for self-esteem, high morale, emotional security, confidence, and feeling valued by others. Thus, aiding clients to increase positive feedback fosters the well-being of individuals and harmonious relationships with others as well.

To enable clients to increase positive feedback, practitioners must be skilled in:

1. Engaging clients in assessing the extent to which they give and receive positive feedback.

2. Educating clients as to the vital role of positive feedback.

3. Teaching clients to express their needs for positive feedback.

4. Teaching clients to discern the needs of others for positive feedback.

5. Cultivating positive perceptual sets.

6. Enabling clients to give and receive positive feedback.

7. Assisting clients to increase levels of positive feedback.

In the following sections, we focus on each of these skills.

Engaging Clients in Assessing the Extent to Which They Give and Receive Positive Feedback

Relationships often flounder because participants fail to meet each other's needs for positive feedback. You can directly explore this dimension of communication by asking clients how often and in what manner they convey positive feedback to sig-

nificant others. Questions you might ask in couple or family sessions to achieve this end include the following:

"How do you send messages that let family members [*or your partner*] know that you care about them?"

"How frequently do you send such messages?"

"How often do you give feedback to others concerning their positive actions?"

In instances of severe marital or family breakdown, clients commonly acknowledge they send positive messages infrequently or not at all. In some instances, they may actually experience only weak positive feelings, but usually they experience more than they express.

Besides exploring how spouses or family members convey positive feedback, you can also explore their desires to receive increased feedback from each other. Questions that elicit such desires include:

"When was the last time you received positive feedback from other family members concerning some action or behavior on your part?"

"Would you like to receive more positive feedback from others in the family? What kind of feedback?"

"Are you satisfied with the number of caring messages you receive from other members of the family? What changes would you like?"

Discussing how clients send positive messages or to what extent they desire increased positive feedback often opens channels for positive communication that have been dammed by repetitive arguments, criticisms, blaming messages, and put-downs.

Educating Clients as to the Vital Role of Positive Feedback

As clients communicate about their needs to receive positive feedback, they begin to appreciate the significance of this dimension in interpersonal relationships. You can expand their awareness of the significance of positive feedback and enhance their motivation to increase the same by further explaining why this dimension is crucial. The logic behind increasing positive feedback is straightforward, and clients generally grasp it readily because it rings true in terms of their own needs and experiences.

Explanations vary according to whether the unit of concern involves parent-child, marital, family, or other interpersonal relationships. The following axioms may apply to one or more of these units, and you can include in an explanation those that seem appropriate.

1. All people need positive feedback to maintain high morale.

2. To exert their best efforts, people, especially children, need encouragement and approval.

3. Unsolicited expressions of love and approval are far more powerful and reassuring than solicited expressions.

4. Satisfaction and happiness in relationships and family life are strongly determined by the degree of positive feedback members give each other.

5. Encouragement and approval are much stronger motivators than criticism and disapproval.

6. People never outgrow the need for love, approval, and encouragement.

7. Feeling taken for granted is a threat to the stability of relationships.

8. Love and respect among family members are indispensable to a harmonious and happy family life.

9. People need positive feedback every day; occasional feedback is insufficient to sustain self-esteem.

10. Individuals, couples, and families fail to achieve their potentials if they do not grow in their capacity to provide and receive positive feedback.

Teaching Clients to Express Their Needs for Positive Feedback

Teaching clients to express their needs involves assisting them to send personalized messages in which they own their feelings and wants. The following are examples of messages that explicitly express needs for positive feedback:

- *Partner:* I've been troubled lately because I haven't felt very important to you. You've been working such long hours, and we haven't had any time together for the last week. I need to know that you still love me.

- *Adolescent:* I've felt really discouraged since I showed you my report card yesterday. I really worked hard this term, and the only thing you seemed to note was the one B. It didn't seem to matter that the rest were A's. Sometimes I wonder if I can please you at all. I need to know that you're pleased with how I'm doing.

In earlier chapters, we discussed how to assist clients to personalize messages. We also illustrated how, through on-the-spot interventions, you can coach clients to formulate authentic messages that clearly express their feelings and needs. Reviewing that discussion will assist you in helping clients to express their needs for positive feedback, as will reading the following case illustration.

Ruth [*to husband*]: I work really hard at keeping the house clean, but you never seem to notice it. All you notice is what I haven't done—like yesterday when you chewed me out for not cleaning the fingerprints off the bathroom door.

Carl: Well, let's face it, you hadn't done it, and you admitted it.

Practitioner: Carl, Ruth was expressing an important need, and I don't want that need to get lost in an argument. Ruth, think for a moment about what you said. What is the need you were referring to?

Ruth: [*Pause*] Do you mean his not noticing what I do?

Practitioner: In a way, yes. What I'm meaning is your need for messages that give you credit for what you do and let you know you're appreciated. Is that what you need?

Ruth: Yes, I do need that. I get so discouraged at times. Like I never really please Carl.

Practitioner [*to Carl*]: She's sharing something that's very important. You both need to feel valued by each other, and that requires getting positive feedback for who you are and what you do. Without positive feedback, partners begin to feel discouraged and insecure, and relationships suffer. [*To both partners.*] To make sure you're aware of each other's needs for positive feedback, both of you need to send clear messages about your needs and to be sensitive to your *partner's* needs. Ruth, I'd like you to start over and express your need to Carl. This time, however, be sure you own your need and send an "I" message. [*Practitioner had previously instructed couple about personalizing messages.*] I'll help you if you'd like.

Ruth: I hope I don't blow it. [*Very deliberately.*] Carl, I need to know you're pleased with me. It seems I can't please you [*voice quivers*]—no matter how hard I try. [*Tears.*]

Practitioner: I know that was hard for you, Ruth, but I was impressed with your message. Your feelings and need came through clearly. [*To Carl.*] What are you feeling now about what Ruth just said?

Carl: I'm feeling like a heel, I guess. I didn't know she felt as strongly as she does.

Practitioner: Can you tell Ruth that?

Carl: This isn't easy. Ruth, I'm sorry. I know I've been overly critical at times. You are a good housekeeper, and I want you to know that I'll try to be less critical.

Practitioner [*to both*]: I'm very pleased with how you just communicated. You've been getting down to some really important needs and feelings. I'd like to point out something else that's also important to getting your needs on the table. That has to do with tuning in to the needs of your partner for positive feedback. That means each of you has to learn to listen for needs that lie behind words, complaints, accusations, and tears. Ask yourself, "What is my partner needing?" By listening for needs, you can prevent a lot of hassles and meet each other's needs more effectively.

Teaching Clients to Discern Others' Needs for Positive Feedback

Enhancing clients' sensitivity to the needs of others for positive feedback involves assisting them to listen attentively. Because others often do not express needs openly and clearly, clients' efforts must extend beyond just listening. They must also learn to "tune in" to needs that are veiled behind the complaints, questions, and actions of others. Because it is difficult for clients to attune to the needs inherent in the messages of others, it is important that you take full advantage of "teachable moments" to help them to learn this skill, as presented in the preceding excerpt.

Notice that the practitioner focuses sharply on Ruth's needs and plays a facilitative role in prompting her to express her need directly to Carl. The practitioner likewise uses the opportunity to advantage by having Carl provide feedback to Ruth, thus performing a vital role in *facilitating positive interaction between the partners*. This is a crucial point, for by serving as catalysts, practitioners enable clients to learn by *actually engaging in positive interaction*, a much more effective mode of learning than merely having clients talk about what they need to do. Notice also that the practitioner addresses the need for learning skills to both members. By not singling out one member, the practitioner avoids appearing to side with one or the other partner. The practitioner could further stress the needs of both participants for positive feedback by centering the exploration on Carl to identify how often and in what ways he receives positive feedback from his wife and then negotiating a mutual task with partners to increase such feedback during the coming week.

Cultivating Positive Perceptual Sets

Before clients can provide positive feedback, they must first be aware of the strengths, positive attributes, and actions of others. Some clients, of course, have perceptual sets that are attuned to the positive attributes and behaviors of others, but others habitually perceive weaknesses and flaws in the personalities and actions of others. As systems, families and couples may also constantly focus on what others are *not* doing or on what they *should* be doing, thereby excluding acknowledgment of positive coping behaviors and efforts. The practitioner, then, has the responsibility of bringing negative perceptual sets to the attention of clients and helping them learn to focus on positive behaviors. Strategies for accomplishing these tasks are delineated in the following subsections.

Sensitizing Couples to Positives   As alluded to earlier, practitioners can set the stage for helping families and couples to develop positive perceptual sets by negotiating an explicit contract specifying that, in addition to focusing on self-defeating behaviors and other obstacles that prevent members from achieving their goals, clients will accord equal weight to accrediting strengths and incremental growth of members. The practitioner then actively intervenes in the early stages of the helping process to highlight strengths and growth and to help clients to incorporate "attention to positives" as part of their normative behavior. The practitioner's subsequent role in this regard is exemplified by the following intervention at the beginning of a third session with a family:

It's likely that if I asked you what went wrong this week, you could probably easily identify a number of incidents. For the next few minutes, though, I'm going to ask you to tell me some of the things that went *right*. This may be hard to do, but I'm going to help you stay with my question because it's important for you as a family to learn to focus on the positive behaviors of members and to identify positive changes that occur.

Practitioners may wish to ask the family (or couple) this question each week until members themselves spontaneously report incidents that involve positive behaviors of other members, thus indicating the family has internalized the value of focusing on positives.

Reviewing Progress and Accrediting Incremental Growth   Practitioners may also increase a family's sensitivity to positives by engaging members in briefly reviewing at each session's end the work that has been accomplished, including incremental growth achieved by individuals or by a family.

Increments of growth are often manifested very subtly in the helping process, and practitioners must therefore make a concerted effort to focus the attention of clients on these positive indicators of progress, as illustrated in the excerpt below from an actual session with a couple. In this session, which involves a husband (an ex-convict) who lacks perceptiveness of his own and others' feelings, the couple discusses an incident that followed the husband's spending $400 to have his motorcycle repaired. Because of the expense, his wife did not share his enthusiasm over having the motorcycle in running order.

Wife: I think you were disappointed because I didn't say more about your getting your motorcycle fixed.

Husband: I was! It hurt me because you weren't happy that I got it fixed and that now you can go riding with me.

Practitioner [*to husband*]: Did you notice anything different about the way you just expressed yourself?

Husband: What, that I'm saying "hurt" and all that shit?

Wife: That's incredible!

Practitioner: That's a big breakthrough, Rick. I don't believe I've ever heard you spontaneously express your feelings.

Husband: I'm just being an old softy. I'm just "washing out." You might as well just run a hose in here and wash me out of the place.

Practitioner: Not so! Rather than being a softy, you're becoming much more aware of your feelings and are learning to express them. I was also pleased that you observed so quickly the change you had made. Your wife also noticed. Did you hear her say, "That's incredible?"

In this excerpt, the practitioner enables the husband to observe his own growth and also accredits the wife's astuteness in noting the subtle changes her husband manifested. Intellectually more capable than her husband, the wife learned in earlier sessions to give her husband positive feedback (and to express feelings). It was striking that the husband (whose ability to think abstractly appeared severely limited) slowly gained skills over a period of five months due in large part to the practitioner's (1) persistent efforts to model and explain skills, (2) heavy focus on his strengths and resources, and (3) concerted effort to acknowledge any signs of incremental growth.

To highlight incremental growth, practitioners may also wish to ask members to contrast their current functioning with their functioning at an earlier time, as illustrated in the following message:

[*To family*]: This is your fourth session. Let's see if you can identify any changes you've made in the way you communicate by contrasting how you related today with the way you related in the first session. I have some observations about that, but first I would like to hear yours.

Employing Tasks to Enhance /Perceptual Sets

Practitioners can also assist clients to develop positive perceptual sets by negotiating tasks that clients can implement between sessions. For example, they can further expand spouses' awareness of the frequency with which they provide positive feedback by negotiating the task of having them keep a daily tally of the number of positive messages they send their partners over a period of one week.[5] Clients (and practitioners) thus not only gain a clear picture of their performance on this dimension but also develop a baseline against which they can later assess their progress in increasing positive feedback. Monitoring also provides advantages because, without explicitly planning to do so, clients often begin to increase the frequency of the desired behavior.

Another task that assists persons to view their partners more positively is to have them compile lists of their partners' positive qualities. Practitioners may ask partners to begin by writing down at least 10 positive qualities and, without discussing their lists, bring them to the following session. In the session, the practitioner asks the spouses to read their lists to each other. This activity is beneficial in affording practice to spouses both in giving and in receiving positive feedback.

After having clients read their lists to each oth-

er, practitioners may ask them to discuss their reactions to hearing the positive feedback. Generally, clients report positive reactions, which provides an opportunity to reemphasize the beneficial consequences of positive feedback. Practitioners can further negotiate tasks of having the partners review their lists daily, with the objective of expanding them on an ongoing basis. A related task is to ask partners to focus not only on their partners' positive attributes but on those of others as well, especially when they find themselves thinking negative thoughts about others. By systematically focusing on the positive attributes of others, clients can gradually achieve more positive perceptual sets.

Enabling Clients to Give and to Receive Positive Feedback

To assist clients in learning to convey positive feedback, practitioners can teach them to personalize messages and guide them in practicing giving positive feedback to others. Practitioners should ask clients to base their practice messages on recent situations during which they experienced positive feelings but did not share them with others. Timely use of this educative intervention assists clients in conceptualizing the elements of positive messages and to develop skill in authentically sharing their positive experiencing.

Practitioners may also need to assist some clients to learn how to accept as well as to give positive feedback. By deflecting positive feedback, in fact, these clients discredit information that could significantly increase their self-esteem.

Assisting Clients to Increase Levels of Positive Feedback

After completing the activities previously delineated, clients are ready to work on the ultimate task of increasing their rates of positive feedback. Practitioners can assist them by negotiating tasks that specify providing positive feedback at higher levels. Clients, of course, must consent to such tasks and determine the rate of positive feedback they seek to achieve. We recommend that practitioners have clients review their baseline obtained earlier and encourage them to set a daily rate that "stretches" their usual level but not to an unrealistic extent. For example, a husband whose mean baseline daily rate in giving positive feedback to his wife is 0.8 might select a beginning level of giving positive feedback twice daily. The client could then gradually increase the number of daily responses until reaching a self-selected optimal rate of five times daily.

As some clients implement the task of increasing positive feedback, they may inappropriately employ insincere positive expressions. Practitioners should caution against this, as such expressions have a hollow ring and create discomfort for both sender and receiver. Practitioners can stress, however, that as clients practice attuning to positives, they will gradually gain a natural facility for perceiving actions or qualities that warrant positive feedback.

In planning with clients to implement this task, it is important to adhere to the task-implementation sequence. In part, this involves anticipating obstacles, two of which are by far the most common. First, clients who have been inhibited in expressing feelings report discomfort with expressing caring messages, explaining, "It just doesn't come naturally to me." Practitioners should respond empathically to clients' discomfort but explain that engaging in new behaviors is bound to be uncomfortable and that if clients will risk themselves and endure the discomfort, they will gradually gain facility and comfort in expressing positive feedback.

The second common obstacle is that others may not respond favorably to clients' increased level of positive feedback and, instead, may question their sincerity. Because some clients have given virtually no positive feedback previously, the skepticism of others is understandable. Practitioners can assist clients to deal with others' skepticism by modeling

and having clients rehearse appropriate coping behavior (including asserting the sincerity of their efforts) and by emphasizing the necessity of persisting in their efforts despite obstacles.

As with all tasks, it is vital to review clients' experiences in succeeding sessions. Clients may have experienced difficulties that warrant exploration, may continue to struggle with awkwardness or discomfort, or may report highly favorable reactions from others. Reviewing outcomes is vitally important, for practitioners can then give encouragement and positive feedback to clients, enable them to savor their successes, and, if warranted, point to the need for additional effort.

As clients implement tasks of increasing their rates of positive feedback, they will need to continue keeping tallies of instances in which they give such responses. Through monitoring, they not only maintain an ongoing record of their progress but also reinforce themselves each time they record a tally. Of course, the ultimate reinforcement derives from improved interactions with others. By giving positive feedback to others, clients increase the likelihood of receiving the same in return.

Tasks for Couples One of many tasks you can employ to increase positive interactions between marital partners involves a strategy developed by Stuart (1980) aimed at increasing mutual demonstrations of caring behaviors by partners. By asking each partner, "Exactly what would you like your partner to do as a means of showing that he or she cares for you?", you assist each partner to identify desired actions that become a resource to the other. As each partner identifies caring behaviors, the other writes them down. You then ask each partner to assume the task of carrying out a specified number of caring behaviors identified by the other, using his or her respective list of positive actions as a resource. Another basic aspect of this activity involves each partner's expressing positive feedback in the form of appreciation when the other partner performs one of the actions from the list.

Tasks and Activities for Families and Couples

A task that cultivates positive feedback among family members involves the activity or game of "Guess Who?" In this game, family members sit in a circle and a parent presents each member with a slip of paper and a pencil. A parent then instructs members of the family to write down something they like about the person sitting on the member's right. (Family members who are unable to write may ask another member to write for them.) The slips are then folded, put into a hat, and mixed up. In succession, each family member draws a slip from the hat, reads it aloud, and members guess which person matches the written description. Family members then shift positions in the circle and repeat the procedure until they have had the opportunity in writing about every other family member. This game assists you in centering the attention of family members on the positive attributes of others. It further provides feedback to each member about strengths and attributes as perceived by other family members.

An exercise that promotes positive feedback among family and group members (which is appropriate in groups only after members have become well acquainted) involves asking the family or group to "spotlight" each member in turn. Other members then give positive feedback about the strengths of the person in the spotlight. If it is necessary to prime the group, you may initiate positive feedback regarding strengths or growth of a member each time the spotlight shifts.

Tasks for Parents   Preliminary to negotiating tasks with parents to increase positive feedback to their children, you can request that parents list functional and dysfunctional behaviors of each child. You then ask parents to choose the three dysfunctional behaviors they would most like to change. The next step is to negotiate a task that involves parents giving positive feedback at opportune times during the week when the specified behavior is *not* occurring (e.g., when the child is *not* fighting with a sibling). Further instruct the parents to give positive feedback when children manifest behaviors the parents would like them to assume *in place of the targeted behaviors* (e.g., when the child *has* told the truth or *did* follow through on an assigned task). Parents are understandably handicapped in using this strategy if children's usual behaviors do not include the behaviors that are desired. For instance, children may never pick up their clothes or do their homework until specifically asked or only after continual nagging. In such instances, you will first need to motivate children by establishing an agreement that they may earn certain rewards in exchange for specified behavior.

Because parental attention to children's behavior is a potent force for modifying or reinforcing behavior, it is vital that you work intensively with parents so that they master the skill of positive feedback and learn to reward their children's positive behaviors systematically. We thus ask parents to reinforce the positive behaviors of children that they earlier identified, incrementally increasing the number of positive responses over a period of time. For example, a child may sometimes relate to siblings in a caring way, display a keen sense of humor that lifts family spirits, or take responsibility seriously. Parents, unfortunately, often take such behaviors for granted. But children need to know what they are *already* doing that pleases parents. If parents want their children to assume particular behaviors, they must give them positive feedback when those behaviors occur. Note the reinforcing property of the following parental messages:

"I want you to know how much I enjoy your sense of humor. Sometimes you absolutely crack me up! It really lightens my day."

"I really like it when you come up and hug me like that. It was such a pleasant surprise, and I could really feel your love coming through. I want you to know that I really love you!"

"When I asked you if you had pushed your little brother down just a minute ago, you said 'Yes.' I appreciated your telling me the truth. I know it was hard for you to do that, knowing that I was angry when I asked. Being honest is very important to me, and I'm glad that you made the choice to tell the truth."

Used consistently by parents, messages such as these have a significant effect in shaping a child's personality and cultivating desired attributes. We cannot overemphasize the importance of taking a *preventive* approach with families by teaching members to emotionally nourish and support each other. Families that implement this approach raise the self-esteem of all members.

STRATEGIES TO MODIFY DYSFUNCTIONAL INTERACTION

Interactional difficulties that clients commonly present include repetitive heated arguments, struggles over power and authority, conflict over issues related to dependence and independence, dissension in making decisions, friction associated with discrepant role perceptions and/or fulfillments, and other forms of defective communication. As we noted in Chapter 11, interpersonal conflicts tend to be redundant; that is, in relations with others, individuals repeat over and over again various types of dysfunctional interaction that predictably lead to the same negative consequences. To assist clients in evolving more functional patterns of communication and interaction, you must be expert in employing appropriate interventions and techniques. In this section, we delineate guidelines and techniques that you can employ in modifying dysfunctional interaction as you work with marital partners, families, groups, and other types of relationships. Note that teaching communication skills to clients is a vital aspect of modifying dysfunctional communications.

Metacommunication

To modify dysfunctional communication, participants must discuss such communication, analyzing their behaviors and emotional reactions as well as the impact of the interaction on their relationship. Such discussions are termed *metacommunication*, for they involve *communication about communication*. When practitioners discuss with clients communication that has just occurred, they too are engaging in metacommunication. Indeed, much of couple, family, and group therapy involves metacommunication. Likewise, when practitioners discuss relational reactions that occur in the context of the helping relationship, they are metacommunicating, for they are clarifying the meanings of messages and actions. Still other examples of metacommunication are messages that clarify intentions (e.g., "I'm only kidding" or "I want to talk with you because I feel bad about the strain between us") or messages that "check out" or seek clarification of others' messages that are vague or ambiguous (e.g., "I'm not sure what you mean by that" or "Let me see if I understood what you were saying").

Skills in metacommunications play a vital role in effective communication, for persons who metacommunicate often avoid needless misunderstandings (by checking out the meanings of messages) and provide feedback that enables others to make choices about modifying ways of communicating that are offensive or abrasive. Moreover, people who metacommunicate well thrash out conflicts with a minimum of antagonism and disruption in their relationships. A major role of practitioners, therefore, is to assist clients to learn to metacommunicate effectively.

Although skills in assisting people to metacommunicate are important with all client systems, they are especially critical in working with families that manifest dysfunctional patterns of communication, including frequent use of discomfirming, incongruent, and double-bind messages. Metacommunication involving these extreme forms of dysfunctional communication is indispensable to obviating their pernicious effects on family members. Families that extensively employ these forms of communication often metacommunicate little, if at all, which means that vulnerable family members are entrapped in processes that produce low self-esteem, blur personal identity, warp perceptions of the world, and foster disordered thinking. It is thus crucial to intervene into these dysfunctional processes and to teach family members to metacommunicate effectively. The following excerpt illustrates use of metacommunication to enhance communication between Anne, age 14, and her mother Ms. T, who acts as a spokesperson for Anne and sends disconfirming messages.

Practitioner: Anne, could you tell me how you've been doing in your gym class? I know you were having a rough time in gym.

Ms. T: It's been *really* rough for her, having to change clothes and shower in front of all the other girls. She feels like she's in a goldfish bowl. I mean—I know what it's like because I went through it when I was in junior high. [*Anne lowers her head and looks at the floor.*]

Practitioner: Excuse me, Ms. T, but you were speaking for Anne. Anne, I'd like to hear from you what it has been like. [*Intervening to counter Ms. T's acting as Anne's spokesperson.*]

Anne [*looking up slightly*]: Well, it has been going a little better, I think. The gym teacher hasn't been after me. In fact she was pretty friendly this last week. And I …[*Ms. T interrupts.*]

Ms. T: But it hasn't been going better, Anne. [*Disconfirming Anne as a separate person.*] When you shower, you just feel everyone's eyes are glued on you.

Practitioner [*to mother*]: I'd like to hear from Anne herself about how she feels about showering. [*To Anne.*] I know your mother's view, but I don't know what your experience has been.

Anne: Actually, it hasn't been like my mother said. It was bad until the past couple of weeks, but I've made friends with a couple of girls, and we shower together. It isn't nearly as bad now.

Ms. T: But you were saying …[*Practitioner interrupts to avert another disconfirming message.*]

Practitioner: Anne, when your mother spoke for you the first time, you looked at the floor as if you were distressed. I wonder if you could tell your mother how you feel when she speaks for you. [*Encouraging metacommunication.*]

Anne: I don't mind, sometimes. But, Mother, you don't always know how I feel. You get your feelings mixed up with mine, and it confuses me. I want to speak for myself.

Ms. T: But, darling, I was just trying to help. I know how hard it's been for you. I mean, you understand that, don't you?

Anne: I guess so, but I wish you wouldn't do it so much.

Practitioner [*to mother*]: I know you're trying to help, Ms. T. But what do you hear Anne telling you? [*Using metacommunication to check out Ms. T's perception.*]

Ms. T.: That she doesn't want me to say how she feels?

Practitioner: Yes. I think Anne's saying that she's needing to be her own person. Is that right, Anne? [*Using metacommunication to check out meaning attribution.*]

Anne: Yes, I want to grow up. I don't want to be a little girl anymore. [*Ms. T squirms.*]

Practitioner [*to both*]: What we've been talking about is very important in improving your communication as well as helping Anne to grow up. [*To Ms. T.*] Though you're meaning to help, your assumptions about Anne's feelings are sometimes inaccurate. If you want to understand Anne, you'll need to ask how she feels rather than assume you know. [*To Anne.*] If you want to help your mother understand, you'll need to remind her not to speak for you when she does. And you'll also need to tell her your real feelings rather than just keeping them inside. I was very impressed with how you did that with your mother just now. I know that was difficult for you.

Notice in the preceding excerpt that the practitioner assertively intervened to prevent the interaction from following its usual destructive course. By not permitting Ms. T to act as Anne's spokesperson, by involving the participants in metacommunicating about the impact on Anne of Ms. T's behavior, and by defining how both can modify their dysfunctional pattern of communication, the practitioner initiated corrective processes. Of course, many such interventions over a period of time are required to produce enduring changes.

Modifying Dysfunctional Family Rules

Dysfunctional family rules can also severely impair the functioning of family members. Because family rules are covert, it follows that changes can occur only by bringing them into the open. The practitioner thus assists family members through meta-communication to acknowledge and consider the impact of rules on family interaction. Openly discussing rules suggests options for replacing them with other processes that better serve the needs of all family members. Practitioners prepare families to consider rules by introducing them to the concept, as illustrated in the following message:

> As we begin work on problems the family is experiencing, we need to know more about how your family operates. Every family has some rules or understandings about how members are to behave. Sometimes these rules are easy to spot. "Each person is to clear his own plate when leaving the table" is a rule that all members of a family might be expected to follow. This is an apparent rule because every member of the family could easily tell me what is expected of them at the end of the meal. But the family's behavior is also governed by other rules that are less easy to identify because they are hidden. Even though members follow these rules, they are often unaware that they exist. In the next few minutes, I'm going to ask you some questions that will help you to understand these two kinds of rules better and to identify some of the ones that operate in your family.

The practitioner can then ask the family to list some apparent rules and coach the family, if needed, by asking questions such as "What are your rules about bedtime?" (or watching television or getting the work done around the house). Once family members have identified some of their common and readily apparent rules the practitioner can then lead them into a discussion of implicit rules by asking them to identify guidelines they follow with regard to any of the dimensions of assessment listed in Chapter 10. For example, the practitioner might ask family members to identify family rules about showing anger or positive feelings or to explore facets of decision making or

power (e.g., "Whom do the kids go to in the family when they want something?"). Rather than engaging the family in a lengthy exploration, practitioners should use the discussion to illustrate the presence of hidden rules that significantly influence their behavior. In the discussion, practitioners should stress that certain rules may undermine opportunities for members to achieve their maximum potential and, in fact, may be destructive to the growth and well-being of both individuals and the family itself.

After explaining the concept of rules to the family, practitioners can utilize this concept in assisting members to identify their patterned ways of interacting. Consider the practitioner's role in this regard in the following excerpt from a third session with Mr. and Mrs. Johnson and their three daughters:

Martha [*age 14*]: You took my blouse again—right out of my closet—and you didn't ask. That really gripes me.

Cynthia [*age 15*]: Well, you borrowed my brush last week, and you still have it.

Father: You girls need to learn to ask to borrow each other's belongings.

Practitioner: Stop for a minute and take a look at what's happening. Martha, what did you notice you were doing?

Martha: She made me really mad.

Practitioner: This is going to take some effort from you because you're still mad, but see if you can stay with me. What were you doing?

Martha: I told Cynthia I was mad at her.

Practitioner: Good! [*To Cynthia.*] Then what did you do?

Cynthia: I told Martha she didn't have any right to complain because she wasn't returning things either.

Practitioner: The two of you then were engaged in what we've earlier referred to as blaming messages—do you see it the same way? [*Girls nod. To father.*] I wonder if you observed what you did when your daughters were involved in their argument?

Father: I was trying to get them to stop arguing and blaming each other—like usual.[6]

Practitioner: We may have the makings of a hidden family rule. Let's explore a little more to find out for sure. [*To family.*] While I'm asking a few questions, let's see if you can figure out what the rule is. [*To 13-year-old Jennifer.*] You weren't involved in this argument. Do you argue with anyone in the family?

Jennifer [*laughs*]: My mother and my sisters.

Practitioner: When you get in an argument with your mother, what happens?

Jennifer: If my dad is there, he tries to stop it. Sometimes he tells my mother to go upstairs, and he'll talk to me.

Practitioner [*to mother*]: When your husband does that, what do you do?

Mother: Sometimes I let him handle the problem with Jennifer or one of the other girls. But when he gets involved like that, it makes me so furious that sometimes he and I end up in a fight ourselves.

Practitioner: We need to do a lot more work to understand what happens in such situations, but for the moment, let's see, father, if you can put your finger on the rule.

Father: I guess I'm always trying to stop everyone from fighting and arguing in the family.

Practitioner: It does appear that you are the family's mediator. I would think that would be a very difficult role to play.

Father: Well, there are no rewards for it, I can tell you that!

Practitioner: There's more to the rule. Who lets father be the mediator?

Martha: We do.

Practitioner: That's right. It isn't father's rule; it's the family rule. It takes the rest of the family to argue and father to break up the fights.

There are many avenues that could be explored in this scenario, but the practitioner chose to narrow the focus by assisting the family to identify one of its major rules. After further exploring specific patterned interactions of the family, the practitioner can introduce questions such as the following that will help the family to weigh whether or not they wish to continue relating under the old rule.

To father:

"How effective are you in actually stopping family members from fighting?"

"What are your worst fears about what might occur in the family if you didn't play that role?"

"Would you like to free yourself from the role of being the family mediator?"

To other family members:

"Do you want father to continue to be the third party in your arguments?"

"What are the risks to your relationship if he discontinues playing the role of mediator?"

"Do you want to work out your own disputes?"

Questions such as these focus on the participation of *all* members in the patterned interaction and assist the practitioner and members to determine the *function* of the behavior in the system. To assist the family to modify their rule, the practitioner will need to teach family members new skills for resolving disagreements. The practitioner will also need to coach the father in declining the role of mediator and to coach others in requesting that he let them manage their own conflicts.

On-the-Spot Interventions

A form of metacommunication, on-the-spot interventions are a potent way of modifying dysfunctional patterns of interaction by intervening immediately when such communication occurs between spouses or family members. On-the-spot interventions are appropriate when clients send fuzzy or abrasive messages; when receivers distort meanings of or fail to respond appropriately to important messages; when actors imply but do not explicitly express wants, needs, or feelings; and when destructive interaction occurs. In implementing on-the-spot interventions, practitioners focus on the destructive impact of the preceding communication (labeling the type of communication so that clients themselves can subsequently identify their dysfunctional behavior) and facilitatively teach and guide participants to implement more effective ways of communication.

This technique is illustrated in the next excerpt, which depicts a practitioner intervening into a "blind alley" argument, one that cannot be resolved because neither party can be proved right or wrong.

Husband: I distinctly remember telling you to buy some deodorant when you went to the store.

Wife: You may have thought you did, but you didn't. I'd have remembered if you said anything about it.

Husband: But you *didn't* remember. I told you for sure, and you're copping out.

Wife [*with obvious irritation.*]: Like hell you did! You're the one who forgot to tell me, and I don't appreciate your telling me I copped out.

Practitioner: Let's stop for a moment and consider what's happening between you. Each of you has a different recollection of what happened, and there's no way of determining who's right or wrong. You were involved in what I call a blind alley argument because you can't resolve it. You just end up arguing over who's right and feeling resentful because you're convinced the other is wrong. This doesn't help you solve your problem but only creates distance in your relationship. Let's go back and start over, and I'll show you a more effective way of dealing with the situation.

After labeling the dysfunctional interaction and guiding clients to communicate constructively, practitioners often subsequently intervene into related dysfunctional interactions but challenge clients themselves to identify their dysfunctional behavior and to modify it accordingly. For example, a practitioner may interrupt interaction, exclaiming, "Wait a minute! Think about what you're doing just now and where it's going to lead you if you continue." If clients fail to discern the nature of their behavior, the practitioner can again label the dysfunctional process and review with them more effective processes. In modifying dysfunctional patterns, the intermediate objective is for clients to arrest their dysfunctional behavior by recognizing it, metacommunicating about it, and substituting newly gained communication skills.

The ultimate goal, of course, is for them to *eliminate* the dysfunctional processes through concentrated efforts between sessions.

Guidelines for Making On-the-Spot Interventions

1. Focus on Process Rather Than Content Practitioners can be infinitely more helpful to clients in enhancing interaction by focusing on interaction processes rather than on the content of conflicts. Conflicts typically are manifested over content issues, but *how clients interact* in dealing with the focal point of a conflict is far more important than the focal point itself. As we illustrated in the preceding excerpt, the issue of who is right in a given dispute is usually trivial when compared to the destructive effects of dysfunctional processes such as belittling, dominating, name-calling, threatening, arguing bitterly, or resorting to violence.

You should usually ignore topics of disputes, focusing instead on assisting clients to learn to listen attentively and respectfully, to employ effective decision making, to own feelings, to examine their own parts in problems, to increase positive feedback and reduce negative feedback, to compromise, to disengage from competitive interaction, and to implement effective conflict-resolution tactics. Clients, of course, will confront countless potentially conflictive situations but will manage them without damaging their relationships if they master effective patterns of communication that preserve mutual respect and self-esteem. Indeed, well-adjusted families differ from poorly adjusted families not in the sheer number of conflictive events but in the fact that the former manage conflict effectively, whereas the latter do not.

2. Give Feedback That Is Descriptive and Neutral Rather Than General and/or Evaluative As you intervene, it is important to present feedback in a neutral manner that does not fault clients and that enables them to pinpoint specific behavior that produces difficulties. Feedback that evaluates their behavior produces defensiveness; general feedback fails to focus on behavior that needs to be changed. To illustrate, consider a situation in which a marital partner glares at his spouse and says: "I've had it with going to your parents' house. You spend all the time there visiting there with your mother and treat me like excess baggage. You can go by yourself in the future." A general and evaluative message would be: "Garth, that message was an example of poor communication. Try again to send a better one." Contrast the preceding message with the following one, which is neutral and behaviorally specific: "Garth, I noticed that when you just spoke to Barbara, you glared at her and sent 'you' messages that focused on what you thought she was doing wrong. I watched Barbara as you spoke and noticed that she frowned and seemed to bristle. I'd like you to get some feedback from Barbara about how your message affected her. Barbara, would you share with Garth what you experienced as he talked?"

In the last message, the practitioner implies the client's message was dysfunctional but avoids making an evaluative judgment, as the practitioner did in the first example. Moreover, by describing specific behavior and eliciting feedback about its impact, the practitioner enhances the possibility that the client will be receptive to examining his behavior and to modifying it. Note that this message also highlights the interaction of *both* participants, as specified in the following guideline.

3. Balance Interventions to Divide Responsibility

Because more than one client is involved in conjoint sessions, practitioners must avoid singling out one person as being the sole cause of interpersonal difficulties. Otherwise, that person may feel the practitioner and others are taking sides and placing the blame on him or her. By focusing on all relevant actors, the practitioner distributes responsibility, models fairness, and avoids alienating one person. Moreover, although one person may con-

tribute more to problems than others, all members of a system generally contribute to difficulties in some degree. The following excerpt illustrates balancing an intervention in a marital therapy session:

Wife: It makes me furious that you won't come home and take care of baby Charly. You agreed for me to go back to work part time and now you won't get off work to take care of him. You think your own career is more important than caring for our child and letting me go back to work.

Husband: I'm new at this job and I just can't take time off now. You know that. Besides, I told you we weren't ready to have a baby now. I really can't get involved in taking care of Charly on work time now.

Practitioner: Both of you seem to have some feelings and needs that are legitimate, but for some reason you seem to be stuck and unable to work things out. [*To wife.*] You resent his not playing his part in child care so you can go ahead with the plan you agreed to about going back to work part-time. [*To husband.*] You feel that since you are on a new job, now is not the time to ask for time off for child care. I'd like to explore what both of you can do to make things better for each other.

In the preceding excerpt, the practitioner responds empathically to the feelings of the participants, thus validating the feelings of each. In so doing, the practitioner remains neutral rather than siding with or against either of the participants. The empathic responses also soften the impact of the participants' attacking messages.

When dysfunctional interactions such as the preceding occur, practitioners may need to address interventions to three or four persons or even the entire family.

4. Balance Interventions to Distribute Time and Focus Equitably

As diverse interactions occur among family members, practitioners must make choices about intervening in processes so that all members have opportunities to focus on their concerns. When intervening in such situations, remember that although it appears that some members of a family are monopolizing the interaction, exploration of the situation usually reveals that less aggressive members are contributing to the problem through their own inactivity. Thus, practitioners must address the responsibility *all* participants have in maintaining the status quo, highlighting *inaction* as well as *action* in their interventions.

5. Direct Messages from Participants to Each Other Because spouses and family members need to learn to communicate effectively with each other, practitioners must facilitate effective communication between them rather than acting as an intermediary. Clients often complain or express feelings to a practitioner that concern a spouse or other family members, and it is easy in such instances to fall into the pattern of communicating with individual members rather than directing them to talk to each other. But clients do not gain essential skill in communicating with each other by talking through the practitioner. Therefore, practitioners should often redirect messages to the parties whom they concern, which is accomplished by utilizing a message such as, "Would you tell your partner, please?"

Sometimes practitioners err by asking members to express directly to others messages that are hostile, blaming, or critical. Such messages may exacerbate an already strained situation and lead to arguing or fighting among participants. Before redirecting messages, then, you must consider the likely consequences of the ensuing interaction. When redirecting messages, actively intervene to facilitate positive interaction by coaching clients to own feelings, to translate complaints to expressions of needs or requests for change, to metacommunicate by clarifying positive intentions, and to avoid harsh tones of voice or hostile facial expressions.

In some instances, when clients begin to talk but do not face one another or maintain eye contact, you may need to interrupt and direct them to face one another and to look each other in the eye, as illustrated in the following message:

"Please stop for just a moment. You were talking to me, not to____ . Will you please start again, but this time talk directly to____ ."

Assisting Clients to Disengage from Conflict

One of the most common (and destructive) types of dysfunctional interaction involves arguments that quickly escalate, producing anger and resentment between participants. Intense competitiveness often is involved, and neither person is willing to let the other be one-up by winning the argument. The content issues involved are secondary to the fact that on a process level each participant is struggling to avoid being one-down, which would mean losing face or yielding power to the other.

To assist clients to avoid competitive struggles, you can use metacommunication about the dysfunctional process, emphasizing that *all* participants lose competitive arguments because of the negative feelings and emotional estrangement that ensue. It is also vital to stress that far more important than winning an argument is safeguarding mutual respect.

Having provided the rationale, you next introduce them to the concept of disengaging from conflicts, which simply means that participants arrest escalating arguments by declining to argue further. A graceful way that spouses or family members can disengage is by making a comment similar to the following: "Listen, it doesn't really matter who's right. If we argue, we just get mad at each other, and I don't want that to happen."

You can further assist couples to arrest arguing between sessions by teaching them to employ code words that signal the need to disengage. We recommend that you challenge partners to develop their own code words, an activity that most clients enjoy. Our clients have developed code words such as "truce," "draw," "peace," and "time out."

Although the process of disengagement is easy to learn, it is not simple for many clients to apply because of their virtually reflexive pattern of responding competitively. You will thus need to intervene frequently at first, gradually transferring responsibility to them for recognizing and disengaging from competitive struggles. Negotiating tasks of applying disengagement in their interaction between sessions is essential in transferring use of this process to their daily lives.

Modifying Dysfunctional Complementary Interaction

The converse of competitive interaction is characterized by submissiveness or passivity on the part of one partner in the face of dominance by the other. Over time, this *complementary* type of relationship often proves dysfunctional to one or both partners. The submissive partner may grow to resent the domineering one and may engage in passive resistance or openly challenge the other partner. Moreover, the domineering partner may weary of assuming the dominant role and/or devalue the passive partner, perceiving the passivity as weakness. In either event, destructive interaction may ensue, culminating in their seeking relationship therapy.

In modifying dysfunctional complementary relationships, it is vital to work with both partners so that you can assist each in adapting to changes that bring the relationship more into balance (assuming the partners have chosen that goal). The submissive partner will need assistance in becoming more assertive, and the dominant partner will need assistance in learning to share power and to encourage and reinforce assertiveness by the submissive partner. By relating to the partners as a system, you avoid the pitfall of severely disrupting the relationship by assisting one partner to make changes that are threatening or unacceptable to the other.

Negotiating Agreements for Reciprocal Changes

During the course of marital and family therapy, a client will sometimes spontaneously propose to make a specific change in behavior if another person will agree to make a reciprocal change. Such conditional proposals reflect the fact that people unconsciously attempt to maintain balance in relationships, a phenomenon described by Lederer and Jackson (1968) as the *quid pro quo*. For example, a marital partner may agree to be more affectionate if the spouse will agree to be less sexually demanding. Or parents may agree to permit their children to watch a favorite television program if the children complete their homework by a specified time. The reason clients are more receptive to making changes when other parties agree to make reciprocal changes are twofold. First, people are more prone to give when they know they are getting something in return. Second, when all involved parties agree to make changes, no single person loses face by appearing to be the sole cause of an interactional problem.

Contracting for reciprocal changes can be a powerful way of inducing change. A particular advantage of reciprocal contracting is that it counters the tendency of many clients to wait for others to initiate changes. Another advantage is that in working on reciprocal tasks, clients are *mutually* involved in a change venture. This mutual involvement may spark collaboration in other dimensions of relationships, an important gain for couples whose interactions have been largely competitive rather than collaborative.

Clients are unlikely to implement reciprocal contracts if they have not moved beyond competitive bickering and blaming each other for their problems. We thus recommend deferring use of this technique (unless clients spontaneously begin to negotiate) until you have assisted them to listen to each other attentively and to express their needs and wants. It is also essential that they demonstrate a commitment to wanting to improve their relationship. This latter condition is especially crucial, for as Jacobson (1978) has pointed out, if clients view their own or others' changes as emanating primarily from meeting stipulations of an agreement, rather than from caring and commitment to the relationship, they are likely to devalue the changes. Therefore, we strongly recommend you have clients explicitly clarify that caring for the other person is the primary factor motivating willingness to make changes (when such appears to be the case). A practitioner's efforts in this regard are illustrated in the following excerpt:

Practitioner [*to husband*]: Could you tell your partner your reasons for agreeing to the change we've discussed?

Husband: I think she must know that.

Practitioner [*to husband*]: Would you check that out with her?

Husband [*to wife*]: You know, don't you?

Wife: I think I do, but I'd like to hear it from you.

Husband: The only reason is because—dammit, you're the most important person in the world to me. [*Choking up.*] I know I haven't shown it, but it's true.

Wife: I appreciate that. It's nice to hear.

Practitioners can employ reciprocal contracts to enhance interaction in diverse problematic situations, as illustrated in the following:

- Husband agrees to visit wife's parents if wife agrees to talk with her mother about not taking over discipline of the children.

- Parents agree to increase allowance if child agrees to save a certain amount of it.

- Wife agrees to have meals on time if husband agrees to stop reading newspaper when called to dinner.

- Husband agrees to express feelings more if wife agrees to listen without interrupting or disagreeing.

In employing reciprocal contracting, it is wise to place maximal responsibility on clients for making proposals. By so doing, you enhance the investment of clients in proposed changes. Moreover, clients often generate innovative and constructive proposals that might not occur to a practitioner. To engage clients in making proposals, you can use a message such as: "It's clear both of you are unhappy with the situation. I'd be interested in hearing each of you make proposals as to what you could do to make it better." With some encouragement, most clients make proposals, but you may need to prompt them by suggesting possible reciprocal actions. As you mutually consider proposals, it is important to guard against encouraging clients to undertake overly ambitious actions. Clients (and naive practitioners as well) are prone to want to effect major changes immediately, which is commendable but unrealistic. Bear in mind that people change by increments and that encouraging them to attempt overly difficult tasks sets them up for failure and disappointment. Moreover, failure in implementing tasks tends to cause clients to lose confidence in the helping process. It is vital, therefore, to encourage modest tasks that are commensurate with clients' capacities and motivation. By successfully accomplishing small reciprocal changes, clients experience the benefits of both giving and getting, which enhances their motivation to attempt additional reciprocal tasks.

Initial task exchanges should be relatively simple and likely to succeed. When intense conflict has marked the interaction, initial tasks may include reciprocal exchanges that do not require face-to-face contact. For example, a child agrees to clean up his room. The mother agrees to purchase the child's favorite brand of cereal.

Another caution you should observe in negotiating reciprocal contracts is that clients should avoid undertaking *multiple* changes at the same time. Multiple tasks dilute efforts and reduce chances for successful accomplishment. Single changes, by contrast, foster concentrated efforts and enhance the likelihood of successful results.

As clients discuss proposals, you should attend carefully to nonverbal messages that suggest misgivings, apprehension, or opposition to carrying out the contract. Clients are sometimes hesitant to express their opposition and may agree to a contract to which they are not actually committed and have no intention of fulfilling. This is particularly true in relationships which include persons with different levels of power such as parent and child. Empathic responsiveness to such nonverbal cues, however, may encourage them to disclose misgivings. By exploring the nature and source of misgivings, you may be able to assist clients to resolve them. If they prove unreceptive to the proposed changes, you can encourage them to identify changes they are willing to make. Our point is that it is critical to avoid contracts and tasks that clients are unlikely to accomplish successfully.

After eliciting or offering one or more feasible proposals for a reciprocal contract and determining that clients are willing to carry out the contract, you assist them to reach an explicit agreement. This agreement specifies tasks clients are to implement before the next session. It is important to plan with clients for implementing the task by following the steps of the task-implementation sequence, delineated in Chapter 13. As you plan with clients for task implementation, it is also vital to stress that each person must exercise *good faith* in carrying out his or her part of the contract, as illustrated in the following message:

"I am pleased that you have both agreed to make the changes we've discussed because the changes can make things better for both of you. To carry out these changes successfully, however, each of you will need to carry out your part no matter what the other does. If you wait for your partner to carry out his or her part first, you may both be waiting for the other to make the first move by the time of our next session. Remember, failure by the other person to keep the contract should be no excuse for you to do likewise. If your partner doesn't keep the agreement, you can take satisfaction in knowing you did your part."

Emphasizing the individual responsibility of all participants in the helping process to fulfill their respective commitments, as in the preceding message, counters the tendency of clients to justify their inaction in subsequent sessions by asserting, "He (or she) didn't carry out his part. I knew he wouldn't, so I didn't do my part."

During the next session, it is vital to follow up on clients' experience in implementing their agreement. If results have been favorable, discussion of their reactions often results in further expressions of positive feedback between participants and leads to discussion of other ways of achieving further positive interaction. If one or more clients have not fulfilled their agreement, you can explore their interactions of the previous week, focusing on obstacles that prevented them from doing so.

Catching the Family's Attention

Used discriminately and in context, creative interventions aid practitioners in interrupting dysfunctional interactions of couples and families. In *101 Interventions in Family Therapy*, Nelson and Trepper (1992) provide a collection of practical and imaginative interventions that can aid the therapeutic process.

Teaching Clients to Make Requests

Most clients have difficulty identifying what they need from others and expressing those needs clearly and fully to others. Many times when communication breaks down it is because clients demand, rather than invite, others to respond to their wishes. Practitioners can make extensive headway in modifying destructive processes of clients by encouraging them to make clear requests to others when they want changes.

Almost always underutilized by clients, requesting is a simple but powerful skill that practitioners can quickly teach clients by introducing them to the following concepts:

- On the flip side of any complaint is an unmet need or want. Ask for what you need, then, instead of complaining about what you are not getting.

- Avoid canceling out positive requests with negative riders: "I know you won't want to do this, but ..."

- Treat your request as a favor others can grant you, not as something to which you are entitled, using language such as: "Would you be willing ...?" or "I'd appreciate..."

- Agree that each party has the right to make any request, but each also has the right to turn down a request. Also agree, because parties are on the same team, that no one will just emphatically say "no" to requests. To requests that don't appeal, make counterproposals ("What if I did this instead?") or ask for others ("Could you propose another avenue for solving the problem?").

- Agree that neither party will say "yes" to a request unless he or she can grant that request without resentment.

Teaching clients how to make clear requests is a form of empowerment, equipping them with an on-the-spot skill to negotiate their differences with others.

Helping Clients Give Up the Past

No relationship over time escapes the accumulation of past hurts. Often those hurts are recycled by couples and families, providing ongoing fodder for fights and arguments. Dwelling on the past, in fact, is one of the most common and destructive problems clients encounter as they attempt to communicate.

Practitioners can aid clients in giving up their habitual focus on the past by asking them not to talk about any problem more than 24 hours old. Declaring a moratorium on the past brings many of the destructive communications of clients to a screeching halt. Practitioners can also ask clients to save their "problem talk" for therapy sessions until they have acquired effective problem-solving strategies, pointing out that it is fruitless to continue in wheelspinning conflict. In later stages of therapy, practitioners might also consider engaging clients in a "past hurts" exercise. In this exercise, clients make individual lists of all the past hurts they still carry with them, no matter how long ago the injuries occurred or how ridiculous they feel about harboring them. Clients then rate their "hurts" on a scale of 1 to 10 (1 = low; 10 = high-intensive hurt) and negotiate together over which past hurts they would be willing to forget or "trade."

MODIFYING MISCONCEPTIONS AND DISTORTED PERCEPTIONS

Clients' cognitions often embody erroneous beliefs that produce dissatisfaction in marital and family relationships, engender resentments toward others, and contribute to dysfunctional interaction. Three common examples of mistaken beliefs manifested in couples, families, and groups are:

1. It's important to get even with people who hurt you or take advantage of you.

2. All people in authority (especially police) exploit their authority to the detriment of others.

3. We must conceal the fact that we have conflict in our family; otherwise, people will think badly of us.

Unrealistic expectations of others and myths are two other forms of misconceptions that contribute to interactional problems. As with rules, myths and unrealistic expectations often are not readily apparent, and practitioners must sometimes infer them by exploring clients' expectations of each other, of marriage, and of family relationships. Myths are also similar to rules in that they govern family operations by shaping beliefs, expectations of spouses, family members, and other relatives. Lederer and Jackson (1968), Glick and Kessler (1974), and Goldenberg and Goldenberg (1991) have identified numerous myths and unrealistic expectations that can profoundly influence interactions in couple and family relationships. Common examples of such myths include the following:

1. Family members should meet all their emotional needs within their family.

2. Partners should know without being told their partners' needs, feelings, and wants.

3. If partners are well matched and love one another, a successful relationship will evolve with no effort.

To eliminate misconceptions and dispel myths, draw them to the awareness of clients, gently assist them to accept the error in the misconceptions, and focus on how they affect couple, family, and group interactions. Because misconceptions and myths commonly protect clients from having to face certain unpleasant realities and to make changes that are perceived as threatening, clients often do not relinquish them without a struggle. To facilitate their making essential changes, you must recognize that making changes entails resolving fears and risking the consequences of learning and implementing new behavior. Responding empathically to these fears and providing emotional support to clients as they struggle with their ambivalence toward change often supply the impetus that clients need to change their patterns of interaction.

To illustrate this process, we consider a family in which an adolescent, age 17, manifests extreme tension and anxiety. During family sessions, it has become apparent that the parents have exerted intense pressure on him to perform well academically and have made it clear they expect him to become a doctor. It has also been apparent that they mistakenly believe the myth that by trying hard enough anyone can become anything he wants. In an effort to reduce the pressure on the son by dispelling the myth and modifying the parents' expectation, the practitioner arranges to meet separately with the parents. The following excerpt is taken from that session.

Practitioner: I've been very concerned that Gary has been making an almost superhuman effort to do well in chemistry and physics but still is floundering in these subjects. I get the impression he believes he has to become a doctor at any price and that one reason he's so uptight is that he realizes he isn't cutting it despite his efforts. It's terribly important to him to meet your expectations, and he's falling short even though he drives himself.

Father: I know he's working hard, but it'll come. He can become a doctor if he really wants to. I could have been a doctor if I had applied myself, but I didn't. I goofed off too much. I don't want Gary to make that mistake.

Practitioner: I can sense your concern for Gary. Still, I've gained the impression that both of you convey to your children the belief that they can become anything they want and that Gary is blaming himself because he's not making it, no matter how hard he tries.

Mother: Don't you think anyone can succeed in anything if they try hard enough?

Practitioner: That belief doesn't square with what we know about differences between people. People have different aptitudes and talents. For example, I couldn't be a dentist, jeweler, surgeon, or pianist or handle many other types of work that require finger dexterity. I couldn't be an engineer or draftsman because I have difficulties in visualizing spatial relationships. Everyone has certain aptitudes and certain limitations. What's important in career planning is discovering what our aptitudes are and making choices that match them. I'll bet both of you can identify talents and limitations you have.

Notice that in seeking to dispel the family myth, the practitioner focused on the destructive impact of the myth on Gary. Notice also that the practitioner authentically disclosed his own limitations. This tactic switched the focus from the abstract to the concrete and provided strong evidence of the error of their belief. The practitioner then further attempted to invalidate the myth by asking them to apply it to themselves.

Practitioners also frequently encounter clients who have distorted perceptions of one another that contribute to dysfunctional interactions. As you will recall from Chapter 10, labeling others is a common form of such perceptual distortions. The effect of labeling is tantamount to that of wearing blinders, for labels obscure perceptions of others' strengths, limitations, feelings, beliefs, interests, goals, attitudes, hopes, and the like. Instead, one's perceptions are limited to attributes and behaviors that are inherent in the label.

When practitioners observe the process of labeling (e.g., "You're lazy," "stupid," "frigid," "rigid," or "undependable"), it is important to intervene, highlighting the negative impact of labeling on the person being labeled (labeling produces defensiveness and resentment) and the fact that labeling limits awareness of the other person, produces friction, and stifles the development of closeness. In focusing on the destructive impact of labeling, the practitioner must be careful to label the process and not the client who has labeled another person. Moreover, it is important to respond empathically to the frustrations the client experiences with the "labeled" person, as illustrated in the following example.

Wife [*to husband*]: I came home so excited about the teacher's report of Jamie's progress. So I tell you, and what do I get? Zip, that's what. You're just a wet blanket!

Practitioner: Just a moment. Let's look at what's happening. [*To wife.*] You're saying you were, and still are, disappointed with Rex's response. I can sense your frustration. But by labeling him as a wet blanket, you're putting him on the defensive, and you're going to get sidetracked. Let's see if we can stay with both of your feelings and understand what both of you are experiencing right now.

After delabeling the other person, the practitioner assists the clients to explore feelings and cognitions and to make specific requests for change.

MODIFYING DYSFUNCTIONAL FAMILY ALIGNMENTS

As we emphasized in Chapter 10, all families develop patterns of affiliation between members that either enhance or impair opportunities for individual growth or the family's ability to carry out operations vital to its survival. Interventions to modify alignments are generally indicated:

1. When bonds are weak between spouses or other family members or when one family member is alienated from others.

2. When there are enmeshed alliances between members that block them from developing appropriate bonds with other members (or outsiders).

3. When two members of a family attempt to cope with dissatisfaction or conflict in their relationship by forming a coalition with a third family member.

This phenomenon, referred to as *triangulation*, most frequently involves marital partners who use a child as a pawn in their struggles.

4. When family members are "disengaged" or alienated from one another, tending to go their own ways with little reliance on each other for emotional support.

5. When members of the family have formed alliances with persons outside the immediate family (e.g., friends and relatives) that interfere with their performing appropriate family roles or providing appropriate emotional support to other family members.

In intervening to modify alignments, the practitioner may endeavor to achieve any of the following:[7]

- To *disassemble* an alliance, which involves breaking it down. For example, a practitioner may assist a single parent to disengage from a destructive relationship with a boyfriend.

- To *develop* alliances, which involves cultivating new alliances or strengthening relationships that are underdeveloped. A practitioner can thus assist a new stepfather and stepson in exploring ways they can develop a relationship or can work with siblings who have been estranged to strengthen their emotional bonds.

- To *reinforce* an alliance, which involves acting to maintain the alliance or to amplify its scope and/or strength. For instance, a practitioner may enable parents to increase their ability to operate as an effective executive subsystem.

- To *loosen* an alliance, which involves helping members who heretofore have been enmeshed to reinvest some of their emotional energy in others.

Before practitioners intervene to modify family alignments, they should involve the family in determining whether and in what ways such changes should take place. The practitioner's first task in this respect is to assist family members to observe the nature of their alignments. This may be accomplished by asking questions that stimulate family members to consider their alignments:

"If you had a difficult problem and needed help, whom would you seek out in the family?"

"Sometimes members of a family feel closer to some

members than to others and may pair up or group together. Which members of your family, if any, group together?"

"In most families, members argue to some extent. With whom do you argue? With whom do other members argue?"

The practitioner can also bring alignments and coalitions to the family's attention as they are manifested in the session. For example:

[*To partner*]: It seems that you're the hub of the family. Most of the conversation seems to be directed through you, while you [*other partner*] seem to be an observer or onlooker to the family's discussion.

As family members become aware of their alignments, the practitioner must assist them in considering whether they wish to become closer to others and to identify obstacles that could prevent that from happening.

Another avenue for enabling family members to observe their alliances and to make decisions concerning possible changes involves asking them to make a drawing on a sheet of paper showing family relationships. Members are instructed to use rectangles in their drawing to represent each person in the family. Rectangles can be of any size and located any place on the paper. Practitioners coach family members to position the rectangles in ways that depict relative closeness and distance among family members. After family members have completed their drawings, the practitioner asks them to draw their family relationships as they would *like* them to be on the other side of the paper. In a subsequent discussion, the practitioner first asks members in turn to share their drawings of existing family relationships and then assists the family to formulate conclusions concerning the nature of alignments and the emotional closeness and distance that members experience in their relationships with others (e.g., "It appears, then, that father and Jeff feel quite close to each other, but that you, Mike, don't feel as close to your father as Jeff does."). The practitioner then asks members to explain their second drawings that show how they would like family relationships to be. During the discussion, the practitioner highlights the desires of members to increase their closeness to others and assists them to formulate goals that reflect changes they would like to make.

Yet another strategy for assisting members to analyze their family structure is to involve them in family sculpting (Constantine, 1978; Jefferson, 1978; Papp, 1976). This technique, which involves having members arrange themselves spatially in a tableau to create a physical representation of the family's relationships, starkly reveals the family's alliances. Since family sculpting is a potent technique for helping families to discern dysfunctional family alignments and to recognize the need to realign their relationships, we suggest that you become adept at using this strategy.

Practitioners' actions to engage the family in discussions related to their family structures often stimulate family members to begin changing the nature of their alignments. Practitioners can also assist members to modify various alignments by employing one or more of the following interventions.

Strengthening Parental Coalitions and Marking Generational Boundaries

In optimally functioning families, strong parental coalitions exist, and generational boundaries are clearly demarcated so that parents neither triangulate children nor permit them to intrude into the parental systems. In working with families that manifest weak parental coalitions, therefore, practitioners face the challenge of assisting partners to strengthen their relationships and to present a united front in their interactions with their children. Otherwise, children learn to relate primarily to the most permissive parent and turn to that parent with requests for privileges, emotional support, and affection. Some such children become adept at playing one parent against the other, which fosters parental divisiveness and produces strain between children and the "excluded" parent. The hazards for the development of such an inimical family climate are especially great in stepfamilies with older children because loyalties and emotional bonding between parents and stepchildren often are lacking. The difficult challenge that confronts such families is to develop unity and cohesiveness when two families have joined together.

Strategies for strengthening marital coalitions include the following:[8]

1. Interspersing conjoint meetings involving only the partners with meetings of the total family and with the children of a subunit. Meeting with only the parents enables practitioners to clarify the need for a united front and to develop relevant tasks aimed at strengthening the parental coalition. Such meetings also enhance the visibility of generational boundaries.

2. Negotiating tasks with partners to engage in some conjoint activities outside the home that exclude children. Parents are to plan activities independent of their children and to implement them, leaving a note informing the children only that they will be gone for a specified time. Upon returning, they are to offer no more than a brief matter-of-fact explanation, and in no event are they to respond defensively. Repeated implementation of such conjoint activities establishes generational boundaries and conveys a clear message to children that parents are united and committed to safeguarding their private domain.

3. Negotiating agreements between parents that they will present a united front in parent-child transactions requiring decision making and/or disciplinary actions. Practitioners assist parents to agree that they will remove themselves from the presence of children to decide upon an appropriate course of action. Parents further agree that when a child approaches only one parent, that parent defers a decision until she or he can discuss the matter with the other and reach a joint decision (exceptions must be made, of course, when an immediate decision is essential). Parents further agree that neither will intervene when the other is disciplining a child, unless it is to support the parent.

4. Negotiating the following agreements among couples that will serve as decision-rules for relating in the marital relationship. Couples may:

- Tell the world when they have something positive to say about the relationship and tell each other when they have something negative to say, with the objective of working out the problem.
- Preserve the privacy and integrity of the relationship by keeping confidential vital details of their intimate life and the partner's personal life.
- Refrain from making the other partner the brunt of jokes or in other ways embarrassing that person in front of others.
- Act as an executive unit in making important financial decisions.
- Act together if there are problems with "outsiders" (e.g., in-laws) to solve the problem in the best interest of everyone concerned, focusing on "what will help" rather than on "who's to blame."

Couples may also adopt guidelines for family relating identified by Larsen (1991) that clarify boundaries of family relationships and significantly reduce family conflict by agreeing to:

- Manage problems of children privately as often as possible, which protects each child's privacy and the integrity of each parent-child relationship.
- Allow each partner to manage his or her own problems with a child without intervention—unless the other partner is being truly hurtful to a child. Critical differences in style are to be ironed out in private conferences.
- Expect that each spouse will handle the parenting problems he or she "owns."
- Eliminate name calling, labeling, screaming, or otherwise emotionally or physically abusing each other.
- Refrain from insisting that one spouse "side" with the other against a child.
- Refrain from letting one child help "parent" another child.
- Refrain from forming alliances with one child against another.

- Refrain from fighting in front of children; from drawing children into disagreements against a spouse; or from forming lasting political alliances with a child against a spouse.

- Refrain from revealing a child's confidences to outsiders.

- Refrain from criticizing or talking negatively about one family member in front of another. This includes not complaining to a child about the other partner or burdening a child with problems belonging to the parental relationship.

Strengthening boundaries is a quest for most families and couples and may be an issue through the entire course of therapy. Practitioners can aid clients in restructuring boundaries and dismantling dysfunctional political alliances with on-the-spot interventions that show the relevance of the preceding decision-rules for relating. When appropriate, practitioners may even review the preceding list with couples or families to aid them in acquiring these relationship strategies.

Utilizing Space

Practitioners may employ space as a tool to facilitate communication and to strengthen and weaken emotional bonds by directing certain family members to sit next to each other (when seeking to strengthen bonds) or placing family members between certain others (when seeking to weaken attachments). Moreover, by having a person who often takes a plaintiff's role sit next to rather than across from a person whom she or he usually complains about or attacks, the practitioner takes the latter "out of the line of fire," thereby disrupting the usual pattern of interaction.

Arranging Sessions for Various Groupings of Family Members

Based on a determination (in consultation with the family) as to which alignments need to be modified, the practitioner may wish to arrange sessions with individuals so as to enhance opportunities of members to make designated changes. If a mother and son are involved in an enmeshed relationship that excludes the father, the practitioner can arrange to see the father and son alone for several sessions to plan ways of developing a closer relationship. During this time, the practitioner continues to meet conjointly with the spouses for the purpose of assisting them to strengthen their marital relationship. *When practitioners endeavor to loosen bonds between clients, they should simultaneously work to strengthen other bonds or to develop other alliances so that clients are not left with unmet emotional needs.*

Formulating Tasks That Strengthen Relationships or Encourage Rearrangements in Alignments

Practitioners can modify various alignments by asking various groupings of family members to assume relevant tasks. For example, when bonds are strong between a father and one son and weak between the father and another son, it is important to preserve the strong bonding in the first relationship while strengthening the bonding in the second. The practitioner may thus formulate a task with the father to spend a specified amount of time daily with *each* son and plan activities involving both sons at least once a week. In another situation, a practitioner may seek to modify a parent-child coalition that is maintained by the mother's encouraging the child to tattle on another child who is excluded from the coalition. To dismantle the coalition, the practitioner can ask the favored child to assume a task of reporting to the mother the *positive* behaviors of the other child during the week. In turn, the practitioner can negotiate with the mother the task of refraining from accepting negative feedback (e.g., "I don't need to know about that. Thank you anyway") and rewarding the favored child for conveying positive information about the other.

KEEPING FAMILIES TOGETHER

In preceding sections, we discussed significant interventions to modify the processes of families and to enhance the functioning of members. At times, however, the stresses on families are so great that traditional ways of treating families are ineffective. In instances in which severely disrupted families are beset with violence, physical or sexual abuse, or children have become emotionally disturbed or delinquent, children are often removed from families.

In response to a rise in the number of seriously disturbed children being removed from their families, family preservation services have emerged as an alternative to immediate out-of-home placement for children and families. Intensive services are provided in crisis at a point when removal of the child is imminent (Maluccio, 1990, p. 17). Such services have a strong congruence with the values underlying this book: the belief that people can change, considering clients as colleagues, a commitment to facilitating empowerment for families, and a view that it is the practitioner's responsibility to instill hope (ibid., p. 20). In addition, the time-limited, crisis-focused nature of the work with an emphasis on tangible, mutually agreed upon goals is consistent with our perspective (Cole & Duva, 1990). Intensive family preservation services include assessment, contracting, organizing linkages to other resource providers and support networks, and counseling. The approach has been adapted for use with many populations including first-generation immigrant families and lesbian households (Faria, 1991; Sandau-Beckler & Salcido, 1991). While intensive family preservation services appear to prevent the placement of some children for some period of time, differences in rates compared to control groups who have not received intensive services appears to diminish over time. Rather than perceiving intensive-home-based services as a panacea for problems of children and families, it is perhaps better to see such services as an important alternative that must be available when problems occur and placement is considered (Wells & Biegel, 1991, pp. 242–249).

NOTES

1 Because of the complexity of family issues and processes, practitioners usually meet with families for sessions of an hour and a half.

2 Notice that the practitioner picked up from where she had left off with the father by utilizing an empathic response that reflected the father's feelings.

3 In this instance, the practitioner employs an additive empathic response to reach for the positive feelings inherent in the client's message, a potent technique for highlighting caring feelings of participants and for facilitating more positive interaction.

4 The practitioner persists to get Jed to talk to his father by repeating her instructions. Clients often need extensive coaching in learning to talk directly to significant others about sensitive topics.

5 A small mechanical hand counter is useful for keeping daily tallies.

6 Notice that the practitioner employed the technique of asking family members to report on their own behavior. This technique assists clients in reflecting on their own (rather than others') contributions to dysfunctional interactions.

7 Several of the items delineated were adapted from a chapter by Aponte and Van Deusen (1981), which discusses structural family therapy.

8 We wish to acknowledge that these strategies are based in part on techniques described by Masson and O'Byrne (1984).

Chapter 17

Intervening in Social Work Groups

As we noted in Chapter 11, social workers operate in a variety of group formats including task, treatment, and support groups. In any group with social work goals, it is the task of the leader to intervene facilitatively to further that group's progress toward goal achievement. In treatment groups, a leader's role is particularly challenging, requiring in-depth, balanced interventions to facilitate growth of both individuals and the group. To add to the complexity of the role, a leader must be astute in sorting through the maze of multilevel communication to bring meaning to the group's experience, to shape the group's therapeutic character, and to provide direction and focus to the group's processes at critical moments. Finally, the leader must formulate all interventions within the context of the stages of development through which a group progresses to reach full maturity. Similarly, in a task group, the leader plays a variety of facilitative roles in assisting the group in meeting its objectives. This chapter focuses primarily on treatment groups with additional content on task groups in the final section.

It is toward the achievement of such ends that we dedicate this chapter. Since the leader's interventions are inextricably related to a group's stages of development, we begin at that point.

STAGES OF GROUP DEVELOPMENT

All groups go through natural stages of development in their progression toward full maturity, varying only in tempo and in the complexity of issues in each stage. Understanding these stages of group development is paramount, assisting leaders to anticipate the thematic behaviors characteristic of each stage and to recognize the significance of behaviors that occur in the group. Comprehension of stages also allows a leader to intervene in appropriate ways to encourage the group's development and the normative behaviors that support its treatment objectives. In addition, the leader is able to remove obstacles that impair the development of the group or the individuals within it and to make tempered choices regarding the level of leader activity necessary at any one time across the lifespan of a group.

Without knowledge of stages, leaders are prone to make errors, such as expecting group members to begin in-depth explorations in initial sessions or concluding that they have failed in their role when groups manifest the turmoil and discord typical of early development. Leaders may also ignore rather than encourage fleeting positive behaviors that herald the group's approaching a more mature stage of development. Further, they may not intervene at critical periods in a group's development to assist groups, for example, to "stay on task," to "count in" all members in decision making, to foster free expression of feelings, or to adopt many other behaviors that are hallmarks of a seasoned group.

Various models of group development provide practitioners frameworks for organizing a large body of observations and group properties and identifying thematic group behaviors. All the models identify progressive steps in group development, although they may organize these steps into four, five, or even six stages. For our purposes we utilize a model developed by Garland, Jones, and Kolodny (1965), which delineates the following five stages:

1. Preaffiliation.
2. Power and control.
3. Intimacy.
4. Differentiation.
5. Separation.

Stage 1. Preaffiliation—Approach and Avoidance Behavior

The frame of reference used by Garland et al. to describe the group's initial stage is that of *approach-avoidance* behavior of members, whose tentativeness toward involvement in the group is reflected in their vacillating willingness to assume responsibility, to interact with others, and to support program activities and events. Hesitancy to participate is also shown by tentative speech, and silence is common as members operate as separate individuals and are preoccupied with their own problems and feelings of uneasiness and apprehension that emanate from their first encounter with the group. Often fearful and suspicious, members tend to be apprehensive regarding the responses of others to their expressions, fearing possible domination, aggression, isolation, rejection, and hostility. Thus, behavior is wary, sometimes even provocative, as members assess possible social threats and attempt to discern the kinds of behaviors the

group wants and expects. Members also tend to identify each other by status and roles and engage in social rituals, stereotyped introductions, and detailed intellectual discussions. They are uncertain as to how the group will benefit them, and their understanding of the group's purpose is fuzzy. At times, members employ testing operations to "size up" other members, to test the group's limits, to find out how competent the leader is, and to determine to what extent the leader will safeguard the rights of members and protect them from feared hurt and humiliation. Members also move tentatively toward the group at times as they seek to define common ground with other members, search for viable roles, and seek approval, acceptance, and respect. Much of the initial communication in the group is also directed toward the leader, and some members may openly demand that the practitioner assume a "take charge" approach by forcefully making decisions regarding group issues and structure and by issuing prompt directives to control the behavior of members.

Stage 2. Power and Control— A Time of Transition

The first stage merges imperceptibly into the second as members, having determined that the group experience is potentially safe and rewarding and worth preliminary emotional investment, shift their concerns to matters related to autonomy, power, and control. The frame of reference for this stage is that of *transition* in that members must endure the ambiguity and turmoil of change from a nonintimate to an intimate system of relationships while they try to establish a frame of reference whereby the new situation becomes understandable and predictable. Moving from a struggle of whether they "belong" in the group, members now become preoccupied with how they "rank" in relation to other members. Turning to others like themselves for support and protection, members evolve subgroups and a hierarchy of statuses, or social pecking order. Gradually, the processes of the group become stylized as various factions emerge and relationships solidify. Conflicts between opposing subgroups often occur in this stage, and members may team together in expressing anger toward the leader, other authority figures, or outsiders. Disenchantment with the group may show itself in hostilities, withdrawal, or in confusion about the group's purposes. Verbal abuse, attacks, and rejection of lower status members may also occur, and isolated members of the group who do not have the protection of a subgroup may discontinue coming to sessions. Attrition in membership may also take place as individuals find outside pursuits more attractive than the conflicted group experience; depleted membership, indeed, may put the group's very survival in jeopardy.

Stage 3. Intimacy—Developing a Familial Frame of Reference

Having clarified and resolved many of the issues related to personal autonomy, initiative, and power, the group moves from the "preintimate" power and control stage to that of intimacy. As the group enters this stage, conflicts fade, personal involvement between members intensifies, and there is growing recognition of the significance of the group experience. Members also experience an increase in morale and "we-ness," a deepening commitment to the group's purpose, and heightened motivation to carry out plans and tasks that support the group's objectives. Mutual trust also increases as members begin to acknowledge each other's uniqueness, spontaneously disclose feelings and problems, and seek the opinion of the group. In order to achieve desired intimacy, however, members may suppress negative feelings that could produce conflict between themselves and others. In contrast to earlier sessions, members express genuine concern for absent members and may reach out to invite them to return to the group.

During this period of development, a group "character" also emerges as the group evolves cul-

ture, style, and a set of values. Clear norms are established, based on personal interests, affection, and other positive forces. Roles also take on form as members find ways of contributing to the group, and leadership patterns become firmly settled. The frame of reference for members is a familial one as members liken their experience to that of their own nuclear families, occasionally referring to other members as siblings or to the leader as the "mother" or "father" of the group.

Stage 4. Differentiation—Developing Group Identity and an Internal Frame of Reference

The fourth stage is marked by tight group cohesion and harmony as members come to terms with intimacy and make choices to draw closer to others in the group. In this stage, group-centered operations are achieved and a dynamic balance between individual and group needs evolves. Members, who participate in different and complementary ways, experience greater freedom of personal expression and come to feel genuinely accepted and valued as their feelings and ideas are validated by others in the group. Gradually, the group becomes a mutual-aid system in which members spontaneously give emotional supplies in proportion to the needs of each individual.

In experiencing newfound freedom and intimacy, members begin to perceive the group experience as unique, and as the group creates its own mores and structure, in a sense it becomes its own frame of reference. Customs and traditional ways of operating emerge, and the group may adopt a "club" name or insignia that accurately reflects the group's purpose. The group's energy is now channeled into carrying out purposes and tasks that are clearly understood and accepted. New roles, more flexible and functional than before, are developed to support the group's activity, and organizational structures (e.g., officers, dues, attendance expectations, rules) may evolve. Status hierarchies also tend to be less rigid, and members may assume leadership roles spontaneously as the need for particular expertise or abilities arises.

By the time the group reaches the differentiation stage, members have accumulated experience in "working through problems" and have gained skill in analyzing their own feelings and those of others in communicating their needs and positions effectively, in offering support to others, and in grasping the complex interrelationships that have developed in the group. Having become self-conscious about their own operations, groups bring conflict out into the open and identify obstacles that impede their progress. All decisions are ultimately the unanimous reflection of the group and are rigidly respected. Disagreements are not suppressed or overridden by premature group action, but rather the group carefully considers the position of any dissenters and attempts to resolve differences and to achieve consensus among members. New entrants serve as catalysts and may express their amazement at the insight shared by older members, who in turn become increasingly convinced of the value of the group. Members may now publicize their group meetings among peers, whereas previously membership in the group may have been linked with secret feelings of shame. Secure in their roles and relationships in the group, members may become interested in meeting with other groups or in bringing in outside culture.

Stage 5. Separation—A Time of Breaking Away

During this phase, members begin to separate, loosening the intense bonds often established with other members and with the leader, and to search for new resources and ties to satisfy needs. Group members are likely to experience a broad range of feelings about leaving the group and the approach of group termination may set off a number of reactions, the diversity of which is reminiscent of the approach-avoidance maneuvers displayed in Stage 1. Members may feel anxiety again, this time in relation to moving apart and breaking bonds that have been formed. There may be outbursts of anger against the leader and others at the thought of the group ending, the reappearance of quarrels that were previously settled, and an increase of dependence on the leader. Denial of the positive meaning of the group experience is not uncommon. These separation reactions may appear in flashes or clusters as members attempt to square their positive feelings about the group with their subconscious feelings of abandonment, rejection, and apprehension over the group's ending.

Termination is also a time of evaluation, of contemplation of the work achieved, and of consolidation of learning. It is a time of finishing unfinished business; of getting and giving focused feedback; and of savoring the good times and the close relationships gained in the group. Members, who have often begun to pull back their group investments and to put more energy into outside interests, speak of fears, hopes, and concerns about the future and about one another. There is often focus on how to apply what has been learned in the group to other situations and talk of reunions or follow-up meetings.

STAGES OF GROUP DEVELOPMENT AND LEADER ROLE

As suggested earlier, the role of the leader shifts and changes with the evolution of the group. Referring to earlier work by Lang (1972), Henry (1992) conceptualizes the leader as enacting certain roles and occupying different locations throughout the group's life span. The shifting *role* of leader is cast along a continuum from primary to variable to facilitative, depending on the needs, capacities, and characteristics of the group's membership and its stage of development. Likewise, the leader occupies a *location* in the group that may be cast along a continuum ranging from central to pivotal to peripheral, depending again on the same variables.

The leader's role—a primary one at the outset of the group—is to select candidates for the group.

The leader is also in a central location in gathering the people who will comprise the group. The leader continues to retain this primacy and centrality during the preconvening phase of the group as he or she brings structure to the group, prethinks its nature and function, conducts pregroup interviews, and negotiates reciprocal contracts with each prospective member. This set of role and location conditions prevails throughout the beginning phase of the group as the leader initiates and directs group discussion, encourages participation, and begins blending the reciprocal contracts with members into a mutual group contract.

As the group evolves to a new level of connectedness, the leader intentionally takes a variable role and occupies a pivotal location with respect to the group. According to Henry (1992):

> As the worker steps back from the central location and primary role, the members begin to supplant some of what the worker has been doing. In the vernacular of cinematography, the worker fades out as the group system comes up. However, because the group's (internal and external) systems are not yet stabilized at full functioning capacity, the worker needs to let the process run at its own speed and sometimes needs to move back in to help keep the system afloat. This is why the worker's role is referred to as variable, and the worker's location as pivotal. This role and location will be part of the mutual contract that is being negotiated at this time. (p. 34)

Henry notes that the leader's variable role and pivotal location continues in the group during the conflict/disequilibrium stage (the Power and Control stage in Garland, Jones, and Kolodny terminology). When the group enters its maintenance or working phase (the Differentiation and Intimacy stages), the leader assumes a facilitative role and occupies a peripheral location. Inasmuch as the group has achieved full capacity to govern itself, the leader is in a resource role rather than a primary role. "He or she will be at the boundary of the system," observes Henry, "because the group is maintaining itself, internal and external systems are 'go,' it conceives of itself as an entity, and it is functioning in a self-directed way" (p. 34).

As the group moves into its separation or termination phase, Henry notes, the leader once again returns to a primary role and central location to supplant the divesting of members, who are launching their own independent courses. In this role the leader aids the group in working through any regression to earlier stages of development and assures the successful ending of the group.

The shifts in role and location can be inferred by studying Table 17-1, which illustrates the evolution of the leader's focus as a group advances through stages of development. Information contained in the table comes from a variety of sources, including Garland, Jones, and Kolodny (1965); Rose (1989); Henry (1992); and Corey and Corey (1992).

INTERVENTION INTO STRUCTURAL ELEMENTS OF A GROUP

The primacy of the leader's role and the centrality of the leader's location is related at one level to the ability of members to assume responsibility for the treatment functions of the group. At another level, these leader positions are related to the relative need to intervene to shape the group's therapeutic character, thereby creating a vehicle for the change process of individuals. In that respect, across stages of group development, the leader pays particular attention to the shaping of the following group elements:

- Cohesion.
- Normative structure.
- Role structure.
- Subgroup structure.
- Leadership structure.

It is, in fact, the evolution of these structures over time that encompasses the phenomenon of group development (Rose, 1989; Yalom, 1985). Because of their importance in determining the relative therapeutic nature and impact of the group, these elements are considered successively in sections that follow.

TABLE 17-1 STAGES. DYNAMICS, AND LEADER FOCUS

STAGE	DYNAMICS	LEADER FOCUS
Preaffiliation	Arms-length exploration	Observes and assesses
	Approach/avoidance	Clarifies group objectives
	Issues of trust, preliminary commitment	Establishes group guidelines
	Intellectualization of problems	Encourages development of personal goals
	Interaction based on superficial attributes or experiences	Clarifies aspirations and expectations of members
	Protection of self; low-risk behavior	Encourages discussion of fears, ambivalence
	Milling around	Gently invites trust
	Sizing up of leader and other members	Gives support; allows distance
	Formulation of individual and group goals	Facilitates exploration
	Leader viewed as responsible for group	Provides group structure
	Member evaluation as to whether group is safe and meets needs	Contracts for help-seeking, help-giving roles
	Fear of self-disclosure, rejection	Facilitates linkages among members
	Uncertainty regarding group purpose	Models careful listening
	Little commitment to goals or group	Focuses on resistance
		Assures opportunities for participation
Power and Control	Rebellion; power struggles	Protects safety of individuals and property
	Political alignments forged to increase power	
	Issues of status, ranking, and influence	Clarifies power struggle
	Complaints regarding group structure, process	Turns issues back to group
	Challenges to leader's role	Encourages expression and acceptance of differences
	Emergence of informal leadership, factional leaders	Facilitates clear, direct, unabrasive communication
	Individual autonomy; everybody for him/herself	Examines nonproductive group processes
	Dysfunctional group roles	Examines cognitive distortions
	Normative and membership crisis; drop-out danger high	Facilitates member evaluation of dissident subgroups
	Testing of leader; other group members Dependence on leader	Holds group accountable for decision by consensus
	Group experimentation in managing own affairs	Clarifies that conflict, power struggles are normal
	Program breakdown at times; low planning Feedback highly critical	Encourages norms consistent with therapeutic group aims
		Consistently acknowledges strengths, accomplishments
		Nondefensively deals with challenges to leadership
		Focuses on "here and now"

Intimacy	Intensified personal involvement	Encourages leadership
	Sharing of self, materials	Assumes flexible role as group vacillates
	Striving to meet others' needs	Aids sharper focus on individual goals
	Awareness of significance of the group experience	Encourages deeper-level exploration, feedback
	Personality growth and change	Encourages acknowledgment, support, of differences
	Mutual revelation, risking	
	Beginning commitment to decision by consensus	Guides work of group
	Beginning work on cognitive restructuring	Encourages experimentation with different roles
	Importance of goals verbalized	Encourages use of new skills inside and outside group
	Growing ability to govern group independently	Assists members to assume responsibility for change
	Dissipation of emotional turmoil	Gives consistent feedback regarding successes
	Member initiation of topics	
	Feedback constructive	Reduces own activity
Differentiation	Here-and-now focus	Emphasizes achievement of goals, exchange of skills
	High level of trust, cohesion	Supports group's self-governance
	Free expression of feelings	Promotes behaviors that increase cohesion
	Mutual aid	
	Full acceptance of differences	Provides balance between support, confrontation
	Group viewed as unique	
	Clarity of group purpose	Encourages conversion of insight into action
	Feelings of security; belonging; "we" spirit	
	Differentiated roles	Interprets; explores common themes
	Group self-directed	Universalizes themes
	Intensive work on cognitions	Encourages deeper-level exploration of problems
	Goal-oriented behavior	
	Work outside of group to achieve personal goals	Assures review of goals, task completion
	Members feel empowered	Stimulates individual and group growth
	Communication open, spontaneous	Supports application of new behaviors outside group
	Self-confrontation	
Separation	Review and evaluation	Prepares for letting go
	Development of outlets outside group	Facilitates evaluation and feelings about termination
	Stabilizing and generalizing	
	Projecting toward future	Reviews individual and group progress
	Recognition of personal, interpersonal growth	Redirects energy of individuals away from group and toward selfing process
	Sadness and anxiety over reality of separation	
	Expression of fears, hopes, anxiety for self and others	Enables individuals to disconnect
	Some denial, regression	Encourages resolution of unfinished business
	Moving apart, distancing	
	Less Intense interaction	Reinforces changes made by individuals
	Plans as to how to continue progress outside group	Administers evaluation instruments
	Talk of reunions, follow-up	

Cohesion

Because the presence of cohesion in a group plays such a central role, leaders must encourage the development of this positive force in groups. In so doing, the leader forges connections between people who are unrelated to each other and tries to expand the interpersonal network of subgroups of people in the group who are too closely related. Further, the leader encourages cohesive behaviors by "pointing out who is present and who is absent ..., by making reference to 'we' and 'us' and 'our,' and by including the group as a whole in his or her remarks in group sessions" (Henry, 1992, p. 167).

Leaders also encourage the development of cohesion by commenting on and thus reinforcing manifestations of the same. Henry identifies signs of cohesiveness that leaders might highlight:

When members return to the group sessions after absence following conflict or disequilibrium, it is a sign of their attraction to the group, to other members, and to what the group does. When the members regroup and reformulate their configuration and stay with that piece of work, it is a sign of their attraction to what the group is doing. When members notice the presence or absence of other members and ask the worker for information about others, it is a sign of their attraction to other members. When people act to take others into account, seeking to be in their shoes when decisions are taken, it is a sign of their attraction to the group. When members take more and more responsibility for what the group does and where it is going and how it is getting there, it is a sign of the attraction that the experience holds for them. (p. 167)

Although these indicators of cohesion are earmarks of advanced stages of group development, they often make fleeting appearances early in a group.

Leaders also increase the attractiveness and cohesion in groups by developing high levels of interaction; by aiding members to successfully achieve goals, fulfill expectations, and meet needs; and by providing opportunities for prestige and access to rewards and resources that individual members alone could not obtain (Toseland & Rivas, 1995).

Ironically, although throughout the group experience leaders seek to increase cohesiveness, they may work to reverse this process during the termination phase, as Garvin (1987) notes:

Members must be helped to become less attracted to the group and, when appropriate, more attracted to alternative relationships. The worker, therefore, also reverses the application of principles for attaining group cohesion. For example, instead of increasing the frequency with which members have contact with one another, this may be reduced by having meetings less often and/or for a shorter time.... The worker may place less emphasis on resolving conflicts within the group and may not call attention to commonalities of experiences or attitudes except as those relate to ways of coping with termination. This may not be true in group psychotherapy, when this type of process is maintained until the very end. (p. 222)

Normative Structure

As a group develops, norms may not evolve that support its treatment objectives. A group, for example, may split into several self-serving factions or subgroups that compete for control. Further, members may develop a habit of socializing rather than focusing on legitimate group tasks. Some members may also repeatedly scapegoat other vulnerable members, harassing those members and blaming them for various group ills. In these and myriad other ways, groups may develop redundant behaviors that undermine the ability of members to aid each other in alleviating problems.

As described in Chapter 11, a vital role of leaders is that of observing evolving group behavior and assessing whether emerging patterns of behavior undermine or support the treatment purposes of the group. Once leaders have determined the impact of emerging patterns, they then intervene to nurture functional group behaviors and to assist the group to modify behaviors destructive to individuals or to the group.

The leader sets the stage for a therapeutic atmosphere and a "working group" by establishing an explicit contract with members in initial sessions that include normative "guideposts" for the group. Guidelines to promote therapeutic behavior such as the following may be generated and recorded in initial sessions and then reviewed in later sessions to assess the group's success in adopting them. These may include:

- Adhering to a decision-by-consensus method of solving problems.
- Personalizing statements and feelings by speaking from an "I" position, e.g., "I (think) (feel) (want)..."
- Keeping the group's focus on the task and mission of the group.
- Keeping group discussion focused primarily on the present rather than on the past.
- Focusing extensively on individual and group strengths and progress.
- Avoiding "gossiping," that is, talking about someone in front of that person.
- Agreeing that the group will "stop action" when there is a breakdown in communication or other problems that interfere with the group's doing its work.

Setting the stage for intervention, the leader emphasizes that it is his or her role in numerous ways to aid the group to observe these contractual guidelines over time, recognizing that adherence to a contract is a process, not an event, and that compliance will occur gradually as the group matures. Significant adherence to these guidelines is a mark, in fact, that the group has achieved full maturity.

In addition to generating structural guidelines that pave the way for the adoption of therapeutic norms, leaders aid members in adopting the following personal guidelines, adapted from Corey and Corey (1992):

- Help establish trust. Initiate discussion of trust issues rather than wait for some other person to take the first risk or to make some gesture of trust.
- Express persistent feelings. Rather than shrouding feelings of boredom, anger, or disappointment, air persistent feelings related to the group process.

- Decide how much to disclose. You are in charge of what, how much, and when you share personal issues.
- Be an active participant, not an observer. Share reactions to what others are saying in the group rather than remaining an unknown entity and thus a possible object of others' flawed observations.
- Listen closely and discriminately. Do not accept others' feedback wholesale or reject it outright, but decide for yourself what does and doesn't apply to you.
- Pay attention to consistent feedback. If a message has been received from a variety of sources, it is likely to have a degree of validity.
- Focus on self. Talk about your role in problems; also avoid focusing on extraneous situations or people outside of the group.

Leaders, of course, often intervene to articulate the need for, or to acknowledge the presence of, the personal normative behaviors that they desire individual members to adopt.

Role Structure/Roles are closely related to norms, as Toseland and Rivas (1995) explain:

Whereas norms are shared expectations held, to some extent, by everyone in the group, roles are shared expectations about the functions of individuals in the group. Unlike norms, which define behavior in a wide range of situations, roles define behavior in relation to a specific function or task that the group member is expected to perform. (p. 68)

Within the group, role dimensions consist of who occupies formal positions (such as chairperson or secretary) and who fills informal positions created through group interactions (such as mediator, clown, rebel, or scapegoat). Leaders may utilize formal group roles in the service of furthering treatment aims such as increasing leadership or other skills. Leaders must also address antitherapeutic roles that evolve in a group, as, for example, focusing on instances in which members criticize other members, manifest excessive dependence on the leader, adopt a "therapist's role," or remain aloof from the group.

Garvin (1986) notes that in later phases of the group members may become locked into dysfunctional roles. For instance:

The "clown" may wish to behave more seriously, the "mediator" to take sides, and passive people to function assertively. The worker, being cognizant of roles that are created out of group interactions, will attend to those that impede either the attainment of individual goals or the creation of an effective group. (p. 112)

Dysfunctional role performance is a critical choice point for intervention. One means of intervening is to use a technique developed by Garvin (1986) to identify informal roles occupied by members. Leaders administer a questionnaire asking members to "vote" on who, if anyone, fulfills group roles such as referee, humorist, nurturer, spokesperson, and "devil's advocate." A subsequent group discussion of results has significant potential for effecting changes in group processes. Another manner of intervening is to simply describe a specific role a member seems to have assumed and to ask that member for observations regarding the accuracy of input. Inquiring as to whether the member would like group feedback preliminary to any moves in that direction reduces defensiveness and gives the member appropriate control over the situation. The strategy of asking members' permission regarding group feedback is potent in instances in which a member might gain from such input.

Another aspect of role performance is aiding members to achieve role attainment, i.e., to fulfill the requirements of roles that they aspire to or are already in, such as student, parent, spouse, employee, friend, or retired person. This may be accomplished by aiding members to assess their own interactions, to practice, and then to apply new ways of interacting and approaching their roles. In this regard, Garvin (1987) suggests steps by which groups can aid members to role play or in other ways simulate the behaviors they seek to possess. Leaders may also draw from Chapter 14 to obtain strategies to enable members to change behavior through behavioral rehearsal and other skill training.

Subgroup Structure

Subgroups inevitably emerge and exist in groups, affecting them in numerous ways, at times facilitating, at other times hindering group processes. Negative subgroups can raise issues of loyalty and exclusion in the group, challenge the leader's authority, and fragment communication as members of a subgroup talk among themselves. The leader, who must intervene in ways to modify the impact of such subgroups, can do so by utilizing strategies such as the following:

- Initiate discussion of the reasons for dissident subgroupings and their impact on the group as a whole. "A frank discussion of the reasons for subgroup formation can often benefit the entire group, because it can reveal problems in the group's goal setting, communication, interaction, and decision-making processes," as Toseland and Rivas (1984, p. 62) indicate.

- Neutralize the effects of negative subgroups through programming or structuring. The leader, for example, might challenge dissident subgroups to work toward a common goal, change seating arrangements, use a "round-robin" approach to get feedback from all members, assign members from different subgroups to work on common group tasks, or use programming materials or exercises to separate subgroup members.

- Create safe positions or roles for marginal members of the group that require minimal activity, but at the same time involve such members in group activity (Balgopal & Vassil, 1983).

- Enable powerful subgroups or individuals to relinquish power or to use it sparingly in the interest of other members. This may be accomplished by encouraging concern for others in the group and also enabling members to grasp that domination of others can be destructive to themselves (Garvin, 1987).

- Appoint powerless members to roles that carry power, such as arranging for group activities, securing resources for the group, or fulfilling significant roles, for example, as observer, chairperson, or secretary.

- Find means to "connect" with dissident subgroups and to demonstrate a concern for their wants (Garvin, 1987).

- Provide ways for such subgroups to attain legitimate power by creating useful roles and tasks in the group.

Leadership Structure

The leader's role in a group can be described as a set of behaviors that facilitate the attainment of group and individual goals and ensure the maintenance of the group. It is the leader's role in the long run to

facilitate the distribution of those behaviors associated with group leadership so that at least some of the rewards and control of leadership accrue to all members. Thus, an important function of the group leader is to gradually eliminate the central leadership role while continuing to maintain focus on the work of the group. The group leader must maintain sufficient responsibility until the members themselves are able to provide guidance to the group. (Rose, 1989, p. 260).

Aiding members to assume leadership behaviors is vital for three reasons, according to Rose. First, members develop vital skills that transfer to other social groups, where leadership is usually highly valued. Second, the more that members exercise leadership, the more likely they are to invest in the group. Third, performance of leadership activities enhances the perceived power or self-efficacy of members, who often experience powerlessness in a wide variety of social situations.

Leaders should expedite the sharing of power with members and the group as a whole. They may do this by (1) encouraging member-to-member rather than member-to-leader communications, (2) asking for members' input into the agenda for the meeting and the direction the group should take in future meetings, (3) supporting indigenous leadership when members make their first tentative attempts at exerting their own influence on the group, and (4) encouraging attempts at mutual sharing and mutual aid among group members during the first meeting (Shulman, 1984).

Group leadership problems occur when a member of the group or vying subgroups attempt to usurp the reins of power. Challenges to leadership (or lack of it) are, in fact, an inherent part of the group's struggle over control, division of responsibility, and decision making (Corey & Corey, 1992). It is important not to label such members because their efforts may be interpreted as attempting to help the group succeed by focusing it on personally meaningful roles (Hurley, 1984). These authors give examples of messages that illustrate control issues:

"I don't want to talk just because you want me to talk. I learn just as much by listening and observing."

"There are several people in here who always get the attention. No matter what I do, I just don't seem to get recognized, especially by the leaders."

"You should pay more attention to Paul. He's been crying several times, and you haven't been taking care of him."

In response to a challenge of leadership, a leader might immediately explore a member's statement through empathic responding, eliciting feedback from other members regarding leadership style, and asking for input (e.g., "What would you have me do differently?"). Another choice, that of authentic responding, is encouraged by Corey and Corey (1992), who emphasize the need of leaders to become aware of their own reactions to a personal challenge as well as to other obstacles manifested by a "resistant group." Leaders, say these authors, often make the mistake of focusing on "problem members" or difficult situations, rather than on how they are affected personally when group processes go awry:

Typically, leaders have a range of feelings: being threatened by what they perceive as a challenge to their leadership role; anger over the members' lack of cooperation and enthusiasm; feelings of inadequacy to the point of wondering if they are qualified to lead groups; resentment toward several of the members, whom they label as some type of problem; and anxiety over the slow pace of the group, with a desire to stir things up so that there is some action. (p. 155)

By ignoring their reactions, leaders leave themselves out of the interactions that occur in the group. Instead, Corey and Corey urge leaders to model a "direct" style of dealing with conflict and resistance, rather than bypassing. Your own thoughts, feelings and observations can be the most powerful resource you have in dealing with defensive behavior. When you share what you are feeling and thinking about what is going on in the group—in such a way as not to blame and criticize the members for deficiencies—you are letting the members experience an honest and constructive interaction with you. (p. 155)

By consistently responding authentically, even when challenged or under attack, the leader encourages the group's eventual wholesale adoption of this mode of representing self, one that is vital to members' dealing effectively with the inevitable differences they encounter among themselves.

LEADER INTERVENTIONS ACROSS STAGES OF GROUP DEVELOPMENT

As previously mentioned, a leader's role must always be pursued within the framework of the group's stages of development. Here, in more detail, key aspects of the leader's role are explicated across the Garland, Jones, and Kolodny (1965) model.

Preaffiliation Stage

Conducting individual interviews to orient potential members to a group experience, as discussed in Chapter 11, is but the beginning of the leader's efforts to prepare members to make effective use of a group. In many ways in initial sessions the leader can prepare members for the experience to come by articulating the basics of group process. These include, for example, the stages of development through which the group will pass; ways in which to create a therapeutic working environment; behaviors and attitudes characteristic of an effective working group; the vital need to establish and adhere to clear group guidelines that lend structure and purpose to the group; and the importance of committing to win-win decisions

regarding group matters. Research, in fact, suggests that direct instruction or teaching regarding group processes tends to facilitate a group's development during early stages (Corey & Corey, 1992; Dies, 1983).

Leaders must also intervene to address initial concerns of members. In early sessions members will be tentative about what it is they hope to get from the group. Most also experience fear and apprehension regarding the group experience. They worry about how they will be received by other members; whether they will be pressured to talk; whether they will be misunderstood or look foolish; whether they are at risk of verbal attack; and whether they indeed want to go through a change process. The leader may aid in explicating and allaying these anxieties by asking all members to share their feelings about coming to the initial group session. One method is to ask members to rate their feelings about being present in the group at that moment on a scale of 1 to 10 in which 1 represents "I don't want to be here" and 10 represents "I'm completely at ease with being in the group." The leader may then ask members to explain the reasons for their ratings.

In focusing on members' fears, leaders need to draw out the feelings and reactions of all members, to validate the importance of their fully disclosing feelings, and to emphasize the need for the group to be a safe place in which such issues can be expressed. Finally, leaders may elicit suggestions for group structuring that address member fears, out of which may flow the formulation of relevant group guidelines.

Leaders can measure the progress of a new group in addressing initial member concerns by administering a questionnnaire developed by Rose (1989) containing items to which members can respond by circling a point on a scale. Examples of items include: How useful was today's session for you? Describe your involvement in today's session. Rate the extent of your self-disclosure of relevant information about yourself or your problem. How important to you were the problems or situations you discussed (others discussed) in the group today? Circle all the words that best describe you at today's session (e.g., excited, bored, depressed, interested, comfortable). How satisfied were you with today's session?

In initial sessions, leaders must review basic information several times regarding the group's purpose, the manner in which the group will be conducted, and its ground rules. Reid (1991, p. 205) emphasizes that none of this information should surprise members. However, reiteration is necessary because "in the beginning, members are often so preoccupied that they do not comprehend the group's purpose, their particular role, the worker's role, and what will be expected of them." If the leader does not make these issues clear early in the group's development, they will come back to haunt the group and hinder its progress.

In preliminary interviews, members contract with the leader for general goals they would like to achieve. In initial sessions the leader must then "wed" individual and group goals. The binding contract thus is expanded from a reciprocal one between leader and individuals to a mutual contract between individuals and group. In the first meeting, Henry (1992, p. 80) notes, the leader engages "all persons present in a discussion that establishes a group way of functioning yet allows each person's initial objectives to be addressed." Henry, who views finding common ground as "an unfolding process," utilizes what she calls a "Goal Questionnaire" to facilitate formulation of the mutual contract. On this questionnaire are two questions to which members respond in writing: (1) "Why do you think all of you are here together?" and (2) "What are you going to try to accomplish together?" Discussion of responses gives the group a beginning point from which to proceed (pp. 83–88).

In the ongoing contractual process in initial sessions, leaders also aid members to refine their general goals. Corey and Corey (1992, pp. 121–22) use examples to illustrate the role of the leader in clarifying global goals:

Member: I want to get in touch with my feelings.
Leader: What kind of feelings are you having difficulty with?
Member: I want to work on my anger.
Leader: With whom in your life are you angry? What do you most want to say?

The leader thus uses the skill of concreteness explicated in Chapter 6 to further the creation of clear and specific goals.

The leader also keeps accomplishment of goals at the forefront of the group. Corey (1990, p. 94) encourages "reading, reflecting, and writing" to aid members to focus on their own themes. He suggests selected books and also asks members to keep a journal, which allows them to record the spontaneous reactions they have during and between sessions. Members are also encouraged to bring to the group the gist of their journal entries, which teaches the value of continuing work between sessions.

Maximizing member productivity and satisfaction requires that leaders attend to how they open and close meetings. Corey and Corey (1992) encourage leaders to draw from the following procedures in opening meetings:

- Give members a brief opportunity to say what they want from the upcoming session.
- Enable members to share accomplishments since the last session.
- Elicit feedback regarding the group's last session and give any reflections you have of the session.

To bring meetings to closure, Corey and Corey (1992) emphasize the need to summarize and integrate the group experience and recommend procedures such as the following:

- Ask members what it was like for them to be in the group today.
- Ask members to identify briefly what they're learning about themselves through their experience in the group. Are they getting what they want? If not, what would they be willing to do to get it?
- Ask members whether there are any topics, questions, or problems they would like to explore in the next session.

- Ask members to indicate what they would be willing to do outside of the session to practice new skills.
- Ask members to give one another feedback, especially regarding positive observations, and relate them to leader reactions and observations.

Developing skills in opening and closing sessions increases the possibility of continuity from meeting to meeting. Such continuity heightens the transfer of insights and new behaviors from the group into daily life.

Power and Control Stage

In the Power and Control stage, the group enters a period in which the group's dynamics, tone, and atmosphere are often conflict ridden. Groups are beset with divisions among individuals and subgroups, complaints and unrest over group goals, process and structure, and challenges to leadership. At the same time, the group is trying out its capacity to manage its own affairs. It is the leader's role to bring the group intact through this stormy period with emerging capacity to cope with individual differences and to manage its own governance. The following are strategies that leaders can employ to discharge this responsibility.

Minimize Changes   During the Power and Control stage, groups with a closed format are particularly susceptible to inner and outer stressors such as a change of leader; moving to a new meeting place; addition or loss of members; or change in meeting time. Traumatic events such as a runaway, a death, an incidence of physical violence in an institutional setting, or acutely disturbing political or natural events at the community or national level may also affect a group.

Such changes or events bring stress to a group at any stage of development. However, they are particularly difficult to manage in the Power and Control stage because members have not yet invested to an appreciable extent in the group and thus become easily disenchanted. Adding new members or changing the group's leader is particularly stressful, causing members to raise their defenses because there are risks involved in revealing themselves when either the leader or member is an unknown entity. The loss of a leader can also be inordinately traumatic to members who have difficulty investing in relationships, affirming their stance that investing in others brings disappointment.

In addition, significant changes in group structure without group involvement may cause members to conclude that the leader or agency has disregard for the impact of decisions on the group and that the group is not important to either. Though changes are sometimes unavoidable, it thus behooves leaders to keep changes to a minimum, to prepare members in advance whenever possible, and to aid them to "work through" their feelings in any regard.

Encourage Balanced Feedback   In the Power and Control stage, leaders must emphasize the need for balanced positive and negative feedback. As they observe that group members are tentatively moving into their first authentic encounters, leaders should intervene in negative interactions to draw the group's attention to providing balanced feedback. They thus remind members of the provision in the contract for focusing on positives as well as negatives, as illustrated in the following excerpt from an early group session with adult members.

Gary [*to Wayne, in irritated voice*]: When you keep machine-gunning me with questions like that, I feel like I'm being interrogated.

Wayne: I didn't know I was coming across like that. Frankly, I just wanted to get to know you better.

Leader [*to Wayne*]: You said in the first session that you'd like to use the group as a way of getting feedback about how you come across to others. I'm wondering if this might be a time for this. Are you game?

Wayne: Yeah. I don't know what's coming, but I really think I do need to know more about how other people perceive me. I was really surprised at what Gary said.

Leader [*to Wayne*]: Good. I can understand you may

have reservations, but I'm also pleased that you're willing to take a risk this early in the group. [*To group.*] Since this is the group's first experience in giving feedback to members, I'd like to remind you of the contract not only to help members identify problems but also to share positive observations you may have. As you do so, I'd like you to personalize your statements. I'll help you do this.

The group's first experiences in giving feedback to members are crucial in setting the tone for all that follows. By intervening to guide the group's first tentative efforts to drop facades and to engage at an intimate level, the leader enables the group to have a successful experience and to incorporate "attention to positives" as a part of its character. As members gain confidence that a group will attend to positives as well as negatives, they will often increase their level of participation and take initiative in soliciting group feedback.

In addition to aiding a group to give positive feedback to individuals, leaders can elicit feedback concerning positive behaviors that have supported the group's accomplishing its task during a session. Such behaviors may include, for example, willingness by members to participate in discussions, to answer questions, and to risk revealing themselves; support shown members; members speaking in turn; the group's giving full attention to the task at hand; acceptance of differing values, beliefs, and opinions; or significant accomplishments by the group or individuals.

If there has been an *absence* of destructive behaviors that have previously retarded the group's progress in other sessions, leaders might highlight the change. Destructive behaviors absent in an adolescent group, for instance, might include whispering, getting out of one's seat, not attending to the person speaking, verbally and physically "hassling" others, playing with objects, introducing tangential subjects, arguing, interrupting, or the like.

Among the leader's roles is that of aiding members to acknowledge and accept positive feedback, as illustrated in the following:

Kim [*to Pat*]: I know you get discouraged sometimes, but I admire the fact you can manage four children

by yourself and still work. I don't think I could ever manage that in a million years.

Pat: I don't always manage it. Actually, I don't do near enough for my children.

Leader: I hear you saying, Pat, that you feel inadequate as a mother—and I'll ask you in a moment whether you'd like to return to those feelings—but right now would you reflect on what you just did?

Pat: I guess I didn't acknowledge Kim's compliment. I didn't feel I deserved it.

Leader: I wonder if others of you have experienced the same feeling when someone has given you positive feedback.

The last response broadens the focus to include the experience of other group members, which may lead into a discussion of the difficulties individuals sometimes encounter in accepting positive feedback.

The leader may wish to help individuals or the entire group to identify dysfunctional cognitive patterns that underlie such discomfort in receiving positive messages (e.g., "I have to do things perfectly" or "Nothing I do can be very good"). The leader may emphasize that the preceding experience illustrates how the group experience can enhance responsiveness to positive feedback.

Increase Effective Communication   Intervening moment by moment to increase the chances of effective communication is particularly vital in the Power and Control stage. Previous chapters have explicated five basic relationship skills that, when possessed by clients, significantly increase their personal efficacy and ability to create satisfying relationships. These skills include: (1) positive feedback; (2) empathic listening (the receiver skill); (3) authentic responding (the sender skill); (4) problem solving and decision making; and (5) requesting (a skill for expressing one's needs). In addition other facets of communication enable members to relate facilitatively as a group, such as taking turns in talking; learning how to explore problems before offering solutions; speaking for themselves, not others; and speaking directly to a person for whom a message is intended. Finally, members benefit from learning to distinguish between effective and noneffective ways of responding and from formulating personal goals to eliminate negative stylistic responses from their communication repertoires, a matter discussed in depth in Chapter 7.

Leaders increase the probability of members adopting effective communications by heavily utilizing and modeling these skills themselves. In addition, leaders aid acquisition of skills by adopting the role of "coach" and intervening to shape the playout of communications in the group, as illustrated in the following:

[*Eliminating negative communications*] I'd like you to shy away from labeling, judging, lecturing, criticism, sarcasm, "shoulds" and "oughts," and the words "always" and "never." As per our group contract, try to give self-reports rather than indirect messages that put down, judge or otherwise focus on another person.

[*Personalizing messages*] That was an example of a "you" message. I'd like you to try again, this time by starting out with the pronoun "I." Try to identify your feelings, or what you want or need.

[*Talking in turn*] Right now several of you are speaking at the same time. Try to hold to the guideline that we all speak in turn. Your observations are too important to miss.

[*Speaking directly to each other*] Right now you're speaking to the group but I think your message is meant for _____. If so, then it would be better to talk directly to him.

[*Exploratory questions*] Switching from closed- to open-ended questions right now could help Liz to tell her story in her own way. (Leader explains difference between these two modes of questioning.)

[*Listening*] Try to listen carefully to what she's saying. Help her to let out her feelings and to get to the source of the problem.

[*Problem exploration vs. problem solving*] When the group offers advice too quickly, members aren't able to share their deeper level feelings or to reveal a problem in its entirety. We may need to allow Richard 5–10 minutes to share his concerns before the group offers any observations. The timing of advice is critical as we try to help members share and solve problems.

[*Authenticity*] Could you risk and tell the group what you're feeling at this very moment? I can see you choking up and I think it would be good for the group to know what you're experiencing.

[*Requesting*] You've just made a complaint about the group. On the flip side of any complaint is a request. Tell the group what would help. Make a request.

Intervening moment by moment to shape the communications of members, as in the instances illustrated above, increases the therapeutic potential of a group.

Create Therapeutic Norms As explicated earlier, leaders must be concerned about the nature of the norms that evolve in the group. It is in the Power and Control stage of a group that many of the group patterns are forming and that the leader can intervene to shape the power structure, the stylistic communications of the group, and ways the group "chooses" to negotiate and solve problems.

In shaping the group's therapeutic norms, leaders need to intervene, for example, in instances when:

- Distractive behavior substantially interferes with the group's task.
- One or more members monopolize the group's air time.
- One or more members are "out of step" with the group process and/or experience strong feelings such as hurt, anger, disgust, disappointment, or disapproval.
- Several members or the entire group begin to talk about one member.
- Behavior of members is incompatible with the governing guidelines set by the group.
- Socializing interferes with the task of the group.
- Members intellectualize about emotionally loaded material.
- One or more members manifest hostility in the form of caustic remarks, jokes, sarcasm or criticism.
- One or more members or the group begin interrogating or ganging up on someone.
- The group offers advice or suggestions to a member without first encouraging that member to fully explore a problem.

- Members ramble or participate in lengthy recitations that ignore self-disclosure of current problems, feelings, thoughts, or reactions.

- There is silence or withdrawal by one or more members or the group itself seems to be "shut down."

- A member adopts a "co-leader" role.

- The group scapegoats one of its members, blaming that member for group problems.

- One member attacks another, who reacts by defending, attacking, or withdrawing.

When members manifest obstacles such as the preceding, it is the leader's role to focus the group's attention on what is occurring in the "here and now." Leaders may simply document what they see by describing specific behaviors or the progression of events that have occurred and then request group input. Once the group focuses on the problem, it is the task of leaders to facilitate discussion and problem solving rather than to take decisive action themselves. The responsibility for resolution needs to rest with the group.

Henry (1992) supports the vital function of leaders in the Power and Control stage in turning issues back to the group, observing:

> When the members are vying for ownership of the group, the wisest intervention for the worker is to join their struggle and to put issues and decisions back to them. The worker does not wholly give up her or his power, but holds back from what had previously been a more directive and active performance. (p. 148)

However, Henry notes, at the end of a particularly conflict-filled episode or session, leaders need to intervene with a proposal to process what has occurred and to lead that processing. In such instances, leaders do not turn issues back to the group but opt, in the interest of closure and resolution, to "clarify what information people carry away from the confrontation, and to see what level of discomfort people are experiencing" (p. 151).

Although leaders need to avoid premature closure on heated issues in a group, they must intervene immediately to refocus process when group members begin to criticize, label, "cut down" others, or argue among themselves. Leaders may make the assumption that letting members verbally "fight it out" when they have conflicts is cathartic or helpful. To the contrary, ample research indicates that aggression begets aggression and that not intervening in conflict only encourages members to continue in the same mode of venting their anger. A leader's passive stance could lead to conflict escalating to the point it breaks out into physical fighting. In instances of serious disruption, a leader's lack of intervention may "prove" to members who are scrutinizing the leader's behavior that it is dangerous to take risks in the group because the leader will not protect them.

It is vital that leaders intervene assertively when dysfunctional group processes warrant such interventions. Otherwise, the leader is in a "one-down" position in the group and loses his or her ability to effect change. Leaders must thus be willing to respond decisively when significant group disruption occurs, if necessary by clapping their hands loudly, standing up, speaking louder than group members, or putting themselves between members who are arguing.

In intervening in group-as-a-whole matters (as contrasted to focusing on individual attitudes or behaviors) leaders increase the effectiveness of their interventions by focusing on a pair, a trio, a foursome, or the group, thus avoiding the singling out of one person or inadvertently getting caught in "siding." In fact, rarely does the destructive or self-defeating behavior of one member or a subgroup not directly affect other members. Rather, such behavior not only affects the group but may also be fostered or reinforced by the group. Intervening to place responsibility on the group for owning its part in maintaining dysfunctional behavior by members or by the group as a whole serves the best interest of all parties.

Consider, for instance, the following leader intervention in an adolescent group: "Mark and Jeannie, you're whispering again and interrupting the group. We need your attention." This message places the responsibility for the distractive behavior solely upon the two members and does not take into account what is happening with the group. As a consequence, the leader's message is more likely to reinforce negative behavior than to encourage positive change for the following reasons:

1. It may polarize the group by aligning the leader with members who are irritated by this behavior ("the good guys") and against the two offending members ("the bad guys").

2. The leader's solution ("we need your attention") circumvents group handling or problem solving of the matter.

3. The leader's blunt intervention fails to attend to the message inherent in the distractible behavior that "this group does not meet our needs at the moment"—a view that may be shared but not expressed by other members.

A guideline to formulating interventions that confront dysfunctional behavior is that the behavior must be analyzed in the context of the group process, with the leader considering how such behavior affects and is affected by group members. This is illustrated by the following message to the same situation:

"I'm concerned about what is happening right now—several of you are not participating; some of you are whispering; one of you is writing notes; a few of you are involved in the discussion. As individuals, you appear to be at different places with the group and I'd like to check out what each of you is experiencing right now."

The preceding message focuses on all group members, neutrally describes behavior that is occurring, and encourages the group process. By not imposing a solution on the group, the leader assumes a facilitative rather than an authoritarian role, the latter being the "kiss of death" to productive group discussion.

Intimacy and Differentiation Stages

The Intimacy and Differentiation stages of a group constitute its working phase. In initial stages of a group's evolution, critical issues at stake were those of trust versus mistrust, the struggle of power, and self-focus versus focus on others. In the working phase, however, issues shift to those of disclosure versus anonymity; honesty versus game playing; spontaneity versus control; acceptance versus rejection; cohesion versus fragmentation; and responsibility versus blaming (Corey & Corey, 1992).

In the working phase, the leader continues to promote conditions that aid members to make healthy choices in resolving issues such as the preceding, for example, by straightforwardly addressing and resolving conflict, openly disclosing personal problems, taking responsibility for their problems, and making pro-group choices.

In the relaxed stance of the working phase, leaders have more opportunities to intensify therapeutic group conditions. Leaders may focus on refining feedback processes, coaching members to give immediate feedback, to make such feedback specific rather than global, to render feedback in nonjudgmental ways, and to give feedback regarding strengths as well as problem behaviors (Corey & Corey, 1992).

Leaders can also enhance individual and group growth by focusing on the universality of underlying issues, feelings, and needs that members seem to share, as Corey and Corey indicate:

> The circumstances leading to hurt and disappointment may be very different from person to person or from culture to culture. But the resulting emotions have a universal quality. Although we may not speak the same language or come from the same society, we are connected through our feelings of joy and pain. It is when group members no longer get lost in the details of daily experiences and instead share their deeper struggles with these universal human themes that a group is most cohesive. (p. 209)

Common themes identified by Corey and Corey include

> fears of rejection, feelings of loneliness and abandonment, feeling of inferiority and failure to live up to others' expectations, painful memories, guilt and remorse over what they have and have not done, discovery that their worst enemy lives within them, need for and fear of intimacy, feelings about sexual

identity and sexual performance, and unfinished business with their parents. (p. 210)

This list is not exhaustive, note Corey and Corey, but "merely a sample of the universal human issues that participants recognize and explore with each other as the group progresses" (p. 210).

In the working phase leaders also support a continuing trend toward differentiation, in which members establish their uniqueness and separateness from others. Leaders do not create these expressions of differences, but rather stimulate or advance them, for example, noting when a member reveals

a heretofore hidden talent, or access to a resource that was previously believed inaccessible, or possession of a needed skill or perspective. A member may articulate a previously unspoken need, or offer an interpretation not thought of by the others, or pose a question that catalyzes or synthesizes a piece of the group's work. (Henry, 1992, p. 183)

The working phase is a time of intensive focus on achieving members' goals. Much of the group's work during this phase is devoted to carrying out contracts developed in initial sessions. Toseland and Rivas (1995) emphasize that leaders should not assume that members continue to be aware of their goals as the group progresses. Rather, a major leader role is to confirm goals periodically and promote organized and systematic efforts to work on them, thus assuring that individuals and leader remain focused on the same issues.

The leader assumes the ongoing responsibility of monitoring the time allocated to each member to work on goals. Toseland and Rivas suggest that the leader help each member to work in turn. Should a group spend considerable time aiding one member to achieve goals, leaders should generalize concepts to other members so that everyone benefits. They should also encourage members to share relevant personal experiences with the member receiving help, thus establishing a norm for mutual aid. In addition, they should check on the progress of members who did not receive due attention and encourage their participation in the next session. These authors state that: "This helps to prevent repeated and prolonged attention to a few members and reduces the possibilities that some members will avoid working on their contracts" (p. 202).

Finally, leaders should establish a systematic method of monitoring treatment goals and tasks in sessions. Without such procedures, monitoring may be haphazard and focused on those who are more assertive and highly involved; those who are less assertive or resistant will not receive the same attention. Without systematic monitoring, tasks to be completed between sessions do not receive the proper follow-up. As Toseland and Rivas (1995) suggest, members are frustrated when they have completed a task between sessions and have no opportunity to report on the results. The expectation of a weekly progress report helps members' motivation to work toward goals between sessions, reduces the necessity of reminding them of their contract agreements, and aids them in gaining a sense of independence and accomplishment.

In the working phase leaders also intensify efforts to aid members to analyze the rationality of thoughts and beliefs that maintain or exacerbate dysfunctional behavior. Group members, say Toseland and Rivas (1984), may

(1) overgeneralize from an event, (2) selectively focus on portions of an event, (3) take too much responsibility for events that are beyond their control, (4) think of the worst possible consequence of future events, (5) engage in either/or dichotomous thinking, and (6) assume that because certain events have led to particular consequences in the past they will automatically lead to the same consequences if they reoccur in the future. (p. 217)[2]

Termination

Termination is a difficult stage for members who have invested heavily in the group; have experienced intensive (and often unheralded) support, encouragement, and understanding; and have received effective aid for problems. Leaders must be astute in sensitively employing interventions to aid members to complete successfully the termination stage, which Mahler (1969) has called a "commencement." To this end we refer you to Chapter 20, which identifies significant termination issues and also change-maintenance strategies that may be utilized with clients in facilitating termination and generalizing changes to the outside world. Here, however, we address aspects of the leader's role that are specific to facilitating planned endings in groups. Leaders may aid groups to complete their "commencement" proceedings by adopting strategies such as the following:

- Ensure that the issues and concerns worked on by the group are representative of those that members encounter outside the group. Also assure that the group is a place where members get honest feedback about how their behavior is likely to be received outside the group and a setting where they may get help in coping with those reactions (Toseland & Rivas, 1995).

- Use a variety of different situations and settings throughout the group experience to aid members to practice and acquire skills, thus better preparing them for the multifaceted situations they encounter outside the group (Toseland & Rivas, 1995).

- Aid members during the last few group sessions to discuss how they will respond to possible setbacks in an unsympathetic environment. Build member confidence in existing coping skills and abilities to solve problems independently. Also teach therapeutic principles that underlie interventive methods, such as those inherent in assertiveness, effective communication, or problem solving (Toseland & Rivas, 1995).

- Share leader reactions to endings as a way of helping members to identify their own conflicted feelings and any sense of abandonment, anger, sadness or loss.

- Reinforce positive feelings of members regarding themselves and the group, including the potency that comes from realizing they are capable of accomplishing goals and assuming responsibility for their own lives; the sense of satisfaction, pride, and usefulness in being able to help others; and the sense of growth and of accomplishment in successfully completing the group experience (Lieberman & Borman, 1979; Toseland & Rivas, 1995).

- Aid review and integration of learning by helping members to put into words what has transpired between themselves and the group from the first to the final session and what they have learned about themselves and others. Also solicit what members were satisfied and unsatisfied with in the group and ways in which sessions could have had greater impact. Finally, ask members to spontaneously recall moments of conflict and pain as well as moments of closeness, warmth, humor and joy in the group (Corey & Corey, 1992).

- Suggest to members several sessions before termination that they consider using the remaining time to complete their own agenda. Leaders may ask the question, "If this were the last session, how would you feel about what you have done, and what would you wish you had done differently?" (Corey & Corey, 1992, p. 229).

- Facilitate the finishing of unfinishing business between members by utilizing an exercise suggested by Henry (1992, p. 124) in which each person, in turn, says in a few short phrases, "What I really liked was the way you …(supply a specific behavior exchanged between the persons, such as 'always gave me positive strokes when I could finally say something that was hard for me to say')," and then, "But I wish we… (supplying a specific wish for a behavioral exchange between the two persons that did not occur, such as 'had made more opportunity to talk to each other more directly')." Use this exercise, Henry recommends, not to generate new issues but to bring closure to the present situation.

- Solicit feedback from the group regarding areas in which members could productively focus once they leave the group. Consider asking members to formulate their own individual change contracts, which may be referred to once the group ends, and request that each member review these contracts with the group (Corey & Corey, 1992).

- Engage individual members in relating how they have perceived themselves in the group, what the group has meant to them, and what growth they have made. Ask remaining members to give feedback regarding how they have perceived and felt about that person, including measured feedback that helps members strengthen the perceptions that they gained during the course of the group (e.g., "One of the things I like best about you is…" "One way I see you blocking your strengths is…" "A few things that I hope you'll remember are …") (Corey, 1990, p. 512).

- Utilize evaluative measures to determine the success of the group and the leader's interventions. Such measures have the following benefits: (1) address the leader's professional concerns about the specific effects of interventions; (2) help leaders improve their leadership skills; (3) demonstrate to agencies or funding sources the efficacy of the group; (4) help leaders assess the member and group progress in accomplishing agreed-upon objectives; (5) allow members to express their satisfactions and dissatisfactions with the group; and (6) give leaders the opportunity to develop knowledge that can be shared with others who are using group methods for similar purposes and in similar situations (Reid, 1991; Toseland & Rivas).

NEW DEVELOPMENTS IN SOCIAL WORK WITH GROUPS

There is increased interest in the use of social work groups for empowerment. For example, Lewis (1991) notes the influences of feminist theory and liberation theology as resources for an empowerment-focused social group work. Feminist theory is egalitarian, participatory, and validates each person's life experience in context. On the other hand, liberation theology focuses on the participation in economic and political action by those persons most vulnerable to injustice (Lewis, 1991). For example, Cox has described how women welfare recipients have learned to advocate for themselves with social services and other agencies through participation in empowerment-oriented groups (Cox, 1991). Meanwhile, other writers are focusing on the special needs of persons of color and immigrant client groups (Congress & Lynn, 1994). Finally, Tolman and Molidor have noted in a review of the research on social work with groups in the decade of the 1980s that cognitive behavioral groups dominated this research with many programs addressing the social skills of children (Tolman & Molidor, 1994).

Work with Task Groups

As described in Chapter 11, a significant aspect of professional social work practice involves performance in task and work groups. In contrast to treatment groups, task groups form to accomplish a purpose, produce a product, or develop policies (Ephross & Vassil, 1988). Hence you are likely to experience participation in task groups throughout your career starting with academic task groups as students and continuing as staff members and eventually leaders of such groups in your practice. Effective participation in task groups is not solely reliant on the skills of the formal leaders of the group. For example, social workers have often been effective participants in interdisciplinary teams through their knowledge of group processes. Social workers can assist task groups particularly in identifying problems to focus on, getting members involved, paying attention to stages of development, and managing conflict.

Problem Identification Leaders can help groups effectively identify problems which the group is capable of solving, that are within the group's domain, and ones which, among many to choose from, would provide a meaningful focus (Toseland & Rivas, 1995). It is useful in this process to help the group avoid responding prematurely with solutions before the problem is well defined. In defining appropriate problems and goals, the group can be helped through techniques such as brainstorming and nominal group techniques to consider an array of possibilities before selecting a focus. Brainstorming includes expression of a variety of opinions without evaluating them. The nominal group technique is one in which members privately list potential problems and rank them (Toseland & Rivas, 1995). The group then proceeds to take one potential problem from each member until all are listed, before proceeding to evaluate and rank them as a group.

Getting Members Involved All members of the group need to have a clear understanding of the functions of the group, to have input into the agenda and decision making. Roles can be assigned such that members will have to depend on each other to get the work of the group accomplished (ibid., 1995). Background papers often need to be circulated to get all members to the appropriate level of information. It is often helpful to conduct the preceding suggested brainstorming exercises in small groups which facilitate member interaction. Recognition of the particular skills, experiences, and perspectives that different members bring can also facilitate more confident sharing by new members.

Awareness of Stages of Development   The stages of group development also occur in task groups though not unidirectionally as some issues will recur, taking the group back to revisit earlier stages. In the preaffiliation stage, individuals enter with varying hopes for the group since common goals have not yet been established. Early development of identity with the group may be influenced by the fact that frequently some members of the group know and work with each other in other capacities. For example, some members of task groups may be colleagues from the same unit, or may have worked together on other projects in the past.

The power and control phase in task groups often occurs around competition for which programs or ideas the group will adopt. Conflict about ideas is to be expected, as it is necessary to well-developed discussions and products and hence should not be avoided. Too often, task groups avoid conflict by evasion, even tabling an issue when enough facts are available to make a decision. Establishing norms at this stage in which differing options are sought and evaluated on their own merits aids the group in accomplishing its objectives. Leaders should attempt, in fact, to stimulate a conflict of ideas while managing and controlling conflict of persons and personalities. Failure to achieve this results in a diminution of the potential contribution of members and a less complete product. Without such healthy conflict, there is danger of "group think," a condition in which alternative views or options are not expressed or taken seriously. Leaders (and members) can assist other members in expressing the reasons behind conflicting opinions, clarifying what information needs to be developed to answer questions raised in the conflicts. Group leaders and members can hence use communication skills described earlier in this book to reframe communications, making them understandable to all parties, reflecting, probing, and making summarizing statements. Group leaders can contribute to a productive working atmosphere by conveying that each member has something to contribute and maintaining civility by not allowing anyone or their ideas to be degraded (Toseland & Rivas, 1995, pp. 306–307).

NOTES

1 We also refer you to Hartford (1971), Henry (1992), and Corey and Corey (1992), sources from which we have drawn information on filling in the Garland, Jones, and Kolodny model.

2 Though it is beyond the scope of this chapter to provide details, techniques abound in the literature to address the preceding issues and other self-defeating client attitudes, including those found in Meichenbaum (1977), Mahoney (1974), and Burns (1980). Both Toseland and Rivas (1995) and Rose (1989) offer specific ways of altering cognitions within a group context.

3 Reid (1991) has reviewed procedures for evaluating outcome in groups, including group testimonials, content analysis of audio- or videotapes, several forms of sociometric analysis, self-rating instruments, and other subjective measures. We refer you to Reid (1991) and to Corey (1990) for further discussion of such vital evaluative measures.

Chapter 18 □ □ □

Additive Empathy, Interpretation, and Confrontation

THE MEANING AND SIGNIFICANCE OF CLIENT SELF-AWARENESS

Self-awareness is a priceless ingredient generally acknowledged as essential to sound mental health. Humans have long known of the profound importance of self-awareness, as reflected by Socrates, the ancient Greek philosopher, in his often-quoted admonition, "Know thyself!" Self-awareness is often sought by voluntary clients and is indispensable to the helping process they seek, particularly during the change-oriented phase. People's efforts to solve problems and to change are effective only if they are properly directed, which in turn depends on accurate awareness of behaviors and circumstances that need to be changed. Indeed, many people experience incessant problems in daily living related to their lack of awareness of forces that produce these problems.

As we employ the term, *self-awareness* refers largely to awareness of forces operating in the present. Practitioners thus assist clients to expand their awareness of needs or wants, motives, emotions, beliefs, dysfunctional behaviors, and of their impact on other people. We do *not* use self-awareness to refer to insight into the etiology of problems, for, as we have noted in earlier chapters, people can and do change without this type of insight. But on occa-

sions, brief excursions into the past may be productive and enlightening, for example, to determine what qualities attracted marital partners to each other, to identify factors that have contributed to sexual dysfunction, to assess the chronicity of problems, to highlight previous successes, and the like. It is important in making such brief excursions, however, to relate elicited information to *present* work and *present* problems, emphasizing to clients that they can change the present, altering current effects of history but not history itself.

Practitioners have numerous tools to assist clients to gain expanded self-awareness, of which additive empathy, interpretation, and confrontation are probably employed most extensively. In this chapter, we define these techniques, specify indications for their use, present guidelines for employing them effectively, and finally, provide skill development exercises.

ADDITIVE EMPATHY AND INTERPRETATION

By now you are aware that empathy on the practitioner's part is critical to the helping process. In earlier chapters, we explained various uses of empathy in the initial phase of the helping process.

During the action-oriented phase, additive levels of empathy are used to expand clients' self-awareness, to cushion the impact of confrontations (discussed later in this chapter), and to explore and resolve relational reactions and other obstacles to change (which we discuss at length in Chapter 19). Bear in mind that practitioners also continue to use reciprocal levels of empathy during the goal-attainment phase because the purposes of empathy in the initial phase continue throughout the helping process. The difference is that additive levels of empathy are employed sparingly in the initial phase but occupy a prominent position during the action-oriented phase.

Additive empathic responses go somewhat beyond what clients have expressed and therefore require some degree of inference by practitioners. For this reason, these responses are moderately interpretive since they interpret to clients forces operating to produce feelings, cognitions, reaction, and behavioral patterns. Indeed, after an exhaustive study of research involving psychoanalysis, Luborsky and Spence (1978) concluded that interpretation, as employed by psychoanalysts, is basically the same as empathic communication. Insight through *interpretation*, it should be noted, is the "supreme agent" in the hierarchy of therapeutic principles that are basic to psychoanalysis and closely related therapies.

Proponents of several other theories (most notably, client centered, Gestalt, and certain existential theories) have avoided the use of interpretation. Still others (Claiborn, 1982; Levy, 1963) maintain that interpretation is essential to the counseling process, regardless of theoretical orientation, and that many behaviors of practitioners (whether intentional or not) perform interpretive functions. Semantic and conceptual confusion has contributed to the divergence in views, but recent writings have tended to sharpen concepts and to reduce vagueness and confusion.

Based on Levy's (1963) conceptualization, Claiborn (1982) posits that interpretation, whatever the theoretical orientation, "presents the client with a viewpoint discrepant from the client's own, the function of which is to prepare or induce the client to change in accordance with that viewpoint" (p. 442). Viewed in this light, interpretation assists clients to view their problems from a different perspective, the desired effect of which is to open up new possibilities for remedial courses of action. This generic view, which emphasizes a *discrepant viewpoint*, is sufficiently broad to encompass many change-oriented techniques identified in different theories, including reframing (Watzlawick et al., 1974); relabeling (Barton & Alexander, 1981); positive connotation (Selvini-Palazzoli, Boscolo, Cecchin, & Prata, 1974); positive reinterpretation (Hammond et al., 1977); additive empathy, and traditional psychoanalytic interpretations. The content of interpretations concerning the same clinical situation thus can be expected to vary according to the theoretical allegiances of practitioners; however, research (summarized by Claiborn, 1982) indicates that "interpretations differing greatly in content seem to have a similar impact on clients" (p. 450).

Levy (1963) classifies interpretations in two categories, *semantic* and *propositional*. Semantic interpretations describe clients' experiences according to the *practitioner's* conceptual vocabulary (e.g., "By 'frustrated,' I gather you mean you're feeling hurt and disillusioned"). Semantic interpretations thus are closely related to additive empathic responses. Propositional interpretations involve the practitioner's notions or explanations that assert causal relationships among factors involved in clients' problem situations (e.g., "When you try so hard to avoid displeasing others, you displease yourself and end up resenting others for taking advantage of you").[1]

Practitioners should avoid making interpretations or additive empathic responses (we are using the terms interchangeably) that are far removed from the awareness of clients. Research (Speisman, 1959) has indicated that moderate interpretations (those that reflect feelings that lie at the margin of the client's experiencing) facilitate self-exploration and self-awareness, whereas deep interpretations engender resistance. Because the latter are remote from clients' experiencing, they appear illogical and irrelevant to clients, who therefore tend to reject them despite the fact that such interpretations may be accurate. The following is an example of such an inept, deep interpretation:

Client: My boss is a real tyrant. He never gives anyone credit, except for Fran. She can do no wrong in his eyes. He just seems to have it in for me. Sometimes I'd like to punch his lights out.

Practitioner: Your boss seems to activate the same feelings you had toward your father. You feel he favors Fran, who symbolizes your favored sister. It's your father who you feel was the real tyrant, and you're reliving your resentment toward him. Your boss is merely a symbol of him.

Understandably, the client would likely reject and perhaps resent this interpretation. Though the practitioner may be accurate (the determination of which is purely speculative), the client is struggling with feelings toward his boss. To shift the focus to feelings toward his father misses the mark entirely from the client's perspective.

The following interpretation, made in response to the same client message, would be less likely to create opposition because it is linked to recent experiences of the client:

"So you really resent your boss because he seems impossible to please and shows partiality toward Fran. [*Reciprocal empathy.*] Those feelings reminded me of similar ones you expressed about two weeks ago. You were talking about how, when your parents spent a week with you on their vacation, your father seemed to find fault with everything you did but raved about how well your sister was doing. You'd previously mentioned he'd always seemed to favor your sister and that nothing you did seemed to please him. I'm wondering if those feelings might be connected with the feelings you're experiencing at work."

In the preceding message, notice that the practitioner carefully documented the rationale of the interpretation and offered it tentatively, a matter

we discuss later under "Guidelines for Employing Interpretation and Additive Empathy."

Because we discussed, illustrated, and provided exercises related to additive empathy in Chapter 5, we shall not deal with these topics in this chapter. Rather, we limit our discussion to uses of interpretation and additive empathy in expanding clients' self-awareness of (1) deeper feelings; (2) underlying meanings of feelings, thoughts, and behavior; (3) wants and goals; (4) hidden purposes of behavior; and (5) unrealized strengths and potentialities.

Deeper Feelings

Clients often have limited awareness of certain emotions, perceiving them only dimly if at all. Moreover, emotional reactions often involve multiple emotions, but clients may experience only the dominant or surface feelings. Further, some clients experience only negative emotions, such as anger, and are out of touch with more tender feelings including hurt, disappointment, compassion, loneliness, fears, caring and the like. Additive empathic responses (semantic interpretations) thus assist clients to become aware of emotions that lie at the edge of awareness, enabling them to experience these feelings more sharply and fully, to become more aware of their humanness (including the full spectrum of emotions), and to integrate emerging emotions into the totality of their experience.

Practitioners frequently employ additive empathic responses directed at expanding clients' awareness of feelings for several purposes, which we identify and illustrate in the following examples:

1. To identify feelings that are only implied or hinted at in clients' verbal messages:

Client [*in sixth session*]: I wonder if you feel we're making any progress. [*Clients frequently ask questions that embody veiled feelings.*]

Practitioner: It sounds as though you're not satisfied with your progress. I wonder if you're feeling discouraged about how it's been going.

2. To identify feelings that underlie surface emotions:

Client: I've just felt so bored in the evenings with so little to do. I went down to the bowling alley and watched people bowl, but that didn't seem to help. Life's just a drag.

Practitioner: I'm getting the impression you're feeling empty and pretty depressed. I wonder if you're feeling lonely and wishing you had some friends to fill that emptiness.

3. To add intensity to feelings clients have minimized:

Client [30-year-old mildly retarded socially isolated woman]: It was a little disappointing that Jana [*her childhood friend from another state*] couldn't come to visit. She lost her job and had to cancel her plane reservations.

Practitioner: I can see how terribly disappointed you were. In fact, you seem really down even now. You'd looked forward to her visit and made plans—it has been a real blow to you.

4. To clarify the nature of feelings clients experience only vaguely:

Client: When Ben told me he wanted a divorce so he could marry another woman, I just turned numb. I've been walking around in a daze ever since, telling myself, "This can't be happening."

Practitioner: It has been a crushing blow to you—you were so unprepared. It hurts so much it's hard to admit it's really happening.

5. To identify feelings manifested only nonverbally:

Client: My sister asked me to tend her kids while she's on vacation, and I will, of course. [*Frowns and sighs.*]

Practitioner: But your sigh tells me you don't feel good about it. Right now the message I get from you is that it seems an unfair and heavy burden to you and that you resent it.

Underlying Meanings of Feelings, Thoughts, and Behavior

Used for this purpose, additive empathy or interpretation assists clients to conceptualize or make meaning of feelings, thoughts, and behavior. Practitioners thus assist clients in understanding what motivates them to feel, think, and behave as they do; to grasp how their behavior bears on their problems and goals; and to discern themes and patterns in their thinking, feelings, and behavior. As clients discern similarities, parallels, and themes in their behavior and experiences, their self-awareness gradually expands in much the same way as single pieces of a puzzle fit together, gradually forming discrete entities and eventually coalescing into a coherent whole. The previous interpretation made to the client who resented his boss for favoring a co-worker is an example of this type of additive empathic response (which also fits into the category of a propositional interpretation).

In a more concrete sense, then, practitioners may employ this type of interpretation or additive empathy to assist clients to discern that they experience troublesome feelings in the presence of a certain type of person or in certain circumstances. For example, clients may feel depressed in the presence of critical people or feel extremely anxious in situations wherein they must perform (e.g., when expected to give a talk or take a test). Practitioners may thus use additive empathy to identify negative perceptual sets and other dysfunctional cognitive patterns that can be modified by employing cognitive restructuring. Clients may attend exclusively to trivial indications of their imperfections and completely overlook abundant evidence of competent and successful performance. Similarly, a practitioner may assist a client to discern a pattern of anticipating negative outcomes of relatively minor events and dreading (and avoiding) the events because of perceiving any of the negative outcomes as probable absolute disasters. One client dreaded visiting a lifelong friend who had recently sustained a severe fall, leaving her partially paralyzed. When the practitioner explored possible negative events that the client feared might occur if she were to visit the friend, she identified the following:

"What if I cry when I see her?"

"What if I stare at her?"

"What if I say the wrong thing?"

Using an additive empathic response, the practitioner replied, "And if you did one of those things, it would be a total disaster?" The client readily agreed. The practitioner then further employed cognitive restructuring to assist her to view the situation in realistic perspective by discussing each feared reaction, clarifying that anyone might react as she feared reacting and that if she were to react in any of the feared ways it would be uncomfortable but certainly not a disaster. They discussed the situation further, concluding that she had a certain amount of control over how she reacted rather than being totally at the mercy of circumstances. Following behavioral rehearsal, her fears of disaster gradually dwindled to manageable proportions.

Practitioners may also employ this type of additive empathy to enhance clients' awareness of perceptual distortions that adversely affect interpersonal relationships. Parents may reject children because they perceive characteristics in them that they abhor. Previous exploration, however, may have disclosed that parents abhor the same qualities in themselves and project their self-hatred onto their children. By assisting clients to recognize how self-perceptions (which may also be distorted) warp their perceptions of their children, practitioners enable them to make discriminations and to perceive and accept their children as unique individuals different from themselves.

Similar perceptual distortions may occur between marital partners, causing spouses to perceive and to respond inappropriately to each other as a result of unresolved and troublesome feelings that derive from earlier relationships with parents of the opposite sex.

Wants and Goals

Another important use of additive empathy is to assist clients to become aware of wants and goals that they imply in their messages but do not fully recognize. Beset by difficulties, people often tend to think in terms of problems and relief from them rather than in terms of growth and change; yet the latter two processes are often implied in the former. When they become more aware of the thrust toward growth implied in their messages, clients often welcome the prospect and indeed may wax enthusiastic. This type of additive empathy not only expands self-awareness, but it also may enhance motivation, as illustrated in the interchange below.

As is apparent in the following excerpt, additive empathic messages that highlight implied wants and goals often result in formulating explicit goals and pave the way to change-oriented actions. Moreover, such messages also play a critical role in arousing hope in dispirited clients who feel overwhelmed by problems and have been unable to discern positive desires for growth manifested in their struggles. This type of message thus plays a key role in the first phase of the helping process and in the change-oriented phase as well.

Client: I'm so sick of always being imposed upon. All of my family just take me for granted. You know, "Good old Ella, you can always depend on her." I'm so fed up with it all I could just chew nails.

Practitioner: Just thinking about it gets your hackles up. Ella, it seems to me that what you're saying adds up to an urgent desire on your part to be your own person—to feel in charge of yourself rather than being at the mercy of others' requests or demands.

Client: I hadn't thought of it that way but you're right. That's exactly what I want. If I could just be my own person.

Practitioner: Maybe that's a goal you'd like to set for yourself. It seems to fit, and accomplishing it would liberate you from the oppressive feelings you've described.

Client: Yes, yes! I'd like very much to set that goal. Do you really think I could accomplish it?

Expanding Awareness of Motives Underlying Behavior

Practitioners sometimes employ interpretations to assist clients to become more fully aware of basic motivations that underlie dysfunctional patterns of behavior. Other people may misinterpret clients' motives, and they themselves may have only a dim awareness of them because of the obscuring effect of their dysfunctional behaviors. Prominent among these motives are the following: to protect tenuous self-esteem (e.g., by avoiding situations that involve any risk of failing), to avoid anxiety-producing situations, and to compensate for feelings of impotency or inadequacy. The following are typical examples of surface behavior and hidden purposes served by the behavior.

1. Underachieving students may exert little effort in school (a) because they can justify failing on the basis of not having really tried (rather than having to face their fears of being inadequate) or (b) because they are seeking to punish parents who withhold approval and love when they fall short of their expectations.

2. Clients may present a facade of bravado to conceal from themselves and others underlying fears and feelings of inadequacy.

3. Clients may set themselves up for physical or emotional pain to expiate for deep-seated feelings of guilt.

4. Clients may engage in self-defeating behavior to validate myths that they are destined to be losers, or to live out life scripts determined by circumstances beyond their control.

5. Clients may avoid relating closely to others to protect against fears of being dominated or controlled.

6. Clients may behave aggressively and/or abrasively because they thereby avoid risking rejection by keeping others at a distance.

Interpretations must be based on substantial supporting information that clients have disclosed previously. Without supporting information, interpretations are little more than speculations that clients are unlikely to accept. Indeed, such speculations often emanate from practitioners' projections and are most often inaccurate. Practitioners who engage in deep and unfounded psychodynamic interpretations might be best described as "armchair psychoanalysts." Their inept interpretations often are calculated to impress others with their erudition, but the actual effect is often quite the opposite. Clients may regard their interpretations as offensive or may question their compe-

tence. The following example illustrates appropriate use of interpretations to expand awareness of underlying motives.

The client, Mr. R, age 33, together with his wife, entered marital therapy largely at his wife's instigation. She complained about a lack of closeness in the relationship and felt rejected because her husband seldom initiated affectional overtures. When she initiated overtures, he typically rebuffed her by pulling back. Mr. R had revealed in the exploratory interviews that his mother had been (and still was) extremely dominating and controlling. He had little warmth for his mother and saw her no more than was absolutely necessary. The following excerpt from an individual session with Mr. R focuses on an event that occurred during the week when the Rs went to a movie. Mrs. R reached over to hold his hand. He abruptly withdrew it, and Mrs. R later expressed her feelings of hurt and rejection. Their ensuing discussion was unproductive, and their communication strained. Mr. R discusses the event that occurred in the theater:

Client: I know Carol was hurt when I didn't hold her hand. I don't know why, but it really turned me off.

Practitioner: So you're wondering why you turn off when she reaches for some affectional contact. I wonder what was happening inside of you at the moment? What were you thinking and feeling?

Client: Gee, let me think. I guess I was anticipating she'd do it, and I just wanted to be left alone to enjoy the movie. I guess I resented her taking my hand. Gee, that doesn't make sense when I think about it. Why should I resent holding hands with the woman I love?

Practitioner: Jim, I think you're asking an awfully good question—one that's a key to many of the difficulties in your marriage. Let me share an idea with you that may shed some light on why you respond as you do. You mentioned you felt resentful when Carol took your hand. Based on the feelings you just expressed, I'm wondering if perhaps you feel you're submitting to her if you respond positively when she takes the initiative and pull back to be sure you're not letting yourself be dominated by her [*the hidden purpose*]. Another reason for suggesting that is that as you were growing up you felt dominated by your mother and resented her for being that way. Even now you avoid seeing her any more than you have to. I'm wondering if, as a result of your relationship with her, you could have developed a supersensitivity to being controlled by a female so that you resent any behavior on Carol's part that even suggests her being in control. [*The latter part of the response provides the rationale for the interpretation.*]

Unrealized Strengths and Potentialities

Another vital purpose served by interpretation and additive empathy is to expand clients' awareness of their strengths and undeveloped potentialities. Clients' strengths are manifested in varied ways, and it behooves practitioners to sensitize themselves to these often subtle manifestations by consciously cultivating a positive perceptual set. This objective is vital, for clients are often preoccupied with their weaknesses. Moreover, becoming aware of strengths tends to arouse clients' hopes and to generate courage to undertake making changes.

Drawing clients' awareness to strengths tends to enhance self-esteem and to foster courage to undertake tasks that involve risking new behaviors. With conscious effort, practitioners can become increasingly aware of clients' strengths, even with clients who possess marked limitations. A mildly mentally retarded and brain-damaged client, for example, lamented to one of the authors that she felt she was a total "zero." In addition to being brain-damaged, she was plagued by numerous phobias, including a fear of leaving home. She commented it had been a major effort for her to canvass the neighborhood soliciting donations for the heart fund. She believed this was a worthy cause, however, and it gave her satisfaction despite the tension and anxiety she experienced. The practitioner replied that her action was evidence of an important strength—namely, her caring about other people to the extent she would make such an effort on behalf of unknown others. He added that caring about others is a precious quality that many people lack and that she certainly was not a "zero" in light of this apparent strength. She beamed and guessed maybe she did have some good qualities.

This case is but one of the countless examples that could be cited for clients' strengths manifested as they report seemingly mundane events.

Guidelines for Employing Interpretation and Additive Empathy

Considerable finesse is required, to employ these skills effectively. The following guidelines will assist you in acquiring this finesse.

1. Use additive empathy sparingly until a sound working relationship has evolved. Because these responses go somewhat beyond clients' awareness of self, clients may misinterpret the motives of a practitioner and respond defensively. When clients demonstrate they are confident of a practitioner's goodwill, they are able to tolerate and often to benefit from additive empathic and interpretative responses. The exceptions to this guideline involve messages that identify (1) wants and goals and (2) strengths and potentialities, both of which are also appropriate in the initial phase of the helping process. Practitioners must avoid identifying strengths excessively in the initial phase, however, for some clients interpret such messages as insincere flattery.

2. Employ these responses only when clients are engaged in self-exploration or have manifested readiness for the same. Clients or groups that are not ready to engage in self-exploration are likely to resist practitioners' interpretive efforts and may interpret such efforts as unwarranted attempts by practitioners to impose their formulations upon them. Exceptions to this guideline are the same as those cited in the preceding guideline.

3. Pitch these responses to the edge of the client's awareness, and avoid attempting to foster awareness that is remote from clients' current awareness or experiencing. Clients generally are receptive to responses that closely relate to their experiencing but resist those that emanate from the practitioner's unfounded conjectures. It is poor practice to at-

tempt to push clients into rapidly acquiring new insights, for many deep interpretations prove to be inaccurate and produce negative effects, including reducing clients' confidence in practitioners, conveying lack of understanding, or engendering resistance. Practitioners should not employ interpretive responses until they have amassed sufficient information to be reasonably confident their responses are accurate and should share the supportive information upon which the interpretation is based.

4.   Avoid making several additive empathic responses in succession. Because interpretation responses require time to think through, digest, and assimilate, a series of such responses tends to bewilder clients.

5.   Phrase interpretive responses in tentative terms. Because these responses involve a certain degree of inference, there is always the possibility of being in error. Tentative phrasing openly acknowledges that possibility and invites clients to agree or disagree. If practitioners present interpretations in an authoritarian or dogmatic manner, however, clients may not feel free to offer candid feedback and may outwardly agree while actually covertly rejecting interpretations. Tentative phrases include, "I wonder if…," "Could it be that your feelings may be related to…?" and "Perhaps you're feeling this way because…"

6.   To determine the accuracy of an interpretive response, carefully note clients' reactions after offering the interpretation. When responses are on target, clients affirm their validity, continue self-exploration by bringing up additional relevant material, or respond emotionally in a manner that matches the moment (e.g., ventilate relevant feelings). When interpretations are inaccurate or are premature, clients tend to disconfirm them (verbally or nonverbally), change the subject, withdraw emotionally, argue or become defensive, or simply ignore the interpretation.

7.   If the client responds negatively to an interpre-

tative response, acknowledge your probable error, respond empathically to the client's reaction, and continue your discussion of the topic under consideration.

To assist you in expanding your skill in formulating interpretive and additive empathic responses, we have provided a number of exercises, together with modeled responses, at the end of the chapter.

CONFRONTATION

Similar to interpretation and additive empathy in that it is a tool to enhance clients' self-awareness and to promote change, confrontation involves facing clients with some aspect of their thoughts, feelings, or behavior that is contributing to or maintaining their difficulties. Confrontation is most likely to be heard when it comes from a source liked and respected by the client. Consequently, confrontations which occur early in contact are often not accurately heard or heeded. Nevertheless, practitioners sometimes have responsibilities to confront clients with law violations and dangers to themselves and others before a helping relationship has developed. Such confrontations should be sparing, given the likelihood that they will not be heeded so early in contact (Rooney, 1992).

In the middle phase of work, practitioners employ confrontation to assist clients to achieve awareness of forces blocking progress toward growth and goal attainment and to enhance their motivation to implement efforts toward change. Confrontation is particularly relevant when clients manifest blind spots to discrepancies or inconsistencies in their thoughts, beliefs, emotions, and behavior that tend to produce or to perpetuate dysfunctional behavior. Of course, blind spots in self-awareness are universal among human beings because all humans suffer from the limitation of being unable to step out of their perceptual fields and look at themselves objectively.

Practitioners have the advantage of viewing clients and their difficulties from an external vantage point, which makes it possible to offer fresh perspectives and corrective feedback when clients' distorted perceptions, avoidance behaviors, and other dysfunctional patterns impede progress. It is this very need for fresh perspectives and corrective input that impels people to seek help when their usual coping patterns prove ineffective.

Additive empathy and confrontation have much in common. Skillful confrontations embody consideration of clients' feelings that underlie obstacles to change. Because fears are often involved in obstacles to change, skill in relating with high levels of empathy is prerequisite to using confrontation effectively. Indeed, effective confrontation is an extension of empathic communication because the focusing on discrepancies and inconsistencies derives from a deep understanding of clients' feelings, experiences, and behavior.

It is important to bear in mind that confrontation is a tool to be used with discretion and not a style of "helping" others. Practitioners who make frequent confrontations generally have failed to master the facilitative conditions or find that their settings do not value them, considering them "soft." Practitioners should focus on the need for confrontation and respectful ways to convey it. Overuse and abusive use that does not convey caring for the client as a person is unethical and ineffective.

It is important for practitioners to have a range of confrontation skills, and not to confront primarily to vent their frustration with lack of progress. Practitioners do better to consider confrontation on a continuum ranging from fostering *self-confrontation* at the lower end to assertive confrontation at the higher end (Rooney, 1992). That is, clients can often be engaged quickly in self-confrontation by asking them questions which cause them to reflect on the relation between their behaviors and their own values. Skillfully designed intake forms can serve a similar function, asking potential clients to reflect on concerns and their perceptions of their causes. Such confrontations are subtle, respectful, and rarely engender strong client opposition. As clients gain expanded awareness of themselves and their problems through self-exploration, they tend to become aware of and to confront discrepancies and inconsistencies themselves. Self-confrontation is generally preferable to practitioner-initiated confrontation because the former is less risky and because clients' resistance to integrate insights is not an obstacle when they initiate confrontations themselves. Clients vary widely in the degree to which they engage in self-confrontation. Emotionally mature, introspective persons engage in self-confrontations frequently, whereas persons who are out of touch with their emotions, who lack awareness of their impact on others, and who blame others or circumstances for their difficulties are least likely to engage in self-confrontation.

Inductive questioning can be a form of confrontation which is more active on the practitioner's part but still conveyed in a respectful manner. The practitioner asks questions which lead the client to consider potential discrepancies between thoughts, values, beliefs, and actions. Also, when the therapist asks a question that relates to facts rather than one that requires the client to label himself or herself, the question is more likely to be effective. For example, asking a client with a chemical dependency problem "Are you powerless over alcohol?" would require the client to essentially label himself as an alcoholic. On the other hand, "Do you ever have blackouts? Do you find it easier to bring up a problem with another person when you have had something to drink? Do you ever find that once you begin drinking you can't easily stop?" are questions that, taken together, raise the possibility that drinking is a problem that might need attention (Citron, 1978).

When a danger is imminent, the practitioner may not be able to rely on the tactful self-confrontation facilitated by inductive questioning, but must rather engage in a more assertive confrontation in which the connection between troubling thoughts, plans, values, and beliefs must be stated in declarative form, connecting them for the client. Such assertive confrontation is a more high-risk technique because clients may interpret confrontations as criticisms, put-downs, or rejections. Paradoxically, the risk of these reactions is greatest among the groups of clients who must be confronted most often because they rarely engage in self-confrontation. These clients tend to have weak self-concepts and are therefore prone to read criticism into messages when none is intended. Moreover, ill-timed and poorly executed confrontations may be perceived by clients as verbal assaults and may seriously damage helping relationships. Using confrontations therefore requires keen timing and finesse. Practitioners must make special efforts to convey helpful intent and goodwill as they employ confrontations. Otherwise, they may engender hostility or offend and alienate clients.

Effective assertive confrontations embody four elements: (1) expression of concern; (2) a description of the client's purported goal, belief, or commitment; (3) the behavior (or absence of behavior) that is inconsistent or discrepant with the goal, belief, or commitment; and (4) the probable negative outcomes of the discrepant behavior. The format of a confrontive response may be depicted as follows:

(want)
I'm concerned because you (believe)
(are striving to)

_____
(describe desired outcome)

but your _____
(describe discrepant action, behavior, or inaction)

is likely to produce _____
(describe probable negative consequence)

This format is purely illustrative. You may organize these elements in varying ways, and we encourage you to be innovative and to develop your own style. For example, you may challenge clients to analyze the effects of behavior that is incongruous with purported goals or values, as illustrated in the following:

[*To male on parole*]: "Al, I know the last thing you want is to have to return to prison. I want you to stay out too, and I think you sense that. But I have to level with you. You're starting to hang out with the same bunch you got in trouble with before you went to prison. You're heading in the

same direction you were before, and we both know where that leads."

Notice that in the preceding confrontation the practitioner begins by making reference to the client's purported goal (remaining out of prison) and expresses a like commitment to the goal. The practitioner next introduces concern about the client's behavior (hanging out with the same bunch the client got in trouble with before) that is discrepant with that goal. The practitioner concludes the confrontation by focusing on the possible negative consequence of the discrepant behavior (getting into trouble and returning to prison). Notice these same elements in the following additional examples of confrontive responses.

[*To father in family session*]: "Mr. D, I'd like you to stop for a moment and examine what you're doing. I know you want the children not to be afraid of you and to talk with you more openly. Right?" [*Father agrees.*] "OK, let's think about what you just did with Steve. He began to tell you about what he did after the school assembly, and you cut him off and got on his case. Did you notice how he clammed up immediately?"

[*To child-abusing mother*]: "Helen, I have a concern I need to share with you. You've expressed your goal of regaining custody of Pete, and we agreed that attending the parents' group was part of the plan to accomplish that goal. This week is the second time in a row you've missed the meeting because you overslept. I'm very concerned you may be defeating yourself in accomplishing your goal."

Because employing assertive confrontation runs the risk of putting clients on the defensive or alienating them, expressing concern and helpful intent is a critical element because it reduces the possibility that clients will misconstrue the motive behind the confrontation. The tone of voice is also vital in conveying helpful intent. If the practitioner conveys the confrontation in a warm, concerned tone of voice, the client will be much less likely to feel attacked. If the practitioner uses a critical tone of voice, verbal reassurance that criticism was not intended is likely to fall on deaf ears. Keep in mind that people tend to attach more credence to non-verbal aspects of messages than to verbal aspects.

Guidelines to Employing Confrontation

To assist you in employing confrontation effectively, we offer the following guidelines:

1. *When a law violation or imminent danger to self or others is involved, a confrontation must occur no matter how early in the working relationship.* Such confrontations may impede the development of the relationship, but the risk of harm to self and others is more important than the immediate effect on the relationship.

2. *Whenever possible, avoid confrontation until an effective working relationship has evolved.* This can occur when a client is contemplating action (or inaction) which impede their own goals, but are not imminent dangers to self or others. Employing empathic responsiveness in early contacts conveys understanding, fosters rapport, and enhances confidence in the perceptiveness and expertise of the practitioner. When a foundation of trust and confidence has been established, clients are more receptive to confrontations and, in some instances, even welcome them.

3. *Use confrontation sparingly.* Keep in mind that confrontation is a potent technique that generally should be employed only when clients' blind spots are refractory to other less risky methods. Some practitioners use confrontation frequently, professing it to be a "high-yield" technique. Research by Lieberman, Yalom, and Miles (1973) involving groups refutes this argument. Their findings indicate that destructive group leaders tend to be highly confrontive and challenging persons who frequently attack members and pressure them for immediate change. Based on their findings, these authors concluded that this type of leadership is associated with negative outcomes. Indeed, poorly timed and excessive confrontations can inflict psychological damage on clients.

Another reason to employ confrontation judiciously is that some clients may yield to forceful confrontation for reasons that are counterproductive. Seeking to please practitioners (or to avoid displeasing them), they may temporarily modify their behavior. But changing merely to comply with expectations of a practitioner fosters passivity and dependence, both of which are anathema to actual growth. Some clients already are excessively passive, and pressuring them for compliance only reinforces their dysfunctional behavior.

4. *Deliver confrontations in an atmosphere of warmth, caring, and concern.* As we have previously emphasized, if practitioners employ confrontations in a cold, impersonal, or critical way, clients are likely to feel they are being attacked. By contrast, if practitioners preface confrontations with genuine empathic concern (as recommended in the paradigm presented earlier), clients are more likely to perceive the helpfulness intended in the confrontation.

5. *Whenever possible, encourage self-confrontations.* Recall from the previous discussion that self-confrontations have decided advantages over practitioner-initiated confrontations. Learning by self-discovery fosters independence and enhances the likelihood that clients will act upon newly gained self-awareness. Practitioners can encourage self-confrontation by drawing the attention of clients to issues, behaviors, or inconsistencies they may have overlooked and by encouraging them to analyze the situation further. For example, the practitioner may directly intervene into dysfunctional interaction and challenge individuals, couples, families, or groups to identify what they are doing. Responses that encourage self-confrontation in such a context include the following:

"Let's stop and look at what you just did."

"What did you just do?"

Other inductive question responses that highlight inconsistencies and foster self-confrontation are as follows:

"I'm having trouble seeing how what you just said (or did) fits with…"

"I can understand how you felt, but how did (describe behavior) make it better for you?"

"What you're saying seems inconsistent with what you want to achieve. How do you see it?"

Still another technique is useful when clients overlook the dynamic significance of their own revealing expressions or when their manifest feelings fail to match their reported feelings. This technique involves asking them to repeat a message, to listen carefully to themselves, and to consider the meaning of the message. Examples of this technique follow:

"I want to be sure you realize the significance of what you just said. Repeat it, but this time listen carefully to yourself, and tell me what it means to you."

[*To marital partner in conjoint interview*]: "Joan just told you something terribly important, and I'm not sure you really grasped it. Could you repeat it, Joan, and I want you to listen very carefully, Bob, and check with Joan as to whether you grasped what she said."

[*To group member*]: "You just told the group you're feeling better about yourself, but it didn't come through that way. Please say it again, but get in touch with your feelings and listen to yourself."

6. *Avoid using confrontation when clients are experiencing extreme emotional strain.* Confrontations tend to mobilize anxiety, and when clients are under heavy strain, supportive techniques rather than confrontation are indicated. Clients who are overwhelmed with anxiety and/or guilt generally are not receptive to confrontation and do not benefit from it. Rather, confrontations may be detrimental, adding to tension that is already excessive.

Confrontation is appropriate for clients who experience minimal inner conflict or anxiety when such reactions would be appropriate in light of their problematic behavior as perceived by others. Self-satisfied and typically insensitive to the feelings and needs of others (whom they cause to be anxious), such clients, popularly referred to as character disorders, often lack the anxiety needed to engender and maintain adequate motivation.

Confrontation, combined with the facilitative conditions, may mobilize the anxiety they need to examine their own behavior and to consider making constructive changes.

7. *Follow confrontations with empathic responsiveness.* Because clients may take offense to even skillful confrontations, it is vital to be sensitive to their reactions. Since clients often do not express their reactions verbally, you will need to be especially perceptive of nonverbal cues that suggest hurt, anger, confusion, discomfort, embarrassment, or resentment. If clients manifest these or other unfavorable reactions, it is important to explore their reactions and to respond empathically to their feelings. Discussing such reactions provides opportunities for clients to ventilate their feelings and for practitioners to clarify their helpful intent and to assist clients to work through negative feelings. If practitioners fail to sense negative feelings or clients withhold expressions of them, the feelings may fester and adversely affect the helping relationship.

It is to be expected that clients will respond to confrontations with a certain degree of anxiety. Indeed, confrontations are employed to produce a temporary sense of disequilibrium that is essential to break an impasse. The anxiety or disequilibrium thus serves a therapeutic purpose in impelling the client to make constructive changes that eliminate the discrepancy that prompted the practitioner's confrontation. Empathic responsiveness following confrontations thus is not aimed at diluting this anxiety but rather at resolving untoward reactions that may derive from negative interpretations of the practitioner's motives for making the confrontation.

8. *Don't expect immediate change after confrontations.* Although awareness paves the way to change, clients rarely succeed in making changes immediately following acquisition of insight. Even when clients fully accept confrontations, corresponding changes ordinarily occur by increments. Known as working through, this change process involves repeatedly reviewing the same conflicts and the client's typical reactions to them, gradually broad-

ening the perspective to encompass more and more situations to which the changes are applicable. Unfortunately, some naive practitioners press for immediate change, sometimes inflicting psychological damage on their clients, as we noted earlier.

Indications for Assertive Confrontation

As we have previously indicated, confrontations are appropriate (1) when law violations or imminent threats to the welfare and safety of self or others is involved; (2) discrepancies, inconsistencies, and dysfunctional behaviors (overt or covert) block progress or create difficulties and (3) when efforts at self-confrontation and inductive questioning have been ineffective in fostering clients' awareness of these behaviors and/or attempts to make corresponding changes. Discrepancies may reside in cognitive/perceptual, emotional, or behavioral functions or may involve interactions between these functions. A comprehensive analysis of types of discrepancies and inconsistencies has been presented elsewhere (Hammond et al., 1977, pp. 286–318); therefore, we merely highlight some of those that most commonly occur.

Cognitive/Perceptual Discrepancies   Many clients manifest dysfunctional behavior that is a product of inaccurate, erroneous, or incomplete information, and confrontations may assist them in modifying their behavior. For example, clients may lack accurate information about indicators of alcoholism, normal sexual functioning, or reasonable expectations of children according to stages of development. Even more common are misconceptions about the self, the most common of which, in the authors' experience, involve self-demeaning perceptions. Even talented and attractive persons may view themselves as inferior, worthless, inadequate, unattractive, stupid, and the like. Such perceptions are often deeply embedded and do not yield to change without extensive working through. Still, confronting with strengths, or raising awareness of other areas of competence, can be

helpful in challenging the self-deprecating view. Other cognitive/perceptual discrepancies include interpersonal perceptual distortions, irrational fears, dichotomous or stereotypical thinking, denial of problems, placing responsibility for one's difficulties outside of oneself, failing to discern available alternate solutions to difficulties, and failing to consider consequences of actions. We focused on these categories of dysfunction in Chapter 9.

Affective Discrepancies   Discrepancies in the emotional realm are inextricably linked to the cognitive/perceptual processes, as emotions are shaped by cognitive meanings clients attribute to situations, events, and memories. For example, one may experience intense anger that emanates from a conclusion that another person has intentionally insulted, slighted, or betrayed one. The conclusion is based on a meaning attribution that may involve a grossly distorted perception of another person's intentions. In such instances, practitioners assist clients to explore their feelings, to provide relevant detailed factual information, to consider alternate meanings, and to realign their emotions with reality.

Affective discrepancies that practitioners commonly encounter include denying or minimizing actual feelings, being out of touch with painful emotions, expressing feelings that are contrary to purported feelings (e.g., claiming to love a spouse or child but expressing only critical or otherwise negative feelings), or verbally expressing a feeling that contradicts feelings expressed nonverbally (e.g., "No, I'm not disappointed," said with a quivering voice and tears in the eyes). Gentle confrontations aimed at emotional discrepancies often pave the way to ventilation of troubling emotions, and many clients appreciate practitioners' sensitivity in recognizing their suppressed or unexpressed emotions. If a client appears unready to face painful emotions, the practitioner should proceed cautiously and may be wise to defer further exploration of them. Confronting the client vigorously may elicit overwhelming emotions and engender consequent resentment toward the practitioner.

Behavioral Discrepancies Clients may manifest many dysfunctional behavioral patterns or lifestyles that create difficulties for themselves and others. Even though these patterns may be conspicuous to others, clients themselves may have blind spots to their patterns or to the impact of the same on others. Therefore, confrontation may be required to expand their awareness of these patterns and their pernicious effects. In Chapter 9 (Table 9-3), we enumerated many of the myriad dysfunctional patterns that practitioners encounter. We will not repeat them here but will highlight certain pervasive categories of dysfunctional behavior.

Irresponsible behavior tends to spawn serious interpersonal difficulties for clients as well as problems with broader society. Neglect of children, weak efforts to secure and maintain employment, undependability in fulfilling assignments, failure to maintain property—these and other like derelictions often result in severe financial, legal, and interpersonal entanglements that may culminate in loss of employment; estrangement from others; and loss of property, child custody, self-respect, and even personal freedom. Irresponsible behavior often pervades the helping process as well, being manifested by tardiness, unwillingness to acknowledge problems, and failure to keep appointments or pay fees. Effective confrontations with such clients require a firm approach couched in expressions of goodwill and concern about wanting to assist the client to avoid adverse consequences of not assuming responsibilities. It is a disservice to clients to permit them to rationalize, deny, and evade responsibility for their actions or inaction. Further, the practitioner must counter their tendency to blame others or circumstances for their difficulties by assisting them to recognize that *only they* can reduce the pressures that beset them.

Other common behavioral discrepancies involve repeated actions that are incongruous with purported goals or values. Adolescents may describe ambitious goals that require extensive training or education but make little effort in school, truant frequently, and otherwise behave in ways entirely inconsistent with their goals. Spouses or parents may similarly espouse goals of improving their marital or family life but persistently behave in abrasive ways that further erode their relationships. Confrontations often must be used to assist them to desist from self-defeating behaviors. In some instances, therapeutic binds (a special form of confrontation discussed in Chapter 19) may be employed to supply additional needed leverage to motivate clients to relinquish destructive and unusually persistent patterns of behavior.

Three other common categories of discrepancies or dysfunctional behavior that warrant confrontation are manipulative behavior, dysfunctional communication, and resistance to change. In groups, certain members may attempt to dominate the group, bait group members, play one person against the other, undermine the leader, or engage in other destructive ploys. The price of permitting members to engage in such behaviors may be loss of certain group members, dilution of the group's effectiveness, or premature dissolution of the group. To avert such undesired consequences, the leader may elicit reactions of other members to such behavior and may assist members to confront manipulators with their destructive tactics. Such confrontations should adhere to the guidelines delineated earlier, and the leader should encourage members to invite offending members to join with them in constructively seeking to accomplish the purposes of the group.

Because dysfunctional communication frequently occurs in individual, conjoint, and group sessions, practitioners encounter abundant opportunities to employ confrontation to good effect. Intervening during or immediately following dysfunctional communication is a powerful means of enabling clients to experience firsthand the negative effect of their dysfunctional behavior (e.g., interrupting, attacking, claiming, or criticizing). By shifting the focus to the negative reactions of recipients of dysfunctional messages, practitioners enable clients to receive direct feedback as to how their behavior offends, alienates, or engenders defensiveness in others, thereby producing effects contrary to their purported goals.

Confrontation is a vital tool in working through clients' opposition both to change and to relating openly in the helping relationship. If individual clients are left to struggle alone with negative feelings about the helping process or the practitioner, their feelings may mount to the extent that they resolve them by discontinuing their sessions. If family members or groups are permitted to oppose change by engaging in distractive, irrelevant, or otherwise dysfunctional behavior, they may likewise lose both confidence in the practitioners (for valid reasons) and motivation to continue. For these reasons, practitioners must accord highest priority to focusing on and resolving resistance. Because of the importance of this matter, we have devoted the entire following chapter to it.

SKILL DEVELOPMENT EXERCISES IN ADDITIVE EMPATHY AND INTERPRETATION

To assist you to advance your skill in responding with interpretation and additive empathy, we provide the following exercises. Read each client message, determine the type of response called for, and formulate a written response you would employ if you were in an actual session with the client. As you formulate your responses, keep in mind the guidelines for employing interpretive additive empathic responses. Compare your responses with the modeled responses provided at the end of the exercises.

Client Statements

1. *White female client* [*to African American female practitioner*]: You seem to be accepting of white people, at least you have been of me. But somehow I still feel uneasy with you. I guess it's just me. I haven't really known many black people very well.

2. *Married woman, age 28:* I feel I don't have a life of my own. My life is controlled by *his* work, *his* hours, and *his* demands. It's like I don't have an identity of my own.

3. *Prison inmate, age 31* [*one week before date of scheduled parole, which was canceled the preceding week*]: Man, what the hell's going on with me? Here I've been on good behavior for three years and finally got a parole date. You'd think I'd be damned glad to get out of here. So I get all uptight and get in a brawl in the mess hall. I mean I really blew it, man. Who knows when they'll give me another date?

4. *Male, age 18:* What's the point in talking about going to Trade Tech? I didn't make it in high school, and I won't make it there either. You may as well give up on me—I'm just a dropout in life.

5. *Widow, age 54:* It was Mother's Day last Sunday, and neither of my kids did as much as send me a card. You'd think they could at least acknowledge I'm alive.

6. *Female secretary, age 21:* I don't have any trouble typing when I'm working alone. But if the boss or anyone else is looking over my shoulder, it's like I'm all thumbs. I just seem to tighten up.

7. *Married female, age 26, who is five pounds overweight:* When I make a batch of cookies or a cake on the weekend, Terry [*husband*] looks at me with that condemning expression, as though I'm not really trying to keep my weight down. I don't think it's fair just because he doesn't like sweets. I like sweets, but the only time I eat any is on the weekend, and I don't eat much then. I feel I deserve to eat dessert on the weekend at least.

8. *Recipient of public assistance* [*disabled male with a back condition caused by recent industrial accident*]: This lying around is really getting to me. I see my kids needing things I can't afford to get them, and I just feel—I don't know—kind of useless. There's got to be a way of making a living.

9. *Depressed male, age 53:* Yeah, I know I do all right in my work. But that doesn't amount to much. Anyone could do that. That's how I feel about everything I've ever done. Nothing's really amounted to anything.

10. *Mother, age 29* [*who has neglected her children*]: I don't know. I'm just so confused. I look at my kids sometimes, and I want to be a better mother. But after they've been fighting, or throwing tantrums, or whining and I lose my cool—I feel like I'd just like to go somewhere—anywhere—and never come back. The kids deserve a better mother.

Modeled Responses for Interpretation and Additive Empathy

1. [*To clarify feelings experienced only vaguely*]: "So I gather even though you can't put your finger on why, you're still somewhat uncomfortable with me. You haven't related closely to that many African Americans, and you're still not altogether sure how much you can trust me."

2. [*Implied wants and goals*]: "Sounds like you feel you're just an extension of your husband and that part of you is wanting to find yourself and be a person in your own right."

3. [*Hidden purpose of behavior, underlying feelings*]: "So you're pretty confused about what's happened. Fighting in the mess hall when you did just doesn't make sense to you. You know, Carl, about your getting uptight—I guess I'm wondering if you were worried about getting out—worried about whether you could make it outside. I'm wondering if you might have fouled up last week to avoid taking that risk."

4. [*Underlying belief after self*]: "Sounds like you feel defeated before you give yourself a chance. Like it's hopeless to even try. Jay, that concerns me because when you think that way about yourself, you are defeated—not because you lack ability but because you think of yourself as destined to fail. That belief is your real enemy."

5. [*Deeper feelings*]: "You must have felt terribly hurt and resentful they didn't as much as call you. In fact, you seem to be experiencing those feelings now. It just hurts so much."

6. [*Underlying thoughts and feelings*]: "I wonder if, in light of your tightening up, you get feeling scared, as though you're afraid you won't measure up to their expectations."

7. [*Unrealized strengths*]: "Paula, I'm impressed with what you just said. It strikes me you're exercising a lot of control by limiting dessert to weekends and using moderation then. In fact, your self-control seems greater than that of most people. You and Terry have a legitimate difference concerning sweets. But it's exactly that—a difference. Neither view is right or wrong, and you're entitled to your preference as much as he's entitled to his."

8. [*Unrealized strength and implied want*]: "Steve, I can hear the frustration you're feeling, and I want you to know it reflects some real strength on your part. You want to be self-supporting and be able to provide better for your family. Given that desire, we can explore opportunities for learning new skills that won't require physical strength."

9. [*Underlying pattern of thought*]: "Kent, I get the feeling that it wouldn't matter what you did. You could set a world record, and you wouldn't feel it amounted to much. I'm wondering if your difficulty lies more in long-time feelings you've had about yourself that you somehow just don't measure up. I'd be interested in hearing more about how you've viewed yourself."

10. [*Underlying feelings and implied wants*]: "So your feelings tear you and pull you in different directions. You'd like to be a better mother, and you feel crummy when you lose your cool. But sometimes you just feel so overwhelmed and inadequate in coping with the children. Part of you would like to learn to manage the children better, but another part would like to get away from it all."

SKILL DEVELOPMENT EXERCISES IN CONFRONTATION

The following exercises involve discrepancies and dysfunctional behavior in all three experiential domains—cognitive/perceptual, emotional, and behavioral. After reading the brief summary of the situation involved and the verbatim exchanges between the client(s) and practitioner, identify the type of discrepancy involved and formulate your next response (observing the guidelines presented earlier) as though you are the practitioner in a real-life situation. Next, compare your response with the modeled one, keeping in mind that the latter is only one of many possible appropriate responses. Carefully analyze how your response is similar to or differs from the modeled response and whether you adhered to the guidelines.

Situations and Dialogue

1. You have been working with Mr. Lyon for several weeks, following his referral by the court after being convicted for sexually molesting his teenage

daughter. Mr. Lyon has been 15 minutes late for his last two appointments, and today he is 20 minutes late. During his sessions he has explored and worked on problems only superficially.

Client: Sorry to be late today. Traffic was sure heavy. You know how that goes.

2. The clients are marital partners whom you have seen conjointly five times. One of their goals is to reduce marital conflict by avoiding getting into arguments that create mutual resentments.

Mrs. J: This week has been just awful. I've tried to look nice and have his meals on time—like he said he wanted, and I've just felt so discouraged. He got on my back Tuesday and…[*Husband interrupts.*]

Mr. J [*angrily*]: Just a minute. You're only telling half the story. You left out what you did Monday. [*She interrupts.*]

Mrs. J: Oh, forget it. What's the use? He doesn't care about me. He couldn't the way he treats me.

Mr. J: [*Shakes head in disgust.*]

3. The client is a slightly retarded young adult who was referred by a rehabilitation agency because of social and emotional problems. The client has manifested a strong interest in dating young women and has been vigorously pursuing a clerk (Sue) in a local supermarket. She has registered no interest in him and obviously has attempted to discourage him from further efforts. The following excerpt occurs in the seventh session.

Client: I went through Sue's checkstand this morning. I told her I'd like to take her to the show.

Practitioner: Oh, and what did she say?

Client: She said she was too busy. I'll wait a couple of weeks and ask her again.

4. Tony, age 16, is a member of a therapy group in a youth correctional institution. In the preceding session, he appeared to gain a sense of power and satisfaction from provoking other members to react angrily and defensively, which tended to disrupt group process. Tony directs the following message to a group member early in the fourth session.

Tony: I noticed you trying to make out with Maggie at the dance Wednesday. You think you're pretty hot stuff, don't you?

5. The client is a mother, age 26, who keeps feelings inside until they mount out of control, at which time she discharges anger explosively.

Client: I can't believe my neighbor. She sends her kids over to play with Sandra at lunchtime and disappears. It's obvious her kids haven't had lunch, and I end up feeding them, even though she's better off financially than I am.

Practitioner: What do you feel when she does that?

Client: Oh, not much, I guess. But I think it's a rotten thing to do.

6. You have been working for several weeks with a family that includes the parents and four children ranging in age from 10 to 17. The mother is a domineering person who acts as spokesperson for the family, and the father is passive and softspoken. A teenage daughter, Tina, expresses herself in the following excerpt.

Tina: We always seem to have a hassle when we visit our grandparents. Grandma's so bossy. I don't like going there.

Mother: Tina, that's not true. You've always enjoyed going to her house. You and your grandmother have always been close.

7. Group members in their fifth session have been intently discussing difficulties of the members in social interaction. One of the members takes the group off on a tangent by describing humorous idiosyncrasies of a person she met while on vacation, and the other group members follow suit by sharing humorous anecdotes about "oddballs" they have encountered.

8. The client is an attractive, personable, and intelligent woman who has been married for three years to a self-centered, critical man. In the fourth session (an individual interview), she tearfully says:

Client: I've done everything he's asked of me. I've lost 10 pounds. I support him in his work. I golf with him. I even changed my religion to please him. And he's still not happy with me. There's just something wrong with me.

9. The clients are a married couple in their early 30s. The following excerpt occurs in the initial interview.

Wife: We just seem to fight over the smallest things. When he gets really mad, he loses his temper and knocks me around.

Husband: The real problem is that she puts her parents ahead of me. She's the one who needs help, not me. If she'd get straightened around, I wouldn't lose my temper. Tell her where her first responsibility is. I've tried, and she won't listen to me.

10. The clients are a family consisting of the parents and two children. Terry, age 15, has been truanting and smoking marijuana. Angie, age 16, is a model student and is obviously her parents' favorite. The family was referred by the school when Terry was expelled for several days. The father, a highly successful businessman, entered family therapy with obvious reluctance, which has continued to this, the fourth session.

Mother: Things haven't been much different this week. Everyone's been busy, and we really haven't seen much of each other.

Father: I think we'd better plan to skip the next three weeks. Things have been going pretty well, and I have an audit in process at the office that's going to put me in a time bind.

Modeled Responses for Confrontation

1. [*Irresponsible and resistant behavior by the client*]: "Ted, I'm concerned you're late today. This is the third time you've been late in a row, and it shortens the time available to us. But my concerns go beyond that. I know you don't like having to come here and that you'd like to be out from under the court's jurisdiction. But the way you're going about things won't accomplish that. I can't be helpful to you and can't write a favorable report to the court if you just go through the motions of

coming here for help. Apparently it's uncomfortable for you to come. I'd be interested in hearing just what you're feeling about coming."

2. [*Discrepancy between purported goal and behavior, as well as dysfunctional communication*]: "Let's stop and look at what you're doing right now. I'm concerned because each of you wants to feel closer to the other, but what you're both doing just makes each other defensive." [*To husband.*] "Mr. J., she was sharing some important feelings with you, and you cut her off." [*To wife.*] "And you did the same thing, Mrs. J, when he was talking. I know you may not agree, but it's important to hear each other out and to try to understand. If you keep interrupting and trying to blame each other, as you've both been doing, you're going to stay at square one, and I don't want that to happen. Let's go back and start over, but this time put yourself in the shoes of the other and try to understand. Check out with the other if you really understood. Then you can express your own views."

3. [*Dysfunctional, self-defeating behavior*]: "Pete, I know how much you think of Sue and how you'd like to date her. I'm concerned that you keep asking her out, though, because she never accepts and doesn't appear to want to go out with you. My concern is that you're setting yourself up for hurt and disappointment. I'd like to see you get a girl friend, but your chances of getting a date are probably a lot better with persons other than Sue."

4. [*Abrasive, provocative behavior*]: "Hold on a minute, guys. I'm feeling uncomfortable and concerned right now about what Tony just said. It comes across as a real put-down, and we agreed earlier one of our rules was to support and help each other. Tony, would you like some feedback from other members about how you're coming across to the group?"

5. [*Discrepancy between expressed and actual feeling*]: "I agree. But I'm concerned about your say-

ing you don't feel much. I should think you'd be ticked off and want to change the situation. Let's see if you can get in touch with your feelings. Picture yourself at home at noon and your neighbor's kids knock on the door while you're fixing lunch. Can you picture it? What are you feeling in your body and thinking just now?"

6. [*Dysfunctional communication—disconfirming Tina's feelings and experiences*]: "What did you just do, Mrs. Black? Stop and think for a moment about how you responded to Tina's message. It may help you to understand why she doesn't share more with you." [*or*] "Tina, could you tell your mother what you're feeling right now about what she just said? I'd like her to get some feedback that could help her communicate better with you."

7. [*Discrepancy between goals and behavior—getting off topic*]: "I'm concerned about what the group's doing right now. What do you think is happening?"

8. [*Misconception about the self—cognitive/perceptual discrepancy*]: "Jan, I'm concerned about what you just said because you're putting yourself down and leaving no room to feel good about yourself. You're assuming that you own the problem and that you're deficient in some way. I'm not at all sure that's the problem. You're married to a man who seems impossible to please, and that is more likely the problem. As we agreed earlier, you have tasks of feeling good about yourself, standing up for yourself, and letting his problem be his. As long as your feelings about yourself depend on his approval, you're going to feel down on yourself."

9. [*Manipulative behavior*]: "I don't know the two of you well enough to presume to know what's causing your problems." [*To husband.*] "If you're expecting me to tell your wife to shape up, you'll be disappointed. My job is to help each of you to see your part in the difficulties and to make appropriate changes. If I did what you asked, I'd be doing both of you a gross disservice. Things don't get better that way."

10. [*Resistance, discrepancy between behavior and purported goals*]: "What you do, of course, is up to you. I am concerned, however, because you all agreed you wanted to relate more closely as family members and give each other more support. To accomplish that means you have to work at it steadily, or things aren't likely to change much." [*To father.*] "My impression is that you're backing off. I know your business is important, but I guess you have to decide whether you're really committed to the goals you set for yourselves."

NOTES

1 Claiborn (1982) presents numerous examples of both types of interpretation as well as a comprehensive discussion of this important topic. Other researchers (Beck & Strong, 1982; Claiborn, Crowford, & Hackman, 1983; Dowd & Boroto, 1982; Feldman, Strong, & Danser, 1982; Milne & Dowd, 1983) have also reported findings comparing the effects of different types of interpretations.

Chapter 19

Managing Individual, Family, and Organizational Barriers to Change

BARRIERS TO CHANGE

Progress toward goal attainment is rarely smooth; rather, the change process is characterized by rapid spurts of growth, plateaus and impasses, and sometimes brief periods of retrogression. Even getting started can be a formidable challenge with involuntary clients and families, such as those with problems of child maltreatment or spouse abuse. The degree and rate of change vary widely, being affected by many variables, most critical of which are variations in the motivation and strengths of clients; the severity and duration of problems; vicissitudes in the helping relationship; environmental forces that support or militate against change; and the responsiveness (or lack thereof) of institutions in providing needed resources. In this chapter we focus on these potential barriers to change and ways of managing them so that they do not unduly impede progress or precipitate premature termination by clients.

First we address the topic of relational reactions and discuss potential barriers that derive from clients, practitioners, transracial and transcultural relationships, and sexual attractions toward clients. Then we focus on managing opposition to change by individuals and families. The last major section is concerned with managing organizational barri-

ers to change. Then the chapter concludes with skill development exercises related to managing relational reactions.

RELATIONAL REACTIONS

The practitioner–client relationship is the vehicle that animates the helping process especially for voluntary clients. Indeed, the quality of the helping relationship critically determines both the client's moment-to-moment receptiveness to the influence and intervention of the practitioner and the ultimate outcome of the helping process. Further, the helping relationship per se may be a source of positive change for many clients, who gain self-respect and feelings of worth in positive helping relationships. For clients whose previous life experiences have been void of sustained caring relationships, the helping relationship may be a corrective emotional experience in the sense of compensating for emotional deprivation experienced in earlier life.

Because of the profound importance of the helping relationship, it is critical that practitioners be skillful both in cultivating relationships and keeping them in repair. In earlier chapters, we discussed qualities and skills in cultivating sound relationships.

Skills in maintaining relationships are equally vital, as feelings that influence the relationship for better or worse constantly flow back and forth between participants in the helping process. Therefore, to maintain positive helping relationships, you must be alert to threats to such relationships and be skillful in managing them. In the following sections, we discuss these factors at length.

RECOGNIZING AND MANAGING THREATS TO HELPING RELATIONSHIPS

Helping relationships that are characterized by reciprocal positive feelings between practitioner and clients are conducive to personal growth and successful problem solving. Practitioners strive to develop positive helping relationships by relating facilitatively with high levels of warmth, acceptance, unconditional caring, empathy, genuineness, and spontaneity, as we discussed earlier. Despite these efforts, however, some clients do not respond positively for a number of reasons that we discuss later. Practitioners, too, may have difficulty responding positively to clients with certain personality attributes and types of problems. Even when a positive relationship evolves, various events and moment-by-moment transactions may pose threats to the continuing viability of the relationship. Practitioners must be vigilant to manifestations that something is going awry in the relationship. Failure to perceive these manifestations and to manage them effectively may result in needless impasses or, even worse, premature termination. In the following discussion, we focus on threats to the relationship that emanate from the client, from the practitioner, and from dynamic mixes of both.

Here-and-Now Reactions

Clients often experience emotional reactions during the course of sessions that create a temporary breach in helping relationships, and if practitioners fail to recognize and handle them skillfully, the reactions may expand into major obstacles in the helping process. The following are typical examples of practitioners' behavior that may engender immediate feelings of hurt, disappointment, anger, fear, rejection, and other like negative emotions:

1. Failing to sense important feelings experienced by clients.
2. Sending messages that clients interpret as criticisms or put-downs.
3. Being inattentive or "tuning out" clients.
4. Failing to acknowledge incremental growth achieved by clients.
5. Employing inept or poorly timed confrontations.
6. Manifesting lapses of memory about important information previously revealed by clients.
7. Being tardy or canceling appointments.
8. Appearing drowsy or fidgety.
9. Disagreeing, arguing, or giving excessive advice.
10. Disapproving of a client's planned course of action.
11. Appearing to take sides against a client (or subgroup) or actually doing so.
12. Dominating discussions or frequently interrupting clients.
13. Giving advice or assignments that clients feel incapable of carrying out.
14. Utilizing power with involuntary clients to interfere in life style areas beyond the range of legal mandates.

Some of the preceding events or circumstances involve mistakes by practitioners; others involve misperceptions by clients. Whatever their source, it is vital to sense and to discuss clients' feelings and thoughts as they are manifested and thus prevent them from escalating. Often clients will not initiate discussion of their negative reactions, and if you are not sensitive to nonverbal cues, the feelings and cognitions will linger and fester. To avert such a development, it is crucial to be perceptive of indicators of negative reactions including the following nonverbal cues: frowning, fidgeting, sighing, appearing startled, grimacing, changing the subject, becoming silent, clearing the throat, blushing, and tightening the muscles. When you discern these or related cues, it is important to shift the focus of the session to the clients' here-and-now feelings and cognitions. You should do this tentatively, checking out whether your perception is accurate. If accurate, proceed sensitively, manifesting genuine concern for the client's discomfort and conveying your desire to understand what the client is experiencing at the moment. Examples of responses that facilitate discussion of troubling feelings and thoughts are:

"I'm sensing you're reacting to what I just said. Could you share with me what it meant to you and what you're thinking and feeling at this moment?"

"You appear distressed right now. I'd like to understand just what you're experiencing and if I may have said or done something that caused your troubled thoughts and feelings."

Keep in mind that discussing negative feelings and cognitions toward a practitioner is extremely difficult for many clients. You can reduce the threat by being warmly attentive and accepting of clients, even though their thoughts and feelings may be entirely unrealistic. By eliciting the client's feelings and thoughts, you have the opportunity to correct a misunderstanding, clarify your intention, rectify a blunder, or identify a dysfunctional belief or pattern of thought. Indeed, some clients benefit from observing a model who can acknowledge imperfections and apologize for errors without appearing humiliated. Moreover, clients may gain self-esteem by realizing that practitioners value them sufficiently to be concerned about their thoughts and feelings and to rectify errors of omission or commission. After productive discussions of here-and-now thoughts and feelings, most clients regain positive feelings and resume working on their problems.

On occasions, however, clients may succeed in concealing negative thoughts and feelings, or you may overlook nonverbal manifestations of them. The feelings may thus fester until it becomes obvious that the client is relating atypically by holding back, being overly formal, responding defensively,

or manifesting other forms of opposition enumerated later in this chapter. Again, it is vital to accord priority to the relationship by shifting focus to what is bothering the client and responding as we recommended earlier. *After you have worked through the negative reaction of the client, it is helpful to negotiate a "minicontract" related to discussing troublesome feelings and thoughts as they occur.* The objective of this renegotiation is to avert similar recurrences in the future and to convey your openness to discussing negative reactions toward you. Learning to express negative feelings and thoughts can be a milestone for clients who typically withhold such reactions to the detriment of themselves and others. The following is an example of a message aimed at negotiating an appropriate minicontract:

"I'm pleased that you shared your hurt with me today. That helped me to understand what you've been thinking and feeling and gave me a chance to explain what I really meant last week. For us to work well together, it is important for both of us to put negative reactions on the table so that we can prevent strains from developing between us. I wonder how you'd feel about our updating our contract to include discussing immediately any troubling thoughts and feelings that might present obstacles in our relationship so that we can explore them together and work them out."

"Pathological" or Inept Practitioners

Although all practitioners commit rectifiable errors from time to time, some practitioners blunder repeatedly, causing irreparable damage to helping relationships and inflicting psychological damage upon their clients. Gottesfeld and Lieberman (1979) refer to such practitioners as *pathological* and point out that "It is possible to have therapists who suffer from as many unresolved problems as do clients" (p. 388). We agree, based on knowledge of practitioners who are abrasive, egotistical, controlling, judgmental, demeaning, rigid, habitually tardy for appointments, sexually promiscuous, patronizing, detached, who create additional difficulties for clients, or foster unhealthy dependency—to mention just a few "pathogenic" attributes. Practitioners with these attributes tend to lose clients prematurely. The majority of voluntary clients discern these attributes and have the good sense to "vote with their feet" by terminating such contacts. Mandated clients suffer greater consequences for deciding to terminate unilaterally. They may be more likely to evade contact or attempt to be transferred to another practitioner. Supervisors should hence be alert when there are several requests for transfer from the same practitioner.

These practitioners are injurious to their clients, their agencies, and the profession. Consequently, other practitioners face a difficult situation in knowing what steps to take when they become aware of injurious practitioners. As Gottesfeld and Lieberman (1979) note: "It is painful to be a helpless observer of a situation that seems to be antitherapeutic for a client. Yet it is also painful and difficult to render a judgment about a professional colleague's competence" (p. 392).

Clearly, both individual practitioners and agencies have a responsibility to protect clients from pathological practitioners. Gottesfeld and Lieberman encapsulate this responsibility in their assertion that "agencies organized to help clients should not accept employee pathology that defeats the system's purpose" (p. 392). Actions to rectify such situations, however, must safeguard the rights of practitioners as well as clients, for unfair judgments may result from biased or inaccurate reports of practitioners' behavior. To protect clients' rights, "a professional's behavior must be open for review through consultation, supervision, or a peer review process" (Gottesfeld & Lieberman, 1979, p. 392). When peer review appears justified, a referral to the closest chapter of the professional organization (NASW) or state licensing or certification board may be in order. Chapters and boards have committees formed to investigate complaints of unethical and unprofessional behavior.

Racial and Transcultural Barriers

Clients may also experience adverse reactions in transracial or transcultural relationships with practitioners who either lack knowledge of the client's culture or lack experience in working with members of a given race or minority group. Similarly, practitioners who are members of ethnic minority groups are more likely to be familiar with values of majority group clients than those clients are accustomed to having minority practitioners. As Proctor and Davis note, Caucasian practitioners tend to know little about the realities of other cultures. Such transcultural conflicts are negatively charged with both sides uncomfortable discussing racial and ethnic differences with Caucasian practitioners fearing rejection and clients of color distrustful of representatives of systems considered oppressive (Proctor & Davis, 1994).

Hence participants in transcultural relationships may experience a mutual strangeness based on limited interaction with members of each others' culture. In such instances, "The void may be filled by stereotyped 'knowledge' and preconception, but the essential unknownness remains" (Gitterman & Schaeffer, 1972). Given these circumstances, mutual defensiveness and guardedness become an obstacle to effective communication. Too often, differences of race and culture are ignored in a form of "color blind" practice designed to avoid conflict (Proctor & Davis, 1994, p. 316).

Empathic communication is a basic skill that tends to bridge the gap often present in transracial and transcultural relationships. Empathically confronting clients' anger and suspiciousness tends to neutralize these negative feelings by demonstrating acceptance and understanding, as we have pointed out previously. Based on modest research evidence, several authors (Banks, 1971; Cimbolic, 1972; Santa Cruz & Hepworth, 1975) recommend that in preparing students to work across racial or ethnic lines, educators should train them to attain high levels of skill in the facilitative conditions of empathy, respect, and genuineness.

Even relating with high levels of the facilitative conditions may be insufficient to bridge the racial gap with certain clients. In analyzing sources of nondisclosure of African American clients, Ridley (1984) has developed a useful typology that identifies "cultural paranoia" as a major barrier to transracial work involving Caucasian practitioners. Some African American clients distrust Caucasians to a degree that effective communication may not be possible; same race practitioners may be preferable in such instances. Of course, cultural paranoia frequently overlaps with involuntary status such that involuntary clients with high levels of distrust often have limited access to same race practitioners.

Another source of negative reactions by African American clients to Caucasian practitioners may be a lack of awareness by the latter to the duality of their feelings toward African Americans. On one hand, as a result of a lack of adequate awareness of the effects of discrimination and oppression upon blacks, practitioners may be insensitive to African American resentment, fear, distrust, and sense of powerlessness. Such practitioners may stereotype African Americans and have a limited capacity for empathizing with them. On the other hand, some Caucasian practitioners may overidentify with African Americans, losing sight of clients' individual problems and erroneously attributing them to racial factors. When this occurs, as Cooper (1973) aptly puts it, "clients tend to lose their individual richness and complexity; there is the danger of no longer treating people—only culture carriers" (p. 76). Clearly then, Caucasian practitioners must empathize with African American clients but not to the extent of overidentifying with them.

Given the potential obstacles that may emerge in transracial and transcultural relationships, one may well wonder if the solution is to match clients with practitioners of the same race or ethnic group. This solution is often not practicable, however, nor is there evidence that matching always works to the clients' advantage. Research studies have indicated that traditional mental health services rendered by Anglo practitioners to Asian Americans and Hispanics are markedly underutilized (Sue & Zane, 1987) and that "regardless of utilization rates, all of the ethnic-minority groups had significantly higher drop-out rates than whites" (p. 37). Further, Sue and McKinney (1975) reported dramatic increases in utilization rates by Asian Americans when a counseling center was established specifically for this ethnic group and culturally relevant services were provided by bilingual therapists. These findings clearly illustrate that it is advantageous to match clients with practitioners of the same race or ethnicity. However, rigorous studies comparing treatment outcomes of racially and ethnically matching helping relationships with transcultural counterparts have not been reported. Moreover, several studies suggest that practitioners have been able to help clients of different races and ethnicity. Whether therapists of the same race or ethnicity could have been more helpful cannot be inferred because these studies lacked control or comparison groups. Based on the dearth of solid information, the most that can be concluded is that client and practitioner racial and ethnic homogeneity promote utilization of services by minority clients and that practitioners who engage in transcultural work, at a minimum, should be knowledgeable about the cultures of their clients and competent in relating with high levels of the facilitative conditions.

Since racial and cultural matching is often not possible, it becomes part of the practitioner's responsibility to become better educated about working with persons who are different culturally and racially from the practitioner. This education includes becoming informed about the history of the groups one works with, both nationally and locally, including the ways such groups have been oppressed and the consequences of that oppression. The education also includes becoming appreciative of the cultural strengths of the groups through becoming familiar with literature, art, and films that accurately portray culture. Finally, it includes a professional education with reviewing journal articles geared toward working with members of a particular culture, and participating in staff training aimed at ethnically sensitive practice.

Difficulties in Trusting and Transference Reactions

Clients vary widely in their capacity to trust. Those whose self-esteem and levels of interpersonal functioning are high may plunge into exploring their problems after only a few moments of checking out the practitioner. Yet despite the latter's goodwill and skills in imparting warmth, caring, and empathy, other clients may be guarded and test a practitioner for weeks or even months before letting down their defenses. As noted in previous chapters, involuntary clients who have not sought a helping relationship should not be expected to readily come to trust practitioners. Attempting to persuade such clients of one's helpful intent is usually counterproductive. Many distrustful clients trust actions before words. That is, practitioners who fulfill commitments or practitioner tasks they have agreed to are more likely eventually to be perceived as trustworthy.

With such clients, practitioners must exercise patience and persistence. Pushing for self-disclosure before trust and a positive relationship are established may alienate them, prolong the period of testing, or precipitate discontinuance of the helping relationship. Because these clients do not enter helping relationships readily and hence often disclose their problems only superficially during early sessions, setting time limits on the duration of the helping process is inappropriate. In fact, it may be necessary to reach out to these clients to maintain their involvement in the helping process. Often they cancel or miss appointments, and unless the practitioner reaches out by phoning them, making a home visit, or writing a letter (the last is the *least* effective), they often do not return. It is important to recognize that many of these clients urgently need help and that their failure to keep appoint-

ments may emanate more from a pattern of avoidance than from lack of motivation. Assisting them to come to terms with fears behind their avoidance behavior thus may be therapeutic, whereas letting them terminate by default contributes to perpetuation of their avoidance behavior.

Unrealistic perceptions of and reactions to a practitioner are known as *transference reactions;* that is, the client transfers to the practitioner wishes, fears, and other feelings that are rooted in past experiences with others (usually parents, parental substitutes, and siblings). Transference reactions may not only impede progress in the helping process but also may create difficulties in other interpersonal relationships. A male may have difficulty trusting all women because he felt rejected and/or abused by his mother or stepmother; similarly, some people resent and rebel against all people in positions of authority, mistakenly perceiving all such people as they perceived an overbearing, punitive, controlling, and exploitative parent.

Transference reactions thus involve overgeneralized and distorted perceptions that create difficulties in interpersonal relationships. Besides being a possible impediment to progress, transference reactions in therapeutic relationships also represent an opportunity for growth. Because the therapeutic relationship is, in effect, a social microcosm wherein clients' interpersonal behavior and conditioned patterns of perceiving and feeling are manifested, in this context clients often recreate here-and-now interactions that are virtually identical to those that plague and defeat them in other relationships. The consequent challenge and opportunity for the practitioner is to assist such clients to recognize their distorted perceptions and to develop finer interpersonal perceptual discriminations so that they can differentiate and deal with the practitioner and others as unique individuals rather than as overgeneralized projections of mental images, beliefs, or attitudes.

The extent to which transference reactions occur during the course of the helping process varies considerably. In time-limited, task-focused forms of intervention, the likelihood of transference reactions is minimal. When treatment extends over a lengthy period of time, focuses on the past, and involves in-depth analysis of intrapsychic processes, transference may play a pivotal role in the helping process. Psychoanalytically oriented therapy and other long-term, insight-oriented therapies, in fact, tend to foster transference, whereas task-centered, behavioral, and crisis interventions do not. Similarly, working with marital partners conjointly tends to discourage transference reactions, whereas working with only one partner may foster transference by the client and overidentification on the practitioner's part. Smith and Hepworth (1967) have written about ways of avoiding pitfalls in working with one marital partner. As for groups,

> Multiple transference reactions may also emerge in groups. An individual can be experienced as a mother by one member, as a father by another, and as a sibling by still another. Similarly, that individual often "finds" parents and siblings in the group. Usually the leader is experienced as a mother or father. As the individual sees how he distorts perceptions in the group, he can begin to appreciate how he distorts other interpersonal relationships. (Strean, 1979, p. 194)

Kinds of clients served also are a significant factor that determines the incidence of transference reactions. In public assistance, child welfare, and correctional settings, for example, many clients come from emotionally deprived backgrounds and have histories of ambivalent involvement with social agencies that predispose them to view social workers with fear and distrust, to react with humiliation and resentment, and to view themselves as helpless. Given these feelings, such clients are caught in a paradoxical situation, for, on the one hand, they have limited coping skills, desire to be assisted with their problems, and have dependency longings; but on the other hand, their fears and negative feelings are powerful deterrents to risking involving themselves with helping professionals. Consequently, many of these clients openly oppose helping efforts or tend to relate in passive, dependent ways that block growth toward competency and independence.

To counter these inimical reactions, practitioners confront the challenge of having clients accept them and their offer of assistance.

Managing Transference Reactions

Whatever the agency setting and the intervention, you will occasionally encounter transference reactions and must be prepared to cope with them. For example, the authors have encountered the following:

1. A client who had great difficulty revealing her problems because the practitioner resembled her brother in appearance.

2. A client (whose father was a harsh and domineering person) who resisted becoming involved in marital therapy because she resented anyone telling her what to do. (The practitioner earlier had clarified that was not his role.)

3. A client who wanted the practitioner to embrace her because it was important to know he cared for her.

4. A client to whom it was important to be the practitioner's favorite.

5. A client who was sure the practitioner couldn't possibly have a genuine interest in her and saw her only because it was his job.

6. A client who misinterpreted a message of the practitioner and almost terminated as a result of feeling put down.

7. A client who accused the practitioner of being in collusion with her husband when the practitioner, in fact, viewed the husband as the major contributor to their marital difficulties.

It is evident that although such reactions derive from the past, they are manifested in the here and now. The question can be raised as to whether transference reactions can best be resolved by focusing on the past to enable clients to gain insight into their origin. We maintain that reactions that derive from past experiences are played out in the present and can usually be resolved by focusing on the inaccurate and distorted perceptions of the present. Some clients, of course, will bring up hurtful experiences and circumstances from the past and brief excursions into the past provide opportunities for emotional catharsis and facilitate understanding of the origin of dysfunctional patterns of thinking, feeling, and behaving.

When it appears clients have experienced traumatic stresses in childhood, such as physical or sexual abuse, gentle probing and exploration of these past experiences may be vital to gaining understanding of and recovery from the detrimental effects of those experiences (Rosenthal, 1988; Wartel, 1991). Focusing on past traumatic experiences of adulthood (such as rape and horrible war experience) may also be essential to healing from the psychic wounds of those experiences.

Except for the circumstances just cited, it is counterproductive to focus extensively on the past, as so doing diverts efforts from problem solving in the present and unnecessarily prolongs treatment. Further, there is no evidence that focusing on the remote origin of unrealistic feelings, perceptions, and beliefs is more effective in modifying them than scrutinizing their validity in the here and now.

To manage transference reactions you must first be aware of their manifestations, of which the following are typical:

1. Relating to the practitioner in a clinging, dependent way or excessively seeking praise and reassurance.
2. Attempting to please the practitioner by excessive compliments and praise or by ingratiating behavior.
3. Asking many personal questions about the practitioner.
4. Behaving provocatively by arguing with or baiting the practitioner.
5. Questioning the interest of the practitioner.
6. Seeking special considerations, such as frequent changes in scheduled appointments for trivial reasons.
7. Attempting to engage practitioners socially by inviting them to lunch, parties, and the like.
8. Having dreams or fantasies about the practitioner.

9. Responding defensively, feeling rejected, or expecting criticism or punishment without realistic cause.
10. Offering personal favors or presenting gifts.
11. Behaving seductively by flirting, wearing revealing clothing, or making affectionate gestures.
12. Regressing or behaving in destructive ways when the practitioner must cancel or miss sessions.
13. Being unusually silent, inattentive, or drowsy in sessions.
14. Being tardy for appointments or striving to stay beyond the designated ending time.
15. Dressing or behaving in ways that diverge markedly from the client's usual style.

When clients manifest the preceding behaviors or other possible indications of transference reactions, it is vital to shift focus to their here-and-now feelings, for such reactions generally cause clients to disengage from productive work and may undermine the helping process. To assist you in managing transference reactions, we offer the following guidelines:

1. Be open to the possibility that the client's reaction is not unrealistic and may be produced by your behavior. If through discussion and introspection you determine the client's behavior is realistic, respond authentically by owning responsibility for your behavior.

2. When clients appear to expect you to respond in antitherapeutic ways, as significant others have in the past, it is important to respond differently, thereby by disconfirming the expectations. Responses that contrast sharply from expectations produce temporary disequilibrium and force the client to differentiate the practitioner from past figures. The client must thus deal with the practitioner as a unique and real person, rather than perpetuating fictional expectations based on past experiences.

3. Assist the client to determine the immediate source of distorted perceptions by exploring how

and when the feelings emerged. Carefully explore antecedents and meaning attributions associated with the feelings. *Avoid attempting to correct distorted perceptions by immediately revealing your actual feelings.* By first exploring how and when problematic feelings emerged, you assist clients to expand their awareness of their patterns of over-generalizing and making both faulty meaning attributions and unwarranted assumptions based on past experience. This awareness can enable them in the future to discriminate between feelings that emanate from conditioned perceptual sets and reality-based feelings and reactions.

4. After clients have discerned the unrealistic nature of their feelings and manifested awareness of the distortions that produced these feelings, share your actual feelings. This can be a source of reassurance to clients who have felt offended, hurt, resentful, rejected, or the like.

5. After you have examined problematic feelings, assist clients to determine whether they have experienced similar reactions in other relationships. You may thus assist clients to discern *patterns* of distortions that create difficulties in other relationships.

The application of these guidelines is illustrated in the following excerpt taken from an actual session (the eighth) of one of the authors with a 25-year-old female who had sought help because of loneliness and discouragement in finding a marital partner.

Client: Boy, the weeks sure go by fast. [*Long pause.*] I don't have much to talk about today.

Practitioner [*sensing the client is struggling with something*]: I gather you didn't really feel ready for your appointment today. [*Empathic response.*] How did you feel about coming? [*Open-ended probing response.*]

Client: I didn't want to come, but I thought I should. Actually it has been an eventful week. But I haven't felt I wanted to tell you about what has been happening. [*Indication of a possible transference reaction.*]

Practitioner: Sounds like you've had some misgivings about confiding certain things in me. [*Paraphrasing response.*] Could you share with me some of your thoughts about confiding these things in me? [*Open-ended probing response/polite command.*]

Client: OK. I've wanted to keep them to myself until I find out how things turn out. I've wanted to wait until it really develops into something. Then I would tell you.

Practitioner: So you haven't wanted to risk it turning out bad and worrying about how I would feel if it did. [*Additive empathy/ interpretation.*]

Client: I guess I've wanted to impress you. I had a date with the fellow we talked about last week. It was wonderful. He's just the opposite of the other creep I told you about. He either has a real line or he's a super guy. I couldn't believe how considerate he was.

Practitioner: You can't be sure yet what he's really like, and you want to be sure he's for real before you tell me about him? [*Additive empathy/interpretation.*]

Client [*with an embarrassed smile*]: Yes! And if it really developed into something, then I could tell you.

Practitioner: And that way you could be sure I'd be favorably impressed? [*Additive empathy/interpretation.*]

Client: Yes! I've felt I wanted you to know someone really good could be attracted to me.

Practitioner: Hmm. Sounds like you've felt I've doubted you have much to offer a man and wanted to prove to me you do have something to offer. [*Additive empathy/ interpretation.*]

Client: Yes, that's true. I have wanted you to think of me as a desirable person.

Practitioner: I'd like to explore where those doubts or fears that I don't see you as a desirable person come from. I'm wondering how you've concluded I don't see you as having much to offer a man. Have I done or said something that conveyed that to you? [*Probing.*]

Client [*thinks for a moment*]: Well—no. Nothing that I can think of.

Practitioner: Yet I gather those feelings have been very real to you. I wonder when you first became aware of those feelings.

Client [*after a pause*]: Well, I think it was when we began to talk about my feelings that guys are just interested in me for what they can get. I guess I wondered if you thought I was a real dud. I wanted you to know it wasn't so, that a desirable person could be attracted to me.

Practitioner: You know, when we were discussing your feelings toward your mother two or three weeks ago you said essentially the same thing. [*Using summarization to make a connection between separate but related events.*]

Client: I'm not sure what you mean.

Practitioner: You had said you felt your mother doubted you would ever marry because you were so cold you couldn't attract a man.

Client [*smiles pensively and nods affirmatively*]**:** You know I never wanted to elope. I always wanted to marry in my hometown and have a big wedding. When I had my ring on my finger, I would turn to mother and say, "See, you were wrong!"

Practitioner: So you've felt you needed to prove to her someone could love you. And that's also what you wanted to prove to me. [*Additive empathy/interpretation.*]

Client: [*Nods affirmatively.*]

Practitioner: I'm interested you've thought maybe I, too, didn't see you as lovable. Could you share with me how you reached that conclusion? [*Practitioner continues to explore the unrealistic nature of her perception and how it pervades other relationships.*]

By sensitively exploring the client's reluctance to attend the session, the practitioner not only resolved an emerging obstacle to productive work but also assisted her to explore further her doubts as to her lovability and to expand her awareness of how these doubts distorted her perceptions of how others viewed her—in this instance, the practitioner. As a result of the exploration, she was able to identify a basic misconception that pervaded her relationships with others and to relate more comfortably with the practitioner.

Countertransference Reactions

Practitioners may also experience adverse relational reactions that can damage helping relationships if not recognized and managed effectively. Just as with clients, these feelings may be realistic or unrealistic. The latter type of reaction, which we discuss first, is the counterpart of transference and is denoted as *countertransference*. This phenomenon involves feelings, wishes, and unconscious defensive patterns of the practitioner that derive from past relationships, interfere with objective perception, and block productive interaction with clients. Countertransference contaminates helping relationships by producing distorted perceptions, blind spots, wishes, and antitherapeutic emotional reactions and behavior. Practitioners who have failed to integrate anger into their own personalities, for example, may be unduly uncomfortable when clients express anger and divert them from expressing such feelings. Other practitioners who have not resolved feelings of rejection by parents may have difficulty relating warmly to clients who are cool and aloof. Still other practitioners who have failed to resolve resentful feelings toward authoritarian parents may overidentify with rebellious adolescents and experience feelings of condemnation for their parents. Marital therapists whose spouses have been unfaithful, controlling, or sexually withholding may also overidentify with clients who have similar problems and be blind to the part these clients play in the marital difficulties they describe. And finally, some practitioners who have excessive needs to be loved and admired may behave seductively or strive to impress their clients.

Before discussing how to manage countertransference reactions, it is first important to identify typical ways they are manifested, which include the following:

1. Being unduly concerned about a client.

2. Having persistent erotic fantasies or dreams about a client.

3. Dreading or pleasurably anticipating sessions with clients.

4. Being consistently tardy or forgetting appointments with certain clients.

5. Feeling protective of or uncomfortable about discussing certain problems with a client.

6. Feeling hostile toward or unable to empathize with a client.

7. Blaming others exclusively for a client's difficulties.

8. Feeling persistently bored or drowsy or tuning out a client.

9. Consistently ending sessions early or permitting them to extend beyond designated ending points.

10. Trying to impress or being unduly impressed by clients.

11. Being overly concerned about losing a client.

12. Arguing with or feeling defensive or hurt by a client's criticisms or accusations.

13. Being overly solicitous and performing tasks for clients that they are capable of performing.

14. Being unusually curious about a client's sex life.

15. Having difficulties accepting or liking certain types of clients (may also be reality based).

Becoming aware of unrealistic feelings toward a client or of reactions such as those just listed are signals that a practitioner should immediately take appropriate corrective measures. Otherwise, the countertransference will limit the practitioner's potential helpfulness, create an impasse, contribute to the client's dysfunction, or otherwise impair the effectiveness of the helping relationship. Ordinarily, the first step in resolving countertransference (and often all that is needed) is to engage in introspection. Introspection involves analytical dialogue with oneself aimed at discovering sources of feelings, reactions, cognitions, and behavior. Examples of questions that facilitate introspection include the following:

"Why am I feeling uncomfortable with this client? What is going on inside me that I'm not able to relate more freely?"

"Why do I dislike [*or feel bored, impatient, or irritated*] with this client? Are my feelings rational or does this client remind me of someone from the past?"

"What is happening inside of me that I don't face certain problems with this client? Am I afraid of a negative reaction on the client's part?"

"What purpose was served by arguing with this client? Was I feeling defensive or threatened?"

"Why did I talk so much or give so much advice? Did I feel a need to give something to the client?"

"What's happening inside me that I'm fantasizing or dreaming about this client?"

"Why am I constantly taking sides with _____ ? Am I overlooking the partner's [*or parent's or child's*] feelings because I'm overidentifying with _____? Could my own similar feelings from the past be blocking my objectivity?

Introspection often assists practitioners to achieve or regain a realistic perspective in their relationships with clients. Discussion of such topics should also be part of consultation with colleagues and supervisors, enabling you to explore your feelings and to gain fresh input. Just as clients are sometimes too close to their problems to perceive them objectively and thus benefit from seeing them from the vantage point of a practitioner, the latter can likewise benefit from stepping out of the relationship and viewing it from the unbiased perspective of an uninvolved colleague, consultant, or supervisor.

Practitioners who repeatedly become enmeshed in countertransference reactions usually have long-standing and unresolved emotional conflicts that continue to pervade their interpersonal relationships. As such, their range of effectiveness is limited and they may cause or contribute to dysfunction in their clients. Some such "pathological" practitioners are able to work through their difficulties by obtaining professional help for themselves. Others are not suited for the profession and for the benefit of themselves, their clients, and the profession should consider making an occupational change.

Realistic Practitioner Reactions

Not all negative feelings toward certain clients involve countertransference reactions. Some clients are abrasive, arrogant, or obnoxious, have irritating mannerisms, or are exploitative of and cruel to others. Even the most accepting practitioner may have difficulty developing positive feelings toward such clients. Practitioners, after all, are human beings and are not immune to disliking others or feeling irritated and impatient at times. Still, repulsive clients are entitled to service and, in fact, often desperately need help because their offensive behavior alienates others, leaving them isolated and confused as to what creates their difficulties.

When practitioners look beyond the offensive qualities of certain clients, they often discover that beneath the facade of arrogance and toughness are desirable, indeed admirable qualities that others rarely, if ever, see. Further, when they gain access to the private worlds of these individuals, practitioners often find persons who endured severe emotional deprivation, physical abuse, and other severe stresses as children and who had little opportunity to learn social skills. Being warmly accepted in spite of their annoying behavior often provides a corrective emotional experience for these clients.

Abrasive clients need far more than acceptance, however. They need feedback about how certain aspects of their behavior are offensive to others, encouragement to risk new behaviors, and opportunities to learn and practice the same. Feedback can be extremely helpful if it is conveyed sensitively and imparted in the context of goodwill. In providing such feedback, you must be careful to avoid evaluative or blaming comments that tend to elicit defensiveness. Examples of such comments are: "You boast too much and dominate conversation" or "You're insensitive to other people's feelings and say hurtful things." Clients are far more likely to be receptive to messages that describe and document their behavior and personalize the practitioner's response to it. An example of a descriptive message that embodies ownership of feelings is: "When you sneered at me just now, I began to feel defensive and resentful. You've done that several times before, and I find myself backing away each time. I don't like feeling distant from you, and I'm concerned because I suspect that's how you come across to others." This message, of course, is highly authentic and would not be appropriate until a sound working relationship has been established.

Sexual Attraction Toward Clients

Romantic and sexual feelings toward clients can be especially hazardous, although such feelings are by no means uncommon. Research findings (Pope, Keith-Spiegel, & Tabachnick, 1986), based on a survey of 585 psychotherapists (psychologists), revealed that only 77 (13%) had never been attracted to any client. The majority (82%), however, had never seriously considered sexual involvement with a client and of the remaining 18%, 87% had considered becoming involved only once or twice. Of the 585 respondents, about 6% had engaged in sexual intimacies with clients.

Most practitioners can thus expect at some point in their careers to experience sexual attraction toward a client. Managing such attraction appropriately, however, is critical. Fortunately, the data indicate that the majority of therapists manage their attractions successfully. Although 83% of those in this study who experienced attraction believed the attraction was mutual, 71% believed that the client was not aware of their attraction. When such was the case they believed the attraction did not have a harmful impact on the helping process. By contrast, therapists who believed clients were aware of their attraction thought the impact was detrimental to the helping process. Although only 6% of those surveyed had engaged in sexual activities with clients, this percentage is alarming, for sexual involvement usually leads to grievous consequences for clients, who often suffer confusion and intense guilt and thereafter have great difficulty trusting professional persons. The consequences of sexual involvement may be devastating for practitioners as well, who, when discovered, may suffer disgrace, be sued for unethical practice, and be ejected from the profession. The proposed revision of the NASW Code of Ethics on this point is unequivocal: "The social worker should under no circumstances engage in sexual activities or sexual contact with current clients, whether such contact is consensual or forced" (Section 1.09 5). Consequently, sexual attraction to clients is normal; acting on that attraction is unethical in a professional relationship.

Effectively managing sexual attractions for clients involves taking the corrective measures identified earlier in relationship to unrealistic feelings and reactions—namely, engaging in introspection and consulting with your supervisor. In this regard, it is noteworthy that in the survey previously cited,

57% of the therapists sought consultation or supervision when they were attracted to a client. We cannot recommend too strongly that you take the same measures under similar circumstances. If allowed to mount unchecked, sexual attraction can lead to the disastrous consequences earlier discussed. Practitioners who frequently experience erotic fantasies about clients are particularly vulnerable to becoming sexually involved and should consider receiving treatment themselves.

A few practitioners have justified engaging in sexual activities with clients on the basis of assisting them to feel loved or helping them to overcome sexual problems. Such explanations are generally thinly disguised and feeble rationalizations for exploiting clients. Typically, such sexual activities are limited to persons considered attractive and relatively youthful. Social workers who engage in sexual activities with clients not only render them a grave disservice but also damage the public image of the profession.

MANAGING OPPOSITION TO CHANGE

Social workers and other helping professionals have been inclined to label client behaviors which oppose the direction in which the practitioner wishes to go as *resistance*. Resistance has been defined as "holding back, disengaging, or in some way subverting change efforts whether knowingly or not without open discussion" (Nelsen, 1975, p. 587) or "as any action or attitude that impedes the course of therapeutic work" (Strean, 1979, p. 70). The resistance concept has tended to be used in a fashion wich holds the client responsible for the opposition.

The first step in avoiding such blaming is to recognize opposition to change as a universal phenomenon, as anyone knows who has attempted to break long-established habits such as being unduly modest, eating excessively, smoking, talking too much or too little, being tardy, or spending freely. The pull of habits is relentless; changing, more-

over, often means yielding gratifications or having to cope head-on with situations that are frightening or aversive. Making changes also often involves risking new behavior in the face of unknown consequences; although the status quo may cause pain and distress, it at least is familiar, and the consequences of habitual dysfunctional behavior are predictable.

As described in earlier chapters, reactance theory provides a fruitful perspective for considering opposition to change. Rather than blaming clients for oppositional behavior, reactance theory leads the practitioner to anticipate objectively the range of responses to be expected when valued freedoms are threatened (Brehm, 1976). For example, some try to regain their freedom directly by attempting to take back what has been threatened. A frequent response is to restore freedom by implication or "find the loophole" by superficial compliance while violating the spirit of requirements. Third, threatened behaviors and beliefs may be more valued than ever before. Finally, the person or source of the threat may be responded to with hostility or aggression (Rooney, 1992, p. 130).

Further, reactance theory lends itself to proactive strategies designed to reduce the opposition. For example, clients who perceive global pressure to change their lifestyle are likely to experience less reactance if those pressures are narrowed in scope with emphasis on behaviors which remain free. Second, reactance is likely to be reduced if the client perceives at least constrained choices (Rooney, 1992). Understanding the client's perspective on the situation and avoiding labeling also reduces reactance (ibid., p. 135).

Resistance and Ambivalence

As noted above, the term *resistance* has connoted deliberate refusal by clients to cooperate. Unfortunately, social workers have often exploited this definition by attributing failure of helping efforts to clients' resistance, when, in fact, failures were often caused by inappropriate or ineffectual helping methods. Leader (1958) conceptualized resistance not as a manifestation of clients' refusal to cooperate but rather as a manifestation of ambivalence about changing. According to Leader, clients' feelings about changing are not unipolar; that is, clients seldom either want to or don't want to change. Rather, opposing feelings coexist; part of the client is motivated to change and another part strives to maintain the status quo. Despite having feelings that oppose change, many clients do change because the thrust to improve their lot in life outweighs the force to maintain the status quo. Leader argues further that social workers are overly concerned about resistance, lamenting that: "If we could only fully recognize that resistance in all phases of life is natural and healthy, perhaps we would be less concerned about its manifestation" (p. 22).

Recognizing clients' ambivalent feelings about changing enables practitioners to assist them to explore their feelings and to weigh advantages and disadvantages of making changes. Indeed, as clients think through their feelings and reassess the implications of maintaining the status quo, the scales often tilt in favor of change. Further, by accepting clients in spite of their opposition to change and by championing their right to self-determination, practitioners may similarly tilt the scales, because clients experience no pressure from the practitioner to change and are therefore free to make up their own minds. This factor is crucial, for pressure by the practitioner often engenders an opposing force or resistance from the client. Viewed in this light, recognizing and accepting oppositional feelings to change prevent such feelings from going underground where they can subtly undermine the helping process. Recognizing, openly discussing, and accepting oppositional feelings thus can liberate a desire and willingness to change.

Preventing Opposition to Change

Opposition to change may emanate from sources other than ambivalence about changing. Clients may misunderstand the nature of service or of a specific intervention and may therefore be reluctant to cooperate fully. Should this occur, it is vital to explain fully the nature of the service or intervention, exploring what is required and where there is room for choice. This should include clarifying roles of the participants, and permitting voluntary clients free choice as to whether or not to proceed. The best way of preventing this type of opposition is to be thorough in formulating contracts, clarifying roles, providing a rationale for specific interventions, inviting questions, eliciting and discussing misgivings, and fostering self-determination.

Other sources include apprehension or fear associated with engaging in behavior that is alien to one's usual functioning or having to face a situation that appears overwhelming. Such fears may be so intense that clients resist carrying out essential actions. Their difficulties may then be compounded by embarrassment over failure to implement the actions, which may produce resistance to seeing the practitioner or discussing the problematic situation further. Again, these forms of opposition can be prevented by anticipating and exploring the fears and preparing the client to carry out the actions through modeling, behavioral rehearsal, and guided practice. Because we discussed these strategies of resolving obstacles to change in Chapter 13 and because Hepworth (1979) has discussed this topic at length elsewhere, we will not discuss them further here.

Transference Resistance

Some clients become enmeshed in major transference reactions that pose an obstacle to progress. A client may idealize the practitioner and attempt to use the helping relationship as a substitute for dependency gratifications that should be obtained elsewhere; such a client may be preoccupied with fantasies about the practitioner rather than focused on goal attainment. Other clients may be disappointed and resentful because a practitioner does not meet their unrealistic expectations. Perceiving the practitioner as uncaring, withholding, and rejecting (as they likewise perceived their parents), these clients may struggle with angry feelings (negative transference) toward the practitioner, which diverts them from working productively on their problems. Unless practitioners recognize and assist such clients to resolve these feelings by discussing them, accepting them, and placing them in realistic perspective, these clients may prematurely terminate, convinced their perceptions and feelings are accurate.

Again we emphasize that transference reactions are relatively infrequent in short-term, task-centered therapies where the practitioner takes an active role, which tends to minimize the possibility of projections. Moreover, time limits and focus on task accomplishment militate against dependency and strong emotional attachment. Long-term and insight-oriented therapies, by contrast, tend to foster dependency and transference.

Manifestations of Opposition to Change

Opposition to change takes many forms, and the frequency with which clients manifest different forms varies according to the type of setting, the personality of the client, and the ethnicity and socioeconomic levels of clients. As we note in a later section, families with multiple problems sometimes manifest opposition by ignoring social workers or by employing confusion and noise. By contrast, middle-class clients, who are more verbal, tend to manifest opposition in communication (for example, by intellectualizing or discussing extraneous matters). The following are common manifestations of opposition:

1. Mental blocking (mind going blank).
2. Lengthy periods of silence.
3. Inattention or mind wandering.
4. Rambling on at length or dwelling on unimportant details.
5. Restlessness or fidgeting.
6. Discussing superficialities or irrelevant matters.
7. Lying or deliberately misrepresenting facts.
8. Intellectualizing (avoiding feelings and problems by focusing on abstract ideas).
9. Changing the subject.
10. Forgetting details of distressing events or of content of previous sessions.
11. Being tardy for or forgetting, changing, or canceling appointments.
12. Minimizing problems or claiming miraculous improvement.
13. Bringing up important material at the end of a session.
14. Not paying fees for service.
15. Not applying knowledge and skills gained in sessions in daily life.
16. Assuming a stance of helplessness.
17. Using various verbal ploys to justify not taking corrective action, including:

    "I couldn't do that; it just wouldn't be me."

    "I just can't!"

    "I've tried that, and it doesn't work."

    "I understand what you're saying, but…"

    "I'm not so different; isn't everyone…?"

Many of the preceding phenomena do not necessarily indicate client opposition to change. If the client continues to work productively, the phenomenon may not warrant special handling. If, however, the client appears to have reached an impasse, it is safe to conclude that opposition is involved and to shift the focus to exploring factors that underlie the opposition.

Opposition may also emerge in family and group sessions. Individual members may manifest any of the preceding phenomena. In addition, members may form subgroups and not invest themselves in the total group process. Other manifestations of resistance in groups include scapegoating individual members, isolating oneself and not participating, attempting to force the leader to assume responsibility that belongs with the group, engaging in social banter, failing to stay on topic, and struggling for power rather than working cooperatively. It is also important to bear in mind that when one family or group member is opposing change may be presenting a concern that others also feel (Nelsen, 1975, p. 591). As with individuals, it is critical when impasses are reached to shift the focus of the group to the dysfunctional processes so that the group does not dissipate its energies in counterproductive activities.[1]

Managing Opposition to Change

Since opposition to change is a universal phenomenon, it is not necessary to become alarmed about every possible manifestation of it. Moreover, focusing on trivial opposition may elicit adverse reactions from clients, such as feeling the practitioner is attempting to scrutinize and analyze their every minute behavior. Ironically, then, overreacting to presumed manifestations of opposition may needlessly engender it. A rule of thumb is that if opposition is not strong enough to impede progress, it is best ignored. Still, opposition can impede progress and, in some instances, damage helping relationships. When clients manifest opposition that blocks progress, it is imperative to grant highest priority to resolving it. When clients are left to struggle with opposition alone, they often resolve it by withdrawing from the helping process.

The first step in managing potential opposition to change is to bring it into the light of discussion by focusing on here-and-now feelings that underlie it. Sensitive and skillful handling is essential because personal feelings toward the practitioner are commonly associated with such opposition, and clients find it difficult to risk sharing these feelings. (Otherwise, they would have shared them already.) Empathy, warmth, and acceptance play a critical role in eliciting clients' untoward feelings because these ingredients foster a nonthreatening interpersonal climate.

In exploring sources of opposition, it is important not to focus on the manifestation per se but rather to cite it as an indication that the client is experiencing troubling thoughts and feelings toward the practitioner or toward what is happening in the helping process. An authentic response that conveys the practitioner's goodwill and concern

that progress has bogged down also reaffirms the practitioner's helpful intent and desire to work out whatever difficulties have arisen. At times, there may be cues as to the sources of difficulties based on the content discussed in a preceding session. For example, the client may have discussed extremely painful material, disclosed personal feelings that involved shame or guilt, or bristled in response to being confronted with personal contributions to a problematic situation. In such instances, the practitioner may open discussion of the feelings, as illustrated in the following: "You appear awfully quiet today, as though you're struggling with some troubling feelings. I know our last session was upsetting to you. Could you share with me what you're feeling about it just now?"

Discussing sources of opposition often reveals fears of where exploring certain personal feelings might lead. Some clients mistakenly fear they are losing their minds and that if they share certain thoughts and feelings, the practitioner will initiate steps to admit them to a mental hospital. Other clients fear the practitioner will condemn them if they disclose hostile feelings toward a child or discuss extramarital affairs. Still other clients fear the practitioner will pressure them to obtain a divorce if they reveal their lack of love for a spouse. With respect to feelings toward the practitioner, some clients fear the former will be hurt or offended if they share negative feelings or that the practitioner will see them as ridiculous and reject them if they share warm and affectionate feelings.

As practitioners initiate exploration of the source of opposition, some clients manifest marked hesitancy about revealing relevant feelings. When this occurs, a technique often successful in cutting through the reluctance is to focus empathically on here-and-now fears about disclosing other troublesome feelings. The practitioner's sensitivity, empathy, and genuineness may well pave the way for the client to risk opening up more. The following illustrates such an empathic response:

"I'm sensing that you're very uncomfortable about discussing your feelings. I may be wrong, but I get the impression you're afraid I would react negatively if you shared those feelings. I can't say for sure how I'd respond, but I want you to know I'd do my best to understand your feelings. Could you share with me what you're feeling at this moment?"

When clients do risk sharing their feelings, it is often therapeutic to accredit their strength for risking and to express reassurance. Such positive responses further cultivate a climate conducive to reciprocal openness, obliterate the feared consequences, and reinforce the client for disclosing risky feelings. The following is an example of such a response:

"I'm very pleased you expressed the anger that has been building up inside you. That took some courage on your part. It's a lot safer to keep those feelings inside, but then they eat at you and create distance in our relationship. I can accept your anger, and your sharing it with me gives both of us an opportunity to talk things out. I'd feel badly if those feelings continued to build and I didn't even know it."

Positive Connotation

This is another technique that is useful in reducing threat and enabling clients to save face, thereby protecting their self-esteem after risking revealing problematic feelings. Positive connotation involves attributing positive intentions to what would be otherwise regarded as a client's undesirable or negative behavior. In using this technique, the practitioner recognizes that the meaning ascribed to behavior can be viewed both positively and negatively, depending on one's vantage point. Viewed as an obstacle to progress, opposition takes on a negative meaning. Viewed from the client's perspective, however, the same behavior may have positive intentions. The following examples clarify this point:

1. A client cancels an appointment and holds back in the following session. Exploration reveals she resented the practitioner's "pressuring her" to follow a certain course of action. The practitioner em-

pathizes with her feelings as evidence of her determination to be her own person.

2. A client has been preoccupied with romantic fantasies about the practitioner and has digressed from working on problems. The practitioner interprets this romantic feeling as evidence he is moving away from his self-imposed isolation and is permitting himself to experience feelings of closeness that he can gradually risk in social relationships.

3. After an extended period of silence and exploration of feelings related to it, a spouse launches into a tirade over how the practitioner took sides with the partner in the previous session. The practitioner labels the client's response as a legitimate effort to be understood and to ensure that the practitioner does not make the marriage worse by drawing erroneous conclusions.

The goal of positive connotation is not to condone the client's opposition or to reinforce distorted perceptions. Rather, the objectives are to minimize clients' needs to defend themselves and to safeguard their already precarious self-esteem and act consistent with a strengths perspective. When using this technique, it is important to assist clients to recognize that their untoward reactions derived from distorted perceptions (if, in fact, they did) and to encourage them to express their feelings directly in the future.

Redefining Problems as Opportunities for Growth

This technique is a close relative of positive connotation because it too involves a form of relabeling. Both clients and practitioners tend to view problems negatively. Moreover, clients often view remedial courses of action as "necessary evils," dwelling on the threat involved in risking new behaviors. Therefore, it is often helpful to reformulate problems and essential tasks as opportunities for growth and challenges to gain liberation from stifling and self-defeating behaviors. Relabeling thus emphasizes the positives; that is, the benefits of change rather than the discomfort, fear, and other costs. In using this technique, it is important not to convey a pollyanna type of attitude, for the fears and threats are very real to clients, and being unduly optimistic may simply convey a lack of understanding on your part. Relabeling does not minimize clients' problems or ignore fears in risking new behaviors. It does enable clients to view their difficulties in a fuller perspective that embodies positive as well as negative factors. The following are examples of relabeling problem situations as opportunities for growth:

1. A teenage foster child who has run away because the foster parent insisted he adhere to certain deadlines in getting in at night resists returning to the foster home because the foster parents "are unreasonable." The practitioner describes returning as a challenge to deal with a problem head-on and to work it out rather than running away from it, which has been the client's pattern.

2. A welfare mother resists seeing a doctor because she fears she has cancer. The practitioner empathizes with her fears but describes having a checkup as also being an opportunity to rule out that frightening possibility or to receive treatment before the disease progresses, should she have cancer.

3. A mildly brain-damaged, socially inhibited young adult expresses fear about seeing a counselor for vocational testing and counseling. The practitioner accepts the discomfort but depicts the situation as an opportunity to learn more about his aptitudes and to expand choices in planning his future.

4. A wife expresses intense apprehension about refusing to submit to her husband's kinky and excessive sexual demands. The practitioner empathizes with her fear but also sees an opportunity for her to gain in strength and self-respect and to present herself as a person to be reckoned with.

Confronting Patterns of Opposition

In some instances, clients fail to progress toward their goals because of the persistence of pervasive dysfunctional patterns of behavior. A client may intellectualize extensively to avoid having to experience painful emotions, such as loneliness or depression. Other clients relate in a distant, aloof manner or in aggressive ways to protect against becoming close to others and risking painful rejec-

tion. Still others may consistently place responsibility on others or on circumstances for their difficulties, failing to examine or acknowledge their part in them. Because such patterns of behavior often create impasses, practitioners must recognize and handle them. Confronting clients with discrepancies between expressed goals and behavior that defeats accomplishment of those goals is often needed to break such impasses. Because we discussed confrontation at length in Chapter 18 we limit our discussion to a special case of confrontation, namely *therapeutic binds*.

Using Therapeutic Binds

Occasionally, practitioners encounter clients who stubbornly cling to self-defeating behaviors despite awareness that these behaviors perpetuate their difficulties. In such instances, placing clients in a therapeutic bind may provide the impetus needed to modify the problematic behaviors. Using a therapeutic bind involves confronting people with their self-defeating behaviors in such a way that they must either modify their behaviors or own responsibility for choosing to perpetuate their difficulties despite their expressed intentions to the contrary. The only way out of a therapeutic bind, unless one chooses to acknowledge no intention of changing, is to make constructive changes. The following are examples of situations in which the authors have successfully employed therapeutic binds:

1. Despite intensive efforts to resolve fears of being rejected in relationships with others, a client continues to decline social invitations and makes no effort to reach out to others. The practitioner confronts her with her apparent choice to perpetuate her social isolation rather than to risk relating to others.

2. A husband who, with his wife, sought marital therapy because of severe marital conflict persists in making decisions unilaterally, despite repeated feedback from his spouse and the practitioner that doing so engenders resentment and alienates her. The practitioner confronts him with how he has apparently decided it is more important to him to wield power than to improve his marital relationship.

3. An adolescent persists in truanting, violating family rules, and engaging in antisocial acts despite his assertion that he wants maximal freedom. The practitioner counters that he or she appears unready to use freedom wisely, because being a law unto himself or herself will only result in the court placing controls on him or her until he or she demonstrates a capacity to set limits for himself or herself.

4. A wife constantly harps on her husband's previous infidelity despite seeking marital therapy to strengthen their relationship. His response to her constant reminders is to withdraw and disengage from the relationship. The practitioner faces her with the contradiction in her behavior, stressing that it is apparently more important to her to punish her husband than to enhance their relationship.

In using therapeutic binds, it is vital to observe the guidelines for confrontation, thereby avoiding "clobbering" and alienating the client. A therapeutic bind is a potent but high-risk technique, and practitioners should use it sparingly, being careful to temper its jarring effect with empathy, concern, and sensitive exploration of the dynamics behind the self-defeating patterns. Above all, practitioners should be sure they are employing the technique to assist the client and not to act out their own frustrations about the client's opposition.

OPPOSITION FROM FAMILIES WITH MANY PROBLEMS

These families pose a special challenge to social workers. They may request service during times of crisis only to withdraw when acute distress is relieved, though their functioning remains submarginal. They pose ongoing problems to the community and often are involuntary clients, referred as a result of complaints from the community for recurrent incidents of child abuse or neglect, family violence, delinquency, and diverse forms of antisocial behaviors. Largely inaccessible to usual methods of intervention, they feel victimized by law enforcement officials, the courts, educators, and child protective services staff, whose interventions they resist as intrusions into their families.

Emotional and economic deprivation are rampant with such families with many problems. Some parents under these conditions are unstable, impulsive, and inconsistent. Practitioners have often had difficulties in forming working relationships with families with many problems, as such family members often view social workers with distrust, ambivalence, and hostility.

Allegations of child neglect or abuse are frequently involved in referrals of these families, and it is thus vital to assess home conditions and family functioning in the natural habitat of the family. Because a major objective of work with these families often is to prevent child placement outside the home, it is also essential to monitor home conditions and family interaction. Some families with multiple problems create barriers through confusion or noise by having radios or television sets blaring or by permitting neighbors to walk in or out of the house during visits by a practitioner. They may attempt to prevent practitioners from observing their usual functioning (by cleaning the house and washing and dressing their children before expected visits).

Home-based interventions are increasingly employed in work with such families, as we discussed in Chapter 16. These interventions are characterized by a strength orientation, focusing on assisting families in coping with their greatest concerns. Home visits greatly aid in helping practitioners see problems and interactions first hand such that they can model and teach different parenting methods. When families realize that practitioners are not attempting to catch them making mistakes, but rather supporting their strengths and efforts to maintain the family, barriers are often reduced. Patience and perseverance demonstrated through continued regular home visits gradually become evidence that practitioners are really concerned about their problems. When practitioners reach this point, they can begin to discuss matters that plague clients, such as threats of eviction, fights with neighbors, and eventually problems in family relationships.

Early indications of making inroads into developing meaningful relationships are efforts by clients to quiet their babies, have older children play outside, excuse themselves from interactions with neighbors, and give up numerous distracting telephone calls. Further, clients begin to save problems for weekly discussion with practitioners rather than cope with them impulsively.

When parents become open to assistance, interventions that address their multiple difficulties can be appropriately employed. Prominent interventions include teaching skills in parenting, budgeting, various homemaking duties, problem solving, communication, conflict resolution, and assertion. Because these families typically are involved with many institutions, coordination of service delivery is essential. Coordination is most effectively ensured by designating one person as a case manager (often a social worker).[2]

Having briefly discussed treatment of families with many problems in general terms, we now shift our focus to specific subgroups of this population that social workers increasingly encounter—namely, families with child maltreatment and spouse abuse. Not all families that manifest abusive behavior are families with many problems, of course, but, as we noted in Chapter 8, the majority of them are. Work with these families is particularly challenging because most of them are mandated to receive service, and the perpetrators of violence or sexual abuse typically deny or minimize the degree of their abusive behavior. We discussed techniques of engaging involuntary clients in Chapter 12, and limit our focus in this chapter to other treatment considerations. We focus successively on work with child physical abuse, child sexual abuse, and spouse abuse.

TREATING CHILD PHYSICAL ABUSE

In recent years, publications about child physical and sexual abuse have proliferated, and we do not presume to do justice to this vast literature. Our approach, rather, has been to briefly review interventions that address the dimensions we identified in Chapter 8 and to refer to selected relevant books and articles. First, we would like to cite authors who have written authoritative books that deal with the general topic of family violence, including child abuse, adolescent abuse, spouse abuse, and in some instances, abuse of the elderly. These authors include: Bolton and Bolton (1987); Gelles and Cornell (1990); Hutchings (1988); and Stith, Williams, and Rosen (1990). We cite additional authors whose publications deal with specific populations or specific dimensions of treatment of abuse in the following sections.

Placement of Children

Existing policies of permanency planning in the United States place an emphasis on removing children from their homes only as a last resort when high risk of repeated abuse poses an imminent threat to the child's safety.

Concrete Services

Because a high percentage of child abuse cases involves impoverished and minority families, the basic needs of these families for income, adequate housing, food stamps, health care, proper hygiene, nutritional meals, and the like are of the highest priority. Case management services are often needed to link these families with essential resources, and focusing on parenting skills, communication problems, and psychological matters without addressing the basic necessities is inappropriate.

Treating the Abused Child

Interventions with abused children consist of individual therapy, group treatment, social skills training, therapeutic day care and temporary shelter care. Howing, Wodarski, Gaudin, and Kurtz (1989) have summarized pertinent research findings regarding these interventions, and much of the following information is based on their summary and discussion.

Individual therapy is preferred by many professionals for the treatment of abused children because it can be adapted to the unique needs and maturational level of each child. With young children, play therapy is widely employed because play offers a natural and appealing way for children to express themselves. An excellent resource for individual therapy with children is the book by James (1989), which not only provides detailed guidelines for evaluation, planning, and treatment of abused children, but also describes creative techniques for forming relationships and assisting children to resolve fears, anxieties, and unrealistic self-blame. In addition to play, these techniques include use of art, drama, and other expressive modes. Malchiodi (1990) has also written a book about art therapy with children from violent homes.

Still another intervention with abused children is bibliotherapy, which entails "treatment through books" (Pardeck, 1990) using carefully selected books. Children are taken through different stages of the bibliotherapeutic process, beginning with the identification and projection phase, followed by the abreaction and catharsis phase, and concluding with the insight and integration stage. Bibliotherapy, like play therapy, has the advantage of using a medium of expression (stories) that is natural and appealing to children. It has been used successfully with children as young as age 6 or 7 (with children this young the practitioner reads the books aloud to the children). Pardeck (1990), who reports the process at length, has cited research studies that support the efficacy of this approach and has provided an annotated list of books useful in bibliotherapy with abused children.

Group Treatment Because of the importance of peer interaction, group approaches are also widely employed with abused children of all ages. Large-scale evaluations of demonstration projects have indicated that such interventions contribute to positive outcomes for both child and adolescent victims of child abuse. The use of group therapy

also has the advantage of being cost efficient, an important feature in light of the elimination of mandatory services for children that occurred in 1981, when block grants to states were introduced. Other advantages of group treatment have been discussed by Howing et al. (1989).

In Chapter 8, we discussed the negative impact of child abuse upon the social relationships of children, which has been documented by a study (Cohn, 1979) indicating that 70% of these children did not relate well with peers. Group social skills training (see Chapter 14) is a promising approach to assist these children to overcome these deficits, but as yet this approach has not been systematically evaluated.

Temporary Shelters and Therapeutic Day Care Programs Evidence indicates that therapeutic day care programs that offer affectional nurturing, stimulation, and monitoring of nutrition and health care produce gains in the functioning of maltreated children (Culp, Heide, & Richardson, 1987). These authors also indicate that girls, in particular, seem to benefit from daily social experiences outside of their families. Similarly, temporary shelter care for abused adolescents produces notable gains, as indicated by studies reviewed by Daro (1988). The disadvantage of both of these types of programs is that they have high costs. However, as Howing et al. (1989) suggest, the cost of such programs could be reduced by using volunteer homes.

Enhancing Family Functioning

Many of the conditions that exist in abusing families also exist in families with no history of abuse. A major factor that apparently accounts for the difference is the higher level of functioning in nonabusing families (Langley, 1991). Employing the interventions discussed in Chapter 16 will enable you to assist families in achieving a higher level of functioning. Moreover, intensive home–based programs (see Chapter 16) strengthen the functioning of families and keep them intact whenever feasible by equipping families with coping skills.

Enhancing Parenting Skills

Structured and time-limited group training programs are increasingly used by family and child welfare agencies to assist parents with deficient parenting skills. Generally these programs embody listening skills, empathic communication, use of positive reinforcement to motivate children, setting and enforcing consistent limits, and employing constructive discipline rather than physical punishment and other aversive measures such as belittling, yelling, nagging, and name-calling. An important by-product of this approach is the support that participants feel from each other and from the instructor or leader. Several large-scale studies have indicated successful outcomes for parent training groups (Howing et al., 1989).

In conducting parent-training groups it is vital to use language commensurate with the educational level of participants and to adapt the principles to situations that correspond to the actual life experiences of participants. Moreover, the efficacy of this approach can be enhanced by making home visits aimed at assisting participants to generalize the skills from the training setting to the home environment. This is particularly essential with disadvantaged clients whose verbal and intellectual skills are limited. It is also important to recognize that training in parenting skills should not be employed as the sole intervention, because other factors (e.g, poverty and social isolation) may be equally or more important. Diverse interventions are required for families with many problems.

Another factor critical to the success of parenting programs is leverage to assure attendance of the parents. Court mandates are often essential to motivate parents (especially fathers) to attend. Studies summarized by Howing et al. (1989) indicate that court mandates increase rates of participation and that behavioral changes for mandated clients are comparable to those for voluntary clients.

Training in Problem Solving

Studies of individual insight-oriented therapies with abusive parents (summarized by Howing et al., 1989) indicate that this approach is less successful than either group therapy or family therapy. This finding is not unexpected, as insight-oriented therapies are generally unsuccessful with clients from the lowest socioeconomic levels. Counseling oriented to basic problem solving, however, has proved to be effective with neglectful parents. Regular home visits and around-the-clock availability appear to be key components in forming effective alliances with neglectful parents. These components are at the heart of the intensive home-based programs described earlier.

Behaviorally Oriented Interventions

In contrast to the sparse evidence supporting insight-oriented therapies are numerous studies (summarized by Howing et al., 1989) that provide evidence of the efficacy of behaviorally oriented interventions. These interventions teach parents to track children's behavior, to reinforce desirable behaviors, and to employ nonphysical methods of discipline. In addition, behavioral techniques that flow from careful assessment may be employed similar to those discussed in Chapters 13 and 14. These include verbal instruction, modeling, role playing, guided practice, stress management, and cognitive restructuring. One caution, however, is that behavioral interventions, like all others, should not be used as the sole intervention. All of the relevant factors in the family's ecosystem must be addressed.

Remedying Social Isolation

With single-parent mothers whose social isolation contributes to their abuse of children, a two-fold approach may be required. Simply seeking to develop a support system may be insufficient because many such mothers lack the skills to develop and maintain supportive relationships. To solve this dilemma, Lovell and Richey (1991) developed an innovative and appealing social skill training program that enables mothers at risk of child abuse to develop skills needed to form and to enhance adult relationships. The 16 weeks of the formal training program were followed by 3 months of post-training case management that consisted of "consulting on an individual basis with group members to help them to achieve and maintain their social network and support goals" (p. 569).

Participants were highly satisfied with the program and the level of participation was higher than the usual rate for involuntary clients. Research has not yet been conducted to determine if the new and expanded friendships actually lead to nonabusive norms and behaviors. The approach is promising, however, and the expanded social relationships alone represent a substantial gain.

Linking isolated clients with self-help groups and support systems also can be a partial remedy to social isolation—at least for the life of the group. Self-help and support groups commonly employed include Parents Anonymous (for child abusers), Parents Without Partners, and Parents United (for sexual abusers).

Anger Control Interventions

Interventions that enable persons to gain control over anger play a key role in most treatment plans for abusive parents. This is readily understandable as underlying anger is common to child abuse incidents. One study (Kadushin & Martin, 1981) revealed that in 85% of the cases studied, the parent's violent reaction was associated with anger triggered by what was perceived as the child's provocative behavior. Obviously, both emotion and cognition are involved, as the parent's emotion emanated from perceptions that the child was deliberately trying to irritate or frustrate the parent. It follows, then, that remedial interventions should be directed to both emotions and cogni-

tions. Most anger control programs, in fact, do just that, embodying the components that play a central role in stress inoculation, namely relaxation training and cognitive restructuring.

An important and relevant study by Whiteman, Fanshel, and Grundy (1987) merits attention. These researchers conducted a well-designed study that tested the efficacy of four different interventions designed to reduce anger responses of parents judged to be at high risk of abusing their children. The interventions used with four groups of randomly selected parents and a control group were as follows: (1) relaxation procedures designed to alleviate stress and arousal associated with the anger response; (2) cognitive restructuring "designed to change the perceptions, expectations, and appraisals of the parent regarding the child as well as the stress encountered by the parent" (p. 470); (3) development of problem-solving skills designed to replace the habitual anger response of the parent; and (4) a composite package consisting of the preceding three modalities.

The outcomes of the four approaches were assessed, using scales that tapped anger toward children and other people and other qualities regarded as critical in successful child rearing. All of the components achieved outcomes superior to those of the control group, and overall, the composite package outperformed the separate modalities. Individually, the cognitive restructuring and problem–solving components were the most potent. The demonstrated efficacy of these modalities is encouraging. We urge you to read this study and to consider using these modalities, all of which we delineated in Chapters 13 and 14.

Adults Abused as Children

Increasingly, those in the helping professions are recognizing the significance and pervasiveness of the effects of child abuse on the functioning of adults; unfortunately, however, the literature has not kept pace with this rapidly expanding awareness. In Chapter 8, we discussed how abuse as a child is commonly linked with severe psychiatric disorders. Many adults victimized as children, however, do not manifest such severe disorders, although less severe, ongoing major effects hinder the functioning of countless others who were abused, and many of them come to the attention of family and mental health agencies.

To determine in initial interviews if childhood abuse has occurred, it is important not to be intrusive and instead to probe gently. Wartel (1991) recommends taking an educative stance by explaining how violent behavior can affect children and can cause subsequent problems in adulthood. Because persons who do remember being victimized commonly experience guilt and shame, Wartel recommends not using the term *abuse* but rather inquiring if the client was hit or beaten frequently, shamed, locked in closets, or subjected to other forms of severe punishment.

If clients affirm that abuse did, in fact, occur, "the abuse needs to be labeled and connected to the symptoms within a cause-effect framework" (p. 159). As children, adults who were abused developed enduring defensive patterns that once served protective functions, but these patterns need to be identified as outmoded and even destructive in adult life. Common patterns include feeling worthless (in fact, seeing oneself as deserving to be abused), having low self-esteem that pervades interpersonal relationships, becoming withdrawn, attempting excessively to please (or avoid displeasing) others, becoming submissive, and being out of touch with one's own needs.

Negotiating goals that involve changing these defensive patterns may be a giant step toward growth and more fulfilling lives. Those who work with these adults need to be warm, accepting and even nurturant, as these clients often not only were physically abused but also deprived of the nurturance, acceptance, and emotional support children need to develop self-respect, confidence, and assertiveness. Fostering the development of self-esteem and the belief that one is entitled to respect are important tasks in the therapeutic process.

These clients also need to ventilate the rage and hurt they feel toward the abuser—feelings that commonly have been kept deeply buried. Expressing these feelings in a warm and accepting environment enables clients to unburden themselves of pent-up emotions and to integrate them as natural human reactions to an intolerable situation.

Most of the publications concerned with assisting adult victims of abuse recommend a psychodynamic approach, as for example, Rosenthal (1988) and Wartel (1991). Therapeutic and support groups can also be especially beneficial in assisting these people to recognize that many others have experienced similar trauma, and in feeling the caring and support of others. Assertiveness groups can also be highly beneficial in overcoming patterns of compliance and subserviency.

TREATING SEXUAL ABUSE

Over the past 20 years, the prevalence of sexual abuse of children has been forcefully brought to public attention, aided by dramatic public disclosures by celebrities that they were sexually abused as children. Awareness by professionals has similarly expanded, accompanied by a virtual deluge of publications in the literature in some of the many books that address this topic in a broad sense.[3]

Reporting Child Abuse

As we discussed in Chapters 4 and 8, social workers are mandated to report child sexual abuse, which means they must break confidentiality with children and adolescents when they have ample reason to believe that abuse has occurred. Damage to the relationship with children by breaking confidentiality can be minimized by carefully explaining in readily understandable language that a report is being made in compliance with the law and for the purpose of protecting the child. Kilgore (1988) recommends explanations similar to: "If you told me you had swallowed poison, I would tell a doctor," or "If you told me you slit your wrists, I would tell your parents." If given in a warm and supportive manner, the action may, in fact, enhance the relationship as the child senses the genuine care and concern of the practitioner.

Protecting the Child

As with physical abuse, the immediate primary concern is to protect the child from continued sexual abuse. In some instances, the parent is ordered from the home by the court. If the parent is a single parent, or if for some other reason removal of the offending parent is not feasible, it may be necessary to place the child in protective custody with a relative, in a shelter home, or other placement.

With respect to decisions about removing the child or offending parent from the home, the trend is to avoid automatic decisions and instead to carefully assess risk factors before reaching a decision. This trend emanates from recognition that breaking up the family can further traumatize the child and the family. One important factor to be weighed is the mother's capacity to protect the child from repeated molestations by the father. Another factor is the child's age and ability to protect herself from further abuse. As we indicated in Chapter 8, Orten and Rich (1988) have developed a risk reabuse scale that considers characteristics of the father, the mother, and the child. Faller (1989) has also provided guidelines to assess risk of sexual reabuse that considers characteristics of the mother, the child, and the degree of abuse.

Treating Victims of Sexual Abuse

Treatment of children who have been victimized involves many of the same factors as those discussed in the preceding section concerned with physical abuse. Because of the trauma experienced, children need a great deal of emotional support, which the therapist can maximize by remaining calm, using the client's language in discussing the molestation, believing the child, and responding sensitively and empathically as the child verbally or nonverbally manifests painful and confusing emotions. It is critical, of course, to warmly accept abused children and to assist them to feel they are worthwhile and have much to offer irrespective of the sexual abuse. It is also important to assist them to believe they are not to blame, even though they may have experienced a degree of pleasure in the sexual activity, and to assist them to view the abusive episodes as resulting from "Daddy's problem."

When fathers or stepfathers are removed from the home, children often blame themselves. To correct their distorted perspective it is helpful to mention that Daddy did wrong and must stay somewhere else until he overcomes his problem. Many children experience a sense of relief when offending parents are removed and rebound remarkably well when their social network responds supportively.

Because young children tend to cope with the trauma of sexual abuse by dissociating the experience, a goal of therapy is "to reconnect the client to his or her dissociated experiences by bringing together the fragmented aspects of the self" (Kilgore, 1988, p. 229). Many different techniques can be employed to accomplish this goal and to enhance the child's damaged self-esteem. Play therapy, art therapy, bibliotherapy, and other forms of expressive therapy are widely used. Gil (1991) and Webb (1991) have written books that describe how to use play therapy with abused and neglected children. The books listed in the first part of this section also discuss these and other techniques. Mandell and Damon (1989) have discussed the use of group therapy, which is frequently employed with sexually abused children. Other references relate specifically to treatment of sexually abused males (see Bolton, Morris, & MacEachron, 1989; Hunter, 1990), a group often overlooked.

Interventions with Mothers

The first consideration in work with mothers of sexually abused children is to assist them to cope with the crisis of learning their spouse or other perpetrator has abused the child. The mother often feels betrayed, angry, and bewildered when confronted by the ugly reality of what has occurred. To assist the mother to cope with the stress of deciding what action to take, whom to tell, what to do about the marriage or other relationship, how to relate to the perpetrating male, and related stresses, crisis intervention is the most appropriate mode of intervention (see Chapter 13). The mother will need emotional support and opportunity to ventilate her emotions before beginning to weigh her options. If memories of being abused in her own childhood are revived, she will need assistance in coping with these painful emotions as well. Longer term counseling may be needed should this occur.

An important task is to aid the mother in taking complete charge of the family and protecting the child by monitoring the relationship between her husband and the child. This may necessitate the father being out of the home for a period of time. Another task is for the mother to establish or reestablish a positive and strong relationship with the daughter "so the mother can mother the child, provide protection, and open communication" (Pittman, 1987, p. 313).

Treating the Family

Although experts are by no means in agreement about employing family treatment with families where sexual abuse has occured, a number see it as the treatment of choice, adding the proviso that the individual needs of children must not be overlooked. Some experts also recommend that family therapy be employed only late in treatment, after reunification has occurred. Howing et al. (1989) have discussed these and other issues in their review of pertinent research findings related to effective interventions for child maltreatment.

An important factor in working with incestual families is that all family members must be included and younger children need to be alerted to "Daddy's problem" so that they can offer protection to one another. No secrets should be permitted, as it has been "family secrets" that contributed to and maintained the problem.

Focus on family alignments is critical. Efforts should be made to strengthen the coalition between the parents (assuming the mother decides to remain in the marriage) and to clearly demarcate generational boundaries. Another major task is to assist the family to define roles clearly so that only parents perform parental roles and children are not expected to perform adult roles that blur generational boundaries and force them into inappropriate interactions with parents (e.g., bathing or sleeping with parents, massaging parents, or wrestling with a parent of the other sex). It is also essential to focus on defining inappropriate sexual behavior and clarifying responsibility of all family members in keeping behavior within acceptable boundaries.

Treating the Perpetrators of Sexual Abuse

Whereas the literature on treatment of victims of sexual abuse is extensive, the literature on treatment of perpetrators is relatively sparse. Editors of one book (Horton, Johnson, Roundy, & Williams, 1989), in fact, refer to the incest perpetrator in the title of their book as "a family member no one wants to treat." Whether professionals do not want to treat perpetrators is debatable, but it appears that many perpetrators either receive no treatment or are ordered by courts to see therapists with limited experience in treatment of sexual abuse (Dawson, 1986; Finkelhor, 1984).

Sexual abusers are generally viewed as difficult to treat because they tend to deny having problems and to resist treatment. Without the leverage of court-mandated treatment, it is unlikely that more than a small percentage would enter treatment. Once in treatment they pose challenges aside from deficient motivation, because many have trouble expressing emotions verbally and do not communicate openly. To bypass their resistance and limited verbal skills, Taylor (1990) introduces nonverbal expression through poetry, prose, art, and collage during the first month of treatment. To avoid the appearance of using gimmicks, the therapist presents these expressive modes as being an integral part of the therapeutic process.

Vital to successful work with perpetrators is providing consistent warmth and acceptance in spite of the repugnant nature of their offenses. This may pose a difficult challenge but is lessened by recognizing that most perpetrators are very needy persons, most of whom were themselves emotionally deprived and many abused as children. As a result, underneath the facade of strength they attempt to project in their families, they struggle with low self-esteem, feelings of inadequacy, and a sense of loneliness. In terms of emotional and sexual maturation, many are little more than needy children masquerading in adult bodies.

Goals in treatment include assisting perpetrators to get in touch with their needs and feelings and to learn to express them in functional ways. Psychodynamically oriented treatment also focuses on unresolved issues from childhood, including emotional deprivation. They are then helped to see the relationship between the frustrations experienced in their own families of origin and their abusive behavior in their current families. By exploring these dynamics, they begin to develop empathy for the child they have victimized, realizing they have subjected the child to traumatic experiences similar to those they themselves experienced. The goal, of course, is not merely to foster insight but to enable the perpetrator to learn new, appropriate ways of interacting in the present and future.

Other approaches have also been employed with perpetrators. Maletzky and McGovern (1990) have discussed behavioral approaches, including aversive conditioning, positive conditioning, and operant conditioning. Dawson (1986) and Frey (1987) have written about group interventions.[4]

Treating Adult Survivors of Sexual Abuse

Because sexual abuse can seriously impair emotional and social development, survivors commonly experience difficulties in adulthood, some of them severe, as we noted in Chapter 8. Typically, it is these difficulties that impel them to seek treatment, and reports of the occurrence of childhood sexual abuse emerge only through gentle but skillful probing during initial interviews or even later during the course of treatment. These survivors enter treatment when the coping skills developed in childhood no longer work. Consequently, their presenting problems commonly include depression (and possibly suicide attempts), mental breakdowns, drug or alcohol abuse, sexual dysfunction, eating disorders, nightmares, phobias, and even hearing voices when no one else is present. They may also enter treatment because of stressors such as threatened or actual divorce, rejections, parent–child problems, serious interpersonal difficulties, or deaths of loved ones.

The traumatic effects of childhood sexual abuse have been divided into four categories by Patten, Gatz, Jones, and Thomas (1989), based on a similar categorization developed by Finkelhor and Browne (1986) to apply to sexually abused children. In brief, these categories are as follows: (1) *traumatic sexualization* (a process that warps both sexual feelings and attitudes and causes them to develop in inappropriate and dysfunctional ways); (2) *stigmatization*, which refers to qualities of badness, shame, and guilt that are conveyed to the abused child, and are incorporated into the self-image (adults abused as children often perceive themselves as "damaged goods"); (3) *betrayal*, which both children and adults feel when they realize they have been exploited and harmed by someone upon whom they were dependent (however, both children and adults often blame themselves also); and (4) *powerlessness* that results from having been overcome contrary to one's will and desires. Effective treatment, it follows, must address the individual effects associated with the above categories.

With respect to treating the effects of traumatic sexualization, Rowe and Savage (1988) have written an informative article clarifying that effects on sexual functioning vary according to the nature of the abuse. They present a typology of types of sexual abuse and discuss the treatment implications of each type.

To overcome the effects of stigmatization, it is important to explore carefully the clients' self-concept, to assist them in identifying the sources of distortions (e.g., being called a "little whore" by the perpetrator), and to convey warm acceptance of them. It is also helpful to gently dispute their self-perceptions of being damaged goods and to negotiate a goal of discarding such negative self-perceptions. To facilitate accomplishing this goal, it is important to assist them to realize that such perceptions were formed when they were not sufficiently mature to place what was happening in realistic perspective. Now, however, they can understand that they were being exploited by a maladjusted parent and that with consistent and determined effort they can gradually replace unrealistic feelings of self-blame and worthlessness with self-respect and self-esteem that is merited and long overdue.

The effects of betrayal often lead to difficulties in trusting other men and in forming genuine intimate relationships. The goal, of course, is to enable them to understand that based on traumatic childhood experiences they have overgeneralized their distrust of the male perpetrator to encompass all adult males. It is realistic to acknowledge that some men are indeed predatory and untrustworthy, but that there are all types of men (and women). The task is to differentiate perceptions of men and to avoid lumping them all into one category. Cognitive restructuring as delineated in Chapter 13 can be highly useful in assisting these women to align their beliefs with reality.

Empowerment techniques are employed to assist incest survivors to overcome feelings of powerlessness. Group approaches are widely used because of the strength women gain by joining with others to identify and overcome effects of sexual abuse. The sense of powerlessness shared by group members emerges as a theme, and members gain strength as they encourage each other to assert their needs and feelings more openly. Hearing reports of success and growth emboldens group members to risk relating with increased assertiveness. Indeed, assertiveness training, as discussed in Chapter 15, is often a major component of support groups for women sexually abused as children. Still another method of empowering these women, described by Nelson (1991), consists of having them "speak out," that is, to make public presentations about their personal histories of having been abused.

Some adult survivors of incest manifest severe problems that require intensive psychotherapy. Many, for example, manifest symptoms of post-traumatic stress disorder and require a more comprehensive approach. With such persons, "Recovery...occurs when a victim is transformed into a survivor who is able to integrate the catastrophe into his or her life history and use it as a source of strength" (Patten et al., 1989, p. 198). Books concerned with therapy for adult survivors of childhood sexual abuse include those by Briere (1989) and Courtois (1988). Another publication (Cruz, Price-Williams, & Andron, 1988) focuses on a subgroup of women who as children were especially vulnerable to sexual abuse, namely developmentally disabled women.

TREATING SPOUSE ABUSE

Our efforts in writing this section were greatly aided by a comprehensive and incisive review reported by Eisikovits and Edleson (1989) of the literature concerned with interventions employed with men who batter women. They organized their review according to an ecological model of understanding the problem. We draw heavily from their review later in our discussion.

Needs of Battered Women

For women who have been battered and are in need of immediate protection, shelters provide an invaluable service. They not only offer a refuge for victims and their children but also provide an environment in which women experience validation for their experiences and receive empathic support that enables them to reevaluate their life circumstances and to consider options. Shelter, of course, is temporary, and battered women may need emergency medical care, legal assistance, employment assistance, and counseling in evaluating possible courses of action. The need for counseling regarding potential income and employment is vital, for without adequate income a woman's self-determination is compromised. Documentation of this dilemma is provided by Caputo (1988), who found that nearly 70% of abused wives remained with perpetrators because of the financial security afforded. This finding largely negates an emerging misconception that battered women remain with partners because of codependency, a belief further refuted by Frank and Golden (1992).

Although most urban centers provide shelter facilities, other resources for battered women are fragmented or nonexistent. Hamlin (1991) has built a strong case for and delineated a model for community-based spouse abuse protection and family preservation teams composed of representatives from law enforcement, medicine, social services, mental health, family services, prosecuting attorneys, shelter care, judiciary, clergy, and agencies that provide employment counseling and substance abuse services. Funded from diverse sources, the team would address both individual case consultation and resource development, arrange for case management services for individual cases, and provide prevention and education services to the community.

Community and State Programs Hamlin's proposal represents an ideal, but some states and communities have developed progressive programs. Minnesota has led the way in developing not only urban programs but also a statewide network of programs, almost half of which are located in areas with low densities of populations. The impetus for the many innovations in the state network came from the dedicated efforts of the Minnesota Coalition for Battered Women, the umbrella for more than 70 programs in the state. Intensive lobbying resulted in changes in state laws and the provision of millions of dollars annually for intervention efforts. Edleson and Frank (1991) have written about Minnesota's experience in developing the network of programs and reported the results of a survey about the operation of 31 such programs.

Need for Federal Policies Because of the pervasiveness of abuse of women, a need exists for coherent federal policies that remedy gender inequities and provide opportunities for women to escape the intolerable circumstances of being abused. Davis and Hagen (1992) have decried the divergencies and inadequacies of federal policies and stressed the need for social workers to recommit themselves to working "to ensure adequate public funding of battered women's short-term shelter needs and services needed to empower women to become self-sufficient" (p. 19).

Children of Abusive Fathers The number of children affected by family violence is large; data from one study (New York Victim Services Agency, 1982) indicated that of abused women with children, 85% reported the children were present when violence occurred. In Chapter 8, we described the adverse affects of violence on children including the fact that many of these children (especially males) grow up to become adult abusers of women.

Although empirical studies have not been reported on the outcomes of interventions with children who have witnessed violence, several publications have dealt with this topic.[5]

System-Oriented Interventions

Of the dozens of articles and books about men who batter that were reviewed by Eisikovits and Edleson (1989), only two reported on interventions with individual men. Work with couples, both in conjoint sessions and in groups, is widely advocated by those oriented to systems theory. The strongest advocates for a systems approach maintain that violence is a product of a dysfunctional system and as such should be resolved in the context of the system. It is important to recall that some feminists oppose this position, taking a linear stance that abuse of women results from the gender-linked factors cited earlier in this chapter and in Chapter 8.

Systems-oriented interventions focus on the dysfunctional reciprocal interactions between partners and assist each partner to see how she/he contributes to conflicts that escalate into violence. Practitioners with this orientation draw heavily from communication/interaction theory, assisting partners to learn to express their needs and feelings in nonattacking ways, to listen attentively, and to learn effective problem-solving skills.

As reported by Eisikovits and Edleson (1989), many systems-oriented practitioners actually include major cognitive/behavioral components in their interventions. The avowed theoretical orientations of practitioners and the interventions they employed thus did not correspond closely. Interventions actually employed, in addition to those listed above, were: training in discerning cues that trigger violence, training in the use of declaring time-out when tensions mount, cognitive restructuring with an emphasis on self-talk that averts and reduces anger, and stress reduction and anger control through training in relaxation procedures and visual imagery.

The outcomes of systems-oriented interventions with couples generally were favorable, but the reported studies employed imprecise outcome criteria and did not include control groups. Thus, firm conclusions are not warranted and the best that can be said is that the findings indicate systems-oriented approaches are promising.

Authors, however, cautioned against using couples treatment under certain circumstances, which varied from author to author. Contraindications for couples therapy included the following situations: (1) when a woman's safety is jeopardized, (2) when abuse is frequent and severe, (3) when chemical dependency exists, (4) when mental illness is present, and (5) when the woman is opposed to couples treatment. In these situations authors recommend that the male be required to undergo treatment (usually group treatment) before beginning couples counseling.

Men's Groups Eisikovits and Edleson (1989) reviewed over 50 studies of group interventions for batterers. Interestingly, in this group of studies they found reference to the influence of gender-role socialization and sociocultural values, which were lacking in literature relating to individual and systemic interventions. (We will discuss these factors later.) Group interventions also emphasized the social learning perspective (i.e., violent behavior is learned and can be replaced by learning alternate coping behaviors).

Most writers argued for a group format in which 5 to 20 men discuss their violence. Underlying this format is the premise that crucial to success is breaking men's social isolation, encouraging mutual self-help, and exposing them to diverse opinions and world views. The reports of men who participated in one such group express reactions that support the rationale: "The men viewed group treatment as a reinforcement for change they were struggling to make and greatly valued the open discussions and closeness of group members. When discussing the group process, the men did not focus on the specific techniques used in the group as much as they did upon the discovery of feelings and how to express them" (Eisikovits & Edleson, 1989, p. 398).

Outcomes of group interventions have shown that group treatment is effective in ending violence in 59 to 84% of those who complete the treatment (Edleson & Syers, 1990). Although ending violence is a marked improvement, questions have been raised about the adequacy of this outcome criterion because it fails to tell the whole story. In many instances of ended violence, the men still made threats which meant that psychological violence continued. Still, overall, group treatment of perpetrators is one of our most potent interventions. Needed future improvements include more systematic integration of ethnic sensitive approaches in such work (Williams, 1994).

An Empirically Based Model   Encouraged by the positive results of group interventions, Edleson and Syers (1990) designed a study to answer two basic questions not answered by other studies: (1) What are the relative effects of self-help groups, educationally focused groups, and composite groups that combine the two preceding formats? and (2) What are the relative effects of different intensities (meetings once per week vs. twice weekly) of time-limited treatment? Three types of experimental groups were thus formed.

The educationally focused format relied heavily on lectures, videotaped and role-played demonstrations, and short group discussions. The format contained five different modules consisting of: (1) "Introduction," (2) "Abuse: How it happens," (3) "Abuse: Its impact on people in my life," (4) "Why has abuse become part of my life?," and (5) "How to change."

The self-help groups were relatively unstructured and provided opportunities for the men to receive lectures if they chose and to discuss issues and events in detail. Typically, portions of the meetings were devoted to educational presentations, followed by personal time for members to tell stories and work on personal problems.

The combined model incorporated aspects of both the educationally focused and self-help groups. Each of the three formats was offered in two intensities: 12 consecutive weekly sessions lasting 2 hours and 15 minutes, and 32 sessions of 2 hours and 15 minutes across 16 consecutive weeks.

Outcome criteria consisted of 29 behaviorally phrased questions that asked the men about varying degrees of violence they had expressed, ranging from threats of violence to actual acts of violence. The same questions were asked at the completion of treatment; at the follow-up interviews six months later the same questions were again asked not only of the perpetrators but of partners as well.

Outcome measures clearly favored the short-term, educationally focused format over the self-help format. Moreover, the less intensive (12 sessions) format achieved results at least equal to the more intensive format (32 sessions). The educational groups surpassed the self-help groups not only in reducing reports of violence but also threats of violence. Self-help groups, therefore, appear not to have the potency of educational groups. Noteworthy is the fact that the short-term, educational format achieved results comparable to the best results reported in earlier studies. Given the transferability and cost effectiveness of this approach, this finding is of great importance to program planners.

ORGANIZATIONAL OPPOSITION TO CHANGE

In agency operations, because direct practitioners deliver services in face-to-face contacts with clients, they are in a critical position to evaluate the impact of agency policies and practices on service delivery. When certain policies or procedures impede service delivery or block the agency from fulfilling its mission in an optimal fashion, front-line workers can identify the impediments and propose remedial changes. In so doing they perform the roles of organizational diagnostician and facilitator/expediter, which we briefly discussed in Chapter 2.

Promoting organizational change is a complex

process and organizational opposition to change is perhaps as common as is opposition to change by individuals, families, and groups. To perform the roles of organizational diagnostician and facilitator/expediter effectively, therefore, practitioners must be armed with knowledge about common sources of organizational opposition so that they can anticipate them and can plan appropriate counter-strategies that will enhance the odds of achieving change. Frey (1990) has developed a useful framework for direct practitioners to assess potential organizational opposition. We present basic elements of Frey's framework in the following sections, together with a brief discussion that synthesizes his and our own commentary.

Before discussing the elements of the framework, however, we would like to stress that some agencies provide a climate conducive to change by encouraging practitioners to identify needed changes and providing mechanisms whereby proposals for change can be initiated. In such settings organizational opposition may be moderated by the receptivity of the organization to proposals for change.

Perceived Advantage

Organizational opposition is likely to be lower to the extent that groups within an organization perceive that adopting the proposal will benefit them. It is important to consider that certain groups within an organization may be positively affected by certain changes and others may be negatively affected. Proposing to increase the time spent in delivering services by purchasing personal computers that can perform much of the paper work may have strong appeal to service providers but be resisted strongly by secretarial staff, some of whose positions may be eliminated. Obviously, the latter are likely to oppose such a proposal.

In assessing the potential benefits of a proposal, it is important to consider the impact on three different groups:

1. The administrators who hold the ultimate authority for accepting or rejecting the proposal.

2. Those who will have responsibility for planning and/or overseeing implementation of the proposal (e.g., middle managers or a task force).

3. Staff persons who ultimately carry out the change (or are affected by it) once it is implemented.

By considering the impact of the potential change on each of these groups, practitioners can weigh benefits against detrimental effects and can plan strategies to counter resistance when the former clearly and substantially outweigh the latter.

Effort

This dimension involves the amount of time and energy required to gain adoption and implementation of a proposed change. To gain favor the benefits of a proposal must outweigh the required efforts, which represent one form of organizational cost. It is axiomatic that the greater the investment of time (including the length of time required) and energy required to implement a proposal, the greater will be the resistance to the proposed change.

Risk

Risk entails potential negative outcomes of implementing a proposal. Because unforeseen problems may develop and unanticipated costs may be incurred, uncertainty that the proposed changes will accomplish the intended objectives is a very real factor. In light of this reality, consideration should be given to what would be entailed in returning to the condition that preceded the change. If return would be difficult and expensive, resistance will be understandably high.

Frey (1990) identifies three types of high-risk proposals including: (1) proposals that cannot be reversed without substantial costs (e.g., purchasing expensive equipment or creating new units), (2) proposals that must be adopted in their entirety rather than implemented in stages, and (3) proposals that are radical and in conflict with the dominant values of the organization, its members, or the public. High-risk proposals such as these types can be expected to engender high levels of opposition.

Sunken Costs

Certain changes require sunken costs (i.e., investments in money, time, or energy that cannot be converted into other types of resources, as, for example, inservice training or costs of consultation), whereas tangible assets such as a building or equipment can be sold and converted into other resources. Proposals that include sunken costs entail greater potential losses and are likely to meet with higher opposition than are proposals with costs that can be partially recovered if the proposal does not produce the desired results. In addition, previous decisions may have entailed sunken costs. If new proposals ignore or do not make use of those resources, organizational opposition may be anticipated.

Understandability

Proposals that are complex and difficult to understand are likely to produce more resistance than proposals that are presented in simple language. To minimize opposition, practitioners should consider their audience and should communicate in clear, understandable language that is compatible with the capacity of the audience to comprehend.

Ability

If proposals for change exceed the capacity of the organization to implement the change, a high level of opposition is likely to result. In the present era of scarce resources, even when consensus exists that a proposed change is highly desirable, opposition is likely if additional funding is required. To overcome opposition in such instances, realistic funding resources must be identified. In some

instances reallocation of existing resources may make proposed changes feasible (e.g., reassigning staff to perform a function accorded higher priority than an existing function).

Depth and Distance

Depth refers to the extent to which adoption of a proposal would change the organization. Citing an article by Patti (1974), Frey delineates three levels of depth. The first involves *peripheral changes* that would alter *rules and procedures* that guide employees in carrying out the agency's policies and programs (e.g., extending hours the agency is open, modifying forms that must be completed, or modifying methods of evaluating employee performance). The next level of depth involves *programmatic changes* that alter ways in which policies or programs are implemented (e.g., changing from open-ended to time-limited service or increasing the use of group interventions). The deepest level involves proposals that would alter the basic goals and objectives of an organization.

The greater the depth of proposed changes, the greater the likelihood of resistance of high intensity. Also, the greater the depth of the proposal, the greater must be efforts aimed at increasing the receptivity of all members of the organization, its funding sources, and its advisory board.

Distance relates to how far removed administrators who ultimately make the decision on the proposal are from the practitioner who proposes the change. The greater the number of administrative levels between the person proposing the change and the administrator who decides, the greater the likelihood of opposition.

Idea and Ideology

Proposals for change that are so innovative that little or no supporting knowledge exists are more likely to be opposed than proposals for which data about costs, effectiveness, and procedures for implementation are available. Obviously, the risk is greater for the former than the latter, and decision makers are understandably reluctant to support higher risk proposals.

Proposals that fit with the ideology of an organization are also likely to encounter less opposition than are proposals that diverge from an organization's ideology. Thus, proposals that involve a liberal ideology are unlikely to be well received in organizations that embrace conservative values and vice versa. The same can be said of other forms of ideology to which organizations may be strongly committed (e.g., gay rights, women's rights, and family planning).

Need

When all or most members of an organization believe that something should be done to remedy a problem, opposition will be lower than when only a few or one group within the organization perceive a need for change. To reduce opposition it is thus important to consider the perceptions of all groups and to couch the proposal so that it is compatible with the goals of all or as many groups as possible.

Generality

Generality refers to the extent of systemic impact that proposed changes would have on an organization. Proposals that would affect all the subsystems of an organization are more likely to be opposed than are changes that affect small subsystems. Similarly, the larger the subsystems that would be affected, the greater the opposition that can be expected. When proposed changes combine high levels of depth and generality, both the basic goals and all members of the organization are affected and opposition will be highest.

OVERCOMING ORGANIZATIONAL BARRIERS

Attainment of clients' goals often requires services provided by social agencies and other community organizations and institutions that are vital strands in the network of resource systems. Unfortunately, however, helping organizations sometimes fall short of delivering fully and effectively the services and resources intended for target populations. Social workers are in a strategic position to identify ways in which these organizations can enhance their responsiveness to clients' needs. In discharging this responsibility, social workers sometimes play the roles of *mediator* and *advocate* in:

1. Increasing accessibility of service.
2. Promoting service delivery in ways that enhance clients' dignity.
3. Ensuring equal access and quality of services to *all* people eligible to receive them.

In the following sections, we discuss each of these activities.

Increasing Accessibility of Services

Social workers have a responsibility to work with administrators within their own agency or with responsible staff of other organizations when services are not accessible to clients. Agencies that offer services only from 8 A.M. to 5 P.M. may make it virtually impossible for working adults to avail themselves of their services. Adopting flexible scheduling practices in agencies that serve families may result in involving increased numbers of working parents, which in turn may produce better outcomes. Providing staff coverage on weekends also makes it possible to respond to clients' crises when they occur, rather than waiting until the following week. Timely intervention provides support when people need it most and are optimally receptive to services.

Another example involves modifying scheduling procedures in health care centers so that patients do not have to wait several hours to be seen. Some clients' conditions or circumstances are such that they are unable to wait for long periods of time. Others become disgusted and leave, failing to receive treatment they vitally need.

Services are not accessible to other people because agencies are not located in proximity to them. Difficulties in arranging transportation and child care may make such services virtually inaccessible to many clients. For these reasons, many family service agencies and community mental health centers have located satellite offices throughout communities rather than having only a central office. Where this is not feasible, it may be necessary to work closely with appropriate public officials to arrange for transportation of clients.

Providing for home visits to large families may circumvent problems of child care, although young children in the home can make it nearly impossible to conduct a productive interview. Some agencies have tried to solve the problem by locating an office in the heart of the area served and providing space for children to play while they wait for their parents.

In locating offices that serve the elderly, as well as other groups who are physically frail, it is important not to place them in areas that have high crime rates. Bendick (1980) has reported that agencies located in these areas are not accessible to the elderly because they fear for their safety and will not risk entering such areas.

Promoting Service Delivery in Ways That Enhance Clients' Dignity

It is unfortunate but true that some people who need services decline to use them because they have been degraded or humiliated by the actions of staff persons, by breaches of confidentiality, or by demeaning procedures. Some large public agencies, for example, make inadequate provisions for privacy, so that interviews are conducted in view of or within earshot of others. Even worse,

some staff persons may be either openly or subtly judgmental of clients, making invidious remarks about their morality, veracity, character, or worthiness to receive public aid. Still other staff members may be brusque or rude or intrude unjustifiably into deeply personal aspects of clients' lives, thereby needlessly subjecting them to embarrassment and humiliation. Such behaviors are not only inhumane but unethical, and practitioners who become aware of such behavior by staff persons should call it to their attention. If the behavior persists, discussing it with responsible administrators or filing a complaint with the local professional organization may be justified.

Another circumstance that strips clients of their dignity may involve requiring them to go to unreasonable lengths to establish eligibility for concrete aid or services. Clients' dignity may also be hurt if practitioners are habitually tardy for appointments, cancel or change scheduled appointments frequently, or don't extend common courtesies.

Ensuring Equal Access to and Equal Quality of Services to Eligible Persons

People may be denied resources to which they are entitled or receive services that are of lesser quality than others receive for at least seven different reasons: (1) institutional racism, (2) discrimination by socioeconomic level, age, or ethnicity, (3) arbitrary decisions of practitioners, (4) lack of knowledge of resources, (5) inability to assert rights, (6) failure of authorities to develop resources mandated by laws, and (7) dysfunctional policies and procedures. In the following sections, we consider each of these factors.

Institutional Racism   Embedded in the fabric of our society to the extent that many people fail to recognize its manifestations, institutional racism often affects service delivery and availability of resources and opportunities in subtle ways. It is therefore vital that practitioners be sensitized to its manifestations so that they can liberate themselves and others from its pernicious effects. The effects of institutional racism range across the entire developmental span beginning with prenatal care and ending with care of the elderly or even burial arrangements. Racism pervades our educational, legal, economic, and political institutions, as well as employment opportunities and health care services.

Social workers have an ethical responsibility to work toward obliterating institutional racism, which is a worthy but formidable challenge. The first step toward meeting this challenge begins with developing awareness of possible traces of racist attitudes within oneself. Practitioners must also analyze policies, procedures, and practices of social agencies and other organizations to assure that all people are treated equitably. Prunty, Singer, and Thomas (1977) have described efforts of mental health practitioners who were assigned to a large integrated public school with the task of assisting school personnel to reduce racial friction and eliminate discriminatory practices. They found subtle evidence of institutional racism, including a disproportionate number of suspensions of black children and frequent assignments of children to instructional groups based on skills (resulting in groups that consisted of either predominately black or white children).

Cross has developed a continuum of agency cultural competence. Many agencies are in the middle of this continuum, carrying out a practice that could be described as "color blind" or insensitive to the effects of policies on minorities. Below this level are agencies which carry our culturally destructive policies. Cross describes here the boarding school policies enforced on Native American families and children earlier in this century which had the express purpose of eliminating Native American culture. Above this midpoint are culturally sensitive and culturally competent practice. These levels require that the agency examine policies for their differential impact on populations served and proactive development of culturally sensitive policies.

Discrimination by Socioeconomic Level, Age, or Ethnicity   Other forms of discrimination may also restrict accessibility of services or result in inferior services. For example, Schofield (1964) and others have shown that psychotherapists (the large majority of whom are middle-class Caucasians) prefer to work with young, attractive, verbal, intelligent patients of the opposite sex. Patients who are poor, less gifted intellectually, elderly, unattractive, and lacking in verbal facility may therefore be assigned to staff of lesser rank or trainees who have little say about patient assignments. Moreover, such patients may be seen less frequently and for shorter periods of time. Whether or not the outcomes are favorable or unfavorable, the fact is that some patients do not have equal access to the resources of such agencies or mental health centers.

Other clients may have unequal access to resources because of ethnicity. We have previously cited evidence (Sue & Zane, 1987) that Asian Americans and Mexican Americans are underrepresented in the use of mental health services in the United States. The most plausible explanations for this underuse of service are that mental health centers tend to be unresponsive to the needs of these minority groups and that language barriers may be a major deterrent to seeking service. Research by Aguilar (1983) has, in fact, verified that the predominant predictor of low utilization of health care by Mexican American women was the characteristics of the health care system. Sue and McKinney (1975) report similar findings concerning underutilization of mental health services by Asian Americans.

Characteristics of service delivery systems that impede utilization by ethnic minority persons include:

- Geographic locations of centers that limit accessibility.
- Few or no staff persons of clients' ethnicity.
- Language barriers.
- Lack of knowledge about and/or insensitivity to clients' values, beliefs, and lifestyles.
- Lack of respect for clients' beliefs in the efficacy of indigenous folk healers.

- Failure to take the time needed to establish rapport and gain confidence of clients.
- Failure to explore clients' beliefs regarding the causes of their problems.
- Failure to reach out to people who are unable to or fail to take the initiative in seeking needed services.
- Excessive red tape or complex procedures that confuse clients.
- Failure to adapt treatment to expectations of clients.

To adapt service delivery systems to the needs of ethnic minority clients, administrators should include representatives of ethnic groups in the process of shaping policies, procedures, and staffing to the unique needs of ethnic minority persons. Moreover, they should develop systems of feedback that assure ongoing input from the ethnic groups they serve by having representatives of ethnic groups on agency boards and by employing periodic follow-up contacts with clients to assess the impact of agency policies and of the service provided. Enlisting volunteers from ethnic groups to serve as interpreters, facilitators, case finders, and investigators can also reduce barriers to service delivery and maintain liaison with ethnic groups. Further recommendations for developing delivery systems that are responsive to health and mental care needs of Hispanics and Native Americans have been made by Guendalman (1983) and Marburg (1983), respectively. Sue and McKinney (1975) also provide convincing information about the potent effects of developing culturally relevant mental health services for Asian Americans.

> An Asian-American Counseling and Referral Service established in Seattle has seen in one year nearly the same number of Asian patients as did the 17 community mental health facilities over a period of three years. The greater responsiveness of Asians to this agency appears to be due to widespread publicity, the use of bilingual therapists and the ability of the therapist to understand the needs and life styles of Asians in the community (ibid., p. 117)

Arbitrary Decisions to Deny Resources to People

This is another factor that restricts the access of some people to resources for which they are eligible. It is an unfortunate reality that some organizations and human service workers are punitive and wield their authority to the detriment of certain clients. At this writing, a revision of the public welfare system is underway which at best will support some recipients in making a transition to work. At worst, needed benefits will be unavailable as we undergo a period in which policies become increasingly punitive to the poor. When clients are arbitrarily denied services or resources, practitioners have a responsibility to serve as an advocate for the client in securing those resources (a role we discussed at length in Chapter 15).

Clients' Lack of Ability or Skills to Assert Their Rights

Some clients lack the physical and/or mental ability to assert their rights and therefore have unequal access to benefits and services. Because they are at a distinct disadvantage in asserting their rights, many such individuals tend to acquiesce to injustices that deprive them of badly needed resources. For example, persons with mental retardation in some cases lack the intellectual capability essential to plan appropriate remedial measures.

Persons with disabilities (particularly those who are homebound) are also likely to need special advocacy services to obtain resources to which they are entitled. Many people with disabilities lack the ability to stand in lines, move from office to office, fill out multiple forms, and engage in other activities typically required to gain services from public clinics or offices. Moreover, homebound persons usually lack access to communication networks that provide inside information about how to remedy some of these problems. Still another obstacle for many persons with disabilities is that they lack clout and find it difficult to disagree with professionals concerning their rights. Weinberg (1983) has described how the rights and dignity of physically disabled persons are typically violated and has recommended remedial interventions social workers can make.

Immigrants and minorities also typically are limited in their ability to assert their rights and historically have tended to submit to injustices rather than to risk becoming embroiled in difficulties.

The frustrations of these people have been graphically described by Cameron and Talavera (1976):

> When non-English-speaking people attempt to locate services, they often end their search in anger and frustration. From the client's point of view, concrete difficulties interfere with their gaining access to services from agencies; arbitrary denial of services; institutional inflexibility; red tape with long delays and silences; undignified or callous treatment; complex forms and procedures of eligibility; long waiting lists; inaccessibility by telephone or in person; a runaround from agency to agency; lack of simple clear directions and explanations.... This list of problems is multiplied many times when the person who needs help cannot speak English. (p. 247)

To assist Spanish-speaking immigrants to cope with the difficulties enumerated above, the Family Service Agency of San Mateo County (California), which serves a substantial population of immigrants from Mexico, established an advocacy program that performs the following services for these people: translates documents, assists in filling out forms, provides information about and makes referrals to social service programs, and mediates problems between clients and other agencies (Cameron & Talavera, 1976, p. 429). Other immigrants and minorities, including Native Americans and Cuban and Asian refugees, sorely need similar services. Because funding for such programs often is unavailable, it usually falls on individual practitioners to perform these advocacy roles.

With respect to immigrants, Golan and Gruschka (1971) have described a model for integrating new immigrants based on extensive experience in Israel. Viewing immigration as a transition state that produces disruption and possible crisis, these authors delineate tasks for immigrants to integrate themselves into new communities, regions, or nations and parallel tasks for communities to absorb them. These tasks embody two dimensions—namely, "material-arrangemental" and "psychosocial" for both the immigrant and the community. The role of the social worker within this model is that of an enabler or catalyst in assisting both immigrant and community to accomplish their respective tasks, thereby minimizing stress and disruption for both parties. Brown (1982), Drachman (1992), and Rubin (1982) have also delineated the many needs of refugees and discussed ways that social workers can respond to these needs.

Lack of Knowledge About or Failure to Use Available Resources   This factor obviously precludes many clients from receiving services they need. Immigrants and minority group members who do not speak English are at a particular disadvantage in this regard, as they are not privy to information about services that tends to circulate by means of gossip networks in broader society. By no means are these the only groups who lack access to information about resources. People who live in rural or geographically isolated areas or have limited reading skills or visual or hearing impairments are also at a distinct disadvantage.

To enhance the accessibility of resources to all persons, both public and private human service organizations often engage in outreach efforts aimed at people who are unaware of or do not voluntarily seek services or resources that could improve their life situations. Toseland (1981) defines outreach as "a social work practice method that attempts to identify clients who are in need of services, alerts these clients to service provisions and benefits, and helps them to use services that are available" (p. 227).[6] Whereas clients commonly take the initiative in contacting social service agencies, practitioners take the initiative in outreach efforts, actively striving to locate, contact, and engage potential clients.

Outreach activities typically involve distributing posters and leaflets, publicizing through mass mailings, advertising in various media, appearing on radio or television, publishing stories in local newspapers, locating information booths in public places, speaking at club meetings, and even canvassing door to door (Bendick, 1980). Effective outreach appears to require personal interaction with potential consumers, for the mass media methods often fail to draw attention of eligible clients most in need of service, many of whom have limited reading skills. As a means of generating face-to-face interaction, Bendick (1980) recommends directing outreach campaigns to other social service professionals, who can subsequently disseminate information about available services and benefits and can refer prospective clients. In rural areas, outreach efforts should also be directed to indigenous caregivers and local officials, for word of mouth through informal communication channels tends to be much more restricted in rural than in urban areas.

Practitioners who engage in outreach efforts must be sensitive to clients' rights to privacy and self-determination. Outreach involves informing people about available services and benefits and striving to enhance their motivation to avail themselves of needed services, but certainly not attempting to impose services upon people.

When employing outreach efforts with minorities who do not have command of English, it is highly preferable to communicate in the native tongue of potential clients. When this is not possible, using indigenous case aides as intermediaries is the next best choice. Potential clients are far more likely to understand explanations of resources, to be receptive to proferred services and benefits, and to ask questions when they can communicate in their own language.

Failure of Authorities to Develop Resources Mandated by Law Sosin (1979) has written a cogent article dealing with this matter in which he points out that enactment of new legislation or regulations does not ensure implementation of the same. Ignoring new laws, in fact, is a widespread phenomenon. Thus, advocacy and social action must sometimes continue even after new laws are enacted as a result of earlier successful efforts.

Because new mandates that involve social welfare issues alter social priorities, resistance by powerful individuals who oppose such changes commonly occurs. Those who bear responsibility for implementing the mandates may minimize social change by ignoring, evading, or subverting a new law, thus denying benefits intended by the law to

potential beneficiaries. Sosin illustrates these forms of resistance and suggests strategies for overcoming them. These strategies are of three types: (1) increasing receptivity to the changes on the part of those who hold the authority for implementing the changes, (2) enhancing the ability of authorities to implement changes when their capacity to do so is deficient for any of several reasons, and (3) exploiting the vulnerability of authorities to sanctions for not implementing the mandates. For each of these remedies Sosin provides guidelines and cautions that will be of value to practitioners.

Dysfunctional Policies and Procedures Rigid, outdated, and otherwise dysfunctional policies and procedures may also have the unintended effects of limiting access to resources for some clients. For example, clients who are illiterate or have limited reading skills are at a decided disadvantage when they must complete numerous forms and procedures to qualify for an agency's services or benefits. Given the fact that 75% of the poverty population reads at an eighth-grade level or lower, this skill deficiency is a major problem as "about 90 percent of the documents drawn from public welfare agencies required more than an eighth–grade level [Bendick & Cantu, 1978], and one third...required college-level reading skills" (Bendick, 1980, p. 272). The obvious implications of this situation are that administrators should reduce red tape to a minimum, simplify forms, and provide aid in completing forms to clients who lack reading skills.

Other procedures cited by Bendick that limit accessibility include the number of visits required at the agency. For rural clients who must travel long distances to agency offices, the numbers of visits required can severely limit accessibility, especially with the current high cost of transportation. For clients who are handicapped or bedridden, the problem is even more severe. To accommodate such persons, either home visits or telephone applications for service or benefits are essential.

Policies may also altogether exclude some

needy persons from obtaining resources. Bendick cites instances in which migrants have been denied food stamps because they could not verify their incomes. Their crew bosses, who were cheating them out of wages and stealing their social security contributions, were reluctant to provide pay stubs that could be used to uncover their schemes. Obviously, more flexible policies are needed to remedy these situations, together with advocacy aimed at eliminating the cheating.

Still another factor that may curtail access to services for some clients involves policies related to fee charging. In times of highly limited resources, agencies may give top priorities for service to clients who can pay larger fees when fee schedules are graduated according to people's incomes. Voluntary agencies, such as family service agencies, may thus exclude the poor from services, even though such agencies were originally conceived to serve clients without regard to financial status. Administrators of such agencies thus find themselves on the horns of a dilemma, for their survival requires an adequate funding base. To resolve the dilemma involves reviewing the agency's purpose with the advisory board and exploring measures that assure continued access of services to the poor. Mobilization of increased external funding may be the only realistic remedy in such situations.

SKILL DEVELOPMENT EXERCISES IN MANAGING RELATIONAL REACTIONS AND OPPOSITION

The following exercises will assist you in expanding your skills in responding appropriately to relational reactions and opposition to change. Study each client message and determine whether a relational reaction or opposition to change might be involved. Then write the response you would give if you were the practitioner. Compare your response with the modeled response provided at the end of the exercises. Bear in mind that the mod-

eled response is only one of many possible appropriate responses.

Client Statements

1. *Client* [*has been discussing feelings of rejection and self-doubt after his fiancé broke their engagement; suddenly he looks down, sighs, then looks up*]: Say, did I tell you I got promoted at work?

2. *Female client, age 23* [*to male practitioner, age 25*]: I've been feeling very close to you these past weeks. I was wondering if you could hold me in your arms for just a moment.

3. *Male client, age 27* [*with irritation*]: I've been coming to see you for eight weeks, and things haven't changed a bit. I'm beginning to question your competence.

4. *Delinquent on probation, age 16:* I think it's ridiculous to have to come here every week. You don't have to worry about me. I'm not getting into any trouble.

5. *Female welfare client:* Sure, you say you want to help me. All you welfare workers are just alike. You don't have the slightest idea what it's like to try to raise children on $500 a month. If you really want to help, increase the dole I get.

6. *Client, age 27* [*to male practitioner*]: I've just never been able to trust men. My old man was alcoholic, and the only thing you could depend on with him was that he'd be drunk when you needed him most.

7. *Male client* [*to female mental health practitioner*]: Sometimes I really felt I was cheated in life, you know, with parents who didn't give a damn what happened to me. I think about you—how warm and caring you are, and—I know it sounds crazy—but I wish I'd had you for a mother. Sometimes I even daydream about it.

8. *Client* [*after an emotion-laden previous session, the client yawns, looks out the window, and comments*]: Not much to talk about today. Nothing much has happened this week.

9. *Male client, age 24* [*in fifth interview*]: I have this thing where people never measure up to my expectations. I know I expect too much, and I always end up feeling let down.

10. *Middle-aged Native American:* It's important to me that you do not think of me according to the

usual stereotype. I'm ambitious and want to do right by my family. I just need a job right now.

Modeled Responses

1. "No, but before you do, I'd like to know more about what you were feeling just a moment ago when you were discussing your breakup with your fiancee. I was sensing that was painful for you to talk about. Could you share what you feel as you think about it?"

2. "I'm complimented you would want me to hold you and pleased you could share those feelings with me. I want you to know I feel close to you too, but if I were to let myself feel romantic toward you, I'd be letting you down. I couldn't be helpful to you if I were involved in that way. I hope you can understand."

3. "I can see you're anxious to get things worked out, and that's a plus." [*Positive connotation.*] "But you're pretty ticked off with me, as though I haven't been doing my job. I'd like to understand those feelings more. What do you feel I should be doing different?" [*Exploring feelings and expectations.*]

4. "You sound pretty angry about having to report to me each week. I can't blame you for that. Still the judge ordered it, and neither of us really has any choice. How do you suggest we make the best of the situation?"

5. "I'm sorry you feel I'm not really interested in helping you. I gather you've had some bad experiences with other caseworkers, and I hope our relationship can be better. I do want you to know, though, that a number of us have been meeting with legislators to help them see the need to increase the amount of grants. I marvel that you do as well as you do on the amount of your grant."

6. "I can understand then that you might find it difficult to trust me—wondering if I'm really dependable."

7. [*With a warm smile*]: "Thank you for the compliment. I gather you've been experiencing my care for you and find yourself longing for the love and care you didn't receive as a child. I can sense your feelings keenly and appreciate your sharing them."

8. "Somehow that doesn't fit with what we talked about last week. You expressed some very deep feelings about yourself and your marriage. I'd like to hear what you've been feeling about what we discussed last time."

9. "I wonder if that's what you're feeling just now in our relationship—that I haven't measured up to your expectations in some way. Could you share with me what you've been feeling in that regard?"

10. "I appreciate your sharing those feelings with me. I gather you've wondered how I do see you. I see you as an ambitious and responsible person, and I want you to know I appreciate those qualities in you."

NOTES

1 In some instances, manifestations of group behaviors that may appear at first to be opposition consist of adjustment reactions of members to excessive changes (e.g., loss of members, canceled sessions, or a move to another meeting place), which tend to frustrate and discourage group members.

2 Several excellent books have been devoted to treatment of families with many problems. Kagan and Schlosberg's (1989) book is particularly useful and instructive, presenting numerous case examples and illustrating the application of a variety of strategies and techniques. Other related books have been authored or edited by McCown and Johnson (1992) and Wood and Geismar (1989).

3 Some of the many books include those authored or edited by Faller

(1990), Finkelhor and Associates (1986), Friedrich (1990), MacFarlane and Waterman (1986), Patton (1991), and Salter (1988).

4 More extensive discussions of treatment of offenders are contained in books by Horton et al. (1989), Ingersoll and Patton (1990), and Salter (1988).

5 Perhaps best known is a book by Jaffe, Wolfe, and Wilson (1990). Relevant articles have been written by Davies (1991); Wilson, Cameron, Jaffe, and Wolfe (1989); and Gibson and Gutierrez (1991).

6 To assist practitioners in implementing outreach services, Toseland (1981) has developed a model consisting of six discrete steps. Toseland delineates each step at length, and we strongly recommend you read this article.

Part 4

The Termination and Evaluation Phase

Chapter 20

The Final Phase: Termination and Evaluation

The third and final phase of the helping process involves termination. Although it has received less attention in the literature than the beginning and middle phases, it is nevertheless vital, for the manner in which the helping relationship and process are concluded strongly influences whether clients maintain the progress they have achieved and continue to grow following formal termination. It is important that practitioners plan for this phase and handle it sensitively and skillfully. In this chapter we focus on various matters that bear on the termination process, identify relevant tasks for both practitioners and clients, and discuss skills essential to managing termination effectively.

TASKS EMBODIED IN TERMINATION

Successful termination involves preparing clients adequately for separation from the practitioner and/or group and accomplishing other tasks that enhance the transition from being a client to being on one's own. These tasks include:

1. Determining when to implement termination.
2. Mutually resolving emotional reactions experienced during the process of separation.
3. Evaluating the service provided and the extent to which goals were accomplished.

4. Planning to maintain gains achieved and to achieve continued growth.

The significance of these tasks and the extent to which they can be successfully accomplished are determined in great measure by the type of termination involved, which we next consider.

TYPES OF TERMINATION

There are essentially five different types of termination, which are as follows:

1. Premature, unilateral terminations by clients.
2. Planned termination determined by temporal constraints associated with an agency's function.
3. Planned termination associated with time-limited modalities.
4. Planned terminations involving open-ended modalities.
5. Termination precipitated by the departure of a practitioner.

As we explained earlier, certain of the tasks identified in the preceding section are irrelevant to some types of termination and highly relevant to others. Determining when to implement termination, for example, is highly relevant to type 4 (above), is of lesser significance to types 2, 3, and

5, and does not apply to type 1. The differential significance of the tasks will become further apparent in the following sections concerned with each type of termination.

Premature, Unilateral Termination

Generally, the preferred way of terminating is for the participants in the helping process to plan the termination mutually because they have accomplished their goals. Unfortunately, some voluntary clients terminate by default, simply failing to appear for appointments, offering perfunctory reasons for termination, and refusing to return to discuss the matter further. Involuntary clients may wish to terminate unilaterally but often find the legal consequences to be prohibitive. Unfortunately, this often means that they continue their presence physically but not psychologically and may attend sporadically, arrive late and leave early. Some clients terminate contact with the practitioner because of circumstances beyond their control, such as illness or death, incarceration, or through transfer to another unit or practitioner.

Other voluntary clients announce at the conclusion of a session that they will not be returning and give the practitioner little opportunity to explore the basis of their decision. In such instances, it is desirable to explain that deciding to terminate is a major decision that should not be made abruptly and that you would like the opportunity to explore with the client factors that led to the decision.

Premature and unilateral terminations may be expressions of unresolved opposition that can be resolved given the opportunity to do so. If there are indications the client may be experiencing negative feelings toward you, it may be productive to share your concern that you may have offended the client and express your desire to discuss the matter further. Should the client be amenable to your invitation, you can attempt to resolve the feelings by following the guidelines discussed in Chapter 19.

Some clients attribute decisions to terminate after one or two sessions to having benefited sufficiently and no longer needing assistance. Recent research (Presley, 1987; Toseland, 1987) has, in fact, indicated that such is often the case and that practitioners have erred in assuming that "premature" terminations generally indicate dissatisfactions by clients and negative outcomes. It is also true, however, that claims of some clients of miraculous improvements may derive from denial of problems or wishful thinking. When there is no basis for believing that actual improvement has occurred, we recommend being candid with clients but exerting no pressure upon them to continue and offering service should they decide to return in the future. A practitioner thus respects the client's right to self-determination but also fulfills a professional obligation to offer expert opinion. The following is a condensed illustration of such a message.

"I wish I could honestly agree with you that you've worked out your difficulties. As I see it, however, we have not made basic changes on the problems that have concerned you and the improvement you are experiencing is likely to be temporary. I believe it's possible that we can yet make a great deal of progress. Still, I respect your right to decide for yourself. I hope you'll feel free to return if you'd like to work further on your difficulties in the future. I'm here to help, and I want you to know I'm still very much interested in you."

The preceding message is authentic, conveys respect and concern, and places responsibility on the client—where it belongs. When we have handled premature terminations in this manner, a number of clients have later returned for additional service, more highly motivated than before. Several clients have even expressed gratitude for our earlier frankness. It is sobering to note that some funding sources consider many terminations that the practitioner may consider premature as appropriate if functioning has been restored. A return for further work in the future is often considered appropriate without concern for dealing with underlying dynamics in the current episode.

Groups may also experience adverse effects from the premature termination of a member. That terminating member may or may not reveal intent to terminate or the practitioner may not be at liberty to share those reasons with the group and hence be unable to provide the group with an opportunity to deal with the loss. In either case, individual members may experience anger toward the "recalcitrant" member who is, in their view, abandoning the group, thereby devaluing the group experience. Other feelings experienced by members toward the departing member may include guilt over their anger, hurt over being "rejected," disturbing doubts that perhaps the group isn't worth their investment after all, a wish to accompany the person who is leaving, and sadness over the loss of a valued relationship. Feelings experienced by the departing member may be similar, including ambivalence about leaving the group, anger at being pressured to remain in the group, guilt over leaving the group, and feelings of loss.

If granted the opportunity to work through the reactions of members, the group can usually absorb the shock of the termination of one member without threat to survival of the group. However, when the group is deprived of this opportunity, premature termination of a member can be harmful to group morale, particularly if the member departed after a negative encounter with others in the group. Likewise, if the group has experienced the loss of other members in a relatively short time, the group's survival may be jeopardized. When a member terminates without discussion, it is imperative to discuss the event with the group (sharing personal feelings in doing so), determine members' perception of the meaning of the event and its impact on the group, and decide with the group whether it wishes to reach out to the absent member. If the group declines, it is important for the practitioner to assume this role.

Feelings similar to those just described may also occur when a group experiences extended absences of individual members or of the group leader, when a group suffers the loss of a member through death or discharge from an institution, or when a member goes AWOL from an institution. Sometimes the group in question is not a formed therapeutic group but rather consists of members who live together in institutions, such as nursing homes or hospitals that provide extended care. Nevertheless, members may experience acute losses when members leave or die, and it is vital for practitioners to assist groups to work through such losses.

Planned Termination Determined by Temporal Constraints

In organizations or agencies whose function involves providing service according to fixed time intervals, termination must be planned accordingly. In school settings, for example, services are generally discontinued at the conclusion of an academic year. In hospitals and other institutional settings, the duration of service is determined by the length of hospitalization, confinement, or insurance coverage. Service may thus extend from several days to several months. Temporal factors are also central in termination when service is provided by social work students, who leave a given practicum setting at the completion of an academic year.

Termination under the circumstances specified in the preceding involves certain factors peculiar to these settings. First, the ending of a school year or of a training period for students is a predetermined time for termination, which reduces the possibility that clients will (1) interpret time limits as being arbitrarily imposed or (2) perceive the practitioner's leaving as desertion or abandonment. Knowing the termination date well in advance also provides ample time to resolve feelings about separation. Nevertheless, this means that in school settings student clients may lose many supports all at one time.

Another factor common to termination determined by temporal constraints related to agency function is that clients' problems may not have been adequately resolved by the ending of a fixed time interval. The predetermined ending time may thus prove to be untimely for some clients; consequently, clients may react intensely to losing service and the helping relationship in midstream. Practitioners are therefore confronted with the dual tasks of working through feelings associated with untimely separation and referring clients for additional services when indicated. We discuss both of these matters in later sections.

A difficulty involving predetermined endings imposed by the close of a school year or training period is that such endings do not convey the same expectations of a positive outcome as do time limits that are imposed by practitioners. In other words, to say "I will see you for eight sessions because that is sufficient time," conveys a far more positive expectation than "I will see you for eight sessions because that is all the available time before school ends." To employ time effectively as a dynamic, it makes good sense to convey a belief that the remaining time is all that is needed, assuming, of course, that such a belief is justified. In the majority of cases this belief is justified, for research indicates that outcomes of interventions ranging from 6 to 10 interviews generally are comparable to those obtained from long-term treatment.

In alluding to termination that coincides with the completion of practicum training, we have made the assumption that students have earlier explained their role as supervised learners and have apprised clients of the date of their departure from the host agency or institution. In making this assumption, we support the position taken by Germain and Gitterman (1980) that students have an ethical responsibility to disclose their role to clients. Aside from purely ethical factors, there are compelling pragmatic reasons for openly sharing this information. First, we have stressed repeatedly in this book the importance of relating genuinely and fostering trust in helping relationships. Concealing one's student status hardly fosters trust or permits one to be fully authentic in a relationship. (Most clients would learn about the student's role in time, anyway.) Further, as the practicum period draws to a close and one must introduce termination, it is most awkward to explain one's reason for leaving an agency without

letting the cat out of the bag. Having to reveal (or further conceal) one's actual role during this critical time may drastically erode trust and credibility and create damage to the helping relationship.

Planned Termination Associated with Time-Limited Modalities

Negotiating time limits in advance strongly affects the termination process. Knowing the ending time from almost the beginning tends to limit the degree of emotional attachment and dependency and hence also limits the degree of loss experienced by clients as a result of termination. And by assuming an active role and by focusing on here-and-now task accomplishment, practitioners further minimize dependency and intense emotional attachment, as we have noted earlier. The emotional reaction to separation thus generally tends to be far less intense than for open-ended service. Nevertheless, clients do form attachments and experience losses in time-limited modalities, and practitioners should be sensitive to termination reactions, which we discuss at length later.

Reid (1978) recommends in the Task-Centered approach that practitioners initiate formal termination in the next-to-last scheduled interview by formulating the last set of tasks to be addressed, which ideally "should be repetitions or modest extensions of previously successful tasks" (p. 179). After reviewing the results of efforts on this set of tasks in the terminal interview, the practitioner then shifts the focus to (1) evaluating clients' accomplishments in relationship to target problems, (2) planning for continued work on the problems, if such is needed, (3) assisting clients to discern how they can apply the problem-solving methods they have learned generally to problems of living, and (4) planning for follow-up sessions. These activities apply to other modalities as well, and we therefore consider them later. Engaging in these activities, however, may lead to reasons for deviating from continuing with the usual process of termination. Making other arrangements may be appropriate if both client and practitioner believe that special disposition is indicated. Other possible dispositions include the following:

1. *Limited extensions of service* can be made to accomplish agreed-upon tasks if it appears that additional time would make it possible for the client to achieve *decisive progress*. There may be legitimate reasons for recontracting for additional sessions, such as not identifying key problems until late in the helping process or anticipating transitional events that bear on the clients' problems (e.g., getting married, being discharged from an institution, regaining custody of a child). The mere expectation that further progress can be achieved by extending the sessions is not a legitimate reason for recontracting nor is the lack of progress. As Reid (1978) indicated, "If little was accomplished during the regular period of service, it is not likely that a few more sessions will add much. Aside from being a waste of the practitioner's and client's time, they may increase the client's sense of failure" (p. 184).

Either clients or practitioners may propose extensions, and if the former make an unsolicited request, Reid recommends usually granting the request, being careful to establish the rationale for the extension. For most clients, the regular contracted period of service suffices, and Reid discourages practitioners from routinely asking clients if they wish additional sessions. Only if practitioners have grounds for believing additional service would accomplish a vital purpose should they suggest extending service.

2. A *successive contract* the same length as the original contract can be negotiated if major problems surface near the end of the contract or were identified earlier but had to be set aside in favor of more pressing problems. In either event, the client may not have had opportunity to tackle a major problem, and a new contract may be warranted, especially if the client achieved substantial progress on other problems during the initial contract peri-

od. Reid cautions, however, that practitioners must be careful to ascertain that the interest in the problem emanates from the client, not the practitioner. If practitioners are sensitive to clients' perceptions and motivation, successive contracts, according to Reid (1978), are very much the exception.

Research reported by Fortune (1985c), however, indicates that less than half of the practitioners who use time limits adhere to those limits. Reasons given most frequently for continuing beyond the planned termination were: incomplete progress toward clients' goals, doubts by practitioners as to the clients' ability to cope independently, desire by clients to continue, and regression by clients. It is also noteworthy that a study of 69 MSW practitioners in central Virginia revealed that time limits were set in only 10% of their cases (Fortune, Pearlingi, & Rochelle, 1991). These findings suggest that open-ended service is overused, even with cases that are excellent candidates for short-term, time-limited service. We would anticipate that current funding limits for extended service may limit such open-ended outcomes.

3. *Terminating in the context of continued care* may also be a disposition when the client has been involved in long-term care and the practitioner's involvement has been but one segment of an overall treatment program. In an institutional setting, for example, a practitioner may be one member of a clinical team, having circumscribed responsibilities for assisting clients to accomplish certain tasks that are a part of a broader treatment program. Other staff members may carry responsibility for coordinating continued efforts of the entire team when the practitioner's role is discharged.

In other situations, a practitioner may carry sole responsibility for working with a client (e.g., in child welfare) in long-term service but may negotiate a task-centered contract for addressing certain problems (e.g., a particular aspect of home management). The task-centered contract thus becomes a subset of a more comprehensive contract. Even though the helping person is the same following completion of the task-centered contract, the practitioner does a terminal interview, evaluates results, and discusses implications of the client's experience for future direction in the ongoing efforts.

4. *Converting from a time-limited to an open-ended modality* is another option open to the practitioner. Although research cited by Reid argues against using this option frequently, there are circumstances in which converting to open-ended treatment is warranted. Although large-scale research studies in the United States (Parad & Parad, 1968) and Britain (Gibbons, Bow, & Butter, 1979) indicate that time-limited interventions (i.e., 12 sessions or less) are preferable for the majority of clients, these same studies indicate that from 15 to 18% of the clients require a longer time. According to Gibbons et al., the clients "who developed into longer term cases tended to have a wider range of problems, usually of great complexity, and to resist the limited focus of the task-centered approach" (p. 209). Further, after the completion of a predetermined number of sessions, some clients request continued services without the limits. In such instances, if another client would not be deprived of service as a result, it may be prudent to respect the client's request rather than to refuse continued service. In any event, the practitioner should conduct an evaluation interview before changing to open-ended service.

While time limits per se are precluded by definition when changing to open-ended service, we recommend, as does Reid, retaining other elements of the task-centered format, including specifying additional goals, formulating a new contract, working on task accomplishment, maintaining focus and continuity, and monitoring progress—elements that are characteristic of all effective helping methods. By continuing to incorporate these elements, practitioners avoid one major hazard of open-ended service—namely, drift or wandering.

5. *Referring the client elsewhere* for additional assistance is an additional option. Locating appropriate resources for specialized assistance, in fact, may be a central task to be accomplished in the context of time-limited modalities. You will recall we discussed referral skills in Chapter 3.

6. Finally, *termination with involuntary clients* is most likely to occur around completion of the terms of a contract and/or court order. It is important to avoid unilaterally extending such contracts because the practitioner believes that something might break down. More useful is a monitoring phase in which the number and frequency of sessions decreases while support systems are called on to assist the client with new concerns. Involuntary clients rarely experience the kind of sadness reported by some voluntary clients at termination. On the other hand, they often experience a sense of accomplishment at achieving difficult tasks and being able to move ahead without an outside agency hovering or interfering in their lives (Rooney, 1992, pp. 252–255).

Planned Termination Involving Open-Ended Modalities

Determining when to terminate is the first major task of termination involving open-ended service. Theoretically, humans can grow indefinitely, and determining when clients have achieved optimal growth is no simple task. Ordinarily it is appropriate to introduce termination when the client has reached the point of diminishing returns, that is, when the gains from sessions taper off to the point of being minor in significance. When practitioners believe that clients have made marked progress, they should be sensitive to expressions indicating the latter share that perception. If the client states that things have been going well for some time and has been wondering about discontinuing, the practitioner may concur and reflect the fact that the client apparently may be feeling ready to consider termination in the near future. If the client affirms that such is the case, it is appropriate to suggest beginning to plan termination together.

Often, clients are hesitant about expressing thoughts about termination, and the practitioner will need to introduce the matter based on impressions gained from indirect manifestations. A client may report having little to talk about and indicate relative freedom from stress. If the client's report is consistent with evidence of marked progress, it is appropriate to suggest reviewing the client's functioning in relationship to extant goals. If the client expresses satisfactory attainment of the goals and the practitioner concurs, the latter can channel the discussion in a natural manner to the topic of termination.

What does research tell us about actual criteria used for termination as reported by practitioners? Research related to this question is scarce, but one study (Fortune, Pearlingi, & Rochelle, 1991) indicates that the criteria cited most frequently by 69 practitioners in Virginia were both positive and appropriate. In order of importance, the criteria actually employed for terminating cases were: (1) client's behavior or coping in the environment improved significantly, (2) client's intrapsychic functioning improved significantly, (3) goals set at or near beginning of treatment were met, (4) client wished to terminate, and (5) changes in the therapeutic content or issues signaled readiness (p. 368). A number of other criteria also led to termination but much less frequently. Summarizing the meaning of these findings, the authors concluded that "practitioners waited for success before terminating and used both internal and external functioning to determine success" (p. 369).

Termination Precipitated by Departure of a Practitioner

On occasions, practitioners must terminate their work with clients or groups because of departure precipitated by reassignment or change of employment. Termination under these circumstances is difficult for both clients and practitioners because many clients need continuing assistance. Emotional reactions are often intense, and time for working through these reactions is often inadequate. Clients who have previously been rejected or abandoned by parents are particularly vulnerable and may experience the practitioner's departure as the latest in a series of painful rejections, each of which has damaged their tenuous self-esteem and constituted further evidence of their lack of worth. Aware of this possible reaction by clients, practitioners too may experience intense emotions, including guilt associated with a sense of failing the client. Because of these feelings, a practitioner may delay introducing termination or may overcompensate for guilt by being overly apologetic, solicitous, and reassuring, thereby making it difficult for clients to express and to resolve their negative feelings.

The primary tasks to be accomplished when a practitioner terminates service because of leaving involve assisting clients to work through their emotions to the extent that time permits and preparing them to transfer to another practitioner. We discuss these tasks in the next section.

REACTIONS TO TERMINATION

Inherent in termination is separation from the practitioner (and group in the case of growth groups). Separation typically involves mixed feelings, which vary in intensity according to the degree of success achieved, the intensity of the attachment to the practitioner, the type of termination, and the previous experiences of the client with separations from significant others. When clients successfully accomplish their goals, they experience a certain degree of pride and satisfaction as the helping process draws to a close. If they have grown in strength and self-esteem, they optimistically view the future as a challenge for continued growth.

Positive Termination Reactions

Most clients in individual, marital, family, and group therapy experience positive emotions in termination. Benefits of the gains achieved usually *far outweigh* the impact of the loss of the helping relationship. Indeed, clients often report an increased sense of mastery, and both practitioners and clients are likely to experience joy over such accomplishments. This is especially true when practitioners have employed a strength-oriented, problem-solving approach. Furthermore, the participants have experienced mutual enrichment from the deep, personal, and authentic human encounter, and, in a very real sense, the self of each person has been expanded by the contacts with the other.

Until very recent years, the literature on termination reactions has stressed that sadness, loss, ambivalence, apprehension, and other negative reactions are associated with termination on the part of both practitioner and client. Research findings (Fortune, 1987; Fortune, Pearlingi, & Rochelle, 1992), however, have refuted these widely accepted beliefs. These findings indicate that in both open-ended and time-limited treatment the common reactions are positive feelings related to success and progress, positive feelings about the therapeutic experience, increased constructive activities outside of treatment, more free time, more financial resources to spend on other activities, and feelings of pride about accomplishments and/or independence gained through treatment. Negative reactions on the part of both clients and practitioners are not common.

Negative Termination Reactions

Clients and practitioners alike commonly experience a sense of loss during the termination process. Indeed, a sense of loss is a universal reaction to the many endings that are a part of life itself (e.g., leaving parents to attend school, advancing from one grade to another, graduating, moving from one home to another, and losing loved ones). This loss may be a deeply moving experience involving the "sweet sorrow" generally associated with parting from a person whom one has grown to value. Clients who have become excessively dependent on a practitioner experience little of the sweetness of termination, however, and view separation as the loss of an irreplaceable person.

Although they are uncommon, negative reactions to termination occur more frequently in open-ended, psychosocial treatment (Fortune, 1987; Webb, 1985). Because the practitioner has played a significant role in the client's life over an extended period of time, a few clients may approach termination with considerable reluctance. Such clients may perceive termination as traumatic and may manifest one or more of several forms of resistance to termination. Levinson (1977) has identified the following termination reactions sometimes encountered in open-ended service and, to a lesser extent, even in time-limited service:

1. Clinging to Therapy and the Practitioner   As we previously noted, some clients tend to use the helping process as a substitute rather than a means to learn how to gain greater fulfillment from life in outside relationships and activities. To avoid fostering such reactions, it is imperative that from the beginning, practitioners stress the goal of achieving independence within the shortest possible time and foster maximal independence by clients. Practitioners who are oriented to this perspective rarely have clients who perceive termination as a major trauma. Other practitioners report the majority of their clients experience severe difficulty in terminating, and one must wonder to what extent they nurture the difficulties by clinging to clients and by focusing on weaknesses, deficiencies, and "pathology" rather than strength and opportunities for growth.

2. Reporting Recurrence of Old Problems   Some clients tend to panic as treatment approaches closure and experience a return of difficulties that have been under control for some time. Other clients whose best functioning is submarginal may manifest more severe reactions by resorting to drastic behaviors, such as attempting suicide. Such actions, however, are infrequent and generally occur only with people who are extremely unstable. When clients manifest recurrences of old problems, it is important not to focus on the problems but rather on the client's fears and uncertainties concerning their lives after termination. After exploring these feelings and empathizing with them, it is helpful to review again the progress the client has made and to accredit the strength and personal resources from which the client can draw. By thinking through their fears and concluding anew that their progress is real, clients often regain a sense of self-efficacy and courage to face the future independently.

3. Introducing New Problems As a ploy to continue the helping relationship, some clients introduce new stresses and problems during the terminal sessions and even during the final scheduled session. Further, clients who normally communicate minimally may suddenly open up, and other clients may reveal confidential information they have previously withheld. Although the practitioner should not minimize the importance of new problems or information, it is vital not to grasp the bait without first exploring feelings about termination. Placed in context, new information and problems often are relatively insignificant.

4. Finding Substitutes for the Practitioner Although finding one or more persons to replace the practitioner may be a constructive way of developing social resources, it may also be a way of locating a person on whom the client can become dependent, thereby compensating for the loss of the practitioner. Clients who seek a nurturing, parental type of confidante are likely attempting to perpetuate dependency at the expense of growth. Should this appear to be the case, the practitioner should assist the client to recognize the pertinent

dynamics and to consider the consequences of making such a choice.

Group members may also seek to compensate for losses of group support by affiliating with other groups and never actually developing enduring social support systems. Some groups attempt to continue without agency involvement with mixed results often including failure and disappointment. We have known of individuals who continually move from one group to the next as each group ends. Such persons resist change and seek the safety and protection afforded in a group context. When leaders are aware that a person is motivated to join a group for this reason, they should consider negotiating a goal to use the group as a vehicle for exploring and resolving fears of relating to others outside growth groups.

Managing Emotions Produced When Practitioners Leave

When termination occurs because a practitioner leaves an agency, clients often manifest other reactions before experiencing sadness. Because the termination is not planned and occurs with little forewarning, reactions are sometimes similar to those that involve other types of sudden crises. A client may thus respond by shutting off thoughts of the impending loss (denial) and relating as though nothing has happened. It is a mistake to interpret the client's business-as-usual demeanor as an indication the client is taking the termination in stride, for the unruffled exterior may represent the calm before the storm. The client's temporary denial of feelings is an attempt to ward off psychic pain associated with a distressing reality that must be faced.

To assist clients in getting in touch with their emotions, it is helpful to reintroduce the topic of termination and to express your desire to assist them in formulating plans to continue working toward their goals after your departure. As you bring up the topic of termination, it is critical to be sensitive to nonverbal cues that manifest emotional reactions. We also recommend employing empathic communication that conveys understanding of and elicits the hurt, resentment, and rejection clients commonly experience when a practitioner leaves. It is vital, however, not to empathize to the extent of overidentifying and losing your capacity to assist the client with negative feelings and to engage in constructive planning. Such planning could include engaging the client in a decision about whether to make a clean break or to include an introductory session attended by both practitioners. The following is an example of a message that expresses genuine concern, conveys empathy, and invites the client to express feelings about termination:

"I can sense that you're having a real struggle with feelings about my leaving. I want you to know how badly I feel about leaving, especially since you still have a way to go before you accomplish your goals. I know it wasn't easy for you to confide in me, and I can understand you'd feel angry over my not seeing you through your difficulties. At least that's how I'd feel if I were in your situation. You've shared a lot with me to this point in your sessions. Could you share with me what you're feeling at this moment?"

When these clients do get in touch with their feelings, anger, resentment, hurt, a sense of betrayal, and feelings of rejection and of worthlessness often emerge. Clients with low self-esteem and a history of being rejected and abandoned experience these feelings most frequently and keenly. Children or adolescents in groups often deal with such feelings by ignoring them or by indirectly attacking or demeaning the practitioner in messages to other members that insinuate the practitioner doesn't really care about them or by directly accusing the practitioner of abandoning them. When these behaviors occur, the practitioner should accept the feelings, empathize with them, and assist the group members to express their feelings directly and to weigh the feelings against the totality of the group's experience to that point. The group practitioner may also respond authentically, highlighting reality factors that foster a more realistic appraisal of the situation, as illustrated in the following message:

"I can understand your being upset and resentful over my leaving. We've grown close over our sessions, and it's hard for me too to lose that closeness. Still, I have a lot of pleasant memories about each one of you that I'll take with me. My leaving can't destroy that nor the progress you've made as a group. Though I'll be gone, you still have each other, and I'm arranging for another leader who can pick up where I leave off."

It is to be expected that members will ventilate additional anger, and the practitioner will need to stay with such negative feelings until they have dissipated. Typically, as they ventilate their anger and are still accepted by the practitioner, members gradually are able to shift to examining their feelings more thoughtfully and to conclude (1) that the practitioner's leaving is not a personal rejection and (2) that though the loss is painful, life must go on. As they resolve these negative feelings, they are then able to express and to bear their sadness and to reexperience positive feelings toward the practitioner.

Occasionally, clients express their anger and hurt over a practitioner's leaving by rejecting a practitioner before the latter can reject them. Members of adolescent groups who either ignore or profess no longer needing the practitioner are, in effect, employing the strategy that the best defense is a good offense. Individual clients often do the same by failing to keep appointments after learning of the practitioner's imminent departure. When clients thus reject the practitioner, it is critical to reach out to them; otherwise, they tend to interpret the failure to do so as evidence the practitioner never really cared about them at all. In reaching out, a personal contact by telephone or home visit is essential, for there must be an opportunity for interaction in which practitioners reaffirm their concern and care and convey empathy and understanding of the client's emotional reaction. Reaching out often succeeds in reengaging the client and averting a devastating termination experience. Some clients, however, will resist the practitioner's overtures and "will steadfastly deny or openly devalue the therapist and the therapy as not having had any influence on their lives" (Levinson, 1977, p. 486).

As members of groups move beyond their negative feelings, practitioners empathize with members' desires to continue the group (e.g., "I know you have grown to care about each other and can understand your desire to keep the group going"). It is important to be firm in adhering to plans for ending a group. When groups sense the plans are firm, members will usually develop more effective means of coping with anger over termination.

Terminations with Unsuccessful Outcomes

Practitioners must occasionally impose termination on clients in open-ended service when clients are hopelessly stalemated despite vigorous and persistent efforts by practitioners to surmount the impasse. Groups also occasionally end with unsuccessful results, and members may be frustrated, disappointed, or angry toward the leader or toward other members. When the helping process ends unsuccessfully, termination should include discussion of (1) factors that prevented achieving more favorable results and (2) clients' feelings about seeking additional help in the future. Managing any of the preceding emotional reactions involves utilizing essentially the same skills and attitudes identified earlier. To work through negative feelings successfully, practitioners will need to maintain focus on the feelings until clients are able to move beyond them. Practitioners will gain enhanced understanding of clients' emotional reactions to termination and be maximally effective in assisting them through these reactions by considering both the nature of previous separations in their lives and their patterns of coping with them. As we have previously noted, clients

who have experienced repeated rejections may mistakenly interpret termination as rejection by the practitioner. Being aware of previous experiences and patterns can assist the practitioner to respond sensitively to clients' feelings and to assist them to recognize how these factors can color current perceptions and feelings. Gaining awareness of their reactions to separation can be extremely valuable to clients, sometimes enabling them to achieve their first nontraumatic separation—a milestone for some clients that prepares them for dealing more effectively with the inevitable separations of the future. Some closure may be attempted by sending a letter to those who fail to return for a final visit.

EVALUATION

Evaluating outcomes of the helping process has assumed ever-increasing significance in direct practice; indeed, the majority of direct practitioners engage in some form of evaluation, as we noted in Chapter 12. If you have systematically obtained baseline measures, clients will be prepared for evaluation at termination. You can further enhance their cooperation by again reviewing the rationale and actively involving them in the process. The following is a brief example of an explanation you might give to a client:

"An important part of termination is to assess the results we have achieved and to identify what helped you most and least during our work together. As an agency, we're committed to improving the quality of our services, and I'm likewise interested in improving services. Feedback from you, therefore, is most important. Your feedback will be of greatest value if you're open and frank in presenting your views. Do you have any questions about evaluation?"

Evaluation consists of three different dimensions: (1) outcome, (2) process, and (3) the practitioner. We consider each of these dimensions in the following sections.

Outcome

Evaluation of outcome involves assessing the results achieved against the goals formulated. Methods of assessing outcome will be determined by the methods utilized during the assessment phase. If no measures were taken, you will need to use an interview or questionnaire to determine clients' views and can then compare their views against your own. (Such a procedure, of course, yields only subjective data and lacks the rigor of quantitative measures.) To assess *general progress*, refer to the goals that were agreed upon and elicit clients' views as to the degree of progress they achieved on each goal. You may wish to ask them to rate the degree of achievement using the following scale:

5. Fully achieved

4. Mostly achieved

3. Moderately achieved

2. Somewhat achieved

1. No progress

Although it is unwise to challenge clients' perceptions, subjectivity can be reduced by asking clients to provide actual examples of recent events that illustrate their attainment of goals. Discussing such events briefly also provides an opportunity for the practitioner and/or group member to accredit accomplishments, which tends to heighten confidence and satisfaction.

In addition to clients' perceptions of their progress, evaluation should include other criteria where practicable. The judgment of other group members and significant others may provide a more balanced and accurate assessment. You can, of course, formulate your own ratings independently using the above scale and then combine yours and clients' ratings to infer outcomes.

Even though you did not obtain baseline measures, using instruments at termination to measure targets of change can still be of value. Comparing measures of depression or self-esteem, for example, against clinical norms enables you to determine if the client's score falls within or outside normal levels, which is very useful information. The limitation, of course, is that you cannot infer that treatment has produced improvement if you did not obtain pretreatment measures.

If goals were discrete (see Chapter 12) or "changes of state" goals (Blythe & Tripodi, 1989, p. 119), evaluation is relatively simple. Either clients achieved the desired changes of state or they did not. Examples of change of state outcomes are as follows: obtained a job, had a medical examination, applied for rehabilitation training, attended all parent training sessions, and received prenatal care. Whether the change of state occurred or not may be readily apparent or may be determined by asking the client if the change, in fact, occurred. When discrete goals involve achieving certain standards of performance (e.g., maintaining certain hygienic standards or properly supervising children), the practitioner may need to render judgments as to whether stipulated conditions were met.

Quantitative Determination of Outcome

If measures were made of the incidence of problem or target behaviors during the assessment process (as suggested in Chapter 11), evaluation consists of comparing baseline measures against the latest measurement. This type of evaluation has the marked advantage of being objective.

An additional advantage of having quantifiable baseline measurements of target behaviors is that the process of evaluating progress and outcome can be aided by use of a computer. Nurius and Hudson (1988) have described the use of a computerized clinical assessment system "that interactively enables workers and their clients to assess client problems and monitor progress over time" (p. 358). According to these authors, computers can eliminate much of the time and effort involved in various aspects of the evaluation process.

Using a graph to depict baseline measures and

measures taken at periodic intervals (as discussed and illustrated in Chapter 12) enables both practitioner and client to visualize the course of progress. Outcome can be determined by "eyeballing" changes in the line that connects measures taken at periodic intervals, including the point of termination. A relatively "flat" line from baseline to termination indicates that little or no progress was achieved. An overall marked drop in the line from baseline to termination indicates marked progress if the goal was to *reduce* or *eliminate* specified targets of change (e.g., angry outbursts, absences from school, putdowns of self). Overall marked elevations in the line, as compared with the baseline, also indicate marked improvement if the goal was to increase the frequency of targets of change (e.g., assertiveness, social contacts, homework assignments completed).

In some instances positive changes from baseline to termination are apparent from inspecting a graph, but it is not clear whether the changes are statistically significant (i.e., the probability that the changes could occur by chance are no more than 5 to 100). Two major statistical procedures can be employed to test the significance of attained differences. One procedure, the Shewart Chart, entails calculating the mean and standard deviations of the measures taken during the baseline period. A line parallel to the horizontal axis is drawn showing the mean of the baseline measures. Two other parallel horizontal lines are drawn above and below the line at points 2 standard deviations away from the line representing the mean. Measures taken during the intervention period and at termination that lie beyond the lines two standard deviations removed from the mean baseline thus are statistically significant at the .05 level.

The second method, known as the celeration line technique, is somewhat more complex and space limitations preclude an adequate explanation. Both of the procedures are explained at length and illustrated in books concerned with evaluating practice by Bloom and Fischer (1982, pp. 442–472) and Blythe and Tripodi (1989, pp. 123–133).

Detailed explanation and illustration of these procedures are beyond the scope of this book.

Process

Another aspect of evaluation relates to clients' perceptions of aspects of the helping process that were useful or detrimental. Feedback about techniques and incidents that enhanced or blocked progress enables practitioners to hone certain skills, eliminate others, and use techniques with greater discrimination. A technique that is useful with an assertive client, for example, may produce an opposite effect with a depressed client. In our opinion, an important aspect of ethical practice is to seek constantly to upgrade one's effectiveness by obtaining and applying systematic feedback about clients' perceptions of the practitioner's implementation of interventions.

On occasions, such feedback can be highly informative, confidence-building, or perhaps humbling. A practitioner may have attributed a positive outcome to a masterfully executed technique only to find the client was helped far more by the former's willingness to reach out and maintain hope when the latter had virtually given up. Group members likewise often identify certain aspects of group process or behavior by other members that were particularly helpful factors the practitioner may have overlooked. Often, it is these subtle or *nonspecfic* factors (Yalom, 1980, pp. 1–2) that likely produce change rather than the precise and calculated interventions of practitioners. The point, of course, is that as we expand our knowledge of nonspecific factors, we can knowingly incorporate them into practice, thereby enhancing our therapeutic effectiveness.

The Practitioner

Some settings facilitate formal feedback by sending out written client evaluation forms which includes not only satisfaction with practitioner service but also evaluates structural issues such as appropriateness of the waiting room, convenience of parking, time elapsed between request and first appointment, friendliness of reception staff, and so on. By soliciting feedback regarding how their own behaviors, attitudes, and attributes may have affected the helping process positively or negatively, practitioners invite criticism, and if requests are genuine, clients are likely to be candid. Practitioners and their employing agencies must welcome criticism and be prepared to respond to it constructively. The resultant feedback can be extremely valuable. Clients typically cite positive more than negative factors. In addition to the "stroking" value of positive feedback, this feedback enables practitioners to be more aware of their strengths and perhaps to tap these strengths more frequently in the future. Negative feedback, although sometimes painful, can also be extremely helpful in bringing to awareness behaviors, attitudes, and mannerisms that may be distractive or antitherapeutic. Just as clients have blind spots, so do practitioners, and criticism illuminates the pathway to growth. As with clients, awareness precedes change.

CONSOLIDATING GAINS AND PLANNING MAINTENANCE STRATEGIES

The aim of the helping process is not only to assist clients in developing solutions to their current problems but also to strengthen them so they can cope with the inevitable future difficulties. Similarly, a major aim of work with groups is not only to assist members to interact successfully within the group context but also to transfer their newly developed interpersonal skills to the broad arena of social relationships. Toward these ends, other vital tasks involved in termination are to assist clients to consolidate the gains they have achieved and to develop plans to maintain these gains. In recent years, these tasks have commanded increasing attention as a result of alarming follow-up research

findings indicating that many clients do not maintain the gains they achieve during the formal helping process. This attention is reflected in the title of an article by Rzepnicki (1991), "Enhancing the durability of intervention gains: A challenge for the 1990's." Failure to maintain gains has been attributed to various factors, including the following:

1. A natural tendency to revert to habitual response patterns (e.g., use of alcohol or drugs, aggressive or withdrawn behavior).
2. Personal and environmental stressors (e.g., family conflicts, pressures from landlords, personal rejection, loss of job, health problems, and deaths of loved ones).
3. Lack of opportunities in the environment for social and leisure activities.
4. Absence of positive support systems.
5. Inadequate social skills.
6. Lack of reinforcement for functional behaviors.
7. Inadequate preparation for environmental changes.
8. Inability to resist peer pressures.
9. Return to dysfunctional family environments.
10. Inadequately established new behaviors.

It follows that in planning maintenance strategies, you must anticipate such forces and prepare clients for coping with them. Rzepnicki (1991) has identified the above forces that erode treatment gains and has delineated a number of counterstrategies designed to prevent these erosive effects.

An important aspect of assisting clients to consolidate gains is to review their problems and to analyze the steps they followed in resolving them. The practitioner's role in this review is to assist clients in grasping the principles of effective problem solving, which involve the basic steps of independent problem solving as defined in Chapter 14. The practitioner then assists them to understand how these principles can be applied to general problems of living. If clients learned independent problem solving and the practitioner guided them to apply this intervention to various problem situations, these clients already have potent and transferable coping skills at their disposal. In termination, the practitioner reviews how they applied this process to discrete problems and reinforces how they can use the process in coping with diverse problems in the future. Other discrete skills that have general application, such as muscle relaxation, cognitive restructuring, self-dialogue, and various interpersonal skills, should be similarly reviewed and practitioners should challenge clients to consider how they can continue to apply these skills to problems of daily living.

Another method of preparing clients to cope with future stresses involves anticipatory guidance, as we discussed in Chapter 13. This approach enables clients to anticipate stresses and negative forces and to plan appropriate countermeasures. Clients formerly engaged in juvenile delinquency, for example, may anticipate being teased, dared, and mocked by peers and can plan to employ self-dialogue and self-reinforcement to resist these forces. In some instances, practitioners may need to actively assist clients to identify forces that militate against maintaining change.

RELAPSE PREVENTION

Although planning maintenance strategies is an important aspect of termination with all clients, it is especially crucial with certain client groups known to be highly vulnerable to relapse or recidivism. These groups include:

1. Clients with drug and/or alcohol addictions.
2. Clients with deficient control of anger and/or sexual impulses (e.g., child and spouse abusers, exhibitionists, pedophiles,[1] and serial rapists).
3. Clients with histories of repeated delinquent or criminal behavior.
4. Clients with entrenched habits of smoking and/or overeating.

Despite successful treatment, members of the above client groups continue to experience urges, impulses, and cravings after termination. The meanings they attach to these impulses and cravings, the ways in which they cope with them, and environmental conditions largely determine whether they will maintain control or will relapse.

During recent years, practitioners and researchers have developed increasingly sophisticated strategies for preventing relapse. Because the factors that interact to produce problems listed above are complex, it follows that effective strategies to prevent relapse must be multidimensional. Such strategies thus typically address intrapersonal, interpersonal, and environmental systems and subsystems. Self-management procedures play a central role and include cognitive restructuring and stress inoculation. Interpersonal strategies include communication, problem solving, and social skills training. Environmental strategies include strengthening family relationships, developing positive social support systems, enhancing educational opportunities, and providing for recreational and other constructive leisure-time activities.

Space limitations preclude discussing relapse prevention strategies for each of the above groups, but before focusing at some length on one group, we wish to call to your attention several excellent publications related to some of the other groups. Brownell, Marlatt, Lichtenstein, and Wilson (1986); Daley (1987, 1991); and Marlatt and Gordon (1985) have authored articles and books that identify various factors that contribute to relapse, discussed beliefs and myths associated with addictions, and delineated models for relapse education and treatment with addicted and impulse-disordered clients.

A Model Relapse Prevention Program

We have chosen to highlight a model of relapse prevention that is empirically based and addresses virtually all of the factors known to contribute to relapse and recidivism of drug-involved delinquents following their discharge from correctional institutions. This population represents a formidable challenge to planning for aftercare and transition to the community because of high rates of relapse to drug use and reversion to delinquency.

Providing effective aftercare following institutionalization, in fact, has been a major concern of the helping professions for many years.

The aftercare model, designated as Project ADAPT (Catalano, Wells, Jenson, & Hawkins, 1989), is based on the social development model of rehabilitation, which organizes factors known to produce or to contribute to problems such as delinquency and drug abuse. The organization of these factors leads to explicit specification of intervention points that enable researchers and practitioners to develop maximally relevant and potent interventions.

Before designing Project ADAPT, Catalano et al. carefully reviewed the literature to identify pretreatment, treatment, and post-treatment factors associated with both relapse and recidivism. Based on an analysis of these risk factors, they then organized those that were subject to change according to the social development model. The risk factors were thus organized as follows (Catalano et al., 1989, pp. 571–572):

- Lack of conventional opportunities or involvement:

    Absence of conventional active leisure activities.

    Lack of involvement in school or work.

    Few non-drug-using or nondelinquent friends.

- Lack of rewards for conventional activities and interactions:

    Lack of family support

    School conflict

    School failure

- Skill deficits:

    Social, Academic

    Self-control (anger, impulsivity, drug use)

    Refusal (of drugs, alcohol, or antisocial activity)

The design of the aftercare program thus was multifaceted, addressing each of the above risk factors. Space limitations preclude discussion of all of the various components of this sophisticated project, but the interventions begin while youth are still in the institution and extend for six months after release from the institution. The interventions are coordinated by a case manager, who begins work with the clients during a ten-week reentry-preparation phase. Efforts during this phase involves goal setting, skill training, and visits to schools, parents' homes, and other sites pertinent to postdischarge activities.

During the six-month aftercare period, the case manager facilitates clients' reentry into the community by working with families (or alternative placements), schools, employment services, and other pertinent systems identified in the above list of risk factors. The case manager also assists clients in enhancing skills needed to develop positive relationships with these systems and assists them to seek out social activities and develop supportive and prosocial social networks. The case manager also plays a major supportive role by reinforcing clients' efforts to form social relationships and to engage in appropriate activities.

In limited space, we cannot do justice to the innovative and exemplary work entailed in the development and implementation of the model just summarized. Empirically based and rigorous in design, the model effectively combines social development theory with ecological systems theory (although the authors make no reference to the latter).

Using Support Systems

Gains achieved in treatment by certain clients may be jeopardized following treatment by limited social skills and deficient natural support systems. In such instances it may be essential in preventing relapse to assist these clients to avail themselves of social, recreational, and self-help groups that can meet their needs for social activities and social support. Senior citizen centers for elderly persons, Parents without Partners for single parents, Parents Anonymous for child-abusing parents, and Recovery Incorporated for former mental patients are potential support groups for the populations cited, to mention just a few such resources. Continued training in social skills may also be required to enable some clients to form meaningful social relationships. Practitioners may also encourage clients to return for additional help should problems appear to be mounting out of control. Although it is important to express confidence in clients' ability to cope independently with their problems, it is equally important to convey your continued interest in them and to invite them to return should they need to do so.

Booster Interviews

Still another strategy of facilitating transition to independent status and of maintaining change is to employ *booster* interviews. This involves holding additional sessions periodically after termination. Booster interviews may be desirable for the majority of clients, but appear to be especially needed by those who have received marital therapy. The findings of one follow-up study (Jacobson, Schmaling, & Holtzworth-Munroe, 1987) indicated substantial erosion of gains achieved through behavioral marital therapy by the time of the follow-up study two years later. Among other findings, it was reported that "couples seemed extremely favorable toward the idea of booster sessions; indeed, some even mentioned the desirability of such sessions spontaneously, prior to the question about them" (p. 194). Based on these findings, the authors cited have reformulated short-term marital therapy to include post-treatment phases that provide for follow-up and booster interviews that are "refresher courses in the tasks taught during phase one of marital therapy" (p. 194). Our experience in using booster interviews for many years is consistent with the findings of the study reported.

Challenging Clients

Another strategy we recommend for preventing relapse is to emphasize to clients that to maintain change (and to continue to grow), they will need to develop appropriate strategies. We know one practitioner who asks clients, "How long do you want to maintain the changes you have made?" Clients invariably respond, "Indefinitely," which provides an excellent opening to stress the need for developing appropriate strategies of maintaining changes. We find clients are impressed when we stress that change is not maintained by chance factors and that people who continue to progress do so by continuing to set personal goals and to monitor their progress regularly. One couple, seen by one of the authors, purchased a journal, which they used as a log for their marriage. This couple schedules regular times with each other to review their progress and to set additional goals to improve their marital relationship. Practitioners could well advise other clients to do likewise.

FOLLOW-UP SESSIONS

Clearly related to evaluation and maintenance of change is the use of follow-up sessions following termination. Wells (1981) recommends that follow-up sessions be included as an integral part of practice with all clients, and we concur with his recommendation.

Follow-up sessions benefit both clients and practitioners.[2] Many clients continue to progress after termination, and practitioners can accredit such gains and encourage clients to continue their efforts. Practitioners can also provide brief additional assistance for residual difficulties during a follow-up session. Follow-up sessions also enable practitioners to assess the durability of changes; that is, to determine whether clients maintain gains beyond the immediate influence of the helping relationship. An additional benefit for clients of planned follow-up sessions is that the impact of termination is cushioned by knowledge of the practitioner's continued interest in them.

To ensure that clients view the follow-up session as an integral part of the helping process, practitioners should introduce the matter early in the helping process and thereafter remind them of the plan from time to time. Presenting the plan in this manner averts the potential pitfall of clients later viewing the follow-up session as an intrusion into their private lives or as an attempt to satisfy the practitioner's curiosity.

Wells recommends that in arranging for the follow-up session, practitioners not set a specific date but rather explain they will contact the client after a designated interval. The practitioner further clarifies that the interval offers the client an opportunity to test out and further consolidate the learning and change achieved during the formal helping period. To enhance clients' positive expectancies, Wells refers to the follow-up session as "a chance to check on your *progress*."

In the follow-up session, the practitioner generally relates more informally than during the period of intervention. After appropriate social amenities, the practitioner guides the conversation to the clients' progress and obtains postintervention measures when appropriate. The follow-up session also provides an excellent opportunity for further evaluation of the practitioner's efforts during the period of intervention. In retrospect, what was most helpful? What was least helpful? Further efforts can also be made to consolidate gains. What was gained from treatment that the client can continue to use in coping with life? And finally, the practitioner can contract for further help if this appears necessary. Follow-up sessions thus enable practitioners to arrange for timely assistance that may arrest deterioration in functioning.[3]

NOTES

1 Pedophiles are adults who sexually molest children.

2 We wish to acknowledge that the content of this section is based largely on material generously provided the authors by Richard A. Wells, who discusses this subject in Richard A. Wells (1994), *Planned Short-Term Treatment,* Second Edition, New York: The Free Press.

3 For additional guidelines to conducting follow-up interviews, we recommend an article by Bernard (1985) about follow-up interviews with psychotherapy patients.

References

Abell, N. (1991). The index of clinical stress: A brief measure of subjective stress for practice and research. *Social Work Research and Abstracts, 27* (2), 12–15.

Abramson, J. (1988). Participation of elderly patients in discharge planning: Is self-determination a reality? *Social Work, 33* (5), 443–448.

Abramson, M. (1985). The autonomy-paternalism dilemma in social work. *Social Work, 27,* 422–427.

Accreditation standards and self-study guides, Council on Social Work Education, (1995).

Aguilar, I. (1972). Initial contact with Mexican-American families. *Social Work, 20,* 379–382.

Aguilar, M. (1983). *Patterns of health care utilization of Mexican-American women.* Unpublished doctoral dissertation, University of Illinois, Urbana-Champaign.

Aguilera, D., & Messick, J. (1982). *Crisis intervention: Theory and methodology* (4th ed.). St. Louis: Mosby.

Akabas, H., Fine, M., & Yasser, R. (1982). Putting secondary prevention to the test: A study of an early intervention strategy with disabled workers. *Journal of Primary Prevention, 2,* 165–187.

Albert, R. (1983). Social advocacy in the regulatory process. *Social Casework, 64,* 473–481.

Alberti, R., & Emmons, M. (1970, 1974). *Your perfect right: A guide to assertive behavior.* San Luis Obispo, CA: Impact Publishers.

Alcabes, A. A., & Jones, J. A. (1985). Structural determinants of clienthood. *Social Work, 30,* 49–55.

Alcalay, R., Ghee, A., & Scrimshaw, S. (1993). Designing prenatal care messages for low-income Mexican women. *Public Health Reports, 108* (3), 354–362.

Allen-Meares, P., & Lane, B. A. (1987). Grounding social work practice in theory: Ecosystems. *Social Casework, 68,* 515–521.

Altman, H. (1982). Collaborative discharge planning. *Social Work, 27,* 422–427.

American Psychiatric Association (1987). *Diagnostic and statistical manual of mental disorders* (3rd ed., rev.), Spitzer, R. L. et al. (Eds.). Washington, DC: American Psychiatric Press.

Anastas, J. W., Gibeau, J. L., & Larson, P. J. (1990). Working families and eldercare: A national perspective in an aging America. *Social Work, 35* (5), 405–411.

Anderson, S., & Grant, J. (1984). Pregnant women and alcohol: Implications for social work. *Social Casework, 65,* 3–10.

Anderson, S., & Mandell, D. (1989). The use of self-disclosure by professional social workers. *Social Casework, 70* (5), 259–267.

Aponte, H. J. (1977). Anatomy of a therapist. In P. Papp (Ed.), *Family therapy: Full length case studies.* New York: Gardner Press.

Aponte, H., & Van Deusen, J. (1981). Structural family therapy. In A. Gurman & D. Kniskern (Eds.), *Handbook of family therapy* (pp. 310–360). New York: Brunner/Mazel.

Applegate, J. S. (1992). The impact of subjective measures on nonbehavioral practice research: Outcome vs. process. *Families in Society, 73* (2), 100–108.

Arnowitz, E., Brunswick, L., & Kaplan, B. (1983). Group therapy with patients in the waiting room of an oncology clinic. *Social Work, 28,* 395–397.

Aronson, H., & Overall, B. (1966). Treatment expectations of patients in two social classes. *Social Work, 11,* 35–41.

Associated Press (1991). Tempe *Daily News Tribune.* (January 9, 1991).

Attneave, C. (1982). American Indians and Alaska native families. In M. McGoldrick, J. Pearce, & J. Giordano (Eds.), *Ethnicity and family therapy* (pp. 55–83). New York: Guilford Press.

Auerback, S., & Moser, C. (1987). Groups for the wives of gay and bisexual men. *Social Work, 32,* 321–325.

Auslander, G. K., & Litwin, H. (1987). The parameters of network intervention: A social work application. *Social Service Review, 61,* 26–29.

Austin, C. D. (1990). Case management: Myths and realities. *Families in Society, 71* (7), 398–405.

Bagarozzi, D., & Anderson, S. A. (1989). *Personal, marital, and family myths.* New York: Norton.

Bagarozzi, D., & Kurtz, L. F. (1983). Administrators' perspectives on case management. *Arete, 8,* 13–21.

Bahou, C., & Gralnick, M. (1989). High–risk conversations: A response to Reamer. *Social Work, 34* (3), 262–264.

Bailey-Dempsey, C., & Reid, W. J. (1995, March). *Paradigm shifting: Preparing social work students for interdisciplinary practice.* Council on Social Work Education. Annual Program Meeting, San Diego, CA.

Balgopal, P., & Vassil, T. (1983). *Groups in social work: An ecological perspective.* New York: Macmillan.

Ballew, J. (1985). Role of natural helpers in preventing child abuse and neglect. *Social Work, 30,* 37–41.

Bandura, A. (1977). Self-efficacy: Toward a unifying theory of behavioral change. *Psychological Review, 84,* 191–215.

Bandura, A., Lipsher, D., & Miller, P. (1960). Psychotherapists' approach-avoidance reactions to patients' expressions of hostility. *Journal of Consulting Psychology, 24,* 1–8.

Banks, G. (1971). The effects of race on one-to-one helping interviews. *Social Service Review, 45,* 137–144.

Banks, G., Berenson, B., & Carkhuff, R. (1967). The effects of counselor race and training upon Negro clients in initial interviews. *Journal of Clinical Psychology, 23,* 70–72.

Barber, J. G. (1995a). Politically progressive casework. *Families in Society: The Journal of Contemporary Human Services, 76* (1), 30–37.

Barber, J. G. (1995b). Working with resistant drug abusers. *Social Work, 40* (1), 17–23.

Barbero, S. L. (1989). Community-based, day treatment for mentally retarded adults. *Social Work, 37* (6), 545–548.

Barker, P. (1981). *Basic family therapy.* Baltimore: University Park Press.

Barozzi, R., & Engel, J. (1985). A survey of attitudes about family life education. *Social Casework, 66,* 106–110.

Barret, R. L., & Robinson, B. E. (1990). *Gay Fathers.* Lexington, MA: Lexington Books.

Barth, R. P. (1985). Beating the blues: Cognitive-behavioral treatment for depression in child-maltreating mothers. *Clinical Social Work Journal, 13,* 317–328.

Barth, R. (1988). Theories guiding home-based intensive family preservation services. In J. K. Whittaker, J. Kinney, E. M. Tracy, & C. Booth (Eds.), *Improving practice technology for work with high risk families: Lessons from the "Homebuilders" social work education project* (pp. 91–113). Seattle: Center for Social Welfare Research, School of Social Work, University of Washington.

Barth, R. P., & Berry, M. (1987). Outcomes of child welfare services under permanency planning. *Social Service Review, 61,* 71–92.

Barth, R. P., & Derezotes, D. (1990). *Preventing adolescent abuse: Effective intervention strategies and techniques.* Lexington, MA: Lexington Books.

Barth, R., & Schinke, S. (1984). Enhancing the supports of teenage mothers. *Social Casework, 65,* 523–531.

Bartlett, H. (1970). *The common base of social work practice.* New York: National Association of Social Workers.

Barton, C., & Alexander, J. (1981). Functional family therapy. In A. Gurman & D. Kniskern (Eds.), *Handbook of family therapy* (pp. 403–443). New York: Brunner/Mazel.

Barusch, A. (1991). *Elder care: Family training and support.* Newbury Park, CA: Sage.

Bassuk, E. L., Rubin, L., & Lauriat, A. S. (1986). Characteristics of sheltered homeless families. *American Journal of Public Health, 76,* 1097–1101.

Bates, M. (1983). Using the environment to help the male skid row alcoholic. *Social Casework, 64,* 276–282.

Bauman, M. (1981). Involving resistant family members in therapy. In A. S. Gurman (Ed.), *Questions and answers in the practice of family therapy* (pp. 16–19). New York: Brunner/Mazel.

Bean, G. J., Stefl, M. E., & Howe, S. R. (1987). Mental health and homelessness: Issues and findings. *Social Work, 32,* 411–416.

Beavers, W. (1977). *Psychotherapy and growth: Family systems perspective.* New York: Brunner/Mazel.

Beck, A. (1974). Phases in the development of structure in therapy and encounter groups. In D. Wexler & L. Rice (Eds.), *Innovations in client-centered therapy.* New York: Wiley.

Beck, A., Kovacs, M., & Weissman, A. (1979). Assessment of suicidal intention. *Journal of Consulting and Clinical Psychology, 47,* 343–352.

Beck, A., Resnik, H., & Lettieri, D. (Eds.). (1974). *The prediction of suicide.* Bowie, MD: Charles Press.

Beck, A., Rush, A., Shaw, B., & Emery, G. (1979). *Cognitive therapy of depression.* New York: Guilford Press.

Beck, A., Ward, C., Mendelson, M., Mock, J., & Erbaugh, J. (1961). An inventory for measuring depression. *Archives of General Psychiatry, 4,* 561–571.

Beck, J., & Strong, S. (1982). Stimulating therapeutic change with interpretations: A comparison of positive and negative connotation. *Journal of Counseling Psychology, 29,* 551–559.

Becvar, D. S., & Becvar, R. J. (1988). *Family therapy: A systemic integration.* Boston: Allyn & Bacon.

Beeman, S. (1993). *Social network structure and interaction among neglecting and nonneglecting mothers.* Unpublished doctoral dissertation, University of Chicago.

Behroozi, C. S. (1992). A model for work with involuntary applicants in groups. *Social Work with Groups. 15* (2/3), 223–238.

Belcher, J. (1988). Rights versus needs of homeless mentally ill persons. *Social Work, 33* (5), 398–402.

Belcher, J., & Ephross, P. (1989). Toward an effective practice model for the homeless mentally ill. *Social Casework, 70* (7), 421–427.

Bell, J. L. (1995). Traumatic event debriefing: service delivery designs and the role of social work. *Social Work, 40* (1), 36–43.

Bendick, M. (1980). Failure to enroll in public assistance programs. *Social Work, 25,* 268–274.

Bendick, M., & Cantu, M. (1978). The literacy of welfare clients. *Social Service Review, 52,* 56–68.

Bennett, C. J., Legon, J., & Zilberfein, F. (1989). The significance of empathy in current hospital based practice. *Social Work in Health Care, 14* (2), 27–41.

Berenson, B., & Mitchell, K. (1974). *Confrontation: For better or worse!* Amherst, MA: Human Resource Development Press.

Berg, R. A., Franzen, M. D., & Wedding, D. (1987). *Screening for brain impairment: A manual for mental health practice.* New York: Springer.

Berlin, S. B., and Marsh, J. C. (1993). *Informing Practice Decisions.* New York: Macmillan.

Bernal, G., & Flores-Ortiz, Y. (1982). Latino families in therapy: Engagement and evaluation. *Journal of Marriage and Family Therapy, 8,* 357–365.

Bernard, H. S. (1985). Follow-up interviews with psychotherapy patients. *Psychotherapy, 22,* 22–27.

Bernier, J. C. (1990). Parental adjustment to a disabled child: A family-systems perspective. *Families in Society, 71* (10), 589–596.

Bernstein, A. (1972). The fear of compassion. In B. B. Wolman (Ed.), *Success and failure in psychoanalysis and psychotherapy* (pp. 160–176). New York: Macmillan.

Bernstein, A. G. (1981). *Case managers: Who are they and are they making any difference in mental health service delivery?* Unpublished doctoral dissertation, University of Georgia, Athens.

Bernstein, B. (1977). Privileged social work practice. *Social Casework, 66,* 387–393.

Bernstein, D., & Borkovec, T. (1973). *Progressive relaxation training: A manual for the helping professions.* Champaign, IL: Research Press.

Berry, M. (1988). A review of parent training programs in child welfare. *Social Service Review, 62,* 302–323.

Bertcher, H., & Maple, F. (1985). Elements and issues in group composition. In P. Glasser, R. Sarri, & R. Vinter (Eds.), *Individual change through small groups* (pp. 180–202). New York: Free Press.

Berwick, D. (1980). Nonorganic failure to thrive. *Pediatrics in Review, 1,* 265–270.

Besharov, D. (1990). *Recognizing child abuse.* New York: Free Press.

Beutler, L. E. (1983). *Eclectic psychotherapy: A systematic approach.* New York: Pergamon Press.

Beutler, L. E., & Clarkin, J. (1990). *Systematic treatment selection: Toward targeted therapeutic interventions.* New York: Brunner/Mazel.

Biegel, D., & Naparstek, A. (Eds.). (1982). *Community support systems and mental health.* New York: Springer.

Biegel, D. E., Sales, E., & Schulz, R. (1991). *Family caregiving in chronic illness.* Newbury Park, CA: Sage.

Biestek, F. (1957). *The casework relationship.* Chicago: Loyola University Press.

Biggs, D. A., & Blocher, D. H. (1987). *Foundations of ethical counseling.* New York: Springer.

Blankertz, L. E., Cnaan, R. A., White, K., Fox, J., & Messinger, K. (1990). Outreach efforts with dually diagnosed homeless persons. *Families in Society, 71* (7), 387–395.

Blechman, E. (1974). The family contract game: A tool to teach interpersonal problem solving. *Family Coordinator, 23,* 269–281.

Blechman, E., Olson, D., Schornagel, C., Halsdorf, M., & Turner, A. (1976). The family contract game: Technique and case study. *Journal of Consulting and Clinical Psychology, 44,* 449–455.

Bloom, M. (1975). *The paradox of helping: Introduction to the philosophy of scientific practice.* New York: Wiley, 231–232.

Bloom, M., & Fischer, J. (1982). *Evaluating practice: Guidelines for the accountable professional.* Englewood Cliffs, NJ: Prentice Hall.

Blum, K. (1991). *Alcohol and the addictive brain: New hope for alcoholics from biogenetic research.* New York: Free Press.

Blythe, B. J., & Tripodi, T. (1989). *Measurement in direct practice.* Newbury Park, CA: Sage.

Bolton, F., & Bolton, S. (1987). *Working with violent families.* Newbury Park, CA: Sage.

Bolton, F., Morris, L., & MacEachron, A. (1989). *Males at risk: The other side of child abuse.* Newbury Park, CA: Sage.

Bonkowski, S., Bequette, S., & Boomhower, S. (1984). A group design to help children adjust to parental divorce. *Social Casework, 65,* 131–137.

Borden, W. (1991). Stress, coping, and adaptation in spouses of older adults with chronic dementia. *Social Work Research and Abstracts, 27* (1), 14–21.

Borkovec, T., & Sides, J. (1979). Critical procedural variables related to the physiological effects of relaxation: A review. *Behavior Research and Therapy, 17,* 119–125.

Boszormenyi-Nagy, I., & Spark, G. (1973). *Invisible loyalties: Reciprocity in intergenerational therapy.* New York: Harper & Row.

Bowen, G. L. (1987). Single fathers in the Air Force. *Social Casework, 68,* 339–344.

Bozett, F. W. (1987). *Gay and lesbian parents.* Westport, CT: Praeger.

Brehm, S. S. (1976). *The Application of social psychology to clinical practice.* New York: Wiley.

Brehm, S. S., & Brehm, J. W. (1981). *Psychological reactance: A theory of freedom and control.* New York: Academic Press.

Breton, M. (1984). A drop-in program for transient women: Promoting competence through the environment. *Social Work, 29,* 542–546.

Breton, M. (1985). Reaching and engaging people: issues and practice principles. *Social Work with Groups, 8* (3): 7–21.

Briar, S. (1964). The family as an organization: An approach to family diagnosis and treatment. *Social Service Review, 38*, 247–255.

Bricker-Jenkins, M. (1992). Building a strengths model of practice in the public social services. In Saleeby, D. (Ed.), *The strengths perspective in social work practice* (pp. 122–135). New York: Longman.

Brickner, P. W., Scharer, L. K., Conanan, B., Elvy, A., & Savarese, M. (1985). *Health care of homeless people.* New York: Springer.

Briere, J. (1989). *Therapy for adults molested as children.* New York: Springer.

Brill, C.K. (1990). *The impact on social work practice of the social injustice content in the NASW Code of Ethics.* Doctoral dissertation, Brandeis University.

Brindis, C., Barth, R. P., & Loomis, A. B. (1987). Continuous counseling: Case management with teenage parents. *Social Casework, 68*, 164–172.

Brown, G. (1982). Issues in the resettlement of Indochinese refugees. *Social Casework, 63*, 155–159.

Brown, J. L. (1988). Domestic hunger is no accident [Guest editorial]. *Social Work, 33*, 99–100.

Brown, L., & Levitt, J. (1979). A methodology for problem-system identification. *Social Casework, 60*, 408–415.

Brown, L., & Zimmer, D. (1986). An introduction to therapy issues of lesbian and gay male couples. In N. Jacobson & A. Gurman (Eds.), *Clinical handbook of marital therapy.* New York: Guilford Press.

Brownell, K., Marlatt, G., Lichenstein, E., & Wilson, G. T. (1986). Understanding and preventing relapse. *American Psychologist, 41* (7), 765–782.

Bruckner, D. F., & Johnson, P. E. (1987). Treatment for adult male victims of childhood sexual abuse. *Social Casework, 68*, 81–87.

Bryer, J. B., Nelson, B. A., Miller, J. B., & Krol, P. A. (1987). Childhood sexual and physical abuse as a factor in adult psychiatric illness. *American Journal of Psychiatry, 44*, 1426–1430.

Bucell, M. (1979). *An empirically derived self-report inventory for the assessment of assertive behavior.* Unpublished doctoral dissertation, Kent State University, Kent, OH.

Budner, S., Chazin, R., & Young, H. (1973). The indigenous nonprofessional in a multiservice center. *Social Casework, 54*, 354–359.

Burman, S., & Allen-Meares, P. (1991). Criteria for selecting practice theories: Working with alcoholic women. *Families in Society, 72*, 387–393.

Burns, D. (1980). *Feeling good.* New York: Avon Books.

Bush, C. T., Langford, M. W., Rosen, P., & Gott, W. (1990). Operation outreach: Intensive case management for severely psychiatrically disabled adults. *Hospital and Community Psychiatry, 41* (6), 647–649.

Butcher, J., & Koss, M. (1978). Research on brief and crisis-oriented psychotherapies. In S. Garfield & A. Bergin (Eds.), *Handbook of psychotherapy and behavior change* (pp. 725–767). New York: Wiley.

Butler, R. (1975). *Why service? Being old in America.* New York: Harper & Row.

Butz, R. A. (1985). Reporting child abuse and confidentiality in counseling. *Social Casework, 66*, 83–90.

Caesar, P. L., & Hamberger, L. K. (1989). *Treating men who batter: Theory, practice and programs.* New York: Springer.

Cain, R. (1991a). Relational contexts and information management among gay men. *Families in Society, 72* (6), 344–352.

Cain, R. (1991b). Stigma management and gay identity development. *Social Work. 36* (1), 67–71.

Camayd-Freixas, Y., & Amaro, H. (1984). *The measurement of Hispanic bilingualism and biculturality in the workplace.* Boston: Massachusetts Department of Social Services, Office of Human Resources.

Cameron, J., & Talavera, E. (1976). An advocacy program for Spanish-speaking people. *Social Casework, 57*, 427–431.

Campbell, J. A. (1990). Ability of practitioners to estimate client acceptance of single-subject evaluation procedures. *Social Work, 35* (1), 9–14.

Canda, E. (1983). General implications of Shamanism for clinical social work. *International Social Work, 26*, 14–22.

Canda, E., & Phaobtong, T. (1992). Buddhism as a support system for Southeast Asian refugees. *Social Work, 37* (1), 61–67.

Caplan, G. (1964). *Principles of preventive psychiatry.* New York: Basic Books.

Caputo, R. (1988). Managing domestic violence in two urban police districts. *Social Casework, 69* (8), 498–504.

Card, D. (1990). *Counseling same-sex couples.* New York: Norton.

Carkhuff, R. (1969). *Helping and human relations: Practice and research.* New York: Holt, Rinehart & Winston.

Carter, B., & McGoldrick, M. (Eds.) (1988). *The changing life cycle—A framework for family therapy* (2nd ed.). New York: Gardner Press.

Catalano, R., Wells, E. A., Jenson, J. M., & Hawkins, J. D. (1989). Aftercare services for drug-using institutionalized delinquents. *Social Service Review, 63* (4), 553–577.

Cates, J. A., Graham, L. L., Boeglin, D., & Tielker, S. (1990). The effect of AIDS on the family system. *Families in Society, 71* (4), 195–201.

Chandler, S. (1985). Mediation: Conjoint problem solving. *Social Work, 30*, 346–349.

Chau, K. L. 1990. A model for teaching cross-cultural practice in social work. *Journal of Social Work Education, spring/summer, 2,* 124–133.

Chelune, G. J. (1979). Measuring openness in interpersonal communication. In G. Chelune & Associates (Eds.), *Self-disclosure.* San Francisco: Jossey-Bass.

Cherbosque, J. (1987). Differential effects of counselor self-disclosure statements on perception of the counselor and willingness to disclose: A cross-cultural study. *Psychotherapy, 24,* 434–437.

Chesler, J., & Davis. S. (1980) Problem pregnancy and abortion counseling with teenagers. *Social Casework, 61,* 173–179.

Cimbolic, P. (1972). Counselor race and experience effects on black clients. *Journal of Consulting and Clinical Psychology, 39,* 328–332.

Cingolani, J. (1984). Social conflict perspective on work with involuntary clients. *Social Work, 29* (September–October), pp. 442–446.

Citron, P. (1978). Group work with alcoholic poly-drug involved adolescents with deviant behavior syndrome. *Social Work with Groups, 1* (1), 39–52.

Claiborn, C. (1982). Interpretation and change in counseling. *Journal of Counseling Psychology, 29,* 439–453.

Claiborn, C., Crawford, J., & Hackman, H. (1983). Effects of intervention discrepancy in counseling for negative emotions. *Journal of Counseling Psychology, 30,* 164–171.

Cnaan, Ram A. (1994). The new American social work gospel: case management of the chronically mentally ill. *The British Journal of Social Work, 24* (5), 533–557.

Cohen, B.-Z. (1985). A cognitive approach to the treatment of offenders. *British Journal of Social Work, 15,* 619–633.

Cohen, C., & Adler, A. (1986). Assessing the role of social network interventions with an inner-city population. *American Journal of Psychiatry, 56,* 278–288.

Cohen, M. B. (1989). Social work practice with homeless mentally ill people: Engaging the client. *Social Work, 34* (6), 505–509.

Cohn, A. H. (1979). Effective treatment of child abuse and neglect. *Social Work, 24,* 513–519.

Cole, E., & Duva, J. (1990). *Family preservation: An orientation for administrators & practitioners.* Washington, DC: Child Welfare League of America.

Community Care Corporation Accreditation Standards and Self-Study Guides (1995). Council on Social Work Education.

Compher, J. (1983). Home services to families to prevent child placement. *Social Work, 28,* 360–364.

Compton, B. R., & Galaway, B. (1994). *Social work processes* (5th ed.). Pacific Grove, CA: Brooks/Cole.

Congress, E. P. (1994). The use of culturagrams to assess and empower culturally diverse families. *Families in Society: The Journal of Contemporary Human Services, 75* (9), 531–538.

Congress, E. P., & Lynn, M. (1994). Group work programs in public schools: ethical dilemmas and cultural diversity. *Social Work in Education, 16* (2), 107–114.

Conklin, C. (1980). Rural care-givers. *Social Work, 25,* 495–496.

Connell, S. (1987). Homelessness. In *Encyclopedia of social work* (Vol. 1, pp. 789–795). Silver Spring, MD: National Association of Social Workers.

Constantine, L. (1978). Family sculpture and relationship mapping techniques. *Journal of Marriage and Family Counseling, 4,* 19–25.

Cook, R. (1988). Trends and needs in programming for independent living. *Child Welfare, 67,* 497–514.

Cooley, R., Ostendorf, D., & Bickerton, D. (1979). Outreach services for Native Americans. *Social Work, 24,* 151–153.

Cooper, S. (1973). A look at the effect of racism on clinical work. *Social Casework, 54,* 76–84.

Coplon, J., & Strull, J. (1983). Roles of the professional in mutual aid groups. *Social Casework, 64,* 259–266.

Corcoran, K., & Fischer, J. (1987). *Measures for clinical practice.* New York: Free Press.

Corcoran, K., & Vandiver, V. (1996). *Maneuvering the maze of managed care: Skills for mental health practitioners.* New York: Free Press.

Corey, G. (1990). *Theory and practice of group counseling.* Pacific Grove, CA: Brooks/Cole.

Corey, M. S., & Corey, G. (1992). *Groups: Process and practice* (4th ed.). Pacific Grove, CA: Brooks/ Cole.

Cormier, W., & Cormier, L. (1979). *Interviewing strategies for helpers: A guide to assessment, treatment, and evaluation.* Pacific Grove, CA: Brooks/Cole.

Coudroglou, A., & Poole, D. (1984). *Disability, work, and social policy.* New York: Springer.

Coulton, C. (1979). A study of the person-environment fit among the chronically ill. *Social Work in Health Care, 5,* 5–17.

Coulton, C. (1981). Person-environment fit as the focus in health care. *Social Work, 26,* 26–35.

Couper, D. P. (1989). *Aging and our families: Handbook for caregivers.* New York: Human Sciences Press.

Courtois, C. A. (1988). *Healing the incest wound: Adult survivors in therapy.* New York: Norton.

Cowan, B., Currie, M., Krol, R., & Richardson, J. (1969). Holding unwilling clients in treatment. *Social Casework, 14,* 146–151.

Cowger, C. D. (1992), Assessment of client strengths. In D. Saleeby (Ed.), *The strengths perspective in social work practice* (pp. 139–147). New York: Longman.

Cowger, C. D. (1994, May). Assessing client strengths: clinical assessment for client empowerment. *Social Work, 39* (3), 262–267.

Cox, E. O. (1991). The critical role of social action in empowerment oriented groups. *Social Work with Groups, 14* (3-4), 77-90.

Cross, T. L., Bazron, B. J., Dennis, K., & Issacs, M. R.(1989). *Toward a culturally competent system of care.* Washington, DC: Georgetown University Child Development Center.

Crotty, P., & Kulys, R. (1985). Social support networks: The views of schizophrenic clients and their significant others. *Social Work, 30,* 301–309.

Cruz, V. K., Price-Williams, D., & Andron, L. (1988). Developmentally disabled women who were molested as children. *Social Casework, 69* (7), 411–419.

Cueller, I., Harris, L. C., & Jasso, R. (1980). An acculturation scale for Mexican-American normal and clinical populations. *Hispanic Journal of Behavioral Sciences, 2* (3), 199–217.

Cull, J. G., & Gill, W. S. (1991). *Suicide Probability Scale (SPS).* Los Angeles: Western Psychological Services.

Culp, R. E., Heide, J., & Richardson, M. T. (1987). Maltreated children's developmental scores: Treatment versus nontreatment. *Child Abuse and Neglect, 11* (1), 29–34.

Curran, J. P., Sutton, R. G., Faraone, S. V., & Guenette, S. (1985). Inpatient approaches. In M. Hersen & A. S. Bellack (Eds.), *Handbook of clinical behavior therapy with adults* (pp. 445–483). New York: Plenum Press.

Curriculum Policy Statement. (1995). Council on Social Work Education.

Cutler, D., & Madore, E. (1980). Community-family network therapy in a rural setting. *Community Mental Health Journal, 16,* 144–155.

Dahl, A. S., Cowgill, K. M., & Asmundsson, R. (1987). Life in remarriage families. *Social Work, 32,* 40–44.

Daley, D. C. (1987). Relapse prevention with substance abusers: Clinical issues and myths. *Social Work, 32,* 138–142.

Daley, D. C. (1991). *Kicking addictive habits once and for all. A relapse prevention guide.* New York: Lexington.

Dane, B. O. (1989). New beginnings for AIDS patients. *Social Casework, 70* (5), 305–309.

Dane, B. O. (1991). Anticipatory mourning of middle-aged parents of adult children with AIDS. *Families in Society, 72* (2), 108–115.

Dane, B. O., & Simon, B. L. (1991, May). Resident guests: social workers in host settings. *Social Work, 36* (3), 208–213.

Dane, E. (1985). *Professional and lay advocacy in the education of handicapped children.* New York: Routledge & Kegan Paul.

Danish, J., D'Augelli, A., & Hauer, A. (1980). *Helping skills: A basic training program.* New York: Human Sciences Press.

Daro, D. (1988). *Confronting child abuse: Research for effective program designs.* New York: Free Press.

Davenport, J., & Reims, N. (1978). Theoretical orientation and attitudes toward women. *Social Work, 23,* 307–309.

Davies, D. (1991). Interventions with male toddlers who have witnessed parental violence. *Families in Society, 72* (9), 515–524.

Davis, L. E., & Gelsomino, J. (1994). An assessment of practitioner cross-racial treatment experiences. *Social Work, 39* (1), 116–123.

Davis, L. V. (1987). Battered women: The transformation of a social problem. *Social Work, 32,* 306–311.

Davis, L. V. (1991). Violence and families. *Social Work, 37* (5), 371–373.

Davis, L. V., & Hagen, J. L. (1992). The problem of wife abuse: The interrelationship of social policy and social work practice. *Social Work, 37* (17), 15–20.

Dawson, R. (1986). Fathers anonymous—A group treatment program for sexual offenders. In B. Schlesinger (Ed.), *Sexual abuse of children in the 1980's: Ten essays and an annotated bibliography* (pp. 70–79). Toronto: University of Toronto Press.

De Anda, D. (1984). Bicultural socialization: Factors affecting the minority experience. *Social Work, 29,* 172–181.

De Anda, D., & Becerra, R. (1984). Support networks for adolescent mothers. *Social Casework, 65,* 172–181.

Delgado, M. (1977). Puerto Rican spiritualism and the social work profession. *Social Casework, 58,* 451–458.

Denton, R. (1989, March). *The religious fundamentalist family: Training for assessment and treatment.* Paper presented to the Annual Program Meeting of the Council on Social Work Education, Chicago.

Denton, W. (1991). The role of affect in marital therapy. *Journal of Marital and Family Therapy, 17* (3), 257–261.

DeShazer, S. (1988). *Clues: Investigating solutions in brief therapy.* New York: Norton.

Devore, W., & Schlesinger, E. (1981). *Ethnic-sensitive social work practice.* St. Louis: Mosby.

Dies, R. R. (1983). Clinical implications of research on leadership in short-term group psychotherapy. In R. R. Dies & R. MacKenzie (Eds.), *Advances in group psychotherapy: Integrating research and practice* (American Group Psychotherapy Association Monograph Series) (pp. 27–28). New York: International Universities Press.

Diorio, W. D. (1992, April). Parental perceptions of the authority of public child welfare caseworkers. *Families in Society: The Journal of Contemporary Human Services, 73* (4), 222–235.

Donovan, D., & Marlatt, G. A. (1988). *Assessment of addictive behaviors.* New York: Guilford Press.

Dore, M. M., & Dumois, A. O. (1990). Cultural differences in the meaning of adolescent pregnancy. *Families in Society, 71* (2), 93–101.

Doster, J., & Nesbitt, J. (1979). Psychotherapy and self-disclosure. In. G. Chelune & Associates (Eds.), *Self-disclosure* (pp. 177–224). San Francisco: Jossey-Bass.

Doster, J., Surratt, F., & Webster, T. (1975, March). *Interpersonal variables affecting psychological communications of hospitalized psychiatric patients.* Paper presented at meeting of Southeastern Psychological Association, Atlanta.

Dougherty, A. M. (1990). *Consultation: Practice and perspectives.* Pacific Grove, CA: Brooks/Cole.

Douglas, H. (1991). Assessing violent couples. *Families in Society, 72* (9), 525–533.

Dowd, E., & Boroto, D. (1982). Differential effects of counselor self-disclosure, self-involving statements, and interpretation, *Journal of Counseling Psychology, 29,* 8–13.

Drachman, D. (1992). A stage-of-migration framework for service to immigrant populations. *Social Work, 37* (1), 61–67.

DuBray, W. (1985). American Indian values: Critical factors in casework. *Social Casework, 66,* 30–37.

Dudley, J. R. (1987). Speaking for themselves: People who are labeled as developmentally disabled. *Social Work, 32,* 80–82.

Duehn, W., & Proctor, E. (1977). Initial clinical interactions and premature discontinuance in treatment. *American Journal of Orthopsychiatry, 47,* 284–290.

Duvall, E. (1977). *Marriage and family development* (5th ed.). Philadelphia: Lippincott.

Dyer, W. (1969). Congruence and control. *Journal of Applied Behavioral Science, 5,* 161–173.

D'Zurilla, T., & Goldfried, M. (1971). Problem solving and behavior modification. *Journal of Abnormal Psychology, 78,* 107–126.

Edleson, J. (1984). Working with men who batter. *Social Work, 29,* 237–242.

Edleson, J., & Frank, M. D. (1991). Rural interventions in woman battering: One state's strategies. *Families in Society, 72* (9), 543–551.

Edleson, J., & Syers, M. (1990). Relative effectiveness of group treatment for men who batter. *Social Work Research and Abstracts, 26* (2), 10–17.

Edwards, A. (1982). The consequences of error in selecting treatment for blacks. *Social Casework, 63,* 429–433.

Edwards, E. (1983). Native-American elders: Current issues and social policy implications. In R. McNeely & J. Colen (Eds.), *Aging in minority groups.* Beverly Hills, CA: Sage.

Ehrlich, E. J., & Moore, P. A. (1990). Delivery of AIDS services: The New York State response. *Social Work, 35* (2), 175–177.

Eisikovits, Z. C., & Edleson, J. L. (1989). Intervening with men who batter: A critical review of the literature. *Social Services Review, 63* (3), 384–414.

Elbow, M., & Mayfield, J. (1991). Mothers of incest victims: Villains, victims, or protectors? *Families in Society, 72* (2), 78–85.

Elkin, I., Shea, T., Watkins, J., & Collins, J. (1986). *Comparative treatment outcome findings.* Presentation of the NIMH Treatment of Depression Collaborative Research Program. Paper presented at the annual meeting of the American Psychiatric Association.

Ellis, A. (1962). *Reason and emotion in psychotherapy.* New York: Lyle Stuart.

Ely, A. (1985). Long-term group treatment for young male schizopaths. *Social Work, 30,* 5–10.

Ephross, P. H. and Vassil, T. V. (1988). *Groups that work: Structure and process.* New York: Columbia University Press.

Epstein, L. (1985). *Talking and listening: A guide to interviewing.* Columbus, OH: Merrill.

Epstein, L. (1988). *Brief treatment: A task-centered approach.* New York: McGraw-Hill.

Epstein, L. (1990). *Brief treatment and a new look at the task-centered approach.* New York: Macmillan.

Erickson, S. (1988). *Family mediation casebook.* New York: Brunner/Mazel.

Ewalt, P. L. (1994, September). Welfare—how much reform? *Social Work, 39* (5), 485–486.

Ezell, M. (1994). Advocacy practice of social workers. *Families in Society, 75,* 1, 36–46.

Falicov, C. (1982). Mexican families. In M. McGoldrick, J. Pearce, & J. Giordano (Eds.), *Ethnicity and family therapy* (pp. 134–163). New York: Guilford Press.

Faller, K. (1989). Decision making in cases of intrafamilial child sexual abuse. *American Journal of Orthopsychiatry, 58,* 121–128.

Faller, K. (1990). *Understanding child sexual treatment.* Newbury Park, CA: Sage.

Faria, G. (1991). Educating students for family-based practice with lesbian families. In *Empowering families* (pp. 15–21). Proceedings of the Fifth Annual Conference on Family Based Services: National Association for Family Based Services, Cedar Rapids, IA.

Faria, G. (1994). Training for family preservation practice with lesbian families. *Families in Society, 75* (7), 416–422.

Farina, A., Burns, G. L., Austad, C., Bugglin, C., & Fischer, E. H. (1986). The role of physical attractiveness in the readjustment of discharged psychiatric patients. *Journal of Abnormal Psychology, 95,* 139–143.

Fatout, M. (1990). Consequences of abuse on relationships of children. *Families in Society, 71* (2), 76–81.

Fauri, D. P., & Bradford, J. B. (1986). Practice with the frail elderly in the private sector. *Social Casework, 67,* 259–265.

Fein, E., & Staff, I. (1991). Implementing reunification services. *Families in Society, 72* (6), 335–343.

Feinstein, B., & Cavanaugh, C. (1976). *The new volunteerism: A community connection.* Cambridge, MA: Schenkman.

Feld, S., & Radin, N. (1982). *Social psychology for social work and the mental health professions.* New York: Columbia University Press.

Feldman, D., Strong, S., & Danser, D. (1982). A comparison of paradoxical and nonparadoxical interpretations and directives. *Journal of Counseling Psychology, 29,* 572–579.

Fiene, J., & Taylor, P. (1991). Serving rural families of developmentally disabled children: A case management model. *Social Work, 36* (4), 323–327.

Filinson, R., & Ingman, S. (Eds.) (1989). *Elder abuse: Practice and policy.* New York: Human Sciences Press.

Fine, M., Akabas, S., & Bellinger, S. (1982). Cultures of drinking: A workplace perspective. *Social Work, 27,* 436–440.

Finkelhor, D. (Ed.) (1984). *Child sexual abuse: New theory and research.* New York: Free Press.

Finkelhor, D., & Associates (1986). *A sourcebook on child sexual abuse.* Newbury Park, CA: Sage.

Finkelhor, D., & Browne, A. (1986). Initial and long-term effects: A conceptual framework. In D. Finkelhor, S. Araji, L. Baron, A. Browne, S. D. Peters, & G. E. Wyatt (Eds.), *A sourcebook on child sexual abuse* (pp. 186–187). Newbury Park, CA: Sage.

Finkelstein, N. (1980). Family-centered group care. *Child Welfare, 59,* 33–41.

Finn, J., & Rose, S. (1982). Development and validation of the interview skills role-play test. *Social Work Research and Abstracts, 18,* 21–27.

First, R. J., Roth, D., & Arewa, B. D. (1988). Homelessness: Understanding the dimensions of the problem for minorities. *Social Work, 33,* 120–124.

Fisch, R., Weakland, J., & Segal, L. (1982). *The tactics of change: Doing therapy briefly.* San Francisco: Jossey-Bass.

Fischer, J. (1976). *The effectiveness of social casework.* Springfield, IL: Charles C Thomas.

Fischer, J. (1978). *Effective casework practice: An eclectic approach.* New York: McGraw-Hill.

Fischer, J., & Corcoran, K. (1994). *Measures for clinical practice* (2nd. ed.). New York: Free Press.

Flaherty, J. A., Gaviria, F. M., & Pathak, D. S. (1983). The measurement of social support: The Social Support Network Inventory. *Comprehensive Psychiatry, 24,* 521–529.

Flapan, D., & Fenchal, G. (1987). *The developing ego and the emerging self in group therapy.* Northvale, NJ: Aronson.

Folberg, J., & Milne, A. (1988). *Divorce mediation: Theory and practice.* New York: Guilford Press.

Fortune, A. E. (1985a). Treatment groups. In A. E. Fortune (Ed.), *Task-centered practice with families and groups* (pp. 33–44). New York: Springer.

Fortune, A. E. (1985b). *Task-centered practice with families and groups.* New York: Springer.

Fortune, A. E. (1985c). Planning duration and termination of treatment. *Social Service Review, 59* (4), 647–661.

Fortune, A. E. (1987). Grief only? Client and social worker reactions to termination. *Clinical Social Work Journal, 15* (2), 159–171.

Fortune, A. E., Pearlingi, B., & Rochelle, C. D. (1991). Criteria for terminating treatment. *Families in Society, 72* (6), 366–370.

Fortune, A., Pearlingi, B., & Rochelle, C. D. (1992). Reactions to termination of individual treatment. *Social Work, 37* (2), 171–178.

Fowler, R. C., Rich, C. L., & Young, D. C. (1986). San Diego suicide study, II: Substance abuse in young cases. *Archives of General Psychiatry, 43,* 962–965.

Frank, P. B., & Golden, G. K. (1992). Blaming by naming: Battered women and the epidemic of co-dependence. *Social Work, 37* (1), 5–6.

Frankel, A. J. (1991). The dynamics of day care. *Families in society, 72* (1), 3–10.

Frankle, H., & Gordon, V. (1983). Helping Selma: A report on a therapist-volunteer relationship. *Social Casework, 64,* 291–299.

Fraser, M., & Hawkins, J. (1984). Social network analysis and drug misuse. *Social Service Review, 58,* 81–87.

Fraser, M. W., Pecora, P. J., & Haapala, D. A. (1991). *Families in crisis: The impact of intensive family preservation services.* Hawthorne, NY: Aldine de Gruyter.

Fredman, N., & Sherman, R. (1987). *Handbook of measurements for marriage & family therapy.* New York: Brunner/Mazel.

Freed, A. (1978). Clients' rights and casework records. *Social Casework, 59,* 458–464.

Freed, A. (1988). Interviewing through an interpreter. *Social Work, 33,* 315–319.

Frey, C. (1987). Minimarathon group sessions with incest offenders. *Social Work, 32,* 534–535.

Frey, G. A. (1990). A framework for promoting organizational change. *Families in Society, 71* (3), 142–147.

Friedlander, M. L., & Schwartz, G. S. (1985). Toward a theory of strategic self-presentation in counseling and psychotherapy. *Journal of Counseling Psychology, 32,* 485.

Friedman, D., & Friedman, S. (1982). Day care as a setting for intervention in family systems. *Social Casework, 63,* 291–295.

Friedrich, W. (1990). *Psychotherapy of sexually abused children and their families.* New York: Norton.

Froland, C., Pancoast, D., Chapman, N., & Kimboko, P. (1981). *Helping networks and human services.* Beverly Hills, CA: Sage.

Gagliano, C. K. (1987). Group treatment for sexually abused girls. *Social Casework, 68,* 102–108.

Gallo, F. (1982). The effects of social support networks in the health of the elderly. *Social Work in Health Care, 8,* 65–74.

Gambe, R., & Getzel, G. S. (1989). Group work with gay men with AIDS. *Social Casework, 70* (37), 172–179.

Gambrill, E., & Barth, R. (1980). Single-case study designs revisited. *Social Work Research and Abstracts, 16,* 15–20.

Gammon, E. A., & Rose, S. (1991). The coping skills training program for parents of children with developmental disabilities. *Research on Social Work Practice, 1* (3), 244–256.

Garbarino, J., & Ebata, A. (1983). The significance of ethnic and cultural differences in child maltreatment. *Journal of Marriage and the Family, 45* (4), 773–783.

Garbarino, J., Stocking, S., & Associates (1980). *Protecting children from abuse and neglect.* San Francisco: Jossey-Bass.

Gardner, R. A. (1971). *Therapeutic communication with children.* New York: Science House Press.

Garfield, R. (1981). Convening the family: Guidelines for the initial contact with a family member. In A. Gurman (Ed.), *Questions and answers in the practice of family therapy* (pp. 5–9). New York: Brunner/Mazel.

Garfinkel, I., & McLanahan, S. S. (1986). *Single mothers and their children.* Washington, DC: Urban Institute Press.

Garland, J., Jones, H., & Kolodny, R. (1965). A model for stages in the development of social work groups. In S. Bernstein (Ed.), *Explorations in group work.* Boston: Milford House.

Garvin, C. (1981). *Contemporary group work.* Englewood Cliffs, NJ: Prentice Hall.

Garvin, C. (1985). Practice with task-centered groups. In A. E. Fortune (Ed.), *Task-centered practice with families and groups* (pp. 45–57). New York: Springer.

Garvin, C. (1986). Assessment and change of group conditions in social work practice. In P. H. Glasser & N. S. Mayadas (Eds.), *Group workers at work: Theory and practice in the 80's.* Totowa, NJ: Rowman & Lillifield.

Garvin, C. (1987). *Contemporary Group Work* (2nd ed.). Englewood Cliffs, NJ: Prentice Hall.

Garvin, C., Reid, W., & Epstein, L. (1976). A task-oriented approach. In R. Roberts & H. Northern (Eds.), *Theories of social work with groups.* New York: Columbia University Press.

Gaylord, M. (1979). Relocation and the corporate family: Unexplored issues. *Social Work, 24,* 186–191.

Gazda, G. M. (1989). *Group counseling: A developmental approach* (4th ed.). Boston: Allyn & Bacon.

Gelles, R., & Cornell, C. P. (1990). *Intimate violence in families.* Newbury Park, CA: Sage.

Gendlin, E. (1967). Therapeutic procedures in dealing with schizophrenics. In C. Rogers, E. Gendlin, D. Kiesler, & C. Truax (Eds.), *The therapeutic relationship and its impact: A study of psychotherapy with schizophrenics.* Madison: University of Wisconsin Press.

Gendlin, E. (1974). Client-centered and experiential psychotherapy. In D. Wexler & L. Rice (Eds.), *Innovations in client-centered therapy.* New York: Wiley.

George, R. M. (1990). The reunification process in substitute care. *Social Service Review, 64* (3), 422–457.

Germain, C. (1973). An ecological perspective in casework practice. *Social Casework, 54,* 323–330.

Germain, C. (1977). An ecological perspective on social work practice in health care. *Social Work in Health Care, 3,* 67–76.

Germain, C. (1979). Ecology and social work. In C. Germain (Ed.), *Social work practice: People and environments* (pp. 1–2). New York: Columbia University Press.

Germain, C. (1981). The ecological approach to people-environmental transactions. *Social Casework, 62,* 323–331.

Germain, C., & Gitterman, A. (1980). *The life model of social work practice.* New York: Columbia University Press.

Getzel, G. S. (1991). Survival modes for people with AIDS in groups. *Social Work, 36* (1), 7–11.

Ghali, S. (1982). Understanding Puerto Rican traditions. *Social Work, 27,* 98–102.

Giannandrea, V., & Murphy, K. (1973). Similarity of self-disclosure and return for a second interview. *Journal of Counseling Psychology, 20,* 545–548.

Gibbons, J., Bow, I., & Butter, J. (1979). Clients' reactions to task-centered casework: A follow-up study. *British Journal of Social Work, 9,* 203–215.

Gibbs, L. & Gambrill, E. (1996). *Critical thinking for social workers.* Thousand Oaks, CA: Pine Forge Press.

Gibson, J., & Gutierrez, L. (1991). A service program for safe-home children. *Families in Society, 72* (9), 554–562.

Gil, E. (1991). *The healing power of play: Working with abused children.* New York: Guilford Press.

Gilbar, O. (1992). Workers' sick fund (kupat holim) hotline therapeutic first intervention: A model developed in the Gulf War. *Social Work in Health Care, 17* (4), 45–57.

Gilbert, N. (1977). The search for professional identity. *Social Work, 22*, 401–406.

Gilbert, N., & Specht, H. (1976). Advocacy and professional ethics. *Social Work, 21*, 288–293.

Gilbert, N., & Specht, H. (1979). Title XX planning by area agencies on aging: Effects, outcomes, and policy implications. *Gerontologist, 19*, 264–274.

Gilbert, N., & Specht, H. (1987). Social planning and community organizations. *Encyclopedia of social work* (Vol. 2, pp. 602–619). Silver Spring, MD: National Association of Social Workers.

Gillman, R. (1991). From resistance to rewards: Social workers' experiences and attitudes toward AIDS. *Families in Society, 72* (10), 593–601.

Gingerich, W. J. (1984). Generalizing single-case evaluation from classroom to practice setting. *Journal of Education for Social Work, 20*, 74–82.

Giovannoni, J., & Billingsley, A. (1970). Child neglect among the poor: A study of parental adequacy in families of three ethnic groups. *Child Welfare, 49*, 196–204.

Gitterman, A. (1996). Ecological perspective: Response to Professor Jerry Wakefield. *Social Service Review, 70* (3), 472–475.

Gitterman, A., & Schaeffer, A. (1972). The white professional and the black client. *Social Casework, 53*, 280–291.

Giunta, C. T., & Streissguth, A. P. (1988). Patients with fetal alcohol syndrome and their caretakers. *Social Casework, 69* (7), 453–459.

Glick, I., & Kessler, D. (1974). *Marital and family therapy.* New York: Grune & Stratton.

Golan, N. (1978). *Treatment in crisis situations.* New York: Free Press.

Golan, N. (1980). Intervention at times of transition: Sources and forms of help. *Social Casework, 61*, 259–266.

Golan, N. (1981). *Passing through transitions: A guide for the practitioner.* New York: Free Press.

Golan, N., & Gruschka, R. (1971). Integrating the new immigrant: A model for social work practice in transitional states. *Social Work, 16*, 82–87.

Gold, M. (1986, November). (As quoted by Earl Ubell.) Is that child bad or depressed? *Parade Magazine, 2*, 10.

Gold, N. (1990). Motivation: The crucial but unexplored component of social work practice. *Social Work, 35*, 49–56.

Golden, G. K. (1991). Volunteer counselors: An innovative, economic response to mental health service gaps. *Social Work, 36* (3), 230–232.

Goldenberg, I., & Goldenberg, H. (1991). *Family therapy: An overview* (3rd ed.). Pacific Grove, CA: Brooks/Cole.

Goldfried, M. (1977). The use of relaxation and cognitive relabeling as coping skills. In R. Stuart (Ed.), *Behavioral self-management* (pp. 82–116). New York: Brunner/Mazel.

Goldstein, E. G. (1983). Issues in developing systematic research and theory. In A. Rosenblatt & D. Waldfogel (Eds.), *Handbook of clinical social work.* San Francisco: Jossey-Bass.

Goldstein, H. (1983). Starting where the client is. *Social Casework, 64*, 267–275.

Gomes-Schwartz, B., Horowitz, J., & Cardarell, A. (1990). *Child sexual abuse.* Newbury Park, CA: Sage.

Gomez, E., Zurcher, L. A. Farris, B. E., & Becker, R. E. (1985). A study of psychosocial casework with Chicanos. *Social Work, 30*, 477–482.

Gomez, M. R. (1990). Biculturalism and subjective mental health among Cuban Americans. *Social Service Review, 64* (3), 375–389.

Gordon, J. (1978). Group homes: Alternative to institutions. *Social Work, 23*, 300–305.

Gordon, T. (1970). *Parent effectiveness training.* New York: P. H. Wyden.

Gordon, W. (1962). A critique of the working definition. *Social Work, 7*, 3–13.

Gordon, W. (1965). Toward a social work frame of reference. *Journal of Education for Social Work, 1*, 19–26.

Gordon, W., & Schutz, M. (1977). A natural basis for social work specializations. *Social Work, 22*, 422–426.

Gottesfeld, M., & Lieberman, F. (1979). The pathological therapist. *Social Casework, 60*, 387–393.

Gottlieb, B. (Ed.) (1981). *Social networks and social support.* Beverly Hills, CA: Sage.

Gottlieb, B. (1985). Assessing and strengthening the impact of social support on mental health. *Social Work, 30*, 293–300.

Gottlieb, B. (Ed.) (1988). *Marshaling social support.* Newbury Park, CA: Sage.

Gould, K. (1988). Asian and Pacific Islanders: Myth and reality. *Social Work, 33*, 142–147.

Graves, B., & Accardo, P. J. (1989). Training in parenting skills for adults with mental retardation. *Social Work, 34* (5), 431–434.

Green, J. (1982). *Cultural awareness in the human services.* Englewood Cliffs, NJ: Prentice Hall.

Greenbaum, L., & Holmes, I. (1983). The use of folktales in social work practice. *Social Casework, 64*, 414–418.

Greif, G. L. (1985). *Single fathers.* Lexington, MA: Heath.

Griffin, R. E. (1991). Assessing the drug-involved client. *Families in Society, 72* (2), 87–94.

Grinnell, R., & Kyte, N. (1974). Modifying the environment. *Social Work, 19*, 477–483.

Gross, E. (1995). Deconstructing politically correct practice literature: The American Indian case. *Social Work, 40* (2), 206–213.

Grunebaum, H. (1986). Harmful psychotherapy experience. *American Journal of Psychotherapy, 40,* 165–176.

Guendalman, S. (1983). Developing responsiveness to the health care needs of Hispanic children and families. *Social Work in Health Care, 8,* 1–15.

Gulati, P., & Guest, G. (1990). The community-centered model: A garden variety approach or a radical transformation of community practice? *Social Work, 35* (1), 63–68.

Gurman, A. (1977). The patient's perception of the therapeutic relationship. In A. Gurman & A. Razin (Eds.), *Effective psychotherapy: A handbook of research.* New York: Pergamon Press.

Gutierrez, L. M. (1990). Working with women of color: An empowerment perspective. *Social Work, 35* (2), 149–153.

Gutierrez, L. M. (1994). Beyond coping: an empowerment perspective on stressful life events. *Journal of Sociology and Social Welfare, 21* (3), 201–219.

Gwyn, F., & Kilpatrick, A. (1981). Family therapy with low-income blacks: A tool or-turn-off? *Social Casework, 62,* 259–266.

Hackney, H., & Cormier, L. (1979). *Counseling strategies and objectives* (2nd ed.), Englewood Cliffs, NJ: Prentice Hall.

Haeuser, A., & Schwartz, F. (1980). Developing social work skills for work with volunteers. *Social Casework, 61,* 595–601.

Hagen, J. L. (1987a). The heterogeneity of homelessness. *Social Casework, 68,* 451–457.

Hagen, J. L. (1987b). Gender and homelessness. *Social Work, 32,* 312–316.

Haley, J. (1963). *Strategies of psychotherapy.* New York: Grune & Stratton.

Hall, M. (1978). Lesbian families: Cultural and clinical issues. *Social Work, 23,* 380–385.

Hamlin, E. R. (1991). Community-based spouse abuse protection and family preservation teams. *Social Work, 36* (5), 402–406.

Hammond, D., Hepworth, D., & Smith, V. (1977). *Improving therapeutic communication.* San Francisco: Jossey-Bass.

Hampton, R. L. (1990). *Black family violence: Current theory and research.* Lexington, MA: Lexington Books.

Handbook of accreditation standards (1995, 5th ed.). Commission on Accreditation, Council on Social Work Education. Alexandria, VA.

Haney, M., & Rabin, B. (1984). Modifying attitudes toward disabled persons. *Archives of Physical Medicine and Rehabilitation, 65,* 431–436.

Haney, P. (1988). Providing empowerment to the person with AIDS. *Social Work, 33,* 251–253.

Hardy, K. (1989). The theoretical myth of sameness: A critical issue in family therapy and treatment. In G. W. Saba, B. M. Karrer, & K. Hardy (Eds.), *Minorities and family therapy* (pp. 17–33). New York: Hawthorne Press.

Harris, M., & Bergman, H. C. (1987). Case management with the chronically ill. *American Journal of Orthopsychiatry, 57,* 296–302.

Hartford, M. (1971). *Groups in social work.* New York: Columbia University Press.

Hartman, A. (1981). The family: A central focus for practice. *Social Work, 26,* 7–13.

Hartman, A. (1993). The professional is political. *Social Work, 38* (4), 365, 366, 504.

Hartman, A. (1994). Diagrammatic assessment of family relationships. In B. R. Compton, & B. Galaway (Eds.), *Social work processes* (5th ed) (pp. 153–165). Pacific Grove, CA: Brooks/Cole.

Hartman, A., & Laird, J. (1983). *Family centered social work practice.* New York: Free Press.

Hartman, C., & Reynolds, D. (1987). Resistant clients: Confrontation, interpretation and alliance. *Social Casework, 68,* 205–213.

Harvey, Y., & Chung, S. (1980). The Koreans. In J. McDermott, Jr., W. Tseng, & T. Maretzki (Eds.), *People and cultures of Hawaii* (pp. 135–154). Honolulu: University of Hawaii Press.

Haynes, K. S., & Mickelson, J. S. (1986). *Affecting change: Social workers in the political arena.* White Plains, NY: Longman.

Hegar, R. L. (1989). Empowerment-based practice with children. *Social Service Review, 63* (3), 372–383.

Henderson, S. (1982). The significance of social relationships in the etiology of neurosis. In C. M. Parkes & J. Stevenson-Hinde (Eds.), *The place of attachment in human behavior* (pp. 205–231). New York: Basic Books.

Henderson, S., Duncan-Jones, P., Byrne, D., & Scott, R. (1980). Measuring social relationships: The interview schedule for social interaction. *Psychological Medicine, 10,* 723–734.

Henry, M. (1988). Revisiting open groups. *Groupwork, 1,* 215–228.

Henry, S. (1992). *Group skills in four-dimensional approach* (2nd ed.). Pacific Grove, CA: Brooks/Cole.

Hepworth, D. (1964). The clinical implications of perceptual distortion in forced marriages. *Social Casework, 45,* 579–585.

Hepworth, D. (1979). Early removal of resistance in task-centered casework. *Social Work, 24,* 317–323.

Hepworth, D. H. (1993). Managing manipulative behavior in the helping relationship. *Social Work, 38* (6), 674–684.

Hepworth, D. H., Farley, O. W., & Griffiths, J. K. (1988). Clinical work with suicidal adolescents and their families. *Social Casework, 69,* 195–203.

Herz, F., & Rosen, E. (1982). Jewish families. In M. McGoldrick, J. Pearce, & J. Giordano (Eds.), *Ethnicity and family therapy* (pp. 364–392). New York: Guilford Press.

Hess, P. (1982). Parent-child attachment concept: Crucial for permanency planning. *Social Casework, 63*, 46–53.

Hill, B., Rotegard, L., & Bruininks, R. (1984). The quality of life of mentally retarded people in residential care. *Social Work, 29*, 275–281.

Hirayama, H., & Cetingok, M. (1988). Empowerment: A social work approach for Asian immigrants. *Social Casework, 69*, 41–47.

Ho, M. (1976). Social work with Asian Americans. *Social Casework, 57*, 195–201.

Ho, M. K. (1987). *Family therapy with ethnic minorities.* Newbury Park, CA: Sage.

Hochschild, A. (1989). *Second shift.* New York: Viking Penguin.

Hoehn-Saric, R., Frank, J., Imber, S., Nash, E., Stone, A., & Battle, C. (1964). Systematic preparation of patients for psychotherapy—I. Effects on therapy behavior and outcome. *Journal of Psychiatric Research, 2*, 267–281.

Hogarty, G. (1989). Meta-analysis of the effects of practice with the chronically mentally ill: A critique and reappraisal of the literature. *Social Work, 34*(4), 363–372.

Holmes, K. (1981). Services for victims of rape: A dualistic practice model. *Social Casework, 62*, 30–39.

Holmes, T., & Rahe, R. (1967). The social readjustment rating scale. *Journal of Psychosomatic Research, 11*, 213–218.

Homma-True, R. (1976). Characteristics of contrasting Chinatowns: 2. Oakland, California. *Social Casework, 57*, 155–159.

Honey, E. (1988). AIDS and the inner city: Critical issues. *Social Casework, 69*, 365–370.

Horton, A. L., Johnson, B. L., Roundy, L. M., & Williams, D. (Eds.) (1989). *The incest perpetrator: A family member no one wants to treat.* Newbury Park, CA: Sage.

Howing, P. T., Wodarski, J. S., Gaudin, J. M., & Kurtz, P. D. (1989). Effective interventions to ameliorate the incidence of child maltreatment: The empirical base. *Social Work, 34*, 330–338.

Hudson, W. (1992). *Walmyr Assessment Scales.* Tempe, AZ: Walmyr.

Hudson, W., & Ricketts, W. A. (1980). A strategy for the measurement of homophobia. *Journal of Homosexuality, 5*, 357–371.

Hull, G., Jr. (1982). Child welfare services to Native Americans. *Social Casework, 63*, 340–47.

Hunt, G., & Paschall, N. (1984). *Volunteers forming effective citizen groups.* Lanham, MD: University Press of America.

Hunter, M. (1990). *The sexually abused male: Vol. 2. Application of treatment strategies.* Lexington, MA: Lexington Books.

Hurley, D. J. (1984). Resistance and work in adolescent groups. *Social Work with Groups, 1*, 71-81.

Hurst, C. E. (1992). *Social inequality: Forms, causes and consequences.* Boston: Allyn & Bacon.

Hurvitz, N. (1975). Interactions hypothesis in marriage counseling. In A. Gurman & D. Rice (Eds.), *Couples in conflict* (pp. 225–240). New York: Jason Aronson.

Hutchings, N. (1988). *The violent family: Victimization of women, children and elders.* New York: Human Sciences Press.

Hutchinson, E. D. (1987). Use of authority in direct social work practice with mandated clients. *Social Service Review, 61*, 581–598.

Hutchinson, J., Lloyd, J., Landsman, M.J., Nelson, K. & Bryce, M. (1983). *Family-centered social services: A model for child welfare agencies.* Oakdale, Iowa: The National Resource Center on Family Based Services, The University of Iowa.

Hutchinson, W., Searight, P., & Stretch, J. (1986). Multi-dimensional networking: A response to the needs of homeless families. *Social Work, 31*, 427–430.

Hystad, N. (1989). *The Alcohol Use Profile.* Two Harbors, MN: Chemical Dependency Publications.

Ingersoll, S. L., & Patton, S. O. (1990). *Treating perpetrators of sexual abuse.* Lexington, MA: Lexington Books.

Ivanoff, A., Blythe, B. J., & Briar, S. (1987). The empirical clinical practice debate. *Social Casework, 68*, 290–298.

Ivanoff, A. M., Blythe, B. J., & Tripodi T. (1994). *Involuntary clients in social work practice: A research-based approach.* New York: Aldine de Gruyter.

Jacob, T., Ritchey, D., Cvitkovic, J., & Blane, H. (1981). Communication styles of alcoholic and nonalcoholic families when drinking and not drinking. *Journal of Studies on Alcohol, 42*, 466–482.

Jacobson, E. (1929). *Progressive relaxation.* Chicago: University of Chicago Press.

Jacobson, N. (1978). A stimulus control model of change in behavioral couples' therapy: Implications for contingency contracting. *Journal of Marriage and Family Counseling, 4*, 29–35.

Jacobson, N., & Margolin, G. (1979). *Marital therapy.* New York: Brunner/Mazel.

Jacobson, N., Schmaling, K., & Holtzworth-Munroe, A. (1987). Component analysis of behavioral marital therapy: 2-year follow-up and prediction of relapse. *Journal of Marital and Family Therapy, 13*(2), 187–195.

Jaffe, P., Wolfe, D., & Wilson, S. K. (1990). *Children of battered women.* Newbury Park, CA: Sage.

James, B. (1989). *Treating traumatized children: New insights and creative interventions.* Lexington, MA: Lexington Books.

James, K., & MacKinnon, L. (1990). The "incestuous

family" revisited: A critical analysis of family therapy myths. *Journal of Marital and Family Therapy, 16* (1), 71–88.

James, P. (1991). Effects of a communication training component added to an emotionally focused couples therapy. *Journal of Marital and Family Therapy, 17* (3), 263–275.

Janis, I., & Mann, L. (1977). *Decision making: A psychosocial analysis of conflict, choice, and commitment.* New York: Free Press.

Jason, L. A., & Burrows, B. (1983). Transition training for high school seniors. *Cognitive Therapy and Research, 7,* 79–92.

Jayaratne, S., & Levy, R. (1979). *Empirical clinical practice.* New York: Columbia University Press.

Jefferson, C. (1978). Some notes on the use of family sculpture in therapy. *Family Process, 17,* 69–75.

Jenkins, S. (1981). *The ethnic dilemma in social services.* New York: Free Press.

Jennings, H. (1950). *Leadership and isolation.* New York: Longmans Green.

Johnson, A. K., & Kreuger, L. W. (1989). Towards a better understanding of homeless women. *Social Work, 34* (6), 537–540.

Johnson, P., & Rubin, A. (1983). Case management in mental health: A social work domain. *Social Work, 28,* 49–55.

Jones, L. (1990). Unemployment and child abuse. *Families in Society, 17* (10), 579–586.

Jones, R. (1983). Increasing staff sensitivity to the black client. *Social Casework, 64,* 419–425.

Jordan, C., & Franklin, C. (1995). *Clinical assessment for social workers.* Chicago: Lyceum Books.

Joseph, M., & Conrad, A. (1980). A parish neighborhood model for social work practice. *Social Casework, 61,* 423–432.

Joyce, K., Diffenbacher, G., Greene, J., & Sorakin, Y. (1983). Internal and external barriers to obtaining prenatal care. *Social Work and Health Care, 9,* 89–93.

Jung, M. (1976). Characteristics of contrasting Chinatowns: 1. Philadelphia, Pennsylvania. *Social Casework, 57,* 149–154.

Kaduchin, A., & Martin, J. A. (1981). *Child abuse: An interactional event.* New York: Columbia University Press.

Kaduchin, A., & Martin, J. A. (1988). *Child welfare services.* New York: Macmillan.

Kadushin, G., & Kulys, R. (1993). Discharge planning revisited: what do social workers actually do in discharge planning? *Social Work, 38* (6), 713–726.

Kagan, R., & Schlosberg, S. (1989). *Families in perpetual crisis.* New York: Norton.

Kane, R. A., & Kane, R. L. (1981). *Assessing the elderly: A practical guide to measurement.* Lexington, MA: Lexington Books.

Kantor, D., & Lehr, W. (1975). *Inside the family: Toward a theory of family process.* San Francisco: Jossey-Bass.

Kaplan, K. (1992). Linking the developmentally disabled client to needed resources: Adult protective services case management. In B. S. Vourlekis & R. R. Greene (Eds.), *Social work case management.* Hawthorne, NY: Aldine de Gruyter.

Katz, D. (1979). Laboratory training to enhance interviewing skills. In F. Clark, M. Arkava, & Associates (Eds.), *The pursuit of competence in social work* (pp. 205–226). San Francisco: Jossey-Bass.

Katz, L. (1990). Effective permanency planning for children in foster care. *Social Work, 35* (3), 220–226.

Kazdin, A. (1979). Imagery elaboration and self-efficacy in the covert modeling treatment of unassertive behavior. *Journal of Consulting and Clinical Psychology, 47,* 725–733.

Kazdin, A., Esveldt-Dawson, K., French, N. H., & Unis, A. S. (1987). Problem-solving skills training and relationship therapy in the treatment of antisocial child behavior. *Journal of Consulting and Clinical Psychology, 55,* 76–85.

Keefe, T. (1978). The economic context of empathy. *Social Work, 23,* 6, 460–465.

Kelen, J. (1980). *The effects of poetry on elderly nursing home residents.* Unpublished doctoral dissertation, University of Utah, Salt Lake City.

Kelly, J. A., & Lamparski, D. (1985). Outpatient treatment of schizophrenics: Social skills and problem-solving training. In M. Hersen & A. S. Bellock (Eds.), *Handbook of clinical behavior therapy with adults* (pp. 485–506). New York: Plenum Press.

Kelly, J., & Sykes, P. (1989). Helping the helpers: A support group for family members of persons with AIDS. *Social Work, 34* (3), 239–242.

Kennard, W., & Shilman, R. (1979). Group services with the homebound. *Social Work, 24,* 330–332.

Kifer, R., Lewis, M., Green, D., & Phillips, E. (1974). Training predelinquent youths and their parents to negotiate conflict situations. *Journal of Applied Behavior Analysis, 7,* 357–364.

Kilgore, L. C. (1988). Effect of early childhood sexual abuse on self and ego development. *Social Casework, 69* (4), 224–230.

Kinney, J., Haapala, D., & Booth, C. (1991). *Keeping families together: The homebuilders model.* Hawthorne, NY: Aldine de Gruyter.

Kiresuk, T. J. & Garwick, G. (1979). Basic goal attainment procedures. In B. R. Compton & B. Galway (Eds.), *social work processes* (2nd ed., pp. 412–421). Homewood, IL: Dorsey Press.

Kirk, S. A., & Kutchins, H. (1988). Deliberate misdiagnosis in mental health practice. *Social Service Review, 62,* 225–237.

Kissman, K. (1991). Feminist-based social work with single-parent families. *Families in Society, 72* (1), 23–28.

Klein, A. (1970). *Social work through group process.* Albany, NY: School of Social Welfare, State University of New York at Albany.

Klier, J., Fein, E., & Genero, C. (1984). Are written or verbal contracts more effective in family therapy? *Social Work, 29,* 298–299.

Komar, Arne A. (1994). Adolescent school crises: structures, issues and techniques for postventions. *International Journal of Adolescence and Youth 5* (1/2), 35–46.

Kopp, J. (1989). Self-observation: An empowerment strategy in assessment. *Social Casework, 70* (5), 276–284.

Koroloff, N. M., & Anderson, S. C. (1989). Alcohol-free living centers: Hope for homeless alcoholics. *Social Work, 34* (6), 497–504.

Koss, M. P., & Harvey, M. R. (1991). *The rape victim: Clinical and community interventions* (2nd ed.). Newbury Park, CA: Sage.

Kratochvil, M. S., & Devereux, S. A. (1988). Counseling needs of parents of handicapped children. *Social Casework, 69* (7), 420–426.

Krona, D. (1980). Parents as treatment partners in residential care. *Child Welfare, 59,* 91–96.

Kruger, L., Moore, D., Schmidt, P., & Wiens, R. (1979). Group work with abusive parents. *Social Work, 24,* 337–338.

Kuhn, D. R. (1990). The normative crises of families confronting dementia. *Families in Society, 71* (8), 451–459.

Kumabe, K., Nishida, C., & Hepworth, D. (1985). *Bridging ethnocultural diversity in social work and health.* Honolulu: University of Hawaii Press.

Kurtz, P. D., Jarvis, S. V., & Kurtz, G. L. (1991). Problems of homeless youths: Empirical findings and human services issues. *Social Work, 36* (4), 309–314.

Kutchins, H., & Kirk, S. A. (1988). The business of diagnosis: DSM-III and clinical social work. *Social Work, 33,* 215–220.

Kutchins, H., & Kirk, S. (1995). Should DSM be the basis for teaching social work practice? No! *Journal of Social Work Education, 31* (2), 159–165.

Kutchins, H., & Kutchins, S. (1978). Advocacy in social work. In G. Weber & G. McCall (Eds.), *Social scientists as advocates* (pp. 13–48). Beverly Hills, CA: Sage.

Kutza, E. A., & Keigher, S. M. (1991). The elderly "new homeless": An emerging population at risk. *Social Work, 36* (4), 288–293.

Laing, R. (1965). Mystification, confusion, and conflict. In I. Boszormenyi-Nagy & J. Framo (Eds.), *Intensive family therapy: Theoretical and practical aspects.* New York: Harper & Row.

Lake, R., Jr. (1983). Shamanism in Northwestern California: A female perspective on sickness, healing and health. *White Cloud Journal of American Indian Mental Health, 3,* 31–42.

Lam, D. H., Brewin, C. R., Woods, R. T., & Bebbington, P. E. (1987). Cognition and social adversity in the depressed elderly. *Journal of Abnormal Psychology, 96,* 23–26.

Lamaze, F. (1958). *Painless childbirth: Psychoprophylactic method.* London: Burke.

Lamb, H. (1982). *Treating the long-term mentally ill.* San Francisco: Jossey-Bass.

Lamb, S. (1986). Treating sexually abused children: Issues of blame and responsibility. *American Journal of Orthopsychiatry, 56,* 303–307.

Land, H. (1988). The impact of licensing on social work practice: Values, ethics and choices. *Journal of Independent Social Work, 2* (4), 87–96.

Land, H., & Harangody, G. (1990). A support group for partners of persons with AIDS. *Families in Society, 71* (8), 471–481.

Lane, F. E. (1986). Utilizing physician empathy with violent patients. *American Journal of Psychotherapy, 40,* 448–456.

Lang, N. (1972). A broad range model of practice in the social work group. *Social Service Review, 46,* 76–89.

Lange, A., & Jakubowski, P. (1976). *Responsible assertive behavior.* Champaign, IL: Research Press.

Langley, P. A. (1991). Family violence: Toward a family-oriented public policy. *Families in Society, 72* (9), 574–576.

Lantz, J. (1978). Cognitive theory and social casework. *Social Work, 23,* 361–366.

Larsen, J. (1975). *A comparative study of traditional and competency-based methods of teaching interpersonal skills in social work education.* Unpublished doctoral dissertation, University of Utah, Salt Lake City.

Larsen, J. (1980). Accelerating group development and productivity: An effective leader approach. *Social Work with Groups, 3,* 25–39.

Larsen, J. (1982). Remedying dysfunctional marital communication. *Social Casework, 63,* 15–23.

Larsen, J. (1991). *I'm a day late and a dollar short and it's okay: A woman's survival guide for the 90's.* Salt Lake City: Deseret Books.

Larsen, J., & Hepworth, D. (1978). Skill development through competency-based education. *Journal of Education for Social Work, 14,* 73–81.

Larsen, J., & Mitchell, C. (1980). Task-centered, strength-oriented group work with delinquents. *Social Casework, 61,* 154–163.

Leader, A. (1958). The problem of resistance in social work. *Social Work, 3,* 19–23.

Lebow, G., & Kane, B. (1992). Assessment: Private case management with the elderly. In B. S. Vourlekis & R. R. Greene (Eds.), *Social work case management*. Hawthorne, NY: Aldine de Gruyter.

Lechnyr, R. (1980a). Hypnosis as an adjunct in crisis intervention. *Behavioral Medicine, 7*, 41–44.

Lechnyr, R. (1980b). Tuning-in patients: Biofeedback instrumentation in clinical practice. *Behavioral Medicine, 7*, 13–23.

LeCroy, C. W. (Ed.). (1983). *Social skills training for children and youth*. New York: Haworth Press.

LeCroy, C. W. (1987). Teaching children social skills: A game format. *Social Work, 32*, 440–442.

LeCroy, C. W., & Rose, S. (1986). Evaluation of preventive interventions for enhancing social competence in adolescents. *Social Work Research and Abstracts, 22*, 8–16.

Lederer, W., & Jackson, D. (1968). *The mirages of marriage*. New York: Norton.

Lee, E. (1989). Assessment and treatment of Chinese-American immigrant families. In G. Saba, B. Karrer, & K. Hardy (Eds.), *Minorities and family therapy* (pp. 99–120). New York: Hawthorne Press.

Lee, K., & McGill, C. (1991). Confronting the lack of resources for patients with AIDS dementia complex. *Social Work, 36* (6), 473–475.

Lehrer, P. (1982). How to relax and how not to relax: A reevaluation of the work of Jacobson. *Behaviour Research and Therapy, 20*, 417–425.

Lemmon, J. A. (1985). *Family mediation practice*. New York: Free Press.

Lester, L. (1982). The special needs of the female alcoholic. *Social Casework, 63*, 451–456.

Levick, K. (1981). Privileged communication: Does it really exist? *Social Casework, 62*, 235–239.

Levine, B. (1967). *Fundamentals of group treatment*. Chicago: Whitehall.

Levinson, D. (1989). *Family violence in cross-cultural perspective*. Newbury Park, CA: Sage.

Levinson, H. (1973). Use and misuse of groups. *Social Work, 18*, 66–73.

Levinson, H. (1977). Termination of psychotherapy: Some salient issues. *Social Casework, 58*, 480–489.

Levy, C. (1973). The value base of social work. *Journal of Education for Social Work, 9*, 34–42.

Levy, C. (1979). *Values and ethics for social work practice*. Washington, DC: National Association of Social Workers.

Levy, E. F. (1992). Strengthening the coping resources of lesbian families. *Families in Society, 73* (1), 23–31.

Levy, L. (1963). *Psychological interpretation*. New York: Holt, Rinehart & Winston.

Lewis, B. (1985). The Wife Abuse Inventory: A screening device for the identification of abused women. *Social Work, 30* (1), 32–35.

Lewis, E. (1991). Social change and citizen action: A philosophical exploration for modern social group work. *Social Work with Groups 14*, 3–4, 23–34.

Lewis, J., Beavers, W., Gossett, J., & Phillips, V. (1976). *No single thread: Psychological health in family systems*. New York: Brunner/Mazel.

Lewis, K. (1980). Children of lesbians: Their point of view. *Social Work, 25*, 198–203.

Lewis, R., & Ho, M. (1975). Social work with Native Americans. *Social Work, 20*, 379–382.

Lie, G-Y, & Inman, A. (1991). The use of anatomical dolls as assessment and evidentiary tools. *Social Work, 36* (5), 396–399.

Lieberman, M. (1980). Group methods. In F. Kanfer & A. Goldstein (Eds.), *Helping people change* (pp. 470–536). New York: Pergamon Press.

Lieberman, M., & Borman, L. (Eds.) (1979). *Self-help groups for coping with crisis*. San Francisco, CA: Jossey-Bass.

Lieberman, M., & Videka-Sherman, L. (1986). The impact of self-help groups on the mental health of widows and widowers. *American Journal of Orthopsychiatry, 56*, 435–449.

Lieberman, M., Yalom, I., & Miles, M. (1973). *Encounter groups: First facts*. New York: Basic Books.

Lister, L. (1987). Contemporary direct practice roles. *Social Work, 32*, 384–391.

Lockhart, L. L., & Wodarski, J. S. (1989). Facing the unknown: Children and adolescents with AIDS. *Social Work, 34* (3), 215–221.

Long, K. A. (1986). Cultural considerations in the assessment and treatment of intrafamilial abuse. *American Journal of Orthopsychiatry, 56*, 131–136.

Longres, J. F. Toward a status model of ethnic sensitive practice. *Journal of Mult-Cultural Social Work, 1* (1), 41–56.

Lopez, D., & Getzel, G. S. (1987). Strategies for volunteers caring for persons with AIDS. *Social Casework, 68*, 47–53.

Lorion, R. (1978). Research on psychotherapy and behavior change with the disadvantaged. In S. Garfield & A. Bergin (Eds.), *Handbook of psychotherapy and behavior change* (pp. 903–938). New York: Wiley.

Lott, J. (1976). Migration of a mentality: The Filipino community. *Social Casework, 3*, 165–172.

Lovell, M. L., & Richey, C. A. (1991). Implementing agency-based social-support skill training. *Families in Society, 72* (9), 563–572.

Low, S. (1984). The cultural basis of health, illness, and disease. *Social Work in Health Care, 9*, 13–23.

Luborsky, L., & Spence, D. (1978). Quantitative research on psychoanalytic therapy. In S. Garfield & A. Bergin (Eds.), *Handbook of psychotherapy and behavior change* (pp. 331–368). New York: Wiley.

Lukton, R. (1982). Myths and realities of crisis intervention. *Social Casework, 63,* 275–285.

Lum, D. (1982). Toward a framework for social work practice with minorities. *Social Work, 27,* 244–249.

Lum, D. (1992). *Social work practice and people of color: A process-stage approach* (2nd ed.). Pacific Grove, CA: Brooks/Cole.

MacFarlane, K., Waterman, J., et al. (1986). *Sexual abuse of young children: Evaluation and treatment.* New York: Guilford Press.

Mackelprang, R., & Hepworth, D. H. (1987). Ecological factors in rehabilitation of patients with severe spinal cord injuries. *Social Work in Health Care, 13,* 23–38.

Mahler, C. (1969). *Group counseling in the schools.* Boston: Houghton Mifflin.

Mahoney, M. J. (1974). *Cognition and behavior modification.* Cambridge, MA: Ballinger.

Malchiodi, C. (1990). *Art therapy with children from violent homes.* New York: Brunner/Mazel.

Malekoff, A., Johnson, H., & Klappersack, B. (1991). Parent-professional collaboration on behalf of children with disabilities. *Families in Society, 72* (7), 416–424.

Maletzky, B. M., & McGovern, K. B. (1990). *Treating the sexual offender.* Newbury Park, CA: Sage.

Maluccio, A. (1979). Perspectives of social workers and clients on treatment outcome. *Social Casework, 60,* 394–401.

Maluccio, A. N. (1990). Family preservation: an overview. in A. L. Sallee & J. C. Lloyd, (Eds.), *Family preservation: Papers from the Institute for Social Work Educators.* Riverdale, IL: The National Association for Family-Based Services.

Maluccio, A. N., Fein, E., & Inger, D. (1995). Family reunification: Research findings, issues and directions. *Child Welfare, 73,* 489–504

Maluccio, A. N., Fein, E., & Olmstead, K. (1986). *Permanency planning for children: Concepts and methods.* New York: Tavistock.

Mandell, J. G., & Damon, L. (1989). *Group treatment of sexually abused children.* New York: Guilford Press.

Mann, B., & Murphy, K. (1975). Timing of self-disclosure, reciprocity of self-disclosure, and reactions to an initial interview. *Journal of Counseling Psychology, 22,* 304–308.

Marburg, G. (1983). Mental health and Native Americans: Responding to the biopsychosocial model. *White Cloud Journal of American Indian Mental Health, 3,* 43–51.

Marckworth, P. (1990). Practice skills and knowledge: Views from the field. In A. L. Sallee & J. C. Lloyd (Eds.), *Family preservation: Papers from the Institute for Social Work Educators* (pp. 29–31). Riverdale, IL: The National Association for Family-Based Services.

Maretzki, T., & McDermott, J. (1980). The Caucasians. In J. McDermott, W. Tseng, & T. Maretzki (Eds.), *People and cultures of Hawaii* (pp. 23–52). Honolulu: University of Hawaii Press.

Marks, I. (1975). Behavioral treatments of phobic and obsessive-compulsive disorders: A critical appraisal. In M. Hersen, R. Eisler, & P. Miller (Eds.), *Progress in behavior modification* (pp. 65–158). Newbury Park, CA: Sage.

Marlatt, G. A. (1988). Matching clients to treatment: Treatment models and stages of change. In D. M. Donovan & G. A. Marlatt (Eds.), *Assessment of addictive behaviors* (pp. 474–483). New York: Guilford Press.

Marlatt, G. A., & Gordon, J. R. (1985). *Relapse prevention: Maintenance strategies in the treatment of addictive behaviors.* New York: Guilford Press.

Marlatt, G. A., & Miller, W. R. (1984). *Comprehensive Drinking Profile.* Odessa, FL: Psychological Assessment Resources.

Marshall, N. L. (1991). The changing lives of young children: Infant child care as a normative experience. *Families in Society, 72* (8), 496–501.

Marshall, N. L., & Marx, F. (1991). The affordability of child care for the working poor. *Families in Society, 72* (4), 202–211.

Marshall, T. K., & Mazie, A. S. (1987). A cognitive approach to treating depression. *Social Casework, 68,* 540–545.

Mass, A. (1976). Asians as individuals: The Japanese community. *Social Casework, 57,* 160–164.

Masserman, J. (1965). Historical-comparative and experimental roots of short-term therapy. In L. Wolberg (Ed.), *Short-term psychotherapy* (pp. 44–66). New York: Grune & Stratton.

Masson, H., & O'Byrne, P. (1984). *Applying family therapy.* New York: Pergamon Press.

Mattaini, M. A. & Kirk, S. A. (1991). Assessing assessment in social work. *Social Work, 36,* 3, 260–266.

May, P., Hymbaugh, K., Aase, J., & Samet, J. (1983). The epidemiology of fetal alcohol syndrome among American Indians of the Southwest. *Social Biology, 30,* 374–387.

Mayadas, N. (1983). Psycho-social welfare of refugees: An expanding service area for social work. *International Social Work, 26,* 47–55.

Mayadas, N., & O'Brien, D. (1976). Teaching casework skills in the laboratory: Methods and techniques. In *Teaching for competence in the delivery of direct services* (pp. 72–82). New York: Council on Social Work Education.

Mayer, J., & Timms, N. (1969). Clash in perspective between worker and client. *Social Casework, 50,* 32–40.

McCarty, P., & Betz, N. (1978). Differential effects of self-disclosing versus self-involving counselor statements. *Journal of Counseling Psychology, 25,* 251–256.

McCown, W., & Johnson, J. (1992). *Therapy with resistant families: A consultation-crisis model.* Binghamton, NY: Haworth Press.

McCreath, J. (1984). The new generation of chronic psychiatric patients. *Social Work, 29,* 436–441.

McDermott, C. J. (1989). Empowering the elderly nursing home resident: The resident rights campaign. *Social Work, 34*(2), 155–157.

McDonald, T., & Marks, J. (1991). A review of risk factors assessed in child protective services. *Social Service Review, 65*(1), 112–132.

McGoldrick, M. (1982a). Ethnicity and family therapy. In M. McGoldrick, J. Pearce, J. Giordano (Eds.), *Ethnicity and family therapy* (pp. 3–30). New York: Guilford Press.

McGoldrick, M. (1982b). Irish families. In M. McGoldrick, J. Pearce, & J. Giordano (Eds.), *Ethnicity and family therapy* (pp. 310–339). New York: Guilford Press.

McGoldrick, M., & Gerson, R. (1985). *Genograms in family assessment.* New York: Norton.

McIntyre, E.L.G. (1986). Social networks: Potential for practice. *Social Work, 31,* 421–426.

McNeely, R., & Badami, M. (1984). Interracial communication in school social work. *Social Work, 29,* 22–25.

McPhatter, A. (1991). Assessment revisited: A comprehensive approach to understanding family dynamics. *Families in Society, 72,* 11–21.

Meenaghan, T. M. (1987). Macro practice: current trends and issues. In *Encyclopedia of social work* (18th ed., pp. 82–89). Silver Spring, MD: National Association of Social Workers, pp. 82–89.

Meichenbaum, D. (1977). *Cognitive-behavior-modification.* New York: Plenum Press.

Meichenbaum, D., & Turk, D. (1976). The cognitive-behavioral management of anxiety, anger, and pain. In P. Davison (Ed.), *The cognitive-behavioral management of anxiety, anger, and pain* (pp. 1–34). New York: Brunner/Mazel.

Meichenbaum, D. C., & Turk, D. C. (1987). *Facilitating treatment adherence: A practitioner's guidebook.* New York: Plenum.

Mercer, S., & Kane, R. (1979). Helplessness and hopelessness among the institutionalized aged. *Health and Social Work, 4,* 90–116.

Merton, R. (1957). *Social theory and social structure.* Glencoe, IL: Free Press.

Meyer, C. (1970). *Social work practice: A response to the urban crisis.* New York: Free Press.

Meyer, C. (Ed.). (1983). *Clinical social work in the eco-systems perspective.* New York: Columbia University Press.

Meyer, C. (1990, April 11). *Can social work keep up with the changing family?* [Monograph]. The fifth annual Robert J. O'Leary Memorial Lecture. Columbus, Ohio: The Ohio State University College of Social Work, 1–24.

Milgram, D., & Rubin, J. S. (1992). Resisting resistance: Involuntary substance abuse group therapy. *Social Work with Groups, 15*(1), 95–110.

Miller, J. L., & Whittaker, J. K. (1988). Social services and social support: Blended programs for families at risk of child maltreatment. *Child Welfare, 67,* 161–174.

Miller, K., Fein, E., Howe, G., Gaudio, C., & Bishop, G. (1984). Time-limited, goal-focused parent aide service. *Social Casework, 65,* 472–477.

Miller, W. R. (1983). Motivational interviewing with problem drinkers. *Behavioral Psychology, 11,* 147–172.

Mills, C., & Ota, H. (1989). Homeless women with minor children in the Detroit metropolitan area. *Social Work, 34*(6), 485–489.

Milne, C., & Dowd, E. (1983). Effect of interpretation style and counselor social influence. *Journal of Counseling Psychology, 30,* 603–606.

Milner, J. S., Halsey, L. B., & Fultz, J. (1995). Empathetic responsiveness and effective reactivity to infant stimuli in high-risk and low-risk for physical child-abuse mothers. *Child Abuse and Neglect, 19*(6), 767–780.

Milofsky, C. (1980). Serving the needs of disabled clients: A task-structured approach. *Social Work, 25,* 149–152.

Mindel, C. H., Habenstein, R. H., & Wright, R. (1988). *Ethnic families in America.* New York: Elsevier.

Minuchin, S. (1974). *Families and family therapy.* Cambridge, MA: Harvard University Press.

Mitchell, M. (1986). Utilizing volunteers to enhance informal social networks. *Social Casework, 67,* 290–298.

Mizio, E. (1974). Impact of external systems on the Puerto Rican family. *Social Casework, 55,* 76–83.

Montero, D., & Dieppa, I. (1982). Resettling Vietnamese refugees: The service agency's role. *Social Work, 27,* 74–81.

Montiel, M. (1973). The Chicano family: A review of research. *Social Work, 18,* 22–29.

Moore, C. (1986). *The mediation process.* San Francisco: Jossey-Bass.

Moore, J. (1983). The experience of sponsoring a parents anonymous group. *Social Casework, 64,* 585–592.

Moore, S. T. (1990). A social work practice model of case management: The case management grid. *Social Work, 35*(5), 444–448.

Morgan, R. (1961). Is it scientific to be optimistic? *Social Work, 6,* 12–21.

Moroney, R. M. (1987). Social planning. *Encyclopedia of social work, II* (pp. 593–602). Silver Spring, MD: National Association of Social Workers.

Moroz, K., & Allen-Meares, P. (1991). Assessing adolescent parents and their infants: Individualized family service planning. *Families in Society, 72* (8), 461–468.

Morrison, B. (1983). Physical health and the minority aged. In R. McNeely & J. Colen (Eds.), *Aging in minority groups.* Beverly Hills, CA: Sage.

Morrissette, P., & McIntyre. S. (1989). Homeless young people in residential care. *Social Casework, 70* (10), 603–610.

Moxley, D. P. (1989). *The practice of case management.* Newbury Park, CA: Sage.

Moynihan, R., Christ, G., & Silver, L. G. (1988). AIDS and terminal illness. *Social Casework, 69,* 380–387.

Mudrick, N. R. (1991). An underdeveloped role for occupational social work: Facilitating the employment of people with disabilities. *Social Work, 36* (6), 490–495.

Mulinski, P. (1989). Dual diagnosis in alcoholic clients: Clinical implications. *Social Casework, 70* (6), 333–339.

Mullen, E. J., & Dumpson, J. R. (Eds.). (1972). *Evaluation of social intervention.* San Francisco: Jossey-Bass.

Napier, A. (1991). Heroism, men and marriage. *Journal of Marital and Family Therapy, 17* (1), 9–16.

National Association of Social Workers. (1973). *Standards for social service manpower.* New York: National Association of Social Workers.

National Association of Social Workers. (1977). 1977 Delegate assembly policy statement—Volunteers and the social service systems. *NASW News, 22,* 39.

National Association of Social Workers. (1980). NASW code of ethics. *NASW News, 25,* 24–25.

National Association of Social Workers. (1981). NASW working statement on the purpose of social work. *Social Work, 26,* 6.

National Association of Social Workers. (1991). *NASW News, 36* (10), 13.

National Association of Social Workers. (1995, September). *Revised code of ethics* (Draft). Washington, DC.

National Committee for Prevention of Child Abuse. (1990, March). *Child abuse fatalities continue to rise: The results of the 1989 annual fifty state survey.* Chicago: Author.

Nelson, J. (1975). Dealing with resistance in social work practice. *Social Casework, 56,* 587–592.

Nelson, M. (1991). Empowerment of incest survivors: Speaking out. *Families in Society, 72* (10), 618–624.

Nelson, T., & Trepper, T. S. (1992). *101 interventions in family therapy.* Binghamton, NY: Haworth Press.

Nelson-Zlupko, L., Kauffman, E. & Dore, M. M. (1995). Gender differences in drug addiction and treatment: implications for social work intervention with substance abusing women. *Social Work, 40,* 1, 45–54.

Neumann, D. (1989). *Divorce mediation: How to cut the cost.* New York: Holt.

New York Victim Services Agency. (1982). *Experiences of women with services for abused spouses in New York City.* New York: Author.

Nezu, A. M. (1985). Differences in psychological distress between effective and ineffective problem solvers. *Journal of Counseling Psychology, 32,* 135–138.

Nezu, A. M., & Carnevale, G. J. (1987). Interpersonal problem solving and coping reactions of Vietnam veterans with posttraumatic stress syndrome. *Journal of Abnormal Psychology, 96,* 155–157.

Nicholson, B., & Matross, G. (1989). Facing reduced decision-making capacity in health care: Methods for maintaining client self-determination. *Social Work, 34* (3), 234–238.

Norton, D. G. (1978). *The dual perspective: Inclusion of ethnic minority content in the social work curriculum.* New York: Council on Social Work Education.

Novaco, R. (1975). *Anger control: The development and evaluation of an experimental treatment.* Lexington, MA: Heath.

Nugent, W. (1991). An experimental and qualitative analysis of a cognitive-behavioral intervention for anger. *Social Work Research and Abstracts, 27* (3), 3–8.

Nugent, W. (1992). The affective impact of a clinical social worker's interviewing style: A series of single-case experiments. *Research on Social Work Practice, 2* (1), 6–27.

Nulman, E. (1983). Family therapy and advocacy: Directions for the future. *Social Work, 28,* 19–22.

Nurius, P. S., & Hudson, W. W. (1988). Computer-based practice: Future dream or current technology. *Social Work, 33,* 357–362.

Nurius, P. S., & Hudson, W. (1993). *Computer assisted practice: Theory, methods, and software.* Belmont, CA: Wadsworth.

O'Connell B. (1978). From service to advocacy to empowerment. *Social Casework, 59,* 195–202.

Office of Policy Development (1988). *Report to the president on the family.* Washington, DC: The White House.

O'Hare, T. (1991). Integrating research and practice: A framework for implementation. *Social Work, 36* (3), 220–223.

O'Leary, K., Shore, M., & Wieder, S. (1984). Contacting pregnant adolescents: Are we missing cues? *Social Casework, 65,* 297–306.

Oritt, E., Paul, S., & Behrman, J. (1985). The perceived Support Network Inventory. *American Journal of Community Psychology, 13* (5), 565–582.

Orlinsky, D., & Howard, K. (1978). The relationship of process to outcome in psychotherapy. In S. Garfield &

A. Bergin (Eds.), *Handbook of psychotherapy and behavior change* (pp. 283–329). New York: Wiley.

Orten, J. D., & Rich, L. L. (1988). A model for assessment of incestuous families. *Social Casework, 69* (10), 611–619.

Palmer, B., & Pablo, S. (1978). Community development possibilities for effective Indian reservation child abuse and neglect efforts. In M. Lauderdale, R. Anderson, & S. Cramer (Eds.), *Child abuse and neglect: Issues on innovation and implementation* (pp. 98–116). Washington, DC: U.S. Department of Health, Education and Welfare.

Panitch, A. (1974). Advocacy in practice. *Social Work, 19,* 326–332.

Panzer, B., Wiesner, L., & Dickson, W. (1978). Program for developmentally disabled children. *Social Work, 23,* 406–411.

Papp, P. (1976). Family choreography. In P. Guerin (Ed.), *Family therapy* (pp. 465–479). New York: Gardner Press.

Paquin, M. (1981). Self-monitoring of marital communication in family therapy. *Social Casework, 62,* 267–272.

Parad, H., & Parad, L. (1968). A study of crisis-oriented planned short-term treatment. *Social Casework, 49,* 346–355.

Pardeck, J. T. (1990). Bibliotherapy with abused children. *Families in Society, 71* (4), 229–235.

Parlee, M. (1979). Conversational politics. *Psychology Today, 12,* 48–56.

Parloff, M., Waskow, I., & Wolfe, B. (1978). Research on therapist variables in relation to process and outcome. In S. Garfield & A. Bergin (Eds.), *Handbook of psychotherapy and behavior change* (pp. 233–282). New York: Wiley.

Parsonnet, L., & O'Hare, J. (1990). A group orientation program for families of newly admitted cancer patients. *Social Work, 35* (1), 37–40.

Parsons, R. J. (1991). The mediator role in social work practice. *Social Work, 36* (6), 483–487.

Parsons, R. J., & Cox, E. O. (1989). Family mediation in elder caregiving decisions: An empowerment intervention. *Social Work, 34* (2), 122–126.

Patten, S. B., Gatz, Y. K., Jones, B., & Thomas, D. L. (1989). Posttraumatic stress disorder and the treatment of sexual abuse. *Social Work, 34* (3), 197–202.

Patterson, D., & Hepworth, D. (1989). *A comparative study of multiple personality disordered and borderline personality disordered inpatients.* Unpublished study. Salt Lake City: University of Utah Graduate School of Social Work.

Patterson, S. L., Germain, C. B., Brennan, E. M., & Memmott, J. (1988). Effectiveness of rural natural helpers. *Social Casework, 69,* 272–279.

Patti, R. J. (1974). Organizational resistance and change. *Social Service Review, 48,* 367–383.

Patton, M. Q. (1991). *Family sexual abuse: Frontline research and evaluation.* Newbury Park, CA: Sage.

Pearlman, M., & Edwards, M. (1982). Enabling in the eighties: The client advocacy group. *Social Casework, 63,* 532–539.

Penka, C. E., & Kirk, S. (1991). Practitioner involvement in clinical evaluation. *Social Work, 36* (6), 513–518.

Perlman, G. (1988). Mastering the law of privileged communication: A guide for social workers. *Social Work, 33* (5), 425–429.

Perlman, H. (1957). *Social casework: A problem-solving process.* Chicago: University of Chicago Press.

Perlman, H. (1968). *Persona: Social role and responsibility.* Chicago: University of Chicago Press.

Peterson, C., Patrick, S., & Rissmeyer, D. (1990). Social work's contribution to psychosocial rehabilitation. *Social Work, 35* (5), 468–472.

Phillips, M. H., DeChillo, N., Kronenfeld, D., & Middleton-Jeter, V. (1988). Homeless families: Services make a difference. *Social Casework, 69,* 48–53.

Pilisuk, M., & Parks, S. H. (1988). Caregiving: Where families need help. *Social Work, 33* (5), 436–440.

Pillemer, K. A., & Wolf, R. S. (Eds.). (1986). *Elder abuse: Conflict in the family.* Westport, CT: Auburn House.

Pincus, A., & Minahan, A. (1973). *Social work practice: Model and method.* Itasca, IL: Peacock.

Pinderhughes, E. (1982). Afro-American families and the victim system. In M. McGoldrick, J. Pearce, & J. Giordano (Eds.), *Ethnicity and family therapy* (pp. 108–122). New York: Guilford Press.

Pinderhughes, E. (1983). Empowerment for our clients and ourselves. *Social Casework, 64,* 331–338.

Pines, B., Krieger, R., & Maluccio, A. (1993). *Together again: Family reunification in foster care.* Washington, DC: Child Welfare League of America.

Pirog-Good, M., & Stets, J. (Eds.). (1989). *Violence in dating relationships: Emerging social issues.* Westport, CT: Praeger.

Pittman, F. (1987). *Turning points: Treating families.* New York: Norton.

Pittman, F. (1991). The secret passions of men. *Journal of Marital and Family Therapy, 17* (1), 17–23.

Polansky, N. A., Ammons, P. W., & Gaudin, J. M., Jr. (1985). Loneliness and isolation in child neglect. *Social Casework, 66,* 38–47.

Ponce, D. (1980). The Filipinos: The Philippine background. In J. McDermott, Jr., W. Tseng, & T. Maretski (Eds.), *People and cultures of Hawaii* (pp. 155–163). Honolulu: University of Hawaii Press.

Pope, K. S., Keith-Spiegel, P., & Tabachnick, B. G. (1986).

Sexual attraction to clients. *American Psychologist, 41,* 147–158.

Potter-Efron, R., & Potter-Efron, P. (1992). *Anger, alcoholism and addiction: Treating anger in a chemical dependency setting.* New York: Norton.

Prager, E. (1980). Evaluation in mental health: Enter the consumer. *Social Work Research and Abstracts, 16,* 5–10.

Presley, J. H. (1987). The clinical dropout: A view from the client's perspective. *Social Casework, 68,* 603–608.

Pridgen, N. H. (1991). Community-based counseling services for deaf and hard-of-hearing individuals. *Families in Society, 72* (3), 174–176.

Proctor, E. (1990). Evaluating clinical practice: Issues of purpose and design. *Social Work Research and Abstracts, 26* (1), 32–40.

Proctor, E. K., & and Davis, L. E. (1994). The challenge of racial difference: skills for clinical practice. *Social Work, 39* (3), 314–323.

Prunty, H., Singer, T., & Thomas, L. (1977). Confronting racism in inner-city schools. *Social Work, 22,* 190–194.

Puryear, D. (1979). *Helping people in crisis.* San Francisco: Jossey-Bass.

Queralt, M. (1984). Understanding Cuban immigrants: A cultural perspective. *Social Work, 29,* 115–121.

Quinn, M. J., & Tomita, S. K. (1986). *Elder abuse and neglect.* New York: Springer.

Rabin, C., Blechman, E. A., Kahn, D., & Carel, C. A. (1985). Refocusing from child to marital problems using the Marriage Contract Game. *Journal of Marital and Family Therapy, 11,* 75–85.

Rabin, C., & Zelner, D. (1992). The role of assertiveness in clarifying roles and strengthening job satisfaction of social workers in multi-disciplinary mental health settings. *The British Journal of Social Work, 22,* 1, 17–32.

Raimy, V. (1975). *Misunderstandings of the self.* San Francisco: Jossey-Bass.

Rapoport, L. (1961). The concept of prevention in social work. *Social Work, 6,* 3–12.

Rapp, C. (1982). Effect of the availability of family support services and decisions about child placement. *Social Work Research and Abstracts, 18,* 21–27.

Rapp, C. A., & Chamberlain, R. (1985). Case management services for the chronically mentally ill. *Social Work, 30,* 417–422.

Rauch, J. B. (1988). Social work and the genetics revolution: Genetic services. *Social Work, 33* (5), 389–395.

Rauch, J. B., Sarno, C., & Simpson, S. (1991). Screening for affective disorders. *Families in Society, 72* (10), 602–609.

Reamer, F. (1988). AIDS and ethics: The agenda for social workers. *Social Work, 33* (5), 460–464.

Reamer, F. (1989). *Ethical dilemmas in social service* (2nd ed.). New York: Columbia University Press.

Reamer, F. (1992). *AIDS and ethics.* New York: Columbia University Press.

Red Horse, J., Lewis, R., Feit, M., & Decker, J. (1978). Family behavior of urban American Indians. *Social Casework, 59,* 67–72.

Register of clinical social workers, Vol. 1 (1976). Washington, DC: National Association of Social Workers.

Reid, K. E. (1991). *Social work practice with groups: A clinical perspective.* Pacific Grove, CA: Brooks/Cole.

Reid, W. (1970). Implications of research for the goals of casework. *Smith College Studies in Social Work, 40,* 140–154.

Reid, W. (1975). A test of the task-centered approach. *Social Work, 22,* 3–9.

Reid, W. (1977). Process and outcome in the treatment of family problems. In W. Reid & L. Epstein (Eds.), *Task-centered practice. Self-help groups and human service agencies: How they work together.* Milwaukee: Family Service of America.

Reid, W. (1978). *The task-centered system.* New York: Columbia University Press.

Reid, W. (1985). *Family problem solving.* New York: Columbia University Press.

Reid, W. (1987). Task-centered research. In *Encyclopedia of social work* (Vol. 2, pp. 757–764). Silver Spring, MD: National Association of Social Workers.

Reid, W. J. (1992). *Task strategies.* New York: Columbia University Press.

Reid, W. J. (1994, June). The empirical practice movement. *Social Service Review, 68* (2), 165–184.

Reid, W., & Epstein L. (1972). *Task-centered casework.* New York: Columbia University Press.

Reid, W., & Hanrahan, P. (1982). Recent evaluations of social work: Grounds for optimism. *Social Work, 27,* 328–340.

Reid, W., & Shyne, A. (1969). *Brief and extended casework.* New York: Columbia University Press.

Remine, D., Rice, R. M., & Ross, J. (1984). management as a practice model. *Social Casework, 68,* 466–470.

Reynolds, C., & Fischer, C. (1983). Personal versus professional evaluations of self-disclosing and self-involving counselors. *Journal of Counseling Psychology, 30,* 451–454.

Rhoades, E. R. (Ed.) (1990). *Minority aging: Essential curricula content for selected health and allied health professionals.* Health Resources and Service Administration, Department of Health and Human Services. DHHS Publication No. HRS (P-DU-90-4). Washington, DC: U.S. Government Printing Office.

Rhodes, M. L. (1986). *Ethical dilemmas in social work practice.* London: Routledge & Kegan Paul.

Rhodes, S. (1977). Contract negotiation in the initial stage of casework. *Social Service Review, 51*, 125–140.

Ridley, R. (1984). Clinical treatment of the nondisclosing black client: A therapeutic paradox. *American Psychologist, 39*, 1234–1244.

Roberts, C. S., Severinsen, C., Kuehn, C., Straker, D., & Fritz, C. J. (1992). Obstacles to effective case management with AIDS patients: The clinician's perspective. *Social Work in Health Care, 17* (2), 27–40.

Roberts-DeGennaro, M. (1987). *Developing case.* New York: Columbia University Press.

Robinson, J. B. (1989). Clinical treatment of Black families: Issues and strategies. *Social Work, 34*, 323–29.

Robinson, V. (1930). *A changing psychology in social work.* Chapel Hill: University of North Carolina Press.

Rogers, C. (1957). The necessary and sufficient conditions of therapeutic personality change. *Journal of Consulting Psychology, 22*, 95–103.

Rogler, L. H., Malgady, R. G., Costantino, G., & Blumenthal, R. (1987). What do culturally sensitive mental health services mean? The case of Hispanics. *American Psychologist, 42*, 565–570.

Ronnau, J. P., & Marlow, C. R. (1995). Family preservation: Poverty and the value of diversity. *Families in Society, 74* (9), 538–544.

Rooney, R. H. (1988). Socialization strategies for involuntary clients. *Social Casework, 69*, 131–140.

Rooney, R. H. (1992). *Strategies for work with involuntary clients.* New York: Columbia University Press.

Rose, S. D. (1989). *Working with adults in groups: Integrating cognitive-behavioral and small group strategies.* San Francisco: Jossey-Bass.

Rose, S. M. (Ed.) (1992). *Case management and social work practice.* White Plains, NY: Longman.

Rose, S. M., & Black, B. (1985). *Advocacy and empowerment: Mental health care in the community.* New York: Routledge & Kegan Paul.

Rose, S. M., Peabody, C., & Stratigeas, B. (1991). Responding to hidden abuse: A role for social work in reforming mental health systems. *Social Work, 36* (5), 408–413.

Rosen, A. (1972). The treatment relationship: A conceptualization. *Journal of Clinical Psychology, 38*, 329–337.

Rosen, A., Proctor, E. K., & Livne, S. (1985). Planning and direct practice. *Social Service Review, 59*, 161–177.

Rosen, P., Peterson, L., & Walsh, B. (1980). A community residence for severely disturbed adolescents: A cognitive-behavioral approach. *Child Welfare, 59*, 15–25.

Rosenfeld, J. (1983). The domain and expertise of social work: A conceptualization. *Social Work, 28*, 186–191.

Rosenstein, P. (1978). Family outreach: A program for the prevention of child neglect and abuse. *Child Welfare, 57*, 519–525.

Rosenthal, K. (1988). The inanimate self in adult victims of child abuse and neglect. *Social Casework, 69* (8), 505–510.

Roth, W. (1987). Disabilities: Physical. In *Encyclopedia of social work* (Vol. 1, pp. 434–438). Silver Spring, MD: National Association of Social Workers.

Rothman, J. (1989). Client self-determination: Untangling the knot. *Social Service Review, 59* (4), 598–612.

Rothman, J. (1991). A model of case management: Toward empirically based practice. *Social Work, 36* (6), 521–528.

Rothman, J., Gant, L. M., & Hnat, S. A. (1985). Mexican-American family culture. *Social Service Review, 59*, 197–215.

Rotunno, M., & McGoldrick, M. (1982). Italian families. In M. McGoldrick, J. Pearce, & J. Giordano (Eds.), *Ethnicity and family therapy* (pp. 340–363). New York: Guilford Press.

Rounds, K. A. (1988). AIDS in rural areas: Challenges to providing care. *Social Work, 33*, 257–261.

Rounds, K. A., Galinsky, M. H., & Stevens, L. S. (1991). Linking people with AIDS in rural communities: The telephone group. *Social Work, 36* (1), 13–18.

Rowe, W., & Savage, S. (1988). Sex therapy with female incest survivors. *Social Casework, 69* (5), 265–271.

Royfe, E. (1960). The role of the social worker in a big brother agency. *Social Casework, 41*, 139–144.

Rubenstein, D., & Timmins, J. (1978). Depressive dyadic and triadic relationships. *Journal of Marriage and Family Counseling, 4*, 13–24.

Rubin, A. (1985). Practice effectiveness: More grounds for optimism. *Social Work, 30*, 469–476.

Rubin, B. (1982). Refugee settlement: A unique role for family service. *Social Casework, 63*, 301–304.

Rubin, S. (1978). Parents' group in a psychiatric hospital for children. *Social Work, 23*, 416–417.

Rueveni, U. (1979). *Networking families in crisis.* New York: Human Sciences Press.

Ryan, N., Puig-Antich, J., Ambrosini, P., Rabinovich, H., Robinson, D., Nelson, B., Ivengar, S., & Twomey, J. (1987). The clinical picture of major depression in children and adolescents. *Archives of General Psychiatry, 44* (11), 854–861.

Rzepnicki, T. L. (1991, March). Enhancing the durability of intervention gains: A challenge for the 1990s. *Social Service Review, 65* (1), 92–111.

Saba, G. W., Karrer, B. M., & Hardy, K. (Eds.) (1989). *Minorities and family therapy.* New York: Hawthorne Press.

Sager, C., Brayboy, T., & Waxenburg, B. (1970). *Black ghetto family in therapy: A laboratory experience.* New York: Grove Press.

Sakai, C. E. (1991). Group intervention strategies with domestic abusers. *Families in Society, 72* (9), 536–542.

Saleeby, D. (Ed.) (1992). *The strengths perspective in social work practice*. New York: Longman.

Salter, A. C. (1988). *Treating child sex offenders and victims*. Newbury Park, CA: Sage.

Saltzman, A. (1986). Reporting child abuse and protecting substance abusers. *Social Work, 31,* 474–476.

Sandau-Beckler, P. A., & Salcido, R. (1991). Family preservation services for first generation Hispanic families in an international border community. In *Empowering families* (pp. 119–129). Proceedings of the Fifth Annual Conference on Family Based Services: National Association for Family Based Services, Cedar Rapids, IA.

Sander, F. (1976). Aspects of sexual counseling with the aged. *Social Casework, 58,* 504–510.

Santa Cruz, L., & Hepworth, D. (1975). Effects of cultural orientation on casework. *Social Casework, 56,* 52–57.

Sarri, R. (1987). Administration in social welfare. In *Encyclopedia of social work* (Vol. 1, pp. 27–40). Silver Spring, MD: National Association of Social Workers.

Satir, V. (1967). *Conjoint family therapy*. Palo Alto, CA: Science & Behavior Books.

Sauer, W. J., & Coward, R. T. (1985). *Social support networks and the care of the elderly*. New York: Springer.

Saunders, D. (1977). Marital violence: Dimensions of the problem and modes of intervention. *Journal of Marriage and Family Counseling, 3,* 43–54.

Schilling, R. F. (1987). Limitations of social support. *Social Service Review, 61,* 26–29.

Schilling, R. F., Schinke, S. P., & Weatherly, R. A. (1988). Service trends in a conservative era: Social workers rediscover the past. *Social Work, 33,* 5–9.

Schinke, S. P., Blythe, B. J., & Gilchrist, L. D. (1981). Cognitive-behavioral prevention of adolescent pregnancy. *Journal of Counseling Psychology, 28,* 451–454.

Schinke, S., Blythe, B., Gilchrist, L., & Smith, E. (1980). Developing intake-interviewing skills. *Social Work Research and Abstracts, 16,* 29–34.

Schneider, L., & Struening, E. (1983). SLOF: A behavioral rating scale for assessing the mentally ill. *Social Work Research and Abstracts, 19,* 9–21.

Schofield, W. (1964). *Psychotherapy: The purchase of friendship*. Englewood Cliffs, NJ: Prentice Hall.

Schopler, J., & Galinsky, M. (1974). Goals in social group work practice: Formulation, implementation and evaluation. In P. Glasser, R. Sarri, & R. Vinter (Eds.), *Individual change through small groups*. New York: Free Press.

Schotte, D. E., & Clum, G. A. (1987). Problem-solving skills in suicidal psychiatric patients. *Journal of Consulting and Clinical Psychology, 55,* 49–54.

Schrier, C. (1980). Guidelines for record-keeping under privacy and open-access laws. *Social Work, 25,* 452–457.

Schrodt, G. R., & Fitzgerald, B. A. (1987). Cognitive therapy with adolescents. *American Journal of Psychotherapy, 41,* 402–408.

Schroeder, H. E., & Black, M. J. (1985). Unassertiveness. In M. Hersen and A. S. Bellack (Eds.), *Handbook of clinical behavior therapy with adults* (pp. 509–530). New York: Plenum Press.

Schwartz, F. (1984). *Voluntarism and social work practice: A growing collaboration*. New York: University Press of America.

Schwartz, G. (1989). Confidentiality revisited. *Social Work, 34* (3), 223–226.

Seagull, E. A. (1987). Social support and child maltreatment: A review of the evidence. *Child Abuse and Neglect, 11,* 41–52.

Segal, U. A. (1991). Cultural variables in Asian Indian families. *Families in Society, 72,* 233–244.

Seligman, M.E.P. (1975). *Hopelessness: On depression, development and death*. San Francisco: W. H. Freeman.

Seligman, M. (1991). Grandparents of disabled grandchildren: Hopes, fears, and adaptation. *Families in Society, 72* (3), 147–152.

Seltzer, M. M., & Bloksberg, L. M. (1987). Permanency planning and its effects on foster children. *Social Work, 32,* 65–68.

Selvini-Palazzoli, M., Boscolo, L., Cecchin, G., & Prata, G. (1974). The treatment of children through brief therapy of their parents. *Family Process, 13,* 429–442.

Selzer, M. L. (1971). The Michigan Alcoholism Screening Test: The quest for a new diagnostic instrument. *American Journal of Psychiatry, 127,* 1653–1658.

Sheafor, B., Horejsi, C. R. and Horejsi, G. A. (1994). *Techniques and guidelines for social work practice* (3rd ed.). Boston: Allyn & Bacon.

Shelby, R. (1992). *If a partner has AIDS: Guide to clinical intervention for relationships in crisis*. Binghamton, NY: Haworth Press.

Shernoff, M. (1990). Why every social worker should be challenged by AIDS. *Social Work, 35* (1), 5–8.

Shimkunas, A. (1972). Demand for intimate self-disclosure and pathological verbalization in schizophrenia. *Journal of Abnormal Psychology, 80,* 197–205.

Shulman, L. (1984). *The skills of helping individuals and groups* (2nd ed.). Itasca, IL: Peacock.

Siegel, M., & Roberts, M. (1989). Recruiting foster families for disabled children. *Social Work, 34* (6), 551–553.

Simon, C. E., McNeil, J. S., Franklin, C., & Cooperman, A. (1991). The family and schizophrenia: Toward a psychoeducational approach. *Families in Society, 72* (6), 323–333.

Simonson, N. (1976). The impact of therapist disclosure

on patient disclosure. *Journal of Transpersonal Psychology, 23,* 3–6.

Sims, A. R. (1988). Independent living services for youths in foster care. *Social Work, 33* (6), 539–542.

Siporin, M. (1975). *Introduction to social work practice.* New York: Macmillan.

Siporin, M. (1979). Practice theory for clinical social work. *Clinical Social Work Journal, 7,* 75–89.

Siporin, M. (1980). Ecological systems theory in social work. *Journal of Sociology and Social Welfare, 7,* 507–532.

Sistler, A. (1989). Adaptive care of older caregiving spouses. *Social Work, 34* (5), 415–420.

Skinner, H. A. (1982). The Drug Abuse Screening Test. *Addictive Behaviors, 7,* 363–371.

Slater, J., & Depue, R. (1981). The contribution of environmental events and social support to serious suicide attempts in primary depressive disorder. *Journal of Abnormal Psychology, 90,* 275–285.

Sluzki, C. (1975). The coalitionary process in initiating family therapy. *Family Process, 14,* 67–77.

Smaldino, A. (1975). The importance of hope in the case work relationship. *Social Casework, 56,* 328–333.

Smith, V. (1979). How interest groups influence legislators. *Social Work, 24,* 234–239.

Smith, V. G., & Hepworth, D. (1967). Marriage counseling with one marital partner: Rationale and clinical implications. *Social Casework, 48,* 352–359.

Solomon, B. (1976). *Black empowerment: Social work in oppressed communities.* New York: Columbia University Press.

Sosin, M. (1979). Social work advocacy and the implementation of legal mandates. *Social Casework, 60,* 265–273.

Sosin, M., & Caulum, S. (1983). Advocacy: A conceptualization for social work practice. *Social Work, 28,* 12–17.

Specht, H., & Courtney, M. E. 1994. *Unfaithful angels: How social work has abandoned its mission.* New York: Free Press.

Specht, H., & Specht, R. (1986a). Social work assessment: Route to clienthood (Part I). *Social Casework, 67,* 525–532.

Specht, H., & Specht, R. (1986a). Social work assessment: Route to clienthood (Part II). *Social Casework, 67,* 587–593.

Speisman, J. (1959). Depth of interpretation and verbal resistance in psychotherapy. *Journal of Consulting Psychology, 23,* 93–99.

Spivack, G., Platt, J., & Shure, M. (1976). *The problem-solving approach to adjustment.* San Francisco: Jossey-Bass.

Spungen, C., Jensen, S., Finkelstein, N., & Satinsky, F. (1989). Child personal safety: Model program for prevention of child sexual abuse. *Social Work, 34* (2), 127–131.

Steinmetz, G. (1992). Fetal alcohol syndrome. *National Geographic, 181* (2), 36–39.

Steinmetz, S. K. (1988). *Duty bound elder abuse and family care.* Newbury Park, CA: Sage.

Stempler, B., & Stempler, H. (1981). Extending the client connection: Using homemaker-caseworker teams. *Social Casework, 62,* 149–158.

Stith, S. M., Williams, M. B., & Rosen, K. (1990). *Violence hits home: Comprehensive treatment approaches to domestic violence.* New York: Springer.

Stokes, J. P. (1983). Components of group cohesion: Intermember attraction, instrumental value, and risk taking. *Small Group Behavior, 14,* 163–173.

Stordeur, R. A., & Stille, R. (1989). *Ending men's violence against their partners.* Newbury Park, CA: Sage.

Strean, H. (1979). *Psychoanalytic theory and social work practice.* New York: Free Press.

Streeter, C. L., & Franklin, C. (1992). Defining and measuring social support: Guidelines for social work practitioners. *Research on Social Work Practice, 2* (1), 81–98.

Strom, K. (1992, September). Reimbursement demands and treatment decisions: A growing dilemma for social workers. *Social Work, 37* (5), 398–403.

Stuart, R. (1980). *Helping couples change.* New York: Guilford Press.

Sue, S., & McKinney, H. (1975). Asian Americans in the community mental health care system. *American Journal of Orthopsychiatry, 45,* 111–118.

Sue, S., & Moore, T. (1984). *The pluralistic society: A community mental health perspective.* New York: Human Sciences Press.

Sue, S., & Zane, N. (1987). The role of culture and cultural techniques in psychotherapy. *American Psychologist, 42,* 37–45.

Surber, R. W., Dwyer, E., Ryan, K. J., Goldfinger, S. M., & Kelley, J. T. (1988). Medical and psychiatric needs of the homeless—A preliminary response. *Social Work, 33,* 116–119.

Tafoya, T. (1989). Circles and cedar: Native Americans and family therapy. In G. A. Saba, B. M. Kerrer, & K. Hardy (Eds.), *Minorities and family therapy* (pp. 71–94). New York: Hawthorne Press.

Taft, Jessie (1937). The relation of function to process in social casework. *Journal of Social Work Process, 1* (1), 1–18.

Taube, P. A., & Barrett, S. A. (Eds.) (1983). (DHHS Publication No. ADM 83-1275). Washington, DC: U.S. Government Printing Office.

Taussig, I. M. (1987). Comparative responses of Mexican-Americans and Anglo-Americans to early goal setting in a public mental health clinic. *Journal of Counseling Psychology, 34,* 214–217.

Taylor, B. (1988). Social skills travel training in social work practice. *Social Casework, 69* (4), 248–252.

Taylor, J. W. (1990). The use of nonverbal expression with incestuous clients. *Families in Society, 71* (10), 597–601.

Thomas, E. (1977). *Marital communication and decision making: Analysis, assessment, and change.* New York: Free Press.

Thomas, E. (1978). Research and service in single-case experimentation: Conflicts and choices. *Social Work Research and Abstracts, 14,* 20–31.

Thomas, E. (1989). Advances in developmental research. *Social Service Review, 63,* 578–597.

Thomlison, R. (1984). Something works: Evidence from practice effectiveness studies. *Social Work, 29,* 51–56.

Thompson, T., & Hupp, S. C. (1991). *Saving children at risk: Poverty and disabilities.* Newbury Park, CA: Sage.

Timberlake, E., & Cook, K. (1984). Social work and the Vietnamese refugee. *Social Work, 29,* 108–114.

Tisdelle, D. A., & St. Lawrence, J. S. (1988). Adolescent interpersonal problem-solving skill training: Social validation and generalization. *Behavior Therapy, 19,* 171–182.

Tolman, R. M. & Molidor, C. E. (1994). A decade of social group work research: Trends in methodology, theory and program development. *Research on Social Work Practice, 4* (2), 142–159.

Tomm, K. (1981). Circularity: A preferred orientation for family assessment. In A. Gurman (Ed.), *Questions and answers in the practice of family therapy* (pp. 84–87). New York: Brunner/Mazel.

Toseland, R. (1977). A problem-solving group workshop for older persons. *Social Work, 22,* 325–326.

Toseland, R. (1981). Increasing access: Outreach methods in social work practice. *Social Casework, 62,* 227–234.

Toseland, R. (1987). Treatment discontinuance: Grounds for optimism. *Social Casework, 68,* 195–204.

Toseland, R. W., Ivanoff, A., & Rose, S. R. (1987). Treatment conferences: Task groups in action. Working effectively with administrative groups. *Social Work with Groups 2,* 79–93.

Toseland, R., & Rivas, R. (1984). *An introduction to group work practice.* New York: Macmillan.

Toseland, R. W., & Rivas, R. S. (1995). *An introduction to group work practice* (2nd ed.). Boston: Allyn & Bacon.

Toseland, R., Rossiter, C., Peak, T., & Smith, G. C. (1990). Comparative effectiveness of individual and group interventions to support family caregivers. *Social Work, 35* (3), 209–217.

Tracy, E. M., & Whittaker, J. K. (1990). The Social Network Map: Assessing social support in clinical practice. *Families in Society, 71* (8), 461–470.

Treatment: An introduction to interpersonal helping in social work practice. New York: Aldine de Gruyter.

Tripodi, T., & Epstein, I. (1980). *Research techniques for clinical social workers.* New York: Columbia University Press.

Truax, C., & Carkhuff, R. (1964). For better or for worse: The process of psychotherapeutic personality change. In (pp. 118–163) *Recent advances in the study of behavior change* . Montreal: McGill University Press.

Truax, C., & Carkhuff, R. (1967). *Toward effective counseling and psychotherapy: Training and practice.* Chicago: Aldine-Atherton.

Truax, C., & Mitchell, K. (1971). Research on certain therapist interpersonal skills in relation to process and outcome. In A. Bergin & S. Garfield (Eds.), *Handbook of psychotherapy and behavior change* (pp. 299–344). New York: Wiley.

Tsui, P., & Schultz, G. L. (1985). Failure of rapport: Why psychotherapeutic engagement fails in the treatment of Asian clients. *American Journal of Orthopsychiatry, 55,* 561–569.

Tsui, P., & Schultz, G. L. (1988). Ethnic factors in group process: Cultural dynamics in multi-ethnic therapy groups. *American Journal of Orthopsychiatry, 58,* 136–142.

Turnbull, J. E. (1988). Primary and secondary alcoholic women. *Social Casework, 69* (5), 290–297.

Turnbull, J. E. (1989). Treatment issues for alcoholic women. *Social Casework, 70* (6), 364–369.

Turner, J. (1984). Reuniting children in foster care with their biological parents. *Social Work, 29* (6), 501–506.

Umbreit, M. S. (1993, January). Crime victims and offenders in mediation: An emerging area of social work practice. *Social Work, 38* (1), 69–73.

U.S. Department of Justice. (1986). *Preventing domestic violence against women.* Washington, DC: Bureau of Justice Statistics.

U.S. Federal Bureau of Investigation. (1988). *Uniform crime reports.* Washington, DC: Author.

VandeCreek, L., Knapp, S., & Herzog, C. (1988). Privileged communication for social workers. *Social Casework, 69,* 28–34.

Van Hook, M. P. (1987). Harvest of despair: The ABCX model for farm families in crisis. *Social Casework, 69,* 273–278.

Vattano, A. (1972). Power to the people: Self-help groups. *Social Work, 17,* 7–15.

Vattano, A. (1978). Self-management procedures for coping with stress. *Social Work, 23,* 113–119.

Videka-Sherman, L. (1987). Research on the effect of parental bereavement: Implications for social work intervention. *Social Service Review, 61,* 102–116.

Videka-Sherman, L. (1988, July–August). Meta-analysis of research on social work practice in mental health. *Social Work, 33–34,* 325–337.

Vigilante, F. W., & Mailick, M. D. (1988). Needs-resource evaluation in the assessment process. *Social Work, 33,* 101–104.

Vincent, J., Weiss, R., & Birchler, G. (1976). A behavioral analysis of problem solving in distressed and nondistressed married and stranger dyads. *Behavior Therapy, 6,* 475–487.

Visher, E. B., & Visher, J. S. (1988). *Old loyalties, new ties.* New York: Brunner/Mazel.

Vogel, E., & Bell, N. (1960). The emotionally disturbed child as the family scapegoat. In N. Bell & E. Vogel (Eds.), *A modern introduction to the family.* New York: Free Press.

Vourlekis, B. S., & Greene, R. R. (1992). *Social work case management.* Hawthorne, NY: Aldine de Gruyter.

Voydanoff, P., & Donnelly, B. M. (1990). *Adolescent sexuality and pregnancy.* Newbury Park, CA: Sage.

Wakefield, J. (1995, March). *Invited presentation at the Council for Social Work Education Annual Program Meeting.* San Diego, CA.

Wakefield, J. C. (1996). Does social work need the ecosystems perspective? Part I. Is the perspective clinically useful? *Social Service Review, 70* (1), 1–32.

Wakefield, J. C. (1996). Does social work need the ecosystems perspective? Part II. Does the perspective save social work from incoherence? *Social Service Review, 70* (2), 183–213.

Wakefield, J. C. (1996). Does social work need the ecological perspective? Reply to Alex Gitterman. *Social Service Review, 70* (3), 476–481.

Walen, S., DiGiuseppe, R., & Wessler, R. (1980). *A practitioner's guide to RET.* New York: Oxford University Press.

Wallace, J. (1989). A biopsychosocial model of alcoholism. *Social Casework, 70* (6), 325–332.

Waltz, T., & Groze, V. (1991). The mission of social work revisited: An agenda for the 1990's. *Social Work, 36* (6), 500–504.

Wartel, S. (1991). Clinical considerations for adults abused as children. *Families in Society, 72* (3), 157–163.

Watson, H., & Levine, M. (1989). Psychotherapy and mandated reporting of child abuse. *American Journal of Orthopsychiatry,*

Watzlawick, P., Weakland, J., & Fisch, R. (1974). *Change: Principles of problem formulation.* New York: Norton.

Weaver, D. (1982). Empowering treatment skills for helping black families. *Social Casework, 63,* 100–105.

Webb, N. B. (1985). A crisis intervention perspective on the termination process. *Clinical Social Work Journal, 13,* 329–340.

Webber, H. S. (1995). The failure of health-care reform: An essay review. *Social Service Review, 69* (2), 309–322.

Weick, A., & Pope, L. (1988). Knowing what's best: A new look at self-determination. *Social Casework, 69,* 10–16.

Weinberg, N. (1983). Social equity and the physically disabled. *Social Work, 28,* 365–369.

Weiner-Davis (1992). *Divorce-busting.* New York: Summit Books.

Weinman, M. L. (1989). Joint case management planning for pregnant teenagers in school. *School Social Work Journal, 14* (1), 1–8.

Weiss, B. S., & Parish, B. (1989). Culturally appropriate crisis counseling: Adapting an American method for use with Indochinese refugees. *Social Work, 34* (3), 252–254.

Weiss, R. (1974). The provisions of social relationships. In L. Rubin (Ed.), *Doing unto others* (pp. 17–26). Englewood Cliffs, NJ: Prentice Hall.

Weiss, R., & Parkes, C. (1983). *Recovery from bereavement.* New York: Basic Books.

Weissman, A. (1976). *Industrial social services: Linkage of problem formulation and problem resolution.* New York: Norton.

Weissman, H. H., Epstein, I., & Savage, A. (1983). *Agency-based social work: Neglected aspects of clinical practice.* Philadelphia: Temple University Press.

Weissman, H. H., Epstein, I., & Savage, A. (1987). Exploring the role repertoire of clinicians. *Social Casework, 68,* 150–155.

Weisz, J. R., Weiss, B., Wasserman, A. A., & Rintoul, B. (1987). Control-related beliefs and depression among clinic-referred children and adolescents. *Journal of Abnormal Psychology, 96,* 58–63.

Wells, C. C., & Masch, M. K. (1986). *Social work ethics day to day.* White Plains, NY: Longman.

Wells, K., & Biegel, D. E. (Eds.)(1991). *Family preservation services: Research and evaluation.* Newbury Park, CA: Sage.

Wells, R. (1975). Training in facilitative skills. *Social Work, 20,* 242–243.

Wells, R. A. (1982). *Planned short-term treatment.* New York: Free Press.

Wells, R. A. (1994). *Planned short-term treatment* (2nd ed.). New York: Free Press.

Wells, R. A., & Gianetti, V. J. (Eds.) (1990). *Handbook of the brief psychotherapies.* New York: Plenum Press.

Wertkin, R. A. (1985). Stress-inoculation training: Principles and application. *Social Casework, 66,* 611–616.

West, L., Mercer, S. O., & Altheimer, E. (1993). Operation Desert Storm: The response of a social work outreach team. *Social Work in Health Care, 19* (2), 81–98.

Whiteman, M., Fanshel, D., & Grundy, J. (1987). Cognitive-behavioral interventions aimed at anger of parents at risk of child abuse. *Social Work, 32* (6), 469–474.

Whitman, B. Y., Graves, B. & Accardo, P. J. (1989). Training in parenting skills for adults with mental retardation. *Social Work, 34* (5), 431–434.

Whitman, B. Y., & Webb, N. B. (1991). *Play therapy with children in crisis.* New York: Guilford Press.

Whitsett, D., & Land, H. (1992). Role strain, coping, and marital satisfaction of stepparents. *Families in Society, 73* (2), 79–92.

Whittaker, J. (1979). *Caring for troubled children.* San Francisco: Jossey-Bass.

Whittaker, J., Garbarino, J., & Associates (1983). *Social support networks: Informal helping in the human services.* Hawthorne, NY: Aldine.

Whittaker, J. K., & Tracy, E. M. (1989). *Social treatment: An introduction to interpersonal helping in social work practice.* New York: Aldine de Gruyter.

Wiehe, V. R. (1990). *Sibling abuse: Hidden physical, emotional and sexual trauma.* Lexington, MA: Lexington Books.

Wile, D. (1978). Is a confrontational tone necessary in conjoint therapy? *Journal of Marriage and Family Counseling, 4,* 11–18.

Williams, O. J. (1994). Group work with African American men who batter: Toward more ethnically sensitive practice. *Journal of Comparative Family Studies, 25* (1), 91–103.

Wilson, J. (1987). Women and poverty: A demographic overview. *Woman and Health, 12,* 21–40.

Wilson, S. K., Cameron, S., Jaffe, P., & Wolfe, D. (1989). Children exposed to wife abuse: An intervention model. *Social Casework 70* (3), 180–184.

Wilson, V. (1990). The consequences of elderly wives caring for disabled husbands. *Social Work, 35* (5), 417–421.

Wiseman, J. C. (1990). *Mediation therapy: Short-term decision making for couples and families in crisis.* New York: Lexington Books.

Wisniewski, J. J., & Toomey, B. G. (1987). Are social workers homophobic? *Social Work, 32,* 454–455.

Withey, V., Anderson, R., & Lauderdale, M. (1980). Volunteers as mentors for abusing parents: A natural helping relationship. *Child Welfare, 59,* 637–644.

Witkin, L. (1973). Student volunteers in a guidance clinic. *Social Work, 18,* 53–57.

Witkin, S. (1991). Empirical clinical practice: A critical analysis. *Social Work, 36* (2), 158–163.

Wolberg, L. (1965). The technique of short-term psychotherapy. In L. Wolberg (Ed.), *Short-term psychotherapy* (pp. 127–200). New York: Grune & Stratton.

Wolff, J. M. (1990). Bite marks: Recognizing child abuse and identifying abusers. *Families in Society, 71* (8), 493–499.

Wong, W. (1983). *Present-day American Samoan family life: A training resource.* University of Hawaii School of Social Work.

Wood, K. (1978). Casework effectiveness: A new look at the research evidence. *Social Work, 23,* 437–458.

Wood, K., & Geismar, L. L. (1989). *Families at risk: Treating the multiproblem family.* New York: Human Services Press.

Wood, W.N.L. (1987). Homosexuality in the family: Lesbian and gay issues. *Social Work, 32,* 143–148.

Wright, R., Saleeby, D., Watts, T., & Lecca, P. (1983). *Transcultural perspectives in the human services: Organizational issues and trends.* Springfield, IL: Charles C Thomas.

Wyatt, G. E., & Powell, G. J. (1988). *Lasting effects of child abuse.* Newbury Park, CA: Sage.

Wyers, N. L. (1987). Homosexuality in the family: Lesbian and gay issues. *Social Work, 32,* 143–148.

Yalom, I. (1980). *Existential psychotherapy.* New York: Basic Books.

Yalom, I. (1985). *The theory and practice of group psychotherapy* (2nd ed.). New York: Basic Books.

Yalom, I., & Lieberman, M. (1971). A study of encounter group casualties. *Archives of General Psychiatry, 25,* 16–30.

Yankelovich, D. (1981). New rules in American life: Searching for self-fulfillment in a world turned upside down. *Psychology Today, 15,* 35–91.

Young, B. (1980). The Hawaiians. In J. McDermott, W. Tseng, & T. Maretzki (Eds.), *People and cultures of Hawaii* (pp. 5–24). Honolulu: University of Hawaii Press.

Yuker, H. E. (Ed.) (1988). *Attitudes toward persons with disabilities.* New York: Springer.

Zastrow, C. (1987). *Social work with groups.* Chicago: Nelson-Hall.

Zastrow, C., & Kirst-Ashman, K. (1990). *Understanding human behavior and the social environment* (2nd ed.). Chicago: Nelson-Hall.

Zborowski, M., & Herzog, E. (1952). *Life is with people: The culture of the shtetl.* New York: Schocken.

Zeiss, A., Lewinsohn, P., & Munoz, R. (1979). Nonspecific improvements effects in depression using interpersonal skills training, pleasant activities schedules, or cognitive training. *Journal of Consulting and Clinical Psychology, 47,* 427–439.

Zingale, D. P. (1985). The importance of empathic responding in the psychotherapeutic interview. *International Social Work, 28,* 35–39.

Zipple, M., & Spaniol, L. (1987). Current educational and supportive models of family intervention. In A. B. Hatfield & H. P. Lefley (Eds.), *Families of the mentally ill.* New York: Guilford Press.

Zung, W. (1965). A self-rating depression scale. *Archives of General Psychiatry, 12,* 63–70.

Zwick, R., & Atkinson, C. C. (1985). Effectiveness of a client pretherapy orientation videotape. *Journal of Counseling Psychology, 32,* 514–524.

Author Index

Subject Index

TO THE OWNER OF THIS BOOK:

We hope that you have found *Direct Social Work Practice: Theory and Skills*, Fifth Edition, useful. So that this book can be improved in a future edition, would you take the time to complete this sheet and return it? Thank you.

School and address: _____

Department: _____

Instructor's name: _____

1. What I like most about this book is: _____

_____

_____

2. What I like least about this book is: _____

_____

_____

3. My general reaction to this book is: _____

_____

4. The name of the course in which I used this book is: _____

_____

5. Were all of the chapters of the book assigned for you to read? _____

   If not, which ones weren't? _____

 6. In the space below, or on a separate sheet of paper, please write specific suggestions for improving this book and anything else you'd care to share about your experience in using the book.

_____

_____

_____

_____

_____

Optional:

Your name: _____ Date: _____

May Brooks/Cole quote you, either in promotion for *Direct Social Work Practice: Theory and Skills,* Fifth Edition, or in future publishing ventures?

Yes: _____ No: _____

Sincerely,

Dean H. Hepworth
Ronald H. Rooney
Jo Ann Larsen

FOLD HERE

NO POSTAGE
NECESSARY
IF MAILED
IN THE
UNITED STATES

BUSINESS REPLY MAIL

FIRST CLASS   PERMIT NO. 358   PACIFIC GROVE, CA

POSTAGE WILL BE PAID BY ADDRESSEE

ATT: *Dean H. Hepworth, Ronald H. Rooney, & Jo Ann Larsen*

Brooks/Cole Publishing Company
511 Forest Lodge Road
Pacific Grove, California 93950-9968

FOLD HERE

Brooks/Cole is dedicated to publishing quality publications for education in the human services fields. If you are interested in learning more about our publications, please fill in your name and address and request our latest catalogue, using this prepaid mailer.

Name: _____

Street Address: _____

City, State, and Zip: _____

FOLD HERE

FOLD HERE

IN-BOOK SURVEY

At Brooks/Cole, we are excited about creating new types of learning materials that are interactive, three-dimensional, and fun to use. To guide us in our publishing/development process, we hope that you'll take just a few moments to fill out the survey below. Your answers can help us make decisions that will allow us to produce a wide variety of videos, CD-ROMs, and Internet-based learning systems to complement standard textbooks. If you're interested in working with us as a student Beta-tester, be sure to fill in your name, telephone number, and address. We look forward to hearing from you!

In addition to books, which of the following learning tools do you currently use in your counseling/human services/social work courses?

_____ **Video** _____ in class _____ school library _____ own VCR

_____ **CD-ROM** _____ in class _____ in lab _____ own computer

_____ **Macintosh disks** _____ in class _____ in lab _____ own computer

_____ **Windows disks** _____ in class _____ in lab _____ own computer

_____ **Internet** _____ in class _____ in lab _____ own computer

How often do you access the Internet? _____

My own home computer is:

_____ Macintosh _____ DOS _____ Windows _____ Windows 95

The computer I use in class for counseling/human services/social work courses is:

_____ Macintosh _____ DOS _____ Windows _____ Windows 95

If you are NOT currently using multimedia materials in your counseling/human services/social work courses, but can see ways that video, CD-ROM, Internet, or other technologies could enhance your learning, please comment below:

_____

_____

_____

Other comments (optional): _____

_____

Name _____

Address _____

Telephone number (optional): _____

You can fax this form to us at (408) 375-6414; e:mail to: info@brookscole.com; or detach, fold, secure, and mail.

FOLD HERE

BUSINESS REPLY MAIL

FIRST CLASS   PERMIT NO. 358   PACIFIC GROVE, CA

POSTAGE WILL BE PAID BY ADDRESSEE

ATTN: ___MARKETING_____

Brooks/Cole Publishing Company
511 Forest Lodge Road
Pacific Grove, California 93950-9968